Congress and the Nation

Sara Miller McCune founded SAGE Publishing in 1965 to support the dissemination of usable knowledge and educate a global community. SAGE publishes more than 1000 journals and over 600 new books each year, spanning a wide range of subject areas. Our growing selection of library products includes archives, data, case studies and video. SAGE remains majority owned by our founder and after her lifetime will become owned by a charitable trust that secures the company's continued independence.

Los Angeles | London | New Delhi | Singapore | Washington DC | Melbourne

Congress and the Nation

VOLUME XIV • 2013–2016

POLITICS AND POLICY IN THE
113TH AND 114TH CONGRESSES

 |

FOR INFORMATION:

CQ Press

An Imprint of SAGE Publications, Inc.

2455 Teller Road

Thousand Oaks, California 91320

E-mail: order@sagepub.com

SAGE Publications Ltd.

1 Oliver's Yard

55 City Road

London EC1Y 1SP

United Kingdom

SAGE Publications India Pvt. Ltd.

B 1/I 1 Mohan Cooperative Industrial Area

Mathura Road, New Delhi 110 044

India

SAGE Publications Asia-Pacific Pte. Ltd.

18 Cross Street #10-10/11/12

China Square Central

Singapore 048423

Print ISBN: 978-1-5443-5066-0

ISSN: 1047-1324

Volume Editor: David Hosansky

Editor, Reference Publishing: Laura Notton

Editorial Assistant: Tamara Tanso

Developmental Editor: Yvette Pollastrini

Production Editor: Tracy Buyan

Copy Editor: Kim Husband

Typesetter: C&M Digitals (P) Ltd.

Proofreader: Lawrence Baker

Indexer: Joan Shapiro

Cover Designer: Candice Harman

Marketing Manager: Carmel Schrire

19 20 21 22 23 10 9 8 7 6 5 4 3 2 1

Summary Table of Contents

Contents

Chapter 7   Energy and Environment

Chapter 8   Agricultural Policy

Chapter 9   Health and Human Services

Chapter 10   Education Policy

Chapter 15   Inside Congress

Chapter 16   The Obama Presidency

Appendix

Tables, Figures, and Boxes

Introduction

During the four-year period of President Barack Obama's second term, the United States appeared in many ways to be enjoying a period of relative prosperity and peace. At the same time, however, Americans contended with deepening socioeconomic struggles, increasingly raw political tensions, and occasional racial violence.

On the positive side of the ledger, the nation continued its slow recovery from the Great Recession of 2007–2009. The economy expanded steadily, investors enjoyed a sustained stock market rally, the housing market rebounded, and workers were so successful in finding jobs that the unemployment rate by the end of Obama's presidency touched down at 4.8 percent, which was less than the historic average. When the Federal Reserve raised interest rates at the end of 2015 for the first time in nine years, it was sending an important signal that the economy had finally recovered from the lingering impacts of the recession.

The situation also appeared to be relatively secure overseas. Although U.S. forces remained engaged, especially in Iraq and Afghanistan, fighting in both nations had largely wound down. Seeking to reduce tensions with long-time adversaries, the White House negotiated a multilateral agreement on Iran's nuclear program and normalized diplomatic relations with Cuba.

At the same time, however, wages rose sluggishly, creating widespread financial insecurity and contributing to a growing gap between the top 0.1 percent of earners and the rest of Americans. Increases in median household income barely made up for the steep losses during the George W. Bush presidency. The economic recovery proved uneven, with urban tech hubs such as Seattle and Denver leaving both traditional manufacturing centers in the Midwest and rural America far behind.

The growing availability of opioids contributed to an epidemic of drug overdoses that swept across the nation, resulting in record numbers of deaths—more than 60,000 in 2016 alone. Resentment toward immigrants and anxiety about terrorism and mass shootings exacerbated the country's sour mood. After police in 2014 shot and killed an African American teenager in Ferguson, Mo., racial tensions erupted into violence, launching the Black Lives Matter movement and heightening scrutiny of racist actions by law enforcement. A landmark Supreme Court decision in 2015 legalizing gay marriage in every state thrilled gay rights supporters but antagonized religious conservatives and others who believed that marriage should only be between a man and a woman. The growing reach of social media exacerbated political and cultural divides, with increasingly discordant exchanges on Facebook, Twitter, and other channels over hot-button issues.

These differences bubbled up to Capitol Hill. Lawmakers reflecting deeply divided constituencies could not even reach agreement on must-pass annual spending bills, let alone more contentious issues such as immigration. Election results reflected the national uneasiness: voters in 2014 repudiated the status quo and backed highly conservative Republican candidates in Congress and state houses and then in 2016 unexpectedly awarded the presidential election to Donald J. Trump, whose grim rhetoric and nativist leanings promised a sharp turnabout from the two terms of the Obama presidency.

These historic events and the political debates they spawned are the subject of this book. *Congress and the Nation, Vol. XIV*, like its predecessor volumes, is framed by a presidential term, but its content is informed deeply by the entire events of Obama's eight years in office.

HOW TO USE THIS BOOK

Readers can access information in several ways. The sixteen chapters are listed in the Summary Table of Contents (page v). An outline of each chapter, including boxes, tables, graphs, and other related material, is provided in the detailed Contents (page vii).

For specific topics, turn to the complete index at the end of the volume (page 691). Throughout the book, page references to related subjects in other chapters are provided. These page "flags" are designed to speed research across an array of subjects.

The Introduction provides an overview of political and legislative activity and a thumbnail description of each chapter's content.

The nation's first African American president, Obama, took office in 2009 at a moment in American history when, paradoxically, there were both high expectations for his presidency and deep concerns over the challenges he faced, especially the most severe economic downturn since the Great Depression.

In some ways, the Obama presidency can be divided into two parts: the first two years, when he enjoyed the backing of a strong Democratic majority in Congress, and the last six years, when Republican gains on Capitol Hill—especially in the House—provided conservatives with greater leverage over national issues. Immediately upon taking office, Obama focused on economic recovery, working with Congress on enactment of major stimulus measures and stricter regulations to prevent another collapse of the financial system. He then pivoted to the contentious issue of health care, winning 2010 passage of his top priority: the Affordable Care Act. The far-reaching bill, passed over the emphatic opposition of congressional Republicans, aimed to provide nearly universal health care to Americans.

But Republicans stormed back in the 2010 elections, winning control of the House for the first time since 2006 and significantly weakening the Democratic majority in the Senate. Fueled by the emergence of a staunchly conservative insurgency known as the Tea Party movement, Congressional Republicans repeatedly tried to repeal the Affordable Care Act, which they derisively called "Obamacare" and regarded as government overreach. They also attempted to scale back financial regulations contained in 2010 legislation known as Dodd-Frank. Perhaps even more ominously for Obama's fortunes, sweeping Republican gains at the state level enabled them to dominate the reapportionment process following the 2010 elections. As a result, heavily gerrymandered legislative districts favored Republican candidates throughout the remainder of the Obama presidency. Many of the districts were either overwhelmingly Republican or overwhelmingly Democratic, reducing the incentive for representatives to reach across the aisle in pursuit of legislative compromises.

Obama won reelection in 2012, becoming the first president since Ronald Reagan to win the majority of the popular vote twice. But his winning margin was narrower than in 2008, reflecting the nation's deep partisan divide, and Democrats failed to retake the House. As a result, Obama entered his second term with the political landscape largely unchanged.

PRESIDENTIAL STRUGGLES

If the yardstick for measuring Obama's second term is how it compared to those of his two immediate predecessors, then it could be judged a success of sorts. Bill Clinton was impeached in his second term, and George W. Bush faced both the natural disaster of Hurricane Katrina and the economic disaster of the 2008 financial collapse. Obama avoided such drama in his second term.

But Obama, handcuffed by a hostile Congress, largely failed to notch major accomplishments. The tone was set in 2013 when he pressed ahead with two top priorities that appeared to have some momentum: immigration and gun control. Latino voters wielded increasing electoral clout, helping to put Obama over the top in key battleground states such as Colorado, and many lawmakers in both parties favored a major overhaul of the immigration system as a way of winning their support. Gun control faced much longer odds in Congress, but public concern over gun violence was rising after a series of mass shootings, including an elementary school shooting in December 2012 that left twenty-six people dead.

Divisions among Republicans, however, stymied immigration reform. In a reprise of congressional battles during the presidency of George W. Bush, many conservatives rejected legislation that would have provided a path to citizenship for undocumented immigrants. Proposed gun regulations fared even worse, with Republicans and some Democrats uniting against any significant measure that, they said, would violate the rights of gunowners and fail to curb gun violence.

Things went from bad to worse for Obama after the midterm elections. Republicans won control of the Senate for the first time since 2006, and they strengthened their House majority. With his presidency coming to an end in just two years, Obama faced scant prospects of winning congressional support for any of his major priorities. Instead he sought to block Republican initiatives to scale back financial and environmental regulations, and he vetoed legislation that would have repealed the Affordable Care Act.

Unable to make much headway on Capitol Hill, Obama instead relied on his presidential authority to sign executive orders on such issues as immigration and environmental protection. He also worked the phone, rallying supporters in an attempt to put pressure on lawmakers. However, this "pen-and-phone" strategy, as he called it, yielded mixed results. The courts blocked executive orders that would have prevented the deportation of millions of undocumented immigrations and reduced carbon emissions from power plants. On the other hand, he was able to raise the minimum wage for federal contractors and prevent them from discriminating against lesbian, gay, bisexual, and transgender individuals. He also rejected the proposed Keystone XL Pipeline, which had drawn opposition from environmentalists.

Obama relied on his executive authority when it came to foreign policy as well. Seeking to end decades of hostility, he made the controversial decision to reopen diplomatic ties with Cuba. The administration also forged an agreement with Iran to freeze that nation's nuclear weapons program, brushing aside concerns by Israel and intense opposition by many in Congress.

Overall, Obama left a mixed legacy on foreign policy. Although he reduced the number of troops in Afghanistan, he fell short in his goal of winding down the war entirely. He initially seemed to underestimate the far-reaching threat posed by the Islamic State, although U.S.-backed forces eventually scored a series of victories against the militants in Iraq and Syria. Obama also imposed sanctions against Russia after it seized Crimea and broadened sanctions against North Korea over its nuclear and ballistic missile programs. The sanctions, however, failed to rein in the aggressive leadership of those nations.

On the domestic front, Obama's presidency reached a low point over an unsuccessful effort to fill the Supreme Court seat left vacant by the February 2016 death of Justice Antonin Scalia, a conservative icon. Presidents had often tangled with the Senate over Supreme Court nominations, dating back to the days of George Washington. But when Senate Majority Leader Mitch McConnell, R-Ky., refused to so much as consider Obama's nominee and declared that it would instead fall to the next president to fill the vacancy, it represented an extraordinary congressional rebuff to the president and an escalation of the ongoing partisan battles over the judicial branch that had already left Obama struggling to fill lower-court judgeships. A stunned White House found itself powerless.

In the months leading up to the 2016 presidential election, Obama threw his energy behind the candidacy of Democratic nominee Hillary Clinton. A Trump victory, he feared, could lead to a reversal of his executive orders on key foreign policy and environmental issues and even endanger his signature accomplishment: the Affordable Care Act. But with Clinton failing to rouse much enthusiasm among Democrats, Trump won a close election despite losing the popular vote. Republicans also held the House and Senate, albeit with slightly reduced majorities. The outcome left Obama's legacy in doubt.

Despite the election results, Obama enjoyed an enduring connection with voters—at least those who were Democrats. He entered his second term with a 54 percent approval rating, according to the Gallup daily national survey. Although it fell to as low as 40 percent in 2014, when Republicans lobbed some of their fiercest criticism at the Affordable Care Act, his approval rating stood at 59 percent when he left office. However, he had the most polarized approval ratings of any president dating to Dwight D. Eisenhower in the 1950s, according to Gallup. Obama averaged 83 percent job approval among Democrats and only 13 percent among Republicans during his administration. That 70 percent gap eclipsed the previous high of 61 percent for George W. Bush—a sign of the growing polarization of American politics.

CONGRESSIONAL DIVISIONS

Persistent political divisions left Congress almost paralyzed at times during Obama's second term. Republicans and Democrats voted against each other at a near-record rate, while intraparty battles among Republicans led to the resignation of House Speaker John Boehner, R-Ohio, and the ouster of his presumed successor, Majority Leader Eric Cantor, R-Va. The seemingly endless battles led to a sixteen-day government shutdown, a highly contentious decision by Senate Democrats to weaken the filibuster, and a breakdown in the process of passing annual spending bills.

The heated differences resulted in unusually low productivity, with lawmakers passing fewer bills than past Congresses and often failing to hold hearings on major issues. Even proposals that ordinarily would have been expected to win bipartisan approval, such as appropriating money to fight an outbreak of the Zika virus in the United States, passed only after major battles. Still, lawmakers were able to work across the aisle to pass several high-profile measures. These included multiyear reauthorizations of major transportation and agriculture policies and substantial changes to education policy.

In the 113th Congress (which held office in 2013–2014), the majorities of the two parties in the House and Senate differed with each other on seven out of every ten roll-call votes. This was the highest percentage of partisan votes in both chambers in the more than six decades of analysis of voting patterns by *Congressional Quarterly*. Partisanship remained high in the 114th Congress (2015–16). In the House, a majority of Republicans and a majority of Democrats opposed each other about three-quarters of the time, a near-record pace. In the Senate, which has a far more bipartisan tradition, majorities squared off 69.3 percent of the time in 2015 for the fourth-highest mark on record.

The partisan battles in the Senate spilled over into the process of confirming Obama nominees, both for judgeships and for administration posts. After months of negotiations, Senate Majority Leader Harry Reid, D-Nev., made the momentous decision in late 2013 to force through a change in Senate rules over heated Republican opposition that would enable most nominees to win confirmation on a simple majority vote instead of needing a sixty-vote supermajority. This led to Obama nominees winning confirmation after waiting for months or even more than a year, but the victory came at a steep price. Republicans warned that they would force through nominees when they regained the White House—a scenario that loomed after Trump won the 2016 presidential election with Republicans in charge of the Senate.

Mitch McConnell proved a highly skilled Senate tactician who was popular with his caucus, both as minority leader in the 113th Congress and then as majority leader after the Republicans took control of the Senate in the midterm elections. He established a rapport with Vice President Joe Biden that enabled the two men to negotiate difficult budget deals. This became critical at several points during Obama's second term, as relations between the administration and House Republican leaders were often too frosty for effective negotiations. Moreover, House leaders, unlike McConnell, had only a shaky hold on their often unruly members.

MAJOR LEGISLATION PASSED BY CONGRESS IN OBAMA'S SECOND TERM

This chart highlights some of the major bills that lawmakers passed during the 113th and 114th Congresses. In addition to the legislation listed here, lawmakers debated controversial measures that did not make it to President Obama's desk, including proposed changes to immigration, the Affordable Care Act, and gun regulations. Those debates are covered in the relevant chapters of this volume.

Congressional action on annual budget and appropriations bills is summarized in the Economic Policy chapter and covered in more detail in the relevant subject chapters. Obama's executive orders on such issues as overseas military activities, agreements with other nations, immigration, and environmental regulations are also covered in the relevant subject chapters.

Economy and Financial Regulation

Dodd-Frank financial regulation (2014). The fiscal 2015 omnibus appropriations bill eliminated a provision in the 2010 Dodd-Frank financial regulation law requiring banks to push out derivatives swaps operations from the portion of the bank that is federally insured.

Puerto Rico debt (2015). Lawmakers agreed to allow Puerto Rico to restructure tens of billions of dollars in debt under the oversight of a federally appointed fiscal board.

Trade

Fast-track authority (2015). Acceding to White House priorities, Congress renewed the president's fast-track trade negotiating authority, known as Trade Promotion Authority. This enabled the chief executive to negotiate foreign trade deals that Congress, instead of amending, could only vote up or down in their totality.

Trade Adjustment Assistance (2015). Passed at the same time as fast-track trade authority, this program offered aid for workers displaced from their jobs by international competition.

Homeland Security

Patriot Act (2015). Congress reauthorized the controversial law that had originally passed after the September 11 attacks. But it cut back on the National Security Administration's ability to collect bulk phone records of Americans' phone calls amid concerns over privacy.

Russian influence (2016). In the fiscal year 2017 intelligence authorization bill, Congress targeted Russia, calling for a new executive-branch entity to counteract "Russian actions to exert covert influence over peoples and governments."

Foreign and Defense Policy

Veterans Administration (2014). Responding to a scandal involving months-long wait times for veterans seeking doctor's appointments at VA medical facilities, lawmakers worked across the aisle to authorize $15 billion for various measures to cut wait times for medical appointments for veterans.

North Korea sanctions (2016). Amid growing concerns over North Korea's nuclear weapons program, Congress imposed sanctions that targeted individuals, foreign financial institutions, and governments that either helped the country evade UN sanctions or helped it proliferate nuclear weapons.

Transportation

Highways and transit (2015). Lawmakers cleared a five-year, $281 billion surface transportation authorization bill to fund and repair roads, bridges, and mass transit systems.

Energy and Environment

Keystone Pipeline (2015). Congress passed legislation to approve the proposed TransCanada Keystone XL pipeline, but Obama vetoed it.

The increasingly conservative bent of the Republican Party was demonstrated dramatically in June 2014 when Eric Cantor, R-Va., became the first majority leader in history to lose a primary, as he was unseated by a tea party favorite who emphasized an antigovernment approach to policy. House Republicans faced more drama the following year with the creation of a new, highly conservative faction called the House Freedom Caucus. With several dozen members and an often uncompromising approach to legislation, it had the ability to prevent Republicans from mustering a majority to pass legislation on the floor. On the other flank of the Republican Party, a group of moderates known as the Tuesday Group tried to steer the party away from highly conservative proposals, although they tended to be more malleable than the Freedom Caucus.

The intractable splits among Republicans left Boehner sometimes needing votes from Democrats to pass legislation. Increasingly frustrated, Boehner resigned in October 2015. He was succeeded by Ways and Means Chair Paul D. Ryan, R-Wis., the one House member who appeared to be able to bring together the disparate wings of his party, at least to some degree.

Despite such conflicts, Congress was able to move forward on several high-profile bills. These included a five-year farm bill that changed government support of farmers and cut spending on food stamps, as well as a five-year transportation measure that authorized $305 billion for road and transit programs. Lawmakers also agreed on a major education measure that provided states with more control over the classroom. The Obama administration

Toxic chemicals (2016). With the backing of both environmental groups and manufacturers, lawmakers passed legislation to speed up the EPA review of toxic chemicals amid concerns that the federal agency had fully tested just 200 of 23,000 chemicals introduced since the law was enacted.

Flint water system (2016). In the final days of the 114th Congress, lawmakers added $170 million to a $11.7 billion water resources bill to help Flint, Mich., repair its drinking water system, which contained dangerous levels of lead.

Agriculture and Food

Farm bill (2014). Congress passed a major, five-year reauthorization of agriculture and nutrition programs, making changes to the system that supports farmers when crop prices fall and reducing funding for food stamps.

Genetically modified organisms (2016). Lawmakers agreed to a national labeling standard for foods that contain genetically modified organisms, stopping state and local governments from imposing their own mandatory labeling laws for GMO products.

Health Care

Medicare (2015). After wrestling with the issue of Medicare payments for years, lawmakers agreed to legislation to provide small annual increases in payments and reward doctors and hospitals for quality rather than the number of patients served. This ended a long-time ritual on Capitol Hill of providing "doc fixes" that assured that doctors and hospitals were not hit with annual Medicare payment cuts.

Zika virus (2016). As the mosquito-borne Zika virus infected thousands of Americans, Congress responded with $1.1 billion for mosquito control and surveillance of the disease, vaccine research, and patient treatment.

Education

Student loans (2013). Amid rising concerns over student debt, lawmakers voted to keep interest rates from rising sharply on the Stafford Direct Student Loan program, which was widely used by college students.

School standards (2015). Replacing the often-criticized 2002 law known as No Child Left Behind, Congress passed a sweeping education measure to give states considerably more leeway and flexibility in how they design their performance standards and tests.

Housing

Home purchasing (2016). With the housing market recovery from the economic downturn, Congress passed legislation to add more home-purchasing options for buyers with low incomes or small down payments while also clamping down on reported abuses by families whose incomes were higher than allowed under guidelines for housing assistance.

Labor and Pensions

Pension plans (2014). Lawmakers agreed to a measure that aimed to protect faltering multiemployer pension plans and bolster the Pension Benefit Guarantee Corporation, which was supposed to protect employer-provided retirement accounts but faced the possibility of high deficits in the coming decade.

Law and Justice

Violence Against Women (2013). Lawmakers agreed to a five-year renewal of the Violence Against Women Act, a law with bipartisan support that was designed to prevent domestic and sexual violence and to help victims.

---

won a rare bipartisan victory when a coalition of Republicans joined a small band of protrade Democrats in 2015 to grant fast-track authority for trade agreements.

LEGISLATION AND POLITICS

This book continues a series begun in 1965 with the publication of *Congress and the Nation, Vol. I*, which covered national government and politics from 1945 to 1964. Subsequent volumes, published every four years, covered the same subjects over the two congresses of each succeeding administration. As with the preceding volumes, this edition is divided into a series of chapters focusing on various substantive subjects such as economic and regulatory policy, commerce, law and law enforcement, and foreign policy. This volume, as with recent ones, contains sixteen chapters, an extensive appendix, and a comprehensive index. Following are brief summaries of the chapters and the highlights of events described in them.

Chapter 1: Politics and National Issues

This chapter is an overview of the four-year period from 2013 to 2016, which encompassed Obama's second presidential term and the 113th and 114th Congresses. It discusses the unusually charged political climate that undermined efforts at compromise in Congress and helped power Republican gains in the midterm elections as well as the presidential election of Donald Trump. The major legislative events noted here are covered in more detail in subsequent chapters.

Chapter 2: Economic Policy

This chapter, in four parts, briefly highlights the national economy from 2013 to 2016 and then describes congressional action on economic and financial regulation, budget and tax policy, and trade issues.

National economy. When Obama first took office in 2009, the nation was facing its most severe economic downturn since the 1930s. The repercussions and sluggish economic growth continued to be felt throughout his second term, even though the recession technically ended in mid-2009. Although the economy continued its upward trajectory from 2013 to 2016, salaries lagged, with much of the job growth coming in low-wage positions. Wealth inequality remained widespread.

Economic and financial regulation. Republicans made repeated efforts to repeal or change the 2010 Dodd-Frank Financial Reform and Consumer Protection Act, which they said amounted to excessive government control of the financial sector. Although their efforts were largely unsuccessful, they made relatively minor changes to the law and delayed the confirmation of Obama's nominee to lead the Consumer Financial Protection Bureau until July 2013, thereby limiting the bureau's ability to implement any final regulations.

Lawmakers also passed legislation allowing Puerto Rico to restructure its debt under the oversight of a federally appointed fiscal board. The island territory, which had borrowed and spent excessively for several years, faced about $72 billion of debt, equivalent to 100 percent of its GDP.

Budget and tax policy. Partisan spending battles in the House and Senate repeatedly tied up the 113th and 114th Congresses. Much of the focus was on the sequester, a series of across-the-board federal spending cuts that had been negotiated during Obama's first term. Liberals resisted cuts to social programs, while conservatives pressed to remove restrictions on defense spending. The battles prevented passage of appropriations bills, caused a sixteen-day government shutdown in 2013 and, at times, threatened to delay increases in the debt ceiling.

In fiscal 2015, fiscal 2016, and fiscal 2017, Congress was unable to pass even one of the regular twelve appropriations bills that fund most government agencies. Lawmakers instead relied on continuing resolutions and omnibus measures. By the end of Obama's second term, Congress had still not found a method to entirely replace or eliminate the sequester.

Trade policy. After more than two years of debate, lawmakers in 2015 acceded to White House priorities by renewing the president's fast-track trade authority. This enabled him to negotiate foreign trade deals that Congress, instead of amending, could only vote up or down in their totality. At the same time, lawmakers reauthorized the Trade Adjustment Assistance program that offered aid for workers displaced from their jobs by international competition.

The U.S. Trade Representative signed the twelve-nation Trans-Pacific Partnership Agreement in February 2016. The agreement was a priority for the administration, but questions over Senate ratification of the deal became a contentious topic in that year's presidential race. As Donald Trump made his opposition to trade deals a major component of his campaign, the Senate declined to ratify the agreement.

Chapter 3: Homeland Security

Although homeland security issues did not always divide lawmakers along partisan lines, the high degree of political animosity made it difficult for the administration to win passage of its priorities. This repeatedly stymied Obama's ongoing attempts to close the U.S. detention facility at Guantanamo Bay, Cuba, which held detainees linked to the September 11 attacks.

Controversy developed in 2013 following revelations that the National Security Agency had engaged in the large-scale collection of data from domestic communications sources. Lawmakers attempted to address this issue on various fronts, including seeking to protect Americans' privacy rights and trying to maintain the NSA's ability to monitor the communications of noncitizens. In a 2015 reauthorization of the Patriot Act, a counterterrorism law passed after the September 11 attacks, they cut back on the National Security Administration's ability to collect bulk phone records of Americans' phone calls.

At the end of 2016, lawmakers turned their attention to Russia, which had meddled in that year's U.S. election and intervened militarily in Syria and Ukraine. In the fiscal year 2017 intelligence authorization bill, Congress targeted Russia, calling for a new executive-branch entity to counteract "Russian actions to exert covert influence over peoples and governments."

Chapter 4: Foreign Policy

Obama faced multiple crises on the international stage, from widening violence in the Middle East to North Korea's growing nuclear capabilities. The president also contended with two U.S.-led wars—one in Iraq and one in Afghanistan—that, while subdued somewhat from their peak, still required significant investment of military and diplomatic resources.

One of Obama's biggest challenges was dealing with the rise of the Islamic State in Iraq and Syria (ISIS), which declared a caliphate in 2014 and held significant territory in Iraq and Syria. The militant group's reach spread across the globe, as numerous attacks were either directly carried out by or inspired by the Islamic State. Wary of becoming involved in a ground war, Obama authorized limited air strikes in Iraq while focusing on providing counterterrorism support to Iraqi forces.

North Korea also rattled nerves in Washington by conducting ballistic missile and nuclear tests in defiance of the international community. Over the years, the United States had imposed sanctions on North Korea, typically under the authority of the president or an executive-level department, such as the Treasury. In 2016, however, Congress imposed its first sanctions on North Korea, targeting individuals, foreign financial institutions, and governments that either helped the country evade UN sanctions or helped it proliferate nuclear weapons.

In a bid to reduce tensions with two long-time adversaries, Obama made the controversial decision to normalize diplomatic relations with Cuba and negotiate a multilateral agreement on Iran's nuclear program. But both initiatives were vulnerable to being reversed by a future administration, as they did not have congressional approval.

Chapter 5: Defense Policy

The Obama administration shifted the nation's focus from long-running wars in Iraq and Afghanistan to countering the emerging threat posed by ISIS, responding to internal unrest in the Middle East, and quelling Russian aggression in former Soviet territories.

Obama had succeeded in withdrawing the last U.S. troops from Iraq in his first term under a schedule negotiated by former President George W. Bush with the Iraqi government. In his second term, Obama oversaw the drawdown of the United States' military presence in Afghanistan after thirteen years of fighting an increasingly unpopular war that cost the lives of more than 2,200 American soldiers. Under an agreement reached with the Afghan government, the United States formally ended combat operations in 2014, but coalition troops remained in the country to help train and support Afghan forces.

The Obama administration focused on training and equipping Afghan and Iraqi soldiers to maintain stability and fight terrorist networks in their own countries. In Iraq, this support became a critical element of the administration's strategy for dealing with the rise of ISIS, which declared a caliphate in 2014. Obama was reluctant to commit the United States to another, potentially long-term ground war, preferring instead to provide assistance from afar and conduct airstrikes against ISIS targets in coordination with U.S. partners.

Chapter 6: Transportation, Commerce, and Communications

After passing a series of short-term extensions over the previous decade, Congress in 2015 cleared a five-year, $281 billion surface transportation authorization bill to fund and repair roads, bridges, and mass transit systems. Critics, however, worried that it would fall short of rebuilding the nation's aging infrastructure.

Lawmakers in 2016 also passed several FAA safety requirements in the wake of terrorist attacks at European airports. But they were unable to finalize a long-term extension of the Federal Aviation Administration, settling instead for two short-term authorization extensions. Congress also cleared two short reauthorizations for the Coast Guard.

Republicans looked for ways to rein in the Federal Communications Commission, particularly regarding its 2011 rule on net neutrality. Lawmakers chose to leave untouched several issues that had become mired in previous partisan disagreements—such as digital piracy —while other issues, such as whether to permit Internet sales taxes, came to a standstill when Congress and the White House again could not resolve differences.

Chapter 7: Energy and Environment

Relying on his executive authority, Obama unveiled a major climate change initiative in 2013 aimed at cutting greenhouse gas emissions from power plants, shoring up coastlines against flooding and sea-level rise, and helping advance an international climate deal. The administration released its Clean Power Plan in 2015, requiring states to reduce carbon dioxide emissions. But the plan swiftly drew court challenges.

The issue of climate change also led to ongoing battles between Congress and the administration over the proposed TransCanada Keystone XL pipeline from Canada to the Gulf of Mexico. Obama vetoed a pipeline approval bill in 2015 and then rejected the pipeline over climate concerns. At the 2015 Paris climate talks, he committed the United States to joining other nations in seeking to reduce carbon emissions as well as taking other steps to limit global warming.

Lawmakers were able to find common ground on a few issues. These included approval of water development legislation, updating a law to regulate toxic chemicals in thousands of household and industrial products, and providing funding to assist Flint, Mich., in fixing its lead-tainted drinking water system.

Chapter 8: Agricultural Policy

Despite partisan differences, lawmakers in 2014 approved a much-delayed farm bill that reauthorized agriculture and nutrition programs. The five-year legislation reduced funding for the food stamp program, officially called the Supplemental Nutrition Assistance Program, and it modified programs designed to protect farmers during times of falling crop prices or reduced revenue.

Two years later, lawmakers overcame protracted differences to pass legislation setting up a national labeling standard for foods that contain genetically modified organisms. Lawmakers said a single standard was needed to prevent the states from setting their own standards, a process that was already underway. The new law stopped state and local governments from imposing their own mandatory labeling laws for GMO products.

Chapter 9: Health and Human Services

Republicans continued their largely futile efforts to weaken or repeal Obama's 2010 signature achievement, the Affordable Care Act. The multiyear battles over the law, known as Obamacare, became so intense that they led to a sixteen-day government shutdown in 2013. When Republicans won control of the Senate in the 2014 midterm elections, they finally were able to muster the votes for outright repeal in the 114th Congress. However, Obama vetoed the repeal legislation, leaving the health care bill intact for the next administration.

Lawmakers were able to make progress on other, less contentious health issues. After wrestling with the issue of Medicare payments for years, lawmakers passed legislation to provide small annual increases in payments and reward doctors and hospitals for quality rather than the number of patients served. This ended a long-time ritual on Capitol Hill of providing "doc fixes" that assured that doctors and hospitals were not hit with annual Medicare payment cuts.

Lawmakers reached agreement on legislation to require more parity in payments for physical and mental health treatment and to focus more attention within the Health and Human Services Department on mental health and drug addiction. They also streamlined the U.S. Food and Drug Administration's drug-approval process and provided $1.1 billion in 2016 to respond to a Zika virus outbreak that had infected thousands of Americans.

Chapter 10: Education Policy

Congress and the White House scored a major accomplishment in 2015 with enactment of a sweeping education measure that replaced the often-criticized 2002 law known as No Child Left Behind and its requirements for standards and testing. The new law, known as the Every Child Succeeds Act, would still require states to measure school performance, but the states would get considerably more leeway and flexibility in how they designed their performance standards and tests.

Policy makers, however, struggled to resolve the issue of mounting student debt, which exceeded a total of $1 trillion and made it difficult for young people to build bank accounts, buy houses, and save for the future. After Congress failed to pass major legislation on the issue, Obama signed an executive order that tied the maximum monthly loan repayments to graduates' incomes so the loans would not consume so much of their disposable pay. Separately, lawmakers passed a measure supported by the president to keep interest rates from rising sharply on the Stafford Direct Student Loan program, which was widely used by college students.

Chapter 11: Housing and Urban Aid

With the housing market stabilizing after the economic shocks of recent years, Congress found little urgency to push for new or expanded housing programs. However, it passed legislation in 2016 to add more home-purchasing options for buyers with low incomes or small down payments. The measure also clamped down on reported abuses of the Section 8 program by families whose incomes were higher than allowed under guidelines for housing assistance.

Through a spending bill in fiscal year 2016, lawmakers also provided funding to help the nation's hardest hit communities deal with lingering remnants of the housing and economic crises. This included more money for tearing down foreclosed, abandoned houses, which housing advocates and industrial state lawmakers said would stabilize neighborhoods and stop the slide in home values and underwater mortgages.

Chapter 12: Labor and Pensions

Congress in early 2013 agreed to a one-year extension of long-term unemployment benefits. But Republicans prevented any further extensions, contending they were not needed at a time of economic recovery. Objecting to Democratic priorities, Republicans also temporarily blocked confirmation for several of Obama's executive-branch nominees, including nominees for the National Labor Relations Board, which oversaw union elections and evaluated charges of unfair labor practices.

On another front, Congress in 2014 passed a measure that aimed to protect faltering multiemployer pension plans and bolster the Pension Benefit Guarantee Corporation, which was supposed to protect employer-provided retirement accounts but faced the possibility of high deficits in the coming decade. The new law allowed some plans to reduce participants' benefits if necessary to remain solvent, and it increased the premiums that companies paid to the PBGC.

Chapter 13: Law and Justice

This two-part chapter discusses law-related issues as well as major Supreme Court decisions.

Democrats won a significant victory in 2013 with a five-year renewal of the Violence Against Women Act, which was designed to prevent domestic and sexual violence and to help victims. Otherwise, however, lawmakers made little headway on law-related issues.

After Latinos voted overwhelmingly for Obama in 2012, Democrats and Republicans alike called for an overhaul of the immigration system, which was a top priority of many Latinos and other recent immigrants. But House Republicans refused to sign off on legislation that would have provided a path to citizenship for many of the estimated 11 million illegal immigrants currently living in the country. Obama tried to take matters into his own hands after the midterm elections, issuing executive orders to protect millions of undocumented immigrants from deportation. But the courts, concerned over executive overreach, blocked the orders from taking effect.

Spurred by a series of mass shootings, including the killings of young elementary school students at the end of 2012, Obama urged Congress to expand the system of background checks and renew bans on some military-style assault weapons. Although senators in 2013 attempted to reach a bipartisan agreement on the issue, proposed legislation fell apart in the face of concerted opposition by gun rights advocates and the influential National Rifle Association.

Obama also struggled to fill vacant judgeships. After Senate Democrats made the controversial decision in late 2013 to change filibuster rules, the president was able to place four judges on the influential U.S. Court of Appeals for the District of Columbia Circuit. In 2016, however, Senate Republicans refused to consider the nomination of U.S. appellate judge Merrick Garland for a vacant Supreme Court seat. In a highly unusual move, they said that the winner of the 2016 election should get to decide the next justice. The gambit paid off when Donald Trump won the election.

The Supreme Court steered a generally conservative course during Obama's second term, despite some significant liberal victories, including a decision guaranteeing same-sex couples the right to marry in every state. In 2016, the justices often split, 4–4, after the death of Antonin Scalia, leaving some key constitutional questions unresolved until the next president could fill the vacant seat.

Chapter 14: General Government

Republicans were outraged by a 2013 report by the Treasury Inspector General finding that the Internal Revenue Service had improperly applied extra regulatory scrutiny to conservative groups. They responded by attempting to limit IRS powers in certain ways, including preventing the agency from targeting individuals or groups based on their ideologies. Some House Republicans wanted to impeach IRS Commissioner John Koskinen, contending he had lied under oath about the tax-exempt reviews and had overseen the destruction of records that would have provided important information to investigators looking into the matter. But the proposed impeachment never gained enough traction for passage.

Republicans also repeatedly took aim at the Consumer Financial Protection Bureau (CFPB), which had been created in 2010 as part of Democratic-backed legislation to reorganize financial oversight organizations. The CFPB was charged with enforcing certain financial regulations to protect the American consumer, but Republicans and financial industry groups argued that it lacked appropriate federal oversight. Throughout the 113th and 114th Congresses, Republicans worked to limit its power, but they largely had to settle for adding provisions to legislation that would require additional reporting on its activities.

Lawmakers also sparred over changes to the United States Postal Service (USPS), a quasi-government agency, which was facing a significant financial crisis. Congress agreed to delay required USPS payments to the Treasury to cover anticipated health care expenses of future retirees. But when the postal service advocated additional steps to alleviate its financial woes, such as closing 3,600 low-revenue locations in mostly rural areas and ending Saturday delivery, Congress prohibited such changes.

Chapter 15: Inside Congress

Partisan battles and ideological differences within Republican ranks stymied efforts to pass much major legislation in the 113th and 114th Congresses. Vote studies showed that polarization neared or exceeded record levels, as more and more members voted along party lines. The partisan gridlock prompted a highly contentious decision by Senate Democrats in 2013 to allow a simple majority of fifty-one senators, rather than a supermajority of sixty, to confirm most judges and other administration nominees.

In addition to partisan battles, ideological divisions widened among Republicans. House Speaker John A. Boehner of Ohio, often unable to exert discipline over his caucus, resigned in 2015. Ways and Means Chair Paul D. Ryan, R-Wis., who was highly regarded by Republicans across the ideological spectrum, took his place. In contrast, House minority leader Nancy Pelosi of California retained a firm grip on her caucus, as did Senate Democratic leader Harry Reid of Nevada and Senate Republican leader Mitch McConnell of Kentucky.

The increasingly rancorous atmosphere in Congress made compromise almost impossible and sank high-profile proposals on immigration and other charged issues. Lawmakers, however, cleared several high-priority measures, and they agreed to keep their salaries frozen as a way of highlighting their concern for fiscal austerity.

Chapter 16: The Obama Presidency

Despite a clear electoral victory over Republican presidential nominee Mitt Romney in 2012, Obama failed to build on that momentum to enact his top priorities, such as immigration reform and gun control. Instead, he resorted to issuing executive orders, which were often blocked by the courts. He spent much of the term fending off Republican attempts to weaken or repeal his major first-term accomplishments, especially on health care and financial regulations.

On the international stage, Obama successfully struck an agreement with Iran to freeze that nation's nuclear weapons program. But he failed to end the war in Afghanistan. Despite his efforts to boost the campaign of Hillary Clinton, his presidency ended with the swearing in of Donald J. Trump, who represented a major threat to Obama's legacy. It was a humbling exit for a man who had made history with his election and who had sought to sign a flurry of landmark bills in the first two years of his presidency that aimed to lift the nation out of its deepest economic crisis in generations and provide health care for millions of Americans.

Appendix

The appendix contains a variety of supplemental materials, including a glossary of congressional terms, an explanation of how a bill becomes law, information about House and Senate committees, Senate cloture votes, presidential vetoes, and major presidential speeches and messages to Congress. In addition, the appendix includes extensive political charts, including presidential, House, Senate, and gubernatorial election returns for the period of Obama's second term.

CONTRIBUTORS

This volume has been prepared under the direction of editors at CQ Press, an imprint of SAGE Publications Inc. The chapters were prepared and edited by a group of veteran reporters and freelance writers, several of whom covered Congress for Congressional Quarterly Inc. and other Washington, D.C., news organizations. The principal contributors were Linda Grimm, Bart Jansen, Ken Jost, Deborah Kalb, Heather Kerrigan, Stephen Koff, Christina Lyons, Peter Urban, and David Hosansky, who also served as volume editor.

CHAPTER 1

Politics and National Issues

Politics and National Issues

President Barack Obama's second term in office was characterized by fierce partisanship and a seeming inability on the part of Congress to come to consensus on even minor issues such as keeping the government funded and open. Despite starting his second term with an optimistic inaugural address that outlined a broad liberal agenda, which involved fixing income and social inequality, the president could get few of his policy priorities even considered in Congress, let alone enacted.

Where there was once some level of bipartisanship, members of the 113th and 114th Congresses appeared stuck in a constant election cycle, yelling past each other on cable news shows and searching for ways to rack up points with their respective base. Inactivity reached a new

---

CONGRESSIONAL LEADERSHIP, 2013–2016

113th Congress

Senate

President Pro Tempore: Patrick Leahy, D-Vt.
Majority Leader: Harry Reid, D-Nev.
Majority Whip: Richard J. Durbin, D-Ill.
Democratic Caucus Vice Chair: Charles E. Schumer, D-N.Y.
Democratic Policy Committee Chair: Charles E. Schumer, D-N.Y.
Minority Leader: Mitch McConnell, R-Ky.
Minority Whip: John Cornyn, R-Texas
Republican Conference Chair: John Thune, R-S.D.

House

Speaker of the House: John Boehner, R-Ohio
Majority Leader: Eric Cantor, R-Va./Kevin McCarthy, R-Calif.[1]
Majority Whip: Kevin McCarthy, R-Calif./Steve Scalise, R-La.[2]
Democratic Caucus Chair: Xavier Becerra, D-Calif.
Minority Leader: Nancy Pelosi, D-Calif.
Minority Whip: Steny Hoyer, D-Ma.
Republican Conference Chair: Cathy McMorris Rodgers, R-Wa.

114th Congress

Senate

President Pro Tempore: Orrin Hatch, R-Utah
Majority Leader: Mitch McConnell, R-Ky.
Majority Whip: John Cornyn, R-Texas
Democratic Conference Vice Chair: Charles E. Schumer, D-N.Y.
Democratic Policy Committee Chair: Charles E. Schumer, D-N.Y.
Minority Leader: Harry Reid, D-Nev.
Minority Whip: Richard J. Durbin, D-Ill.
Republican Conference Chair: John Thune, R-S.D.

House

Speaker of the House: John Boehner, R-Ohio/Paul Ryan, R-Wisc.[3]
Majority Leader: Kevin McCarthy, R-Calif.
Majority Whip: Steve Scalise, R-La.
Republican Conference Chair: Cathy McMorris Rodgers, R-Wa.
Minority Leader: Nancy Pelosi, D-Calif.
Minority Whip: Steny Hoyer, D-Md.
Assistant Democratic Leader: James E. Clyburn, D-S.C.

NOTES:

1 Cantor resigned from Congress on August 1, 2014; succeeded by Kevin McCarthy.

2 McCarthy succeeded by Steve Scalise on August 1, 2014.

3 Boehner resigned from Congress on October 29, 2015; succeeded by Paul Ryan.

low in 2013 when Congress managed to pass and enact only seventy-two pieces of legislation, marking it as one of the least productive Congresses in modern history. The political brinksmanship culminated in 2016 with the surprise election of President Donald Trump over his Democratic opponent, former senator and Secretary of State Hillary Clinton. Because Trump had provided few concrete policy proposals and failed to fully embrace the Republican agenda, Congressional leadership was left questioning how well they would be able to work with the new commander in chief, and Democrats were left wondering what Trump's repudiation of Obama's major legislative victories—such as the Affordable Care Act—would mean for the nation.

2013

The Legislative Year

The 113th Congress was on shaky footing from the start, with Democrats in control of the Senate and Republicans holding the House. The congressional split left lawmakers generally unwilling to negotiate to find common ground, something made more difficult by the growing voice of the tea party in the Republican caucus. These far-right, limited-government conservatives fought their party's leadership at every turn, seeking ways to vastly cut or offset government spending. This resulted in a sixteen-day shutdown of the federal government in October that was predicated on a disagreement over the 2010 Patient Protection and Affordable Care Act (ACA), President Obama's landmark piece of health care legislation.

The failure to pass a federal budget was only one in a long list of issues on which Democrats and Republicans could not reach a consensus. Highly charged debates abounded over the debt ceiling, immigration, and gun control. Congressional Republicans were also quick to criticize the Obama administration over two early scandals during the president's second term. The first involved apparent civil liberties violations. According to Britain's *The Guardian* newspaper, the National Security Agency (NSA) was carrying out top-secret surveillance programs that collected information on electronic communications in bulk without individual warrants. Some of these activities were not necessarily linked to anyone conducting illegal activity. The issue was challenged in court, and the Court of Appeals for the Second Circuit ruled in 2015 that the NSA had exceeded the scope of its authority under the Patriot Act. However, because Congress had allowed the challenged provisions of the Patriot Act to lapse, the NSA was given six months to amend its surveillance activities.

The administration also drew fire when a report by the Internal Revenue Service (IRS) Inspector General came to light in 2013, revealing that conservative groups had been improperly targeted for additional scrutiny when applying for 501(c)(4) tax-exempt status. A directive circulated throughout the IRS advised that staff should specifically watch for applications containing the words "tea party," "Patriots," and "9/12 Project." Use of the list was discontinued in late 2012, but Republicans demanded that those responsible be held to account. Lois Lerner, head of the division in charge of tax-exempt status reviews, left her position, and was later held in contempt of Congress, a largely symbolic charge, over her refusal to testify during two separate hearings. The battle over the IRS would stretch on into 2015, when the House attempted, unsuccessfully, to impeach IRS Commissioner John Koskinen. Although Koskinen became commissioner after the incidents in question occurred, Republicans claimed that he lied while testifying about the matter before Congress—while under oath—and that he oversaw the destruction of key records that could have provided important findings.

The biggest news in Washington in 2013, however, was Congressional inaction—or at most limited action—especially as it related to the high-profile issues of immigration, gun control, the debt ceiling, and the federal budget. On March 1, as required by the Budget Control Act of 2011 (and a subsequent bill to delay action), President Obama signed an executive order setting in motion a series of defense and domestic budget cuts known as the sequester. The across-the-board reductions were brought on by an inability of Congress in 2011 to decide how to offset an increase in the debt ceiling and by the subsequent 2012 failure to agree on more targeted cuts to stave off the sequester.

Members floated a variety of ideas throughout 2013 to stop the automatic cuts. Republicans sought deeper cuts to nondefense programs and entitlement program changes, while Democrats wanted to entirely replace the sequester and increase federal spending, which they intended to offset with tax increases for corporations and the wealthiest Americans. In March, the president signed into law a cromnibus bill (so called because it combined elements of an omnibus spending package with a continuing resolution) that included greater flexibility for the managers of some programs—primarily related to the military and the Food and Drug Administration—to distribute funds in the way they saw fit in an effort to ease sequester cuts. This raised Democratic objections, because Republicans had not offered similar flexibility to other agencies. By the close of 2013, the sequester was still in place.

Twice in 2013, Congress was forced to consider increasing the debt ceiling, the limit on how much the government can borrow to pay its debts. Once in January and again in October, House and Senate Republicans and Democrats struggled to reach consensus on increasing the debt limit, with Republicans working to match any increase with spending cuts and Democrats seeking a clean bill. If it were to default on its payments, the government faced a downgrade of its credit rating (which had already happened two years earlier during the 2011 fight over the debt ceiling) and decreased investor confidence, not to mention an inability to fund its long-term obligations to programs such as Social Security and military benefits. In both instances, the two parties managed to find common ground and temporarily raise the debt ceiling, allowing for further negotiation on the issue at a later time.

On immigration and gun control, Congress faced pressure from the public to act, but Democrats and Republicans found themselves too far apart to enact meaningful legislation. The Senate passed a bill in June 2013 to create a path to citizenship for illegal immigrants

CONGRESS IN 2013

The first session of the 113th Congress began on January 3, 2013. The House was in session on 160 days for a total of 767 hours and adjourned January 3, 2014. The Senate was in session on 156 days for a total of 1,095 hours and adjourned January 3, 2014.

Members introduced 2,280 bills and resolutions during the year, a record low since 2008. Congress cleared 72 bills that became public law. President Barack Obama did not veto any bills during the 113th Congress. *(See public laws table, p. 12; presidential vetoes, p. 647.)*

The House took 640 roll-call votes (excluding quorum calls) in 2013, 305 fewer than in 2011. The Senate took 291 recorded votes during the year, 56 more than in 2011. *(See recorded votes table, p. 13.)*

already in the United States who met certain qualifications. The bill also enhanced border security and adjusted the U.S. visa system. At the time, Sen. Chuck Schumer, D-N.Y., leader of the so-called Gang of Eight (four Democrats and four Republicans who had negotiated the bill), said it had generated so much support that the House would be unable to ignore it. However, the House did not even consider the Senate's legislation, instead moving four immigration-related bills out of committee, none of which received a floor vote.

Similarly, on gun control, despite a spate of mass shootings in 2012 and 2013, Congress could not find common ground. Democrats and Republicans in the House and Senate proposed a variety of bills, some of which attempted to expand gun rights, while others looked to enhance background checks and renew an expired assault weapons ban. Nothing had enough support to pass both houses, so the president instead opted to issue more than two dozen executive actions on gun control.

Perhaps the greatest illustration in the stark divide in Congress came on October 1, 2013, when nonessential federal government operations shut down for sixteen days and an estimated 800,000 federal employees were furloughed. Although the House had passed a budget to keep the government open through December 15, it contained policy riders that were nonstarters in the Senate, such as a complete defunding of the Affordable Care Act (ACA). The Senate amended the bill and removed the ACA language, but the House refused to pass it. It was not until nearly midnight on October 16 when the two parties formulated the Continuing Appropriations Act of 2014 to keep the federal government funded through January 15, 2014. The compromise legislation also

addressed the debt ceiling, raising it through February 2014 without any associated budget cuts.

RECORD LOW NUMBER OF LAWS ENACTED BY CONGRESS

In the 2012 presidential election, Republicans took control of the House of Representatives, but Democrats maintained their control of the Senate and even gained two seats. This almost ensured that the partisan bickering that had marred congressional activity for the previous two decades would continue and set the body up for what became a record-breaking year in its inability to agree to and enact legislation. What Congress was able to accomplish in 2013 was limited in scope and often focused more on just keeping the government funded and open than working toward long-term solutions to address the nation's issues.

Many of the debates in Congress were characterized by the ongoing breakdown of what is known as "regular order," the standard process of moving bills from committee or subcommittee through the holding of floor votes. That process is intended to build consensus among lawmakers and allow both parties to provide input for legislation before the chambers. Regular order was almost never exercised in 2013, as Republicans in the House and Senate made nearly every bill that came up for consideration about either offsetting spending increases or attempting to eliminate provisions of the Patient Protection and Affordable Care Act (ACA). The House voted multiple times to outright repeal the president's landmark legislation, and also attempted to attach policy riders to appropriations bills that would limit the ability of agencies to implement their portions of the law. These unrelated fights derailed legislation—including some that was bipartisan in nature—on issues ranging from energy efficiency to the president's authority to oversee Keystone XL pipeline permits to a reauthorization of the farm and nutrition bills.

PRESIDENTIAL PRIORITIES REMAIN STALLED

Three weeks after President Obama delivered his inaugural address, he stood before a joint session of Congress to give the first State of the Union address of his second term. He outlined a list of domestic priorities, including reinvigorating the economy, improving the U.S. education system, and growing the middle class. President Obama called on the newly divided Congress to set aside their partisan differences and work together to meet the needs of the nation. He asked that Republicans and Democrats partner on passing a budget that makes smart investments in the country's future without relying on the brinksmanship that strains the U.S. economy.

One of the key issues facing the economy in the near term was the sequester implemented under the Budget Control Act of 2011. These across-the-board automatic spending cuts were originally set to take place on January 2, 2013, but just one day prior, Congress voted to delay implementation for two months. However, the body failed to find a compromise on a way to replace or lessen the impact of the sequester, other than some tactics used in the fiscal 2013 budget that allowed a handful of agencies greater ability to shift funds in order to accommodate the cuts. Democrats and Republicans were at odds over how else to address the sequester, with Democrats calling for new taxes to replace the automatic cuts, while Republicans thought the burden could be made up through entitlement reform and non–defense-appropriation reductions. The president backed Democrats, asking why cuts should be made to education and Medicare budgets in order to protect special interest tax breaks. He added, "Why is it that deficit reduction is a big emergency justifying cuts in Social Security benefits, but not closing some loopholes? How does that promote growth?" The president would change his tune slightly in April when the White House released the president's annual budget request, one that included some entitlement program changes that both Democrats and Republicans balked at.

Other major priorities addressed by the president were immigration and gun control. Although there was bipartisan agreement in Congress that those issues were vital and should be addressed with haste, there was little consensus on how that should be done. Both Republicans and Democrats had an interest in immigration reform, because both parties were dependent on the growing fraction of Hispanics in the United States to support them in elections. In the State of the Union address, Obama asked Congress to develop a bipartisan immigration bill that would penalize those in the country illegally while still providing them a path to citizenship. On gun control, the president asked for legislation that included background checks at gun shows, a ban on semi-automatic weapons, a limit on the size of magazines, and new policies to prevent guns from being sold to criminals. The president made clear that he did not want to infringe on the Second Amendment rights of Americans, while also noting that a majority of citizens support some kind of gun control legislation.

Despite a threat from the president that he would act unilaterally by executive order if Congress were unable to reach a compromise on any of his priorities, the body took no decisive action on most of the president's key issues. In fact, lawmakers found themselves so deadlocked by the end of the year that they were unable to keep the government funded for fiscal 2014, and a sixteen-day federal government shutdown resulted.

CONGRESSIONAL GRIDLOCK FURTHER DISAFFECTS AMERICANS

Despite some minor victories celebrated on Capitol Hill, the gridlock over major issues resulted in an ever-decreasing opinion of Congress among the American public. In the final three months of the year, Congressional disapproval averaged 84 percent in two dozen nationwide polls. In one, conducted by CNN from December 16 to 19, 73 percent of the 1,035

Table 1.1 Partisanship in Congress, 2013–2016

The table shows the percentage of times that the majority of one party voted against the majority of the other during President Barack Obama's second term. In the 113th and 114th Congresses, nearly three of every four votes split the two parties in the House. Even in the Senate, with a more bipartisan tradition, the two parties differed on about two-thirds of votes during most of the second Obama administration. These were among the highest percentages of party unity votes since *Congressional Quarterly* began this study in 1953.

	2013	2014	2015	2016
Party Unity (% of votes in which majority of party voted together)				
House Democrats	88	90	92	91
House Republicans	92	91	92	93
Senate Democrats	94	93	91	91
Senate Republicans	86	84	89	86
Partisan Votes (% of total)				
House	68.6	72.6	75.1	73.4
Senate	69.8	66.7	69.3	46.0

respondents said Congress had done nothing during the year to address the nation's problems, while two-thirds considered the 113th Congress the worst in their lifetimes. Congress had a similarly low opinion of itself, with Senate Majority Leader Harry Reid, D-Nev., joking that the current Congress was less popular than a cockroach. But the two parties differed on who was responsible. Republicans frequently placed the fault with Democrats, but Democrats said it was a result of obstructionism on the part of Republicans. House Speaker John Boehner, R-Ohio, would concede that both parties bore some of the blame and that many factors had slowed progress in Congress.

Minor victories came throughout the year. They included the January votes to appropriate emergency relief and long-term assistance funds to states affected by Superstorm Sandy. Even that came with a delay, however, because members from affected states had pushed leadership to bring a bill to the floor providing the funding in December 2012, but the body moved instead to recess before a vote could be held. Growing discontent within the Republican caucus and across the aisle forced House Speaker John Boehner, R-Ohio, to move forward on a funding package when the 113th Congress convened in January. In the end, the total recovery package from the federal government reached more than $60 billion and included $9.7 billion for the National Flood Insurance Program to help handle claims related to the storm. The funds provided were awarded only to the Northeast, despite the storm's vast reach. (*See discussion of Sandy disaster bill in Chapter 2, pp. 63–65.*)

The body twice voted on raising the debt ceiling, the limit on how much the government can borrow to pay its debts, once in January and again in October to stop the nation from defaulting, which may have resulted in another embarrassing downgrade of the U.S. credit rating. Those votes did not come without a fight, however. Republicans and Democrats in the House and Senate struggled to reach consensus on increasing the debt limit because Republicans sought to match any increase with spending cuts, while

Democrats wanted a clean bill. To win Republican votes, the January increase was written in a way that did not place a cap on how much the Treasury could borrow, instead giving it discretion to borrow what was necessary to avoid a default. This open-ended plan meant that spending cuts could not be set to match a specific number that did not exist. In addition, a provision was added to defer lawmaker salaries unless each chamber adopted a fiscal 2014 budget resolution by the statutory deadline of April 15, which they both ultimately did. The October increase was added to the Continuing Appropriations Act, a bill that extended current funding levels to federal agencies through January 15, 2014, and raised the debt ceiling until February 7, 2014, thus guaranteeing another fight on the issue during the second session of the 113th Congress. *(See discussion of debt ceiling limit in Chapter 2, pp. 65–66.)*

The body also managed to pass a defense authorization bill, albeit at the last minute. Every year since 1961, Congress has passed the bill, typically with broad bipartisan support, to provide basic needs for the military and cover any wars or overseas commitments. Intense partisanship made the authorization process increasingly difficult, and Congress came very close to not passing a bill before the close of 2013. Disagreements revolved primarily around process rather than the bill's content, with Democrats pushing for a quick vote and Republicans seeking time to review the hundreds of amendments that were offered. Because the bill stalled in the Senate, the House and Senate Armed Services Committees could not officially conference on the measure, so they instead met informally to write a new bill that both chambers accepted late in December. *(See discussion of fiscal 2014 defense authorization in Chapter 5, pp. 185–187.)*

Lawmakers also counted among their achievements the reauthorization of the Violence Against Women Act, a student loan program overhaul, new rules for compounding pharmacies and tracking pharmaceuticals, and a repeal of the ban on organ transplants for HIV-infected patients.

NO REAL WINNERS

Although Congress had a plethora of issues to consider, it focused most of its time on funding bills and authorizations. Both parties were forced to accept concessions, and neither got everything they wanted. For example, in late December, Congress debated a budget agreement to raise discretionary spending caps for fiscal 2014 and 2015, intended to help lessen the impact of the sequester. Although Democrats sought tax increases and Republicans wanted at least some type of entitlement reform, neither was included, nor did the bill fully replace the sequester, something President Obama had supported.

Partisan politics came to a head in November, when Senate Democrats acted unilaterally to invoke the so-called nuclear option, essentially a rule change eliminating the ability of the Senate minority to filibuster presidential nominees that required Senate confirmation (Supreme Court justices were not included in the bill). Prior to the rule change, breaking a filibuster to vote on a motion to close debate and consider the nomination required a sixty-vote supermajority, but the rare parliamentary move allowed filibusters to be stopped by a simple majority vote, which the Democrats had in 2013. Sen. Reid invoked the measure in an attempt to break the stalemate that had ensued over President Obama's nomination of multiple federal judges and other office holders. Reid said he was doing so because the Senate must change in order to survive. Republicans warned that the decision would come back to haunt them once they were again in the minority, while parliamentary analysts said the decision impacted the character of the Senate, which has traditionally enjoyed greater bipartisanship and civility than the House. *(See "Senate Democrats Confirm Judges after Weakening Filibuster" box in Chapter 13, pp. 395–396.)*

Neither the House nor the Senate could move through either vital legislation or seemingly mundane issues. And at times the deadlock was not just between the two parties but within them as well. House Republican leaders faced a rebellion from their own members during an attempt to reauthorize the bill that covers farm and nutrition programs. They tried a number of tactics to get it passed, including splitting the bill into parts in order to go to conference with the Senate to resolve any disagreements over the bill. But at the end of

Table 1.2 Age Structure of Congress, 1949–2015

Year	House	Senate	Congress
1949	51.0	58.5	53.8
1951	52.0	56.6	53.0
1953	52.0	56.6	53.0
1955	51.4	57.2	52.2
1957	52.9	57.9	53.8
1959	51.7	57.1	52.7
1961	52.2	57.0	53.2
1963	51.7	56.8	52.7
1965	50.5	57.7	51.9
1967	50.8	57.7	52.1
1969	52.2	56.6	53.0
1971	51.9	56.4	52.7
1973	51.1	55.3	52.0
1975	49.8	55.5	50.9
1977	49.3	54.7	50.3
1979	48.8	52.7	49.5
1981	48.4	52.5	49.2
1983	45.5	53.4	47.0
1985	49.7	54.2	50.5
1987	50.7	54.4	52.5
1989	52.1	55.6	52.8
1991	52.8	57.2	53.6
1993	51.7	58.0	52.9
1995	50.9	58.4	52.2
1997	51.6	57.5	52.7
1999	52.6	58.3	53.7
2001	55.4	59.8	54.4
2003	54.0	59.7	55.5
2005	55.0	60.4	56.0
2007	56.0	61.2	57.1
2009	57.2	63.1	58.2
2011	56.7	62.2	59.5
2013	57.0	62.0	59.5
2015	57.0	61.0	59.0

NOTE: The table shows average age of members at the beginning of each Congress.

the year, the measure remained stalled. The House, was, however, able to pass four of twelve regular appropriations bills.

Spending issues were the same in the Senate where, despite issuing a fiscal 2014 budget for the first time in three years by the required deadline, they only managed to get one free-standing appropriation bill to the floor, that which covered the departments of Transportation and Housing and Urban Development. Leadership ultimately decided not to hold a vote on the bill after Republicans threatened a filibuster.

PARTISANSHIP HAMPERS PROGRESS

Some congressional scholars were quick to rate the first year of the 113th Congress as one of the worst in terms of productivity. Edward Carmines, the research director at the Center on Congress at Indiana University, said the current Congress was at a fifty-year low in terms of the number of bills enacted, the substance of what was debated and passed, and the issues that were ignored. However, there is vast evidence that partisan tension had been worse in the past than it was in 2013. In the late nineteenth and early twentieth centuries, partisanship was rampant, and it took a world war to force members of Congress to seek bipartisan solutions for the good of the country. But by the late twentieth and early twenty-first centuries, that goodwill had eroded, and another era of divided government was ushered in.

According to a *Congressional Quarterly* analysis, 2013 marked the first time in more than sixty years that the percentage of partisan votes in the House and Senate had been so high, with the two parties differing on around seven out of every ten roll-call votes. Leadership on both sides decried outside influence on Congress for encouraging their members to vote in ways that did not reflect the spirit of compromise they were sometimes trying to reach.

This partisanship slowed progress to a crawl. It can be difficult to measure the impact or productivity of Congress, because what Republicans and Democrats view as success is starkly different, and merely counting the number of laws enacted does not account for those that take extreme compromise and partisan wrangling, versus those that rename federal buildings for a war hero. The president signed a total of seventy-two new statutes in 2013, every one that crossed his desk, which marked the smallest number since before World War II. The previous low was set just two years earlier, in 2011, at ninety. The Senate met for fewer days than was typical for a nonelection year and held fewer roll-call votes than in all but one nonelection year since 2003. Although the House met frequently, it ended its days earlier than usual and also took fewer roll-call votes.

The Political Year

Seven special elections were held in 2013, two in the Senate and five for the House. None of the races shifted the balance of power in either body, nor did any single seat change party hands.

Massachusetts Sen. John Kerry resigned his Senate seat in February 2013 following his confirmation as U.S. Secretary of State. Kerry had held the seat since 1985, and it was widely anticipated that another Democrat would replace him. Gov. Deval Patrick appointed Mo Cowan, his former chief of staff, to serve as interim senator until a special election could be held. Rep. Ed Markey, representing Massachusetts' 7th Congressional District, won the Democratic nomination in the April primary, defeating Rep. Stephen Lynch of Massachusetts' 8th Congressional District. Three Republicans sought their party's nomination: former Navy SEAL Gabriel Gomez, former U.S. Attorney for the District of Massachusetts Michael Sullivan, and state Rep. Daniel Winslow. Gomez easily won the nomination, with 51 percent of the vote compared to Sullivan's 36 percent and Winslow's 13 percent. Markey defeated Gomez in the June election, winning 55 percent of the vote.

In New Jersey, Sen. Frank Lautenberg died from complications of pneumonia in June 2013. Lautenberg had been the oldest member of the Senate and the chamber's only remaining World War II veteran. He had already announced in February 2013 that he would not seek reelection when his term was up the following year.

Table 1.3 Presidential Vote by Region

Democrat Barack Obama in 2012 won reelection by a comfortable margin, taking 65.9 million votes to former governor Mitt Romney's 60.9 million for a margin of just under 5 million votes, or 3.9 percentage points. The regional vote shows Republican Romney dominating the southern states, and Democrat Obama in full command of the eastern and western regions and splitting the midwestern region but winning the vote-heavy states of Michigan, Ohio, Illinois, Minnesota, and Wisconsin.

In 2016, Democrat Hillary Clinton won the popular vote against Republican Donald J. Trump by 2,868,686 votes, but was projected to receive fewer electoral votes. In a major upset in December, the Electoral College gave the election to Trump, 304–227 votes, the second time in fifteen years the candidate with the popular vote lost the presidential election. *(See Political Charts Appendix, 2016 Presidential Election, p. 662.)*

	2012			
	Popular Votes		*Electoral Votes*	
Region	*Obama*	*Romney*	*Obama*	*Romney*
East	59%	21%	112	5
Midwest	51	38	80	38
South	44	54	42	133
West	54	43	98	30
National	51	47	332	206

	2016			
	Popular Votes		*Electoral Votes*	
Region	*Trump*	*Clinton*	*Trump*	*Clinton*
East	19%	24%	26	91
Midwest	25	22	88	30
South	38	30	160	13
West	18	24	30	93
National	46	48	304	227

Table 1.4 Incumbents Reelected, Defeated, or Retired, 1946–2016

Year	Retired	Total Seeking Reelection	Defeated in Primaries	Defeated in General Election	Total Reelected	Percentage of Those Seeking Reelection	Year	Retired	Total Seeking Reelection	Defeated in Primaries	Defeated in General Election	Total Reelected	Percentage of Those Seeking Reelection
House							Senate						
1946	32	398	18	52	328	82.4	1946	9	30	6	7	17	56.7
1948	29	400	15	68	317	79.3	1948	8	25	2	8	15	60.0
1950	29	400	6	32	362	90.5	1950	4	32	5	5	22	68.8
1952	42	389	9	26	354	91.0	1952	4	31	2	9	20	64.5
1954	24	407	6	22	379	93.1	1954	6	32	2	6	24	75.0
1956	21	411	6	16	389	94.6	1956	6	29	0	4	25	86.2
1958	33	396	3	37	356	89.9	1958	6	28	0	10	18	64.3
1960	27	405	5	25	375	92.6	1960	4	29	0	1	28	96.6
1962	24	402	12	22	368	91.5	1962	4	35	1	5	29	82.9
1964	33	397	8	45	344	86.6	1964	2	33	1	4	28	84.8
1966	23	411	8	41	362	88.1	1966	3	32	3	1	28	87.5
1968	24	408	4	9	395	96.8	1968	6	28	4	4	20	71.4
1970	30	401	10	12	379	94.5	1970	4	31	1	6	24	77.4
1972	40	392	14	13	366	93.4	1972	6	27	2	5	20	74.1
1974	43	391	8	40	343	87.7	1974	7	27	2	2	23	85.2
1976	47	384	3	13	368	95.8	1976	8	25	0	9	16	64.0
1978	49	382	5	19	358	93.7	1978	10	25	3	7	15	60.0
1980	34	398	6	31	361	90.7	1980	5	29	4	9	16	55.2
1982	31	387	4	29	354	91.5	1982	3	30	0	2	28	93.3
1984	22	409	3	16	390	95.4	1984	4	29	0	3	26	89.7
1986	38	393	2	6	385	98.0	1986	6	28	0	7	21	75.0
1988	23	408	1	6	401	98.3	1988	6	27	0	4	23	85.2
1990	27	407	1	15	391	96.1	1990	3	32	0	1	31	96.9
1992	65	368	19	24	325	88.3	1992	7	28	1	4	23	82.1
1994	48	387	4	34	349	90.2	1994	9	26	0	2	24	92.3
1996	49	384	2	21	361	94.0	1996	13	21	1	1	19	90.5
1998	33	402	1	6	395	98.3	1998	4	30	0	3	27	90.0
2000	32	405	3	6	396	97.8	2000	5	29	0	6	23	79.3
2002	35	398	8	8	382	96.0	2002	5	28	1	3	24	85.7
2004	29	404	2	7	395	97.8	2004	8	26	0	1	25	96.2
2006	27	404	2	22	380	94.1	2006	4	29	1	6	23	79.3
2008	32	403	4	19	380	94.3	2008	5	30	0	5	25	83.3
2010	36	397	4	54	339	85.4	2010	12	25	3	2	21	84.0
2012	39	391	13	27	351	89.8	2012	10	23	1	1	21	91.2
2014	41	392	4	14	374	95.4	2014	7	28	0	5	23	82.1
2016	43	392	5	8	379	96.7	2016	5	29	0	2	27	93.1

SOURCES: Norman J. Ornstein, Thomas E. Mann, and Michael J. Malbin, *Vital Statistics on Congress 2001–2002* (Washington, DC: American Enterprise Institute, 2002); *CQ Weekly*, selected issues; Richard Scammon, Alice McGillivray, and Rhodes Cook, *America Votes 24* (Washington, DC: CQ Press, 2001) various editions; Harold W. Stanley and Richard G. Niemi, *Vital Statistics on American Politics, 2013–2014* (Washington, DC: CQ Press, 2013); *Vital Statistics on American Politics, 2015–2016* (Washington, DC: CQ Press, 2016).

NOTE: The column titled "Retired" does not include persons who died or resigned before the election except in the case of deaths, for candidates whose name remained on the ballot. Some numbers in the table involved incumbents defeated in primaries but who won as independents in the general election. For details on these and other special cases, consult footnotes in Stanley/Niemi, *Vital Statistics on American Politics, 2015–2016.*

The heavily Democratic state held primaries in August 2013 and the special election in October. Newark Mayor Cory Booker defeated Rep. Rush Holt of New Jersey's 12th Congressional District, Rep. Frank Pallone of the 6th Congressional District, and General Assembly Speaker Sheila Oliver to win the Democratic nomination. The former mayor of Bogota, New Jersey—Steve Lonegan—won the Republican nomination over Dr. Alieta Eck. Booker won the election with nearly 55 percent of the vote, making him the first African American senator from New Jersey.

In the House, Rep. Jesse Jackson Jr. resigned his seat in November 2012, citing health problems including an ongoing battle with bipolar disorder. At the time, Jackson was also facing a federal investigation of allegations that he

had misused campaign funds for personal purchases. Jackson had represented Illinois' 2nd Congressional District since 1995. The special election to fill Jackson's seat was held in April 2013. Robin Kelly, Chief Administrative Officer for Cook County, beat sixteen other candidates to win the Democratic primary, while ex-convict Paul McKinley won the Republican primary by less than 1 percent. Kelly easily defeated McKinley, and Green Party candidate LeAlan Jones, with about 71 percent of the vote.

South Carolina 1st Congressional District Rep. Tim Scott was appointed by Gov. Nikki Haley to fill the Senate seat vacated by Jim DeMint in December 2012. Scott resigned his seat in Congress the following month. A crowded Republican primary to replace Scott featured sixteen candidates and culminated in a runoff between former Gov. Mark Sanford—who previously represented the 1st Congressional District—and former Charleston County Councilman Curtis Bostic. Sanford defeated Bostic with 57 percent of the runoff vote. He went on to win 54 percent of the vote in the special election, beating out Democratic candidate Elizabeth Colbert Busch, the director of business development for Clemson University's Restoration Institute, and Green Party candidate Eugene Platt, a James Island Public Service Commissioner.

Rep. Jo Ann Emerson resigned from her seat representing Missouri's 8th Congressional District in December 2012 to become CEO of the National Rural Electric Cooperative Association. Under Missouri law, the state Republican and Democratic Parties can choose their own nominees without holding a primary. The Republican Party selected state Rep. Jason Smith as its candidate, while the Democratic Party chose state Rep. John Hodges. Also on the special election ballot were Libertarian Party candidate Bill Slantz and Constitution Party nominee Doug Enyart. Constituents in the heavily Republican district elected Smith with 67 percent of the vote.

After Rep. Markey vacated his seat to complete outgoing Sen. John Kerry's term, a special election was held to select the next representative for Massachusetts' 5th Congressional District. The Democratic primary featured seven candidates, with state Sen. Katherine Clark emerging as the winner with 32 percent of the vote. Lawyer Frank Addivinola won the Republican primary with 49 percent of the vote, defeating two other candidates. Clark defeated Addivinola with more than 65 percent of the vote, keeping the seat solidly within Democratic control and marking more than ninety consecutive congressional losses by Republicans in Massachusetts.

Alabama 1st Congressional District Rep. Jo Bonner resigned from his seat in May 2013 to become the vice chancellor of government relations and economic development for the University of Alabama system. Real estate agent Burton LeFlore won the Democratic primary with 70 percent of the vote, defeating Lula Albert-Kaigler. Nine Republicans sought their party's nomination, with former state Sen. Bradley Byrne and businessman Dean Young emerging as the leading candidates and advancing to a runoff vote. Byrne won the nomination with 52 percent of the runoff vote, compared to Young's 47 percent. Reflecting the district's heavily conservative constituency, Byrne handily defeated LeFlore with 70 percent of the vote.

Citing frustrations with increased partisanship in Washington, D.C., Rep. Rodney Alexander announced in August 2013 that he would not seek reelection. Rodney resigned from his seat representing Louisiana's 5th Congressional District the following month to become secretary of the state's Department of Veterans Affairs. Louisiana holds nonpartisan qualifying primaries rather than individual party primaries, meaning all fourteen candidates for Alexander's seat competed in a single primary in October 2013. The top two vote getters advance to the general election. In this case, state Sen. Neil Riser and businessman Vance McAllister—both Republicans—advanced to the November election. There was some controversy surrounding Riser's candidacy, with other candidates accusing Alexander and Gov. Bobby Jindal of giving Riser advance notice of Alexander's resignation. These allegations were driven in part by Riser's filings with the Federal Election Commission, which were dated before Alexander announced his resignation. McAllister ultimately defeated Riser with 60 percent of the vote.

2014

The Legislative Year

Because 2014 included a midterm election, it was all but certain that it would be another year of low productivity for Congress. Congress did agree to one major measure in 2014, passing a thirteen-month extension of the debt limit. As in 2013, the debate revolved around Republicans seeking an offset to the $17.3 trillion limit, while Democrats rejected any such attempt. Wanting to avoid a default in an election year—and under their watch—House Republicans ultimately dropped their demands. But they appeared to fully intend to use the fight as a campaign issue.

President Barack Obama, frustrated by the Congressional lack of progress, repeatedly exercised his executive authority on issues ranging from discrimination in the workplace to illegal immigration. In April, the president signed an executive order and presidential memorandum that gave employees of federal contractors the freedom to discuss their wages with colleagues and required employers to make their compensation structures more transparent. The intent of the action was to help close the wage gap between men and women. In July, the president signed another action aimed at federal contractors, as well as federal employees, this time extending hiring protections to gender identity and sexual orientation. In November, the president signed his most controversial executive actions to date that addressed the issue of the estimated 11 million illegal immigrants living in the United States. The executive orders included provisions to improve border security and defer the deportations for certain groups of illegal immigrants already in the United States.

Republicans used the president's executive orders in their midterm campaigns as an example of executive overreach and highlighted the need to send more Republicans to Washington to act as a check on the president's power. Both parties also placed a heavy focus on which was better suited to help the middle class. The biggest surprise during the midterms came during primary season, when House majority leader Eric Cantor of Virginia was defeated by David Brat, a college professor. Cantor was the first sitting majority leader to lose his primary reelection campaign, and he went on to resign both his leadership position and his House seat.

By the time the votes were counted, Republicans had kept control of the House and won back control of the Senate. They were able to hold all of their current seats in the Senate and win nine new ones, including the unseating of Democratic incumbents in Alaska, Arkansas, Colorado, Louisiana, and North Carolina. In the House, Republicans held their largest number of seats since 1928, at 247. Republicans planned to use their new power to push through conservative priorities, including a repeal of the Affordable Care Act.

113TH CONGRESS'S SECOND LOW-PRODUCTIVITY YEAR

The second year of the 113th Congress was again marred by inaction on the part of lawmakers, who frequently could not reach consensus either between or within their own parties. Republicans in particular found themselves on shaky footing as the ultra-conservative tea party members within their own caucus rebelled against leadership. They faced a leadership shakeup in the House

---

CONGRESS IN 2014

The second session of the 113th Congress began January 3, 2014. The House adjourned January 2, 2015. The Senate adjourned December 16, 2014. The House was in session on 135 days for a total of 704 hours. The Senate was in session on 136 days for a total of 908 hours.

A total of 1,432 bills and resolutions were introduced in the two chambers in 2014, 848 fewer than in 2013. Congress signed 224 bills into public law. For the fourth year in a row, President Barack Obama issued no vetoes. *(See public laws table, p. 12; presidential vetoes, p. 647.)*

The House took 563 roll-call votes (excluding quorum calls) in 2014, 382 fewer than in 2011. The Senate took 366 recorded votes, 131 more than in 2011. *(See recorded votes table, p. 13.)*

Table 1.5 Number of Public Laws Enacted, 1975–2016

Year	Public Laws	Year	Public Laws
1975	205	1996	245
1976	383	1997	153
1977	223	1998	241
1978	410	1999	170
1979	187	2000	410
1980	426	2001	136
1981	145	2002	241
1982	328	2003	198
1983	215	2004	300
1984	408	2005	169
1985	240	2006	248
1986	424	2007	161
1987	242	2008	321
1988	471	2009	125
1989	240	2010	258
1990	410	2011	90
1991	243	2012	193
1992	347	2013	72
1993	210	2014	224
1994	255	2015	115
1995	88	2016	214

Table 1.6 Recorded Vote Totals

Following are the recorded vote totals between 1955 and 2016. The figures do not include quorum calls or two House roll calls in 2011 and 2012 that were vitiated. The numbers, while high during President Barack Obama's first term, did not set records. The highest total for the Senate was 688 recorded votes in 1976. The highest number in the House was 1,177 in 2007. Also in 2007 Congress set a new record for the highest number of recorded votes ever taken in a single year: 1,619. But the 95th Congress (1977–1979) still held the record for the most votes taken in a single Congress: 2,691.

Year	House	Senate	Total
1955	76	87	163
1956	73	130	203
1957	100	107	207
1958	93	200	293
1959	87	215	302
1960	93	207	300
1961	116	204	320
1962	124	224	348
1963	119	229	348
1964	113	305	418
1965	201	258	459
1966	193	235	428
1967	245	315	560
1968	233	281	514
1969	177	245	422
1970	266	422	688
1971	320	423	743
1972	329	532	861
1973	541	594	1,135
1974	537	544	1,081
1975	612	602	1,214
1976	661	688	1,349
1977	706	635	1,341
1978	834	516	1,350
1979	672	497	1,169
1980	604	531	1,135
1981	353	483	836
1982	459	465	924
1983	498	371	869
1984	408	275	683
1985	439	381	820
1986	451	354	805
1987	488	420	908
1988	451	379	830
1989	368	312	680
1990	510	326	836
1991	428	280	708
1992	473	270	743
1993	597	395	992
1994	497	329	826
1995	867	613	1,480
1996	454	306	760
1997	633	298	931
1998	533	314	847
1999	609	374	983
2000	600	298	898
2001	507	380	887
2002	483	253	736
2003	675	459	1,134
2004	543	216	759
2005	669	366	1,035
2006	540	279	819
2007	1,177	442	1,619
2008	688	215	903
2009	987	397	1,384
2010	660	299	959
2011	945	235	1,180
2012	656	251	907
2013	640	291	931
2014	563	366	929
2015	703	339	1,042
2016	621	163	784

SOURCE: "Résumé of Congressional Activity," *Congressional Record— Daily Digest,* various issues, Eightieth Congress (1947) through 114th Congress (2016).

when majority leader Rep. Eric Cantor, R-Va., was defeated in a primary election by a little-known but a fiercely conservative college professor named David Brat. Cantor went on to resign his leadership position and eventually his Congressional seat ahead of the November 2014 general election. Rep. Kevin McCarthy, R-Calif., the party whip, was elected majority leader, and Steve Scalise, R-La., took over as party whip.

Even more important than the House leadership shakeup was the November 2014 midterm election that resulted in Republicans expanding their majority in the House and taking control of the Senate for the first time in eight years. With the Democrat in the White House becoming increasingly unpopular among the public, Republicans saw this as their mandate to begin undoing many of Obama's landmark achievements from the first six years of his presidency, including the Patient Protection and Affordable Care Act (ACA) and the Dodd-Frank Wall Street Reform and Consumer Protection Act. In fact, despite spending most of the first ten months of the year holding lengthy hearings and considering legislation that would ultimately go nowhere, during the lame-duck session following the midterm election, the House and Senate proposed more than 100 new laws and passed a significant omnibus spending measure. The American people, however, maintained their dismal view of Congress, with around 80 percent disapproving of the job Congress had done throughout 2014, according to Gallup.

REPUBLICANS TARGET THE IRS

In March 2013, the Treasury Inspector General released a report finding that the Internal Revenue Service (IRS) had improperly applied extra regulatory scrutiny to conservative groups seeking 501(c)(4) tax exempt status. According to the report, such scrutiny was directly linked to a 2010 IRS directive that required additional review of applications for 501(c)(4) status bearing words such as "tea party," "Patriots," and "9/12." Republicans responded by attempting to undermine the IRS in a variety of ways, including attempting to limit the agency's ability to implement the provisions of the ACA, for which it was responsible, and conducting a symbolic vote to hold former IRS official Lois Lerner in contempt of Congress for her refusal to testify at two congressional hearings. Congress then turned its focus to IRS Commissioner John Koskinen, who took on his role after the scandal came to light. Republicans claimed that the commissioner had lied under oath about the tax-exempt reviews and had overseen the destruction of records that would have provided important information to investigators looking into the matter. The House moved to impeach Koskinen but never gained enough traction for passage. In 2015, the Justice Department would announce that its investigation resulted in no findings that any IRS official had acted in such a politically biased manner to support criminal prosecution and that no IRS official had attempted to obstruct justice. The Justice Department did, however, note that it found evidence of mismanagement and poor judgement that should be corrected. *(See discussion on "House Holds IRS Official in Contempt" in Chapter 14, pp. 455–457.)*

SENATE CONSIDERS OBAMA NOMINEES

In late 2013, Democrats in the Senate exercised the so-called nuclear option, changing Senate procedural rules to require only a simple majority, rather than the traditional sixty votes, to break a filibuster and move to end debate to consider a presidential nominee. This rule change essentially meant that most executive branch and judicial nominees could be confirmed with only fifty-one votes. That proved beneficial to many of Obama's nominees who had been trapped in the Senate awaiting confirmation, but some still faced extensive battles.

These included Antonio Weiss, who was nominated as undersecretary of the Treasury for domestic finance. In this position, Weiss would have been responsible for managing the country's debt portfolio and communicating with Congress about the budget. Weiss's nomination was opposed by the more liberal members of the Senate because of his ties to Wall Street as a former investment banker for Lazard. Sen. Elizabeth Warren, D-Mass., led the opposition, citing Weiss's involvement in corporate inversions, the act through which U.S. corporations merge with foreign companies and move their headquarters offshore to reduce their U.S. tax burden. She expressed that Weiss would be too deferential to the finance industry and lacked the regulatory experience necessary for the role. Weiss was unable to garner enough votes for confirmation during the 113th Congress and asked Obama not to resubmit his nomination during the 114th Congress, saying that he wished to avoid the "lengthy confirmation process" his nomination would have caused. Weiss instead became an unofficial advisor to the Treasury. *(See discussion of Antonio Weiss in Chapter 16, pp. 520–521.)*

Another failed nomination was that of Debo P. Adegbile, former NAACP Legal Defense Fund attorney, who Obama named to head the Justice Department's Civil Rights Division. Adegbile drew criticism for his involvement in the representation of Mumia Abu-Jamal, who was convicted of murdering a Philadelphia police officer in 1981. Some Democrats expressed frustration with the White House for moving ahead with Adegbile's nomination, knowing that it put some members of the caucus in a difficult position. Democrats in traditionally Republican states—where law and justice are hot button issues—who were facing a tough reelection battle crossed the aisle to vote "no" on a procedural measure that would clear the way for a final confirmation vote on Adegbile's nomination. Sen. Patrick Toomey, R-Pa., said the vote was good for the country and affirmed that the criminal justice system should not be abused to support a personal agenda. Adegbile withdrew his name from consideration and returned to private practice. *(See discussion of Debo P. Adegbile in Chapter 16, p. 521.)*

Democrats were successful, however, in confirming Obama's choice to lead the Federal Reserve Board, Janet L. Yellen. Yellen was the first woman to hold the job. All but eleven Republicans opposed Yellen's nomination, with many voting in opposition over unrelated spats with the White House. Sen. Lindsey Graham, who was one of eighteen senators that could not reach Capitol Hill to vote due to inclement weather, had promised to vote against Yellen over his personal campaign to get more information from the Obama administration about the 2012 attack on the U.S. diplomatic compound in Benghazi, Libya.

TWO HOUSE REPUBLICANS FACE SCANDAL

Two Republican members of the House—Reps. Michael Grimm of New York and Vance McAllister of Louisiana—were felled by scandal in 2014. Grimm was subject to an investigation into his campaign finances and was also caught on camera threatening to throw a reporter off the balcony of the rotunda of the Cannon House office building for asking a question about the situation. In April, Grimm was indicted for filing false tax returns, hiring undocumented immigrants to work at a restaurant he owned, health care fraud, and lying under oath, among other charges. Grimm, who denied any wrongdoing, pushed aside calls for his resignation, insisting that he would keep his seat and run for a third term in November. Grimm went on to win his reelection bid with 53 percent of the vote against Democrat Domenic Recchia. In December, Grimm pleaded guilty to a single count of tax fraud but again refused to step down, noting that his plea related to something that had happened before he was elected to Congress. Ultimately, Grimm stepped down just days later and in 2015 was sentenced to eight months in prison.

Louisiana's McAllister was elected in a special election in November 2013. In April 2014, Louisiana newspapers published surveillance footage of the married McAllister kissing a married staff member. McAllister quickly issued a statement apologizing and asking for the forgiveness of his family, staff, and constituents. Initially, McAllister said he would serve out the remainder of the term but would not seek reelection. However, two months after the surveillance footage surfaced, he decided that he would in fact seek reelection in November. McAllister lost that bid, coming in fourth.

CONGRESS STRUGGLES TO PASS A BUDGET BILL

On the heels of a sixteen-day government shutdown in October 2013, Democrats and Republicans appeared anxious to avoid a similar situation in 2014. Reflecting that, the fiscal 2015 budget proposal Obama sent to Congress in April contained few of his ambitious agenda items and focused more on keeping the government moving forward.

The $3.9 trillion budget differed from Obama's previous budget proposal in that it contained neither lofty Democratic goals nor potential areas on which the two parties could negotiate. Instead, the budget was closely aligned with the agreements negotiated between the House and Senate in December 2013 that set a fiscal 2015 discretionary spending cap of $1.014 trillion. Congress in February passed a thirteen-month extension of the debt limit, and in May the House adopted a budget resolution, but it was never marked up by the Senate Budget Committee, which saw it as unnecessary because the December budget agreement already set a spending level for the year.

For the fifth year in a row, Congress was unable to finish any of the twelve regular appropriations bills and was instead forced to put everything into a year-end omnibus spending bill that was sent to President Obama for his signature in mid-December. The last time the House and Senate had completed action on an individual appropriation bill was in 2009, when Democrats held the House, Senate, and presidency. Even before losing their House majority in 2010, the appropriations process was already on shaky ground.

Even so, House and Senate leadership entered the 2014 budget negotiations with optimism, holding hearings, marking up bills, and passing some appropriations bills. However, once they reached summer and attention turned more toward the midterm election battles, work on the appropriations bills stalled. After the election, and without time to pass all twelve appropriations bills, Congress started fervently working to pass an omnibus spending measure to keep the government running and avoid another shutdown.

It was nicknamed the cromnibus because it combined a short-term continuing resolution for the Department of Homeland Security with an omnibus appropriation for most of the remaining government agencies. Congress narrowly passed the $1.1 trillion bill in December, following tense floor debate and hours of vote whipping, the process of party leadership encouraging their members to vote in a specific way. The Department of Homeland Security had its budget funded only through February, and the hope among budget negotiators was that this would force the new Congress—which would be completely Republican controlled—to act to limit immigration executive orders the president issued in November 2014 and that would defer the deportation of millions of illegal immigrants already in the country. *(See discussion of omnibus package in Chapter 2, pp. 85, 96–97.)*

DEFENSE, VA SCRAMBLE

Lawmakers once again found themselves scrambling to finalize a defense authorization bill before Congress adjourned at the end of 2014, even though the House passed its version of the fiscal 2015 measure in May. The Senate Armed Services reported its version of the bill in late May. However, remaining floor time in both chambers was limited in the weeks before summer recess and the session break for the midterm elections. Most of the available time was consumed by deliberations over spending bills needed to keep the government open past the end of fiscal 2014. The House and Senate Armed Services Committees were unable to begin a formal conference committee, and unofficial negotiations began taking place.

The chairs and ranking members of the House and Senate Armed Services Committee began closed-door negotiations in November on a compromise bill that could gain approval by both chambers. The group was known as the "Big Four." Their deliberations were guided by input from other Armed Services Committee members who had met in September to outline their priorities for the final legislation.

In the first week of December, the Big Four released the details of their compromise bill, which authorized $577.1 billion for the Department of Defense and defense-related programs for fiscal 2015. A base budget of $495.5 billion was authorized, in addition to $17.9 billion for national security programs within the Energy Department, which generally involve maintenance of the United States' nuclear arsenal. Lawmakers also authorized $63.7 billion in OCO funding, including an administration-requested budget of $5.1 billion to help train the Iraqi Army and sustain U.S. personnel conducting intelligence and military operations in the region to continue the fight against the Islamic State of Iraq and the Levant (ISIL).

To help expedite its consideration and approval, the compromise bill's language was added as a substitute amendment to another piece of legislation that was previously approved by the House and Senate. That bill sought to exempt volunteer firefighters and other emergency responders from counting toward the number of employees that triggers the employer mandate under the Patient Protection and Affordable Care Act of 2010. Lawmakers also added about 100 provisions related to public lands that had been under consideration for more than a year to the updated bill, in an effort to push their approval forward. These provisions had been negotiated separately by leaders of the House Natural Resources and Senate Energy and Natural Resources committees. The inclusion of these provisions prompted several attempts by Sen. Tom Coburn, R-Okla., to have the public lands language stripped from the final bill via amendment. However, the Senate rejected all of these proposed measures. Ultimately, the final defense authorization bill was signed by President Obama on December 19. *(See discussion of fiscal 2015 defense authorization in Chapter 5, pp. 190–193.)*

Quick Congressional action was also required for the Department of Veterans Affairs (VA), which came under fire in April when Dr. Sam Foote, a doctor at the Carl T. Hayden VA Medical Center in Phoenix, Ariz., filed a complaint with the VA inspector general alleging that the hospital was falsifying information about how long veterans were waiting for appointments to be scheduled to cover up its excessive wait times. Dr. Foote's allegations included claims that some veterans died while waiting for care.

To address public concern, Congress passed legislation authorizing $15 billion in spending to help cut wait times for medical appointments. A third of the funding was intended to support the hiring of additional doctors and nurses and upgrades to medical facilities, while $10 billion would help subsidize private health care for veterans who met certain criteria. The bill was signed into law on August 7. *(See discussion of emergency VA spending authorization in Chapter 5, pp. 193–194.)*

REPUBLICANS SEEK FINANCIAL, TRADE CHANGES

Since its passage in 2010, Republicans had repeatedly sought to repeal or change the Dodd-Frank Wall Street Reform and Consumer Protection Act. The law was passed in the wake of the recession to reorganize financial oversight bodies to better protect the economy and to establish new regulations governing how banks are structured. It included the creation of two new oversight bodies, the Consumer Financial Protection Bureau (CFPB) and the Financial Services Oversight Council, both of which would be housed within the Federal Reserve, outside of traditional Congressional appropriations.

In December 2014, Republicans cleared a change to the Dodd-Frank law as part of the fiscal 2015 omnibus bill. Specifically, they added a policy rider that would repeal a provision of the law that required banks to separate the part of their operations that deal with derivatives from the part of the institution that is federally insured. The original provision was meant to ensure the federal government was not insuring potentially risky transactions but was strongly opposed by the financial industry and even the Department of the Treasury. Led by Sen. Elizabeth Warren, opponents to the rider staged a last-minute attempt to remove the provision from the spending bill. The question Americans should ask themselves, Warren said, is whether Washington works for all people or only those with the resources to hire lobbyists and lawyers. *(See Dodd-Frank in Chapter 2, pp. 51–54.)*

The Internet Tax Freedom Act, the law that blocks state and local governments from taxing Internet access, was up for renewal in 2014. Supporters of the law frequently argued that not only did the law prevent taxes on Internet service, it also codified a Supreme Court decision that prohibited states from collecting sales taxes for online purchases if the retailer does not have a physical presence in the state where the purchase is made. Because of this, the renewal of the Internet Tax Freedom Act was tied up in debate with questions about taxing Internet sales, an issue Congress considered at length but failed to act on in 2013. *(See discussion of moratorium on Internet tax in Chapter 2, pp. 83–84.)*

In 2014, those in the House who opposed a 2013 Senate-passed bill known as the Marketplace Fairness Act, which would force online retailers with more than $1 million in annual sales to collect sales taxes on all purchases, threatened to allow the Internet Tax Freedom Act to expire at the end of 2014. Republican House leadership declined to delay the extension and floated the idea of making the law permanent, something Senate Democrats said they would oppose. In July, a bill was introduced in the Senate to extend the Internet Tax Freedom Act until November 1, 2024, while also requiring online retailers to collect sales taxes. The bill never received a full Senate vote, and despite House Republicans pushing leadership to consider a bill to allow states to collect sales taxes on Internet purchases, they never did so. Ultimately, Congress used the cromnibus fiscal 2015 spending bill to add a provision extending the moratorium on state and local Internet sales taxes until October 1, 2015.

MINOR LEGISLATIVE VICTORIES

House and Senate leadership started the year optimistic that they could pass a six-year highway and transit authorization, but that quickly fell apart over disagreement about how big the bill should be, where the funding would come from, and a time frame for funding the measure. The Highway Trust Fund, which finances most federal government spending on highways and mass transit projects, was set to run out of money on August 1. So in July, the two houses of Congress worked to write a short-term extension but were unable to agree to a bill until July 31. Many Democrats and the White House backed the measure, leading to its passage.

Doctors were hopeful that the second year of the 113th Congress would result in a permanent fix to the formula that dictates Medicare reimbursement rates and requires automatic reductions in the rate if spending exceeds the rate of inflation. Congress has frequently passed temporary patches to the law, but those in the health care sector have urged Congress to develop a permanent fix to provide greater security to doctors. Democrats and Republicans pushed for legislation that would address the situation but that would be offset by spending cuts elsewhere; however, they couldn't agree on where those cuts should be made. Instead, they passed their seventeenth law since 2003, known as the "doc fix," to temporarily protect doctors from the mandated cuts. *(See discussion of doc fix in Chapter 9, pp. 302–303.)*

More than a year after it expired, in early 2014, Congress passed a five-year farm bill. The final legislation eliminated direct and "countercyclical" payments to farmers and instead provided new forms of crop insurance. To win Republican votes, the bill also included reduced spending on Supplemental Nutrition Assistance Program (SNAP) benefits and changed the subsidies for cotton producers and dairy farmers.

The House passed legislation that would allow the Keystone XL pipeline to move forward, but the Senate fell one vote short and left the matter unresolved. Similarly, while the House was able to pass bills that would ease the regulatory burden related to leasing onshore and offshore federal lands for energy exploration and extraction, opposition from Democrats in the Senate prevented the bills from moving forward. Congress did, however, manage to retroactively extend tax breaks for renewable fuels and alternative energy industries that had expired at the end of 2013.

The Political Year

SPECIAL ELECTIONS HAVE LITTLE IMPACT ON CONGRESSIONAL MAKEUP

There were eight special elections to fill five House and three Senate seats, but only two of those were held outside of election day, November 4. Republicans were victorious in five of the races, and Democrats won three, but there was no change of party in any of the eight races. Republicans held the Senate seats in South Carolina and Oklahoma, which had been vacated through resignation, while Democrats held the Hawaii Senate seat vacated by Daniel Inouye upon his death in December 2012. In the House, Democrats retained control of two Florida seats along with one each in New Jersey and North Carolina. Republicans held a seat in Virginia that previously belonged to House Majority Leader Eric Cantor. Cantor chose to step down from leadership and resign from Congress after his primary defeat in August.

THREE SENATE SPECIAL ELECTIONS

In December 2012, Sen. Inouye died after a bout with a respiratory illness. He had served nearly five decades in Congress and before his death indicated his wishes that Rep. Colleen Hanabusa take his place. By law, the Hawaii governor is given the opportunity to name a temporary successor to a Senate seat until a special election can be held, and Governor Neil Abercrombie chose instead the state's lieutenant governor, Brian Schatz. Schatz had previously run for the U.S. House of Representatives, although he lost to Mazie Hirono, who herself went on to secure the state's second Senate seat in 2012. Schatz held the seat until November 2014, when the state would hold an election to fill the remaining two years of Inouye's term. In the Democratic primary ahead of the special election, Schatz faced off against Hanabusa and won by a slim margin of 48.5 percent to 47.8 percent, a difference of fewer than 2,000 votes. Schatz had no issue holding off Republican challenger Campbell Cavasso in the special election, winning nearly 70 percent of the vote.

In South Carolina, Sen. Jim DeMint resigned in December 2012 to instead take a position as president of the Heritage Foundation. Governor Nikki Haley tapped U.S. Rep. Tim Scott to take DeMint's place on December 17, 2012. Scott was the first African American Republican to represent South Carolina in Congress in a century and the first African American senator from the South since Reconstruction. Scott held the seat until a special election was held in 2014, and he was unopposed in the Republican primary to fill the remainder of DeMint's term. In the general election, Scott won 61.1 percent of the vote to county councilperson Joyce Dickerson's 37.1 percent.

In January 2014, Sen. Tom Coburn, who was battling prostate cancer, announced that he would retire at the end of the 113th Congress, two years prior to the end of his term. Noting that his decision was not about his health, Coburn said he was convinced he should shift his focus elsewhere for the good of his family. The primary ahead of the special election to fill the rest of Coburn's term featured Rep. James Lankford, a former youth pastor and chair of the House Republican Policy Committee, Oklahoma state House Speaker T. W. Shannon, a tea party favorite, and five other candidates. Lankford won with more than 57 percent of the vote to Shannon's 34.4 percent, thus avoiding a runoff. He went on to defeat state Sen. Connie Johnson in November, 67.9 percent to 29 percent.

FIVE HOUSE SPECIAL ELECTIONS

When Rep. C. W. Bill Young, R-Fla., former chair of the powerful House Appropriations Committee, died in October 2013, he was the longest-serving House Republican. The Republican primary to fill the 13th Congressional district seat featured attorney David Jolly, a staff member of

Table 1.7   Black Members of Congress, 1947–2016

Congress	Senate	House
80th (1947–1949)	0	2
81st (1949–1951)	0	2
82nd (1951–1953)	0	2
83rd (1953–1955)	0	2
84th (1955–1957)	0	3
85th (1957–1959)	0	4
86th (1959–1961)	0	4
87th (1961–1963)	0	4
88th (1963–1965)	0	5
89th (1965–1967)	0	6
90th (1967–1969)	1	5
91st (1969–1971)	1	9
92nd (1971–1973)	1	12
93rd (1973–1975)	1	15
94th (1975–1977)	1	16
95th (1977–1979)	1	16
96th (1979–1981)	0	16
97th (1981–1983)	0	17
98th (1983–1985)	0	20
99th (1985–1987)	0	20
100th (1987–1989)	0	22
101st (1989–1991)	0	24
102nd (1991–1993)	0	26
103rd (1993–1995)	1	39
104th (1995–1997)	1	38
105th (1997–1999)	1	37
106th (1999–2001)	0	37
107th (2001–2003)	0	36
108th (2003–2005)	0	39
109th (2005–2007)	1	40
110th (2007–2009)	1	40
111th (2009–2011)*	0	39
112th (2011–2013)	0	42
113th (2013–2014)	2	41
114th (2015–2016)	2	44

NOTE: House totals reflect the number of members at the start of each Congress and exclude nonvoting delegates.

*President-elect Barack Obama of Illinois resigned his Senate seat in November 2008. African American Roland W. Burris assumed the seat on January 15, 2009.

Young's but a relative unknown in the Florida political arena; state Rep. Kathleen Peters; and Iraq War veteran Mark Bircher. Jolly easily won the right to face former gubernatorial nominee Alex Sink, who was unopposed for the Democratic nomination, in the March 2014 special election. Democrats and political action committees (PAC) spent a significant amount of money in favor of Sink, who held the fundraising advantage to Jolly. At the time, it was the most expensive special congressional election in history. The national Republican Party questioned how Jolly was running his race, characterizing it as one full of inept fundraising and poorly coordinated campaigning. Jolly was also subject to intense media scrutiny given that he finalized his divorce from his wife right after the primary and was quickly dating someone fourteen years his junior. The polls showed a close race in the lead-up to Election Day, but in the end, Jolly beat out Sink with 48.5 percent of the vote to her 46.6 percent. A Libertarian candidate, Lucas Overby, received 4.8 percent. Because Young's term expired at the end of 2014, Jolly ran again in the November general election where he faced Overby and no Democrat. Jolly was the victor with more than 75 percent of the vote.

The 19th Congressional District in Florida also held a special election in 2014 to fill the seat vacated by Rep. Trey Radel, a Republican, who resigned after being arrested for purchasing cocaine from an undercover police officer. In the Republican primary, Curt Clawson, a retired CEO of an automotive wheel manufacturing company, defeated three other candidates with 38 percent of the vote. In the June special election, Clawson easily defeated his Democratic opponent, April Freeman, 67 percent to 29.3 percent. In the November general election, Clawson, who was backed by the Tea Party Express, the largest of the tea party PACs, won reelection, again defeating Freeman by more than 30 points. According to *CQ Roll Call*, Clawson was the twenty-ninth richest member of Congress.

In New Jersey's 1st Congressional District, Rep. Robert Andrews, a Democrat, announced his intent to resign in February 2014 because he was under investigation by the House Ethics Committee for funding a family trip to Scotland with campaign donations. The district is widely considered a safe Democratic seat, and on the same day Andrews announced his resignation, Donald Norcross, a state senator and former laborer, announced his intent to run. Norcross was popular among Democrats both in New Jersey and nationwide and raised a significant amount of money in the race. He defeated his opponent, Republican Garry Cobb, a former linebacker for the Philadelphia Eagles, 57.4 percent to 39.4 percent.

Rep. Melvin Watt resigned from his seat representing North Carolina's 12th Congressional District in January 2014 to take the position of director of the Federal Housing Finance Agency. The district is heavily Democratic, and Watt had held the seat for more than two decades. The Democratic primary to replace him featured five candidates. The frontrunner was Alma Adams, a former college professor and member of the

state legislature, who was able to secure 44 percent of the vote, thus avoiding a runoff. Her next closest opponent, state Sen. Malcolm Graham, received less than 24 percent. Adams defeated Republican challenger Vince Coakley with more than 75 percent of the vote. When she was sworn in, Adams became the 100th woman in the current Congressional class, beating the previous record of ninety-nine.

The most surprising special election was in Virginia's 7th Congressional District. The seat was held by Rep. Eric Cantor, former House Minority Whip and current House Majority Leader. Cantor was defeated in the June 2014 Republican primary by professor David Brat, who became the first person to oust a sitting majority leader in a primary. Despite winning 55.5 percent of the vote to Cantor's 44.5 percent, Brat spent only $200,000 to Cantor's more than $2 million. After his defeat, Cantor resigned his leadership position on July 31 and was replaced by Rep. Kevin McCarthy of California. Cantor went on to resign his House seat on August 18, saying he wanted to ensure the constituents in his district had a voice during the lame-duck session. Virginia Gov. Terry McAuliffe called a special election to allow a candidate to be seated immediately rather than leaving the position open until January 2015.

Table 1.8 Women in Congress, 1947–2016

Congress	Senate	House
80th (1947–1949)	1	7
81st (1949–1951)	1	9
82nd (1951–1953)	1	10
83rd (1953–1955)	1	12
84th (1955–1957)	1	17
85th (1957–1959)	1	15
86th (1959–1961)	1	17
87th (1961–1963)	2	18
88th (1963–1965)	2	12
89th (1965–1967)	2	11
90th (1967–1969)	1	10
91st (1969–1971)	1	10
92nd (1971–1973)	1	13
93rd (1973–1975)	1	16
94th (1975–1977)	0	17
95th (1977–1979)	2	18
96th (1979–1981)	1	16
97th (1981–1983)	2	19
98th (1983–1985)	2	22
99th (1985–1987)	2	22
100th (1987–1989)	2	23
101st (1989–1991)	2	28
102nd (1991–1993)	3	29
103rd (1993–1995)	7	48
104th (1995–1997)	8	48
105th (1997–1999)	9	51
106th (1999–2001)	9	56
107th (2001–2003)	13	59
108th (2003–2005)	14	59
109th (2005–2007)	14	64
110th (2007–2009)	16	71
111th (2009–2011)	17	75
112th (2011–2013)	17	72
113th (2013–2014)	20	80
114th (2015–2016)	20	84

NOTE: House totals reflect the number of members at the start of each Congress and exclude nonvoting delegates.

In the special election, Brat faced off against his colleague at Randolph-Macon College, Democrat John Trammell. Brat was victorious with more than 60 percent of the vote.

REPUBLICANS MAKE BIG GAINS IN THE MIDTERM ELECTIONS

When voters across the country went to the polls on November 4, 2014, they were voting for nearly 150 ballot measures, all 435 seats in the House of Representatives, thirty-six Senate seats, thirty-six governors, and forty-six state legislatures, in addition to local races. Historically speaking, Democrats were expected to lose. Since the Great Depression, midterm elections held in the sixth year of a president's two terms have frequently resulted in losses in Congress for the president's party. In addition, midterm electorates tend to feature a higher percentage of white and older Americans, and both are groups that often favor Republicans. Both parties, however, were faced with a public that was strongly anti-incumbent. According to a Gallup

poll conducted in late April, only 22 percent of registered voters felt most members of Congress deserved reelection, while 72 percent said they did not. Gallup said the "deserved reelection" figure was tracking as one of the lowest measured in an election year. Of their own members of Congress, 50 percent of poll respondents felt they deserved reelection, which Gallup said was similar to data recorded in 1992, 1994, 2006, and 2010, all years of high Congressional turnover.

Democrats were also working against a dim view of the Democratic president, who had a 42 percent approval rating in the last nationwide Gallup poll taken before November 4. Heading into election night, political analysts estimated that turnout would be low, as is typical of a non-presidential-election year, and they were right. Turnout was less than 37 percent, the lowest for a midterm since 1942. Campaign spending was at an all-time high, which analysts considered a direct reflection of the Supreme Court's *Citizens United* ruling in 2010 that gave corporations and labor unions the ability to spend virtually unlimited sums of money on campaign advertisements and other means to encourage support of or opposition to specific candidates.

The elections were ultimately a major victory for the Republican Party, which took control of the Senate for the first time in eight years and expanded its majority in the House to the largest since 1947–48. The party also won a majority of the state legislative and gubernatorial races.

In the Senate, the biggest wins for Republicans came in Kansas and Georgia, their two most vulnerable seats. In Kansas, Republican Sen. Pat Roberts held off independent Greg Orman with an 11-point victory, and in Georgia, David Perdue avoided a runoff with 53 percent of the vote to Democrat Michelle Nunn's 45 percent. In the House, Democratic losses were in the double digits, and the party lost almost every competitive and open seat.

After the election, House Speaker John Boehner, R-Ohio, and soon-to-be Senate Majority Leader Mitch McConnell, R-Ky., wrote a *Wall Street Journal* op-ed outlining their priorities for the incoming Congress and promising to support the middle class through job creation and a repeal of the Affordable Care Act. They also indicated a desire to avoid the vast partisan divide and brinksmanship that had plagued recent Congresses. Members, McConnell said, know they were not elected just to fight with other elected officials. Both McConnell and Boehner were also searching for greater unity within their own party, a possibility given that many of the new members were backed by the Republican establishment rather than the tea party.

Republicans were already promising to use the power of the purse to push back against some of Obama's key programs, including weakening the Dodd-Frank Wall Street Reform and Consumer Protection Act and the Affordable Care Act and pushing through stalled legislation on the Keystone XL pipeline. President Obama remained hopeful there were areas on which the White House could work with the House and Senate, including on creating jobs, expanding exports, and increasing trade but admitted that the two parties would not

Table 1.9 Hispanic Members of Congress, 1947–2016

Congress	Senate	House
80th (1947–1949)	1	1
81st (1949–1951)	1	1
82nd (1951–1953)	1	1
83rd (1953–1955)	1	1
84th (1955–1957)	1	1
85th (1957–1959)	2	0
86th (1959–1961)	2	0
87th (1961–1963)	2	1
88th (1963–1965)	1	3
89th (1965–1967)	1	4
90th (1967–1969)	1	4
91st (1969–1971)	1	5
92nd (1971–1973)	1	6
93rd (1973–1975)	1	6
94th (1975–1977)	1	6
95th (1977–1979)	0	5
96th (1979–1981)	0	6
97th (1981–1983)	0	7
98th (1983–1985)	0	10
99th (1985–1987)	0	11
100th (1987–1989)	0	11
101st (1989–1991)	0	11
102nd (1991–1993)	0	11
103rd (1993–1995)	0	17
104th (1995–1997)	0	17
105th (1997–1999)	0	18
106th (1999–2001)	0	18
107th (2001–2003)	0	19
108th (2003–2005)	0	24
109th (2005–2007)	2	23
110th (2007–2009)	3	23
111th (2009–2011)*	3	24
112th (2011–2013)	2	24
113th (2013–2015)	4	33
114th (2015–2017)	3	34

NOTES: Totals reflect the number of members at the start of each Congress and exclude nonvoting delegates.

*Democrat Ken Salazar of Colorado, a member of the Senate when the 111th Congress convened, resigned on January 21, 2009, to become secretary of the Interior. His replacement, appointed by the Colorado governor, was not Hispanic.

always agree. But on those issues, the president said, he would keep pushing for the position he felt would be best to support the country and grow the middle class.

REPUBLICANS TAKE CONTROL OF THE SENATE

The most closely watched races in the lead-up to the 2014 midterm election were in the Senate, where thirty-six seats were up for grabs. Republicans needed a net gain of six seats to claim the majority and retake control of the body for the first time since 2007. It was clear on election night that Republicans would have at least a slight majority in the Senate, but just how significant their control would be was dependent on multiple races that faced delayed results and recounts, including a runoff in Louisiana. In that race, Sen. Mary Landrieu's defeat by Bill Cassidy left Republicans with fifty-four seats in the Senate. The party held all its current seats and won nine new ones including unseating incumbents in Alaska, Arkansas, Colorado, Louisiana, and North Carolina.

McConnell, who was easily reelected to his own seat, said the election was a clear message to both Congress and the White House about what the American people want. While voters are not happy with the positions of the administration, McConnell said, they also dislike the gridlock and dysfunction in Washington.

TEA PARTY, POLITICAL DYNASTIES LOSE INFLUENCE

The tea party movement, made up of the most fiscally conservative Republicans, began in 2009 following the end of the Great Recession. The group supported policies such as limited government, a reduction of the national debt, and lower taxes. The tea party gained influence during the 2010 midterms when it put up its candidates against mainstream, establishment Republicans and won. Their movement waned quickly, however, and the Republican faction won only 25 percent of contested Senate races in 2012 while losing around 20 percent of the House seats it originally had won in 2010. By the 2014 election, they were even less successful. Of the challengers fielded to run against eight Republican incumbents, none of them succeeded.

In Georgia, a reliably red state, Republican Saxby Chambliss was retiring after two terms in office. Republicans chose David Perdue, a former CEO of Reebok and Dollar General, in the primary election, while Democrats picked Michelle Nunn, the daughter of a former senator and CEO of the nonprofit Points of Light Foundation. Both candidates sought to portray themselves as someone who could set aside partisan divides to get things done in Washington, and early polls showed a close race. However, Perdue, who promised to bring his business experience to the seat, defeated Nunn by nearly 8 percentage points.

In New Hampshire, former governor and incumbent Sen. Jeanne Shaheen, a Democrat, was challenged by former Massachusetts Sen. Scott Brown, a Republican. Brown held former Sen. Edward Kennedy's seat before losing it, and in his move to New Hampshire, where he owned a vacation home and had family ties, he struggled to shift the perception that he was an outsider. Shaheen used this to focus her campaign on local issues and what she had done, both in the governor's mansion and the Senate, to serve the state. Shaheen defeated Brown by more than 3 percentage points.

OBAMA PROVES DETRIMENTAL TO DEMOCRATS

History shows that the president's party typically loses seats in Congress during a midterm election. Since 1934, only two presidents—George W. Bush and Franklin Roosevelt—have seen their parties gain seats in both the House and Senate. In 2014, Democrats were defending twenty-one of the thirty-six Senate seats up for reelection, and seven of those were in states carried by Mitt Romney, the Republican candidate for president, in 2012. Obama inadvertently made himself and fellow Democrats a target, noting on October 2 that while he was not on the ballot, his policies were. Conservative groups seized on this and spent millions to back Republican candidates and remind voters about what they saw as Obama policies that were failing Americans, such as the Affordable Care Act. Sensing his unpopularity, in the months prior to the election, Obama did not campaign for candidates who were in conservative-leaning districts, rather focusing on holding safe seats and instead sending more popular surrogates such as his wife to lend support.

Republicans flipped Senate seats in Alaska, Arkansas, Colorado, Iowa, Louisiana, Montana, North Carolina, South Dakota, and West Virginia. No Republican incumbent lost a seat. The most endangered Republican was Sen. Thad Cochran of Mississippi, whose biggest fight came in the primary. Cochran faced off against state Sen. Chris McDaniel, who tried to paint Cochran as a big-spending liberal. Neither candidate won more than 50 percent of the primary vote, leading to a runoff. Cochran touted his experience and how it had benefited the state and courted African American voters, who proved a crucial component of Cochran's ultimate victory. Cochran won the primary by around 7,000 votes and easily defeated Democrat Travis Childers in the November general election.

Sen. Pat Roberts also faced a closer-than-expected race in Kansas against Greg Orman, who was running as an independent (the Democratic nominee withdrew from the race in support of Orman). Orman had previously filed as a Democrat to run unsuccessfully against Roberts in 2008, and Roberts used that to closely tie his opponent to the unpopular president. Roberts ultimately defeated Orman by double digits.

In Colorado, Obama's unpopularity resulted in Democratic incumbent Sen. Mark Udall losing to Rep. Cory Gardner, a rising GOP star who gave up a safe seat to run for Senate. A Quinnipiac poll conducted in the state in February showed that nearly 60 percent of Colorado voters did not approve of Obama's work, a surprise given that the president won the state in both 2008 and 2012. Instead of making a case based on what he had done for the state, Udall focused the race on Gardner's positions on abortion and birth control, which did not resonate with voters, and Udall lost by approximately 40,000 votes. Similarly, in Arkansas, Sen. Mark Pryor was defeated by first-term Rep. Tom Cotton, who based his campaign on Pryor's support of the president's health care law. Exit polls in the state showed that 40 percent of voters cast their ballot in opposition to the president and his policies.

In Iowa, Rep. Bruce Braley was unable to hold on to the seat being vacated by retiring Democratic Sen. Tom Harkins. Braley's lackluster campaign could not compete against that of state Sen. Joni Ernst, who quickly gained prominence within the Republican Party for a quirky campaign ad in which she explained that growing up on a pig farm made her qualified to cut pork-barrel spending in Washington. Although polls were close in the lead-up to the election, Ernst won by more than 8 percentage points.

REPUBLICANS HOLD THE HOUSE

In the House, Democrats were also predicted to lose seats in the midterm, based both on history and on the president's unpopularity. Since the 1950s, the president's party has lost seats during the sixth year of a two-term presidency, except in 1998. Ultimately, 2014 would prove no different, with Republicans gaining a net of 13 seats to reach 247 total seats held, the most since 1928. Only two Republican incumbents lost in 2014, Lee Terry of Nebraska and Steve Southerland II in Florida, both of whom had largely caused their own losses through off-color statements. Democratic leadership took the loss in stride. House minority leader Nancy Pelosi, D-Calif., said the results did not indicate a wave of approval for either Democrats or Republicans. Pelosi went on to explain that the problem for Democrats was not the president or their policies but rather that two-thirds of voters did not cast a ballot.

Democrats were initially hopeful that they could utilize the 2013 sixteen-day federal government shutdown and the quest to defund the Affordable Care Act against Republicans. Rep. Steve Israel, D-N.Y., head of the Democratic Congressional Campaign Committee, said that the shutdown inspired Democrats to run for office because they wanted to change the direction of the current Congress and serve as a buffer to Republican ideologies. However, in early 2014, those predictions were not coming true. In March, a special election to replace Republican C.W. Bill Young after his death was held in a Florida district that Obama had won narrowly in 2012. Democrats put up Alex Sink, the party's nominee for governor in 2010, while Republicans chose lobbyist David Jolly, who was in the process of divorcing his wife to marry a woman fourteen years his junior. Jolly won with 48.5 percent of the vote. Israel cautioned Democrats against reading into the vote, noting that special elections are not necessarily an indicator of future public sentiment. In 2014, however, they certainly appeared to be.

REPUBLICAN PRIMARY UPSETS

There were two major Republican primary upsets in 2014. On May 27, 2014, Rep. Ralph Hall, R-Texas, became the first House incumbent to lose a primary that year. Hall, who was first elected as a Democrat, had held his seat since 1980 and was the oldest sitting member of the House. He was defeated by John Ratcliffe, a former mayor and U.S. attorney, by approximately 4 percentage points. Ratcliffe ran unopposed in the November general election.

The bigger surprise, however, came in June when House Majority Leader Eric Cantor fell to professor Dave Brat. Brat campaigned primarily on the issue of immigration and Cantor's support of providing a path to citizenship for those brought to the United States illegally as children, noting that Cantor was more liberal on immigration than any other Republican. Brat went on to win the general election in November.

REDISTRICTING BENEFITS REPUBLICANS

Despite making few gains at the national level in 2010, Republicans won control of many state legislatures that year, which gave them the opportunity to lead the redistricting process following the decennial census. That benefit became clear on election night in 2014, when some newly drawn districts resulted in a greater vote share for Republicans. Back in 2012 in North Carolina, Rep. Mike McIntyre, a Democrat, had been reelected to his seat representing the state's 7th Congressional District after defeating state Sen. David Rouzer. McIntyre won his ninth term only after a recount confirmed his slim margin of victory in the district that had not been represented by a Republican in Congress since 1868. Following McIntyre's retirement, in 2014, Rouzer faced off against Democrat Jonathan Barfield for the open Congressional seat and won by more than 22 points. The race is frequently cited as evidence of party-serving gerrymandering.

However, the Republican wave was so significant that even in states where redistricting was handled by Democrats or done in a bipartisan fashion, Republicans came out on top. In Illinois, where Democrats controlled the redistricting process, Republicans defeated two Democratic incumbents, while in Iowa, a state that requires both parties to participate in district mapping, Democratic candidates Pat Murphy and Staci Appel both lost.

DEMOCRATS WEIGHED DOWN BY OBAMA, PERSONAL SCANDALS

The president's unpopularity was second only to that of Congress, and Obama proved to have little clout in pulling Democrats, especially those in competitive districts, across the finish line. Some Democrats chose to retire rather than face difficult reelection battles, including Jim Matheson in Utah and McIntyre in North Carolina. Both of those seats ultimately went to Republicans. Eleven Democratic incumbents lost to Republican challengers, including long-serving members Nick Rahall II of West Virginia and John Barrow of

Georgia. Rahall was first elected in 1976 and was defeated by Evan Jenkins by nearly 11 points. Barrow, a conservative Democrat, lost by nearly 10 percentage points to Rick Allen. In the Syracuse, New York, district, two-term incumbent Democrat Dan Maffei lost to challenger John Katko by 19 percentage points. Six-term Rep. Timothy Bishop lost in New York's 1st District to Lee Zeldin. Both Maffei and Bishop represented districts that Obama had easily carried in 2012.

Bishop was not just hampered by the president's unpopularity. He was also under investigation by the Justice Department over allegedly seeking a campaign donation from a constituent for whom he had previously helped get a fireworks permit. The investigation was closed without any action two months prior to the election, but the National Republican Campaign Committee continued to target Bishop with ads about the donation. In a rebuttal, the Democratic Congressional Campaign Committee said Bishop's opponent favored privatizing entitlement programs such as Social Security.

José Antonio Garcia Jr., in Florida's 26th District, was also subject to a federal investigation into his 2010 campaign and the alleged funding of a third-party candidate intended to siphon votes from his opponent. In the 2014 race, Garcia's Republican opponent, Carlos Curbelo, seized on a ramp-up of the criminal investigation of those tied to Garcia's 2010 campaign, while Garcia used a strategy similar to Bishop's and tied Curbelo to entitlement reforms that would not benefit Floridians. Curbelo went on to win by 3 percentage points.

Even Democrats in districts that were considered safe had closer-than-expected races. In the final weeks of the campaign, Republican groups began spending heavily in districts that might be flipped in what became the Republican tsunami. In October, Crossroads GPS, a conservative advocacy group backed by prominent Republicans, spent $1 million on television ads to target Democrat Steven Horsford in Nevada. Despite being in what the *Rothenberg Political Report/Roll Call* considered a "Safe Democratic" district, Horsford lost to Republican Crescent Hardy. In New York, Rep. Louise Slaughter won with only 871 votes in a district Obama carried in 2012 with nearly 60 percent of the vote. In Minnesota, incumbent Collin Peterson won by a narrow margin, as did Dave Loebsack in Iowa.

STATE BALLOT INITIATIVES

Despite handing both houses of Congress to Republicans, voters were far more liberal leaning in their opinions on nearly 150 ballot measures. According to an analysis by *The Washington Post*, in some states, citizens voted in favor of liberal ballot measures but against Democrats. For example, in Alaska, the Republican candidate for governor won his race against incumbent Mark Begich by 3.2 percent, but the initiative to legalize marijuana won by 4.6 percent, indicating that voters were 7.8 percentage points more liberal on marijuana legalization than their choice for governor. This ran contrary to early 2014 political commentary indicating that

liberal ballot measures would help carry Democrats to victory in competitive and open races.

A variety of ballot measures were considered across the country, including legalizing recreational marijuana, abortion rights, gun control, and prohibition. Spending on ballot measures reached more than $1 billion, and most of that money went toward stopping referenda from being added to the ballot. The number of ballot initiatives was lower than usual, reflecting the effort to keep measures off the ballot, as well as a desire to push some issues until the presidential election in 2016, when turnout would be higher.

Legalization of Marijuana

Two states—Alaska and Oregon—and the District of Columbia included questions for voters on their 2014 ballots about legalizing the recreational use of marijuana; notably, the D.C. measure did not include legalization of the sale of marijuana but would permit possession of a small amount for personal use if the drug were acquired elsewhere. All three measures succeeded, and Alaska and Oregon were poised to become the third and fourth states, after Colorado and Washington State, to legalize recreational marijuana. In Washington, D.C., despite passing by a more than 2-to-1 margin, Congress had the opportunity to vote to reject the referenda, which it did under a December 2014 spending agreement to keep the government funded through September 2015. D.C. leaders expressed shock at the addition of the policy rider, but Rep. Andy Harris, R-Md., who had proposed a similar amendment during budget negotiations in the summer, said the Constitution provided Congress the power to determine what happens in a federal district.

In Florida, voters were considering whether to legalize marijuana specifically for medical use. The ballot measure was closely watched, because similar referenda across the country tend to increase the vote share of liberal-leaning individuals. With the Republican-turned-Democrat-turned-Independent former Governor Charlie Crist on the ballot seeking a Senate seat, many speculated that this would increase his chance of victory. Florida law requires a 60 percent majority to enact a referendum, and the medical marijuana initiative received only 57 percent of the vote. Crist also lost to Republican Rick Scott by around 1 percent.

Minimum Wage Hikes

Backed by President Obama, Democrats in the House and Senate frequently floated proposals to raise the federal minimum wage to above $7.25 per hour. Unable to gain any traction with Republicans, the president used his executive authority to increase the federal contractor minimum wage to $10.10 per hour and encouraged state leaders to take action on the issue. According to the president, raising the minimum wage had support from all sides of the political sphere.

In November 2014, five states—Alaska, Arkansas, Illinois, Nebraska, and South Dakota—included minimum wage hikes on their ballots. These measures are typically popular with voters on both sides of the aisle. The one Democratic-led state in the group, Illinois, had the largest minimum wage increase to $10 per hour. Arkansas and South Dakota were seeking an increase to $8.50 per hour, while Alaska wanted to increase its minimum wage from $8.75 to $9.75 per hour by 2017, after which point it would be tied to inflation. If passed, Nebraska's minimum wage was set to rise to $9 per hour by January 1, 2016. All five states approved the minimum wage ballot measures by double-digit margins.

Gun Control

Voters in Alabama and Washington considered gun-related measures on their November 2014 ballots. In Alabama, a question was posed about whether the state should create a law to make it difficult to restrict gun ownership. The measure would change the state's constitution to include the language, "Every citizen has a fundamental right to bear arms in defense of himself or herself and the state. Any restriction on this right shall be subject to strict scrutiny." The measure received significant support from the National Rifle Association (NRA), and the amendment passed with 72.4 percent of the vote.

Washington had two competing gun-control measures on the ballot. One asked voters if the state should require background checks before a gun purchase can be made at a gun show or in a private transaction. The second asked if the state should prevent extensive background checks for gun purchasers. Ahead of Election Day, lawmakers admitted that they were unsure what would happen if both measures were approved. Ultimately, voters approved the initiative expanding background checks with 59 percent of the vote and rejected the other 55 percent to 44 percent.

Abortion Rights

Colorado, North Dakota, and Tennessee considered abortion measures in November 2014. In Colorado, voters were asked if fetuses should be included in the state's criminal code under the definition of "person." The so-called personhood amendment would essentially define life as beginning at conception. Opponents of the measure said passage would outlaw abortion in the state, while supporters disagreed, arguing that the measure's intent was not to outlaw abortion but to charge someone with an act of homicide if a fetus were killed, either along with the mother or separately, for example, in a car accident. Voters rejected the amendment 64.8 percent to 35.2 percent.

North Dakota voters considered a somewhat similar amendment that asked whether the state constitution should be amended to read that there is an "inalienable right to life" beginning at the moment of conception. This would have made North Dakota the first state to enshrine in its constitution a definition of life beginning at conception. The measure failed, 64.1 percent to 35.9 percent.

In Tennessee, Amendment 1 would add language to the state constitution allowing the legislature to change, repeal, or enact laws on abortion, even in cases of rape or incest, and when the mother's life was in danger. Opponents said the measure would eventually lead to legislators banning all abortions. The measure passed 52.6 percent to 47.4 percent.

State Hunting Initiatives

Alabama, Maine, and Mississippi all included initiatives related to hunting on their ballots. In Alabama and Mississippi, voters overwhelmingly passed measures to amend the state constitution to declare hunting a right and the preferred method of animal population control. The vote in Maine was somewhat closer, and voters were considering whether dogs and bait should be banned from use during bear hunting. There, the referendum was rejected 53.4 percent to 46.6 percent.

Voting

Voters in Connecticut, Missouri, and Montana all considered initiatives related to the act of voting. In Connecticut and Missouri, the question posed was how early voters should be allowed to cast a ballot. In Connecticut, the expansion of early voting and absentee ballot access was rejected, 52 percent to 47 percent. Missouri voters rejected a six-day window for early voting. In Montana, the initiative asked whether the state should end same-day voter registration and instead require voters to register no later than the Friday before an election. Voters rejected the change 56.9 percent to 43.1 percent.

Gubernatorial Races

Nationwide, voters were selecting the governors of thirty-six states, with Republicans defending twenty-two seats and Democrats fourteen. Republicans had a net gain of two seats, while Democrats had a net loss of three seats. An Independent won one seat. Republican pickups came in Arkansas, Illinois (an incumbent defeat), Maryland, and Massachusetts. Only two incumbent Republican governors lost their 2014 races: Pennsylvania's Tom Corbett and Alaska's Sean Parnell, who was replaced by an Independent.

The biggest surprise of the night came in Maryland, where Republican Larry Hogan and Democratic Lt. Gov. Anthony Brown faced off to replace Gov. Martin O'Malley, a Democrat. Brown received heavy support from the outgoing governor, along with national political heavyweights such as President Obama, First Lady Michelle Obama, and former President Bill Clinton. But he struggled to differentiate himself from O'Malley, who had grown increasingly unpopular as his two terms in the governor's mansion came to an end. Brown also focused more on the negative impact of a possible Hogan victory than on his own positions and priorities. But what truly hurt Brown, and what catapulted Hogan to victory, was low Democratic turnout in the state's population centers such as Baltimore and Montgomery County.

2015

The Legislative Year

In 2015, President Obama was facing a new political reality with Republican majorities in both the House and the Senate. The parties found little to agree on, and with the 2016 presidential election season getting an early start and five senators throwing their hats into the ring, there was little hope at the start of the year for any major progress on a number of issues that had been dogging the legislative body for years. Where the president and Congress did find space to work together was on so-called fast-track authority, which allows the president to negotiate trade deals without the threat of a Congressional amendment or filibuster. President Obama sought the authority, which had expired in 2007, to facilitate finalization of the Trans-Pacific Partnership (TPP), a trade deal with twelve primarily Pacific Rim countries. Despite Democratic opposition over a belief that multilateral trade deals tend to hurt Americans by killing jobs and suppressing wages, the Republican majority in both chambers pushed the bill forward to passage.

President Obama faced a series of legal challenges to his November 2014 executive actions on illegal immigration, including a lawsuit filed by twenty-six states alleging that deferring deportation ran afoul of federal rulemaking requirements. Two federal courts ruled that the president had exceeded his executive authority, and, given that Congress had still failed to pass comprehensive immigration reform, the administration subsequently appealed the decisions to the Supreme Court.

The state and local levels proved somewhat more active than Congress, as tense debates over religious freedom and civil liberties played out and began creating battle lines for the 2016 election. In March, Indiana Governor Mike Pence, who would in 2016 be the Republican vice presidential nominee, signed a religious freedom law aimed at protecting citizens from being compelled to provide services for same-sex weddings or other such events with which they disagreed on religious grounds. The move immediately drew criticism from civil liberties groups, and the governor quickly signed a second bill clarifying the original law but did not go so far as to extend antidiscrimination protections to the LGBTQ community. Arkansas Governor Asa Hutchinson was presented with a similar religious freedom bill in March but, given the controversy in Indiana, asked the legislature to develop something more palatable, which he eventually signed into law in April. In Kentucky, a county clerk refused to issue marriage licenses to any couple over her objection to being required to give such licenses to same-sex couples, which she said was a violation of her faith. The American Civil Liberties Union (ACLU) filed suit against Davis, and a federal judge ruled that she could disagree with the Supreme Court's ruling granting marriage rights to same-sex couples but that she would not be excused from doing her job, which required providing marriage licenses. The clerk continued to deny marriage licenses for same-sex couples and spent five days in jail for this reason.

PARTISANSHIP PREVENTS SIGNIFICANT CONGRESSIONAL ACTION

Despite early predictions, Congress had a relatively productive year that culminated in the passage of a $1.15 trillion omnibus spending bill. The body was also able to extend tax breaks, overhaul the Elementary and Secondary Education Act, and enact a multiyear authorization for highway and transit programs, the first time Congress had done so in a decade. Congress also granted the president fast-track authority to expedite trade agreements, enacted legislation reducing the government's surveillance powers, ended a ban on exporting crude oil, reauthorized the Export-Import Bank, and confirmed two of President Obama's nominees for the positions of Secretary of Defense and Attorney General.

However, the bitter partisan divide remained, and the two parties frequently sparred over who had been more obstructionist in the minority. There was also dissent in the Republican Party, which was grappling with how to handle the newly formed Freedom Caucus, a far-right group of legislators that was sympathetic to the tea party movement. The group demanded input in the Republican caucus's agenda, and discontent among members forced the resignation of Speaker John Boehner, R-Ohio, who was succeeded by Rep. Paul Ryan, R-Wis., chair of the Ways and Means Committee.

CONGRESS IN 2015

The first session of the 114th Congress began January 6, 2015. The House adjourned December 18, 2015. The Senate adjourned on December 18, 2015. The Senate was in session for a total of 1,073 hours over 168 days. The House was in session 804 hours over 157 days.

Members introduced 2,823 bills and resolutions in 2015, compared with 4,604 in 2010 and 9,079 in 2009. Congress cleared 115 bills that were enacted into law, 109 fewer than in 2014. President Barack Obama issued five vetoes during this session. *(See public laws table, p. 12; presidential vetoes, p. 647.)*

The House took 703 roll-call votes in 2015, the highest since 2009. The Senate took 339 recorded votes, 27 fewer than in 2014. *(See recorded votes table, p. 13.)*

REPUBLICANS REJECT OBAMA INITIATIVES

The 114th Congress began with a protracted fight over President Obama's executive actions on immigration. In November 2014, amid a failed congressional effort to pass comprehensive immigration reform, the president issued a series of executive orders that sought to address the status of the millions of immigrants in the country illegally. The executive actions enhanced border security and enforcement and also deferred deportations of certain undocumented immigrants who had been in the country for at least five years and expanded a similar program for those who were brought to the United States illegally as children. Republicans immediately questioned the constitutionality of the orders and promised to fight back when the new session of Congress convened. *(See discussion of Obama executive orders in Chapter 13, pp. 394, 396.)*

Some Republicans sought to use the annual Homeland Security appropriations bill as a means to roll back Obama's orders, because the bill covers both the Department of Homeland Security and other agencies that are responsible for enforcing immigration laws. Senate Democrats refused to back the plan, and without enough Republican votes to overcome Democratic resistance, Republicans in both chambers instead agreed on a clean funding bill that did not include any policy riders related to immigration. *(See discussion of Homeland Security appropriations for FY 2016 in Chapter 3, pp. 139–141.)*

In his sixth State of the Union Address in January, President Obama, who was facing a Republican majority in both Houses of Congress for the first time, laid out his priorities for the year, but there was little expectation that Republicans would support any of them. Primarily, the president focused on growing the economy and expanding the middle class. Unlike the president's 2014 address, his 2015 speech did not include threats to take executive action if Congress failed to act on his proposals, but the president did remind Congress that he was firmly in charge of the government. The president hinted many times throughout his speech at the need for greater bipartisanship, especially in relation to domestic challenges. President Obama said he had spoken to many members of Congress who were tired of politics as usual in Washington. "Imagine if we did something different . . . a better politics isn't one where Democrats abandon their agenda or Republicans simply embrace mine. A better politics is one where we appeal to each other's basic decency instead of our basest fears," Obama said in his State of the Union address.

In February, the president unveiled his fiscal 2016 budget, to which Republicans paid little attention. The more than $4 trillion budget was intended to end the sequester—something Obama called bad for both security and economic growth—largely by increasing taxes on the wealthiest Americans and corporations. Obama's budget would provide for a 7 percent increase in defense and domestic discretionary program budgets.

Republicans instead wanted to find ways to cut both taxes and the deficit and hoped to enact all twelve individual appropriations bills rather than being forced to adopt an omnibus package. This was predicated on their ability to adopt a final budget resolution to grant them use of the budget reconciliation process, a procedural tool that allows budget-related legislation to move through the Senate without the threat of a filibuster. Talks on using the reconciliation process broke down ahead of the summer recess because Democrats rebelled against a Republican proposal to use a budget account for overseas military operations in order to circumvent the sequester caps on discretionary defense spending while also failing to increase funding for nondefense programs.

When Congress reconvened, it was stuck in a stalemate made more difficult by the far-right members of the Republican caucus demanding that any continuing resolution used to avoid a government shutdown come October 1 had to include a provision that would deny funding to Planned Parenthood. It was only after Speaker John Boehner, R-Ohio, announced that he would resign his leadership position and Congressional seat that behind-the-scenes budget talks resumed.

The resulting budget agreement came just three days before Boehner's final day in Congress and included a suspension of the debt limit to allow the Treasury to borrow as much as it saw fit to avoid a default and also partially suspended sequestration levels for two years for both defense and nondefense spending. Despite Republicans' animosity toward their leaders and the overall plan, because all Democrats in the House and Senate backed the measure, along with one-third of Republicans in each chamber, the measure was able to pass.

By the end of the year, however, the two chambers had still not reached an agreement on any of the twelve individual appropriations bills and were again forced to complete a year-end omnibus measure. The $1.15 trillion bill passed on December 18 and was quickly signed by the president. Everyone had reason to be unhappy with both the process and the resulting bill. Republicans felt that they hadn't garnered enough concessions on issues like limiting Obama's environmental agenda and reducing the number of Syrian refugees allowed into the country. Democrats, on the other hand, scoffed that the agreement ended a ban on crude oil exports and didn't provide fiscal relief for Puerto Rico, which was on the verge of bankruptcy.

REPUBLICANS, DEMOCRATS FIND CONSENSUS IN HIGHWAY BILL

Where Democrats and Republicans could find common ground was on a highway bill, which the body passed in early December to provide a five-year, $305 billion authorization for highway and mass transit programs. When debating the measure, the early question was about how to financially support the Highway Trust Fund in an age of declining revenue from the federal fuel tax. Democrats supported increasing the gas tax or indexing it to inflation, which they argued could have offset the existing Highway Trust Fund shortfall. Republicans have generally opposed such a measure, and the more conservative members of the caucus would prefer that the federal government get out of the business of funding highways and transportation programs and instead leave that to the states.

The conference committee elected to transfer $70 billion from the General Fund to the Highway Trust Fund and then offset that transfer primarily through revenue from the Federal Reserve. Approximately $53 billion came from the central bank's surplus fund, while another $6.9 billion came from slashing a dividend paid by the Federal Reserve to banks with more than $10 billion in assets. The bill also authorized Amtrak and the Export-Import Bank, the body responsible for helping facilitate and finance exports of U.S. goods and services.

It was that latter provision that drew criticism from many on the right, especially those who were running for president. Conservatives see the bank as a form of corporate welfare and over the course of two years had blocked its reauthorization. Moderate Republicans partnered with Democrats in 2015, however, to use a discharge petition to force a vote on the floor. The vote succeeded and allowed the reauthorization to be attached to the far more popular highway bill. Those who opposed the bank's reauthorization proposed a number of amendments to the highway bill to restrict the bank's operations; all were defeated. Those Republicans who opposed the bank vowed to fight on. *(See discussion of surface transportation reauthorization in 2015–2016 in Chapter 6, pp. 225–228.)*

PRESIDENT OBAMA'S NOMINEES CONFIRMED

President Obama's two most high-profile 2015 nominees were former federal prosecutor Loretta Lynch as Attorney General and former deputy defense secretary and chief Pentagon weapons buyer Ashton Carter as Secretary of Defense. Carter was popular among Democrats and Republicans alike and was easily confirmed by the Senate 93–5. He gained Republican support during his confirmation hearing for his willingness to break with White House policy when he thought the strategy was wrong. However, Sen. John McCain, R-Ariz., was more practical in his assessment, noting that while Carter might be willing to disagree with the administration, he likely would not influence the president's decisions.

The Lynch nomination proved more difficult. Lynch was a former U.S. attorney in the Eastern District of New York, and although Republicans respected her credentials and felt she had the right experience for the job, her nomination became mired in a fight over President Obama's immigration executive actions that, among other things, stalled the deportation of millions of illegal immigrants. Nearly six months of debate and posturing followed Lynch's nomination to replace outgoing Attorney General Eric Holder, but on April 23, 2015, Lynch was confirmed by a 56–43 vote. She became the first black woman to hold the position.

CONGRESS BACKS FAST-TRACK TRADE AUTHORITY

Throughout much of his second term, President Obama had urged Congress to renew the authority that provides a president the ability to negotiate trade agreements without the threat of Congressional filibusters or amendments (Congress retains the ability to approve or reject any trade deal). So-called "fast-track" authority had been available to every president from 1974 to 2007, when Congress allowed the provision to lapse. In 2015, the president pushed Congress to reconsider to allow him to finish negotiations on the Trans-Pacific Partnership (TPP), a major trade agreement with eleven primarily Pacific Rim nations, and the Transatlantic Trade and Investment Partnership, an agreement with the European Union.

The president faced strong backlash from Democrats, backed by labor unions, who argued that trade agreements negotiated utilizing fast-track authority result in the loss of American jobs and reduced wages. Richard Trumka, president of the American Federation of Labor and Congress of Industrial Organizations (AFL-CIO), said that previous trade agreements had resulted in the outsourcing of jobs and lower wages.

President Obama was, however, able to find partners among Republican leaders in Congress to bring to committee the Bipartisan Congressional Trade Priorities Act of 2014, introduced in the Senate on January 9, 2014. The legislation would remain in effect until July 1, 2018, at which point Congress would again need to reauthorize it. The legislation never made it out of the committee, but following the midterm elections, the president made another push to approve a bill for the negotiating power necessary to finish the TPP. This time, a trade authority bill was introduced in the Senate, with a companion introduced in the House on the same day. The Trade Promotion Authority bill would provide the president fast-track authority but would also require that Congress receive detailed updates on any trade negotiations. In the House, the bill passed by only 10 votes, and in the Senate, it passed 60–38. The TPP was ultimately signed into law in February 2016, while the negotiations were ongoing on the Transatlantic Trade and Investment Partnership. *(See discussion of fast-track negotiating in Chapter 2, pp. 113–114, and Trans-Pacific Partnership in Chapter 2, pp. 115–117.)*

CONGRESS SEEKS COMPROMISE ON EDUCATION, ABORTION, MEDICARE

Members of Congress found consensus on an education bill that reauthorized the 1965 Elementary and Secondary Education Act while doing away with many of the provisions of the No Child Left Behind law passed during the administration of President George W. Bush. The new education policy would provide states more say in their education policy by removing accountability mandates and excessive testing. The bill prohibited the Secretary of Education from setting national academic standards, which were unpopular among conservative states-rights advocates, who felt that individual states were best capable of determining how to hold their schools and teachers accountable for academic performance.

In negotiating the deal, Democrats sought some concessions from Republicans to ensure that an equitable education system remained, especially in districts that are poor or primarily minority. The 1965 law being reauthorized specifically sought to use federal funds to even out the differences in school funding between rich and poor school districts to ensure all students received a quality public education.

Although it took nearly twelve months, on December 10, 2015, President Obama signed the Every Student Succeeds Act, reauthorizing the 1965 law. Provisions in the act ensured equitable access to high-quality education no matter an individual's living situations, required that students be taught to academic standards meant to help them succeed in careers and college, required annual statewide assessments, and sustained the Obama administration's investments in early childhood education programs. *(See discussion of No Child Left Behind in 2015–2016 in Chapter 10, pp. 334–337.)*

After a slew of undercover videos were released allegedly showing Planned Parenthood employees discussing and extracting aborted fetal tissue for medical research, many Republicans renewed their calls to prohibit federal funds from flowing to Planned Parenthood. Members argued that the group was profiting from selling fetal tissue, while Planned Parenthood said it was only compensated for storage and transportation of such items, which is legal under U.S. law. Antiabortion members attempted to defund Planned Parenthood in a stand-alone bill, which failed, and through an amendment to the fiscal 2016 government spending bill, which the president said he would veto. The year ended without any resolution on Planned Parenthood funding.

Congress did, however, reach an agreement on ending the scheduled Medicare reimbursement cuts to doctors. The Sustainable Growth Rate formula was developed under the 1997 Balanced Budget Act and dictated how Medicare doctors would be reimbursed. The formula increased payments to doctors when the rate of growth of spending on their services ran below inflation and cut payments when the growth in spending exceeded inflation. Since 2003, Congress had stepped in each year to implement what was known as a "doc fix" to block any payment reductions but was unable to agree on a permanent fix. In April 2015, Congress finally managed to permanently end the cuts by repealing the Sustainable Growth Rate formula.

CHARGES FILED AGAINST HOUSE AND SENATE MEMBERS

Criminal charges and ethics investigations brought down two House members and left one senator scrambling to keep his seat. Rep. Aaron Schock, R-Ill., resigned his seat on March 17 following an ethics investigation into alleged improper spending of his House member budget. Under review were charges related to concert tickets, charter planes, overseas personal travel, mileage reimbursements, and a $40,000 expense to redecorate his office to look like a set from the popular television show *Downton Abbey*. Announcing his resignation, Schock said the questions about his conduct had distracted from the work he was trying to do for his constituents. In November 2016, Schock was indicted on twenty-four counts, including theft of government funds, making false statements, and filing false tax returns.

Another 2015 indictment came against Rep. Chaka Fattah, D-Pa., and four of his associates related to his 2007 campaign for mayor of Philadelphia. Fattah was charged with bribery, racketeering, money laundering, bank fraud, mail and wire fraud, and filing false statements. Fattah denied the charges against him, saying he had never participated in any illegal activity as an elected official. In June 2016, Fattah was convicted in the case and stepped down from his seat shortly thereafter. Fattah had already lost the Democratic primary for his seat in the spring of 2016.

On the Senate side, Sen. Robert Menendez, D-N.J., was indicted on April 1 on federal corruption charges related to helping an associate work around government roadblocks to benefit his business and personal ventures. In return, Menendez received a number of paybacks, including large campaign contributions. Menendez pleaded not guilty and said he was prepared to fight the charges. Menendez refused to step down from his Senate seat but did temporarily step aside from his position as ranking member on the Foreign Relations Committee. (The Menendez trial subsequently took place in 2017, and the jury deadlocked.)

The Political Year

The first year of the 114th Congress also served as the kickoff of the 2016 presidential race. Republicans and Democrats began throwing their hats in the ring for the nomination in earnest in the spring of 2015, including five members of the Senate, and by August, Republicans were holding their first presidential candidate debate; Democrats followed shortly thereafter in October. The early primary season highlighted the stark divide between the two parties and the splintering that was happening within the Republican Party between its more moderate members and the far right.

By the end of the year, the 2016 presidential campaign was in full swing, and the field had narrowed to twelve Republican and three Democratic candidates. Wealthy real estate developer Donald Trump emerged as the Republican front runner. Trump was popular among Americans disaffected by traditional party politics and who appeared willing to take a chance on a nontraditional candidate. On the Democratic side, former senator and Secretary of State Hillary Clinton was fighting off an unexpectedly strong challenge by Sen. Bernie Sanders, I-Vt. Their battle showed that it was not only Republicans who had warring factions within their own party but also the Democrats, where sharp differences existed around what strategies were most important for growing the middle class and how the party's priorities should stack up.

LOUISIANA SENATOR LOSES GUBERNATORIAL BID

In November 2015, Sen. David Vitter, R-La., announced that he would not seek reelection to his Senate seat after his twelve-point loss in the Louisiana governor's race. Vitter said he had already decided ahead of the election that he wanted to pursue new opportunities. On election night, he told voters that he was ready to get to work in the Senate, but only for one more year.

Vitter's political life began in 1991, when he ran successfully for the Louisiana state House seat formerly held by Ku Klux Klan leader David Duke, who was resigning to run for governor. Eight years later, Vitter replaced Rep. Robert Livingston in his U.S. House seat after Livingston resigned over an extramarital affair. In 2004, Vitter ran for an open Senate seat and became the first popularly elected Republican senator in Louisiana history.

During his eleven years in the Senate, Vitter served as a member of the Banking, Housing, and Urban Affairs Committee and as chair of the Small Business and Entrepreneurship Committee. On the Banking committee, Vitter reached across the aisle to partner with Sen. Sherrod Brown, D-Ohio, to infuse greater security into the financial sector and limit the government safety net for certain banking operations. Vitter and Brown sponsored a bill aimed at ending the perception that the government would always bail out troubled banks. Vitter reprised the underlying idea of the bill in May 2015 when he proposed an amendment to a financial regulatory relief bill that would set minimum equity requirements for banks holding more than $500 billion in assets.

As chair of the Small Business and Entrepreneurship Committee, Vitter was a leading voice on efforts to deny federal funds to so-called sanctuary cities, areas with laws or ordinances in place that limit cooperation with federal immigration enforcement activities. Vitter seized on an instance in San Francisco in which an illegal immigrant was charged with murdering a woman named Kathryn Steinle. The illegal immigrant had previously been held by San Francisco authorities but was released ahead of the murder.

Vitter was viewed as the most likely successor to outgoing Republican governor Bobby Jindal.   In the gubernatorial race, Vitter was one of many candidates to enter the state's "jungle primary," a nonpartisan race that places all eligible candidates on one ballot. If no single candidate receives more than 50 percent of the vote, the top two vote getters move on to a runoff election. In the October primary, Vitter finished second to state Rep. John Bel Edwards, a Democrat, but neither topped the 50 percent threshold to avoid a runoff. The runoff was scheduled for November 21. Ahead of the vote, Edwards used a 2007 scandal against Vitter, in which his phone number was found in the records of the D.C. Madam, Deborah Palfrey. An ad ran two weeks before the election claiming that "Vitter chose prostitutes over patriots."

Interestingly, Vitter had apologized back in 2007 when the scandal came to light, asking for forgiveness for his "very serious sin," and the situation did not hurt him in his 2010 Senate reelection bid, which he won by 19 points. In 2015, however, the issue proved fatal. *The Washington Post* explained this as a combination of a difficult primary fight, Obama not being on the ballot, Edwards's conservative bent, and the fact that voters in Louisiana tend to worry more about their governor than their senators. Curt Anderson, a Republican adviser to Gov. Jindal, said voters take the governor's race more seriously than the race for Senate. On November 21, Edwards easily won with 56.1 percent of the vote to Vitter's 43.9 percent.

REPUBLICANS HOLD SEATS IN THREE SPECIAL ELECTIONS

Three special elections were held for House seats in 2015, and all were held by Republicans. These three seats were vacated by Rep. Michael Grimm of New York, Rep. Aaron Schock of Illinois, and Rep. Alan Nunnelee of Mississippi. Both Grimm and Schock resigned under pressure, while Nunnelee's seat was vacated at the time of his death.

New York

In New York's 11th District, Dan Donovan, a Republican and former District Attorney, and Democrat Vincent Gentile, a city council member from Brooklyn, faced off in the May 5 special election to replace Rep. Grimm, who had plead guilty to tax fraud. Donovan staked his election on the importance of keeping a Republican in the seat, given that the party was in control of the U.S. House. Throughout his campaign, Donovan portrayed himself as being in lockstep with Republicans in Washington. This included staking a position as a tough critic of President Obama and his policies. According to Donovan, if New York Mayor Rudolph Giuliani, a Republican, had been elected in 2008 rather than Obama, the United States would have a better standing in the world. However, the 11th District is the only New York City–area congressional seat held by a Republican, so those seeking to replace Grimm needed to seek some balance with the Democrats. For Donovan, that came in the form of illegal immigration. Donovan said he would seek a change to current immigration policy that would make it easier for those following U.S. law to become citizens. His message was a bit less clear on how to deal with those brought to the United States illegally as children and their parents. While indicating that he did not want to break up families, Donovan said he supported a pathway to citizenship for some, coupled with fines and penalties, but that those cases should not be considered ahead of those seeking to apply for citizenship through the proper, legal channels.

Donovan, a former District Attorney, faced questions throughout the campaign about his office's handling of the Eric Garner case. Garner was killed in July 2014 while being held in a chokehold by a New York City police officer. Donovan's office was responsible for presenting evidence to the grand jury that was considering whether they would proceed with criminal charges against the officer; the grand jury ultimately decided not to pursue those charges. Donovan's office also fought to prevent the release of the trial proceedings. Donovan was asked if Congress should take up the question of the excessive use of force by police but said he felt local governments were better situated to determine what was best for their communities.

Gentile, a relative unknown in the district, had an uphill battle from the start, and the Democratic Congressional Campaign Committee basically wrote off the race as a loss. He did receive backing from Mayor Bill de Blasio, although the mayor was an unpopular figure in the district. Throughout the two months of his campaign, Gentile touted his experience from eleven years as assistant district attorney in Queens, six years in the state Senate, and three terms on city council. Gentile stressed that voters should not expect someone without any legislative experience to be an effective legislator, just as they would not choose a grocer to become an astronaut. Donovan ultimately won the seat with nearly 59 percent of the vote.

Mississippi

In Mississippi's 1st District, Rep. Alan Nunnelee died on February 6 due to a complication from brain surgery. Thirteen candidates vied to replace Nunnelee in the May 12 special election, but no candidate reached the 50 percent threshold needed to win outright. Thus, the top two vote getters—Republican District Attorney Trent Kelly and Democrat Walter Zinn—faced each other in a runoff on June 2.

The seat had been comfortably in Democratic hands for more than five decades before Republicans claimed it in 1994. Since that time, the district has become deeply conservative, and Democrats held the seat only once, from May 2008 to January 2011, before Nunnelee won. Kelly was the clear front runner from the start and had the support of Nunnelee's widow and a large base of voters from his time as district attorney. Kelly described himself as a religious man who believes in protecting the country, shrinking the size of government, and supporting small businesses. This resonated well in the district, and Kelly was also able to tout his credentials as an Iraq War veteran and colonel in the Army National Guard. Kelly was endorsed by the National Rifle Association and the National Right to Life Committee, powerful forces in deep red Mississippi.

Despite Kelly's anticipated dominance, it was Zinn who took first place in the May 12 race, although with less than 20 percent of the vote. Zinn was the only Democrat running to replace Nunnelee. An attorney well known in local Democratic circles, Zinn served as an aide to two former Jackson mayors and worked for former Rep. Roger Wicker, D-Miss. Zinn said that he had spent his career committed to helping the most qualified candidates get elected to public office and advocating for what the citizens of Mississippi needed most. Zinn, however, fell well short of Kelly in the June 2 runoff and received only 30 percent of the vote.

Illinois

In March, Rep. Aaron Schock, R-Ill., resigned from his seat amid a federal investigation into possible misuse of funds for personal travel and office redecoration. A special election was set for September 10 to replace Schock. State Senator Darin LaHood, son of Obama's Secretary of Transportation Ray LaHood, won the July 7 Republican primary with 69 percent of the vote. In the deeply conservative district, the primary was widely viewed as paramount to the general election, and there was little question that LaHood would win in September.

LaHood's family is well connected in the Illinois district he sought to represent. His father was a staff member for former House Minority Leader Rep. Robert Michel, and Ray LaHood went on to replace Michel when he retired in 1994. LaHood was an intern and legislative assistant for House members and served as an aide on the powerful Appropriations Committee. LaHood said he was running to create a better future for the citizens of Illinois and that he would do so by working to reduce the national debt, increase transparency in government, and repeal the Affordable Care Act.

Challenging LaHood on September 10 was Army Reserve officer Rob Mellon. Mellon had previously sought election to the U.S. House in 2014 but was defeated in the Democratic primary. Mellon was bested by LaHood's fundraising prowess and high-profile endorsements and secured only 31 percent of the vote.

SENATORS VIE FOR PRESIDENTIAL NOMINATION

Five senators—four Republicans and one Independent—were among the twenty-three major party candidates vying for their respective parties' presidential nominations. The race to replace outgoing President Obama began in earnest in 2015, and by the close of the year, four of the declared senators—Republicans Ted Cruz of Texas, Rand Paul of Kentucky, and Marco Rubio of Florida and Independent Bernie Sanders of Vermont (who caucused with the Democrats)—remained in the running. Only Republican Lindsey Graham of South Carolina, who failed to gain any traction among the large pool of candidates, dropped out before the end of the year.

Ted Cruz

Cruz, who had been in the Senate for only two years, announced on Twitter his intent to run. "I'm running for President and I hope to earn your support!" he wrote on March 23. Cruz had made a name for himself in the Senate for his staunch opposition to Democrats and President Obama's policies. His attempt to differentiate himself from his Senate Republican colleagues by holding firm on hardline conservative issues rather than seeking compromise irritated some in leadership and came to a head in July 2015 when, on the Senate floor, Cruz accused Senate Majority Leader Mitch McConnell, R-Ky., of lying. The issue was whether McConnell had coerced Cruz into voting for a trade bill under the false assurance that McConnell would not provide reauthorization for the Export-Import Bank. McConnell, however, went on to attach reauthorization for the body to a surface transportation bill.

Cruz, who was elected in 2012 on the back of the tea party, became known primarily for talking. He conducted lengthy orations, including holding the Senate floor in September 2013 for twenty-one hours and nineteen minutes to speak on the necessity of defunding the Affordable Care Act. The speech was not technically a filibuster because he did not have the support of a majority of his colleagues and was ultimately required by Senate rules to yield the floor to a vote on a spending package to fund the federal government through mid-November. But that did not stop Cruz from using his time to rail against the president, take questions from other senators, and read *Green Eggs and Ham* to his children, who were watching at home.

The son of a Cuban immigrant who was born in Canada and raised in Houston, Texas, Cruz was politically active from an early age. He held various government positions including Solicitor General of Texas, Director of the Office of Policy Planning at the Federal Trade Commission, and Associate Deputy Attorney General at the Justice Department. Cruz also spent time as a policy advisor during former President George W. Bush's 2000 campaign. He returned to private practice before setting up a 2012 run for the Senate. *The Washington Post* called Cruz's defeat of sitting Lt. Gov. David Dewhurst in the Republican primary "the biggest upset of 2012."

Cruz remained in the Republican presidential nominee race until May 2016, when he exited following a series of primary losses to billionaire businessman Donald Trump. Announcing his withdrawal from the race, Cruz said he had promised early on only to remain in the race if there was a path to victory for his campaign. At the time he left the race, Cruz had been mathematically eliminated from securing the nomination.

Rand Paul

Sen. Rand Paul, R-Ky., was the second senator to throw his hat into the ring. On April 7, he announced that he was running to "return our country to the principles of liberty and limited government." Paul, the son of Rep Ron Paul, R-Texas, who ran unsuccessfully three times for president, said he would bring his own brand of "conservative constitutionalism" to the voters. The senator classified himself as a libertarian and maintained as one of his platforms the need to limit the power of the government to only what it is constitutionally mandated to do.

Paul frequently reached across the aisle to partner with Democrats on issues related to criminal justice reform, especially as it related to penalizing drug offenders. Paul also went toe to toe with Republicans over the military and foreign policy, arguing that the United States should support stability abroad rather than sewing chaos by not fully considering all outcomes before an action is taken. In 2013, Paul led

the effort to stall or reduce aid to Egypt in the wake of the overthrow of its government. Two years later, he again broke with Republicans, opposing sanctions on Iran during negotiations on the Joint Comprehensive Plan of Action (JCPOA).

On March 6, 2013, Paul held the Senate floor for thirteen hours in an effort to delay a confirmation vote on John Brennan, who was nominated by President Obama for the position of Central Intelligence Agency (CIA) director. Paul promised to oppose Brennan's nomination in February over questions about whether the Obama administration would ever use an unmanned aerial drone to kill an American citizen on U.S. soil. The attorney general responded to Paul, noting that it was not the intent of the administration to do so but that the devices could be used in the event of "an extraordinary circumstance." That did not satisfy Paul, who called the response "more than frightening." Upon taking the floor, Paul said he would speak until all Americans and their leaders understood that no citizen of the United States should be killed by a drone on American soil without being found guilty of a crime through the normal judicial process. Two years before, Democrats had already invoked the "nuclear option" to revise the rules of Senate proceedings and require only a simple majority to end debate on a nomination and move to a confirmation vote rather than the previously required sixty votes. Immediately after Paul yielded the floor, Sen. Dick Durbin, D-Ill., motioned to end debate on Brennan's nomination.

Paul remained in the race until February 3, 2016, exiting after receiving only 4.5 percent of the vote during the Iowa caucuses. In a statement, he said he stood ready to fight for liberty and would continue to pursue limited government, privacy rights, criminal justice reform, and a more reasonable foreign policy.

Marco Rubio

Sen. Rubio of Florida, the son of Cuban immigrants, entered the presidential race on April 13. "Grounded by the lessons of our history, but inspired by the promise of our future, I announce my candidacy for president of the United States," he said in front of a crowd of supporters in Miami. Rubio said that while his candidacy might appear a longshot to those in other nations, the United States is a place where anyone—even the son of an immigrant bartender and maid—can become president.

Rubio was first elected to public office at the age of twenty-six, when he won a seat as city commissioner in West Miami. He went on to serve nine years in the Florida legislature, in 2007 assuming the role of Speaker of the House. He was the first Cuban American to hold that position in Florida history. In 2010, Rubio faced off against former Florida Gov. Charlie Crist in the Republican Senate primary. Crist and Rubio had frequently clashed during Rubio's time as speaker, and Crist was an early favorite to win the seat. Rubio, however, embraced the tea party ideals that were growing in popularity among conservatives and was carried to victory. After winning the primary, Rubio worked to downplay his ties to the tea party to better align himself with the general population of Florida voters.

Although initially viewed as the conservative answer to Obama's meteoric rise, Rubio struggled to gain traction on some of his policies, such as immigration. He favored offering a path to citizenship for those in the country illegally, a position with which many in the Republican Party strongly disagreed. In 2013, Rubio was part of the Gang of Eight senators who wrote a bill to overhaul the U.S. immigration system. The Senate passed that bill, which enhanced border security, revised employment-based immigration, and expanded the use of the E-Verify employment system. It also included a provision allowing illegal immigrants in the country to apply for probationary legal status and eventually seek citizenship. The House never considered the measure.

Rubio had, however, embraced traditionally Republican positions on issues such as the Affordable Care Act, and he refused to appropriate funds to implement the law, a move that led to the sixteen-day government shutdown in October 2013. Rubio was a defense and foreign policy hawk and frequently voted to support measures that provided additional funds to counter the Islamic State of Iraq and the Levant (ISIL). Rubio also staunchly opposed President Obama's moves to normalize relations with Cuba. Early in his political rise, Rubio frequently shared that his parents had fled Cuba to escape the rule of dictator Fidel Castro. However, he later had to walk back those remarks after it came to light that his parents had emigrated to the United States two years before Castro took power.

Rubio exited the presidential race in March 2016 after losing his home state of Florida to Trump. Rubio said that while his campaign was on the right side of the issues, it was not on the side of victory in 2016.

Bernie Sanders

Sanders was the lone senator to seek the Democratic presidential nomination. He informally declared his candidacy in April and officially announced his bid on May 26. "After a year of travel, discussion and dialogue, I have decided to be a candidate for the Democratic nomination for president," Sanders wrote in an email to supporters. He said his campaign would be based on addressing income inequality, tightening financial rules in the banking sector, amending campaign finance laws to reduce the influence of money in politics, and addressing climate change.

Sanders entered politics in the early 1970s when he founded the Liberty Union Party in Vermont, his attempt at promoting candidates and policies that were neither solely Democratic nor Republican and not backed by corporate interests. He ran twenty times for positions ranging from mayor of Burlington, Vermont, to governor and Congress, but never once as a Democrat. In 1980, Sanders was elected mayor of Burlington, a position he held until 1989, when he chose not to seek reelection. In 1990, Sanders was elected as Vermont's only member of the U.S. House. He served until 2007, when he was elected senator.

Sanders, a self-described "Democratic socialist" was seventy-three when he entered the race, and his bid was considered a long shot, given some of his far-left positions. Sanders outlasted most of the other Democrats in the race including former Rhode Island Governor Lincoln Chafee, former Maryland Governor Martin O'Malley, and former Sen. Jim Webb of Virginia. He vowed to stay in the race until the Democratic convention in July to give a voice to the more progressive wing of the Democratic Party.

Sanders drew his support primarily from voters who characterized themselves as "very liberal" yet "independent." They tended to be younger, with at least some college education, and Sanders was widely popular on college campuses. Sanders's supporters at times complained that the system had been stacked against their candidate in favor of his key primary opponent, former Secretary of State Hillary Clinton. That was borne out just ahead of the Democratic convention in July, when emails from the chair of the Democratic National Committee, Debbie Wasserman Schultz, were leaked indicating that she had favored Clinton over Sanders. Schultz was forced to resign her position. The situation resulted in some Sanders convention delegates promising to walk out of the Philadelphia meeting en masse, although at the urging of Sanders, that did not come to fruition.

Clinton was ultimately chosen as the party's nominee on the first ballot at the convention on July 26, with 59.7 percent of the vote to Sanders's 39.2 percent.

Lindsey Graham

South Carolina senator Lindsey Graham was the last senator to enter the race and the first senator to exit after only seven months. When announcing his run on June 1, 2015, Graham said he wanted to be elected to address the problems of the United States "honestly and realistically, for the purpose of solving them, not hiding them or taking political advantage of them."

Much of Graham's campaign was focused on funding for the military and combating the rise of "radical Islam." Graham said terrorist groups were stronger and more capable of attacking the United States than they were on September 11, 2001, and that as president he would ensure their power was diminished. Graham frequently touted his national security experience and sought to increase the number of troops in Iraq and Syria to combat the Islamic State and other terrorist organizations. Graham said he wanted as many as 10,000 troops deployed to destroy the Islamic State.

Graham's campaign failed to gain footing among the front-runner candidates, and given the large field, he was relegated to second-tier debates that all but killed any chance he may have had at the nomination. In suspending his bid on December 21, Graham said he would return to the Senate to work toward his primary goal of securing the United States. In his last undercard debate before exiting the race, Graham urged voters to choose a candidate worthy of representing the United States, and noted he was not sure that was either Trump or Clinton.

2016

The Legislative Year

The lack of progress in Congress in 2016 was expected given the upcoming presidential election, lame-duck White House, and members doing their best to avoid any controversial votes that would hamper their reelection chances back home. Democrats and Republicans reached consensus on just enough issues to keep the government functioning, and even that required the passage of a series of continuing resolutions to keep the government funded and avoid a shutdown. Congress had no chance of passing its twelve separate appropriations bills, and even the use of an omnibus spending package was beyond their reach. Republicans tried to begin the year by achieving a top conservative priority, with both houses passing a repeal of the Affordable Care Act as a reconciliation measure, but the president vetoed it, and Republicans lacked the support to override the veto.

Among the body's achievements for the year were a formal authorization for the State Department, something Congress had failed to do during the past fourteen years, a defense authorization bill, a revision to the 1976 Toxic Substances Control Act, a reauthorization of the Water Resources Development Act, passage of a package of biomedical innovation bills (a pet project of Senate Majority Leader Mitch McConnell, known as the 21st Century Cures Act), bailout legislation for Puerto Rico, an energy policy bill, and a law requiring the labeling of foods with genetically modified ingredients. Although Congressional activity was halting, the year did bring about the resurgence of the gun control debate after forty-nine people were killed in a nightclub in Orlando, Florida, in the worst mass shooting in American history. Because the club was frequented by those in the LGBTQ community, President Obama labeled the shooting as a terror attack and hate crime. A week after the shooting, Senate Democrats held a twelve-hour filibuster in support of four gun control measures, all of which failed. A week after that, Rep. John Lewis, D-Ga., led a sit-in on the House floor calling for commonsense reform. But the year ended without any meaningful action on gun control.

President Obama used his final year in office to cement his legacy and deliver on some of the promises he had made over the course of the prior seven years. In September, the president ratified the Paris climate agreement, a successor to the Kyoto Protocol, intended to limit global climate change. This marked the first time the United States had ever ratified an international climate change accord, and the Paris Agreement entered into force just days before the November 8 election. In October, President Obama again exercised his executive authority to ban drilling on millions of acres of federal land in the Arctic and Atlantic Oceans. He also designated land in Nevada and Utah as national monuments to prohibit mining and drilling in those protected areas.

But Obama had less success in filling a vacancy on the Supreme Court after Justice Antonin Scalia died in February. The president nominated Merrick Garland, a chief judge for the United States Court of Appeals for the District of Columbia Circuit who was regarded as a moderate liberal. Senate Majority Leader Mitch McConnell, R-Ky., refused to bring the nomination before the Senate for consideration, arguing that during an election year, it would be more appropriate to wait until the new president was seated and allow that individual to choose a judge. McConnell was also gambling on a Republican winning the White House. Outraged Democrats lacked leverage to overcome McConnell's decision. The lack of a ninth justice for a majority of 2016 left the court deadlocked on a number of issues. *(See discussion of the Supreme Court in Chapter 16, p. 521.)*

BUDGET RESOLUTION CONSIDERED

The White House said that President Obama's $4.23 trillion fiscal 2017 budget proposal included proposals that would win Republican backing, including funding for the drug epidemic and expanded tax credits. Republicans were dismissive and barely considered the president's proposal in their own budget negotiations.

House Republicans started the year working on a budget resolution, although they did not necessarily need one because they had already passed a two-year budget deal in October 2015 that set topline spending limits for fiscal 2017 and that would have formed the basis of appropriations bills

---

CONGRESS IN 2016

The second session of the 114th Congress began on January 4, 2016. Both chambers adjourned on January 3, 2017. The Senate met on 165 days for a total of 780 hours. The House met on 131 days for a total of 633 hours.

A total of 1,466 bills and resolutions were introduced in 2016, compared with 6,903 in 2011 and 4,604 in 2010. Congress cleared 214 bills that were signed into public law. President Barack Obama issued five vetoes. *(See public laws table, p. 12; presidential vetoes, p. 647.)*

The House took 621 roll-call votes in 2016, 82 fewer than in 2015, and the lowest number of roll calls in the House since 2006. The Senate took 163 recorded votes in 2016, 176 fewer than in 2015. *(See recorded votes table, p. 13.)*

MONEY IN ELECTIONS

More than $8.8 billion was raised for the presidential and congressional elections between January 1, 2015, and December 31, 2016, according to a report from the Federal Election Commission (FEC). Of that total, $8.6 billion was spent—about $3.1 billion by the presidential and congressional candidates, $1.5 billion by political parties, and nearly $4 billion by outside political action committees (PACs) and other interest groups.

The Democratic National Committee and Republican National Committee spent similar amounts funding campaigns throughout the election cycle, at $347 million and $323 million, respectively. The Democratic Congressional Campaign Committee far outspent the National Republican Congressional Committee, $216.4 million to $160.6 million, and the same was true of the party's Senate political committees, with Democrats spending $177.4 million to the Republican's $133.9 million. Being outspent at the House and Senate level did not appear to matter, because Republicans maintained their control of both houses of Congress.

Presidential Race

Despite winning the election, Donald Trump's campaign was outraised by Democratic rival Hillary Clinton. According to the FEC report, Trump raised $350,668,436 to Clinton's $585,669,599. Trump contributed a significant amount of money to his own campaign, around $66 million, compared to Clinton's personal funds that totaled slightly more than $1.4 million.

Neither candidate accepted public financing for either the primary cycle or the general election. Each candidate was eligible for about $96 million in funds for the general election, but the tradeoff is that if a candidate accepts these funds, they cannot accept any private contributions or spend their own money (party, PAC, and individual expenditures would still have been allowable). Former Governor Martin O'Malley, who ran for the Democratic nomination, and Green Party candidate Jill Stein were the only two who accepted public financing during the 2016 election cycle.

Super PACs, formed after the 2010 Supreme Court rulings in *Citizens United* and *Speechnow.org v. FEC*, played a significant role in the 2016 campaign. These "independent expenditure-only" groups, otherwise known as Super PACs, are banned from coordinating their activity with any specific candidate or campaign, but they can raise and spend virtually unlimited amounts of money to indirectly support or oppose a candidate. The super PACs spent more than $1.8 billion in the 2016 election cycle, more than any other type of PAC.

Congressional Races

According to the FEC, House and Senate candidates running in the 2016 election cycle raised $1.6 billion and spent $1.6 billion between January 1, 2015, and December 31, 2016. Of the 217 candidates vying for the Senate, $594.5 million was raised and $625.3 million was spent (money spent in excess of receipts is primarily rollover funds from a candidate's past campaign). The race for the U.S. Senate in Pennsylvania, which featured incumbent Sen. Pat Toomey and Democrat Katie McGinty, was the most expensive of the year and, in fact, the most expensive in history, at around $170 million disbursed, according to FEC data.

Of the 1,400 candidates seeking a seat in the House, $1 billion was raised, of which more than $970 million was spent. Of note, those totals include the seven special elections conducted in 2015 and 2016. Four House races topped more than $20 million in spending by the candidate and outside groups, including Virginia's 10th District, the Minnesota 8th District, the Florida 18th District, and the Pennsylvania 8th District.

---

negotiations. Internal divisions quickly put a new budget resolution out of the question, because House Budget Committee members were unable to find enough spending cuts to satisfy fiscal hawks while sowing seeds of compromise for Democrats. The bill never made it out of committee.

WATER CONCERNS

Water Resources Development Act (WDA) bills are typically passed every two years, but partisan squabbling has prevented that from happening, and since 2000, only two reauthorization bills were signed into law. An update to the WDA did draw some compromise in 2016, and Congress was able to authorize nearly $11.7 billion for infrastructure projects with additional funds allocated to Flint, Michigan, to repair its drinking-water system in the wake of a lead poisoning scandal. The WDA bill authorized thirty new Army Corps of Engineers projects and modified eight existing projects. *(See discussion on water resources development in Chapter 7, pp. 260, 262.)*

On another water-related issue, a Congressional resolution to nullify the Waters of the United States regulation that outlines the types of bodies of water projected by the 1972 Clean Water Act was vetoed by the president. Senate Republicans failed to override the veto.

DEFENSE AUTHORIZATION BILL PASSED

Lawmakers managed to avoid a presidential veto of their fiscal 2017 defense authorization bill, though one was threatened by the White House after the chambers' committees reported out their draft bills. Many of the most contentious provisions that President Obama objected to—including House language that would effectively undo an executive order prohibiting sex- and gender-based discrimination by federal contractors—were removed from the bill or modified as the measure progressed through floor deliberations and conference. While the final conference report preserved some provisions that the White House strongly opposed, such as ongoing restrictions on the transfer of Guantanamo Bay detainees, both the House and Senate approved the compromise measure with veto-proof majorities.

Completion of the fiscal 2017 authorization bill marked Congress's fifty-fourth consecutive year of passing the annual defense policy measure. The final bill authorized a total of $611.2 billion in spending, of which $543.4 billion was approved for base defense spending and $67.8 billion was allowed in OCO funds. The bill also included a 2.1 percent military pay raise and a reorganization of the Pentagon's acquisition, technology, and logistics arm, creating instead two undersecretaries, one for acquisition and sustainment and another for research and engineering. *(See discussion of the fiscal defense authorization in Chapter 5, pp. 205–209.)*

The House passed two variations of a fiscal 2017 intelligence authorization bill, but the Senate failed to act before the end of the year. Ultimately, the Intelligence Authorization Act, which provides guidelines for the intelligence community, was tacked onto the fiscal 2017 omnibus appropriation. The legislation included language targeting Russia due to both its military incursion in Ukraine and Syria, and the U.S. intelligence community announcement that it had evidence of Russian interference in the 2016 presidential election. The legislation created a group within the executive branch that would counter "Russian actions to exert covert influence over peoples and governments."

STATE DEPARTMENT REAUTHORIZED

In April 2016, the Senate took up State Department authorization legislation originally proposed by Senate Foreign Relations Committee Chair Bob Corker, R-Tenn., and Ranking Member Ben Cardin, D-Md., in June 2015. Behind-the-scenes negotiations between Corker and Senators Marco Rubio, R-Fla., and Ted Cruz, R-Texas, enabled the bill to proceed after nearly a year of delay. As part of the deal, Rubio agreed to allow a vote to proceed on Obama's nomination of Roberta Jacobson as ambassador to Mexico, which had stalled in 2015 due to her role in normalizing U.S.–Cuba diplomatic relations. In return, Corker agreed to hold a committee vote on Rubio's proposed legislation to renew sanctions against Venezuelan officials over human rights violations. Rubio also agreed to help Cruz persuade the House to pass a measure renaming a street in front of the Chinese embassy in honor of prodemocracy leader and political prisoner Liu Xiaobo.

In the final bill, U.S. embassy security was a top priority, and $4.8 billion was authorized for security upgrades, maintenance, and construction. Lawmakers also required the State Department to determine high-risk, high-threat overseas posts; prioritize funding and security for those high-risk sites; and develop a joint contingency plan with the Department of Defense to secure U.S. embassies during crises. The legislation made changes to the line of communications between the State Department and Congress by ordering the Secretary of State to deliver monthly briefings regarding the opening or reopening of positions at any foreign embassies deemed high risk and by making the Assistant Secretary for Diplomatic Security accountable to the Secretary of State. Other security provisions included increasing the authority of the Department of State to penalize staff for security violations, mandating an annual review of and a report by the secretaries of State and Defense on Marine Security Guard units assigned to foreign diplomatic areas, and approving a transfer of up to 20 percent of Administration of Foreign Affairs appropriations to enhance embassy security. *(See discussion of the fiscal 2017 State Department authorizations in Chapter 4, pp. 167–169.)*

In other areas of foreign affairs, Congress imposed new sanctions on North Korea following its alleged hydrogen bomb test, satellite launch, and a threat from the regime of Kim Jong Un that the nation had a weapon capable of reaching the U.S. mainland. The passage of the sanctions bill was seen as a result of impatience in Congress with the administration's failure to take a stronger stance on the rogue regime. The law sanctioned foreign financial institutions and governments that either helped the country evade UN sanctions or helped it proliferate nuclear weapons.

RELIEF FOR PUERTO RICO

After failing in 2015 to reach an agreement on Puerto Rican debt restructuring, in 2016 Congress reached an agreement to allow Puerto Rico to restructure its $72 billion debt to help it avoid financial collapse. Puerto Rican officials asked Congress in 2015 to allow the island to declare bankruptcy and restructure debt in the same manner U.S. states can, but Republican lawmakers refused such proposals and argued that doing so would hurt U.S. investors. In October 2015, the Obama administration released its own proposal, asking Congress to provide the island a mechanism for debt restructure, in addition to developing a mechanism for independent fiscal oversight of the plan, reforming their Medicaid program, and allowing Puerto Ricans to qualify for the Earned Income Tax Credit. House and Senate legislation reflecting this language failed.

In May 2016, the Puerto Rico Oversight, Management, and Economic Stability Act (PROMESA) was introduced in the House, and granted Puerto Rico the ability to restructure $70 billion of its debt and placed a hold on lawsuits brought by creditors. It also established an oversight panel that would monitor progress. Although the legislation had support from both parties, there were a few, such as Sen. Robert Menendez, D-N.J., who said the bill amounted to treating the people of Puerto Rico "like subjects, not citizens." There was also opposition from the island's creditors, who ran an advertising campaign claiming that American taxpayers were bailing out Puerto Rico.

Obama urged Congress to pass the legislation before Puerto Rico was due to make its next debt payment on July 1, which the Puerto Rican government had already admitted it could not do. The House passed PROMESA on June 9, and the Senate followed on June 29. When President Obama signed the bill into law on June 30, he acknowledged that it would not solve all of Puerto Rico's financial challenges but that it was an important step to put the country on the path to stability. *(See discussion of Puerto Rico assistance in Chapter 2, pp. 56–58.)*

CHEMICAL LAW UPDATED

On June 22, 2016, the Frank R. Lautenberg Chemical Safety for the 21st Century Act was signed into law. It amended the 1976 Toxic Substances Control Act, which regulates household and industrial chemicals. The new law had the backing of both environmental groups and manufacturing trade associations. The law created a mandatory requirement for the Environmental Protection Agency (EPA) to evaluate existing chemicals with clear and enforceable deadlines, called for risk-based chemical assessments, increased public transparency of chemical information, and provided a consistent source of funding to the EPA to carry out the requirements of the law. President Obama said the legislation would protect the most vulnerable members of society from dangerous chemicals.

FAA STAYS OPEN

In July, the House and Senate reached an agreement on keeping the Federal Aviation Administration (FAA) open at existing funding levels through fiscal 2017, with the expectation that a longer-term reauthorization would be worked out in the 115th Congress. The extension also included safety measures and provisions related to drones.

The agreement followed a proposal submitted by House Transportation and Infrastructure Chair Bill Shuster, R-Pa., that would reauthorize the FAA for six years while also dividing air traffic control from the FAA and instead creating a federally chartered nonprofit that would take over air traffic control duties. Shuster's bill provided $69 billion in total, $51 billion for fiscal years 2017 to 2019, and another $18 billion for fiscal years 2020 to 2022, the smaller budget meant to reflect the air traffic control spinoff. House leaders never brought the legislation to a floor vote, and it was a nonstarter in the Senate.

BIOMEDICAL INNOVATION

Senate Majority Leader McConnell frequently touted the 21st Century Cures Act as one of his key legislative priorities. The package of biomedical innovation bills had been debated for more than two years and would alter the way products gained Food and Drug Administration (FDA) approval and establish a shorter path for new medical devices to reach the marketplace. The intent of the legislation was to get innovative treatment to patients faster and more efficiently.

As signed into law on December 13, 2016, the legislation changed the leadership structure at the Substance Abuse and Mental Health Services Administration and required greater transparency from the National Institutes of Health. It also created and reauthorized grants for state and community mental health care. The FDA was given expanded authority to recruit and retain experts in the field and expedited product development programs.

The law provided $4.8 billion to the National Institutes of Health over the next decade to address President Obama's cancer initiative and gave $500 million to the FDA and $1 billion to states to help fight prescription drug abuse. *(See discussion of streamlining drug approval in Chapter 9, pp. 316–318.)*

REGULATORY UNDOING

Continuing their campaign to undo the 2010 Dodd-Frank Wall Street Reform and Consumer Protection Act, in 2016 House committees approved bills that would repeal the law as well as one that would move the Consumer Financial Protection Bureau (CFPB) into the regular appropriations process (as written in the Dodd-Frank law, CFPB is funded by the Federal Reserve, which is not subject to annual Congressional appropriations). Neither measure made it to the floor. The full House did succeed in passing legislation that would remove twenty-seven banks from the "too big to fail list," but the Senate did not act. Banks included on the list are subject to enhanced federal scrutiny of their operations.

Republicans also found a way to stymie the work of the Export-Import Bank, which is responsible for financing and facilitating the export of U.S. goods and services. Congress had reauthorized the body in 2015, despite protests from Republicans who saw it as corporate welfare. But in 2016, the bank had only two seats on its five-member board filled. By law, it can only approve financing of more than $10 million with at least three members. Sen. Richard Shelby, R-Ala., chair of the Senate Banking Committee, refused to consider any nominees to fill the remaining seats on the board due to his deeply held belief that the bank was focused more on corporate welfare than on supporting the American economy.

The Political Year

Nearly all of 2016 was consumed by the presidential race that pitted former Secretary of State Hillary Clinton against billionaire businessman Donald Trump. Clinton and Trump frequently traded barbs on the campaign trail and during a series of three debates, with each straying from their policies and priorities to instead criticize each other's past misdeeds. Trump focused primarily on Clinton's handling of the 2012 attack on U.S. government facilities in Benghazi, Libya, that led to the death of four Americans, as well as her use of a private email server during her time as secretary of state and sexual assault allegations lobbed at Clinton's husband, former president Bill Clinton. Clinton primarily attacked Trump over his brash comments about women and a recording of him suggesting that he can sexually assault them because he is famous. Clinton also called out Trump for his views that she considered racist and xenophobic.

Throughout much of 2016, Clinton held a narrow but clear lead in the polls. But her campaign was stunned on October 28 when Federal Bureau of Investigation (FBI) director James Comey sent a letter to Congress indicating that the agency was reviewing new emails it had discovered related to Clinton's private email server. It was not until November 6, two days before the election, that Comey said the review was complete and that it had not changed the FBI's earlier assessment that there were no charges to be brought against Clinton. The Comey letter helped provide late momentum to the Trump campaign, the polls narrowed, and Clinton never recovered. Clinton largely failed to connect with voters on a personal level, and her well-crafted policy plans did not resonate in an antiestablishment year. Trump, despite his lack of experience in government, ran up enormous margins in rural areas to counter Clinton's overwhelming strength in cities. He was able to overcome Clinton's edge in the popular vote by narrowly carrying three swing industrial states with a total of 46 electoral votes: Pennsylvania, Michigan, and Wisconsin. Trump was ultimately elected president with 304 electoral votes to Clinton's 227, although Clinton received almost 3 million more votes than Trump. She was the fifth candidate in U.S. history to win the popular vote but lose the electoral vote.

In November and December, Trump began to assemble his transition team and choose candidates for top roles in the White House. The president-elect drew quick criticism for the slow pace at which his team was working, as well as his choice of his children to take on some advisory positions. Reince Priebus, former chair of the Republican National Committee, was picked as chief of staff, and Steve Bannon, former executive editor of the right-wing *Breitbart News*, was tapped as chief strategist and senior counselor. Cabinet choices included Sen. Jeff Sessions, R-Ala., as attorney general, Lt. Gen. Michael Flynn as national security adviser, and Rep. Mike Pompeo, R-Kan., to take over as director of the Central Intelligence Agency (CIA). Trump's cabinet would be one of the wealthiest in U.S. history.

A prominent issue after Trump's election was the rise of fake news and its spread on social media. Concerns about the inability of many in the American public to discern real, fact-based news from fake news reached a fever pitch in

December when U.S. intelligence agencies announced that they had uncovered a misinformation campaign perpetrated by Russian intelligence officials. According to their assessment, the operatives specifically sought to undermine the Clinton campaign while bolstering Trump. In response, President Obama opted to place additional sanctions on Russian businesses and individuals. The Trump campaign dismissed the concerns, but questions about Russia's involvement with his victory continued into 2017.

In Congress, Republicans lost two seats in the Senate but still held their slim majority at fifty-two. Similarly, in the House, Republicans maintained their majority but had a net loss of six seats. The new House majority was also shifted further to the right ideologically than in previous Congresses. This set up a difficult battle for Speaker of the House Paul Ryan, R-Wis., to reach a consensus within his caucus between mainstream Republicans and the forty-member-strong Freedom Caucus, a group of far-right libertarian, isolationist, and small-government conservatives who had pushed out former Speaker John Boehner, R-Ohio.

Trump's antiestablishment rhetoric and seeming lack of a solid legislative agenda also left Congressional leadership wondering how they would work with the new administration. Trump rarely offered solid ideas for achieving his priorities, instead asking his supporters to trust him. Even after Election Day, those promises did not amount to policies or a cohesive legislative agenda.

SPEAKER BOEHNER'S CONGRESSIONAL SEAT IS FILLED

On September 25, 2015, in a meeting with House Republicans, Speaker John Boehner, R-Ohio, announced that he intended to step down from his leadership position and resign from the House prior to the end of his term. Boehner said he told his wife the night prior that he might step down and that by the next morning he was convinced it was the right day to do so. Boehner was the first speaker to willingly leave the post since 1986.

Boehner had struggled as speaker since he assumed the position in 2011 given the fiercely partisan climate. The situation worsened as the presidential primary election began and Republicans running for the seat became more vocally critical of their leaders. Anti-Boehner sentiment grew with the establishment of the Freedom Caucus, whose ultraconservative members seemed prepared to reject any bill before the House. The expectation was that Boehner would be replaced as speaker by House Majority Leader Kevin McCarthy, R-Calif., but the most conservative in the caucus rejected the idea, and McCarthy took himself out of the running. Ultimately, Rep. Paul Ryan, R-Wis., took over the position of speaker in October.

The special election to replace Boehner for the last seven months of his term was held on June 7, 2016. The race featured Democrat Corey Foister, Republican Warren Davidson, and Green Party candidate James Condit. There was little question that Davidson would win in Boehner's heavily Republican district. Davidson was also a favorite of the Freedom Caucus, who helped him beat out fourteen other candidates in the March 15 primary.

Davidson was critical of Republicans in the House and Senate, asking whether the party would hold fast to its ideologies or if it instead simply wanted to oppose Democrats. He specifically pointed to examples of Republicans not blocking what he saw as the president's abuse of power in issuing executive orders, such as those related to immigration that stalled the deportation of millions of immigrants.

Davidson's roots were in manufacturing. His father started the West Troy Tool and Machine company in 1987, and Davidson worked there before starting his own company in 2002. He bought his father's tool company in 2005 and in 2014 merged his company with another but maintained a management role. Davidson also chaired the Dayton Region Manufacturers Association. Given his experience, manufacturing, or more specifically the loss of U.S. manufacturing jobs, was a topic Davidson frequently addressed on the campaign trail. Davidson countered Trump's pessimistic view of manufacturing, saying the sector was healthy and had been growing since the end of the recession.

Davidson was also critical of candidate Trump's proposal to impose a 45 percent tariff on Chinese manufactured goods that were imported into the United States, arguing that the president did not fully grasp the negative impact that might have on the economy. He added that imports from overseas are not the reason for the loss of U.S. manufacturing jobs but rather technological innovations. Instead, Davidson sought to address the nation's tax code to draw more foreign investment.

Davidson was passionate about the military and helping American veterans, having served in the Army. The first bill he would propose in Congress, Davidson said, would be one to require members of Congress to have the same health benefits as those offered to military veterans served by the Veterans Affairs system. On foreign intervention and nation-building activities, Davidson was critical of past U.S. efforts and wary of becoming involved in protracted nation-building efforts.

Davidson's opponents never made much headway in the lead-up to the special election. On June 7, Davidson walked away with nearly 77 percent of the vote.

CLINTON AND TRUMP ACCEPT NOMINATIONS

The campaign for president began in earnest in early 2015 and featured a field of nineteen Republicans and five Democrats vying for their respective parties' nominations. By early 2016, only four candidates remained: Trump, Sen. Ted Cruz, R-Tex., Sen. Bernie Sanders, I-Vt., and Clinton.

On March 1, 2016, known as Super Tuesday because it is the day on which most states hold their primaries and caucuses, it became clear that the only candidates who had a clear path to victory were Trump, for the Republicans, and Clinton, for the Democrats. Trump took seven states on that date to Cruz's three (Sen. Marco Rubio, R-Fla., won Minnesota). Trump told supporters on March 1 he considered himself "the presumptive nominee" and used the opportunity to attack Clinton, saying if she were a male, she would receive hardly any votes. Trump officially became the presumptive nominee on May 3 after all the other Republican candidates suspended their campaigns. On the Democratic side, Clinton won seven states on Super Tuesday, while Sanders won four. In her victory speech, Clinton said she intended to unify the party and ensure her policies created an America that seeks to support rather than divide. Despite being far shy of earning enough delegates to become the presumptive nominee, Sanders vowed to remain in the race until the Democratic convention in July.

The Republicans held their nominating convention in Cleveland, Ohio, from July 18 to 21, 2016. In light of Trump's divisive rhetoric that had become a hallmark of his campaign, a number of prominent Republicans declined to attend, including former presidents George W. Bush and George H.W. Bush, former presidential candidate Sen. John McCain, R-Ariz., and Ohio Governor John Kasich. Headed into the convention, there were questions raised about whether delegates were legally bound to support the candidate for which their state had voted, and a newly formed group called Democrats Unbound put forth a proposal before the convention's rules committee to allow delegates to unbind themselves from Trump. The committee rejected the proposal and instead instituted a rule specifically requiring delegates to vote based on the preference of their state's primary or caucus. Trump was ultimately nominated on the first ballot, and Indiana Governor Mike Pence was nominated as the party's vice presidential candidate. At his convention speech, Trump said the meeting was occurring at a moment of crisis in America and that any candidate who did not understand that "is not fit to lead our country."

One week later, Democrats convened in Philadelphia to choose their presidential candidate. In the days leading up to the event, Democrats found themselves mired in controversy over leaked emails from the head of the Democratic National Committee, Debbie Wasserman Schultz, that indicated the party had been biased toward Clinton. This led to talk among Sanders supporters of walking out in protest of the Clinton nomination, but that never came to fruition. Clinton went into the event with enough delegates to become the nominee, but Sanders maintained his promise not to admit defeat until all the votes had been counted. Clinton was selected on the first ballot with 59.7 percent of the vote. Sen. Tim Kaine, D-Va., was selected as the vice presidential nominee. In her acceptance speech, Clinton, the first female presidential candidate nominated by a major political party, spoke about her accomplishments fighting for women and children and also used the opportunity to criticize Trump. "He wants to divide us from the rest of the world, and from each other," Clinton said.

GENERAL ELECTION BATTLE

Clinton, who had been in the national spotlight as first lady, senator, Secretary of State, and 2008 presidential contender, and Trump, an author and real estate developer, could not have been more starkly different. Trump rested his campaign on nationalist, populist proposals and making America "great again." He promised to be tough on immigration and crime, renegotiate trade deals, end government regulations, lower taxes, and take a more aggressive stance on foreign policy. Among his most popular proposals were building a wall along the U.S.–Mexico border (which he said Mexico would pay for), ending the Affordable Care Act (ACA), and creating a database of Muslims living in the United States. Mainstream Republicans found Trump's rhetoric difficult to embrace but did get behind talk of repealing the ACA. Clinton stuck to familiar Democratic issues such as free college tuition at in-state public institutions for many Americans, comprehensive immigration reform that would create a legal path to citizenship for those in the country illegally, expansion of the ACA, a higher minimum wage, expanded background checks on gun sales, and more jobs for the middle class.

While Clinton was frequently criticized for her seemingly robotic personality and inability to connect with people, Trump was the champion of those who felt left behind by Washington politicians on both sides of the aisle. He frequently told supporters that the political system in the country was tilted toward the elites, calling it a "rigged system" and promising to "drain the swamp" of the ruling class once elected.

Trump was able to convince his supporters in rural America, especially the parts of the country that had lost jobs in industries such as manufacturing and coal, that only he could help bring back the jobs that had been "taken" by nations such as China and Mexico. Clinton, he said, was part of the political establishment that was responsible for killing jobs in America. Trump said that by renegotiating what he considered bad trade deals such as the North America Free Trade Agreement (NAFTA), jobs would begin flowing back into the country. According to Trump, these renegotiations would begin on day one. He also promised to punish companies that moved operations overseas.

Both candidates performed poorly in the polls. According to a Real Clear Politics average from October 28 to November 7, 2016, Clinton had a 54.4 percent unfavorable rating, while Trump's was at 58.5 percent. Those numbers were likely exacerbated by near around-the-clock coverage of scandals plaguing the two candidates. Clinton was still under fire for using a private email server and email address during her time as secretary of state and was called before Congress to testify at a hearing in which they were debating whether Clinton violated federal law when she deleted some

33,000 emails from the server. The Federal Bureau of Investigation (FBI) concluded in July 2016 that there was no reason to bring charges against Clinton. That did not stop Trump supporters from frequently chanting "lock her up" during Trump campaign rallies in response to what they saw as Clinton's wrongdoing. In what is widely considered a turning point in the election, on October 28, FBI Director James Comey announced to Congress that his agency was in the process of analyzing new emails from Clinton's server that had recently been discovered. On November 6, just two days before the election, Comey said the emails reviewed would not change the FBI's assessment that there were no charges to be brought against Clinton.

Candidate Trump was derided for violence perpetrated by his supporters during campaign rallies, which in his rhetoric Trump appeared to encourage. Often, the violence was directed at nonwhite Americans and led Clinton to say that many of Trump's supporters were within "the basket of deplorables. They're racist, sexist, homophobic, xenophobic, Islamophobic—you name it." Trump's campaign used this as a rallying cry. The biggest Trump scandal broke on October 7 when a 2005 video was released by the *Washington Post* in which Trump was heard suggesting to an *Access Hollywood* host that he had sexually assaulted women. "When you're a star," Trump said, "they let you do it. You can do anything." Some Republicans urged Trump to step aside, while Trump defended the statements as "locker room talk."

TRUMP CLAIMS VICTORY

Although nationwide polling favored a Clinton victory, albeit by a small margin, it became readily apparent as the polls closed on election night that Trump had the better path to victory. Early on the morning of November 9, Clinton called her opponent to concede after Wisconsin was called for Trump, pushing him past the requisite 270 electoral votes needed to secure the presidency. In his victory speech, Trump said it was time for Republicans, Democrats, and independents to come together and address their divisions. In Clinton's concession speech, she said the election showed that the nation was more deeply divided than many thought, but she said everyone must accept the outcome of the race and provide Trump the opportunity to lead. President Obama sought to bring Americans together and repair the divide that the 2016 election had caused. In the White House Rose Garden the day after the election, Obama said he was "rooting" for Trump's success because we all want what is best for the country. Nevertheless, the results clearly alarmed Obama, who now faced the prospect of his key achievements, including the Affordable Care Act, being repealed or significantly rolled back by a Republican administration and Congress.

Although Trump received 304 electoral votes to Clinton's 227, Clinton was well ahead in the popular vote, winning 65,853,625 to Trump's 62,985,106. That had occurred only four other times in history—George W. Bush in 2000, William Henry Harrison in 1888, Rutherford B.

Hayes in 1876, and John Quincy Adams in 1824. The Clinton campaign submitted recount petitions in Michigan, Pennsylvania, and Wisconsin. The Republican Party and Trump asked the courts to intervene to stop the recount effort. Michigan's recount was halted on December 7 when a judge ruled that there was not enough evidence to indicate tampering with voting machines; Pennsylvania's recount never began; and although the Wisconsin recount proceeded, the outcome did not flip the state for Clinton.

The Electoral College is required to convene after a presidential election to formally select the president and vice president, which they did on December 19. In the weeks leading up to the meeting, there were intense lobbying campaigns encouraging Republican electors to vote against the outcome in their states. Individual state law governed whether electors could unbind themselves from the outcomes. A number of lawsuits were filed in 2016 to unbind electors in states that required them to respect the will of the state's voters, but none was successful. Forty electors requested an intelligence briefing before the December 19 vote on potential Russian interference in the election, but that request was rejected. Although Trump was officially chosen as president by the Electoral College, there were seven faithless electors who cast their ballots in opposition to state outcomes: four Clinton delegates from Washington State, one Clinton delegate from Hawaii, and two Trump Texas delegates. One elector from Georgia and another from Texas resigned instead of voting for Trump and were replaced by alternates, and three Clinton delegates from Minnesota, Colorado, and Maine were replaced after refusing to cast a ballot for Clinton. As required by law, the results of the election were certified by Congress on January 6, 2017, and Trump was inaugurated on January 20.

REPUBLICANS HOLD THE SENATE

Despite early predictions that Democrats might be able to take back control of the Senate, down-ballot candidates tended to ride Trump's coattails, and Democrats were unable to reach the net gain of five seats they needed for control. Thirty-four Senate seats were up for grabs in 2016, twenty-four of which were held by Republicans. Democrats picked up momentum in the late summer and early fall, but Senate races tightened in the final weeks of campaigning, along with the presidential race.

Some races Democrats hoped to win ended up going to the Republicans. In Wisconsin, Democrats thought former senator Russ Feingold would defeat incumbent Sen. Ron Johnson. But it was Johnson who was victorious with 50 percent of the vote to Feingold's 47 percent. For the first time since 1984, Wisconsin also swung for a Republican president. In Pennsylvania, Republican Sen. Pat Toomey held off a strong challenge from Democrat Katie McGinty, and the state also went for Trump, choosing a Republican president for the first time since 1988. Democrats succeeded in flipping a seat in Illinois, when Rep. Tammy Duckworth, an Iraq War veteran, defeated incumbent Mark

Kirk. And they also flipped a New Hampshire Senate seat when Governor Maggie Hassan defeated incumbent Republican Sen. Kelly Ayotte by just more than 1,000 votes. They also narrowly held onto the seat being vacated by Senate Minority Leader Harry Reid. The winner of that race, Catherine Cortez Masto, would be the first Latina in the Senate.

In the end, Republicans had fifty-two seats in the new Congress, Democrats held forty-six, and two seats went to Independents, who typically caucus with the Democrats. With a smaller majority, Senate leadership knew it needed to keep the entire caucus together to pass any legislation. Senate Majority Leader Mitch McConnell, R-Ky., said he spoke with Senate Minority Leader Chuck Schumer, D-N.Y., and the two intended to work together for the good of the country. McConnell's lame-duck-session priorities included restoring regular order, a potential elimination of the nuclear option, and ensuring that the government was funded.

REPUBLICANS MAINTAIN CONTROL IN THE HOUSE

There was little expectation headed into November 8, 2016, that Democrats could regain control of the House, which required a thirty-seat pickup. Although they were able to chip away at the Republican majority, Democrats took only 194 seats to the Republicans' 241. Political analysts and Republicans themselves were shocked, however, at the sweep of both houses of Congress and the presidency, and Speaker Paul Ryan, R-Wis., saw it as a mandate for the Republican agenda named "A Better Way." Ryan said America was ready for Republicans to take the country in a different direction. What congressional Republicans did not know, however, was how the president intended to work with Congress and whether he would support the House Republican agenda after his inauguration in 2017. But Ryan said the Republican Congress stood ready to work with the administration to improve the lives of Americans.

Although Republicans held a smaller majority in the House following the 2016 election, the members who were elected were farther right than previous House members, setting up a likely battle within the Republican caucus come 2017. The caucus would require unity to push through its agenda. Democrats hoped that they could use this to their advantage, not by stalling progress in the House but by partnering with the body's more moderate Republicans. While Democrats criticized the Republican caucus for being held hostage by the far-right Freedom Caucus, Republicans remained hopeful that having one of their own in the White House would spur their members into action.

This partnership between the House and the president would be dependent on whether Ryan and Trump could set aside their rocky campaign-season relationship. Even after Trump clinched the Republican nomination, Ryan refused to give an endorsement and ultimately refused to campaign with Trump after a video surfaced showing the nominee joking about sexually assaulting women. "Women are to be championed and revered, not objectified," Ryan said of the situation. Trump turned on the House Speaker, tweeting that Ryan was "a weak and ineffective leader." Ryan sought to avoid being pulled deeper into the issue and focused his attention on ensuring the House remained in Republican hands, which seemed an indication that Ryan assumed Democrat Hillary Clinton would win the presidency. It was not until the final week of the campaign, as polls started to tighten, that Ryan began backing Trump's election.

STATE AND LOCAL ELECTIONS

In addition to voting for president and members of the House and Senate, voters around the country were also selecting members of eighty-six out of ninety-nine state legislatures, choosing eleven governors (plus a special election in Oregon), and voting on 154 statewide ballot measures and hundreds of local referenda. Riding the coattails of the Republican sweep at the federal level, Republicans in the states were also highly successful on November 8. In the eighty-six state legislative chambers holding elections, Republicans were able to flip 138 seats, while Democrats flipped ninety-five. As a result, six of the ninety-nine state legislative chambers switched party control. Democrats gained control of the Nevada House and Senate and the New Mexico House, while Republicans took control of the Kentucky House, Iowa Senate, and Minnesota Senate. In the gubernatorial elections, more Republicans were sent to the governors' mansions than at any time since 1922. With the results combined, Republicans controlled the state House, Senate, and governor's seat in twenty-five states, while Democrats had that trifecta in only six states.

The most notable statewide election was in North Carolina, where incumbent Governor Pat McCrory faced off against Attorney General Roy Cooper. The two gained national prominence in March 2016 when McCrory signed what became known as a "bathroom bill," which banned transgender individuals from using the bathroom corresponding to the gender with which they identify rather than their gender at birth. McCrory saw it as a safety issue, but Cooper, in his role as attorney general, refused to defend the law against any legal challenges. The bathroom bill was a key issue for North Carolina voters, who handed Cooper a slim victory. The McCrory campaign requested a recount on November 23, alleging that ballots cast for Cooper were done so fraudulently. McCrory did not concede the race until December 5.

STATE BALLOT MEASURES

Among the most popular issues on the 2016 ballot were marijuana, the minimum wage, LGBTQ rights, the death penalty, health care, tobacco taxes, and gun ownership. A record seventy-six of the statewide ballot measures considered were the result of initiatives brought by citizens. Marijuana was one of the most popular ballot issues and was featured in nine

Table 1.10 House of Representatives Vote by Region

After being in the minority since 2006, the Republican Party took control of the House in 2010 and retained it for the remainder of Barack Obama's presidency. Republican gains in the 2010 elections were driven both by the continued reverberations of the sharp economic downturn in 2008 as well as by effective attacks against Democratic initiatives, especially the controversial overhaul of health insurance. Republicans also captured a number of governorships and statehouses, giving them control over redrawing congressional districts in a number of key battleground states, such as North Carolina, Pennsylvania, and Wisconsin. This helped them defend their majority in 2012, despite Obama winning reelection, and hold the House in the 2014 and 2016 elections. Obama's loss of the House was hardly unusual: the House flipped from Democratic to Republican two years into the presidency of Democrat Bill Clinton, and then flipped back to Democratic six years into the presidency of Republican George W. Bush. GOP strength was anchored in southern states and supported by solid, if less overwhelming, majorities in the midwestern region. Democrats generally won election in compact urban districts, while Republicans were more popular in sprawling rural districts.

	South			West		Midwest		East			Total House		
	R	D	I	R	D	R	D	R	D	I	R	D	I
2000	81	55	1	43	50	57	48	40	59	1	221	212	2
2002	85	57	0	46	52	61	39	37	57	1	229	205	1
2004	91	51	0	45	53	60	40	36	58	1	232	202	1
2006	85	57	0	41	57	51	49	25	70	0	202	233	0
2008	80	62	0	35	63	45	55	18	77	0	178	257	0
2010	102	40	0	43	55	65	35	32	63	0	242	193	0
2012	108	41	0	39	63	59	35	28	62	0	234	201	0
2014	109	40	0	41	61	57	36	34	56	0	241	194	0
2016	109	40	0	39	63	57	36	31	59	0	236	199	0

SOURCE: Compiled from Rhodes Cook, *America Votes 30* and *America Votes 31* (Washington, DC: CQ Press, 2013 and 2017).

NOTES: R: Republican, D: Democrat, I: Independent. The following groups of states make up the four regions. South: Alabama, Arkansas, Florida, Georgia, Kentucky, Louisiana, Mississippi, North Carolina, Oklahoma, South Carolina, Tennessee, Texas, and Virginia. West: Alaska, California, Colorado, Hawaii, Idaho, Montana, Nevada, New Mexico, Oregon, Utah, Washington, and Wyoming. Midwest: Illinois, Indiana, Iowa, Kansas, Michigan, Minnesota, Missouri, Nebraska, North Dakota, Ohio, South Dakota, and Wisconsin. East: Connecticut, Delaware, Maine, Maryland, Massachusetts, New Hampshire, New Jersey, New York, Pennsylvania, Rhode Island, Vermont, and West Virginia.

states and dozens of municipalities. Voters were asked about medical use, recreational use, cultivation, and sales. Voters in Arkansas, Florida, Montana, and North Dakota all opted to legalize marijuana for medical use. In California, the first state to legalize medical marijuana, voters approved the legalization of recreational marijuana use for citizens twenty-one and older. Similar measures were considered and approved in Maine, Massachusetts, and Nevada, while Arizona voters declined to permit recreational use of marijuana.

Gun control was another of the more popular issues, with California, Maine, and Nevada all considering the expansion of background checks. In California, voters approved a measure that would require a background check prior to the purchase of ammunition. In Nevada, it became illegal for a private firearm sale or transfer to occur without a licensed dealer first conducting a background check. Voters in Maine took a different approach and voted down a measure that would have required a background check for the purchase or transfer of a firearm through a nonlicensed dealer. In Washington State, voters overwhelmingly approved an initiative that would allow the courts to temporarily stop those with mental illness or a history of violent or criminal behavior from accessing a gun if such an order was requested by a set list of individuals, including relatives or police.

Raising the minimum wage was both a state and local issue in 2016. Four states—Arizona, Colorado, Maine, and Washington—all considered raising the state minimum wage. In Arizona, Colorado, and Maine, voters approved increasing the minimum wage to $12 per hour by 2020, while Washington State voters elected to raise their minimum wage to $13.50 by 2020. South Dakota voters rejected a measure that would have lowered the minimum wage to $7.50 per hour for workers under the age of eighteen.

Three states—California, Nebraska, and Oklahoma—considered questions related to the death penalty. California voters considered two separate measures, one that would repeal the death penalty and one that would speed up the time frame from conviction to execution. The former was rejected but the latter approved. Oklahoma, which was subject to a Supreme Court case on the state's use of a new drug cocktail during a botched lethal injection, asked voters if the state should be allowed to use any legal method to carry out an execution. Voters approved it by a wide margin. In Nebraska, where the legislature in 2015 voted to repeal the death penalty, voters chose to overturn that law and keep the death penalty available.

Sales taxes—specifically those on cigarettes and soda—were considered in California, Colorado, Missouri, North Dakota, and a variety of cities. California voters overwhelmingly approved a measure that would increase cigarette taxes by $2 per pack, the proceeds of which would be directed to health care and tobacco control programs, while voters in Colorado, Missouri, and North Dakota all rejected increasing cigarette taxes. Voters in three California cities and Boulder, Colorado, all approved taxes on soda and other sugar-sweetened drinks.

REPUBLICANS, DEMOCRATS LOOK AHEAD TO THE NEXT CONGRESS

McConnell was keen on delivering victories in the Senate that members could utilize during their 2018 midterm reelection campaigns. Even before votes were tallied in November 2016, Republicans were talking to their supporters about how strong Republican support for senators in 2016 could set them up for a sixty-vote supermajority in 2018 that would all but guarantee Republicans could push through any legislation that crossed their desks.

The first battle likely to hit the House in the 115th Congress would be over the debt ceiling, the federal government's limit on how much it can borrow to pay for its obligations. The borrowing authority was set to expire in March, and in order to avoid a default, Congress would need to either raise or suspend the limit. The Treasury said it could avoid a default by using extraordinary measures, which it had been exercising for the previous two years.

At the start of the new term, the new Congress would also be considering a new Supreme Court Justice. McConnell's most notable decision in 2016 was refusing to consider President Obama's nominee to replace Supreme Court Justice Antonin Scalia, who died in February of that year, arguing that it was irresponsible for the Senate to consider a nominee during a presidential election year. McConnell said that it should instead fall to the next president to choose someone to fill the court's vacancy. Trump's election vindicated McConnell's strategy. Under existing Senate rules, however, Democrats could filibuster any Trump nomination because Supreme Court justices did not fall under the 2013 procedural change that allowed simple majorities to defeat filibusters for judicial- and executive-branch nominees. McConnell seemed keen to avoid adding Supreme Court justices to the list of nominees for whom the nuclear option could be used.

Republicans also wanted to leverage their majorities in the House and Senate, as well as having a Republican in the White House, to move forward on their major priorities, including repealing the Affordable Care Act (ACA), cutting the federal deficit, overhauling the U.S. tax code, and making changes to entitlement programs. Republicans planned to begin the Trump presidency with a massive budget reconciliation bill, for which they would rely on a special congressional rule to pass it with a simple majority in both chambers. Republicans hoped it might include tax cuts, a repeal of the ACA, and welfare reform that would turn the Medicaid program into a block grant to the states.

What Republicans worried about, however, was how Trump's more clearly defined initiatives would divide Republicans, especially those related to immigration and trade. Trump frequently promised on the campaign trail to build a wall along the 2,000-mile southern U.S. border and also promised to remove the United States from trade deals with which he disagreed. Still, Republicans were certain they could find other areas on which they agreed with the president, especially when it came to tax cuts and deregulation. Democrats, on the other hand, felt they had a partner in Trump on issues such as infrastructure spending. During his campaign, Trump had promised to make significant investments in America's roads, bridges, and transit systems. Infrastructure, it seemed, was a key component of Trump's plan to create more American jobs. Democrats also seemed hopeful that they could leverage Trump's victory to spur action among their base that would lead them to victory in the 2018 midterms and beyond.

CHAPTER 2

Economic Policy

Economic Policy

President Barack Obama's second term was somewhat quieter on the economic front than his first, which had been characterized by a significant expansion of federal spending to fund the ongoing recovery from the 2007–2009 recession. However, the political brinksmanship that had grown increasingly common in Washington, combined with the Republicans taking control of the Senate as well as the House in 2015, hampered the president's ability to accomplish many of his agenda items. Instead, Congress was focused primarily on simply keeping the government funded and open.

PRESIDENT OBAMA'S ECONOMIC RECORD

By many measures, the economy continued its upward trajectory during President Obama's second term in office. Real gross domestic product (GDP) grew at an annual rate of 2.3 percent, monthly job growth averaged 215,900, annual growth in real hourly wages averaged 1.3 percent, and the S&P 500 Index rose by an annual rate of 11.2 percent. That economic expansion was made possible not only through cooperation in Congress on his various economic policies but also by appointing Janet Yellen as chair of the Federal Reserve. In her position, Yellen maintained the expansionary monetary policy relied on by former Fed Chair Ben Bernanke immediately after the recession began, thus allowing the economy to continue to climb while increasing consumer confidence. In December 2015, Yellen led the Fed as it decided to raise interest rates for the first time in nine years, sending a signal to investors that the economy had finally overcome the impact of the recession and could now withstand higher borrowing costs.

By the time his presidency came to an end in January 2017, the unemployment rate had fallen to 4.8 percent, below the historical norm, and down from a peak of 10.2 percent in October 2009. However, much of the job growth came in low-skill, low-wage service-sector and temporary positions, and wealth inequality remained widespread. From January 2009 through 2016, median household income was up 5.3 percent, the fastest growth on record, but that barely made up for the 4.2 percent loss during President George W. Bush's term in office. Under Obama, average weekly earnings rose 4 percent for all workers after inflation but only 3.7 percent for nonsupervisory and production workers.

Economic improvement relied heavily on deficit spending, something that drew frequent criticism from the president's Republican foes in Congress. According to the Center on Budget and Policy Priorities, despite decreasing in his second term, by the end of his presidency, Obama's total deficits reached $6.785 trillion, higher than those of any other president. Federal debt owed to the public rose 128 percent over the course of Obama's two terms.

Halting Budget Negotiations

President Obama's second four years in the White House were dominated by spending fights with Congress that were predicated on the enactment of the sequester (the across-the-board defense and nondefense spending cuts set in motion by the Budget Control Act of 2011). The president made frequent attempts to work with Congress to eliminate the sequester by finding other areas for cuts or revenue increases, but the parties were too far apart. Most

REFERENCES

Discussion of economic policy for the years 1945–1964 may be found in *Congress and the Nation Vol. I*, pp. 337–458; for the years 1965–1968, *Congress and the Nation Vol. II*, pp. 119–182, 253–305; for the years 1969–1972, *Congress and the Nation Vol. III*, pp. 53–145; for the years 1973–1976, *Congress and the Nation Vol. IV*, pp. 49–149; for the years 1977–1980, *Congress and the Nation Vol. V*, pp. 205–287; for the years 1981–1984, *Congress and the Nation Vol. VI*, pp. 27–120; for the years 1985–1988, *Congress and the Nation Vol. VII*, pp. 27–136; for the years 1989–1992, *Congress and the Nation Vol. VIII*, pp. 31–161; for the years 1993–1996, *Congress and the Nation Vol. IX*, pp. 31–148; for the years 1997–2001, *Congress and the Nation Vol. X*, pp. 33–170; for the years 2001–2004, *Congress and the Nation Vol. XI*, pp. 35–167; for the years 2005–2008, *Congress and the Nation Vol. XII*, pp. 51–59; for the years 2009–2012, *Congress and the Nation Vol. XIII*, pp. 47–72.

ECONOMIC LEADERSHIP

Treasury Secretary

Throughout President Obama's first term, the Treasury Department was led by Timothy Geithner, a former president of the Federal Reserve Bank of New York. During his time with the Obama administration, Geithner oversaw the reforms of the Troubled Asset Relief Program (TARP), the bailout fund established during the 2007–2009 financial crisis, and was instrumental in developing and defending the 2010 Dodd-Frank Wall Street Reform and Consumer Protection Act, a significant overhaul of the financial regulatory system.

Geithner retired from his position in January 2013. To replace Geithner, President Obama nominated Jack Lew, his chief of staff, and former director of the Office of Management and Budget under both Obama and former president Bill Clinton. Lew was not expected to face much opposition in the Senate, given that he had already been confirmed three times for previous positions. However, he did face tough questioning when he sat before the Senate Finance Committee for hearings on his nomination on February 13, 2013, especially from Republicans who found his ideologies too liberal and his spending of federal funds excessive.

Questions from the panel primarily revolved around Lew's time at Citigroup, where he oversaw wealth management and alternative investment units from 2006 to 2008, shortly before the financial institution was forced into accepting a taxpayer-funded bailout. Sen. Orrin Hatch, R-Utah, asked whether Lew was privy to conversations about Citigroup's financial challenges. Lew admitted that he was aware that the funds held by Citigroup that led to its near collapse were struggling, but he made the point that he was not responsible for the funds, nor did he recall all of the conversations in which he took part. Lew was also questioned about whether he should have accepted the $1 million bonus he received from Citigroup just a day before the bailout was accepted, to which Lew responded that he was compensated for the work he did and whether it was the right decision should be left "for others to judge."

Lew did have support from some Republicans on the committee, who saw him as an integral part of overhauling the U.S. tax code. Lew noted during his hearing that he worked on the tax code changes passed in 1986 as a staff member for then–House Speaker Tip O'Neill, D-Mass. Lew expressed a desire to exercise his power as Treasury Secretary to eliminate tax loopholes and change both the corporate and individual tax structures in a revenue-neutral way.

Ultimately, Lew was easily passed out of committee on February 26, 2013, by a vote of 19–5, and was confirmed by the full Senate one day later, 71–26. Twenty Republicans joined the Democrats in support of Lew's nomination. All but one of the no votes came from Republicans; the other was cast by Sen. Bernie Sanders, I-Vt.

Early in his tenure, Lew urged Congress to raise the debt ceiling when they returned from recess in early 2014 to avoid a federal government default. Although Republicans initially balked at passing a clean bill, in February 2014, they were able to do so. Lew, however, was unsuccessful in two areas he spoke about at his confirmation hearing: eliminating the sequester and overhauling the U.S. tax code. Lew served in President Obama's administration until President Donald Trump's inauguration.

Federal Reserve

Ben Bernanke, who was first appointed chair of the Federal Reserve by President Bush in 2006, remained on with the Obama administration until January 2014, when his second term expired. Bernanke was credited by President Obama for his work during the 2007–2009 financial crisis for helping the country avoid a second Great Depression. Under Bernanke's leadership, the Fed kept interest rates low to help restart the economy after the economic downturn and also undertook a policy known as quantitative easing in which the Fed made public its long-term strategy to help investors better plan for future interest rate increases and policy changes. Despite high praise from the president, Bernanke faced criticism from Democrats and Republicans alike. The former felt that he had not done enough to address the persistently high unemployment rate after the end of the recession, while Republicans believed his pattern of holding down interest rates would result in a significant increase in the key rates once the economy recovered, which could destabilize the markets.

When Bernanke's term expired, President Obama nominated Janet Yellen to take his place. At the time, Yellen was vice chair of the Federal Reserve and had previously served as president and chief executive officer of the Federal Reserve Bank of San Francisco and chair of the White House Council of Economic Advisers under President Clinton. Questioning during her nomination hearing focused on decisions made at the Fed to hold off on interest rate increases while the

Republicans found the cuts too deep for the defense budget and sought instead further cuts to domestic spending, especially entitlement programs. This was a nonstarter for Democrats, who instead wanted to see tax increases on corporations and the wealthiest Americans to offset sequester cuts. The 2013 budget fights resulted in a sixteen-day government shutdown, and although Congress managed to avoid another similar crisis through the remainder of economy came out of the financial crisis. Ultimately, Yellen was confirmed 56–26 by the Senate on January 6, 2014, making her the first woman to hold the position of chair of the Federal Reserve. This marked the narrowest confirmation in history for the Federal Reserve chair position.

Yellen's term started on shaky footing in March 2014 when she gave a news conference that caused a market selloff because traders thought her remarks indicated the Fed planned to begin tightening and raising interest rates soon. A year and a half later, in December 2015, she oversaw the Fed as it decided to increase its key interest rate for the first time since 2006. The move initially drew sharp criticism, but Yellen is widely regarded as one of the most successful Fed chairs. When she left office in early 2017, U.S. employment had declined 2.6 percentage points under her leadership, more than under any other modern Fed chair, and no other Fed chair had seen the S&P 500 climb as far as quickly as it did under Yellen's leadership.

Office of Management and Budget

During President Obama's second term, he had three directors of the Office of Management and Budget (OMB). The first was Jeffrey Zients, who served in an acting capacity after Lew was nominated and confirmed as Treasury Secretary. Zients was replaced by Sylvia Mathews Burwell in April 2013. Burwell helped establish the National Economic Council under President Clinton's direction and served as staff director for the organization until 1995. She went on to serve as Clinton's deputy chief of staff, before moving to the Office of Management and Budget, where she served as a deputy director under Lew. Burwell spent time working in the nonprofit sector, including a stint as chair of the Wal-Mart Foundation, before Obama nominated her as director of OMB. Burwell's nomination had bipartisan support, and she was easily confirmed in the Senate 96–0. In her role at OMB, Burwell oversaw the sixteen-day October 2013 federal government shutdown, and, once the government reopened, was responsible for working closely with Congress on a two-year budget deal to avoid future shutdowns.

On April 11, 2014, Burwell was nominated by President Obama to become Secretary of the Department of Health and Human Services, and Shaun Donovan, currently serving as director of the Department of Housing and Urban Development, was nominated to take her place at OMB. Donovan was confirmed by the Senate on July 10, 2014, by a vote of 75–22. As head of OMB, Donovan took up the mantle as

White House representative in the perpetual federal spending fights. He frequently found himself at odds with congressional Republican leadership and chided them for what the White House saw as unnecessary cuts to certain spending areas and unrelated policy riders attached to spending bills that would either derail their passage or draw a veto from the president.

National Economic Council

The National Economic Council was established by President Clinton to coordinate White House economic policies. Gene Sperling, a presidential assistant for economic policy under both Presidents Clinton and Obama and a former council chair, was chosen in 2011 to again lead the body. In his role, Sperling represented the White House in congressional budget negotiations and helped design and support the president's economic initiatives. Sperling left the council in March 2014 and was replaced by Jeffrey Zients. Zients worked in the White House from near the start of President Obama's first term as deputy director of OMB, Chief Performance Officer (he was the first person to hold the position), and acting director of OMB. Zients's ascension to the position of National Economic Council chair was temporarily delayed so he could lead a team tasked with fixing the Healthcare.gov website, which he is widely credited with saving. During his time with the National Economic Council, Zients was instrumental in negotiating with Congress to extend expiring taxes that impacted working families and businesses, strengthen trade enforcement, and improve U.S. job training programs.

Council of Economic Advisers

The Council of Economic Advisers is a three-member body responsible for providing economic advice to the president and producing the annual White House economic report. It experienced significant turnover during Obama's first term, with three different council chairs. Alan B. Kruger, a Princeton economics professor, took over as chair in August 2011 and served into Obama's second term. When he stepped down in 2013, he was replaced by Jason Furman. Furman at the time was serving as deputy director at the White House National Economic Council. Although Furman was considered left of center, he had strong bipartisan support and was approved by voice vote on August 1, 2013. He frequently sought to advise the president to work toward compromises that could pass Congress rather than supporting only liberal agendas.

President Obama's second term, the two parties were unable to pass any regular appropriations bills and were instead forced to fund the government through last-minute stopgap spending measures and omnibus packages.

Protecting Dodd-Frank

In negotiations with Congress, President Obama and his economic team spent a significant part of his second term protecting the 2010 Dodd-Frank Wall Street Reform

A LOOK AT THE ECONOMY

Economic Growth
Annual Percentage Change

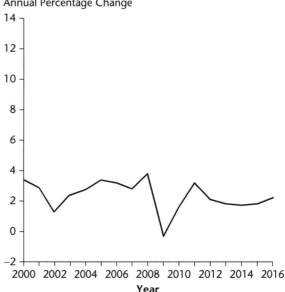

Growth: Annual changes in real GDP, measured in chained 2012 dollars.

SOURCE: Commerce Department, Bureau of Economic Analysis.

Economic growth sagged during President George W. Bush's first term (2001–2005), which was marked by a mild recession followed by a mild recovery. Economic growth in his second term (2005–2009) slowed gradually until December 2007, when the country entered a deep recession. By 2010, the economy was growing again, albeit slowly, under the stewardship of President Barack Obama. Annual growth did not return to the level of 3 percent or higher that the nation had sometimes achieved in the first decade of the century.

Unemployment
Annual Percentage Average

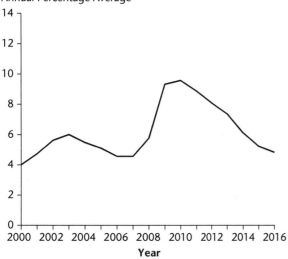

Unemployment: Annual rate of unemployment for all civilian workers (does not include the military).

SOURCE: Labor Department, Bureau of Labor Statistics.

Unemployment experienced a slight uptick in the early 2000s before settling at about 5 percent. As a deep recession took hold in 2008, unemployment began to rise, reaching a high point of 10.6 percent in January 2010 before steadily falling during the rest of the Obama presidency. By Obama's last year in office, it had dropped to less than 5 percent.

Inflation
Annual Percentage Change

Inflation: Annual change in the consumer price index for all urban consumers, expressed as an annual average rate.

SOURCE: Labor Department, Bureau of Labor Statistics.

Inflation stayed relatively consistent and tame during the first years of the 2000s. It rose somewhat before the 2008 recession but never approached the double-digit levels of 1979–1980. During President Obama's first term, the aftershocks of the sharp economic downturn meant that deflation was at times a larger concern than inflation. Prices rose annually during Obama's second term but at a mild rate.

Interest Rates
Annual Percentage Average

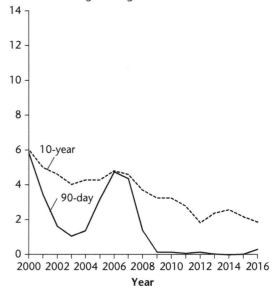

Interest Rates: Annual average for ninety-day Treasury bills and ten-year Treasury notes, adjusted for constant maturities.

SOURCE: Federal Reserve; Federal Reserve Bank of St. Louis.

Interest rates on short- and long-term Treasury securities fell in 2003 to their lowest levels in almost thirty years then rose slightly as the Fed tried to engineer a "soft landing" for the booming housing market. In late 2008, interest rates fell again and remained low as the Fed intervened in an effort to stimulate the slumping economy. They remained low through the Obama presidency.

and Consumer Protection Act. Dodd-Frank reformed how the financial industry is regulated by creating new oversight bodies, such as the Consumer Financial Protection Bureau (CFPB) and making changes to how banks are structured and scrutinized, especially those deemed "too big to fail," to help protect the country against another economic collapse. Republicans voted with near unanimity against the measure and frequently criticized it as a prime example of federal overreach without adequate oversight. The House and Senate struggled to reach consensus during the 113th and 114th Congresses on how to change Dodd-Frank, even after Republicans took control of the two chambers following the 2014 midterm elections. Republicans were forced to accept mostly minor changes to the 2010 law and failed to enact the sweeping revisions or outright repeal they sought.

Chronology of Action on Economic and Regulatory Policy

Repealing or changing the Dodd-Frank Financial Reform and Consumer Protection Act was paramount to the Republican agenda during President Obama's second term. Action in the House drew little notice in the Senate given Democratic control through 2014 and the threat of a White House veto. Where Republicans in both chambers did have some success in amending Dodd-Frank was through the annual appropriations process. In particular, they eliminated through the fiscal 2015 omnibus a Dodd-Frank provision requiring banks to separate swaps and other risky operations from the portion of the bank that is federally insured. The Treasury Department supported the change and had actually opposed including that language in the original Dodd-Frank law.

Republicans were unable, however, to make changes to one of their primary targets, the structure of the CFPB. As written in the 2010 law, the CFPB was situated under the Federal Reserve, which is not subject to the annual appropriations process and is instead funded with interest, thus limiting the influence Congress can have over the body. In addition, CFPB was set up to be led by an individual director who could only be removed by the president for cause. Republicans felt that whoever was installed in the director's seat was ultimately set up to act as a dictator, and they instead preferred that a five-member panel lead CFPB. Although they did not change CFPB's structure, the Senate did delay the confirmation of Obama's nominee to lead CFPB, former Ohio Attorney General Richard Cordray, until July 2013, thus limiting the CFPB's ability to implement any final regulations.

Lawmakers also agreed to legislation that allowed Puerto Rico to restructure its debt under the oversight of a federally appointed fiscal board. The territory, which had borrowed and spent excessively for several years, faced about $72 billion of debt, equivalent to 100 percent of its GDP. As its government defaulted repeatedly on scheduled debt payments, Puerto Rico Gov. Alejandro García Padilla urged Congress to allow the territory to declare bankruptcy and restructure its debt under Chapter 9 of the U.S. Bankruptcy Code. Despite concerns on both sides of the aisle, lawmakers ultimately passed a bipartisan bill to help the territory in 2016 after failing to agree on legislation in 2015.

Congress also tackled several additional issues, including changes related to the Commodity Futures Trading Commission and small business legislation.

REFERENCES

Discussion of economic policy for the years 1945–1964 may be found in *Congress and the Nation Vol. I*, pp. 337–458; for the years 1965–1968, *Congress and the Nation Vol. II*, pp. 119–182, 253–305; for the years 1969–1972, *Congress and the Nation Vol. III*, pp. 53–145; for the years 1973–1976, *Congress and the Nation Vol. IV*, pp. 49–149; for the years 1977–1980, *Congress and the Nation Vol. V*, pp. 205–287; for the years 1981–1984, *Congress and the Nation Vol. VI*, pp. 27–120; for the years 1985–1988, *Congress and the Nation Vol. VII*, pp. 27–136; for the years 1989–1992, *Congress and the Nation Vol. VIII*, pp. 31–161; for the years 1993–1996, *Congress and the Nation Vol. IX*, pp. 31–148; for the years 1997–2001, *Congress and the Nation Vol. X*, pp. 33–170; for the years 2001–2004, *Congress and the Nation Vol. XI*, pp. 35–167; for the years 2005–2008, *Congress and the Nation Vol. XII*, pp. 51–59; for the years 2009–2012, *Congress and the Nation Vol. XIII*, pp. 73–110.

Discussion of financial regulation activity for the years 1945–1964 may be found in *Congress and the Nation Vol. I*, pp. 337–386; for the years 1965–1968, *Congress and the Nation Vol. II*, pp. 253–279; for the years 1969–1972, *Congress and the Nation Vol. III*, pp. 135–145; for the years 1973–1976, *Congress and the Nation Vol. IV*, pp. 107–117; for the years 1977–1980, *Congress and the Nation Vol. V*, pp. 253–265; for the years 1981–1984, *Congress and the Nation Vol. VI*, pp. 83–93; for the years 1985–1988, *Congress and the Nation Vol. VII*, pp. 109–136; for the years 1989–1992, *Congress and the Nation Vol. VIII*, pp. 113–161; for the years 1993–1996, *Congress and the Nation Vol. IX*, pp. 109–148; for the years 1997–2000, *Congress and the Nation Vol. X*, pp. 120–144; for the years 2001–2004, *Congress and the Nation Vol. XI*, pp. 123–144; for the years 2005–2008, *Congress and the Nation Vol. XII*, pp. 136–162; for the years 2009–2012, *Congress and the Nation Vol. XIII*, pp. 73–110.

2013–2014

House Republicans largely focused on Dodd-Frank but could not overcome the resistance of Senate Democrats to major changes in the law. The Senate, after a prolonged debate, confirmed Obama's choice to lead the CFPB.

Dodd-Frank

Making changes to the 2010 Dodd-Frank Wall Street Reform and Consumer Protection Act was a top priority for Republicans, who had strongly opposed Dodd-Frank since it was signed into law in 2010. They claimed that the bill amounted to government overreach that lacked adequate oversight. In 2013, House Republicans attempted to roll back provisions of the act a number of times and were successful in passing six bills, but with President Obama in the White House and Democratic control of the Senate, their attempts never became law. The Senate in 2013 confirmed a director to lead the Consumer Financial Protection Bureau (CFPB), a body created by Dodd-Frank. The nomination had been stalled as the two parties argued over Senate rules.

In 2014, two changes to Dodd-Frank were signed into law. One gave regulators the authority to exempt insurers from the law's capital requirements given that their business models vary significantly from those of other financial institutions such as banks. The other change, which was backed by the Treasury, removed language from Dodd-Frank that required banks to separate their derivatives and swaps operations from the portion of the bank that is federally insured. That change was included in the fiscal 2015 omnibus legislation.

BACKGROUND

On July 21, 2010, President Obama signed into law the Dodd-Frank Wall Street Reform and Consumer Protection Act, one of his administration's landmark achievements. Named for its primary congressional sponsors, Sen. Chris Dodd, D-Conn., and Rep. Barney Frank, D-Mass., the bill was intended to reform the structure responsible for policing the financial industry to provide government regulators broader capacity to avoid another recession like the one that took place from 2007 to 2009 and resulted in multiple bank bailouts. When President Obama signed Dodd-Frank, he said the law ensured that the financial system would work for all Americans by ensuring everyone was held to the same system and no one was allowed to unfairly skirt financial regulations.

The severe recession that hit the nation from 2007 to 2009 was sparked primarily by declining home values and a jump in the number of foreclosures. A significant number of these foreclosures were for homes financed with adjustable-rate, subprime mortgages that essentially extend financing to buyers who have credit issues. In return, the buyer accepts a high interest rate. The problem did not impact solely the housing market but also major banks that were trading in derivatives that included credit default swaps, mortgage-backed securities, and collateralized debt obligations. These risky trading operations quickly hampered the banks' ability to issue new lines of credit, resulting in less money flowing into the markets. The stock market plummeted, and the nation landed in its worst recession since the 1930s.

After a declaration from Federal Reserve Chair Ben Bernanke that banks such as Bear Stearns, JPMorgan Chase, Lehman Brothers, insurance giant AIG, and mortgage giants such as Fannie Mae and Freddie Mac were "too big to fail," the federal government stepped in and injected greater liquidity into the market. This $700 billion bailout came with the creation of the Troubled Asset Relief Program (TARP), and shortly thereafter, Congress also approved a new $787 billion stimulus package aimed at restarting the economy. On June 17, 2009, President Obama announced a proposal to introduce new reforms into the financial system to further the work done by his predecessor, President George W. Bush, to shore up the economy.

Debate in Congress over Dodd-Frank in 2009 centered around the creation of a consumer watchdog agency, known as the Consumer Financial Protection Bureau (CFPB), which would be housed within the Federal Reserve. The CFPB was dedicated to educating and enforcing certain financial regulations to protect the American consumer. Republicans and financial industry groups were vocal in their opposition to CFPB from the start, arguing that the body was given sweeping powers that lacked appropriate federal oversight. In the House, an amendment that was strongly backed by business groups was proposed to eliminate CFPB from the bill. That amendment failed 223–208, despite some support from Democrats. The House would go on to pass the Dodd-Frank bill 223–202 on December 12, 2009. The Senate moved slowly and did not approve its version of the legislation until May 20, 2010, by a 59–39 vote. During reconciliation, language was softened regarding the banning of derivative trading by commercial banks, and a new rule was added banning proprietary trading. The final conference bill passed the House on June 30 and the Senate on July 15.

Final provisions of the 848-page document included

- creation of the CFPB, which would later be led by former Ohio Attorney General Richard Cordray
- creation of the Financial Stability Oversight Council that would analyze and respond to threats in the financial system
- the ability of the Federal Deposit Insurance Corporation (FDIC) to seize and liquidate troubled financial firms headed toward bankruptcy
- a ban on utilizing taxpayer dollars to bail out corporations
- increased federal insurance on bank deposits

- a transfer of powers from the Office of Thrift Supervision to the Office of the Comptroller of the Currency, Federal Reserve, and FDIC
- improved regulation of derivatives trading, including the removal of some derivatives trading operations from the portion of a banking institution that is federally insured
- new protection for investors

2013 HOUSE ACTION

All legislative attempts to limit Dodd-Frank in 2013 came from the House. Six bills were passed out of committee but never made it to the floor. These included HR 1135, passed on June 19 by a vote of 36–21, which would eliminate a requirement for publicly traded companies to disclose the compensation of their chief executives during every Securities and Exchange Commission (SEC) filing. Three bills passed out of the House Financial Services Committee on November 21. H Rept 113–345, passed by a vote of 31–21, would replace the CFPB director with a five-member commission. Republicans argued that this was necessary to provide Congress with greater control over the body's activities. By a 32–24 vote, the committee approved HR 3519—H Rept 113-347, which would make the consumer bureau an independent agency subject to regular congressional authorization and appropriations. As signed into law, CFPB was an arm of the Federal Reserve, a body that is not subject to annual congressional appropriations but is instead funded by interest collected. Also on November 21, the committee passed by 32–25 HR 3193—H Rept 113-346 to make it easier for other financial regulators to block CFPB action. Two other attempts, HR 2385—H Rept 113-249, would alter the pay scale for those employed at the CFPB, while HR 2571—H Rept 113-344; HR 3183 would limit the information the CFPB was able to collect on consumers.

Of the measures that were passed on the House floor, one included HR 1062—H Rept 113–60, which would require the SEC to conduct a cost-benefit analysis on any regulation it intended to issue and again after that regulation had been in effect for two years. The House passed the bill on May 17 by a vote of 235–161, but it was never taken up in the Senate. On June 12, the House passed four bills to change or clarify provisions of Dodd-Frank related to derivatives and financial swaps, financial instruments with value based on an underlying asset or instrument. One of those bills, HR 1256—H Rept 113–103, which passed 301–124, would prevent the Commodity Futures Trading Commission (CFTC) from moving forward with the tough derivative rules it had proposed that would be applied to cross-border derivative trading. Those voting in favor of the bill felt that the CFTC, in cooperation with the SEC, should not be able to enforce the regulations outside of the United States if the foreign entities were already complying with similar rules imposed by another Group of 20 nation.

One week later, the House voted on HR 1613—H Rept 113–101, which passed 256–171. The legislation would exempt companies that extracted natural resources from the Dodd-Frank regulation that required disclosure of payments to foreign governments. The concern, among those who supported the legislation, was that oil and natural gas companies might be kept out of contracts if Mexico did not want to disclose royalty payments received.

On October 29, the House passed HR 2374—H Rept 113–228 by a vote of 254–166. The legislation would temporarily prohibit the Department of Labor from issuing a regulation on the fiduciary responsibility of financial advisers to put their clients' interests first when providing information on retirement accounts. Supporters of the bill thought that the regulation could prevent consumers from being able to access sound financial advice. The White House threatened to veto the bill if it reached the president's desk, viewing it as a significant hit to consumer protection. One day later, the House passed HR 992—H Rept 113–229, which would require banks to separate derivatives and swaps from the part of the bank that is federally insured. The measure passed 292–122.

Finally, on December 4, 2013, the House passed HR 1105—H Rept 113–276 by a vote of 254–159. The bill would have exempted advisers from registering and filing reports with the SEC if their funds had not borrowed and did not have an outstanding principal amount exceeding twice their capital commitments. Republicans and Democrats who backed the bill said that these investment funds had nothing to do with the 2007 to 2009 financial crisis and should therefore not be subject to new regulations. The White House again threatened a veto.

Republicans in the House also attempted to use the appropriations process to limit the impact of Dodd-Frank. Again, they took aim at the CFPB and attempted to bring it under the regular congressional appropriation process, and while a funding measure with that language passed out of the House Appropriations Committee, it was not included in the final fiscal 2014 omnibus package (HR 3547—PL 113-76). The House Appropriations committee also included measures that would limit funding to the SEC and CFTC, despite their expanded responsibilities under Dodd-Frank. Those, too, were left out of the final omnibus.

CFPB DIRECTOR CONFIRMATION

The Senate was finally successful in 2013 in confirming a director to lead the CFPB. Without one in place, the regulatory body had been unable to fully implement new regulations.

Confirmation of President Obama's nominee Richard Cordray, former Ohio Attorney General, got caught up in both Republican concerns about the CFPB and a partisan battle over the use of filibusters. Overcoming a filibuster in the Senate and ending debate required a sixty-vote majority. Majority Leader Harry Reid, D-Nev., warned over the course of the Cordray fight that he would consider invoking what was known as the nuclear option, which meant changing Senate rules to limit filibusters by allowing them to be ended by a simple majority vote. On July 11, 2013, Reid filed a motion to limit debate on Cordray's nomination. This was followed by a closed-door meeting during which Republicans agreed to allow the nomination to proceed by a simple up-or-down vote.

On July 16, 2013, the Senate voted 66–34 in favor of Cordray's nomination, thus strengthening the authority of the CFPB.

2014 HOUSE ACTION

Republicans revived their attempts to change provisions in Dodd-Frank in 2014. One of the first pieces of legislation was HR 3193, a bill passed in February that would overhaul the structure and funding of the CFPB by bringing the body under normal federal appropriations. As it was written into the Dodd-Frank law, the CFPB fell under the Federal Reserve, from which it received its funding. The bill would also replace the CFPB director with a bipartisan five-member commission appointed by the president and confirmed by the Senate (the Senate considered similar legislation in committee, but it never made it to the floor), would require CFPB to obtain consumer permission before collecting personal information, and would authorize the chair of the Financial Stability Oversight Council to set aside any CFPB regulation if a majority of the council's ten voting members found it inconsistent with the safety of U.S. financial institutions. The White House issued a veto threat, saying the bill made the economy vulnerable to another financial crisis.

On May 17, 2014, the House passed HR 1062, the SEC Regulatory Accountability Act, by a vote of 235–161. The bill required the Securities and Exchange Commission (SEC) to conduct and submit to the Office of Management and Budget a cost-benefit analysis for any rule it was preparing to implement, including those related to Dodd-Frank. Under current law, the SEC was exempt from these reporting requirements. The Senate did not take up consideration of the bill. The next House-passed measure was HR 1256, the Swap Jurisdiction Certainty Act, approved by a vote of 301–124. The legislation would direct the SEC and Commodity Futures Trading Commission to jointly issue rules on cross-border derivatives trades involving both U.S. and non-U.S. individuals.

In June, the House passed HR 1613, the Outer Continental Shelf Transboundary Hydrocarbon Agreements Authorization Act, by a vote of 256–171. Within the bill, the Dodd-Frank provision requiring a disclosure of payments made by resource extraction companies to a foreign government was eliminated.

In October 2014, the House passed two additional Dodd-Frank rollback bills. The first, HR 2374, the Retail Investor Protection Act, passed 254–166 on October 29. The bill would delay the implementation of regulations being written by the Department of Labor until the SEC finalized its rules on when brokers, dealers, and investment advisors must act as a fiduciary. Then, on October 30, the House passed HR 992, the Swaps Regulatory Improvement Act, by a vote of 292–122. The bill would amend Dodd-Frank to repeal the law's swaps provision that requires banks to separate out their derivatives operations from the portion of the bank that is federally insured. Seventy Democrats joined all but three Republicans to support the bill. Former Rep. Barney Frank, D-Mass., the Dodd-Frank law's namesake, warned that eliminating the swaps provision would only result in future bank bailouts. The banking industry, backed by the Treasury Department, heavily supported the bill. The derivatives swaps separation language from that bill was rolled into the fiscal 2015 omnibus (PL 113-235).

In December, one other Dodd-Frank change was passed into law. On December 10, the House passed S 2270, which the Senate had approved six months earlier by unanimous consent. The bill would allow regulators to exempt large insurers such as AIG and Prudential from the Dodd-Frank bank capital requirements. Lawmakers generally agreed that, because insurers had different business models than banks, they should not face the same regulations. The bill was signed into law (PL 113-279) by the president on December 18, 2014.

COMMODITY FUTURES TRADING COMMISSION

In 2014, the House and Senate undertook a number of activities related to the Commodity Futures Trading Commission (CFTC), the body responsible for regulating commodity and financial futures and options. This included Senate confirmation of three commission members, although that still left the CFTC understaffed, and a House attempt at reauthorizing the group. The Senate never took up consideration of the reauthorization.

CONFIRMATION OF NEW CFTC MEMBERS

The CFTC is overseen by a five-person commission, whose members are nominated by the president and confirmed by the Senate. In June 2014, three members—Timothy Massad, Sharon Bowen, and J. Christopher Giancarlo—were confirmed and sworn in. Massad was also chosen as the chair.

Massad formerly worked for the Treasury Department, including as assistant secretary for financial stability. Some advocacy groups worried that he would not be as tough a regulator as his predecessor, but during his confirmation hearing before the Senate Agriculture Committee, Massad said he planned to vigorously enforce the laws governing futures, swaps, and options markets. He also intended to implement the CFTC's Dodd-Frank provisions and a new position limits rule that restricts how large a share of any market a single trader can have. Along with Massad, both Bowen, a law partner at Latham & Watkins LLP and the acting chair of the Securities Investor Protection Corporation, and Giancarlo, the executive vice president at interdealer broker GFI Group, promised to shield nonfinancial end users of the commodity markets—such as farmers and manufacturers—from excessive regulation under Dodd-Frank while also guarding against market manipulation. Statements from the three nominees made them popular with both Democrats, who wanted to ensure Dodd-Frank was fully implemented, and Republicans, who wanted to verify that any regulations would fairly treat nonfinancial firms.

CFTC REAUTHORIZATION

In April 2014, the House Agriculture Committee considered the Consumer Protection and End User Relief Act (HR 4413), which would reauthorize the CFTC and make changes to the Dodd-Frank Wall Street Reform and Consumer Protection Act (PL 111-203), a popular target among Republicans. Provisions from three House-passed measures were added to the bill's language. These included

- HR 634, the Business Risk Mitigation and Price Stabilization Act of 2013, a bill that exempted nonfinancial bodies that were entering into a swap or security-based swap from meeting certain requirements, if the swap was intended to offset losses or gains in other investments
- HR 677, the Inter-Affiliate Swap Clarification Act, which would amend Dodd-Frank to exempt certain swap and security-based swap transactions from some regulatory requirements, but only if the parties conducting the transaction meet specific qualifications, such as completing their financial statements with a parent company or affiliate

- HR 742, the Swap Data Repository and Clearinghouse Indemnification Correction Act of 2013, a measure that would eliminate a portion of Dodd-Frank that prevented the CFTC from sharing information with regulatory agencies before those agencies agreed to indemnify the CFTC for expenses related to any litigation that might result from the information being shared. Both Democrats and Republicans felt the provision hindered the market transparency the Dodd-Frank law sought to enhance.
- HR 1256, the Swap Jurisdiction Certainty Act, which would effectively block the CFTC regulation on cross-border derivatives trading by requiring the CFTC and SEC to issue rules on the matter.

The reauthorization bill would provide appropriations for the CFTC through 2018. It was also intended to ensure that nonfinancial end users of derivatives would be exempt from the Dodd-Frank derivatives rules. It would place additional requirements on the CFTC, such as one calling for a cost-benefit analysis before any new rule could be implemented. Democrats contended that the latter provision was an attempt by Republicans to slow new regulations from taking effect, thus hampering the CFTC's ability to carry out its Dodd-Frank responsibilities. Republicans said the measure would ease the regulatory burden placed on financial and nonfinancial institutions.

The bill had strong bipartisan backing and easily cleared the committee. It passed the full House on June 24 by a vote of 265–144, with 44 Democrats lending their support. The bill was referred to the Senate Agriculture committee, which did not take any action in 2014.

2015–2016

With control of the House and Senate, Republicans were poised to use their new majority to make changes to one of their primary targets: the Dodd-Frank Wall Street Reform and Consumer Protection Act. The House passed, or at least considered in committee, a number of changes including those that would bring the Consumer Financial Protection Bureau (CFPB) under the regular congressional appropriations process and give Congress more control over the Financial Stability Oversight Council (FSOC). The Senate also considered a couple pieces of legislation, but none had enough support for passage.

While the House and Senate could not find much room for compromise on major changes to Dodd-Frank during the 114th Congress, they were able to include a policy rider in an unrelated piece of legislation to relax derivatives regulations for nonfinancial institutions. Congress failed to reach consensus on two other topics, stopping so-called patent trolls from frivolous lawsuits and helping small businesses raise capital. Both issues had components that drew bipartisan support, but a complete piece of legislation on either issue could not garner the necessary support.

Congress also responded to a fiscal crisis in Puerto Rico by clearing legislation that allowed lawmakers in both parties to raise concerns, with Democrats worried about antilabor provisions and Republicans warning it could set a precedent for future taxpayer bailouts. Senate Majority Leader Mitch McConnell, R-Ky., said it would not cost taxpayers any money, and Treasury Secretary Jacob Lew said the territory could face chaos without an agreement.

Dodd-Frank

Signed into law by Obama in 2010, the Dodd-Frank Wall Street Reform and Consumer Protection Act was intended to reform the structure responsible for policing the financial industry to provide government regulators broader capacity to avoid another recession like the one that took place from 2007 to 2009 and resulted in multiple bank bailouts. Republicans strongly opposed the legislation as an example of government overreach and complained that the law lacked adequate oversight. But their efforts to roll back Dodd-Frank provisions in the 113th Congress largely fell short.

2015 ACTION

In 2015, with control of both chambers of Congress, Republicans renewed their attempts to change Dodd-Frank. These included passage of a number of measures that made major changes to Dodd-Frank, including those that would bring the Consumer Financial Protection Bureau (CFPB) under the regular appropriations process to provide Congress more leeway in controlling the body's operations. The bills were never considered in the Senate. Similarly, a measure introduced in the Senate Banking Committee that would rewrite banking laws never made it to the floor. Republicans

also tried to add policy riders to the fiscal 2016 omnibus, including a measure raising the threshold for systemically important financial institutions above the $50 billion level and easing some mortgage lending requirements. The White House threatened to veto the omnibus if the Dodd-Frank riders were included, so they were pulled before the House and Senate voted on the final bill funding the government.

The House also passed but the Senate did not take up HR 3189 to make changes to the Federal Reserve, by giving Congress greater input into the Fed's monetary policy and rolling back some of its emergency powers. Both the White House and the Federal Reserve thought the provisions of the bill were dangerous for the economy, and although the Senate was willing to negotiate on some changes to the Fed's power, they were unwilling to consider the strong language included in the House bill.

Lawmakers were successful in including a policy rider in the Terrorism Risk Insurance Act (PL 114-1) that would relax the derivatives regulations for nonfinancial institutions while still requiring them to meet regular reporting requirements to the Commodity Futures Trading Commission.

2016 ACTION

Republicans specifically sought to outright repeal Dodd-Frank, but short of that, they wanted to exert more control over the CFBP and put Congress in charge of the budget for the Financial Stability Oversight Council (FSOC). (The FSOC was created by Dodd-Frank to bring together banking, housing, and insurance regulators to track whether conditions were arising that would threaten the economy.) The House Financial Services Committee approved three bills to roll back specific provisions of Dodd-Frank, none of which were considered by the full House. These included

- HR 1486, passed 33–20, which would bring the CFPB under the regular appropriations process; it would also eliminate the position of director, which many Republicans believed gave too much power to one individual, and replace it with a five-member commission
- HR 4894, passed 34–22, to eliminate the Orderly Liquidation Authority (OLA) provided to large banks. OLA allows the FDIC to resolve a failing financial institution to prevent a domino effect leading to the failure of other financial companies; under the House bill, even those institutions deemed "too big to fail" would be required to go through bankruptcy court to resolve their financial issues
- HR 5983, passed 30–26, to fully repeal Dodd-Frank and replace it with new legislation, the Financial CHOICE Act; the new act would rename the CFPB, replace its director with a five-member panel, and subject it to regular appropriations and would allow banks to opt out of existing regulations if they maintained a 10 percent capital ratio.

The full House approved one Dodd-Frank change, which was attached as a policy rider to an appropriations bill. The Financial Services appropriations bill (HR 6392) began in a House Appropriations subcommittee and contained a number of policy riders, including one that would bring the CFPB and Office of Financial Research into the regular appropriations process and eliminate the requirement that large banks receive extra scrutiny. The appropriations bill passed the house on July 7, 239–185, with the Dodd-Frank riders included. The administration promised to veto the bill if it reached the president's desk. The Senate, however, never considered the bill, and Congress was in turn forced to use continuing resolutions to fund the government into 2017, thus negating the Dodd-Frank riders.

The Senate considered only one Dodd-Frank–related bill (S 3318) that would bring the CFPB into the regular congressional appropriations process. The bill bypassed committee and was put on the Senate calendar on September 14. Few Republicans were willing to take it up, despite similar legislation being considered in the House, because the White House would likely have vetoed the bill.

Puerto Rico Assistance

By 2015, U.S. territory Puerto Rico was facing a major financial crisis after years of overborrowing and overspending. The island had approximately $72 billion worth of debt, mostly in the form of municipal bonds, and its public debt had ballooned to 100 percent of its GDP. Puerto Rican officials, led by Governor Alejandro García Padilla and Resident Commissioner Pedro Pierluisi, aggressively lobbied the federal government to allow the territory to declare bankruptcy and restructure its debt under Chapter 9 of the U.S. Bankruptcy Code. While Congress deliberated Puerto Rico's proposal and other options for economic assistance, the government defaulted on scheduled debt payments on three separate occasions.

After several attempts to reach agreement on assistance for Puerto Rico failed in 2015, Congress passed a bipartisan bill in the summer of 2016 that allowed the island to restructure its debt under the oversight of a federally appointed fiscal board. While the bill secured support on both sides of the aisle in both chambers, lawmakers remained concerned about some of its provisions. Democrats opposed the oversight board's creation and objected to provisions lowering the minimum wage for some Puerto Rican workers and blocking them from a new overtime rule. Republicans expressed concerns that allowing Puerto Rico to restructure its debt would open the door to similar requests from U.S. states and that it could lead to a future taxpayer-funded bailout of the island territory.

The bill's passage followed an intense lobbying campaign by outside groups, the Puerto Rican government, and Obama administration officials. The Center for Individual Freedom—a group reportedly backed by Puerto Rico's creditors, who were concerned debt restructuring would decrease the value of their investments—launched an ad campaign describing the bill as a bailout. Lawmakers including Senate Majority Leader Mitch McConnell, R-Ky., refuted this assertion, saying that the bill in fact prevented a bailout and would help Puerto Rico avoid future financial crises. Lawmakers also faced pressure from several Puerto Rican civil society organizations that opposed the oversight board's establishment, claiming it would supersede the will of Puerto Rican citizens to "move towards full self-government." A coalition of these organizations sent an open letter to the Senate in June 2016, calling on them to oppose the bill, which they characterized as a "limitation of democracy." Treasury Secretary Jacob Lew made several trips to Capitol Hill to encourage lawmakers to support the bill, warning that there would be "chaos" if an agreement was not reached. Padilla also met with lawmakers.

BACKGROUND

The roots of Puerto Rico's financial crisis can be traced to several federal and domestic policies. In 2006, Congress repealed a federal tax credit that exempted U.S. companies from paying taxes on income originated in U.S. territories. The tax credit had encouraged many mainland companies, particularly those in the manufacturing sector, to establish a presence in Puerto Rico; once the incentive was removed, many of these companies withdrew from the island. Meanwhile, high corporate taxes on domestic companies had discouraged the growth of Puerto Rico–based businesses, meaning there were few local companies that could fill the void created by departing businesses. The resulting lack of jobs pushed many Puerto Ricans to leave the island in search of employment, further reducing the territory's tax revenue. Puerto Rico was further disadvantaged by having to comply with U.S. minimum wage laws, which can make labor more expensive in the territory than on other nearby islands. It also pays higher import costs due to U.S. laws requiring goods sent between U.S. ports to be transported on U.S.-built ships with a crew comprised of U.S. citizens and permanent residents.

Puerto Rico has traditionally relied heavily on deficit financing and the issuance of bonds to fund the government. These bonds are exempt from federal, state, and local taxes, making them more attractive to investors. Puerto Rico experienced significant demand for its bonds between 2006 and 2014, enabling the government to borrow and spend beyond its means. In 2015, Puerto Ricans held an estimated $20 billion of the commonwealth's debt, and nearly 60 percent of the debt was held in Americans' retirement accounts. The more bonds the government issued, the more interest payments it was required to make. Bond interest rates also increased in 2013 due to declining investor confidence; in fact, Standard & Poor's downgraded Puerto Rico's bonds to junk bond status (a designation reserved for the riskiest of bonds) in 2014.

The Puerto Rican government tried to address the island's debt concerns by imposing a new gross receipts tax, raising the retirement age, increasing sales tax, reinstating higher corporate tax rates, and cutting summer and Christmas bonuses for public workers. Other actions taken by the government included selling assets from its worker's compensation fund, liquidating pension system assets, and suspending set-asides for future payments of general obligation bonds. Austerity measures were also introduced and included transitioning the government's largest pension fund from a defined benefit plan to a defined contribution plan, freezing collective bargaining agreements, implementing a hiring freeze, and cutting expenses. However, many of these actions further diminished the government's revenue and ability to repay creditors.

Without enough resources to repay creditors, Puerto Rico defaulted on its public debt, failing to pay $58 million of a $493 million debt payment due in August 2015. This was followed by two subsequent defaults in January and May 2016. Puerto Rican officials repeatedly called for Congress and the Obama administration to agree to allow the island to declare bankruptcy and restructure its debts, which is an option for municipalities in U.S. states (as Detroit demonstrated in 2013).

Lawmakers in Congress made several attempts to pass a legislative solution to Puerto Rico's financial crisis in 2015 but failed to agree on a bill before the end of the year. Republicans generally did not support allowing Puerto Rico to declare bankruptcy, arguing that it would hurt U.S. investors and that other options were available. Investment fund managers also lobbied aggressively against extending Chapter 9 to Puerto Rico, claiming it would violate the terms of investors' bond agreements and would create unanticipated risks for bond holders. Puerto Rican officials sought to add a policy rider to the fiscal 2016 omnibus that would allow debt restructuring, but this language was not included in the final bill. The omnibus did provide some funding for the Treasury Department to provide technical assistance to Puerto Rico. At the end of the year, House Speaker Paul Ryan, R-Wis., instructed the committees with jurisdiction over Puerto Rico to find a "responsible solution" by March 31.

House Action

On May 18, Rep. Sean Duffy, R-Wis., introduced the Puerto Rico Oversight Management and Economic Stability Act (HR 5278) in the House. The bill was an updated version of a similar bill (HR 4900) that Duffy had introduced on April 12. The House Natural Resources Committee had conducted a hearing and heard opening statements for a markup of that bill on April 13 but postponed further markup. Most of the provisions in the two bills were the same, though several measures had been revised, added, or removed.

Known as PROMESA, the bill would establish a seven-member Fiscal Oversight and Management Board to oversee the development of budgets and fiscal plans for the Puerto Rican government. Members would be appointed by both congressional leaders and President Obama. The members would have the power to approve fiscal plans drafted by Padilla and approve and enforce annual budgets, including by ordering reductions in spending if necessary. The board would also be authorized to review laws, contracts, rules, regulations, and executive orders for compliance with the approved fiscal plan. Other authorities included the certification of agreements between creditors and debtors, subpoena issuance, and imposition of penalties.

The bill would also give Puerto Rico the ability to restructure $70 billion of its debt and placed a hold on creditor lawsuits. It included language allowing the federal minimum wage to be lowered to $4.25 per hour for Puerto Rican workers age twenty-four or younger for a period of no more than four years. Additionally, the bill would establish expedited procedures for approving "critical" energy and infrastructure projects that could help boost the commonwealth's economy and would create the position of Revitalization Coordinator to designate projects that are critical.

PROMESA was referred to the House Natural Resources Committee as well as the Judiciary, Education and the Workforce, and Small Business Committees on May 18. The Natural Resources Committee held its markup on May 24 and May 25. The original draft of the bill remained largely intact following markup, with many of the agreed-upon amendments making technical corrections or calling for various studies on the Puerto Rican government and economy. For example, Reps. Sam Graves, R-Ga., and Jared Polis, D-Colo., required the Government Accountability Office to report to Congress on the debts of U.S. territories and subnational governments' debt policies. Another amendment from Graves added language emphasizing that the bill would not authorize the payment of federal funds for any liability of a territorial government or instrumentality. Graves also co-introduced an amendment with Rep. Don Beyer, D-Va., that empowered the oversight board to investigate how the island's government bonds were sold to small investors.

The committee approved the revised bill by a vote of 29 to 10 on May 25 and reported it to the full House on June 3. The Judiciary, Education and the Workforce, and Small Business Committees discharged the bill and did not conduct separate markups.

PROMESA passed the House on June 9 by a vote of 297 to 127 following roughly three hours of debate. A total of eight amendments were considered. A proposal by Rep. Norma Torres, D-Calif., seeking to strike the minimum wage provision from the bill was the only amendment to fail. A package of changes proposed by Natural Resources Committee Chair Rob Bishop, R-Utah, and adopted by voice vote made several changes related to the oversight board, including accelerating deadlines for appointing board members, modifying funding for the board, and enabling the board to rescind laws enacted by the Puerto Rican government between May 4, 2016, and the date by which all board members were appointed. Other agreed-upon amendments were relatively minor, with several requiring various debt-related reports to Congress.

Senate Action

Per a House Rules Committee rule (H Res 770), the text of the House-approved bill was inserted into an unrelated Senate-passed bill (S 2328). The revised bill was received in the Senate on June 27 and passed by a vote of 68–30 two days later.

Sen. Robert Menendez, D-N.J., was a vocal opponent of the bill and spoke critically of the bill for more than four hours on the Senate floor before the vote. Menendez particularly objected to establishment of the oversight board, arguing the bill treated Puerto Ricans "like subjects, not citizens." He proposed an amendment that would strip the minimum wage and overtime provisions from the bill, allow Puerto Rico to "opt in" to the oversight board, and expand the board by adding two governor-appointed island residents. However, his amendment fell when members voted 68–32 to invoke cloture. Thirteen Democrats and Sen. Bernie Sanders, I-Vt., were among those who voted in favor of cloture. Sanders previously said the bill eliminated the powers of elected officials in Puerto Rico.

Final Action

Remarking on PROMESA's passage, President Obama echoed the sentiments of some in Congress that the bill was flawed but was nonetheless a step in the right direction. While noting that the bill was not perfect, Obama said the legislation was critical to economic recovery and future growth.

Padilla welcomed the bill's passage, but he also recognized its imperfections, telling a Puerto Rican radio station that certain aspects, such as the implementation of a control board, were not preferred but were necessary to address the nation's debt.

The president signed the bill on June 30 (PL 114-187).

SMALL BUSINESSES

On December 5, 2016, the House approved a package of bills that had already passed individually during the 114th Congress with bipartisan support. These bills were intended primarily to help small businesses raise capital. The previously passed individual bills had not been considered in the Senate, and supporters, such as Rep. Scott Garrett, R-N.J., chair of the House Financial Services Subcommittee on Capital Markets and Government Sponsored Enterprises, hoped that a larger package of bills would receive more attention. Garrett touted the package as a bipartisan solution to extend legislation passed in 2012 (PL 112-106) to change securities laws and help small businesses raise capital. Included in the package of bills were

- HR 4168, passed in February 2016, 390–1, requiring the Securities and Exchange Commission (SEC) to consider and respond to recommendations related to its government business forum on capital formation
- HR 2187, passed in February 347–8, to add securities professionals, attorneys, and accountants to the definition of accredited investors who can take part in investments currently restricted to those meeting specific wealth and income standards
- HR 3784, passed by voice vote in February, creating a small business advocate position
- HR 4854, passed 388–9 in July, to define qualifying venture capital funds as those with less than $10 million and/or 250 investors
- HR 4855, passed 394–4 in July, to relax registration requirements imposed on crowd-funded shares
- HR 5322, passed by voice vote in July, eliminating from the Investment Company Act the exemption for investment companies in Puerto Rico, the Virgin Islands, and other U.S. possessions.

Chronology of Action on Budget and Tax Policy

The 113th and 114th Congresses were dominated almost entirely by budget fights between Republicans and Democrats in the House and Senate. On January 2, 2013, Congress passed and the president signed a bill temporarily delaying the start of the sequester, a series of across-the-board federal spending cuts that hit defense and nondefense budgets equally. The cuts were born out of the inability of Congress to reach an agreement in 2011 on how to offset the increase in the debt ceiling and the subsequent 2012 failure to determine how to replace the sequester with more targeted cuts. Although some of the most fiscally conservative on the Hill saw the sequester as a means to keep government spending in check, most Republicans felt it was too harsh on defense. Their efforts to raise spending focused on increasing defense spending at the detriment of domestic programs such as Medicaid and the Supplemental Nutrition Assistance Program (SNAP). Democratic proposals focused on replacing the sequester and subsequently increasing federal spending. A majority of their proposals would offset the increase by raising revenue through eliminating certain tax breaks for corporations and wealthy individuals. With Congress unable to determine how to overcome the sequester in a way that would pass in both chambers, on March 1, 2013, President Obama issued an executive order setting the sequester in motion. Throughout the president's second term, Congress would go on to make a number of adjustments to the sequester, mainly by extending its time frame to allow for a delay in the cuts and by adding workaround funding for defense by appropriating more money to Overseas Contingency Operations (OCO), an uncapped fund primarily used for war-related needs.

Partisan bickering in 2013 culminated in a sixteen-day federal government shutdown in October. The shutdown was based on a disagreement over the 2010 Patient Protection and Affordable Care Act (ACA), President Obama's landmark piece of health care legislation. The Republican-led House passed a stopgap measure to keep the government funded through December 15, but the bill would entirely defund the ACA. That was a nonstarter in the Democratic-controlled Senate, where debate resulted in a twenty-one-hour marathon speech by Sen. Ted Cruz, R-Texas, against the president's signature law. The Senate went on to amend the House spending

REFERENCES

Discussion of tax policy for the years 1945–1964 may be found in *Congress and the Nation Vol. I*, pp. 397–442; for the years 1965–1968, *Congress and the Nation Vol. II*, pp. 141–182; for the years 1969–1972, *Congress and the Nation Vol. III*, pp. 77–96; for the years 1973–1976, *Congress and the Nation Vol. IV*, pp. 83–106; for the years 1977–1980, *Congress and the Nation Vol. V*, pp. 231–251; for the years 1981–1984, *Congress and the Nation Vol. VI*, pp. 63–82; for the years 1985–1988, *Congress and the Nation Vol. VII*, pp. 75–107; for the years 1989–1992, *Congress and the Nation Vol. VIII*, pp. 87–112; for the years 1993–1996, *Congress and the Nation Vol. IX*, pp. 83–107; for the years 1997–2000, *Congress and the Nation Vol. X*, pp. 87–119; for the years 2001–2004, *Congress and the Nation Vol. XI*, pp. 86–122; for the years 2005–2008, *Congress and the Nation Vol. XII*, pp. 60–135; for the years 2009–2012, *Congress and the Nation Vol. XIII*, pp. 111–190.

Discussion of federal budget policy for the years 1945–1964 may be found in *Congress and the Nation Vol. I*, pp. 387–395; for the years 1965–1968, *Congress and the Nation Vol. II*, pp. 127–140; for the years 1969–1972, *Congress and the Nation Vol. III*, pp. 63–75; for the years 1973–1976, *Congress and the Nation Vol. IV*, pp. 57–81; for the years 1977–1980, *Congress and the Nation Vol. V*, pp. 211–230; for the years 1981–1984, *Congress and the Nation Vol. VI*, pp. 33–61; for the years 1985–1988, *Congress and the Nation Vol. VII*, pp. 33–74; for the years 1989–1992, *Congress and the Nation Vol. VIII*, pp. 37–86; for the years 1993–1996, *Congress and the Nation Vol. IX*, pp. 37–82; for the years 1997–2000, *Congress and the Nation Vol. X*, pp. 40–86; for the years 2001–2004, *Congress and the Nation Vol. XI*, pp. 44–85; for the years 2005–2008, *Congress and the Nation Vol. XII*, pp. 60–135; for the years 2009–2012, *Congress and the Nation Vol. XIII*, pp. 117–190.

MAJOR ACTIONS ON BUDGET AND TAX POLICY

Following is a chronology of the major actions on budget and tax policy taken during the 113th and 114th Congresses.

2013

January 2: Congress passes, and President Obama signs, a bill temporarily delaying the start of the sequester (PL 112-240).

January 3: Congress passes legislation increasing federal borrowing authority of FEMA. It is signed by President Obama on January 6 (PL 113-1).

January 23: House passes legislation raising the debt ceiling. The bill passes the Senate on January 31 and is signed by President Obama on February 4 (PL 113-3).

January 28: Congress approves a Hurricane Sandy supplemental spending bill. It is signed by President Obama on January 29 (PL 113-2).

February 11: Debt limit extension passes the House and is followed by Senate passage on February 12. It is signed by President Obama on February 15 (PL 113-83).

March 1: President Obama signs an Executive Order putting the sequester into effect.

March 6: House passes a "cromnibus" extending government funding through September and providing full-fiscal 2013 appropriations for select agencies. An amended version passes the Senate on March 20, followed by the House on March 21. It is signed by President Obama on March 26 (PL 113-6).

April 10: President Obama submits his fiscal 2014 budget request.

September 29: House passes a bill guaranteeing military pay during the anticipated government shutdown. It is passed by Senate and signed by President Obama on September 30 (PL 113-39).

October 1: Sixteen-day federal government shutdown begins.

October 9: House passes a bill guaranteeing payout of military death benefits during shutdown. It passes the Senate and is signed by President Obama on October 10 (PL 113-44).

October 16: Congress passes a bill raising the debt ceiling and extending fiscal 2013 funding levels through January 2014. It is signed by President Obama on October 17 (PL 113-46).

December 12: House passes a short-term continuing resolution incorporating the Bipartisan Budget Act of 2013. It is passed by Senate on December 18 and signed by President Obama on December 26 (PL 113-67).

2014

January 15: House passes the fiscal 2014 omnibus. It is passed by the Senate on January 16 and signed by President Obama on January 17 (PL 113-76).

March 4: President Obama submits his fiscal 2015 budget request.

September 17: House passes a continuing resolution to keep the government funded through December 11. It is passed by the Senate on September 18 and signed by President Obama on September 19 (PL 113-164).

December 11: House passes the fiscal 2015 cromnibus spending bill. It is passed by the Senate on December 13 and signed by President Obama on December 16 (PL 113-235).

December 12: House passes a continuing resolution that passes the Senate and is signed by President Obama on December 13 (PL 113-203).

2015

February 2: President Obama submits his fiscal 2016 budget request.

September 30: Congress approves and the president signs a ten-week continuing resolution to keep the government temporarily funded through December 11 (PL 114-53).

October 28: House passes a budget agreement allowing for an increase in discretionary spending limits. The bill passes the Senate on October 30 and is signed by President Obama on November 2 (PL 114-74).

December 18: House and Senate pass the fiscal 2016 omnibus package. The bill includes an extension of expiring tax cuts that passed the House and Senate on December 17. The omnibus is signed into law by President Obama the same day (PL 114-113).

2016

February 9: President Obama issues his fiscal 2017 budget request.

June 9: House passes the PROMESA Act to provide financial relief to Puerto Rico. The Senate passes the legislation on June 27, and it is signed by President Obama on June 30 (PL 114-187).

September 28: House and Senate pass a fiscal 2017 continuing resolution to fund the government through December 9. It is signed by President Obama on September 29 (PL 114-223).

December 8: House approves a second fiscal 2017 continuing resolution to fund the government through April 28, 2017. The Senate approves the measure on December 9 and it is signed by President Obama on December 10 (PL 114-254).

Table 2.1 Federal Budget, Fiscal 1960–Fiscal 2016 (billions of dollars)

Year	Revenues	Outlays	On-budget Surplus or Deficit	Social Security	Total Surplus or Deficit	Public Debt
1960	$92.5	$92.2	$510.0	$-0.2	$301.0	$236.8
1961	94.4	97.7	-3.8	0.4	-3.3	238.4
1962	99.7	106.8	-5.9	-1.3	-7.1	248.0
1963	106.6	111.3	-4.0	-0.8	-4.8	254.1
1964	112.6	118.5	-6.5	0.6	-5.9	256.8
1965	116.8	118.2	-1.6	0.2	-1.4	260.8
1966	130.8	134.5	-3.1	-0.6	-3.7	263.7
1967	148.8	157.5	-12.6	4.0	-8.6	266.6
1968	153.0	178.1	-27.7	2.6	-25.2	289.5
1969	186.9	183.6	-507.0	3.7	3.2	278.1
1970	192.8	195.6	-8.7	5.9	-2.8	283.2
1971	187.1	210.2	-26.1	3.0	-23.0	303.0
1972	207.3	230.7	-26.1	2.7	-23.4	322.4
1973	230.8	245.7	-15.2	0.3	-14.9	340.9
1974	263.2	269.4	-7.2	1.1	-6.1	343.7
1975	279.1	332.3	-54.1	0.9	-53.2	394.7
1976	298.1	371.8	-69.4	-4.3	-73.7	477.4
1977	355.6	409.2	-49.9	-3.7	-53.7	549.1
1978	399.6	458.7	-55.4	-3.8	-59.2	607.1
1979	463.3	504.1	-39.6	-1.1	-40.7	640.3
1980	517.1	590.9	-73.1	-0.7	-73.8	711.9
1981	599.3	678.2	-73.9	-5.1	-79.1	789.4
1982	617.8	745.7	-120.6	-7.4	-128.1	924.6
1983	600.6	808.4	-207.7	-0.1	-207.8	1,137.3
1984	666.4	851.9	-185.3	-0.1	-185.4	1,307.1
1985	734.0	946.4	-221.5	9.2	-212.3	1,507.3
1986	769.2	990.4	-237.9	16.7	-221.2	1,740.6
1987	854.3	1,004.1	-168.4	18.6	-149.7	1,889.8
1988	909.2	1,064.5	-192.3	37.1	-155.2	2,051.6
1989	991.1	1,143.8	-205.4	52.8	-152.6	2,190.7
1990	1,032.0	1,253.0	-277.6	56.6	-221.0	2,411.6
1991	1,055.0	1,324.2	-321.4	52.2	-269.2	2,689.1
1992	1,091.2	1,381.6	-340.4	50.1	-290.3	2,999.7
1993	1,154.3	1,409.4	-300.4	45.3	-255.1	3,248.4
1994	1,258.6	1,461.8	-258.8	55.7	-203.2	3,433.1
1995	1,351.8	1,515.7	-226.4	62.4	-164.0	3,604.4
1996	1,453.1	1,560.5	-174.0	66.6	-107.4	3,734.1
1997	1,579.2	1,601.1	-103.2	81.4	-21.9	3,772.3
1998	1,721.7	1,652.5	-29.9	99.2	69.3	3,721.1
1999	1,827.5	1,701.8	1.9	123.7	125.6	3,632.4
2000	2,025.2	1,789.0	86.4	149.8	236.2	3,409.8
2001	1,991.1	1,862.8	-32.4	160.7	128.2	3,319.6
2002	1,853.1	2,010.9	-317.4	159.7	-157.8	3,540.4
2003	1,782.3	2,159.9	-538.4	160.8	-377.6	3,913.4
2004	1,880.1	2,292.8	-568.0	155.2	-412.7	4,295.5
2005	2,153.6	2,472.0	-493.6	175.3	-318.3	4,592.2
2006	2,406.9	2,655.1	-434.5	186.3	-248.2	4,829.0
2007	2,568.0	2,728.9	-342.2	181.5	-160.7	5,035.1
2008	2,524.0	2,982.5	-641.8	183.3	-454.6	5,803.1
2009	2,105.0	3,517.7	-1549.7	137.0	-1412.7	7,544.7
2010	2,162.7	3,457.1	-1371.4	77.0	-1294.4	9,018.9
2011	2,303.5	3,603.1	-1366.8	67.2	-1299.6	10,128.2
2012	2,450.2	3,537.1	-1148.9	61.9	-1087.0	11,281.1
2013	2,775.1	3,454.6	-719.0	39.5	-679.5	11,982.7
2014	3,021.5	3,506.1	-514.1	29.5	-484.6	12,779.9
2015	3,250.0	3,688.4	-465.8	27.3	-438.5	13,116.7
2016	3,268.0	3,852.6	-620.2	35.5	-584.7	14,167.7

SOURCE: Executive Office of the President, Office of Management and Budget, *Budget of the United States Government, Fiscal Year 2018, Historical Tables* (Washington, DC: US Government Printing Office, 2018), Table 1.1.

Table 2.2 Deficit History, Fiscal 1929–Fiscal 2016 (billions of dollars)

Fiscal Year	Receipts	Outlays	Surplus or Deficit (–)	Surplus/ Deficit as % of GDP
1929	$3.9	$3.1	$0.7	—
1933	2.0	4.6	-2.6	-4.5%
1939	6.3	9.1	-2.8	-3.2
1940	6.5	9.5	-2.9	-3.0
1945	45.2	92.7	-47.6	0.5
1950	39.4	42.6	-3.1	-1.1
1955	65.5	68.4	-3.0	-0.8
1960	$92.5	92.2	0.3	-0.1
1965	116.8	118.2	-1.4	-0.2
1969	186.9	183.6	3.2	-0.3
1970	192.8	195.6	-2.8	-0.3
1975	279.1	332.3	-53.2	-3.4
1980	517.1	590.9	-73.8	-2.7
1981	599.3	678.2	-79.0	-2.6
1982	617.8	745.7	-128.0	-4.0
1983	600.6	808.4	-207.8	-6.0
1984	666.4	851.9	-185.4	-4.8
1985	734.0	946.4	-212.3	-5.1
1986	769.2	990.4	-221.2	-5.0
1987	854.3	1,004.1	-149.7	-3.2
1988	909.2	1,064.5	-155.2	-3.1
1989	991.1	1,143.8	-152.6	-2.8
1990	1,032.0	1,253.0	-221.0	-3.9
1991	1,055.0	1,324.2	-269.2	-4.5
1992	1,091.2	1,381.6	-290.3	-4.7
1993	1,154.3	1,409.4	-255.1	-3.9
1994	1,258.6	1,461.8	-203.2	-2.9
1995	1,351.8	1,515.7	-164.0	-2.2
1996	1,453.1	1,560.5	-107.4	-1.4
1997	1,579.2	1,601.1	-21.9	-0.3
1998	1,721.7	1,652.5	69.3	0.8
1999	1,827.5	1,701.8	125.6	1.4
2000	2,025.2	1,789.0	236.2	2.4
2001	1,991.1	1,862.8	128.2	1.3
2002	1,853.1	2,010.9	-157.8	-1.5
2003	1,782.3	2,159.9	-377.6	-3.4
2004	1,880.1	2,292.8	-412.7	-3.5
2005	2,153.6	2,472.0	-318.3	-2.6
2006	2,406.9	2,655.1	-248.2	-1.9
2007	2,568.0	2,728.9	-160.7	-1.2
2008	2,524.0	2,982.5	-458.6	-3.2
2009	2,105.0	3,517.7	-1412.7	-10.1
2010	2,162.7	3,457.1	-1294.4	-9.0
2011	2,303.5	3,603.1	-1299.6	-8.7
2012	2,450.2	3,537.1	-1087.0	-7.0
2013	2,775.1	3,454.6	-679.5	-4.1
2014	3,021.5	3,506.1	-484.6	-2.8
2015	3,250.0	3,688.4	-438.5	-2.4
2016	3,268.0	3,852.6	-584.7	-3.2

SOURCE: Executive Office of the President, Office of Management and Budget, *Budget of the United States Government., Fiscal Year 2020, Historical Tables* (Washington, DC: US Government Printing Office, 2018). Tables 2.1, 2.2.

NOTE: GDP: gross domestic product.

legislation to remove the ACA provision and sent it back to the House, where Republicans refused to pass it in its current form. The bill volleyed between the House and Senate, but the two chambers were unable to reach a compromise by September 30, the end of the federal fiscal year. Closed-door negotiations over the course of two weeks produced a clean bill that would both fund the government until January 15,

Figure 2.1 Federal Budget Receipts

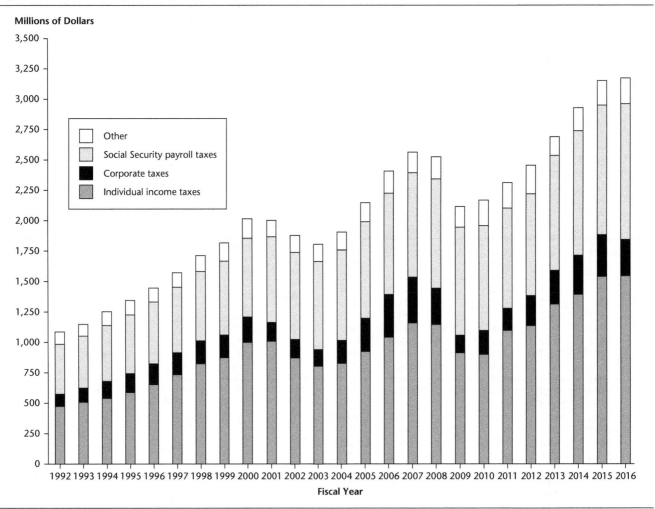

SOURCE: Executive Office of the President, Office of Management and Budget, *Budget of the United States Government, Fiscal Year 2018, Historical Tables* (Washington, DC: U.S. Government Printing Office, 2018), Table 2.1.

2014, while also raising the debt ceiling through February 2014 without matching budget cuts. Included in the continuing resolution was a requirement that the House and Senate establish a conference committee to work out a budget agreement that would provide the framework for funding the government for the remainder of fiscal 2014. What resulted was a deal negotiated primarily by House Budget Committee Chair Paul Ryan, R-Wis., and Senate Budget Committee Chair Patty Murray, D-Wash. That agreement was to be used to develop the final fiscal 2014 spending bill, and it raised discretionary spending caps for both domestic and defense programs, offset by cuts elsewhere and an

extension of the sequester. *(See discussion on Affordable Care Act in Chapter 9, p. 292.)*

Although the agreement established by Ryan and Murray staved off another federal government shutdown in early 2014, it did not have much lasting impact beyond that time. In fiscal 2015, fiscal 2016, and fiscal 2017, Congress was unable to pass even one of the regular twelve appropriations bills that funds most government agencies and was instead forced to rely on continuing resolutions and omnibus measures. By the end of President Obama's second term, Congress had still not found a method through which to entirely replace or eliminate the sequester.

2013–2014

The 113th Congress began with the passage of more than $60 billion in funding to support recovery in the Northeastern United States from Superstorm Sandy, which ravaged the East Coast in late 2012. Passage of that bipartisan piece of legislation would be one of Congress's biggest achievements in 2013 and 2014, as the remainder of the term was characterized by partisan squabbling and a struggle to keep the federal government open.

In the fall of 2013, ultra conservative members of the House Republican caucus held up passage of fiscal 2014 federal government funding legislation, refusing to vote for any budget bill that did not fully repeal the Affordable Care Act. That fight resulted in a sixteen-day shutdown of the federal government that was only overcome with passage of a massive spending bill, known as an omnibus. To avoid another shutdown, Democrats and Republicans came together to agree on spending levels for the next two fiscal years, but that work failed to restore regular order in the budget process, and Congress again was forced to pass omnibus legislation for fiscal 2015.

Congress did temporarily resolve some other significant issues before it. This included raising the debt ceiling, the limit on how much the federal government can borrow, three times to avoid a default. The House and Senate also temporarily extended expiring tax breaks but were unable to reach their bigger goal of a full overhaul of the U.S. tax code.

Supplemental Appropriation for Sandy Recovery

On January 28, 2013, three months after Superstorm Sandy swept across New York and New Jersey, Congress approved a $50.5 billion supplemental spending bill (HR 152—PL 113–2) that would provide both immediate relief to victims and long-term financial support for rebuilding damaged infrastructure. The Senate had pushed forward a bill late in December 2012 for $60.4 billion in immediate aid, but the body moved instead to recess before a vote could be held. Growing discontent within the Republican caucus and across the aisle forced House Speaker John Boehner, R-Ohio, to move forward on a funding package when the 113th Congress convened in January. In the end, the total recovery package from the federal government reached more than $60 billion and included $9.7 billion for the National Flood Insurance Program to help handle claims related to the storm. The funds provided were awarded only to the Northeast, despite the storm's vast reach.

BACKGROUND

On October 29, 2012, Superstorm Sandy made landfall near Atlantic City, New Jersey, causing record storm surges along the East Coast and devastating rain, wind, and snow. At the time, it was one of the costliest storms in the history

Table 2.3 Growing Public Debt

The public debt is the amount owed to the public, American or foreign, through individual or institutional purchase of government securities such as bonds. The remainder of the federal debt is the amount the government has borrowed from government trust funds such as Social Security. The latter is an intragovernmental transaction but is still an obligation that must be paid someday and carries interest the same as debt owed to the general public.

	Public Debt (millions of dollars)			
Fiscal Year	Total Public Debt	As a % of GDP	Total Federal Debt	As a % of GDP
1990	$2,411.6	40.8%	$3,206.3	54.2%
1991	2,689.0	44.0	3,598.2	58.9
1992	2,999.7	46.6	4,001.8	62.2
1993	3,248.4	47.8	4,351.0	64.0
1994	3,433.1	47.7	4,643.3	64.5
1995	3,604.4	47.5	4,920.6	64.9
1996	3,734.1	46.8	5,181.5	64.9
1997	3,772.3	44.5	5,369.2	63.3
1998	3,721.1	41.6	5,478.2	61.2
1999	3,632.4	38.2	5,605.5	58.9
2000	3,409.8	33.6	5,628.7	55.5
2001	3,319.6	31.4	5,769.9	54.6
2002	3,540.4	32.5	6,198.4	57.0
2003	3,913.4	34.5	6,760.0	59.7
2004	4,295.5	35.5	7,354.7	60.8
2005	4,592.2	35.6	7,905.3	61.3
2006	4,829.0	35.3	8,451.4	61.8
2007	5,035.1	35.2	8,950.7	62.5
2008	5,803.1	39.3	9,986.1	67.7
2009	7,544.7	52.3	11,875.9	82.4
2010	9,018.9	60.9	13,528.8	91.4
2011	10,128.2	65.9	14,764.2	96.0
2012	11,281.1	70.4	16,050.9	100.1
2013	11,982.7	72.6	16,719.4	101.2
2014	12,779.9	74.2	17,794.5	103.3
2015	13,116.7	73.3	18,120.1	101.2
2016	14,167.7	77.0	19,539.4	106.1
2017*	14,823.8	77.4	20,354.4	106.2

SOURCE: Executive Office of the President, Office of Management and Budget, *Budget of the United States Government, Fiscal Year 2018, Historical Tables* (Washington, DC: U.S. Government Printing Office, 2018), Table 7.1.

NOTE: GDP: Gross domestic product. *Estimate.

of the United States. More than 100 were killed across the twenty-four states impacted, and tens of thousands of buildings, homes, and other pieces of vital infrastructure were destroyed. Ahead of the storm, governors in Connecticut, Delaware, Maryland, New Jersey, New York, North Carolina, Rhode Island, and Virginia issued voluntary and mandatory evacuation orders and declared states of emergency.

New York and New Jersey bore the brunt of the storm. Millions lost power, public transportation systems and roads were closed, airlines canceled thousands of flights, and even the New York Stock Exchange trading floor was closed for two days, marking the first time since 1888 that the stock market closed unexpectedly on two consecutive days. Newspapers and television news outlets were flooded with images of the iconic Seaside Heights boardwalk in New Jersey and parts of its wooden roller coaster floating in the ocean.

In December 2012, the Senate moved to provide aid to victims of Sandy and the states impacted, passing a proposal for $60.4 billion in relief. But the bill stalled in the House, where Democrats and Republicans could not agree on the size of an aid package, and the most fiscally conservative Republicans called for offsets in other parts of the budget. Democrats and Republicans blasted Boehner for failing to get his caucus in line behind the package. Sen. Kirsten Gillibrand, D-N.Y., called on Boehner to face the families in New York and New Jersey who were most impacted by the storm but said he likely did not have the dignity to do so.

The storm created an unlikely partnership between President Obama and Republican New Jersey Governor Chris Christie, who was highly critical of the president's first term, saying during the 2012 Republican presidential convention that it was essential that better leaders be sent to the White House. The pair would end up appearing frequently together to tour the damage, and they praised each other's efforts to help the affected areas. The president promised that the states impacted would receive the assistance required and said that if a request was made, his administration would figure out a way to approve it. Christie ignored the backlash from his own party for partnering with the president, noting that the recovery in New Jersey was more important than partisan politics.

LEGISLATIVE ACTION

On January 2, 2013, Speaker Boehner announced that he would allow a vote on the floor to provide aid to the region impacted by Superstorm Sandy. The first bill to reach the floor of the House was HR 41, which would temporarily increase the borrowing authority of the Federal Emergency Management Agency (FEMA) to handle claims made after the storm through the National Flood Insurance Program. The concern among lawmakers was that the program was running out of money and might be unable to cover all the claims made following Superstorm Sandy. HR 41 would increase federal borrowing authority from $20.725 billion to $30.425 billion to cover the cost of such claims. The bill was introduced on the House floor on January 3 and came to a quick vote the following day when it was approved overwhelmingly under suspension of the rules, 354–67. Because it was listed as an emergency requirement, HR 41 was able to skirt the funding offset requirement under the Statutory Pay-As-You-Go Act of 2010 and receive the support it needed from conservatives. The Senate took up the bill the same day and passed it without amendment by voice vote. President Obama signed the legislation on January 6 (HR 41—PL 113-1).

While the flood insurance program faced little resistance, there was greater debate over a proposed $50.5 billion supplemental disaster appropriation (HR 152), introduced in the House on January 4. The bill would provide $17 billion in immediate emergency assistance for areas most heavily impacted by the storm, including $5.4 billion to FEMA to provide direct aid, another $5.4 billion for transportation system repairs in New York and New Jersey, $3.9 billion for the Department of Housing and Urban Development (HUD), and funds for the Army Corps of Engineers, Coast Guard, and other agencies responsible for repairs and cleanup.

Progress was slowed by amendments seeking to offset the cost of the bill and another attempting to provide additional funding. The first, introduced by Rep. Mick Mulvaney, R-S.C., Rep. Tom McClintock, R-Calif., Rep. Jeff Duncan, R-S.C., and Rep. Cynthia Lummis, R-Wyo., would offset the $17 billion in immediate disaster assistance with cuts elsewhere in the federal budget. Specifically, the proposal included an across-the-board 1.63 percent cut to all federal discretionary appropriations. Mulvaney said his amendment was not a delay tactic but that he instead wanted to be fiscally responsible and find a way to cover the cost. The measure failed on January 15 by a vote of 162–258. To provide fiscally conservative Republicans some cover in their vote for the $17 billion package, a substitute amendment was introduced that reflected the language of the full House bill and that would limit the disaster funding provided to $17 billion and no more. That amendment was adopted by a vote of 327–91.

Another Republican-proposed amendment was introduced by Rep. Rodney Frelinghuysen, R-N.J., to provide an additional $33.5 billion for recovery and disaster mitigation. The amendment would provide $12.2 billion for HUD community development, $6.1 billion for the FEMA Disaster Relief Fund, $5.5 billion for transportation, $4 billion for Army Corps of Engineers projects, and $2 billion for highway repair. The amendment had strong support from representatives from the East Coast but not many Republicans. Despite that, it was adopted 228–192, with only 38 Republicans voting in favor.

Other amendments included in the final bill limited distribution of fisheries disaster money, increased appropriations to the National Cemetery Administration, provided clarification on spending by the Army Corps of Engineers, restricted how money from the bill was used, and required FEMA to disclose all disaster relief grants received. The House passed the final, $50.5 billion supplemental appropriation on January 15 by a vote of 241–180, with 49 Republicans joining Democrats in support of the measure.

The Senate took up consideration of the bill on January 28. Sen. Mike Lee, R-Utah, proposed one amendment that would offset the total cost of the aid package with a decrease in federal discretionary spending by 0.49 percent over the course of nine years. Senate Democrats, who controlled the chamber, were strongly opposed to any offset, and Lee's amendment was handily defeated, 35–62. With the amendment rejected, Sen. Charles Schumer, D-N.Y., urged the Senate to quickly move forward on passing the final bill, noting in a floor speech that the families impacted by the storm were desperately waiting for congressional action. The Senate passed the House measure without amendment, 62–36, with all 36 "no" votes cast by Republicans. President Obama signed the measure into law on January 29, 2013 (PL 113-2).

Debt Ceiling Limit

Twice in 2013 Congress was forced to consider increasing the debt ceiling, the limit on how much the government can borrow to pay its debts. Once in January and again in October, House and Senate Republicans and Democrats struggled to reach consensus on increasing the debt limit, with Republicans working to match any increase with spending cuts and Democrats seeking a clean bill. If it were to default, the government faced a downgrade of its credit rating (which had already happened during a 2011 fight over the debt ceiling) and decreased investor confidence, not to mention an inability to fund its long-term obligations to programs such as Social Security and military benefits. In both instances, the two parties managed to find common ground and temporarily raise the debt ceiling, allowing for further negotiation on the issue.

BACKGROUND

Before 1917, if the federal government wanted to issue debt, it required congressional approval to do so. That year, Congress set the first debt ceiling at $11.5 billion to fund the war effort and to provide the Treasury greater autonomy to issue bonds. Since 1960, Congress has voted dozens of times under both Democratic and Republican administrations to raise the debt ceiling, the maximum amount the government can borrow. These borrowed funds primarily cover previously incurred debts such as Social Security payments, interest on bonds, and appropriations.

A debt ceiling increase is typically done only if the United States is in danger of default. A default can result in a stoppage of Social Security and military benefit payouts, a decrease in foreign investment, and an overall loss of confidence in the financial systems of the United States. The country has technically only defaulted once, in 1979, when negotiations on an increase came down to the wire and a glitch at the Treasury resulted in some Treasury notes not being paid in full. This instance is generally not considered a true default.

In 2011, the Treasury announced that it had until May 16 before it would default but that it could likely take extraordinary measures to shift payments and stave off a default until early August. Republicans and Democrats in Congress struggled to reach consensus, with Republicans demanding spending cuts to cover any increase and Democrats preferring to deal with the debt ceiling and budget negotiations separately. On July 31, negotiators reached a deal that would raise the debt ceiling and be coupled with a $2.4 trillion spending cut over the next ten years. A congressional super committee was established to determine how those cuts would be made, and the debt ceiling agreement included language that if the committee could not reach a consensus or if Congress did not enact the recommendations, automatic across-the-board spending cuts would be made to defense and domestic budgets. The super committee was ultimately unable to make any recommendations, and the more than $1.2 trillion in cuts, known as the sequester, were set to go into effect in January 2013.

JANUARY LEGISLATIVE ACTION

By the time sequester cuts were set to go into effect, the debt ceiling had reached $17.1 trillion. The Treasury announced that it had technically breached the ceiling at the close of 2012 but that it was using all the tools at its disposal to prevent a default. Due to opposition from President Obama and Democrats who controlled the Senate, the proposal to raise the debt ceiling (HR 325) was written in such a way that it would give the Treasury discretion to borrow what was necessary to avoid a default rather than relying on past tactics and permitting borrowing only up to a certain amount. The open-ended nature helped Republicans set aside their demands for spending cuts to match the increase. The Treasury was given until May 18 to borrow what it needed, and the following day, the debt ceiling would be reset at the total amount it had accumulated.

To win Republican votes, HR 325 also included a provision that would defer lawmaker salaries unless each chamber adopted a fiscal 2014 budget resolution by April 15. This was primarily aimed at the Senate, which had not adopted a budget during the previous three years. In the end, both the House and Senate met the deadline for developing budget plans. On January 23, the House passed HR 325 by a vote of 285–144. A total of eighty-six Democrats voted in favor and thirty-three Republicans voted against the measure.

In the Senate, five amendments to the legislation were proposed and each was tabled. One, offered by Sen. Rob Portman, R-Ohio, and Sen. Jon Tester, D-Mont., would allow discretionary spending to continue for 120 days past the expiration of an appropriations bill, after which point, without a new budget in place, the appropriation would continue but with a 1 percent across-the-board reduction. Another amendment Portman proposed would have codified a requirement of Congress to find spending cuts equal to the debt ceiling increase over the next decade. Sen. David Vitter, R-La., proposed a similar amendment, and both were rejected along party lines. A fourth amendment was proposed by Sen. Pat Toomey, R-Pa., that would require the treasury to prioritize debt securities, Social Security benefits, and military personnel pay in any instance when the debt limit could not be increased and the Treasury was forced to operate only on incoming funds. That, too, was rejected along party lines. The final rejected amendment, proposed by Sen. Rand Paul, R-Ky., was unrelated to the debt ceiling and would prohibit the sale of certain military weapons to Egypt following a coup in the country. The Senate would ultimately vote 64–34 to pass the House measure without amendment. Twelve Republicans joined Democrats in voting for the bill, while one Democrat voted in opposition.

On February 4, 2013, President Obama signed the bill (HR 325—PL 113-3) suspending the debt ceiling until May 19, when it would rise to a level "necessary to fund commitment incurred by the Federal Government that required payment." This amounted to nearly $16.7 trillion by May 19.

In May, the House passed legislation (HR 807) similar to Toomey's Senate amendment. Prioritizing certain payments, Republicans said, would avoid a default because a failure to pay federal workers or contract creditors would not leave the nation in default, but not paying debt holders such as military families and Social Security beneficiaries would. The House passed the measure 221–207, but Democrats in the Senate and strong opposition from the White House prevented it from moving any further.

OCTOBER LEGISLATIVE ACTION

Despite the earlier debt ceiling increase to approximately $16.7 trillion, in August, the Treasury again announced that it would likely default on October 17. Although the Treasury would have an estimated $30 billion to pay some obligations, the Treasury Secretary and congressional leaders worried that coming so close to another default would negatively impact financial markets and consumer confidence. This time, not only was Congress contending with a potential default, but it also faced a government shutdown without consensus on a budget deal to keep the government funded. Democrats again took the tack that the budget and debt ceiling should be handled separate of one another and refused to pass a debt limit increase that included spending cuts.

Republicans requested a number of concessions from Democrats, ranging from the privatization of social programs such as Medicare and Social Security, to tax reform, an increase in the retirement age, and reductions in the Supplemental Nutrition Assistance Program (SNAP). Democrats in Congress, backed by the president, stood firm in their desire to avoid any cuts on top of those already enacted under the sequester. In an effort to find some common ground, President Obama proposed that if Republicans would allow for the passage of a clean debt ceiling increase, he would encourage his party to negotiate on spending issues.

The first House proposal, made in September 2013, raised the debt ceiling for one year. To gain approval from both parties, it also delayed the implementation of the Affordable Care Act (ACA), a frequent source of ire for Republicans, called for votes on tax reform to be held before the close of 2013, and pushed for construction on the Keystone XL pipeline to begin. That measure never received

a vote. The second House proposal would raise the debt ceiling until November 22 but kept the government shutdown in place. This bill also never made it to the floor.

In the end, the two parties were able to reach consensus on the Continuing Appropriations Act, a bill that both extended current funding levels through January 15, 2014, and raised the debt ceiling until February 7, 2014. The Senate attached the agreement to an unrelated House-passed measure (HR 2775) and passed the bill 81–18, and the House approved it without amendment, 285–144. Eighty-seven Republicans, including House Speaker John Boehner, R-Ohio, joined the Democrats and voted in favor of passage. President Obama quickly signed it into law (HR 2775—PL 113-46).

Although the debt limit increase enacted in October 2013 expired on February 2014, the Treasury told Congress that it could use "extraordinary measures" to avoid a default but likely only until the end of the month. On February 11, the House passed S 540, a bill extending the debt limit until March 15, 2015. To avoid any procedural issues, the House had substituted the debt-limit language for the text of previously passed Senate legislation renaming an air traffic control center in New Hampshire. Only twenty-eight Republicans joined nearly all Democrats in support of the measure. The clean bill, which included no spending offsets or other policy riders, drew criticism from many Republicans and conservative groups.

Democrats in the Senate pushed for quick consideration and passage of the legislation to avoid any uncertainty in U.S. financial markets, and on February 12, the Senate cleared the legislation by a vote of 55–43. A motion to close debate on the bill passed 67–31 after Sen. Ted Cruz, R-Texas, demanded that the sixty-vote threshold be used so Republicans could unite in their opposition to a debt limit extension that included no spending offsets or other conditions to address federal spending. Senate Republican leadership worked with its members to ensure there would be enough members of their caucus to vote with the Democrats to end debate.

Fiscal 2013 Budget

Congress struggled throughout 2012 to reach an agreement on a fiscal 2013 budget. In September 2012, one month ahead of the end of the federal fiscal year, Congress passed a six-month continuing resolution to keep the government funded at fiscal 2012 levels and to give themselves more time to pass the twelve regular appropriations measures for the year. That ultimately proved unsuccessful, given that Congress was also grappling with the fiscal cliff—the combination of expiring tax provisions, a need to raise the debt ceiling to avoid default, and the upcoming start to the across-the-board budget cuts brought on by the sequester—which postponed any work on most other legislation, including fiscal 2013 funding. Ultimately, in March 2014, the House and Senate quickly passed what was called a "cromnibus" because it combined elements of

BUDGET CONTROL ACT OF 2011

The battles over the sequester, which repeatedly roiled Congress during Obama's second term, could be traced back to a 2011 legislative compromise known as the Budget Control Act.

In May 2011, the United States had reached its debt ceiling, the limit on how much the government can borrow to pay its previously incurred debts such as Social Security. The Treasury Department was able to exercise extraordinary measures at its disposal to stop a default until August 2, before which time Congress would need to reach an agreement to raise the debt ceiling or risk the ramifications of default, namely a stoppage on certain payments, diminishing investor confidence in the U.S. economy, and a potential credit rating downgrade. Republicans and Democrats disagreed over how to address the issue, with Republicans seeking a decrease in spending to offset the debt ceiling increase, while Democrats wanted a clean bill that did not require cuts elsewhere. The compromise bill, the Budget Control Act of 2011 (PL 112-25), would raise the debt limit by up to $2.4 trillion, made in two separate installments, but required that it be offset by matching spending cuts.

In the first installment, the debt ceiling was immediately increased by $900 billion, which was offset by caps on discretionary spending. For the second part of the increase to go into effect, the bill established a twelve-member Joint Select Committee on Deficit Reduction tasked with recommending where cuts should be made to offset the second increase and proposing the corresponding legislation to do so. The so-called super committee was given until November 2011 to present its recommendations, which Congress would then have until December 23, 2011, to approve. If the committee failed to reach a conclusion by the deadline, the debt ceiling would still be raised, but instead of Congress having a say in how the offsets were allocated, across-the-board spending cuts would automatically be made every year for the next nine years. The cuts, known as the sequester, would be evenly split between defense and domestic spending.

The committee ultimately failed to release any recommendations, and the sequester was set to go into effect on January 2, 2013. In total, $1.2 trillion would be cut from federal spending between 2013 and 2021, and Congress was forced to negotiate within these new limits when setting federal spending each year. This set off annual budget fights as Democrats, backed by the White House, sought to eliminate the sequester and offset the spending with tax increases on corporations and high-income individuals, a nonstarter with Republicans who wanted to maintain the sequester but rebalance its limits by providing some of the domestic funds to defense. The Budget Control Act also put in place discretionary spending caps that required Congress to work within set limits, and if they were exceeded, additional mandatory budget cuts would be made.

Since 2011, Congress modified the sequester four times, either delaying its implementation or raising spending caps. The first one came on January 1, 2013, one day before the sequester would take effect. The mandatory cuts were set to begin at the same time as some tax cuts would expire, spurring action in Congress to avoid what became known as the fiscal cliff. The final compromise bill (PL 112-240) delayed the start of the sequester to March 1, 2013, and renewed some of the expiring tax cuts. The delay slightly rolled back spending cuts from $109 billion for the year to $85 billion, which was offset by a combination of new spending cuts in fiscal 2013 and 2014 as well as new revenue generated through changes to retirement savings account rules. A total of $43 billion in cuts was made to military operations, although none of the reduction impacted military personnel. Domestic discretionary spending was reduced by $26 billion. No cuts were made to programs run by the Department of Veterans Affairs. Mandatory spending was reduced by $16 billion, with $11 billion coming from Medicare and the remaining $5 billion primarily through a reduction in agriculture programs and unemployment benefit extensions.

A second change was implemented in December 2013 within the two-year budget agreement (PL 113-67) reached between leaders of the House and Senate Budget committees. That change raised discretionary spending caps for fiscal 2014 and 2015 by a total of $63 billion. To make up for the increase, the mandatory spending limits were extended from 2021 to 2023. The bill also made cuts to mandatory programs and raised nontax revenue. Two months later, in February 2014, Congress extended the sequester on mandatory programs from 2023 to 2024. This was done to offset savings lost through a repeal (PL 113-82) of a reduction in military pension cost-of-living increases.

A fourth change was made in the October 2015 two-year budget agreement (PL 114-74) to raise discretionary spending caps by $80 billion over the next two fiscal years. That increase would be offset with spending cuts and other revenue increases.

an omnibus spending package with a continuing resolution. This bill (HR 933—PL 113-6) funded the government through September 30, 2013, and provided Congress time to begin working on its fiscal 2014 budget.

House Action

Negotiation in the House happened relatively quickly and behind closed doors. The final bill was introduced by House Appropriations Chair Harold Rogers, R-Ky., just two days ahead of the floor vote on the measure. In the interest of time, it was not considered by the committee but instead went straight to the full House. Rogers said that the provisions included in the bill would stave off the risk of a government shutdown by providing funding for the remainder of the fiscal year while ensuring defense agencies were funded at an adequate level to protect national security and properly equip troops. HR 933, which passed the House by a vote of 267–151 on March 6, incorporated two full-year funding bills for Defense and Military Construction–VA accounts while freezing funding for other departments at fiscal 2012 levels. The aggregate discretionary spending in the cromnibus totaled $1.2 trillion, or $984 billion after taking the sequester into account.

The budget provided for Defense and Military Construction–VA was not increased in the bill, nor did the bill's creators attempt to eliminate the sequester for defense and veteran programs beyond what was stipulated in the Budget Control Act of 2011. However, the bill did provide greater flexibility to the managers of programs covered under Defense and Military Construction–VA to distribute funds in the way they best saw fit. This raised Democratic objections, because Republicans had not offered similar flexibility to other agencies to help them offset the cuts in the sequester.

Democrats were also frustrated that the spending bill did not appropriate the necessary funds for the Centers for Medicare and Medicaid Services (CMS) to implement the federal health insurance exchanges, known as the marketplace, that were set to go live in October 2013. In light of the automatic sequester cuts, Democrats felt that a funding increase for CMS was vital to ensure the system was working properly and that Americans could begin enrolling in coverage. The White House did not strongly object to the way the bill was written and offered praise to negotiators for respecting the spending caps in the Budget Control Act but expressed concern that there were likely improvements that could have been made.

Senate Action

While HR 933 was debated on the floor, the Senate announced that it would take a slightly different approach to fiscal 2013 funding and would increase the number of full-year appropriation bills to five, adding Agriculture, Commerce-Justice-Science, and Homeland Security. House Speaker John Boehner, R-Ohio, warned Senate Appropriations Chair Barbara Mikulski, D-Md., that if the Senate chose to add an excessive number of policy riders or provisions or use any budget gimmicks, they were risking a government shutdown. Boehner said the House was prepared to move a clean continuing resolution, and Mikulski told reporters that she had no intent of introducing any changes that would be unpalatable in the House and wanted to avoid a government shutdown. Senators saw little issue with the addition of the three full-year funding bills because many had been pre-conferenced earlier with the House.

Debate on the Senate floor began on March 13, and around 100 amendments were proposed. Senate leaders worked together to shrink that total to something more manageable to ensure they did not run up against the expiration of the continuing resolution passed in September 2012. Only a few of those amendments considered were actually adopted. These included one approved by voice vote introduced by Sen. Mark Pryor, D-Ark., to add $55 million for the Agriculture Department's Food Safety and Inspection Service to help limit the impact of the sequester on their work. This amendment won passage because it was offset by a cut in the Department of Agriculture school equipment grant program and an account for deferred maintenance on department facilities. Other amendments included those banning some spending on political science research at the National Science Foundation, requiring the continuation of tuition assistance programs within military departments, a prohibition on the Environmental Protection Agency (EPA) enforcing a regulation on farmers to prevent oil spills, and one that would block funding of infrastructure projects in Guam. Amendments rejected included those that would block spending on the ACA, bar the Department of Homeland Security from using funding for projects unrelated to homeland security, and reduce spending for biofuel production.

In the Senate version, Interior-Environment received the most significant decrease in funding, at $800 billion, while programs funding transportation and housing had the largest increases. Prior to voting on the funding package, Sen. Mikulski introduced a comprehensive substitute amendment that would incorporate all the Senate's changes into the House version of the bill. The amendment passed 70–29. The Senate passed its final amended version of the House bill on March 20, by a vote of 73–26. Twenty Republicans joined all but one Democrat in voting for the bill. The total cost for the final Senate version was almost exactly in line with the House version.

House leadership noted that they were happy with the changes made by the Senate, although Democrats continued to express concern over the sequester, and it passed on March 21 as amended in the Senate by a vote of 318–109. The president signed HR 933—PL 113-6 on March 26.

FISCAL 2013 BUDGET PROVISIONS

Most federal departments were funded at fiscal 2012 levels through the continuing resolution portion of the bill, so discretionary appropriations in the final budget increased only slightly from $1.039 trillion in fiscal 2012 to $1.043 trillion in fiscal 2013. That was lower than the $1.047 trillion enacted in the six-month continuing resolution due to the fiscal cliff deal passed in December 2012, which delayed the sequester's implementation until March. That total included the funding subject to the spending caps included in the Budget Control Act of 2011 but not the spending exempt from those caps, including funding for efforts in Iraq and Afghanistan, emergency disaster assistance, and smaller appropriations that improve the integrity of other government programs.

Because President Obama was required under the 2012 fiscal cliff deal to enact the sequester on March 1, before the House and Senate passed the fiscal 2013 funding measure, the sequester was applied to the final bill, lowering the $1.043 billion discretionary spending total to $984 billion. Most of the sequestered funds came from Defense, as called for in the Budget Control Act.

The final fiscal 2013 spending bill provided full-year spending for Agriculture, Commerce-Justice-Science, Defense, Homeland Security, and Military Construction-VA. The accounts covered by the seven other annual appropriations bills—Energy-Water, Financial Services, Interior-Environment, Labor-Health and Human Services-Education, Legislative Branch, State-Foreign Operations, and Transportation-Housing and Urban Development—were covered through a continuing resolution at fiscal 2012 levels with some minor adjustments. These adjustments were intended to provide relief to the covered agencies to deal with the impact of the sequester and included a $1.3 billion increase for embassy security, as well as additional funds for Head Start and child care block grants. Full-year funding provisions included:

- $139.3 billion for Agriculture, a 2 percent increase from fiscal 2012 before the sequester. A vast majority of the funding was allocated to mandatory programs such as crop price supports and nutrition assistance; the $20.5 billion provided in discretionary appropriations was up 6 percent from the prior fiscal year. The Supplemental Nutrition Assistance Program, commonly referred to as food stamps, took a 4 percent hit, but the bill did preserve the $55 billion bump for the Agriculture Department's Food Safety and Inspection Service to ensure the sequester did not impact food inspections.
- $59.5 billion was allocated for Commerce-Justice-Science, including $50.2 billion in discretionary spending, 5 percent lower than fiscal 2012 before the sequester. Increased funding was provided to the National Oceanic and Atmospheric Administration, FBI cybersecurity programs, the National Institute of Standards and Technology, the National Science Foundation, and the Community Oriented Policing Services Program. The Justice Department received a 45 percent cut in administrative funding, while the Commerce Department's U.S. Economic Development Administration, charged with promoting innovation to prepare the nation to compete in the global economy, took a 51 percent hit.
- $605.3 billion was provided for Defense before the sequester was added, which included $518.1 billion in base appropriations for the Pentagon. Both the operations and maintenance readiness accounts and Overseas Contingency Operations (OCO) received

small increases. The sequester cut most accounts covered under Defense by 7.8 percent.

- $46.6 billion went to programs funded under Homeland Security before the sequester, including $6.7 billion in emergency disaster relief. The bill provided $39.6 billion in discretionary spending, which was in line with the fiscal 2012 total. The bill included $10.4 billion for Customs and Border Protection, up 2 percent from fiscal 2012, $5.4 billion for Immigration and Customs Enforcement, a decrease of 2 percent from the prior year, and $5.2 billion for the Transportation Security Administration, down 6.5 percent from the prior year.
- $147 billion before the sequester went to Military Construction-VA, of which $71.9 billion was discretionary. Most of the appropriated funds—$134 billion—were for veterans' programs, including health care. A total of $10.6 billion went to military construction.

Internet Sales Tax Bill Halted

In April 2013, the Senate voted to approve a bill that would require Internet retailers to collect the service and use tax on any purchase made, regardless of the physical location of the buyers. The company would then be required to distribute these taxes to the appropriate taxing authority based on the buyer's location. The bill included an exemption for small retailers with less than $1 million in sales each year. Opposition to the legislation came primarily from a coalition of smaller retailers along with eBay, who saw the bill as an unnecessary regulation and one that would essentially cap growth for small businesses that sought to remain below the $1 million mark to avoid collecting taxes. Amazon led support for the bill with other large online retailers, who felt the bill provided greater certainty in their sales tax collection and prevented them from complying with the patchwork of state laws that had cropped up in the past two decades. Ultimately, the House failed to vote on the Senate legislation or the companion version submitted in the House, and no further action was taken, leaving states to take the lead on passing laws that would ensure the collection of online sales taxes.

BACKGROUND

As a growing number of Americans complete at least some of their purchases online, sales tax implications have come into question, especially because the retailer frequently does not have a physical presence in the state in which the buyer made the purchase, therefore making it difficult for a state to collect sales tax. The Supreme Court ruled on the issue in 1992 in the case of *Quill Corp v. North Dakota*, deciding that the retailer is not required to charge state and local sales tax to a buyer if that company does not have a physical location in the state where the customer makes the purchase. However, buyers were responsible for voluntarily making a tax payment directly to the state for any of those purchases, making it unlikely that a state would receive 100 percent of the tax due.

While buyers benefit from the tax savings, which can typically range anywhere from 5 to 10 percent if they make their purchase from Internet sellers, state and local governments lose out. In 2009, the University of Tennessee conducted a study that revealed these taxing authorities lose out on an estimated $11 billion per year. Although those specific figures have been called into question, there is broad agreement that states and localities are losing at least some of their expected sales tax revenue each year to online retailers. Multiple states attempted to rectify the situation by passing their own laws requiring online retailers to collect sales tax on all sales made within their jurisdiction, but this created a patchwork of requirements that retailers found difficult to keep pace with. In turn, states and physical and online retailers pushed for Congress to step in.

Senate Action

The first bill to come before the Senate in 2013 was S 336, the Marketplace Fairness Act, introduced by Sen. Mike Enzi, R-Wyo. (a companion version was introduced at the same time in the House). The bill would require Internet retailers to collect sales tax from any purchase, regardless of the buyer's location. It was referred to the Committee on Finance on February 14 and had bipartisan backing from a group of fifty-seven lawmakers. The bill had provisions that appealed to both Democrats and Republicans, including the preservation of states' rights, something popular with Republicans, while Democrats viewed it as a way to protect smaller businesses from the onslaught of larger online retailers.

A test vote was held on the measure in March during fiscal 2014 budget negotiations. A nonbinding amendment was attached that reflected the goals of S 336. It easily passed 75–24 on March 22. Sen. Max Baucus, D-Mont., chair of the Senate Finance Committee, strongly opposed the amendment, arguing that his committee had not been given proper time to consider S 336 and that it forced non–sales tax states such as Montana to essentially have a sales tax even if they do not want one.

Given his opposition, Baucus did not act to take up S 336 in his committee. With S 336 stalled but with strong backing for the idea, in April 2013, the Senate took up consideration of another iteration of the Marketplace Fairness Act (S 743). Introduced by Sen. Enzi, S 743 would force Internet retailers to collect sales and use taxes on all purchases regardless of the physical location of the buyer. With the help of Senate Majority Leader Harry Reid, D-Nev., the bill reached the floor without going to committee.

Floor debate centered around whether small Internet retailers should be subject to the burden of collecting sales taxes and distributing them to the various taxing authorities across the country. The argument was raised by Sen. Jeanne Shaheen, D-N.H., that those smaller companies were put at a disadvantage and that the bill would make it more difficult for them to compete against larger Internet sellers. Small retailers, she said, did not need the additional burden of complying with taxing regulations, and she noted that the bill would be specifically harmful for retailers in states where sales tax is not collected for any purchase, whether online or in person.

In the bill was a provision that exempted any retailer earning less than $1 million in online sales from the requirement of collecting sales taxes. Shaheen said that the provision provided some protection, but it ultimately placed a ceiling on corporate growth. According to Shaheen, as businesses reached the $1 million cap, they would be forced to consider whether it was worth the bureaucratic burden to comply with forty-six different state sales taxes. Small companies, a handful of senators from non–sales tax states (including Alaska, Delaware, Montana, and Oregon), and a few online retailers such as eBay backed Shaheen's opposition. According to a report by the Small Business Administration, exempting these smaller retailers meant that at least 40 percent of online sales would remain untaxed, resulting in billions still lost in sales tax revenue. On the other side were online corporate giants such as Amazon, which, given its rapid growth that required distribution centers across the country, was already paying taxes in other states and supported the Enzi bill. The money that poured in from lobbyists supporting the bill led Sen. Ted Cruz, R-Texas, to note that the bill had forced both Democrats and Republicans to cozy up with giant corporations.

The Senate voted 69–27 on May 6 to approve the Marketplace Fairness Act. Five Democrats joined twenty-two Republicans in voting "no."

House Action

In the House, conservative support was necessary if any Internet sales tax bill was to pass. A number of the body's fiscal conservatives refused to support the Senate measure or the companion House bill (HR 684), arguing that it amounted to little more than a tax increase and did nothing to simplify sales tax systems across the country or lift the burden on online retailers. The sponsor of the House bill, Rep. Steve Womack, R-Ark., urged the House to take up the bill in committee or on the floor to allow for debate and for any changes to be made that would alleviate member concerns instead of just ignoring the issue outright. House Speaker John Boehner, R-Ohio, who received multiple letters from House conservatives opposing the measure, indicated that he was in no rush to move any online sales tax bill forward. Discontent grew louder in the summer of 2013, when a group of more than 500 online retailers, known as the eMainStreet Alliance, lobbied against the legislation and sought a small online business exemption that was more significant than what the Senate had passed.

The House Judiciary Committee in September decided to start over on the sales tax issue and issued a list of principles it required to send any such bill to the floor. These included creating a level playing field for businesses big and small, devising a simpler tax system, preventing the application of unnecessary taxes, allowing tax competition, maintaining sovereignty in state tax activity, protecting consumer data, and not creating any new taxes that would apply to online sales. Rep. Bob Goodlatte, R-Va., hoped that these principles would form the basis of any new legislation. However, neither the committee nor the full House considered either the Senate's Marketplace Fairness Act or any similar legislation in 2013.

Without federal action, dozens of states worked to pass their own "Amazon laws" requiring the collection of sales tax. This resulted in significant confusion among online retailers and purchasers, and many of those laws have been challenged in court, and some were struck down.

Fiscal 2014 Budget Request

On April 10, 2013, two months later than it was statutorily required, President Obama submitted to Congress his annual budget request for fiscal 2014. The $3.778 trillion proposal was delayed primarily by the funding and debt ceiling debates that played out in December 2012 and spilled into the start of the year, coupled with the beginning of the across-the-board sequester spending cuts required by the Budget Control Act of 2011. In a Rose Garden ceremony announcing his budget request, the president said that any budget produced by Congress must eliminate "the foolish across-the-board spending cuts" required by the sequester and raise taxes on the wealthiest Americans and largest corporations.

Primarily, the White House included in the budget request proposals the president had made in the past that were aimed at increasing economic growth and job creation as the nation continued to climb out of the 2007 to 2009 recession. To do this while bringing the national debt under control, the president favored tax increases over spending cuts. However, he did include spending proposals that appealed to Republicans, namely an overhaul of the nation's safety net programs. Obama called the entitlement cuts less than ideal but said he was willing to compromise and hoped that Republicans would use them as an opportunity to demonstrate how serious they are about addressing debt and deficits.

This gave Democrats pause, but some Republicans expressed optimism that there would be room to work with the White House. Sen. Johnny Isakson, R-Ga., said it would be interesting to see how the conversation about entitlement reform would progress between congressional leaders and the White House. Republican leadership in the House and Senate, however, dismissed the olive branch as a technicality. Rep. Paul Ryan, R-Wis., said the White House offer to use the chained Consumer Price Index (CPI) to decrease Social Security cost-of-living adjustments was not the fundamental reform that was needed but rather a clarification that would not save money. Ultimately, few of the president's proposals were likely to make it into a final budget package given heavy Republican opposition.

By the time he submitted his request, debate had already begun on fiscal 2014 spending in both houses of Congress, thus limiting the impact of the president's proposals. In the House, Republicans on the powerful Budget Committee were working on a fiscal 2014 budget that would leave the sequester in place, repeal the Patient Protection and Affordable Care Act (ACA), partially privatize Medicare for those under age fifty-five, and make significant cuts to Medicaid and other safety-net programs. Their aim was to balance the budget over the next decade without raising taxes. In the Senate, Democrats were attempting to eliminate the sequester by raising more revenue through increased taxes. Neither the House nor the Senate version under consideration included any changes to Social Security.

Further complicating the congressional response to Obama's proposal, the White House Office of Management and Budget (OMB) was unable to use fiscal 2013 enacted numbers to develop its fiscal 2014 budget proposal because Congress did not finish its fiscal 2013 budget work until March 2013. This made it difficult to measure the president's proposal against current funding levels. In developing the proposal, OMB had relied on the fiscal 2012 enacted budget coupled with the White House fiscal 2013 budget request. The Obama budget also did not take into consideration the impact of the sequester. Instead, it proposed alternative savings of $1.8 trillion for the $1.2 trillion sequester over the next nine years. Combined, this made it hard for budget watchdogs to estimate the impact of the president's budget proposal. According to the bipartisan Committee for a Responsible Federal Budget, the president's budget had the potential to save somewhere between $160 billion and $1.8 trillion. They further estimated that spending would either fall by as much as $600 billion or increase by as much as $700 billion.

Entitlement Reform

Democratic presidents have traditionally stayed away from proposing or enacting significant changes to entitlement programs such as the Supplemental Nutrition Assistance (SNAP) program, Medicare, and Social Security. Until 2013, Obama was no different. However, his fiscal 2014 budget proposal included a different method for calculating the CPI, which likely would reduce cost-of-living adjustments for Social Security beneficiaries, veterans, and other Americans who receive government payments. Moving from the standard Consumer Price Index to what is referred to as chained CPI would slow benefit increases. Economists noted that chained CPI is a more accurate calculation of cost-of-living adjustments, but retiree advocates believe it places undue burden on older Americans who face higher health care expenses. Obama also proposed additional means testing for Medicare benefits to ensure that those at the higher end of the income spectrum pay more for coverage.

Obama's proposal reflected an offer he had made to Republicans in December to avoid a larger fight over the budget and debt ceiling, which was rejected. By April 2013, Republican leadership felt no different, with Senate Minority Leader Mitch McConnell, R-Ky., calling the cuts too modest to offset Obama's proposed tax increases. Democrats expressed disappointment in the president's budget proposal. Sen. Bernie Sanders, I-Vt., vowed to use any tools necessary to block cuts to entitlement program benefits, and even Republicans questioned the president's offer, with Rep. Greg Walden, R-Ore., calling it an attack on the nation's seniors.

New Taxes, Spending, and Deficit Reduction

President Obama made a number of new spending requests that reflected traditionally Democratic priorities. This included Preschool for All, an initiative that would provide incentives to states to expand early education programs to low- and middle-income families. Along with other early childhood initiatives, it was estimated that these programs would increase spending by $77 billion. The president also asked for $50 billion in new funding for infrastructure projects, such as repairing roads, bridges, airports, and mass transit systems. Another $166 billion was set aside specifically for surface transportation- and infrastructure-related job creation programs. President Obama's budget request included $149.5 billion in discretionary and mandatory spending for the Department of Veterans Affairs (VA), which included an increase in the budget of the Veterans Benefits Administration, the VA arm charged with administering financial and other benefits to veterans and their dependents, to $2.5 billion.

To cover the cost of his spending proposals, the president primarily relied on tax increases that the White House projected would raise about $1.4 trillion. This included an increase on taxes for the wealthiest Americans. Some of this would be achieved by limiting deductions for high-income earners to 28 cents on the dollar and enactment of the "Buffett rule" that requires households earning more than $1 million per year to pay an effective tax rate of 30 percent. Another proposal likely to have the greatest impact on high-income households was the restoration of the estate tax to 2009 levels by 2017, which would raise $72 billion. President Obama also called for the cigarette tax to double, which was estimated to raise $78 billion, and capped tax-free retirement accounts at $3.4 million, which would likely bring in $9 billion. The president did include tax cuts in his budget proposal, but those were aimed at small companies and low-income families.

In issuing his budget proposal, the president stated that his goal was to improve the economy while reducing the deficit. The White House concluded that if the president's budget were enacted (including the cancellation of the sequester), the deficit would fall from an estimated $973 billion in fiscal 2013 to $439 billion in 2023. The White House cautioned that the debt would continue to grow in dollar terms but that as a percentage of the gross domestic product (GDP) it would shrink. Fiscal analysts were mixed in their belief that the president's budget would have such a significant impact on the deficit. The Committee for a Responsible Federal Budget expected that the Congressional Budget Office would decide that the president's budget led to only a modest downward trajectory over the next decade.

The president also assumed in his budget that GDP would expand by 2.3 percent in 2013 and 3.2 percent in 2014, which many economists thought unlikely. Those estimates would assume that the United States was officially out of the recession and back on the average GDP growth track that the United States had enjoyed since the end of World War II. The Congressional Budget Office estimated that GDP growth was more likely 1.4 percent in 2013 and 2.6 percent in 2014, while the Blue Chip economists who make regular macroeconomic forecasts landed in the middle of the two, at 2.1 percent for 2013 and 2.7 percent in 2014.

Budget Resolutions

2013 marked the first time in four years that both the House and Senate passed a budget resolution for the next fiscal year by the statutory deadline. The two chambers were incentivized to do so by the debt limit increase legislation (HR 325—PL 113-3) passed at the end of January, which would escrow the salaries of members in either chamber if it failed to adopt a budget resolution by the deadline. The resolution carries little force but is often seen as a blueprint of how the parties intend to shape the budget, and it provides negotiators some guidelines for priority funding areas. However, given the other pressing issues facing Congress—preventing an across-the-board tax increase, raising the debt ceiling, and delaying the sequester—the budget agreements never came into play. In fact, by September, the two chambers were so bitterly divided on a number of issues, most notably the Patient Protection and Affordable Care Act (ACA), which Republicans sought to dismantle, they could not reach a spending agreement by the end of the fiscal year and a sixteen-day government shutdown ensued. The chairs of the House and Senate Budget Committees came together to work out a year-end deal that altered spending caps and the sequester. That budget agreement (H J Res 59—PL 113-67) was essentially a gentleman's agreement between the two chambers to come back to Washington in January 2014 and negotiate in good faith to keep the government open and funded through the remainder of fiscal 2014.

House Action

The House adopted its budget resolution in early 2013. H Con Res 25, which was written primarily by House Budget Committee Chair Paul Ryan, R-Wis., was debated in committee on March 13 and reflected core conservative principles of spending reductions, primarily for domestic programs, and a drive toward a balanced budget. The committee considered and rejected all but one of twenty-three Democratic amendments, most of which were based on the Democratic priority of providing additional funding to nondefense programs. Amendments proposed by Democrats included those seeking to increase spending for entitlement programs, particularly Medicaid and the Supplemental Nutrition Assistance Program (SNAP), which Republicans wanted to turn into a block grant. The one amendment accepted by the committee that was proposed by a Democrat came from Rep. Gwen Moore, D-Wis., and would ensure that no part of a child support payment could go toward administrative costs. The final budget resolution was approved 22–17 on a party-line vote.

The House debated H Con Res 25 from March 19 through March 21, during which time it considered only five amendments and rejected all of them. All five were full substitute amendments, including:

- A substitute to replace the Ryan resolution with the Senate Democratic budget, rejected 134–261
- A substitute offered by the Congressional Black Caucus, rejected 105–305, that called for more spending on infrastructure, education, and community redevelopment with a goal of reducing unemployment and poverty
- A substitute from the Congressional Progressive Caucus, rejected 84–327, to replace the Ryan resolution with its own budget that would reduce the deficit by $2.7 trillion over the next ten years by raising taxes on corporations and wealthy individuals
- A substitute from the Republican Study Committee, rejected 104–132, that called for $7.7 trillion in spending cuts over the next ten years and balancing the budget by fiscal 2017; in a political maneuver, most Democrats voted "present" to force Republicans to vote against the substitute and ensure it would not pass
- A substitute amendment to replace Ryan's text with the House Democratic budget, rejected 165–253, that would balance the budget by 2040 and replace the sequester with revenue increases and spending cuts.

The full House passed the Ryan resolution on March 21, 221–207, without any Democratic support. The budget blueprint called for a discretionary appropriation cap of $967 billion in fiscal 2014. That total reflected the limits set by the Budget Control Act of 2011. Ryan's resolution, however, would allow more money for defense than provided for under the sequester by reining in nondefense spending to offset the increase. Domestic discretionary spending was set at $414 billion, around $55 billion less than allowed under the Budget Control Act, with the savings transferred directly to the Pentagon. Moving that $55 billion into defense coffers essentially wiped out the impact of the sequester on the defense budget. The resolution also repealed the ACA, overhauled the tax code, and called for balancing the budget within the next decade. Savings in the resolution were primarily drawn from cuts to domestic programs.

Senate Action

On March 22, the Senate Budget Committee adopted its budget resolution (S Con Res 8), its first in three years, by a 12–10 party-line vote. The Senate plan, authored by Sen. Patty Murray, D-Wash., took a decidedly different tack than the House. It called for capping discretionary spending at $1.058 trillion in fiscal 2014 and would eliminate the sequester. Unlike the House, Murray called for a budget reconciliation bill, legislation used for expedited consideration of spending-related bills without threat of a filibuster and with limited amendments. Murray said the reconciliation bill should produce $975 billion over the next decade in additional tax revenue. The Senate committee rejected a variety of Republican-offered amendments, including those that would change spending and revenue levels offered in the resolution.

The full Senate debated its budget resolution from March 21 through March 23 and considered more than 100 amendments, of which only a few inconsequential ones were adopted. Many of the roll-call votes on the amendments that were rejected were simply symbolic and reflected existing party positions, including:

- A motion to recommit the budget resolution as rewritten to reach a balanced budget within ten years; the motion was rejected 46–53
- An amendment including the House Republican budget, rejected 40–59
- An amendment to strike reconciliation instructions that call for higher taxes, rejected 45–54.

Some of the adopted amendments, most of which had no practical effect, included an amendment endorsing the 2.3 percent medical device tax required under the ACA, which was adopted 79–20. The Senate also approved, by a 62–37 vote, an amendment endorsing construction of the Keystone XL oil pipeline. With all amendments considered, on March 23, the Senate adopted S Con Res 8 by a vote of 50–49 without any Republican support and four Democrats joining Republicans to vote "no."

Conference Negotiations

Given the vast differences between the House and Senate budget resolutions, conference negotiations stalled almost immediately. Work was further complicated because the president was delayed in releasing his annual budget request. In the end, House Republicans refused to form a budget conference committee, and Senate Republicans rejected Democratic efforts to appoint conferees. Instead, Ryan called for meetings between him and Murray to agree to a framework for negotiations before the conference committee would begin its work. The two chambers continued to struggle through the summer to decide how to proceed on the budget, but that changed in October after a sixteen-day government shutdown. Included in the legislation reopening the government (PL 113-46) was a provision requiring that a budget conference committee meet and, by December 13, reach a budget agreement.

Negotiations were primarily conducted by Ryan and Murray, and the pair quickly realized that they had to limit their expectations for what would appear in the final deal to ensure it was palatable to members of both parties. The prospects of a ten-year budget resolution conference agreement instead gave way to a compromise, short-term deal to set discretionary spending levels, address the sequester, and provide a simple solution for finalizing fiscal 2014 appropriations without the threat of another shutdown.

On December 10, Ryan and Murray announced their final agreement. It split the difference between the House and Senate budget resolution totals and set a fiscal 2014 discretionary spending cap of $1.012 trillion and a slightly higher level for fiscal 2015 of $1.014 trillion. The fiscal 2014 total allowed for $491.5 billion for nondefense and $520.5 billion for defense programs. The agreement pared back the scope of the sequester for fiscal 2014 and 2015 and provided both domestic and defense programs each around $22 billion extra, which was offset by $63 billion in alternative savings. That savings offset extended until 2023 the sequester cuts for mandatory spending programs. Additional savings came through the adjustment of aviation security fees and federal civilian and military retirement programs.

The agreement was inserted into the dormant short-term continuing resolution (H J Res 59) that had been considered in both the House and Senate ahead of the October shutdown. In the Senate, two procedural hurdles needed to be cleared ahead of a final vote, one cloture motion to break a filibuster and a move to make offering amendments to the bill easier. The cloture motion passed 67–33, while the procedural move was rejected 46–54. The Senate voted 64–36 in favor of the final spending deal on December 17. The House passed the deal in bipartisan fashion 332–94 on December 24 in its final roll-call vote of the year.

OMNIBUS APPROPRIATIONS

The 2013 congressional agenda was almost completely dominated by appropriations battles. A fight over discretionary spending caps, the sequester, and the debt limit hampered negotiations on the twelve regular individual appropriations bills. But it was a Republican miscalculation on the willingness of Democrats to negotiate on the Patient Protection and Affordable Care Act (ACA) that led to a sixteen-day government shutdown in October. That budget ended with a continuing resolution, signed into law on October 17, to keep the government open until mid-January 2014 to allow negotiators more time to reach an agreement for fiscal 2014 spending. That agreement included language requiring that a conference committee meet to develop a budget framework that would set spending levels for fiscal 2014 and 2015 and avoid a government shutdown when the continuing resolution expired in January. Eventually, Congress was forced to wrap all twelve appropriation bills into a large omnibus spending measure that was enacted on January 16, 2014, marking the fourth consecutive year Congress was forced to pass omnibus legislation.

INDIVIDUAL APPROPRIATION BILLS

House and Senate appropriators worked through the spring and summer of 2013 on language for the twelve individual spending bills that fund a majority of the government. The two chambers, however, were $91 billion apart in spending levels. This was because the House wanted to honor the sequester cuts while also allocating more to defense spending than was permitted under the Budget Control Act of 2011 and which would come from cuts to domestic programs. Senate Democratic negotiators, who were closely aligned with the White House, rejected the House proposals. On May 21, the House Appropriations Committee approved bottom-line allocations for its twelve bills and began sending them to the floor. The president threatened to veto all the bills due to the cuts to domestic spending and policy riders, and even some House Republicans disagreed with their own caucus because they were seeking a higher spending limit. Ultimately, the House Appropriations Committee approved only ten regular bills; left out were one covering the Interior Department and one financing the departments of Labor, Health and Human Services, and Education.

The Senate Appropriations Committee approved bottom-line numbers for its twelve spending bills on June 20, which totaled $1.058 trillion, a level equal to the spending cap required under the 2011 Budget Control Act and as revised by the January 2013 legislation on the fiscal cliff. Democrats remained hopeful that in negotiations with the House, they could shrink the sequester, and they refused to consider House language that would assume the sequester was in effect. The committee approved eleven of the twelve bills, leaving out the one funding the Interior Department.

LIMITED FLOOR ACTION

The House managed to pass four individual appropriations bills, one financing military construction for the Pentagon and Department of Veterans Affairs (HR 2216), one for the Department of Homeland Security (HR 2217), one for the Department of Energy civilian activities and water projects (HR 2609), and one for military activities at the Department of Defense (HR 2397). The Senate did not pass any of its bills, with Republicans united in opposition to the $1.058 trillion spending measure. Without sixty votes needed to invoke cloture and close debate on the bills, there would be no action.

The appropriations process came to a halt in July when Republicans in the House staged a revolt over what they saw as a constrained funding level for an appropriations bill funding the departments of Transportation and Housing and Urban Development, and the bill was pulled from the House floor. Senate Republicans blocked a cloture vote on a similar measure.

Following the August recess, both chambers appeared at an impasse, with Republicans attempting to force Democrats to accept lower spending levels and Senate Democrats refusing to yield. Republicans were also seeking to prevent the Patient Protection and Affordable Care Act (ACA) from fully taking effect ahead of the October 1, 2013, opening of the state and federal insurance exchanges. House Republicans made the first attempt at combining a continuing resolution with a slowing of ACA implementation under HJ Res 59. The House passed three different versions of the continuing resolution, each of which would provide funding for the government through December 15 at the House appropriation level and with specifications in place about the implementation of the ACA. The White House issued a veto threat for each iteration. The first version, which passed 230–189 on September 20, eliminated all mandatory and discretionary appropriations that financed the ACA. The Senate took up the bill, and debate ended with a twenty-one-hour marathon speech given by Sen. Ted Cruz, R-Texas, against the ACA. Ultimately, the body invoked cloture and voted 54–44 to strip out the ACA language and provide appropriations at a higher level through November 15. On September 27, the Senate sent the amended bill back to the House. Two days later, on September 29, the House voted 231–192 to clear a measure funding the government through December 15 while delaying all aspects of the ACA for one year and voiding a tax on medical devices. The Senate voted 54–46 on September 30 to table the House amendments and send the bill back to the House. Then, on September 30, the House voted 228–201 to amend the bill again and delay for one year only the individual mandate, the ACA provision that required all Americans to have health insurance. The Senate again voted 54–46 to table the House amendments and sent the bill back. Without fiscal 2014 funding in place, the federal government shut down nonessential operations on October 1.

The shutdown marked the seventeenth lapse in government funding in U.S. history. More than 800,000 federal employees were furloughed, and all nonessential government functions were discontinued, including the national parks, funding for the Women, Infants, and Children (WIC) program, and flu programs run by the Centers for Disease Control and Prevention (CDC). Essential services, including payouts to military families, and Social Security and food stamp recipients were continued, as were programs deemed vital to national security and public safety. The shutdown lasted a total of sixteen days and cost the country an estimated $24 billion, according to Standard & Poor's. The Congressional Budget Office reported that the shutdown had significantly impacted the economy because it delayed infrastructure projects that were job creators, delayed import and export license applications, delayed loans to homeowners and small businesses, and reduced travel and tourism.

CONTINUING RESOLUTION

As the shutdown began, Republicans and Democrats took turns blaming the opposing party for failing to pass a budget. The House passed seventeen specific appropriations bills that would reopen certain parts of the government, of which the Senate considered and passed two (HR 3210—PL 113-39 and HJ Res 91—PL 113-44), both of which guaranteed that military pay and death benefits would continue to be paid out. By the second week, leadership on both sides appeared ready to negotiate on a bill that would reopen the entirety of the federal government; rank and file, however, seemed to disagree, seeking policy concessions that would appeal to the party's bases. On October 10, congressional leaders met with the president, intent on developing a plan that would temporarily fund the government and delay the debt limit debate as long as the president agreed to accept some spending cuts. The meeting produced no consensus.

This gave way to closed-door negotiations between Senate Democratic and Republican leaders, which began on October 14. A tentative continuing resolution was announced on October 15 that would reopen the government for three months through January 15, 2014, at the fiscal 2013 postsequester level, would allow for the debt limit to increase until February 7, 2014, to stave off a default, and would give back pay to the 800,000 federal workers who were furloughed during the shutdown. The bill also made a change to the ACA to require that those seeking insurance subsidies provide income verification. The Senate voted 81–18 on October 16 to attach the continuing resolution to HR 2775, an unrelated House-passed bill. The House cleared the bill a few hours later, 285–144, with 87 Republicans joining Democrats to vote for passage. The president signed the Continuing Appropriations Act of 2014 into law on October 17.

OMNIBUS BILL

The October agreement that reopened the government called for a panel of members from both chambers to meet to develop a budget agreement that would set spending levels for fiscal 2014 and 2015. Negotiations were focused on ensuring the bill would meet discretionary spending caps set in place by the sequester and would also be palatable to members of both parties in the House and Senate. On December 10, Ryan and Murray announced that the group had a framework that would allow for the resumption of fiscal 2014 funding discussions to allow Congress enough time to put a spending deal in place to meet the January 15, 2014, expiration of the October continuing resolution.

The budget agreement set a fiscal 2014 and 2015 discretionary spending cap of $1.012 trillion, allowing $520.5 billion for defense and $491.5 billion for nondefense programs, while also cutting the automatic sequester for the next two fiscal years by a total of $63 billion. The terms of the agreement were added to HJ Res 59 (PL 113-67), the short-term continuing resolution signed into law on December 26.

At the start of the new year, appropriators were still working to finalize a fiscal 2014 budget before the continuing resolution expired. To provide time to conclude negotiations, on January 14, the House passed a stopgap measure extending the deadline to January 18, which the Senate passed on January 15. Negotiations concluded on January 13, 2014, when a full-year appropriation package was released that included details for all twelve regular spending bills. The language was inserted into HR 3547, a previously passed and unrelated measure. The House passed the omnibus on January 15 by a vote of 359–67, and the Senate cleared it one day later 72–26. The bill was signed into law on January 17. The final omnibus kept in place the $1.012 trillion cap on discretionary spending agreed to in December and provided an additional $98 billion in spending not subject to the cap, most of which was for Overseas Contingency Operations spending.

Fiscal 2015 Budget Proposal

During his first five years in office, President Barack Obama used his annual budget proposal to outline an ambitious agenda he thought was best to address the nation's challenges. By 2014, however, with a Congress deadlocked on a variety of issues and with spending capped by the Budget Control Act of 2011, the 2014 White House budget reflected instead the president's frustration and included few visionary goals. The $3.9 trillion budget plan closely followed the December 2013 budget agreement negotiated by Rep. Paul Ryan, R-Wis., chair of the House Budget Committee, and Sen. Patty Murray, D-Wash., chair of the Senate Budget Committee. According to the Office of Management and Budget (OMB), over ten years the president's plan would increase outlays as a share of gross domestic product from 21.1 percent in fiscal 2014 to 21.5 percent in fiscal 2024. Tax receipts would grow from 17.3 percent to 19.9 percent over the same time period. Debt would peak at 74.6 percent of GDP in fiscal 2015 before falling to 69 percent in 2024. Notably, the White House relied on a fiscal outlook rosier than that of the Congressional Budget Office (CBO). The president's budget projected 3.1 percent GDP growth in fiscal 2014, while the CBO assumed 2.7 percent growth. From 2018 through 2024, OMB projected 2.4 percent growth to CBO's 2.2 percent.

Obama's budget proposal offered a blueprint for how the White House felt it could address its priorities within the spending limits set by the December 2013 budget deal. It was widely viewed as Obama's most realistic budget, in that it included few of his more liberal policy goals, instead favoring those areas where Republicans and Democrats could find common ground. Of course, the president did offer some proposals that were nonstarters with Republicans, including an end of sequestration in 2016 to be replaced with $1.2 trillion in alternative deficit reduction. According to the Office of Management and Budget, if sequestration was not eliminated, "funding levels for 2016 and beyond will continue to preclude the investments needed to protect our nation or enable our economy to achieve its full potential," OMB wrote in the budget proposal. The president also added a supplemental discretionary and defense spending request totaling $56 billion for what he called an Opportunity, Growth, and Security initiative. This, the president said, was intended to increase spending on programs such as preschool education, research, job training, and weapons system modernization. Such spending would be offset by a combination of spending cuts elsewhere and the end of certain tax breaks. Republicans dismissed the funding request—and the proposal to end sequestration—as little more than an election-year talking point for Democrats.

ENTITLEMENT REFORM

In his fiscal 2015 budget proposal, the president dropped a provision he had previously included, a rollback of the Social Security cost-of-living increases. The plan would reduce the federal deficit and had many supporters in the Republican Party but few Democratic backers. The past proposal would have utilized what many believe is a more accurate measure of inflation to determine the cost-of-living adjustments in exchange for tax increases. It was the latter provision that Republicans were unwilling to consider. Although it was left out of his fiscal 2015 budget proposal, the president did note that he was still willing to consider it if Republicans would eliminate some tax breaks for corporations and the wealthiest Americans. However, despite the president's ongoing willingness to negotiate, leaving entitlement reform out of the budget request was largely seen as acknowledgment from the administration that the debate had reached an impasse.

The president did receive credit for issuing a proposal that reduced the budget deficit to 1.6 percent of gross domestic product by 2024, as well as put debt on track to shrink as a share of the economy after fiscal 2015. The president's proposal made this possible through savings in Medicare, Medicaid, and other health programs, as well as $650 billion in savings over the next decade through tax changes targeting the wealthy. In outlining his plan, the president said it was necessary for the country to decide whether it would continue protecting tax breaks for the rich or if it instead wanted to expand opportunity for every American by investing in programs that grow the economy and create jobs. However, even the White House admitted that the president's budget would likely receive little consideration in the current Congress, especially with the House controlled by Republicans and Democrats facing tough reelection battles across the country.

A president's budget is generally dismissed out of hand by members of the opposition party, and Obama's fiscal 2015 proposal was no different. Specifically, Republicans took aim at the president's limited vision and his failure to consider the rapidly growing federal spending on entitlement programs. According to Republicans, a CBO report said programs such as Medicare, Medicaid, and Social Security were not sustainable in the long run without spending cuts, tax increases, or both. Democrats shot back, criticizing Republicans for protecting tax breaks for the wealthy over a better fiscal solution for entitlement reform.

DEMOCRATIC PRIORITIES

The president's budget included a number of Democratic priorities that were repeated from earlier White House proposals and which were primarily used in 2014 as talking points for members of the House and Senate running for reelection, given that they had little chance of being taken up by the Republican-controlled House. These included forty-five new manufacturing institutes, universal preschool, new job training programs, an early Head Start initiative, and an extension of emergency unemployment insurance. The White House sought to cut taxes for low- and middle-income families, partly by extending the Earned Income Tax Credit for adults without children, the cost of which would be covered by redrawing tax provisions that benefit high-income earners. Although Republicans have typically shied away from cutting any tax credits, there was potential for this particular proposal to gain traction in Congress, where the extension of the Earned Income Tax Credit already had Republican support.

SPENDING BY DEPARTMENT AND MAJOR AGENCY

Agriculture

Reductions in the Department of Agriculture's spending had already been made under the recently enacted five-year farm bill (PL 113-79), but the administration sought additional cuts. In its fiscal 2015 budget proposal, the White House requested $23.2 billion in discretionary funds, matching the fiscal 2013 budget but lower than the fiscal 2014 enacted level of $24.1 billion; total budgetary authority would fall from $158 billion in fiscal 2014 to $146 billion in fiscal 2015. The reduction was primarily made up of a decrease in mandatory spending for crop subsidies and crop insurance. The administration also proposed the closure or consolidation of 250 Farm Service Agency offices, to be replaced by regional service centers. Thirty-one of the offices proposed for consolidation or closure did not have full-time staff at the time Obama's budget was released. The administration argued that the purpose was to provide for better-staffed centers to aid with economic development. It was unlikely these proposals would gain any traction, because Congress had refused to consider them when it passed the five-year farm bill. The administration, however, said it was again including these proposals because it wanted to provide for consistency in its ideas for cutting spending in some areas to fund other initiatives.

The president's budget also included a proposal to change how the Food for Peace program purchases food, allowing foreign food aid programs to purchase 45 percent of their food overseas from local or regional producers rather than importing U.S.-grown goods. The White House had made this proposal while Congress was debating the farm bill, and it was rejected. The budget included $75 million for three new agricultural research institutes that would study crop science, pollinator health, biobased product manufacturing, and antibiotic resistance.

The president requested an extra $1 billion for the USDA's Forest Service to combat wildfires in the west. The budget would allow both the Forest Service and the Interior Department to draw disaster money from a special fund held by the Federal Emergency Management Agency (FEMA), with a goal of reducing the amount of borrowing done from internal funds being used for other vital services such as thinning forests.

Commerce

The Commerce Department would receive a 6 percent budget increase under President Obama's fiscal 2015 budget request, rising from the $8.3 billion fiscal 2014 enacted level to $8.8 billion, well above the $7.6 billion fiscal 2013 budget. The focus of the increase was on advances in skill training, manufacturing technology (including the forty-five new innovation hubs), broadband telecommunications, and advanced weather data. The National Oceanic and Atmospheric Administration (NOAA) received a 3 percent bump to $3.3 billion in the Obama budget; the National Telecommunications and Information Administration, an 11 percent increase to $51 million; and the National Institute of Standards and Technology would receive $680 million, an increase of 4 percent. The president also included an additional $281 million, increasing the total to $753 million, to develop cost-saving methods for the 2020 decennial census.

Corps of Engineers

The White House proposed only $4.5 billion for the Army Corps of Engineers, down from $5.5 billion in fiscal 2014 and $9.9 billion in fiscal 2013. Spending for the Harbor Maintenance Trust Fund, which covers dredging and port maintenance, would decrease to $947 million from $1.1 billion, despite an expected increase in user fees charged to shippers. The Obama administration also proposed changing the 20-cents-per-gallon diesel tax charged to barge operators with a per-vessel fee. The industry, along with some Republicans, supported instead an increase in the diesel fee. The money would fund inland waterway maintenance, improvements, and new construction projects.

Defense

The president's fiscal 2015 budget included a decrease in core funding for the Department of Defense, as well as funds for Overseas Contingency Operations (OCO). The former would receive $495.6 billion in the president's budget request and the latter $79.4 billion. The budget was one of the first the White House submitted that reflected the reality of the sequester spending caps and instead prioritized the needs of the military as it carried out the wars in Iraq and Afghanistan. The Pentagon sought to modernize its current fighting force in return for cutting back the number of soldiers and reining in pay and benefits. The number of active-duty troops was expected to decrease from 510,000 in fiscal 2014 to between 440,000 and 450,000 or perhaps lower if sequester cuts continued.

The proposal drew sharp criticism from Republican defense hawks who placed the blame for cuts on President Obama. Sen. James Inhofe, R-Okla., who led the Armed Services Committee, said the administration's misguided budget priorities left the military in a situation where it had to cut budgets and leave American soldiers without the advanced weapons, technology, and manpower they required. Some Democrats agreed that the cuts, especially those proposed for reduction in force size and compensation, would be difficult to support but said the fiscal responsibility to fund and prioritize spending rested with Congress, not the president.

The Pentagon requested $199 billion for operations and maintenance, up $4 billion from the prior fiscal year, funds that are primarily used for readiness and training. The president also requested $91 billion for procurement accounts, down $3 billion from fiscal 2014, with most cuts impacting the Army and Navy, while the Air Force received a slight increase. Programs facing cuts or terminations included the Army's Ground Combat Vehicle, to be replaced with $131 million in science and technology funding to determine what would be feasible for the next infantry fighting vehicle. The Pentagon also proposed limiting to thirty-two the number of Littoral combat ships it would buy; to appease lawmakers, the Navy would research alternatives for a surface combatant program. The Pentagon continued to push for the retirement of the A-10 Warthog support aircraft fleet, which it said would save $3.5 billion over five years. This was a nonstarter for lawmakers, who in their 2014 defense authorization prohibited the Air Force from retiring the program.

The fiscal 2015 budget sought to slow the growth of costs related to military pay and benefits. The White House proposed a 1 percent increase in basic pay, a 1.5 percent increase for housing allowance, and an increase of 3.4 percent for subsistence. The proposal also requested that Congress increase some health care copays, something Congress regularly rejected. According to the Pentagon, failure to accept the compensation and health care package would cost $2.1 billion in fiscal 2015 and $30 billion over the next five years.

Education

In his fiscal 2015 budget request, President Obama sought to expand competitive education grants and expand prekindergarten programs to more Americans. The expansion resulted in an increase to $68.6 billion from the fiscal 2014 enacted budget of $67.3 billion. The expansion of education grants had in the past been met with skepticism from both sides of the aisle, with Republicans viewing it as a way to impose federal guidelines on state education policy and Democrats believing it would result in some states

or districts losing out on funding. The fiscal 2015 proposal was titled the Race to the Top Equity and Opportunity program and was specifically designed to ensure greater equality in the nation's poorest school districts. According to the White House, the plan would link state and local data on school finances, student achievement, and human resources to pair the best teachers, administrators, and coursework with underserved students. To fund the program, the president asked for $300 million.

To fund preschool development competitive grants, the president requested $500 million while continuing his call for a universal preschool program to be funded by an increase in the federal tobacco tax. To fund the latter, the administration proposed spending $1.3 billion in fiscal 2015 and $75 billion over the next decade. As for higher education, the president called for funding programs to lower the cost of college and ensure a greater number of Americans finish the college programs they begin. Republicans criticized the president's requests as adding to an already confusing and costly litany of education programs, which instead should be streamlined.

Energy

For the Department of Energy, the president opted to increase the discretionary budget by 2.6 percent to a total of $27.9 billion. The White House intended for the extra funds to be used toward research and development of renewable energy technologies that would address climate change and ensure U.S. energy independence. The Energy Department Energy Efficiency and Renewal Energy Office would see its spending increase by 24 percent over the previous fiscal year to $2.3 billion. The Advanced Research Projects Agency–Energy program would also receive a significant bump of 16 percent to $325 million. Funding to secure the U.S. energy grid would increase almost threefold to $23 million; a program for integrating the number of sources of renewable energy into the grid would receive $56 million. Another large increase would go to projects focusing on advanced manufacturing. Funding for this area would increase by nearly 50 percent to $305 million.

Funding for wind energy research received a boost of 16 percent over fiscal 2014 levels, up to $115 million, and geothermal research would receive an additional 22 percent, reaching $62 million. Both solar energy and hydrogen fuel research would see their funding reduced, by 4 percent and 12 percent, respectively. The White House also proposed to eliminate $4 billion per year in fossil fuel subsidies.

The budget set aside funds for research and development to safely store and dispose of nuclear waste from commercial reactors and would increase nuclear weapons spending to $8.3 billion. U.S. efforts to prevent the proliferation of nuclear weapons would be cut by nearly 20 percent to $1.6 billion. Programs to safely process, secure, and dispose of nuclear waste from Cold War–era weapons facilities increased to $5.6 billion.

Environmental Protection Agency

The fiscal 2015 White House budget set aside $7.9 billion for the Environmental Protection Agency (EPA), down from $8.2 million in fiscal 2014. Those cuts would primarily be to programs that help states and localities pay for clean water projects, with remaining funds focused on the highest-priority areas. Budget increases were included for federal partnership grants that help states and tribal governments protect public health and the environment, and the EPA said it would also have enough funding to continue working toward the president's goal of reducing carbon pollution. The president also included in his request $20 million for states to implement his climate action plan to cut carbon pollution and prepare for the impact of climate change.

Food and Drug Administration

The president's fiscal 2015 budget request included $2.6 billion in budget authority for the Food and Drug Administration (FDA), along with $4.7 billion in total resources that included spending covered by fees. This equated to an 8 percent increase over the fiscal 2014 enacted level. Most of the extra funds were intended to implement the Food Safety Modernization Act (PL 111-353), which was passed in 2011 without a designated funding source. The FDA estimated that it required up to $450 million to implement provisions in the law but thus far had not received the appropriation from Congress. The White House budget also included $25 million for oversight of compounding pharmacies, pharmacies that fill prescriptions for medications that cannot be met by commercially available drugs. In 2012, a Massachusetts-based compounding pharmacy issued tainted drugs that caused a meningitis outbreak that killed dozens of people. The FDA, state boards of pharmacy, and the Drug Enforcement Administration regulate varying parts of a compounding pharmacy's activities, but FDA oversight has been called into question after a 1997 law extending its authority over these pharmacies was struck down by the Supreme Court. Since then, the FDA had been operating under guidance it issued saying it could regulate compounding pharmacies but only under certain circumstances. Congress passed a law in late 2013 that would give the FDA more power to oversee the operations of these pharmacies.

Health and Human Services

The Department of Health and Human Services would see its discretionary budget decrease to $77.1 billion in fiscal year 2015 from the fiscal 2014 enacted level of $79.8 billion. The White House proposal fully funded ongoing implementation of the Patient Protection and Affordable Care Act (ACA) and did not make any notable changes to Medicare or Medicaid but did increase by less than 1 percent the budget for the National Institutes of Health, which drew criticism from public health advocates who argued the small increase, which did little to make up for sequester cuts, was slowing medical breakthroughs.

A total of $629 million was allocated to federal marketplace exchanges that would allow Americans to register for health insurance. The funding included money for information technology, outreach, in-person assistance, and call center operations. The White House estimated the Centers for Medicare and Medicaid Services, which was responsible for implementing a significant portion of the ACA, would collect $1.2 billion in user fees from insurance issuers and from the law's reinsurance and risk adjustment programs.

Given that it was an election year and the president had little bargaining room with Republicans in control of the House, he offered no major structural changes to the Medicare and Medicaid programs, instead opting to revamp his earlier proposal calling for an increase in the premiums for Medicare Parts B and D for wealthier beneficiaries. His budget also called for new Medicare enrollees to make a copayment for home health services for the first time ever, while those new enrollees who chose a supplemental Medigap plan with low cost-sharing requirements would be assessed a surcharge. Obama said his changes would extend the solvency of the Medicare health insurance trust fund by approximately five years. Overall, changes to federal health programs would save $402 billion over the next decade. As for Medicaid, the budget proposal would extend payment increases for primary care services for one year and allow for more providers to be added to the program. The White House budget also created a Medicaid demonstration project to encourage more states to provide psychosocial interventions for children in foster care as opposed to prescribing medication and requested funds for improving mental health services for youth in psychiatric residential treatment facilities. Other changes proposed to the Medicaid program included limiting the reimbursement for durable medical equipment and changing hospital allotments for sites that serve a disproportionately large share of uninsured or underinsured patients.

Homeland Security

The president's Homeland Security request, which does not include disaster relief funding, totaled $38.2 billion, in line with fiscal 2013 funding, but a decline from the fiscal 2014 enacted level of $39.3 million. Funding, however, would increase for Customs and Border Protection (CBP), a nod to a Republican precondition for considering an immigration system overhaul that CBP receive an additional 2,000 officers. The president also conceded to Republicans' $124 million to expand the E-Verify federal online employment checking system. Funding for Immigration and Customs Enforcement fell to $5 billion, with the administration seeking alternatives to detention for illegal immigrants. Around 10 percent would be cut from the programs specifically for detaining captured illegal immigrants, and the president renewed his call for decreasing the number of beds available for detained illegal immigrants to 30,539, from the current 34,000.

Other agencies included within the Department of Homeland Security, such as the Transportation Security Administration (TSA) and Coast Guard, would experience reductions in their budgets under the White House proposal. TSA would receive $700 million less than in fiscal 2014 and the Coast Guard $200 million less. The Federal Emergency Management Agency (FEMA) discretionary budget would increase slightly to $10.2 billion. The Disaster Relief Fund, which FEMA uses to pay for large disasters, would receive an increase to $7 billion, and firefighter grants would increase to $680 million. The White House renewed its attempt to restructure state and local grant funds managed by FEMA, something unpopular in Congress. The fiscal 2015 budget request eliminated a grant account funded at $1.3 billion in fiscal 2014 and a training grant account funded at $5 billion, replacing them with a joint account valued at around $1 billion.

Housing and Urban Development

In President Obama's fiscal 2015 budget, the Department of Housing and Urban Development (HUD) would see its budget shrink to $32.6 billion in discretionary funds, lower than the $33.7 billion enacted fiscal 2014 level and far lower than the $38 billion allocated to the department in fiscal 2013. One area of reduction was a $280 million cut from the Community Development Block Grant and HOME Investment Partnership programs, which the administration said would improve program operations by eliminating small grants and encouraging more regional coordination and high-impact investments.

Despite a rollback, the president did prioritize programs that target very low-income Americans to help them receive housing by holding steady the payments those individuals receive to cover the cost of living in rental units. Another $2.4 billion was allocated to reduce chronic homelessness, and $1 billion was set aside to expand the housing supply available to extremely low-income families. If Congress chose to enact President Obama's supplemental Opportunity, Growth, and Security initiative, HUD would receive an additional $280 million for a grant program that revitalized distressed neighborhoods, $125 million for improving the employment opportunities available to those living in public housing, and $75 million for grants that provide tax breaks and other assistance for troubled neighborhoods. Other funding targeting low-income individuals and neighborhoods included $1 billion more for the Housing Choice Voucher program that allows low-income families to find housing in a neighborhood of their choice, $15 billion for the Project Rebuild Program to aid communities blighted by foreclosures, and $45 million to support households with elderly or disabled members by helping them find affordable housing to meet their needs.

One area the president's budget did not touch on was how to address the ongoing problems with mortgage giants Fannie Mae and Freddie Mac, which were still in government conservatorship after the 2007–2009 financial crisis. Lawmakers had considered a number of solutions, but none had enough support to clear the House and Senate. Both Fannie Mae and Freddie Mac were due to make payments to the government in 2014 that would exceed their bailout amount. The assessments were initially supposed to be used to fund the Housing Trust Fund, but the payments were suspended by the Federal Housing Finance Agency.

Intelligence Operations

In President Obama's fiscal 2015 budget, intelligence agencies such as the Central Intelligence Agency (CIA), National Security Agency (NSA), and the Director of National Intelligence would see their budgets reduced by about $3.4 billion, or 7 percent when compared with fiscal 2013 postsequester levels. The White House said the cuts to nonmilitary accounts would come primarily through workforce reductions and shrinking or eliminating low-priority programs to instead focus on the areas with the greatest return on investment. The National Intelligence Program and Military Intelligence Program together cover the sixteen U.S. intelligence agencies. The former was set to receive $45.6 billion in discretionary funds, up from fiscal 2013, the last year during which the administration declassified the figures. The Military Intelligence Program would receive $13.3 billion, less than the administration's fiscal 2014 request. Neither of the requests for these programs included funds for war-related activities. Proposed reductions in intelligence activities would be hampered even further once the sequester was considered.

Interior

President Obama's fiscal 2015 request for the Department of the Interior stood at $11.7 billion, matching the fiscal 2013 level and $200 million above the fiscal 2014 enacted budget. Much of the department's budget was dedicated toward the National Park Service, and Obama slated $1.2 billion over the next three years to upgrade some of the nation's parks and landmarks. Along with the regular $30 million appropriation for national parks, the money would specifically fund restoration for high-priority projects such as stabilizing the Alcatraz Island Cellhouse at Golden Gate National Recreation Area in California. Obama's proposed $200 million for the centennial initiative, a program started by his predecessor George W. Bush to restore the national parks in advance of the Park Service's 100th anniversary, would come from the supplemental $56 billion Opportunity, Growth, and Security initiative. According to the White House, the additional funds to support national parks would create thousands of jobs and volunteer and training opportunities. The president said that the supplement would help departments such as the Department of the Interior overcome sequester cuts, but Republican appropriators had already rejected including the supplement in any fiscal 2015 budget.

Other highlights of Obama's fiscal 2015 Interior funding proposal included a new long-term funding source for land and water conservation, a restructuring of wildlife suppression programs, and additional money to review and permit renewable energy projects located on federal lands. According to the White House, the president's budget would produce $2.5 billion in new revenue over the next decade through an overhaul of the management of oil and gas resources located on federal lands and waters.

Justice

The Justice Department discretionary budget rose slightly from $27.2 billion in fiscal 2014 to $27.4 billion in fiscal 2015. The White House was hoping Congress would appropriate the additional funds for two of the president's priority areas: gun control and a reduction in criminal penalties. To cover these programs, the president also proposed making cuts to programs such as the State Criminal Alien Assistance Program that pays states to temporarily hold illegal immigrants who commit crimes.

According to the Justice Department, $173 million of the president's budget request would go toward criminal justice reform efforts that aim to decrease the federal prison population by funding programs that focus on avoiding recidivism by helping inmates transfer back into society. The administration also promised to continue working with Congress to eliminate mandatory minimum sentences for low-level drug offenders and provide judges more flexibility to reduce time spent in prison in favor of rehabilitation programs.

As it relates to gun control, the Obama budget provided an increase in funds for agencies that oversee the country's gun laws. The Department of Justice said the resources would help keep guns out of the wrong hands by improving the criminal background check system and enhancing gun ownership enforcement programs. They also intended to use funds to reduce gun violence by encouraging states to share records more readily with the federal government to improve background checks, improve school security, and provide more training for active shooter situations.

Labor

Discretionary funding for the Department of Labor in the White House budget was set at $11.8 billion, equal to fiscal 2013 but slightly under the fiscal 2014 level of $12 billion. The president used his budget to renew calls for more money to help struggling workers and streamline access to federally funded job training programs. This included $2 billion to fund programs that let people keep unemployment benefits while they work short-term contracts and $4 billion in mandatory funds for grants that help businesses hire the long-term unemployed. The supplemental $56 billion initiative the president proposed would provide additional money to the Labor Department to create jobs for younger workers. Republicans criticized the budget for excessive government intervention and spending that would ultimately hurt workers.

NASA

The White House proposed a $152 million boost in discretionary funding for the National Aeronautics and Space Administration (NASA) that would go primarily toward research and development of commercial spaceflight capabilities. If Congress agreed to the $56 billion supplemental funding package proposed by the White House, NASA would also see $250 million to help private space companies. The goal of the White House, backed by NASA, was to end U.S. reliance on Russia to get astronauts and supplies to the International Space Station; the supplemental funds could potentially result in launches from the United States beginning in 2017. Without additional spending, the budget would decrease around $100 million from the fiscal 2014 enacted level, with cuts to the joint U.S.-Germany Stratospheric Observatory for Infrared Astronomy program that observes magnetic fields, comets, and star-forming regions. The budget would allow NASA to stay on track for its 2018 launch of the James Webb Space Telescope, move ahead with a project to redirect an asteroid, and begin work on a potential mission to one of Jupiter's moons.

State

In the president's fiscal 2015 budget, the State Department was allocated $42.6 billion in base discretionary funds, nearly equal to spending in fiscal 2014, and another $5.9 billion for Overseas Contingency Operations (OCO), a decrease from $6.5 billion the previous year. The funding package reflected the administration's desire to shift away from spending in war zones such as Iraq and Afghanistan and instead redirect funds to address humanitarian crises in places such as Syria, where the Islamic State of Iraq and the Levant (ISIL) was growing in strength. The White House also requested $4.6 billion to upgrade diplomatic security and protect U.S. personnel overseas, down from $5.4 billion allocated in fiscal 2014. The president revived his attempt to modify how food aid is delivered through the Food for Peace program by requesting that 25 percent of food be locally sourced rather than purchased from U.S. producers and shipped overseas. The administration had previously requested that Congress allow 45 percent of food to be purchased locally in an effort to improve program flexibility and affordability for the groups using the funds.

Transportation

The president's $14 billion proposal for discretionary spending for the Department of Transportation would go toward funding a plan to invest more in infrastructure but would require Congress to pass the four-year surface transportation authorization and overhaul corporate taxes. There was little expectation that, especially in an election year, Congress would do either. The total $91 billion in discretionary and mandatory funds for the Transportation Department increased spending on transit and rail programs by 81 percent. This included new spending on intercity rail services including improvements to the Amtrak Northeast Corridor and money for long-distance Amtrak routes. Formula grants for transit projects received a significant boost from $8.6 billion in fiscal 2015 to $13.9 billion in fiscal 2015 and would include funds for rapid-transit bus corridors and repairs to existing transit systems.

Under Obama's budget request, airports would be permitted to increase their passenger facility fee from $4.50 to $8 to finance airport improvements. It also proposed a $100-per-flight takeoff fee for most aircrafts to more equitably distribute the cost of air traffic across the entire system. The Airport Improvement Program would receive a budget of $2.9 billion, but guaranteed funding for large hubs would be eliminated. Only around $1 billion was requested to support the transition to a satellite-based air traffic control system, while funding for underserved rural airports would increase.

Treasury

The Department of the Treasury would receive $13.8 billion in discretionary funds in the White House fiscal 2015 budget, up over the fiscal 2014 enacted level; it was expected that $1.4 billion would be offset by receipts. The biggest gains were for agencies responsible for implementing the 2010 Dodd-Frank Wall Street Reform and Consumer Protection Act. This included a 30 percent boost for the Commodity Futures Trading Commission and a 26 percent increase for the Securities and Exchange Commission. The proposed funding was likely to gain little traction among Republicans, who had worked to roll back provisions of Dodd-Frank and hamper agencies from implementing the law's provisions for which the agency is responsible. The administration's budget also continued to wind down the Troubled Asset Relief Program that had bailed out the banking and auto sectors after the 2007–2009 financial crisis and included a fee assessed on banks and financial firms with more than $50 billion in assets, known as a financial-crisis responsibility fee, that was expected to raise $56 billion over 10 years.

Veterans Affairs

The Department of Veterans Affairs (VA) was set to receive a 3 percent boost from the fiscal year 2014 enacted level to $65.3 billion in discretionary funds. If the estimated $3.1 billion in collections from health insurers is added in, the total rose to $68.4 billion. Overall, both mandatory and discretionary spending under the White House proposal totaled $163.9 billion, a 6.5 percent increase from fiscal 2014. Funding included $56 billion for VA medical care programs, $7 billion for expanded mental health services, $138.7 million to streamline the claims intake system and convert data into electronic systems, and $173.3 million for a web-based claims processing platform. The White House also made a $58.7 billion fiscal 2016 advance request for VA medical care programs, which ensures continuity of services in the event of a lapse in funding.

Tax Break Package

At the end of 2013, more than fifty tax breaks expired, impacting industries from biofuel producers to the real estate sector. Congress needed to intervene to address the provisions that had sunset and was able to reach an agreement to retroactively implement the tax breaks but only for 2014. Despite general agreement that a larger overhaul of the nation's tax system was needed, Democrats and Republicans could not find consensus on how to do so in 2014. Democrats sought to raise revenues and aid deficit reduction, partly through increasing taxes on the wealthy and large corporations, while Republicans proposed a tax cut for corporations and revenue-neutral changes to the tax code.

CAMP PLAN

In February 2014, House Ways and Means Committee Chair Dave Camp, R-Mich., released a blueprint detailing his proposal for overhauling the U.S. tax code. In unveiling his plan, Camp said the purpose was to provide the American people with a simpler, fairer tax code. The Camp plan would cut tax rates for both individuals and corporations while eliminating or scaling back many tax breaks. The corporate tax rate would be cut to 25 percent, while the seven individual tax brackets would be reduced to two, at 10 percent and 25 percent. Camp's plan included an asset tax on large financial institutions, something first championed by President Obama, and eliminated the mortgage interest deduction, intended to help low- and middle-income Americans. The Joint Committee on Taxation estimated that the plan would generate $700 billion in revenue over the next decade. The plan did not receive the backing of Republican leaders and was never considered in 2014.

TAX BREAK BILLS

In April, the Senate Finance Committee approved S 2260 to renew nearly all of the fifty-five tax breaks that expired at the end of 2013. Sen. Patrick Toomey, R-Pa., offered an amendment that would eliminate tax credits for production of wind and solar energy, as well as those for biofuel, biodiesel, and renewable diesel production. Toomey's amendment also eliminated tax credits for energy-efficient appliances and electric motorcycles. According to Toomey, providing these tax credits gave an unfair advantage to certain energy companies over the others. Sen. Chuck Grassley, R-Iowa, noted that oil and gas companies were already benefiting from tax credits, and eliminating those for renewables would be unfair. The amendment was rejected 6–18, with six Republicans voting in support. S 2260 ultimately stalled on the Senate floor.

In the House, HR 4438 was approved 274–131, which extended dozens of tax credits for two years. The bill also permanently extended research and development tax credits without providing an offset for the cost, estimated at $156 billion over the next decade. The House Ways and

Means Committee in May approved twelve bills that would make permanent several temporary tax credits, including those for business and charities. The twelve bills were approved on party-line votes, with Democrats unanimous in their disapproval of the measures for both their permanency and lack of offset.

The biggest point of contention in the Ways and Means Committee was over a bonus depreciation provision, which allows businesses to deduct a certain amount of the costs of specific equipment in their first year of operation, as well as the remaining costs over a fixed depreciation schedule. The effort was supported by Republicans and the business community that felt it would encourage greater investment. Democrats believed that making the provision permanent would negate its efficacy. Ultimately, the committee approved HR 4718 by a vote of 23–11, which made permanent the 50 percent bonus depreciation at an estimated cost of $287 billion over ten years.

The House Ways and Means Committee also approved HR 2807 by a vote of 23–14, which made permanent a tax credit for farmers and ranchers that allowed them to claim a larger percentage of any donated property for conservation as taxable income. Rep. Richard Neal, D-Mass., proposed an amendment to HR 2807 that would have extended the tax credit for only two years, but it was rejected 10–26. Another amendment, proposed by Rep. Jim McDermott, D-Wash., and rejected 23–14, would have extended the deduction for state and local general sales taxes for two years. Under the amendment, the credit would be offset by limiting the deductions available to oil and gas companies.

The committee approved by a vote of 23–14 HR 4619 to permanently extend preferential tax treatment of charitable donations from Individual Retirement Accounts (IRAs). The proposal made donations for IRAs and Roth IRAs by those over age seventy tax exempt, at a cost of $8.4 billion. The committee also approved HR 4719 by a vote of 23–14, to make permanent a tax credit for corporations and small businesses that donate any food inventory. The bill increased the allowable write-off from 10 percent to 15 percent of income. The committee approved an amendment to HR 4719 proposed by Rep. Camp that would allow companies to receive credit for food donations made after the 2013 credit expiration.

HR 3134, which extended the due date for individuals claiming a tax break on charitable contributions to federal, state, and local governments, passed 23–12. The proposal permanently allowed individuals to make these charitable deductions for nearly four months after the end of a calendar year, until the April 15 tax filing deadline. The committee also approved HR 4691, by a vote of 23–10, to advance a permanent modification to the excise tax on the investment income of private foundations. The bill replaced the existing two-tier tax structure on charity investment income with a single 1 percent excise tax.

HOUSE PASSAGE

In June, the House passed HR 4457, which would permanently extend the small business expensing allowance, and HR 4453 to permanently extend preferential treatment of the built-in gains for S corporations. Democrats criticized Republicans for passing the legislation without any offset, as had been agreed to in the December 2013 budget agreement (PL 113-67). The House also passed HR 4718, the 50 percent bonus depreciation of business equipment tax credit, by a vote of 258–160. This measure made permanent a provision that allowed a company to claim an accelerated Alternative Minimum Tax credit instead of taking the bonus depreciation. Rep. Neal made a motion to recommit to cap the credit's extension at two years, as he had proposed during debate in the House Ways and Means Committee. Neal's motion also included a restriction on tax breaks for multinational corporations that move operations offshore. The procedural motion was opposed. Democrats expressed outrage over the issue, because Camp had included in his tax overhaul blueprint an elimination of the bonus depreciation. The House also passed HR 4719 and HR 2807, making permanent the tax deductions for donations of food and land, respectively.

Part of the Republican strategy in permanently extending the expired tax breaks, rather than just extending them for two years, was to lower revenue expectations to make future spending growth seem more expensive and increase deficit projections. This essentially gave them talking points when attempting to label the Democrats as out-of-control spenders. Permanent tax breaks were a nonstarter for most Democrats, especially because there was no offset.

TAX BREAK EXTENSION

With the tax break extension package stalled in the Senate, House and Senate leadership began considering the option of passing a one-year extension of the tax credits after the midterm election. The House voted on December 3, 2014, on HR 5771, a $41.6 billion bill that would retroactively extend the expired tax credits through the end of 2014, passing it by a wide margin of 378–46. HR 647, which created tax-free savings accounts for families with disabled children, was also rolled into the tax credit extender bill. The Senate cleared the package on December 16, by a vote of 76–16. Republicans remained frustrated by the lack of activity on a full overhaul of the U.S. tax code and vowed to use their new Senate majority in 2015 to seek consensus on such a measure.

Moratorium on Internet Tax

Lawmakers failed to pass legislation on Internet taxation. Instead, they agreed on appropriations language to extend the moratorium on state and local Internet access taxes until October 1, 2015.

In 2012, the House had failed to consider the Marketplace Fairness Act (S 743), passed in the Senate 69–27, which would have required Internet retailers to collect sales and use tax on all purchases, regardless of where the buyer was located and whether or not the retailer had a physical location in the same state. That bill had strong support from large online retailers such as Amazon, which, because it had distribution centers in multiple states, was wrestling with the challenge of following a patchwork of state laws to ensure taxes were properly collected. Smaller Internet retailers strongly objected, despite a provision in the bill that required compliance only for companies that had more than $1 million in sales per year. The small businesses saw the requirements as overly burdensome and considered the $1 million threshold a cap on growth. States without a sales tax in place also objected, fearing that it was a violation of states' rights by essentially forcing those states to accept the tax. Although the House tried to restart negotiations on a revised version of the Senate bill, it never came to fruition in either 2013 or 2014. The House did weigh in, however, on taxing Internet access, a popular bipartisan issue that was mired in 2014 in the debate over online sales taxes.

BACKGROUND

In 1998, Congress enacted the Internet Tax Freedom Act, which blocked state and local governments from taxing Internet access for three years. The act prevented governments from adding a sales tax to the fee paid by customers to their Internet service providers. A provision was included in the law that allowed any state already taxing Internet access prior to October 1, 1998, to continue doing so. The Internet Tax Freedom Act was extended prior to each time it was set to expire. The law was set to expire at the end of 2014. Supporters of the law frequently argued that not only did the law prevent taxes on Internet service, it also codified the Supreme Court's *Quill Corp. v. North Dakota* decision that prohibited states from collecting sales taxes for purchases made online or through a mail order catalog if the retailer did not have a physical presence in the state where the purchase was made. Thus, the renewal of the Internet Tax Freedom Act was frequently tied up in debate with questions about taxing Internet sales.

In 2014, this debate was particularly acute, and those in the House who opposed the Senate-passed Marketplace Fairness Act threatened to allow the Internet Tax Freedom Act to expire at the end of 2014. They then planned to renew it at the start of 2015. The intent was to prevent any agreement from being made prior to the end of the 113th Congress that would combine the two provisions. Republican leadership in the House declined to delay the extension of the Internet Tax Freedom Act and floated the idea of making the law permanent. Sen. Mike Enzi, R-Wyo., who sponsored S 743 in 2013, and supporters of his measure said they would oppose such a move.

LEGISLATIVE ACTION

On July 15, 2014, Enzi proposed S 2609, the Marketplace and Internet Fairness Act, which would extend the Internet Tax Freedom Act until November 1, 2024, and would also require online retailers that did not qualify for a small-seller exemption to collect sales and use taxes on any online purchase. Sen. Lamar Alexander, R-Tenn., argued on the Senate floor in support of the bill, calling it important for respecting states' rights and necessary for them to collect vital sales tax dollars. The bill never received a full Senate vote.

In the House, in 2013, Rep. Bob Goodlatte, R-Va., proposed HR 3086, the Permanent Internet Tax Freedom Act, that would amend the Internet Tax Freedom Act and make the ban on Internet access taxation permanent. It would also remove the grandfather clause that allowed seven states to maintain their taxes on some Internet services. The bill was reported out of the Judiciary Committee on July 3, 2014, and the House passed the measure by voice vote less than two weeks later. The companion bill proposed by Sen. Ron Wyden, D-Ore., the Internet Tax Freedom Forever Act (S 1431), was introduced in the Senate in August 2013 but never received a floor vote.

House Republicans pushed leadership to take up a bill that would allow states to collect sales taxes on Internet purchases. A bill never came for a vote, and ultimately Congress would use the cromnibus fiscal 2015 spending bill (HR 83—PL 113-235) signed into law on December 16, 2014, to extend the moratorium on state and local Internet access taxes until October 1, 2015.

Overseas Tax Avoidance Schemes

In an effort to lower their U.S. tax liability, domestic companies have been known to merge their operations with foreign firms and then set up a joint headquarters abroad. This drew the ire of congressional members in 2014, but they were unable to pass any legislation halting these tax inversions by the end of the congressional term. No bill made it out of the Senate Finance Committee, but the debate claimed one victim, Antonio Weiss, whom President Obama nominated as undersecretary of the Treasury for Domestic Finance. Weiss was involved in at least one inversion during his work for asset management firm Lazard. When the new Congress convened in 2015, Weiss asked President Obama not to resubmit his nomination in order to avoid a protracted debate.

Debate over inversion gained traction in May, after pharmaceutical company Pfizer sought to take over AstraZeneca, a British firm. Although the deal fell apart, tax experts said it was an example of the steps domestic companies are willing to take to lower their tax liability. President Obama tried a number of times to propose, through his annual budget request to Congress, methods to rein in the use of inversions and tax-driven mergers, as the Pfizer deal was. The president suggested amending a 2004 provision of the jobs bill (PL 108-357) that requires domestic owners controlling more than 60 percent of a new foreign-based company to be hit with tax penalties on the gains in the inversion transaction. If U.S. shareholders owned more than 80 percent, the company was still considered a U.S. entity for tax purposes. The president argued that the 60 percent threshold for ownership fees had not stopped companies from moving overseas, so he instead proposed lowering the 80 percent shareholder limit to 50 percent. The president wanted these companies to qualify as inversions if they had substantial business activities in the United States or if the company was primarily managed in the United States. Republicans disregarded any of the president's attempts to strengthen the rules that limit inversions, saying that they unfairly targeted companies instead of addressing the true concern, the corporate tax rate in the United States, which at 35 percent was the highest in the world.

In the Senate, Democrats on the Finance Committee began drafting legislation to stop companies from acquiring overseas firms as a means to avoid U.S. taxes. Republicans dismissed the idea, saying Democrats should focus less on making inversions more difficult and more on helping companies view the United States as an ideal headquarters location by lowering the corporate tax rate. Republicans preferred changing the global tax system, which taxes foreign profits and domestic profits at the same 35 percent rate, to a territorial tax system that did not tax profits earned outside the United States. No bill moved out of committee in 2014.

Although members on both sides of the aisle expressed concern about tax inversions, corporate taxes make up only 10 percent of federal revenues, and the multinational attempts to avoid corporate taxes were a fraction of that. According to the Joint Committee on Taxation, a bill proposed in the House (HR 4679) to stop inversions would save $19.5 billion over the next decade, or just 0.05 percent of the $40.6 trillion in federal revenue expected over that time period.

Budget Resolution

At the end of 2013, Congress passed a two-year budget agreement that set spending levels for fiscal 2015 and amounted to a handshake agreement between the two chambers of Congress and the White House not to shut down the government when funding ran out in January 2014. Although not entirely necessary given that appropriators already had their parameters within which to work—a discretionary budget cap of $1.014 trillion—the House still passed a budget resolution in May 2014, at the urging of Budget Committee Chair Paul Ryan, R-Wis., who was seeking to outline a more conservative roadmap for the coming fiscal year. The Senate did not consider the House agreement.

TEN-YEAR BUDGET AGREEMENT

Ryan's ten-year budget agreement was released on April 1 and sought to balance the budget and reduce the federal deficit by cutting $5.1 trillion in spending over the next decade. To do so, Ryan relied on cuts to a number of federal programs, most notably entitlement programs such as Social Security and the Supplemental Nutrition Assistance Program (SNAP). Perhaps most significantly, the plan called for repealing the 2010 Patient Protection and Affordable Care Act (ACA). Ryan maintained the $1.014 trillion discretionary spending cap set by the December 2013 budget agreement, but after the next fiscal year, his plan called for shifting more than $50 billion per year from domestic to defense priorities while reforming a variety of domestic programs. According to the Congressional Budget Office (CBO), the Ryan plan would eliminate the deficit by fiscal 2024 if expected economic growth from the policy changes were taken into consideration. By 2024, according to the CBO, the United States would have a $5 billion surplus. Ryan's plan left almost no room for compromise with the Democrats, so it ultimately acted as little more than a platform for the coming midterm elections and an outline for how Republicans intended to govern if they took back the Senate in the fall.

Ryan's budget plan did not call for raising taxes to balance the budget and reduce the federal deficit, something Democrats had pushed for, but would instead overhaul the existing U.S. tax code and lower tax rates for both individuals and corporations. Here, the Ryan budget offered few specifics beyond eliminating the Alternative Minimum Tax and consolidating the number of existing tax brackets. Ryan also intended to overhaul entitlement programs by changing many of them into block grants for the states. According to Ryan, those changes would save $875 billion over ten years. Medicare would largely be left untouched for those already fifty-five and older, but it would gradually evolve into a premium-support system for future retirees that would give beneficiaries a federal subsidy, which they could then use to choose among both private-sector health plans and the existing Medicare program.

House Action

The House passed Ryan's plan 219–205 on April 10, 2015, with twelve Republicans joining all Democrats to vote against it.

The House rejected several alternatives that were offered, including one by Budget Committee Ranking Member Chris Van Hollen, D-Md. The Democratic alternative was similar to Ryan's in that it maintained the $1.014 trillion discretionary spending cap for fiscal 2015 and the distinct separation between defense and nondefense spending. Where it differed, however, was that it sought to reduce the deficit by raising taxes on corporations and the very wealthy, and it made fewer cuts to domestic programs. The plan would eliminate portions of sequestration, specifically from nondefense discretionary spending in 2016, and also added funding for President Obama's priority areas such as early childhood education and transportation. Under the Democratic alternative, by the end of the decade, the United States' deficit would fall to 2.3 percent of gross domestic product. The Democrats' plan also maintained the ACA. It was rejected by the full House, 163–261.

The Republican Study Committee, a group of conservative lawmakers first formed to review legislation and act as a check on party leadership, proposed an alternative to Ryan's budget plan that would reduce discretionary spending to fiscal 2008 levels in an attempt to balance the budget by fiscal 2018. Under the Study Committee's plan, discretionary spending would be capped at $950 billion in fiscal 2015 and then frozen at that level until the budget was balanced, after which point it would be allowed to grow with inflation. Included in the plan was a repeal of the ACA, a conversion of Medicaid and the Children's Health Insurance Program (CHIP) into a single block grant, and a gradual increase in the eligibility age for both Medicare and Social Security. The plan also sought to reduce the size of the federal workforce through attrition and convert the Supplemental Nutrition Assistance Program (SNAP), commonly referred to as food stamps, into a block grant. The proposal was rejected 133–291 by the full House.

OMNIBUS PACKAGE

Buoyed by the budget agreement negotiated between the House and Senate in December 2013 that set funding caps for fiscal 2014 and 2015, there was hope early in 2014 that Congress could return to regular order and pass individual appropriations bills by the September deadline. However, ongoing partisan bickering, a midterm election, and a lengthy battle over fiscal 2014 funding forced Congress in 2014 to pass its fifth-straight omnibus package to fund the federal government.

APPROPRIATIONS TIMETABLE

In March 2014, appropriators outlined a timetable for passing all twelve regular appropriations bills, with markups beginning in May and floor action taking place over the summer ahead of the August recess. This timeline was based on close adherence to the budget deal worked out in December 2013 that set limits on defense and domestic spending, at $521.4 billion and $492.5 billion, respectively.

In the Senate, activity slowed when Republican appropriators rejected 302(b) allocations, which cap spending for each appropriation bill, set by Appropriations Committee Chair Barbara Mikulski, D-Md., arguing that they did not adhere to the spirit of the budget deal. Senate leadership also suspended debate on a minibus (HR 4660) that would fund portions of the government because Republicans and Democrats could not decide on how best to handle the amendment process. In the House, the prospect of passage became less likely when House Appropriations Chair Harold Rogers, R-Ky., decided to pass the individual bills

through regular order, which allowed any member to introduce amendments and which would invite dozens of proposed changes and bog down debate.

The Obama administration then complicated the situation in July when it requested a $3.7 billion supplemental appropriation to address a growing number of unaccompanied minors appearing at the U.S.–Mexico border, along with authority to increase the speed of screening and deporting those children without any legal option to remain in the United States. As the year drew closer to recess and the election, Congress ran out of opportunities to pass any appropriation or the White House supplement.

CONTINUING RESOLUTION AND OMNIBUS

Following the August recess, negotiators worked on assembling a continuing resolution (HJ Res 124) that would fund the government from October 1 into December, allowing the body to push off a fight on a larger budget deal until after the midterm election. The bill was slightly delayed ahead of filing due to a last-minute request from the White House to include funding that would train and equip Syrian rebels to defend against the Islamic State of Iraq and the Levant (ISIL). The House passed an amendment to the continuing resolution providing for that short-term funding requested by the president, by a vote of 273–176; they then went on to pass the full continuing resolution 319–108. The following day, the Senate passed the House measure with the Syria amendment intact, 78–22, and the president signed the continuing resolution into law.

After the midterm election, House and Senate negotiators began work on a cromnibus spending bill, so-called because it combined omnibus appropriations for most agencies with a short-term continuing resolution for the Department of Homeland Security (DHS) through February 27, 2015. Short-term funding for DHS was a political move by Republicans to force a showdown with the president on immigration once the 114th Congress convened with Republicans in control of both the House and Senate. *(See discussion of Obama executive orders in Chapter 13, pp. 394, 396.)*

In the House, Republican leadership delayed the vote for a few hours to ensure they had enough members for passage. Pelosi wrote to her caucus that the delay provided them leverage to argue for changes to the bill, including the removal of provisions making changes to Dodd-Frank and campaign finance laws. The White House, however, issued a statement in support of the cromnibus, although it did note its objection to some policy riders, such as those on Dodd-Frank, which would repeal the portion of the law requiring a bank to separate its derivative swaps operations from the federally insured portion of the bank, and a provision changing campaign finance language to increase limits on how much an individual can contribute to a national party each year to fund certain activities. Support from the president provided Democrats cover to vote for the bill, even as they came under pressure from Pelosi to oppose the various policy riders. Ultimately, the House barely passed the cromnibus (HR 83), 219–206, after hours of tense debate and vote whipping. The House also passed, by unanimous consent, a two-day continuing resolution (HJ Res 130) to provide the Senate additional time for debate and consideration of the bill.

In the Senate, passage was preceded by a second continuing resolution (HJ Res 131), a five-day extension of existing federal funding already passed in the House, to ensure the body had the votes to avoid a government shutdown. Debate on the omnibus primarily centered on the provision agreed to in the House that would eliminate language in the Dodd-Frank Wall Street Reform and Consumer Protection Act requiring banks to separate their derivative swaps operations from the portion of the bank that is federally insured. Unlike in the House, Democratic leadership encouraged members to support the omnibus with that rider intact, calling the bill a hard-fought compromise that was better than another short-term continuing resolution or a shutdown.

FINAL OMNIBUS PROVISIONS

The final measure signed by the president adhered to the $1.013 trillion spending cap set under the December 2013 budget agreement, including $521.3 billion for defense and $492.4 billion for nondefense spending. Also included in the bill was $64 billion in uncapped war funds for Overseas Contingency Operations (OCO). Other provisions in the bill included:

- funding to combat the Ebola crisis domestically and abroad
- increased spending for Pell grants, the Commodity Futures Trading Commission, and the Securities and Exchange Commission
- smaller budgets for the Environmental Protection Agency and Internal Revenue Service
- a cost-of-living increase for federal workers
- a ban on federal funds being utilized for abortions
- a ban on federal and D.C. funding being used to implement a referendum on the decriminalization of marijuana within the District of Columbia
- a lifting of the ban on the Export-Import Bank and Overseas Private Investment Corporation financing overseas coal plants
- $948 million for the office within the Department of Health and Human Services that houses and cares for unaccompanied migrant children
- $5.6 billion for disaster funding
- a limit on health insurance coverage requirements for U.S. expatriates.

2015–2016

The 114th Congress faced many of the same budget issues that had plagued the previous session, but those challenges were heightened by the upcoming 2016 presidential election. Congress was successful in again extending expiring tax breaks. The two parties did not reach their larger goal of a tax code overhaul, but a plan for one was outlined by Republicans. Despite concerns in both parties, the body also managed to enact financial assistance to address the fiscal crisis in Puerto Rico that would allow the island to restructure its debt.

Table 2.4 Taxes and Other Revenues as Percentage of Gross Domestic Product, 1935–2017

Fiscal Year	Individual Income	Corporate Income	Social Insurance	Excise	Other	Total
1935	0.7%	0.8%	—	2.0%	1.5%	5.1%
1940	0.9	1.2	1.8%	2.0	0.7	6.7
1945	8.1	7.1	1.5	2.8	0.5	19.9
1950	5.6	3.7	1.6	2.7	0.5	14.1
1955	7.1	4.4	1.9	2.2	0.5	16.1
1960	7.6	4.0	2.7	2.2	0.7	17.3
1965	6.9	3.6	3.1	2.1	0.8	16.4
1970	8.6	3.1	4.2	1.5	0.9	18.4
1975	7.6	2.5	5.2	1.0	0.9	17.3
1980	8.7	2.3	5.6	0.9	0.9	18.5
1985	7.8	1.4	6.2	0.8	0.9	17.2
1990	7.9	1.6	6.4	0.6	0.9	17.4
1991	7.7	1.6	6.5	0.7	0.8	17.3
1992	7.4	1.6	6.4	0.7	0.9	17.0
1993	7.5	1.7	6.3	0.7	0.7	17.0
1994	7.5	2.0	6.4	0.8	0.8	17.5
1995	7.8	2.1	6.4	0.8	0.8	17.8
1996	8.2	2.2	6.4	0.7	0.8	18.2
1997	8.7	2.1	6.4	0.7	0.7	18.6
1998	9.3	2.1	6.4	0.6	0.8	19.2
1999	9.2	1.9	6.4	0.7	0.9	19.2
2000	9.9	2.0	6.4	0.7	0.9	20.0
2001	9.4	1.4	6.6	0.6	0.8	18.8
2002	7.9	1.4	6.4	0.6	0.7	17.0
2003	7.0	1.2	6.3	0.6	0.7	15.7
2004	6.7	1.6	6.1	0.6	0.6	15.6
2005	7.2	2.2	6.2	0.6	0.6	16.7
2006	7.6	2.6	6.1	0.5	0.7	17.6
2007	8.1	2.6	6.1	0.5	0.7	17.9
2008	7.8	2.1	6.1	0.5	0.7	17.1
2009	6.3	1.0	6.2	0.4	0.7	14.6
2010	6.1	1.3	5.8	0.5	1.0	14.6
2011	7.1	1.2	5.3	0.5	0.9	15.0
2012	7.1	1.5	5.3	0.5	0.9	15.3
2013	8.0	1.7	5.7	0.5	0.9	16.8
2014	8.1	1.9	5.9	0.5	1.1	17.5
2015	8.6	1.9	5.9	0.5	1.1	18.2
2016	8.4	1.6	6.1	0.5	1.2	17.8
2017*	8.7	1.7	6.1	0.5	1.1	18.1

SOURCE: Executive Office of the President, Office of Management and Budget, *Budget of the United States Government, Fiscal Year 2018, Historical Tables* (Washington, DC: U.S. Government Printing Office, 2018), Table 2.3.

NOTE: The "Social Insurance" category includes Social Security, Medicare, railroad, and other retirement programs, and unemployment insurance. The "Other" category principally includes estate and gift taxes and customs duties.

* Estimate.

Similarly to 2013 and 2014, 2015 ended in the passage of omnibus legislation to keep the federal government funded. The following year, highly charged debate in the lead-up to the election meant that Congress failed to pass any individual appropriations bills or even another omnibus. Instead, the body passed two continuing resolutions at the close of 2016, ultimately passing the fiscal 2017 funding battle to the next Congress.

Fiscal 2016 Budget Request

Released on February 2, 2015, President Obama's fiscal 2016 budget request proposed a total of $4.066 trillion in spending. Notably, the proposal sought to lift—rather than adhere to—discretionary spending caps imposed by the Budget Control Act of 2011 (PL 112-25) in order to provide a roughly 7 percent increase, or an additional $75 billion, for defense and domestic spending. Specifically, the administration requested $38 billion more in defense spending and $37 billion more in nondefense spending than the levels set by the law for fiscal 2015. Together, defense and nondefense discretionary funds totaled $1.091 trillion under the president's budget. To help pay for the increased discretionary budgets, the president proposed approximately $2 trillion worth of tax increases over ten years, most of which would impact wealthy Americans and corporations. An estimated $277 billion of this revenue would be used to provide tax breaks to the middle class, while the remainder would be used to offset higher discretionary spending, provide targeted tax breaks, and reduce the deficit. When he announced the proposal, President Obama effectively issued a veto threat by declaring that he would not accept a budget from Congress that locked in sequestration cuts long term, nor would he accept increases in defense spending without similar increases in nondefense domestic spending.

The president's proposal also included about $1.8 trillion in deficit reduction, to be achieved through $400 billion in health care savings, a projected $160 billion in savings that could be generated by overhauling the immigration system, and higher taxes on the wealthy, among other measures. These were less ambitious deficit-cutting measures than those proposed by the administration in earlier budgets, and officials acknowledged they likely would not make a dent in the growing interest costs of the United States' $18 trillion federal debt. Administration officials estimated that interest costs would more than triple from $229 billion in 2015 to $785 billion in 2025. According to the White House Office of Management and Budget (OMB), the proposal would keep the deficit below 2.5 percent of the gross domestic product during the ten-year period it covered. OMB estimated the proposal would result in total spending of about $50.3 trillion over those ten years, compared to $44.7 trillion in revenue, meaning that about $5.6 trillion in deficits would accumulate.

Administration officials expressed hope that the president's proposal would provide a starting point for negotiations with Republicans that could result in a budget deal such as the Bipartisan Budget Act of 2013 (PL 113-67). However, Republicans generally dismissed the proposal and criticized the president for proposing more spending and higher taxes. They also objected to several of the items highlighted by the administration, such as the imposition of a 14 percent tax on about $2 trillion in offshore corporate profits to cover an anticipated funding shortage for the Transportation Department. Republicans further argued that the proposal would cause the nation's gross debt—which includes the cost of programs, such as student loans, that are not counted against the deficit—to rise to $26.3 trillion in 2025. Leadership and rank-and-file members pledged to take a different approach than the president and come up with a budget that would eliminate the deficit in ten years. Republicans also said they would push the president to agree to spending cuts and no tax increases to keep discretionary spending levels from triggering sequestration's across-the-board cuts.

SPENDING BY DEPARTMENT AND MAJOR AGENCY

Agriculture

President Obama's budget request for the Department of Agriculture (USDA) included a proposal to consolidate the department's and the Food and Drug Administration's (FDA) food safety functions into a new food safety entity within the Department of Health and Human Services (HHS). The proposal reflected the president's broader push to reorganize federal agencies. Consolidating the food safety functions would be possible, the administration claimed, because the two agencies had adopted more proactive approaches to preventing food-borne illness that could be more easily aligned than their past, reactive

Table 2.5 Annual Caps on Spending

Fiscal Year	Caps in Trillions of Dollars	Year-to-Year Change
2011	$1.050	
2012	1.043	−0.7%
2013	1.047	0.4
2014	1.066	1.8
2015	1.086	1.9
2016	1.107	1.9
2017	1.131	2.2
2018	1.156	2.2
2019	1.182	2.2
2020	1.208	2.2
2021	1.234	2.2

NOTE: The table shows the annual caps for each fiscal year and the percentage change from the previous year. The caps essentially amounted to an actual freeze for fiscal 2012 and fiscal 2013 and a "real" or inflation-adjusted freeze for the remaining eight years.

Discretionary Spending Caps

Fiscal Year	BCA (Billions)	Actual (Billions)
2012	$1.043	1.043
2013	1.047	1.043 (American Taxpayer Relief Act of 2012)
2014	0.973	1.012 (Bipartisan Budget Act of 2013)
2015	0.994	1.014 (Bipartisan Budget Act of 2013)
2016	1.016	1.067 (Bipartisan Budget Act of 2015)
2017	1.040	1.070 (Bipartisan Budget Act of 2015)
2018	1.066	1.208 (Bipartisan Budget Act of 2018)
2019	1.093	1.244 (Bipartisan Budget Act of 2018)
2020	1.120	1.118 (Bipartisan Budget Act of 2018)
2021	1.146	1.145 (Bipartisan Budget Act of 2018)

SOURCES: Congressional Budget Office, *Final Sequestration Report for Fiscal Year 2012* (January 2012), Table 2; *Final Sequestration Report for Fiscal Year 2018* (April 2018), Table 2.

stances. The administration also wanted to consolidate USDA's rural business programs with similar offices and programs within the Department of Commerce, Small Business Administration, U.S. Trade Representative, and Export-Import Bank.

The president requested a total of $24.4 billion in discretionary spending on agriculture in fiscal 2016, which was about $500 million less than the Department of Agriculture received for fiscal 2015. A controversial proposal included in the request was a ten-year, $16 billion cut to subsidies for crop insurance. Farm state lawmakers, including Senate Agriculture Committee Chair Pat Roberts, R-Kan., have repeatedly opposed such cuts, claiming the subsidies provide critical assistance to America's farmers. The president also sought authority to use 25 percent, or about $350 million, of funding allocated to the international Food for Peace program for local or regional food purchases closer to areas of need, as well as for food vouchers and cash transfers.

Army Corps of Engineers

The Army Corps of Engineers stood to receive about $1.2 billion less than its fiscal 2015 budget under President Obama's proposal. Approximately $200 million would be cut from the Corps' operations and maintenance budget, which would shrink to $2.7 billion, while the Harbor Maintenance Trust Fund's budget would be cut by 17 percent.

The president's proposal provided $86 million for the Comprehensive Everglades Restoration Plan; $39 million for the Emergency Management program to respond to natural disasters; $31 million to help communities develop plans to mitigate flood risks; and $411 million for restoration of significant aquatic ecosystems, such as the Chesapeake Bay and California Bay-Delta. He also proposed a new annual per-vessel fee for the use of inland waterways, which the administration estimated would generate $113 million in revenue for the Corps.

Commerce

For the Commerce Department, the president sought $9.8 billion for fiscal 2016. Republicans generally balked at the $1 billion increase over the fiscal 2015 enacted level, although they supported some of the activities included in the president's proposal.

President Obama's request included $306 million for research and development of industrial technology. Nearly half that funding would be used to increase the National Network for Manufacturing Innovation's budget to support its existing nine manufacturing institutes and the creation of seven new institutes, with additional financial support to come from the Departments of Commerce, Agriculture, Defense, and Energy. In addition, the administration sought $1.9 billion in mandatory funding for another twenty-nine manufacturing institutes.

Other requests included $141 million to support a network of sixty manufacturing extension partnership centers and $15 million to encourage advanced manufacturing technology partnerships. The president proposed increasing the International Trade Administration's budget by about 8 percent, for a total of $497 million, to strengthen trade enforcement and help American exporters challenge unfair overseas competition. The National Oceanic and Atmospheric Administration (NOAA) would receive a 7 percent increase under the president's proposal, bringing its total budget to $3.4 billion for fiscal 2016. The administration also sought to move NOAA to the Interior Department.

Defense

The significant base defense budget increase sought by the administration for fiscal 2016 was driven in part by a proposed 13 percent increase in spending on procurement and research and development. Of the $534.3 billion requested for fiscal 2016, $107.7 billion would go to procurement, while $69.8 billion would be designated for research and development activities. Deputy Defense Secretary Robert Work said the increases were necessary to support modernization of the United States' defenses and its capabilities to combat a wide variety of current and emerging threats.

Within the procurement budget, the Defense Department requested the purchase of fifty-seven F-35 Joint Strike Fighters; sixteen P-8 Poseidons; five E-2D Advanced Hawkeye aircraft; and twelve KC-46 aerial refueling tankers. The administration sought $5.4 billion for two Virginia-class attack submarines; $3.2 billion for two Arleigh Burke-class destroyers; and $1.6 billion for three Littoral Combat Ships. Another $4.5 billion was requested for the Army's modernization of its helicopters, and $1.2 billion was requested for continued development of a next-generation bomber. Research and development work on a replacement for Ohio-class ballistic submarines would be funded to the tune of $1.4 billion.

Some cost savings were proposed, including the retirement of the A-10 Warthog, which was expected to save $428 million in fiscal 2016, as well as a new Base Realignment and Closure round. Congress has repeatedly rejected such proposals. The administration also proposed slowing the growth of the basic allowance for military housing, consolidating Tricare health care plans, imposing annual fees for Tricare for Life coverage, and adjusting pharmacy co-pays. Officials estimated these adjustments could generate $18.2 billion in savings over the next five years. Military pay—which the administration proposed increasing by 1.3 percent in fiscal 2016—and benefits were expected to be a major focus of congressional spending deliberations in 2015 following the Military Compensation and Retirement Modernization Commission's January report to Congress on its recommendations for updating military benefits.

President Obama requested $50.9 billion for Overseas Contingency Operations (OCO) in fiscal 2016, compared to the $64.2 billion fiscal 2015 enacted level. The request included $5.4 billion for airstrikes, intelligence gathering, and equipping Iraqi security forces and Syrian moderates to combat the Islamic State. The Counterterrorism Partnership Fund, which helps U.S. allies fight terrorism, would receive $2.1 billion. Another $3.8 billion was requested to train and equip Afghan security forces; $789 million was sought for the European Reassurance Initiative; and $1.7 billion in spending was proposed for the Coalition Support Fund.

Education

Increased spending on child care comprised a significant portion of the president's requested $70.7 billion fiscal 2016 budget for the Department of Education, which would mark a $3.6 billion increase over the fiscal 2015 enacted level. A $266 million increase was sought for child care and development block grants, bringing the total funding for this program to $2.7 billion, while $100 million was requested to help states and local governments develop and implement new child care models that focused on providing high-quality care during parents' working hours. The administration also proposed tripling the child care and dependent tax credit for families with children under the age of five and making the full child care tax credit available to families making up to $120,000 per year. Administration estimates said these tax code changes would benefit 6.7 million children in 5.1 million families. In addition to the discretionary funding requests, the proposal included $82 billion in mandatory funding over ten years to help lower- and middle-class families pay for child care.

Other requests included $2 billion for preschool programs and $1 billion for teacher recruitment. An increase of $1 billion was sought for Title I grants to low-income schools, bringing the total Title I budget to $15.4 billion. The administration said the Title I program had helped increase low-income students' high school graduation rate and boosted the number of minority students attending college. President Obama also requested $1.4 billion to pay for the first year of his initiative to provide free community college to students of families that earn $200,000 or less per year. Administration officials estimated that federal investment in the community college initiative would eventually cover three-quarters of the program's cost, based on anticipated enrollment and calculations of projected graduate earnings.

Energy

For the Department of Energy, the president sought $29.9 billion for fiscal 2016, or a 9.4 percent increase over fiscal 2015 enacted levels. Major line items included $2.72 billion for energy efficiency and renewable energy programs—a 41 percent boost over 2015. Funding for natural gas technologies would increase by 76 percent to $44 million and be used for programs including development of technology for monitoring and reducing emissions from midstream natural gas infrastructure, such as pipelines and bulk transportation. Spending for electricity delivery and energy reliability would increase by 84 percent to $270 million and would include a doubling of funding for smart grid research ($30 million). The administration also sought $117 million for research on capturing carbon dioxide, $11 million for a tribal energy loan guarantee program, and $325 million for the Advanced Research Projects Agency–Energy.

President Obama requested $1.03 billion for the Nuclear Regulatory Commission for fiscal 2016, which was about $20 million less than the independent agency had received in fiscal 2015. The total would include $793 million for nuclear reactor safety and $226 million for nuclear materials and waste efforts. Administration officials also noted that the commission needed about 141 fewer full-time employees due to a reduced workload.

Environmental Protection Agency

For the Environmental Protection Agency (EPA), President Obama sought $8.6 billion in fiscal 2016 funding. The agency received $8.1 billion in fiscal 2015.

The president's request included funding for a new Clean Power State Incentive Fund to distribute about $4 billion over several years to states that develop their Clean Power Plan implementation strategies faster and aim for deeper, more rapid greenhouse gas reductions from power plants. The administration said the funding could be distributed through programs such as grants for infrastructure investments in energy-efficient technologies. Officials said the fund would be similar to the $3 billion block grant program administered by the Department of Energy that helped states and local governments collaborate on development and administration of energy efficiency projects.

Other line items included $239 million for EPA efforts to write climate-focused rules and guidelines, of which $25 million would go to help states write Clean Power Plan implementation plans. Another $769 million was sought for scientific research, including EPA efforts to identify air quality benefits linked with climate mitigation and adaptation policies.

Food and Drug Administration

The president sought $2.7 billion for the FDA in fiscal 2016, which represented a $120 million increase over fiscal 2015. Another $2.2 billion in expected user fees would bring the total FDA budget to $4.9 billion.

The total request included $109.5 million for implementation of the Food Safety Modernization Act (PL 111-353). Under that law, the FDA was working to shift from a reactive stance in which it focused on responding to food-borne illness to a preventive approach. The law also gave the FDA new authority to enforce prevention- and risk-based food safety standards and better respond to problems when they occur. The FDA was further tasked with building a new integrated national food safety system. The budget proposal relied on an additional $160 million in user fees to fund the law's implementation.

President Obama sought $33.2 million in new spending to support medical product initiatives, to include $15 million for combating antibiotic resistance and $9.7 million for his Precision Medicine Initiative.

Health and Human Services

The president requested $80.3 billion for HHS for fiscal 2016. The agency had received $83.4 billion in fiscal 2015, though that total included a portion of the additional $5.4 billion lawmakers appropriated to fight the Ebola virus.

Several of the proposals included in the president's budget reflected a renewed focus on emergency preparedness and health threats following the Ebola outbreak. For example, $646 million was requested for Project BioShield Act programs. Project BioShield is designed to safeguard against naturally occurring biological threats and attacks. Another $110 million was requested to support international and domestic responses to public health emergencies, while $522 million was sought to help develop medical countermeasures against biological, nuclear, chemical, and radiological agents.

President Obama also requested $2.3 billion for the Ryan White HIV/AIDS Program, which supports organizations providing HIV-related services to people with insufficient health coverage. The AIDS Drug Assistance Program that provides access to antiretroviral medicine would receive $900 million. Programs combatting prescription drug abuse would get an increase of $99 million in funding.

For the National Institutes of Health (NIH), the administration sought a $1 billion increase, bringing the agency's total budget to $30.3 billion for the year. NIH's National Cancer Institute also stood to receive $70 million of $215 million requested to advance the president's Precision Medicine Initiative, which seeks to leverage genomics to fight diseases such as cancer and diabetes.

A budget of $7.07 billion was requested for the Centers for Disease Control and Prevention, down from $8.71 billion in 2015. The administration also sought $948 million to provide shelter for unaccompanied migrant children detained at the border until they are placed with sponsors, as well as a contingency fund of an additional $100 million.

Homeland Security

Despite ongoing disagreements between the president and Congress over immigration policy, his proposed fiscal 2016 budget for the Department of Homeland Security was generally on par with what congressional appropriators were considering. The total request of $41.2 billion in discretionary spending included $5.9 billion for Immigration and Customs Enforcement and $10.7 billion for Customs and Border Protection (CBP). Administration officials said the 7 percent increase in CBP's budget would help pay for an increased operational force of 21,000 Border Patrol agents and about 24,000 other officers. Another $4 billion was requested for the department's Citizenship and Immigration Services, which was charged with implementing the administration's new deferred action program for adults who have been in the United States for five years and are parents of U.S. citizens or lawful residents. The E-Verify program, used by employers to confirm workers are in the United States legally, would receive $120 million.

President Obama requested $5.9 billion for the Transportation Security Administration. He also proposed reinstating security fees on airlines and raising passenger fees from $5.60 on a one-way trip to $6. The administration projected this increase would generate annual revenue of $195 million. For the Secret Service, the president sought $1.9 billion, of which $86.7 million would be designated for implementing the Protective Mission Panel's recommendations for correcting internal issues at the agency and tightening security around the White House compound, following various scandals and security lapses at the agency.

About $1 billion was requested for the Federal Emergency Management Agency (FEMA), and the president repeated his proposal to consolidate various FEMA-administered grants into one National Preparedness Grant Program. Congress has opposed this proposal because lawmakers prefer grant money be given directly to local agencies, and some have expressed concerns that certain grants may be overlooked if they are combined into one broader program. Another $7.4 billion was sought for the Disaster Relief Fund, while $2.2 billion was requested to provide grants to state and local governments for disaster preparation and response.

Housing and Urban Development

For the Department of Housing and Urban Development (HUD), the president requested $41 billion, which was $6 billion more than the department had received in fiscal 2015. The proposal included $2.1 billion for the Housing Choice Voucher program that helps very low-income families afford housing in neighborhoods of their choosing. The administration estimated this funding would restore approximately 67,000 vouchers that had been eliminated in 2013 due to sequestration and would help about 2.4 million families find housing.

Republicans objected to President Obama's proposal to reduce Federal Housing Administration (FHA) mortgage insurance premiums. The administration claimed the reduction would result in 250,000 new homebuyers over three years. However, Republicans argued that it would encourage more of the risky lending that led to the 2008 financial crisis. The president also sought authority to charge lenders a new FHA fee to offset administrative and staffing costs and help increase the number of loans reviewed for quality assurance. The administration estimated the new fee would generate annual revenue of about $30 million. Congress had rejected a similar request in 2014.

The proposed HUD budget included $100 million for the Jobs-Plus program to offer job training and financial incentives for public housing residents, with up to $15 million of that funding potentially going to Native American populations. According to the administration, the proposed Jobs-Plus money would offer aid to 20,000 individuals, about four times as many as in 2015. Additionally, the budget sought to create an Upward Mobility Project initiative that would allow communities to pool money they had received through four HUD and HHS block grant programs to promote economic development, reduce poverty, and help families become more self-sufficient.

Interior

The Interior Department would receive $12.9 billion for fiscal 2016 under the president's budget, or an increase of about $800 million over fiscal 2015. The funding request included a new, $50 million program that would focus on building coastal community resilience to climate change. The administration said the program would be modeled on the competitive grant program created to aid recovery from Superstorm Sandy in 2012.

The administration also sought to change the federal government's revenue-sharing agreement with Gulf States, through which Alabama, Louisiana, Mississippi, and Texas receive a percentage of the fees paid by fuel companies drilling in the Gulf of Mexico. The administration said it wanted to redirect those payments to national programs providing resource, watershed, and conservation benefits. Doing so would provide more than $3 billion in revenue from 2016 to 2025, officials estimated. Gulf State lawmakers were outraged by the proposal, with some claiming it amounted to a raid of their states' finances.

Other requests included $805 million for the department's wildfire fighting efforts. Of this, about $200 million would be provided by a proposed discretionary cap adjustment; those funds would be used to cover the costs of fighting the most severe wildfires. President Obama also wanted to permanently authorize the Land and Water Conservation Fund at $900 million annually, with mandatory spending supporting the program partially in fiscal 2016 and entirely by fiscal 2017. The fund's authorization was set to expire in September 2015.

Justice

The administration sought $28.7 billion for the Department of Justice in fiscal 2016, or approximately $1.3 billion more than its 2015 spending level. This total included $97 million for a new initiative to build and sustain trust between law enforcement and the communities they serve in response to recent high-profile police shootings in Ferguson, Missouri, and Staten Island, New York. The funding would be used to expand training and oversight for law enforcement, increase the use of body cameras, and launch ten pilot sites where community and law enforcement would interact.

An additional $7 million was requested for U.S. attorneys to use to establish civil rights enforcement attorneys in districts across the country. The Justice Department's Civil Rights Division would receive an extra $16 million over fiscal 2015 funding levels to enforce the Voting Rights Act, fight human trafficking, and for other enforcement activities.

Other proposed increases included an additional $20 million for the Federal Bureau of Investigation to enhance its cybersecurity programs and an extra $110 million for the Bureau of Prisons' re-entry programs, which seek to reduce recidivism by helping inmates transition back into society. One notable cut the president proposed was a reduction of $185 million for a program that reimburses states for costs of imprisoning illegal immigrants who commit crimes.

Labor

President Obama requested an 11 percent increase in the Department of Labor's budget for fiscal 2016, for a total of $13.2 billion. This included $3.5 billion for training and employment services provided through the Employment and Training Administration—an 8 percent increase from 2015. The president also called for full implementation of the Workforce Innovation and Opportunity Act (PL 113-128), aimed at streamlining job training and placement programs. Another $200 million was requested to support technical training programs. Job Corps would receive a 2 percent budget increase under the president's proposal. The boost would help pay for piloting a training program for younger Americans and expansion of the organization into New Hampshire and Wyoming. President Obama also requested $16 billion in mandatory spending over ten years for training and credentialing grants to help jobless workers find positions in high-growth sectors such as health care and information technology.

To support the administration's goal of enhancing enforcement of the minimum wage, overtime, and other labor standards, the president requested a 21 percent increase in the Wage and Hour Division's budget, for a total of $277 million. Additionally, the president proposed a strengthening of labor-related penalties, including a $5,000 penalty per violation for employers who intentionally keep fraudulent wage and hour records or no records at all.

NASA

The National Aeronautics and Space Administration (NASA) would receive a $500 million boost under the president's budget proposal, for a total of $18.5 billion in discretionary spending for fiscal 2016. The total request included a 3 percent increase in funding for exploration activities, which covers NASA's development of the Orion crew vehicle and Space Launch System rocket for future missions to Mars, as well as its collaboration with the private sector to transport astronauts to the International Space Station. President Obama also requested $1.9 billion for NASA's Earth sciences missions. He continued to target a 2018 launch for the James Webb Space Telescope, which is the successor to the Hubble Space Telescope.

State

The president's base fiscal 2016 funding request for the State Department was $46.3 billion. Of that total, $5.6 billion would provide humanitarian assistance, $1.1 billion would go toward diplomatic engagement with Iraq, and $3.5 billion would be used to help stabilize the Middle East, fight ISIL and support the Syrian opposition. The State Department would receive $390 million for its portion of the Counterterrorism Partnership Fund, which seeks to improve international counterterrorism partnerships and address the root causes of terrorism. The president sought $1 billion to help Central American countries improve their living conditions and thereby reduce the number of migrants coming to the United States from countries such as El Salvador, Guatemala, and Honduras.

The OCO would receive $7 billion, about 25 percent less than what Congress appropriated for fiscal 2015. For the first time, the president's proposal included using OCO funds to help Eastern European countries purchase U.S. weapons as a deterrent against Russian aggression in the region. Ukraine, Georgia, and Moldova would all receive funding via the Foreign Military Financing program.

Transportation

Although President Obama sought a relatively minor increase in the Department of Transportation's discretionary budget for fiscal 2016 ($14.3 billion, compared to $13.8 billion in fiscal 2015), he proposed a more than $22 billion increase in the department's total budget authority. Specifically, the president sought $94.5 billion in overall funding, up from $72.1 billion in fiscal 2015.

One of the most significant and controversial components of the president's budget was a proposed one-time, 14 percent tax on about $2 trillion in corporate profits being held overseas to avoid U.S. income taxes. Administration officials estimated the tax could generate $238 billion, which would be used to supplement insufficient gas tax receipts and help pay for a new, six-year highway authorization bill that would cost $478 billion. The existing surface transportation authorization was set to expire at the end of May 2015.

If the corporate tax proposal was implemented, the Highway Trust Fund would receive about $40.1 billion, in addition to approximately $39.6 billion generated from fuel taxes. The administration wanted the fund to spend about $60.5 billion in fiscal 2016, meaning that approximately $20 billion would be left in the fund at the end of the year. The Federal Transit Administration's budget would also increase, from $11 billion to $18.4 billion. Most of that increase would be used for capital investment in mass transit systems.

The administration also proposed moving highway grant programs, highway safety, passenger rail, and most public transit spending from the Department of Transportation's discretionary budget to the Highway Trust Fund, which would then be renamed the Transportation Trust Fund. Doing so would create some room on the discretionary side of the budget, the administration said. Others noted the shift would allow the administration to protect some contentious programs from congressional action, such as TIGER grants. This competitive grant program provides funding for state and local transportation projects, but Republicans claim the grants are not administered properly and tend to favor liberal-leaning areas and big cities.

Additionally, President Obama sought to create two new bond programs to spur greater private investment in transportation projects. The first, called America Fast Forward bonds, would be modeled on the Build America Bonds, a taxable bond program launched in the 2009 stimulus. The second, known as Qualified Public Infrastructure Bonds, would be a tax-exempt form of municipal bonds modeled on existing Private Activity Bonds.

Treasury

The Department of Treasury would receive $13.5 billion in discretionary funding for fiscal 2016 under the president's proposal, as compared to the $12.2 billion it received in 2015. Budget increases of $200 million and $72 million, respectively, were sought for the Securities and Exchange Commission and the Commodity Futures Trading Commission. Both agencies are involved in the implementation of Dodd-Frank Act regulations, making them a perennial target for Republican cost-cutting proposals.

President Obama requested $12.9 billion for the Internal Revenue Service (IRS), which was $2 billion more than Congress had appropriated for fiscal 2015. Republicans had pushed to scale back funding for the IRS since it was revealed that some agents had targeted conservative organizations seeking 501(c)(3) status for additional scrutiny.

Veterans Affairs

President Obama proposed a roughly 8 percent increase in the Department of Veterans Affairs' (VA) budget for fiscal 2016, to total $70.2 billion. The increase was tied to VA projections that it would treat more patients during the year. Officials estimated that 6.9 million patients would be served by VA facilities in fiscal 2016, and 7 million would be treated in fiscal 2017. Iraq and Afghanistan War veterans were expected to comprise a growing portion of the patient population during this time.

The president proposed diverting some of the $10 billion that Congress had set aside to subsidize non-VA medical care through the new Veterans Choice Program, created by a 2014 law (PL 113-146), for what the administration described as essential investments in priorities for the VA system. OMB Director Shaun Donovan said the administration wanted to have the option to shift the funds to other priorities if it turned out that there was low demand for non-VA care. He said the money would only be tapped if not fully spent by the Choice Program and that it would be spent to help VA facilities better meet patient demand. The VA had begun sending Choice Program vouchers to potentially eligible veterans in November 2014.

The vast majority of the requested discretionary funds ($63.3 billion) were for advance fiscal 2017 appropriations for VA medical care accounts. Most of the VA's discretionary funds are appropriated in advance to protect against potential shutdowns or gaps in funding. Another $95.3 billion in mandatory spending was included in the budget. Most of this funding was earmarked for veterans' benefits programs.

Fiscal 2016 Budget Resolution

With a majority in both houses of Congress for the first time since the mid-2000s, Republicans began 2015 with an ambitious plan to adopt a budget resolution and enact all twelve regular appropriations bills rather than being forced into using an omnibus spending package to stave off a government shutdown. Adopting a budget resolution would allow Republicans to use the budget reconciliation process to push through budget-related bills with a limitation on amendments and no threat of a Senate filibuster. S Con Res 11, the congressional budget resolution, allowed the House and Senate to send to the president legislation that would repeal most of the president's landmark health care legislation, the 2010 Patient Protection and Affordable Care Act (ACA).

The so-called regular appropriations process broke down before the summer recess, however, because Democrats united in their opposition to Republican proposals that defense spending be increased above discretionary spending caps set by the 2011 Budget Control Act, without any increase in domestic spending. A new spending fight arose when Congress needed to keep the government funded past the September 30 end of the fiscal year. Hard-line conservatives refused to pass any continuing resolution that did not include the defunding of Planned Parenthood. The stalemate was only broken when Speaker John Boehner, R-Ohio, announced that he would resign at the end of October, giving the more conservative wing of the party that opposed his leadership an opportunity to vote for a new speaker. Announcing his resignation also provided Boehner the political cover he needed to negotiate with the White House on a number of issues, and the partnership was instrumental in a late-October budget agreement (HR 1314—PL 114-74) that increased defense and nondefense spending above the levels set by the sequestration and suspended the debt limit, the maximum amount the government can borrow to pay previously incurred debts, until March 2017. That budget agreement paved the way for Congress to pass an omnibus appropriations bill (HR 2029—PL 114-113) for fiscal 2016 that was coupled with a package of tax credit extenders and modifications.

Budget resolutions are nonbinding and do not require presidential approval, but they do set budgetary limits for Congress, including spending caps that appropriators must follow when negotiating legislation to set the budget for the coming fiscal year. With a majority in both the House and Senate, Republicans set out to write one that would outline their spending priorities for the next decade while also balancing the budget. The division within their own party between fiscal conservatives and defense hawks made it difficult to develop an agreement that would both cut federal spending and provide defense funding over what was allowed under the Budget Control Act.

House Action

The House fiscal 2016 budget resolution was released on March 17 by House Budget Committee Chair Tom Price, R-Ga. The plan would balance the budget within the next ten years, primarily through spending cuts, a full repeal of the ACA, a conversion of Medicaid and the Supplemental Nutrition Assistance Program (SNAP) into a block grant for the states, and a restructuring of Medicare into a program that would provide beneficiaries a subsidy that would allow them to choose private health coverage. Democrats objected to any changes to entitlement programs and offered a variety of amendments aimed at eliminating those measures from the budget plan, but all were rejected by the Republican-controlled committee. Price's plan gave direction to the thirteen authorizing committees to develop savings legislation that would modify mandatory spending programs. His budget resolution adhered to the sequester spending caps set by the Budget Control Act but provided $90 billion in uncapped defense funds for Overseas Contingency Operations (OCO). A portion of these OCO funds would be contingent on finding spending cuts to offset the increase. Defense hawks threatened to vote against the budget on the House floor unless higher defense funding was provided. To gain the votes needed for passage, during markup, Republican leadership proposed an amendment that would provide another $2 billion in defense OCO funds and remove the required offset, but that was still not enough to gain the votes necessary because the most fiscally conservative in the party refused

to increase the federal deficit. The amendment was never formally offered, but the Budget Committee passed the Price budget blueprint (H Con Res 27) on March 19 by a party-line vote of 22–13. House leadership promised to address the defense-deficit concern when the bill was on the floor.

To address the issue, Republican leaders initially considered modifying the budget resolution through a self-executing floor rule within the rules package. Under this scenario, if the rules package was approved and the bill proceeded to the floor, the change would automatically be made, and members would vote on the modified budget plan rather than the original marked-up version from the Budget Committee. Deficit hawks objected to such a plan and said they would vote down the rule. House leadership instead decided to put up both the original committee measure and a version with the leadership-supported changes as substitute amendments. Under this scenario, whichever version received more votes would be the version adopted. The House ended up voting on six substitutes. The original Budget Committee version was rejected 105–319, while the leadership proposal was adopted 219–208. Final passage came on March 25, when the House adopted its budget resolution that provided an extra $2 billion in defense OCO funding and eliminated the need for an offset, passed 228–199.

Senate Action

The Senate Budget Committee considered its own budget plan, unveiled on March 18 by Chair Mike Enzi, R-Wyo. The Senate version was similar to that being considered in the House in that it would also balance the budget within ten years through spending cuts, a repeal of the ACA, and entitlement program modifications. The proposal also cut nondefense discretionary spending after fiscal 2016 but kept in place the Budget Control Act cap for defense and nondefense spending. However, instead of following the House method of adding additional defense funds through the OCO, the Senate instead chose to pursue a deficit-neutral reserve fund that would allow the budget cap to be raised if the House and Senate agreed later in the year to roll back sequestration.

The Senate panel considering the budget plan adopted an amendment by a vote of 12–10 that would add defense funding to the OCO that matched the president's request for defense. President Obama had been seeking since the implementation of the Budget Control Act a way to eliminate or avoid sequestration for both domestic and defense programs, and adding funds to the uncapped OCO was one way to do so. The additional defense spending in the amendment was offset through funding reductions later in the ten-year budget. Of the fifty amendments that were proposed, those written by Democrats that would prevent spending cuts and changes to entitlement programs were rejected. The Budget Committee adopted its budget resolution (S Con Res 11) 12–10.

The full Senate considered the budget plan the following week, culminating in a fifteen-hour series of votes on amendments to the budget plan, as well as the plan itself. Amendments were offered on a variety of topics, including environmental policy, foreign affairs, and education. A total of 135 amendments were adopted on the final day of consideration. Rejected amendments included one to give appropriators greater spending authority for fiscal 2016 to increase defense spending above the discretionary cap and another that would partially roll back both the defense and nondefense sequester by two years, paid for by closing tax loopholes. Senate leadership sought to avoid amendments such as these to prevent passage of a bill that was too dissimilar to the House version, which would have made conference negotiations difficult. However, the Senate did approve an amendment that would roll back sequester spending by two years and pay for it through spending cuts and revenue increases. The Senate voted for final passage on March 27, adopting the budget resolution by a 52–46 vote.

Conference Negotiations

There were two primary issues during conference negotiations between the House and Senate, including what rules would be used for reconciliation and whether there were restrictions that needed to be considered with relation to the extra funds for the OCO account. Although both the House and Senate budgets provided additional uncapped OCO funds for Pentagon needs, the Senate provision required sixty votes to spend OCO funds above the $58 billion level in fiscal 2016 and $59.5 billion in fiscal 2017. On the rules, Republican senators wanted to adhere to their original proposal and use the expedited reconciliation process—where filibusters are prohibited—only to repeal the ACA instead of for deficit reduction efforts, as the House had proposed. Doing so, Republican senators argued, would take public attention away from the effort popular among their base to repeal the ACA.

Another issue was Senate-passed language eliminating the Changes in Mandatory Programs (CHIMPS), a budget tool that can be used by appropriators to increase discretionary spending. CHIMPS allows appropriators to replace spending restrictions on mandatory programs scored as budget savings, which can be used to offset additional discretionary funding. Critics say that it amounts to little more than budget gimmicks that never produce savings. Sen. Bob Corker, a member of the conference committee who sponsored the CHIMPS language and was a strong supporter of the sixty-vote requirement for OCO funding, refused to sign the final agreement reached by conferees until April 29. When he signed the plan, Corker issued a statement indicating his desire to make further progress on CHIMPS and the OCO funding in next year's budget process.

The final fiscal 2016 budget agreement (S Con Res 11) was adopted in the House on April 30 by a vote of 226–197 and in the Senate on May 5, 51–48, marking the first time

the two chambers adopted a final budget resolution since 2009. Included in the agreement were provisions that would

- balance the budget within ten years by cutting $5.3 trillion in spending, mostly from mandatory programs, entitlement reform, and through a repeal of the ACA
- keep in place the sequester spending caps in fiscal 2016, allowing for $523 billion in base defense spending and $493.5 billion in nondefense spending
- provide $96 billion in OCO funding, although the Senate provision requiring sixty votes to spend over the OCO levels was dropped
- issue reconciliation instructions to the Senate Finance and Health, Education, Labor and Pension committees, as well as the House Ways and Means, Education and the Workforce, and Energy and Commerce committees; it also gave flexibility for the reconciliation process to be used for a legislative response to an expected Supreme Court ruling related to the ACA
- freeze CHIMPS at $19.1 billion in fiscal 2016 and reduce it again to $15 billion by fiscal 2019 rather than phasing CHIMPS out entirely
- maintain a House reserve fund for increased defense spending and the Senate reserve fund, allowing for increased defense and nondefense spending.

FISCAL 2016 SPENDING

Having Republican control in both the House and Senate did not ease budget work for fiscal 2016, and in fact it took the announcement by Speaker John Boehner, R-Ohio, that he would resign at the end of October 2015 for bipartisan negotiations to move forward. Work on a funding bill was decidedly different than in previous years, because Congress was facing the reenactment of full sequester cuts for discretionary spending for both defense and nondefense programs. A December 2013 budget deal reached by the House and Senate partially rolled back cuts set by the Budget Control Act of 2011 only for fiscal 2014 and 2015, forcing Congress in 2015 to determine how to deal with those cuts and whether to further change sequestration to allow more funding for defense and/or nondefense programs.

Republicans and Democrats differ on their opinion of the sequester, with some right-wing budget hawks viewing the automatic cuts as a means to keep federal spending in check, while Democrats have sided with the president in their belief that the cuts were never meant to take effect and should be reversed to provide adequate funding levels to both defense and nondefense programs. Republicans have primarily sought to increase spending for defense, arguing that any cuts to that budget impact national security.

In President Obama's fiscal 2016 budget request, he sought to increase both defense and nondefense spending by a combined $75 billion, by rolling back sequestration completely through 2021 and offsetting the increased spending through mandatory spending cuts and the end of certain tax breaks. The president's budget provided a total of $561 billion for defense, $38 billion more than the limit set by the sequester. The Pentagon told Congress that national security would be threatened if lawmakers did not provide at least the level requested by the president.

Republicans agreed that the additional funds were vital and in their fiscal 2016 budget resolution (S Con Res 11) provided $96 billion through the uncapped Overseas Contingency Operations (OCO) fund, which is used primarily for war-related activities. The resolution that passed both chambers set discretionary spending limits of $523 for nonwar defense spending and $493.5 billion for nondefense spending that appropriators would be held to as they negotiated fiscal 2016 spending bills. These totals met the sequester-reduced funding levels, which frustrated appropriators who hoped that the sequester would again be rolled back to provide extra room for negotiation and additional funds for vital programs. The White House, angry that the budget agreement failed to eliminate or reduce the impact of the sequester, issued a veto threat against any spending bill or other legislation that would adhere to the Republican budget framework. Democrats in the Senate announced that they would oppose any sequester-based spending bills. This essentially allowed Democrats to filibuster any of the chamber's spending bills and prevented the Senate from considering any individual appropriations bills.

The House was able to use the budget framework to pass six of the twelve regular appropriations bills by late July, but passage was inconsequential given that there would be no movement in the Senate. The House and Senate left for August recess without any progress on funding the government for fiscal 2016.

DEBT LIMIT

Further complicating negotiations on spending was the need to again raise the debt limit, the cap on how much the federal government can borrow to pay its previously incurred debts and avoid a default. In February 2014, Congress passed a bill that suspended the debt limit through March 15, 2015, effectively resetting it to $18.113 trillion, and the Treasury Department said it could likely use extraordinary measures at its disposal to avoid a default until November 2015. Before that point, Congress would need to act to increase the debt ceiling. As they had in the past, Republicans sought to tie any debt limit increase to spending cuts elsewhere, but Democrats and the White House refused to negotiate on any such measure.

BOEHNER RESIGNATION AND FINAL NEGOTIATIONS

In late September, Speaker Boehner, a frequent foe of more hardline conservatives in the House, announced that he would leave Congress in October. Initially, that announcement paved the way for the House to adopt a clean continuing resolution (one that did not include a provision defunding Planned Parenthood as demanded by some Republican members) to prevent a government shutdown and provide more time for spending negotiations.

Budget deal negotiations continued behind the scenes between leaders in the House and Senate and the White House. That resulted in a late-October bipartisan agreement to roll back sequestration for another two years to increase defense and nondefense spending caps, as well as raise the debt limit to avoid a default. The bill also included a provision to keep the Social Security disability trust fund solvent until 2022, prevent significant increases in certain Medicare premiums for some beneficiaries, and make other changes to some health care programs. The increase in spending was offset by cuts to some entitlement programs, fee increases, and other revenue raisers.

Republicans opposed the agreement because it increased discretionary spending, had been negotiated in secret, and was not considered by any committee. On October 28, the House passed the agreement as a substitute to unrelated Senate-passed legislation (HR 1314) by a vote of 266–167; the Senate voted two days later, 64–35. On final passage in the House and Senate, all Democrats voted in support, while two-thirds of Republicans voted against it. The budget deal provided for the enactment of a full-year omnibus fiscal 2016 appropriations bill.

BUDGET AGREEMENT PROVISIONS

Included in the October budget agreement was a suspension of the debt ceiling through March 15, 2017, at which point the debt limit would be reset at the total amount of debt that had been accumulated through that date. It also increased the fiscal 2016 discretionary spending cap by $50 billion and the fiscal 2017 cap by $30 billion above sequestration levels. Those increases were evenly divided between defense and nondefense programs, with the new caps for fiscal 2016 set at $548.1 billion for defense, while nondefense was set at $518.5 billion. Funding for the OCO, which is not subject to the sequester cap, was set at $73.7 billion each year. The non-OCO increases were completely offset, primarily through Social Security, Medicare, and other health care changes, as well as a modification of IRS auditing rules and changes to the federal crop insurance program. The measure also

- kept the Social Security disability trust fund solvent until 2022
- prevented an increase in Medicare Part B premiums in 2016 for some beneficiaries
- repealed an ACA requirement that large employers automatically enroll certain employees in their health plans.

OMNIBUS APPROPRIATIONS PACKAGE

Republicans were hopeful early in the year that they would be able to use the regular appropriations process and pass the twelve individual spending measures to keep the government funded. However, by summer, Democrats refused to consider any spending bills that kept in place the discretionary defense and nondefense spending limits set by the Budget Control Act of 2011.

To overcome the cuts required by the sequester, Democrats instead pushed for another budget agreement similar to that reached in December 2013 between Rep. Paul Ryan, R-Wis., chair of the House Budget Committee, and Sen. Patty Murray, D-Wash., chair of the Senate Budget Committee. That agreement circumvented the budget control act and provided slightly more funding for defense and nondefense programs. Republicans, however, were seeking to raise spending by $38 billion, but only for the Pentagon Overseas Contingency Operations (OCO) account that was not subject to sequester spending caps.

To avoid a government shutdown and allow larger spending limit discussions to continue, on September 30, Congress passed a ten-week continuing resolution (PL 114-53) that would keep the government open through December 11. The continuing resolution adhered to the spending limits set by the Budget Control Act, providing for an annualized budget of $1.017 trillion for both defense and nondefense programs. Budget agreement discussions continued into the fall, and on October 26, 2015, Congress and the White House agreed to increase discretionary spending limits above those set by the Budget Control Act by $80 billion over the next two years, $50 billion in fiscal 2016 and $30 billion in fiscal 2017, evenly divided between defense and nondefense spending. The agreement (HR 1314—PL 114-74) would also suspend the debt limit until March 2017 to allow the government to avoid default. Despite objections from fiscal conservatives who viewed the offsets as budgetary gimmicks, the measure passed the House October 28, 2015, and the Senate agreed to the legislation two days later. It was signed into law on November 2.

House and Senate negotiators used the top-line budget agreement numbers as they continued to work on allocating funds for government agencies and programs by the December 11 deadline set by the September 30 continuing resolution. Two additional short-term continuing resolutions were passed to fund the government for a total of eleven days after the December 11 deadline to provide additional time to finalize the $1.15 trillion omnibus package.

For the sixth year in a row, in 2015 Congress was forced to pass an omnibus spending bill to fund the government instead of passing the twelve individual spending bills that cover most federal agencies. Although the omnibus easily passed the House 316–113 and Senate 65–33 on December 18, neither party was particularly happy with the outcome. Both Democrats and Republicans felt that provisions they had long fought for were not included in the legislation. For example, Republicans were unable to include any limits on President Obama's environmental policies, provide enough pro-life policy riders, limit the number of Syrian refugees allowed into the United States annually, or restrict government spending. Democrats were also concerned about what was left out of the bill, such as support for Puerto Rico's financial crisis, and the inclusion of other riders such as the lift on a decades-old ban on crude oil exports. As signed on December 18, 2015, the bill would fund the government through the remainder of fiscal 2016.

The final bill included a package of tax break intenders, reauthorized the 9/11 first responder health care program, and lifted the ban on crude oil exports. The increases in spending were offset by spending cuts, revenue increases, and tax compliance provisions. In a big win for Republicans, the final bill also repealed the requirement of the Patient Protection and Affordable Care Act that required large employers to automatically provide health insurance to their employees. The bill provided relief to Medicare beneficiaries who would have been hit with rising premiums and made changes to the Social Security disability insurance trust fund to prevent the exhaustion of funds.

Budget Reconciliation

In April, the House and Senate agreed to a final budget resolution, a nonbinding plan that sets budgetary limits appropriators must adhere to when developing spending legislation. Included in this bill were specific instructions providing for the reconciliation process, which allows for expedited consideration of budget-related legislation in the Senate with limited amendments and without the threat of a filibuster. The final budget resolution allowed for reconciliation to be used to repeal the Patient Protection and Affordable Care Act (ACA), President Obama's landmark legislation, specifically by directing two Senate committees and three House committees to develop repeal legislation. The final budget resolution also provided for reconciliation to be used for a legislative response to an expected Supreme Court decision related to ACA federal health insurance subsidies. Opponents of the law's provisions argued that subsidies could only be used for health insurance policies purchased on the exchanges set up by the states, not the federal government. Republicans felt the court would strike down the subsidies and deal a major blow to the law, so they wanted the ability to pass a subsidy replacement plan to prevent millions of Americans from losing their insurance until Congress could come up with permanent legislation to replace the ACA. On June 25, however, the Supreme Court upheld the use of subsidies on both the state and federal exchanges in *King v. Burwell.*

Given the Supreme Court decision, questions were raised about how reconciliation should be used, with some rank-and-file members supporting using reconciliation for something other than repealing the ACA. Added to the uncertainty of how Congress would proceed was a June estimate by the Congressional Budget Office that repealing the ACA would add hundreds of billions of dollars to the deficit over the next decade and even more after that point. Budget reconciliation rules require that the legislation produced by the committees instructed to develop repeal legislation reduce the deficit. In addition, the Senate was hampered by the Byrd rule, which prohibits reconciliation legislation that increases the deficit in any year after the budget resolution's ten-year window. Waiving that prohibition would require sixty votes. The Byrd rule also bars including extraneous matter in reconciliation provisions where the impact to the budget is more a side effect than the intent.

With Sen. Mitch McConnell, R-Ky., announcing in July that Republicans would use reconciliation to strike down the ACA rather than for other means, discussions focused on how to remove portions of the law while following Senate reconciliation rules and adhering to the budget resolution's deficit reduction requirements. According to Republican leadership, full repeal was not necessary, because if they removed specific provisions, the law would crumble on its own.

House Action

As House leaders began to mark up legislation in September, a new challenge presented itself. Some members of the Republican caucus were attempting to defund Planned Parenthood after videos emerged that purported to show officials from the organization discussing the sale of fetal tissue harvested after abortions for medical research. Those seeking to defund Planned Parenthood refused to vote for a stopgap continuing resolution to keep the government funded beyond the September 30 end of the fiscal year unless such a provision was included. To avoid a government shutdown, Republican leadership instead proposed adding a funding prohibition to the reconciliation legislation, which was amendable to their members.

The three House committees tasked with reconciliation related to the ACA—Ways and Means, Energy and Commerce, and Education and the Workforce—marked up the House legislation the week of September 28. The portion considered by Ways and Means, which passed 23–14, repealed the individual and employer mandates that require Americans to have health insurance and employers of a certain size to offer it to their employees or face penalties. The legislation also repealed the tax on high-cost employer health insurance plans, as well as the 2.3 percent tax on medical devices. By voice vote, the panel also approved a repeal of the law's Independent Payment Advisory Board (IPAB) that would recommend to Congress changes that should be made to Medicare that would result in savings.

The legislation approved by the Energy and Commerce committee defunded the ACA's Prevention and Public Health Fund, which is used to issue grants to public and private organizations for public health activities. It was within this legislation that Planned Parenthood was defunded for one year. The savings would be used to increase funding for community health centers. The

Education and the Workforce committee's portion, approved 22–15, repealed the ACA provisions that required large employers to automatically enroll all new full-time employees in a health insurance plan.

The House Budget Committee, which is responsible for packaging the committee-approved reconciliation pieces for floor consideration, approved the consolidated version (HR 3762) on a party-line 21–11 vote. The full House passed the measure on October 23 by a vote of 240–189. Because the CBO estimated that the package would add at least $5 billion to the deficit after 2025 because costs of repealing the IPAB would eventually exceed savings from the remainder of the bill, a provision in the House rules package automatically deleted the IPAB from the legislation upon its acceptance. This would allow the Senate to consider the legislation without violating its own reconciliation governing rules. Before the legislation was sent to the Senate, the House also modified the bill to delete the portion that repealed the requirement for large employers to automatically enroll new staff in a health insurance plan because that repeal was already enacted in separate legislation.

Senate Action

In the Senate, Republican leadership needed to ensure that any legislation it passed would conform to Senate reconciliation rules and also needed to ensure they could find enough votes for passage. Three Republican senators had already announced that they planned to vote against the legislation because it did not offer full repeal of the ACA, and some moderate Republicans announced opposition over the defunding of Planned Parenthood. To find additional portions of the ACA to repeal to gain Republican votes, leadership consulted the Senate Parliamentarian. The Parliamentarian ruled that repealing the individual and employer mandate violated the Byrd rule and would need sixty votes to waive, as did the repeal of the tax on high-cost health insurance plans.

Instead of asking the two committees designated under the budget agreement to develop a plan for repealing portions of the ACA, the Senate sent the House bill directly to the floor. Under Senate rules, reconciliation legislation can be debated for no more than twenty hours, at which point only a limited number of amendments can be considered. The Republican strategy to avoid sending its own legislation to the House for consideration and conference rested on an amendment being offered immediately after debate to address areas where the House bill violated the Byrd rules. Then any other amendments would be considered and a final substitute would be offered on the floor that eliminated any Byrd rule concerns and expanded the amount of the law that would be repealed. After seven hours of votes on amendments, on December 3, the Senate passed the House-amended version of the legislation 52–47. Among the rejected amendments was one removing the provisions defunding Planned Parenthood. In the measure passed by the Senate, more than a half-dozen ACA provisions would be repealed or effectively repealed, including the individual and employer mandate, expansion of Medicaid, the Prevention and Public Health Care Fund, and federal subsidies for individuals buying insurance on the exchanges. The Senate circumvented the Byrd rule on the individual and employer mandate issue by setting the penalty to $0 for those who failed to comply with the regulations. Additionally, more than a dozen taxes that financed the law would be repealed, including the medical device tax, the 3.8 percent tax on net investment income above certain levels, and the 0.9 percent payroll tax used for Medicare's hospital program. It also maintained the House repeal of the tax on high-cost health plans. Republican leadership initially intended to circumvent the Byrd rules by restoring the tax in 2025, but no senator raised a point of order related to the amendment making the repeal permanent, so it was included in the legislation in its original House-passed form.

Final Passage and Veto

House and Senate Republican leadership knew President Obama would veto the legislation, but it was their opinion that by sending the bill to the White House and forcing the veto, Republicans would head into an election year in a way that made clear they could repeal the law with a Republican-controlled Congress and a Republican in the White House. The House postponed the vote until January 2016 so it would occur during election year. On January 6, 2016, the House voted 240–181 in favor of the Senate-amended legislation, and President Obama issued his veto two days later. On February 2, the House failed to meet the two-thirds threshold required to override a veto, only reaching a vote of 241–186.

Tax Cut Extensions and Tax Code Overhaul

For decades, Congress has attempted to complete a full overhaul of the U.S. tax code, a system that politicians and Americans agree is overly complicated. However, in the 114th Congress, the two parties remained far apart on the best methods for fixing the tax system, and they chose to focus instead on extending popular tax cuts. At the close of 2015, Congress passed an omnibus spending package to fund the federal government. Included in that legislation were provisions extending a number of tax breaks that, according to the nonpartisan Committee for a Responsible Federal Budget, would cost more than $800 billion once the cost of borrowing to finance the deficit was considered. The permanent and short-term tax break extensions included the Earned Income Tax Credit, the refundable child tax credit, research and experimentation credits, and a $500,000 cap on small business expensing. The legislation also delayed taxes in the 2010 Patient Protection and Affordable Care Act (ACA), including an excise tax on medical devices and a levy on high-cost employer health plans, and suspended the tax on insurers that had taken effect in 2014.

Obama and congressional leaders proposed additional tax changes in 2016. Although no legislation was passed, the Internal Revenue Service issued several significant rules changes.

Members of both parties typically come together to extend various tax breaks, a public relations win with both individuals and businesses. The two parties have frequently expressed a desire to completely overhaul the U.S. tax code and make these temporary tax breaks permanent to streamline and inject greater predictability into the tax system. However, the parties disagree on whether taxes should be reduced for the wealthy and corporations or if the overhaul should be revenue neutral or raise revenues to help offset the federal deficit. Without agreement on a broader overhaul, in 2014 and again in 2015, Congress instead chose to pass bills that would extend some expiring tax cuts and make others permanent.

Republicans focused the 2015 tax extender negotiations on making permanent certain provisions impacting businesses, including the research and development tax credit and small business expensing provisions, while Democrats instead wanted to expand credits for families, such as the Earned Income Tax Credit, child tax credit, and American Opportunity Tax Credit. Democrats sought to index these credits to inflation to extend the opportunity of low-income families to receive the credits. Republicans wanted to match the indexing with program integrity safeguards to prevent fraud, including requiring that Social Security numbers be provided to claim the tax credits, a move intended to prohibit undocumented immigrants from receiving them. Democrats would not support such a provision. Republicans also expressed concern that the tax extender package lacked adequate offsets.

2015 AGREEMENT

The final tax agreement wrapped into the omnibus was not an outright win for either party. Democrats opposed the tax extenders because most of the credits that would be made permanent benefited businesses, while the family tax credits were not indexed to inflation. Some Democrats also expressed concern about the cost of the tax extenders, estimated at upward of $622 billion in debt and deficits over the next decade. Lack of an offset would put pressure on future Congresses to cut spending elsewhere to reduce debt and deficit levels. Republicans, meanwhile, were unhappy that many of the policy riders they supported were not included and did not like that the overall omnibus measure reflected higher funding levels for defense and nondefense programs. Ultimately, however, the House approved the tax extender portion of the omnibus legislation on December 17, 2015, by a vote of 318–91, and the Senate passed it on December 18, 65–33.

The package retroactively renewed tax credits that expired at the end of 2014, allowing them to be claimed when individuals and corporations filed their tax returns in 2016, and made some credits permanent while extending and modifying others. Included in the tax package portion of the omnibus were permanent extension of:

- the research and development tax credit, which was also expanded to allow certain small businesses to claim it against Alternative Minimum Tax liability and allow some startup companies to use it as an offset of the employer's payroll tax liability
- the small business expensing credits
- various charitable tax credits
- some family and middle-class tax credits, including the refundable child tax credit, the Earned Income Tax Credit, and the American Opportunity tax credit
- the deduction for state and local sales tax credits.

The package also

- suspended for 2016 and 2017 the ACA medical device tax
- modified tax treatment of real estate investment trusts (REITs)
- modified Internal Revenue Service (IRS) policies related to taxpayer rights and the process for applying for tax-exempt status, a nod to the IRS scandal in which the body was inappropriately targeting conservative groups applying for such status
- allowed 529 college saving plan funds to be used for the purchase of computers and related equipment.

2016 PROPOSALS FOR TAX REFORM

Projections that Congress would pursue a tax overhaul in 2016 proved overly ambitious, especially during a heated presidential campaign. Although House Speaker Paul Ryan, R-Wis., unveiled Republicans' plan for sweeping tax reform in June, the proposals were framed as a blueprint for the next Congress and new president to follow, and no related legislation was introduced.

Aside from this blueprint, discussion of tax code changes during the year largely focused on the corporate tax structure for multinational corporations, particularly what Senate Finance Committee Chair Orrin Hatch, R-Utah, dubbed "the inversion problem." The United States has a top corporate tax rate of about 35 percent, making it one of the highest statutory rates in the world (corporations may pay between 15 percent and 35 percent depending on the amount of taxable income earned during the year). This has led some multinational companies to close their U.S. locations or shift operations overseas to take advantage of lower corporate tax rates in other countries. In some cases, companies have merged with other foreign-based companies located in countries with lower tax rates specifically for the purpose of reducing or avoiding U.S. taxes. This practice is known as inversion.

Companies typically invert in two ways. If a foreign company buys a U.S. company, the newly merged entity can reincorporate abroad, and the U.S. company is dissolved.

A U.S. company may buy or merge with a foreign business and choose to use that business's overseas location as the merged company's new headquarters. In either case, the newly created company is not obligated to pay U.S. tax on foreign profits.

OBAMA ADMINISTRATION ACTION

In his budget proposal for fiscal 2017, President Obama included several tax-related measures, such as the maintenance of higher taxes imposed on wealthy individuals by the fiscal 2013 omnibus. He also proposed additional tax increases for the wealthiest taxpayers—a measure previously rejected by Republicans. Other tax proposals included implementing a 19 percent minimum tax on foreign business earnings and a one-time 14 percent tax on $2.1 trillion in tax-deferred offshore corporate profits to help fund domestic infrastructure projects and other programs. Hatch and Senate Majority Leader Mitch McConnell, R-Ky., strongly opposed the latter measure, arguing that offsets should be considered by the next Congress as it pursued a tax code rewrite.

In April, the Treasury Department and the Internal Revenue Service (IRS) issued new "temporary and proposed regulations to further reduce the benefits of and limit the number of corporate tax inversions." The rules included an adjustment to the ownership threshold for inversions. Per rules issued by the Treasury Department in 2012, a company could invert if it had "substantial business operations" in the country where its new parent was to be located that equaled at least 25 percent of the company's operations. Firms could also invert if the original U.S. stockholders owned less than 80 percent of the new, post-merger firm (some restrictions on inversion apply between the 80 percent and 60 percent ownership bracket, but the company is still considered foreign). According to the Treasury Department, some foreign companies had circumvented the inversion threshold by acquiring several smaller American companies over a short period of time, thereby increasing the size and assets of the foreign company, which in turn enabled them to make another, larger acquisition of a U.S. company without triggering inversion limits. The 2016 rules excluded any assets acquired by a foreign company via purchases of U.S. companies within the last three years from ownership percentage calculations, which would effectively shrink the percentage of foreign ownership as compared to U.S. ownership.

The new rules also allowed the IRS to reclassify certain intercompany loans from a parent company to a subsidiary to treat them like stock transactions, thereby eliminating the subsidiary's ability to claim tax deductions for interest payments. This change was designed to target a tactic known as "earnings stripping," which enables inverted corporations to further minimize tax payment obligations. The new foreign parent company or one of its foreign affiliates will make a loan to the U.S. affiliate. The interest income of the foreign entity is taxed at a lower rate due to its location in a lower-tax country, while the U.S. affiliate can claim interest deductions that are significantly higher than the taxes paid by the foreign entity.

Treasury Secretary Jacob Lew said that while the new rules were important, it was vital that Congress move forward with anti-inversion legislation as soon as possible.

Lawmaker reaction to the rules was mixed. Democrats called for their full implementation while Congress continued to negotiate a broader package of restrictions on corporate inversions. Republicans, including Hatch and House Ways and Means Committee Chair Kevin Brady, R-Texas, warned that they would take legislative action to block the rules. Brady argued that the rules would cause "real economic damage" by forcing U.S.-based companies to forgo future mergers or other deals that could help them restructure operations and cut costs in order to maintain the interest deduction. Business groups including the National Association of Manufacturers and the U.S. Chamber of Commerce also expressed concerns about the rules, writing to the chairpersons and ranking members of the House Ways and Means and Senate Finance Committees in June to say they would create "further obstacles to much needed investment, job creation and economic growth." The groups claimed the rules would force businesses to abandon certain internal financing options in favor of "more expensive external debt."

GOP TAX REFORM PROPOSALS

On June 24, Ryan released a new tax plan, developed in coordination with Brady, as part of Republicans' "A Better Way" policy agenda. The two lawmakers framed the plan as a foundation for tax reform debate in the next Congress and made clear that they wanted input from the American people on the plan.

The plan's major components included:

- consolidation of the seven individual tax brackets into three, with rates of 12 percent, 25 percent, and 33 percent
- increases in the standard deduction and a larger child and dependent tax credit
- estate tax repeal
- elimination of the individual and corporate alternative minimum tax
- creation of a separate, lower tax rate of 25 percent for small businesses
- lowering the corporate tax rate to 20 percent
- allowing families and individuals to deduct 50 percent of the dividends, capital gains, and interest received from stocks and mutual funds.

House Action

Several House members introduced legislation aimed at addressing pieces of the tax code, including those related to corporate taxes, but none progressed beyond referral to committee.

For example, Rep. Sander Levin, D-Mich., introduced the Stop Corporate Earnings Stripping Act of 2016 (HR 4581) on February 23. The bill would have limited the tax deduction available to certain foreign-controlled U.S. multinational corporations for excess interest on company debt. Levin also sponsored the Protecting the U.S. Corporate Tax Base Act of 2016 (HR 5261), which sought to revise the rules for taxing earnings and determining stock ownership of certain controlled foreign corporations, including by changing the inversion ownership threshold to 50 percent U.S. ownership. The Corporate EXIT Fairness Act (HR 5125), introduced by Rep. Lloyd Doggett, D-Texas, on April 29, would have required U.S. multinational corporations or partnerships to pay tax on their deferred overseas profits before they reincorporate or organize in a foreign country. It would also have allowed any stock of a controlled foreign corporation in connection with a corporate expatriation to be treated as sold for its fair market value as of the date of expatriation and thereby subject to U.S. taxation.

Fiscal 2017 Budget Proposal

In the last budget proposal of his administration, President Obama adhered to fiscal 2017 discretionary spending caps agreed to as part of the fiscal 2015 budget deal. Released on February 9, the president's budget proposed a $4.23 trillion budget for fiscal 2017, which would be partly funded by an anticipated $3.64 trillion in revenue. Administration officials projected that actual spending would total $4.15 trillion, resulting in an estimated deficit of $503 billion.

According to the White House Office of Management and Budget (OMB), the president's proposed budget would increase outlays by $296 billion while increasing revenue by $308 billion, as compared to the fiscal 2016 budget. The proposal was projected to cost $52.63 trillion between 2017 and 2026, or $26 billion less than the $52.89 trillion that the administration estimated would be spent if existing laws and policies remained in effect. Over that same period, OMB estimated the plan would raise $46.52 trillion in revenue, or $3.38 trillion more than the $43.137 trillion that was projected to be raised under current laws and policies. The administration said that additional revenue would be generated from economic growth spurred by the proposed budget, closing tax breaks, and increasing some taxes.

OMB further estimated that President Obama's proposed budget would lower the deficit by $2.9 trillion over ten years by achieving $378 billion in health care savings, generating $955 billion from ending tax breaks for wealthy individuals, and making changes to immigration laws that would result in $170 billion saved. If the budget were fully adopted, OMB projected the deficit would remain below 3 percent of the gross national product over ten years and that the national debt would be 75.3 percent of the gross domestic product (GDP) in 2026. Under current laws, OMB projected the national debt would grow to 87.6 percent of GDP during the same time period.

President Obama's budget reflected a roughly 5 percent increase in spending compared to fiscal 2016. Almost all of this increase was attributed to mandatory spending for programs including Social Security and Medicaid. Discretionary spending only increased by about 0.8 percent. The ten-year plan also included proposals for repealing sequester-lowered discretionary spending caps and across-the-board cuts to mandatory spending programs, beginning in fiscal 2018.

In announcing the proposal, administration officials sought to highlight provisions they believed could win bipartisan support in Congress, such as proposed funding for cancer research, combatting the opioid epidemic, and expanded tax credits. Republicans, however, were scathing in their criticism, even before the budget was released, with some declaring it would go nowhere in Congress. In fact, Budget Committee Chairs Rep. Tom Price, R-Ga., and Sen. Michael Enzi, R-Wyo., said they would not hold their committees' usual hearings on the president's budget proposal.

White House press secretary Josh Earnest criticized the decision to forgo hearings, saying the budget was critical to the United States' economy and national security and that Republicans should at least have a conversation with the administration about it. OMB Director Shaun Donovan attempted to counter Republicans' criticisms by noting many of Obama's fiscal 2015 proposals became law, including increased discretionary spending caps.

SPENDING BY DEPARTMENT AND MAJOR AGENCY

Agriculture

The U.S. Department of Agriculture (USDA) would receive $24.2 billion under President Obama's fiscal 2017 budget request, a $1.5 billion decrease from fiscal 2016. The total USDA request included $127 million for a new national program that would provide summer meals to the approximately 22 million children who receive subsidized lunches during the school year. The White House said the goal of the program was to feed 20 million children each year by fiscal 2026 at a projected total cost of $12 billion.

The president's budget request also included increased funding for agriculture research. Funding for the Agriculture and Food Research Initiative would double from $350 million in fiscal 2016 to $700 million in fiscal 2017. The program is used to provide research, education, and extension grants for agricultural sciences. Another $1.2 billion was requested to fund the Agricultural Research Service, which conducts research on topics ranging from climate change resilience and vulnerability to soil health, avian flu, and antimicrobial resistance.

One budget item that was expected to face considerable opposition from lawmakers representing farm states was the president's proposal to cut $18 billion from federal subsidies for private crop insurance over the next ten years. Farm state lawmakers had successfully defeated a push by their colleagues in Congress to include language cutting $3 billion from the crop insurance program in the fiscal 2016 omnibus.

Army Corps of Engineers

Congress had repeatedly objected to President Obama's budget proposals for the Army Corps of Engineers as unrealistically low, and the fiscal 2017 request was no exception. The president sought $4.6 billion in discretionary funding for the Corps, which was 23 percent less than the amount Congress had appropriated for fiscal 2016. Proposed cuts to the Corps' budget included decreasing spending on studies and construction by $808 million. This reduction was nearly 65 percent larger than a similar cut proposed for fiscal 2016. Additionally, the administration proposed to reduce Corps operations and maintenance spending by $432 million.

Other proposals included the imposition of a new revenue-generating mechanism: an annual per-vessel fee for barge and towboat operators to use inland waterways. The administration argued this fee was necessary because the fiscal 2016 increase in the diesel fuel excise tax would not generate enough revenue to pay for future capital investments. The single biggest construction item in the proposed Corps budget was $225 million for the Olmsted Locks and Dam on the Ohio River.

Commerce

President Obama proposed providing $9.8 billion to fund the Commerce Department in fiscal 2017, which was $1 billion more than the fiscal 2016 enacted level. More than $2 billion of this total would be dedicated to manufacturing institutes. Three existing institutes would receive $42 million, while another $1.9 billion would be used to develop new institutes that would convene researchers, companies, and entrepreneurs to develop new, broadly applicable manufacturing technologies. The Census Bureau would receive $1.6 billion to upgrade its data collection systems ahead of the 2020 Census—an investment Commerce officials estimated could generate $5 billion in savings by lowering the per-household cost for conducting the count.

Defense

The total defense budget requested by the president represented a roughly $2.5 billion increase over fiscal 2016 enacted levels. His $582.7 billion request comprised $523.9 billion in base defense funding and $58.8 billion for Overseas Contingency Operations. Even before the White House's budget was released, House Armed Services Committee members wrote to the House Budget Committee that at least $15 billion more in defense spending would be needed for fiscal 2017. Republicans also pledged to provide more funding for the OCO; administration officials generally acknowledged that it was all but certain OCO spending would grow.

The president's proposal largely punted on major decisions about personnel levels, force structure, and new weapons programs. Although $11.2 billion would be cut from weapons programs, those funds would mostly be diverted from program plans rather than actual spending. The administration proposed cutting planned spending on twenty-four Blackhawk helicopters, nine Apache helicopters, and seventy-seven Marine Corps Light Tactical Vehicles, but virtually no other cuts to major programs were proposed. In some instances, cuts in certain areas were balanced by increases elsewhere. For example, while the administration sought to cut the Air Force's planned purchase of F-35s by five planes, it increased the number of planes to be purchased by the Navy and Marine Corps by thirteen, thereby resulting in a net increase. The budget reflected a slight decrease in the number of active-duty soldiers and sailors, but no more than was already planned. Further, while Pentagon officials once again asked Congress to close unnecessary bases, an additional $6 billion was provided for operations and maintenance spending for fiscal 2017, in part to keep excess bases running, because they did not expect lawmakers to grant the request.

Some defense programs would see significant funding increases under the president's proposal. The European Resistance Initiative would receive $3.4 billion in funding, or four times more than the fiscal 2016 level of $800 million. The program seeks to deter Russian aggression by providing more weapons, training, and a continuous Army presence on U.S. allies' territories. Funding to continue fighting the Islamic State in the Levant (ISIL) would double to $7.5 billion in fiscal 2017 and would include $200 million specifically for fighting extremists in Africa.

Education

Regarding education policies, the president's fiscal 2017 budget request reflected a focus on early learning and schools serving lower-income neighborhoods. His requested $69.4 billion included $15.4 billion in funding for Title I education grants to schools that serve the poorest students. Although the requested amount represented a $450 million increase for Title I grants over fiscal 2016, it did not necessarily equate to new funding for schools. States were expected to direct the increased Title I funds to activities that had previously been paid for by School Improvement Grants. Those grants had been eliminated by the Every Student Succeeds Act in 2015 (PL 114-95).

Preschool Development Grants would receive $350 million under the president's budget, or $100 million more than was allocated in fiscal 2016. Another $500 million would be given for Student Support and Academic Enrichment Grants, which provide funding to states and school districts to support student achievement, including programs expanding access to science and math courses and increasing the use of technology in the classroom. Head Start, which provides early childhood support services to low-income children, would receive $9.6 billion, or $434 million more than it received in 2016. This amount included $292 million to expand access to programs that offer longer school days and school years.

Two new programs were also included in the budget request. One program, named Computer Science for All, sought to provide $4 billion in funding over three years to help states increase access to K–12 computer science and other science, technology, engineering, and math courses. Another program would use $1 billion to provide incentives, such as increased compensation, to help attract and retain teachers for high-need schools.

Energy

Energy Department funding requested by President Obama reflected the administration's recent commitment to Mission Innovation, an international effort by top carbon-emitting countries to double investment in research and development of clean energy systems by 2020. The initiative had been announced in November 2015, on the heels of the historic Paris Agreement. The president's budget included a request for $7.7 billion in funding for clean energy research, of which about 80 percent would go to the Energy Department.

Outside of research and development funding, the president requested $2.9 billion for the Office of Energy Efficiency and Renewable Energy, which was $800 million more than the office received under fiscal 2016 enacted spending levels. Another $1.3 billion was requested for investments in clean transportation infrastructure and technology, and $4 billion was sought for loan guarantee authority to promote projects that would reduce greenhouse gas emissions. The president's total request for Energy Department discretionary spending amounted to $30.2 billion, or $600 million more than the department received for fiscal 2016.

Environmental Protection Agency

President Obama requested $8.3 billion in discretionary spending for the EPA in fiscal 2017, a minor increase over the agency's $8.1 billion budget for fiscal 2016. The total included $2 billion for states to fund wastewater treatment and water delivery systems, reflecting the administration's desire to prevent future contaminations of drinking water following the Flint, Michigan, water crisis. The president also sought $235 million for programs to reduce carbon emissions, including the Clean Power Plan rule, although the U.S. Supreme Court granted a stay of that rule the same day the budget request was released.

Food and Drug Administration

For the Food and Drug Administration (FDA), President Obama requested $4.8 billion in discretionary spending. The $80 million increase over the FDA's fiscal

2016 budget was to come from a combination of $2.75 billion in Congress-appropriated funds and $2.1 billion in new user fees from drug makers, medical devices, and tobacco products.

The president's request included $75 million for the administration's "moonshot" initiative to develop a cure for cancer. This funding would be used to create a virtual center for evaluating cures and diagnostic tests, to be partially staffed by FDA scientists. Other requested items included $25 million in new spending for food safety and $180 million in new user fees on food facilities and food importers.

Health and Human Services

For the Health and Human Services Department, President Obama requested $78.3 billion in funding—roughly $8 billion less than the department's enacted fiscal 2016 budget. The president's inclusion of $300 million for the Title X family planning program, representing a $13 million increase over fiscal 2016 funding levels, drew opposition from Republican lawmakers. Planned Parenthood derives a portion of its funding from the Title X program, and conservative members of Congress have repeatedly attempted to eliminate any federal support for that organization.

Other proposals were less controversial. The president requested a $1 billion increase for the National Institutes of Health (NIH), which would raise the agency's total budget to $33.1 billion in fiscal 2017. NIH had previously received a $2 billion budget boost in fiscal 2016. Administration officials said the additional funding would help NIH provide about 10,000 new grants in areas including brain research and precision medicine. The National Cancer Institute would also receive more funding under the president's request, which proposed a $5.9 billion budget for the organization. The 13 percent increase was intended to support the institute's research on a cure for cancer. A supplemental request of $1.8 billion in emergency funding to help fight the Zika virus, most of which would be given to the Health and Human Services Department, was also included in the president's budget proposal.

Homeland Security

Funding to enhance cybersecurity programs was a focus of the president's $47.3 billion budget request for the Homeland Security Department. Approximately $19 billion of that total would be dedicated to cybersecurity, representing a 35 percent increase over fiscal 2016 cybersecurity funds. This amount included $471 million for the National Cybersecurity Protection System, which maintains the EINSTEIN program that protects government networks from online threats. Nearly $275 million would go to the Continuous Diagnostics and Mitigation Program to provide hardware, software, and services that bolster security of .gov websites.

Border security continued to be a major component of the proposed Homeland Security budget. The president's request included $7 billion for salaries and benefits for roughly 21,000 Border Patrol agents and almost 24,000 Customs and Border Protection officers. OMB estimated that 2,070 new officers would be supported through a proposed increase in user fees. Customs and Border Protection would also receive $529 million to support its intelligence activities, while $353 million would be spent on security technology and infrastructure along the northern and southern borders. Immigration and Customs Enforcement would receive $2.2 billion to maintain nearly 31,000 detention beds, though Republicans in Congress were expected to push for more funding in this area.

Other funding requests in the president's proposed Homeland Security budget included $197.5 million for inspection and enforcement efforts overseas, including the Immigration Advisory Program, which seeks to prevent travelers identified as being high risk from getting on flights to the United States. The administration also sought funding to bolster community partnership programs that it views as critical to countering violent extremism at home.

Housing and Urban Development

The Department of Housing and Urban Development's (HUD) budget would essentially remain flat under the president's fiscal 2017 proposal, with the agency receiving $38 billion as compared to $37.8 billion in fiscal 2016. Initiatives seeking to end homelessness were highlighted in the budget proposal, such as HUD's Opening Doors program, which seeks to end family homelessness by 2020. The program would receive $11 billion over 10 years under the president's request, the majority of which would be allocated to providing project-based rental assistance for the elderly, families, and people with disabilities. Approximately $400 million of this total was requested as advance appropriations for fiscal 2018. The Local Housing Policy Grants program—which offers grants to states, localities, and regional coalitions to support efforts to increase available housing—would receive $300 million under the president's proposal, and another $25 million would be dedicated to testing projects that help homeless youth.

Intelligence Operations

The exact spending levels sought by the president in his budget proposals are classified. However, Director of National Intelligence James Clapper announced that the National Intelligence Program would receive $53.9 billion in fiscal 2017 if the president's request was granted. The National Intelligence Program accounts for the majority of the United States' intelligence spending, and Clapper's announcement signaled the administration's interest in boosting overall intelligence spending to levels not seen since fiscal 2012. The program received $50.5 billion in fiscal 2014 by comparison, and the president's fiscal 2015 request for program funding was $49.4 billion.

A summary of the administration's intelligence request explained that the fiscal 2017 budget request sought to place a greater focus on emerging threats, better integrating intelligence agencies, and helping the military adapt to countering the new challenges faced by the United States. For example, Defense Department officials indicated that intelligence efforts to thwart asymmetrical warfare tactics— such as those employed by Russia, China, and North Korea— would be emphasized in the administration's requested budget.

Declassified portions of the budget request showed the president was seeking $35 million to improve cyberintelligence integration, analysis, and planning; $26.9 million for language training; and funding to maintain the U-2 spy plane. The administration had previously requested to phase out the aircraft.

Interior

Interior Department funding would remain flat at $13.2 billion under the president's proposal. However, that total included a new allocation of $2 billion for the Coastal Climate Resilience Fund. This ten-year program seeks to provide resources to coastal communities to help them respond to the effects of climate change. The president proposed offsetting this new funding by repealing a 2006 law that established an offshore oil and gas revenue sharing agreement that directed a significant portion of the federal revenue derived from oil drilling in the Gulf of Mexico to Alabama, Louisiana, Mississippi, and Texas. These states received nearly $2 million through this agreement in fiscal 2015. Gulf state lawmakers vowed to do everything in their power to prevent the law's repeal.

President Obama's budget also called for the permanent reauthorization of the Land and Water Conservation Fund, which is co-administered by the USDA and the Department of the Interior. He requested $475 million in discretionary spending and $425 million in mandatory spending for the fund in fiscal 2017 while outlining a plan to transition to mandatory-only spending beginning in fiscal 2018. Congress had ignored a similar plan put forward by the president in his fiscal 2016 budget request, opting instead to provide only a three-year authorization and $450 million for the fund.

For the National Park Service, the president sought an increase of $206 million over fiscal 2016 to fund restoration and visitor projects planned as part of the service's centennial celebration. He also proposed providing $100 million in annual mandatory funding beginning in fiscal 2018.

Justice

President Obama's request for the Justice Department also largely maintained fiscal 2016 spending levels, with a discretionary budget of $29 billion proposed. While overall spending totals would essentially remain flat, the request did seek more than twice the fiscal 2016 budget for a program that would allow the Federal Bureau of Investigation (FBI) to circumvent encryption of messages and other information on cell phones. This program would receive nearly $70 million in funding in fiscal 2017 if his request was granted.

Other requests included $500 million per year over ten years for an initiative to reduce what the administration characterized as unnecessarily long sentences and unnecessary incarceration and to help build community trust in police. As part of its ongoing efforts to secure gun law reforms, the administration also sought funding for 230 new employees to enhance the criminal background check system for gun purchases and make it available twenty-four hours per day. Another $1.4 billion was requested to build a new FBI headquarters.

Labor

The president's budget request for the Labor Department reflected a focus on job training programs to further reduce unemployment, especially among youth. At the time the budget proposal was released, the unemployment rate was at an eight-year low of 4.9 percent. However, administration officials acknowledged that the unemployment rate was much higher for youth aged sixteen to twenty-four (12.2 percent in the summer of 2016). Requested funds included $5.5 billion in mandatory spending to create a pathway to the workforce for youths and young adults and $1.8 billion for Job Corps—a $66 million increase over fiscal 2016— which provides job training to approximately 50,000 young people every year. Another $2 billion in mandatory spending was requested for the Apprenticeship Training Fund to help employers and states create apprenticeship programs, and $6 billion was sought to support employment training, apprenticeship programs, and partnerships with private companies. In total, the Labor Department would receive $12.8 billion for fiscal 2017, or roughly $600 million more than its fiscal 2016 enacted level.

NASA

For NASA, the president requested $19 billion in fiscal 2017 funding, including $8.4 billion to support commercial development of rockets and spacecraft that could transport American astronauts to the International Space Station and on deep-space missions. Another $5.6 billion was requested for NASA's science branch, which oversees the Hubble Space Telescope, global land-imaging measurements, and the agency's mission to Jupiter's moon Europa. The president sought $790 million to support NASA's research into more efficient aircraft, which was 23 percent more than was appropriated for such activities in fiscal 2016, and $827 million for space technology programs.

State

President Obama requested a total of $52.2 billion for the State Department for fiscal 2017, of which $14.9 billion would go to the OCO. These totals roughly matched the department's fiscal 2016 funding.

Proposals to bolster counterterrorism efforts and deter Russian influence were expected to be well received in Congress. The president sought $4.1 billion to help the United States' Middle East allies fight ISIL, combat the organization's recruitment efforts, and provide humanitarian assistance in the region. This request included development funds for countries such as Jordan that are hosting large numbers of Syrian refugees to help them provide social services to displaced individuals. Public diplomacy efforts and economic assistance for European, Eurasian, and Central Asian countries facing potential threats from Russia would receive $953 million under the president's request. This funding would be used to support activities such as fighting local corruption, strengthening the rule of law, promoting European integration, and improving defense capabilities, with a focus on programs in Georgia, Moldova, and Ukraine.

Other proposals were expected to be controversial. These included the president's request for $6.2 billion in humanitarian assistance for refugees, internally displaced persons, and people affected by humanmade and natural disasters. The administration said this funding would help resettle 100,000 refugees from around the world in the United States—an initiative facing opposition by Republican lawmakers. The president also sought $1 billion for developmental aid to Central America in an effort to reduce the number of migrants trying to enter the United States from countries such as Honduras and El Salvador. The Feed the Future initiative, which helps improve agricultural productivity, food security, and nutrition in developing countries, would receive $978 million.

The president's request for the State Department also included $984 million for the Global Climate Change Initiative. The program helps developing countries prepare for the effects of global warming and would receive a total of $1.3 billion under President Obama's proposed budget. The State Department portion of that funding included $500 million in contributions to the United Nations Green Climate Fund, to which Republicans were likely to object. Republicans had attempted but failed to include language blocking U.S. funding to the Green Climate Fund during fiscal 2016 budget negotiations.

Transportation

President Obama requested $12 billion in discretionary spending for the Transportation Department for fiscal 2017. While this appeared to mark a decrease from the fiscal 2016 enacted level of $14.3 billion, it did not reflect the major increase in mandatory spending sought by the administration.

The president proposed increasing the department's mandatory budget from $76 billion in fiscal 2016 to $98.1 billion in fiscal 2017 to implement the administration's 21st Century Clean Transportation Plan. According to the White House, the plan sought to increase U.S. investment in clean transportation infrastructure by roughly 50 percent in addition to adjusting existing investment strategies to focus on cutting carbon emissions, reducing oil consumption, and creating new jobs. Resources from other federal agencies, including the Energy Department, the National Aeronautics and Space Administration (NASA),

and the Environmental Protection Agency (EPA), would be combined to help support this increase in funding. Additionally, the administration proposed implementing a new $10.25-per-barrel fee on domestic and imported oil, to be paid by oil companies, to help finance the program. Administration officials estimated the new fee would generate $319 billion for the Transportation Department over ten years and said this funding could be supplemented by increased revenue from a proposed corporate tax overhaul. Taxes on motor fuel have historically been a primary source of funding for the Transportation Department, but because these taxes have not increased since 1993, they no longer provide enough funds for the department's programs. The administration argued the new fee on oil barrels would help close this funding gap. Republicans generally opposed making such a significant shift in the structure of the Transportation Department's budget because Congress is not able to control mandatory spending.

Under the president's request, the new mandatory spending level would include $7.5 billion to fund new grant and formula programs at the Federal Highway Administration (FHA), such as the Transportation Investment Generating Economic Recovery grant program and the New Starts transit grants. These programs have traditionally been funded through general appropriations. The FHA's total budget would also increase by about $8.5 billion, while the Federal Transit Administration would receive an additional $11.8 billion and the Federal Railroad Administration would receive an increase of $1.7 billion.

Treasury

President Obama requested $13.1 billion for Treasury Department operations for fiscal 2017, representing a 4 percent increase over fiscal 2016. The department's total budget request amounted to $15.5 billion.

Of that total, $12.28 billion would go to the Internal Revenue Service (IRS), with a portion of that funding designated to improve customer service. Republicans had been reluctant to grant the president's requests for additional IRS funding following revelations that some agency employees had improperly targeted conservative organizations seeking 501(c)(3) status.

The president also sought increased funding for the Securities and Exchange Commission (SEC) and the Commodity Futures Trading Commission (CFTC), both of which regulate Wall Street. The SEC would receive an 11 percent increase, bringing its budget to $1.8 billion, while the CFTC would see a 31 percent increase, for a total budget of $330 million. Administration officials said the increased funding was intended to help both entities better enforce Dodd-Frank regulations, which Republicans had repeatedly sought to repeal.

Veterans Affairs

An increased budget request for the Department of Veterans Affairs (VA) reflected officials' estimates that VA facilities would treat a greater number of patients in fiscal 2017 and a desire to expand mental health services. The VA projected it would treat 7 million patients in its hospitals in 2017 and that outpatient visits would grow by about 3 percent over 2016.

In total, the president requested $181.2 billion in VA funding for fiscal 2017, as compared to the $162.7 billion enacted level for fiscal 2016. Nearly $104 billion of that total was for fiscal 2018 advance appropriations for VA medical programs. Approximately $75 billion in discretionary spending was sought, with the rest of the budget comprised of mandatory funds. The administration requested $7 billion to expand veterans' mental health services, including treatments for post-traumatic stress disorder and sexual trauma, as well as $664 million for medical research.

Fiscal 2017 Continuing Resolutions

At the beginning of 2016, Republican leadership in the House and Senate vowed to return to regular order in the annual budget process by passing a budget resolution for fiscal 2017. Some also expressed a desire to include reconciliation instructions in the budget resolution, though they did not indicate the specific policies that might be pursued through the reconciliation process. Budget reconciliation enables Congress to make changes to mandatory spending programs and tax policies as outlined in a budget resolution. It was last used by Democrats in 2010 to facilitate enactment of the Patient Protection and Affordable Care Act (PL 111-148). The process can be employed only if both chambers adopt a final budget resolution that includes reconciliation instructions.

It was not necessary for Congress to pass a budget resolution in 2016. Instead, lawmakers could have approved individual appropriations measures based on the top-line numbers included in a two-year budget agreement (PL 114-74) reached by President Obama and former House Speaker John Boehner, R-Ohio, in October 2015. That agreement raised the discretionary spending caps for fiscal 2016 and fiscal 2017, with fiscal 2017 caps set at $552 billion for defense and $518.5 billion for nondefense spending. However, House Budget Committee Chair Tom Price, R-Ga., and Senate Budget Committee Vice Chair Todd Rokita, R-Ind., set an ambitious timeline for having a budget resolution adopted in the House by late February or mid-March. Democrats, including House Budget Committee Ranking Member Nita Lowey, D-N.Y., urged Republicans to adhere to the 2015 budget deal, noting that any attempts to reduce discretionary spending below the agreed-upon caps could result in yet another budget stalemate and potentially a government shutdown.

Price indicated his intent to maintain the higher discretionary caps for fiscal 2017 but faced opposition from many of the most conservative House Republicans, including members of the House Freedom Caucus, who wanted to cut spending. Others said they were open to following

the budget deal, but only if other concessions were made, such as an agreement to reallocate some of the funds, take action to address the growing cost of entitlements, or implement budget process reforms. Concerns about the growing deficit also posed a challenge for budget resolution passage. Republicans had repeatedly pledged to pass a budget that would eliminate the deficit within ten years. With the Congressional Budget Office projecting the total deficit would grow to $9.4 trillion over the next ten years, a fiscal 2017 budget resolution would have to make even deeper spending cuts than those included in the fiscal 2016 budget resolution in order to achieve Republicans' goal.

Additional tension was created by Republicans' immediate dismissal of President Obama's fiscal 2017 budget request, released in early February. Price and Senate Budget Committee Chair Michael Enzi, R-Wyo., broke with years of precedent and announced they would not conduct their committees' usual hearings on the administration's proposal. White House officials and congressional Democrats decried the move as a breach of decorum and tried, unsuccessfully, to highlight items within the proposed budget that might appeal to Republicans.

While Price worked to find a compromise that most Republicans could agree to, the House Energy and Commerce and Ways and Means Committees both pursued cost-cutting legislation aimed at easing conservatives' opposition to discretionary spending increases. On March 15, the Energy and Commerce Committee approved a bill (HR 4725) that would cut about $25 billion in health care spending over ten years. To achieve these savings, the bill would reduce federal support for the Children's Health Insurance Program (CHIP), scale back the government's contributions to states for Medicaid, and close a loophole allowing lottery winners to receive Medicaid coverage, among other measures. The bill was staunchly opposed by Democrats and was never taken up on the House floor. The following day, the Ways and Means Committee reported a bill (HR 4723) seeking to recover health insurance subsidy overpayments. This bill did not see floor action, either.

On February 10, House Speaker Paul Ryan, R-Wis., announced that House appropriators would mark up their fiscal 2017 spending bills using the discretionary levels agreed to in the 2015 budget deal. By the end of the month, Republicans on the House Budget Committee had agreed on a resolution that sought to offset the $30 billion increase in discretionary spending with various options for cutting mandatory spending.

On March 16, the committee approved the resolution (H Con Res 125) by a vote of 20–16. All fourteen of the committee's Democrats voted against the measure, as did two Republican members. Democratic amendments offered during markup—including those seeking to provide billions of additional dollars for safe drinking water programs, raise the minimum wage, and remove resolution language allowing Medicare beneficiaries to shop for a plan on a health insurance exchange—were defeated by party-line votes. One amendment offered by Rep. Scott Garrett, R-N.J., a member of the Freedom Caucus, called for tens of billions of dollars in mandatory spending cuts to be attached to a must-pass bill that would force the Senate to consider the measure. This amendment was adopted at the end of markup, by a vote of 22–14. Leadership had already agreed to bring a "sidecar" bill to the House floor that would seek to cut mandatory spending by at least $30 billion over two years and $150 billion over ten years. Efforts to win conservatives' support for the budget resolution ultimately failed, however, with lawmakers stating they simply could not vote for higher discretionary spending levels as the deficit continued to balloon, and the House failed to meet the statutory April 15 deadline for budget adoption. Without a budget resolution in place, the House was prohibited from taking floor action on appropriations bills until May 15, per House rules.

Meanwhile, Senate Majority Leader Mitch McConnell, R-Ky., attempted to jumpstart his chamber's budget process by recycling pieces of House-passed fiscal 2016 spending bills that were still sitting in the Senate. The first appropriations bill produced from these efforts (S 2804) sought to fund energy and water projects for fiscal 2017 and moved quickly through committee to reach the Senate floor in mid-April. Progress on the measure quickly ground to a halt following adoption of an amendment by Sen. Tom Cotton, R-Ark., that would have prevented the Department of Energy from using funds to purchase heavy water from Iran. The White House threatened to veto the bill, claiming the amendment would disrupt the U.S.–Iran nuclear deal, and Democrats acted to block the bill's progress. The Senate would later pass the measure without Cotton's amendment, but the stumbling block was a sign of the partisan disagreements that would continue to derail budget negotiations throughout the year.

By the time Congress returned from a two-week recess at the end of April, some lawmakers were already acknowledging that a continuing resolution may be necessary to keep the government open past the end of fiscal 2016.

PREELECTION CONTINUING RESOLUTION

The budget process continued to fall apart as lawmakers in both chambers pursued standalone appropriations measures for fiscal 2017. As in prior years, negotiations were hampered by partisan disagreements over spending levels and various policy riders, such as a proposal by Democrats to add language prohibiting discrimination against LGBT workers in federal contracts to the House's Energy-Water spending bill. The appropriations process came to a grinding halt when Senate Democrats blocked the defense spending bill over concerns that Republicans would not pass other bills to fund domestic priorities.

Lawmakers began discussing a continuing resolution in June. However, Republicans disagreed over whether the resolution should last through December 2016 or into early 2017. On September 28, the Senate passed a ten-week continuing resolution (HR 5325) to fund the government through December 9 by a vote of 72–26. The Veterans Affairs–Military Construction spending bill that had passed both chambers but stalled in conference provided the legislative vehicle for the resolution, which was inserted into the bill language. The House cleared the measure by a vote of 342 to 85 later the same day, and it was signed by President Obama on September 29 (PL 114-223). In addition to fully funding military construction and veterans' programs through fiscal 2017, the resolution included $500 million in flood relief for Louisiana and other states, $1.1 billion in emergency spending to fight the spread of the Zika virus, and temporary funding to address the opioid epidemic.

Conservative lawmakers and outside groups criticized the measure's short timeline, with many conservatives preferring a spring 2017 end date that would allow the new administration and new Congress to make spending decisions for the remainder of the fiscal year.

POSTELECTION CONTINUING RESOLUTION

After the election, Republicans began pursuing another resolution that would fund the government through the first few months of 2017. The measure (HR 2028) was overwhelmingly approved by the House on December 8 by a vote of 326–96. The Senate approved the measure the next day by a vote of 63–36. It was signed by the president on December 10 (PL 114-254).

As adopted, the resolution funded the government until April 28, 2017. It provided $1.07 trillion in discretionary spending, as set by the 2015 budget deal. The resolution's funding provisions only applied to eleven of Congress's annual appropriations bills, since full-year funding for the Department of Veterans Affairs and military construction had already been authorized by the previous continuing resolution. Most programs and activities saw a roughly 0.2 percent cut in their fiscal 2016 budgets so that overall funding could be maintained at the fiscal 2017 cap. Overseas Contingency Operations (OCO), disaster relief funding, Social Security Administration continuing disability reviews, and the Department of Health and Human Services' health care fraud and abuse control activities were not subject to this across-the-board cut.

Due to the uncertainty surrounding budget negotiations and final spending totals for the remainder of the fiscal year, the resolution permitted payments for entitlements and other mandatory spending to be made up to thirty days past its expiration date. It also directed agencies to take the most limited funding action possible to continue existing projects and activities, meaning that no new projects or multiyear contracts should be initiated. Additionally, the resolution prevented programs that typically distribute full-year payments at the beginning of the fiscal year from doing so and stipulated that any program with high initial rates of operation should limit those activities.

The measure provided some departments and agencies with funding flexibility to ensure that certain activities were carried out. For example, it allowed flexible apportionment of funding for the Transportation Security Administration, Immigration and Customs Enforcement, Customs and Border Protection, and the Secret Service to maintain their staffing levels. Flexible apportionment was also permitted for the Agricultural Credit Insurance Fund to fund approved loans for farmers planning for spring planting season. Additionally, the measure continued the funding authorities for certain programs—such as the Temporary Assistance to Needy Families block grant program and the Supplemental Nutrition Assistance Program—that are usually financed by appropriations bills.

The measure provided $10.1 billion for the OCO, which was $1.6 billion less than the White House had requested. Of that total, $5.8 billion was allocated to the Department of Defense. These funds included $5.1 billion to support counterterrorism operations, such as the ongoing fight against ISIL, and $652 million for the European Reassurance Initiative. The remaining $4.3 billion in OCO funds were given to the State Department and the United States Agency for International Development (USAID). A $1.6 billion portion of this total was designated for embassy security.

In addition to OCO funds, the Department of Defense received $4.3 billion for operations and maintenance, $724 million for procurement and munitions, and $170 million for Joint Improvised Explosive Device Defeat Fund and research and development. A total of $290 million was provided for assistance to the Kurdish Peshmerga helping to fight ISIL. Personnel-related appropriations included $145 million for U.S. troops in Afghanistan, Iraq, and Syria, as well as other personnel supporting counterterrorism operations. Another $120 million was appropriated to support rotational troop deployments to Europe related to the European Reassurance Initiative.

The State Department also stood to receive $1.2 billion for economic and stabilization assistance, which includes programs that counter Russian influence, support for the Iraq sovereign loan guarantee, and community-based programs that help combat the spread of terrorist organizations. Another $916 million was allocated for humanitarian assistance to displaced individuals, while $404 million was provided for security assistance activities including civilian police training and explosive ordinance removal.

Funding for natural disaster relief formed an important piece of the resolution. Emergency supplemental funding of $2.7 billion was appropriated for Hurricane Matthew and flood recovery efforts in Louisiana, West Virginia, Texas, North and South Carolina, and Florida. Another $1.4 billion was designated as disaster relief spending, meaning that it would be counted toward the annual disaster funding cap rather than the discretionary spending cap. A total of $1 billion was appropriated for the Army Corps of Engineers' flood and coastal storm protection projects and dredging activities. Similarly, the Federal Highway Administration Emergency Relief program received $1 billion to repair damaged highways. The measure appropriated $206.1 million to the Department of Agriculture's emergency watershed protection and conservation programs to help mitigate the costs of damage to farms and ranches, nonindustrial private forests, and watersheds. NASA was given $75 million to repair hurricane-damaged facilities at the Kennedy Space Center in Cape Canaveral, Florida.

In response to the water crisis in Flint, Michigan, lawmakers authorized $170 million to be used to repair and rebuild the city's drinking water infrastructure, including the replacement of lead water service lines. The total appropriation included $20 million to create a lead exposure registry and an advisory committee that would review programs, services, and research on lead poisoning prevention. The Centers for Disease Control and Prevention's Childhood Lead Poisoning Prevention Program received $15 million to conduct screenings and referrals for children with elevated blood lead levels, while the Department of Health and Human Services' Healthy Start Program received the same amount to help reduce infant mortality and improve perinatal outcomes. The Flint-related funding was offset by a $170 million cut to CHIP.

Other noteworthy appropriations included $872 million for programs authorized by the 21st Century Cures Act (PL 114-255), which had just cleared Congress on December 7. These funds included $352 million for the National Institutes of Health Innovation Account disease research initiatives and $500 million for antiopioid addiction grants to states. Another provision authorized $45 million to temporarily extend health benefits for retired coal miners under the United Mine Workers Association 1993 Benefit Plan, which were scheduled to expire on December 31, 2016.

Additionally, the resolution included a measure allowing expedited Senate consideration of legislation waiving a waiting requirement that would prevent President-elect Donald Trump's nominee for secretary of defense, Marine Corps Gen. James Mattis, from taking office. Under existing law, a member of the military had to wait seven years between leaving active duty and becoming the defense secretary. Mattis had only been retired for about five years when he was nominated. The expedited process outlined by the resolution would only apply to Mattis's nomination, since the bill stipulated it could only be used for the first person nominated as defense secretary after the resolution's enactment who has been retired for at least three years.

Chronology of Action on Trade Policy

Trade issues seemed a likely area for President Obama to find agreement with Capitol Hill, particularly Republicans, but his agenda divided both parties in both chambers and led to fierce lobbying by a range of business groups and labor unions.

Obama placed a high priority on securing renewed fast-track trade authority that would allow him to negotiate foreign trade deals without the possibility that Congress could amend any agreement. Such authority, which Congress had granted to several of his predecessors, limited Congress to taking simple up or down votes on negotiated deals. Administration officials said such authority was needed to gain the trust of other countries that wanted to be sure agreements would not be later unraveled or altered and necessitate renegotiation.

But many Democrats and Republicans were hesitant to grant approval of fast-track authority while the administration withheld details of negotiations with even other nations on a Trans-Pacific Partnership Agreement, and with the European Union on another potential pact. Further, many Democrats were reluctant to grant fast-track authority unless they also could guarantee reauthorization of the Trade Adjustment Assistance (TAA) program that offered aid for workers displaced from their jobs by international competition. President Obama also wanted both TAA and fast-track renewal.

After more than two years of debate, lawmakers in 2015 extended the authorization for TAA and renewed fast-track trade authority, moving bills in tandem so they reached the president's desk together.

Congress did extend authorization for the Export-Import Bank, an institution that provided loans and financial guarantees for U.S. exports, but only after more than two years of debate that divided conservative and moderate Republicans, as well as the business community. But even after the 2015 reauthorization, the bank was left limited in its ability to issue loans because the Senate refused to vote on the nomination of a new board member, which was necessary to bring the board to a quorum.

REFERENCES

Discussion of trade action for the years 1945–1964 may be found in *Congress and the Nation Vol. I*, pp. 172–207; for the years 1965–1968, *Congress and the Nation Vol. II*, pp. 49–116; for the years 1969–1972, *Congress and the Nation Vol. III*, pp. 119–134; for the years 1973–1976, *Congress and the Nation Vol. IV*, pp. 125–137; for the years 1977–1980, *Congress and the Nation, Vol. V*, pp. 267–276; for the years 1981–1984, *Congress and the Nation Vol. VI*, pp. 95–112; for the years 1985–1988, *Congress and the Nation Vol. VII*, pp. 139–166; for the years 1989–1992, *Congress and the Nation Vol. VIII*, pp. 165–200; for the years 1993–1996, *Congress and the Nation Vol. IX*, pp. 151–184; for the years 1997–2000, *Congress and the Nation Vol. X*, pp. 147–170; for the years 2001–2004, *Congress and the Nation Vol. XI*, pp. 145–167; for the years 2005–2008, *Congress and the Nation Vol. XII*, pp. 197–213; for the years 2009–2012, *Congress and the Nation Vol. XIII*, pp. 191–202.

Table 2.6 Trade Balances (millions of dollars)

Year	Current Account	Goods	Services	Other
2000	$-416,317	$-446,942	69,605	$-38,981
2001	-396,697	-422,512	60,173	-34,358
2002	-457,800	-475,842	57,678	-39,635
2003	-518,657	-542,273	51,728	-28,113
2004	-629,327	-666,364	61,466	-24,430
2005	-739,796	-784,133	76,219	-31,882
2006	-798,478	-838,788	86,389	-46,079
2007	-713,389	-822,743	123,677	-14,323
2008	-681,343	-833,957	131,655	20,959
2009	-381,636	-510,550	126,893	2,021
2010	-449,471	-650,156	150,777	49,908
2011	-457,725	-744,139	187,301	99,113
2012	-440,416	-741,475	206,819	94,240
2013	-349,200	-702,200	240,400	112,600
2014	-373,900	-751,500	261,100	116,500
2015	-434,400	-761,800	261,500	65,900
2016	-451,700	-752,500	247,700	53,100

SOURCE: Bureau of Economic Analysis, Department of Commerce, "U.S. International Transactions."

NOTE: The current account balance includes the balances on trade in goods, services, and net unilateral transfers such as private remittances. Income and transfers make up the "Other" column.

Meanwhile, the U.S. Trade Representative signed the twelve-nation Trans-Pacific Partnership Agreement in February 2016, but questions over Senate ratification of the deal became a contentious topic in that year's presidential race. President-elect Donald Trump made his opposition to trade deals a major component of his campaign and vowed he would withdraw the United States from the agreement after he took office in 2017. He also vowed to halt negotiations with the European Union on the Transatlantic Trade and Investment Partnership, which were ongoing at the end of Obama's administration, and to renegotiate the North American Free Trade Agreement, which he said had hurt U.S. workers and businesses.

2013-2014

The Obama administration during the 113th Congress was repeatedly frustrated by lawmakers' inaction on several of his trade priorities, including fast-track trade negotiation authority, reauthorization of the Trade Adjustment Assistance Act to ensure expanded assistance for displaced workers, reauthorization of the Export-Import Bank, and support for ongoing negotiations on two major trade deals.

The issues divided both parties on both sides of Capitol Hill and became intertwined in prolonged debate.

In Obama's State of the Union speech on February 12, 2013, he said he intended to complete negotiations on a Trans-Pacific Partnership that year. At the same time, he announced new talks on a Transatlantic Trade and Investment Partnership with the European Union, "because trade that is free and fair across the Atlantic supports millions of good-paying American jobs." Negotiations were not complete at the end of the 113th Congress and resumed in 2015.

With little information about the exact details of those potential deals, conservative Republicans and many Democrats refused to grant the president fast-track trade authority. Many Republicans also believed that the TAA program was too costly and ineffective.

Senate Finance Chair Max Baucus, D-Mont., wanted to move measures on both fast-track authority and trade adjustment assistance. But he resigned his seat on February 6, 2014, after he was confirmed as ambassador to China. The gavel was then handed to Ron Wyden, D-Ore., who had long been a supporter of trade but was concerned about some aspects of the pending TPP negotiations—including intellectual property protections. He accused the Obama administration of too much secrecy in trade talks.

The administration announced September 19, 2014, that it would proceed with a labor enforcement case against Guatemala under the Central American Free Trade Agreement. Some said the announcement was aimed at easing concerns of critics who said Obama had been too soft on trade. Sen. Wyden called the action important because labor rights were a pillar of our nation's trade policy.

Still, lawmakers declined to move on measures to renew fast-track trade authority, and they allowed a 2011 law that had expanded the TAA program to expire. Congress provided a temporary reauthorization, through June 2015, for the Export-Import Bank after being unable to resolve differences over the effectiveness of the bank and the fairness and transparency of its lending practices.

At the end of 2014, as McConnell prepared to lead the new Senate Republican majority, he said he wanted to make progress on trade issues—including fast-track, the TPP, and supporting bilateral investment with China.

Fast-Track Negotiating

Lawmakers in both parties and both chambers declined to move on measures to renew fast-track trade negotiation authority, which would have allowed the president to strike trade deals that could not be amended or filibustered by Congress. Most lawmakers were concerned about a lack of transparency in ongoing U.S. talks regarding a multination trade deal and a potential trade partnership with the European Union, making them wary of relinquishing control over the details of such deals.

Under fast-track trade authority, first granted in 1974 and later renamed Trade Promotion Authority or TPA, a trade agreement must receive an up or down vote by Congress, without amendment, within 90 days of being submitted by the White House. Supporters argued such authority made it easier for the president to negotiate deals with other nations that could be assured any final agreement would not later be changed in Washington. Congress had never rejected a trade agreement submitted that way, although trade deals with Colombia, Panama, and South Korea had required some accommodations for some lawmakers.

TPA had lapsed in the mid-1990s when lawmakers were concerned about abrogating their authority to regulate commerce with foreign powers. The most recent grant of authority (PL 107-210) was cleared in 2002 and expired in 2007.

2013 DEBATE

At the start of the 113th Congress, business groups lobbied Congress and the White House to renew fast-track authority so the president could move forward in opening markets around the world.

On March 1, 2013, the administration released a 2013 trade policy agenda that included reestablishing fast-track authority. Throughout Obama's first term in office, Republicans had criticized the president for not requesting a renewal of the authority, and business groups said it was evidence that Obama placed little priority on trade. Sen. Orrin G. Hatch of Utah, the top Republican on Finance, called the authority "the linchpin" of U.S. trade policy.

But some congressmen, like Sander M. Levin of Michigan, top-ranking Democrat on the House Ways and Means Committee, did not want to clear fast-track until negotiations on the Trans-Pacific Partnership (TPP) were complete so they could make sure they liked the agreement before Obama signed off on it.

Senate Finance Committee Chair Max Baucus, D-Mont., was eager to renew fast-track authority. "Fast-track authority will help us conclude the TPP negotiations, and that will bring concrete benefits for American ranchers, farmers, businesses and workers," he said at an April 24 hearing.

In April, Baucus floated the idea of linking TPA with a renewal of the Trade Adjustment Assistance (TAA) program that aided workers who had lost their jobs due to global trade. During a Senate Finance Committee hearing the previous month, he had called the programs "two sides of the same coin—making trade work." A similar deal was made when Congress renewed fast-track trade authority in 2002.

Sen. Sherrod Brown, D-Ohio, said he might support such a deal, but organized labor opposed it. "TAA is an ongoing program that workers are going to need in response to all of our current trade policy," Celeste Drake, a trade policy advisor for the AFL-CIO, told *CQ Roll Call* in April. "It doesn't sort of make up for" future agreements that might cost U.S. jobs.

On June 13, 2013, Sens. Rob Portman, R-Ohio, and Maria Cantwell, D-Wash., wrote in a *CQ Roll Call* column that fast-track trade authority would "support American job creation and keep our nation competitive in the global economy while not costing taxpayers any money." They said it not only would allow the president to negotiate trade deals that could not be amended by Congress but also would "outline principles and framework for trade negotiations, while ensuring continued congressional consultation. TPA principles have guided U.S. bilateral negotiations with countless countries from Chile to Australia, helping us knock down barriers to exports."

On November 13, 2013, 151 Democrats signed a letter to the White House saying they would oppose renewing fast-track authority unless the administration agreed to consult with lawmakers before negotiating on trade matters. "Beyond traditional tariff issues, these [issues] include policies related to labor, patent and copyright, land use, food, agriculture and product standards, natural resources, the environment, professional licensing competition, state-owned enterprises and government procurement policies, as well as financial, healthcare, energy, e-commerce, telecommunications and other service sector regulations," the letter said.

Twenty-two House Republicans also wrote to Obama opposing fast-track authority. "By requiring the House to vote on a bill given a preset period of time, it takes the floor schedule out of the hands of the House majority and gives it to the president," they wrote in a November 12 letter.

Rep. Devin Nunes, R-Calif., chair of the House Ways and Means trade subcommittee, had told *CQ Roll Call* in July that lawmakers "have absolutely no reason to say they are not informed, because if they want to spend the time, dedicate the resources, and go down to USTR and ask for meetings," U.S. negotiations "will bend over backwards."

Labor unions said they were concerned about the possibility of trade negotiations jeopardizing U.S. jobs. They pointed to reports showing that free-trade deals such as the North American Free Trade Agreement of 1994 (PL 103-182) had led to U.S. job losses and wage stagnation. A 2011 Commerce Department report, for example, concluded that large multinational companies had cut 2.9 million jobs in the United States during the previous decade while adding 2.4 million jobs overseas.

"We're not against trade, we're just against trade that keeps costing us jobs," said Leo Gerard, international president of the United Steelworkers.

2014 MEASURES IGNORED

Baucus and Sen. Orrin Hatch of Utah, ranking Republican on the Finance Committee, introduced a fast-track renewal measure (S 1900) on January 9, 2014. "Exporting is such a large percent of our economy and offers such good-paying jobs that, frankly, I am perplexed more Americans don't want to work harder to get trade agreements passed so we can export more and get more good-paying jobs in America," Baucus said when introducing the measure.

House Ways and Means Committee Chair Dave Camp, R-Mich., introduced a companion measure (HR 3830), which ranking Democrat Sander Levin of Michigan said would not give Congress a large enough role in overseeing trade agreements.

During his State of the Union address, Obama said fast-track authority should be one area where the two parties could cooperate "to protect our workers, protect our environment, and open new markets to new goods stamped 'Made in the USA.' China and Europe aren't standing on the sidelines. Neither should we."

But Sen. Majority Leader Harry Reid, D-Nev., immediately announced that any proposal to renew TPA would not move in the Senate that year. "I'm against fast track. . . . Everyone knows how I feel about this. . . . Everyone would be well advised not to push this right now," he told reporters January 29, 2014.

Sen. Sherrod Brown, D-Ohio, and other Finance Committee Democrats wrote to U.S. Trade Representative Michael Froman on January 9, 2014, saying they would not support legislation that did not "provide mechanisms that enable Congress to hold USTR more accountable through the negotiation process or give USTR greater authority to negotiate basic standards on good governance and human rights."

Union-backed Democrats also vowed not to allow a trade bill to pass in 2014. "More fast-track authority to push a trade deal that's bad for American workers and consumers is a nonstarter," Rep. Rosa DeLauro, D-Conn., said during a January 29 conference call organized by Public Citizen's Global Trade Watch. A poll released January 30 by the Democratic firm Hart Research Associations and the Republican firm Chesapeake Beach Consulting showed 62 percent of voters opposed fast-track trade authority for the president.

With midterm elections nearing, Obama did not work hard to sell Congress and the public on fast-track or the TPP deal. And Wyden, taking over the Senate Finance Committee after Baucus's resignation in early 2014, said he was in no hurry to act on fast-track while details remained vague on discussions about TPP as well as those on the Transatlantic Trade and Investment Partnership (TTIP) being negotiated at the time between the European Union and the United States.

On September 10, 2014, about 550 organizations, led by the Sierra Club, AFL-CIO, and Public Citizen, wrote to Wyden, urging him to replace the traditional fast-track

U.S.–CHINA BILATERAL INVESTMENT TREATY

Treasury Secretary Jacob J. Lew in July 2013 announced the administration was restarting a so-called strategic and economic dialogue with China that aimed to complete a bilateral investment treaty. Discussions continued during the remainder of President Obama's administration, but lawmakers who supported the talks became more skeptical amid reports of China cybersecurity threats to U.S. companies.

Since 1979, total U.S. trade with China had increased from $2 billion to $562 billion, and the United States listed China as its second-largest trading partner, third-largest export market, and largest source of imports. U.S. negotiators hoped a treaty would improve the investment climate for American companies in China by improving legal protections and procedures to resolve disputes. They also wanted China to pledge to treat U.S. investors the same as Chinese investors.

Negotiations on a Bilateral Investment Treaty had started in 2008 but had paused while the Obama administration and lawmakers reevaluated the usefulness of such treaties, according to Rep. Kevin Brady, R-Texas. "We sort of pulled the truck to the side of the road, took a look at the engine, made some adjustments. But now it's really time to get back on down the road, and it's an important tool," Brady said at a House Ways and Means Committee hearing on July 18, 2013, according to *CQ Roll Call*.

Michael Froman, the U.S. trade representative, said in July that, for the first time, China already had promised to make it easier for U.S. companies to invest in more sectors in China, but details had yet to be worked out.

House Republicans, meanwhile, urged the treaty be completed alongside Trans-Pacific Partnership (TPP) negotiations, even though it would only be up to the Senate to ratify any final deal. Many observers saw TPP as a counterbalance to China's growing economic power and questioned whether the concessions China had made so far in that investment treaty might indicate it wanted to sign onto the TPP deal.

Meanwhile, critics of China warned about the country's economic and currency policy, which created an unfair playing field for U.S. industries—particularly high-tech manufacturing, finance, and energy—and suggested China might be unwilling to change those policies as part of any deal.

As the largest Republican majority in decades prepared to take over Congress in 2014, many analysts were optimistic about improved U.S.–China relations and progress on a bilateral investment treaty. Supporters of trade expansion included incoming Senate Majority Leader Mitch McConnell of Kentucky and House Speaker John A. Boehner of Ohio.

Fifty-one American business executives signed a letter, written by the U.S.–China Business Council, that said, "There are few other commercial outcomes that would gain as much support from business leaders in both the United States and China."

(Continued)

---

authority model with "a new system for negotiation and implementing trade agreements that provides for more congressional and public accountability."

Lawmakers briefly discussed bringing up a bill during the lame-duck session but kept it off the table.

After the 2014 midterm election, House Speaker John Boehner, R-Ohio, said he might not list renewal of fast-track authority as a priority for the 114th Congress, and he criticized Obama for not making a strong request to Congress for working harder to woo GOP and Democratic votes on a potential measure.

"I've made clear that not only [does] the president have to ask for it, but he has to work to build bipartisan support to get it passed," Boehner said during a December 5 press conference, according to *CQ Roll Call*.

Trade Adjustment Assistance

Congress in 2013 let expire a 2011 law that had expanded a five-decades-old program of assistance to U.S. workers whose jobs were adversely affected by free trade. The program was a priority among Democrats, but Republicans fought against renewing a program they said was ineffective.

Trade adjustment assistance programs had been created in 1962 to aid workers who had lost jobs in the wake of U.S. trade deals with other countries. After the start of the recession, the programs had been expanded under the 2009 economic stimulus law (PL 111-5) to cover service-sector workers and increase a health care tax credit for unemployed workers.

Those changes expired in 2011, and Congress then renewed many of them (PL 112-40) along with approval of Colombia, Panama, and South Korea trade pacts. Democrats at that time had insisted on a reauthorization of TAA in exchange for their vote on the long-stalled trade deals, and all of them supported the final measure. The program's benefits were slightly pared down to address conservatives' concerns that the program was becoming too expensive, though a majority of House and Senate Republicans still voted against it.

That extension was scheduled to expire at the end of 2013, after which the TAA programs would revert to pre-2009 status.

Renewal of the expanded program was a top priority for Democrats in 2013. Senate Finance Chair Baucus vowed to renew it and initially dangled the idea of linking it to fast-track trade authority. But labor unions did not like that

(Continued)

The executives urged Obama to press China's President Xi Jinping for a list of market barriers his country would be willing to relax. They said if China would "open markets to American manufacturers, agriculture producers, and service providers, you will find the business community fully engaged and supportive of your leadership to gain Senate approval of the treaty."

Rep. Rick Larsen, D-Wash., co-chair of the U.S.–China Working Group, said he was confident the Chinese would reduce its list of barriers.

In July, the two countries agreed to a timetable for reaching agreement on major issues. In November 2014, Froman offered some optimism when announcing an agreement with China —applauded by the U.S. Chamber of Commerce and the National Association of Manufacturers—to eliminate tariffs on high-tech products. The deal, made through the World Trade Organization (WTO), would eliminate tariffs in fifty-four economies, including the United States and China. It was the first WTO agreement to eliminate tariffs on high-tech products since 1996.

However, Obama and many lawmakers of both parties remained concerned about cybersecurity issues related to China. Earlier in 2014, the Justice Department had indicted five Chinese military hackers for "economic espionage and other offenses directed at six American victims in the U.S. nuclear power, metals and solar products industries."

In a November 20, 2014, report to Congress, the U.S.–China Economic and Security Review Committee suggested lawmakers sanction Chinese firms "that benefit from trade secrets or other information obtained through cyber intrusions or other illegal means." China immediately pulled out of cybersecurity talks planned for the following summer.

Former Armed Services Committee Chair Carl Levin, D-Mich., and his successor Sen. John McCain, R-Ariz., cosponsored a measure that would have required the president to block imports of products using stolen U.S. technology or made by companies alleged to have been conducting criminal activity.

Obama told the Business Roundtable in December 2014, "We are pressing [China] very hard on issues of cybersecurity and cyber theft, mostly in the commercial area. . . . It is indisputable that they engage in it, and it is a problem."

Negotiations on the investment treaty continued in 2015, with both sides submitting their first so-called negative list proposals that outlined areas not open to negotiation. They presented revised, narrowed lists the following year, and the treaty was discussed at the September 2016 G-20 Summit in Hangzhou, China. But no final agreement was announced, and the BIT was not completed by the end of Obama's second term. Incoming President Donald Trump was unclear about his position on such a treaty.

---

idea and conservative Republicans increasingly argued that the TAA program was ineffective and too inexpensive.

In July 2013, Baucus introduced a bill (S 1357) that would have renewed the expanded TAA programs throughout 2020. But the bill was not considered in committee after his resignation, and no companion House bill had been introduced.

In 2014, midterm elections complicated the thinking of Democrats, who knew that their control of the Senate was at stake. Many Democrats hoped to push through a renewal during the lame-duck session of Congress after the elections, but that hope did not come to fruition.

With the expiration of the 2011 TAA Extension Act, the program operated under sunset provisions that limited eligibility for service workers, dropped a health coverage tax credit approved in a 2002 reauthorization, and ended case management services. Unemployed workers were eligible for the program only if their firms had shifted their production or outsourced their jobs to a country with which the United States had a free trade agreement. Congress included funding for the TAA program in the fiscal 2015 omnibus spending measure (HR 83—PL 113-235) cleared in December.

Trans-Pacific Partnership

The Trans-Pacific Partnership was a top priority for the administration as it sought to pivot foreign policy toward Asia to counter China's growing economic power, but Congress was increasingly skeptical of the deal, as U.S. negotiators revealed few details of the talks. Lawmakers on both sides of the aisle, who ultimately would be asked to sign off on any trade agreement, raised a range of concerns about the potential deal's effects on workers and businesses and refused to move on Obama's other legislative priorities regarding trade until they obtained more information.

Meanwhile, negotiations among the twelve participating countries failed to conclude before the end of the 113th Congress, as the Obama administration had hoped.

Negotiations initially included ten other countries: Vietnam, Brunei, Chile, Canada, Malaysia, Mexico, New Zealand, Peru, Australia, and Singapore. In April 2013, Obama welcomed Japan into the group, raising concerns among automakers, insurers, and agricultural interests, along with unions and some domestic manufacturers. Japan's involvement particularly jeopardized the support of the auto industry for TPP.

U.S. TRADE NEGOTIATOR

U.S. Trade Representative Michael Froman helped President Obama achieve one of his top trade priorities: completion of the twelve-nation Trans-Pacific Partnership agreement before he left office, but not in time to save it from election-year politics and its expected demise due to opposition from the incoming Trump administration in early 2017.

Froman faced intense bipartisan pressure on Capitol Hill as negotiations dragged out through the 113th and 114th Congresses and few details were made public. Members of both parties criticized him for holding secret negotiations even while pressuring lawmakers to approve fast-track trade negotiating authority that would allow the president to secure a deal that could not be amended by Congress.

When Obama nominated Froman, his former law school classmate, Froman had been serving as deputy White House national security adviser for international economic affairs. He had helped complete trade agreements with Colombia, Panama, and South Korea—all of which the George W. Bush administration had negotiated under fast-track trade authority.

The Senate's consideration of his nomination was neither partisan nor controversial.

The Senate Finance Committee approved the nomination by voice vote on June 11, 2013, after minimal discussion. A week later, the Senate confirmed his nomination by a 93–4 vote. Democrats Carl Levin of Michigan, Joe Manchin II of W.Va., Elizabeth Warren of Mass., and Bernard Sanders, I-Vt., opposed the confirmation.

Warren said she was concerned about the transparency of ongoing trade negotiations—particularly the Trans-Pacific Partnership (TPP). "The American people have the right to know more about our negotiations that will have a dramatic impact on our working men and women, on our environment, on our economy, on the Internet," Warren said before the Senate vote, according to *CQ Roll Call*.

She was particularly concerned about the possibility of such deals to allow big banks to bypass U.S. financial regulations. Froman had said during his June 6 confirmation hearing, according to *CQ Roll Call*, "There's nothing that we are going to do through a trade agreement to weaken our financial regulation, to roll back Dodd-Frank or to roll back the efforts that the administration and Congress have worked on for the last four years to reform our financial . . . system."

Froman, a native of Marin County, Calif., had earned a bachelor's degree in public and international affairs at Princeton University, a Ph.D. in international relations at Oxford University, and a law degree at Harvard Law School. Before joining the Obama administration, he had held several executive positions at Citigroup and, earlier in his career, had served in the Treasury Department during the Clinton administration.

Froman replaced U.S. Trade Representative Ron Kirk, who had served in the role during Obama's first term.

Many observers feared Japan would negotiate the end of a 2.5 percent U.S. tariff on Japanese cars and a 25 percent tariff on Japanese trucks sold in the United States without any concessions to the U.S. industry in the Japanese market. Such a move would further hurt the U.S. auto industry, they said. The United States had recorded a $76.3 billion trade deficit with Japan in 2012—led only by the deficit with China—and automotive products made up more than two-thirds of the deficit. The deficit at that time was up from $31 billion from twenty years earlier.

Dozens of House and Senate Democrats in March had complained about Japan's barriers to the U.S. auto industry and warned in a letter to Obama that the American auto industry—which was still struggling to recover from the recent recession—would suffer even more if Japan was allowed to join the negotiations.

"These long-standing, economically harmful practices are not susceptible to cursory negotiation at this stage, three years into the U.S. involvement in the TPP negotiations and close to the administration's target date of concluding talks by the end of this year," stated the March 14 letter. Reps. Dave Camp and Sander M. Levin of Michigan, chair and ranking Democrat on the Ways and Means Committee, also raised concerns.

The auto industry sent a warning: "Adding a complicated trading partner to the negotiations will certainly delay TPP's conclusion and may keep it from ever coming to fruition," said Matt Blunt, president of the American Automotive Policy Council, which represented U.S. car makers.

But Froman, Obama's deputy national security adviser for international economic affairs, who would soon be nominated as the new U.S. Trade Representative (USTR), said April 12, "Having Japan in TPP and contributing to the high standards of TPP is good for the U.S., it's good for the Trans-Pacific Partnership as a whole, and it's very good for the multilateral trading system itself."

Labor unions, meanwhile, were increasingly opposing TPP negotiations because they feared a deal would hurt U.S. jobs and they worked to block renewal of the president's fast-track trade authority.

There were other concerns that hampered congressional backing for TPP negotiations. Elizabeth Warren, D-Mass., said she feared a deal might provide large banks a way to gut existing regulations put in place five years earlier by the Dodd-Frank Wall Street Reform and Consumer Protection Act (PL 111-203), a 2010 financial services reform law that aimed to avert a Wall Street meltdown like the collapse that ignited the Great Recession. Rep. Mark Pocan, D-Wisc., feared a deal might enable other countries to bypass "Buy American" requirements Congress had imposed during the recession.

In September, U.S. reports showed a rise in the U.S. trade deficit, reaching $39.1 billion in July, and supporters of fast-track and the TPP—led by the U.S. Chamber of Commerce and the North American Manufacturers Association—urged action on such trade deals to open new markets. But opponents of such trade deals said the report only proved that past deals had hurt jobs and exports.

In mid-November 2013, 151 Democrats signed a letter to Obama requesting that he consult lawmakers before negotiating various issues within the TPP, and they threatened to withhold fast-track authority otherwise.

"We will oppose 'Fast Track' Trade Promotion Authority or any other mechanism delegating Congress' constitutional authority over trade policy that continues to exclude us from having a meaningful role in the formative stages of trade agreements and throughout negotiating and approval processes."

2014 TALKS

Froman, confirmed as USTR in June 2013, said during a House Ways and Means Committee hearing April 3, 2014, he would proceed with TPP negotiations regardless of Congress's continued inaction on fast-track authority. He also said he hoped to complete a deal that year even while admitting resolving major issues with Japan—such as market access for autos and agricultural goods—was proving difficult. He said congressional members were given information and allowed to provide feedback all along the way.

"Done right, trade policy creates opportunities for American workers, farmers and ranchers; manufacturers and service providers; innovators, creators, investors and businesses," Froman said during the hearing.

But the administration saw that negotiations on TPP would not be finished by the end of the year as Obama had hoped. In November, TPP-participating nations said they were making major progress and hoped to release an agreement in 2015. Negotiations had yet to be finalized on a range of other issues apart from automobiles and agricultural products, such as how to address state-owned enterprises, labor and human rights standards, and market barriers.

Following the GOP gains in the mid-term elections, which put Republicans back in control of the Senate, Senate Republican Leader Mitch McConnell said he told Obama, "Send us some trade agreements."

But several House Democrats—including DeLauro; George Miller of California, ranking Democrat on the House Education and the Workforce Committee; Loretta Sanchez of California; and Pocan—maintained their opposition to a TPP deal, saying it did not appear to include meaningfully enforceable labor protections.

U.S.–EU Trade Deal

President Obama in his February 2013 State of the Union address to Congress announced his administration would begin negotiating a new trade agreement with the European Union in hopes of boosting economic growth on both sides of the Atlantic.

The business community, which in previous years had criticized Obama for a lack of ambition in opening new trade deals, applauded the announcement. "We have long called for such a pact to eliminate tariffs, ensure compatible regulatory regimes, and address investment, services, and procurement," said Myron Brilliant, senior vice president for international affairs at the U.S. Chamber of Commerce.

A High-Level Working Group of U.S. and EU officials had started working in November 2011 to determine ways to improve the transatlantic relationship as trade had remained stagnant. According to the Census Bureau, the United States reported a $125.9 billion trade deficit with Europe in 2012. The overall value of trade had grown less than 4 percent since 2008. The group had been expected to issue a formal report at the end of 2012 but had yet to complete it.

In late summer 2013, the United States began negotiating a Transatlantic Trade and Investment Partnership (TTIP) with several European countries. But negotiators faced difficult obstacles to agreement, including U.S. labeling requirements for imported wines, which many European countries did not like, and the EU's restrictions on genetically modified food products from the United States. DuPont thus far had been unable to obtain EU approval for its genetically engineered soybeans, for example.

Negotiators also would have to overcome differences in general regulatory approaches; the United States used a more science-based approach, while the EU had a more risk-averse approach that resulted in banning new technologies whose risks might be uncertain.

Senate Finance Chair Baucus and ranking member Hatch had raised with the administration their concerns about access for U.S. agricultural exports and intellectual property protections under the deal, along with other issues. U.S. agribusiness groups warned they would lobby against any agreement that did not ease Europe's food safety standards.

Rep. Maxine Waters, D-Calif., asked the administration not to include financial services provisions in the agreement, warning such provisions could undermine regulatory efforts in the United States and other countries to address cross-border oversight. Specifically, Waters and other Democrats feared a trade deal could override certain provisions of the Dodd-Frank financial law in favor of international laws. For example, the deal could affect rules on technology development that would override U.S. rules.

Sen. Pat Roberts, R-Kan., raised concerns that the EU was attempting to use the potential deal to protect European producers' use of so-called geographical indicators in names, such as Parmigiano Reggiano cheese made in Italy, and Feta cheese, originating from the eastern Mediterranean region. EU rules protected such geographical indicators for member countries.

German Chancellor Angela Merkel was a strong proponent of the negotiations, saying she wanted to see something in place by 2015. She saw the deal in part as an opportunity to boost energy cooperation across the Atlantic and to make her country more independent from energy supplies from Russia.

Negotiations on TTIP were briefly threatened in 2014 after reports of extensive U.S. surveillance overseas—specifically a National Security Administration surveillance on Merkel's cell phone. Lawmakers worked to allay her concerns, and she resumed her faith in a trade agreement.

Export-Import Bank

Congress provided a temporary reauthorization, through June 30, 2015, for the Export-Import (Ex-Im) Bank while they worked to resolve differences over the effectiveness and legitimacy of the institution that provided about $20 billion annually in direct loans, financing, and loan guarantees for foreign buyers to support the purchase of U.S. products overseas.

The Republican party was particularly divided during heated debates on renewing the bank's charter. The business community, including groups such as the Chamber of Commerce and the National Association of Manufacturers, pushed for a multiyear reauthorization of the bank. More conservative groups such as Club for Growth and Heritage Action for America pushed for an end to the bank.

Several U.S. corporations, such as Boeing, relied on the bank to help promote sales overseas and depended on Ex-Im Bank financing when loans were hard to obtain. The business community had generally long believed the bank helped promote U.S. goods abroad, and typically the bank faced little opposition on Capitol Hill.

But Republicans in 2012 had started arguing the bank's activities distorted the free market. A three-year reauthorization (PL 112-122) was cleared in May 2012, with unanimous Democratic support, but Republicans from both chambers were split.

DEBATE

In 2013, debate over the role of the Export-Import Bank initially delayed the confirmation of Fred Hochberg as president of the bank. He had held the held the position since 2009, but his term expired on January 20, 2013, and he needed to be renominated and confirmed. The Club for Growth led opposition to Hochberg's confirmation. But on June 6, the Senate Banking Committee approved his nomination by a vote of 20–2, with Republicans Tom

Coburn of Oklahoma and Patrick J. Toomey of Pennsylvania voting no by proxy. The Senate confirmed his nomination by a vote of 82–17 on July 17.

At the start of 2014, House Speaker Boehner said reauthorization of the Export-Import Bank was a priority, with its expiration looming on September 30. Rep. Kevin McCarthy, R-Calif., had supported the bank's continuance. But when House Majority Leader Eric Cantor lost a June 10, 2014, primary in Virginia, McCarthy was in line for the leadership position and switched his position on the bank. McCarthy, who had voted in 2012 to extend the bank's authority, said he would allow its charter to expire because its job was something the private sector could do.

Several other House Republicans also opposed extending the bank's charter, saying the bank provided excessive government intervention in the free-market by picking winners and losers.

"There is probably no better poster child of the Washington insider economy and corporate welfare than the Export-Import Bank," House Financial Services Committee Chair Jeb Hensarling, R-Texas, said in a speech before the Heritage Foundation on May 20, 2014. "Its demise would clearly be one of the few achievable victories for the Main Street competitive economy left in this Congress. I believe it is a defining issue for our party and our movement."

In early April, Financial Services Committee ranking Democrat Maxine Waters of California pressed for reauthorization, saying the bank had supported 1.2 million private-sector jobs over the previous five years. According to *CQ Roll Call*, Waters said during a committee discussion that the bank was self-sustaining and the previous year had recorded a profit of more than $1 million, which benefited U.S. taxpayers.

However, in a statement released April 25, Hensarling warned about a risk to taxpayers, noting the bank's inspector general reported in 2012 that the bank's risk-management framework and governance structure "are not commensurate with its size, scope and strategic ambitions of the institution."

In April 2014, Hochberg criticized the bank's conservative opponents. "There's a vocal minority out there who can't stomach the thought that the government might have a role to play in empowering U.S. businesses to compete across the globe," he said. He said such criticism was costing U.S. businesses and cited as an example a small renewable energy company in California that reported losing a $57 million order in the Philippines after a South Korean company said the United States might not get financing.

But, according to *CQ Roll Call*, Club for Growth President Chris Chocola said April 24, "The Export-Import Bank is nothing more than a taxpayer-backed slush fund that benefits a few politically connected companies more than anyone else, and it's time to shut it down."

In May, thirty conservative groups released a statement opposing reauthorization, saying the bank "tilts the playing field away from mid-sized and small businesses in favor of large, politically connected corporations." The statement mentioned a study by the trade association Airlines for America that estimated bank loans to foreign airlines "have killed up to 7,500 jobs" at U.S. air carriers. Boeing was a top beneficiary of the credit agency's financing, and Delta had long argued the bank unfairly supported that company.

Boeing, along with the National Association of Manufacturers and the U.S. Chamber of Commerce, said the bank helped level the playing field against foreign governments that finance exports abroad. At the time, Boeing was seeking a loan guarantee from the bank to further a sale of widebody jets to a Chinese airline, and a former bank official, Jonny Gutierrez, was under investigation for accusations that he was receiving kickbacks for helping arrange Ex-Im financing.

On July 30, 2014, Sen. Joe Manchin, D-W.Va., offered a bipartisan bill (S 2709) that would have reauthorized the bank for another five years. But senators did not take action on the measure.

SHORT-TERM RENEWAL

With Congress preparing to recess for the 2014 midterm elections, lawmakers in September included an extension of the Export-Import Bank's authorization through June 30, 2015, in a stopgap spending bill (H J Res 124) that continued funding the government through December 11, 2014.

Conservative groups Heritage Action and the Club for Growth urged lawmakers to vote against the spending measure because it included the bank's reauthorization. Heritage said the bank was the poster child for cronyism and corporate welfare, and the organization said it would keep track of those who voted to reauthorize it.

The Senate cleared the bill September 18 by a vote of 78–22. The House passed the bill September 17 by a vote of 319–108. The president signed the measure into law (PL 113-164) on September 19.

In October, Rep. Gary G. Miller, R-Calif., vice chair of the Financial Services Committee, and Rep. Maxine Waters of California, the panel's top Democrat, introduced a draft bill to provide a five-year reauthorization of the bank and make several changes aimed at protecting taxpayers from potential undue risk and to satisfy lawmakers who wanted the bank reformed. But lawmakers did not act on the measure before the end of the session, and Hensarling vowed he would let the bank's charter expire the following June.

"With no further action or consideration expected during this Congress, I look forward to the bank's expiration and working with members to make our exporters more competitive by advancing pro-growth tax, energy, regulatory and liability policies," he said in an October 14 statement.

2015–2016

More than two years of debate on several trade issues came to an end with Congress's passage of measures to grant the president fast-track trade negotiating authority, reauthorize an expanded trade-assistance program for displaced workers, and reauthorize the controversial Export-Import Bank.

The 114th session of Congress had opened with expectations that the GOP and President Obama could find agreement on trade, particularly on fast-track, as the party could benefit from such legislation, particularly as Republicans hoped to retake the White House in 2016. But many conservative Republicans as well as some Democrats remained opposed to deals on fast-track trade and Trade Adjustment Assistance reauthorization. Many lawmakers continued to say they wanted more details of ongoing Trans-Pacific Partnership negotiations.

Republicans worked to move fast-track and TAA in tandem to boost chances of Democratic support, leading to complicated procedural maneuvering that ultimately moved the measures to the president's desk as part of unrelated trade bills.

Congress also cleared a four-year reauthorization of the Export-Import Bank after attaching it to a must-pass highway reauthorization measure.

Meanwhile, U.S. Trade Representative Michael Froman signed the TPP with eleven other nations in early 2016, but many business groups, labor unions, and lawmakers from both sides of the Hill indicated opposition to Senate ratification. Presidential campaign politics that year doomed any chance the Senate would consider ratifying the bill before the November election.

Fast-Track Authority, Trade Adjustment Assistance

Congress in 2015 renewed the president's Trade Promotion Authority, or fast-track negotiating authority, to allow the president to negotiate agreements with the promise that Congress would not amend them before giving them an up or down vote. A coalition of Republicans and a few protrade Democrats provided bipartisan support for the measure, which extended the authority for three years and imposed new requirements for the administration to consult with congressional committees and advisory groups before agreeing to any trade deal.

House and Senate Republicans maneuvered passage of the measure in tandem with a renewal of the Trade Adjustment Assistance program, which helped workers displaced from their jobs due to international competition, with hopes of ensuring Democratic support. Congress ultimately reauthorized the Trade Adjustment Assistance Act until 2021. The Reauthorization Act of 2015 made the trade assistance program again similar to the 2011 program, reversing changes that occurred in 2014 as a result of lapsed extension. The measure reinstated eligibility for service workers, as well as the health care tax credit and case management services. It also reinstated eligibility for workers who had lost their jobs as a result of outsourcing to any country—not just those with which the United States had a free-trade agreement.

Unions, environmental groups, and others had continued to oppose fast-track reauthorization, just as they did during the previous session of Congress. Sen. Bernie Sanders, I-Vt., who was campaigning for president, and others worried that the Trans-Pacific Partnership deal that the administration was negotiating with eleven other countries was a job-killing trade deal that should be stopped and did not want to grant the president leeway to agree to a deal Congress could not amend.

The president had restated his desire for fast-track in his 2015 State of the Union address, hoping to ease negotiations on TPP as well as talk with the European Union about the Transatlantic Trade and Investment Partnership. The White House said the other participating nations would be more willing to make concessions in the deal if they knew it would not later be changed by Congress.

But Rep. Sander M. Levin said in January he was hesitant to extend fast-track authority, known as Trade Promotion Authority or TPA, without knowing whether TPP was on the right track. But Ways and Means Chair Paul Ryan, R-Wis., hoped to move swiftly, as did Senate Finance Chair Orrin Hatch, R-Utah.

A COMBINED EFFORT

Sen. Ron Wyden of Oregon, ranking Democrat on the Senate Finance Committee, and House Ways and Means Chair Paul Ryan, R-Wisc., agreed to move in tandem bills reauthorizing TPA and TAA.

Sen. Hatch on April 16, 2015, introduced a bill (S 995) to extend fast-track authority for the president. The Finance Committee approved the bill on April 22 by a vote of 20 to 6, with seven of twelve Democrats supporting the measure. The committee also reported to the floor, by a vote of 17–9, a measure to reauthorize the Trade Adjustment Assistance program for six years, and authorize $450 million for job training for workers adversely affected by trade.

In the House, the Ways and Means Committee approved Ryan's measure to reauthorize TPA (HR 1890) on April 23 by a vote of 25–13, with two Democrats voting yes. The committee added provisions intended to make human rights a principal objective of negotiations and discourage Europe from taking so-called antitrade actions against Israel—provisions that brought the House bill in line with the Senate bill.

At the same time, Ryan maneuvered a bill on a Trade Adjustment Assistance renewal (HR 1892) out of committee without a recommendation from Democrats, who threatened to vote against it. The measure would have renewed the program until June 30, 2021, authorized $450 million for the program, and made service industry workers eligible for the program. Democrats objected to a provision to fund the program in part from a sequestration cut in Medicare.

Both bills then moved in tandem to the Senate and House floors. Senators ultimately passed fast-track renewal on May 22 as part of an unrelated measure (HR 1314) that included language from S 995. The vote on the overall bill was 62–37, with fourteen Democrats and a majority of Republicans supporting it.

During debate, senators rejected an amendment by Sens. Rob Portman, R-Ohio, and Debbie Stabenow, D-Mich., that would have required U.S. negotiators to seek enforcement against currency manipulation. The vote was 48–51. The Senate approved language by Hatch and Wyden to make enforceable rules on currency exchange a principal negotiating objective of any trade deal.

In the House, Democrats voted down a broad trade package on June 12 that was similar to the Senate-passed measure. But under rules guiding floor consideration of the bill, members voted separately on each section. The House passed the section addressing TPA by a vote of 219–211 but defeated language on the Trade Adjustment Assistance program by a 126–302 vote. At the last minute, Minority Leader Nancy Pelosi, D-Calif., said she would sacrifice TAA if that would enable fast-track language to move.

Ultimately, House and Senate Republican leaders chose to separate fast-track language from language on the TAA, with the House to vote first and Senate to clear it. But the president said he would sign TPA legislation only if he got a reauthorization of trade adjustment assistance as well.

BILLS MOVE SEPARATELY

After agreeing to consider fast-track language separately from a reauthorization of TAA, the House on June 18 passed fast-track reauthorization language, 218–208, as part of an unrelated tax measure (HR 2146). The bill had support from 190 Republicans and 28 Democrats.

At the same time, the Senate planned to revive a measure to reauthorize TAA. Senate Majority Leader McConnell filed for cloture to end debate on a House-passed trade preferences bill (HR 1295) after getting Senate support to amend it with the TAA provisions. That bill also included a fix for a contentious $700 million cut to Medicare spending in 2024 that some had sought to offset costs for the TAA program.

On June 24, the Senate passed by voice vote the combined measure and sent it back to the House. That same day, it also cleared, by a 60–38 vote, the House tax bill (HR 2146) that included renewal for fast-track trade authority. Rep. Sander M. Levin of Michigan, ranking Democrat on Ways and Means, said the fight over fast-track authority was a prelude to a vigorous debate on TPP.

Under the measure, fast-track authority was granted to the president for U.S. trade agreements entered into before July 1, 2018, but allowed for the president to extend the authority for agreements entered into before July 1, 2021, unless Congress passed a resolution barring such an extension. Under the bill, before the administration agreed to any trade deal, the U.S. Trade Representative would have to consult appropriate trade advisers, relevant committees, and new congressional advisory groups authorized by the legislation.

On June 25, the House took up the Senate amended version of the trade preferences bill (HR 1295) that included provisions for trade adjustment assistance. The House voted 286–138 to pass the bill, with many Democrats providing support because of the Medicare fix. In the end, only 6 Democrats opposed the bill reauthorizing Trade Adjustment Assistance, compared to 144 two weeks earlier.

The bill reauthorized TAA through 2021. As under previous authorizations, workers eligible for the program could receive up to 117 weeks of income support and another 13 weeks of assistance under certain circumstances. An applicant would have to show the need for further training and demonstrate they had met the goals of a training program, which could include opportunities for part-time training and training before they were laid off.

Voting against the bill, Rep. Stephen F. Lynch, D-Mass., said his constituents wanted jobs, not trade assistance.

On June 29, the president signed the tax bill measure (HR 2146), which included fast-track renewal, into law (PL 114-26), and he signed the trade preferences bill (HR 1295) that included TAA reauthorization into law (PL 114-27).

Export-Import Bank

Congress renewed the charter for the Export-Import Bank, the export financing agency, for another four years as part of a surface transportation law (PL 114-94) cleared in December 2015—nearly six months after the authority (PL 113-164) approved by the previous Congress had lapsed. But the Senate delayed confirmation of one board member, leaving it without a quorum that it needed to approve loans.

Debate over the bank's reauthorization, advocated by Democrats and moderate Republicans and opposed by conservatives, had started two years earlier. The debate also divided business groups such as the U.S. Chamber of Commerce against more conservative groups such as Club for Growth and Heritage for America.

As the bank neared the end of its authorization on June 30, bank President Fred P. Hochberg campaigned for its renewal. He announced March 6, 2015, that the United States had exported $189.4 billion of goods and services that January. "At Ex-Im Bank, we will continue to support American exporters so they can introduce their goods and services to new global markets and create more middle-class jobs here at home," he said.

During the bank's lapse of authority, General Electric and Boeing said they were suffering from the loss of export financing and would move some jobs overseas to benefit from support of comparable foreign agencies. Such announcements further pressured lawmakers to come to an agreement.

Conflict over the bank's renewal was overcome only by combining the charter's renewal with a highway reauthorization bill that conservative Republicans wanted.

Senate Action

At the start of the 114th Congress, as the House began considering a reauthorization measure (HR 597) for the Export-Import Bank, Senate Banking Chair Richard C. Shelby, R-Ala., announced he had problems with the financing agency and was not inclined to renew its charter. He said the Export-Import Bank's programs represented corporate welfare, adding that his committee had more pressing priorities.

Shelby's committee held a hearing on the bank in early June, during which time the Chamber, NAM, and other supporters said tens of thousands of U.S. jobs were at stake, while bank opponents said it only subsidized a few wealthier corporations. The chair said the committee lacked consensus on whether to reauthorize it and refused to consider legislation.

Meanwhile, in May, a bipartisan bloc of senators led by Sen. Maria Cantwell, D-Wash., negotiated a promise from the leadership for a vote the following month on the bank's reauthorization in exchange for their support for a bill renewing fast-track trade authority for the president.

Mark S. Kirk, R-Ill., and Heidi Heitkamp, D-N.D., had drafted a five-year reauthorization for the bank, which they hoped to attach to a bill moving on the floor. Initially the Senate, in a 65–31 vote, approved their language as an amendment to the defense authorization bill on the floor. But Kirk and Heitkamp immediately withdrew the amendment from the controversial defense bill, hoping to find a bill that would more likely land on the president's desk.

Senate leaders then eyed the six-year highway reauthorization bill heading to the floor, leading senators such as Shelby to try to block the highway bill from a vote due to his opposition to the Ex-Im Bank. On July 26, a bipartisan coalition, in a 67–26 vote, defeated a filibuster of an amendment to the highway bill to reauthorize the bank. The next day, the Senate voted, 64–29, to adopt the amendment to the highway bill, which would grant a four-year reauthorization of the bank's charter, until September 30, 2019. The Senate on July 30 passed the underlying bill by a vote of 65–34.

House Action

Rep. Stephen Fincher, R-Tenn., on January 28, 2015, introduced a measure (HR 597) that would have overhauled and extended the bank's authorization for five years. Fincher said his bill aimed to make the bank's practices more transparent.

On April 15, at a joint hearing of House Financial Services and Oversight and Government Reform subcommittees, conservative Republicans harshly criticized the bank and admonished Export-Import Bank President Fred Hochberg for lobbying for its renewal. That month, a former bank employee was charged with fraud.

"Perhaps, maybe a little more time managing the store rather than posing for photo ops and lobbying for your reauthorization would lead to fewer indictments," Financial Services Chair Jeb Hensarling, R-Texas, said during the hearing.

Hensarling vowed to block the bill's renewal and held the bill in committee without a vote for months. Rep. Stephen Fincher, R-Tenn., then led an effort—supported by House Democrats and moderate Republicans—to gather the necessary 218 signatures on a discharge petition to get the bill out of committee. That allowed Fincher to bypass the opposition of conservative Republicans, including that of Rep. Paul D. Ryan, R-Wis., an opponent of the bank who hoped to rise in leadership ranks with the retirement of Speaker John A. Boehner, R-Ohio, at the end of the session. Bank supporters wanted to move a bill before Boehner retired.

On October 27, the House passed the bill, 313–118. The bill was supported by 127 Republicans and 186 Democrats. But Senate Majority Leader Mitch McConnell, R-Ky., said the Senate would not take up the House stand-alone measure, preferring to attach it to a highway reauthorization bill as the Senate had done the previous July.

The House Transportation and Infrastructure Committee on October 22 had approved a six-year highway bill (HR 3763), but that measure did not include a provision for the bank's renewal. Debate on the House floor began in early November, and the bank's supporters defeated a series of amendments intended to restrict the bank's operations.

Conference Agreement

Negotiators ironing out differences between the two chambers' surface transportation reauthorization bills included the Senate's language reauthorizing the Export-Import Bank in a conference report.

The House on December 3 voted 359–65 to adopt the conference report on that bill (HR 22), which included the four-year renewal, reduced the value of individual loans it could issue from $140 billion to $135 billion, increased small business lending requirements, mandated the bank to hire a chief risk officer, and required the Government Accountability Office to conduct an annual audit on the bank's fraud control measures.

The Senate cleared the measure the same day by a vote of 83–16, and Obama signed the bill into law (PL 114-94) on December 4.

LACK OF QUORUM

By 2016, membership on the five-seat board for the Export-Import Bank had dwindled to two members, and

Republican opponents of the bank's renewal blocked action on President Obama's nominees to the board through the rest of the session.

Senate Banking Committee Chair Richard C. Shelby, R-Ala., who had opposed the bank's renewal in 2015, released a statement May 20, 2016, saying he would not approve any nominees for the board. "Nearly 99 percent of all American exports are financed without the Ex-Im Bank, which demonstrates that the Bank is more about corporate welfare than advancing our economy," the statement said.

Without a quorum, the bank could not approve transactions of more than $10 million. Bank president Hochberg said about 75 percent of the bank's about $20 billion in annual loans and financial guarantees were valued at more than $10 million.

President Obama nominated Patricia M. Loui-Schmicker to a second term on the board in March 2015. The Senate had unanimously confirmed her nomination to the board in 2011, but after she waited ten months for the Banking committee to hold a hearing on her nomination, she withdrew her name.

The president on January 11, 2016, then nominated John Mark McWatters, a former counsel for House Financial Services Chair Hensarling, to serve on the Export-Import Bank board.

Trans-Pacific Partnership

U.S. Trade Representative Michael Froman in February 2016 signed the Trans-Pacific Partnership (TPP) agreement with eleven other nations, but it was not considered by the Senate for ratification before the end of the session. By late 2016, the United States' future participation in the deal appeared dim, as President-elect Trump vowed to withdraw from the agreement as soon as he took office the following January.

The TPP included the United States, Australia, Brunei, Canada, Chile, Japan, Malaysia, New Zealand, Peru, Mexico, Singapore, and Vietnam. The Obama administration said the agreement would reduce or eliminate 18,000 tariffs, encourage digital trade, help small U.S. businesses that want to export, and remove nontariff barriers to U.S. exports.

Tufts University researchers reported the agreement would result in 448,000 lost jobs in the United States by 2025—the majority of the overall 771,000 jobs the deal would cost all twelve countries combined. The Peterson

Institute for International Economics reported the agreement would affect about 540,000 jobs over ten years, with workers in import-related industries to lose jobs and workers in export-related industries likely to gain.

After Froman signed the deal in a ceremony in Auckland, New Zealand, Obama faced challenges in finding support in Congress. Most Democrats opposed the deal, as did a growing number of Republicans, particularly as the presidential and congressional general election campaigns heated up. Senate Majority Leader Mitch McConnell, R-Ky., said senators would reject the agreement if the president tried to force them to vote before the November 8 election.

On April 1, the Obama administration sent Congress a one-page document calling for several changes to various laws that would be needed to move forward on potential legislation to implement the TPP. The document called for changes to provisions of the 1985 omnibus budget reconciliation law (PL 99-272), the Tariff Act of 1930 (PL 71-361), and the Trade Agreements Act of 1979 (PL 96-39).

The National Farmers Union, the nation's second-largest general farm group, and a coalition of 161 groups sent a letter to lawmakers in April urging them to oppose TPP. They said it would hurt smaller U.S. farmers and ranchers because the deal would allow for greater market access to imports. Several major agricultural organizations backed the trade deal because it would provide tariff reductions and greater access to foreign markets for their exports.

Other opponents of TPP pointed to a growing U.S. trade deficit with South Korea in the wake of a 2012 trade agreement with that country. Several government watchdog groups and House lawmakers said exports of machinery and of computer and electronic products to South Korea, for example, had fallen 22.6 and 6.6 percent, respectively.

Ultimately, the presidential campaign impeded Obama's efforts to gain congressional and public support for TPP.

Obama had some hope that Congress might approve the Trans-Pacific Partnership during the lame-duck session following the 2016 elections. But Congress already was facing a national backlash against trade deals, and President-elect Trump had campaigned strongly against TPP and vowed to withdraw the United States from the deal. House Ways and Means Chair Kevin Brady had been a strong supporter of TPP but ruled out any chance the chamber would vote on the deal. Senate Majority Leader Mitch McConnell also dismissed the possibility of a Senate vote.

CHAPTER 3

Homeland Security

Homeland Security

The four years of President Barack Obama's second term saw a series of controversial homeland security issues dominate the headlines. The Department of Homeland Security (DHS), created in response to the terrorist attacks of September 11, 2001, includes a wide variety of agencies covering topics from immigration enforcement to antiterrorism efforts to disaster relief. Many of the topics under debate had carried over from previous years, during the presidency of George W. Bush and also during Obama's first term.

While opinions on homeland security issues did not always break down along strict partisan lines, the high degree of political animosity during the 113th and 114th Congresses often made it difficult for lawmakers to enact legislation in this area. Janet Napolitano, Obama's first Homeland Security secretary, who left her post in 2013, and her successor, Jeh Johnson, often faced tough going when pushing for administration priorities on Capitol Hill, particularly once the GOP took control of the Senate following the 2014 midterm elections. The House was in Republican hands during the entire four years.

One of the biggest issues on the homeland security front involved revelations in 2013 that the National Security Agency (NSA), part of DHS, had engaged in the large-scale collection of data from domestic communications sources. These revelations, by former defense contractor Edward Snowden, who leaked material to journalists, sparked anger and concern on Capitol Hill and around the country. Lawmakers, in response, attempted to address this issue on various fronts, including seeking to protect Americans' privacy rights and trying to maintain the NSA's ability to monitor the communications of noncitizens.

The Patriot Act, a counterterrorism law passed after the September 11 attacks, had produced controversy over the years, and in 2015, Congress again took up the measure, which was due for reauthorization, eventually reauthorizing it through 2019. The new version of the legislation cut back on the NSA's ability to collect bulk phone records of Americans' phone calls, one response to the Snowden revelations.

One issue that had always proven difficult but seemed ratcheted up during this time period was immigration. In November 2014, President Obama moved to create extra protections for undocumented immigrants, a plan that many Republicans greeted with disfavor. Controversy over this issue made its way into congressional consideration of the fiscal year 2015 homeland security appropriations bill, which faced delays because of arguments over immigration policy.

Then, in November 2015, in the wake of terrorist attacks in Paris, GOP leaders sought to push legislation designed to restrict refugees from Syria and Iraq from entering the United States. The measure passed in the House but was opposed by President Obama and ultimately was blocked by Democrats in the Senate.

Throughout his presidency, Obama had sought to close the U.S. detention facility at Guantanamo Bay, Cuba, which held detainees linked to the September 11 attacks. This issue continued to fester during Obama's second term, as lawmakers debated the procedures under which these prisoners could be released or transferred. Ultimately, Congress approved legislation detailing various requirements pertaining to the detainees, and after vetoing one iteration of the measure, Obama signed a second version. But the facility was not closed down.

Lawmakers also approved a controversial cybersecurity measure. The legislation, a compromise among previous versions of the bill, encouraged private companies to voluntarily share cyberthreat information with one another and with the government. While the bill's supporters said it would boost the country's defenses against cyberattacks, critics said it was lacking in privacy safeguards.

REFERENCES

Discussion of homeland security policy for the years 2001–2004 may be found in *Congress and the Nation Vol. XI*, pp. 175–225; for the years 2005–2008, *Congress and the Nation Vol. XII*, pp. 217–261; for the years 2009–2012, *Congress and the Nation Vol. XIII*, pp. 205–219.

At the end of 2016, lawmakers turned their attention to Russia, which had meddled in that year's U.S. election and intervened militarily in Syria and Ukraine. In the fiscal year 2017 intelligence authorization bill, Congress targeted Russia, calling for a new executive branch entity to counteract Russian actions to exert covert influence over peoples and governments.

HOMELAND SECURITY LEADERSHIP

During President Barack Obama's second presidential term, two people served as Secretary of Homeland Security: Janet Napolitano, who held the position during Obama's first term and remained into his second, and Jeh Johnson, who took over the department after Napolitano's departure in 2013 and remained there through the rest of Obama's presidency.

Obama had selected Napolitano, then serving her second term as the Democratic governor of Arizona, on December 1, 2008, to run the department. She had worked on the issue of illegal immigration as governor, signing into law a measure that imposed tough sanctions on employers who intentionally hired illegal immigrants. In addition, her state was the first to establish its own homeland security strategy. And she was the first governor to call for a National Guard presence along the U.S. border with Mexico. But she did not back President George W. Bush's plan to erect a border fence.

The Senate confirmed Napolitano on January 20, 2009, by voice vote. As secretary of a department that had been created less than a decade before, she faced various crises, including the ongoing terrorism threat, illegal immigration, a drug war along the U.S. border with Mexico, and continuing scrutiny of the Federal Emergency Management Agency (FEMA), a component of the Department of Homeland Security (DHS). Napolitano backed the idea of a path to citizenship for people living illegally in the United States. But the rate of deportation of illegal immigrants rose during her time at DHS.

She left her post at the end of August 2013 to lead the University of California system.

Obama picked Johnson, the former general counsel at the Pentagon, on October 18, 2013, to be his second secretary of Homeland Security. Johnson had worked on a variety of issues at the Defense Department during his tenure from 2009 to 2012, including the repeal of the don't ask, don't tell policy on gays serving in the military and the effort to shutter the U.S. detention facility at Guantanamo Bay. The Senate approved Johnson's nomination on December 16, 2013, by a vote of 78–16. The bipartisan nature of Johnson's support was something of an anomaly during a time of bitter partisan fighting over Obama's nominees. Johnson had backing from the three previous secretaries of Homeland Security, Napolitano, Michael Chertoff, and Tom Ridge; the latter two had served under GOP President George W. Bush.

Johnson, born in New York on September 11, 1957, graduated from Morehouse College and Columbia Law School. He spent many years as a corporate lawyer with the firm of Paul, Weiss and also served as general counsel of the U.S. Air Force from 1998 to 2001 and as an assistant U.S. Attorney for the Southern District of New York from 1989 to 1991.

As secretary of Homeland Security, he, like his predecessor, faced a host of controversial issues, including border security, cybersecurity, and terrorism. Among the threats he focused on was the Ebola outbreak in several African countries in 2014. Johnson's department announced travel restrictions on passengers arriving in the United States whose trips had begun in Ebola-affected countries; these travelers were subject to additional screening and precautionary measures. Johnson also was involved in implementing Obama's controversial November 2014 executive orders focusing on protecting undocumented people who arrived here as children, as well as those residents whose children were American citizens or legal permanent residents. After Obama left office, Johnson returned to Paul, Weiss to practice law.

Chronology of Action on Homeland Security

2013–2014

The biggest issue relating to homeland security during the 113th Congress involved revelations that the National Security Agency (NSA) had been engaging in widespread data collection from domestic communications sources. The initial reports in media sources in June 2013 caused a furor on Capitol Hill and throughout the country. Lawmakers' initial reactions ranged from angry calls to prosecute the leaker, former defense contractor Edward Snowden, to fury over concerns that Americans' privacy could have been breached.

As the year progressed, lawmakers sought to introduce measures that would maintain the NSA's ability to monitor noncitizens' communications and also measures to protect privacy rights of Americans. Disputes over the NSA surveillance program affected congressional consideration of other, more routine intelligence matters. In 2013, Congress failed to pass a fiscal 2014 intelligence authorization bill, something members had managed to accomplish the previous several years. This resulted in lawmakers' having to approve two intelligence authorization bills in 2014, one for the remainder of the 2014 fiscal year, which ended September 30, and one for the 2015 fiscal year.

The first two years of President Obama's second term saw Republicans in control of the House and Democrats in charge of the Senate. While homeland security issues did not always break down along party lines, the tone of partisan animosity on Capitol Hill was an additional factor weighing on lawmakers.

One issue that had always proven difficult but seemed to become more so during this period was immigration. In November 2014, President Obama took action to create additional protections for undocumented immigrants, a plan that met with disapproval from many Republicans. Repercussions from this issue carried over into congressional consideration of the fiscal year 2015 homeland security appropriations bill, which faced lengthy delays due to disagreements over immigration policy.

Revelations About NSA Program

News in June 2013 that the National Security Agency was engaged in widespread data collection from domestic communications sources caused a commotion on Capitol Hill. Reactions from lawmakers varied from furious calls to prosecute the leaker to revulsion that Americans' privacy could have been violated.

While lawmakers proposed a variety of changes to those laws in response to the NSA's surveillance programs, Congress did not end up passing legislation to limit the NSA's surveillance activities, although public anger about the revelations was increasing. Lawmakers found themselves divided over the programs' legality, and the divisions cut across party lines. Only one of the four committees with jurisdiction over the issues in question approved a bill before the end of 2013, and that measure did not make it to the floor. Instead, lawmakers added language to the fiscal 2014 omnibus appropriations bill, requiring the agency to provide them with information about its collection of phone records.

The issue proved so tough to resolve that Congress was unable to complete action on routine bills to authorize the government's intelligence activities.

BACKGROUND

Reports on June 5 and June 6, 2013, in the *Guardian* newspaper and *The Washington Post* provided the first evidence that the NSA was mining domestic phone and Internet transmissions. The early stories reported that the NSA was obtaining bulk telephone records to parse metadata through computers. A data-mining program, known as PRISM, was reported to be tapping into the databases of nine U.S. communications companies. The stories indicated that the metadata program was used to collect information on the time, duration, and routing of phone calls but not on their actual content.

The person providing the details of the NSA surveillance program to the *Guardian*, the *Post*, and other news organizations was Edward Snowden, 29, a defense contractor who had worked at an NSA facility in Hawaii. He fled to Hong Kong prior to the disclosures and later moved to Russia under a grant of temporary asylum.

Amidst ongoing revelations throughout the year, calls emerged for legislation to maintain the NSA's ability to monitor the transmissions of noncitizens, even when they occurred inside the United States, as well as legislation to protect the privacy of Americans.

To justify the NSA activities, the executive branch had used several laws falling under the jurisdiction of the Judiciary and Intelligence committees, including the 2001 anti-terrorism Patriot Act law (PL 107-56), the Foreign Intelligence Surveillance Act (FISA) (PL 95-511), and a 2008 FISA update (PL 110-261).

Many lawmakers, in the wake of the initial revelations, called for Snowden to be prosecuted for the security leaks. Among those were Sen. Dianne Feinstein, D-Calif., and Rep. Mike Rogers, R-Mich., the respective chairs of the Senate and House Intelligence committees. A few lawmakers, on the other hand, said Snowden should go free, and more members started seeking changes in the laws used to authorize the surveillance.

As time passed, while some lawmakers continued to call for Snowden's prosecution, attention turned away from Snowden and toward questions about the degree to which the NSA's activities amounted to possibly illegal surveillance of U.S. citizens.

2013 ACTION

On the House side, congressional anger about the NSA revelations bubbled up in late July, during House consideration of the fiscal 2014 Defense appropriations bill (HR 2397). Two representatives from Michigan, Justin Amash, a conservative Republican, and John Conyers Jr., a liberal Democrat, offered an amendment designed to bar spending for domestic data collection activities, except in very narrow circumstances. The administration lobbied to protect the NSA program, and lawmakers narrowly defeated the amendment on a close bipartisan vote of 205–217. The close vote showed the level of public concern over the revelations. Ninety-four Republicans and 111 Democrats voted against the surveillance program, meaning that more than half the Democrats in the House turned against Obama's handling of the NSA's activities.

The top three Republicans in the House, Speaker John A. Boehner of Ohio, Majority Leader Eric Cantor of Virginia, and Majority Whip Kevin McCarthy of California, voted against the amendment, as did the chamber's top two Democrats, Minority Leader Nancy Pelosi of California and Minority Whip Steny H. Hoyer of Maryland.

House Intelligence Chair Rogers took the lead in opposing the amendment, referring to the September 11, 2001, terrorist attacks and the questions raised at the time about the United States' ability to detect that type of threat. But Amash and his allies described the amendment as a referendum on civil liberties.

Meanwhile, as the year progressed, both intelligence committees set to work on legislation designed to increase privacy protections and transparency while also keeping the NSA's ability to conduct surveillance. But as additional elements of the NSA program continued to come to light, Senate Judiciary Committee Chair Patrick J. Leahy, D-Vt., and former House Judiciary Chair Jim Sensenbrenner, R-Wis., worked to prepare legislation that would have permanently ended the telephone data collection and put additional restraints on other NSA operations. They introduced bills in each chamber (S 1599, HR 3361) on October 29 that would have curtailed the NSA's ability to monitor domestic communications.

In September, Sen. Ron Wyden, D-Ore., introduced legislation (S 1551) to end the phone data collection program. He was joined by Richard Blumenthal, D-Conn., Mark Udall, D-Colo., and Tom Udall, D-N.M., plus Republican Rand Paul of Kentucky, demonstrating the common ground that was developing between libertarians and liberals on the issue.

By the end of 2013, the Senate Intelligence Committee was the only panel to approve NSA-related legislation. On October 31, in a closed-door markup, the committee approved a bill (S 1631), sponsored by Feinstein, on a vote of 11–4, that would have allowed the NSA to collect phone or electronic communication records if the data did not include the content of the communications.

The bill would have allowed data collection subject to a ninety-day order by the Foreign Intelligence Surveillance Court created by the FISA law. In addition, the bill would have placed a five-year limit on the retention of bulk communication records. It also would have required the FISA court to limit the number of NSA personnel who had access to the agency's database of call records. It would have set up a criminal penalty of up to ten years in prison for people who accessed communications data acquired under a FISA court order without authorization.

2014 ACTION

January 17, 2014, Obama called for an end to the NSA's bulk collection of phone records and asked Congress to approve legislation requiring government agents to get a court order before demanding that a phone company pull records for individual numbers. Lawmakers would address those issues in a reauthorization of the Patriot Act in 2015 (Patriot Act, pp. 136–137).

The fiscal 2014 omnibus appropriations bill, enacted in January 2014, included language requiring the agency to provide Congress with details on the bulk collection of phone records. The NSA was instructed to provide lawmakers with a series of reports. One was to describe records the NSA had acquired over the past five years and the number of records reviewed. Another was to describe all bulk collection activities, including their start date, their cost, the records collected, and the agency's future plans. A third was to list terrorist activities disrupted with the aid of the data collection program.

INTELLIGENCE AUTHORIZATION EFFORTS

During the 113th Congress, revelations about the National Security Agency's surveillance practices roiled the intelligence committees, leading to delays during 2013 in their work on an intelligence authorization bill. Ultimately, lawmakers failed to clear an intelligence authorization measure in 2013, but they managed to clear two the following year.

2013 ACTION

While lawmakers had managed to send an intelligence authorization to the president for his signature the past four years, they ran into trouble in 2013 as they attempted to work on a fiscal 2014 bill.

The House and Senate Intelligence Committees each succeeded in approving an authorization bill for the country's intelligence-gathering operations, but neither the House nor the Senate ended up voting on the measures.

During the previous year, lawmakers succeeded in keeping the fiscal 2013 bill relatively free of controversy. But disclosures that started emerging in June 2013 about the National Security Agency's surveillance of domestic telephone calls were among the concerns that disrupted the legislative schedules of the intelligence committees. Both committees were preoccupied with these controversial disclosures by former intelligence contractor Edward Snowden about the NSA's widespread data collection. In addition, lawmakers were concerned about prospects of a military strike on Syria and covert-action proposals from the Obama administration about arming Syrian rebels.

Members of the intelligence committees found themselves facing criticism in the wake of the NSA revelations. Many lawmakers complained that they did not understand how far the executive branch had stretched the 2001 antiterrorism law called the Patriot Act (PL 107-56), the 1978 Foreign Intelligence Surveillance Act (PL 95-511), and the 2008 update of FISA (PL 110-261) to permit the bulk collection of Americans' phone records. These lawmakers blamed the intelligence committees, saying they were not doing their jobs properly. Lawmakers and outside experts argued that Congress should change the way it oversaw the spy agencies.

But the two committee chairs, Rep. Mike Rogers, R-Mich., and Sen. Dianne Feinstein, D-Calif., defended themselves, including the production of documents showing that other lawmakers had been invited several times to review documents and attend briefings on the same NSA programs they said they learned about only from media reports. With all of the controversy swirling around the committees, both panels were late in beginning deliberations on the authorization bills.

Due to concerns about the NSA data collection, it was likely that debate on the House or Senate floor on an intelligence authorization bill would attract NSA-related amendments that the leadership did not want to consider. The House had already debated and rejected an amendment to end the NSA program during its consideration of the fiscal 2014 defense appropriations bill (HR 2397).

On the Senate side, the Intelligence Committee focused on the authorization measure after approving an NSA bill in late October. The committee approved the measure (S 1681) on a vote of 13–2 during a closed-door meeting November 5. Unclassified portions of the bill were released two days later. Authorized spending levels remained classified.

The bill looked at the issue of the disclosure of the number of deaths and injuries outside active war zones resulting from the use of targeted lethal force, such as drone strikes. It would have required an unclassified report from the president on the number of combatants and civilians killed or injured. It included an exception for Afghanistan until the end of combat operations there and for any countries identified in a future declaration of war or authorization of military force.

The bill would have required an independent analysis when U.S. officials considered launching a lethal strike overseas against an alleged American terrorist. The provision was sponsored by Sens. Angus King, I-Maine, and Marco Rubio, R-Fla. It came in response to protests over drone strikes against U.S. citizens abroad who were accused of terrorism.

In addition, the bill would have extended whistleblower protections to intelligence workers who informed the Director of National Intelligence (DNI), agency heads, inspectors general, or congressional intelligence committees about mismanagement, illegal behavior, waste, fraud, or abuse.

On the House side, the House Intelligence Committee approved its authorization bill (HR 3381) by voice vote in a closed-session meeting November 21. Spending levels in the bill were classified, but President Obama had requested a total of $70.8 billion for intelligence activities for fiscal 2014, and Chair Rogers said the bill would have set spending levels slightly below that.

Rogers and ranking committee Democrat C. A. "Dutch" Ruppersberger of Maryland said the bill would have provided an increase of $75 million to improve protection of classified information following Snowden's disclosures. The lawmakers' statement also said the bill would have permitted additional spending to collect intelligence on unnamed hostile countries, to pay for additional counterintelligence positions, to pay for the DNI's plan to consolidate and modernize computer systems, and to maintain Navy intelligence, surveillance, and reconnaissance programs and those devoted to tracking medical, scientific, and environmental information.

The House bill would have required spy agency employees to be reevaluated more often than the existing five-year requirement to maintain their top-secret security clearances. It would have required spy agencies to share possibly damaging information about an employee switching employers, and it would have required agency contractors handling classified information to maintain security plans in accordance with standards set by the DNI.

Committee leaders in both the House and Senate had expected to be able to resolve any differences in the bills without problems.

2014 ACTION

Congress had failed to enact a fiscal year 2014 intelligence authorization bill by the end of 2013, although the new fiscal year had begun on October 1. So during 2014, Congress enacted two intelligence bills—one for the remainder of fiscal 2014, and one for fiscal 2015.

The most controversial intelligence-related issue on the congressional agenda, the government's mass collection of telephone data, was dealt with in other legislation.

In June, the House approved a bill (HR 3381) by Jim Sensenbrenner (R-Wis.) designed to end the National Security Agency's (NSA) collection of telephone metadata, including the numbers dialed, the times of the calls, and their duration. The Senate never took the bill up.

Later that month, the House included an amendment in its Defense authorization bill (HR 4870) that would bar funds from being used to query metadata collected by the U.S. intelligence community with U.S. citizens' personally identifiable information. It also barred the NSA from using funds on "backdoor" surveillance, requiring or requesting the redesign of a product to facilitate the electronic surveillance of a person who uses it.

Then, in mid-November, senators seeking to impose privacy protections on intelligence agencies fell short of ending debate on a bill by Patrick J. Leahy (D-Vt.) (S 2685) designed to prohibit intelligence agencies from engaging in the bulk collection of domestic telephone and Internet metadata. The bill would have codified a proposal by the Obama administration to basically privatize the NSA's phone metadata program by leaving the information in phone company computers, to be used by the government only if it could demonstrate that such a search was needed to fight terrorism.

Meanwhile, lawmakers turned to the intelligence authorization bill, which sets classified funding levels for sixteen intelligence agencies and intelligence-related activities, as well as covert action programs connected to counterterrorism missions and research and development programs.

In May, the House Intelligence Committee got to work on an intelligence authorization bill (HR 4681) for both fiscal years 2014 and 2015. The House passed it the same month, approving the legislation May 30 on a vote of 345–59.

The House bill ordered continuous background monitoring of government and contract workers with access to classified information, in an effort to avoid leaks such as those by former contractor Edward Snowden. The bill also set up a method for contractors to report breaches of their networks to government intelligence entities. In addition, intelligence contractors were ordered to institute network security plans meeting standards established by the Director of National Intelligence. The bill also called for a cost-benefit analysis of technology upgrades to the security clearance process.

The Senate approved its version of a fiscal 2014 authorization bill (S 1681) on June 11 by voice vote. Senators also agreed that if the bill were enacted into law, the Senate would adopt a resolution clarifying the responsibility of Senate committees in providing advice and consent on intelligence agency posts. Civilian nominees would receive consideration first by the Select Committee on Intelligence, military nominees by the Armed Services Committee.

The Senate bill allocated funds to deploy information technology detection systems to protect against insider threats in the intelligence community; this was seen as a response to the Snowden leaks. In addition, the bill gave the Director of National Intelligence (DNI) more power to strengthen the government's process to investigate and reinvestigate people with security clearances to obtain classified information. The bill also mandated an annual report on the number of deaths and injuries from drone strikes, and it required a review process for when a U.S. individual is targeted with lethal force. It also required the attorney general to give the House and Senate Intelligence Committees a list of every legal opinion on spy agency activities.

On June 24, the House passed the Senate version of the bill by voice vote and sent it to President Obama, who signed it on July 7. Among the provisions in the bill was one requiring the NSA's inspector general to be appointed by the president. The bill also required that the directors of the NSA and the National Reconnaissance Office and the NRO inspector general be subject to Senate confirmation. It instructed the DNI to provide Congress, within a month of the bill's enactment and every ninety days thereafter, with a comprehensive assessment of chemical weapons stockpiles in Syria.

Later that month, on July 29, the Senate Intelligence Committee approved a fiscal 2015 bill. The House had already passed a fiscal 2015 bill (HR 4681) that had been combined with its 2014 bill, and committee leaders from both chambers had been negotiating over the legislation.

The November 2014 election resulted in a Republican takeover of the Senate and an expanded GOP House majority. Nevertheless, despite potential complications for the postelection lame-duck session, the Senate passed an amended version of HR 4681 on December 9 by voice vote. The House cleared the measure the following day on a vote of 325–100, and President Obama signed it into law on December 19.

Under this bicameral agreement, certain intelligence employees would need to sign written agreements requiring at least annual reporting of employment with a foreign government in the two-year period after leaving an intelligence entity. The bill also required the DNI to write "a comprehensive national intelligence strategy to meet national security objectives" in 2017 and every four years thereafter. In addition, the bill required the DNI to give Congress, within 180 days of enactment, a report on U.S. counterterrorism strategy regarding al Qaeda and the Islamic State.

Also included in the bill was a requirement that all supervisory posts at U.S. diplomatic facilities in Russia be filled within a year of enactment by American citizens who have passed background checks. U.S. diplomatic facilities built or upgraded in Russia and former Soviet countries bordering Russia would be required to include a facility for viewing classified information.

Fiscal 2014 Homeland Security Appropriations

During 2013, the appropriations process for fiscal year 2014—which began on October 1, 2013—faced many stumbling blocks, including a sixteen-day government shutdown that ended on October 16. The homeland security appropriations were ultimately included in an omnibus package (HR 3547—PL 113-76) that was approved by both houses of Congress in January 2014 and signed into law by President Obama.

In the omnibus measure, border enforcement manpower remained at an all-time high, but the Coast Guard and the Transportation Security Administration, both parts of the Homeland Security Department, were targeted for cuts. Overall, the department received $39.3 billion in discretionary budget authority.

Both the House and Senate Appropriations committees had approved their own homeland security bills. The bills were not that different from each other, although they differed on some policy provisions, such as those affecting immigration.

On the House side, the House Appropriations Committee approved its version of the bill (HR 2217) on May 22 by voice vote. The full House took up the bill and on June 6 approved the measure on a vote of 245–182.

The House bill called for $39 billion in discretionary appropriations, about $603 million less than the fiscal 2013 enacted level and $39 million less than the administration's request. This version of the bill would have provided almost $1 billion more than the department received

in fiscal 2013, postsequester. The bill provided more than $10.6 billion for Customs and Border Protection, plus about $2.1 billion from customs user fees. It provided $5.4 billion for Immigration and Customs Enforcement (ICE), plus $345 million in user fees. It gave $4.8 billion for the Transportation Security Administration (TSA), plus $2.1 billion through passenger user fees, and $9.9 billion for the Coast Guard.

On the Senate side, the Appropriations Committee, on a vote of 21–9, approved its version of the bill on July 18. It provided $39.1 billion in discretionary spending, including $10.4 billion for Customs and Border Protection (plus fee income), $5.1 billion for Immigration and Customs Enforcement (plus fee income), $4.9 billion for the TSA (plus fee income), and $10.1 billion for the Coast Guard. The Senate bill did not reach a full Senate floor vote.

Both measures included $5.6 billion in mandatory disaster assistance. In addition, the House bill contained a provision requiring U.S. Immigration and Customs Enforcement (ICE) to maintain 34,000 beds for detained immigrants waiting to be deported, while the Senate bill favored the administration's call for 31,800 beds.

The House bill sparked White House opposition. As lawmakers debated the bill on the House floor, they approved an amendment blocking some administration directives on immigration enforcement. These included a June 15, 2012, memo providing temporary legal status to Dreamers, those younger than thirty-one who were brought to the United States before turning sixteen; did not have a criminal record; and were in school, had graduated, or had served in the military. The House passed the amendment June 6 on a vote of 224–201 that mostly fell along party lines. The White House put out a statement after the amendment's adoption saying it would not become law. In addition, the White House issued a Statement of Administration Policy objecting to some elements of the House bill and threatening a veto over the overall limit on discretionary appropriations.

Ultimately, the House and Senate approved an omnibus package that included homeland security funding in January 2014. The House passed the measure on January 15, the Senate on January 16, and President Obama signed it on January 17.

Under the omnibus, Customs and Border Protection saw a boost. The Border Patrol was given funding to preserve its staffing level of 21,370 agents, but funding for customs processing and inspections was increased to allow for 24,800 customs officers, up about 3,430. Lawmakers from the Southwest and trade groups had argued that delays from lengthy customs lines at the border between the United States and Mexico were hurting U.S. companies.

Included in the omnibus was an initiative, originally proposed by Texas and Arizona business groups, for a five-year pilot program that would let Customs and Border Protection partner with companies, allowing them to finance border infrastructure improvements, including roads and buildings, to upgrade land port facilities, or to reimburse the agency for services. Customs and Border Protection also received money to upgrade a threat-targeting system for terrorists and other potential dangers.

ICE got $5.3 billion, $159 million less than the 2013 enacted level but $272 million more than the administration had requested. The measure followed the House proposal for 34,000 detention beds.

The Secure Communities Program, which allowed agency officials to check fingerprints taken during local police bookings against those in immigration databases, and the E-Verify workforce eligibility system received almost $25.3 million.

The measure continued funding the immigration enforcement local partnership program called 287(g), but the money would be stopped if the department's inspector general determined that program rules had been broken. The program aimed to allow local law enforcement to search for incarcerated illegal immigrants and to allow specially trained local officer teams to arrest illegal immigrants within their jurisdictions. But 287(g) had led to concerns about racial profiling, and the Obama administration had halted agreements giving authority to make arrests.

The omnibus called for a $5 million increase, to $294 million, for the Criminal Alien Program, designed to identify incarcerated illegal immigrants who had committed serious crimes.

It also included a GOP proposal to cap the TSA's screener workforce at 46,000, or about 1,000 fewer than the 2013 employment figure. The workforce had been capped at 25,000 when the agency was created in 2001, and GOP lawmakers had expressed concern about its growth. The omnibus provided $158 million, $5 million more than the White House's request, for the TSA to hire private companies to undertake security functions at airports.

The TSA's overall funding was set at $4.9 billion, a cut from almost $5.2 billion in 2013. It was given money to continue training pilots to carry firearms, an effort the administration wanted to cut back or eliminate, arguing that stronger cockpit doors eliminated the need.

In addition, the omnibus gave $10 billion to the Coast Guard, turning aside the department's plan to cut back some of the Coast Guard's operations and spend more on upgrading its aging fleet. The omnibus provided money for materials for an eighth new National Security Cutter and for the construction of six Fast Response Cutter patrol boats. The Coast Guard also would receive fourteen C-27J patrol aircraft from the Air Force.

The administration's request for $6.2 billion for FEMA disaster relief was included in the bill, as was increased spending for first-responder grants. The omnibus offered a total of $1.5 billion for various state and local government grants.

Also included was $792 million for cybersecurity, which was $35.5 million more than the previous year. The Secret Service received $1.6 billion, $39 million more than requested. It was told to set aside $7.5 million to expand cybercrime training for judges, prosecutors, and local law enforcement.

The administration had requested $106 million for a project consolidating Homeland Security headquarters at the former St. Elizabeths Hospital campus in Washington; the bill provided $35 million.

Fiscal 2015 Homeland Security Appropriations

Disagreements between congressional Republicans and the Obama administration over immigration halted progress on homeland security spending bills for fiscal year 2015, which began on October 1, 2014. Ultimately, the measures were pushed off until early 2015 and the start of a new Congress. The Department of Homeland Security operated under a continuing resolution until February 27, 2015.

Ironically, both parties agreed in general on spending levels for homeland security agencies.

The House Homeland Security Appropriations Subcommittee had approved the House version of the homeland security spending bill May 28 by voice vote. Lawmakers turned aside most of the $1.04 billion in cuts that the White House had proposed for the department, bringing discretionary funding levels to $39.2 billion, $50 million less than the fiscal 2014 level and almost $888 million above the administration's request. While Republicans felt the bill put a priority on enforcement and operations, Democrats argued that it put arbitrary minimum standards on Immigration and Customs Enforcement (ICE) detention beds and lacked funding for cybersecurity operations.

The measure provided $8.5 billion for the Coast Guard, almost $316 million more than Obama had requested but almost $47 million less than the fiscal 2014 level. Under the bill, funding for ICE and for Customs and Border Protection (CBP) saw increases. CBP would get $10.8 billion, $98.3 million more than the White House request and $220 million more than the previous year's level. ICE's funding was set at $5.5 billion, $466.2 million more than Obama's request and more than $211 million above the 2014 level.

The full House Appropriations Committee approved the measure by voice vote on June 11.

On the Senate side, the Senate Homeland Security Appropriations Subcommittee approved its funding bill by voice vote June 24. The measure included $39 billion in discretionary spending and suggested a $2 rise in customs fees to cover additional immigration detention resources, partly to handle the sudden increase in unaccompanied child migrants.

The full Senate Appropriations Committee signed off on the bill, also by voice vote, two days later, on June 26. The committee added a provision allowing the Federal Emergency Management Agency (FEMA) more leeway in fiscal 2015 to cover costs of preventing future wildfires in areas stricken by disaster.

Overall FEMA funding in the measure totaled $10.7 billion, $359 million above the administration's request and $786 more than the previous year's level. The legislation called for $5.5 billion for ICE, $149 more than Obama's request and $106 million below 2014's level. The CBP would get $12.6 billion, $18 million less than the budget request and $480 million more than the fiscal 2014 level.

In early December 2014, already a couple of months into the fiscal 2015 year, appropriators followed through on a plan for a stopgap spending bill, included in the omnibus appropriations measure (HR 83), that would freeze funding levels for the Homeland Security Department through February 27. This deprived several agencies of the spending increases they had hoped for. The House passed HR 83 on December 11, on a vote of 219–206, and the Senate cleared it December 13 on a vote of 56–40. President Obama signed it on December 16.

Once the new Congress began in January 2015, with both chambers controlled by Republicans following GOP gains in the November 2014 midterms, House Republicans introduced a new full-year appropriations bill for Homeland Security (HR 240) and amended it in an effort to block immigration actions by President Obama that GOP lawmakers opposed. The Senate failed four times in February to move past procedural votes on the House bill, so GOP leaders went ahead without the controversial provisions.

At first, House Republicans refused to take up the new version, deciding instead to push for extra time with more stopgap legislation. But a vote in the House on a three-week spending measure (H J Res 35) failed, 203–224, when nearly all Democrats, joined by 52 Republicans, voted against the proposal. The House advanced a one-week stopgap measure (PL 114-3) two hours before funding would run out.

During the one-week period, House GOP leaders concluded that it would be unlikely for them to come up with the votes to approve another short-term spending measure and conceded that the Senate's stance left them with a choice: to set a funding shutdown in motion or to pass the base bill without the immigration language. In early March, House lawmakers, under a rarely used procedural rule, called a vote on agreeing to the Senate's changes to the legislation. This cleared the funding measure, more than five months after the 2015 fiscal year had begun.

2015–2016

As partisan tensions deepened in the run-up to the 2016 presidential election, one topic that continued to fester was immigration policy. In November 2015, following terrorist attacks in Paris, the Republican leadership tried to restrict refugees from Syria and Iraq from entering the United States. The measure passed in the House but was opposed by President Obama and ultimately was blocked by Democrats in the Senate.

The U.S. military facility at Guantanamo Bay, Cuba, which Obama had vowed to close, proved to be another difficult issue. The facility held detainees linked to the September 11, 2001, attacks, and questions swirled around the procedures under which these prisoners could be released or transferred. Congress eventually approved legislation in 2015 spelling out various requirements relating to the Guantanamo detainees. After vetoing one version of the bill, Obama signed a second version.

The 114th Congress also saw passage of a controversial cybersecurity measure. The measure, a compromise among previous iterations of the legislation, encouraged private companies to voluntarily share cyberthreat information with the government and with one another. While the bill's supporters argued it would strengthen the country's defenses against cyberattacks, critics said it would not do enough to safeguard privacy.

In addition, Congress in 2015 reauthorized the Patriot Act, a post–September 11 counterterrorism law, through 2019. The bill curtailed the National Security Agency's ability to collect bulk phone records of Americans' phone calls, another issue that had roiled American politics during the previous Congress.

At the end of 2016, lawmakers focused on Russia, which had meddled in that year's U.S. election and intervened militarily in Syria and Ukraine. In the fiscal year 2017 intelligence authorization bill, Congress targeted Russia, creating an entity within the executive branch to counter "Russian actions to exert covert influence over peoples and governments."

Patriot Act Reauthorization

The National Security Agency's ability to collect bulk phone records of Americans' phone calls was curtailed under legislation reauthorizing the post–September 11 counterterrorism law called the Patriot Act. The House passed the legislation (HR 2048), also known as the USA Freedom Act, which reauthorized the Patriot Act through 2019, on May 13, 2015. The Senate, after a difficult debate, followed suit on June 1, and President Obama signed the measure (PL 114-23) into law on June 2.

The issue of NSA surveillance of Americans' phone records had jumped into the spotlight back in 2013, after former government contractor Edward Snowden leaked information to journalists about the subject, and controversy had swirled around it ever since. Some argued that the surveillance was necessary to protect the country from terrorism, while others argued that people's privacy was being violated.

The bill, called the USA Freedom Act, had met with criticism from Senate Majority Leader Mitch McConnell, R-Ky., who had taken the post in January following the GOP takeover of the Senate after the 2014 midterm elections. McConnell proposed a series of amendments to the bill, which he argued were necessary for national security reasons. All of them ended up being voted down in the course of Senate debate on the measure, marking a major defeat for McConnell.

In April, McConnell had introduced a different bill (S 1035) to extend for five years the provisions in the Patriot Act that were fundamental to maintaining the NSA's surveillance authority. But many other lawmakers, including Democrats and libertarian Republicans, had concluded that the post–September 11 surveillance programs went too far.

The House, meanwhile, was moving ahead on the USA Freedom Act (HR 2048), passing its bill on a vote of 338–88 on May 13. Almost two weeks earlier, on April 30, the House Judiciary Committee had approved the bill, voting overwhelmingly, 25–2, for the measure. During the committee's debate, it turned back five amendments, including one by Rep. Ted Poe (R-Texas) that sought to end an NSA program under which the agency collected content of emails and phone calls between U.S. citizens and foreigners.

McConnell hoped to at least push for a compromise with the House leadership. But opponents of the Patriot Act extension, led by Sen. Rand Paul, McConnell's fellow Kentucky Republican, were eager to slow down the legislation's progress in the Senate.

McConnell gave up on the idea of a five-year extension of the Patriot Act but wanted to convince his GOP colleagues to give him time to come up with something more to his liking than the USA Freedom Act. But when a two-month extension (S 1357) came up for a vote, it failed, with only forty-five senators supporting it.

During Senate debate over the USA Freedom Act, McConnell proposed a series of amendments to the legislation. One would have eliminated a requirement in the bill that the Foreign Intelligence Surveillance Court, which grants warrants in terrorism cases in secret, empanel privacy and civil liberties experts to argue against the government position before the court. Democrats argued that the amendment was designed to weaken the bill's civil liberties protections.

Another McConnell amendment would have required that the national intelligence director certify that the phone company databases were searchable in real time before the transition from NSA storage of the call records to phone company stewardship could be finalized.

Ultimately, the Senate approved the bill on a vote of 67–32.

The legislation changed the rules for domestic surveillance by prohibiting the National Security Agency's bulk collection and storage of phone metadata. It also limited collection of other bulk data. It required the NSA to get approval from the Foreign Intelligence Surveillance Court to study the calling records of individual target phone numbers on a case-by-case basis before the request could be made to a phone company.

In addition, it limited the associated calling records of a phone number that could be examined to only two "hops" from the suspect's number. This basically codified proposals that President Obama had made back in 2014.

The bill also redefined the type of information that could be subject to search queries under surveillance programs. It imposed additional requirements for surveillance oversight. It also extended the Patriot Act Section 215 (relating to "tangible things" to be produced during an investigation), roving wiretap, and "Lone Wolf" surveillance authorities through December 2019.

Fiscal 2016 Cybersecurity and Intelligence Authorization

At the end of 2015, Congress combined a contentious cybersecurity information-sharing bill and a fiscal 2016 intelligence authorization bill and included them in a year-end omnibus appropriations bill (HR 2029) approved in December.

Privacy advocates and many big technology companies had opposed the cybersecurity bill, although many lawmakers on both sides of the aisle supported the measure. This measure proved more controversial than the intelligence authorization bill (HR 4127).

In the omnibus, lawmakers combined a compromise version of two cybersecurity bills (HR 1560 and HR 1731) that the House had approved in the spring with a version the Senate had passed on October 27 (S 754). The compromise measure encouraged private companies to voluntarily share cyberthreat information with the government and with one another. Companies that participated would get liability protection.

Backers of the bill argued it would help shore up the country's defenses against cyberattacks, but the bill's critics maintained it would not do enough to safeguard privacy and was basically a surveillance measure. Information-sharing legislation had been a flashpoint for debate, particularly since former national security contractor Edward Snowden's revelations about government surveillance.

In June, another security breach had alarmed lawmakers, a massive intrusion into the Office of Personnel Management's networks, believed to be the work of Chinese hackers. It compromised the personal information of more than 22 million current and former government workers. As a result, lawmakers were eager to demonstrate that they were trying to do something about cybersecurity threats.

Civil liberties and technology advocacy organizations criticized the bill's content and the process under which it was negotiated. One reason for their frustrations was that the bill they had favored, the House Homeland Security Committee version, seemed to be sidelined during negotiations in favor of the Intelligence Committee's bill.

Meanwhile, lawmakers had been working on a fiscal 2016 intelligence authorization measure. On December 1, the House approved a revised version of the bill (HR 4127), which included changes made in negotiations between House and Senate intelligence committee leaders. The vote on the measure was 364–58.

The version of the bill that ended up in the omnibus was virtually identical to this House version. It included various reporting requirements about the recent Iran nuclear deal, the fight against the Islamic State, and some actions and policies of Russia and China.

The bill required the DNI to report on how much money Iran had received in sanctions relief since the 2013 interim agreement on Tehran's nuclear program went into effect. The report was to include information on how Iran had used the money and whether it was being funneled toward terrorist activity, supporting Syrian President Bashar al-Assad, or developing a nuclear weapon.

In January, the White House had asked for $53.9 billion for the National Intelligence Program, the major part of intelligence spending. The administration asked for another $17.9 billion for the Military Intelligence Program, making the total $71.8 billion. The legislation funded the intelligence community at slightly below that figure.

Fiscal 2017 Intelligence Authorization

Although the House approved two versions of a fiscal 2017 intelligence authorization bill in 2016, the authorization was not actually enacted until the following year, as part of an omnibus appropriations measure.

Perhaps the most important provision in the intelligence measure involved Russia, a country many lawmakers saw in a suspicious light after Russia had meddled in the 2016 election and intervened militarily in Ukraine and Syria. The bill targeted Russia, creating a presidentially appointed group within the executive branch to counter "Russian actions to exert covert influence over peoples and governments."

The bill also contained a provision that required the secretary of state, the FBI, and the Director of National Intelligence (DNI) to establish an "advance notification regime" to govern and limit travel by accredited Russian diplomatic staffers. In addition, the bill required the DNI to create a report assessing Russia's war-fighting doctrine and the extent to which Russian flights under the Open Skies Treaty contributed to that doctrine. The treaty permitted signatories to conduct observation flights over each other's territory. It had gone into effect in 2002.

The administration had requested $70.3 billion for the intelligence community for fiscal 2017, including $53.5 billion for the National Intelligence Program and $16.8 billion for the Military Intelligence Program. Those figures did not include classified parts of the budget.

On April 29, the House Intelligence Committee marked up its bill, unanimously approving the measure (HR 5077).

Among its provisions was one requiring the DNI to post online, within 180 days of the bill's enactment, a list of logos and symbols connected with foreign terrorist groups. The DNI would also be required to declassify information on "past terrorist activities," including any role in the killing of U.S. troops or citizens, by detainees at the military prison at Guantanamo Bay.

In addition, the bill asked for a report from the DNI on the travel of foreign fighters to "terrorist safe havens" and another report on cybersecurity threats to U.S. seaports and maritime shipping.

In mid-April 2016, the Senate Intelligence Committee started to discuss its version of the intelligence bill. On June 7, the committee reported a bill (S 3017) to the Senate. However, several senators, concerned about a provision critics said would expand government surveillance powers, put holds on the measure.

House Intelligence Committee leaders, trying to work around these problems and get something done by the end of the year, introduced a new version of their bill. This new bill (HR 6393) included elements of the Senate measure, including the creation of a presidentially appointed group tasked with countering Russian efforts "to exert covert influence."

The bill also attempted to limit the travel of accredited Russian diplomatic staff to within twenty-five miles of their official post and required the DNI to produce a report assessing Russia's warfighting doctrine.

The bill did not include language from the Senate version that would have aimed at the intelligence community's ties with Hollywood and the entertainment industry by requiring the agencies to tell Congress at least thirty days before their organization works with TV or movie producers, writers, and others on a project.

The House approved the revised intelligence bill on November 30, but the Senate did not act on the legislation.

In early May 2017, House and Senate leaders finally succeeded in overcoming the impasse over intelligence policy and attached the authorization that the Senate had approved early in the year (S 133) to a must-pass omnibus spending bill (HR 244). In addition to the Russia-related provisions, the measure required intelligence agencies to tell Congress before working on TV or movie projects.

Guantanamo Prison Releases

With Republicans in charge of both houses of Congress during the 114th Congress, the question of the U.S. military prison at Guantanamo Bay, Cuba, where terrorists picked up after September 11 were detained, became a flashpoint. Obama believed the prison hurt the image of the United States and had pledged before he was president to close the facility. In the last couple of months of 2014, he transferred prisoners out of Guantanamo at a more rapid pace, part of his goal of closing the place down.

But many Republicans believed releasing the terrorists was putting U.S. security in jeopardy, although the administration of George W. Bush also had released or transferred prisoners from the facility.

In January 2015, Senate Armed Services Committee Chair John McCain, R-Ariz., said his panel would work on legislation that would prohibit any transfers to Yemen for two years and would suspend transfers of medium- and high-risk detainees from the prison. McCain and Sen. Lindsey Graham, R-S.C., the chair of the Judiciary subcommittee on crime and terrorism, had said they would support closing Guantanamo but expressed concern over what they considered the administration's lack of leadership on the issue and its inability to come up with a feasible alternative.

The Senate bill, S 165, also included language that required the administration to come up with a plan for transferring detainees from Guantanamo to a maximum-security prison within the United States. The committee approved the language, but the plan would need to meet congressional approval, which would be difficult in a Republican-controlled Congress. If Congress chose to accept the plan, existing prohibitions on domestic transfers would end, and new certifications relating to the foreign transfers of detainees would revert to the less restrictive standards already in place. But if Congress turned the plan down, the tighter standards and the ban on domestic transfers would remain in place.

On February 12, the Senate Armed Services Committee marked up the legislation (S 165) behind closed doors. The White House threatened a veto of the bill.

On the House side, the House Armed Services Committee marked up a fiscal 2016 defense authorization bill (HR 1735) in April 2015 that included strong new language forbidding movement of detainees to the United States. It also prohibited the transfer or release of prisoners to high-risk foreign countries and required the Secretary of Defense to meet multiple certification requirements before prisoners could be transferred abroad. The provisions were seen as a response to the administration's decision in May 2014 to transfer five Taliban prisoners from Guantanamo to Qatar in exchange for captured Army Sgt. Bowe Bergdahl.

Under the House bill, among other requirements, a detainee could not be moved unless the administration certified that the host nation was not a state sponsor of terrorism and was not facing a threat that would hinder its ability to hold the prisoner. The certification would need to be given to Congress at least thirty days before any transfer. The bill also barred the transfer of detainees to designated combat zones and continued year-on-year bans on transferring prisoners to the United States for imprisonment and on funds to construct or modify facilities in the United States for the holding of the detainees.

Congress eventually approved a defense authorization bill on October 7 that would have repealed less stringent requirements on detainees that had been implemented under a fiscal 2014 defense authorization law (PL 113-66) and returned to stricter standards. Under the agreement, the transfer of detainees to Yemen, Somalia, Syria, or Libya was prohibited. Detainees could not be transferred to the United States, and any construction or modification of U.S. facilities for the housing of detainees was prohibited. The legislation called for the Pentagon to provide a plan within ninety days of enactment on the current and future detention of people held under the 2001 authorization for use of military force (PL 107-40).

Obama chose to veto the defense bill. He signed a second version of the bill (S 1356), which prohibited the transfer of Guantanamo detainees to Yemen, Somalia, Syria, or Libya, as well as the transfer of detainees to the United States, and prohibited the construction or modification of facilities in the United States for housing detainees. Under this second bill, the administration had to produce a plan within ninety days of enactment on how and where it would hold current and future enemy combatants.

Senate Blocks Refugee Restrictions

Terrorist attacks in Paris on November 13, 2015, affected congressional approaches to the ongoing issue of how many refugees to accept from Syria and Iraq. In the wake of the attacks, House Republicans attempted to restrict refugees from those countries through legislation (HR 4038) that had the backing of House leaders.

House Speaker Paul D. Ryan, R-Wis., and Majority Leader Kevin McCarthy, R-Calif., had a GOP task force tackle the issue of refugees in the days following the Paris attacks. The task force included some important committee chairs, including Rep. Michael McCaul, R-Texas, chair of the Homeland Security committee. McCaul introduced the bill, which would require FBI approval for all refugee resettlement applications from Syrian and Iraqi asylum seekers. On November 19, the House easily passed the measure on a vote of 289–137.

But President Obama had threatened a veto of the measure, and many senior congressional Democrats opposed it. Although the bill ostensibly would not prevent the president from admitting Syrian refugees, it added a layer of certification that had the potential to slow the process, which already took eighteen to twenty-four months.

Under the measure, new Syrian and Iraqi refugees would not be allowed entry into the United States until the FBI and the Director of National Intelligence jointly told Congress that the refugees were not a security threat. In addition, the measure required Homeland Security to give monthly reports to Congress on the number of Syrian and Iraqi refugees admitted and the number denied admission. It also required the department's inspector general to undertake "risk-based" reviews of all Syrian and Iraqi refugee certifications.

However, the measure faced obstacles in the Senate and, to the dismay of many conservatives, was not included in the measures added to the year-end omnibus appropriations package. The omnibus bill did include legislation (HR 158) that required enhanced security checks in the visa waiver program. The House had approved that measure on a vote of 407–19.

Fiscal 2016 Homeland Security Appropriations

Appropriating money for homeland security programs was a complicated process in 2015, the first year of the 114th Congress. The process ultimately involved two steps: one bill for seven months of fiscal 2015 and another for fiscal 2016.

Republicans, who already had control of the House in the 113th Congress, won control of the Senate as well in the 2014 midterm elections. After the elections, members had started negotiations on an omnibus spending bill designed to complete the fiscal 2015 appropriations process. The fiscal 2015 year had already begun on October 1, 2014, but lawmakers had not completed their work.

However, the omnibus efforts hit a roadblock in mid-November when President Obama announced executive actions on immigration that the White House said would prevent the deportation of nearly 5 million illegal immigrants. The initiative (Deferred Action for Parents of Americans and Lawful Permanent Residents, or DAPA) called for government immigration enforcement activities to focus on national security threats, serious criminals, and recent border crossers *(See discussion of DAPA in Chapter 13, p. 414.)*

Obama's plan created a new deferred-action category for illegal immigrants who had lived in the United States for more than five years and were parents of children who are U.S. citizens or lawful permanent residents. The plan also expanded a previous Obama program, Deferred Action for Childhood Arrivals (DACA), created in 2012, to apply to children who entered the United States before January 1, 2010. Obama's actions were the subject of lawsuits, and the issue of immigration continued to roil politics, especially as the 2016 presidential campaign got underway.

Conservatives, angered by Obama's move, wanted to use the omnibus package to force a confrontation with the president on the immigration issue. But GOP leaders tried to forestall the showdown until the new GOP-controlled Congress began its work in January 2015.

Congress ended up enacting a fiscal 2015 omnibus appropriations bill (PL 113-235) providing full, detailed spending for the rest of fiscal 2015 for eleven of the twelve appropriations measures—all but Homeland Security, which was funded by a continuing resolution through February 27, 2015. This approach was seen as a way to give members the opportunity to respond to Obama's immigration actions in a second, seven-month fiscal 2015 appropriations bill. The Department of Homeland Security includes agencies that enforce immigration laws as well as those that protect against terrorists entering the country.

In early 2015, the House agreed to take up a fiscal 2015 Homeland Security Appropriations bill that had been negotiated in December by Senate Democrats and House Republicans as part of the broader omnibus. The measure (HR 240) was unveiled on January 9. Again, many conservative lawmakers saw this bill as a way to express their displeasure with Obama's immigration moves. The House passed the bill on January 14, on a vote of 236–191, adding five controversial Republican amendments seeking to block or roll back the president's orders.

The five amendments were

- an amendment by Rep. Robert B. Aderholt, R-Ala., that would bar the use of any funds to implement various administration policies on immigration or to grant any federal benefit to any illegal immigrant as a result of those policies. The House adopted the amendment, 237–190.
- an amendment by Rep. Marsha Blackburn, R-Tenn., to bar the use of any funds after January 9, 2015, to consider new, renewal, or previously denied applications under Obama's 2012 DACA program or any succeeding executive policy. This amendment passed on a narrow 218–209 vote.
- an amendment by Rep. Ron DeSantis, R-Fla., to prioritize immigration enforcement actions against illegal immigrants convicted of any offense involving domestic violence, sexual abuse, child molestation, or child exploitation. This amendment was approved 278–149.
- an amendment by Rep. Matt Salmon, R-Ariz., that expressed the sense of Congress that the administration should not pursue policies that disadvantage the hiring of U.S. citizens and those lawfully present in the country by making it economically advantageous to hire workers who came to the country illegally. This amendment passed on a vote of 253–171.
- an amendment by Rep. Aaron Schock, R-Ill., expressing the sense of Congress that the administration should stop putting the interest of immigrants who entered the country legally behind those who arrived illegally. The amendment was approved 260–167.

But in the Senate, Democrats stood firm in their opposition to the immigration amendments, blocking consideration of the homeland security measure in a series of procedural votes. Republicans grew concerned that if an impasse ensued, they would be blamed for another government shutdown.

In late February and early March, both chambers worked to clear a final fiscal 2015 appropriations measure without the immigration riders. The bill provided a total of $47.8 billion for the Department of Homeland Security. It included $39.7 billion in discretionary spending subject to budget caps, $6.4 billion for emergency disaster relief that was not subject to the regular caps, and $213 million for Overseas Contingency Operations within the Coast Guard. The total figure was a $1.2 billion increase over the previous year and $1.6 billion more than the president's request.

In the fiscal 2015 bill was $12.6 billion for Customs and Border Protection, $7.2 billion for the Transportation Security Administration, $6.3 billion for Immigration and Customs Enforcement, and $1.7 billion for the Secret Service.

After a series of maneuvers and complications, both houses of Congress approved the measure, and President Obama signed it (PL 114-4) into law on March 4, bringing an end to the saga of the fiscal 2015 homeland security spending measure.

Meanwhile, Congress needed to work on a fiscal 2016 homeland security appropriations bill. The Obama administration had requested $41.4 billion in adjusted net discretionary budget authority for homeland security programs.

The Senate Appropriations Committee reported its version of the bill on June 18, voting for the measure 26–4. The bill included $40.2 billion in adjusted net discretionary budget authority, $1.2 billion below the president's request but $500 million over the previous year's total. The House Appropriations Committee approved its version of the bill on July 14, on a 32–17 vote. This measure called for $39.3 billion.

But the appropriations process for fiscal 2016 disintegrated during a partisan fight over the display of the Confederate flag on federal lands, and the homeland security bill was not considered by either chamber. Finally, in December 2015, congressional leaders negotiated an omnibus spending measure combining all twelve appropriations bills. The measure (PL 114-113) was approved by the House and Senate on December 18, and President Obama signed it the same day.

The bill appropriated $41 billion in discretionary funding subject to spending caps, $160 million in Overseas Contingency Operations funding, and $6.7 billion in disaster relief funding. It increased funding for Customs and Border Protection by 4 percent over the previous year, Coast Guard funding by 7 percent, and TSA funding by 3 percent. It reduced funding for ICE by 2 percent.

Among other provisions, the measure included $216 million to consolidate DHS's headquarters at the St. Elizabeths campus in Washington, D.C.

Fiscal 2017 Homeland Security Appropriations

Legislation to fund homeland security programs for fiscal 2017 failed to make it to either the House or Senate floor in 2016. Lawmakers did not even manage to combine the various appropriations bills into one omnibus package. Instead, they passed two continuing resolutions, one to keep the government operating through the end of the fiscal year on September 30, 2016, and one that extended spending through March 2017.

Both the House and Senate Appropriations Committees had passed versions of homeland security appropriations legislation earlier in the year.

Back on May 24, 2016, the Senate Homeland Security Appropriations Subcommittee approved a draft fiscal 2017 spending bill. On May 26, the full Senate Appropriations Committee approved, 30–0, a Homeland Security spending package for the coming fiscal year.

The package called for $49.7 billion in spending for fiscal 2017, about $307.7 million above the previous year's enacted level and about $740.4 million over the Obama administration's request.

The bill included $11.4 billion for the Federal Emergency Management Agency, the department's biggest component; $11.2 billion for Customs and Border Protection; $10.4 billion for the Coast Guard; $5.96 billion for Immigration and Customs Enforcement; and $5.08 billion for the Transportation Security Administration.

On the House side, the House Homeland Security Appropriations Subcommittee, by voice vote, approved a draft fiscal 2017 spending bill on June 9. The full House Appropriations Committee approved its bill June 22 by voice vote. The measure provided $41.1 billion for homeland spending. The total did not include an additional $7.3 billion for the Federal Emergency Management Agency for disaster relief funds.

CHAPTER 4

Foreign Policy

Foreign Policy

In President Barack Obama's second term, he faced competing crises on the international stage—from the ongoing civil war in Syria to the deepening reach of the Islamic State of Iraq and the Levant (ISIL) to North Korea's growing nuclear capabilities. The president was also contending with two U.S.-led wars—one in Iraq and one in Afghanistan—that, while subdued somewhat from their peak, still required significant investment of military and diplomatic resources.

Midway through his second term, Democrats lost control of the Senate, ceding the legislative majority to Republicans and all but guaranteeing that the president would have little opportunity to act through Congress to fulfill his international priorities. Despite their majority, Republicans frequently found themselves unable to reach an agreement to prevent the president's policies from taking effect. Republicans were keen, for example, to stop the president from normalizing diplomatic relations with Cuba and prevent the United States from signing on to a multilateral agreement on Iran's nuclear program. Legislative attempts, however, failed to produce any actionable strategies to thwart Obama's efforts on these issues.

MIDDLE EASTERN CONFLICTS

The ongoing civil war and humanitarian crisis in Syria raised tensions across the Middle East as allies of President Bashar al-Assad, like Iran, faced off in what became a proxy war against nations backing the rebels, including Saudi Arabia. The scenario led the United States to wade cautiously into the conflict, but in 2013, after the United Nations confirmed that the Assad regime had used chemical weapons against civilians, the president was forced to act. UN Secretary General Ban Ki-moon pressured member nations to come together to find a solution—diplomatic or otherwise—to force Assad to end the civil war. Because Russia and China, two permanent members of the Security Council, thwarted efforts to sanction or take official action against Assad, the United States raised the option of U.S. unilateral airstrikes targeting chemical weapons facilities. Ultimately, the United States did carry out an air campaign against the Assad regime, backed by its international partners including France and the United Kingdom.

A host of peace talks were attempted in 2014, 2015, and 2016 to end the Syrian crisis, many of which were led by the United Nations. Despite involvement from dozens of countries, progress was halting, and the parties struggled to reach a ceasefire agreement given the rebels' commitment to a transitional government and new elections and Assad's refusal to relinquish his power. In 2015, the United Nations passed a resolution calling for the rebels and the Assad government to meet and develop a roadmap toward a peaceful transition of power and resolution of the conflict. Those talks never came to fruition. The international body tried again in 2016, but talks quickly faltered. The United States and Russia successfully worked on a ceasefire agreement that was implemented in late February 2016, but it collapsed by the summer, and a second ceasefire also quickly failed. The United States subsequently decreased its involvement in diplomatic efforts, leaving Russia and Turkey to take the lead. They secured a third temporary

REFERENCES

Discussion of foreign policy for the years 1945–1964 may be found in *Congress and the Nation Vol. I*, pp. 91–232; for the years 1965–1968, *Congress and the Nation Vol. II*, pp. 49–116; for the years 1969–1972, *Congress and the Nation Vol. III*, pp. 853–948; for the years 1973–1976, *Congress and the Nation Vol. IV*, pp. 847–912; for the years 1977–1980, *Congress and the Nation Vol. V*, pp. 31–95; for the years 1981–1984, *Congress and the Nation Vol. VI*, pp. 123–197; for the years 1985–1988, *Congress and the Nation Vol. VII*, pp. 169–251; for the years 1989–1992, *Congress and the Nation Vol. VIII*, pp. 203–297; for the years 1993–1996, *Congress and the Nation Vol. IX*, pp. 187–250; for the years 1997–2000, *Congress and the Nation Vol. X*, pp. 173–231; for the years 2001–2004, *Congress and the Nation Vol. XI*, pp. 229–300; for the years 2005–2008, *Congress and the Nation Vol. XII*, pp. 270–327; for the years 2009–2012, *Congress and the Nation Vol. XIII*, pp. 223–259.

ceasefire to allow civilians to leave and humanitarian aid workers to gain access to stranded civilians, at the same time as Assad's forces reclaimed control of the capital city of Aleppo.

In nearby Egypt, the United States found itself in another quandary. The 2011 Arab Spring uprising that swept across the Middle East and Northern Africa resulted in the end of Hosni Mubarak's thirty-year grip on power. A subsequent democratic election installed as president Mohammed Morsi, who used his authority to punish his detractors. Morsi was overthrown by the military in 2013. The White House refused to refer to the overthrow as a coup, a word that carries significant weight in how the United States has to handle its relationship with the country. If Obama had declared the overthrow a coup, it would have triggered language in the Foreign Assistance Act that prevents assistance—with the exception of humanitarian aid—from going to any country "whose duly elected head of government is deposed by military coup or decree." That could have weakened the United States' relationship with Egypt, which it has long viewed as a key ally and stabilizing force in the Middle East.

The Egyptian military, under its leader Abdul Fattah el-Sisi, did hold a constitutional referendum and presidential elections in 2014. Unsurprisingly, Sisi won the election with 97 percent of the vote. International election observers said the poll was marred by irregularities and did not stand up to democratic norms. The new president quickly concentrated power in the executive and pushed back parliamentary elections indefinitely. Sisi's reign has been characterized by continuing indifference toward international calls for a full transition to democracy, and he instead prefers to use the media as a mouthpiece of the state while brutally cracking down on any opponents.

The biggest Middle Eastern victory for the Obama administration came in 2015 when, after two years of delays, the talks between China, France, Germany, Russia, the United Kingdom, the United States, and Iran produced the Joint Comprehensive Plan of Action (JCPOA), a multilateral agreement intended to reduce Iran's nuclear activities in exchange for a lifting of sanctions. Although members of both parties noted that the agreement was flawed, Democrats were more likely to side with the president, believing this was the best diplomatic outcome that could be expected. Republicans, on the other hand, were highly critical of the deal and worked to pass legislation either stopping its implementation or limiting its power. Ultimately, by the end of Obama's presidency, Congress was unable to reach an agreement to stop the JCPOA from taking effect.

THE ISLAMIC STATE

Perhaps one of the biggest challenges of Obama's second term was how to deal with the rise of the Islamic State. The group, which has roots in the fall of Saddam Hussein, declared a caliphate in 2014. Since that time, it has been growing in power, especially in Iraq and Syria, where it claimed significant portions of territory, including some of the largest cities in Iraq. The United States was cautious in its response, and President Obama frequently reiterated his concern that the United States could become engaged in another long-term ground war. He preferred, instead, to maintain the U.S. commitment to training Iraqi soldiers, offering counterterrorism support, and providing military equipment to the Iraqis to fight the militant group.

In 2014, the president announced in a televised address that the United States would be taking its strongest action to date, launching airstrikes against key ISIL strongholds in Iraq, in an effort to protect humanitarian aid workers and its own interests in the country. Thousands of strikes would be carried out by the United States and its international partners throughout 2014 and 2015 in both Iraq and Syria. The president also authorized a limited, nonmilitary engagement that included additional humanitarian aid and intelligence assistance, along with a few hundred support troops. The president relied on the 2001 and 2002 Authorization for the Use of Military Force (AUMF) to conduct these activities, despite pushback from critics that those pieces of legislation did not provide broad capability to the president to carry out military activity against Islamic State terrorists. In 2015, President Obama submitted to Congress draft legislation requesting a new AUMF, with the specific goal of fighting terrorism around the globe. Weighed down by partisan infighting, however, Congress was unable to pass new AUMF legislation, but it did succeed in providing the president additional funds to fight ISIL as part of a defense appropriation.

ISIL's impact was not limited to the devastation it wrought across Iraq and Syria. The militant group's reach spread across the globe. Dozens of attacks were either directly carried out by or inspired by the Islamic State, resulting in hundreds killed and thousands more injured. A glut of attacks in France and Belgium increased Western involvement in the fight against ISIL but also raised concerns around the European Union about whether the nations should continue to accept Syrian refugees and whether their traditionally open borders should be subject to more stringent citizenship verification or closed altogether.

The Islamic State's rise also led to a serious humanitarian crisis, with millions internally displaced and millions of refugees flooding into the neighboring nations of Jordan, Turkey, and Lebanon. Aid workers trying to reach those stranded by the fighting in their home countries were hampered by both the Syrian government and rebel groups that prevented assistance from reaching civilians. For those who had managed to escape, the United Nations pled with its member states to support the nations that were struggling with the influx of Iraqi and Syrian citizens, but the coffers frequently came up short.

ISIL ATTACKS

The Islamic State of Iraq and the Levant, alternately known as ISIL, ISIS, and the Islamic State, is a terrorist group rooted in the 2003 fall of Saddam Hussein's government in Iraq. It came to worldwide prominence about a decade later as it used the power vacuum in neighboring Syria to increase its ranks and begin claiming territory in the region. The militant group is responsible for dozens of deadly attacks in Iraq and Syria that have killed thousands of civilians. But in 2014, after its leader Abu Bakr al Baghdadi declared a caliphate, the Islamic State's reach spread across the globe. Since then, the group has carried out or inspired more than 100 attacks in dozens of countries, leaving thousands dead and injured. Because of their involvement in the fight against terrorism in the Middle East, a growing number of those attacks have occurred in Western nations. Although not all of the attacks are directed by ISIL leaders, many involve perpetrators that pledge their allegiance to the terrorist group.

France has borne the brunt of many of the deadliest Western attacks either directed or inspired by ISIL. From January 7 to 9, 2015, a spate of related attacks in and around Paris killed seventeen, twelve of whom were gunned down in the offices of the French satirical magazine *Charlie Hebdo*. On November 13, a coordinated attack in central Paris killed 130 civilians in cafes and a music venue. The following year, more than eighty were killed in Nice, France, after a truck drove through a Bastille Day festival. Each occurrence was followed by a claim of responsibility by the Islamic State and resulted in increased airstrikes by French forces against ISIL strongholds.

Neighboring Brussels, Belgium, where the central city was shut down in November 2015 as the masterminds of the Paris attacks were sought out, was the site of the nation's deadliest terror attack on March 22, 2016. Thirty-two civilians were killed by two bombs in the Zaventem airport and a suicide attack at the Maalbeek metro station. Belgium, and specifically the Molenbeek neighborhood, are frequently touted in the media as a hotbed of terrorist activity. The country has had more of its citizens per capita join ISIL than any other European nation, and the Molenbeek neighborhood, where the 2015 Paris attackers were found, was also home to a man who attacked a Paris-bound train in 2015 and the gunman who killed four at a Brussels museum one year earlier. Many blame the high rate of poverty and limited opportunity for the residents of the overcrowded Brussels municipality for breeding a propensity for violence.

In the United States, fourteen were killed and more than twenty injured on December 2, 2015, at a San Bernardino, California, public health facility by a man and his wife who pledged allegiance to ISIL on Facebook. Although the Federal Bureau of Investigation (FBI) announced that its investigation had found no direct links to any terrorist cell, it did treat the situation as a terrorist attack. ISIL called the shooters two of its followers. Six months later, on June 12, 2016, fifty were killed in an ISIL-inspired shooting at a gay nightclub in Orlando. The shooter told police negotiators that he was inspired by U.S. airstrikes against ISIL and called on the country to stop bombing Syria and Iraq. It was later learned that the FBI had twice investigated the shooter for alleged terrorist links prior to the attack.

NORTH KOREAN WEAPONS PROGRAM

Defying the international community and sanctions imposed by the United Nations, United States, and European Union, North Korea continued to enhance its weapons programs, conducting ballistic missile and nuclear tests. In 2016 alone, the reclusive nation carried out more than a dozen missile and rocket tests, including at least two fired by submarine. Since it revealed its nuclear program in 2002 and withdrew from the Nuclear Non-Proliferation Treaty, multiple attempts have been made to reach an agreement with the North Korean government to abandon its nuclear program in exchange for the lifting of economic sanctions and additional aid. These talks have repeatedly failed, and international response to the growing frequency and strength of the weapons tests have had little impact on the state. China, a key ally and trading partner of North Korea, has typically stood in the way of any harsh sanctions while at the same time denouncing the nation's nuclear ambition.

The United States imposed unilateral sanctions against North Korea over its nuclear program beginning in 1992 (the Treasury Department has been issuing its own financial sanctions regarding trade issues since the 1950s). The U.S. sanctions differ from those levied by the United Nations in that they often target more individuals and businesses and place more specific restrictions on economic activity. Until recently, these sanctions were typically imposed by the president or an executive-level department, such as the Treasury. In 2016, however, Congress imposed its first sanctions on North Korea. Passed with bipartisan support, and quickly signed into law by the White House, the North Korea Sanctions and Policy Enhancement Act of 2016 (HR 757—PL 114–122) sanctioned individuals, foreign financial institutions, and governments that either helped the country evade UN sanctions or helped it proliferate nuclear weapons.

North Korea also drew international ire for the treatment of its citizens. In 2014, the United Nations released a report detailing extensive human rights violations being carried out by the government of leader Kim Jong Un. According to the report, the regime was responsible for crimes against humanity including "extermination, murder, enslavement, torture, imprisonment, rape, forced abortions and other sexual violence," persecuting citizens based on their political and religious views, and causing "prolonged starvation." North Korea rejected the report's findings, but when it appeared that the United Nations might refer it to the International Criminal Court or impose additional sanctions, the government began pivoting toward the international community, reopening talks with South Korea, releasing American detainees, and appearing before the United Nations. The U.S. Department of State released its own human rights report in 2016, identifying officials who were allegedly responsible for torture, forced labor, arbitrary arrests, and extrajudicial killing. Based on the report's findings, for the first time ever, the Treasury Department imposed direct sanctions on Kim while also levying sanctions against fifteen other individuals and entities for their involvement in human rights abuses.

Chronology of Action on Foreign Policy

2013–2014

At the start of Obama's second term, Congress was characterized more by what it did not do than what it did do. With a Republican-controlled House and Democratic-controlled Senate in 2013, and then a Republican majority in both houses after the 2014 elections, the ability to reach consensus on any issue was severely limited. Where Democrats and the White House expended their political capital, it was primarily for domestic rather than foreign issues.

Most of the foreign activity considered by Congress in the first two years of Obama's second term had to do with appropriating funds for efforts abroad. Egypt, for example, is the largest recipient of U.S. foreign aid of any country other than Israel, and the United States has been keen to ensure the nation remains a key, strategic ally in the region. A few attempts were made to cut back or slow aid to Egypt after its democratically elected president was overthrown by the military, but those were rejected in favor of supporting the relationship. Although Congress maintained the annual level of funding ($1.3 billion for military aid and $250 million in economic assistance), it did impose conditions that Egypt would need to meet for the money to be released, including working toward presidential elections and a referendum on a new constitution.

Congress also authorized funds for the president for ongoing operations in Iraq and Syria, primarily intended to support action against the Islamic State. Despite a request from the White House, funds for Syria were authorized only for action against the Islamic State and were barred from being used by the rebels to fight against the government of President Bashar al-Assad. Since the 2011 Arab Spring uprising, Assad had refused to step down and had undertaken increasingly violent means to quash the rebels, including the use of chemical weapons. In Iraq, the president submitted to Congress a draft Authorization for the Use of Military Force (AUMF) aimed at fighting terrorist organizations abroad, but Congress balked at passing such legislation because members disagreed over whether there should be a time limit attached to such a measure, if it should be geographically targeted, and whether it should focus on one terrorist group or allow for a broader scope.

Congress made some headway toward passing legislation that would increase economic and human rights sanctions against Iran over the continued growth of its nuclear program. A sanctions bill (HR 850) passed the House almost unanimously, despite urging from the White House to hold off on the legislation as it pursued multilateral, diplomatic talks to halt Iran's nuclear ambitions. Companion legislation was proposed in the Senate but stalled in committee and never reached a floor vote. Renewed attempts were made in the Senate to attach sanction amendments to the FY 2014 defense authorization bill; however, they were rejected in favor of utilizing the fast-track process to ensure the bill passed before the end of the year.

Fiscal 2014 State-Foreign Operations Funding

Partisan disagreements on divisive policy riders, economic and multilateral assistance to foreign countries, and a $10 billion discretionary funding gap between the House and Senate Appropriations Committee budgets prevented consensus on a stand-alone fiscal 2014 appropriations bill for the State Department and foreign operations. Disagreement over the spending measure contributed to a protracted and contentious federal budget negotiations process that continued three months past the October 1 start of the fiscal year. Senate Democrats and House Republicans were sharply divided over the handling of budget cuts and decreased spending levels set by the Budget Control Act of 2011 (S 365—PL 112–25), while Republicans also sought to halt the scheduled rollout of President Obama's landmark legislation, the Patient Protection and Affordable Care Act (ACA).

Without approved funding measures in place by the start of the fiscal year, lawmakers sought a continuing resolution (CR) to keep the government running through December 15. However, Republican inclusion of language designed to severely limit ACA implementation met strong Democratic resistance, including the threat of presidential veto. The measure failed to pass, and the government shut down for sixteen days, from October 1 to October 17.

FOREIGN POLICY LEADERSHIP

New team members were appointed to nearly every foreign policy leadership position within the Obama administration during the president's second term, though all were familiar faces at the White House and within their respective agencies. James R. Clapper Jr. remained the director of national intelligence until January 2017.

State Department

U.S. Ambassador to the United Nations Susan Rice and Senate Foreign Relations Committee Chair John Kerry, D-Mass., were widely viewed as the two leading candidates to replace outgoing Secretary of State Hillary Clinton. However, Rice ultimately withdrew her name from consideration after being assailed by Republicans for remarks she made about the attack on the U.S. consulate in Benghazi, Libya, that later proved inaccurate. The president's subsequent nomination of Kerry was well received by his colleagues in the Senate, where he had represented the Commonwealth of Massachusetts since 1985. A 2004 presidential candidate, Kerry was also engaged by the administration during Obama's first term to serve as a diplomatic envoy to Pakistan, Afghanistan, and Syria.

Kerry's nomination was unanimously approved by the Senate Foreign Relations Committee on January 29, 2013, along with a resolution honoring the senator for his four years of service as committee chair. Hours later, the full Senate voted overwhelmingly to confirm Kerry by a vote of 94–3. Senators Ted Cruz, R-Texas, John Cornyn, R-Texas, and James Inhofe, R-Okla., cast the three no votes. Inhofe expressed a concern about Kerry's focus on global warming, while a spokesman for Cornyn said Kerry had a history of embracing liberal ideologies that did not reflect the opinions of a majority of Texans.

Kerry was sworn in as secretary of state on February 1, 2013. Assessments of Kerry's tenure typically cite the successful negotiation of the Iran nuclear deal and the development of the Paris Climate Agreement as his key accomplishments, while the United States' ineffective response to the crisis in Syria is generally considered to be his greatest failure.

William J. Burns continued to serve as the deputy secretary of state until November 3, 2014, at which point Undersecretary for Political Affairs Wendy R. Sherman became the acting deputy. Anthony Blinken, former principal deputy national security advisor, assumed the deputy title in January 2015.

United Nations

Susan Rice succeeded Tom Donilon as national security advisor—a position that does not require Senate confirmation—on July 1, 2013. Rosemary DiCarlo, the deputy permanent representative to the United Nations, was tapped to serve as acting ambassador until Samantha

Power was confirmed on August 1 by a vote of 84–10. Power previously served on the National Security Council as a special assistant to the president and the senior director for multilateral affairs and human rights. She had also served as a senior foreign policy advisor during the president's 2008 campaign.

Power had a reputation for being critical of U.S. foreign policy and faced several challenges from Republican senators during her confirmation hearing. In her testimony, Power backed away from past comments about the United States abetting massive crimes against humanity and Israel's human rights abuses toward the Palestinians and sought to reassure senators she believed the United States was "the greatest country on earth."

Central Intelligence Agency

Perhaps the most controversial change to Obama's foreign policy team was the January 2013 nomination of John Brennan as director of the CIA. The post had been temporarily filled by Deputy Director Michael Morell since David H. Petraeus's resignation in November 2012, following revelations that he had had an extramarital affair.

A nearly twenty-five-year veteran of the CIA, Brennan had been an intelligence advisor during Obama's campaign and was serving as assistant to the president for homeland security and counterterrorism at the time of his nomination. Despite his years of experience, both Democrats and Republicans raised concerns about Brennan's nomination, citing controversial policies implemented by the administrations for which he worked. During his confirmation hearing on February 7, Brennan faced questions about his support for the CIA's use of enhanced interrogation techniques under former President George W. Bush, drawing criticism for declining to describe waterboarding as torture, although he said the technique would never be used under his directorship. Brennan was also asked about the Obama administration's drone program, which he defended by stating that drone strikes were only used when "there is no other alternative."

A confirmation vote was delayed for weeks as lawmakers sought government documents offering further details about the administration's drone strikes and the Benghazi attack. In addition, Sen. Rand Paul, R-Ky., staged a thirteen-hour filibuster the day before the vote, calling for a statement from the administration that drones would not be used to kill American citizens who are suspected of terrorism on U.S. soil. Attorney General Eric Holder sent Paul a letter stating that the president did not have the authority to use a weaponized drone to kill an American who was not engaged in combat on American soil, which the senator claimed was a victory for civil liberties. The Senate ultimately confirmed Brennan by a vote of 63–44 on March 7.

Outlays for International Affairs

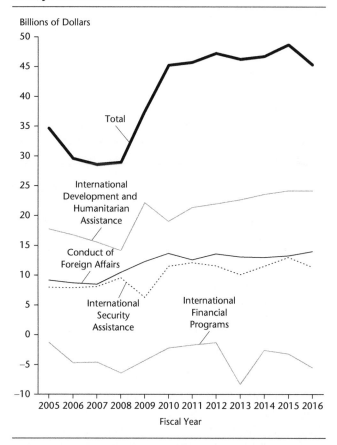

SOURCE: Office of Management and Budget, *Historical Tables, Budget of the United States Government: Fiscal Year 2018* (Washington, DC: U.S. Government Printing Office, 2018), Table 3.2.

NOTE: Total line includes some expenditures not shown separately.

Closed-door meetings between Sen. Harry Reid, D-Nev., and Sen. Mitch McConnell, R-Ky., produced a deal on October 15 to reopen the government through January 15, 2014; to increase the debt ceiling to allow the Treasury Department to borrow whatever was needed to cover the government's obligations through February 7, 2014; and to pay federal workers who had been furloughed because of the shutdown. While not included in subsequent legislation, Reid and McConnell's agreement also included the formation of a conference committee to produce a final agreement on the fiscal 2014 budget resolution, with a deadline of December 13, 2013. With bipartisan support, the Senate attached the debt limit deal and the CR to an unrelated House bill (HR 2775), which quickly passed the House and was signed into law by President Obama on October 17.

Conferees began meeting periodically in an effort to jumpstart the budget negotiation process and resolve spending differences ahead of the December 13 deadline. However, they made little progress, in part because statutory changes to the sequester and spending caps were needed to appease lawmakers on both sides of the aisle. As a result, Senate Budget Committee Chair Patty Murray,

D-N.Y., and House Budget Committee Chair Paul Ryan, R-Wisc., focused on working together to write and present a bipartisan budget agreement (HJ Res. 59) that raised discretionary spending levels and reduced sequestration cuts for fiscal years 2014 and 2015. Funding for the State Department and foreign operations, along with eleven other appropriations bills, were ultimately rolled into a fiscal 2014 omnibus measure (HR 3547–PL 113–76) negotiated under the terms of this bipartisan agreement.

House Action

Neither the House nor the Senate was willing to match the amount of State Department and foreign operations funding requested by the Obama administration in its proposed fiscal 2014 budget. The Republican-controlled House was particularly eager to slash nonwar spending. In July, the House Subcommittee on State, Foreign Operations, and Related Programs put forward a draft bill (HR 2855–H Rept 113–185) sponsored by subcommittee Chair Kay Granger, R-Texas, that provided the State Department with a $34.1 billion base discretionary budget—$13.8 billion less than the president had requested.

The bill would have reduced funding for overseas aid and multilateral assistance (the latter by more than half) but provided $6.5 billion for war-related activities, counterterrorism efforts, and humanitarian relief for refugees. The bill also sought to restore the controversial Mexico City Policy, which forbids U.S. aid to international groups providing abortion-related services, including counseling and referrals. A frequent political football, this policy has been repealed and reinstated several times since its introduction in the 1980s and was a regularly contested issue in budget negotiations during the Obama presidency. Similarly, the House bill prevented assistance to the United Nations Population Fund (UNPF), a program focused on safe childbirth and accessible birth control, and limited U.S. aid to international family planning and reproductive health programs to $461 million, equivalent to the fiscal 2008 funding level. The House Appropriations Committee reported the measure on July 30, but no further action was taken by the full House.

Senate Action

Chair Patrick Leahy, D-Vt., sponsored the Senate State, Foreign Operations, and Related Programs Subcommittee's draft appropriations bill (S 1372–S Rept 113–81), under which base discretionary programs would receive almost $10 billion more than the House had appropriated. The bill also increased multilateral aid to $3.5 billion, provided $39.5 million to the UNPF, and allocated $670 million for global family planning and reproductive health programs.

The Senate Appropriations Committee reported the measure to the full Senate on July 25. The committee also voted 19–11 to repeal the Mexico City Policy by statute, rather than rely on presidential action to curb it. No further action was taken by the full, Democrat-led Senate.

Final Omnibus

Working under the terms of the Ryan-Murray agreement, appropriators reached compromises on all twelve regular spending bills and announced the details of full-year fiscal 2014 appropriations on January 13. The omnibus spending bill they proposed met the $1.012 trillion discretionary spending cap set by the December deal and provided another $98 billion in funding that was not subject to the spending cap. Nearly $92 billion of the uncapped funds were allocated to the war-related Overseas Contingency Operations (OCO) fund.

House Appropriations Committee Chair Hal Rogers, R-Ky., said the bill was a reflection of the need to realign the nation's funding priorities by putting money where it is most useful while working to reduce overall federal spending.

The fiscal 2014 omnibus (HR 3547—PL 113–76) passed the House on January 15, 2014, cleared the Senate a day later, and was signed into law by President Obama on January 17. The final bill provided $49.2 billion in funding for the State Department and foreign assistance programs—a $4.3 billion decrease from fiscal 2013. However, the reduction only affected the OCO fund. Base discretionary funding increased by $400 million (before the sequester was taken into account) and totaled $42.5 billion.

The bill allocated $1.1 billion in aid for Afghanistan, half the amount requested by the White House, and stipulated payment would be withheld until the Afghan government agreed to sign a bilateral security agreement, provide better security for State Department and U.S. Agency for International Development (USAID) personnel, and cooperate on the release of detainees. Appropriators also continued assistance to Israel ($3.1 billion for military aid to Israel) and Jordan ($1 billion, including $300 million in military financing).

Funding for embassy security totaled $1.9 billion, $1.7 billion less than the previous fiscal year due to significant carryover in unspent appropriations. The final bill also prohibited aid to Libya until the Secretary of State could certify the Libyan government's cooperation with the investigation into the 2012 attack on a U.S. diplomatic compound in Benghazi that left four Americans, including the U.S. ambassador to Libya, dead.

The bill preserved $1.3 billion in U.S. military assistance to Egypt. However, the omnibus required the Secretary of State to certify that Egypt remained a U.S. security partner and continued to uphold obligations under the 1979 Egypt-Israel Peace Treaty before any funds could be disbursed. Further, Egypt was required to hold a constitutional referendum before receiving an initial portion of the appropriated funds, with the remaining funds to be provided once parliamentary and presidential elections were held. Another $250 million was allocated for economic aid to Egypt.

Congress approved $8.4 billion for global health programs, including $6 billion to combat HIV/AIDS overseas, $330 million for USAID programs, and $665 million to fight malaria.

International financial institutions received $2.6 billion, including $1.9 billion for the World Bank—an amount about equal to the fiscal 2013 level. However, the bill denied the Obama administration's request for $315 million for the International Monetary Fund to meet the U.S. quota commitment to the body and help shore up a still-unstable world economy.

Though significantly less than the amount requested by the White House, funding for international peacekeeping efforts and disaster assistance was approved at the level of $1.8 billion each. Other major provisions included

- $1.3 billion in aid to Syrian refugees through the OCO fund
- $1.3 billion for international organization membership
- $1.3 billion for counternarcotic assistance
- $298 million for nuclear nonproliferation efforts
- $159 million for humanitarian demining programs
- $51 million to promote Internet freedom
- $3.5 million for the U.S. Commission on International Religious Freedom
- $37 million for the U.S. Institute of Peace

Aid to Egypt

As lawmakers in the Republican-controlled House and Democratic-controlled Senate debated funding levels for the range of foreign assistance programs to be included in the fiscal 2014 budget, one piece drew a higher level of scrutiny than normal: the annual allocation of $250 million in economic and $1.3 billion in military aid to Egypt. The Congressional effort to reduce or stall aid to Egypt was led by Sen. Rand Paul, R-Ky., who introduced two amendments during debate over the 2014 budget. Both were tabled, although his efforts—coupled with suggestions from the Senate Foreign Relations Committee—did result in specific conditions being set before the aid could be disbursed.

BACKGROUND

Egypt has long been one of the largest recipients of U.S. assistance, totaling more than $78 billion from 1946 to 2016. A majority of this spending is for military aid, and much of it goes toward purchasing equipment for the Egyptian Armed Forces from U.S. defense contractors. Federal officials have long argued that Egypt is strategically important to U.S. interests elsewhere in the Middle East and that the Egyptian military, in particular, is a stabilizing force in the region. Given the questionable human rights records of past Egyptian governments and the country's failure to fully embrace democratic norms, occasional attempts have been made to restrict aid or set conditions on disbursement. These efforts have either been tabled in Congress or bypassed by the president.

Vocal support of a reduction in aid grew louder after 2012, when Mohammed Morsi took power in what was considered the nation's first fully democratic election. Morsi's victory followed the 2011 Arab Spring uprising that swept across the Middle East and Northern Africa and resulted in the resignation of Egyptian President Hosni Mubarak. Morsi's rule was quickly characterized by a violent crackdown on his detractors.

Morsi's government was overthrown on July 3, 2013, by the Egyptian military. The White House refused to refer to the overthrow as a "coup." Such a declaration has consequences for U.S. foreign aid and would have triggered language in the Foreign Assistance Act that prohibits providing financial assistance—with the exception of humanitarian aid—to a country whose democratically elected head of state is overthrown by coup or decree. The Commander-in-Chief of the Egyptian Armed Forces, Abdel Fattah el-Sisi, ultimately claimed power and went on to rule similarly to his predecessor, attempting to quash all opposition to his government, resulting in the arrest and murder of thousands of Egyptian citizens.

The Obama administration responded to the violence in Egypt by canceling joint military exercises and announcing that a full review of all U.S. aid to the country would be completed. While the review was underway, a scheduled transfer of warplanes, helicopters, tanks, and missiles was temporarily halted, as was a $260 million cash transfer. The president expressed his desire to sustain the U.S. relationship with Egypt but noted it would be impossible to maintain the status quo while Egypt's government failed to protect its citizens. The move was quickly condemned by the Egyptian military, which stated the Obama decision was not based in fact. The Obama administration would not release the military equipment to Egypt until 2015 and at the same time fully eliminated the ability of the nation to purchase weapons from the United States on credit, thus obligating Congress to appropriate any future military aid.

Senate Committee Action

In December, Sen. Robert Menendez, D-N.J., and Sen. Bob Corker, R-Tenn., introduced the Egypt Assistance Reform Act of 2013 (S 1857) in the Senate Foreign Relations Committee. The legislation would place restrictions on providing aid to Egypt if it did not meet certain conditions, including

- Ongoing implementation of the 1979 Egypt–Israel peace treaty
- The implementation of counterterrorism measures, including the destruction of tunnels between Egypt and the Gaza strip, preventing smuggling into the Gaza Strip, and securing the Sinai Peninsula
- Continued authority for the United States military to utilize Egyptian airspace and territorial waters
- Showing support for a transition to a civilian-run, fully democratic government and progress toward regular free and fair elections
- Protecting the political and economic freedom of all Egyptians, including respect for freedom of expression and due process of law
- Continued commitment to the Treaty on the Non-Proliferation of Nuclear Weapons

The bill also called on the Secretary of State to submit a revised strategy for modernizing assistance to and cooperation with Egypt and would codify in the Foreign Assistance Act anticoup language setting restrictions on aid to any nation where a coup d'état occurs rather than maintaining the existing requirement that the language be included in annual appropriation bills. Provisions were provided in the bill that would allow the president to waive many of the restrictions on aid issuance.

Sen. Menendez said the legislation reaffirmed the U.S. partnership with Egypt while sending a message that the money should be used to support the people of Egypt and their pursuit of democratic norms and economic stability.

The legislation was reported out of committee on December 18, 2013. Concerns raised about considering the bill focused on immediate security challenges in the region that could be exacerbated if aid to Egypt was withheld, along with resistance from members of Congress representing districts where the weapons sold to Egypt are produced. Ultimately, the bill was not taken up by leadership and did not receive a floor vote.

Senate Floor Action

In January, Sen. Paul proposed an amendment to HR 325, a debt limit bill, "to prohibit the sale, lease, transfer, retransfer, or delivery of F-16 aircraft, M1 tanks, or certain other defense articles or services to the Government of Egypt." Paul said it would be a mistake for the United States to show its support for Egypt through the transfer of military equipment after Morsi supporters had attacked the U.S. embassy and burned the U.S. flag. Sen. John McCain, R-Ariz., led the opposition to the amendment, arguing that failure to support Egypt would have a negative impact on the decades-long partnership between Egypt and the United States and that it could threaten Israel's security by weakening the influence the United States has over the Egyptian military. Ultimately, Paul's amendment was tabled by a 79–19 vote.

Paul reprised his attempt at weakening U.S. aid to Egypt in July, with a proposed amendment to the fiscal year 2014 Transportation, Housing and Urban Development, and Related Agencies Appropriations Act (S 1243). The amendment would "redirect certain foreign assistance to the Government of Egypt as a result of the July 3, 2013, military coup d'état." Paul argued that the White House was wrong in its failure to classify Morsi's ouster by the Egyptian military as a coup. Paul insisted the Obama administration was ignoring the rule of law by providing ongoing aid to the country. Again, Paul's amendment was killed by a vote of 86–13.

On January 16, 2014, by a vote of 72–26, the Senate approved the fiscal 2014 omnibus measure (HR 3547—PL 113–76) that maintained $1.3 billion in annual military aid and $250 million in economic aid for Egypt. Under the appropriation, the Secretary of State was required to

RUSSIA ANNEXES CRIMEA

Russia maintained a close relationship with Ukraine immediately after the fall of the Soviet Union in 1991, but that began to sour as Ukraine sought greater ties to the West. In 2010, pro-Russian Viktor Yanukovych was elected president, and while he allowed Russian troops to train in the country and station themselves in the Crimean Peninsula, he also spent many years negotiating a free trade agreement with the European Union, much to the dismay of Russian leader Vladimir Putin. Late in 2013, Putin convinced Yanukovych to walk away from the deal, which sparked months of deadly protests in Ukraine as citizens clashed with security forces.

In February 2014, protesters demanded that Yanukovych step down and promised to take up arms if he failed to leave office. In response, Yanukovych and many of his top aides fled the country. The Ukrainian parliament subsequently impeached the president, and he was replaced by a pro-European interim government led by Oleksandr Turchynov. The new administration was quickly recognized by the United States and European Union, while Putin declared it an illegitimate government and characterized the impeachment as a coup d'état.

While most Ukrainians celebrated the installation of the new government and the promise of revived negotiations with the European Union, in the Crimean Peninsula, where the population is made up primarily of ethnic Russians, protests broke out. In response, in late February 2014, Russia began moving additional troops into Crimea, and the peninsula's parliament voted to dissolve its government and called for a referendum on the peninsula's autonomy. On March 16, 2014, an overwhelming majority of Crimean voters turned out in support of Crimea becoming part of the Russian Federation. The Crimean parliament subsequently voted to respect the will of the voters and secede from Ukraine, and the Russian government agreed to annex the territory. The interim Ukrainian government moved to abolish Crimea's parliament to vacate the referendum, but that was largely ignored in both Crimea and Russia.

In March, the United States and the European Union began issuing sanctions against Russia over its annexation of Crimea and continued troop movement into Ukraine in support of Ukrainian separatists around the country. The initial round of sanctions froze assets held by Russian government officials and banned certain Russian leaders from traveling into the United States or European Union. President Barack Obama said that the sanctions would be lifted only if Russia moved its troops out of Crimea. The United States extended its sanctions in late April, prohibiting business transactions for specific Russian officials and companies within the United States. New sanctions were enacted in July, following the downing of Malaysia Airlines Flight 17 over Ukraine (reportedly by pro-Russian separatists using surface-to-air missiles provided by Russia), and again in September.

Congress struggled throughout 2014 to agree on legislation that would both sanction Russia and provide aid for Ukraine, despite bipartisan support for some type of action. Sen. Robert Menendez, chair of the Senate Foreign Relations Committee, cautioned that the U.S. response could have significant global consequences. It was not until mid-December that the House and Senate passed a series of bills to add another round of sanctions targeting Russia's energy, defense, and financial sectors, while also authorizing the sale of arms, services, and training to Ukraine. Menendez said the legislation was intended to send a direct message to Russia's president that Ukraine's sovereignty must be respected and its territory restored. Sen. Bob Corker, R-Tenn., while noting the danger in the initial hesitation in the U.S. response, said the bill demonstrated the commitment to the sovereignty of Ukraine while ensuring Putin was penalized for his actions.

The Russian government responded by issuing sanctions of its own against U.S. leaders and also called for a one-year embargo on imports of most agricultural products from any nation that had enacted sanctions against Russia. The retaliation had the greatest impact on the European Union, which exports a significant amount of produce, meat, and dairy to Russia.

Putin continued to reject international allegations that Russia had done anything wrong in annexing Crimea and also denied that it was supporting pro-Russian separatists in Ukraine despite photographic evidence to the contrary. The increase in tensions between Russia and the West resulted in a significant decline in foreign investment in the country, creeping inflation, and an economy teetering on the brink of recession.

---

certify that Egypt was both sustaining its strategic partnership with the United States and continuing to meet its obligations under the 1979 Egypt–Israel Peace Treaty. That certification would allow economic aid to be released provided that at least $35 million be utilized for higher education programs and would provide the president authority to release the remaining military assistance in two installments, one after the nation's constitutional referendum in January 2014 and the second after presidential elections, also scheduled to take place in 2014. These were the toughest conditions set on military aid to Egypt to date, and members of Congress were quick to note after the omnibus passage that they would not hesitate to reduce or cut off future aid if Egypt failed to follow through on the conditions set and continue moving toward a fully democratic government.

Iran Sanctions

Congress began pursuing new legislation to increase economic and human rights sanctions related to Iran's nuclear program early in 2013. Facing pressure from the pro-Israel lobby, the House Foreign Affairs Committee took up a draft sanctions bill introduced by Chair Ed Royce, R-Calif., and Ranking Member Eliot Engel, D-N.Y., in February. The proposed bill sought to sanction individuals and companies engaged in "significant financial transactions" with the Central Bank of Iran and other Iranian financial institutions and expand the list of Iranian government officials and economic sectors subject to further sanctions, among other measures.

The House's push for tougher sanctions occurred as Obama administration officials engaged in negotiations aimed at reaching an agreement with Iran that would limit the country's nuclear activity in exchange for economic relief. Despite the administration's urging that Congress hold off on additional sanctions while negotiations were underway, the House moved forward, approving the Royce-Engel bill in July. Companion legislation was proposed in the Senate but was delayed in committee and did not come to a floor vote. A subsequent attempt in the Senate to attach Iran sanctions to the FY 2014 defense authorization bill also failed.

BACKGROUND

The United States has repeatedly sought to leverage economic sanctions to pressure Iran to suspend its nuclear activities amid suspicions that Iran is building nuclear weapons rather than trying to generate electricity, as its government claims. Prior to 2013, the United States had also been involved in several multilateral efforts to reach a diplomatic solution to the nuclear dispute, but none of those attempts had been successful.

In February 2013, a new round of talks began between representatives from the United States, United Kingdom, Russia, China, France, Germany, and Iran. U.S. and Iranian officials also met directly in a series of secret talks that started in March. The June election of Hassan Rouhani, a moderate reformer who supported a nuclear agreement with the international community, to succeed hardline conservative President Mahmoud Ahmadinejad helped facilitate the talks' progress.

On November 24, negotiators reached a six-month interim deal. Under the Joint Action Plan, Iran agreed to begin limiting some of its nuclear activities in return for approximately $7 billion of sanctions relief from the United Nations, United States, and European Union while negotiators continued working on a longer-term agreement. President Obama described the deal as the most significant progress of his administration's diplomatic efforts to date, stating that it would help chart a path toward a more secure world.

Lawmakers had mixed reactions to the deal, with Republicans and some Democrats claiming the agreement would make it more likely for Iran to achieve nuclear weapons in the future and calling for tougher sanctions. Royce, for example, said he had concerns that the agreement would not ensure protections for the United States and its allies because it allows Iran to maintain some of its nuclear-weapons capability. Sen. Robert Menendez, D-N.J., also urged caution. He noted his belief that sanctions should not be reduced, nor should the United States hesitate to impose new sanctions if Iran failed to uphold the agreement. The Obama administration and deal supporters argued that increased sanctions would violate the terms of the interim agreement and jeopardize further negotiations.

House Committee Action

The Nuclear Iran Prevention Act of 2013 (HR 850) was introduced by Royce and Engel on February 27 and was unanimously approved by the Foreign Affairs Committee on May 22. By that time, roughly three-fourths of all House members had signed on as cosponsors.

The bill called for amending prior sanctions—such as the Comprehensive Iran Sanctions, Accountability, and Divestment Act of 2010—to include provisions that

- enabled the president to sanction individuals and companies engaged in "significant financial transactions" with the Central Bank of Iran or other blacklisted Iranian financial institutions, as well as banks making transactions in foreign currencies on behalf of blacklisted Iranian financial institutions
- authorized the president to restrict foreign aid to countries that allow certain goods, services, and technology to be diverted to Iran in order to prevent items originating from the United States from being provided to Iran
- expanded the list of Iranian government officials responsible for human rights violations and called on the president to impose sanctions on these people
- authorized state and local governments to divest assets from, prohibit investment of assets in, prohibit the issuance of business licenses to, or impose transparency requirements on individuals who conduct transactions with any person or sector subject to Iran-related sanctions
- allowed the president to exempt from sanctions individuals from countries that significantly reduced their trade with Iran as a way of creating a de facto commercial embargo
- required countries that buy Iranian oil to reduce their purchases by one million barrels per day within one year to obtain a "significant reduction" exemption from sanctions

- expanded the list of blacklisted Iranian sectors (i.e., those facilitating nuclear proliferation activities) to include automotive and mining in addition to energy, shipping, and shipbuilding, and authorized the president to determine whether construction and engineering sectors should be added as well.

The committee also adopted an amendment by Royce that added severability language to the bill, thereby allowing most of the bill's provisions to remain law if any section of it were deemed unconstitutional.

House Floor Action

Following Rouhani's election, on July 1, 2013, the House Foreign Affairs committee collectively sent a letter to President Obama cautioning that Rouhani's victory had "done nothing to suggest a reversal of Iran's pursuit of a nuclear weapons capacity" and urging the president to strengthen sanctions. Weeks later on July 18, another group of 131 lawmakers, including several House Foreign Affairs members, sent a separate letter to President Obama calling for negotiations with Rouhani, stating that the United States must be "careful not to preempt this potential opportunity by engaging in actions that delegitimize the newly elected president and weaken his standing relative to hardliners within the regime who oppose his professed 'policy of reconciliation and peace.'" The diversity of opinions in the House and administration appeals to delay sanctions legislation did not prevent the chamber from bringing the Royce-Engel bill to the floor. The full House passed the bill without amendment on July 31, 2013, by a vote of 400–20. Rep. Jim McDermott, D-Wash., was among the lawmakers who spoke against the bill, expressing his concern that it limited the opportunity to negotiate diplomatically.

Senate Action

The same day the House Foreign Affairs Committee approved the Royce-Engel bill, the Senate adopted a nonbinding resolution (S Res 65) supporting the full implementation of U.S. and international sanctions on Iran. The resolution also affirmed the strong relationship between the United States and Israel and called on the Obama administration to provide diplomatic, military, and economic support if Israel had to take military action to defend itself against Iran's nuclear program. Iranian leaders have frequently expressed a desire to eliminate Israel, including Ayatollah Ali Khamenei's January 15, 2001, statement that "It is the mission of the Islamic Republic of Iran to erase Israel from the map of the region." As a result, Israeli leaders have ardently opposed the Iranian nuclear deal, with Prime Minister Benjamin Netanyahu describing the agreement as a historic mistake that will threaten the survival of Israel.

A companion bill to HR 850 (S 1001) had been introduced the day prior by Senators John Cornyn, R-Texas, and Mark Kirk, R-Ill. The bill was referred to the Senate Banking, Housing, and Urban Affairs Committee, where it stalled after Chair Tim Johnson, D-S.D., agreed to delay consideration until multilateral negotiations with Iran concluded. Senators Kirk and Menendez later drafted a separate sanctions bill (S 1881) with many of the same provisions as S 1001, in case Iran violated any agreement resulting from the negotiations. The bill also included a provision authorizing the president to suspend sanctions against Iran for 180 days if he certified to Congress every 30 days that Iran was in compliance with the agreement, among other requirements. However, the bill was not introduced until December 19, days before the Congressional session ended, and was not considered by the Senate.

Menendez also led an effort to amend the FY 2014 defense authorization bill (S 1197) to include increased Iran sanctions. The effort stalled due to disagreement over the handling of proposed amendments. The House and Senate Armed Services Committees ultimately agreed on a new version of the defense bill (HR 3304) that omitted any Iran sanctions language and was approved on December 19 under procedures that did not allow for amendment votes. That version of the defense bill was passed into law on December 26.

Fiscal 2015 State-Foreign Operations Funding

Despite initial progress by House and Senate appropriators, stand-alone measures for fiscal 2015 State Department and foreign operations funding stalled once the chambers' respective bills were voted out of committee. A $2.7 billion difference between House and Senate proposals for war-related spending through the OCO fund was the primary issue that prevented lawmakers from reaching an agreement. The OCO fund, established during President George W. Bush's administration to provide war-related funds to both the State and Defense Departments, has long been a source of disagreement among lawmakers. OCO funds are not subject to sequestration cuts or spending caps, enabling lawmakers to circumvent budget limits by shifting money to the OCO from other accounts. In 2014, Senate Democrats attempted to leverage these exemptions to increase available discretionary funds by moving part of the military's base budget to the OCO fund. The OCO budget is currently used to respond to humanitarian crises and support programs in Iraq, Afghanistan, and Pakistan as well as in North Africa, the Middle East, and other areas undergoing political transition.

With midterm elections approaching, both the House and Senate floors became bogged down with partisan arguments over politically charged amendments dealing with domestic and international policies on issues such as reproductive rights, health care, and climate change. Some Republicans also pushed to delay spending discussions until early 2015 to allow the newly elected Congress to set appropriations, but this movement failed to gain traction.

Following the August recess, House and Senate leaders worked to piece together a continuing resolution to fund the government through December 11 and begin laying the groundwork for a fiscal 2015 omnibus. The resolution (HJ Res. 124—PL 113–64) cleared the House on September 17 with one amendment—requested by the White House—that temporarily authorized the provision of U.S. military training and equipment to Syrian rebels to help them defend against Islamic State attacks. The Senate passed the measure the following day.

The final $1.013 trillion cromnibus (HR 83—PL 113–235) included appropriations for most government agencies through the end of fiscal 2015 along with a short-term continuing resolution funding the Department of Homeland Security. The House passed the consolidated spending package on December 11 with a 219–206 vote, despite heavy Democratic opposition due to the late addition of provisions increasing the limit on individuals' annual giving to national political parties and rolling back part of the Dodd-Frank regulatory overhaul.

With the threat of another shutdown looming, the House and Senate passed a second continuing resolution (HJ Res. 130—PL 113–202) to give the Senate time for floor debate on the omnibus measure. The final fiscal 2015 omnibus cleared the Senate by a vote of 56–40 on December 13 and was signed by President Obama three days later.

House Action

On June 17, the House Subcommittee on State, Foreign Operations, and Related Programs approved a draft bill (HR 5013) put forward by Chair Kay Granger, R-Texas. The bill provided $15.6 billion in both base discretionary spending and war-related funding, including about $5.9 billion for the OCO. This was $926 million less than the White House had requested and $128 million below the fiscal 2014 level.

The bill included a measure restricting foreign aid to countries that accepted detainees transferred from the Guantanamo Bay detention center. This was an apparent response to President Obama's trade of five Taliban prisoners in exchange for the safe return of Sgt. Bowe Bergdahl, who was captured in 2009 by the Taliban in Afghanistan after leaving his post. Republicans claimed the president's trade constituted a violation of the law that required the president to notify lawmakers at least thirty days prior to any transfer of Guantanamo detainees; the White House had not informed Congress until after the exchange was complete. Assistance to Ukraine and the Baltic states was increased in response to Russia's military incursions into Ukraine, including its annexation of the Crimean peninsula in spring 2014.

The full House Appropriations Committee reported the measure on June 27 after rejecting Democrats' attempts to decrease military aid for Egypt and boost funds for reproductive health. These efforts included a motion by Rep. Debbie Wasserman Schultz, D-Fla., to remove language restoring the contentious Mexico City Policy that was defeated.

The committee did accept a Granger-sponsored amendment that provided aid for Mexico and Central American countries to enhance border security, combat human trafficking, and help repatriate and reintegrate their citizens.

Senate Action

On June 17, the Senate State, Foreign Operations, and Related Programs subcommittee approved a $48.3 billion spending bill (S 2499) sponsored by Chair Patrick J. Leahy, D-Vt. The bill included $8.6 billion in war-related funding via the OCO, reflecting an effort by Senate Democrats to move a portion of the military's base budget to the OCO to allow for increased domestic spending elsewhere.

The full Senate Appropriations Committee approved the bill two days later, following a vote to permanently repeal the Mexico City Policy. No further action was taken on the measure.

MAJOR PROVISIONS

While slightly less than President Obama's initial $53 billion request, the final omnibus (HR 83—PL 113–235) provided the State Department with a total budget of nearly $52 billion, of which $42.5 billion was provided for base discretionary spending. The OCO received nearly $9.3 billion in funding, a 20 percent increase from FY 2014 and $1.5 billion more than the White House had requested.

A total of $5.4 billion was allocated to upgrade U.S. embassy security, surpassing the Obama administration's request by $46 million. The additional funds would allow for the implementation of the twenty-nine recommendations put forward by the Benghazi Accountability Review Board. Much like the fiscal 2014 omnibus, the 2015 legislation again denied financial assistance to Libya until the State Department could confirm the Libyan government's cooperation with the Benghazi investigation.

Congress agreed to provide $2.5 billion in emergency funding to respond to the Ebola epidemic in West Africa. The total was $370 million less than requested by the White House, but lawmakers stated it was enough to meet immediate needs.

Appropriators continued military and economic aid for Egypt at the fiscal 2014 levels of $1.3 billion and $250 million, respectively. They also provided $1 billion in economic, crisis, and military aid to Jordan for its hosting of nearly 600,000 Syrian refugees and its support for U.S. operations against the Islamic State.

A measure was included to withhold funds from Afghanistan unless certain conditions, such as enactment of a Bilateral Security Agreement with the United States, were met. The bill also contained a rider discontinuing aid to Palestine if the country became a member of the United Nations or any of its agencies without a preexisting agreement with Israel, or if the Palestinian Authority attempted to bring Israel before the International Criminal Court.

Funding for U.S. contributions to the United Nations Green Climate Fund was not included in the bill, despite

U.S. WAR CASUALTIES, 2001–2016

War in Iraq

Year	Killed in Action	Noncombat Deaths	Wounded in Action
2001	0	0	0
2002	0	0	0
2003	315	171	2,420
2004	713	133	8,002
2005	673	171	5,944
2006	704	116	6,411
2007	764	139	6,112
2008	221	92	2,045
2009	74	74	678
2010	19	41	328
2011	34	20	219
2012	0	1	0
2013	0	0	-
2014	0	4	-
2015	1	7	-
2016	7	12	-
Total	**3,525**	**981**	**32,231***

NOTE: Figures include Operation Iraqi Freedom (2003–2016) and Operation New Dawn (2010–2016). *Accounts for the 72 total wounded in action for the years 2013–2018.

War in Afghanistan

Year	Killed in Action	Noncombat Deaths	Wounded in Action
2001	3	8	33
2002	18	31	74
2003	17	28	99
2004	25	27	217
2005	66	32	268
2006	65	33	403
2007	83	34	748
2008	132	23	795
2009	271	40	2,145
2010	438	62	5,249
2011	360	54	5,216
2012	237	76	2,963
2013	91	41	-
2014	39	17	-
2015	10	11	-
2016	9	1	-
Total	**1,864**	**518**	**18,519***

NOTE: * Accounts for the 309 total wounded in action for the years 2013–2018.

SOURCE: Defense Casualty Analysis System, U.S. Department of Defense (https://dcas.dmdc.osd.mil/dcas/pages/casualties.xhtml).

the Obama administration's promise to provide $3 billion in support. A Joint Explanatory Statement accompanying the omnibus explained that Congress did not provide for such contributions in the bill because the White House had not made an official request for any funds for the climate program for fiscal 2015.

The bill supported continued operation of the Overseas Private Investment Corp., the government's private sector financial institution that provides funding and advocacy for U.S. businesses in emerging markets, and the Export-Import Bank, the United States' official export credit agency created to promote and facilitate the export of American goods and services. The Export-Import Bank's charter had expired on June 30, 2015.

Funding for Operations in Iraq and Syria

Congressional action on U.S. activity in Iraq and Syria in 2014 was primarily focused on the rise of the Islamic State of Iraq and the Levant (ISIL), a group borne out of the fall of the regime of Iraqi leader Saddam Hussein in 2003. ISIL sought to take control of wide swaths of land in Iraq and neighboring Syria, with the intent of establishing an Islamic caliphate. However, partisan squabbling over the United States' level of involvement in combatting the terrorist group, and how any intervention would be authorized, limited Congress's ability to act.

IRAQ

When President Obama took office, he vowed to bring U.S. involvement in the Iraq war to a close. The president pulled all U.S. combat troops out by 2011 while maintaining a few thousand soldiers in the country for the purposes of training Iraqi forces and providing logistical and intelligence support, a majority of which was focused on combatting ISIL.

The Iraqi government struggled to slow ISIL's capture of strategic locations across the country, and by January 2014, the group had taken control of some of Iraq's largest cities, including Fallujah, Ramadi, and Mosul. In response, the United States provided Apache helicopters, Hellfire missiles, and surveillance unmanned aerial vehicles (UAVs), in addition to ramping up its training and counterterrorism units in the area. Diplomatic efforts focused on encouraging the Iraqi government to develop a holistic plan to fight ISIL by partnering with local tribal fighters to encourage greater support for the movement against the terrorist group.

In August 2014, President Obama announced in a televised address that he had authorized U.S. airstrikes against ISIL in Iraq in order to secure U.S. interests in the country and protect humanitarian aid workers. This resulted in some public criticism that the president required Congressional approval for such military action, but Obama stated that he was operating under the 2001 al Qaeda authorization for the use of military force (AUMF) approved after the September 11 terrorist attacks.

In response to the criticism, on December 11, 2014, the Senate Foreign Relations Committee passed along party lines an AUMF (SJ Res 47) that would authorize the president to use military force against ISIL for no more than three years unless the bill was reauthorized. The bill prohibited U.S. ground forces from being used in any operation except in limited circumstances. Republicans on the committee strongly opposed both the time limit set and the prohibition on ground troops. The committee's ranking member, Sen. Bob Corker, R-Tenn., suggested that it would be better if the Senate discussed the limitations with the president and waited for the White House to submit its own AUMF language. The bill did not receive full consideration in the Senate.

Republicans in Congress remained highly critical of Obama's strategy in Iraq, arguing that it would be of little lasting benefit, and repeatedly called on the president to increase the number of troops in Iraq. While admitting that he had underestimated ISIL's power, the president continued to refuse to commit more U.S. soldiers to operations against the group.

The only action passed by the full Congress in 2014 in relation to Iraq was to provide the president $5 billion through the Overseas Contingency Operations budget in the omnibus spending package to carry out military operations (HR 83—PL 113-235). Approximately $1.6 billion of these funds would be specifically for training and equipping Iraqi forces that had been decimated by ISIL.

SYRIA

Syria had been the site of a brutal civil war since the 2011 Arab Spring uprisings and subsequent calls for the resignation of President Bashar al-Assad. Assad refused

---

AUMF

Shortly after the September 11, 2001, terrorist attacks, Congress passed a joint resolution (PL 107-40), the Authorization for the Use of Military Force (AUMF). The law allowed then-President George W. Bush "to use all necessary and appropriate force against those nations, organizations, or persons he determines planned, authorized, committed or aided the terrorist attacks that occurred on September 11, 2001, or harbored such organizations or persons, in order to prevent any future acts of international terrorism against the United States by such nations, organizations or persons." This authorization was utilized by President Bush to carry out the invasion of—and subsequent war in—Afghanistan.

In October 2002, a second AUMF was passed (PL 107-243) that gave the president the ability "to use the Armed Forces of the United States as he determines to be necessary and appropriate in order to (1) defend the national security of the United States against the continuing threat posed by Iraq; and (2) enforce all relevant United Nations Security Council resolutions regarding Iraq." That authorization was utilized by President Bush for the war in Iraq.

Following in the footsteps of his predecessor, President Obama utilized the language in the 2001 and 2002 AUMF to carry out military operations against terrorist groups both in and outside of Iraq and Afghanistan. Neither AUMF provides a broad scope under which the president can operate, and many have argued in favor of a new AUMF to support ongoing U.S. actions abroad, specifically those that target organizations that didn't exist at the time of the September 11 attacks, including the Islamic State.

In response, in 2014, the White House argued that due to ISIL's relationship with al Qaeda and Osama bin Laden, in addition to its history of carrying out attacks against U.S. citizens and ongoing U.S. combat operations that date back to 2014 when ISIL first affiliated itself with al Qaeda, the president could utilize the 2001 AUMF to target ISIL.

Critics point to two key concerns in this argument: first that ISIL did not come to power until 2004, three years after the 2001 AUMF was written, and that al Qaeda has denounced ISIL, thus weakening the link between the two terrorist groups.

In 2014, the Senate Foreign Relations Committee considered a new AUMF (SJ Res 47) that restricted the use of ground forces to combat ISIL and placed a three-year time limit on the bill, unless it was reauthorized. Notably, it did not include a geographic restriction on where the United States could carry out operations, and an amendment in support of one was struck down. The bill was never taken up by the full Senate. Other proposals that were never considered by the full Senate in 2014 similarly sought to define the boundaries under which military operations could be undertaken and primarily limited that to Iraq and Syria.

In 2015, the Obama administration delivered draft language to Congress on a new AUMF to be utilized for airstrikes and limited operations against the Islamic State. Despite previously arguing that he did not require such authorization, growing concern among the public and in Congress over the ever-expanding use of the 2001 AUMF forced action. The draft language did not allow for the use of ground forces, would terminate three years after passage (unless reauthorized), and while noting that ISIL controls significant portions of Iraq and Syria, it did not place any geographic boundaries or even limit the use of force to ISIL. Instead, the language indicated that "the term 'associated persons or forces' means individuals and organizations fighting for, on behalf of, or alongside ISIL or any closely-related successor entity in hostilities against the United States or its coalition partners."

Congress, however, found itself unable to act, stalled by partisan debate about what a new AUMF should authorize, whether time limits and geographic restrictions should be imposed on its use, and whether the use of ground forces can be constrained.

and instead violently cracked down on protesters. Civilian rebel groups formed across the country and frequently clashed with the state's military. The violence resulted in tens of thousands killed and millions displaced either internally or in neighboring nations such as Jordan and Turkey.

U.S. involvement was tepid from the start, especially after the conflict devolved into a proxy war between Iran, which threw its support behind Assad, and Saudi Arabia, which backed the rebels. The United States did carry out limited airstrikes but refused to send ground troops or get involved in a more significant capacity, preferring instead to work through the United Nations or other allies on diplomatic resolutions to the conflict.

In 2014, Congress took its biggest action to date in the Syrian conflict, authorizing $500 million to be transferred to the Counterterrorism Partnerships Fund through the fiscal 2015 defense authorization (HR 3979—PL 113-291) and 2015 omnibus appropriations (HR 83—PL 113-235). Together, the two pieces of legislation provided funds for training, equipment, supplies, and stipends for Syrian rebels in their fight against the Islamic State. An early version of the funding bills passed in the House included White House–backed language allowing the Syrians to utilize the money not only to fight ISIL but also to defend themselves against attacks by the Syrian regime. In the final conference version, however, the authorization, which would sunset on December 31, 2016, could be used for:

- defending the Syrian people from attacks by ISIL
- securing territory controlled by the Syrian opposition
- protecting the United States, its allies, and Syrians from threats posed by terrorists operating in Syria
- promoting a negotiated settlement to end the Syrian conflict.

The law stipulated that the money could only be provided to "appropriately vetted" groups, specifically those unaffiliated with terrorist organizations and committed to a peaceful and democratic Syria, and that the money could not be used to purchase shoulder-fired missiles.

2015-2016

In the last two years of President Obama's term, he and the Republican-controlled Congress frequently clashed over priorities, but even where they agreed, action was halting. Both parties, for example, appeared to believe that there was a need to better structure the United States' response to the Islamic State. The president called for a new Authorization for the Use of Military Force (AUMF) in 2015 specifically targeted to fighting ISIL and other terrorist groups and giving Congress some say in the president's power to wage war. Congress failed to act, however, due to disagreement about how such legislation would be structured.

On other topics, given the impending 2016 presidential election, Congressional activity was limited both to provide cover to members up for reelection and to allow the incoming administration to set a new policy course. Where action did happen, it was focused more on domestic issues than international affairs.

One area of foreign policy activity was in relation to the Joint Comprehensive Plan of Action (JCPOA), a multilateral agreement between the United States, China, France, Germany, Russia, the United Kingdom, and Iran, aimed at reducing Iran's nuclear capabilities in exchange for lifting certain economic sanctions. Although Democrats agreed that the measure had flaws, they sided with the president in arguing that it was likely the best diplomatic solution they would get to curb Iran's nuclear buildup. Republicans, however, were highly skeptical of the plan and feared that it had the potential to destabilize the entire region and harm U.S. allies such as Israel. Sen. Lindsey Graham, R-S.C., called the agreement a dangerous move in the Middle East, while House Speaker John Boehner, R-Ohio, promised to do anything necessary to stop the JCPOA from moving forward.

In 2015, the House introduced HR 1191, the Iran Nuclear Agreement Review Act. The legislation would give Congress sixty days to review the terms of the final JCPOA and then approve or disapprove of the United States signing on. The measure passed the House and Senate with little resistance and was signed into law by President Obama on May 22 (PL 114-17). Once the JCPOA was finalized, Congress was provided its requisite review period, and Senate Republicans mounted an effort to reject the deal. However, without the sixty votes needed to stop a Democratic filibuster, Republicans fell short, and the JCPOA took effect on October 18, 2015.

As sanctions against Iran began being lifted in January 2016, Congressional Republicans renewed their efforts to fight back against provisions in the JCPOA. The House passed a measure (HR 3662) that would require the president to make certain certifications to Congress that Iran was following through on its part of the agreement before sanctions could be lifted. The White House threatened to veto the measure, but ultimately, it was not taken up in the Senate. The Senate also failed to act on a series of House-passed measures dealing with Iranian access to the U.S. dollar, sanctions for specific business sectors, and a prohibition on the use of U.S. funds to purchase material to make nuclear warheads.

Congress did come together in bipartisan fashion with the support of the White House to impose new sanctions on North Korea. Throughout 2016, the reclusive nation carried out many missile tests, launched a satellite, and potentially tested a hydrogen bomb. The North Korean government also ramped up its rhetoric that its nuclear weapons had the potential to reach the U.S. territory of Guam and potentially the U.S. mainland. With near-unanimous support, both houses of Congress passed the North Korea Sanctions and Policy Enhancement Act of 2016, and it was signed into law on February 18, 2016 (HR 757—PL 114-122). The legislation allowed for sanctions to be levied against individuals, foreign financial institutions, and governments that helped North Korea evade UN sanctions or aided the nation with the proliferation of weapons of mass destruction.

Fiscal 2016 State Department Authorizations

In 2015, the Senate Foreign Relations and House Foreign Affairs Committees pledged their commitment to passing a State Department authorization bill for the first time since 2002.

Before the thirteen-year lull, Congress had previously enacted fifty-three consecutive authorization bills, which were necessary to guide formal congressional policy and establish oversight of the State Department. Without authorization legislation, the State Department was forced to operate off policies passed more than a decade ago. Foreign operations and policy priorities have instead generally been dictated by funding levels established in annual appropriations measures.

Following a markup session on June 9, the Senate Foreign Relations Committee unanimously approved a draft authorization bill (S 1635) sponsored by Corker and Ranking Member Ben Cardin, D-Md. "This effort takes a modest but important step toward reestablishing oversight of the State Department through an annual authorization," said Corker of the legislation in a June 9, 2015, press statement.

The bill was limited in scope, with a focus on streamlining State Department operations, authorizing funding for department programs, and enhancing embassy security. Additional provisions authorized multilateral aid, including funds for international peacekeeping organizations and U.S. educational and cultural programs. The bill did not include provisions for bilateral or developmental assistance to any foreign nations, nor did it authorize military action against the Islamic State.

The legislation also increased State Department reporting requirements to include a mix of reports on internal and external matters such as embassy construction and security, activities and operations of Foreign Service posts, sexual abuse during peacekeeping missions, and the employment of U.S. citizens by the United Nations and other international organizations. On this point, Sen. Chris Murphy, D-Conn., noted his concern about the undue burden these responsibilities would create for the State Department, which already faced the possibility of extremely reduced funding due to sequestration. Sen. Cardin countered this concern, explaining the strategies and reports would help the committee move toward a broader State Department authorization bill in 2016.

Corker had planned to attach the authorization as an amendment to the annual National Defense Authorization Act (S 1376), which was then under consideration on the Senate floor. However, a host of competing priorities—including debate surrounding the Iran nuclear deal, ongoing refugee crisis, defense authorizations, and budget negotiations—prevented the State Department authorization bill from progressing beyond the committee, and the House did not take any related action.

Fiscal 2016 State-Foreign Appropriations

Funding for the State Department and foreign operations was once again incorporated into an omnibus bill after ongoing disagreements over federal spending levels derailed the fiscal 2016 appropriations process. In the summer, Senate Democrats pledged to block any bills adhering to spending limits set by the 2011 Budget Control Act (S 365—PL 112-25), while congressional Republicans, buoyed by midterm election victories, rejected calls for a bipartisan agreement to increase spending. Divisions over policy riders, including the contentious Mexico City Policy and a proposal to withhold a portion of State Department funding until certain internal practices were improved, prevented lawmakers from reaching consensus on a stand-alone appropriations bill.

The final State Department–foreign operations bill was attached as an amendment to the Military Construction and Veterans Affairs and Related Agencies Appropriations Act of 2015 (HR 2029) by the Senate, along with the other remaining fiscal 2016 appropriations bills. The massive omnibus package (HR 2029—PL 114-113) totaled $1.15 trillion in spending.

House Action

The House Subcommittee on State, Foreign Operations, and Related Programs reported a $47.8 billion draft bill unanimously on June 3. The total was $6.1 billion less than the White House had requested and $1.4 billion under the fiscal 2015 level. It included $40.5 billion in base discretionary funding and $7.3 billion in war-related (OCO) spending.

The bill also included several controversial provisions, such as the restoration of the Mexico City Policy forbidding U.S. aid to international groups providing abortion-related

services, including counseling and referrals. Another measure sought to hold in reserve 15 percent of the State Department's funding until the department began to improve responsiveness to open records requests for information and better retain employee emails and communications. These provisions appeared to be in direct response to former Secretary of State Hillary Clinton's use of a private email server to conduct official State Department business. Other measures cut multilateral assistance to the World Bank, international climate change programs, and United Nations agencies.

After adding a manager's amendment—a package of noncontroversial, technical amendments that are agreed to by both sides in advance—the House Appropriations Committee approved the draft bill by voice vote on June 11. Amendments proposed by Democratic members to restore funding to climate change programs, the World Bank, and United Nations agencies, as well as their attempts to remove policy riders prohibiting U.S. aid to abortion-related services and restricting funding for a new U.S. embassy in Cuba, were voted down.

Senate Action

The Senate Subcommittee on State, Foreign Operations, and Related Programs presented its unanimously approved draft bill (S 1725—Rept 114–79) without amendment on July 7. As is customary, the $49 billion total included both discretionary and emergency funds. The Senate Appropriations Committee approved the measure on July 9, after voting 17–13 to remove the Mexico City Policy from the final bill.

Conference and Final Action

On September 30, the last day of fiscal 2015, with the threat of another government shutdown looming, Congress passed a ten-week continuing resolution to keep the government open through December 11 and allow budget negotiations to continue. Ultimately, congressional leaders and the White House reached an agreement at the end of October to temporarily increase federal spending limits by $80 billion over two years, suspend the debt limit until March 2017, and provide $73.5 billion for the Overseas Contingency Operations (OCO) fund, each for fiscal years 2016 and 2017.

While the October deal provided a new framework for appropriators to resume budget negotiations, lawmakers struggled to reach consensus ahead of the December 11 deadline. A second continuing resolution was approved to extend the deadline for a final budget deal through December 16. Still a third continuing resolution was necessary to provide an extension through December 22 or the enactment of fiscal 2016 appropriations, whichever occurred first.

After weeks of closed-door meetings, Congress announced, on December 18, a $1.15 trillion omnibus bill and tax break extensions package. The House and Senate approved the bill

(HR 2029), and it was signed by President Obama (PL 114–113) the same day.

MAJOR PROVISIONS

The State Department received a $52.8 billion operational budget for fiscal 2016. This marked a $3.4 billion increase from fiscal 2015 and was $5 billion and $4 billion higher, respectively, than the funding initially sought by House and Senate appropriators. The omnibus included $14.9 billion in funding for the OCO, which was almost $5 billion more than in fiscal 2015.

The measure also included $3.1 billion to help address humanitarian crises resulting from conflict, which was $605 million more than the president had requested. Of this total, $2.1 billion was provided through the OCO and was primarily intended to support Syrians who had fled to Lebanon, Turkey, Jordan, and other neighboring countries.

Congress set aside $750 million to respond to the swell of unaccompanied children coming to the United States from Central America and to implement response and prevention strategies with a focus on upgrading U.S. border security and migrant reintegration. Aid also went to improving security and social services in Central American countries.

The bill continued restrictions on aid to the Palestinian Authority from fiscal 2014. Appropriators provided military assistance in the form of $3.1 billion for Israel and allocated aid to Egypt, Jordan, and Ukraine in the amounts of $1.45 billion, $1.3 billion, and $658 million, respectively.

Appropriators approved a package of reforms to increase the amount of core funding for the International Monetary Fund (IMF) and to expand the voting share of emerging countries, such as China, to better reflect their growing share of the world economy. The United States had authored the changes, which all major participating countries had agreed to in 2010, but opposition from Republican lawmakers had prevented reform implementation until 2015.

While the final omnibus did not reinstate the Mexico City Policy, it did contain a provision known as the Helms Amendment that prevents U.S. assistance from being directly used to provide foreign abortions. Additionally, the bill included a compromise measure prohibiting State Department or USAID appropriations from being used to pay for private servers and email accounts. The measure also required both agencies to ensure departing employees turned over all communications.

Other major provisions included

- $8.5 billion for global health programs ($322 million more than requested by the White House), including combatting HIV/AIDS ($6 billion total)
- $3.1 billion for humanitarian crises resulting from conflict, including the Syrian civil war
- $575 million for bilateral family planning assistance, at the fiscal 2015 level
- $32.5 million for the United Nations Population Fund, $2.5 million under the fiscal 2015 level

Relationship with Cuba

When President Obama first took office, he made a goal of normalizing the U.S. relationship with Cuba, including full restoration of diplomatic and economic ties. Throughout his second term, this included the development of a framework for working with the island nation and subsequent changes to U.S. policies toward Cuba that opened up more travel and investment opportunities. The lifting of most economic sanctions, however, would fall to Congress, and the body, although it did not put up much resistance to Obama's other normalization efforts, did not move forward on lifting economic restrictions, including a stringent trade embargo.

BACKGROUND

The United States and Cuba have had a strained relationship since 1959, when Fidel Castro came to power by toppling the U.S.-backed government of General Fulgencio Batista. Castro's government increased ties to the Soviet Union and raised taxes on the import of American goods, resulting in economic sanctions from the United States, including a complete embargo on all trade. The 1961 Bay of Pigs invasion marked the end of any remaining diplomatic ties, and even since the fall of the Soviet Union, the United States has failed to lift its embargo against Cuba. Congress even moved to strengthen economic restrictions in 1992 and 1996. The island nation was added to the U.S. list of state sponsors of terrorism in 1982.

Castro's 2008 replacement by his brother, Raúl, sparked hope that the United States might begin to soften its relationship with Cuba. When President Obama assumed office in 2009, he quickly began undoing some of the restrictions put in place by his predecessor, President George W. Bush, and began allowing Americans with Cuban relatives to make unlimited visits to Cuba and to send financial aid to the nation. He also eased restrictions on wireless providers, permitting them to establish cell phone and television service in Cuba. The Obama administration hinted that it hoped these changes would reduce Cuban dependence on the Castro regime. Congressional Republicans, including Cuban-American Sen. Marco Rubio, R-Fla., argued that the efforts by the Obama administration to restore the economic and diplomatic relationship with Cuba, when the nation had made no effort to democratize and frequently violated the human rights of its citizens, were a concession to tyranny.

Furthering these efforts, in 2013 and 2014, administration officials met with Cuban leaders to explore the potential of normalizing the relationship between the two countries. The secret, eighteen-month process produced a framework plan to restore full diplomatic ties as long as specific concessions were met, including the release of dozens of political prisoners.

In January 2015, the Obama administration began implementing the first portions of the agreement when it scaled back travel restrictions. U.S. citizens would no longer be required to obtain a government license to travel to Cuba but would still need to meet certain requirements, including participating in an educational activity or conducting research. That same month, some economic sanctions were lifted, allowing for U.S. corporate investment in some small Cuban companies, shipment of building materials to private Cuban businesses, and use of American credit and debit cards by travelers to Cuba. By July, the United States and Cuba reopened their embassies in Havana and Washington, D.C., respectively.

Congressional Action

When they took power following the 2014 midterm elections, Republican leaders in both the House and Senate promised to attempt to block some of the president's normalization plans, including the reopening of the U.S. embassy in Havana. However, by the close of 2015, the body offered little opposition, but it also took no action to lift economic sanctions against Cuba. Doing so would require the repeal of the Helms-Burton Act of 1996 (PL 104–114) that prohibits lifting economic sanctions against Cuba until the government provides full democratic rights to its citizens.

Republicans did propose policy riders to the fiscal 2016 omnibus appropriations bill (HR 2029), including:

- a prohibition on U.S. companies doing business with Cuban military and intelligence organizations
- a travel ban on U.S. citizens for educational purposes that are not part of a degree program
- a ban on the import of property seized by the Cuban government
- a ban on U.S.-flag airlines and cruise companies prohibiting them from operating in Cuba.

The policy riders were ultimately not included in the final omnibus spending bill (HR 2029—PL 114–113), but neither were some provisions that would have aided the administration's cause, including fully lifting the travel ban, allowing U.S. banks to offer credit for agricultural exports to Cuba, and ending the licensing requirement for U.S. ships to load or unload goods on the island. Congress also failed to overrule the State Department's decision to remove Cuba from the list of state sponsors of terrorism. Congress had been given its requisite forty-five-day review period, beginning on April 14, 2015, following the State Department's announcement of its intent to change the list. By the close of the allotted time, no joint resolution had been passed overturning the decision, thereby allowing Secretary of State John Kerry to remove Cuba on May 29.

Iran Nuclear Deal

As negotiations of a nuclear agreement with Iran entered their second year, members of Congress remained sharply divided over whether a potential deal would be a diplomatic victory or a significant concession to an untrustworthy government. Unable to prevent negotiations from moving forward, lawmakers instead sought to grant themselves authority to review and approve the terms of a final agreement. The Iran Nuclear Agreement Review Act of 2015 (HR 1191—PL 114–17) cleared both the House and Senate with little resistance and was signed by the president in May.

BACKGROUND

Throughout 2014 and early 2015, the United States joined Russia, China, the United Kingdom, France, and Germany in ongoing negotiations with Iran to arrive at a long-term nuclear agreement to replace the interim Joint Plan of Action. On April 2, 2015, after several deadline extensions, the parties agreed to a preliminary framework that established parameters for a final deal. This was followed by the signing and release of the Joint Comprehensive Plan of Action (JCPOA) on July 14, 2015.

Under the agreement, Iran reaffirmed it would not seek, develop, or acquire nuclear weapons and agreed to limits on its nuclear program. These included restrictions on the number and type of uranium-enriching centrifuges Iran could maintain, as well as the amount of enriched uranium it could stockpile. Iran also committed to allowing the International Atomic Energy Agency (IAEA) to monitor agreement implementation and have a long-term presence in the country. In return, once the UN Security Council had endorsed and the IAEA had verified Iran's implementation with the requirements of the JCPOA, the United States and the European Union would begin lifting sanctions against Iran. Billions of dollars in oil revenue would also be released from Iran's frozen offshore accounts.

Opinion of the JCPOA was sharply divided, with many U.S. lawmakers highly skeptical that Iran could be trusted to comply with the agreement. Members of Congress also expressed concern about what Iran would do with the sanctions relief money it received and questioned whether Iran would simply ramp up its nuclear activity as provisions of the deal expired. In both the House and Senate, lawmakers called for an opportunity to review and approve the deal. In early March, House Foreign Affairs Committee Chair Ed Royce, R-Calif., and Ranking Member Eliot Engel, D-N.Y., released a letter to the president reminding him that Congress had to approve any agreement before congressionally imposed sanctions could be lifted and that this would require passing legislation. This was followed by forty-six Senate Republicans signing an open letter to Iranian leaders warning that any agreement might not last beyond Obama's second term unless it was approved by Congress.

Senate Committee Action

On January 29, 2015, the Senate Banking, Housing and Urban Affairs Committee voted 18–4 to approve a bill (S 269) sponsored by Senators Bob Menendez, D-N.J., and Mark Kirk,

R-Ill., that would have imposed tougher sanctions on Iran. The approved bill also included a nonbinding amendment expressing the sense of Congress that a final nuclear agreement with Iran should get an up-or-down vote. The measure did not proceed to the Senate floor, however, because Menendez and nine other Democrats did not want the bill to be considered before negotiators had reached a framework agreement.

The following month, Senate Foreign Relations Committee Chair Bob Corker, R-Tenn., and Menendez, the ranking committee member, introduced the Iran Nuclear Agreement Review Act of 2015 (S 615). The bill required President Obama, within five days of a final agreement being reached, to submit to Congress the full text of the agreement, a verification assessment report prepared by the Secretary of State, and certification that the deal meets the United States' nonproliferation objectives, among other assurances. It then gave Congress sixty days to review and vote to approve or disapprove of the agreement, during which time the White House was prohibited from lifting any statutory sanctions. If Congress approved the deal or took no action by the end of the sixty-day period, sanctions could be lifted. The bill was reported out of committee favorably on April 14, 2015.

Senate Floor Action

The Senate unanimously agreed to attach S 615 as an amendment to HR 1191, the Protecting Volunteer Firefighters and Emergency Responders Act, which had passed the House on March 17, 2015. The bill was approved by a vote of 98-1 on May 7. Lawmakers on both sides of the aisle generally acknowledged that Corker's proposal provided the best possible opportunity for Congress to have any official input on the JCPOA.

House Action

As promised by leadership, the House quickly took up consideration of Senate amendments to HR 1191 and voted 400-25 to accept the revised bill on May 14, 2015. President Obama signed the bill into law on May 22 (PL 114-17).

In accordance with the new law, the State Department provided all details and documents of the JCPOA to Congress on July 19, 2015, with the official congressional review period beginning on July 20. The same day, more than sixty former national security leaders submitted a letter to Congress urging lawmakers to approve the deal. Congress did not pass a resolution disapproving the JCPOA by the sixty-day deadline, allowing officials to proceed with implementation. The JCPOA formally took effect on October 18, following its approval by the United Nations, European Union, and Iran's parliament.

Iran Sanctions Blocked in 2016

Days before the IAEA verified Iran's implementation of the JCPOA, lawmakers in the House revived their efforts to influence the terms of the deal and impose new economic sanctions on Iran. Although the House succeeded in passing four separate sanctions-related measures, Senate Democrats blocked all of them from progressing further. With no congressional roadblocks in place, the United States began lifting sanctions against Iran on January 16, the date of IAEA compliance verification. Most of those lifted were secondary sanctions, or those that apply to non-U.S. individuals and other countries doing business with Iran.

House Action

On January 13, 2016, the House voted 191-106 to pass a bill (HR 3662) seeking to cripple the JCPOA by requiring President Obama to make certain certifications to Congress before sanctions could be lifted. Specifically, the bill would have prohibited the president from removing a foreign financial institution—including Iranian entities—from the Treasury Department's list of designated nationals and blocked persons until he certified to Congress that the institution had not knowingly facilitated a significant transaction or provided significant financial services to the Iranian Revolutionary Guard Corps, a foreign terrorist organization, or a person whose property or property interests were blocked in connection with Iran's nuclear program. The president would also have to certify that the institution no longer engaged in illicit or deceptive financial transactions or other activities. Additionally, the bill stipulated that the president could not remove foreign individuals from the designated nationals and blocked persons list until he certified that the individual had not knowingly assisted in or provided support to a terrorist organization or engaged in activities or transactions that had materially contributed to Iran's nuclear program.

The vote was later vacated and rescheduled following complaints by lawmakers that House leadership had not provided enough time to cast their vote (140 members missed the vote). The bill was brought up for another vote on February 2, when it passed 246-181. The White House threatened to veto the measure; however, it never made it to the president's desk because the Senate did not take action.

The House next passed a series of sanctions bills on July 14 in what was largely viewed as a move providing political cover to Republicans returning home for the August recess; the bills allowed them to tell constituents they were taking action against Iran's ballistic missile development and support for terrorist groups. House Majority Leader Kevin McCarthy, R-Calif., told the *Washington Post* that Republicans intended to penalize Iran for its activities, something he felt the White House would not do.

The trio of bills included a measure (HR 5631) sponsored by McCarthy that would have required the president to determine whether specific Iranian business sectors—including the chemical, computer science, construction, electronic, metallurgy, mining, research, and telecommunications industries—had supported the country's ballistic missile program. If any person or business within one of these sectors had provided such support, then the president would have been required to sanction the entire sector. This bill passed by a vote of 246-179.

A second bill (HR 4992), sponsored by Foreign Affairs Committee Chair Ed Royce, R-Calif., codified Iranian access to the U.S. dollar and clarified that U.S. dollars held by foreign financial institutions could not be used in offshore transactions on behalf of Iranian banks and businesses. The measure passed 246–181, despite warnings from the Treasury Department that it could weaken the dollar's standing as the world's preferred currency reserve.

The third and final measure (HR 5119) was sponsored by Rep. Mike Pompeo, R-Kan. It would have prohibited the use of U.S. funds to purchase Iranian heavy water, a material used to make nuclear warheads. Pompeo's bill was a response to an Energy Department announcement that it would buy thirty-two tons of heavy water from Iran—which had agreed to reduce its stockpile of the material under the terms of the JCPOA—for $8.6 million. The bill was approved by a vote of 249–176. The Senate took no action on these bills other than to refer them to committee for consideration.

While no new congressional sanctions were approved in 2016, the House and Senate did vote to renew the Iran Sanctions Act (PL 104–172), which was set to expire at the end of the year. Originally passed in 1996, the act implemented a series of nuclear-related and nonnuclear sanctions against Iran and authorized the president to impose and/or waive sanctions. The White House deemed renewal unnecessary, stating that the president already had the authority to impose sanctions, and argued that it might undermine the nuclear deal's success. However, lawmakers claimed the act's extension would provide the president with an important tool to ensure Iran's compliance with the JCPOA—or to act quickly to reimpose sanctions if Iran violated the terms of the agreement.

On November 15, the House voted 419 to 1 to renew the act and extend sanctions for ten years (HR 6297). The Senate unanimously approved the measure on December 1. President Obama declined to sign the bill but still allowed it to become law (PL 114–277) on December 15.

North Korea Hydrogen Bomb: U.S. Sanctions

Early in 2016, lawmakers united to pass new sanctions against North Korea following reports that the government had conducted its first successful underground test of a hydrogen bomb—a weapon significantly more powerful than an atomic bomb—and launched a satellite into space.

BACKGROUND

North Korea withdrew from the Nuclear Non-Proliferation Treaty, an international agreement aimed at stopping the spread of nuclear weapons, in 2003, a year after making its weapons program public. The government announced its first test of a nuclear device in 2006, leading to an initial round of UN Security Council sanctions seeking to limit the country's ballistic missile program.

The international community, including the United States, has repeatedly implemented various sanctions packages in response to North Korea's continued nuclear activities. However, sanctions have yet to prove an effective deterrent, due in part to a lack of enforcement by the UN Security Council. North Korea has also found ways to evade the sanctions, particularly through its close relationship with China. Approximately 80 percent of North Korea's trade is conducted with China—a major factor in the Chinese government's resistance to harsh sanctions despite its opposition to North Korea's nuclear program. Additionally, smuggled goods are known to cross China's border into North Korea. Some of this trade is allegedly run by or involves kickbacks to North Korea's Communist Party and military officials.

North Korea has persisted in testing various missiles and related weapons technology every year since its nuclear program was revealed. In 2016, in addition to the hydrogen bomb test and satellite launch, North Korea conducted many different missile tests, including two launched from submarines. The submarine-based tests, in particular, raised new concerns that North Korea may be able to launch an attack against the United States or other distant targets without needing to develop long-range missile technology.

Congressional efforts to respond to these actions with additional sanctions would be followed by the Obama administration's announcement in March of fresh sanctions against five North Korean government entities, including the National Defense Commission, and twelve individuals for their involvement in the country's nuclear and weapons programs. Then in July, the Treasury Department imposed the United States' first-ever sanctions against North Korean leader Kim Jong Un, in addition to sanctioning fifteen other individuals and entities involved in censorship and human rights abuses.

House Action

The House approved a new sanctions measure (HR 757) on January 12, 2016, by a vote of 418–2. The bill had been introduced by Rep. Ed Royce, R-Calif., and approved by the House Foreign Affairs Committee in February 2015 but had not progressed further and received little attention; North Korea's hydrogen bomb test revived interest in the measure.

The bill authorized the president to sanction individuals who knowingly engaged or attempted to engage in significant activities with North Korea that materially contributed to the "proliferation of weapons of mass destruction." It also authorized sanctions against individuals, foreign financial institutions, and governments that help North Korea evade UN Security Council sanctions—a measure expected to impact primarily China.

The bill required the Treasury Department to determine whether North Korea should be designated as a "primary money laundering concern," which would effectively cut North Korean banks off from the U.S. financial system. Additionally, the bill allowed individuals involved in censorship or serious human rights abuses by the government to be sanctioned.

Senate Action

The approved House bill was received in the Senate on January 19 and was referred to the Foreign Relations Committee. The committee unanimously approved the measure, with several amendments, by voice vote on January 28.

One of the amendments attached by the committee required that sanctions be imposed on individuals involved in North Korea's mining, steel, and aluminum sectors, which provide the country with significant revenue. The committee also amended the bill to mandate sanctions against those selling or buying minerals such as coal and steel from North Korea. It was anticipated that this particular measure could create tension in U.S.–China relations given that Chinese businesses are among the biggest importers of North Korean minerals.

Other changes amended the House bill to include sanctions against individuals who knowingly engage in significant activities that help North Korea undermine cybersecurity measures, as well as new reporting requirements and sanctions on individuals involved in the government's human rights abuses.

The full Senate passed the bill 96–0 on February 10, 2016.

Final Action

The House accepted the Senate's amendments and approved the revised legislation on February 12 by a vote of 408–2. President Obama signed the bill on February 18 (PL 114–122).

Fiscal 2017 State Department Authorizations

In April 2016, the Senate took up State Department authorization legislation (S 1635) originally proposed by Senate Foreign Relations Committee Chair Bob Corker, R-Tenn., and Ranking Member Ben Cardin, D-Md., in June 2015.

Behind-the-scenes negotiations between Corker and Senators Marco Rubio, R-Fla., and Ted Cruz, R-Texas, enabled the bill to proceed after nearly a year of delay. As part of the deal, Rubio agreed to lift his hold on President Obama's nomination of Roberta Jacobson as ambassador to Mexico, which had stalled in 2015 due to her role in normalizing U.S.–Cuban diplomatic relations. In return, Corker agreed to hold a committee vote on Rubio's proposed legislation to renew sanctions against Venezuelan officials over human rights abuses. Rubio further agreed to help Cruz persuade the House to pass a measure renaming a street in front of the Chinese embassy in honor of prodemocracy leader and political prisoner Liu Xiaobo, a Nobel Peace Prize laureate who called for reforms and openly campaigned against China's communist one-party system.

Rubio also encouraged Cruz to move forward on legislation authorizing and funding the State Department. Following the 2015 announcement of the nuclear deal with Iran, Cruz had sent a letter to President Obama indicating his intention to block all nominees for the Department of State and hold any legislation that reauthorized funds for the Department of State unless the administration pledged to delay the UN Security Council's approval of the agreement until after Congress completed its review.

Senate Action

The Department of State Authorities Act, Fiscal Year 2017 (S 1635) was approved by the full Senate on April 28, 2016, by unanimous consent.

Major provisions of the bill included a requirement that the State Department create and implement a plan to leverage U.S. influence at the United Nations to reduce sexual exploitation by peacekeepers. The bill also made explicit the applicability of the Leahy Law—stipulating U.S. foreign assistance and military training be withheld from any country or entity found to have committed human rights violations—to UN peacekeeping missions. These measures sought to make UN peacekeeping missions more accountable following reports that some UN peacekeepers had sexually abused the civilians they were supposed to be protecting.

Additionally, the bill ordered a Government Accountability Office report on overhauling the formula used to determine U.S. contributions to peacekeeping missions and directed the president to seek reimbursement of contributions that had not been spent. Another provision permanently implemented the annual withholding of 15 percent of U.S. funds from international organizations, such as the United Nations, that failed to protect whistleblowers from recrimination.

Other measures established more competitive pay levels for local embassy staff members; increased flexibility for the State Department to retain noncareer appointed individuals for more than five years; granted Diplomatic Security agents arrest authority in cases of physical security incidents in the United States and subpoena authority to investigate visa and passport fraud as well as other protective duties; and restricted the consular fee system to fully cover service costs with fees charged. Prior to the bill's passage, a package amendment striking language related to a compensation fund for Americans held hostage in Iran between 1979 and 1981, endowing the Ambassador at Large for International Religious Freedom with the primary responsibility for religious freedom training, and including various other technical changes was added via unanimous consent.

House Committee Action

The authorization bill was referred to the House Foreign Affairs Committee and amended before being reported by unanimous consent on May 26, 2016.

The House committee amendment was designed to improve diplomatic security with measures, including authorizing the State Department to award local guard contracts based on best value rather than lowest price, by which the department had been constrained in the past.

This change was based on findings during the Benghazi investigation that the local guards hired were ineffective and chosen based on cost. Other measures adopted included increased communication between the Assistant Secretary of State for Diplomatic Security and the Secretary of State and designation of the Assistant Secretary as directly accountable to the Secretary.

Finally, the committee approved an amendment proposed by Representative Jeff Duncan, R-S.C., establishing a policy requiring the United States to "strongly consider" a United Nations member state's voting record before entering into any agreement with that country. This provision was in response to some nations, such as Haiti, benefiting from U.S. aid despite voting against the United States at the United Nations.

House Floor Action

The amended authorization legislation was not taken up by the full House until December. On December 5, House Foreign Affairs Committee Chair Ed Royce, R-Calif., moved to suspend the rules and pass the bill. Debate ensued and was followed by a vote on Royce's motion, which passed 374–16.

The final House bill included a clause inserting language requiring the Special Envoy to Monitor and Combat Anti-Semitism to report to Congress on U.S. efforts to combat anti-Semitism in Europe within 180 days of the enactment of the authorization. The legislation also included changes addressing how officials at the USAID's Office of the Inspector General receive payment, providing greater work flexibility for State Department personnel to serve abroad, and giving permission for the department to develop a plan to recruit private-sector professionals.

Conference and Final Action

The Senate consented unanimously to the House's amendments to the authorization bill on December 10, 2016, the night before Congress adjourned for the year. President Obama signed the bill (S 1635—PL 114–323) on December 16.

MAJOR PROVISIONS

U.S. embassy security remained a top-priority issue in the final bill, which authorized a $4.8 billion budget for security upgrades as well as embassy maintenance and construction where current facilities do not meet security needs.

Lawmakers also sought to improve diplomatic security by requiring the State Department to determine high-risk, high-threat overseas posts; prioritize funding and security for those high-risk sites; and develop a joint contingency plan with the Department of Defense to secure U.S. embassies during crises. The legislation made changes to the line of communications between the State Department and Congress by ordering the Secretary of State to deliver monthly briefings regarding the opening or reopening of

positions at any foreign embassies deemed high risk and by making the Assistant Secretary for Diplomatic Security accountable to the Secretary of State.

Other security provisions included

- increasing the authority of the State Department to penalize staff for misconduct and security violations
- enhancing embassy security by approving a transfer of up to 20 percent of Administration of Foreign Affairs appropriations
- mandating an annual review of and a report by the secretaries of State and Defense on Marine Security Guard units assigned to foreign diplomatic areas

The bill set pay levels for State Department personnel, determined service requirements for Foreign Service members, and put forward measures to promote economic literacy and diversity within the department.

The authorization bill mandated the State Department to craft and implement a strategy to halt sexual exploitation and abuse by UN peacekeepers within 180 days of the bill's enactment, to include improved training and accountability mechanisms such as creation of an ombudsperson position and a standing claims commission. The Leahy Law clarification and 15 percent withholding of U.S. contributions to international organizations that do not protect whistleblowers were also included in the final bill.

Other UN-related provisions include

- greater transparency about how the UN determines the reimbursement rate for countries providing troops and police personnel and how that rate may be better adjusted
- an annual report by the Office of Management and Budget on U.S. funds to the UN for peacekeeping missions
- a report by the Secretary of State to Congress on the costs of U.S. troop deployment versus a UN peacekeeping mission

Other general provisions included

- reducing misconduct, abuse, fraud, and waste within the State Department by ordering offices to report allegations to the Office of the Inspector General
- extending Radio Free Asia to be broadcast throughout the entire area (not just North Korea, Tibet, China, Cambodia, Laos, Vietnam, and Burma)
- creating exchange programs to assign State Department employees through the Transatlantic Diplomatic Fellowship program with NATO or the European Union to assist foreign governments and international organizations and vice versa
- mandating an annual report by the Secretary of State to make transparent how UN entities fulfill geographic quotas when filling personnel posts

- an expression by Congress that all U.S. passports and their components should be made and compiled within the United States by U.S. entities holding the proper security clearances
- establishing a United States International Drug Policy Commission to refine current counternarcotic efforts by comparing U.S. policies and programs with international policies and programs
- State Department notification to Congress within fifteen days of authorizing a reward for information, actions, or assistance in preventing or pursuing terrorist acts against the United States based on the Rewards for Justice program established in 1984

Fiscal 2017 State-Foreign Appropriations

Claims of obstruction and dysfunction came from both sides of the aisle during the fiscal 2017 budget and appropriations process, which was paralyzed by the 2016 presidential campaign and partisan policy battles. Ultimately, Congress did not send any appropriations bills to the White House, and the Department of State, Foreign Operations, and Related Programs bill was one of the five spending bills that never made it to the House or Senate floor.

Senate Subcommittee Action

The Senate Subcommittee on State, Foreign Operations, and Related Programs approved a nearly $52.1 billion fiscal 2017 spending bill (S 3117) on June 28, 2016. Senators agreed to withhold amendments until the full Appropriations Committee had an opportunity to consider the bill.

Providing $687 million less than what the White House had requested but $100 million more than the subsequent House bill, the subcommittee bill's total comprised approximately $37.2 billion in base funding and almost $14.9 billion for the OCO account.

The bill allocated more than $8.3 billion to international security assistance ($6.5 billion in base funding and nearly $1.9 billion in OCO funding), about $215 million more than requested by the Obama administration. State Department operations would receive $5 billion, which was $157 million more than requested. The subcommittee increased funding for USAID operations by $92 million, bringing USAID's total annual funding to $1.4 billion. The bill also provided $6.1 billion for embassy security.

The subcommittee bill slashed funding for international financial institutions by $277 million, banned financial assistance to the United Nations Population Fund (UNFP), and limited U.S. funds to international reproductive health and family planning programs to $461 million.

The subcommittee boosted funding for Middle East and North Africa programs by providing about $3.4 billion in aid to Israel and $44.5 million for the Multinational Force and Observers in the Sinai Peninsula, which monitors implementation of the 1979 Israel–Egypt peace treaty. These totals were $300 million and $10 million higher, respectively, than the amounts requested by the Obama administration. Additionally, the bill authorized $1.3 billion in security assistance and $75 million in economic assistance to Egypt.

Seed money of $25 million was allocated for a new Near East and Africa Relief and Recovery Fund. Championed by Chair Lindsey Graham, R-S.C., the fund was created to support programs that address the basic needs—such as food, water, electricity, sanitation, and health care—of areas that had been liberated from, or were under the influence of, extremist organizations.

Another measure provided $28 million for grants and cooperative agreements that support girls and women in predominantly Muslim nations at risk from extremism and conflict. The bill stipulated that funds would be made available to programs that promote tolerance and pluralism, develop and disseminate early-warning and response systems, provide psychosocial services, establish safe houses or other centers of empowerment and protection, document crimes and support investigations of those crimes, and increase the participation and influence of women in politics.

While the bill contained $3.1 billion to support the State Department's migration and refugee assistance account, appropriators reduced the amount of assistance for internally displaced peoples by $400 million.

Senate Committee Action

The full Senate Appropriations Committee approved the subcommittee's draft bill on June 29, 2016, with amendments regarding issues of family planning, climate change response, and the anti-Israel boycott. An amendment from Senator Jeanne Shaheen, D-N.H., to increase funding for international family planning programs by $124 million was adopted by a 17–13 vote, bringing the total to $585 million. The measure also allocated $37.5 million to the UNFP and removed language forbidding U.S. aid from directly supporting abortion-related services, including referrals and counseling. According to Sen. Shaheen, the services are responsible for helping people around the world and were important to continue funding.

Another measure put forward by Senator Jeff Merkley, D-Ore., that provided $500 million to the U.N. Green Climate Fund, was adopted by voice vote. The program, for which the base bill had denied funding despite a White House request for $750 million, exists to help developing countries prepare for and mitigate the effects of climate change.

Despite Democratic opposition, the committee also adopted, by a vote of 21–9, an amendment by Senator Mark Kirk, R-Ill., allowing U.S. state and local governments to divest from organizations or other entities that participate in or support the boycott of Israel.

An amendment to deny military funding to Saudi Arabia unless the country demonstrated it had taken precautions to mitigate civilian casualties in the fight against terrorism failed in a 14–16 vote.

House Subcommittee Action

Following a markup session during which debate on partisan policy riders was suspended, the House Subcommittee on State, Foreign Operations, and Related Programs unanimously approved its version of the fiscal 2017 spending bill (HR 5912) on July 6, 2016. The bill provided a total of $52 billion in funding, which was $700 million less than the White House's requested amount.

Subcommittee appropriators continued refugee aid at the fiscal 2016 level ($3.1 billion) but capped funding intended for the resettlement of refugees within the United States at $394 million (the fiscal 2015 level). Global health security efforts, including money to respond to the Zika virus, would receive $200 million under the House bill.

The bill reduced multilateral assistance by $900 million, bringing the total to $1.7 billion, and cut funding for programs designed to address international climate change and activities supporting reproductive health and family planning. Programs affected by these cuts included the U.N. Green Climate Fund, the Intergovernmental Panel on Climate Change, the UNFP, and the U.N. Educational, Scientific, and Cultural Organization (UNESCO).

The subcommittee increased spending for embassy security to $6.1 billion and boosted funding for international security assistance. A total of $9.1 billion was provided for base and OCO funding.

House Committee Action

The full House Appropriations Committee reported HR 5912 to the full House on July 15, 2016. Republicans defeated several Democratic attempts to attach amendments to increase spending levels for certain programs, including an amendment from Rep. Nita Lowey, D-N.Y., seeking to boost funds for refugee resettlement. Amendments allocating money to the U.N. Green Climate Fund and increasing funding for bilateral and multilateral assistance for family planning activities also failed.

Conference and Final Action

Despite initial progress in the House and Senate committees, neither bill saw floor action. By the summer, with budget negotiations stalled in both chambers, it had become abundantly clear lawmakers would need to adopt a continuing resolution to avoid a shutdown and continue funding the government through the start of the fiscal year on October 1. Republicans disagreed on how long the resolution should delay negotiations, with many eager to punt deliberations into 2017, and possibly as late as March, after the election.

The Senate passed a ten-week continuing resolution (HR 5325—PL 114-223) by a vote of 72-26 on September 28, 2016, funding the federal government through December 9. The measure cleared the House with little resistance on the same day and was signed by the president on September 29.

Following Donald Trump's election to the presidency in November, Republican leaders renewed their efforts to push fiscal 2017 spending discussions into the spring, allowing a new Congress and a new administration to restart the process.

A second and final continuing resolution (HR 2028—PL 114-254) cleared the Senate with a 63-36 vote on December 9, 2016, replacing the September stopgap resolution. Written by conservative leaders, the $1.07 trillion measure would continue funding the federal government through April 28, 2017. The resolution passed the House with a 326-96 vote.

MAJOR PROVISIONS

The final measure incorporated eleven of the twelve appropriations bills Congress had been unable to complete and provided the State Department and USAID with $160 million in discretionary funding and an additional $4.3 billion in OCO funds.

Other relevant provisions included

- $1.2 billion for economic and stabilization assistance, including countering Russian influence, ISIL and other terrorist groups, and support for the Iraq sovereign loan guarantee
- $916 million for humanitarian assistance, including refugee aid
- $404 million for global security assistance and for peacekeeping and stabilization operations in the Middle East and Africa

Foreign Aid: Transparency and Food Assistance

In 2016, Congress passed two bills aimed at improving the effectiveness and transparency of U.S. foreign aid. The legislation was backed by a number of humanitarian agencies that are the beneficiaries of U.S. foreign assistance. The bipartisan bills were developed in cooperation with the Obama administration, with the intent of furthering the president's efforts to enhance existing programs by eliminating micromanagement and ensuring greater return on investment from foreign aid programs.

FOREIGN AID TRANSPARENCY

In October 2015, Rep. Ted Poe, R-Texas, introduced the Foreign Aid Transparency and Accountability Act of 2016 (HR 3766) in the House Foreign Affairs Committee. The legislation sought to codify previous actions undertaken by the Bush and Obama administrations by requiring the submission of reports on the effectiveness of foreign aid programs. Although the legislation did not add any new evaluation programs, it would ensure that the administration's efforts would continue into the future to allow foreign aid dollars to flow with greater efficacy to more evidence-based practices.

Within eighteen months of the bill's passage, President Obama would be required to submit a report outlining the goals, metrics, and evaluation plans for U.S. foreign assistance programs. These guidelines would direct the more than twenty federal agencies responsible for administering a portion of U.S. foreign aid dollars as to how to undertake their evaluation programs, including how to establish annual monitoring agendas, develop metrics for measuring success, create a clearinghouse for disseminating data and lessons learned to allow for benchmarking of future programs, and distribute internal and public reports.

The Government Accountability Office would subsequently analyze the Obama administration's guidelines and assess how they are being utilized across the federal government. The Department of State was instructed to post on its ForeignAssistance.gov website any information on covered foreign assistance programs received from federal departments or agencies each quarter.

The intent of the legislation was to provide greater insight to lawmakers, foreign aid recipients, and the public on how this money is spent, where it is most effective, and where it has fallen short of program goals. Rep. Ed Royce, R-Calif., chair of the House Foreign Affairs Committee, criticized previous attempts at evaluating the efficacy of foreign aid programs, noting that they were frequently graded on what was delivered rather than outcomes achieved, such as lives saved through medical interventions.

The legislation was reported out of the House committee on November 5, 2015, and was approved by a voice vote on December 8, 2015. The Senate's companion bill, sponsored by Marco Rubio, R-Fla., included two amendments to the House version. One of the amendments changed the title, while the other

- provided additional time for the GAO to report out to Congress
- required agencies to post data on ForeignAssistance. gov from fiscal year 2015 through the current fiscal year (rather than the original bill's requirement that data go back to fiscal year 2012)
- called on USAID and the State Department to coordinate the data collection for ForeignAssistance.gov and Explorer.USAID.gov no later than fiscal year 2018

- required that "covered assistance" for which data must be collected include assistance provided under the International Narcotics and Law Enforcement account

The amended legislation was passed by unanimous consent in the Senate on June 28, 2016, and subsequently agreed to under suspension of the rules in the House on July 5, 2016. The president signed the bill into law on July 15, 2016 (HR 3766—PL 114–191).

FOOD SECURITY

The Senate took the lead on a separate bill, S1252, the Global Food Security Act. This bipartisan legislation was aimed at enhancing the U.S. commitment to ending hunger, poverty, and child malnutrition while increasing food security around the world by codifying the Obama administration's Feed the Future initiative. According to co-sponsor Johnny Isakson, R-Ga., the bill was vital to national security interests, based on a premise that access to affordable food has a significant impact on economic productivity and livelihood.

The legislation called on the president to develop a strategy for addressing hunger and food security around the world and then issue a report to Congress annually on the effectiveness of that plan. The president's strategy was required to include metrics, measurable goals, and an evaluation plan and would provide a platform for regular consultation and collaboration with stakeholders and Congressional committees.

The legislation also amended the Foreign Assistance Act of 1961 to give the president greater authority to provide emergency food assistance through vouchers and cash transfers to local and regional groups to help them procure food following humanmade or natural disasters when U.S. commodities cannot reach the impacted location fast enough.

S 1252 was reported out of the Senate Foreign Relations Committee on March 15 and easily cleared a Senate floor vote on April 20, 2016. On July 6, the House passed the bill under suspension of the rules, and the president signed it into law on July 20 (PL 114–195). Notably, the final bill authorized $7 billion in funding for food security programs but did not require the funds to be spent, providing greater leeway to the agencies administering food aid.

CHAPTER 5

Defense Policy

Defense Policy

The transition in defense priorities that began when President Barack Obama took office in 2009 continued through his second term as the United States shifted its focus from long-running wars in Iraq and Afghanistan to countering the emerging threat posed by the Islamic State in Iraq and the Levant (ISIL), responding to internal unrest in the Middle East, and quelling Russian aggression in former Soviet territories.

WINDING DOWN WARS

Obama had succeeded in ending Operation Iraqi Freedom during his first term, withdrawing the last U.S. troops from Iraq in December 2011 according to a schedule negotiated by former President George W. Bush with the Iraqi government. In his second term, Obama oversaw the drawdown of the United States' military presence in Afghanistan after thirteen years of fighting an increasingly unpopular war that cost the lives of more than 2,200 American soldiers.

U.S. officials reached an agreement with the Afghan government in 2012 that provided a framework for an ongoing relationship between the two countries and required the execution of a Bilateral Security Agreement (BSA) to more clearly define the United States' role in Afghanistan after 2014. BSA negotiations were repeatedly delayed by former Afghan President Hamid Karzai, but two years after they began, a final agreement was signed with the new administration of Ashraf Ghani. Per the agreement, combat operations would end in 2014, but approximately 12,500 to 13,500 coalition troops would remain in the country to help train and support Afghan forces. The official end of the combat mission was announced on December 28, 2014.

With both wars concluded, the Obama administration shifted its priorities in the region to training and equipping Afghan and Iraqi soldiers to maintain stability and fight terrorist networks in their own countries. In Iraq, the provision of military equipment and counterterrorism support, in addition to training, became a critical element of the United States' strategy for dealing with the rise of ISIL, which declared a caliphate in 2014. The group has since claimed increasingly broad swaths of territory in the Middle East, particularly in Iraq and Syria. Obama was reluctant to commit the United States to another, potentially long-term ground war, preferring instead to provide assistance from afar and conduct airstrikes against ISIL targets in coordination with U.S. partners.

DEFENSE SPENDING

Another element of transition that continued during Obama's second term involved significant cuts to defense spending, which had been growing steadily each year since 2001. Delayed implementation of congressionally mandated sequestration—across-the-board budget cuts from which the Defense Department was not exempt—occurred in March 2013, trimming defense spending for the remainder of fiscal 2013 by nearly 8 percent across all programs and accounts and resulting in a twenty-two-day furlough of the Pentagon's 800,000 civilian employees.

Spending levels set for subsequent fiscal years by the Budget Control Act of 2011 (PL 112-25)—under which the 2013 sequestration had been imposed—became a primary source of partisan disagreements during appropriations negotiations in Congress and created a major obstacle to

REFERENCES

Discussion of defense policy for the years 1945–1964 may be found in *Congress and the Nation Vol. I*, pp. 237–334; for the years 1965–1968, *Congress and the Nation Vol. II*, pp. 827–890; for the years 1969–1972, *Congress and the Nation Vol. III*, pp. 191–252; for the years 1973–1976, *Congress and the Nation Vol. IV*, pp. 153–197; for the years 1977–1980, *Congress and the Nation Vol. V*, pp. 125–176; for the years 1981–1984, *Congress and the Nation Vol. VI*, pp. 201–257; for the years 1985–1988, *Congress and the Nation Vol. VII*, pp. 273–340; for the years 1989–1992, *Congress and the Nation Vol. VIII*, pp. 335–412; for the years 1993–1996, *Congress and the Nation Vol. IX*, pp. 253–323; for the years 1997–2000, *Congress and the Nation Vol. X*, pp. 235–311; for the years 2001–2004, *Congress and the Nation Vol. XI*, pp. 303–366; for the years 2005–2008, *Congress and the Nation Vol. XII*, pp. 331–401; for the years 2009–2012, *Congress and the Nation Vol. XIII*, pp. 263–316.

Figure 5.1 Outlays for National Defense

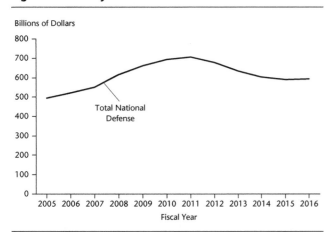

SOURCE: Executive Office of the President, Office of Management and Budget, *Budget of the United States Government, Fiscal Year 2018, Historical Tables* (Washington, DC: U.S. Government Printing Office, 2018), Table 3.2.

NOTE: Most of the expenditures, approximately 97 percent, were for military activities of the Department of Defense. Atomic energy defense activities accounted for most of the remainder.

passage of standalone funding measures. Lawmakers failed to pass independent defense appropriations measures for fiscal years 2014, 2015, 2016, and 2017, though defense budgets were incorporated into omnibus bills along with other annual spending packages. Each of these agreements was reached after the start of the new fiscal year; in 2013, the government shut down for sixteen days while lawmakers deliberated the terms of an omnibus.

Two-year bipartisan budget agreements reached in 2013 and 2015 were critical to facilitating defense appropriations negotiations and avoiding another sequester. Together, the agreements raised discretionary spending caps above sequestration levels for fiscal years 2014 through 2017, dividing the increases equally between defense and nondefense spending. In fiscal 2014, for example, the Defense Department could receive up to $22 billion more in funding for its base defense budget than would otherwise have been possible under existing spending caps. Both deals also suspended statutory limits on the public debt.

Adjustments to discretionary spending levels did not stop lawmakers from attempting to circumvent spending caps and provide additional money for the base defense budget through Overseas Contingency Operations (OCO) funding. OCO funds are shared by the Departments of Defense and State and are meant to cover war-related operational costs, particularly those incurred by the wars in Iraq and Afghanistan. War funding has historically been requested and authorized through emergency and supplemental appropriations, but beginning in 2010, base defense budgets and OCO funding were addressed simultaneously.

The Budget Control Act of 2011 helped cement this change and created an opportunity to provide larger overall defense budgets by exempting OCO funds from spending limits. Since then, lawmakers have repeatedly authorized more OCO funds than what the administration has requested and allocated a growing portion of those funds to base defense programs and accounts instead of war-related activities. This practice has generally been decried by Democrats, who have particularly taken issue with the allocation of OCO funds for weapons, aircraft, and ship procurements not requested by the Defense Department. Disagreements over OCO funding featured prominently in defense authorization and appropriations negotiations during Obama's second term, even prompting threats of a presidential veto.

ORGANIZATIONAL REFORMS

Change for the Defense Department also came via a variety of internal reforms required by Congress. The fiscal 2017 defense authorization bill called for an organizational restructuring that eliminated the undersecretary of defense for acquisition position, delegating the role's responsibilities among the armed services and the newly created positions of undersecretary for acquisition and sustainment and undersecretary for research and engineering. Further changes to the department's acquisition system sought by lawmakers included measures opening contracts to commercial vendors and establishing a preference for fixed-price contracts over those that reimburse contractors for their costs. The same bill also placed limitations on the number of National Security Council staff the president could have, cut the number of general officer positions in the military, and called for the separation of Cyber Command from the U.S. Strategic Command.

The Department of Veterans Affairs was also subject to reform efforts, including lawmakers' requirement that certain construction funds be withheld until the VA secured a non-VA federal entity, such as the Army Corps of Engineers, to serve as the agent for each major construction project. Significant cost overruns on several VA projects, particularly a new medical center outside of Denver, Colo., prompted the change, amid criticisms by lawmakers that VA officials were mismanaging the projects at great cost to American taxpayers. Another VA scandal, this time involving the cover-up of months-long wait times for veterans to schedule medical appointments, led Congress to create the Veterans Choice program. While short term, the program was significant in that it allowed veterans to obtain private health care if they faced excessive wait times for a VA appointment or they lived more than forty miles from the nearest VA medical facility.

A-10 WARTHOG

At least one Defense Department program that proved resistant to change was the revered A-10 Warthog. The Air Force has repeatedly sought to retire its fleet of the close-air support aircraft, with officials estimating that removing the A-10 from service would save roughly $4.2 billion over five years. Despite facing pressure to find cost savings where they could in the defense budget, lawmakers proved resistant to the Air Force's proposal and repeatedly included language in defense authorization and appropriations measures that prohibited the A-10's retirement. Sen. Kelly Ayotte, R-N.H., led the charge to keep the plane in service, arguing that the low-flying aircraft were critical to supporting combat troops on the ground.

To overcome congressional resistance to their plan, Air Force officials proposed a phased retirement for the A-10 that would pull the planes out of service over a period of several years. When this failed to win lawmakers over, officials lowered the number of planes they proposed to retire in the first year of the phased plan and packaged their counter proposal with a warning that keeping the A-10 flying would negatively impact Congress's pet F-35 Joint Strike Fighter project—the Pentagon's most expensive program. Lawmakers were skeptical of the Air Force's claim that it did not have enough maintenance personnel to support both programs at once. However, they ultimately agreed that a small number of A-10s could be placed in "backup inventory status," which is not retirement, while the Defense Department evaluated the Air Force's capacity to maintain the A-10s along with its other aircraft.

Chronology of Action on Defense Policy

2013–2014

Nearly all the 113th Congress's defense-related work in 2013 and 2014 involved setting policy priorities for the Defense Department and providing appropriations for its various programs and accounts.

In 2013, for the first time in roughly fifty years, lawmakers faced a significant possibility of failing to approve a defense authorization bill in 2013 due to concerns about process rather than disagreements on substance. Although a draft bill progressed relatively quickly through the House and the Senate Armed Services Committee, it stalled in the Senate when Republicans objected to Democrats' attempts to limit floor debate and consideration of proposed amendments. Facing an end-of-year time crunch, House and Senate committee members launched informal negotiations to develop a compromise measure, which cleared both chambers and was signed by the president in December.

Lawmakers found themselves in a similar situation in 2014. By the time the authorization bill had passed the House and been approved by the Senate Armed Services Committee, there was little time available to consider it on the Senate floor around the summer and midterm election recesses, and lawmakers had to prioritize their work on spending measures to keep the government open past the end of the fiscal year. Committee leaders were once again forced to negotiate a compromise measure outside of the formal conference process, with the final bill signed into law one week before Christmas.

Appropriations also proved challenging for Congress. Defense spending measures had once been considered "must-pass" legislation. However, lawmakers were unable to approve freestanding appropriations bills in either year due to Congresswide disagreements over discretionary spending levels. Each year, the full House and the Senate Appropriations Committee cleared their respective versions of defense spending packages, only to see those proposals get bogged down in the Senate. Similarly, congressional gridlock prevented independent appropriations bills for the VA and military construction projects from clearing both chambers, despite the annual measure's popularity and efforts on both sides of the aisle to

keep it free of controversial provisions. Defense and VA spending was instead incorporated into the omnibus bills negotiated for fiscal years 2014 and 2015.

Lawmakers did succeed in approving an emergency spending bill that authorized $15 billion in funding to address a medical scandal at the VA. Reports surfaced in the spring of 2014 that officials in VA medical facilities were falsifying records to cover up excessive wait times for veterans seeking to schedule appointments and that some veterans had died waiting for appointments. An audit ordered by VA Secretary Eric Shinseki confirmed that a majority of VA medical facilities kept "secret waiting lists" of veterans whose appointments had not been scheduled while reporting shorter wait-time data to the VA. Shinseki later resigned due to significant pressure from lawmakers and veterans' groups.

Fiscal 2014 Defense Appropriations

By August 2013, the House and the Senate Appropriations Committee had approved separate, freestanding appropriations bills to fund the Defense Department and military operations. However, neither measure progressed further due to a breakdown in budget negotiations across Congress.

Staunch partisan disagreements between Senate Democrats and House Republicans over budget cuts and decreased spending levels set by the Budget Control Act of 2011 (PL 112-25) for fiscal 2014 stymied negotiations, leading to a sixteen-day government shutdown in the fall. Senate leadership eventually agreed to a deal (HR 2775) that reopened the government through January 15, increased the debt limit, set discretionary spending levels, and called for the House and Senate Budget Committees to adopt a joint budget resolution by December 13. Senate Budget Committee Chair Patty Murray, D-Wash., and House Budget Committee Chair Paul Ryan, R-Wisc., subsequently collaborated to produce a bipartisan budget resolution (H J Res 59—PL 113-67) that raised the caps on discretionary spending and reduced sequestration cuts for

DEFENSE LEADERSHIP

Secretary of Defense

In stark contrast to the lengthy tenure of President Obama's first secretary of defense, Robert M. Gates, who filled the role for nearly five years across two presidential administrations, Obama's three subsequent selections for the cabinet-level post each served for two years or less.

Gates's successor, former CIA Director Leon Panetta, retired from the office in February 2013 after nineteen months on the job. Panetta's time as secretary of defense was largely consumed by efforts to rein in department budgets to meet reduced spending levels mandated by Congress in the 2011 Budget Control Act. His ability to get the Joint Chiefs of Staff to agree, however reluctantly, to abide by Congress's $487 billion cut to defense spending over ten years was widely viewed as one of his major accomplishments. Panetta also initiated the administration's reversal of a policy preventing women from serving in combat roles, a formal process that began in January 2013 and concluded in December 2015.

To succeed Panetta, Obama nominated Chuck Hagel, a former Republican senator for the state of Nebraska and a Vietnam War veteran. Despite his conservative background, Hagel was not a popular pick among Republicans in Congress, who expressed concerns about his opposition to sanctions against Iran and willingness to engage with groups such as Hamas, which the State Department has designated a terrorist group, and Hezbollah. Hagel was also criticized as not showing strong enough support for Israel, and his description of pro-Israel lobbying groups on Capitol Hill as "the Jewish lobby" was controversial.

Many political observers were surprised by how acrimonious Hagel's confirmation process became, with Republicans scouring his past remarks and financial records for opportunities to discredit him and staging a filibuster of his nomination. Hagel was ultimately confirmed on February 26, 2013, by a largely party-line vote of 58–41, which was the smallest margin a defense secretary had received during a confirmation vote since the position was created in 1947.

Less than two years later, in late November 2014, Hagel announced he had submitted his resignation to the president. There were conflicting reports about why Hagel was resigning. Some said the president's priorities for the Defense Department had shifted—from restructuring the military and cutting costs to fighting the emerging threat from ISIL and helping combat the Ebola outbreak in West Africa—and so it had been determined that different leadership was needed. Others suggested Hagel was being pushed out due to internal disagreements about national security policy and strained relations with other members of Obama's senior team, including National Security Adviser Susan Rice.

The president announced Ashton B. Carter, a physicist and former Defense Department official, as his nominee to replace Hagel in December. Carter was widely regarded for his experience within the department, as he first worked in the Pentagon during the Clinton administration before serving as the top weapons buyer during Gates's tenure and eventually becoming the deputy defense secretary. He was also considered an expert on nuclear weapons and military technology.

Unlike Hagel, Carter sailed through the confirmation process, gaining the Senate's approval in a 93–5 vote on February 12, 2015, roughly one week after his confirmation hearing. He was sworn in on February 17.

Carter would inherit a host of challenges from his predecessors, from managing mandatory defense budget cuts to leading the fight against ISIL and setting U.S. policy for handling the drawn-out Syrian Civil War. He also continued the department's push to update personnel policies by finalizing the process for opening all combat roles to women in 2015 and announcing in June 2016 that transgender individuals would be allowed to openly serve and enlist in the military.

Chair of the Joint Chiefs of Staff

Marine Corps Commandant Gen. Joseph Dunford was nominated by President Obama on May 5, 2015, to replace retiring Chair of the Joint Chiefs of Staff Gen. Martin E. Dempsey. Dempsey had served as chair for four years and was scheduled to step down in September. In announcing Dunford's nomination, Obama described the general as one of the "most admired officers in our military," noting that the United States had "achieved key milestones" in Afghanistan under his leadership of the Marines. He also praised Dunford's proven ability "to give me unvarnished military advice based on his experience on the ground."

Dunford had been serving as commandant since October 17, 2014, having previously served as assistant commandant from 2010 to 2012. A Boston native and veteran of the Korean War, Dunford was commissioned as an officer in 1977 and advanced quickly through the military's ranks. He had, for example, risen from a one-star brigadier general to a four-star general in about three years; generals typically spend several years in each rank. Dunford had attended the U.S. Army Ranger School, Marine Amphibious Warfare School, and the U.S. Army War College. He also held master's degrees from Georgetown University and Tufts University in government and international relations, respectively.

(Continued)

DEFENSE LEADERSHIP (Continued)

Dunford's nearly forty-year military career included considerable experience in Iraq and Afghanistan. He led the 5th Marine Regiment during the Iraq War and was the commander of the International Security Assistance Force and United States Forces in Afghanistan from February 2013 to August 2014. While serving in Afghanistan, Dunford had overseen the drawdown of U.S. troops and the transfer of ongoing security responsibilities from NATO to Afghan forces. Additionally, Dunford previously served as the Assistant Division Commander of the 1st Marine Division; Marine Corps Director of Operations; Marine Corps Deputy Commandant for Plans, Policies and Operations; and the commander of Marine forces for U.S. Central Command.

The nomination was well received by lawmakers on both sides of the aisle, with Senate Armed Services Committee Chair John McCain, R-Ariz., praising the "outstanding selection." Dunford's July 9 confirmation hearing before the committee took place without controversy. The general spoke of the "need to restore readiness and modernize the joint force" while managing fiscal challenges and budget uncertainty to ensure the military was equipped to deal with a variety of evolving challenges, including potential cyber threats. He warned that if Congress did not act to change existing budget law and allowed sequestration cuts, it could have "catastrophic consequences" on the military's ability to "support the current strategy that we have to protect our nation."

Dunford told the committee that Russia posed the greatest threat to the United States' national security, citing its nuclear power and recent aggression in Ukraine. "If you want to talk about a nation that could pose an existential threat to the United States, I'd have to point to Russia," Dunford said. "And if you look at their behavior, it's nothing short of alarming." Yet Dunford also emphasized the importance of maintaining a relationship with Russia's military "to mitigate the risk of miscalculation and begin to turn the trend in the other direction in terms of trust." He identified China as his second top concern, due to its growing military capabilities and strength in the Pacific, but he also noted that China was not necessarily a current threat. The general told lawmakers that he was comfortable with the administration's strategy for fighting ISIL, explaining how it involved nine different lines of effort managed by various federal agencies. Dunford said the two lines managed by the Defense Department—denying the enemy sanctuary and the building up of Iraqi and Syrian forces—were buying time for other efforts, managed by agencies including the State and Treasury Departments.

Dunford's nomination was held up for about two days due to a hold placed on it by Sen. Kirsten Gillibrand, D-N.Y. She was seeking unrelated documents from the Defense Department about sexual assaults at the largest base for each branch of the military, as well as at four military training facilities. Gillibrand had been pushing to remove the prosecution of military sexual assault cases from the military's chain of command in favor of assigning prosecution to independent attorneys. She lifted her nomination hold after receiving assurances from Defense Secretary Ashton Carter that the department would fulfill her request.

Aside from this brief delay, Dunford was easily confirmed by the Senate on July 29 via voice vote. He was sworn in as chair of the Joint Chiefs of Staff on October 1, 2015.

Afghanistan Command

Obama's second term also involved several changes in the command of the International Security Assistance Force (ISAF) in Afghanistan. In 2011, Obama had named Marine Corps Gen. John Allen to succeed Army Gen. David H. Petraeus when Petraeus became the CIA director. However, Allen later became ensnared in the same personal scandal that prompted Petraeus's resignation in November 2012. The FBI investigation that revealed Petraeus's extramarital affair with his biographer, Paula Broadwell, also resulted in the discovery of thousands of "potentially inappropriate" emails sent from Allen to Jill Kelley, a volunteer social liaison for military families at MacDill Air Force Base in Tampa, Fla. Kelley's complaint to an FBI acquaintance about harassing emails she had been receiving, which were later traced to Broadwell, kicked off the investigation that eventually led to Petraeus's fall from grace.

At the time the Allen-Kelley emails were revealed, the general was preparing for a Senate confirmation hearing to consider his nomination to become the next NATO Supreme Allied Commander in Europe. Allen's nomination was subsequently placed on hold. Although he was cleared of any wrongdoing in January 2013, Allen forfeited his nomination for the top NATO post and announced his intent to retire from the military the following month, citing his wife's deteriorating health.

Marine Corps Gen. Joseph Dunford Jr. was tapped to replace Allen, assuming the Afghanistan command on February 10, 2013. During his tenure, Dunford oversaw the drawdown of U.S. troops and the transfer of ongoing security responsibilities from NATO to Afghan forces. He left the post in August 2014 following his confirmation as Marine Corps commandant.

The final Afghanistan commander to serve under Obama, Army Gen. John Campbell, was also the last ISAF commander. Obama announced the end of U.S. combat operations in Afghanistan on December 28, 2014. U.S. allies had also drawn down their forces in the country, leaving a small force of about 13,500 U.S. and allied service members in Afghanistan to help train local security forces and support counterterrorism operations.

fiscal 2014 and 2015. In terms of defense spending, this agreement created the potential for the Pentagon to receive $22 billion more in base defense spending than it would have if fiscal 2014 sequester cuts had not been pared back.

The budget agreement provided a framework for appropriators to incorporate provisions of twelve regular spending bills into an omnibus measure for fiscal 2014 (HR 3547—PL 113-76). The omnibus deal was announced on January 13, 2014. Despite lingering partisan differences on policy issues ranging from education and health care to climate change and financial regulations, the House approved the omnibus by a significant margin (359–67) on January 15, and the Senate approved the bill the following day by a vote of 72–26. The president signed the omnibus on January 17. (See "Omnibus Appropriations" in Chapter 2, p. 74.)

House Action

The House Appropriations Committee approved its freestanding defense appropriations bill (HR 2397) by voice vote on June 17. The bill recommended appropriations of $512.5 billion for the base defense budget and $85.7 billion for Overseas Contingency Operations (OCO), a fund that supports war-related and counterterrorism activities in countries including Pakistan, Iraq, and Afghanistan. Spending caps do not apply to the OCO, though the fund is subject to sequester. Several measures included in the bill sought to restrict the president's authority, including one provision that would have limited Obama's ability to order furloughs of the Defense Department's civilian employees. This particular item was proposed in response to extensive furloughs that had been ordered in fiscal 2013.

The full House passed the bill (HR 2397—H Rept 113-113) by a vote of 315 to 109 on July 24. Nearly all Republicans voted in favor of the bill, as did about half of the House Democrats. Seventy amendments were proposed and considered during floor debate, of which forty were adopted. Concerns about the National Security Agency's (NSA) blanket collection of phone records and implications for Americans' privacy were a key part of the House debate. One amendment added to the spending bill—after receiving 409 votes in favor—prohibited the NSA's use of funds to "target a U.S. person or acquire and store the content of a U.S. person's communications," including phone calls and emails. However, another amendment seeking to end authority for the blanket collection of records under the Patriot Act was narrowly defeated by a vote of 205–217. NSA surveillance continued to be a contentious issue during subsequent fiscal years' spending negotiations.

The final House bill would have provided $512.4 billion in base defense spending, which was $4 billion less than the administration requested and $5 billion less than the fiscal 2013 enacted level. The bill would also have provided $85.6 billion in OCO funding. At a total of roughly $598 billion, the bill would have exceeded fiscal 2014 spending limits—as set by the Ryan-Murray budget bill—and would have triggered a $28 billion sequester cut had it been signed by the president.

Senate Action

On August 1, the Senate Appropriations Committee approved its bill (S 1429) by a vote of 22–8. The funding levels agreed to by the Senate panel were slightly different than those authorized by the House bill. The Senate committee recommended total appropriations of about $594.4 billion for defense, of which $516.6 billion was allocated for base defense spending. The remaining $77.6 billion was allocated to the OCO.

The bill did not see floor action since it soon became clear that an omnibus or other Congresswide budget agreement would be needed to overcome disagreements over fiscal 2014 appropriations.

Final Omnibus

Defense-related spending comprised roughly half of the final $1.012 trillion omnibus. The bill provided a base defense budget of $486.9 billion, roughly the same as the fiscal 2013 base defense budget after sequestration cuts.

The base defense budget included $159.9 billion for operations and maintenance funds, covering readiness programs, flight time and battle training, equipment and facility maintenance, and base operations given priority for appropriators. A portion of operation and maintenance funds ($447 million) was allocated to Cyber Command. Another $157 million was provided for sexual assault prevention and response programs.

For procurement, appropriators provided $92.9 billion, while $64 billion were allocated for research and development activities. These totals were $6.2 billion and $4.5 billion less than the administration's request, respectively.

The omnibus made a series of cuts to funding for specific weapons, vehicles, and equipment, though some of these cuts were offset by additional funds for other programs. The bill reduced funding for research, development, and procurement of the F-35 Joint Strike Fighter, but the Pentagon said it would still be able to purchase the twenty-nine aircraft it wanted. Procurement accounts for the Air Force C-130J cargo plane were cut by $60 million, but appropriators allocated $92 million more than requested for research and development of a long-range bomber. The bill cut $81.4 million from the Army's MQ-1 Predator drone request but gave the Air Force $77 million to buy eight more MQ-9 Reaper drones than planned. Additional budgets were provided to convert Army Stryker vehicle hulls into a more survivable "double-V" configuration ($45 million); upgrade the Abrams tank ($90 million); purchase a second Virginia-class submarine for the Navy ($1.2 billion); and modernize and continue operating seven guided-missile cruises and two amphibious dock landing ships the

Navy had suggested be retired early ($2.2 billion). Appropriators also granted the Navy's request for $1.8 billion to purchase four littoral combat ships, even though structural and mechanical issues and cost overruns have plagued the program since its inception. Some reductions that appeared to be cuts were really delayed expenditures for weapons programs. For example, $204 million was cut from the Army's Warfighter Information Network–Tactical Increment II due to testing issues, and another $400 million was cut from the Navy's Air and Missile Defense Radar, Next–Generation Enterprise Network, and Next–Generation Jammer due to contract protests.

Another $85.2 billion was provided for the OCO. Critics of the bill said the amount of funding allocated to the OCO was artificially high, particularly since military operations in Afghanistan were winding down, and was basically providing a slush fund for the Defense Department to cover unrelated expenses. Appropriators countered that the OCO funding was needed to pay for personnel requirements, operational needs, new aircraft to replace combat losses, combat vehicle safety modifications, and maintenance of facilities and equipment.

Figure 5.2 Outlays for Veterans

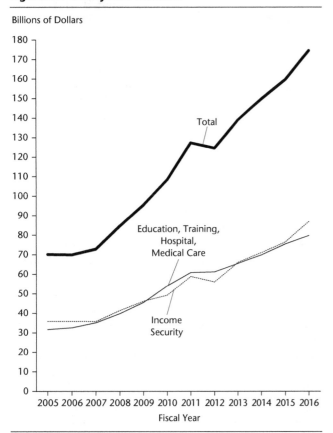

Billions of Dollars

SOURCE: Executive Office of the President, Office of Management and Budget, *Budget of the United States Government, Fiscal Year 2018, Historical Tables* (Washington, DC: U.S. Government Printing Office, 2018), Table 3.2.

NOTE: Total line includes expenditures not shown separately.

Other major provisions included

- a 1 percent pay increase for service personnel, as requested by the administration;
- $20 million for suicide prevention;
- $25 million to implement new Special Victims Counsel programs to provide legal assistance to victims of sexual assault;
- an exemption for medically retired personnel and their survivors from a cost-of-living adjustment reduction for working-age military retirees receiving a pension;
- a prohibition on the transfer of detainees from Guantanamo Bay to U.S. soil and the modification of any U.S. facility to hold those detainees;
- a requirement that the NSA submit the details of its bulk collection of phone records to Congress.

Fiscal 2014 Veterans Affairs–Military Construction Funding

The annual appropriations bill funding the Department of Veterans Affairs (VA) and military construction is generally one of the least controversial spending measures considered by Congress. The bill provides funding for veterans' health, benefits, and disability claims adjudication, as well as Defense Department accounts that cover base closures, military construction, and housing for service members' families. It is a politically popular measure among lawmakers, who typically try to shield the programs it supports from the partisan disagreements that arise elsewhere in the budget process.

Although the full House and the Senate Appropriations Committee quickly approved their respective VA–military construction spending bills in the summer of 2013—with a mere $1.1 billion difference in discretionary spending between them—these measures were ultimately folded into the fiscal 2014 omnibus (HR 3547—PL 113-76).

The omnibus provided a total of $159.2 billion for mandatory and discretionary spending on veterans' benefits and health care, military construction projects, and family housing. Discretionary spending comprised $73.3 billion of that total—$1.4 billion more than the fiscal 2013 enacted level but $1.4 billion less than the White House requested.

House Action

On May 28, the House Appropriations Committee approved by voice vote a bill (HR 2216) providing $157.7 billion for the VA and military construction, of which $73.3 billion was discretionary spending.

The bill included $55.6 billion in advance fiscal 2015 appropriations for VA medical programs. Lawmakers are required by law (PL 111-81) to provide one year of advance appropriations for certain VA medical accounts in annual spending measures to help protect against budget lapses. The VA would also receive $290 million to assist in the reduction of backlogged claims. Some of these funds were

GUANTANAMO BAY DETENTION CENTER

The detention center at the U.S. Naval Station at Guantanamo Bay, Cuba, was a recurring topic of congressional deliberations over defense authorization and appropriations measures between 2013 and 2016. Lawmakers repeatedly included language in these bills that limited the Obama administration's options for repatriating or transferring to third-party countries detainees deemed safe to release and prohibited the use of Defense Department funds to build or modify a facility on U.S. soil for the purpose of housing detainees.

The detention center was opened by former President George W. Bush shortly after the September 11, 2001, attacks to house "unlawful combatants," or those suspected of having ties to al Qaeda or the Taliban. The facility became a flashpoint of controversy following the Justice Department's determination that detainees held at Guantanamo Bay were outside the U.S. court system's jurisdiction and the president's creation of a new military commission system to prosecute detainees. This decision drew sharp criticism from human rights groups because military commissions typically require defendants to forgo certain rights they would otherwise enjoy in civilian courts, including the right to habeas corpus. The prison was also plagued by allegations of abuse, torture, and poor living conditions.

When Bush left office, 245 detainees remained at the facility; more than 500 others had been released to their home countries or transferred to a third-party country. President Obama inherited responsibility for the prison upon taking office in 2009. As a candidate, Obama promised that closing the detention center would be a priority of his administration. He moved quickly to make good on that promise, signing an executive order calling for the detention center to be closed within a year on his second day in office. Obama claimed the detention center provided a proof point for terrorist networks' recruiting efforts and sullied U.S. alliances, all while costing taxpayers millions of dollars a year.

It soon became clear that closing Guantanamo Bay would not be an easy political feat to accomplish. Republicans opposed its closure, arguing that it would create a threat to national security and pointing to intelligence community reports indicating that some recently released detainees had rejoined al Qaeda or other terrorist organizations. Congress denied administration requests for funding to facilitate the prison's closure and began placing restrictions on detainee transfers, including instituting a ban on detainees' relocation to the United States, as early as the fiscal 2011 defense authorization.

Obama's efforts to continue clearing detainees out of the facility were also hampered by internal resistance at the Defense Department. Some military officials were reluctant to free detainees out of concern that they might end up fighting U.S. troops once they had been released. Department policies also required multiple levels of approval, including evaluation by a periodic review board, before detainees could be transferred. Further, some officials reportedly created administrative roadblocks to transfer agreements being negotiated by the State Department. For example, some officials allegedly refused to provide photographs, complete medical records, and other basic documentation to foreign governments that were willing to take detainees. Others restricted visits by representatives of these foreign governments to Guantanamo Bay or limited the time they had to interview detainees.

As Obama's second term drew to a close, the administration made a concerted effort to speed the detainee transfer process. Upon taking office in February 2015, Defense Secretary Ashton Carter pushed to finalize the transfer of detainees whose release had been approved years earlier but who were waiting on the secretary's signature. By law, the defense secretary is required to personally guarantee the safety of all detainee transfers. In July 2015, the National Security Council imposed a new deadline for recommending detainee transfers: After the State Department completed negotiations with a third-party country, six agencies were given one week to review and sign off on the proposed agreement before it went to Carter for final approval. Defense Department officials also conducted visits to several U.S. sites to evaluate their potential to hold detainees, either indefinitely or until they could be brought to trial. These sites included military prisons in Leavenworth, Kan., and Charleston, S.C., as well as civilian facilities in Colorado and Illinois. Meanwhile, the State Department successfully negotiated detainee transfer agreements with twenty-four countries by early October.

Then in November, Congress included a measure in its final fiscal 2016 defense authorization bill requiring the administration to submit, within ninety days of the bill's approval, a plan for holding current and future Guantanamo Bay detainees, to include identification of one or several facilities that could house the prisoners. On February 23, 2016—the deadline stipulated by the fiscal 2016 defense authorization—President Obama submitted his plan for closing the detention center to Congress. "Keeping this facility open is contrary to our values," he said in an address announcing the plan. "It undermines our standing in the world. It is viewed as a stain on our broader record of upholding the highest standards of rule of law."

(Continued)

GUANTANAMO BAY DETENTION CENTER (Continued)

The nine-page plan explained the administration's intent to move thirty to sixty detainees to facilities on U.S. soil. At the time of the president's announcement, the Guantanamo Bay facility held ninety-one detainees, of whom thirty-five had been recommended for transfer if security conditions were met, ten had been charged or convicted by a military commission, and forty-six had neither been charged nor approved for transfer. Administration officials estimated there would be fewer than sixty detainees remaining at the facility by the end of the year once already-approved transfers were completed.

The administration estimated that closing the prison, moving detainees, and building or modifying a suitable long-term holding facility in the United States would cost between $290 million and $475 million. However, officials also projected that closing the facility would save up to $85 million per year.

Republicans immediately rejected the president's plan as too vague. "His proposal fails to provide critical details required by law, including the exact cost and location of an alternate detention facility," said House Speaker Paul Ryan, R-Wisc., referencing a section of the report that says thirteen facilities in the United States could house detainees without identifying those locations. Lawmakers generally acknowledged that the plan was unlikely to gain congressional approval, saying that it lacked the necessary support, particularly during a presidential election year. Indeed, the fiscal 2017 defense authorization bill approved by Congress and signed by Obama in December maintained language that limited the administration's options by prohibiting the transfer of detainees to U.S. soil. In announcing his proposed plan, the president left open the possibility that he could act unilaterally to close the prison via executive order before his term ended, but he declined to do so.

---

allocated to pay for a paperless claims processing system and digital scanning of medical and benefits records.

The bill also included $8.2 billion for military construction, which was $427 million less than the White House requested. However, the committee roughly met the administration's request for family housing, providing $1.5 billion for these accounts. Other provisions barred the administration from building facilities in the United States to house detainees transferred from Guantanamo Bay and from using appropriated funds to support a new round of base realignments and closures. The Obama administration objected to these restrictions.

The committee's bill passed the House by a vote of 421–4 on June 4. Fifteen amendments were adopted by the House during its consideration of the bill, including one that cut the salaries of VA officials by 25 percent until the agency was able to reduce the number of pending disability compensation claims. The VA defines pending claims as those waiting 125 days or more for processing. At the time of the House debate, the VA had approximately 817,000 unprocessed disability claims, roughly two-thirds of which had been pending for more than 125 days. The amendment required the VA to cut its backlog by at least 40 percent by mid-2014.

Senate Action

The Senate Appropriations Committee approved an amended version of the House bill on June 20 by a vote of 23–6. All the committee's Democrats voted in favor of the bill. The Republicans who voted against the measure largely did so because they opposed the overall discretionary spending levels set by the Senate, not the specific appropriations included in the VA–military construction

bill. HR 2216 was the first appropriations bill considered by the Senate Appropriations Committee in 2013, which meant it was also the first opportunity for Republicans to express their opposition with their votes.

The amended bill increased the House's allocation for discretionary spending by $1.1 billion; it also provided an additional $120 million for military construction.

FINAL OMNIBUS

The $1.012 trillion omnibus provided $149.1 billion for the VA, a $13 billion increase over the fiscal 2013 enacted amount. Most of this increase was earmarked for mandatory spending accounts. However, the discretionary budget did increase by about $2.3 billion to a total of $63.2 billion.

The Veterans Health Administration received $55.6 billion in funding, about $45 billion of which was for advance medical services appropriations for fiscal 2015. The Veterans Benefits Administration, which oversees programs providing financial assistance to veterans and their dependents and survivors, received $84.8 billion. Of that amount, $71.5 billion was appropriated for pensions and benefits while $13.1 billion was provided for other veterans' benefits, such as education assistance and vocational training.

To help address the VA's backlog of disability claims, the omnibus provided $90 million for overtime pay for claims processors and $140 million for information technology upgrades to support the paperless claims system. Another $88 million was set aside for the Board of Veterans Appeals. The omnibus also provided $323 million to help the VA develop an electronic health record system in coordination with the Defense Department but mandated that 75 percent of these funds be withheld until the two agencies submitted to Congress a plan for system development that included a budget and performance benchmarks.

For military construction, the omnibus provided $7.9 billion, which was $278 million less than the fiscal 2013 enacted level. Funds for active military, reserve, and National Guard family housing were also cut from fiscal 2013, totaling $1.5 billion. The omnibus preserved committee language prohibiting the use of military construction funds to build or make changes to any military facility in the United States for the purpose of housing Guantanamo Bay detainees.

Fiscal 2014 Defense Authorization

Every year since 1961, Congress has passed a defense authorization bill—generally with broad bipartisan support—that provides for basic military needs as well as any wars and other overseas commitments. While these bills were generally approved with broad bipartisan support, intense partisanship had made the authorization process increasingly difficult, and in 2013, Congress came very close to not passing a defense bill before the end of the year.

Disagreements over process rather than content became a major obstacle to the bill's passage. Senate Democrats tried to limit debate on their version of the bill and push for a quick vote in the days before Thanksgiving. This angered Republicans, who claimed they would not have enough time to give enough consideration to the hundreds of amendments that had been offered on the bill, and Democrats' motion was ultimately rejected.

With the bill stalled in the Senate, the House and Senate Armed Services Committees were unable to convene a formal conference committee to resolve differences between the two chambers' bills. Committee leaders instead began meeting informally after the Thanksgiving break to write a new, streamlined bill (HR 3304) for both chambers to consider. The House passed the new bill on December 12, followed by the Senate on December 19. President Obama signed the bill into law on December 26 (PL 113-66).

House Committee Action

On June 6, the House Armed Services Committee approved its draft defense authorization bill (HR 1960) after a sixteen-hour markup session that involved consideration of more than eighty amendments. The bill authorized $638.5 billion in spending for defense-related accounts—$52 billion more than the total spending allowed by the Budget Control Act of 2011 (PL 112-25) limits. However, the committee rejected a proposal by Rep. Jim Cooper, D-Tenn., that would have enabled the Defense Department to shift $20 billion among various accounts to accommodate sequester cuts triggered by the total budget. The total included $85.8 billion for Overseas Contingency Operations (OCO), a fund used to pay for war-related activities and counterterrorism efforts. Most of the OCO funding authorized by the bill was intended to pay for the ongoing war in Afghanistan.

Noteworthy provisions included language calling on the president to consider all options for removing Syrian President Bashar al-Assad from office and requiring Defense Secretary Ashton Carter to outline related military tactics, such as establishment of a no-fly zone, providing Syrian rebels with heavy military equipment, and conducting limited airstrikes against select infrastructure targets. The bill also would have prevented administration officials from reducing the U.S. nuclear arsenal below 800 missiles unless the president certified Russia's compliance with the terms of the New Strategic Arms Reduction Treaty (New START) that had been ratified in 2010 and expressed "high confidence" in intelligence community assessments of China's nuclear capabilities.

Other measures sought to address growing concerns about sexual assault in the military by preventing commanders from dismissing court-martial decisions for all but minor offenses and from lessening guilty findings in sexual assault cases. One amendment considered by the committee was a proposal from Rep. Michael Turner, R-Ohio, to require the filing of incident reports within eight days of a sexual assault victim's filing of a "restricted" report. Restricted reports allow victims to confidentially disclose an assault and receive medical treatment and legal assistance without launching an official investigation. This amendment was adopted and included among the bill's other sexual assault provisions.

The committee rejected an amendment from Rep. Adam Smith, D-Wash., that would have eliminated the bill's prohibition on the transfer of detainees held at the Guantanamo Bay, Cuba, naval base to the United States or its territories. Committee members approved a separate measure that Rep. Robert Andrews, D-N.J., proposed to withhold $186 million in funding for the detention center until the president had submitted a report to Congress on possible locations to which detainees could be transferred.

Additionally, the committee adopted another amendment put forward by Turner that would have directed the Missile Defense Agency to build a third U.S. missile interception site and make it operational by fiscal 2018. Only one of the committee's Democrats voted for this amendment; the others questioned the need for a third site, which had not been requested by the Defense Department, and objected to its estimated cost.

House Floor Action

Despite a veto threat from the White House, the House passed HR 1960 on June 14 by a vote of 315 to 108. Floor debate included consideration of a variety of amendments. Among those rejected by the House was a proposal by Rep. Chris Van Hollen, D-Md., to reduce OCO funding by $5 billion, and a separate amendment from Rep. Rick Nolan, D-Minn., to cut the total defense authorization by $60 billion. Lawmakers also rejected an amendment by Smith that would have required the Guantanamo Bay detention center to be closed by the end of 2014.

Senate Committee Action

The Senate Armed Services Committee approved its own defense authorization bill (S 1197) on June 13 by a vote of 23–3. Unlike the House bill, the Senate would have allowed the administration to move Guantanamo Bay detainees to the United States for trial or continued detention or to transfer them to another country.

Among the bill's financial provisions was the authorization of $9.3 billion for missile defense programs, which was $150 million more than the administration requested, and included funding for deployment of advanced radar within the United States to detect incoming ballistic missiles. It did not include authorization for a third missile defense site, as the House bill did. The committee bill would have lowered the cap on reimbursements to contractors from $750,000 to $487,000; provided a 1 percent pay raise for military personnel; and increased the budget for construction of the *Gerald R. Ford* aircraft carrier to $12.9 billion. Another provision required the chief of naval operations to report to Congress on how the Navy planned to use its new littoral combat ships and how survivable the ships were for anticipated missions.

One of the most significant provisions considered by the committee was language added by Sen. Kirsten Gillibrand, D-N.Y., that would have removed decisions about whether to pursue prosecution of sexual assaults and other felony-level crimes from the military chain of command. Instead of having commanders make these determinations, such decisions would be left to military lawyers. Had this provision been maintained, it would have represented one of the most sweeping changes ever made to the military's justice system. However, the committee adopted an amendment by Sen. Carl Levin, D-Mich., that struck this language. Instead, Levin's amendment would require the next officer in the chain of command to review a commander's decision not to send a sexual assault case to trial and would have made retaliatory action against a victim a crime.

Senate Floor Action

Although S 1197 was reported to the Senate and placed on the Senate's calendar on June 20, floor debate did not begin until November 14, and the first full day of debate did not occur until November 19. At that point, there was considerable concern among lawmakers that Congress would not have enough time to finalize the authorization bill before the year ended, leading to a push in the Senate to hurry the authorization along.

On November 21, Senate Majority Leader Harry Reid, D-Nev., moved to invoke cloture, which would have ended debate and prompted a vote on passage. Republicans refused to support cloture, demanding that twenty-five of their amendments be considered before final votes were cast. Among these amendments was a proposal to impose new sanctions on Iran, despite ongoing negotiations between the United States, Iran, Russia, China, and several European allies to reach a deal limiting Iranian nuclear

activity. Another contested proposal sought to prohibit the government from paying the employer's share of health insurance premiums for lawmakers and their aides. Republicans also delayed consideration of a package of thirty-nine amendments—including already agreed-upon, bipartisan amendments—until their changes were debated. Democrats countered that there was not enough time left in the year to give full consideration to every amendment.

Conference and Final Action

Republican and Democratic leaders of the House and Senate Armed Services Committees began meeting privately to negotiate the terms of a new authorization bill after Congress's Thanksgiving break. The group of four lawmakers did not disclose any details of their negotiations until December 9, when they briefed reporters on the major components of the draft bill.

The bill authorized a total of $632.8 billion in fiscal 2014 spending. The total included $625.1 billion in discretionary funds, which was more than half of the federal government's discretionary spending for the year. A base defense budget of $526.8 billion was authorized, as well as $80.7 billion for the OCO, most of which was intended to fund the ongoing war in Afghanistan. Another $17.6 billion was authorized for national security programs at the Energy Department, which mostly entail the maintenance of the U.S. nuclear arsenal. Notably, while the bill permitted the operation of military and related programs at these spending levels, no funds were appropriated until Congress approved the fiscal 2014 omnibus, which included appropriations for defense.

Other financial elements of the authorization involved personnel-related costs and funding for major weapons systems. The bill authorized a force of 1.36 million active-duty Army, Navy, Air Force, and Marine Corps personnel, marking a reduction in force of about 40,000 individuals from fiscal 2013. It also granted the Obama administration's request for a 1 percent military pay raise, as opposed to the 1.8 percent increase that would otherwise have been provided by existing law. The administration had estimated that providing a smaller pay increase would help to save $600 million in fiscal 2014 and $3.5 billion over the next five years, in addition to matching a 1 percent pay raise for civilian federal workers.

Approximately $9.5 billion was authorized for missile defense programs, which was $358 million more than the administration had requested, and prohibited the use of these funds for the Medium Extended Air Defense System—a collaborative effort with Germany and Italy that had been cancelled. The bill authorized $14.7 billion for major Navy vessels—$656 million more than the administration requested—and increased the budget for the *Gerald R. Ford* aircraft carrier to $12.9 billion. It limited future *Ford*-class aircraft carriers to a budget of $11.5 billion. Another $8 billion was authorized for the development and procurement of the F-35 Joint Strike Fighter.

Additional measures prevented the Air Force from retiring its Global Hawk Block 30 unmanned aerial reconnaissance system and the A-10 Warthog ground support aircraft.

Other key components of the authorization bill dealt with several major issues facing the Defense Department. In May, the Defense Department estimated that about 26,000 instances of unwanted sexual contact had occurred within the military in 2012, but only about 10 percent of these incidents had been reported, based on anonymous surveys and sampling research. The department also found, in its annual report on sexual assault, that 3,374 incidents of sexual assault had been reported in 2012. Both numbers represented an increase over 2011 totals, which were about 19,300 and 3,100, respectively. As a response to these findings, the authorization bill included more than twenty-four different provisions related to preventing and reporting sexual assault. These measures removed commanders' ability to dismiss court-martial findings or change a guilty verdict to one of lesser offense; required civilian review of any cases commanders declined to prosecute; made retaliation against victims who reported sexual assault a crime under the Uniform Code of Military Justice; and made dishonorable discharge mandatory for any service member convicted of sexual assault. The bill also allowed sexual assault victims to apply for a permanent change of station or unit transfer, eliminated the five-year statute of limitations for reporting sexual assault, and required the military to establish special counsels for victims of sexual assault and rape.

Regarding the detention center at the naval base in Guantanamo Bay, Cuba, the bill maintained language prohibiting the transfer of detainees to U.S. soil. It also continued a prohibition on the construction or modification of military facilities in the United States for the purpose of housing the detainees. It did, however, relax requirements for transferring detainees to foreign countries, permitting such transfers if a review board determined the detainee was no longer a threat to the United States or if the transfer was court ordered.

Another section of the bill dealt with New START. These provisions allowed the Defense Department to begin planning and preparing to meet the terms of New START, which required the United States and Russia to reduce their nuclear arsenals by 2018. The bill also permitted the department to use half of the funds allocated for environmental assessments to meet the treaty's terms, with the remaining half to be released when a force structure plan was completed.

The compromise authorization language was added to a separate measure (HR 3304) that had already passed both the House and Senate and enabled the president to award Medals of Honor to Vietnam War soldiers Bennie G. Adkins and Donald P. Sloat. The Medal of Honor provisions were preserved in the final bill language, with the addition of a third Medal of Honor for Civil War artillery officer Alonzo H. Cushing.

The House passed the bill by a vote of 350–69 on December 12. The measure was considered under a suspension of the rules, which meant only forty minutes were allowed for debate and no amendments were offered.

The bill, as passed in the House, was received in the Senate on December 15. Senators narrowly rejected a motion by Sen. John Cornyn, R-Texas, that would have allowed amendments. Cornyn expressed the continued frustration felt by some Republicans that the Senate only had two days to debate the bill and would not have the opportunity to consider amendments. "We're tired of getting jammed," said Cornyn, the second-ranking Republican in the chamber. "Is it really more important for the Democrats to jam us with non-essential, non-urgent nominees than to take care of the people who've sacrificed so much for this country?" Reid pushed back by arguing that "the bill before us is not a Democratic bill and it's not a Republican bill. It is a bipartisan, bicameral defense bill." Cloture was invoked by a vote of 71 to 29 on December 18, and the bill was approved the following day by a vote of 84–15.

Fiscal 2015 Defense Appropriations

Although House and Senate appropriators pursued and had some success in passing standalone defense appropriations measures for fiscal 2015, the overall backlog of and Congresswide partisan disagreements over spending bills prevented any freestanding legislation from gaining approval. Lawmakers clashed on everything from reproductive rights to climate change to health care, while some Republicans also sought to push budget negotiations to early 2015, in hopes of capitalizing on expected midterm gains.

Deadlocked once again, Congress passed a continuing resolution (HJ Res 124—PL 113-64) in mid-September to keep the government open through December 11 while appropriators worked to piece together another omnibus spending package. The resulting bill (HR 83) provided $1.013 trillion to fund most government agencies, including the Defense Department, through the end of fiscal 2015. A total of $554.2 billion was appropriated for defense and war-related spending.

The House narrowly passed the omnibus on December 11 with a 219-to-206 vote. This was followed by Senate passage on December 13, by a vote of 56 to 40; a second continuing resolution was required to give the chamber time to vote. The bill was signed by President Obama on December 16 (PL 113-235).

House Action

The House Defense Appropriations Subcommittee approved a draft bill (HR 4870) by voice vote on May 30, totaling $570.4 billion. The bill included $165 billion for operations and maintenance—$4.8 billion more than fiscal 2014 funding but $1.4 billion less than the administration's request. It also provided $1.6 billion for seven KC-46A tankers, $5.8 billion for thirty-eight F-35 Joint Strike Fighters, and $975 million for twelve EA-18G Growler aircraft. The aircraft appropriations provided for purchases of four and seven more planes, respectively, than the totals included in the House-passed fiscal 2015 defense authorization legislation. Similarly, the subcommittee provided funding for a 1.8 percent pay raise for service members. This exceeded the 1 percent increase requested by the Obama administration, though it matched the pay raise recommended by the authorization bill.

The House Appropriations Committee marked up the bill on June 10, with notable amendments including the addition of language demanding assurances from the administration that it would not circumvent the law requiring the Defense Department to give Congress thirty days' notice before transferring detainees. This amendment was offered in response to lawmakers' concerns that the president broke the law when he agreed to release five Guantanamo Bay detainees to Qatar in exchange for the Taliban's return of Army Sgt. Bowe Bergdahl. The Taliban captured Bergdahl in 2009, one month after he was deployed to Afghanistan. U.S. officials had been engaged in negotiations with the Taliban since 2012; Bergdahl was ultimately released in May 2014. He would later be charged with one count of desertion with intent to shirk important or hazardous duty and one count of misbehavior before the enemy.

The amended bill was approved by voice vote following the markup.

The bill proceeded to the House floor, where it was debated for three days before a final vote on June 20. Lawmakers were concerned about a National Security Agency (NSA) surveillance program that involved the bulk collection and monitoring of millions of phone calls, text messages, emails, and other communications, including those of U.S. citizens, without obtaining individual warrants. This program included a collaborative effort with the Federal Bureau of Investigation called PRISM to directly tap into the servers of companies such as Google and Facebook to collect bulk information. The scope of this program was revealed in 2013 as a result of leaked information provided by former NSA contractor Edward Snowden, leading to a renewed public outcry that such surveillance was a violation of privacy and could be abused. Administration officials argued that the NSA's activity was permitted by the 2008 FISA Amendments Act as long as one of the parties to the communications was reasonably believed to be a foreigner outside of the United States and if the information collected was for a valid intelligence purpose.

Reps. Thomas Massie, R-Ky., Jim Sensenbrenner, R-Wisc., and Zoe Lofgren, D-Calif., sponsored an amendment to the House bill that would prohibit the use of funds to conduct warrantless searches of Americans' communications in government databases and would block the NSA and the Central Intelligence Agency from requiring companies to create "back doors" to their software and hardware that would give intelligence officials direct access to communications. The amendment was adopted by a vote of 293–123.

The House approved the amended bill by a vote of 340–73.

Senate Action

Nearly one month later, on July 15, the Senate Defense Appropriations Subcommittee approved its version of the spending bill by voice vote. Two days later, it was approved by the Senate Appropriations Committee, also by voice vote.

The bill provided a total of $542.7 billion in funding, including $58.3 billion for the OCO. One of its most notable provisions authorized the administration to train and equip vetted members of the Syrian opposition. Lawmakers on both sides had expressed deep reservations about including this measure. Other noteworthy provisions included $25 million for a competition to develop a new domestic rocket engine, thereby ending the United States' reliance on Russian engines; $338 million to maintain the fleet of A-10 Warthog close-air support planes, despite the Air Force's plan to retire the aircraft; and $351 million for Israel's Iron Dome air defense system.

The backlog of appropriations bills in the Senate meant that the bill never saw floor action.

FINAL OMNIBUS

As in fiscal 2014, defense spending comprised about half of all funds appropriated by the omnibus, with a total of $554.2 billion set aside for defense and war spending.

About $64 billion was allocated to the OCO and included $5 billion for military operations against ISIL in Iraq and Syria, as well as $4.1 billion for training and sustainment of Afghan security forces. Cooperative counter-terrorism programs—including those in place with Jordan, Yemen, and Libya—received $1.3 billion, which was $4 billion less than the Defense Department requested. The European Insurance Initiative received $810 million, $175 million of which was required to be spent in support of Baltic nations and Ukraine. The OCO amount also included funding for military participation in Ebola-fighting efforts in West Africa. The total OCO appropriation represented a $21.2 billion decrease in funding as compared to fiscal 2014.

The omnibus provided $490.2 billion for the base defense budget, which was $500 million less than the Defense Department's request but $3.3 billion more than the fiscal 2014 spending level. It granted the administration's request for a 1 percent pay raise for military personnel and provided $88 million for the basic housing allowance. A competition to develop a new rocket engine was given $220 million, with an additional $125 million allocated for another competitive space launch in fiscal 2015.

Many of the bill's provisions involved funding or other measures related to the development and procurement of military vehicles and weapons programs. These included a prohibition on the use of funds to retire the A-10 aircraft, as desired by the Air Force, and provision of $337.1 million to keep them flying for another year. The Air Force estimated that retiring the planes would save $4.2 billion over five years, but lawmakers countered that the planes were needed to protect ground troops. The bill also denied the Navy's plan to take eleven cruisers out of service for modernization. Instead, the bill directed the Navy to modernize two ships per year, beginning in fiscal 2016. Another $848.5 million was provided to refuel the USS *George Washington* aircraft carrier. Defense Department officials sought to delay that project until they had a better sense of the department's long-term budget forecast.

Other provisions included

- $1 billion for a down payment on the LPD-28 amphibious ship—funding not requested by the Pentagon
- $1.5 billion to buy fifteen E/A-18G Growler electronic attack aircraft
- $224 million for the Air Force and Navy; $255 million for the Navy to buy two more F-35s each, expanding the F-35 Joint Strike Fighter program
- funding for three littoral combat ships for the Navy
- additional funding for ground vehicles, including $72 million for the Improved Recovery Vehicle, $28.5 million for the Bradley Fighting Vehicle, $120 million for the Abrams tank, and $79 million for the Stryker vehicle development and production.

Additionally, the omnibus included language prohibiting the administration from using funds to transfer Guantanamo Bay detainees to the United States or to modify or build a facility to house those detainees.

Fiscal 2015 Veterans Affairs–Military Construction Funding

Although lawmakers reached broad bipartisan agreements on freestanding VA–military construction appropriations bills for fiscal 2015, partisan bickering across Congress and sharp disagreements over spending limits and sequester cuts led to yet another omnibus bill.

Signed by President Obama on December 16 (PL 113-235), the omnibus provided about $169.2 billion for the VA and military construction. Approximately $162.2 billion was allocated for VA accounts, with the rest given to military construction, family housing, base realignment, and closure accounts.

House Action

The House Military Construction–Veteran Affairs Appropriations Subcommittee approved HR 4486 on April 3, providing $165 billion in funding. Of this total, $6.6 billion was allocated for military construction—a $3.2 billion decrease from fiscal 2014 but full funding for the administration's request. The Defense Department was prohibited from using any of these funds to build or modify military facilities in the United States for the purpose of housing Guantanamo Bay detainees.

The subcommittee provided a $158.2 billion budget for the VA, covering mandatory and discretionary spending. The Veterans Benefits Management System, the paperless IT system designed to speed up processing of disability claims, received $173 million. Additional funding of $20 million was provided for digital scanning of health and benefits files, a centralized mail initiative, and staff overtime to increase the capacity of benefits workers and reduce the claims backlog. At the time of the vote, the VA had reduced its backlog of claims pending from 817,000 in June 2013 to 344,000. The official benchmark for backlogged claims was 125.

The bill included $344 million to develop electronic health records, though only 25 percent of those funds would be made available unless the VA provided cost estimates for the program and updates on efforts to ensure interoperability with Defense Department records to Congress. VA medical services, facilities, support, and compliance received $58.7 billion in advance appropriations for fiscal 2016. By law (PL 111-81), certain VA medical care accounts are appropriated a year in advance to ensure continuity of services.

Other provisions allocated $62 million for Arlington National Cemetery, $63.4 million for the Armed Forces Retirement Home, and $31.4 million for the U.S. Court of Appeals for Veterans Claims.

The House Appropriations Committee approved the bill by voice vote with no amendments on April 9. The full House approved the bill by a vote of 416 to 1 on April 30. Two dozen amendments were offered and sixteen adopted prior to the final vote. Amendments approved by lawmakers provided funding for the planning, design, and construction of an additional missile defense site capable of providing protection from a long-range ballistic missile attack; increased backlog-reduction funds for the Veterans Benefits Administration Account; prohibited funds from being used to propose, plan, or execute a new round of Base Realignment and Closure; and increased funding for the VA inspector general to investigate the alleged misrepresentation of appointment times and the deaths of veterans at the VA hospital in Phoenix, Ariz.

Senate Action

The House bill was received in the Senate on May 1 and sent to the Committee on Appropriations Subcommittee on Military Construction and Veterans Affairs, and Related Agencies on May 20. Two days later, the Senate Appropriations Committee approved HR 4486, without amendment, unanimously. The bill did not see any action on the Senate floor.

FINAL OMNIBUS

The final omnibus package included $162.2 billion in funding for the VA, of which $94.2 billion was mandatory spending. About $79 billion in mandatory spending was allocated to pensions and benefits, while $15 billion was provided for readjustment benefits such as education assistance and vocational training. The bill also authorized advance appropriations for compensations and pensions, readjustment benefits, and veterans' insurance and indemnities beginning in fiscal 2017. Advance appropriations for Veterans Health Administration medical accounts for fiscal 2016 totaled $58.7 billion.

To aid in the further reduction of the VA's backlog of disability claims, the omnibus provided $2.5 billion for claims processing support. The VA was expected to eliminate its claims backlog by the end of 2015. Also related to claims, the Board of Veterans Appeals received $99 million to handle appeals of Veterans Benefit Administration claim ruling.

Funding for the VA inspector general was increased by $5 million. Lawmakers provided this additional funding to support an investigation into allegations that VA officials had covered up excessive wait times for appointments at VA medical facilities. Another measure required the VA to submit a report on its construction expenditures and savings and limited the agency's ability to adjust the scope of these projects amid concerns about cost overruns on several medical facility projects.

The omnibus continued funding for the VA to work with the Defense Department to develop interoperable electronic health records that would facilitate the seamless transfer of medical information between the two departments. A total of $344 million was allocated for this program. However, only 25 percent of the funds were made available to the VA until the agency met the bill's reporting requirements, which included quarterly briefings for appropriators on the schedule, benchmarks, and expenditures for the electronic health records program.

The VA's budget would be supplemented by $15 billion in emergency medical funds per legislation approved by Congress in August. Although that measure authorized the emergency spending, funds were not formally appropriated until the omnibus was passed.

For military construction and family housing for active military, reserve, and National Guard service members, the omnibus provided $6.6 billion. This was a decrease of $3.3 billion from the fiscal 2014 enacted spending level, which appropriators said was due to a reduced need for military construction. The bill maintained the prohibition against the use of military construction funds to build or modify facilities in the United States with the intent to house Guantanamo Bay detainees.

Fiscal 2015 Defense Authorization

Lawmakers once again found themselves scrambling to finalize a defense authorization bill before Congress adjourned at the end of 2014, even though the House passed its version of the fiscal 2015 measure in May. The Senate Armed Services reported its version of the bill in late May. However, remaining floor time in both chambers was limited in the weeks before summer recess and the session break for the midterm elections. Most of the available time

was consumed by deliberations over spending bills needed to keep the government open past the end of fiscal 2014.

As had been the case in 2013, because the Senate did not pass a version of the defense authorization bill, the two chambers' Armed Services Committees were unable to conduct formal conference committee negotiations. Instead, committee leadership held informal negotiations to arrive at an agreement that both chambers eventually adopted.

House Committee Action

The House Armed Services Committee unanimously approved its draft defense authorization bill (HR 4435) on May 8 after a day-long markup period. The bill authorized $521.3 billion in defense funding. The total included $79.5 billion for the OCO, but this figure was meant to be a placeholder until the Obama administration submitted its formal budget request for OCO funding to Congress. That request was pending the ratification of an agreement with the government of Afghanistan about the U.S. troops who remained in the country past the end of the year.

Notably, the committee decided not to grant Defense Department requests to limit personnel compensation and benefits to achieve cost savings, specifically, proposed cuts to housing allowances, TRICARE prescription coverage, and commissary benefits. In a report accompanying the approved bill, the committee wrote, "While the committee recognizes the need for compensation reform, it believes such reforms must be examined holistically before proceeding with wide-impacting changes and it looks forward to reviewing the recommendations provided by the congressionally directed Military Compensation and Retirement Modernization Commission." Allocations for military benefits would become a key point of contention between the House and Senate during the informal conference negotiations.

About eighty amendments were offered and debated during the committee's markup, several of which went against administration requests to adjust some military branches' personnel and programs. For example, the original draft of the bill partially granted the Defense Department's request to retire the Air Force's A-10 Warthog by permitting the fleet of planes to be kept in "Type-1000" storage, meaning they would be preserved in near-flight-ready condition and could easily be recalled to service. Air Force officials had estimated that retiring the aircraft would save $4.2 billion over the next five years. However, the committee later adopted an amendment offered by Rep. Ron Barber, D-Ariz., that prevented the planes' retirement and authorized $635 million in funding to keep the planes flying.

Similarly, the committee adopted an amendment from Reps. Joe Wilson, R-S.C., and Bill Enyart, D-Fla., that effectively rejected the Army's plans for a major force restructure. The Army had proposed retiring its fleet of 600 Kiowa scout helicopters and approximately 200 other aircraft while shifting 192 AH-64 Apache helicopters from the Army National Guard to the active force. The National

Guard's helicopters would in turn be replaced with about 111 Black Hawk utility helicopters. The Wilson-Enyart amendment, approved by voice vote, prohibited the transfer of Apache helicopters. It also prevented the Army from reducing its active-duty roster below 490,000 in fiscal 2015, while the National Guard was required to maintain an end strength of at least 350,000 troops.

Another agreed-upon amendment offered by Seapower Subcommittee Chair J. Randy Forbes, R-Va., barred the Navy from retiring any cruisers or dock landing ships. The Navy had proposed removing half of its fleet of Ticonderoga-class cruisers from service.

Among the amendments rejected by the committee were several measures put forward by Ranking Member Adam Smith, D-Wash., that would have authorized the Obama administration to close the controversial Guantanamo Bay detention center and transfer the detainees it housed to facilities in the United States. The committee also rejected a proposal by Rep. Jackie Speier, D-Calif., that would have removed decisions to prosecute sexual assault cases and other major crimes from the military chain of command, with an exception for crimes unique to the military. Speier offered an alternative proposal that would only have removed commanding officers' prosecutorial discretion for sexual assault cases, but that amendment was also voted down by committee members. Sen. Kirsten Gillibrand, D-N.Y., had unsuccessfully attempted to include similar language in the Senate version of the fiscal 2014 defense authorization bill the year prior.

House Floor Action

The House easily passed the committee-approved bill on May 22 by a vote of 325–98. Nearly 170 amendments were considered during the course of debate, though some controversial amendments—including a proposal by Smith to authorize a new Base Realignment and Closure process in 2017—did not make it to the floor due to rules limiting debate.

As in 2014, Smith offered an amendment pushing for closure of the Guantanamo Bay detention center, this time calling for a framework that would result in facility closure by the end of 2016. Smith reiterated Democrats' argument that it was too expensive to keep the facility open and that there was no reason why Guantanamo Bay detainees could not be transferred to U.S. soil when other terrorists were being held in maximum-security prisons. Republicans countered that the detention center was a national security asset and that housing detainees domestically was politically unpopular. Smith's amendment was defeated by a vote of 177–247.

House members also rejected a proposal by Rep. Adam Schiff, D-Calif., to repeal the 2001 Authorization for the Use of Military Force (AUMF) one year after the fiscal 2015 defense authorization passed. Schiff argued that the AUMF was outdated and could no longer provide a sufficient legal foundation for U.S. counterterrorism activities in the Middle East. The amendment was voted down, 191–233.

In the wake of Russia's recent annexation of Crimea, lawmakers included several provisions in the authorization bill that restricted the United States' contact and cooperation with the Russian military. House members took these limitations one step forward when they adopted, by a vote of 233–191, an amendment from Rep. Doug Lamborn, R-Colo., that restricted funding available to implement the 2010 New START nuclear arms reduction treaty until Defense Secretary Chuck Hagel certified that Russia was no longer occupying Ukrainian territory and was in compliance with both the Intermediate-Range Nuclear Forces Treaty and the Treaty on Conventional Armed Forces in Europe. *(See "Russia Annexes Crimea" box in Chapter 4, p. 154.)*

Senate Action

The Senate Armed Services Committee's multi-day, closed door markup of its version of the defense authorization bill (S 2410) ended on May 22, when committee members voted 25–1 to approve the measure. Sen. Mike Lee, R-Utah, was the only dissenter.

The bill would have authorized $514 billion for fiscal 2015, split into $496 billion for Defense Department base spending and $17.7 billion for the Energy Department's national security programs. Unlike the House, Senate committee members opted against including an authorization for OCO funds while the administration's budget request was pending.

The Senate bill included several notable breaks with the House-approved bill. A bipartisan agreement incorporated into the measure called for the president to submit a plan to Congress for closing the Guantanamo Bay detention center and transferring detainees to U.S. soil but gave Congress the authority to reject that plan. This provision was amended during markup to place a one-year limit on the transfer of detainees to Yemen.

In addition, the Senate partially granted the Army's request to transfer Apache helicopters from the National Guard. Up to forty-eight helicopters could be transferred under the Senate bill, with additional transfers placed on hold until an independent commission examined and reported to Congress on the future force and structure of the Army's active, reserve, and National Guard components. The bill called for this report to be submitted in 2016.

The Senate also granted the Defense Department's request to increase pharmacy copays for prescriptions filled outside of military treatment facilities and to limit an increase in troops' housing allowance below the rate of inflation. Committee members expressed their reluctance to agree with these requests, writing in their report on the bill that while "undesirable," the proposals were "necessary to produce a DOD budget that provides sufficient funding to address readiness and modernization deficits, authorizes a sufficiently sized and trained force to meet national defense objectives, and adheres to congressionally mandated budget levels." Related to this sentiment, the committee-approved bill expressed the sense of the Senate that sequestration had adversely impacted the defense budget, with language calling for deficit-neutral, bipartisan legislation increasing budget caps for national defense while providing offsets.

Like the House, the Senate bill favored keeping the A-10 Warthog in service, authorizing $320 million to keep the aircraft flying in fiscal 2015. It also authorized the Navy secretary to transfer up to $650 million in unobligated funds from underperforming programs to support refueling of the USS *George Washington* aircraft carrier.

Despite achieving committee approval of a draft authorization bill earlier than in 2013 and before the midyear mark, the Senate still had little floor time available to debate the measure due to the chamber's scheduled recesses for the summer and the midterm elections. Armed Services Committee Chair Carl Levin, D-Mich., and Ranking Member James Inhofe, R-Okla., tried to push for speedy consideration of the bill, in part by calling on their colleagues in June to file any amendments to the bill by the July Fourth recess. Offering amendments early, they said, would help the committee streamline chamber deliberations by enabling them to review and clear as many proposals as possible for inclusion in managers' packages, as well as determine which proposals were likely to be more contentious and should therefore be scheduled for earlier debate.

Levin and Inhofe were unsuccessful, however, as lawmakers prioritized passage of fiscal 2015 funding measures in hopes of avoiding another government shutdown.

Conference and Final Action

With further progress on a defense authorization held up by another impasse in the Senate, the chairpersons and ranking members of the House and Senate Armed Services Committee began closed-door negotiations in November on a compromise bill that could gain approval by both chambers. Known as the "Big Four," the group's deliberations were guided by input from other Armed Services Committee members who had met in September to outline their priorities for the final legislation.

In the first week of December, the Big Four released the details of their compromise bill, which authorized $577.1 billion for the Department of Defense and defense-related programs for fiscal 2015. A base budget of $495.5 billion was authorized, in addition to $17.9 billion for national security programs within the Energy Department, which generally involve maintenance of the United States' nuclear arsenal. Lawmakers also authorized $63.7 billion in OCO funding, including an administration-requested budget of $5.1 billion to help train the Iraqi Army and sustain U.S. personnel conducting intelligence and military operations in the region to continue the fight against ISIL.

Military benefits were the biggest area of disagreement between House and Senate participants in the Big Four talks, with Senate representatives willing to agree to some of the administration's requested cuts and limitations, while House representatives rejected them. In the end, lawmakers

agreed to a 1 percent decrease in the basic housing allowance for 2015 and did not provide for future adjustments to raise or further lower this benefit. They also authorized a one-time, $3 increase in pharmacy copays for retail prescriptions and mail-order nongeneric prescriptions filled through TRICARE, in lieu of the Pentagon's longer-term benefit reduction request. The bill required that all nongeneric prescription maintenance medications be filled through military treatment facility pharmacies or the national mail-order pharmacy program beginning October 1, 2015. In an explanatory statement accompanying the bill, lawmakers said they were deferring further adjustments to TRICARE copays until the Military Compensation and Retirement Modernization Commission provided its report to Congress. Lawmakers also authorized a 1 percent pay increase for military personnel in fiscal 2015 while freezing the monthly basic pay for all general and flag officers.

The agreement prohibited the A-10 Warthog's retirement and authorized $334 million in funding to cover the cost of maintaining the planes in their current flying status. However, it also said the Air Force could potentially place up to thirty-six aircraft in "backup inventory status," which is a reduced operational status, if an independent assessment determined that it was necessary to retire the Warthogs to ensure sufficient manpower was available to keep the F-35 Joint Strike Fighter program on track to achieve "initial operational capability" in fiscal 2016 and maintain other aircraft. The Air Force had argued that it needed to reassign maintenance crews from the A-10 squadrons to the F-35, which it could not do if the Warthogs remained in service.

Other provisions authorized new procurement expenditures for various military vehicles and weapons programs. These included

- $13.5 billion for 109 Navy aircraft;
- $12.3 billion for 114 Air Force planes;
- $8.1 billion for procurement, research, and development of the F-35 Joint Strike Fighter;
- $450 million for five new EA-18G Airborne Electronic Attack aircraft;
- $2.2 billion for a new KC-46A aerial refueling tanker;
- $15.7 billion for Navy shipbuilding, including $1.4 billion for three littoral combat ships, $2.7 billion for two DDG-51 destroyers, and $795 million for USS *George Washington* refueling;
- $9 billion for ballistic missile defense.

The bill maintained, for at least one year, the ongoing prohibition on closure of the Guantanamo Bay detention center and use of funds to build or alter any U.S. facilities for the purpose of housing transferred detainees.

The funding amounts included in the bill would account for more than half of the federal government's discretionary spending for fiscal 2015, though it authorized $48 billion less than the fiscal 2014 defense policy bill.

Per congressional procedure, while the authorization bill stipulated spending levels for military operations and related programs, funding for these activities was not officially provided until passage of the fiscal 2015 omnibus package.

To help expedite its consideration and approval, the compromise bill's language was added as a substitute amendment to another piece of legislation (HR 3979) that was previously approved by the House and Senate. That bill sought to exempt volunteer firefighters and other emergency responders from counting toward the number of employees that triggers the employer mandate under the Patient Protection and Affordable Care Act of 2010. Lawmakers also added about 100 provisions related to public lands that had been under consideration for more than a year to the updated bill in an effort to push their approval forward. These provisions had been negotiated separately by leaders of the House Natural Resources and Senate Energy and Natural Resources committees. The inclusion of these provisions prompted several attempts by Sen. Tom Coburn, R-Okla., to have the public lands language stripped from the final bill via amendment. However, the Senate rejected all these proposed measures.

The House passed HR 3979 on December 2 by a vote of 300 to 119. The Senate cleared the bill on December 12, voting 89–11 in favor of the compromise measure. It was signed by the president on December 19 (PL 113-291).

Emergency VA Spending Authorization

In April 2014, a scandal erupted surrounding months-long wait times for veterans seeking doctor's appointments at VA medical facilities. Dr. Sam Foote, a doctor at the Carl T. Hayden VA Medical Center in Phoenix, Ariz., filed a complaint with the VA inspector general alleging that the hospital was falsifying information about how long veterans were waiting for appointments to be scheduled to cover up its excessive wait times. Dr. Foote's allegations, which he also shared with a local newspaper, *Arizona Republic,* included claims that some veterans died while waiting for care. The hospital had been touting its significant reduction in wait times, even though veterans were still waiting up to twenty weeks to have an appointment scheduled.

More than 9 million veterans are enrolled in health care through the VA and rely on VA medical facilities for access to doctors and other providers. The VA had, in 2011, set a goal of scheduling medical appointments within fourteen days of a patient's or a provider's desired appointment date. An electronic wait time tracking system was deployed in 2012 to help address wait time concerns. However, the VA inspector general and the Government Accountability Office reported to Congress in 2013 that wait times remained unacceptably high.

Dr. Foote's allegations outraged lawmakers, veterans' groups, and the public. VA Secretary Eric Shinseki ordered the Veterans Health Administration to conduct a nationwide audit of scheduling and access management practices at all VA medical centers and outpatient clinics. Conducted between May 12 and June 3, the audit revealed that 70 percent of the VA's 731 medical facilities kept "secret waiting lists" of veterans whose appointments had not been scheduled while reporting manipulated wait time data to the VA that made it appear as though these appointments had been scheduled and wait times were much shorter. About 13 percent of scheduling staff interviewed by auditors confirmed that they had been directed to enter fake appointment dates into the VA's scheduling system to hide excessive wait times. The audit also concluded that 63,869 of the veterans who had enrolled in VA health care since 2004 still had not been seen for an appointment and that 57,426 veterans were waiting to have appointments scheduled at the time the audit was conducted.

Congress launched its own investigation into the allegations, summoning Shinseki to Capitol Hill twice to testify before lawmakers. On May 15, Shinseki told senators that he was angry about the matter and pledged to work with VA staff to find ways to address the problem. The following day, Shinseki announced the resignation of Dr. Robert Petzel, the VA undersecretary for health. Pressure soon mounted on Shinseki to resign, particularly after 100 lawmakers signed a letter calling for the secretary to step down. Shinseki ultimately submitted his resignation to President Obama on May 30. VA Deputy Secretary Sloan Gibson became interim secretary; he later revealed that at least eighteen veterans had died while waiting for care at the Phoenix facility, adding further fuel to the scandal. The president's nominee to replace Shinseki, Robert A. McDonald, a veteran and former CEO of Procter and Gamble, was easily confirmed by the Senate in July.

Veterans' groups blamed Congress for the scandal, arguing that lawmakers failed to provide sufficient funding for the department while also expanding the VA's mandate. "Until the Congress and the administration commit to providing truly sufficient resources to hire adequate staff and establish real capacity, the problems being reported around the country will only get worse," Carl Blake, national legislative director of the Paralyzed Veterans of America, told the Senate Veterans' Affairs Committee. "The administration and Congress both bear the responsibility of these problems." Blake's organization joined with American Veterans, Disabled American Veterans, and Veterans of Foreign Wars to develop their own VA budget proposal, which totaled about $5.5 billion more than what Congress had appropriated over the last ten years.

In response to the growing scandal, lawmakers passed an emergency VA funding measure authorizing $15 billion in spending to help cut wait times for medical appointments. A third of the funding was intended to support the hiring of additional doctors and nurses and upgrades to medical facilities, while $10 billion would help subsidize private health care for veterans who met certain criteria. The bill was signed into law on August 7 (PL 113-146).

Senate Action

On June 5, Sens. John McCain, R-Ariz., and Bernie Sanders, I-Vt., announced a bipartisan VA health care bill (S 2450) with support from Senate Majority Leader Harry Reid, D-Nev. The draft bill's major provisions authorized the VA to hire additional doctors and nurses and to lease twenty-six new medical facilities in eighteen states. It also permitted veterans to seek private health care if they experienced wait times longer than the VA's stated goal or lived more than forty miles away from a VA facility. This provision was set to remain in place for two years, at which time it would be reevaluated. The bill further allowed for the immediate firing of VA officials. Additionally, the bill authorized payment of in-state tuition for all qualifying veterans at public colleges and universities, as well as tuition assistance for spouses of soldiers who died in the line of duty.

The sponsoring senators estimated that the bill would cost less than $2 billion and that these funds would be classified as emergency appropriations, meaning they would not have to be offset with cost savings, per existing budget rules, and would not be subject to discretionary spending caps.

The Senate moved to insert the bill language into HR 3230, the Pay Our Guard and Reserve Act, which the House had passed in October 2013. That bill made continuing appropriations for fiscal 2014, for any period during which interim or full-year appropriations were not in effect (e.g., during a government shutdown), to provide pay and allowances to reserve members who performed inactive-duty training during the year. Using an already-passed House bill as the legislative vehicle for VA emergency funding allowed the Senate to circumvent potential disagreements with the House over the chambers' respective constitutional powers. The Senate also changed the bill title to the Veterans' Access to Care through Choice, Accountability, and Transparency Act of 2014 before approving it by a vote of 93–3 on June 11.

House Action

A message on the Senate's action was sent to the House on June 11. One week later, the House took up consideration of the revised bill. Members agreed by voice vote to concur on the Senate's amendment to the bill title and to the bill text, but they also further amended the bill to incorporate language from two other previously passed House bills, HR 4810 and HR 4031, that authorized some private care options for veterans and easier firing of senior VA officials for poor performance, respectively.

Conference and Final Action

A conference committee was convened in late June by members of the House and Senate Veterans' Affairs Committees. It was the first conference on veterans' health issues held in fifteen years.

A primary concern raised during the conference was the projected cost of the bill. The Congressional Budget Office (CBO) estimated that the McCain-Sanders bill would cost $35 billion over ten years while also creating the potential for veterans to seek additional care that could cost another $50 billion per year. By comparison, the House bill was estimated to cost $44 billion over a five-year period while potentially incurring another $54 billion per year if veterans sought additional health care.

Lawmakers were surprised by the hefty price tags, since their projections suggested much lower costs. Conference committee members challenged the CBO's estimates, calling them exorbitant and arguing that they did not account for the number of veterans who would choose to drop their health care coverage to enter the VA health system.

Conferees eventually agreed to authorize $15 billion in emergency funding, with $10 billion recommended to provide private health care subsidies for veterans. The private health care option was authorized for a period of three years. The remaining $5 billion was authorized for hiring medical providers and upgrading health care facilities. The bill stipulated that the VA could roll unused appropriations from one fiscal year into the next. An updated CBO analysis estimated that the revised bill would add $10 billion to the deficit over ten years.

Some lawmakers expressed concern that the private health care provisions of the emergency funding measure would simply create another entitlement program that Congress would get locked into funding repeatedly and would cost more than anticipated. However, the conference report easily passed the House on July 30 by a vote of 420–5 and the Senate on July 31 by a vote of 91–3. The president signed the bill on August 7.

2015–2016

Although a new Congress convened on Capitol Hill in 2015, it brought with it the partisan bickering and disagreements over spending that had plagued the previous Congress.

Defense, VA, and military construction appropriations once again had to be folded into continuing resolutions and omnibus spending packages for fiscal years 2016 and 2017. Deliberations over the fiscal 2017 VA–military construction appropriations measure provided an unexpected backdrop for congressional drama: House floor debate was interrupted when Democrats staged a sit-in demanding a vote on gun control legislation. It also provided a forum for politically charged debate on controversial issues ranging from LGBTQ rights to the future of the Guantanamo Bay detention center.

Additionally, lawmakers used the appropriations measure as a vehicle to provide supplemental funding to combat the spread of the Zika virus, which had been deemed a public health emergency by the World Health Organization and had reached the continental United States. While the House and Senate were initially far apart on their proposed approaches to funding disease-fighting measures, the two chambers finally agreed to provide $1.1 billion to organizations including the Centers for Disease Control and Prevention, the National Institutes of Health, and the Biomedical Advanced Research and Development Authority to study the virus, develop testing and treatments, and educate the public about preventive measures.

In hopes of avoiding further year-end scrambles to get defense authorization bills done, both the House and Senate pushed for earlier passage of the annual policy-setting measure in 2015 and 2016. In 2015, Obama made good on his promise to veto the bill lawmakers sent to his desk in October. The president objected to the authorization of $38 billion more OCO funding than he had requested and for programs that should be covered by the base defense budget. Obama also took issue with lawmakers' continued inclusion of language limiting his ability to transfer prisoners being held at the Guantanamo Bay detention center or achieve his long-stated goal of closing the facility. Following finalization of a subsequent two-year agreement that raised spending caps, lawmakers moved quickly to revise the authorization bill, clearing a new version that was signed by the president in November.

The White House also threatened to veto Congress's authorization bill for fiscal 2017. A primary concern was lawmakers' inclusion of language that would effectively roll back the president's executive order prohibiting federal contractors from discriminating against employees on the basis of sexual preference or gender identity. While this and other measures cited as concerns by the White House were removed during conference, the president remained strongly opposed to other provisions, including the preservation of

language limiting his options for dealing with Guantanamo Bay detainees. Defense Secretary Ashton Carter also wrote a strongly worded letter to the White House Office of Management and Budget expressing significant concerns about Congress's "micromanagement" of defense priorities while simultaneously encouraging Obama to sign the authorization bill. Veto-proof majorities in the House and Senate made presidential approval a near certainty, and the bill was eventually signed in December.

Fiscal 2016 Defense Appropriations

Congress's inability to pass standalone appropriations measures continued in 2015, with spending bills for fiscal 2016 ultimately folded into a $1.14 trillion omnibus. Before reaching an omnibus agreement, Congress passed a ten-week continuing resolution (PL 114-53) on the last day of September in order to avert another government shutdown. The omnibus was approved by the House and Senate and signed by the president on December 18 (PL 114-113). Funding for the Department of Defense and war-related programs comprised about half of the total omnibus allocation.

House Action

As in recent prior years, the House successfully adopted a freestanding defense bill before budget negotiations broke down. The Defense Appropriations Subcommittee approved draft appropriations legislation (HR 2685) by voice vote on May 20, recommending a total of $578.6 billion in funding. This was $800 million more than the Obama administration's requested amount and $24.4 billion more than the fiscal 2015 enacted spending level. The total appropriation included $88.4 billion for the OCO, as well as procurement funds such as $88.4 billion for F-35 Joint Strike Fighters, $16.9 billion for nine Navy ships, and $1.6 billion for 102 UH-60 Black Hawk helicopters.

Notably, the bill prohibited the transfer of funds into a National Sea-Based Deterrence Fund that the House proposed creating as part of the fiscal 2016 defense authorization. The fund was meant to support the development and procurement of a new ballistic missile submarine. At the time, the Navy planned to begin replacing its current Ohio-class ballistic missile submarines with the new class of submarine. However, appropriators were concerned that building the new submarine could consume a significant portion of the Navy's shipbuilding budget, forcing the branch to cut back on other planned ship procurements.

The House Appropriations Committee approved the draft bill by voice vote on June 5, after adopting an amendment stating that Congress had a constitutional duty to debate whether a new Authorized Use of Military Force (AUMF) was needed to authorize the United States' use of military force against ISIL. The Obama administration had been using the 2001 and 2002 AUMFs, passed shortly after the September 11 terrorist attacks to give then-President George W. Bush the legal authority to wage war in Iraq and Afghanistan, to carry out military operations against ISIL, as well as other terrorist groups in and outside of the two countries. Some lawmakers argued that the existing AUMFs did not provide a broad enough scope to allow the administration to conduct these operations and called for a new AUMF that could better support ongoing counterterrorism activities. *(See "AUMF" box in Chapter 4, p. 159.)*

Floor debate on the measure began in the whole House around 3:45 p.m. on June 10 and continued until nearly 2:00 a.m. on June 11, then resumed for several hours later that afternoon. Nearly seventy amendments were considered during that time, of which thirty-six were agreed to. Much of the debate centered around lawmakers' lingering concerns about the NSA's bulk collection of electronic communications, including phone calls, without obtaining individual warrants. Despite assurances from administration officials that the NSA's surveillance did not target U.S. citizens, some lawmakers remained concerned about the potential for the NSA to collect and search Americans' communication records without first obtaining a warrant from the U.S. Foreign Intelligence Surveillance Court and the implications of such searches for Americans' privacy. One of the amendments adopted by the House, by a vote of 255–174, prohibited the use of funds for "back door" warrantless tracking of U.S. citizens' communications.

The House also agreed 321–111 to delete bull language prohibiting fund transfers to the National Sea-Based Deterrence Fund. A separate amendment, adopted by voice vote, made $3.5 billion of defense appropriations available for transfer to the fund.

Senate Action

The Senate Appropriations Committee on June 11 approved its draft appropriations bill (S 1558) by a vote of 27–3. While containing measures similar to the House bill, it called for slightly lower funding levels. The bill recommended appropriations totaling approximately $576 billion for defense and war-related activities. Nearly $87 billion of that total was allocated to the OCO. Before approving the measure, the committee rejected, by a vote of 14–16, a Democratic proposal to shift roughly $37.5 billion from the OCO to the base defense budget.

The bill did not progress to the Senate floor for consideration.

FINAL OMNIBUS

A total of $572.7 billion in defense funding was appropriated by the final omnibus, which was $18.5 billion more than fiscal 2015 defense funding. The bill provided $514.1 billion for the base defense budget, which also represented an increase over fiscal 2015 of $23.9 billion. Operations and

maintenance accounts received $167.4 billion, while $69.7 billion was allocated for research and development, and $110.8 billion was provided for procurement. Military personnel were to receive a 1.3 percent pay raise under the bill.

The procurement funds once again included appropriations for weapons and vehicles that the Defense Department did not request or said it did not need. For example, appropriators provided $10 billion to procure sixty-eight F-35 Joint Strike Fighters, which was $1.4 billion and eleven planes more than the department's request. Nearly $1 billion was provided for a Navy destroyer, $600 million was allocated to purchase seven Growler electronic warfare planes, and about $500 million was provided to continue the military's use of the A-10 Warthog. Other procurement funds included

- $2.4 billion for the Air Force to buy aerial-refueling aircraft;
- $736 million for a new stealth bomber with the capability to carry nuclear weapons;
- $5.3 billion for construction and long-lead components for the next boats in the Virginia class of submarines, which will replace Los Angeles–class submarines;
- $228 million to develop a next-generation rocket propulsion system, though the Defense Department could continue using foreign-made engines until the new system became available.

Funding for various programs and partnerships with U.S. allies was also included in the omnibus. Of the $10 billion provided for missile defense programs, $488 million was allocated to cooperative defense missile programs with Israel. A new counterterrorism partnership fund intended to help Middle Eastern and African countries combat terrorism received $1.1 billion. The administration requested $2.1 billion, but lawmakers opted not to fully fund the request due to concerns that the program could become a slush fund for the Defense Department. To continue the Defense Department's European Reassurance Initiative, which involves prepositioning U.S. military equipment and increasing training with European allies and partners, the omnibus provided $789 million in funding. This initiative is part of the United States' planning and preparation for a response to potential Russian aggression in the region.

The OCO received $58.6 billion from the omnibus, including $715 million for training and arming the Iraqi Army and $3.7 billion for training and equipping Afghan security forces. The OCO allocation also included $250 million in assistance to the Ukrainian military and national security forces. Other bill language authorized the provision of lethal weapons of a defensive nature to Ukrainian security forces. No direct funding was provided for the Syria Train and Equip program, which the Defense Department had implemented to arm and train "moderate" rebels to help fight ISIL and put pressure on President Bashar al-Assad's government. Department officials had earlier reported to Congress that the program had only produced five active fights after spending $500 million.

The omnibus maintained restrictions on efforts to close the Guantanamo Bay detention center or use funds to build or modify any U.S. facility with the intent to hold detainees. The bill also prohibited the transfer or release of detainees to Libya, Somalia, Syria, or Yemen.

Fiscal 2016 Veterans Affairs– Military Construction Appropriations

Both the House and Senate succeeded in passing the politically popular and generally uncontroversial annual appropriation for the VA and military construction in 2015. However, the breakdown in negotiations for other spending measures meant that fiscal 2016 funds were once again folded into an omnibus bill at the end of the year.

The VA–military construction bill (HR 2029) actually provided the legislative vehicle used to pass the massive omnibus package, which totaled $1.15 trillion in spending. It included $162.7 billion in VA funding and $79.9 billion for military construction, family housing, and base and veterans' services. The bill cleared both the House and Senate on December 18 and was signed by the president the same day (PL 114-113).

House Action

HR 2029 was put forward by the House Military Construction–Veterans Affairs Subcommittee on April 15. The draft bill provided a total of $171.1 billion in funding. The VA was to receive $163.2 billion, divided into $94.5 billion for mandatory spending and $68.6 billion for discretionary spending. For military construction, the bill allocated $7.6 billion, including $532 million that would be placed into the OCO. The House Appropriations Committee approved the bill by voice vote on April 22 after adding a few noncontroversial amendments, including one proposed by committee Democrats that increased funding for VA medical research.

The Obama administration threatened to veto the committee-approved bill due to the provision of military construction funds for the OCO, which would be exempt from spending caps. Despite this threat, House members rejected during floor debate three bipartisan amendments that would have removed the OCO funding. Two dozen amendments were approved by the House, including one from Rep. Doug LaMalfa, R-Calif., that redirected $5 million from the VA's general administration budget to the Veterans Benefits Administration account to help address backlogged disability claims. The Veterans Benefits Administration received another budget boost from an amendment proposed by Rep. Paul Gosar, R-Ariz., which provided an additional $3.2 million for information technology systems used to reduce the backlog. Gosar's proposal to include language prohibiting the use of funds to create or maintain unofficial

recordkeeping systems at the VA—a response to the 2014 appointment wait time scandal—was also approved.

The revised bill passed the House on April 30 by a vote of 255–163.

Senate Action

The Senate Appropriations Committee made several amendments to the House bill before approving it on May 21 by a vote of 21–9. As amended, the committee-adopted bill included a slightly higher discretionary funding level of $77.6 billion, compared to the House-provided $76.6 billion. At $163.8 billion, it provided less VA funding than the House but increased military construction funding to $8.1 billion. The committee also added language proposed by Sen. Steve Daines, R-Mont., that would have made it easier for veterans to access medical marijuana.

The full Senate did not consider the committee-approved bill until the fall due to Democrats' months-long threat that they would filibuster all fiscal 2016 appropriations bills. A manager's package of amendments increasing VA funding for prosthetic research and requiring the VA to study the link between combat and suicide rates among service members and veterans was adopted during floor debate. Senators also approved amendments requiring the U.S. comptroller general to conduct audits relating to the timely access of veterans to hospital care, medical services, and other health care provided by the VA and to report to Congress on the VA's recruitment and retention of health care providers.

Final Omnibus

The fiscal 2016 omnibus provided $162.7 billion in funding for the VA, of which $91.3 billion was mandatory spending and $71.4 billion was discretionary spending. The Veterans Benefits Administration received $91.4 billion for the year, including $76.9 billion for pensions and compensation benefits and $14.3 billion for veterans' readjustment benefits, such as education assistance and vocational training.

Advance appropriations of $63.3 billion were provided for Veterans Health Administration medical care accounts for fiscal 2017. A total of $505 million was allocated to the VA–Defense Department interoperable electronic health records program, though only 25 percent of these funds would be released before the VA met Congress's quarterly reporting requirements. An additional $10 million was provided for the VA inspector general. The base VA funds provided by the omnibus were supplemented by $4.8 billion in expected emergency funding for fiscal 2016. The bill did not include language easing access to medical marijuana for veterans.

The omnibus provided $8.2 billion for military construction and family housing, a $1.6 billion increase from the fiscal 2015 level. However, it required that some construction funds be withheld until the VA reached an agreement with a non-VA federal entity to serve as the agent for each major construction project. Lawmakers included this restriction in response to the mishandling of funds involved in construction of the new Denver VA Medical Center in Aurora, Colo. Project delays and cost overruns caused the project budget to balloon, with officials estimating in March 2013 that construction costs would end up totaling $1.73 billion—more than five times the original estimate of $328 million. This high price tag made the medical center the most expensive construction project in VA history. The project was temporarily shut down in December 2014 after a federal judge ruled the VA was in breach of contract with Kiewit-Turner, the company hired to build the medical center. Kiewit-Turner reportedly warned VA officials that the plans the department submitted would cost more than $1 billion to complete; the company had been given a budget of about $600 million when the contract was awarded in 2010. Rep. Jeff Miller, R-Fla., chair of the House Veterans' Affairs Committee, said the project was "the biggest construction failure in VA history" and called for the VA officials responsible for the project's mismanagement to be fired. Some lawmakers argued that responsibility for construction oversight should be removed from the VA's remit and given to the Army Corps of Engineers, which oversees other construction projects for the federal government.

The final omnibus did not include any funding specifically for the OCO. It maintained ongoing prohibitions against using funds to build or change facilities in the United States to hold detainees transferred from Guantanamo Bay.

A Joint Explanatory Statement accompanied the omnibus and included recognition of the VA's reduction in its backlog of pending disability claims, noting that the department was on track to clear the backlog completely. Lawmakers directed the VA to provide Congress with an integrated master plan for modernizing its appeals process, including plans to ensure interoperability with the Veterans Benefits Management System, because the clearing of the claims backlog prompted an increase in appeals, which were in turn at risk of becoming backlogged.

Fiscal 2016 Defense Authorization

After two consecutive years of barely passing defense authorization bills before session adjournment, the House and Senate both succeeded in approving their own versions of a fiscal 2016 bill by June 2015. Several months later, the House–Senate conference committee announced a final conference report that was adopted by both chambers in early October. However, the bill would go no further.

President Obama had threatened to veto the measure while it was still being deliberated in the House, criticizing lawmakers' authorization of $38 billion more in funding for the OCO than the administration had requested, as well as their rejection of cost-saving measures proposed by the Pentagon and limitations placed on the transfer of detainees held at the Guantanamo Bay military prison. The OCO funding proved to be the primary issue for the White House: Lawmakers intended the funds to be used

for programs that would otherwise be covered by the Defense Department's base budget but shifted them to the OCO to circumvent statutory spending caps. At the same time, lawmakers declined to provide similar increases in funding for nondefense programs.

The president followed through on his threat on October 22. During a brief public veto ceremony, Obama said the authorization bill "falls woefully short" in adhering to sequestration spending caps and other measures and called on Congress to "do this right."

Congress later reached a two-year budget agreement (PL 114-74) with the White House that raised defense and nondefense spending caps by $25 billion each in fiscal 2016 and provided an extra $8 billion for defense spending through the OCO. With new budget guidelines in place, lawmakers moved quickly to revise the defense authorization bill and push it through the House and Senate. The updated measure cleared Congress on November 10, the day before Veterans Day. Senate Armed Services Chair John McCain, R-Ariz., called the final revised bill "the most significant reform legislation that has been passed in 30 years" and an "example of working not only on both sides of the aisle, but on both sides of the Capitol."

House Committee Action

The original House version of the authorization bill (HR 1735) was approved by the Armed Services Committee at 4:30 a.m. on April 29 by a vote of 60–2. The vote followed a marathon eighteen-and-a-half-hour markup, during which more than 300 amendments were offered. The full committee's deliberations stood in stark contrast to the subcommittee process, during which each subcommittee marked up and approved its respective section of the bill in roughly fifteen minutes or less.

As approved by the committee, the bill authorized $515 billion in national defense funding, including $495.5 billion for the base defense budget and $19 billion for national security programs within the Energy Department. Another $89.2 billion was authorized for the OCO, a total that exceeded the administration's request by about $38.3 billion. Most of the additional funds were designated for operations and maintenance accounts typically covered by the base defense budget. Committee Chair Mac Thornberry, R-Texas, said the additional OCO funding helped the committee meet the administration's total defense budget request but noted "it is certainly not the ideal budget."

One of the bill's most significant policy provisions involved a major shift in the military retirement system's structure. The bill combined the existing defined benefit pension system—which only paid out pensions to those who had served in the military for at least twenty years—with a matching Thrift Savings Plan that was similar to a civilian 401(k). This in turn extended retirement benefits to servicemembers who did not meet the twenty-year pension threshold. The change would be effective for anyone who enlisted in the military after October 1, 2017. Those who were currently serving in the military were exempt from the changes but could opt in to the new combined system. The shift in retirement benefits would implement one of the fifteen recommendations for updating military benefits presented by the Military Compensation and Retirement Modernization Commission in its January 2015 report to Congress. Established by Congress in the fiscal 2013 defense authorization bill, the commission called for a revised retirement system that helped more service members save for retirement earlier in their careers and facilitated a smoother transition to civilian life. Prior to the bill's approval, Rep. Chris Gibson, R-N.Y., offered an amendment that would have stripped the retirement change from the bill in lieu of a requirement that the Defense Department explore the proposed modification further and report to Congress, but the committee rejected the measure.

The bill also authorized $682.7 million to keep the Air Force's A-10 Warthogs flying for another year, despite the service's request that the aircraft be retired. During markup, Rep. Seth Moulton, D-Mass., proposed an amendment that would have permitted the Air Force to retire 164 of its 283 active A-10s and reassigned the funds previously used to maintain the retired aircraft to purchasing counter-IED equipment and MQ-9 Reaper drones. This amendment was rejected by a vote of 26–37. The committee approved an amendment offered by Rep. Martha McSally, R-Ariz., that added language prohibiting the plane's retirement to the bill. McSally's district is home to the Davis-Monthan Air Force Base, where eighty Warthogs are housed.

Language limiting the transfer of Guantanamo Bay detainees to the United States or to designated combat zones such as Afghanistan and Yemen was included in the bill, as was a measure requiring the administration to make certain certifications to Congress before detainees could be transferred. The committee once again rejected an effort by Ranking Member Adam Smith, D-Wash., to remove these provisions and allow the administration to close the Cuba-based detention center.

The bill also prohibited the use of funds for the development, installation, or sustainment of fixed-site radiological portal monitors and related equipment in foreign countries. Rep. Jim Cooper, D-Tenn., had proposed and then withdrawn an amendment in subcommittee that would have struck this language; he attempted to offer a similar amendment during the full committee markup. Cooper acknowledged that the portals, which are used to detect nuclear material crossing borders, were not completely effective but argued that they were useful in "detecting loose nukes" and serving as a deterrent to weapons smugglers. The committee rejected his proposal, 27–35.

The bill barred a new round of base realignment and closures (BRAC), the last of which was conducted in 2005. Instead, it required the defense secretary to provide Congress with a twenty-year structure plan for each branch of the military and a worldwide inventory of existing defense infrastructure to help determine whether force adjustments may be needed. The bill also blocked the Navy from retiring its Ticonderoga-class cruisers and mandated that modernization of two such cruisers begin only once "sufficient materials are available." The Navy was required to complete modernization of the ships in two years, with the option to request a six-month extension. Navy officials had expressed concerns that this would not be enough time to complete modernization, which they estimated could take an additional four years.

Another provision called for an independent review of the F135 engine, which is used by the F-35 Joint Strike Fighter, following an engine fire earlier in 2015 that grounded the jets and delayed the program's progress. It authorized the administration to provide lethal defensive weapons to the Ukrainian military, recommending $200 million in related funding, in response to Russia's annexation of Crimea. "This committee views this Ukraine assistance authority as part of a larger policy to reassure U.S. allies and partners in Europe and to deter further Russian aggression in both conventional and unconventional forms," the committee report accompanying the bill stated. The bill provided $185 million for development of a U.S. rocket propulsion system by 2019, with the goal of ending reliance on Russian engines.

Notably, the bill did not include language granting the Pentagon's request to increase TRICARE fees and prescription copayments to generate cost savings, nor did it include provisions authorizing a pay increase for military personnel, though committee aides said service members would receive a default 1.3 percent pay raise.

Other amendments considered by the committee during markup included language from Rep. Ruben Gallago, D-Ariz., calling on the defense secretary to review military eligibility statutes and determine if illegal immigrants deemed eligible for the Department of Homeland Security's Deferred Action for Childhood Arrivals program were also eligible to enlist in the military. This measure was adopted and incorporated into the bill text. Rep. Jackie Speier, D-Calif., mounted a second, unsuccessful attempt to remove prosecutorial decision making for sexual assault cases from the chain of command. The committee-approved bill did include several provisions related to sexual assault in the military, including measures requiring standardized training for special counsels for sexual assault victims and development of a Defense Department plan for improving sexual assault prevention and response for male victims.

House Floor Action

The House passed its defense authorization bill on May 15 by a vote of 269–151. Thornberry and Smith engaged in some debate over the OCO funding prior to the bill's passage. Smith objected to the additional OCO funding and urged his colleagues to vote against the legislation. Thornberry pointed out that the authorization bill did not appropriate any funds, so "if there's a better way to deal with our budget issues in the appropriations bill, there's lots of time this year to do that." He said the question for the House was "will we vote against a defense authorization bill—not an appropriations bill, the defense authorization bill—and prevent it from moving a step ahead?"

Several packages of amendments were adopted by the House, with one notable measure from Rep. Doug Lamborn, R-Colo., prohibiting the use of funds to implement the New START nuclear treaty until the president certified that Russia was no longer illegally occupying Ukrainian territory and that Russia was in compliance with the Intermediate Nuclear Forces and the Conventional Armed Forces in Europe Treaties.

Senate Action

On the Senate side of Capitol Hill, the Armed Services Committee approved its version of the defense authorization bill (S 1376) on May 14 by a vote of 22–4. The Senate bill authorized $612 billion in spending, including an additional $38.9 billion in base budget operations and maintenance funding to be provided through the OCO. Unlike the House, the Senate bill permitted the transfer of OCO funds above the administration's $50.9 billion request to the base defense budget if a budget deal was reached that raised defense and nondefense spending caps "in proportionally equal amounts."

The Senate also diverged from the House in its approach to the Guantanamo Bay detention center. It would permit the facility's closure if the president provided and Congress approved a detailed plan for how and when that would be completed and where detainees would be transferred.

The Senate bill included the same shift in military retirement benefits as the House bill. It also specifically authorized a 1.3 percent pay raise for uniformed personnel, as well as $8.4 billion for military construction, family housing, and related projects. It prohibited another BRAC round as well.

Other provisions authorized $300 million to provide lethal weapons to Ukraine and $600 million to train and equip vetted Syrian rebels. Another $200 million was recommended for the military to assess the cyber vulnerabilities of each branch's online platforms. Like the House, the Senate rejected calls to retire the A-10 Warthog and authorized $355 million to keep the planes in service in fiscal 2016. The Navy was authorized to receive $800 million to start buying parts for the next Virginia-class attack submarine, $400 million for a down payment on a new Arleigh Burke destroyer, and $199 million to support procurement of a new amphibious assault ship dubbed LHA-8. The Senate bill also allowed for the procurement of some jets that were not included in the president's budget request but that the services had asked Congress to provide if funds should become available. Those included twelve F-A-18E/F Super Hornet jets for the Navy and six more F-35s for the Marine Corps.

After two consecutive years of failing to pass a preconference defense authorization bill, the full Senate approved the policy package on June 18 by a vote of 71 to 25. The chamber debated the bill for two weeks, with sixty amendments proposed on the Senate floor. Most of these were not controversial and were adopted by unanimous consent. Amendments that were rejected by senators included a measure offered by Senate Armed Services Committee Ranking Member Jack Reed, D-R.I., seeking to limit the availability of authorized OCO funds until spending caps were adjusted.

Conference

The House voted to begin conference on June 25, and the Senate followed suit on July 9. Reed moved to instruct Senate conferees to insist that the final conference report move the extra $38 billion in OCO funding to the base defense budget, but his motion failed by a vote of 44–52.

Conferees worked for four months to resolve differences between the House and Senate bills, including those surrounding the Guantanamo Bay detention center, military procurement processes, and personnel policies. Disagreements over military benefits were a primary focus of conference negotiations. The Senate wanted to slowly reduce the growth of the military's basic housing allowances, thereby increasing service members' share of housing costs by 4 percent, and to limit eligibility for multiple housing subsidies. House lawmakers did not propose any changes to the existing housing benefit.

At the conclusion of the conference, on September 29, House and Senate representatives had reached a final deal that maintained the authorization for additional OCO funds. It also preserved language prohibiting the transfer of Guantanamo Bay detainees to Yemen, Somalia, Syria, or Libya and the use of funds to build or modify U.S. facilities to hold them. Lawmakers would instead require the Defense Department to submit, within ninety days of the authorization's enactment, a plan for the current and future detention of individuals held under the 2001 Authorization for Use of Military Force (PL 107-40), including a "specific facility or facilities that are intended to be used" for holding detainees. The agreement would gradually reduce the military housing subsidy by 1 percent per year over four years. It did not include language authorizing a specific pay raise amount for military personnel.

The conference report was adopted by the House on October 1 by a vote of 270–156 and was approved by the Senate six days later, with a 70–27 vote.

Revised Authorization Bill

Following Obama's veto and the new budget agreement established between Congress and the White House, lawmakers moved quickly to revise and reapprove the fiscal 2016 defense authorization. The revised bill (S 1356) largely maintained the original bill's policy provisions. However, it authorized $5 billion less in funding, for a total of $607 billion in defense spending. McCain and Thornberry were credited with negotiating the $5 billion in cuts that brought the bill in line with spending caps. The committee chairs found $1 billion in fuel savings, cut $250 million from Army readiness and $192.6 million from Army National Guard readiness, reduced the authorization for training and equipping Syrian rebels by $125 million, and saved $230 million by delaying the contract award for the Long Range Strike Bomber. The authorization for OCO funding was also reduced to $58.8 billion—considerably closer to the administration's initial request.

The new blended military retirement system was preserved in the revised bill. Lawmakers provided for a one-time increase in certain TRICARE pharmacy copays to help offset the costs of changing retirement benefits. The Senate's proposal to gradually decrease the military housing subsidy by 1 percent over four years was also included. A specific pay raise was not authorized, meaning an across-the-board 1.3 percent increase would likely be approved.

The bill preserved language prohibiting the transfer of Guantanamo Bay detainees to certain countries and prevented the use of funds for building or modifying facilities on U.S. soil for the purpose of holding those individuals. It also maintained the requirement for the administration to produce a plan for how and where it would house current and future enemy combatants. The bill authorized $406 million to train and equip the Syrian opposition, $200 million to provide weapons to Ukraine, and $715 million for Iraqi forces fighting ISIL, though some of these funds were withheld until the secretaries of state and defense determined that the Iraqi government was meeting certain conditions for political reconciliation with the Kurds and Sunnis. Other provisions limited contacts between U.S. and Russian officials on New START implementation, restricted purchases of Russian-made rocket engines, and prevented the retirement of the A-10 Warthogs.

The House passed the revised authorization bill on November 5 by a vote of 370–58, followed by Senate passage on November 10 with a 91–3 vote. The president signed the bill into law on November 25 (PL 114-92).

Fiscal 2017 Defense Appropriations

Defense appropriations legislation was one of only six spending bills that made it to the House floor for debate in 2016. Although the measure was approved, a companion bill in the Senate did not progress beyond the committee stage.

Budget negotiations across Congress had stalled by the summer, with lawmakers concluding that a continuing resolution would be needed to keep the government open through the end of fiscal 2016. In fact, two continuing resolutions became necessary. The first passed the House and Senate on September 28 and provided funding through December 9. The measure was signed by the president on September 29 (HR 5325—PL 114-223). After the presidential election in November, which resulted in a win for Republican nominee Donald Trump, Republicans revived an earlier push to delay budget negotiations until the

spring of 2017 to allow the new administration—and a new Congress—to finish the process. Lawmakers approved a second continuing resolution on December 9. That measure (HR 2028—PL 114-254) provided $1.07 trillion to continue funding the government through April 28, 2017.

House Action

The draft appropriations bill (HR 5293) put forward by the House Defense Appropriations Subcommittee recommended a budget of $575.8 billion for the Defense Department and war-related spending. The base defense budget comprised $517.1 billion of that total, which was $3 billion above the fiscal 2016 level but $587 million less than the administration's request. The remaining $58.6 billion was allocated to the OCO.

Notably, the subcommittee included language requiring that $15.7 billion of the OCO funds be used for programs that are typically covered by the Defense Department's base budget. For example, the bill provided $9.6 billion in OCO funding for the procurement of military hardware, including $3 billion to purchase seventy-four F-35 Joint Strike Fighters and sixteen F/A-18E/F Super Hornets. The bill also required the OCO funds to be spent by April 30, 2017. Shifting funds typically included in the base defense budget to the OCO was something of an accounting trick that allowed appropriators to provide billions of dollars more than the White House requested to buy new weapons, maintain existing ones, operate military facilities, and conduct training exercises, all while circumventing discretionary spending caps. Democrats were strongly opposed to these measures, in part because placing an effective expiration date on the OCO funds meant that the next Congress would have to approve a new war spending bill by the deadline—or sooner if military activity increased—to provide enough funds to last the remainder of the fiscal year.

The subcommittee provided a 2.1 percent pay raise for military personnel; the White House had requested only a 1.6 percent raise. It also required the military to maintain a higher number of uniformed personnel, calling for 28,000 active-duty personnel and 25,000 more reservists. Other provisions included $8 billion for operations and maintenance of military equipment and facilities; $282 million for cancer research; $450 million for medical facility upgrades; $125 million for traumatic brain injury and psychological health research; and $296 million for sexual assault prevention and response.

Lawmakers said they had identified savings in other areas of the budget that would help offset spending increases. These included $1.5 billion in savings from lower-than-expected fuel costs, $573 million saved due to favorable economic conditions, and $1.95 billion in savings from rescissions of unused prior-year funding.

The House Appropriations Committee approved the bill, with amendments, by voice vote on May 19. Spending levels remained the same, as did language requiring a portion of OCO funds to be applied to nonwar spending and used by the end of April. Amendments adopted by the committee included a measure proposed by Rep. Rodney Frelinghuysen, R-N.J., that rescinded a 2014 Defense Department policy that scaled back reimbursements for employees' long business trips. The committee also agreed to a nonbinding measure offered by Rep. Barbara Lee, D-Calif., that said Congress should debate a new Authorization of the Use of Military Force for the fight against ISIL.

President Obama threatened to veto the bill because of the budget and spending requirements, but the House passed the bill on June 16 by a vote of 282–138 with those provisions still in place. Members even rejected an amendment from Rep. Mick Mulvaney, R-S.C., that would have blocked OCO funds from being used for anything other than war-related activities. The amendment was easily defeated in a 306–112 vote, with some lawmakers arguing it was necessary to tap OCO funds to pay for some military needs that would not fit into the base budget.

Members also rejected an amendment that would have barred the government from conducting warrantless surveillance of Americans' digital communications when that data crossed the U.S. border. It also would have prevented the government from requiring device manufacturers to include encryption "back doors" so that communications could be easily and directly accessed for surveillance purposes. The House had previously endorsed such language, but the amendment was voted down with a count of 222–198.

The final bill maintained language preventing the use of funds to transfer detainees out of the Guantanamo Bay detention center. Two amendments approved by the House also prohibited the use of funds to survey, assess, or review alternatives to the detention center and blocked funding for salaries and expenses for the offices of the special envoy for Guantanamo Bay and the principal director for detainee policy.

Other amendments approved by the committee included one blocking the use of funds to modify military installations to temporarily detain unaccompanied immigrant children and another eliminating funding for reconstruction projects in Afghanistan. The House overwhelmingly rejected an amendment that would have blocked funding for drug interdiction and counterdrug activities in Afghanistan. Another amendment that sought to strike a provision preventing funds from being used to propose, plan, or execute a new Base Realignment and Closure round was also defeated.

Senate Action

On May 24, the Senate Defense Appropriations Subcommittee approved its defense appropriations bill (S 3000) by voice vote. The bill provided a total of $574.6 billion of funding, which kept it within the fiscal 2017 limits established by the 2011 Budget Control Act of 2011. It was also $1.7 billion less than the White House requested.

The bill total included $515.9 billion for the base defense budget and $58.6 billion for the OCO. The subcommittee did not take the same approach as the House,

and neither shifted base budget funding to the OCO or provided details on how much, if any, OCO funds should be spent on programs unrelated to war efforts. The bill also included a 1.6 percent pay raise for military personnel, per the administration's request.

The subcommittee trimmed $15.1 billion from various line items in the Obama administration's budget request to increase funding for other accounts, such as

- adding $1 billion to the Navy shipbuilding budget to speed up procurement of a new heavy icebreaker for the Coast Guard;
- adding $1.1 billion for procurement of other unrequested ships, including one additional Arleigh Burke–class destroyer and one littoral combat ship;
- $979 million for twelve Navy F/A-18E/F Super Hornet fighter jets, none of which had been requested, although the Navy wanted them;
- $507 million for four additional F-35 Joint Force Striker Jets for the Marine Corps;
- $367 million for fifteen more Black Hawk helicopters than requested;
- quadrupling the requested funding for Israeli missile defense, providing just under $601 million;
- adding $900 million to the budget request for the National Guard and Reserve Equipment Account;
- adding $915 million for medical research programs that were not requested;
- $397 million, which was $100 million over request, for new launch vehicles or rocket engines.

The Senate Appropriations Committee unanimously approved the bill on May 26 after adopting a package of amendments, one of which added language directing the Defense Department to quickly assign aircraft to bolster security at U.S. ground-based nuclear missile fields. Officials had said that the military's old UH-1N Huey helicopters were no longer able to provide adequate support to personnel assigned to those sites.

Fiscal 2017 Veterans Affairs– Military Construction Appropriations

While usually a popular bill that quickly passes through the annual appropriations process, in 2016, the VA–military construction spending package provided an unexpected vehicle for politically charged debate on several hot-button issues ranging from the detention center in Guantanamo Bay, Cuba, to LGBT rights.

Both the House and Senate managed to pass their own versions of the freestanding appropriations bill on May 19. Significant differences between the two chambers' plans for combatting the spread of the Zika virus were a major focus of the resulting conference committee. The House adopted the final conference report on June 23, largely along party lines and after a day-long delay due to

Democrats' staging a sit-in on the House floor to call for increased gun control.

However, VA–military construction funds for fiscal 2017 were ultimately bundled into a continuing resolution (HR 2028—PL 114-254) signed into law on December 10 that provided a $1.07 trillion budget to fund the government through April 28, 2017.

House Committee Action

On March 23, the House Military Construction–VA Appropriations Subcommittee approved its draft fiscal 2017 appropriations bill (HR 4974). The House Appropriations Committee followed suit on April 13, unanimously approving the measure by voice vote. The committee bill recommended nearly $184.2 billion in funding—an increase of approximately $13 billion over the fiscal 2016 enacted level. All this increase was seen in VA appropriations, which comprised $176 billion of the bill's total and were about $13.4 billion higher than in fiscal 2016. Military construction and family housing appropriations totaled $7.8 billion, a decrease of $305 million from fiscal 2016. In sum, the bill recommended $81.6 billion in discretionary spending and $102.5 billion in mandatory spending.

Approximately $66.3 billion and $103.9 billion in advance appropriations for fiscal 2018 were provided for VA medical care and mandatory benefits programs, respectively. The bill granted the administration's request for $2.8 billion for the Veterans Benefits Administration's general operating budget, which included funds for converting to paperless claims, centralizing mail intake, and hiring additional staff to assist with claims processing. It also included direction for the VA to continue working to address its backlog of disability claims, with a goal of clearing the backlog by the end of 2016. The Board of Veterans Appeals received $156 million to help mitigate its growing caseload—a direct result of the VA's continued work to reduce its disability claims backlog.

Disagreement over a Democratic proposal to attach emergency supplemental funding to help combat the Zika virus dominated the committee's deliberation over the bill. Rep. Nita M. Lowey, D-N.Y., offered an amendment granting the administration's request for $1.9 billion in Zika funds, declaring it "unacceptable" that Congress had not yet acted in response to the global health crisis. A major outbreak of the mosquito-borne virus had begun in Brazil in May 2015 and spread quickly, reaching sixty countries and territories by the fall of 2016. The virus has been linked to microcephaly and other congenital defects, as well as neurological disorders, and the World Health Organization (WHO) declared it a Public Health Emergency of International Concern in February 2016. With no vaccine available, officials around the world focused on preventive measures and issued a variety of travel and other advisories for pregnant women and those living in Zika-affected areas. The first cases of locally transmitted Zika in the United States were confirmed in Miami, Florida, in July 2016,

prompting the Centers for Disease Control and Prevention to issue its first-ever guidance on travel within the continental United States.

Committee Chair Harold Rogers, R-Ky., opposed Lowey's amendment, arguing that the administration had not provided enough information about where and how the emergency funds would be spent. He noted that committee staff were working on a draft supplemental funding bill to help prevent the disease's spread but said the bill could not move forward without further details from the administration. Rogers ultimately proposed a substitute amendment directing the administration to use unobligated Ebola funding for the Zika response while the committee continued to work on a supplemental measure. This amendment was adopted instead of Lowey's.

House Floor Action

The full House passed the bill on May 19 by a vote of 295–129, after considering about thirty amendments. The most politically charged deliberations surrounded an amendment offered by Rep. Patrick Maloney, D-N.Y., that would have prevented discrimination against federal contractors based on their sexual orientation or gender identity. The amendment was narrowly defeated by a vote of 212–214, but Democrats claimed Republicans manipulated the outcome by holding the vote open longer than usual so they could persuade members who voted in favor of the amendment to change their vote. Some lawmakers yelled "Shame!" repeatedly on the floor while votes were being cast. "We had a vote where equality and justice and inclusion won," said House Minority Whip Steny Hoyer, D-Md., after the vote. "And they spent five or 10 minutes twisting arms, turning them around, so that they could defeat the Maloney motion for nondiscrimination."

Other amendments rejected by the House included four separate proposals to remove OCO funding from the bill.

Notable amendments that were adopted included a measure from Rep. Jared Huffman, D-N.Y., preventing the VA from using funds to fly Confederate flags in national cemeteries on the two days per year this is permitted: Memorial Day and the southern Confederate memorial day. Huffman said he had anticipated "various parliamentary maneuvers" and "some drama" in response to his proposal, given the tension and divisiveness of debate surrounding similar measures proposed in 2015. However, no major opposition surfaced, and the amendment passed 265–159.

The House adopted by voice vote an amendment from Rep. Paul Gosar, R-Ariz., prohibiting the Veterans Benefit Administration from using funds to implement a memo that purportedly facilitated some employees' manipulation of appointment scheduling wait time data—as revealed by a VA whistleblower in 2015—or to create or maintain any record-keeping system other than those approved by the VA. Lawmakers also agreed to an amendment from Rep. Earl Blumenauer, D-Ore., allowing the VA to prescribe medical marijuana in states with legal programs.

Senate Committee Action

While the House worked to adopt its VA–military construction spending package, Senate appropriators were drafting their own funding measure. On April 14, the Senate Appropriations Committee unanimously approved S 2806, which recommended total funding of $190 billion. Of this total, $7.9 billion was allocated for military construction and family housing, including $172 million for the OCO, with the remaining $177.4 billion given to the VA. This marked a $14.7 billion increase in the VA's budget as compared to fiscal 2016. The bill's nearly $104 billion in mandatory funding included $66.4 billion in advance appropriations for fiscal 2018 VA medical care.

Prior to passage, committee members adopted an amendment put forward by Sens. Steve Daines, R-Mont., and Jeff Merkley, D-Ore., prohibiting the use of funds to interfere with veterans' participation in state-approved medical marijuana programs. Similar language had been approved by the committee in 2015 but was not included in the fiscal 2016 omnibus. Sen. Patty Murray, D-Wash., proposed an amendment permitting the VA to cover the cost of fertility treatment, including in-vitro fertilization, and counseling for veterans who suffered service-related injuries that prevented them from having children. Murray noted that active-duty service members, civilian federal employees, and lawmakers could get such treatments covered, but veterans could not. The measure was adopted by a vote of 23–7. The committee also agreed, by a vote of 20–10, to adopt an amendment from Sen. Christopher Murphy, D-Conn., allowing former members of the Merchant Marine to be designated as "veterans" and be eligible for medals, though they would not be eligible to receive VA benefits such as health care or homelessness assistance. "All they are seeking is to be recognized as veterans before they pass," Murphy said.

The committee's most intense debate was spurred by an amendment from Sen. Richard Durbin, D-Ill., which sought to remove the long-running policy rider preventing construction, renovation, or expansion of any facility in the United States for the purpose of housing detainees transferred from the military prison in Guantanamo Bay, Cuba. Durbin argued that the United States was wasting money keeping the facility open to hold just ninety detainees, noting that hundreds of convicted terrorists are held in U.S. maximum-security facilities. He said the roughly $600 million it cost to keep the Guantanamo Bay detention center running would be better spent on further reducing the VA's backlog of disability benefit claims. Sen. Mark Kirk, R-Ill., objected to Durbin's proposal, claiming that detainees would have a greater chance of being released if they were transferred to U.S. soil. "If he comes to the continental United States, he would get all lawyered up and would have a likelihood of getting out," he said. Sen. Lamar Alexander, R-Tenn., also argued against the amendment, saying it was hypocritical of Durbin to add a controversial provision to the bill when Democrats had repeatedly called

for appropriations bills to remain noncontroversial until they reach the Senate floor. "We've got a whole barrel of controversial amendments we can start putting on appropriations bills and we can start with this bill," he said. Alexander moved to table the amendment, and the committee agreed by a vote of 16–14.

Senate Floor Action

Senate leadership combined the committee bill with HR 2577 for floor consideration. HR 2577 provided fiscal 2016 appropriations for the Departments of Transportation and Housing and Urban Development. It had been passed by the House in June 2015 and approved by the Senate Appropriations Committee but did not go further. The Zika Response and Preparedness Act was also added to the legislative package by amendment. Approved by a vote of 68–30, the Zika measure appropriated $1.1 billion in emergency funding through September 30, 2017, to help combat the virus. Lawmakers included language in the measure that required a portion of funds to be spent fighting Zika in Puerto Rico, where the CDC had documented more than 400 cases.

Before the Senate approved the package of bills on May 19 by a vote of 89–8, lawmakers spent time debating an amendment offered by Sen. John McCain, R-Ariz., that would have extended the Veterans Choice program for three years. Established in 2015 as part of an emergency VA health care spending bill, the program allowed veterans to get private health care if wait times for VA appointments were too long or they lived more than forty miles from the nearest VA medical facility. McCain's amendment would have provided $7.5 billion in emergency spending to extend the program. Senate Budget Committee Chair Michael Enzi, R-Wyo., raised a point of order (a claim from the Senate floor that a chamber rule was being violated) against the amendment because the funds were designated as emergency spending, meaning it did not have to be offset. If the Senate could not find offsets for emergency spending, "we won't be able to help our veterans or our military or our education or anything else," Enzi said. McCain countered that the program had been a success and provided 1.4 million appointments for veterans who otherwise would have waited for delayed care. Senators voted 84–14 to waive Enzi's point of order. However, the amendment was ultimately dismissed when Sen. James Lankford, R-Okla., raised a separate point of order claiming McCain's proposal was not germane to the debate.

Conference and Final Action

A conference committee charged with reconciling differences between the House and Senate bills convened on June 15, with the conference report filed one week later. The two chambers did not vary significantly on the details of VA–military construction appropriations, but they were far apart on Zika funding.

The day before the House passed HR 4974, it approved HR 5243, a stand-alone Zika aid bill that provided $622 million in assistance for the remainder of fiscal 2016. The final conference report hewed closer to the Senate's approach, providing $1.1 billion for Zika funding. The total included $476 million for the CDC to conduct mosquito control, disease surveillance, lab work, and public education efforts. The National Institutes of Health received $230 million for vaccine research and development, while the Biomedical Advanced Research and Development Authority received $85 million to develop new rapid diagnostic tests to detect the virus. Another $40 million was allocated for community health centers in Puerto Rico and U.S. territories, and $95 million was given for the Social Services Block Grant to use in the territories as well. The State Department and USAID received $175 million for the last three months of fiscal 2016. Conferees included $750 million in offsets to the Zika funding: $107 million was taken from Ebola-fighting funds; administrative funds for the Department of Health and Human Services were reduced by $100 million; and $543 million had been set aside, but never used, to create health exchanges in the U.S. territories. *(See Zika Virus Response in Chapter 9, pp. 319–320.)*

The conference report provided $176.9 billion in VA funding, including $66.4 billion in advance appropriations for fiscal 2018 medical programs. Nearly $53 billion was provided for other medical services, such as $7.9 billion for mental health services and $173 million for suicide prevention efforts. Another $2.9 billion was allocated to help the VA process its backlog of disability claims, and $260 million was given to modernize the VA's electronic health record system. Language regarding the display of Confederate flags was not maintained in the conference report.

Military construction projects received $7.9 billion. That total included $1.27 billion for military family housing, $304 million for military medical facilities, $246 million for education facilities, and $178 million for the NATO Security Investment Program. It also included $172 million in OCO funding.

The House adopted the conference report at 3:12 a.m. on June 23, following Democrats' gun control sit-in. No debate was allowed, and the measure was approved primarily along party lines by a vote of 239–171. Senate Majority Leader Mitch McConnell, R-Ky., made several attempts to invoke cloture on the conference report and prompt a vote, but these efforts failed, and the Senate did not approve it.

Fiscal 2017 Defense Authorization

Lawmakers managed to avoid a presidential veto of their fiscal 2017 defense authorization bill, though one was threatened by the White House after the chambers' committees reported out their draft bills. Many of the most contentious provisions that President Obama objected to—including House language that would effectively undo an executive order prohibiting sex- and gender-based discrimination by federal contractors—were removed from the bill or modified as the measure progressed through floor deliberations and conference.

While the final conference report preserved some provisions that the White House strongly opposed, such as ongoing restrictions on the transfer of Guantanamo Bay detainees, both the House and Senate approved the compromise measure (S 2943—H Rept 114-840) with veto-proof majorities. Defense Secretary Ashton Carter and Under Secretary of Defense for Acquisition, Technology, and Logistics Frank Kendall expressed considerable concerns about congressional "micromanagement" and misguided reforms in the final bill, but Carter encouraged the president to sign the measure, which he did on December 23 (PL 114-328).

Completion of the fiscal 2017 authorization bill marked Congress's fifty-fourth consecutive year of passing the annual defense policy measure. The final bill authorized a total of $611.2 billion in spending, of which $543.4 billion was approved for base defense spending and $67.8 billion was allowed in OCO funds.

House Committee Action

The House Armed Services Committee approved HR 4909 on April 27, following brief markups completed by the subcommittees on their respective bill sections from April 19 to 21. The full committee's markup took more than sixteen hours to complete and did not conclude until 2:34 a.m.

Perhaps the most contentious proposal considered by the committee during markup was an amendment offered by Rep. Steve Russell, R-Okla., that would allow corporations that contract with the federal government to claim religious exemptions from antidiscrimination rules. Democrats claimed the measure would effectively nullify an executive order issued by President Obama in 2015 that prohibited federal contractors from discriminating against employees based on sexual orientation or gender identity. Russell and Republican supporters argued that the measure would protect contractors' First Amendment rights. The amendment was narrowly approved by a vote of 33–29.

The committee also adopted—by a one-vote margin—an amendment offered by Rep. Duncan Hunter, R-Calif., requiring both men and women to register for the Selective Service, in the event a future military draft was needed. The U.S. military has consisted entirely of volunteer enlisted individuals since 1973, but men aged eighteen to twenty-six years old have still been required to register for a potential draft. Since women have traditionally been excluded from serving in combat roles, they also have not been required to sign up with the Selective Service. However, in December 2015, the Defense Department announced it was opening all combat roles to women, leading some lawmakers to call for women to be included in the draft. Others opposed the change in policy, saying more time was needed to evaluate it and consider whether the draft should be abolished entirely. Hunter even voted against his own amendment, saying he simply wanted to provide a congressional forum for debate on the matter. This language was stripped during floor debate in the House.

One of the draft bill's provisions authorized $294 million for the United States to build its own, new rocket engine, thereby ending reliance on Russian-made engines. During markup, the committee approved language put forward by Ranking Member Adam Smith, D-Wash., that allowed some of that funding to be spent on a new launch vehicle to accompany the rocket. An amendment by Rep. Mike Coffman, R-Colo., was also adopted and authorized the Air Force's continued use of eighteen Russian-built RD-180 rocket engines while an alternative was being developed.

Committee members rejected another effort by Smith to lift restrictions on the transfer of detainees held at the Guantanamo Bay military prison. In fiscal 2016, Congress had required the administration to submit a detailed plan for the facility's closure and subsequent relocation of the suspected terrorists it housed. The administration fulfilled this requirement. However, Committee Chair Mac Thornberry, R-Texas, observed that the plan was only about seven pages long and "didn't say very much."

The committee weighed several proposed amendments related to alternative energy sources. Members approved, 33–29, an amendment offered by Rep. Tim Walz, D-Minn., that deleted bill language preventing the Agriculture Department from helping the Defense Department procure alternative fuels or award credits to any entity that provided alternative fuels to the military. They rejected two Republican-sponsored measures that sought to sidetrack the department's promotion of alternative energies and green technologies.

The final bill adopted by the committee authorized a total of $610 billion in spending. Funding approved for the OCO included $18 billion that lawmakers designated for weapons procurement and personnel-related spending rather than war and counterterrorism activities, which the OCO is supposed to finance. These funds were only to be available through the first five months of fiscal 2017. Democrats continued to object to Republicans' use of the OCO to circumvent spending caps on the base defense budget, under which procurement and personnel matters typically fall, and particularly opposed the authorization of OCO funds for items not requested by the Defense Department. "At some point, we are going to have to live within our means, a means we decided to provide," said Smith. Democrats also expressed concern that the short-term nature of the OCO funds would force the next president to pursue a supplemental war spending bill early in his or her term.

The bill prohibited the use of fiscal 2017 funds to conduct a new BRAC. While similar measures had been included in previous defense authorization bills, its inclusion in the fiscal 2017 measure was notable because the Pentagon had recently reported that it had 22 percent more infrastructure than it needed. Defense Department officials said they could make better use of the $2 billion a year they were spending to maintain the excess overhead. The bill also requested a series of reviews by the Government Accountability Office on issues including whether the Marine Corps version of the F-35 Joint Strike Fighter was ready to deploy; how the Defense Logistics Agency intended to prevent future purchases of defective parts; sustainment of major weapons systems; and spending on military bands.

In consideration of emerging threats, the bill directed the Defense Department to develop strategies for countering propaganda and messaging from ISIL and other adversaries with the goal of disrupting their recruitment efforts. Similarly, lawmakers called on the department to review the military's use of social media and devise strategies for improving its use of such platforms to disseminate messaging. Another provision authorized funding to develop a new security clearance IT architecture in response to a 2015 data breach at the Office of Personnel Management that compromised the personal information of more than 20 million federal employees.

The bill authorized $20.6 billion for Navy shipbuilding, which was $2.3 million above the administration's request. It prevented the Navy from using any funds to downsize the number of shipyards working on the littoral combat ship program until the service certified that this would be done through a competitive process. It also prohibited the Navy from retiring cruisers or placing more than six of the ships in long-term modernization status. The Navy had planned to put four cruisers in modernization by end of fiscal 2017 and seven cruisers in phased modernization in fiscal 2018—an approach the service said was more cost effective than Congress's preferred plan. However, lawmakers were concerned that the Navy would not have enough cruisers to meet operational needs if it implemented its own plan.

Additionally, the bill authorized $2.2 billion for a first-installment payment on the new B-21 bomber. The Air Force shared plans for a total fleet of 100 aircraft, but lawmakers asked Air Force Secretary Deborah Lee James to submit a report to Congress estimating the number of bombers needed to meet combatant commander requirements, suggesting they might want to fund additional planes in the future.

Other major provisions included

- a requirement for the Missile Defense Agency to start designing, developing, and testing a space-based antimissile system;
- authorization for the energy secretary to use force, if necessary, to defend U.S. nuclear weapons facilities against drone attacks;
- a requirement that the Air Force designate a single officer to command and control nuclear forces;

- the mandated development, by the Defense Department, of a new missile defense strategy that included offensive capabilities;
- eased restrictions on special immigrant visas for Afghans who supported U.S. missions in Afghanistan and faced threats to life at home as a result.

House Floor Action

The full House passed an amended version of the committee-reported bill on May 18 by a vote of 277–147. The final measure authorized a total of $602.2 billion in spending.

The vote followed two days of debate and consideration of 181 amendments, though only minor changes were made to the committee bill. Most of the changes agreed to by the House added language requiring various reports from the Pentagon or expressing the sense of Congress on a variety of issues, and most of these amendments were adopted by voice vote as part of "en bloc" amendment packages. The Republican-dominated Rules Committee had adopted guidelines for the bill's consideration that did not allow floor debate on the requirement that women register for the draft or language concerning the religious exemptions for federal contractors, which were two of the most contentious aspects of the bill.

In a floor speech prior to the vote, Smith called on his colleagues to reject the bill because of its authorization to use OCO funds for growing the services' ranks, procuring new weapons, and making facilities improvements. Smith characterized the bill as "a fiscal path to nowhere" and said Congress should be making difficult defense choices now rather than starting to fund programs that might not be fiscally sustainable long-term and would eventually be cut. Thornberry countered that the use of war funding for base defense programs was necessary because statutory budget caps had negatively impacted military readiness. "My view is: help the troops now," he said.

Among the amendments debated on the floor was a proposal from Thornberry to require the president to seek Senate confirmation of the national security advisor if at any point the NSC staff exceeded 100 people. Thornberry's measure argued that a large NSC was "no longer advisory and should be publicly accountable to the American people through Senate confirmation of its leadership and the activities of the council subject to direct oversight by Congress." A complimentary amendment from Rep. Jackie Walorski, R-Ind., made the Freedom of Information Act applicable to the NSC upon Senate confirmation of the national security adviser. Both amendments were adopted by voice vote.

A separate amendment from Walorski pertaining to the Guantanamo Bay detention center was also adopted by voice vote. That measure required the United States to sign a memorandum of understanding with any country to which it planned to transfer detainees and to provide those agreements to Congress to increase transparency around prisoner transfers. Rep. Mike Pompeo, R-Kan., successfully proposed an amendment requiring the director of national intelligence to consider declassifying and making public intelligence reports on the past terrorist activities of detainees transferred or released from the military facility.

Lawmakers rejected two attempts by Democratic lawmakers to adjust the base defense and OCO funding amounts. One such amendment from Reps. Jared Polis, D-Colo., and Barbara Lee, D-Calif., sought to cut the base defense budget by 1 percent, with exceptions for some programs. Separately, Rep. Keith Ellison, D-Minn., proposed shifting $9.4 billion in the OCO fund back to war-related spending accounts rather than using that money for procurements not requested by the administration.

Senate Committee Action

The Senate Armed Services Committee approved its version of the authorization bill (S 2943) following a closed-door markup session on May 18. The bill authorized $602 billion in funding, including $59 billion for the OCO. Committee Chair John McCain, R-Ariz., said the committee decided not to tap OCO funds to make up for base defense budget shortfalls, though he suggested he would seek additional funding during floor debate.

One of the most significant components of the bill represented a major overhaul of the United States' defense bureaucracy. The bill capped the number of National Security Council (NSC) staff at 150 amid lawmakers' concerns about the NSC's expansion under Obama and resulting increase in influence on defense operations and policymaking. (Prior to Obama's presidency, the NSC traditionally had fewer than twenty advisors. During Obama's tenure, this had increased to an estimated 400 staff.) "In addition to the growth in size, and largely enabled by it, we have seen an expansion of the NSC staff's role into tactical and operational issues," read a summary of the bill. "This provision seeks to push the NSC staff toward prioritizing the strategic mission that led Congress to create it in the first place, while maintaining executive privilege for its activities."

The bill also cut the number of civilian Senior Executive Service positions within the Defense Department by 25 percent. Another 25 percent of one-, two-, and three-star general officer positions were eliminated, and the number of four-star positions was reduced from forty-one to twenty-seven. Committee members said the officer count had "become increasingly out of balance with the size of the force it leads." Some sixty provisions within the bill also sought to revamp the department's acquisition system. These included measures opening Defense Department contracts to commercial vendors, streamlining government data requests, expanding rapid prototyping, and establishing a preference for fixed-price contracts over those that reimburse contractors for their costs.

Like the House Armed Services Committee, the Senate committee included a requirement that women register for the draft, with an effective date of January 1, 2018. It also called for a commission to explore whether the Selective Service was still needed. This component of the bill divided senators as it had divided lawmakers in the House. Sen. Ted Cruz, R-Texas, said he could not "in good conscience vote to draft our daughters into the military." Others positioned the change as an extension of women's equality. "Given where we are today, with women in the military performing virtually all kinds of functions, I personally think it would be appropriate for them to register just like men do," said Senate Majority Leader Mitch McConnell, R-Ky.

Other personnel measures included a 1.6 percent pay raise; modest increases in annual enrollment fees for working-age military retirees and incremental increases in pharmacy copays over the next nine years; and elimination of the "widow's tax," a measure allowing husbands and wives of military personnel who die from service-related injuries and conditions to collect additional benefits. The committee also proposed revisions to the Uniform Code of Military Justice to streamline the posttrial process, reform sentencing for guilty pleas and plea agreements, and provide greater transparency to the military justice system.

About $10.5 billion was authorized for the F-35 Joint Strike Fighter program, of which $8.5 billion was intended to procure sixty-three new jets. The bill also disbanded the joint office established to provide oversight for the program, giving the Air Force and Navy direct responsibility for the F-35 to ensure "proper alignment of responsibility and accountability." Committee members authorized funds for the B-21 bomber but cut $302 million from the spending levels approved by the House. They extended the prohibition on the A-10 Warthog's retirement until the F-35, which is supposed to replace the Warthog, undergoes initial operational testing and evaluation.

Within the Navy's proposed shipbuilding budget, the bill authorized $5 billion for two Virginia-class submarines and provided for advance procurement for future boats; $1.6 billion for the next amphibious assault ship, including incremental funding authority for fiscal 2017 and 2018; $1.5 billion for the Ohio-class submarine replacement program; and $3.3 billion for two Arleigh Burke–class destroyers. The bill required the Navy to report to Congress on the mission packages it had developed for the troubled littoral combat ships.

Unlike the House, the Senate committee bill only permitted the Air Force to continue using eight of the Russian-made RD-180 rocket engines while a U.S. alternative was developed. However, it allowed up to half of the funds authorized for development of a U.S. launch vehicle or launch propulsion system to be used to offset potential increase in launch costs as a result of the limitations on Russian engine use.

For operations and maintenance, the committee authorized $140 billion, including $2 billion for programs such as cyberreporting and depot maintenance that military officials had identified as priorities but were not included in the administration's budget request. The bill did not approve the use of funds for a new BRAC.

Senate Floor Action

The Senate approved its version of the authorization bill on June 15 with an 85–13 vote. Floor debate became acrimonious when some senators who were unable to get votes on their amendments blocked votes on other amendments. Amendments that were not voted on included those increasing the number of visas for Afghans employed as interpreters for the U.S. military, removing prosecution of major crimes from the military chain of command, barring the indefinite detention of Americans arrested in the United States on charges of terrorism, and authorizing State Department programs.

The Senate did consider and adopt by unanimous consent an amendment offered by Sen. Bill Nelson, D-Fla., that allowed the Air Force to continue using eighteen Russian rocket engines through 2022 while a U.S. alternative was developed. The White House had cited the Senate's original provision limiting the Air Force to nine rockets as one of the reasons the president might veto the measure.

Conference and Final Action

Conference began in the second half of July, and conferees expressed a goal of finalizing a compromise measure by late September. However, disagreement over the handling of one peripheral issue delayed talks, extending the conference timeline beyond the November election.

The issue in question dealt with the designation of the sage grouse as an endangered species. House Natural Resources Committee Chair Rob Bishop, R-Utah, who was also a member of the Armed Services Committee, had long championed a measure banning the bird's addition to the Endangered Species List. He successfully argued that such language should be added to the House's version of the defense authorization because the increased protections the sage grouse would receive as an endangered species would interfere with military training in the western United States. The Senate bill did not include this language, which the White House also objected to in an earlier statement threatening to veto the authorization measure. Conferees ultimately agreed to drop the sage grouse provision.

Differences between the two chambers' approaches to fiscal 2017 OCO funding also proved controversial during conference. Conferees eventually reached a compromise in which the House authorization of $18 billion in OCO funds for base-budget programs was slashed to $8.3 billion. About $5.1 billion of this total was authorized for requests from the administration, while the remaining $3.2 billion represented spending directed by Congress. Most of these funds were intended to support the hiring of new servicemembers. The final bill mandated an increase in military "end strength," or the maximum number of personnel the military is required to have by the end of the fiscal year: 16,000 active Army troops, 3,000 active Marines, and nearly 4,000 active Air Force personnel.

Another contentious item during conference was the Russell amendment allowing contractors to claim religious exemptions from federal rules prohibiting discrimination based on sexual orientation or gender identity. This language was cited by the White House as a primary concern driving the president's veto threat. A statement issued in May by the White House Office of Management and Budget said the measure "would undermine important protections put in place by the President to ensure that Federal contractors and subcontractors do not engage in discriminatory employment practices" and that the administration strongly objected to its inclusion. Conferees agreed to delete this provision.

The final conference report (H Rept 114-840) was released on November 30. It authorized a total of $611.2 billion in discretionary budget authority, which was equal to the overall defense budget requested by the administration, though the allocation of funds to specific accounts and programs varied. Lawmakers agreed to a $543.4 billion base defense budget and $67.8 billion for the OCO. Unlike the original House bill, the conference agreement authorized OCO funding for the full fiscal year.

In terms of organizational restructuring, the bill permitted the National Security Agency director to continue serving as the chief of Cyber Command as well, but it did require the separation of Cyber Command from the U.S. Strategic Command. It limited the number of nonadministrative positions within the NSC to 209 and established a chief management post within the Defense Department. As part of lawmakers' desired acquisition reform, the bill eliminated the position of undersecretary of defense for acquisition and began transferring the undersecretary's authority to approve most major defense development projects to the services. It also divided remaining responsibilities between two new positions: the undersecretary of acquisition and sustainment and the undersecretary of research and engineering. Lawmakers argued these changes were needed because the acquisition office had grown too big and was trying to do too much while placing more of an emphasis on compliance than innovation. Frank Kendall, the sitting undersecretary for acquisition, sharply opposed these changes and other acquisition reforms as a "serious mistake."

Personnel-related provisions of the bill authorized a 2.1 percent military pay raise, which was half a percent higher than the administration-requested and Senate-passed increase. The bill also closed a loophole that had enabled the Defense Department to give families of military reservists who died when they are not on active duty a much smaller financial benefit than families whose loved ones died on active duty. Another measure required the department to review California National Guard members who had been asked to repay excessive bonuses. Following the objections of Republicans in both chambers, language requiring women to register for the Selective Service was not included in the final bill. Instead, the bill called for an assessment of whether the draft is still a realistic and cost-effective option for the military.

The bill created a new Counter ISIL fund that included the president's requested $920 million for training and equipping Iraqis and $250 million for training and equipping Syrians. Another $4.3 billion was authorized for Afghan security forces training. Lawmakers authorized $350 million to provide lethal weapons to Ukraine and required the Defense Department to report on Russian compliance with the Intermediate Range Nuclear Force Treaty. It also limited contacts between U.S. and Russia/Russia-related nonproliferation programs.

Other provisions included

- $10 billion for missile defense programs;
- creation of a two-tier TRICARE program for new service members;
- $14.4 billion for Navy aircraft and $14.7 billion for Air Force planes, including $10 billion for F-35 research and development, modifications, and procurement of sixty-three new planes;
- $18.9 billion for Navy shipbuilding;
- $7.9 billion for military construction and family housing;
- $105 million for international humanitarian assistance.

Both the House and Senate overwhelmingly approved the conference report. The House voted 375–34 to pass the bill on December 2, followed on December 8 by the Senate, which sent the measure to the president by a vote of 92–7.

In an unusual move, Defense Secretary Ashton Carter urged the president to sign the bill while also submitting a lengthy letter to Shaun Donovan, director of the White House Office of Management and Budget, declaring that "there are many reasons to veto" the authorization. Carter decried Congress's "micromanagement" of the Defense Department, as well as the bill's "extensive disregard of the advice of the Department's senior civilian and uniformed leaders, and the failure to address the real and long-term fiscal needs of the Department." He characterized lawmakers' proposed organizational changes as "rushed, poorly understood" and said they were "particularly inappropriate" given the upcoming presidential transition. Carter added that Congress was treading "dangerously close to subsuming the president's prerogative as commander in chief" and that the reforms included in the bill "should not be unilaterally decided and dictated—in extreme detail—by Congress."

Despite the administration's strong opposition to a number of provisions that remained in the bill after conference—including the long-standing prohibition on Guantanamo Bay detainee transfers—the president signed it into law on December 23 (PL 114-328).

CHAPTER 6

Transportation, Commerce, and Communications

Transportation, Commerce, and Communications

As the recession began to ease through President Barack Obama's second term, businesses and consumers expected lawmakers would be able to address a series of transportation and communications issues. Congress did approve a long-term highway reauthorization measure—achieving a goal that had eluded Capitol Hill since 1987—but partisan disagreements and Republicans' efforts to restrain the administration's regulatory power impeded lawmakers' ability to resolve many other major issues.

In 2012, Obama laid out a vision for transportation infrastructure with a broad, four-year surface transportation plan while congressional leaders envisioned a six-year measure. However, as in previous years, neither the White House nor lawmakers on Capitol Hill could determine a long-term, guaranteed way to pay for such programs. After clearing several stopgap measures, the House and Senate ultimately agreed to a five-year, $281 billion measure that relied on a series of short-term government revenue streams. Critics said the bill would not help adequately rebuild the country's crumbling infrastructure.

The bill did include some provisions to address the safety of rail transport of certain hazardous materials in the wake of a series of fatal accidents involving trains carrying crude oil from fracking operations in North Dakota. However, despite a series of high-profile and fatal highway accidents, Democrats and Republicans had more difficulty coming to terms on a 2011 transportation rule that set new restrictions on commercial truck drivers to reduce driver fatigue and improve highway safety. Ultimately, they suspended and then forced a repeal of the rule unless the administration could prove the rule would improve highway safety.

While Congress was unable to finalize a long-term extension of the Federal Aviation Administration—approving two short-term authorization extensions instead—it did clear several FAA safety requirements in the wake of terrorist attacks at European airports in early 2016.

Congress also cleared two short reauthorizations—covering three years—for the Coast Guard but did not grant the president's request to have a majority of the U.S. food aid for refugee relief overseas be bought in countries closer to where it was needed. The maritime industry argued it needed the guaranteed cargo as other business had dwindled. Lawmakers did grant the president's request for funding for a new polar icebreaker to help the United States compete with Russia and defend its interests in the Arctic.

Meanwhile, Republicans continued to seek ways to rein in the Federal Communications Commission's authority, particularly regarding its 2011 rule on net neutrality. Lawmakers chose to leave untouched several issues that had become mired in previous partisan disagreements—such as digital piracy—while other issues, such as whether to permit Internet sales taxes, came to a standstill when lawmakers and the White House again could not resolve differences.

Meanwhile, a measure was quietly cleared to the president's desk to require that the financial disclosures of legislative- and executive-branch staff be made available online. Lawmakers moved the legislation after a report

REFERENCES

Discussion of transportation, commerce, and communications policy for the years 1945–1964 may be found in *Congress and the Nation Vol. I*, pp. 517–562, 1159–1185; for the years 1965–1968, *Congress and the Nation Vol. II*, pp. 227–251, 281–305, 779–823; for the years 1969–1972, *Congress and the Nation Vol. III*, pp. 147–187, 659–700; for the years 1973–1976, *Congress and the Nation Vol. IV*, pp. 146–147, 433–451, 505–555; for the years 1977–1980, *Congress and the Nation Vol. V*, pp. 291–362; for the years 1981–1984, *Congress and the Nation Vol. VI*, pp. 261–286, 289–329; for the years 1985–1988, *Congress and the Nation Vol. VII*, pp. 357–413; for the years 1989–1992, *Congress and the Nation Vol. VIII*, pp. 415–464; for the years 1993–1996, *Congress and the Nation Vol. IX*, pp. 327–398; for the years 1997–2000, *Congress and the Nation Vol. X*, pp. 318–338; for the years 2001–2004, *Congress and the Nation Vol. XI*, pp. 371–405; for the years 2005–2008, *Congress and the Nation Vol. XII*, pp. 405–440; for the years 2009–2012, *Congress and the Nation Vol. XIII*, pp. 319–359.

TRANSPORTATION, COMMERCE, AND COMMUNICATIONS LEADERSHIP

Transportation Secretary

President Barack Obama in April 2013 nominated two-term Charlotte Mayor Anthony Foxx to be the next Transportation Secretary to replace outgoing secretary Ray LaHood, a former House member representing Illinois. Obama called Foxx one of the most successful mayors Charlotte had ever seen.

Many transportation lobbyists praised Foxx for expanding and improving existing infrastructure in Charlotte, where he entered politics in 2005 as a City Council member before being elected mayor in 2009. He also won national attention for his role in bringing the 2012 Democratic National Convention to Charlotte.

Foxx had once worked as an aide for the House Judiciary Committee, then worked in the Justice Department.

The committee, in a 23–0 vote, approved Foxx's nomination and sent it to the floor for a confirmation. The Senate confirmed his nomination, 100–0, on June 27. He served until January 2017.

Commerce Secretary

Penny Pritzker, a Chicago businesswoman, served as secretary of Commerce during President Obama's second term. She had worked as Obama's 2008 presidential campaign fundraising chief and served on the President's Council on Jobs and Competitiveness and Economic Recovery Advisory Board.

Pritzker founded and led the PSP Capital Partners private investment firm and Pritzker Realty Group. She had overseen her family's 50 percent stake in Superior Bank, a thrift and subprime mortgage lender in Illinois that collapsed in 2001. As part of a settlement with federal regulators, the family agreed to pay $460 million over fifteen years to the Federal Deposit Insurance Corp., but the FDIC reduced that amount in 2011 by $144 million.

Pritzker also was a member of the Chicago Board of Education and a board member of the Hyatt Hotels chain.

During her confirmation hearing before the Senate Commerce, Science, and Transportation Committee, Pritzker faced questions about how she would scale back spending in the Commerce Department and protect the National Weather Service, as well as about her personal finances. Sen. John Thune of South Dakota, the panel's ranking Republican, asked her to explain her holdings in overseas trusts and about her role in managing her family's investment in Superior Bank. She said she had not been managing the bank prior to its collapse in 2001.

Meanwhile, UNITE HERE, an AFL-CIO affiliate that represented workers for Hyatt Hotels Corp., complained Pritzker had not done enough to improve working conditions.

The committee, in a 23–0 vote, approved Pritzker's nomination and sent it to the floor for a confirmation. The Senate backed Pritzker's nomination in a 97–1 vote. Bernard Sanders, I-Vt., cast the only vote against her nomination.

Pritzker, who served as secretary until January 2017, replaced acting Secretary Rebecca M. Blank, who left to be chancellor of the University of Wisconsin-Madison.

Federal Communications Commission Chair

President Barack Obama on May 1, 2013, nominated Tom Wheeler, a veteran cable and wireless industry lobbyist, to replace Julius Genachowski as chair of the Federal Communications Commission.

"If anybody is wondering about Tom's qualifications, Tom is the only member of both the cable television and the wireless industry hall of fame. So he's like the Jim Brown of telecom, or the Bo Jackson of Telecom," Obama said when he announced the nomination on May 1. "That's because for more than 30 years, Tom's been at the forefront of some of the very dramatic changes that we've seen in the way we communicate and how we live our lives. . . . Tom knows this stuff inside and out."

Wheeler led the National Cable and Telecommunications Association from 1979 to 1984, then headed various technology startups and oversaw the top wireless industry trade group. He had served as managing director of Core Capital Partners since 2005. His background was similar to that of Genachowski, who also had spent more than a decade working in the media and telecommunications industry.

The telecommunications industry applauded the choice, while liberals urged a more progressive selection and someone who would question large media mergers. Sen. Bernard Sanders, I-Vt., said in a statement, released the same day, that "the American people deserve to know where he stands on one of the most important issues facing our nation: the fact that more and more of our media are owned and controlled by fewer and fewer multinational media conglomerates." He also questioned yet another appointment of a former head of a major industry lobbying association.

Wheeler faced little resistance during his confirmation hearing, and on July 30, the Senate Commerce, Science, and Transportation Committee approved his nomination by voice vote. The Senate confirmed the nomination by unanimous consent on October 29.

Wheeler served until January 2017, but the commission faced some criticism—particularly from industry officials and Republican lawmakers—during his tenure. He had inherited from his predecessor the task of addressing legal and political challenges to the FCC's rule on net neutrality.

GOP leaders in the House were particularly concerned about regulations on the Internet. "If you prize Internet freedom, don't let government break the Internet," Louisiana Rep. Steve Scalise, chair of the Republican Study Committee, said January 23, 2013.

Republicans had long been trying to advance legislation to change how the FCC operates by requiring, for example, the commission to identify specific consumer harm and more cost-benefit analyses before issuing new regulations. Rep. Marsha Blackburn, R-Tenn., called for a telecommunications law overhaul that would rein in the Federal Communications Commission and reduce wireless industry regulations.

Oregon Rep. Greg Walden, chair of the Energy and Commerce Subcommittee on Communications and Technology, in 2013 circulated two draft bills designed to overhaul how the FCC does business, but neither moved amid the fierce partisan gridlock on Capitol Hill. They were similar to bills the House had passed in previous Congresses but that the Senate had refused to take up. The first bill would have required the FCC to take more steps to justify new regulations of the telecommunications markets and limit the types of conditions the agency could place on mergers. It also would have required the commission to specify how the rule aims to correct a market failure and to identify whether the issue would be addressed by further technological advances. The second bill would have consolidated or eliminated several of the agency's reporting requirements.

Henry A. Waxman of California, ranking Democrat on the full committee, said the first bill would only give industry more opportunities to take the FCC to court.

The FCC gained bipartisan approval when it voted unanimously on July 14, 2016, to approve a rule to provide more broadband spectrum for fifth-generation, or 5G, wireless technology that could be used for applications such as autonomous cars.

Wheeler said after the FCC vote that "5G will connect the Internet of Everything." He said he believed the vote to be one of the most important decisions the FCC made that year. He told members of the House and Energy and Commerce days earlier that the proposal would put the United States on the path to becoming the world leader in wireless.

The rule would open up nearly 11 gigahertz of spectrum for a mix of licensed use, unlicensed use, and sharing.

The agency said in a July 14 press release that the rule would allow wireless broadband operations "in frequencies above 24 GHz, making the United States the first country in the world to make this spectrum available for next generation wireless services."

Figure 6.1 Outlays for Transportation

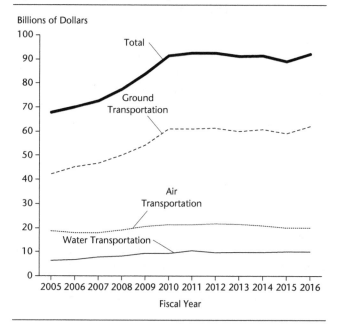

indicated such public disclosures of financial information could endanger the security of the nation or individuals. The House and Senate also easily cleared legislation to bar the use of automated software that circumvents online security measures on ticket-selling websites. But measures to require government agencies to obtain a warrant to access individuals' emails failed to clear both chambers.

SOURCE: Executive Office of the President, Office of Management and Budget, *Budget of the United States Government, Fiscal Year 2018, Historical Tables* (Washington, DC: U.S. Government Printing Office, 2018), Table 3.2.

NOTE: Total line includes some expenditures not shown separately.

Chronology of Action on Transportation, Commerce, and Communications

2013–2014

Lawmakers during the 113th Congress passed a short-term authorization extension of surface transportation programs, falling short of promises among congressional leaders for a long-term reauthorization. As in previous years, refueling the Highway Trust Fund—which was primarily dependent on gas taxes—was a major stumbling block for lawmakers. Democrats and Republicans on the Hill became mired in debate about whether to pull revenue from other areas of the federal budget to shore up the trust fund.

A series of accidents involving trains carrying crude oil from fracking operations in North Dakota raised concerns within the administration and Congress about the need to improve safety standards for oil shipments by rail. The Transportation Department proposed new rules in mid-2014, which included a two-year phaseout of older tank cars, and Congress cleared legislation directing the department to quickly finalize its rules. That measure also included funding for railroad research, including the transport of crude oil.

But many lawmakers, particularly Republicans, sought to rein in the Transportation Department's rulemaking activity in other areas. Many Republicans raised concerns about a new rule that required commercial truck drivers to take a break of at least thirty-four hours, including two nights, after each workweek. The administration and safety groups said the rule would make highways safer by reducing driver fatigue, but the industry argued it would force more truck drivers to be on duty during the daytime when highway traffic was heaviest and, therefore, accidents would be more likely. Ultimately, lawmakers blocked for one year implementation of the department's new rules.

Lawmakers also ended the FAA's furlough of air traffic controllers in spring 2013 by shifting funds to cover spending cuts forced by a 2011 budget law.

Congress fell short of approving a long-term reauthorization of the Coast Guard, ultimately approving a one-year authorization measure.

The House and Senate agreed to a one-year extension of a moratorium on Internet access taxes, but the chambers did not agree on legislation that would have permitted states to collect taxes on online sales. Proposed legislation that would have required a warrant to obtain an individual's emails from an Internet service provider also failed to move, while Congress—without debate—quietly moved legislation to nullify a requirement that financial disclosures by government staff be made public on the Internet.

Surface Transportation Reauthorization

Congress in mid-2014 passed a short-term extension of the authorization for surface transportation programs and postponed debate on a long-term reauthorization amid fierce partisan disagreements.

As in previous Congresses, lawmakers could not resolve how to maintain the dwindling Highway Trust Fund that had provided funding for most surface transportation programs and projects since 1956. The fund was primarily financed by gas taxes, but that revenue had been dwindling as people were driving less and buying more fuel-efficient or hybrid cars. Lawmakers also had not increased the tax since 1993; the tax lingered at 18.4 cents per gallon for gasoline and 24.4 cents per gallon for diesel.

An NBC/*Wall Street Journal* poll in November 2014 found that 75 percent of respondents supported spending more on roads and highways across the nation. However, lawmakers still did not want to advance an unpopular gas tax increase and again had difficulty finding alternative sources of revenue. Since 2008, Congress had moved about $74 billion from the general fund and other money to replenish the Highway Trust Fund. Congress previously had passed a two-year reauthorization measure (PL 112-141) that expired September 30, 2014.

LONG-TERM MEASURE STYMIED

President Obama, in his State of the Union address on February 12, detailed his plan for a four-year, $302 billion surface transportation reauthorization. His Grow America Act, which he sent to Congress later that month, called for refilling the Highway Trust Fund with tax revenue collected as a result of luring corporate overseas profits back to the United States. The measure also would have boosted transit spending, combined rail programs into the Highway Trust Fund, and put another $87 billion into the fund to repair aging bridges, transit systems, and other facilities.

The administration also proposed removing a ban on tolls for existing interstate highways in order to allow states to raise revenue. Congress had banned the tolls in 1956 when the Eisenhower administration created the interstate highway system. The plan also included proposals to

- alter long-standing bus and trucking pay scales;
- authorize an increase—from $35 million to $300 million—the amount in the civil penalties that the National Highway Traffic Safety Administration could levy against automakers that failed to quickly act on vehicle recalls;
- empower the Transportation Department to impose wage standards for some commercial truck and bus drivers;
- require that truck drivers who are paid on a cents-per-mile basis also be paid at least the standard hourly minimum wage for time spent on duty but not driving;
- implement a strategy to reduce risk on railroads through more capital improvements, better enforcement, and safety programs that identify risks.

With the latter provision, the administration had hoped to resolve concerns following several accidents in both the passenger and freight rail industries in the previous year, including a derailment of a passenger train on December 1 on a line connecting Poughkeepsie, New York, with Manhattan's Grand Central Stations, resulting in the death of four passengers while another sixty-one passengers were injured. The previous May, seventy-two passengers were injured when two Metro cars collided after a train derailment near Fairfield, Connecticut, injuring sixty people.

Transportation Secretary Anthony Foxx lobbied Congress to take up the plan, but to no avail.

House Transportation and Infrastructure Committee Chair Bill Shuster, R-Pa., said he hoped to push through Congress a new highway reauthorization bill before the 2012 authorization (PL 112-141) expired at the end of September 2014. But he did not introduce a formal measure.

Meanwhile, the Senate Environment and Public Works Committee leader introduced a six-year authorization bill (S 2322) that would have maintained existing funding authorization levels but added inflationary costs—or $16 billion a year more than what was provided by the Highway Trust Fund. Chair Barbara Boxer, D-Calif., said Finance Chair Ron Wyden, D-Ore., suggested funding could be tied to a tax overhaul.

The Environment and Public Works Committee approved the bill (S 2322) on May 15. But then both House and Senate transportation panels turned their attention to a short-term,

stopgap measure because the fund was expected to be depleted by August 1, when states would face a 28 percent reduction in their federal transportation funding.

COMMITTEE ACTION

House and Senate tax-writing committees on July 10 approved by voice vote separate bills that would raise nearly $11 billion to shore up the Highway Trust Fund through May 2015.

The House Ways and Means on July 10 approved by voice vote a $10.8 billion bill (HR 5021), introduced by Ways and Means Chair Dave Camp, R-Mich., to keep the highway trust fund solvent through May 2015. Under the bill, the Highway Trust Fund would be replenished short term (about ten months) with about $6.4 billion from changes to pension rules and $3.5 billion from an extension of customs user fees over ten years. The bill also would transfer $1 billion from a separate trust fund for underground oil leak cleanups.

House Transportation member Tom Petri, R-Wis., raised concerns about the offsets in Camp's proposal. "[W]e are playing games with the budget by using offsets unrelated to transportation and others that will not be realized until 2024 to fund our current needs. That only kicks the can down the road," Petri said July 9 after Camp's proposal was unveiled, according to CQ Roll Call. House Majority Whip Kevin McCarthy, R-Calif., said GOP leaders hoped to find a long-term solution for highway and transit program funding.

The Senate Finance Committee approved a draft bill that would rely on the same offsets to a lesser degree and would add tax compliance provisions. For example, the bill would require more information on tax returns related to mortgage interest.

Previously, Senate Finance Chair Wyden and ranking Republican Orrin G. Hatch of Utah had pushed an $8 billion measure to extend the trust fund to the end of 2014. But Camp said such a bill would not pass the House. "Any effort that just goes to the end of this year will only lead to another backroom deal during the lame-duck session where only very few members are present or have any say in the matter," Camp said on July 8 in a written statement when introducing the bill.

The Senate rejected several Democratic amendments to limit the extension to the end of the year, hoping that would force Congress to move on a long-term solution before the next session began.

House Action

A coalition of sixty-two infrastructure advocacy groups—such as the American Road and Transportation Buildings Association, the American Trucking Associations, U.S. Chamber of Commerce, and others—wrote a letter to House members on July 14, 2014, urging them to quickly pass the bill to "prevent a shutdown of federal highway and public transportation investments across the country."

But Transportation Secretary Foxx criticized lawmakers for not moving on a long-term solution. He and eleven former transportation secretaries wrote to lawmakers on July 21, 2014, urging them to clear a six-year bill. "We are hopeful that Congress appears willing to avert the immediate crisis. But we want to be clear: This bill will not 'fix' America's transportation system. For that, we need a much larger and longer-term investment," they wrote. "Never in our nation's history has America's transportation system been on a more unsustainable course."

Heritage Action and Club for Growth, two conservative business groups, mobilized against the House bill because it failed to provide a comprehensive overhaul of the highway and transit program. "Rather than continue down this path of bailout after bailout, Republicans should begin enacting serious reforms," Heritage Action president Michael Needham wrote in a blog post.

Petri acknowledged the desire for a long-term bill but said that it was the only option they had that day for passage.

The House passed the measure (HR 5021) on July 15 by a vote of 367–55, sending it to the Senate for consideration.

Senate Action

The Senate on July 29 passed HR 5021 by a vote of 79–18 after shortening the duration of the stopgap measure.

The Senate initially adopted, 71–26, a proposal by Wyden that would have provided $10.8 billion for the trust fund through May 2015, with some slightly different offsets from the House approved. Then the Senate approved, 66–31, a proposal that would have shortened the duration of the fix until mid-December and would have eliminated some of the offset provisions.

The Senate then sent the bill back to the House and urged House Speaker John A. Boehner to put it on the floor. However, the Congressional Budget Office determined that a technical error in the Senate bill would leave it underfunded by about $2.4 billion.

Final Action

On July 31, the House voted 272–150 to reject the Senate amendments and send it back to the other chamber for reconsideration. The Senate backed off its changes and quickly cleared the bill the same day by a vote of 81–13. President Obama signed it into law (PL 113-159) on August 8.

Many observers continued to criticize Congress's failure to pass a long-term fix for the Highway Trust fund. "The mere fact that lawmakers punted—instead of summoning the courage to craft a long-term, sustainably financed solution to the Highway Trust Fund—is perfectly emblematic of this Congress," Dennis Slater, president of the Association of Equipment Manufacturers, said in a statement released July 31.

Crude Oil Transports

Several fatal incidents involving trains carrying crude oil led Congress in 2014 to require the Transportation Department to more quickly finalize plans to phase out older tanker cars that had been built before new federal safety regulations had been instituted for the transport of crude oil from fracking operations. Lawmakers also approved additional funding for railroad research, including research into rail lines carrying crude oil.

BACKGROUND

In 2013, safety and transportation experts began to raise concerns about the possibility that petroleum produced from hydraulic fracturing might be more hazardous to ship by train than conventional crude oil. Several instances of severe corrosion in tanker cars had been reported, leading the American Petroleum Institute to investigate whether the oil shipments were properly classified. In July, for instance, oil tanker cars exploded in Lac-Mégantic, Quebec, destroying almost thirty buildings and killing nearly fifty people in the town, which lies near the U.S.–Canada border along Maine and New Hampshire. The tankers had been carrying oil from North Dakota, where drillers were using fracking to tap reserves under the Bakken shale formation.

Fracking involves the injection of water, sand, and chemicals to crack shale and free oil and gas. Some experts believed the chemicals used in the process might mix with the crude oil and make it more corrosive and combustible.

After an accident in 2009, the Association of American Railroads devised rules aimed at improving safety on new DOT-111 cars, named for the Transportation Department code that sets the standards for their construction. In 2013, the Pipeline and Hazardous Materials Safety Administration was developing regulations covering rail transport of hazardous materials. The rules were to include new standards for the DOT-111 tanker cars.

In November, another explosive derailment of oil tanker cars occurred in Alabama. Subsequently, the Association of American Railroads voluntarily recommended the phaseout or retrofitting of more than 92,000 tanker cars to improve the safety of trains transporting crude oil. The group had updated its standards for the cars, which account for about 70 percent of active tankers in the United States, to require thicker shells for the tanks, among other things. However, the upgraded standards had not required changes to cars built before the rules were issued. The association suggested the standards be applied retroactively to older cars.

North Dakota Republican Sen. John Hoeven and Louisiana Democrat Mary L. Landrieu, a member of the Energy and Natural Resources Committee, urged the Pipeline and Hazardous Materials Safety Administration to quickly move to implement a regulation to satisfy that recommendation.

Sen. Charles E. Schumer, D-N.Y., and Maine Democratic Reps. Michael H. Michaud and Chellie Pingree had asked the administration to consider phasing out the DOT-111 cars since they were not constructed with the new chemical-based oil drilling methods considered. The Transportation Department moved to do so, targeting a March 2015 completion date for a new rule.

On December 30, 2013, another oil train exploded near Casselton, North Dakota, after being struck by a derailed grain train. In early January, Hoeven called administration officials to his office, and Transportation Secretary Foxx called on the railroad and oil and gas industries to work with the department to improve safety standards.

Meanwhile, Senate Energy Committee Chair Wyden and Transportation Committee Chair Jay Rockefeller called for a federal investigation into the safety of crude oil shipments by rail. Rail shipments of crude oil and other petroleum products in the United States had increased by about 48 percent during the first half of 2012 compared with the same period a year earlier, largely due to increased oil production in the Bakken formation, according to the Association of American Railroads.

PROPOSED RULES

In July 2014, the Transportation Department released proposed rules aimed at making the transport of oil safer, in part by overhauling specifications for new tanker cars. The proposal would define "high-hazard flammable trains" as those carrying twenty or more tank cars full of crude oil, ethanol, or other explosive liquids. It would phase out within two years the older DOT-111 tank cars—which were used to move most of the oil from fracking operations in North Dakota—and require tank cars built after October 1, 2015, to meet new design standards.

The Department of Transportation (DOT) also sought new braking equipment and potential requirements such as spreading locomotives throughout a train carrying hazardous materials to ensure braking power was distributed along the line.

The rules would require railroads to continue to comply with a federal order, issued the previous spring, that they notify responsible state emergency officials about the routes for trains hauling hazardous materials. The department also sought industry feedback on proposed speed limit options for high-risk cargoes.

At the same time the DOT released its proposed rules, it released an analysis of Bakken crude oil data that indicated that the oil from fracking operations in North Dakota tended to be more volatile than other crude oil. Federal officials had been seeking to determine whether companies had been mislabeling the oil to make it appear less flammable, thus leading to improper packaging.

"We've confirmed so far that Bakken crude oil is on the high end of volatility compared to other crude oils," Transportation Secretary Foxx told reporters July 23, according to *CQ Roll Call*.

But the American Petroleum Institute rejected the finding. "The best science and data do not support recent speculation that crude oil from the Bakken presents greater than normal transportation risks," said API President and CEO Jack Gerard in a July 23, 2014, statement.

The Pipeline and Hazardous Materials Safety Administration said it hoped to issue a final regulation by March 2015 but in December 2014 said it might not make that deadline due to the volume of comments on its proposals.

Final Action

At the end of 2014, lawmakers included in the fiscal 2015 omnibus spending bill (HR 83) some provisions directing the Transportation Department to finalize a phaseout of the DOT-111 oil tanker cars by January 15, 2015, six weeks ahead of the scheduled completion date.

The broad spending bill also included $39 million for railroad research, including $2 million for rail lines carrying crude oil and $2 million for research into technologies using liquefied natural gas in rail transport.

The House passed the bill, 219–206, on December 11, and the Senate voted 56–40 on December 13 to clear the spending package after overcoming bipartisan resistance on various provisions in the bill unrelated to crude oil transport. The president on December 16 signed the measure into law (PL 113-235).

Truck Drivers' Workweek

As part of an omnibus spending bill, Sen. Susan Collins, R-Maine, added a provision to block for one year a new Department of Transportation rule that mandated truck drivers take off at least thirty-four hours—including at least two nights—between workweeks. The trucking industry had pushed for the delay, saying the new rule had not been properly studied and would result in more daytime driving. Safety advocates, however, said the rules would reduce the time drivers could be on the road and thereby reduce risks of driver fatigue and make roads safer.

BACKGROUND

The Federal Motor Carrier Safety Administration had finalized a rule December 27, 2011, that required commercial truck drivers to take a mandatory thirty-minute break from driving during the first eight hours of their workday and a thirty-four-hour break once a week. The thirty-four-hour break had to include two nighttime periods from 1 a.m. to 5 a.m., and drivers could only take a thirty-four-hour break (restarting their official workweek) every 168 hours.

Safety groups said the rule did not sufficiently increase safety, while the trucking industry criticized the one-size-fits-all approach.

The agency implemented the rule in mid-July 2013 after launching a field study as mandated by the 2012 surface transportation reauthorization law (PL 112-141). The industry and several House leaders objected that the agency implemented the rule before the study was complete—researchers had missed a March 31 deadline for the study's completion—and before the D.C. Circuit Court issued a decision on a challenge of the rules by the American Trucking Association and other industry groups.

In September 2013, fifty House Republicans and one Democrat, Michael H. Michaud of Maine, called on Transportation Secretary Foxx to finish the study.

Researchers submitted their final report—based on a field study—to the agency that month, and the study was released publicly on January 1, 2014. The report said having at least two nighttime breaks from 1 a.m. until 5 a.m. before restarting a work period helps mitigate drivers' fatigue.

"Given that driver fatigue has been documented to be a risk factor for truck crashes, the new restart rule can thus be expected to help improve safety on U.S. roads," the report concluded. Still, the American Trucking Association and Collins said they feared the rules would force more drivers to operate in daytime hours, when more passenger vehicles are on the road and thus increasing the risks for crashes.

Senate Action

The Senate Appropriations Transportation-HUD Subcommittee on June 5, 2014, included an amendment by Sen. Susan Collins, R-Maine, to its 2015 spending bill (S 2438) to delay for one year the Transportation Department's rule on truck drivers' workweeks while its provisions were reevaluated. The panel adopted the amendment, 21–9.

Foxx urged Senate and House Appropriations chairs Barbara A. Mikulski, D-Md., and Harold Rogers, R-Ky., not to include the amendment in the omnibus bill for fiscal 2015. In a December 5, 2014, letter to the appropriators, Foxx wrote that the rule was "essential for the safety of our truck drivers and the safety of families and loved ones who share the road with them." Months earlier, on July 17, the White House had issued a statement that Collins's suspension of the rules' enforcement would boost "the number of hours a truck driver could work from the seventy-hour maximum average on the books today, to eighty-two hours a week."

Other opponents of Collins's amendment cited a reported lack of sleep by a cargo truck driver involved in a highway crash on June 7, 2014, that severely injured comedian Tracy Morgan and killed another passenger in Morgan's vehicle.

The Teamsters union and safety groups backed the rules, but the trucking industry again said the agency did not do enough research before finalizing them.

Several Senate Democrats prepared to undo the provision on the Senate floor. Months later, with time running out to keep the government funded, House and Senate negotiators turned to an eleven-bill omnibus spending package. They included the Collins provision in their compromise omnibus spending measure, suspending until September 30, 2015, the main provisions of the rule mandating that drivers' breaks include two nighttime periods and that drivers could only restart their official workweeks every 168 hours.

Final Action

The House passed the bill in a 219–206 vote late on December 11, 2014. Senate passage followed on December 13 with a vote of 56–40. The president signed the measure into law December 16.

Coast Guard Reauthorization

In early December 2014, Congress cleared legislation that reauthorized the U.S. Coast Guard for one year and required

at least half of all government-subsidized humanitarian food aid shipped overseas to be carried in U.S.-registered vessels. Food-aid groups and farmers had long desired to ship food commodities cheaply, while the U.S. maritime shipping industry wanted guaranteed cargo.

House Measure

The House Transportation and Infrastructure Committee on February 11, 2014, approved a bill (HR 4005), introduced by Coast Guard and Maritime Transportation Subcommittee Chair Duncan Hunter, R-Calif., that would have reauthorized the Coast Guard for two years. The bill would have authorized $8.7 billion annually for fiscal years 2015 and 2016, maintaining the existing level.

Rep. Bill Shuster, R-Pa., said the bill—which was reported to the full House on March 25—would protect small-vessel operators from unnecessary regulations, require the Coast Guard to review its needs in light of existing budget restraints, and require the Coast Guard to report on its fleet of medium-endurance cutters. The bill also would remove a restriction on the length of time for which the Department of Homeland Security could call Coast Guard reservists to active duty during a disaster. It also would require the Coast Guard to report to Congress on its strategy to maintain ice-breaking capabilities in the polar regions.

Under the bill, injured foreign seamen would be able to sue foreign passenger vessel operators for personal injury in the United States only if they did not have the right to sue in either their native country or where the vessel was registered, and provided they were permanent residents of the United States or injured in U.S. waters. The panel rejected, 22–33, an amendment by John Garamendi, D-Calif., that would have eliminated the provision and would have removed a provision extending a cap on penalties that cruise ships would owe seamen for not paying them.

The committee approved a manager's amendment to require the Government Accountability Office to report on the number of maritime jobs that would be created if domestically built U.S. vessels were required to carry liquefied natural gas exports. The amendment also would increase, from 50 percent to 75 percent, the minimum portion of U.S.-procured cargo for humanitarian food aid exports that must be shipped via private commercial vessels. The provision was intended to keep the administration from shifting to a model in which more food staples were purchased in regions closer to people in need—a move the Obama administration advocated as a way to reduce by weeks the transport time for such aid and to provide a market for farmers in developing nations.

In addition, the bill would exempt commercial vessels shorter than 79 feet, and without ballast tanks, from having to obtain EPA permits regarding incidental discharges.

The House passed the measure—named for retiring North Carolina Republican Howard Coble—on April 1 by voice vote. The bill would set the Coast Guard's strength at 43,000 active-duty personnel for fiscal years 2015 and 2016 while reducing the number of authorized commissioned officers from 7,200 to 6,700. There were 6,576 officers as of September 1, 2013.

Bennie Thompson of Mississippi, ranking Democrat on the Homeland Security Committee, complained the legislation did not address port and maritime security and was not first considered by the Homeland Security Committee. "Every day, the men and women of the Coast Guard work to protect our ports and waterways from terrorist attack and other dangers," he said on the chamber floor on April 1.

The legislation also would authorize $25 million for each of the two fiscal years for the Federal Maritime Commission, an independent regulatory agency, and limit commissioners to two terms.

House–Senate Deal

The House bill stalled in the Senate, and the Senate Transportation Committee wrote a new authorization bill (S 2444) that did not include the provisions mandating that 75 percent of U.S. food aid be transported on U.S.-flagged vessels.

However, shipping companies continued to tell lawmakers they needed assurances of food aid cargo to offset a decline in their business, largely due to a drop in military transports. "In order for the major carriers to have faith in maintaining their ships in U.S. flag fleet they need to have a reliable stream of cargo and this provides a reliable stream of cargo," Don Marcus, president of the International Organization of Masters, Mates & Pilots, told the House Transportation and Infrastructure panel on September 10.

The Obama administration continued to urge that more food be purchased closer to where it was needed rather than ship it from the United States.

The House Transportation and Infrastructure Committee and the Senate Commerce, Science, and Transportation Committee announced a deal on December 2 on a bill to reauthorize the Coast Guard for one year. The bill would require strict enforcement of the provision governing transport of food aid overseas by U.S.-registered vessels.

The House passed the measure (HR 5769) on December 3 by a vote of 413–3.

The Senate passed its measure (S 2444) by unanimous consent on December 10 after Republican Bob Corker of Tennessee and Democrat Chris Coons of Delaware blocked the cargo preference enforcement provisions. They said it would unnecessarily increase costs for shipping the food. The Senate's measure left the cargo preference requirement at 50 percent but required the Transportation Department to review cargo shipped by federal agencies to ensure the agencies complied with the rule.

The House subsequently approved the Senate version by voice vote, and the president signed it into law (PL 113-281) December 18, 2014.

FAA Furloughs

Congress in April 2013 cleared legislation to end an intense political battle over the furlough of several air traffic controllers and resulting flight delays.

The Federal Aviation Administration (FAA) had started to furlough air traffic control employees that month to meet spending reduction targets that were mandated by the 2011 Budget Control Act (PL 112-25). Known as sequestration, the law required agencies to cut nondefense discretionary spending by 5.3 percent that fiscal year.

The furloughs resulted in flight delays, and Republicans went on Twitter to blame President Obama, while Democrats accused Republicans of refusing to reopen broader budget negotiations. As both parties faced public outrage about snarled airports, Senate Commerce, Science, and Transportation Chair Jay Rockefeller, D-W.Va., and ranking Republican John Thune of South Dakota joined with Susan Collins, R-Maine, and Mark Udall, D-Colo., to find a solution to end the furloughs.

The Senate on April 25—five days after the furloughs began—passed by unanimous consent a bill (S 853) to allow Transportation Secretary Ray LaHood to transfer up to $253 million from other FAA accounts and unspent airport improvement grants through the end of the fiscal year to avoid further furloughs and traffic control tower closings.

The House, the next day, under suspension of the rules, passed an identical bill (HR 1765) by a vote of 361–41. Under a Senate consent agreement, the House bill was deemed cleared for the president.

House Republicans blamed the administration for mismanaging implementation of sequestration, arguing that the administration needlessly created air traffic problems. "We are taking this action to end the administration's political games" that "threatened" passenger safety and rights, Tom Latham, R-Iowa, said on the House floor on April 26.

Minority Whip Steny Hoyer, D-Md., said on the House floor on April 26 that he opposed the bill "because it fails to address the whole impact of sequester." Rick Larsen, D-Wash., also said on the floor during the vote, "This is a band-aid, and sequestration needs a triple-bypass surgery."

Obama signed the bill into law (PL 113-9) on May 1, but he said it was just a short-term solution to a single problem and that he hoped for a more comprehensive agreement that would forestall all automatic budget cuts before the end of the fiscal year.

Cell Phone Calls on Planes

Lawmakers urged the Transportation Department to issue rules barring cell phone use during airline flights but did not finalize legislation on the issue while the administration sought public input.

House

The House Transportation and Infrastructure Committee on February 11, 2014, approved by voice vote a bill (HR 3676) that would require the Department of Transportation to devise regulations to bar passengers from talking on their cell phones during domestic flights. Flight personnel and law enforcement agents would be exempt from the rules.

Committee Chair Bill Shuster, R-Pa., had introduced the bill before the Federal Communications Commission in December 2013 proposed allowing airlines that had planes equipped to block interference with ground networks to decide whether to permit cell phone usage. The ban had long been maintained to address concerns that cellular phones could interfere with aircraft navigation systems.

Shuster and ranking Democrat Nick J. Rahall II said they were concerned about a disruption to passengers if cell phone use was permitted. Shuster said he supports letting passengers use cell phones to access the Internet but that loud phone conversations would bother fellow passengers. "When it comes to cellphones on planes, tap—don't talk," Shuster said in a statement released February 11, 2014.

FCC Chair Tom Wheeler had said in a prepared statement during a hearing of the House Energy and Commerce Committee's subcommittee on Communications and Technology on December 12, 2013, "I do not want the person in the seat next to me yapping at 35,000 feet any more than anyone else." However, he added, "I firmly believe that if we are serious about eliminating regulations which serve no purpose, the decision is clear."

Administration

The mobile phone industry urged the Federal Communications Commission to lift the prohibition and allow airlines to decide for themselves whether to allow voice calls in flight. CTIA-The Wireless Organization, which represented the nation's cellular providers, said in a statement released December 12 that the FCC should first determine whether "it is technically feasible to operate devices without causing harmful interference to avionics or to wireless networks on the ground."

The Federal Aviation Administration in October 2013 had announced it would begin to allow in-flight use of personal electronics but would continue the ban on voice calls.

Meanwhile, Transportation Secretary Foxx considered whether to continue a ban on in-flight calls, saying his department would base its decision on whether allowing phone calls would be "fair to consumers." In February 2014, the department announced it was seeking public comment on whether to propose a rule to ban voice calls during flights. It continued to seek public and industry input for more than two years.

Sens. Dianne Feinstein, D-Calif., and Lamar Alexander, R-Tenn., members of the Senate Appropriations Committee, in March urged Foxx to move forward with a ban.

Sen. Alexander also introduced a bill (S 1811) to ban the use of cell phones on planes, but the chamber did not act on it.

Meanwhile, Senate appropriators, in the June 5, 2014, committee report accompanying the fiscal 2015 Transportation–Housing and Urban Development spending bill, said they wanted the Department of Transportation to ban cell phone use on planes. "The approval of voice communication over mobile wireless devices during commercial airline flights would be problematic for many of the two million Americans who fly each day and challenging for the airlines," the committee report said.

Internet Sales Taxes

The Senate in 2013 passed legislation that would have permitted states to collect taxes on online sales from out-of-state retailers, but House members failed to resolve differences on the issue, and debate stalled.

Retail store chains, as well as state governments seeking new forms of tax revenue, had long lobbied for a federal law to permit them to impose Internet sales taxes, even if the online company did not have a physical presence in their state. The Senate bill aimed to counter a 1992 Supreme Court decision in *Quill Corp. v. North Dakota* that said a company had to have a physical presence in a state before the state could tax its sales.

Some states, including New York, had ruled that an online seller only needs to have an affiliate in a state—which provided links to a seller's Internet page, for example—to be subject to sales tax collection. The Supreme Court in December 2013 refused to consider a challenge by Amazon and Overstock to a federal court decision that upheld New York's law.

Senate Action

Senate Majority Whip Richard J. Durbin, D-Ill., and Wyoming Republican Michael B. Enzi, on April 16, 2013, introduced a measure (S 743) to allow states to collect sales taxes from most online retailers.

The bill would have allowed states to collect sales taxes from online retailers with more than $1 million in annual sales. Under existing law, online retailers only had to pay state sales taxes in states where the retailer had a physical presence, although typically such taxes were never collected. Meanwhile, many states and localities reported a severe drop in sales tax revenue as shoppers have moved to online retail.

Online companies such as eBay opposed the measure, calling it an attempt to stifle competition. Finance Committee Chair Max Baucus, D-Mont., also strongly opposed the bill, saying businesses would have to hire lawyers and accountants to comply and therefore it would be expensive. Over objections by Baucus and Orrin G. Hatch of Utah, ranking Republican on Finance, Senate Majority Leader Harry Reid, D-Nev., bypassed the committee and brought the bill directly to the floor for a vote.

On April 25, the chamber agreed, 63–30, to limit debate and proceed to the bill. Behind the scenes, several potential amendments threatened agreement on the measure. Baucus and Wyden blocked attempts to move the amendments—primarily because they had not been vetted in committee—including a proposal by Susan Collins, R-Maine, that would delay implementation of the bill for one year.

The Senate on May 6, 2013, passed the bill in a 69–27 vote after adopting a manager's amendment to address several objections. The manager's amendment would have delayed the bill's implementation for six months, barred states from imposing sales tax requirements on remote sellers that are any different from those required of in-state retailers, and exempted retailers making $1 million or less in remote sales.

House

In the House, Rep. Steve Womack, R-Ark., had introduced legislation (HR 684) to allow states to impose taxes on Internet sales and allow states to force out-of-state websites to collect taxes. But House Judiciary Chair Robert W. Goodlatte, R-Va., said he was concerned retailers affected by the bill would have no representation in states in which they are not based.

But Sen. Alexander said the equal protection clauses in the Constitution should protect retailers from discriminatory treatment by states.

Meanwhile, Virginia passed a law that would trigger an increase in the wholesale gasoline tax from 3.5 percent to 5.1 percent in 2015 if Congress did not grant states the authority to collect Internet sales taxes.

In September, Goodlatte released a one-page outline listing seven government principles for handling Internet-related fees and taxes, including a desire to avoid discriminatory taxes. But he never introduced a full bill, and the committee never acted on legislation.

On July 16, 2014, Enzi included provisions of his bill in another bill (S 2609) that would have combined the sales tax provision with an extension of an Internet access tax moratorium for ten years, until November 2024. But there was little appetite in the House to pass such a combined measure.

Internet Access Tax Moratorium

Congress extended to October 1, 2015, a moratorium on Internet access taxes that had been set to expire in November 2014. The extension was approved after House Majority Leader Reid dropped plans to combine the measure with legislation to allow states to tax online retail sales.

HOUSE AND SENATE ACTION

On June 18, 2014, the House Judiciary Committee approved, 30–4, a bill (HR 3086) that would have extended permanently a moratorium on state and local Internet access taxes. The existing moratorium was set to expire November 1. The bill included a provision to eliminate an exemption that allowed seven states to tax some Internet services.

Several Democrats opposed making the moratorium permanent because, they said, the Internet had changed significantly since the moratorium had initially been set in 1998 under the Internet Tax Freedom Act (PL 105-277) to jumpstart online commerce.

The original moratorium included a grandfather clause to give states that were then taxing Internet access some time to transition to other sources of revenue, bill sponsor Robert W. Goodlatte, R-Va., chair of the Judiciary Committee, said during the June 18 hearing. "For those that still haven't, it has been sixteen years, time enough to change their tax codes. If the revenue [that] grandfathered states now reap is truly essential, it should be straightforward for the state to recoup it through a different form of taxation."

In July, the House passed the measure by voice vote. Sen. Ron Wyden, D-Ore., had offered a companion bill (S 1431), but it did not move in the Senate as it became entangled in the debate on taxing online sales. Meanwhile, Reid pushed for a short-term extension of the Internet access tax moratorium—through December 21—to be included in another measure (S 2735), which did not move.

Final Action

An extension of the moratorium was temporarily extended to December 11 as part of a budget resolution (HJ Res 124) that Congress cleared on September 19 and signed into law (PL 113-164). The moratorium then was extended until October 1, 2015, as part of the omnibus spending bill (HR 83) that Obama signed into law December 16 (PL 113-235).

Email Privacy Safeguards

Senate Judiciary Chair Patrick J. Leahy, D-Vt., and Rep. Kevin Yoder, R-Kan., in 2013 introduced legislation that would have required a warrant for government officials to obtain an individual's emails from an Internet service provider. But neither bill made it through Congress.

The Senate Judiciary Committee on April 25, 2013, approved by voice vote Leahy's bill (S 607) to amend a 1986 privacy law known as the Electronic Communication Privacy Act (PL 99-508) and require government officials to obtain a search warrant before accessing any electronic data.

Under existing law, unopened emails sent in the previous 180 days required a warrant, while older and already opened messages required a subpoena. The bill would have required the government agency to obtain a warrant from a judge to obtain electronic communications stored by an Internet provider.

The bill also included a provision that would have required the government to notify individuals within ten days of obtaining a search warrant for their emails.

Interest groups across the partisan spectrum supported the measure. The committee had approved a similar bill near the end of the 112th Congress, which never made it to the Senate floor for a vote. Likewise, Leahy's bill was not taken up by the full Senate before the end of the 113th Congress.

Yoder's bill (HR 1852) drew 272 cosponsors but remained locked up in the House Judiciary subcommittee.

STOCK Act Revisions

Congress in 2013 nullified a provision of a law that required that financial disclosures of legislative and executive branch staff be made available to the public on the Internet. The change was in response to a report that warned that posting the information could endanger national security.

The law (PL 112-105), called the STOCK Act—or Stop Trading on Congressional Knowledge—required legislative- and executive-branch staff members who are paid more than $119,553 annually to disclose any assets, liabilities, and financial transactions worth more than $1,000. The information would be posted in a searchable and downloadable online database.

The law was expected to prevent public officials from using for personal benefit any nonpublic information they learned as a result of their jobs. The 112th Congress swiftly passed the measure in the wake of a CBS *60 Minutes* story about public officials' stock trading habits. Critics, however, said they feared staff members would be vulnerable to cybercrimes if they were required to post such information online.

The Senior Executives Association led a coalition of groups that filed suit against the section of the law requiring Internet posting of senior executive branch officials' financial disclosure forms. In March, the National Academy of Public Administration released a report indicating that public disclosures of financial information could endanger national security or staff members' safety.

Senate Majority Leader Harry Reid, D-Nev., responded on April 11 by introducing a measure (S 716) to scale back the law. His bill would exempt congressional and executive branch staff from disclosing information but would leave intact requirements for the president, vice president, members of Congress, congressional candidates, and individuals in Senate-confirmed positions. The bill would delay the implementation date of the mandate to January 2014 and repeal the law's requirement that the public be allowed to search, sort, and download financial disclosure information on the Internet.

The STOCK Act would still require lawmakers, judges, and top officials to report stock and securities transactions within forty-five days and report their home mortgages. Another provision, also left intact, expanded the list of crimes for which members of Congress would lose their congressional pension benefits.

The Senate quickly passed the bill, by unanimous consent, the same day it was introduced and without discussion. The House quietly cleared the measure the next day, also by unanimous consent. President Obama signed the measure into law (PL 113-7) on April 15.

2015–2016

The 114th Congress ended years of debate by passing a major, five-year authorization of surface transportation programs. The $281 billion bill relied on a variety of methods for shoring up the Highway Trust Fund and provided a measure of long-term certainty for state and local transportation officials.

Lawmakers also approved two short-term authorization extensions for the Federal Aviation Administration to keep programs operating through September 2017. Lawmakers were unable to come to terms on a longer-term agreement when House Transportation Chair Shuster proposed transferring management of the nation's air traffic control system to a private, nonprofit corporation. But both parties, with prompting from the administration, easily agreed to include several additional safety requirements in the wake of terrorist attacks at European airports in early 2016.

Agreement also was reached to repeal a Transportation Department rule on commercial truck drivers' workweeks until the department could prove it would make highways safer.

Lawmakers also cleared a two-year reauthorization for the Coast Guard, including funds for a new polar icebreaker to help the United States defend its interests in the Arctic where Russian activity had increased.

The House and Senate agreed to permanently ban Internet access taxes but failed to reach agreements on a measure to lift a ban on Internet sales taxes. Lawmakers could not agree on whether to require government agencies to obtain a warrant to access individuals' emails but easily cleared legislation to bar the use of automated software that circumvents online security measures on ticket-selling websites.

Surface Transportation Reauthorization

After passing a series of short-term extensions over the previous decade, Congress in 2015 cleared a five-year, $281 billion surface transportation authorization bill to fund and rebuild roads, bridges, and mass transit systems. In a December 1, 2015, statement, the House and Senate transportation committee leaders of both parties said the bill—called the FAST Act for Fixing America's Surface Transportation—would provide "long-term certainty for states and local governments" and ensure "improvements to the programs that sustain our roads and bridges and passenger rail system."

A long-term measure previously had eluded lawmakers due to disagreements over how to shore up the Highway Trust Fund. While some transportation advocates called for an increase on motor fuels taxes, which had not increased since 1993, Congress turned to other solutions, such as changing customs user fees and pulling funds from the Federal Reserve. Some conservative groups repeatedly called for the federal government to withdraw its involvement in transportation programs and hand it completely over to states, but House Transportation and Infrastructure Committee Chair Shuster

rejected that idea. About half of states' funds for maintaining roads comes from the federal government.

The Obama administration again proposed a one-time, 14 percent tax on earnings held by U.S. corporations overseas to raise an estimated $238.4 billion. But Ways and Means Chair Ryan rejected the idea.

The bill also included a provision to reauthorize for four years the Export-Import Bank, which finances U.S. exports by lending to foreign buyers.

Senate Committee Action

The Senate Environment and Public Works Committee on June 24, 2015, approved, 20–0, a six-year, $278 billion surface transportation reauthorization measure (S 1647) that did not include provisions for paying for the measure.

The bill would have changed elements of the 2012 MAP-21 authorization—known as Moving Ahead for Progress in the 21st Century Act or MAP-21 (PL 112-141)—by adding a $2 billion authorization for a freight program, shortening environmental reviews for projects, and granting Congress final authority over a new grant program for high-priority projects.

A Congressional Budget Office report said the highway portion of the bill would have cost $157 billion from 2016 through 2020.

The Senate Commerce, Science, and Transportation Committee on July 15 approved, in a 13–11 vote, a bill (S 1732) that included the highway and passenger rail safety provisions of the six-year highway reauthorization bill. Senate Finance Chair Orrin Hatch, R-Utah, however, warned that the overall package could require tax hikes that Republicans would oppose, and he pushed for a three-year measure with a project cost of about $40 billion.

STOPGAP BILLS

First Extension. As lawmakers deliberated on how to fund a six-year bill, the existing authorization for highway programs was set to expire July 31. The House on July 15 passed, in a 312–119 vote, a five-month extension (HR 3038) to keep the highway and transit programs operating until December 18. The bill, sponsored by Ryan and Shuster, would have provided the Highway Trust Fund with $8 billion from tax compliance measures and reduced spending of Transportation Security Administration fees in 2025 and 2026.

Sen. McConnell, however, resisted moving on the House bill and urged immediate action on the six-year reauthorization bill (S 1647), which was attached to a swiftly moving House bill (HR 22) that aimed to encourage businesses to hire military veterans. On July 21, he announced Republican and Democratic leaders had reached an agreement on a six-year bill that would include $40 billion in general revenue to cover the Highway Trust Fund for about three years and a three-year package of revenue raisers that would be determined later.

When the Senate did not take up the House's five-month extension (HR 3038), the House passed a three-month extension (HR 3236) on July 29 before leaving for the August recess. The Senate agreed to the House's short-term extension in a 91–4 vote on July 30, and the president signed it into law (PL 114-41) on July 31.

SECOND EXTENSION

While lawmakers continued to work toward a longer-term agreement, the chambers had to pass another extension. The House on October 27, 2015, approved a three-week authorization extension (HR 3819) to the Senate, which included a three-year extension—from December 31, 2015, to December 31, 2018—of the deadline for railroads to install new train safety technology known as positive train control. Congress had mandated the new technology as part of a 2008 law (PL 110-432) after a train collision in a Chatsworth neighborhood of Los Angeles killed twenty-five people and injured another 130 people. The National Transportation Safety Board said new technology could have prevented the accident.

Railroad officials said they would have to shut down service if they did not get an extension on a deadline to install new train safety technology, and Rep. Shuster said a variety of groups, including farmers relying on fertilizer shipments and drinking water systems needing chlorine shipments, were anxious about the uncertain rail service.

The Senate cleared the measure by voice vote, and the president signed it into law (PL 114-73) on October 29.

House Action

The House Transportation and Infrastructure Committee on October 22 approved a $330 billion, six-year authorization bill (HR 3763) by voice vote. The Congressional Budget Office estimated that fuel tax revenue, however, would leave the Highway Trust Fund about $85 billion short. Shuster said he hoped Ways and Means Chair Ryan would find a new revenue source.

The committee approved by voice vote an amendment by Rep. Reid Ribble, R-Wis., that would allow fire trucks and other emergency vehicles weighing up to 86,000 pounds, or forty-three tons, to travel on interstate highways—up from 80,000 pounds or 40 tons. The panel also approved by voice vote a manager's amendment to establish corridors along major national highways for electric, hydrogen, and natural gas vehicle fueling and recharging stations.

The House on November 4 passed its measure as an amendment to the Senate-passed six-year reauthorization measure (HR 22) in a 363–64 vote, including it with a package of amendments to the Senate bill and agreeing to go to conference with the Senate to iron out differences between the chamber's bills.

House–Senate Negotiations

The Senate on November 10 agreed by unanimous consent to go to conference with the House to resolve differences between their six-year reauthorization bills.

The House highway bill (HR 3763) would authorize about $339 billion, while the Senate bill (HR 22) would authorize $367 billion. The biggest challenge continued to be reaching agreement on a package of offsets to fully fund the bill. When they were unable to reach such an agreement, the conferees shortened the authorization to five years with an estimated $305 billion of funding to be provided with available offsets.

SHORT-TERM EXTENSION

While negotiators hammered out differences between the two chambers' bills, the House and Senate provided another short-term authorization extension (HR 3996)—until December 4—for highway and transit programs. The House passed the measure by voice vote on November 16, and the Senate granted voice-vote approval on November 19. The president signed the measure into law (PL 114-87) the next day.

FINAL LONG-TERM AGREEMENT

The House on December 3 adopted the conference report on the bill (HR 22—H Rept 114-4) in a 359–65 vote, and the Senate followed suit that night in an 83–16 vote—just one day before the existing authorization was to expire. Obama signed the bill into law (PL 114-94) on December 4, 2015.

The bill authorized the transfer of more than $70 billion from Treasury's general fund and $300 million from the Leaking Underground Storage Tank Trust Fund to cover projected shortfalls in the Highway Trust Fund through fiscal year 2020 and to fully fund the measure's estimated cost. The gas tax also was extended through September 30, 2022. The measure was estimated to increase highway spending to states by 5 percent over existing levels and transit spending by 8 percent over existing levels.

The measure also reauthorized Amtrak and restructured its funding, renewed the charter for the Export-Import Bank, and rolled back a reduction in the crop insurance program that had been targeted as an offset for the previous month's budget deal.

Other major provisions of the Fixing America's Surface Transportation (FAST) Act included the following.

Highway Programs

The measure authorized a gradual increase of guaranteed spending from the Highway Trust Fund, from $42 billion in fiscal 2016 to $46 billion in fiscal 2020.

The measure also converted the Surface Transportation Program into a block grant program, under which states and municipalities could decide how to spend funds and required that higher funding be distributed to areas with higher populations.

A new competitive grant program was created by the bill for national freight and highways projects to improve the nation's freight corridors.

Public Transportation

The measure authorized $11.8 billion for Federal Transit Administration programs for fiscal 2016, rising to $12.6 billion by fiscal 2020. It also created a new competitive grant program to upgrade aging bus fleets.

Financing and Offsets

In addition to continuing the gas tax, the measure extended the retail sales tax on heavy highway vehicles—such as trucks, trailers, and certain tractors—and manufacturers' excise tax on heavy-vehicle tires as well as an annual use tax on heavy vehicles.

To offset the cost of the bill's transfer from the general fund to replenish the Highway Trust Fund, the measure included provisions to reduce spending or raise revenues. It included, for example,

- a cap on the size of the Federal Research Surplus Fund, at $10 billion;
- a reduction of the Federal Reserve's 6 percent dividend rate paid to large banks with more than $10 billion in consolidated assets;
- a sale of oil from the Strategic Petroleum Reserve in 2016, 2017, and 2023 through 2025;
- an indexing of the U.S. Customs service user fees to inflation;
- an increase of motor vehicle safety penalties to $21,000 per violation per day from $5,000 per violation per day and an increase of the maximum penalty to $105,000 from $35,000. The measure also required civil penalties to be deposited into the Highway Trust fund rather than the Treasury general fund.
- authority for the State Department to deny passport applications or revoke passports of individuals with more than $50,000 of unpaid federal taxes.

Highway Safety and Crude Oil Transport

The agreement consolidated nine grant programs of the Federal Motor Carrier Safety Administration into four.

It also required the National Highway and Traffic Safety Administration to study marijuana-impaired driving and whether to set an impairment standard.

Environmental Review

The measure retained provisions under the previous surface transportation authorization to improve coordination and expedite environmental reviews to accelerate the approval of transportation infrastructure projects. The measure included some process modifications.

It also established a pilot program under which a limited number of states would conduct environmental reviews if their laws were equivalent to federal standards.

Crude Oil and Hazardous Materials

The agreement set new requirements to improve the safety of moving crude oil on railroads. Such requirements included protective thermal blankets for new oil tank cars, the testing of advanced braking technology for crude oil railway cars, and a requirement that railroads notify state emergency responders about hazardous material being transported through the state.

In addition, the Pipeline and Hazardous Materials Safety Administration would have to develop rules requiring each rail carrier that transports certain flammable liquids to maintain an oil spill response plan.

The Government Accountability Office also would have to evaluate electronically controlled pneumatic brake systems, including their safety benefits compared to conventional braking systems.

Amtrak Authorization

The agreement reauthorized Amtrak (the National Railroad Passenger Corporation) for five years. It also restructured Amtrak funding according to its major lines of business to provide greater transparency and accountability. Accordingly, it authorized a new Northeast Corridor Improvement Fund account and a new National Network account, the latter to cover expenses related to Amtrak's state-supported and long-distance routes.

It also included provisions to promote the development of more passenger rail service in the United States. For example, it created three competitive grant programs for the construction of rail infrastructure and intercity rail passenger service.

Congestion Mitigation

The agreement prioritized the spending of funds from the Congestion Mitigation and Air Quality Improvement Act in areas where vehicle emissions significantly contribute to air quality programs.

Tribal Transportation Self-Governance

The agreements established a program under which Indian tribes would receive and administer transportation funds for their own jurisdictions. To participate, an Indian tribe was required to sign an agreement with the federal government that included an annual funding authorization and identification of programs, services, functions, and activities the tribe would administer.

Safety Standards

The measure authorized the Department of Transportation to assume state safety oversight activities for a rail system if the system operates in more than two states and the state had failed to provide adequate oversight. The department also could withhold up to 25 percent of urbanized area formula grant funding from states that do not comply with federal safety laws.

Public Transportation Innovation

Under the measure, $28 million was authorized annually for the research and development of new transportation projects, including the deployment of low- or zero-emission vehicles. The Transportation department was required to designate up to two facilities at higher education institutions to conduct testing and analysis of components for such low- or no-emission vehicles.

Seniors and Individuals with Disabilities

The measure authorized $263 million to $286 million annually for services to improve the mobility of seniors and individuals with disabilities.

It also authorized a pilot grant program for innovative projects to improve the coordination of transportation services and nonemergency medical transportation and authorized $2 million to $3.5 million for the program annually.

Truck Driver Hours

At the end of the 114th Congress, lawmakers cleared a bill that would repeal—unless the Transportation Department could prove highways would be safer—a 2011 Transportation Department rule that set new restrictions on commercial truck drivers' workweeks. The lawmakers cleared the conditional repeal after extending a suspension on the rules it had issued at the end of the previous Congress.

The 2011 Transportation Department rule—initially implemented in 2013—mandated that truck drivers take a thirty-minute break from driving during the first eight hours of their workday and a thirty-four-hour break once a week. The thirty-four-hour break had to include two nighttime periods from 1 a.m. to 5 a.m., and drivers could only take a thirty-four-hour break (restarting their official workweek) every 168 hours. Previously drivers had to take at least thirty-four hours off after working sixty hours in a seven-day period.

Several lawmakers and industry groups raised concerns that the rules would instead make roads less safe because truck drivers would be forced to be on the road during more daytime hours, when highways were more likely to be congested with passenger traffic. They also said the rules were implemented before the department had completed a congressionally mandated study on the rule's effectiveness.

The agency in mid-2013 issued a report concluding that a field study backed up its conclusions that the rules would make highways more safe by reducing driver fatigue. However, in July 2015, the Government Accountability Office released a report concluding the agency did not meet certain research standards when conducting the study.

In 2015, Congress in the fiscal 2016 Transportation appropriations measure (PL 114-113) extended the suspension on truck driver hours it had issued in the 2015 omnibus appropriations bill.

In 2016, a provision in a stopgap spending bill (HR 2028) would repeal the DOT rules unless the Department "demonstrated statistically significant improvement in all outcomes related to safety, operator fatigue, driver health and longevity, and work schedule." The provision still would require a thirty-four-hour break but let truck drivers decide when to use their breaks.

Safety advocates said repealing the rule would make highways less safe, while the trucking industry said it would allow truckers to drive fewer daytime hours.

The provision was included in the stopgap spending bill that the House passed on December 8, 2016, in a 326–96 vote and the Senate cleared the next day in 63–36 vote. The president signed the bill into law (PL 114-254) on December 10.

Coast Guard Reauthorization

Congress on February 1, 2016, cleared a bill (HR 4188) to reauthorize the Coast Guard and the Federal Maritime Commission for two years, as well as to finance a new polar icebreaker to help the United States defend its interests in the Arctic.

President Obama in September 2015 had proposed expediting the purchase of an icebreaker from 2022 to 2020 and acquiring more icebreakers to enable the United States to operate year-round and protect American interests in the Arctic from Russia. The loss of ice due to climate change had increased commercial activity in the region, with Russia operating a fleet of more than forty icebreakers while the U.S. had two functioning icebreakers—the 399-foot *Polar Star* and the 420-foot *Healy*.

"The growth of human activity in the Arctic region will require highly engaged stewardship to maintain the open seas necessary for global commerce and scientific research, allow for search and rescue activities, and provide for regional peace and stability," the White House said in a September 1, 2015, statement. "Accordingly, meeting these challenges requires the United States to develop and maintain capacity for year-round access to greater expanses with polar regions."

The Homeland Security Department in 2013 projected expanding the fleet to six vessels, and the Congressional Research Service estimated the cost of each icebreaker to be between $900 million and $1 billion.

House Action

Republicans Duncan Hunter of California and Bill Shuster of Pennsylvania and Democrats Peter A. DeFazio of Oregon and John Garamendi of California introduced a two-year, $8.7 billion Coast Guard reauthorization bill (HR 1987) in April 2015.

The House Transportation and Infrastructure Committee on April 30 approved, by voice vote, the measure, which included provisions that aimed to modernize aging fleets.

The measure also included provisions intended to encourage involvement of the U.S. Merchant Marine—a fleet of U.S.-owned and -operated vessels—to participate in the country's liquefied natural gas export trade. "Very simply put, if we're going to export one of our great national assets, natural gas, then we ought to also use that export to enhance another extremely important national strategic asset, which is our merchant marine," said Rep.

John Garamendi, D-Calif., during the committee's April 30 meeting, according to *CQ Roll Call.*

Rep. Janice Hahn, D-Calif., introduced and later withdrew an amendment that would have created a compensation fund for World War II survivors who were Merchant Marines.

The House passed the measure by voice vote, under suspension of the rules and without amendment, on May 18, 2015. The measure was then sent to the Senate, but the Senate did not act on it.

Senate Action

The Senate Commerce, Science, and Transportation Committee on June 25 approved a similar two-year Coast Guard reauthorization bill (S 1611), sponsored by Committee Chair John Thune, R-S.D., that would maintain funding at $8.7 billion annually and seek to update the Coast Guard's fleet as well as its command structure.

The bill included the text of another bill (S 834), also sponsored by Thune, that would have reauthorized through fiscal 2023 the Sport Fish Restoration and Boating Trust Fund, which collected about $600 million annually from fees on fishing and boating equipment and used the revenue for conservation and boat safety programs.

The committee adopted by voice vote an amendment to authorize $14 million over two years to develop a new ice-breaker. The bill moved to the floor, but the Senate did not act on it, and bill managers from both chambers and both parties negotiated a new measure (HR 4188) that was sent to the full House and Senate for approval.

Final Action

Lawmakers negotiated a bipartisan measure (HR 4188) that reauthorized the U.S. Coast Guard and Federal Maritime Commission (FMC) through the end of fiscal 2017. It authorized $8.7 billion annually for the Coast Guard and $24.7 million annually for the FMC. The bill also authorized funding to begin acquiring a new polar icebreaker and mandated a study of alternative icebreaking operations.

The House passed the measure by voice vote on December 10, 2015.

The Senate passed that bill by voice vote on December 18, 2015, after quickly adopting a substitute amendment that included technical changes. The House cleared the Senate version on February 1, and the president signed the measure into law (PL 114-120) on February 8.

Among its major provisions, the bill:

- authorized $4 million in fiscal 2016 and $10 million in fiscal 2017 to begin acquiring a new polar icebreaker;
- required the Department of Homeland Security to evaluate the icebreaker *Polar Sea* and determine whether it would be cost-effective to reactivate that icebreaker;
- required the department to submit a report by the National Academy of Sciences to compare various options for conducting icebreaking operations,

including transferring *Polar Sea* to a private entity and leasing it back;

- created a pilot program to evaluate a "radio gateway" that would allow multiagency collaboration and secure communications using commercially available, off-the-shelf technology;
- required the creation of a new master's degree education program in maritime operations for members and employees, as well as a training course on the working of Congress;
- required the Coast Guard to produce a long-term major acquisitions plan for each of the next twenty-one fiscal years, including the numbers and types of cutters and aircraft that would be decommissions, ships and planes to be acquired, and the funding necessary.
- required the Coast Guard to determine the effectiveness of the oil spill response in the Great Lakes;
- required the Transportation Department to devise guidelines and a plan to promote the transport of liquefied natural gas to the United States on U.S.-flagged vessels.

FAA Reauthorization

Congress during the 114th Congress approved two short-term authorization extensions for the FAA—maintaining authorization for programs through September 2017, while putting off a longer-term reauthorization until the 115th Congress.

Debate on a long-term bill was particularly complicated by an effort by House Transportation Chair Shuster to transfer management of the nation's air traffic control system from the FAA to a private, nonprofit corporation supported by airlines and other airport users.

House Action

House Transportation Chair Shuster on February 3, 2016, introduced a six-year, $69 billion FAA reauthorization bill (HR 4441), which included a provision that would have transferred the air traffic control operation of FAA to a separate corporate entity, which could issue bonds and borrow money in the private sector. With the ability to raise funds, the provision's supporters said, the FAA could obtain capital to fund projects such as a new navigation system known as Next Gen. Under the bill, the FAA would have retained safety oversight.

"Separating air traffic control into an independent, not-for-profit corporation and leaving behind the regulatory [and] the safety aspect in government, is something that we need to do. . . not only to improve the travel and movement of commerce, but also for our manufacturers to get out from under this red tape," Shuster said when introducing the bill February 3. Otherwise, he said, "I believe they will lose their competitive edge, and America will lose its lead in the world in aviation."

But appropriators from both parties and chambers, as well as lobbyists from the general aviation industry, balked at the spin-off proposal.

Peter A. DeFazio of Oregon, ranking Democrat on the Transportation and Infrastructure Committee, and Rep. Rick Larsen of Washington, ranking Democrat on the aviation subcommittee, said the provisions would stymie progress on the underlying bill, which had broad support. Several of the bill's other provisions aimed to expedite the FAA process for certifying aircraft and other equipment, establish an advisory committee, create new performance objectives, and integrate drones into the national airspace, for example.

The House Transportation and Infrastructure Committee approved the bill (HR 4441) on February 11 by a vote of 32–26. Republicans Sam Graves of Missouri and Todd Rokita of Indiana joined Democrats in opposing the bill. The panel rejected, in a 25–34 vote, an alternative by DeFazio that would have restructured the FAA's procurement and personnel practices and would have moved the Airport and Airway Trust Fund out of reach of appropriations and budget directives. He said he aimed to ensure revenue collected from passengers would be invested in the aviation system, but Shuster said that under DeFazio's bill, the trust fund would become a sort of ATM for the FAA administrator.

The panel adopted, 33–26, an amendment by Delegate Eleanor Holmes Norton, D-D.C., that would ban vaporizers and electronic cigarettes on passenger flights.

House Ways and Means Committee Chair Kevin Brady, R-Texas, blocked the six-year reauthorization from moving directly to the floor when he announced his panel had jurisdiction over the FAA spin-off proposal.

Shuster put his six-year-reauthorization on hold as leaders began to consider a short-term renewal to avoid a shutdown of FAA services on April 1.

Short-Term Authorization

Senate Action. Senate Commerce, Science, and Transportation Committee Chair Thune and ranking Democrat Bill Nelson of Florida on March 9 introduced a two-year, $33.1 billion reauthorization measure (S 2658). The committee on March 16 approved the bill, which included provisions related to unmanned aircraft, the FAA's equipment certification process, aircraft control system technology, and consumer protection. The bill did not include a provision for a spin-off of air traffic control, as included in Shuster's six-year reauthorization measure.

The committee approved by voice vote an amendment by Thune that would create FAA guidelines for sharing cybersecurity information between the airline industry and government regulators on a voluntary basis.

The committee rejected amendments by Edward J. Markey, D-Mass., that would have allowed the Transportation Department to impose certain airline fees and required airlines to disclose to the FAA any cyberattacks on aircraft systems.

House Action

In the House, meanwhile, Shuster put on hold his long-term reauthorization while he and Brady on March 10, 2016, introduced a bill (HR 4721) to extend the FAA's authorization through July 15, 2016—without the provision on the air traffic control spin-off. The House passed the bill on March 14 under suspension of the rules. The bill would have authorized through March 31, 2017, the taxes used to raise revenue for the Airport and Airway Trust Fund and the authority for money to be released from that fund. "Without this bill, the authority to collect aviation fees will lapse, depriving the trust fund of more than $300 million per day," Shuster said on the House floor before passage.

The Senate on March 17 passed an amended version of the House bill to extend authorization through July 15 of that year. Under the Senate bill, the authority for taxes used to raise revenue for the trust fund would be extended only through July 15, 2016. The House on March 21 cleared the measure. Obama signed the short-term extension into law (PL 114-141) on March 30.

Second Short-Term Reauthorization

Senate Action. On April 6, the Senate agreed by voice vote to proceed to a $33.1 billion bill (HR 636) to reauthorize aviation programs through fiscal 2017. The bill contained provisions that would have directed the agency to craft new metrics to streamline certification of new aircraft technology and to require the FAA to work with NASA to develop an air traffic control system for drones, or unmanned aircraft systems. The bill would give the FAA authority to create safety regulations for drone operations and manufacturers. The bill also would keep the U.S. air traffic control system under the authority of the FAA; Thune said he wanted to avoid the contentious issue, which could stall the FAA reauthorization.

The bill also included consumer protection provisions, including a provision that would require airlines to standardize information displays about fees and a proposed study of airport accessibility for individuals with disabilities.

On April 19, the Senate passed its two-year reauthorization measure by a vote of 95–3, after nearly two weeks of debate that led to the adoption of several amendments. On April 7, the Senate adopted, by a vote of 85–10, an amendment by Thune to require the Transportation Security Administration to improve vetting of airport employees and develop practices for employee security screening. The amendment included language from a bill (S 2361) that the Senate Commerce, Science, and Transportation Committee had adopted in March.

Senators also approved, 91–5, an amendment by Martin Heinrich, D-N.M., that would increase the number of TSA security teams that could be stationed at airports, train stations, and port facilities.

On the same day, the Senate adopted five amendments en bloc by voice vote, including:

- a proposal by Pennsylvania Sens. Bob Casey and Patrick J. Toomey to require commercial airlines to create another barrier in front of cockpit doors;
- an amendment by Wyden that would direct the FAA to conduct a review of heads-up guidance displays for airplane pilots;
- an amendment by Collins that would clarify regulations affecting weather observers under contract with the FAA;
- an amendment by Jon Tester, D-Mont., to require the Government Accountability Office to determine the feasibility and cost to use advanced imaging technology at airports; and
- an amendment by Dean Heller, R-Nev., to require the FAA to explore incorporating drone-related occupations into its Veterans Employment Program, which helps military veterans transition into the civilian workforce.

The Senate adopted twelve more amendments on April 11, including a proposal by John Hoeven, R-N.D., to extend the unmanned aircraft system program.

House Action

Meanwhile, Shuster could not convince House leaders to bring his six-year reauthorization bill (HR 4441) to the floor for a vote.

On July 6, nine days before the FAA's authority was set to expire, the leaders of the House and Senate transportation committees agreed to move forward a bill to reauthorize FAA programs through September 2017. The agreement did not include Shuster's provision to spin off the agency's air traffic control duties.

On July 11, the House adopted by voice vote a resolution (H Res 818) that would carry out the agreement, using HR 636 as the vehicle to extend the authorization another fourteen months. The measure included security provisions the House had passed in separate bills, including language from a bill (HR 4698) that would require the FAA to check on security practices in overseas airports that service direct flights to the United States.

The bill also increased the number of bomb-sniffing dog teams at airports, directed the TSA to work with the private sector to market its trusted traveler program known as TSA PreCheck, and set more ground rules for drone use near airports and critical infrastructure.

Under the bill, spending was maintained at the existing level of about $13.6 billion annually, including $3.35 billion for the Airport and Airways Trust fund. Taxes on fuel and tickets were kept at existing levels, as was a $4.50-per-flight segment cap on passenger facilities charges that airports can use to fund local projects.

Final Action

The Senate on July 13 voted 89–4 to clear the legislation (HR 636), which the president signed into law (PL 114-90) on July 15.

Thune said the bill was not as broad as he would have liked but that its safety provisions were imperative after terrorist attacks at European airports earlier in the year.

Internet Access Tax Moratorium

The Senate on February 11, 2016, voted to permanently ban Internet access taxes after a moratorium was consistently extended over twenty years.

On June 9, 2015, the House approved the Permanent Internet Tax Freedom Act (HR 235), which permanently banned state and local taxation of Internet access and barred multiple or discriminatory taxes on online commerce. A companion bill (S 431) was introduced in the Senate but did not move.

Sen. Hatch later that year said he would push to include a permanent ban on Internet access taxes in a spending bill to cover the remainder of the fiscal year. Instead, language from the measure was included in the conference report on the Trade Facilitation and Trade Enforcement Act (HR 644). Several lawmakers objected to its inclusion in the trade bill because they had hoped to combine the Internet access tax ban with an online sales tax mandate. Opposition was largely led by supporters of Sen. Enzi's bill (S 698) to authorize state collection of online sales taxes.

Nevertheless, the House passed the measure on December 11, 2015, in a 256–158 vote. The Senate passed the measure on February 11, 2016, in a 75–20 vote.

FCC Commissioner Ajit Pai said in a statement released the same day, "This confirms a national consensus that state and local taxes on Internet access should be taken off the table once and for all. These taxes would make . . . broadband more expensive, reducing consumers' ability and willingness to get online. This, in turn, would reduce private sector investment in deploying broadband, especially in rural areas, and inhibit entrepreneurship."

Obama signed the measure into law (PL 114-125) on February 24.

Internet Sales Tax

Lawmakers continued to debate whether to lift a ban on Internet sales taxes but failed to agree on a measure. A similar effort had failed in the previous session. Meanwhile, multiple states sought court rulings to give them power to enforce sales tax laws.

Senate

Sen. Michael B. Enzi, R-Wyo., in March 2015 introduced a bill (S 698) to allow states to collect taxes on Internet sales, but it languished through that year and the next. Sen. Lamar Alexander in November 2016 urged the House to pass a bill and send it to the Senate, and thus enable Majority Leader McConnell to fulfill a commitment he had made earlier in the year.

McConnell had committed in February to a vote in order to expedite the completion of a conference report on a customs and trade measure (PL 114-125). Minority Whip Richard Durbin, D-Ill., had been calling for the language of Enzi's Internet sales tax bill to be included in that customs and trade package, which contained another provision to permanently extend a moratorium on Internet access taxes.

House

Rep. Jason Chaffetz, R-Utah, introduced a bill (HR 2775) on June 15, 2015, that would allow states to collect taxes on Internet sales by companies that did not have a physical presence in the state. But Chaffetz's bill, which would have based sales taxes on the location of the buyer, could not gain sufficient traction, and Judiciary Chair Goodlatte released his own proposal to ensure out-of-state sellers would only have to deal with home-state tax collectors and auditors. Under his proposal, sales taxes would have to be based on the rate in effect in the seller's home state on all online transactions, with proceeds funneled to the buyer's home state.

An alliance of 107 Internet and direct-mail businesses, such as Direct Marketing Association and NetChoice, a coalition of Internet sellers, supported Goodlatte's bill, but the proposal did not gain support among lawmakers.

"Only Congress can bring certainty and rationality to this situation. What's needed is a simple solution that works for all stakeholders," the alliance said in a letter to Goodlatte.

House Majority Leader Kevin McCarthy refused to bring either proposal directly to the floor, urging the committee to resolve differences between the proposals.

Email Privacy Safeguards

The House in April 2015 passed a measure (HR 699) that would have required government agencies to obtain a warrant to access emails, but a similar measure stalled in the Senate amid opposition from law enforcement agencies. A portion of the measure was included in the fiscal 2016 omnibus spending bill enacted in December 2015 and required government agencies funded under the Financial Services section of the bill to obtain a warrant to obtain information from Internet service providers.

House Action

The House Judiciary committee on April 13 voted 28–0 to approve the bill (HR 699) introduced by Rep. Kevin Yoder, R-Kan., that would have updated the Electronic Communications Privacy Act of 1986 (PL 99-508) to address when and how law enforcement agencies could access emails.

Under existing law, access rules depended on how long the email had been stored and whether it was stored in the cloud, which is a network of remote servers. The bill would have required law enforcement to obtain a warrant regardless of how long and where the emails had been stored.

The committee approved, by voice vote, a substitute amendment to Yoder's original bill that removed language that would have required law enforcement agencies to notify the targets of investigations when they issued a warrant to an Internet service provider for that individuals' online communications. However, the providers would be allowed to tell their customers about the warrant unless barred from doing so by a court, according to Goodlatte.

On April 27, the House passed the bill by a 419–0 vote.

Senate Action

Several members of the Senate Judiciary Committee voiced support for a similar bill (S 356), introduced by Sen. Mike Lee, R-Utah, as did several technology trade groups. But privacy advocates raised concerns, particularly about the removal of the requirement that individuals targeted in investigations be notified.

"The result is that Americans have no guarantee that they will even know when the government accesses their most sensitive information, be they intimate photos, financial documents, or even personal emails," ACLU legislative counsel Neema Singh Guliani said in a statement released July 9.

Meanwhile, several federal agencies, including the Securities and Exchange Commission, raised concerns about a provision in the bill that would have required that they obtain a warrant to access information directly from a service provider. Government officials said civil agencies do not have the authority to obtain warrants. But Sen. John Cornyn, R-Texas, said exempting civil agencies would have been unconstitutional.

When the Senate Judiciary Committee took up the bill, Chair Charles E. Grassley, R-Iowa, granted a request by Lee to delay a vote while members tried to reach agreement on potential changes. Several members and outside groups were particularly concerned about an amendment by Cornyn to expand the ability of the FBI to use national security letters to obtain information about online communications. National security letters are used by intelligence agencies to obtain information about online customers without a court order.

Cornyn said during a committee meeting May 26, when the bill was scheduled to be considered, that the amendment was a response to a concern raised by FBI Director James B. Comey that "an oversight" in the statutes was "needlessly hamstringing our counterintelligence and counterterrorism efforts."

Another amendment aimed to create an emergency exception to the warrant requirement without allowing communications service providers to challenge the request. More than a dozen technology companies wrote in a May 25 letter to Senate Judiciary leaders that existing exceptions already worked, and that the amendment would leave providers "no ability to resist or challenge potentially unreasonable or unlawful demands."

Disagreement on those provisions derailed debate on the bill, and it never reached a vote by the panel.

Final Action

A portion of language from Yoder's bill was tucked into the fiscal 2016 spending bill (HR 2029) in December 2015. That language would require government agencies funded under the Financial Services title to obtain a warrant to request information from Internet service providers. Yoder and Rep. Jared Polis, D-Colo., had pushed for the language, which would apply to the IRS, the Securities and Exchange Commission, and the Federal Trade Commission.

Ban on Ticket-Scalping "Bots"

At the end of the 114th Congress, lawmakers cleared legislation to bar the use of automated software known as "bots" to circumvent online security measures and buy tickets sold online.

Event organizers typically limit the number of tickets a person may buy in order to give more people a chance to attend. To circumvent the restriction, some individuals use bots—which automatically and continuously check ticket-seller websites and buy tickets under multiple names and credit card numbers—to buy a large number of tickets to a popular event. Such individuals then resell the tickets at a premium. Many say that practice had led to escalating entertainment ticket prices.

Sen. Jerry Moran, R-Kan., introduced the measure (S 3183) on July 13, 2016. The Senate Commerce, Science, and Transportation Committee approved the bill by voice vote on September 21, and the Senate passed it by unanimous consent on November 30.

The House on December 7 cleared the measure by unanimous consent, and President Obama signed it into law (PL 114-274) on December 14.

FCC and Internet Access

Republicans and Democrats continued a long battle over "net neutrality," a concept intended to ensure that providers of Internet access did not control how consumers used the Internet and did not discriminate against any content providers. But ultimately the Federal Communications Commission's (FCC's) rules mandating an "open Internet" were allowed to stand.

The FCC in 2010 had issued an Open Internet Order that included three rules governing transparency, blocking, and unreasonable discrimination. It created an Open Internet Advisory Committee to ascertain the effects of the rules and to make further recommendations. Republicans contended that former FCC Chair Julius Genachowski had overstepped his authority by instituting the rules, which came under immediate legal challenge.

The rules also came under court challenge. In early 2014, a federal court struck down most of the FCC's 2010 Open Internet rule that barred the throttling of speed and traffic. The court said the FCC could regulate Internet service providers under Section 706 of the Telecommunications Act (PL 104-104), as the FCC had, but it must allow broadband companies to offer content providers faster speed at a higher price and practice other forms of so-called discrimination provided they did so within a "commercially reasonable" standard.

The FCC then began drafting a new proposal aimed at complying with the court's decision. Its new rule, adopted February 26, 2015, still required Internet service providers such as Comcast and Verizon to treat online traffic equally. The FCC had moved its regulations to Title II of the 1934 Communications Act, which the agency uses to regulate telephone companies and other carriers. The rules banned slowing down and blocking content as well as allowing paid prioritization.

FCC Chair Wheeler said after the committee's February 26 vote that net neutrality would ensure that small companies could reach consumers online without having to pay providers and that providers would not block online speech they found objectionable. He said the Internet is "simply too important to be left without rules and a referee on the field."

Internet service providers pledged to sue, and Republican lawmakers vowed to block the FCC from implementing its rule. Many critics said the regulation would lead to decreased investment by Internet service providers in expanding and improving their networks.

House Action

The House Appropriations Committee approved, by voice vote, a financial services spending bill (HR 2995) on June 17, 2015, that would have barred the FCC from spending money to implement its net neutrality regulations until all legal challenges were resolved. It also would have reduced the FCC budget by $25 million to $315 million and required the FCC to make public all proposed regulations for twenty-one days before the commission voted on them.

Senate Action

The Senate financial services spending bill (S 1910), approved by the Senate Appropriations Committee in a 16–14 vote on July 23, would have reduced funding for the FCC by $20 million to $320 million, barred the FCC from regulating rates under its net neutrality order, and nullified a rule on joint sales agreements by grandfathering in all existing agreements.

Final Agreement

Ultimately, the fiscal 2016 omnibus spending measure (HR 2029), cleared by Congress and signed by the president on December 18, did not limit the FCC's enforcement of its Internet neutrality rules. It did, however, put on hold the commission's 2014 rule aimed at ensuring diversity in media ownership.

Court Ruling

AT&T and Verizon, through their trade group USTelecom, asked a three-judge panel of the U.S. Court of Appeals for the District of Columbia Circuit to overturn the rules. In a 2–1 ruling, the panel on June 14, 2016, upheld the net neutrality rules.

Interstate Commerce

The House Judiciary Committee on June 17, 2015, approved two measures related to interstate commerce, but neither made it to the House floor.

One measure (HR 2584), introduced by Steve Chabot, R-Ohio, would have barred state business activity taxes on companies engaged in interstate commerce unless they have a physical presence inside a state for more than fourteen days. The committee approved the measure, 18–7, after rejecting an amendment that would have postponed the effective date of the measure to January 1, 2026.

Another bill (HR 1643), introduced by Rep. Lamar Smith, R-Texas, would have barred multiple or discriminatory state and local taxes on digital goods or services. The bill was approved by voice vote on the same day.

CHAPTER 7

Energy and Environment

Energy and Environment

After a first term focused on health care and the economy, President Barack Obama stepped up his efforts on energy and the environment during his second term. Despite his concerns about climate change and related energy and environment issues, however, Obama often faced unyielding resistance in Congress. With Republicans in charge of the House in the 113th Congress and of both chambers in the 114th, any legislative proposal backed by the White House faced a difficult path on Capitol Hill.

The president and Democrats in Congress often found themselves on the defensive, working to block Republican efforts to loosen energy and environmental regulations the GOP saw as harmful to the economy. Obama often relied on executive actions to achieve his priorities, drawing intense criticism from Republican leaders, who viewed his approach as presidential overreach.

Amid the increasingly divisive atmosphere in Washington, even legislation with bipartisan support often fell short. Still, lawmakers were able to push a few pieces of legislation across the finish line. These included passage of two major water infrastructure bills and the reauthorization of a law regulating toxic chemicals.

CLIMATE CHANGE

At a June 2013 speech at Georgetown University, Obama unveiled a first-ever climate strategy aimed at cutting greenhouse gas emissions from power plants, shoring up coastlines against flooding and sea level rise, and helping advance an international climate deal. The plan would rely less on a divided Congress and more on executive powers and the bully pulpit—what the White House would dub his "pen-and-phone" strategy to achieve its ambitious goals. Obama believed this strategy would help him advance his priorities without relying on lawmakers to reach consensus.

Rather than take up Obama's climate strategy, Republicans worked against it. The House passed legislation in the 113th Congress that would have delayed or prevented the Environmental Protection Agency (EPA) from regulating so-called greenhouse gas emissions from power plants as anticipated. The Democratic-controlled Senate, however, declined to take it up, and the EPA released proposed emission standards for new and existing "electric generating units" in 2014.

Concerns over emissions of greenhouse gases, blamed for warming the planet, also affected energy legislation. The House approved bills in the 113th Congress to expand offshore oil and natural gas drilling and to rescind Obama's authority over the proposed TransCanada Keystone XL pipeline from Canada to the Gulf of Mexico. Those efforts failed to win Senate approval, although a Senate vote on the Keystone XL pipeline fell just one vote short of the sixty needed to move ahead with the bill.

With GOP frustrations mounting, House Republicans ahead of the midterm elections scheduled a vote on a package of thirteen energy-related bills they had previously approved as a way to highlight their chamber's efforts to increase domestic fossil fuel production. The bill passed—and was again ignored in the Senate.

The story was much the same in the 114th Congress. Emboldened by their gains in the midterm elections, lawmakers cleared a pipeline approval bill (S 1) in January

REFERENCES

Discussion of environmental and energy policy for the years 1945–1964 may be found in *Congress and the Nation Vol. I*, pp. 771–1095; for the years 1965–1968, *Congress and the Nation Vol. II*, pp. 463–528; for the years 1969–1972, *Congress and the Nation Vol. III*, pp. 745–849; for the years 1973–1976, *Congress and the Nation Vol. IV*, pp. 201–320; for the years 1977–1980, *Congress and the Nation Vol. V*, pp. 451–530, 533–597; for the years 1981–1984, *Congress and the Nation Vol. VI*, pp. 333–400, 403–482; for the years 1985–1988, *Congress and the Nation Vol. VII*, pp. 417–495; for the years 1989–1992, *Congress and the Nation Vol. VIII*, pp. 467–532; for the years 1993–1996, *Congress and the Nation Vol. IX*, pp. 401–476; for the years 1997–2001, *Congress and the Nation Vol. X*, pp. 341–414; for the years 2001–2004, *Congress and the Nation Vol. XI*, pp. 409–444; for the years 2005–2008, *Congress and the Nation Vol. XII*, pp. 443–505; for the years 2009–2012, *Congress and the Nation Vol. XIII*, pp. 363–404.

Figure 7.1 Outlays for Natural Resources and Environment

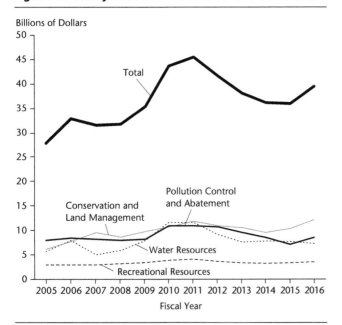

SOURCE: Executive Office of the President, Office of Management and Budget, *Budget of the United States Government, Fiscal Year 2018, Historical Tables* (Washington, DC: U.S. Government Printing Office, 2018), Table 3.2.

NOTE: Total line includes some expenditures that are not shown separately.

Rob Portman, R-Ohio, and Jeanne Shaheen, D-N.H., to update model building energy codes and establish energy-savings programs and guidelines in federal buildings. The bill (S 2262) was widely supported, but debate stalled in 2013 when it attracted a slew of amendments from senators looking for opportunities to advance their own proposals through the Senate.

A few pieces of legislation, however, made it into law.

One rare success was approval of a long-term water development bill (PL 113-121) to provide authorization for dozens of waterway and environmental projects handled by the Army Corps of Engineers. Partisan fights had kept Congress from enacting such a bill for seven years. Congress also passed a law (PL 113-23) to speed regulatory approval of hydropower plants that produced between 5,000 and 10,000 kilowatts. The industry argued that it was taking up to five years to get approval for these small-sized plants under regulations more suitable for larger projects.

In year-end action in 2014, Congress approved legislation retroactively extending more than fifty expired tax breaks, including a $9.6 billion continuation of the wind energy production tax. But the legislation was only for 2014, as lawmakers postponed until 2015 more ambitious efforts to redraw and make permanent tax credits.

2015, only to run into an Obama veto. The Republican-controlled Congress also passed resolutions attempting to block the EPA from regulating greenhouse gas emissions (SJ Res 24) and establishing emission performance standards for new plants (SJ Res 23). (It also passed a resolution, SJ Res 22, to redefine which waterways were covered under the Clean Water Act.)

The Obama administration continued to use its authority to address climate change, with the EPA issuing its Clean Power Plan in 2015 to require individual states to meet specific standards with respect to reduction of carbon dioxide emissions. Later in the year, Obama rejected the Keystone XL pipeline, saying the project would have undercut America's image as a global leader on climate change. He then attended the Paris climate talks in December 2015, where he committed the United States to join other nations in seeking to reduce carbon emissions as well as take other steps to limit global warming.

None of those actions sat well with Republicans in Congress. On the day Obama announced his support for the Paris Climate deal, the House voted in favor of Senate joint resolutions to block EPA action on greenhouse gas emissions. Obama subsequently vetoed the resolutions.

BIPARTISAN SUPPORT

Congress struggled even when there was broad bipartisan agreement for legislation such as efforts by Sens.

Figure 7.2 Outlays for Energy

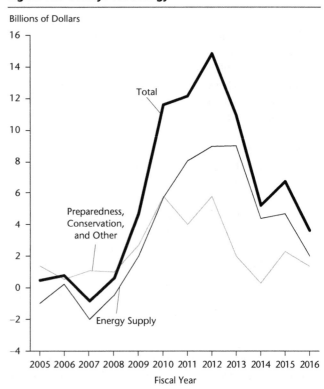

SOURCE: Executive Office of the President, Office of Management and Budget, *Budget of the United States Government, Fiscal Year 2018, Historical Tables* (Washington, DC: U.S. Government Printing Office, 2018), Table 3.2.

NOTE: Total line includes some expenditures that are not shown separately.

In the 114th Congress, lawmakers and the administration were able to agree on legislation (HR 2576—PL 114-182) to update a forty-year-old law regulating toxic chemicals in thousands of household and industrial products. The update to the Toxic Substances Control Act of 1976 (PL 94-469) addressed concerns over the slow pace of EPA review of toxic chemicals: the federal agency had fully tested just 200 of 23,000 chemicals introduced since the law was enacted and only banned five.

Congress also came together at the end of the 114th Congress to pass a water resources development bill authorizing $11.7 billion for infrastructure projects overseen by the Army Corps of Engineers. The deal also included funding to assist Flint, Michigan, in fixing its lead-tainted drinking water system.

FUNDING BATTLES

Appropriations bills were hardly exempt from partisan disagreements. House Republicans sought to sharply reduce funding for the EPA and reduce the agency's staff. Obama and Senate Democrats were able to parry the deepest cuts.

Funding for the EPA rose slightly in real dollars from $7.9 billion in fiscal 2013 (Obama's final first-term budget) to $8.06 billion in fiscal 2017 (his final second-term budget). EPA staffing was the same in both fiscal years at 15,408.

In contrast, EPA funding had hit its high-water mark during Obama's tenure in fiscal 2010 at nearly $10.3 billion and staffing in fiscal 2011 at 17,359.

ENERGY AND ENVIRONMENT LEADERSHIP

Energy Secretary

President Barack Obama nominated Ernest Moniz, a nuclear physicist from the Massachusetts Institute of Technology, to replace Steven Chu as head of the Department of Energy on March 4, 2013. Chu was energy secretary from January 21, 2009, until April 22, 2013, when he resigned to return to Stanford University as professor of physics and professor of molecular and cellular physiology.

Moniz previously served as Under Secretary of Energy under President Clinton and then directed MIT's Energy Initiative focused on developing energy independence. At his confirmation hearing, he said he would pursue an "all of the above" energy strategy that supports both traditional and alternative energy sources while calling for a robust research-and-development program at the Energy Department for low carbon options to mitigate climate change. Moniz's qualifications drew praise from senators on both sides of the aisle. Even though other Obama nominees sparked fierce partisan battles, he was confirmed by a 97–0 vote on May 16, 2013.

Moniz played a crucial role in negotiating technical details of the Iran nuclear deal, signed on July 14, 2015, that he said would provide a significant barrier to prevent Iran from building a nuclear weapon. The agreement between Iran, the United States, and other nations was intended to curb Iran's progress toward developing nuclear weapons in exchange for lifting economic sanctions.

Interior Secretary

Sally Jewell, who was chief executive of REI, an outdoor gear retailer, was nominated on February 6, 2013, to replace Ken Salazar as head of the Department of Interior, an agency that western Republicans complained was too restrictive on energy and other commercial development on public lands during Obama's administration. Salazar served from January 20, 2009 to April 12, 2013. He was named a partner of the international law firm WilmerHale in June 2013.

At her confirmation hearing, before the Senate Energy and Natural Resources Committee, Jewell suggested Obama's all-of-the-above energy strategy included increased oil and gas production on public lands managed by the Interior while also stressing that a balance must be struck for wildlife preservation and recreation. Jewell noted her own love of the outdoors as well as her early career as a petroleum engineer.

She was confirmed by an 87–11 vote of the Senate on April 10, 2013.

During her tenure, she issued a secretarial order on March 20, 2014, expanding recreational, education, volunteer, and career opportunities for young people on public lands in support of Obama's 21st Century Conservation Service Corps. And in 2015 she helped launch Obama's Every Kid in a Park initiative, making every fourth-grade student and their families eligible for a free one-year pass to every national park.

Environmental Protection Agency Administrator

Gina McCarthy, who since 2009 served as the chief air quality regulator at the Environmental Protection Agency, was tapped on March 4, 2013, to replace EPA administrator Lisa Jackson as the Obama administration prepared to issue rules limiting carbon emissions from coal-fired power plants. Her confirmation faced intense Republican opposition over claims EPA rulemaking was ideologically driven without regard for economic consequences.

(Continued)

ENERGY AND ENVIRONMENT LEADERSHIP (Continued)

Jackson served from January 22, 2009, to February 19, 2013. She joined Apple in May 2013 as the corporation's environmental director.

At her confirmation hearing before the Environment and Public Works Committee on April 11, 2013, McCarthy said she believed greenhouse gas emissions contribute to global warming and that an increased focus and commitment to addressing climate change is perhaps the greatest obligation to future generations.

The Senate confirmed her on July 18, 2013, by a vote of 59–40. Sen. Joe Manchin of Virginia was the lone Democrat in opposition.

Chronology of Action on Energy and Environmental Policy

2013–2014

Republicans were unable to gain much ground on their legislative initiatives to expand domestic energy production in a divided 113th Congress as Democrats resisted efforts to promote fossil fuels at what they saw as a risk to the environment and a threat to climate change. The clashes were particularly heated over the controversial Keystone XL pipeline.

The House Natural Resources Committee introduced and approved a package of bills under the GOP's "American Energy Initiative" aimed at expanding oil, gas, and coal production to lower energy costs for consumers and create additional jobs. Natural Resources Committee Chair Doc Hastings, R-Wash., touted the panel's success as the bills went on to clear the House. Democratic Whip Steny Hoyer of Maryland, however, complained the GOP had ignored climate change and instead repeatedly voted for measures benefitting the oil and gas and coal industries.

The bills stalled in the Senate, where Democrats held the majority and persisted in blocking legislation they deemed would harm the environment.

Democrats and Republicans also tangled over several environmental issues, including opening a nuclear waste repository at Yucca Mountain and blocking the administration's efforts on listing the greater sage grouse as endangered.

Congress was able to overcome the partisan stalemate on a few issues. Lawmakers approved a long-term water development bill (PL 113-121) that had eluded them for seven years. The bill authorized dozens of waterway and environmental projects handled by the Army Corps of Engineers without the use of Congressional earmarks.

Congress also passed a law (PL 113-23) to speed regulatory approval of smaller hydropower plants.

Keystone XL Pipeline

The Keystone XL pipeline remained at the forefront of the energy debate in the 113th Congress. Supporters repeatedly criticized Obama for foot dragging as TransCanada awaited action on a presidential permit application the company initially submitted in 2008 to construct the pipeline to transport crude oil from Alberta's tar sands to Gulf Coast refineries.

Frustrated by the delays, proponents won House passage of a bill in May 2013 that would have rescinded Obama's authority over the Keystone XL pipeline and granted the remaining permits necessary to construct it. Even though senators demonstrated bipartisan support for constructing the pipeline, they could not muster the needed sixty votes to pass legislation.

2013 LEGISLATIVE ACTION

Although the House readied a series of bills designed to expedite approval of the pipeline, House leaders focused their efforts on the bill (HR 3) to rescind the president's authority to issue permits for the northern portion of the cross-border infrastructure project that Rep. Lee Terry, R-Neb., proposed. Three committees gave their approval before the full House took up the legislation.

The northern leg of the pipeline would have run from an oil terminal near the tar sands to a market hub in southern Nebraska. The administration had already approved the southern section of the project, which ran to refineries on the Gulf Coast.

The Energy and Commerce Committee approved the measure in April 17, 2013, by a vote of 30–18. Democrats Gene Green of Texas, Jim Matheson of Utah, and John Barrow of Georgia joined all Republicans in support of the measure.

The panel rejected, by a vote of 16–31, an amendment by Illinois Democrat Jan Schakowsky that would have prevented it from taking effect unless the Energy and Commerce Committee found that operation of the pipeline would reduce the price of gasoline in the United States. The panel also rejected, by a 13–31 vote, an amendment by New Mexico Democrat Ben Ray Luján that would have required all crude oil transported by the pipeline to be used domestically.

The Natural Resources Committee followed suit a week later, approving the bill by a vote of 24–17. Jim Costa of California was the only Democrat to vote with all Republicans in support of the bill.

The Transportation and Infrastructure Committee approved it in May 17 by a vote of 33–24. Cheri Bustos of Illinois and Sean Patrick Maloney of New York were the only Democrats to vote with all Republicans in support of the bill.

In the face of a presidential veto threat, the House passed the bill (HR 3) by a vote of 241–175 on May 22, with 19 Democrats joining all Republicans in support.

Republicans rejected, by roll-call votes, eight attempts by Democrats to modify the bill. One amendment, rejected by a vote of 177–238, would have removed provisions deeming the northern route approved.

Democrats took particular issue with provisions that would have deemed the State Department's 2011 environmental-impact statement sufficient to satisfy National Environmental Policy Act (PL 91-190) requirements and that would have required the secretaries of the Interior and the Army to issue the necessary permits for the construction and operation of the pipeline. The House rejected, on a vote of 177–238, an amendment offered by Nick J. Rahall of West Virginia to address the issue.

Proposals to accelerate action on the pipeline progressed much more slowly in the Senate than in the House.

In March, during consideration of the chamber's fiscal 2014 budget resolution (S Con Res 8), senators adopted an amendment that merely expressed support for the pipeline. The vote was 62–37, and although it was nonbinding, it suggested that more than 60 senators were in favor of the project, enough to break a filibuster against a future Keystone bill or amendment.

The Senate never considered either HR 3 or a similar bill (S 582) sponsored by Sen. John Hoeven of North Dakota. A nonbinding resolution (S Con Res 21) to declare the pipeline in the national interest that Hoeven and Landrieu sponsored was also ignored.

Keystone supporters in the Senate set their sights on a bipartisan energy efficiency bill (S 1392), sponsored by Jeanne Shaheen, a New Hampshire Democrat, and Rob Portman, an Ohio Republican. The bill was dragged down on the Senate floor by disputes over unrelated amendments and was eventually pulled in September. At the end of the year, Shaheen said she was hopeful about returning to the energy efficiency bill in 2014 and that she was working with Hoeven and Landrieu to incorporate unspecified Keystone language.

2014 LEGISLATIVE ACTION

The House and Senate held votes in 2014 to approve the pipeline with a majority in each chamber in favor of moving ahead with the project. The Senate, however, fell one

vote short of the sixty needed to overcome parliamentary hurdles, and so the matter was left unresolved.

With the success of the Republicans in the 2014 midterms, there would be a new Republican majority in the Senate in 2015, and GOP leaders vowed early action on the pipeline.

For much of 2014, Senate Majority Leader Harry Reid's strategy was to protect his Democratic members up for reelection from having to cast votes on politically sensitive amendments. His maneuvers came in response to Republicans' attempts to force Democrats such as Louisiana's Mary L. Landrieu and North Carolina's Kay Hagan, who were in tight 2014 races, to take exactly those politically difficult votes.

Landrieu, the chair of the Senate Energy and Natural Resources Committee, had pushed for a vote on the Keystone XL pipeline bill in May in connection with an energy efficiency bill (S 2262), which fell a few votes short of the sixty needed to end debate.

But the outcome of the Louisiana Senate election on November 4 made it politically useful both for Landrieu and for her principal Republican opponent, Rep. Bill Cassidy, to have a chance to flaunt their support for the pipeline, which would provide new input for Louisiana refineries geared to process heavier grades of oil, such as the oil sands output from Canada that would travel through the pipeline.

In the November 4 balloting, Cassidy got 41 percent to Landrieu's 42 percent, with another Republican, Rob Maness, getting 11 percent. Since no candidate won a majority, Cassidy and Landrieu would face each other in a December 6 runoff. That, in turn, set the stage for votes on Keystone XL in both the House on November 12 and the Senate six days later.

The House, which had already passed legislation to expedite the construction of the pipeline on eight different occasions, voted 252–161 to approve it. No Republican members voted against it, while thirty-one Democrats, including seven from Texas and one from Louisiana, voted for it.

Under the Senate's agreement, the bill, sponsored by Hoeven, would need sixty votes for passage, a tally Landrieu said she thought she had. But the pipeline's Senate supporters fell one vote short. All forty-five Senate Republicans voted for it, as well as Landrieu and thirteen other Democrats, including three who had been defeated on Election Day: Hagan, Mark Begich of Alaska, and Mark Pryor of Arkansas.

The bill would have immediately allowed TransCanada to construct, operate, and maintain the pipeline and cross-border facilities. The 2014 environmental impact statement issued by the State Department would be declared sufficient to satisfy all requirements for review under the National Environmental Policy Act and the Endangered Species Act.

Offshore Drilling

Congressional efforts to expand opportunities for offshore oil and natural gas drilling stalled in the 114th Congress as the Republican-led House approved a bill to expedite production off the Atlantic and Pacific coasts. The Senate, however, was unable to agree on a measure to boost revenue sharing for coastal states with offshore oil and natural gas wells.

President Obama issued a five-year offshore leasing plan in 2013 that placed more than 85 percent of offshore areas off-limits to energy production and included the lowest number of lease sales ever offered in a plan.

In response, the House Committee on Natural Resources on June 12 approved a measure to expedite oil and natural gas production off the Atlantic and Pacific coasts over strong objections from Democrats and the White House. The bill (HR 2231—H Rept 113-125) was approved by a vote of 23–18, with New Jersey Republican Jon Runyan voting with all Democrats in opposition.

It would have directed the Interior secretary to implement a five-year oil and gas leasing program and required that at least 50 percent of each area of the outer continental shelf be made available for leasing. It also would have narrowly expanded revenue sharing with the states to encourage more coastal areas to support drilling off their shores.

Supporters said the bill would open new crude oil and gas reservoirs, create 1.2 million long-term jobs, and generate $1.5 billion in revenue. Chair Doc Hastings, R-Wash., said the legislation would generate jobs and safely increase energy production.

But the White House, in a statement threatening a veto, said the bill would have exposed the outer continental shelf to environmental destruction while ignoring state and local concerns, threatened commercial and recreational fisheries, and interfered with military operations off the coastlines. They also complained it would have imposed unrealistic deadlines for regulatory reviews, which would have undermined existing environmental laws.

During committee debate, Rush D. Holt, D-N.J., criticized Republicans for not including safety changes recommended by the commission that investigated the 2010 *Deepwater Horizon* oil spill in the Gulf of Mexico.

Raúl M. Grijalva, D-Ariz., offered an amendment, rejected 14–25, that would have levied increased fines for safety infractions and would have required drilling operations to comply with heightened safety standards for blowout preventers, well casing, and cementing—all of which were issues in the *Deepwater Horizon* spill.

Lawmakers on both sides of the aisle voiced parochial concerns, taking issue with provisions that would have permitted drilling off their state coastlines. Democrat Alan Lowenthal sought to bar new drilling leases off the California coast, saying there was resounding opposition to offshore drilling in his state. Runyon wanted New Jersey voters to decide by referendum whether to allow drilling off its coast.

Hastings dismissed both amendments as unnecessary, saying the bill limited drilling off California to areas that were reachable only from existing infrastructure. He noted that New Jersey—like every other state—had jurisdiction over just the first three miles of the outer continental shelf, while anything beyond that was under federal control. Both measures were defeated.

Republicans Jeff Duncan of South Carolina and Rob Wittman of Virginia highlighted their states' interest in promoting offshore drilling, saying the bill was essential to boosting employment and economic growth.

The bill cleared the House in June by a vote of 235–186 after an amendment offered by Alan Grayson, D-Fla., seeking to preserve state authority over offshore drilling was defeated by a vote of 209–210. The House also rejected amendments to prohibit oil and gas leases near the site of the 1989 *Exxon Valdez* disaster in Alaska and near the 1969 Santa Barbara oil spill.

An amendment by Paul Broun, R-Ga., seeking a sixty-day deadline on the judicial review of claims arising from projects in the leasing program, was approved by the House, 217–202. The measure would have also placed restrictions on appeals and instituted a "loser pays" requirement on individuals or entities filing suit in most circumstances.

An amendment by Bill Cassidy, R-La., to double to almost $1 billion the annual cap on offshore oil and gas leasing revenue shared with adjacent states, was adopted by a vote of 238–185.

In the Senate, a bipartisan group worked on a bill to boost revenue sharing for coastal states with offshore oil and natural gas wells, but the measure did not progress to committee or floor consideration as they struggled to find offsetting budget savings.

Some coastal states with offshore oil and natural gas reserves had tried for years to expand areas for drilling and receive a larger share of the royalties. Because state control extended, under existing law, to three miles offshore, they kept all the royalties. From three to six miles, states generally received about a quarter of oil and gas royalties, and beyond six miles, existing law allowed some revenue sharing for new drilling projects.

Louisiana Democrat Mary L. Landrieu had long argued that coastal states were given unfair and unequal treatment compared with states that had oil, natural gas, and coal production on public lands within their borders. Typically, those states received almost half of the money the federal government took in from producers.

Landrieu teamed up with Lisa Murkowski of Alaska, the ranking Republican on the Senate Energy and Natural Resources Committee, to promote an increase in offshore revenue sharing. Their bill (S 1273) would have directed as much as 37.5 percent of the revenue from offshore energy production in federal waters—both fossil fuel and renewable—to coastal states' coffers. It also would have gradually raised the annual $500 million cap on revenue sharing.

The bill ran into difficulty because the Congressional Budget Office estimated that it would have cost $6 billion over ten years, mostly because it would have sped up higher royalty payments that Gulf Coast states were already slated to begin receiving in fiscal 2017.

No further action occurred on the legislation in 2014, although the Obama administration continued work toward developing a final offshore leasing program for 2017–2022. As part of that effort, Interior Secretary Sally Jewell and Bureau of Ocean Energy Management Director Abigail Ross unveiled a "draft proposed program" in January 2015 that included potential lease sales in eight planning areas including the Gulf of Mexico, the Alaskan coast, and the Mid- and South Atlantic. Jewell characterized it as a balanced proposal that would make available nearly 80 percent of the undiscovered technically recoverable resources, while protecting other areas.

Energy Efficiency

A bipartisan bill intended to improve the energy efficiency of buildings and manufacturing processes failed in the 113th Congress as political skirmishes in the Senate in 2013 and 2014 kept it from reaching a floor vote.

Sens. Rob Portman, R-Ohio, and Jeanne Shaheen, D-N.H., had spent the better part of three years trying to require the Energy Department to update model building energy codes and establish energy-savings programs and guidelines in federal buildings.

As agreed to in committee, the legislation would have encouraged states to update their building codes to require more energy-efficient materials and construction techniques; to provide incentives for manufacturers to improve the efficiency of their production lines; and to establish energy-saving guidelines for federal buildings. While an attractive idea to most lawmakers, the bipartisan legislation (S 2262) was also a magnet for other proposals.

In recent years, few energy-related bills had been considered on the floor. So when a rare opportunity emerged for lawmakers to propose germane amendments, they could hardly resist.

Senate floor debate on the bill began in September 2013, but deliberations stalled after senators offered a series of unrelated amendments. In the absence of an agreement to limit votes on amendments—and with the chamber headed toward a showdown over fiscal policy that did not allow for extended floor time—the bill was pulled from the floor, leaving sponsors hoping for a chance to return to the measure in 2014.

The bill returned to the floor in May 2014, where Majority Leader Harry Reid of Nevada took procedural steps to block amendments, a move that irritated Republicans seeking votes on other energy-related proposals. After a cloture motion failed, further action on the bill came to a halt.

In May, the Energy and Natural Resources Committee approved by voice vote a version of the Shaheen-Portman bill (S 761—S Rept 113-37) that included a provision to finance efficiency upgrades in commercial buildings. Two months later, the lawmakers introduced a revised version (S 1392) that dropped the finance title, and that was the bill that went to the floor.

Three Republicans on the panel—Jeff Flake of Arizona, Mike Lee of Utah, and Tim Scott of South Carolina—asked to be recorded as opposed to the bill.

Before approving the bill, the committee adopted by voice vote an amendment by Portman to offset the cost of financing efficiency upgrades in commercial buildings by redirecting money from the Energy Department's Zero Net Energy Commercial Buildings Initiative. It would have transferred $200 million in fiscal 2013, $130 million in fiscal 2014, and $100 million each year from fiscal 2015 through fiscal 2017.

Portman's amendment also specified that model building standards outlined by the bill were to be voluntary and nonbinding.

Other senators said they wanted to broaden the bill on the floor to address other energy efficiency matters. For example, Debbie Stabenow of Michigan wanted to make the bill "technology neutral," noting that it would have allowed only natural gas and electric vehicles to qualify for energy-efficiency incentive programs.

Al Franken of Minnesota, chair of the panel's Subcommittee on Energy, said he intended to offer a floor amendment to allow all vehicles to qualify for energy-efficiency programs. Other lawmakers expressed interest in adding provisions relating to weatherization and in extending grants to nonprofit groups interested in undertaking energy efficiency initiatives.

Meanwhile, the House took no action on a bill (HR 1616) that had been introduced in April, at the same time as S 761—and that was identical to the version introduced in the Senate. House sponsors David B. McKinley of West Virginia and Peter Welch of Vermont said they were waiting to see the outcome of the Senate bill before considering their companion version.

During the summer, efforts by Reid and the measure's sponsors to find time for floor debate were repeatedly thwarted by more pressing business and by the threat of a wholesale amendment process.

Supporters tried to find a way to limit the number of potential amendments once the measure reached the floor, and to that end, Shaheen and Portman introduced S 1392, their revised version of the committee-approved bill, at the end of July. The new bill dropped a provision to finance efficiency upgrades in commercial buildings.

One potential fight arose when John Hoeven of North Dakota and Joe Manchin III of West Virginia introduced a bill (S 1020) to make major revisions in energy efficiency standards for federal buildings. They made clear that they would offer it as an amendment to S 1392.

The Hoeven-Manchin measure would have rewritten a section of a 2007 energy law (PL 110-140) that required federal buildings to stop using energy produced from fossil fuels by 2030 and extended the phase-out of fossil fuels. Hoeven's state was experiencing a boom in oil and natural gas production, and Manchin's state was a major coal producer. They called existing law requirements unworkable and noted that the Energy Department had yet to issue implementation regulations.

Led by the American Institute of Architects, more than a dozen green-building advocates that supported the existing standards urged Shaheen and Portman to oppose the amendment.

Hoeven was also a leading advocate of building the controversial 1,700-mile Keystone XL oil pipeline, which the Obama administration had delayed approving. Along with Mary L. Landrieu, D-La., Hoeven said he planned to offer an amendment either to allow Congress to approve its construction or to express that the pipeline was in the national interest.

During floor debate in September, senators filed more than sixty amendments to the bill including a handful that were not germane to energy issues.

Progress on the bill came to a halt when Louisiana Republican David Vitter demanded a vote on his amendment to deny employer contributions to health insurance for members of Congress and their aides under the president's 2010 health care law (PL 111-148, PL 111-152). Vitter's amendment was a sticking point for several other measures in September.

Democratic leaders sought a deal to give Vitter a vote on his amendment but complained that Republicans kept demanding additional concessions. After more than a week

of fitful debate—and no votes—Majority Leader Harry Reid of Nevada pulled the bill off the floor to focus on a continuing resolution for fiscal 2014, which was to begin October 1, and on an impending government shutdown.

When the Senate finished business for the day on September 19—after a week of occasional floor debate but no real action and no movement to resolve the impasse over amendments—the energy-efficiency bill was essentially dead for the year. The chamber never came back to it, despite hopeful noises from the sponsors.

Shaheen expressed frustration "that a small group of senators" delayed action on the bill, which was backed by environmental groups and business organizations alike. She and Portman planned to incorporate about a dozen energy efficiency amendments that had been proposed on the floor in September and had bipartisan support, in an effort to bring the measure back in the second session of the 113th Congress.

2014 LEGISLATIVE ACTION

Portman and Shaheen tried to convince their Senate colleagues to limit the number of amendments to the bill. Several Republican provisions were included into the Portman-Shaheen bill (S 1392), and Minority Leader Mitch McConnell of Kentucky sought votes on other energy-related amendments, including a provision to expedite liquefied natural gas exports and another to restrict rules on carbon emissions by coal-fired power plants.

But Majority Leader Harry Reid took procedural steps to block amendments, saying he had already compromised with Republicans to keep contentious amendments out of the debate by allowing a separate vote on a stand-alone measure (S 2280) to approve the Keystone XL pipeline project.

That did not satisfy most of the Republicans, and when a cloture motion was called in May, only two of them, Portman

SUPERSTORM SANDY AID

Among the first actions President Barack Obama took after his second term began was to sign into law a $50.5 billion supplemental spending bill (HR 152—PL 113-2) to provide both immediate—and more controversially—long-term assistance for victims of Superstorm Sandy.

The long-term funding, which drew criticism from fiscal conservatives, was directed toward rebuilding impacted coastal communities with an eye toward resiliency—a term used to denote construction able to withstand future storms that climate change likely would make more severe.

After sweeping across parts of the Caribbean, Sandy struck the East Coast, including densely populated areas of

New York and New Jersey, on October 29, 2012. Sandy was responsible for killing at least 147 people, including more than 70 in the United States, and causing tens of billions of dollars in damage.

Less than three months later, Obama issued an executive order that among other things would "identify resources and authorities that can contribute to strengthening community and regional resilience as critical infrastructure is rebuilt" to withstand future extreme weather events.

A year later, the Obama administration noted that the federal government was working with state and local governments to make the Sandy-affected region more resilient,

(Continued)

SUPERSTORM SANDY AID (Continued)

not only through building taller and stronger barriers but utilizing the best information and innovations to deal with increasingly severe storms. This goal served as a guiding principle of President Obama's Climate Action Plan, according to John P. Holdren, director of the White House Office of Science and Technology Policy.

Congress had in the past acted quickly to provide emergency aid after similar catastrophes, but Sandy struck as the 2012 presidential campaign was nearing its end and lawmakers were struggling with the federal budget.

Many conservatives in Congress were reluctant to sign on to such an expensive aid package, much of which would not be spent for months or years. Some objected to paying to make infrastructure more resilient to the future effects of big storms, arguing that such projects fell outside the realm of traditional disaster assistance. Others wanted offsetting budget cuts for at least part of the aid package to keep it from adding so much to the deficit.

New York and New Jersey lawmakers, in particular, had pushed for the aid immediately after the storm hit, and the Senate passed a bill on December 28—two full months after the storm—to provide $60.4 billion for recovery efforts, including almost $10 billion to shore up the financially threatened flood insurance program. But House Speaker John A. Boehner, R-Ohio, facing a fractious caucus, put off action until the new Congress convened in 2013. Boehner's decision to adjourn the 112th Congress without acting angered fellow Republicans from the Northeast, including New Jersey Gov. Chris Christie. Rep. Peter T. King, R-N.Y., went so far as to urge Republican financial backers in his state to withhold contributions to the party until Congress passed aid legislation.

Over the year-end holidays and into January, pressure continued to build from New York and New Jersey and other states hit hard by the storm. When the new Congress convened in 2013, Sandy aid was again atop the list of priorities.

House Action

As its first legislative business after convening, the House voted on January 4 for a noncontroversial first piece of the aid package (HR 41—PL 113-1), which increased the borrowing authority of the National Flood Insurance Program by $9.7 billion. More than two-thirds of Republicans and all Democrats supported the bill, which passed 354–67.

The flood insurance program had been reauthorized and overhauled the previous year (PL 112-141) but was running out of money to pay claims, and many lawmakers and Americans were already unhappy with premium increases enacted in 2012. The borrowing increase was not intended to address broader concerns about the program. The Senate

cleared the borrowing increase by voice vote the same day, and the president signed it January 6.

It took the House an additional eleven days to pass a $50.5 billion supplemental disaster appropriation, one of the largest infrastructure measures since the 2009 economic stimulus law (PL 111-5).

The bill as it came to the floor would have provided just $17 billion in emergency assistance to address the immediate needs of locales damaged by the storm. South Carolina Republican Mick Mulvaney, a fiscal conservative, sought to offset the emergency spending by imposing an across-the-board reduction in federal discretionary appropriations. The amendment failed, 162–258.

The House then adopted by a 228–192 vote an amendment offered by Rodney Frelinghuysen, R-N.J., to add $33.5 billion in short- and long-term recovery aid and disaster mitigation spending. Only thirty-eight Republicans supported the addition of $12.2 billion for HUD community development activities, $6.1 billion for FEMA's Disaster Relief Fund, $5.5 billion for transit support, $4 billion for Corps of Engineers projects, $2 billion for repair of federal-aid highways, and other smaller amounts.

The House then passed the bill by 241–180 on January 15, with 49 Republicans in favor and 1 Democrat opposed. Combined with the earlier flood insurance measure, the disaster aid package roughly matched the estimated $60.4 billion passed by the Senate the previous December.

Senate Action

Almost two weeks after the House action, the Senate took up the disaster bill.

Utah Republican Mike Lee sought to offset the additional spending, as Mulvaney had attempted in the House, through an across-the-board reduction in federal discretionary spending. The Senate rejected his amendment by a vote of 35–62, with all 35 "yea" votes coming from Republicans. All Democrats and 10 Republicans voted "nay."

The Senate cleared the aid measure by 62–36 with only Republicans opposed. Northeastern senators praised the bill as long overdue. *(See discussion of Supplemental Appropriation for Sandy Recovery in Chapter 2, pp. 63–65.)*

Aftermath

The law included a huge infusion of money for transit systems damaged by the storm—of the $10.9 billion allotted to the Federal Transit Administration, about half could be spent on long-term resiliency projects.

Federal Transit Administration (FTA) made available $6.8 billion for Hurricane Sandy recovery projects mostly in New York and New Jersey. New York received

$4.6 billion, New Jersey received $711 million, and the Port Authority of New York and New Jersey got $1.5 billion. Smaller amounts went to Pennsylvania, Rhode Island, Massachusetts, and Connecticut.

FTA also provided $3.2 billion for competitive resilience projects that again went mostly to New York (nearly $1.6 billion) and New Jersey (nearly $1.4 billion), while much smaller amounts went to Massachusetts, Connecticut, New Hampshire, Pennsylvania, and the District of Columbia.

The Department of Interior also received $829.2 million to rebuild and repair coastal assets and strengthen natural ecosystems vulnerable to coastal storms, rising sea levels, flooding, and erosion. The department also worked with the National Fish and Wildlife Foundation to distribute $100 million in Sandy supplemental funding to fifty-four projects in the Sandy-impacted region through a competitive grant program that received 375 applications requesting more than $563 million through the Hurricane Sandy Coastal Resiliency Competitive Grants Program.

The selected projects (again mostly in New York and New Jersey) were expected to restore more than 6,600 acres of marsh and wetlands, 225 acres of beach and dune, and more than 200 miles of rivers and streams.

The National Oceanic and Atmospheric Administration (NOAA) also received $2.56 million to support recovery planning efforts at the regional, state, and local levels. Using a competitive process, six projects from New York, New Jersey, and Connecticut were selected in July 2014. Among those included was $410,000 for a pilot project to research, plan, and create strategic green infrastructure projects for Staten Island and Jamaica Bay in New York.

and New Hampshire's Kelly Ayotte, supported ending debate to move toward passage of the bill. Needing a 60-vote majority to succeed, the cloture motion fell on a 55–36 vote.

Natural Gas Exports

The boom in hydraulic fracturing, or fracking, continued to transform the natural gas market in the United States. Members of Congress from energy-producing states sought support from colleagues for legislation to speed regulatory approvals and spur additional exports of liquefied natural gas (LNG).

At the Senate Energy and Natural Resources Committee's first hearing on the topic in March 2014, Chair Mary L. Landrieu, D-La., noted that a healthy oil and gas industry is important for job creation. The LNG issue had become entwined with the Ukraine crisis early in 2014. Russian military aggression in Ukraine and its annexation of Crimea were followed by the Russian utility company Gazprom shutting off Ukraine's natural gas supply because the country refused to pay inflated prices. Officials from Eastern Europe made the case to lawmakers that the Ukraine crisis should spur action because approval of increased exports of LNG could immediately help alleviate Europe's dependence on Russian gas.

A week prior to the March 25, 2014, hearing, Landrieu and eight other U.S. officials were denied entry into Russia for opposing that nation's actions against Ukraine. At the hearing, she said being sanctioned by President Putin was a "badge of honor" and that she looked forward "to playing a role to bring energy security and independence to America and our democratic allies around the world."

Landrieu was not alone in seeking to expand LNG exports. Rep. Bill Cassidy, R-La., who was challenging Landrieu in the Senate race, sought to bar the Energy Department from considering lifecycle greenhouse gas emissions when evaluating applications for LNG exports to avoid what he described as adding an unneeded layer of legal risk and uncertainty to an already extensive and difficult process.

The House on July 10, 2014, voted, 232–187, to amend an Energy–Water spending bill with Cassidy's proposal over objections from Energy and Commerce Ranking Democrat Henry A. Waxman of California. He raised concerns about the potential impacts of LNG exports on climate change.

Sen. John Barrasso of Wyoming also offered an amendment to a Ukraine aid bill (S 2124) which would have required approval of LNG exports to Ukraine and NATO members. Majority Leader Harry Reid of Nevada would not agree to allow a vote on Barrasso's amendment, and a House version of the bill (HR 4152), without Barrasso's amendment, was signed into law on April 3, 2014.

Another Democratic senator up for reelection in 2014, Colorado's Mark Udall, sponsored a bill that would allow for the export of natural gas to World Trade Organization members without requiring an Energy Department determination that the exports are in the public interest. Such automatic approval had been limited to free-trade partners with the United States.

Udall's challenger, Rep. Cory Gardner, R-Colo., offered a competing bill (HR 6—H Rept 113-477) that would have required an expedited process for the Energy Department to approve applications for LNG exports that he argued was needed to fix a backlog of applications being unnecessarily delayed. It passed the House on June 25, 2014, 266–150.

Gardner's bill would give the Energy Department just thirty days to issue a final verdict, whereas Udall's bill would have required a decision within forty-five days.

In the House, critics of Gardner's bill said it could take years for natural gas exports to reach Ukraine and were concerned that the measure would cause domestic natural gas prices to rise. Rep. Rush D. Holt, D-N.J., proposed having the Energy secretary make a public-interest determination in how LNG exports would affect gas prices, jobs, and manufacturing before approving any applications, but his amendment was defeated on a voice vote.

Although the Senate did not take up Gardner's House-passed bill, the Senate Energy and Natural Resources Committee was poised to vote on a bill (S 2638) that would expedite Energy Department consideration of LNG export applications, requiring a determination within forty-five days of an application's submission.

Landrieu had scheduled a November 13 meeting to consider the bill that Senator John Hoeven, R-N.D., had introduced. Hoeven, however, pulled it after Energy Secretary Ernest J. Moniz voiced concerns about the bill with respect to how it would affect the National Environmental Policy Act (PL 91-190) process that the Federal Energy Regulatory Commission must carry out before the department can make a decision on a proposed terminal.

Energy Bill Package

Ahead of the November 2014 elections, House Republican leaders scheduled a vote on a package of thirteen energy-related bills the House had previously approved but were ignored in the Senate, as a way to highlight their chamber's efforts to increase domestic fossil fuel production.

Doc Hastings of Washington, the Republican chair of the Natural Resources Committee, hammered that point home during debate in September, saying the House had passed dozens of energy bills that the Senate had failed to take up, including a number from the House Natural Resources Committee, on which the Senate had failed to act. Peter DeFazio of Oregon, the ranking Democrat on the committee, said it would not do any good to keep sending the same bills to the Senate.

The final vote on September 18 on the omnibus energy bill (HR 2) was 226–191. The handful of crossover votes from each party included members who were in difficult reelection races such as West Virginia Democrat Nick J. Rahall II and Georgia Democrat John Barrow, both of whom voted for the GOP bill and both of whom lost their seats in November.

Among the bills included in the package were the following:

- HR 4899, which passed the House by a 229–185 vote in June, sought to increase domestic oil and gas production on federal lands and offshore. It would have required that at least 25 percent of eligible federal land be made available each year for leasing and that the review of drilling permits be streamlined. It would have required the Interior Department to make available for oil and gas exploration and development at least 50 percent of the unleased coastal areas that have the most potential for energy production and required

that drilling be allowed more immediately off the coasts of California, South Carolina, and Virginia.
- HR 2728, which passed 235–187 in 2013, would have prohibited the Interior Department from enforcing federal rules on hydraulic fracturing for natural gas in states that have their own fracking oversight rules. It also would have required the EPA to take certain actions in conducting its study of the impact of fracking on drinking water—including setting a deadline for release of a final report.

The Senate, as expected, did not take up the House package.

EPA Carbon Rules

The Environmental Protection Agency proposed the first national limits on carbon dioxide emissions by existing power plants in June 2014, prompting Democrats from conservative-leaning states with economic interests in oil, gas, and coal to distance themselves from President Obama's marquee plan to address climate change.

A year earlier, President Obama had announced a Climate Action Plan directing the EPA to establish federal standards to reduce carbon emissions from new and existing fossil fuel–fired power plants. He was now looking ahead to cementing a global response to climate change at the 21st Conference of Parties, or COP21, in Paris in 2015 with a goal of limiting global warming to between 2.7 and 3.6 degrees Fahrenheit above preindustrial temperatures.

The Democrats joined Republican critics in vowing to fight implementation of the rule aimed at reducing carbon emissions from existing power plants by 30 percent in 2030 compared to 2005 levels. Other Democrats, as well as health and environmental groups, praised the rulemaking.

Louisiana Sen. Mary L. Landrieu, chair of the Energy and Natural Resources Committee, voiced her opposition to the rulemaking by EPA. She said it was important to reduce atmospheric levels of carbon but not through EPA regulations. Instead, she said in a June 2014 interview with the New Orleans *Times-Picayune*, it should be up to Congress to set the terms, goals, and timeframe to build on progress the industry had already made to reduce carbon emissions that were already at their lowest levels in twenty years.

Cassidy, expressing the general view of most Republicans, argued the rule would be too costly to the economy, raising energy costs and costing jobs. Fitting the familiar pattern in 2014 of the House passing legislation that the Senate would never debate or vote on, the House Energy and Commerce Committee—anticipating EPA's rulemaking—advanced in February a bill (HR 3826—H Rept 113-365) that would have limited the EPA's ability to regulate greenhouse gas emissions from fossil-fueled power plants under the Clean Air Act.

Top Democrats on the Energy and Commerce Committee opposed the bill when it came before the panel in February, saying it would significantly impair their ability to address climate change because those plants accounted for roughly a third of the nation's carbon dioxide emissions. They argued the bill's requirement that EPA could only require coal-fired power plants to install pollution controls already in wide use would effectively block the agency from imposing any controls.

Rep. Nick Rahall, a Democrat, was an original cosponsor along with fellow West Virginian David McKinley, a Republican. Rahall had described the EPA efforts as disastrous for his state, claiming they would wreak havoc on its economy.

The House voted 229–183 to approve the bill, which would have nullified the EPA's rules for new electric power plants and only have allowed the agency to set national standards for new plants that have already been broadly adopted by industry. It also would have blocked EPA regulation of existing power plants unless Congress later allowed the EPA to do so. Rahall was among the ten Democrats to vote in favor.

The Senate did not take up the bill, and in the $1.1 trillion omnibus spending bill at the end of the year (HR 83), which was signed by the president on December 16, Democrats were able to exclude GOP language blocking implementation of the EPA's carbon rules.

Rahall went on to defeat in the 2014 midterm elections. Landrieu lost to Cassidy in the Senate run-off election held on December 6 in Louisiana.

Water Projects

For the first time since 2007, Congress approved a long-term water development bill that was signed into law (PL 113-121) to provide authorization for dozens of waterway and environmental projects.

The conference version of the bill (HR 3080—H Rept 113-449) authorized projects that would result in federal spending of $5.4 billion through fiscal 2019 and $12.3 billion over the next decade, according to Congressional Budget Office estimates.

Under normal circumstances the Water Resources Development Act, known familiarly as WRDA, is supposed to be completed every two years to authorize spending for dozens of waterway and environmental projects handled by the Army Corps of Engineers. Partisan fights, however, had kept Congress from enacting such a bill in seven years.

The Senate Committee on Environment and Public Works met on March 20, 2013, to consider the Water Resources Development Act of 2013 (S 601) that was introduced two days earlier by Chair Barbara Boxer, D-Calif., and Sen. David Vitter of Louisiana, the ranking Democrat. The bill was based largely on a discussion draft the committee had received in 2012 that was the subject of a committee hearing on November 15, 2012. The committee also held oversight hearings in January 2013 on the Harbor Maintenance Trust Fund and in February 2013, on implementation of Corps water resources policies.

The committee voted 18–0, on March 20, in favor of the bill that would authorize the Army Corps of Engineers (Corps) to construct water projects for mitigating storm damage, restoring ecosystems, and reducing erosion on inland and intracoastal waterways. The legislation also would authorize the agency to establish grant programs to assist local and state governments with levee safety and rehabilitation programs. It would also authorize the Corps and the Environmental Protection Agency (EPA) to provide loans or loan guarantees to state and local governments and certain nongovernmental entities to complete water infrastructure projects.

The bill passed the Senate on May 15, 2013, by a vote of 83–14. Several amendments were considered. Among them, the Senate voted 67–32 in favor of an amendment offered by Sen. Sheldon Whitehouse, D-R.I., to create the National Endowment for the Oceans to promote the protection and conservation of ocean, coastal, and Great Lakes ecosystems. The Senate rejected an amendment proposed by Sen. Tom Coburn, R-Okla., to curb federal subsidies for ongoing beach replenishment projects. It failed on a 43–53 vote.

In the House, the Transportation and Infrastructure Committee took up its water resources development bill (HR 3080) on September 19, 2013, eight days after it was introduced by the committee leaders from both parties. The committee approved the bill by voice vote, although some Democrats voiced concerns that proposals to speed the approval process for Corps projects may have gone too far in diminishing environmental and judicial reviews. The House version, unlike the Senate, established a three-year deadline for the Corps to conduct feasibility studies, some of which had in the past dragged on for fifteen or more years. Concerns were also raised that the bill did not fully address financing challenges facing the Harbor Maintenance Trust Fund and the Inland Waterways Trust Fund.

The bill passed the House, 417–3, on October 23 under a closed rule that allowed for a limited number of amendments. Most of those considered addressed specific water development projects already underway. Rep. Peter DeFazio, D-Oregon, proposed an amendment to delay the implementation of the bill's environmental streamlining provisions until sufficient funding was in place to reduce the current backlog of Corps projects to less than $20 billion. DeFazio argued that lack of funding is the major culprit in delaying projects and not environmental impact studies. His amendment failed on a largely party-line vote, 183–236.

The House and Senate established a conference committee to report out a final version of the bill to be presented to the House and Senate for an up-or-down vote.

The House voted 412–4 on May 22 to adopt a conference report on the bill that would authorize spending on thirty-four port, inland waterway, and environmental restoration projects. The measure also introduced an authorization process that retained congressional authority over project approvals without using earmarks. The

Senate followed two days later, approving it by a vote of 91–7. The president signed it on June 10.

Fiscal conservatives, including Sen. Tom Coburn of Oklahoma, complained that the bill did not go far enough in reducing the $80 billion backlog of pending projects that the Army Corps of Engineers cannot afford to complete and that the system created to consider new projects left too many opportunities for politics and parochialism to play a role.

Heritage Action and Taxpayers for Common Sense had spoken out against the bill, saying it fell far short of reforms needed to rein in excess spending. In particular, they worried that Congress would feel compelled to approve projects that local authorities submitted under the bill.

The legislation changed how local sponsors seek federal support for their projects. Rather than requesting earmarks directly from lawmakers, as was the case with the 2007 authorization (PL 110-114), they would present projects to their regional Corps of Engineers post for review. After positively reviewing a project, the corps would submit annual reports to Congress, which would hold hearings on the projects.

Proponents saw the measure as an improvement that should speed maintenance, repairs, and needed improvements for projects that have been delayed because of backlogs within the Army Corps of Engineers.

The conference bill authorized state-specific seaport, levee, and environmental restoration projects, as well as instituted broader changes, such as enabling the Army Corps of Engineers to use resilient construction techniques. And it adjusted spending formulas for an Ohio River lock project to increase the federal share, freeing up more money out of an industry-financed trust fund to upgrade other river locks and dams for barge traffic.

Senators touted the package as a way to boost fiscal responsibility with infrastructure projects, such as through provisions that create a process for the Army Corps of Engineers to speed up project planning and construction. The bill revoked authorization of $18 billion in old projects considered obsolete. Lawmakers and industry groups described it as a "jobs bill," both for the construction work it would generate and for the trade competitiveness it could bring. Bob Stallman, president of the American Farm Bureau Federation, said maintaining infrastructure that supports the nation's waterway transportation was vital to agriculture.

Sage Grouse

With the Fish and Wildlife Service expected to decide in 2015 whether to declare the greater sage grouse as endangered, or at least threatened, under the Endangered Species Act (PL 93-205), Republican opponents turned to the purse strings to slow the process down.

A fiscal 2015 spending bill adopted at the end of 2014 (HR 83—PL 113-235) included language barring the Fish and Wildlife Service from making an endangered species listing decision on the sage grouse, whose habitat spans 257,000 square miles across eleven Western states and encompasses lands suitable for oil and gas production.

Environmental advocates had been pressing for nearly a decade for an endangered designation, citing threats to the bird's habitat brought about by livestock grazing and invasive weeds, drought, and urban and energy development. The government believed the bird's numbers had declined by 30 percent since the mid-1980s, to as few as 200,000, and that its historic range had been cut by more than half.

Meanwhile, many Western states and their GOP allies in Congress were lobbying the Interior Department to let state conservation plans protect the bird—an option that environmentalists were less than happy with.

The debate over the grouse was just the latest fight triggered by a 2011 legal settlement between environmental groups and the Fish and Wildlife Service, in which the agency agreed to a timetable for making decisions on whether to list as threatened or endangered hundreds of species that had languished for years on a candidate list. The settlement was a big victory for the conservationists, who had accused the government of neglecting its responsibilities under the 1973 Endangered Species Act.

In July, the House Natural Resources Committee reported out a bill (HR 4315—H Rept 113-537) that the panel's chair had introduced to require the agency to reveal publicly on the Internet all of the data it considers when making listing decisions.

Chair Doc Hastings of Washington said the bill needed an update to reflect changes in technology. The Internet, he noted, was in its infancy stages when the last major revision to the law took place in 1988. Posting data to support major decisions related to the Endangered Species Act would increase transparency and data quality, he said.

Committee Democrats argued against it, saying it would just slow down the process of listing endangered species and make it harder for the agencies to focus on species recovery.

The measure would require the government to publish online the data that was used to justify listing a species as endangered or threatened under the Endangered Species Act. It would require that the data be made available to states before making such determinations.

The bill contained the text of a measure (HR 4316) that would have required the public disclosure of litigation fees for lawsuits related to the Endangered Species Act; a second measure (HR 4317) that would have required that the evidence used to make endangered species determinations include data provided by state, local, and tribal governments; and legislation (HR 4318) that would have limited the awarding of attorneys' fees when litigants prevail in suing the federal government under the act.

The White House issued a veto threat. Nevertheless, the bill was approved later that month in the House by a vote of 233–190. Fourteen Democrats, including five from Western states, joined 219 Republicans in voting for the bill. Eight Republicans, most of them from the Northeast, joined 182 Democrats in voting against it.

The Senate did not take it up.

Yucca Mountain Nuclear Waste

As had become custom in recent years, House Republicans failed to make headway on efforts to open a nuclear waste repository at Yucca Mountain, less than 100 miles northwest of Las Vegas, as Senate Majority Leader Harry Reid of Nevada stood in the way.

In July, the House passed a $34 billion fiscal 2015 Energy–Water spending bill (HR 4923—H Rept 113-486) that included $150 million for continued work on the Yucca site, as well as $55 million for the Nuclear Regulatory Commission's work on Yucca's license application, which a court had ordered to continue while funds were available.

The bill passed, 253–170, with 11 Republicans in opposition, including Rep. Joe Heck of Nevada. Rep. Mark Amodei, a Republican whose district included the Yucca site, voted for it. Amodei, however, had joined the Nevada delegation in support of an amendment from Rep. Dina Titus, a Nevada Democrat, to remove the $150 million for Yucca and block further action on the project. Her amendment was defeated, drawing only ninety-six votes in support.

The White House threatened to veto the spending bill, objecting to the funding levels for renewable and fossil research as well as environmental policy riders and restrictions on nonproliferation cooperation with Russia.

The Department of Energy in 1986 had recommended Yucca Mountain as a national repository for an anticipated 100,000 tons of spent nuclear fuel generated by commercial utilities and highly radioactive waste the government produced in the manufacture of nuclear weapons. Congress a year later agreed to focus solely on the Nevada site.

Mismanagement, technical setbacks, and underfunding in Congress engineered by Reid delayed the project. Reid used his position as Senate leader to reduce or block authorization of funding for the project. Obama, who as a candidate for president promised to kill the project, followed through, proposing instead a blue-ribbon commission that recommended a new strategy to locate and develop alternative nuclear waste sites.

During the House debate, Texas Republican Joe L. Barton offered but later withdrew an amendment that would have authorized a pilot program for interim storage of nuclear waste and allowed any interested states to submit competitive proposals for the program. Barton said interim storage would allow the federal government to meet its obligation to secure high-level nuclear waste while it seeks a long-term permanent solution that could still include Yucca Mountain.

As Congress wrapped up business for the year, a $1.1 trillion spending bill (HR 83) that would keep most of the government funded through the end of fiscal 2015 was adopted. Reid made sure that there was no funding for the Yucca

Mountain site in it. Reid's hand was further strengthened by the retirement of NRC Chair Allison M. Macfarlane. Her designated replacement, NRC member Stephen Burns, had ties to Gregory B. Jaczko, a former Reid staffer and staunch Yucca opponent, who was NRC chair prior to Macfarlane.

Republicans favoring Yucca Mountain were encouraged by the release in October of a 781-page Nuclear Regulatory Commission (NRC) staff analysis of a plan that the Department of Energy submitted for a license in 2008, which concluded the Yucca site "with reasonable expectation" could satisfy licensing rules.

Sen. Lisa Murkowski of Alaska said the NRC study shows the Nevada site is a safe, worthwhile investment that should be allowed to move forward. Pressing the issue, however, would have to wait until 2015, when after the midterm elections Republicans would gain the majority in the Senate and Murkowski would become chair of the Senate Energy and Natural Resources Committee.

Interior and Environmental Appropriations

FISCAL 2014

The fiscal 2014 spending bill for the Interior Department and environmental programs cleared on January 15, 2014, as part of a broader bill to fund the federal government through the remainder of the fiscal year. President Barack Obama signed the legislation (HR 3547—PL 113-76) the next day.

The omnibus bill included $30.1 billion in discretionary funding that represented a $291 million increase over fiscal 2013 funding levels, surpassing the administration's request by a marginal amount. The bill reduced spending for EPA by about $143 million, or 1.7 percent, less than that of fiscal 2013. The funding loss was far less than what House Republicans had sought. The Interior Department budget was increased over fiscal 2013.

The appropriations bill funded the Environmental Protection Agency (EPA), Interior Department as well as its Bureau of Land Management, National Park Service, and Bureau of Indian Affairs. It also covered the Agriculture Department's Forest Service and the Department of Health and Human Services' Indian Health Service.

The appropriations process extended more than three months beyond October 1, the start of the fiscal year, and included a sixteen-day partial government shutdown. House and Senate appropriators crafted the omnibus under the terms of a bipartisan two-year budget agreement (HJ Res 59—PL 113-67) negotiated in December 2013 that pared back cuts imposed by the sequester and raised caps on discretionary spending first set in the 2011 debt limit law (PL 112-25).

Neither chamber's Appropriations Committee was able to approve a stand-alone Interior–Environment spending bill for fiscal 2014.

House Committee Action

The House Interior–Environment Appropriations Subcommittee voted 7–4 along party lines on July 23 to approve a draft bill that included $24.3 billion in discretionary spending, or $5.7 billion less than the administration requested.

The EPA would have faced a 34 percent reduction in funding under the subcommittee bill, which provided $5.5 billion for the agency, or $2.8 billion less than in fiscal 2013. The largest cut, $2.1 billion, would have come out of grants for state and tribal environmental and infrastructure programs, while environmental programs and management would have been trimmed $539 million.

The bill would have also blocked EPA from: implementing regulations aimed at limiting greenhouse gas emissions by power plants, limiting sulfur content of gasoline, and changing the definition of navigable waters or fill material under the Clean Water Act (PL 95-217).

Rep. Mike Simpson of Idaho, chair of the subcommittee, said the prohibitions were included to address concerns raised over the number of regulatory actions being pursued by agencies in the absence of legislation and without clear congressional direction.

Rep. James Moran of Virginia, the ranking Democrat on the subcommittee, walked out of the markup meeting in protest after delivering an opening statement in which he said the draft bill was an "embarrassment" to the subcommittee and complained that provisions within it would prevent EPA from implementing clean air regulations and limit its ability to provide clean water.

The full Appropriations Committee took up the draft bill on July 31 but adjourned before completing a markup after Democratic committee members persisted in seeking to amend the draft bill. Republicans said they planned to reconvene the markup after the August recess but did not.

Before the markup ended, the panel had adopted on a 27–20 party-line vote an amendment offered by Rep. John Culberson, a Republican from Texas, to bar the EPA from using a formula to calculate the social cost of carbon emissions. The appropriators also rejected on a 17–29 vote, mostly along party lines, a Democratic amendment to strike several of the bill's environmental policy riders.

Senate Committee Action

The Senate Appropriations Committee never began consideration of its version of the legislation, although a draft proposal was released on August 1 by the Republican and Democratic leaders of the Appropriations Interior and Environment Subcommittee, Sen. Lisa Murkowski of Alaska and Sen. Jack Reed of Rhode Island, respectively.

The draft document, which they said they hoped would serve as a starting point for further discussions, would have provided $30.1 billion, or $96 million more than the administration requested. It would have appropriated $8.5 billion for the EPA, about $328 million more than requested and $138 million more than in fiscal 2013.

Final Action

Three months after the fiscal year began, the House voted 359 to 67 to approve the fiscal 2014 omnibus appropriations bill (HR 3547—PL 113-76), and the Senate followed suit a day later, voting 72 to 26 in favor. President Barack Obama signed it into law on January 17.

The omnibus included only a handful of the limits on the EPA sought by House Republicans to address concerns the administration was acting without congressional input on climate change. It prohibited the EPA from issuing regulations or requiring clean-air permits for greenhouse gas emissions from livestock and banned the agency from imposing reporting requirements on greenhouse gas emissions. It also required the administration to report to Congress on all federal agency expenditures for climate change programs in fiscal 2013 and 2014.

The omnibus, which funded federal agencies through the end of fiscal 2014 (September 30, 2014), adhered to the $1.012 trillion discretionary spending limit agreed to in the Bipartisan Budget Act of 2013.

MAJOR PROVISIONS

Interior Department

The department received nearly $10.5 billion, a slight increase over fiscal 2013 appropriations but $337 million less than the administration requested. The total was $2.3 billion more than the House subcommittee draft but only $271 million less than the Senate draft.

Departmental funding included the following:

- $1.1 billion for the Bureau of Land Management, an increase of just $7 million above the fiscal 2013 enacted level.
- $2.6 billion for the National Park Service, an increase of $29 million but $74 million less than Obama sought. Most of the money, $2.3 billion, was for park operations.
- $1.5 billion for the Fish and Wildlife Service, $32 million less than in fiscal 2013 and $114 million less than the administration requested.
- $2.5 billion for the Bureau of Indian Affairs, $31 million less than the administration requested. Most of the funds provide for operation of American Indian programs administered by the Bureau of Indian Affairs and the Bureau of Indian Education.

Environmental Protection Agency

The EPA received $8.2 billion, which roughly matched the administration request. It was $281 million less than the Senate draft proposal but $2.7 billion more than the amount proposed by the House subcommittee. It included $3.5 billion for EPA state and tribal assistance grants, $381 million more than the administration request, although still $44 million less than was provided a year earlier. The Superfund hazardous waste cleanup program was financed at $1.1 billion, $91 million less than requested and $88 million less than the enacted 2013 level. The administration's $300 million request for the Great Lakes Restoration Initiative was fully appropriated.

Forest Service

The agency, part of the Agriculture Department, received almost $5.5 billion, roughly $291 million more than enacted for fiscal 2013 and $639 million more than requested. The total included $3.1 billion for wildland fire suppression, $1.5 billion for the maintenance of the National Forest System, $333 million for capital improvements, $230 million for state and private forestry projects, and $44 million for land acquisition.

Indian Health Service

Part of the Department of Health and Human Services, the agency received $4.4 billion, an increase of $78 million over fiscal 2013 and $4 million more than the administration requested.

Wildfires

The bill also appropriated nearly $4.1 billion for preventing and fighting wildfires, a $559 million increase from fiscal 2013, or 16 percent. The bill included $130 million to purchase two aircraft to replace two Korean War–era firefighting planes used for large-scale fire suppression. Within the $4.1 billion total was $1.5 billion in emergency funding that was offset by a $4.2 billion rescission of unused funding from the Advanced Technology Vehicle Manufacturing loan program, originally funded as a stimulus project in 2009. The remaining $2.7 billion was marked for deficit reduction.

FISCAL 2015

A stand-alone spending bill for the Interior Department and environmental programs was not considered on the House or Senate floor as Republicans, and some Democrats, clashed with the White House and Democratic leaders over the EPA's ability to regulate carbon emissions.

Instead, Congress turned in December to an omnibus spending package (HR 83—PL 113-235) that included eleven of the twelve annual appropriations bills. The $30.1 billion provided for Interior–Environment represented a compromise between House and Senate draft proposals. House appropriators had recommended $200 million less, while Senate appropriators recommended $300 million more.

The EPA received $8.1 billion, the same level Senate appropriators offered in their draft bill in August, which was about $600 million more than proposed in July by House appropriators (HR 5171—H Rept 113-551). The compromise, however, included House Republican requests to continue to reduce EPA staffing, which they said would hold employee numbers to the lowest level since 1989.

The Interior received nearly $10.8 billion, about $300 million more than in fiscal 2014 but $100 million less than the administration requested.

The broader spending package was signed by President Obama on December 16. Ahead of the midterm elections, lawmakers had approved a three-month continuing resolution to avoid a partial government shutdown that would otherwise have occurred at the start of the 2015 fiscal year on October 1.

House Committee Action

The House Appropriations Committee on July 8 unveiled a $30.2 billion bill for the Interior Department and environmental programs that provided an increase in spending to combat a predicted dangerous wildfire season in the West due to a persistent drought.

The draft bill was approved a day later by the Interior–Environment Appropriations Subcommittee by a voice vote. It proposed to cut spending in half for the EPA's budget and congressional affairs offices and the office of Administrator Gina McCarthy as punishment for failing to answer committee questions about how the agency was spending its money.

Rep. Harold Rogers of Kentucky, the Republican committee chair, said the committee would not tolerate getting inaccurate or incomplete spending information from agencies it funds.

The draft bill provided $7.5 billion for the EPA, a 9 percent reduction from fiscal 2014 levels, and would hold staffing levels at 15,000. The subcommittee bill also proposed to block the EPA from regulating greenhouse gas emissions from new and existing power plants.

The House Appropriations Committee voted 29–19, along party lines, to approve the $30.2 billion funding bill (HR 5171), an increase of $162 million above the fiscal year 2014 enacted level and a reduction of $409 million below the administration's request.

It included a one-time payment of $442 million for Payments in Lieu of Taxes (PILT), which provide funds to local communities with large areas of federal land to help offset losses in property taxes.

Rogers noted that the bill would rein in agency rulemaking that he said goes beyond what Congress has authorized and he claimed often is harmful to the economy.

The bill would have blocked the administration from implementing a Clean Water Act rule or a listing of sage grouse as endangered or threatened. The committee also rejected attempts to designate some wildfire funding as emergency spending. The proposed water rule that would be blocked by the bill would define what waters are regulated under the pollution law (PL 95-217).

The legislation was not considered on the House floor.

Senate Committee Action

As in the first year of the 113th Congress, the Senate Appropriations Committee never began consideration of its version of the legislation, although a draft proposal was released in August by the Republican and Democratic leaders of the Appropriations Interior and Environment Subcommittee.

The draft document, which they said they hoped would serve as a starting point for further discussions, would have provided $30.7 billion with spending levels across the agencies generally consistent with the House proposal. The Senate appropriators, however, diverged from the House on wildfire spending, setting aside $4.3 billion to combat western wildfires, with nearly $1.2 billion of the total considered emergency funding without offsets.

No further action was taken on the Senate draft proposal.

Final Action

After the midterm elections, lawmakers returned to work with the federal government funded through a short-term continuing resolution. House and Senate leaders agreed to largely stick to funding levels the chambers had in common in their respective Interior–Environment Appropriations proposals.

On December 11, the House voted 219–206 to approve an omnibus spending package (HR 83—PL 113-235) that included eleven of the twelve annual appropriations bills. The Senate followed two days later, voting 56–40 to approve the bill, and President Obama signed it on December 16.

The Interior–Environment account saw its funding stay relatively steady. Democrats agreed, however, to GOP demands for some policy provisions by including language prohibiting funding for the Fish and Wildlife Service to make an Endangered Species Act listing decision on the sage grouse. The package also contained a rider blocking the EPA from regulating, under a 1976 chemicals law, the lead contained in ammunition or fishing tackle. Left out of the bill were Republican proposals targeting the EPA's ability to regulate carbon emissions from power plants and limit its jurisdiction under the Clean Water Act.

MAJOR PROVISIONS

Interior Department

The department received nearly $10.8 billion, an increase over fiscal 2014 appropriations of $10.5 billion, but not as much as the administration requested.

Departmental funding included the following:

- $1.1 billion for the Bureau of Land Management, an increase of $14 million above the fiscal 2014 enacted level.
- $2.6 billion for the National Park Service, the same amount requested by the administration.
- $1.4 billion for the Fish and Wildlife Service, $12 million more than in fiscal 2014.
- $2.6 billion for the Bureau of Indian Affairs, $70 million more than in fiscal 2014.

Environmental Protection Agency

The EPA received nearly $8.2 billion, which was $20 million less than it received in fiscal 2014.

Forest Service

The agency, part of the Agriculture Department, received almost $5.1 billion, roughly $423 million less than enacted for fiscal 2014.

Indian Health Service

Part of the Department of Health and Human Services, the agency received $4.6 billion, an increase of more than $200 million over fiscal 2014.

Water and Energy Appropriations

FISCAL 2014

Congress appropriated $34.1 billion in fiscal 2014 for the Department of Energy, the Army Corps of Engineers, the Interior Department's Bureau of Reclamation, and other agencies as part of a broader funding bill for the federal government that cleared on January 15, 2014.

The following day, President Obama signed the legislation (HR 3547—PL 113-76), although he had sought more funding for energy efficiency and renewable energy programs than was provided. The Water–Energy title fell almost $1 billion short of the administration's request but provided nearly $800 million more than presequester fiscal 2013, not including supplemental appropriations for disaster relief.

The appropriations process extended more than three months beyond October 1, the start of the fiscal year, and included a sixteen-day partial government shutdown. House and Senate appropriators crafted the omnibus under the terms of a bipartisan two-year budget agreement (HJ Res 59—PL 113-67) negotiated in December 2013 that pared back cuts imposed by the sequester and raised caps on discretionary spending first set in the 2011 debt limit law (PL 112-25).

House and Senate appropriators were sharply divided over how they should address renewable and conventional energy sources, approving separate fiscal 2014 Energy–Water bills that reflected those differences.

The House bill (HR 2609—H Rept 113-135) would have provided $30.4 billion in fiscal 2014, while the Senate bill (S 1245—S Rept 113-47) had $34.8 billion for Energy–Water programs—close to the administration's request and roughly $1.5 billion more than enacted for fiscal 2013.

The House approved its bill on July 10, voting mostly along party lines, 227–198. The Senate Appropriations Committee passed its bill in June on a bipartisan 24–6 vote, but it did not advance any farther.

Conflicts between the two bills began with spending on renewable energy and science research. The House bill would have financed renewable energy programs under the Energy Department at $983 million, roughly half the fiscal 2013 amount. The House bill also would have limited spending on high-risk energy research, to $50 million, compared with $265 million appropriated for 2013. At the same time, it would have provided $450 million for the development of coal, natural gas, and oil energy technologies.

The Senate committee moved in the opposite direction. Its bill called for increasing spending on energy efficiency and renewable programs to $2.4 billion, $476 million more than in fiscal 2013, and would have provided $329 million more than the House for high-risk energy research.

The Senate bill would have provided $5.2 billion for the Energy Department's Office of Science, which financed biological, energy, and scientific-computing research. The total was about $500 million more than the House bill and $277 million more than enacted for 2013.

Omnibus Highlights

Negotiators on the omnibus (HR 3547) agreed to provide $562 million for research on coal, natural gas, oil, and other fossil energy technology, an amount roughly $28 million greater than the fiscal 2013 level and $141 million more than the administration wanted.

The bill increased spending on renewable energy and efficiency by $95 million above the 2013 level, but that figure remained $896 million short of the administration's request. It also provided $889 million for nuclear energy research and development, an increase of $36 million over the 2013 level and $154 million more than the administration requested.

Negotiators zeroed out a requested $20 million to develop new technologies for the interconnection between electric transmission and distribution grids. And they added $5.5 million to the $38 million requested to develop cybersecurity protections for energy transmission systems.

They also provided $110 million for small modular reactor licensing technical support, 57 percent more than the administration sought. The package also included $62 million to keep afloat a financially troubled uranium enrichment project in Ohio that was intended to produce nuclear fuel for power plants and low-enriched uranium used to produce tritium for nuclear weapons.

The omnibus set the appropriation for high-risk energy research at $280 million, a $15 million increase from fiscal 2013 and far more than the House proposed, but $99 million short of the administration's request, which had been endorsed by the Senate committee.

Army Corps of Engineers spending was increased to $5.5 billion, about $487 million above fiscal 2013. The appropriation included more than $1 billion from the Harbor Maintenance Trust Fund, an increase from the typical annual appropriation from that fund of about $700 million. The omnibus also called for general-fund financing of 75 percent of the cost of the Olmsted lock and dam project on the Ohio River, up from the previous 50 percent ceiling. The remaining 25 percent was to come from the Inland Waterways Trust Fund. The larger contribution from the general fund allowed for an increase in the number of projects financed by the inland waterways fund.

Negotiators dropped the House bill provision that would have provided an additional $25 million for the Yucca Mountain project, but $13 million from fiscal 2013 remained available.

FISCAL 2015

Controversial policy riders to the Energy–Water bill helped sink the fiscal 2015 appropriations process in the Senate. Wrap-up funding for the bill was ultimately included in an omnibus package in December (PL 113-235).

President Obama had sought a 2.6 percent increase in spending for the Energy Department to fuel his goal of increasing renewable energy production. His proposal called for a dramatic increase in research and development of renewable energy technologies while slashing subsidies for fossil fuels research.

The plan was not well received among House Republicans. The Appropriations Committee in June approved a $34 billion bill (HR 4923—H Rept 113-486) that would decrease spending on renewable energy by $1.8 billion and increase fossil-fuel research to nearly $600 million. Over the objections of Democrats, the bill included provisions to allow guns to be carried on Army Corps of Engineers land and prevent the Environmental Protection Agency from completing a rule to redefine national waters subject to the Clean Water Act (PL 95-217).

The House took up the bill in July, rejecting several amendments from Democrats that would have set funding for renewable energy to fiscal 2014 levels. It also rejected measures from Republicans that would have cut the entire $1.8 billion renewable program, including one that would have cut fossil fuel and nuclear funding as well. Instead, they included an amendment to prohibit greenhouse gas research. The bill passed on July 10 by a vote of 253–170.

President Obama already had threatened to veto the bill—the administration objected to restrictions on cooperation with Russia on nonproliferation programs and cuts in funding for renewable energy programs, as well as environmental policy riders. The White House also opposed a requirement in the bill to continue construction of a mixed oxide plutonium processing plant in South Carolina, which it intends to put on hold while searching for cheaper alternatives.

In the Senate, energy and water appropriations had not progressed much beyond the draft bill stage, as Republicans threatened to use it to force a vote on the administration's carbon emissions regulations.

Still, the Senate Energy and Water Development Appropriations subcommittee approved its draft version of a $34.2 billion bill on June 17. The bill included $28.36 billion for the Energy Department, a 4 percent increase from 2014 levels, including $5.09 billion for the Office of Science, $2.1 billion for energy efficiency and renewable energy programs, and $280 million for the Advanced Research Projects Agency–Energy.

The full committee scrapped a scheduled vote because of the contentious proposed amendment and a preliminary veto threat from the White House.

Omnibus Highlights

The fiscal 2015 omnibus spending package (PL 113-235) included $34.7 billion for energy and water funding. It included $1.9 billion for renewable energy and increases on fossil fuel and nuclear programs. It also included policy riders that would restrain several of the Obama administration's Clean Water Act policies but did not provide new funding for the Yucca Mountain nuclear waste repository. Lawmakers stopped short of blocking the EPA rule.

The bill did not block the Obama administration's efforts to define the Waters of the United States subject to jurisdiction under the Clean Water Act, as the House pushed. But it included related policy riders aimed at protecting farmers from the so-called WOTUS rule. It did not include a provision to allow guns to be carried on Army Corps of Engineers land that had been sought by some House Republicans.

The bill included $10.2 billion for Energy Department programs, a slight increase compared with fiscal 2014.

Spending for research on advanced coal, natural gas, oil, and other fossil energy technologies was set at $571 million, a 1.5 percent increase from fiscal 2014 levels, while renewable energy development remained at $1.9 billion and science research remained at $5.1 billion. Funding for nuclear energy research and development increased by 2.7 percent to $914 million.

The Army Corps of Engineers received $5.5 billion—slightly more than the fiscal 2014 enacted level—which included $2.3 billion for navigation projects and studies.

2015–2016

After Republican gains in the 2014 midterm elections, incoming Senate Majority Leader Mitch McConnell pointed to the Keystone XL oil pipeline as being at the top of the list of issues he expected to tackle now that Republicans controlled both chambers.

Meanwhile, President Barack Obama said in a December 2014 interview with NPR that he was prepared to uncap his veto pen if Republicans sent him bills he found objectionable. "I suspect there are going to be some times where I've got to pull that pen out. And I'm going to defend gains that we've made in health care; I'm going to defend gains that we've made on environment and clean air and clean water," he said.

True to McConnell's goal, the Senate approved a Keystone bill (S 1) in January to speed the approval process for the pipeline. After clearing the House, it landed in the Oval Office, where Obama vetoed it. Republicans did not have a two-thirds majority in either chamber to override a veto.

Obama would later veto Republican-led resolutions seeking to block the Obama administration from regulating carbon emissions from power plants or broadening the scope of waterways that fall under federal regulation.

While at loggerheads over climate change issues, the 114th Congress was able to come together on legislation (HR 2576—PL 114-182) to update a forty-year-old law regulating toxic chemicals in thousands of household and industrial products. Lawmakers also agreed to a water resources development bill authorizing $11.7 billion for infrastructure projects overseen by the Army Corps of Engineers that included assistance to Flint, Michigan, in fixing its lead-tainted drinking water system. And they turned to the appropriations process to lift a ban on the export of crude oil.

Energy Policy

An energy policy bill that had been the subject of two years of debate and negotiations did not make it to the House floor before the 114th Congress ended because conferees were not able to reach an agreement on the House and Senate bills.

The bill passed by the Senate (S 2012) would have streamlined permitting for the export of liquefied natural gas, permanently reauthorized the Land and Water Conservation Fund, and established new energy efficiency standards for buildings. The House version (HR 8) focused more on energy infrastructure, including more extensive natural gas pipeline permitting.

All of those elements were dropped in the conference talks, according to House and Senate negotiators. The compromise left mostly provisions related to natural resources, such as forest fire management and rules for the use of public lands.

Sen. Lisa Murkowski of Alaska, the chair of the Energy and Natural Resources Committee, and Sen. Maria Cantwell of Washington, the ranking Democrat, said conferees had reached an agreement in principle on a framework for the conference report but that House leaders appeared to have concluded that time had run out.

The House passed a broad energy bill in December, but partisan differences over energy policy kept it from going further. In fact, Democrats' support for the measure had disintegrated during an Energy and Commerce Committee markup when Republicans added more provisions to slow or halt a transition from the use of fossil fuels, especially coal, in U.S. power plants.

The White House had already issued a veto threat against the bill (HR 8), arguing it would undermine efforts to improve renewable technology infrastructure and efficiency improvements.

Among other provisions, the bill would streamline the export of liquefied natural gas, expedite gas pipeline permits, and direct federal agencies to coordinate better on power grid reliability issues and to incorporate smart grid and efficiency technologies into the overall electricity infrastructure.

A less ambitious Senate bill (S 2012) never got past a markup in the Energy and Natural Resources Committee. It also would streamline permitting for gas exports, raise energy-efficiency standards for commercial and federal buildings, indefinitely reauthorize the Land and Water Conservation Fund, and require infrastructure upgrades to ensure grid reliability and security.

It turned out, though, that the biggest energy policy development in Congress in 2015—lifting the ban on the export of crude oil—was accomplished on the omnibus appropriations bill in December.

2015 House Action

The House Energy and Commerce subcommittee on energy and power approved a draft energy bill on July 22 that committee leaders said they hoped would be a starting point for further bipartisan compromise after the August recess. The draft, approved by voice vote, aimed to shore up the reliability of energy infrastructure, encourage energy efficiency upgrades, and enhance cooperation with other North American countries to make the continent self-sufficient on energy needs.

Subcommittee Chair Edward Whitfield of Kentucky and committee Chair Fred Upton of Michigan said the full panel would not mark up the legislation until September to allow members time to negotiate. Democrats expressed cautious optimism about the process but warned that their support was far from guaranteed.

The measure reflected the beginnings of compromise in some areas. It would allow industries and environmentalists concerned about proposed efficiency standards for furnaces more time to negotiate with Energy Department regulators—a change from the original draft, which would have delayed the rule until an advisory panel studied costs.

Frank Pallone Jr., the ranking Democrat on the Energy and Commerce subcommittee, said he would not object to that language at the time, but other provisions troubled him, including one that would change the Federal Energy Regulatory Commission (FERC)'s involvement in forward capacity markets that are designed to ensure sufficient electricity for a reliable grid. That language was still in the works.

Upton and Pallone had agreed to include a number of the Energy Department's recommendations from its Quadrennial Energy Review, they said, such as modifications to the Strategic Petroleum Reserve and the Oil Spill Liability Trust Fund.

The leaders had agreed to include authorizations for infrastructure spending, Pallone said, naming leaky gas pipelines as an area of focus. Hydropower licensing changes were also under discussion, he said.

Though committee members worked through the spring and summer on a consensus draft of energy legislation, an early September vote was delayed by conflicts over provisions on fossil fuels and climate change, and just before a September 29 Energy and Commerce markup, top Democrats withdrew their support over fossil fuels provisions that Republicans had added earlier in the day.

At the opening of a markup, Upton acknowledged the difficulty in reaching bipartisan consensus on many issues, but he hoped the panel would approve a bill that would be supported by the White House. Pallone, however, was pessimistic that Obama would support the bill being offered by Republicans because it failed to address climate change.

Whitfield said negotiations had broken down over provisions sought by Republicans, including one to require the FERC to review the effects of major EPA regulations.

Another GOP addition to the bill would allow the public to comment on Energy Department building codes, and still another would repeal a 2007 energy law provision barring the use of fossil fuels, such as coal and natural gas, to power federal buildings after 2030.

Energy and Commerce approved the revised legislation the next day, September 30, by a 32–20 vote. Just three Democrats on the panel voted for the bill—Gene Green of Texas, Jerry McNerney of California, and Kurt Schrader of Oregon. Most objected to provisions they said favored fossil fuels and would undercut President Obama's climate agenda.

Democrats warned that Republican provisions added in a revised draft bill would undermine its chances of becoming law, such as a directive that would require FERC to study the impacts of major regulations issued by the EPA and mandate the repeal of a law requiring federal buildings to use non–fossil fuel energy by 2030.

The bill also included language that would order FERC to analyze regional electricity markets, and to make recommendations to Congress for reforms, based on whether the markets "properly value" reliable baseload coal electricity,

Whitfield said. Rep. Joseph P. Kennedy III of Massachusetts offered an amendment to remove the provision, but it was rejected, 22–26.

Rep. Mike Pompeo, R-Kan., won inclusion of an amendment that would require state public utility commissions to publicly report whether utility rates include grid costs that are avoided by rooftop solar power users. Pallone also criticized the amendment, which was adopted by voice vote, as a move to slow the installation of home solar panels.

House GOP leaders hoped to bring the energy bill to the floor the week after Thanksgiving, and on November 18, Upton made even more changes to the measure, filing a manager's amendment with the Rules Committee to strike eight sections of the bill, mainly those endorsed by Democrats. They included sections dedicated to hydropower production and efficiency incentives, 21st Century Workforce programs, carbon capture and sequestration technologies, and the use of energy and water efficiency measures in federal buildings.

Republican leaders also attached two bills from the Natural Resources Committee. One bill (HR 2295) would allow natural gas pipeline rights-of-way through all federally owned lands, while the second (HR 2358) would allow pipeline owners to clear brush, trees, or other vegetation from electrical transmission and distribution facilities on federal land.

The House passed the energy bill on December 3 by a vote of 249–174, mainly along party lines. The bill had originally moved with bipartisan support, but Republican-backed language added to the bill in committee resulted in the collapse of Democratic support. Only nine members of the minority backed it when it cleared the House.

2015 Senate Action

Murkowski and Cantwell unveiled an energy bill (S 2012) in the Senate in July focused on a wide range of national energy issues. They said it would save energy, expand domestic supplies, facilitate investment into critical infrastructure, protect the grid, boost energy trade, improve the performance of federal agencies, and renew programs that have proven effective in a fiscally responsible manner.

The Energy and Natural Resources Committee marked up the bill (S 2012—S Rept 114-138) over the course of three days, considering fifty-nine amendments, of which thirty-four were adopted, nine were rejected, and fifteen were offered and withdrawn. The committee voted 18–4 on July 30 to recommend the Senate approve the bill.

The bill included electric grid modifications, enhanced cybersecurity safeguards, streamlining the process for natural gas export projects, reauthorizing weatherization programs, development of renewable and traditional energy and resources, better interagency coordination of energy/water initiatives, and a permanent reauthorization of the Land and Water Conservation Fund and Historic Preservation Fund, according to the committee. It was not considered by the Senate before the end of 2015.

Congressional Action 2016

The Senate spent two weeks in January debating its energy bill (S 2012), but Democrats were unwilling to move it forward without the Republican majority first allowing them to consider an amendment unrelated to energy policy that would provide federal financial support to help Flint, Michigan, fix its lead-tainted water crisis. Republicans, careful to stress that they were eager to help Flint, said the cost was too great and would establish a precedent of federal assumption of state and local responsibilities.

The Democrats delayed the bill's passage for two months until lawmakers found a different vehicle—the 2016 update to the Water Resources Development Act (S 2848)—to carry the Flint aid package. In April, the Senate finally passed the bill (S 2012) with overwhelming support, 85–12.

Murkowski and Cantwell lauded the open debate process that allowed for more than sixty amendments to be considered from both sides of the aisle, including an amendment they crafted that combined a package of thirty discrete lands and water bills of particular interest to Western states. The final bill, they noted, included priorities sponsored or cosponsored by eighty members of the Senate. Cantwell said it would modernize the electricity grid, make investments in emerging efficiency technologies, and improve cybersecurity.

The energy bill suffered a second setback in May when the House amended the bill to include additional partisan legislation that had drawn strong Obama administration opposition, including veto threats. It passed the House on a 241–178 vote on May 25, setting up the potential for the House and Senate to go to conference.

The Obama administration had opposed measures in the House bill to ease protections for some endangered species as a way to address the California drought. There had been decades of regulatory and legal battles fought in northern California pitting efforts to protect endangered salmon and delta smelt against water infrastructure projects. The administration had also opposed measures to speed up environmental reviews of logging on federal lands and to ease the process for getting permits for natural gas pipelines on federal land, which only added to the reluctance of Senate Democrats to go to conference with the House package.

But in the end, the 2016 election may have been the final nail in the bill's coffin.

House Republicans grew increasingly reluctant to complete the measure before President-elect Donald Trump, who supported the development of fossil fuels—which the Obama administration and Democrats sought to limit—took office in January 2017.

Keystone Pipeline

The Obama administration in November rejected the proposed Keystone XL pipeline from Canada, winding up for the time being, at least, a seven-year campaign by TransCanada Corporation and its allies in Congress to build the $8 billion conduit to connect Alberta's oil sands to Nebraska and then through existing pipelines to Gulf Coast refineries.

Republicans in Congress had tried, through legislation earlier in the year, to force the administration to grant the project permission to cross the Canadian border, but even with the backing of some Democrats, they did not have the votes to override President Barack Obama's veto on February 24, 2015.

TransCanada, a Calgary-based pipeline and power company, asked the U.S. government on November 2 to put on hold its long-standing application for the Keystone XL pipeline. The State Department, which must approve of any such cross-border projects, instead rejected the pipeline application—a position supported by the president.

Obama rejected a permit for the Keystone pipeline on November 6, 2015, remarking at the White House that the project's "overinflated role in our political discourse" had "obscured the fact that this pipeline would neither be a silver bullet for the economy, as was promised by some, nor the express lane to climate disaster proclaimed by others."

In January, the Nebraska Supreme Court had ruled against a group of landowners who had challenged the constitutionality of a state law that had allowed Republican Gov. Dave Heineman to unilaterally approve the Keystone XL pipeline's route across the state, which included some environmentally sensitive areas.

Even though the state law was upheld, TransCanada in October changed course and applied for a route permit from Nebraska's Public Service Commission and then asked the State Department to delay its review while it sought that state approval.

Congressional Action

The Keystone pipeline had been a major issue during the midterm elections, with many Republican candidates supporting its approval as a benefit to the economy. Within days of taking control of the Senate in January, Sens. John Hoeven, a North Dakota Republican, and Joe Manchin, a West Virginia Democrat, introduced legislation (S 1) requiring approval of the Keystone pipeline project. The bill was identical to legislation that failed to pass the Senate by one vote in the 113th Congress.

The Energy and Natural Resources Committee promptly approved the bill, 13–9, on January 8. The same day, the House passed its own version of the legislation (HR 3) by a 266–153 vote. Although twenty-eight Democrats joined the Republican majority in support, the tally remained short of what would be needed to override a veto.

The House debate echoed familiar arguments for and against the Keystone pipeline. Republicans maintained that the pipeline was necessary to establish North American energy security and to aid Canada as an ally. Democrats said that building the pipeline would do little to move the

United States away from the use of oil when greenhouse gas emissions need to be curbed to avoid the worst impacts of climate change.

The full Senate passed the bill 62–36, on January 29, with nine Democrats supporting the legislation, again, not enough to override a veto.

In speaking out against the bill, Sen. Maria Cantwell of Washington, the ranking Democrat on the Energy and Natural Resources Committee, focused on the concerns of landowners in Nebraska—many of whom oppose the proposed route—about the risk of spills. She only briefly mentioned the potential climate impact of the project.

The House cleared the Senate version of the bill, 270–152, on February 11. Obama made good on his veto threat later that month.

"Through this bill, the United States Congress attempts to circumvent longstanding and proven processes for determining whether or not building and operating a cross-border pipeline serves the national interest," Obama said in his veto message on February 24.

The Senate attempted to override the veto but fell five votes short of the 67 majority needed on a 62–37 vote on March 4. Eight months later, the administration rejected TransCanada's application, with Obama stressing U.S. leadership in fighting global climate change.

TransCanada said it might reapply for permission to build the pipeline, and Republican leaders in Congress vowed that the long fight over the project was not over.

Yucca Mountain Nuclear Waste

With a majority in both chambers, Republicans hoped to revive plans for a nuclear waste repository at Yucca Mountain but once again could not overcome opposition from Sen. Harry Reid of Nevada, now in the minority, but who retained the support of President Obama on this issue.

In response to stepped up interest in Yucca, Nevada lawmakers in March introduced legislation in the House (HR 1364) and Senate (S 1825) to safeguard the state from an unwanted repository by requiring the federal government to get approval from the state's governor, local governments, and Indian tribes before building any nuclear waste dump. Reid proposed a second bill in July to require the same approvals before the Department of Energy (DOE) could spend any funds in connection with testing or evaluating a facility. None of the bills advanced.

Meanwhile, the House Appropriations Committee in 2015 included funds to restart the Yucca program in a fiscal 2016 energy–water bill (HR 2028—H Rept 114-91) that was approved by voice vote. During House debate, Rep. Dina Titus of Nevada sought to strip $150 million from nuclear waste disposal funding. Her amendment was defeated on a voice vote, and the bill (HR 2028) passed by a vote of 240–177 in May.

Senate appropriators in May sought to create a pilot program for consolidated nuclear waste storage as proposed by

Sen. Lamar Alexander of Tennessee, the chair of the Energy–Water subcommittee, and Sen. Dianne Feinstein of California, the ranking Democrat. Funding for their pilot program was included in the fiscal 2016 bill for Energy–Water (HR 2028—S Rept 114-54), as well as language to allow DOE to store nuclear waste at private facilities, such as those proposed in Texas and New Mexico.

The appropriations process stalled between the House and Senate, leaving congressional leaders to negotiate an omnibus bill for Congress to consider as it headed toward its year-end recess.

In a December 18, 2015, interview with the *Las Vegas Review-Journal* ahead of the vote on the omnibus, Reid pointed gleefully to the fact that no additional funding was included in the final package that emerged from negotiations between Republican and Democratic leaders in the House and Senate. "Notice there is nothing in these bills for Yucca Mountain," Reid chuckled, according to the newspaper.

Meanwhile, the DOE in December launched a "consent-based" siting process to ensure that communities, tribes, and states were comfortable with the location of future storage and disposal sites before they are constructed. Exactly how the process will work had not been determined, but as a first step, it planned to develop a pilot interim storage facility to accept used nuclear fuel from reactors that have been shut down.

2016 Congressional Action

The legislative dance played out again in 2016 with no funds committed for Yucca Mountain. House appropriators supported a fiscal 2017 bill (HR 5055—H Rept 114-532) that included $150 million within Nuclear Waste Disposal to support Yucca and $20 million within the Nuclear Regulatory Commission to support the licensing application. Senate appropriators again backed a pilot program for consolidated nuclear waste storage in its bill (S 2804—S Rept 236).

The Senate bill did not advance, while the House bill came to the floor in May for debate but failed to pass on a roll-call vote that gained only 112 votes in support. Congress struggled again with the entire appropriations process, ending the 114th Congress with federal agencies being funded on a stopgap measure (PL 114-254)—largely maintaining fiscal 2016 spending levels—that would remain in effect through March 28, 2017, giving the next Congress and administration some breathing room to negotiate a final package.

Clean Water Rule

Republican congressional leaders could not muster the votes they needed to block a controversial new clean water regulation from taking effect in August, though the 2015 rule was tied up in legal challenges that kept it from going into effect.

The Waters of the United States regulation, first proposed in April 2014 and finalized in May 2015, was meant to clarify what bodies of water and wetlands are subject to the jurisdiction of the EPA and the Corps of Engineers under the 1972 Clean Water Act (PL 95-217), which was enacted to protect the nation's waters from pollution.

The law was meant to safeguard "navigable waters," which the rule defined broadly as "the waters of the United States, including the territorial seas." Government agencies and the courts have been left to figure out just what these "waters" are and how far up a river system the federal protection extends.

EPA Administrator Gina McCarthy told a House–Senate hearing in February 2015 that the rule, shorthanded as WOTUS, was intended to narrow, not expand, the agency's jurisdiction over bodies of water. The rule, she said, was designed to clarify uncertainty for state regulators, businesses, and agriculture caused by Supreme Court rulings in 2001 and 2006. The ruling included different tests for determining which bodies of water are subject to regulation under the Clean Water Act.

Republican opponents from states with large farming and ranching interests saw the proposal differently. They feared the rule change would mean virtually every stream, pond, and puddle could be subject to regulation under the Clean Water Act.

Republican Sen. James M. Inhofe of Oklahoma, chair of the Environment and Public Works Committee, had said in February that he read the proposal as being so broad that virtually no land would fall outside of federal regulation. Similarly, Republican Sen. John Barrasso of Wyoming said an EPA map he saw at a January 2016 hearing showed almost all of his home state would be subject to regulation under the Clean Water Act.

Opponents of the rule in Congress turned to several legislative options in the 114th Congress to thwart the rule including stand-alone legislation, the appropriations process, and utilizing the Congressional Review Act, which was included as part of the Contract with America Advancement Act of 1996 (PL 104-121). Under the latter process, Congress can make it so a rule cannot take effect or stay in effect if it passes a joint resolution disapproving the rule. The president may veto resolutions of disapproval, and Congress may override the veto.

The process had been used successfully only once—in 2001, in the early weeks of the George W. Bush administration: Congress disapproved of a workplace regulation of the Clinton administration, and Bush signed the resolution of disapproval. Once a regulation is disapproved of by Congress in this fashion, it cannot be revived "substantially the same." Also, the law is a blunt instrument—Congress cannot disapprove of part of a regulation; it's the whole rule or nothing.

House Action

The House Transportation and Infrastructure Committee on April 15, 2015, approved legislation (HR 1732—H Rept 114-93) that would order the EPA and Corps of Engineers to withdraw the proposed WOTUS rule and start over. The vote was 36–22, Democrats Sean Patrick Maloney of New York and Cheri Bustos of Illinois having joined Republicans in backing the measure.

The committee approved by voice vote an amendment by Rep. Jared Huffman, D-Calif., affirming that the federal government would continue to defer to state authority on the development of water law, water rights, and the legal system under which states mediate disputes over water use. Huffman said the language was necessary for Western states, where water rights are key to local and state economies.

The panel voted 33–23 to reject an amendment by Del. Eleanor Holmes Norton, D-D.C., that would have protected the authority of the EPA and the Army Corps of Engineers to regulate surface water available for public water supplies. The committee's counsel, responding to a question from Chair Bill Shuster, R-Pa., said the language of the amendment was broad and could conceivably apply to water molecules.

The full House passed the WOTUS bill on May 12. The 261–155 vote, though, would not be enough to override President Obama's expected veto if the measure ever reached him.

Republican lawmakers, however, argued that the bill still sent a message against regulatory overreach. Democrats argued that Congress should not act until the final rule was published.

Senate Action

The Senate Environment and Public Works Committee approved a measure (S 1140—114-84) in July 2015 by voice vote to revoke the WOTUS rule. It also spelled out categories of waters to be included or excluded in a revised rule the agencies would need to issue by the end of 2016. Republican leaders, however, failed to round up the necessary sixty-vote majority needed to take up the bill on the floor. The cloture vote was 57–41.

Instead, party leaders turned to a resolution of disapproval (S J Res 22) that was adopted by the Senate on November 4 by a vote of 53–44. Fifty Senate Republicans and Democrats Joe Donnelly of Indiana, Heidi Heitkamp of North Dakota, and Joe Manchin III of West Virginia voted for passage of the disapproval resolution. Susan Collins of Maine was the only Republican to vote against the resolution.

The House adopted it on January 13, 2016, by a vote of 253–166. President Obama, however, vetoed the resolution on January 19. On January 21, a procedural vote in the Senate to override the veto failed.

Water Resources Development

In the waning days of the 114th Congress, lawmakers came together to pass a water resources bill authorizing nearly $11.7 billion for infrastructure projects and $170 million to help Flint, Michigan, repair its drinking water system

NATIONAL MONUMENTS BATTLE

Seeking to bolster his environmental legacy in his final weeks in office, President Barack Obama used authority granted to him under the 1906 Antiquities Act to designate expansive new national monuments in Nevada and Utah that were opposed by leading Republicans in those states.

In all, Obama designated twenty-nine new monuments and enlarged five others during his two terms in office, using the authority more than any previous president to protect the public lands from human damage caused by mining, logging, or road building.

The limits on commercial use of public lands has been hotly contested by western conservatives in Congress, where large swaths of their state lands are under federal control. Calls from them to limit presidential authority under the Antiquities Act has grown since President Bill Clinton designated the Grand Staircase–Escalante National Monument in 1996, expressing concern that the area could be damaged by a large coal mining operation.

The debate played out in Congress on March 26, 2014, when the House took up legislation proposed by Natural Resources Committee Chair Rob Bishop of Utah to modify presidential authority to designate national monuments. His bill (HR 1459) would have restricted the president to no more than one designation per state during a four-year term and required a National Environmental Policy Act review for any designation greater than 5,000 acres.

Of the twenty-nine new national monuments designated by Obama, fourteen were smaller than 5,000 acres, including a February 2015 designation of a quarter-acre in Chicago as the Pullman National Monument and a September 2012 designation of 4,726 acres in Colorado as the Chimney Rock National Monument.

On the floor, Rep. Doc Hastings, R-Wash., argued on March 26 that the modification was needed given Obama's willingness to circumvent Congress on a variety of issues. He warned that national monument designations could significantly block public access and limit public recreation and economic activities.

"Major land use decisions such as this should not be made behind closed doors and should fully involve the local citizens whose livelihoods would be directly affected by such action," he said. "The American people and their elected leaders deserve to have a say in which of their lands deserve special protections as national monuments and which should, instead, be allowed to contribute to the full range of recreational, conservation, economic, and resource benefits that carefully managed multiple-use lands provide."

Rep. Raúl M. Grijalva, D-Ariz., argued against what he called diluting this popular tool and questioned the sincerity of Republican opponents who claimed they wanted more public input into designating national monuments.

"If the majority is truly concerned about public input or congressional review of national monuments and conservation of Federal land, why don't they consider bills to establish new monuments, parks, heritage areas, or wilderness?" he said on the House floor on March 26. "Nearly 100 conservation designation bills have been introduced in the last two Congresses. Four have become law," he said.

The House voted 222–201, mostly along party lines, to approve the bill (HR 1459). Only three Democrats supported it. The Senate did not consider it.

A year later, the House would again debate limiting presidential authority under the Antiquities Act when President Obama designated in July 2015 new national monuments in California, Nevada, and Texas. During debate on a funding bill (HR 2822) for the Interior Department, a Nevada Republican proposed an amendment to block new monuments where there is local opposition.

Rep. Crescent Hardy's proposal specified certain counties in California, Arizona, New Mexico, Oregon, and Utah for exclusion from the Antiquities Act. It passed by a 222–206 vote that fell largely along party lines.

On December 28, 2016, President Obama designated about 2,100 square miles in Utah as the Bears Ears National Monument, citing the land's "extraordinary archaeological and cultural record" and its "sacredness" to many Native American tribes as important for conserving. He also designated 463 square miles in Nevada as the Gold Butte National Monument, saying it was worthy of protection because of its "diverse and irreplaceable scientific, historic, and prehistoric resources."

The end-of-year designations left no time for the 114th Congress to weigh in, but Bishop and other Republican opponents vowed that they would act after the 115th Congress was seated and then President-Elect Donald Trump was sworn into office.

"The President was never meant to set aside millions of acres against the express wishes of local communities and their elected representatives," Sen. Orrin Hatch, R-Utah, said in a statement following Obama's December 28 declaration.

that had been tainted with lead. President Barack Obama signed the bill into law (PL 114-322) on December 16.

In a flurry of late-session action, the House renamed S 612 the Water Infrastructure Improvements for the Nation Act and replaced the underlying text with language that included authorizing infrastructure projects, help for Flint, provisions to address California's prolonged drought, and several water settlement agreements with Native Americans. The amended bill passed, 360–61, on December 8, 2016.

To address lead in drinking water, the bill directs the EPA to establish a grant program for projects and activities that reduce lead in drinking water, including replacement of lead service lines and corrosion control. And it requires the EPA to establish a voluntary program for testing for lead in drinking water at schools and child care programs under the jurisdiction of local education agencies.

The Senate agreed to the House amendments, voting 78–21 in favor on December 10.

The $11.7 billion in infrastructure authorization represented a reauthorization of the Water Resources Development Act, known familiarly as WRDA, that historically is redone every two years, but partisan fights had caused only two to be signed since 2000. The 2014 bill (PL 113-121) was the first to be enacted in seven years. Included in the 2016 authorization were thirty new Army Corps of Engineers navigation, natural disaster management, and ecosystem restoration projects, along with modifications to eight existing projects.

The Corps needed about $19.7 billion to complete water and other projects already authorized. At current funding rates of about $1 billion a year, those projects would take about twenty years to complete, Chief of Engineers Lt. Gen. Thomas P. Bostick told the Senate Environment and Public Works Committee in March.

Congressional Action

In April 2016, the Senate Environment and Public Works Committee approved, on a 19–1 vote, an early version of WRDA (S 2848—S Rept 114-283). The next month, the House Transportation and Infrastructure Committee approved its bill (HR 5303—H Rept 114-785, Pt. 1).

Transportation and Infrastructure Committee Chair Bill Shuster of Pennsylvania and Rep. Peter DeFazio of Oregon, the ranking Democrat on the panel, released a joint press statement saying the bill would address the infrastructure needs of the nation's ports and waterways through the regular legislative process.

In September, the House approved its bill (HR 5303) by a vote of 399–25 and the Senate approved its bill (S 2838) by a vote of 95–3, setting up negotiations for a final bill.

A key issue to resolve was authorizing funding to address the drinking water crisis in Flint caused by lead and other contaminants leaching from the city's pipes.

The Senate bill included up to $100 million in grants to assist states with drinking water emergencies, which only Flint qualified for at the time, and $70 million to subsidize loans for water infrastructure projects. It also included $50 million in grants to help small and disadvantaged communities comply with drinking water standards, $30 million in grants to reduce lead exposure among children, and $20 million to develop a national lead exposure registry.

The House bill did not include Flint funding. Rep. Dan Kildee of Michigan had proposed inserting $100 million in paid-for Flint aid into the House version, but the proposal was rejected during a House Rules Committee hearing.

Negotiations over a final version of the bill included the Flint aid, and the House passed the water resources bill 360–61 on December 8.

In the Senate, a late-entry provision for drought-stricken California drew opposition from Barbara Boxer of California, ranking Democrat on the Environment and Public Works Committee. She threatened to try to block the bill after her fellow California Democrat Dianne Feinstein and House Majority Leader Kevin McCarthy, a Republican from the state, had agreed to include a provision to relax environmental regulations in order to allow more water to be pumped for drought-stricken central and southern California from federal and state water projects.

Boxer spoke against the bill on the floor saying it was opposed by salmon fisheries on the West Coast as well as environmental groups.

Other Democrats objected to a provision to require that drinking water projects authorized in the bill use U.S.-made iron and steel for fiscal 2017, saying the "Buy America" provision should have been extended indefinitely.

A similar provision applying to clean water projects was made indefinite in the 2014 water resources bill.

In addition to those who voted against the measure over environmental and labor concerns, senators from Alabama voted "no" due to a provision that wades into a water dispute between their state and neighboring Georgia.

The vote was 78–21. It followed soon after the chamber cleared a continuing resolution late on December 9 (HR 2028) that avoided a government shutdown at the end of the day. Passage of both measures was needed to deliver funding to Flint to help it repair its drinking water system.

Toxic Chemical Regulations

President Barack Obama in June 2016 signed the first update of the nation's toxic chemicals review law in forty years, ending years of debate on Capitol Hill over how best for the federal government to regulate toxic chemicals found in thousands of household and industrial products.

The Toxic Substances Control Act of 1976 (PL 94-469) allowed chemicals to be used in products unless the EPA proved they were dangerous, but in the forty years since it was enacted, the federal agency had fully tested just 200 of the 23,000 chemicals introduced and banned just five.

The new law (PL 114-182) was intended to step up the pace of the EPA's reviews and increase the number of chemicals it restricts. The measure had bipartisan backing and was endorsed by both environmental groups and manufacturing trade associations. It passed the House in May by a vote of 403–12 and cleared the Senate on a voice vote in June.

Congressional Action

Early in the 114th Congress, Sens. David Vitter of Louisiana and Tom Udall of New Mexico reintroduced the Frank R. Lautenberg Chemical Safety for the 21st Century Act (S 697), named in honor of the late New Jersey Democrat who had been a longtime advocate for updating the 1976 Toxic Substances Control Act (TSCA).

In May 2013, Lautenberg and Vitter had introduced legislation (S 2009) that represented the first bipartisan TSCA reform proposal. However, Lautenberg died soon after the bill's introduction, and it did not become law. Udall then stepped in to work with Vitter on the issue. Their bill passed the Environment and Public Works Committee on April 28, 2015, by a vote of 15–5.

The bill (S 2009—S Rept 114-67) would set safety standards for tens of thousands of unregulated chemicals and offer new protections to children, pregnant women, and others who are vulnerable to the effects of toxic chemicals. While an improvement over the current law, Barbara Boxer of California and four other Democrats on the committee opposed it, saying it fell short of what is needed to protect the public from harmful chemicals.

Massachusetts Sen. Ed Markey offered a number of critiques but primarily raised concerns that states would have less ability to intercede in the absence of federal action to protect public health and the environment for their residents. He noted that Massachusetts and eleven other states had regulated BPA, a chemical used in some plastic containers, because of federal inaction.

The Senate's version of the bill would establish a four-year mandatory deadline for industry compliance with EPA regulations while expediting EPA regulation on ninety chemicals, such as asbestos, that are known to be dangerous. The legislation also would raise to $25 million, from $18 million, the cap on fees the industry pays to offset the EPA's costs in conducting the reviews.

Udall issued a fact sheet highlighting that the bill would ensure EPA considers health and environmental impacts to determine whether a chemical should be allowed to be sold or manufactured.

In the House, the Energy and Commerce Committee reported out the TSCA Modernization Act (HR 2576—H Rept 114-176) that was approved on June 3, 47–0, and later that month, an amended version passed the House by a 398–1 vote.

The amended measure would set two-year deadlines for the EPA to complete the risk assessments the industry had requested for chemicals and three-year deadlines for agency-initiated studies to be completed, with opportunity for extensions.

New Jersey Rep. Frank Pallone Jr., the Energy and Commerce Committee's top Democrat, said changes made to the bill would ensure that the EPA could set a schedule to complete company-requested risk assessments if the requests exceeded the agency's capacity to process.

Under the amended bill, the EPA would wait to collect fees from the manufacturers that requested the assessments until regulators began the risk evaluation. Lawmakers hoped that companies making chemicals that have raised concerns among retailers or individual states would take their substances directly to the EPA for study so that there would be certainty in the marketplace, all while taking the financial burden off the agency.

Illinois Republican John Shimkus, who led the House TSCA effort, said he could think of no better seal of approval for a chemical manufacturer than having the EPA perform an objective risk evaluation.

The amended bill also reiterated that the EPA must ignore costs and other nonrisk factors when determining whether a substance posed an "unreasonable risk" to public health or the environment. Current law requires the agency to consider the "least burdensome" approach to regulation, a clause that stymied the EPA's 1989 attempt to ban most uses of asbestos.

The Senate amended and passed the House version of the bill on December 17 by voice vote. According to Udall, there were not many differences between the bills, but the House's version was much narrower.

The Obama administration backed most of the Senate's proposal, with EPA Administrator Gina McCarthy writing that "the lack of a workable safety standard, deadlines to review and act on all existing chemicals, and a consistent source of funding are all fundamental flaws in TSCA that should be addressed."

In 2016, House and Senate leaders hammered out a compromise bill that would limit the EPA's ability to preempt state oversight of commercial chemicals, although it would have more authority than under current law. The House voted 403–12 to approve the compromise bill, and in June it passed the Senate by voice vote, though one senator remained skeptical.

Sen. Rand Paul of Kentucky spoke against it, saying the federal government was overreaching its authority.

But other senators praised it. Sen. Jim Inhofe of Oklahoma said it would provide regulatory certainty that would encourage new manufacturing investments as well as protect public health, strengthen transparency and oversight of the EPA, and protect small businesses from unnecessary bureaucratic requirements.

GMO FOOD LABELING

Congress in mid-July 2016 passed legislation backed by the food industry to override state laws and establish a national labeling standard for genetically engineered foods: those that contain genetically modified organisms, or GMOs.

The GMO labeling bill (S 764) was prompted by a Vermont law that went into effect on July 1 requiring the labeling of food and beverage products made from genetically modified crops or ingredients. Similar laws, vociferously opposed by the agriculture and food industries, had been approved in the Connecticut, Maine, and Alaska state legislatures but were yet to be implemented.

The state laws were nullified on July 29 when President Barack Obama signed the GMO labeling bill into law (PL 114-216). It also barred state and local governments from passing mandatory labeling laws for genetically modified food products, beverages, and ingredients.

For the House, support for the Senate bill was an about-face. A year earlier, lawmakers voted 275–150 for a voluntary federal GMO labeling bill (HR 1599), an approach favored by the nation's largest food and beverage companies. Grocery Manufacturers Association President Pamela Bailey argued that a national voluntary system would be better than a patchwork of state laws that she said could potentially confuse consumers and also increase prices.

Reps. Mike Pompeo, R-Kan., and G. K. Butterfield, D-N.C., first introduced a similar bill (HR 4432) in the 113th Congress to preempt individual state food labeling laws with a single, voluntary nationwide labeling program similar to the organic certification program now run by the U.S. Department of Agriculture. The bill failed to clear the Energy and Commerce Committee.

They introduced the voluntary federal GMO labeling bill (HR 1599) in the 114th Congress, this time forging a partnership with the Agriculture Committee, most of whose members view biotechnology and the genetically modified seeds it produces as scientific advancements that improve crop productivity and hardiness.

The House Agriculture Committee approved the bill on a voice vote on July 14, 2015, with a substitute amendment by Rep. Rodney Davis of Illinois, designating the Agriculture Department to administer a certification process and national voluntary labeling for non–genetically modified and genetically modified food and ingredients. The non-GMO certification review would have been similar to the organic certification program the Agriculture Department already operates.

Davis said report language to accompany the legislation would address lingering questions and concerns of lawmakers or interest groups.

The bill would have codified the Food and Drug Administration's position that genetically modified foods and ingredients do not require labeling because they are as safe as those produced through conventional agriculture. About 70 to 80 percent of processed foods sold in the United States contain a genetically modified ingredient, usually corn or soybeans.

The bill (HR 1599) passed the House in July, 275–150, over objections from some Democrats. Rep. James McGovern of Massachusetts, a member of the Rules and Agriculture committees, said he supported mandatory federal GMO labeling but argued the bill left too much of the labeling to the discretion of the food industry.

The bill was left to languish in the Senate Agriculture, Nutrition, and Forestry Committee for the rest of the year. But, on July 7, 2016, the Senate voted 63–30 in favor of replacing the underlying language of S 764, a bill to reauthorize the National Sea Grant College program, with a measure to establish a mandatory federal labeling system for genetically modified foods.

Senate Minority Leader Harry Reid, D-Nevada, had spoken against bringing a GMO bill to the floor under this process, arguing that a major issue such as this should be subject to committee review and open to amendments.

Agriculture Committee Chair K. Michael Conaway of Texas and ranking Democrat Collin C. Peterson of Minnesota said they preferred the House bill, which their committee helped write. But they gave the Senate-passed bill tepid support because they said it would prevent a proliferation of conflicting and costly state laws. Peterson explained the political reality was that Senate Democrats would not support a voluntary approach.

The House agreed to approve the Senate-passed bill on July 14 by a vote of 306–117.

BILL PROVISIONS

The legislation directed the Agriculture Department to establish a process for disclosure of foods and ingredients produced through biotech genetic modification. Small food manufacturers, which had yet to be defined, also would be able to direct consumers to websites or telephone numbers for information.

The bill gave larger companies three options for telling consumers if they are buying a GMO food product: on-label information, a symbol to be developed by the USDA, or bar codes or other digital means that consumers can scan with smartphones.

Agriculture Secretary Tom Vilsack championed the idea of using machine-readable markings, such as a QR code that can be read by a smartphone, as a balance between providing consumers with information some may want and concerns by food and agriculture groups that labeling products as GMO-produced would drive consumers away. Food processors and retail companies argued that the Food and Drug Administration has consistently said current science finds that GMO foods are safe and do not merit labeling because of the way they were produced.

Critics and opponents of the legislation said they would try to address shortcomings in the bill when the Agriculture Department does the rulemaking required to establish the federal labeling process. They note that the legislation did not give USDA enforcement authority for companies that knowingly fail to identify GMO products. The department does not have the authority to recall a product for failing to include a bioengineered disclosure.

Interior and Environmental Appropriations

FISCAL 2016

Lawmakers struggled again to approve a fiscal 2016 spending bill for the Interior Department and environmental programs but this time found something other than climate change to battle over, as a debate over the Confederate flag in the House brought down the entire appropriations process.

As in previous sessions, lawmakers were compelled to pass several continuing resolutions to keep the government funded past the start of the new fiscal year on October 1, 2015. They eventually agreed to a broader spending package (HR 2029—PL 114-113) that included all twelve annual appropriations bills, which President Obama signed on December 18, 2015, the same day it was approved in the House, 315–133, and in the Senate, 65–33.

House and Senate leaders agreed to largely stick to funding levels the chambers shared in common in their respective proposals, with some modifications. The omnibus bill provided $32.2 billion for the Environmental Protection Agency (EPA), Interior Department, as well as its Bureau of Land Management, National Park Service, and Bureau of Indian Affairs. It also covered the Agriculture Department's Forest Service and the Department of Health and Human Services' Indian Health Service.

The $32.2 billion was $1.7 billion more than the fiscal 2015 level but $1.1 billion less than requested by the administration. The EPA did not see an increase in funding, but Interior Department agencies received a $926 million increase, and other agencies were increased by $822 million.

House Committee Action

The House Interior–Environment Appropriations Subcommittee on June 16, by voice vote, approved a $30.2 billion bill (HR 2822) that proposed cutting overall funding for the EPA by 9 percent compared to fiscal 2015 levels, down to $7.4 billion. The agency's staffing levels would be held to 15,000, the lowest since 1989.

The subcommittee draft bill also proposed to block the EPA from issuing greenhouse gas regulations for new and existing power plants, a key component of the administration's "Clean Power Plan," which sought to reduce carbon dioxide emissions from electrical power generation by 32 percent within twenty-five years relative to 2005 levels.

Rep. Betty McCollum of Minnesota, a Democrat, offered an amendment in committee to fund 30 percent of wildfire suppression costs under disaster relief accounts. Although supported by most Appropriations Committee members, leaders argued against it saying it would circumvent the Budget Committee, which has jurisdiction over the issue. The amendment was rejected by voice vote.

The bill included $452 million for the Payments in Lieu of Taxes program (PILT) that was not included in the president's request. The subcommittee did not include a new cap adjustment for wildfires. The president had proposed a new $1.1 billion discretionary cap adjustment because a persistent drought in the West had meant a dangerous fire season ahead.

The full Appropriations Committee reported the bill a week later, on June 16. During the committee markup, Democrats succeeded in attaching three amendments to the spending proposal to limit Confederate imagery at national cemeteries in response to the recent shooting deaths of nine people at a historically black church in Charleston, S.C. A website associated with the young gunman included a manifesto detailing his beliefs on race, as well as several photographs showing him posing with emblems associated with white supremacy, including the Confederate battle flag.

The stand-alone Interior–Environment bill (HR 2822—H Rept 114-170) was brought to the House floor in early July. Republican leaders sought to revise the amendments to allow Confederate flag imagery to continue to be displayed in some circumstances. Democrats pushed back, and on July 9, Speaker John A. Boehner announced the measure was being pulled from floor consideration until the flag issue was resolved. Republican leaders declined to bring any other spending bills to the House floor, fearing Democrats would attach similar Confederate flag amendments to those measures.

Before pulling the bill, the House had weighed in on an Obama administration plan recommending that the coastal plain within the Arctic National Wildlife Refuge be designated as wilderness—a move that would permanently remove the area from oil development.

The Comprehensive Conservation Plan, released on April 3, 2015, would have little actual impact given the remote location and existing prohibitions on energy development there, but the issue was still a flashpoint for Alaskan Republicans. Rep. Don Young of Alaska proposed an amendment to HR 2822 prohibiting funds to be used to implement the plan. His amendment was adopted by voice vote on July 7.

Senate Committee Action

The Appropriations Interior and Environment Subcommittee on June 16 approved, by voice vote, a $31.1 billion spending proposal (S 1645) for the covered agencies but did not include discretionary funding for PILT. The overall total was $900 million more than the House version.

The major funding difference was over Wildland Fire Management. The Senate committee proposed $1.1 billion, a $654 million increase over fiscal 2015. The House proposed $408 million for fiscal 2016, a $246 million cut from the previous year.

The bills reported by the Senate and House committees contained less money than the president sought—the

Senate bill was $2.2 billion less, while the House bill was $3.1 billion less.

Final Action

To prevent a government shutdown, lawmakers passed several continuing resolutions to keep the government funded past the start of the new fiscal year on October 1 and in December agreed to a broader spending package (HR 2029—PL 114-113) that included all twelve annual appropriations bills.

House and Senate leaders largely stuck to funding levels the chambers had in common in their respective proposals for the Interior Department and environmental programs and settled on a top-line figure of $32.2 billion for those agencies. The total represented a $1.7 billion increase over fiscal 2015 but was $1.1 billion less than the administration requested.

The bill included $452 million for the PILT program and additional Wildland Fire Management funding but did not adjust the discretionary spending limits in law or emergency funding for this purpose, both of which had been proposed. The measure did fully fund operations to fight wildfires at the ten-year average cost.

Republican efforts to try to block the Obama administration's climate change regulations from going forward were largely discarded in the final deal. But the measure did prohibit the sage grouse being placed on the Endangered Species List and blocked funding for the EPA to regulate the lead contained in ammunition or fishing tackle under the Toxic Substances Control Act of 1976 (94-469).

MAJOR PROVISIONS

The major provisions of the bill are as follows:

Interior Department

The department received $12 billion, a $1.3 billion increase over fiscal 2015 and roughly $70 million less than the president requested.

Departmental funding included the following:

- $1.2 billion for the Bureau of Land Management, roughly matching what the administration requested.
- $1.5 billion for the Fish and Wildlife Service, nearly $70 million more than in fiscal 2015 but about 65 million less than the administration requested.
- $2.8 billion for the National Park Service, a $237 million increase over fiscal 2015 but nearly $150 million less than the administration requested. The bill also allowed for some public–private partnerships ahead of the National Park Service's 100th anniversary in 2016 and continued to prohibit the construction of a memorial to honor Dwight D. Eisenhower because of disagreements over its design.
- $2.8 billion for the Bureau of Indian Affairs, or $195 million above fiscal 2015 but about $130 million less than the administration requested.

Environmental Protection Agency

Funding for the EPA was held at the fiscal 2015 level of $8.1 billion, roughly $450 million less than the administration requested.

Forest Service

The agency, part of the Agriculture Department, received nearly $5.7 billion, about $120 million less than the administration's request but $600 million more than fiscal 2015.

Indian Health Service

Part of the Department of Health and Human Services, the agency received $4.8 billion, an increase of $165 million over fiscal 2015 but about $300 million less than the administration requested.

FISCAL 2017

The final year of the Obama administration found Congress struggling again with the appropriations process as they completed only one of the twelve appropriations bills for fiscal 2017, which began on October 1, 2016. Agencies were largely maintained at fiscal 2016 levels through a series of stopgap measures designed to avoid a partial government shutdown. The last of these measures (PL 114-254) extended through March 28, 2017, to give the next administration and Congress time to negotiate a final package.

While a final spending deal was not struck in the 114th Congress, the House and Senate did consider spending bills for the Interior Department and environmental programs that once again found Democrats and Republicans at odds over environmental and public lands issues.

House Committee Action

The House Interior–Environment Appropriations Subcommittee on May 25 approved a $32.1 billion bill (HR 5538) by voice vote, roughly $1 billion below what the administration requested and $64 million less than was provided in fiscal 2016.

Republicans on the panel said they intended to use the measure to cut down the administration's authority to implement some key regulations aimed at combating human-caused climate change. Rep. Ken Calvert of California, the Republican chair of the panel, said they were concerned over the number of regulatory actions being pursued by EPA without clear congressional direction. But Rep. Betty McCollum of Minnesota, the ranking Democrat on the panel, said the legislation would undermine environmental laws, endanger public health and safety, and deny the impact climate change is having on the planet.

The measure proposed to reduce the EPA budget to just under $8 billion, a $164 million cut from fiscal 2016, and contained language to prohibit the implementation of the Waters of the United States rule and the Stream Protection

Rule that was in the works at the time. It also blocked the EPA from starting, finalizing, or implementing any rules aimed at controlling methane emissions in existing, rebuilt, or new oil and gas facilities.

The measure was taken up by the House Appropriations Committee on June 15, where it was approved, 31–18. Much of the committee's debate focused on requests by Democrats for emergency funding to deal with an outbreak of the Zika virus in the Americas and lead-tainted water in Flint, Michigan.

A $1.9 billion emergency funding allocation sought by the Obama administration to address the Zika virus outbreak was rejected, 19–28. The World Health Organization (WHO) declared on February 1, 2016, the outbreak was a public health crisis of potentially global reach but nine months later, WHO said the Zika outbreak no longer constituted a global health emergency.

Democrats also wanted $385 million in emergency funding to replace, repair, and upgrade drinking water systems in Flint, Michigan, where, in 2015, elevated levels of lead were found in the blood of children who drank from the system. The request was rejected, 20–29.

Though those amendments were rejected, the bill was to provide funding for cities across the country to address lead in their drinking water. It would boost the clean water and drinking water State Revolving Fund's budget by $207 million to $2.1 billion and allocate $50 million for water infrastructure programs. Rep. Dan Kildee of Michigan, a Democrat, said those provisions would help Flint and other cities to provide clean drinking water.

House Floor Action

The House on July 14 voted 231–196 to approve the Interior–Environment spending bill after three days of late-night debates on more than 130 proposed amendments. A structured rule approved by the House Rules Committee limited debate time, helping pave the way for a quicker vote before the summer recess.

Over the three days, lawmakers passed mostly Republican amendments including measures to block the White House from implementing and forcing rules to control hydraulic fracturing on public and Native American lands; to prevent actions to designate the Mexican gray wolf, the sage grouse, or the jumping mouse as endangered species; and to prevent the EPA from enforcing some of its air pollution polices.

The House again voted on an amendment to prohibit funds to be used to implement an Obama administration plan that recommended designating the coastal plain of the Arctic National Wildlife Refuge as wilderness. It passed 231–196. Three months earlier, the House rejected—on separate legislation—a proposal to designate the coastal plain as wilderness. That amendment fell on a 176–227 vote.

Lawmakers also approved an amendment by Kildee to allow states dealing with drinking water emergencies, like in Flint, Michigan, to tap into their Drinking Water Revolving Funds to resolve the issues.

The bill would have cut funding for the EPA to $7.98 billion, a reduction of $164 million from fiscal 2016 levels and $291 million below the White House's request for the agency. It also included additional funding to control and combat wildfires.

Senate Committee Action

The Senate Interior–Environment Appropriations Subcommittee voted by voice on June 14 to approve a $32 billion spending bill (S 3068) that also dealt harshly with the EPA.

The measure would cut the EPA's budget to $8.1 billion, or $31.2 million less than fiscal 2016 enacted levels, as Republicans on the panel said they planned to stop its "overreach."

Sen. Lisa Murkowski of Alaska, the Republican chair of the panel, said cuts in the bill targeted EPA regulatory actions that go beyond what Congress has authorized.

The measure would have boosted funding for clean water projects with about $2.4 billion for the Clean Water and Drinking Water revolving fund, an increase of $113 million from fiscal 2016. It would also provide $2.9 billion for the National Park Service, $63 million above fiscal 2016.

Two days later, the full Appropriations Committee took up the bill, voting, 16–14, along party lines to approve it after Democrats unsuccessfully sought to strip some Republican-backed policy riders from the measure.

On party-line votes, the committee rejected amendments offered by Sen. Tom Udall of New Mexico to strike riders in the bill that would bar funding for water pollution rules and any designation of the greater sage grouse as endangered. The panel did approve by voice vote an amendment by Udall to allocate additional funding for wildfire suppression and one by Sen. Bill Cassidy, a Republican from Louisiana, to establish a commission that would advise the Interior secretary before issuing regulations on royalty-related issues in mining.

The approved bill included policy riders to prohibit implementation of the Waters of the United States rule, block the administration from listing the greater sage grouse as an endangered species, and included a provision to remove from the endangered list the gray wolf in Wyoming and the Great Lakes.

The bill was not taken up on the Senate floor.

Water and Energy Appropriations

FISCAL 2016

As in recent years, Congress turned to an omnibus spending package (PL 114-113) to complete work on fiscal 2016 appropriations including the energy–water title.

The $37.2 billion for energy and water programs represented a $3 billion boost from fiscal 2015 levels and about

$2 billion more than House and Senate appropriators originally allocated.

President Obama had requested an increase for renewable energy programs and less for fossil fuels research, a position opposed by House Republicans. In the end, both renewable energy and fossil fuel dollars were raised.

The bill also did not include a provision to block the WOTUS rule that would extend federal authority under the Clean Water Act to certain tributaries and wetlands.

House Action

The House Appropriations Committee approved a $36.1 billion energy–water funding bill (HR 2028—H Rept 114-91) by voice vote on April 22, 2015, that provided $1.7 billion for renewable energy and $605 million for fossil fuel research, a decrease for renewables and an increase for the latter.

The House took up the bill the next month, rejecting several amendments proposed by Democrats to restore renewable energy to fiscal 2015 levels, as well as across-the-board spending reductions sought by fiscal conservatives. The House did agree to amendments related to a severe drought in California, including one to block the Bureau of Reclamation from purchasing available water for release into California rivers to benefit fish populations.

The bill was approved by a vote of 240–177.

Senate Action

The Senate Appropriations Subcommittee on Energy and Water Development proposed a $35.4 billion fiscal 2016 budget plan that would have provided a $1.2 billion increase over fiscal 2015 but $668 million less than the administration requested.

The draft bill also included a pilot program for consolidating nuclear waste storage that had been proposed by Alexander and Sen. Dianne Feinstein of California, the ranking Democrat on the subcommittee, but it never advanced, as the Senate appropriations process once again was sidelined over partisan policy issues.

OMNIBUS HIGHLIGHTS

The fiscal 2016 omnibus spending package (PL 114-113) included $37.2 billion for energy and water programs, a $3 billion boost from fiscal 2015 levels, and about $2 billion more than House and Senate appropriators originally allocated.

It provided $29.7 billion for the Energy Department, including the restoration of $40 million in climate change research that was initially cut by House appropriators. The Army Corps of Engineers received about $6 billion, including $1.7 billion for flood and storm damage reduction activities. The Interior Department's Bureau of Reclamation got $1.26 billion, including more than $100 million to address the drought in the West.

The bill also provided money for the Nuclear Regulatory Commission and several other independent agencies that have generally enjoyed bipartisan support.

The bill increased spending for research on advanced coal, natural gas, oil, and other fossil energy technologies to $632 million, an 11 percent increase from fiscal 2015 levels, raised renewable energy development research to $2.1 billion, an 8 percent increase, and provided $5.4 billion for science research, a 6 percent increase.

The Army Corps of Engineers received $6 billion, a 9 percent increase compared to fiscal 2015. It included $1.9 billion for general water project construction.

The measure included $3.6 million for the Nuclear Waste Technical Review Board but no new funding for the proposed Yucca Mountain nuclear repository outside Las Vegas. Senate Minority Leader Harry Reid, D-Nev., has stalled the repository for years through the budget process. It also did not include a nuclear waste pilot program proposed by Alexander and Feinstein.

FISCAL 2017

The final year of the Obama administration found Congress struggling again with the appropriations process as they completed only one of the twelve appropriations bills for fiscal 2017, which began on October 1, 2016. Agencies were largely maintained at fiscal 2016 levels through a series of stopgap measures designed to avoid a partial government shutdown. The last of these measures (PL 114-254) extended through March 28, 2017, to give the next administration and Congress time to negotiate a final package.

As in recent years, Congress failed to reach agreement on a stand-alone Energy–Water bill, but this time the process was derailed in the House rather than the Senate.

The Senate, for the first time in seven years, overwhelmingly passed an energy and water development funding bill for fiscal 2017 (S 2804). The House, however, rejected its $37.4 billion proposal (HR 5055) after it became bogged down by nonrelated amendments on the Iran nuclear agreement, so-called sanctuary cities, and the North Carolina transgender bathroom law.

Senate Action

The Senate Appropriations Committee approved on April 14 by a vote of 30–0, a $37.5 billion Energy–Water bill that would boost funding by $355 million above fiscal 2016 enacted levels and $261 million over the president's budget request.

The bill, however, largely ignored the president's call for a gradual increase in clean energy research and development funding under the "Mission Innovation" banner—an effort by leading carbon-emitting nations to increase spending on research and development of energy sources that release fewer climate-warming gasses into the atmosphere. Obama sought $7.7 billion for low-carbon energy research across twelve agencies in fiscal 2017, 76 percent of which would go to DOE.

The Senate appropriators included $5.4 billion for science research and roughly $2 billion for energy efficiency and renewable energy programs, equal to fiscal 2016 levels.

They also provided $11.2 billion for energy programs, up $157 million from fiscal 2016—including prioritization of "all-of-the-above" strategies for U.S. energy independence—and included $6 billion for the Army Corps of Engineers, an increase of $11 million over existing levels.

When the Senate took up the bill in May, it approved by voice vote an amendment by Jeff Flake, R-Ariz., that would direct the Army Corps of Engineers to help states and other federal agencies pay for certain environmental reviews for their water projects.

The bill stumbled after Sen. Tom Cotton of Arkansas, an opponent of the 2015 Iran nuclear deal, sought an amendment to prevent the use of fiscal 2017 funds by the Energy Department for the planned purchase from Iran of heavy water, a byproduct of nuclear fuel processing.

The White House said the amendment would disrupt the U.S.–Iran nuclear deal and would force President Barack Obama to veto the spending bill. Following the White House's lead, Democratic senators said they would not allow the bill to advance as long as the amendment remained a threat, resulting in three rejected cloture votes on Alexander's substitute.

The Senate, however, passed the bill on May 12 by a vote of 90–8 after senators reached a unanimous-consent agreement sought by Alexander to bypass procedural floor votes and waive cloture debate time.

House Action

The House Appropriations Committee on April 19 approved by a voice vote a $37.4 billion energy and water development funding bill (HR 5055) for fiscal 2017, rejecting once again an Obama administration request for a major boost in funding for clean energy research and development. The committee instead directed additional funding toward the Army Corps of Engineers projects and development of "all-of-the-above" energy strategies including both traditional and renewable sources. The Corps of Engineers received the biggest boost compared to the administration's budget request. The bill would fund the Corps at $6.1 billion, an increase of $100 million over fiscal 2016.

While no Democrats objected to the bill advancing to full committee, the party's leading appropriators criticized controversial policy riders attached to the bill.

Rep. Nita Lowey of New York, the top Democrat on the committee, said the bill should not include significant changes to the Clean Water Act or include changes to gun laws.

The policy riders, which had been included in previous House Energy–Water bills, had caused partisan strife in recent years. One of the most controversial this year would prevent an expansion of federal regulatory power under the Clean Water Act. The Army Corps and the EPA jointly issued a Waters of the United States (WOTUS) regulation that would extend federal authority under the act to additional tributaries and wetlands.

Appropriations Chair Harold Rogers, R-Ky., said the policy riders were needed to address regulatory overreach that is putting too great a burden on crucial industries.

An amendment from Democrats Rosa DeLauro of Connecticut and Betty McCollum of Minnesota would have directed $765 million in emergency aid to Flint, Michigan, to fix water infrastructure and provide services for families and children affected by lead poisoning. The proposal was rejected on a voice vote after Republicans made the case that the aid was not germane to the Energy–Water measure and belonged in other bills, such as the Interior–Environment title.

But the debate turned fiery when Republicans questioned Democrats' motives in bringing the amendment. Texas Republican John Culberson called the move a publicity stunt, drawing loud objections from Democrats.

On the House floor in May, lawmakers considered a number of amendments that eventually tanked the bill. The vote on passage failed 112–305.

Lawmakers had adopted Republican-sponsored provisions dealing with the federal government's response to the North Carolina bathroom law, the Iran nuclear deal, and cities granting "sanctuary" to undocumented immigrants. They also added an amendment offered by Sean Patrick Maloney, D-N.Y., to prohibit discrimination on the basis of sexual orientation or gender identity in federal contracts. The Maloney amendment drew strong opposition from conservatives.

Just 106 Republicans voted in favor of the bill, while 130 voted against it. There were only six Democratic votes in favor as well, with 175 opposed.

CHAPTER 8

Agricultural Policy

Agricultural Policy

President Barack Obama's second term saw continued partisan conflict between the White House and Congress. Obama, a Democrat, faced tough going in the GOP-controlled House throughout these four years, and his party's losses in the 2014 midterm elections resulted in a Republican takeover of the Senate. Nevertheless, Congress was able to push through a much-delayed multi-year farm bill in 2014. In addition, lawmakers approved a measure designed to label food products containing genetically modified organisms.

During Obama's first term, Congress had failed to pass a farm bill by the time the bill was set to expire, September 30, 2012. Farm programs eventually had been extended through October 1, 2013, but it took until early 2014 for lawmakers, facing a deeply partisan environment, to approve a new five-year farm bill.

As they debated the farm bill, one issue that particularly stymied lawmakers was the food stamp program, officially called the Supplemental Nutrition Assistance Program (SNAP). Many Democrats maintained that given the difficult economic times facing numerous Americans, the program should not be cut. But among those seeking cuts to the program were a number of conservative Republicans.

The Republican House leadership chose to split the farm bill in two, with one measure containing the nutrition programs and another containing the farm legislation. But the Senate, controlled by Democrats in 2013–2014, kept the measures as one, and in the end, members voted for a single bill.

The House approved the farm bill legislation on January 29, 2014, by a vote of 251–166, and the Senate passed it on February 4. President Obama signed it into law (PL 113-79) on February 7.

Figure 8.1 Outlays for Agriculture

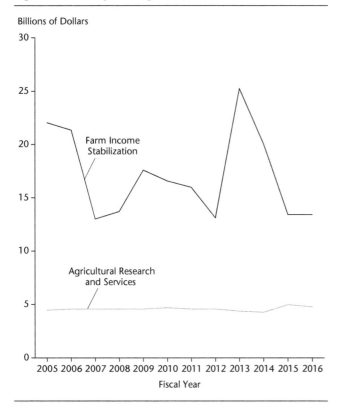

Billions of Dollars

Farm Income Stabilization

Agricultural Research and Services

Fiscal Year

SOURCE: Executive Office of the President, Office of Management and Budget, *Budget of the United States Government, Fiscal Year 2018, Historical Tables* (Washington, DC: U.S. Government Printing Office, 2018), Table 3.2.

REFERENCES

Discussion of agricultural policy for the years 1945–1964 may be found in *Congress and the Nation Vol. I*, pp. 665–767; for the years 1965–1968, *Congress and the Nation Vol. II*, pp. 555–597; for the years 1969–1972, *Congress and the Nation Vol. III*, pp. 331–352; for the years 1973–1976, *Congress and the Nation Vol. IV*, pp. 717–740; for the years 1977–1980, *Congress and the Nation Vol. V*, pp. 365–395; for the years 1981–1984, *Congress and the Nation Vol. VI*, pp. 485–516; for the years 1985–1988, *Congress and the Nation Vol. VII*, pp. 499–539; for the years 1989–1992, *Congress and the Nation Vol. VIII*, pp. 535–557; for the years 1993–1996, *Congress and the Nation Vol. IX*, pp. 479–505; for the years 1997–2000, *Congress and the Nation Vol. X*, pp. 417–431; for the years 2001–2004, *Congress and the Nation Vol. XI*, pp. 447–468; for the years 2005–2008, *Congress and the Nation Vol. XII*, pp. 509–528; for the years 2009–2012, *Congress and the Nation Vol. XIII*, pp. 407–415.

Another important agriculture-related measure approved during President Obama's second term involved the labeling of genetically modified food products.

Congress passed legislation setting up a national labeling standard for genetically engineered foods—those that include genetically modified organisms (GMOs). The bill (S 764) was signed into law (PL 114-216) by President Obama on July 29, 2016.

Interested parties had been debating the issue of how best to label GMO foods for a while, and members of Congress felt the need to step in to prevent the states from setting their own standards, a process that was already underway.

The food industry preferred the idea of one national standard rather than a variety of laws. The new federal law stopped state and local governments from passing their own mandatory labeling laws for GMO products.

Chronology of Action on Agricultural Policy

2013–2014

The 113th Congress notched a major achievement with passage of the five-year farm bill. After the previous farm bill had expired on September 30, 2012, lawmakers had to extend many farm-related programs through October 1, 2013. It took until early 2014 for Congress, mired in various arguments over the legislation and operating in a difficult partisan climate overall, to finally clear the sweeping bill.

One particular sticking point was the food stamp program, officially called the Supplemental Nutrition Assistance Program (SNAP). With many Americans facing tough economic times, Democrats tended to argue that the program should remain intact. Conservative Republicans, meanwhile, were among those seeking steep cuts to the food stamp program.

In the Republican-controlled House, the GOP leadership eventually opted to split the farm bill in two, separating the nutrition programs into a separate measure from the other farm legislation. The Democratic-controlled Senate, meanwhile, retained the nutrition programs in the overall farm bill. The Senate approach ultimately prevailed.

The House approved the farm bill legislation on January 29, 2014, by a vote of 251–166, the Senate followed suit on February 4, and President Obama signed it into law on February 7.

The SNAP program saw an $8.6 billion cut over ten years under the new law, more than the $4 billion that the Democratic-controlled Senate originally sought in its farm bill but much less than the $40 billion cut proposed by many House Republicans. In addition, the law made changes to risk management programs for farmers and to federal support for dairy farmers.

Meanwhile, during the 113th Congress, appropriations for agriculture-related programs were included in omnibus-funding bills that combined the agriculture measures with other measures. Due to partisan gridlock, action on these spending bills often ground to a halt, and lawmakers were forced to resort to stopgap spending measures to keep the government functioning.

Farm Bill

The most important piece of agricultural legislation passed during President Barack Obama's second term was a much-delayed five-year farm bill. The previous farm bill had expired back on September 30, 2012. Under a last-minute deal approved in January 2013, many farm-related programs were extended through October 1, 2013. But amidst battles over various issues connected to the legislation, it took until early 2014 for lawmakers to approve a new farm bill.

One of the most difficult battles centered on the food stamp program, officially called the Supplemental Nutrition Assistance Program (SNAP). Some members, particularly conservative Republicans, wanted steep funding cuts in the program. Supporters of the food stamp program, meanwhile, argued it should not be cut, especially given tough economic times for many Americans. Other issues included country-of-origin food labeling for beef, poultry, and pork and federal support for dairy farmers.

Lawmakers, operating in a difficult partisan environment, worked on the bill throughout 2013. Ultimately, the House approved the farm bill legislation on January 29, 2014, on a vote of 251–166. The Senate approved the conference report on February 4, and President Obama signed it into law on February 7.

NINE-MONTH EXTENSION

The year 2013 seemed to be heading toward a repeat of the year 2012, when Congress had failed to make progress on a farm bill. In 2012, the House Agriculture Committee and its chair, Frank D. Lucas, R-Okla., approved a five-year farm bill containing $35 billion in savings over ten years. But Republican leaders opted against bringing the bill to the House floor. Under the 2012 House bill, requirements for SNAP eligibility would have been changed to save the government about $16 billion over ten years, but GOP leaders said a majority of their party, members who wanted more savings, would not support the bill. The Senate, meanwhile, had approved a bipartisan farm bill in 2012. Lucas and Senate Agriculture Committee chair Debbie

AGRICULTURE LEADERSHIP

Tom Vilsack served as secretary of agriculture for almost the entire eight years of Barack Obama's presidency, becoming the longest-serving member of Obama's cabinet. Obama, then president-elect, picked Vilsack, the former Democratic governor of Iowa, for the post in December 2008. Vilsack had vied for the Democratic presidential nomination against Obama and others but had dropped out of the race in February 2007. Vilsack subsequently opted to support Obama's chief rival, Hillary Rodham Clinton, backing her in the key Iowa caucuses, which took place in January 2008. After Obama defeated Clinton in the caucuses and eventually won the party's presidential nomination, Vilsack enthusiastically backed Obama.

The Senate Agriculture Committee held Vilsack's confirmation hearings on January 14, 2009. He promised to implement the 2008 farm bill, promote renewable energy programs, improve the department's record on civil rights issues, and implement standards for junk food sold in schools. The Senate confirmed him by voice vote on January 20, Inauguration Day.

Vilsack was born on December 13, 1950, in Pittsburgh, Pa. Adopted as an infant, he grew up in Pittsburgh and went on to graduate from Hamilton College and Albany Law School. He moved to Mount Pleasant, Iowa, the hometown of his wife, Christie, where he practiced law and got involved in politics, serving as mayor of Mount Pleasant and as a state senator.

He won the first of his two terms as governor in 1998 in a come-from-behind victory seen as an upset, becoming the first Democrat elected governor of Iowa in three decades. In 2002, he won reelection and was mentioned as a possible running mate for John Kerry, the 2004 Democratic presidential nominee. Having said he would serve only two terms as governor, Vilsack did not run again in 2006. He was known during his gubernatorial terms for his support of corn-based ethanol production and biotechnology, and Obama mentioned Vilsack's backing of biotech and renewable energy as important reasons for selecting him to head the Agriculture Department.

The reaction to Vilsack's nomination among members of Congress was favorable overall. However, because Vilsack hailed from a corn-growing state, some on Capitol Hill expressed concern that he would not be as supportive of farmers from other parts of the country. At the time, another Iowa Democrat, Tom Harkin, chaired the Senate Agriculture Committee.

When Vilsack took over the department in 2009, the farm economy, like the economy as a whole, was facing difficulties. Vilsack, at his confirmation hearings, maintained that the department's food assistance programs were especially important given the economic downturn.

During the four years of Obama's first presidential term, Vilsack's tenure as agriculture secretary was fairly low-key. But a controversy developed in July 2010 when an Agriculture Department employee, Shirley Sherrod, who is African American, was forced to resign her post as rural development director in Georgia after a misleading video clip seemed to show that she was biased against a white farmer. After it became clear that the footage was only part of a longer set of remarks showing Sherrod's opposition to racial bias, Vilsack offered a public apology to Sherrod. He offered her a new job with the department, but Sherrod declined. The episode proved embarrassing for Vilsack, Obama, and the department.

While Democrats controlled Congress during the first two years of Obama's presidency, Republicans took control of the House following the 2010 midterm elections. The Obama administration's relationship with Capitol Hill, already frayed given the outspoken GOP minority, worsened with the arrival in January 2011 of a large group of tea party–backed conservatives focused on slashing government spending. During House consideration of the 2012 multiyear farm bill, Vilsack worried about the cuts to food stamps proposed in the House bill. While many Democrats opposed the magnitude of those cuts, some Republicans wanted even bigger cuts, and the dispute contributed to Congress's inability to pass a farm bill on time.

When Obama won a second term in November 2012, Vilsack decided to stay on as secretary of agriculture. In January 2016, Obama placed Vilsack—who reportedly felt he did not have enough to do and was thinking about quitting—in charge of the administration's initiative focusing on the growing opioid crisis, a problem that hit hard in many rural areas. Vilsack traveled around the country, often recounting to audiences that his mother was a drug and alcohol addict.

In the summer of 2016, Vilsack's name made headlines as speculation mounted that Democratic presidential nominee Hillary Clinton might choose him as her running mate. The two had known each other for many years, and the idea of a Midwesterner with ties to rural communities seemed a good fit. In the end, Clinton opted for Tim Kaine, a Democratic senator from Virginia.

Vilsack, by then the longest-serving member of the Obama administration, departed from his post a week early, on January 13, 2017. On January 17, the U.S. Dairy Export Council, an organization promoting dairy products in the global market, announced that Vilsack would become its president and CEO, effective February 1, 2017.

Stabenow, D-Mich., attempted to come up with a compromise that could be attached to broader fiscal policy legislation, but they failed to bridge the differences between their respective bills.

Farm and nutrition programs had been extended for three months, in October 2012, to provide more time for negotiations. At the end of the 112th Congress, as part of legislation averting a "fiscal cliff" of tax increases for almost all Americans and postponing automatic spending cuts, lawmakers enacted another farm bill extension running through the end of September 2013. This fiscal-cliff bill cleared Congress on January 1, 2013.

Senate Majority Leader Mitch McConnell, R-Ky., and Vice President Joseph R. Biden Jr. were instrumental in forging the 2013 farm bill extension. It scrapped most of the work the Agriculture committees had done and extended only some expiring programs. In addition, it authorized some assistance for farmers and livestock producers affected by weather-related disasters. But it did not authorize all the disaster aid that had been requested.

Direct farm payments, a target of spending cuts by farm bill negotiators from both the House and Senate, were left intact in the extension. But the extension converted mandatory spending for some programs to discretionary accounts, giving appropriators more latitude to set spending levels. In addition, the extension ameliorated concerns that the cost of milk might jump significantly because the federal dairy program would revert to a law enacted right after World War II, requiring the Agriculture Department to buy surplus milk at inflated prices. Many expected the higher costs to eventually make their way to grocery stores.

Stabenow spoke on the floor, objecting to the extension, arguing that she and Lucas had not been consulted. Still, Stabenow and Lucas voted for the bill, considered very important by many lawmakers because of its tax cut and spending provisions. It passed overwhelmingly in both chambers.

House and Senate Committee Action

Once the 113th Congress was underway, House and Senate farm bill writers went back to work. In mid-May, the House and Senate agriculture committees approved similar bills. The Senate Agriculture Committee on May 14 approved S 954, a five-year bill to reauthorize and overhaul farm and nutrition programs. The bill passed on a 15–5 vote, with Senator Kirsten Gillibrand, D-N.Y., who did not approve of the bill's proposed cuts in food benefits, joining four Republicans in opposition. The following day, the House Agriculture Committee approved its five-year measure, HR 1947, on a 36–10 vote. Most lawmakers from each party supported the bill, with two Republicans and eight Democrats in opposition.

The Congressional Budget Office estimated that the Senate bill would cost $955 billion over ten years, saving $17.9 billion compared with existing law. Of that savings total, only $3.9 billion was expected from changes to nutrition programs, with the rest coming from farm programs.

The House bill would cost about $940 billion and would save $33.4 billion, $20.6 billion of which would come from changes to food stamps and other nutrition aid.

As approved in committee, both bills covered traditional "program" commodities—corn, wheat, sorghum, barley, oats, upland cotton, rice, and soybeans and other oilseeds. The bills were quite similar in their broad strokes when it came to agriculture provisions. The biggest difference between them involved their approaches to SNAP and other nutrition programs.

Both bills would have eliminated the direct-payments program that was part of the 2002 farm bill (PL 101-171), under which payments were made to producers and landowners based on their historical participation in commodity price and income support programs, regardless of whether they continued to grow anything on the land. Continued payments to those who did not plant subsidized crops drew opposition to the program from both sides of the aisle.

Both bills would have revised and renamed some existing programs. The countercyclical price program, which paid farmers when the season average of market prices fell below a target price set by the government, would have been eliminated, but both bills would have kept a version of countercyclical assistance. The Senate called its program Adverse Market Payments; the House version was called Price Loss Coverage. In both cases, the target prices were written into the legislation.

The Senate bill's target price program accommodated the desires of Southern growers, although its target price levels were lower than those found in the House bill and lower than what rice and peanut growers requested. The House bill dropped a reference price for cotton from its version of a new crop insurance program that would have become the primary government support program for cotton farmers.

Both bills sought to eliminate the Average Crop Revenue Election (ACRE), created in the 2008 farm bill. It offered farmers a state-level revenue guarantee if they gave up the direct and countercyclical programs.

Both bills would have continued marketing-assistance loans, used to permit farmers to hold off selling some of their production at harvest, when market prices were usually at their lowest.

The House and Senate bills would have expanded crop insurance benefits in an effort to help offset reductions in direct payments to farmers. But the chambers' approaches differed, which was seen as another possible stumbling block to future compromise.

Both bills would have created a new dairy support program including a supply management plan opposed strongly by milk processors and by House Speaker John A. Boehner, R-Ohio.

Senate Floor Action

On June 10, the Senate approved S 954 by a vote of 66–27, making no major changes to the committee-approved bill. Forty-six Democrats, 18 Republicans, and both independents voted for the bill, while 25 Republicans and 2 Democrats—Jack Reed and Sheldon Whitehouse, both of Rhode Island—opposed it.

During floor debate, supporters of the food stamps program defeated proposals to modify SNAP, the country's largest domestic food aid program. By a near-party-line vote of 40–58 on May 21, the Senate rejected an amendment by Pat Roberts, R-Kan., that would have further cut food stamps eligibility by limiting the types of low-income benefits that would have automatically qualified recipients for the food program. The Senate also voted down an amendment by Gillibrand that would have undone the SNAP changes proposed in the bill and offset the $4 billion cost by limiting some reimbursements to crop insurance providers. The vote, also on May 21, was 26–70, with all the support coming from Democrats.

The Senate, on a vote of 45–54, rejected an amendment by Jeanne Shaheen, D-N.H., on May 22, to overhaul U.S. sugar subsidies. Her amendment sought to reduce sugar price supports and tariff restrictions and to allow the Agriculture Department to suspend or modify marketing allotments based on consumer interests and domestic competition.

Senators also voted to reduce by 15 percent crop insurance premium subsidies provided to farmers with an average adjusted gross income of more than $750,000, provided that a USDA study showed that the reduction would not harm other growers. The amendment, by Richard Durbin, D-Ill., was approved 59–33 on May 29.

The Senate also adopted, on a near-party-line vote of 48–38, an amendment by Patrick J. Leahy, D-Vt., to create a pilot program to provide ultra-high-speed broadband service to rural areas, with downstream transmission capacities of 1 gigabit or higher.

House Floor Action

Opposition from House Democrats and small-government conservatives doomed the House farm bill, HR 1947, when it came to the House floor. On June 20, the House rejected the bill on a 195–234 vote seen as a major defeat for GOP leaders Boehner and Cantor, who had backed the legislation along with Lucas. Sixty-two Republicans opposed the bill. Only twenty-four Democrats backed it.

The main reason Democrats opposed the bill was its cutbacks in food stamps. The legislation called for saving more than $20 billion from SNAP. Peterson pointed to House passage of an amendment by Steve Southerland II, R-Fla., which would have allowed states to impose new work requirements on SNAP recipients, as a key reason for Democratic opposition to the bill. The House adopted the amendment on June 20, on a near-party-line vote of 227–198, just before the vote on passage of the overall bill. Six Republicans opposed the amendment and just one Democrat supported it. In addition, an amendment by Richard Hudson, R-N.C., which would have allowed states to require drug testing of SNAP applicants, was adopted by voice vote June 19. Another amendment, by Diane Black, R-Tenn., which would have terminated a

U.S.–Mexico program educating immigrants about SNAP, was approved by voice vote the same day.

Among other amendments the House considered were the following:

- An amendment by Robert W. Goodlatte, R-Va., to strike the bill's dairy market stabilization program, designed to prevent an oversupply of milk, was approved June 20 by a vote of 291–135. Boehner and dairy producers backed the amendment, while Lucas opposed it. It also would have replaced existing support payments with an option for farmers to enroll annually in a new insurance program based on market prices.
- An amendment by Ron Kind, D-Wis., which would have ended crop insurance premium subsidies for farmers with incomes above $250,000 annually and capped yearly per-person premium subsidies at $50,000, was rejected June 20, on a vote of 208–217.
- An amendment by Foreign Affairs Chair Ed Royce, R-Calif., and ranking Democrat Eliot Engel of New York, which would have allowed up to 45 percent of "Food for Peace" appropriations to be used to purchase food produced in or close to recipient countries rather than from U.S. producers, was rejected June 19 on a vote of 203–220.

Food stamps remained a contentious issue, with many Democrats arguing against the cuts to SNAP and many conservative Republicans saying the cuts should be deeper still.

At that point, Majority Leader Eric Cantor, R-Va., split the House bill in two. One dealt with farm programs and the other with nutrition programs, including SNAP. The tactic marked the first time in four decades that the two bills had moved separately.

The farm-programs-only bill (HR 2642) came to the House floor in mid-July. It faced a veto threat from President Obama, in part because of the separation of agriculture and nutrition issues. The bill passed narrowly, on a vote of 216–208, with no Democrats supporting it. In an emotional debate over the bill, Democrats argued that removing the bill's food stamps provisions exposed the GOP majority's indifference to the plight of low-income families. The bill's provisions were more or less the same as the agriculture language in the rejected HR 1947. It was estimated to save $12.9 billion over ten years when compared with existing law.

The nutrition-only bill, HR 3102, which would have saved about $39 billion, also faced a veto threat from Obama. The House approved it on September 19, on a vote of 217–210, also with no support from Democrats. Fifteen Republicans opposed the bill. Unlike the farm-programs-only bill, the nutrition bill was not just taken from HR 1947, the earlier combination farm bill. It included additional provisions designed to reduce spending on food stamps.

In addition to curtailing rules that made people eligible for food stamps based on noncash aid or services they received from other programs for low-income people, the bill would have eliminated an employment waiver for

SNAP recipients living in areas with unemployment rates of 10 percent or higher. Under existing policy, states had the flexibility to continue benefits for childless, single, able-bodied adults younger than fifty for longer than three months out of every thirty-six months.

The nutrition title in HR 1947 had been estimated to save $20.5 billion over ten years, mostly by limiting food stamps eligibility. The new bill's savings of $39 billion represented about 5 percent of the program's cost over a decade, according to the Congressional Budget Office (CBO). The main difference was the provision eliminating the work requirement waiver. The CBO also estimated that were the bill to be enacted, 3.8 million people would have been removed from the SNAP rolls in 2014.

In late September, the House voted to combine the two measures and go to conference with the Senate on HR 2642.

CONFERENCE MEETS

In the fall of 2013, Congress was focused on matters other than the farm bill, with lawmakers enmeshed in a fiscal policy fight that led to a sixteen-day government shutdown beginning October 1. But House leaders, aware that farm programs would expire September 30, moved to expedite a conference committee with the Senate in an effort to resolve the various differences in the chambers' versions of farm legislation.

After the House passed the farm-programs-only bill, HR 2642, on July 11, 2013, the Senate returned it to the House on July 18, amending it with the text of the Senate-passed bill, S 954. At the time, the Senate asked for a conference committee, but the House failed to reply.

On September 28, the House voted to add the text of HR 3102, its nutrition bill, to HR 2642. The decision to combine the bills came in a resolution, H Res. 361, which passed the House on a near-party-line vote of 226–191.

Two days later, the Senate took up HR 2642 again and once more opted to amend it with the text of S 954 and return it to the House, asking for a conference. On October 11, the House, by voice vote, agreed to form a conference committee. The negotiations did not inspire high expectations, especially considering the two chambers' different approaches to food stamps eligibility, and there were few signs of progress as the conference committee continued to meet through the fall.

And yet, as members were getting ready to adjourn for the year, the top four conferees—Lucas, Peterson, Stabenow, and Sen. Thad Cochran, R-Miss.—said they had been able to resolve differences in various crucial areas and expected to have a framework for agreement in early 2014.

Given that the farm programs had expired again, the House passed a bill (HR 3695) by voice vote on December 12 that would have extended the programs through January 2014. But the Senate failed to consider the bill.

BILL APPROVED

On January 29, 2014, the House approved the conference report by a vote of 251–166. The Senate cleared it by a vote of 68–32 on February 4, and President Obama signed the legislation (HR 2642—PL 113-79) on February 7. The final bill eliminated direct and "countercyclical" payments to farmers in favor of new forms of crop insurance. In addition, it cut spending on food stamps, reduced subsidies for cotton producers, and changed the method of subsidizing dairy farmers. Lucas stated that the bill reflected necessities in an era of fiscal retrenchment.

In the House vote, the sixty-two Republicans voting against the conference report included small-government conservatives. The 103 Democratic opponents included progressives who argued that the cuts in nutrition assistance were too steep. But a bipartisan majority, who saw the need to reauthorize farm supports and continue food assistance to the poor, even at a reduced level, mobilized to pass the bill.

The Congressional Budget Office estimated that the bill would cost $956 billion over ten years and would reduce the deficit by $16.6 billion over the same period, or $23 billion when factoring in already enacted sequester savings. Spending on crop insurance programs would rise by $5.7 billion, according to the CBO, while there would be cuts of $8.6 billion to food stamps, $14.3 billion from commodity programs, and $4 billion from conservation programs.

At the start of 2014, one area sparking debate was mandatory country-of-origin labeling for beef, poultry, and pork. Meat processors argued that the country-of-origin rules were unwieldy. Under World Trade Organization rules, Mexico and Canada had challenged those labeling requirements, and this exposed U.S. agribusinesses to potential retaliatory tariffs. Ultimately, the law was silent on country-of-origin labeling regulations.

KEY PROVISIONS

Risk Management for Farmers

The new farm law repealed three major payment systems and replaced them with two programs designed to protect farmers when crop prices fall dramatically or when farmers' revenue drops.

The programs repealed were as follows:

- Direct payments, which gave farmers fixed annual assistance not coupled to crop prices or yields;
- Countercyclical payments, which were paid to farmers when crop prices were less than a target price Congress set in the farm bill; and
- Average Crop Revenue Election, or ACRE, which guaranteed revenue for participating farmers based on market prices and average yields for their commodities.

The two new risk-management programs were:

- The Price Loss Coverage (PLC) program, which was intended to help farmers when prices for a commodity crop, such as corn, wheat, or soybeans, show deep, multiyear declines. Payments would be triggered when a crop's mid-season market price drops below an official reference price.

- The Agriculture Risk Coverage (ARC) program, which would cover a portion of a farmer's revenue losses when crop prices fall to 86 percent of the average of the middle three of the previous five years.

The CBO estimated that the Price Loss Coverage program would cost about $13.1 billion through fiscal 2023, and the Agriculture Risk Coverage would cost $14.1 billion.

In contrast, direct payments would have been worth $40.8 billion over that period, countercyclical payments would have totaled $1.5 billion, and ACRE payments would have been $4.7 billion.

Under the law, cotton producers, who were not eligible for the PLC or the ARC programs, would have access to a supplemental crop insurance system, the Stacked Income Protection Plan (STAX). It was designed to provide assistance without violating World Trade Organization (WTO) rules. The WTO had ruled that the old system unfairly subsidized U.S. cotton producers. STAX would cost $3.3 billion through fiscal 2023, according to a CBO estimate.

The law put new limits on how much federal assistance an individual farmer can receive per year: $125,000 per person or $250,000 per couple. Any Agriculture Risk Coverage (ARC) or Price Loss Coverage (PLC) payments count toward the cap, as well as benefits from marketing loans, another aspect of the safety net that gives farmers a cushion to sell their crops when it is most advantageous. (Farmers can default without penalty, but they forfeit the crops to the government.)

Farmers with adjusted gross incomes above $900,000 would not be eligible to receive benefits under federal commodity and conservation programs. Under the old law, the limit was $1 million.

Dairy Programs

Federal support for dairy farmers was one of the more difficult issues to resolve as lawmakers tried to finish work on the bill. Speaker John A. Boehner of Ohio, along with other Republican leaders, opposed a dairy supply management proposal, arguing that it would be too heavy-handed in its impact on the industry. Under that proposal, participating farmers would reduce milk output to avoid surpluses that could lower prices. The proposal was not included in the final bill, but other changes affecting the dairy industry were included.

Three programs were reauthorized: Dairy Forward Pricing, which allows pools of milk producers to lock in contracts with buyers for future deliveries; Dairy Indemnity Payments, which compensate dairy producers when the government tells them to remove contaminated raw milk from the market; and Dairy Promotion and Research.

A new voluntary insurance program replaced four previous programs. The new plan was designed to protect farmers against losses if milk prices drop too close to feed costs.

The four repealed programs were:

- the Dairy Product Price Support Program, which purchased dairy products with the intention of bringing parity—a measure of the purchasing power of agricultural commodities in relation to their purchasing power in the decade before World War I—to the industry;
- the Dairy Export Incentive Program, which ensured that dairy producers at least broke even on exports;
- the Milk Income Loss Contract Program (MILC), which compensated producers when domestic prices fell below a target level; and
- the Federal Milk Marketing Order Review Commission, which was authorized under the 2008 farm law but never convened.

Nutrition Programs

The SNAP program saw an $8.6 billion cut over ten years under the new law, which represented a net $8 billion in savings on nutrition programs given that the law increases funding for programs that provide commodities to food banks and food pantries, and that provide SNAP beneficiaries with more purchasing power at farmers' markets. The cut was twice the $4 billion that the Democratic-controlled Senate originally sought in its farm bill (S 954) but was much less than the $40 billion cut proposed by many House Republicans.

The law also aimed to curb the ability of states to use nominal payments under the Low Income Home Energy Assistance Program (LIHEAP) to help poor people qualify for more SNAP benefits, since the two programs have been connected.

Illegal immigrants, major lottery prizewinners, traditional college students, convicted murderers, and violent sex offenders were no longer eligible for food stamp benefits.

Fiscal 2013 Agriculture Appropriations

In March 2013, Congress cleared an appropriations measure (HR 933—PL 113-6) financing government activities for the rest of fiscal year 2013, which ended September 30. The measure incorporated five full-year spending bills and preserved prior-year spending levels for agencies and programs covered by the other seven regular bills.

In September 2012, Congress had enacted a six-month continuing resolution (PL 112-175), which kept the government operating under fiscal 2012 spending levels through March 27, 2013. The idea was to give members more time to work on individual spending bills.

Agriculture spending under the bill totaled $139.3 billion, which was 2 percent more than fiscal 2012 before taking the ongoing spending sequester into account. Mandatory programs, including crop price supports and nutrition assistance, accounted for more than 85 percent of the money. Discretionary appropriations came to $20.5

billion, 6 percent over the 2012 figure. Food stamp spending saw a cut of 4 percent. In the measure was $55 million designed to prevent furloughs under the sequester of meat, poultry, and egg inspectors for the Food Safety and Inspection Service.

The House passed HR 933 on March 6 by a vote of 267–151, and the Senate passed an amended version of the bill on March 20 on a 73–26 vote. The House cleared the amended bill on March 21, 318–109, and President Obama signed it into law on March 26.

Fiscal 2014 Agriculture Appropriations

Neither the House nor the Senate saw floor action on a stand-alone agriculture appropriations bill for fiscal year 2014, which began on October 1, 2013. But each chamber's appropriations committee approved a measure. The Senate version (S 1244) would have given $20.9 billion in discretionary budget authority. The House version (HR 2410) called for $19.5 billion, less than both the postsequester fiscal 2013 level and the administration's request. President Barack Obama threatened to veto the House version, citing plans by Republican lawmakers to cut nutrition spending for women and infants by $214 million and cut the budget of the Commodity Futures Trading Commission (CFTC), which regulated the derivatives market.

The House Appropriations Committee approved HR 2410 by voice vote on June 13. One of the issues involved the CFTC's funding level. The administration had requested $315 million for the agency, while the bill called for $195 million, more or less in line with the previous year's appropriation after the sequester. In the Senate, the CFTC funding was located in the Financial Services appropriations bill (S 1371), which suggested a funding level matching that of the administration.

House Democrats opposed the lower CFTC funding level and also spoke out against the committee's $6.7 billion allocation for the Special Supplemental Nutrition Program for Women, Infants and Children, a program supporting pregnant women, nursing mothers, and their children. The $6.7 billion represented a lower level than that enacted in fiscal year 2013 and was $487 million less than Obama's request.

The House committee also sought to reduce spending on Food for Peace grants below the fiscal 2013 level and turned aside an administration effort to move the program to the U.S. Agency for International Development. The measure also would have reduced spending on food safety programs, which provided funding for inspections of meat, poultry, and eggs.

The Senate Appropriations Committee approved its version of the legislation on June 20 by a vote of 23–6. The bill's $20.9 billion in discretionary appropriations was more than the fiscal 2013 postsequester level and the almost $20 billion requested by the administration. Six Republicans voted against the measure, saying it violated statutory spending caps.

Under the Senate measure, the Food and Drug Administration would receive $2.6 billion, approximately $97 million more than the previous year. That figure included $53 million to continue implementing a 2011 food safety overhaul (PL 111-353) and $19 million for medical-product safety. The bill also included $7.1 billion for WIC, about $415 million more than the House-passed measure, and $1.5 billion for the Food for Peace program, slightly more than the previous year.

Congress ended up including all twelve appropriations measures in an omnibus spending bill, which passed the House on January 15, 2014, and cleared the Senate January 16. President Obama signed the measure into law on January 17, 2014.

Under the omnibus bill, the WIC appropriation totaled $6.7 billion, marking a defeat for Democrats who had sought a higher level of funding for the program. The fiscal 2014 figure marked a reduction of $153 million from the previous year and was $426 million below Obama's request. Supporters of the lower funding level said it provided enough for all eligible participants.

The FDA received almost $2.6 billion in discretionary appropriations, about $95 million more than the previous year. Including spending from user fees, the FDA's 2014 budget was $4.4 billion.

The Agriculture Department's Food Safety and Inspection Service got just over $1 billion, $19 million below the 2013 level but a little more than what the administration had requested. Lawmakers said the amount would pay for 8,000 inspectors and other front-line workers at about 6,200 facilities.

The omnibus ended up increasing CFTC spending to $215 million, about $10 million more than the 2013 level but far below the administration's $315 million request.

Fiscal 2015 Agriculture Appropriations

Once again, appropriations for agricultural programs ended up in an omnibus bill for fiscal year 2015. In May 2014, the Senate and House appropriations committees each approved a fiscal 2015 agriculture appropriations bill, but the measures did not end up progressing to final floor votes. The fiscal 2015 omnibus spending package, which Congress cleared on December 13, 2014, included a total of $147.6 billion for the Agriculture Department and the Food and Drug Administration. That figure was $1.9 billion more than the previous year's funding and $17.9 billion less than the administration had requested. The bill's total included $126.5 billion in mandatory spending and $20.6 billion in net discretionary spending subject to budget caps. The net discretionary total was $305 million less than that of the previous year. Also included was $25 million in emergency funding for FDA activities responding to the Ebola crisis.

In early April 2014, the Obama administration requested $20 billion in discretionary budget authority for the Agriculture Department and $122 billion in mandatory spending, more than half of which would go to the

Supplemental Nutrition Assistance Program (SNAP), which provides monthly food benefits for low-income people. The FDA budget request included $2.58 billion in appropriations and the authority to spend $2.16 billion in user fees collected from food and drug companies.

On the House side, the House Agriculture Appropriations Subcommittee approved a draft bill on May 20 that would provide $20.9 billion in discretionary spending, a figure approximating the totals of the previous year, for the Agriculture Department, the Food and Drug Administration, and the Commodity Futures Trading Commission (CFTC). Included in the bill was a total of $142.5 billion for Agriculture mandatory and discretionary spending, $1.5 billion less than the administration's request and $3 billion less than 2014 enacted levels. The full House Appropriations Committee approved the measure (HR 4800) on May 29. The measure reached the House floor but was pulled without a final vote after several amendments had been adopted.

On the Senate side, the Senate Agriculture Appropriations Subcommittee approved its own bill on May 20, which included $20.58 billion in discretionary funding for fiscal 2015—slightly lower than the House version, which included the CFTC. The bill included $2.588 billion for the FDA, $36 million above the previous year. The full Senate Appropriations Committee approved the bill (S 2389) on May 22.

Barbara Mikulski, D-Md., the Senate Appropriations chairwoman, bundled the bill with the Transportation-HUD and Commerce-Justice-Science measures but failed to get unanimous consent to start floor debate on the bundled "minibus" bill. Disagreements between Democrats and Republicans over amendments caused Senate Majority Leader Harry Reid, D-Nev., to withdraw the spending measure.

Eventually, with the end of the fiscal year approaching on September 30 and little progress made on passing appropriations bills, Congress approved a continuing resolution to keep the government funded into December. The stopgap spending measure (HJ Res 124), designed to give lawmakers time to put together a future omnibus bill, provided $1.012 trillion. The House approved the measure on September 17 by a vote of 319–108, and the Senate cleared the resolution the following day by a vote of 78–22.

On December 11, the House passed HR 83, the omnibus appropriations bill, on a vote of 219–206. The Senate cleared the measure on December 13 by a vote of 56–40, and President Obama signed the bill on December 16.

Among the items in the final omnibus legislation for fiscal year 2015 were:

- $1 billion for the USDA's Food Safety and Inspection Service, $854 million for the Animal and Plant Health Inspection Service, $1.1 billion for the Agricultural Research Service, $1.3 billion for the National Institute of Food and Agriculture, and $6.6 billion for the Women, Infants, and Children (WIC) supplemental nutrition program.
- $2.6 billion in direct appropriations for the Food and Drug Administration, including $27.5 million for work implementing the 2010 Food Safety Modernization Act.
- $859 million in discretionary funding for conservation programs and reductions of $136 million in mandatory spending from the Environmental Quality Incentives Program and $7 million from the Conservation Stewardship Program.

2015–2016

The 114th Congress did not see a great deal of action on the agriculture front, but lawmakers did pass legislation in July 2016 that set up a national labeling standard for genetically engineered foods. President Obama signed it into law (PL 114-216) on July 29, 2016.

The labeling of genetically engineered foods—those that include genetically modified organisms (GMOs)—had been under discussion for a while, and this legislation was an effort by Congress to circumvent state efforts to set their own GMO standards. Vermont had already established its own mandatory labeling law, which had gone into effect on July 1, 2016.

The food industry liked the idea of a national standard rather than multiple state laws. The new federal law, which prohibited state and local governments from passing their own mandatory labeling laws for GMO products, overrode the Vermont law and other such legislation pending in the states.

In addition, lawmakers acted in late 2015 to reverse a cut of $3 billion in crop insurance payments that had been part of a two-year budget agreement. Lawmakers had promised the agriculture industry that they would figure out a way to make the reversal happen.

GMO Food Labeling

One important piece of food-related legislation during the 114th Congress set up a national labeling standard for genetically engineered foods—those that include genetically modified organisms (GMOs). The bill (S 764) was signed into law (PL 114-216) by President Barack Obama on July 29, 2016.

The issue of how to label GMO foods had been percolating for a while, and the legislation marked a congressional attempt to circumvent state efforts to set their own standards. Vermont had established its own mandatory labeling law, which had gone into effect July 1, and GMO legislation was pending in Connecticut, Maine, and Alaska.

The food industry preferred the idea of one national standard rather than a patchwork of GMO-related laws. The new federal law, which forbade state and local governments from passing their own mandatory labeling laws for GMO products, overrode the Vermont law and killed the not-yet-enacted laws in the three other states.

House Action

House approval of this legislation marked a turnaround from the chamber's approach the previous year. On July 23, 2015, the House voted in favor of a voluntary federal GMO labeling bill (HR 1599) by a margin of 275–150. The bill would have prevented states from forcing food companies to label products with GMO ingredients. The impetus behind the bill was the Vermont law. The food and agriculture industries had lobbied against state ballot initiatives dealing with GMO food labeling.

The voluntary bill had backers on both sides of the aisle, including Agriculture Chair K. Michael Conaway of Texas and ranking Democrat Collin C. Peterson of Minnesota, although its approval relied heavily on Republicans, with 230 supporting it along with 45 Democrats. The bill would have codified the position of the U.S. Food and Drug Administration that there is no need to label GMO foods and ingredients because they are just as safe as conventionally produced food. Approximately 70 to 80 percent of processed foods sold in the United States included a GMO ingredient, usually soybeans or corn.

The House Agriculture Committee approved the bill by voice vote on July 14. It included a substitute amendment by Rodney Davis, R-Ill., which designated the Agriculture Department to administer a certification process and national voluntary labeling for non–genetically modified and genetically modified food and ingredients. The certification review for non-GMO items would have resembled the Agriculture Department's organic certification process.

The bill had been introduced in the 113th Congress by Reps. Mike Pompeo, R-Kan., and G. K. Butterfield, D-N.C., but it failed to make it out of the Energy and Commerce Committee. The food and biotech industries supported the legislation. The members filed the bill again, partnering with the Agriculture Committee. Many committee members see biotech and genetically modified seeds as positive developments that improve crop hardiness and productivity.

The bill's opponents argued that consumers should know how their food was produced and that mandatory labeling should be enacted at the state or federal level. Organic food groups and consumer groups backed the idea of mandatory labeling.

Senate Action

On the Senate side, a voluntary federal labeling law (S 2609) stalled in March 2016. Agriculture Chair Pat Roberts, R-Kan., and Senate Majority Leader Mitch McConnell, R-Ky., tried to win sixty votes to move Roberts's legislation forward but failed to do so, leaving the matter hanging.

The bill, backed by the food industry, would have halted Vermont's mandatory GMO labeling law. Roberts argued that there was no need for mandatory labeling because the FDA had deemed GMO foods safe. The food industry, meanwhile, expressed concern that if various state labeling laws went into effect, it would result in an increase in food prices and industry costs. But with a 48–49 defeat on a March 16 vote, Roberts was unable to proceed, and the Senate departed for its spring break with the issue unresolved. Forty-five Republicans and three Democrats voted for cloture, or limiting debate, on the measure.

Roberts joined with Debbie Stabenow, D-Mich., the ranking Democrat on the Agriculture Committee, who had opposed the voluntary approach, to reach a compromise. The legislation (S 764), supported by the food industry, sought to override state laws and establish a national labeling standard for foods with GMO ingredients.

Both the House and Senate approved the bill in July 2018, and President Obama signed it into law on July 29, 2016.

MAJOR PROVISIONS

The legislation ordered the Agriculture Department to set up a process for disclosure of foods and ingredients produced through biotech genetic modification. Small food manufacturers, which had yet to be defined, would be able to direct consumers to telephone numbers or websites for information.

The legislation provided bigger companies with three options for informing consumers about whether they are buying a GMO food product: on-label information, a symbol to be developed by the USDA, or bar codes or other digital means that consumers can scan with smart phones. Agriculture Secretary Tom Vilsack supported the idea of scannable markings, seeing it as a compromise between giving consumers information that some of them may want and assuaging concerns by food and agriculture groups that labeling products as GMO produced would repel customers.

Using a definition in the legislation, the USDA would determine which products should be labeled. The bill directed the department to set up a GMO disclosure process within two years after the enactment of the law.

Crop Insurance

In late 2015, soon after approving a two-year budget agreement (PL 114-74), Congress made good on a promise to the agriculture industry that lawmakers would figure out a way to reverse a cut of $3 billion in crop insurance payments that had been used to help offset the cost of the budget pact.

The budget agreement, approved by Congress in late October, raised discretionary spending limits by $80 billion but included the cut in crop insurance payments. Congressional leaders then opted to use some of the $70 billion in anticipated offsets for a five-year highway and transit bill to cover the cost of reversing the crop insurance payment cuts.

Sens. Jeff Flake (R-Ariz.) and Jeanne Shaheen (D-N.H.) raised a point of order against using the surface transportation bill to undo the crop insurance offset for the budget deal. But they were on the losing side, as the bill's managers warned that any such changes could result in the collapse of the highway agreement.

House Agriculture Chair K. Michael Conaway, R-Texas, offered praise to Speaker Paul D. Ryan, R-Wis., Majority Leader Kevin McCarthy, R-Calif., and Transportation and Infrastructure Chair Bill Shuster, R-Pa., for including the provision that repealed the crop insurance cut.

The budget agreement capped the rate-of-return payments to private crop insurance companies at 8.9 percent, a drop from 14.5 percent. Savings from the Agriculture Department's renegotiation of contract terms with companies would have gone to deficit reduction rather than into the crop insurance program, as required by the 2014 farm bill (PL 113-79).

Members of the House and Senate Agriculture committees argued that cutting $3 billion over ten years from the Agriculture Department's return-on-investment payments to participating insurance companies would result in a cut in services to farmers. The lawmakers said that smaller profit margins might result in consolidation among crop insurance companies, thus resulting in less competition.

Three trade associations for the crop insurance industry—the Crop Insurance and Reinsurance Bureau, American Association of Crop Insurers, and the National Crop Insurance Service—had issued a statement encouraging Congress to approve the conference report and pass the highway bill. But other organizations, such as the Environmental Working Group, said lawmakers' concerns and the industry's claims about the budget agreement's possible effects were overblown.

In early December, the highway bill was approved by both houses of Congress and signed into law by President Obama.

Fiscal 2016 Agriculture Appropriations

Continuing the pattern of recent years, Congress ended up including fiscal year 2016 funding for agriculture programs in an omnibus spending package rather than in a stand-alone bill. Congress cleared the omnibus measure on December 18, 2015. It contained a total of approximately $141 billion for the Agriculture Department and the Food and Drug Administration (FDA), which was a drop from fiscal year 2015 levels and less than the administration had requested.

Most of the money, 85 percent, or about $119 billion, was mandatory funding for domestic food programs, crop insurance, and the Commodity Credit Corporation. Discretionary funding made up about $21.8 billion, about $925 million above the previous year's totals. The discretionary spending provided for WIC, the FDA, the Commodity Futures Trading Commission, rural development, farm assistance, food safety inspections, foreign assistance, conservation, and animal and plant health.

The House and Senate Appropriations Committees each approved agriculture spending bills in July 2015, but neither bill ended up being scheduled for floor action. On the House side, appropriators approved a measure July 8, by voice vote, that totaled $143.9 billion in discretionary and mandatory spending. Senate appropriators, on July 16, approved their version of the bill by a vote of 28–2. It called for $143.8 billion in combined mandatory and discretionary funding.

The final omnibus bill approved in December included a variety of provisions. It increased funding for the FDA by $132 million over the previous year's level, which raised the amounts provided for food safety and medical-product safety activities. Rural development funding was $2.8 billion, $386 million more than the previous year.

Funding for the Supplemental Nutrition Assistance Program (SNAP) and the Special Supplemental Nutrition

Program for Women, Infants, and Children (WIC) was reduced, but there was a decrease in enrollment in the programs. Child nutrition programs saw a raise of $850 million over the previous year's level.

Mandatory country-of-origin labeling for beef and pork products was repealed, which avoided more than $1 billion in retaliatory tariffs by Canada and Mexico. The Food Safety and Inspection Service saw an increase of $4 million, bringing its total to $1.02 billion. The Commodity Futures Trading Commission received $250 million, the same as in fiscal 2015.

A policy rider designed to exempt e-cigarettes from tougher regulatory oversight was not included in the bill.

Fiscal 2017 Agriculture Appropriations

In the spring of 2016, the House and Senate Appropriations Committees approved fiscal year 2017 appropriations bills. But the measures never made it to the floor. In fact, unlike the pattern of recent years, Congress did not even pass a year-end omnibus appropriations bill at the end of 2016. Instead, lawmakers approved two continuing resolutions that kept the government functioning.

On the House side, the House Agriculture Appropriations Subcommittee on April 13 approved a spending bill for fiscal year 2017, covering the Agriculture Department, the Food and Drug Administration, the Commodity Futures Trading Commission, and related agencies. The bill included $21.3 billion in discretionary funding, $451 million lower than fiscal year 2016's enacted level, and $281 million less than the administration's fiscal 2017 request. The bill would have funded the CFTC at $250 million, the same as had been enacted the previous year. The bill would have provided the FDA with $2.7 billion in discretionary funding, an increase of $33 million over fiscal 2016, most of which would go to food safety activities. The bill provided the agency with $2.7 billion in discretionary funding and would approve the collection of $64 million extra in user fees over fiscal 2016. The total FDA budget for discretionary and user fees came to $4.78 billion.

The bill included $126.4 billion in mandatory funding, most of which would go to SNAP, formerly known as food stamps. SNAP would get $79.7 billion for fiscal 2017.

In addition, the bill would cut more than $113 million from the Environmental Quality Incentives Program and reduce the number of acres the Conservation Stewardship Program could enroll, resulting in a cumulative cut in funding of more than $300 million.

The House Appropriations Committee marked the bill up on April 19 and approved it by voice vote. The amendments adopted included exempting e-cigarette products already on the market from premarket review by the FDA, as well as reinstating a ban on the Agriculture Department finishing controversial regulations designed to give poultry and livestock farmers under contract for meatpacking and poultry companies legal remedies to challenge what they saw as unfair treatment.

The committee voted along party lines, 30–20, in favor of an amendment by Chair Harold Rogers, R-Ky., that reaffirmed his position that the Obama administration use available money originally provided to combat the Ebola virus to respond immediately to the Zika virus. The administration had requested emergency Zika funding for fiscal 2016 and 2017.

The committee voted 31–19 to approve the e-cigarette amendment, by Reps. Tom Cole, R-Okla., and Sanford D. Bishop Jr., D-Ga. It would effectively shield e-cigarette vapor products currently on the market from the FDA's premarket approval process and could potentially allow future e-cigarette products to use a less stringent premarket pathway.

The committee voted 26–24 on the amendment to stop the Agriculture Department from issuing draft and final rules on marketing and contract regulations for poultry and livestock.

On the Senate side, the Senate Agriculture Appropriations Committee approved a bill May 17 that would increase funding for agricultural research, fund an Agriculture Department post in Cuba, and put money into programs for military veterans interested in agriculture.

The subcommittee, by voice vote, approved the bill, which included $21.3 billion in discretionary funding—$250 million below the 2016 enacted level—and $126.5 billion in mandatory funding. President Obama had requested $21.33 billion in discretionary spending.

The FDA would be funded at about $2.75 billion in discretionary funding, $39 million above the fiscal 2016 enacted level, and the bill would allocate $40.2 million for the FDA's work on implementing the Food Safety Modernization Act (PL 111-353), $15 million above the president's request.

Included in the bill was $1.5 million to meet the administration's request to pay for Agriculture Department staffers in Cuba.

On May 19, the full Senate Appropriations Committee voted 30–0 to approve the bill. Senate appropriators voted to deny funding for the Agriculture Department to finalize a proposed rule that would make stores ineligible to accept food stamps if they do not meet new requirements to carry a diversity of foods.

Among other provisions, the committee approved an amendment by voice vote, offered by Sen. Lisa Murkowski, R-Alaska, that would require labeling of genetically engineered salmon to include those words or "GE" in their label.

Neither of these measures, the House version or the Senate version, saw a vote in the full chamber. On September 28, two days before a partial government shutdown would have happened, the Senate passed a ten-week continuing resolution to fund the government through December 9. The Senate voted 72–26 for a legislative-branch spending bill that included the continuing resolution. The House cleared the measure on a vote of 342–85 (PL 114-223).

In December, both chambers approved a continuing resolution (HR 2028), replacing the earlier stopgap law. The new measure would fund the government until April 28.

CHAPTER 9

Health and Human Services

Health and Human Services

Ever since President Barack Obama's signature accomplishment, the Patient Protection and Affordable Care Act, became law in 2010 (PL 111–148, PL 111–152), congressional Republicans had attacked it on scores of occasions, seeking changes, carve-outs, or full repeal. The long but unending slog showed how determined Republicans were to repeal or replace the law that required most Americans to have health insurance, mandated that insurers cover an array of essential health services and treatments, and established income-based taxpayer subsidies to help individuals and families pay premiums.

The health law, commonly known as Obamacare, was anathema to the free-market and small-government ideals of the GOP. House Republicans often had the votes to weaken or overturn the law, but the Senate proved tougher because it had only a narrow Republican majority that often could not overcome procedural blockades. Finally in December 2015 and early January 2016, House and Senate Republicans mustered majorities for repeal.

Then Obama swiftly vetoed the repeal bill.

The repeated attempts to pass a bicameral, veto-proof bill turning back the ACA could sum up the focus of the 113th and 114th Congresses when it came to health care. No issue except abortion saw anywhere near this level of debate and attention.

Yet as prominent as the health care battles were, lawmakers in the 113th and 114th sessions found time to address other important, albeit more limited, health and human services issues. They got results, too, displaying occasional flashes of bipartisanship.

For example, early in 2013, some of the most liberal and conservative senators, including Democrat Barbara Boxer of California and Republican Tom Coburn of Oklahoma, worked together to end a twenty-five-year ban on organ transplants from people with HIV to others with the same condition. By Thanksgiving that year, their efforts were signed into law (S 330—PL 113-51), without objection from a single House or Senate member. This was expected to save the lives of as many as 1,000 HIV-infected patients a year.

Congress also was able to end the ritual of providing "doc fixes," or assuring that doctors and hospitals were not hit with annual Medicare payment cuts, although this took a few years (HR 2—PL 114-10). Medicare is the federal health insurance program for people age sixty-five and older, and to guard against rising bills from doctors and hospitals, Congress in 1997 passed a budget-related provision that capped annual hikes for the health care providers serving Medicare patients.

Doctors and hospitals soon complained their government payments for treatment would lag their costs, and they fought back year after year, saying if Congress did not provide more money, they might have to stop accepting new Medicare patients. So lawmakers wrote exceptions—seventeen in all—and each was known as a temporary "doc fix." In 2015, the House and Senate passed legislation to permanently change the payment schedule, providing small annual increases in payments for several years and adopting a new system intended to reward doctors and hospitals for quality rather than basing payment on a formula that had factored in the quantity of patients served and a measure of inflation.

The House and Senate also passed legislation to require more parity in payments for physical and mental health

REFERENCES

Discussion of health policy for the years 1945–1964 may be found in *Congress and the Nation Vol. I*, pp. 1122–1194; for the years 1965–1968, *Congress and the Nation Vol. II*, pp. 665–707; for the years 1969–1972, *Congress and the Nation Vol. III*, pp. 551–580; for the years 1973–1976, *Congress and the Nation Vol. IV*, pp. 323–375; for the years 1977–1980, *Congress and the Nation Vol. V*, pp. 601–653; for the years 1981–1984, *Congress and the Nation Vol. VI*, pp. 521–556; for the years 1985–1988, *Congress and the Nation Vol. VII*, pp. 547–606; for the years 1989–1992, *Congress and the Nation Vol. VIII*, pp. 561–610; for the years 1993–1996, *Congress and the Nation Vol. IX*, pp. 513–569; for the years 1997–2000, *Congress and the Nation Vol. X*, pp. 429–503; for the years 2001–2004, *Congress and the Nation Vol. XI*, pp. 471–529; for the years 2005–2008, *Congress and the Nation Vol. XII*, pp. 531–578; for the years 2009–2012, *Congress and the Nation Vol. XIII*, pp. 419–464.

Outlays for Medicare and Medicaid

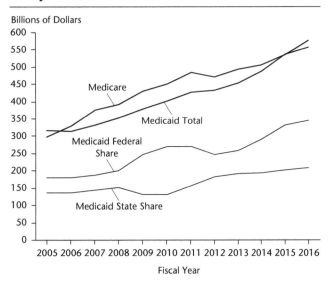

Billions of Dollars

SOURCES: Medicare: Office of Management and Budget, *Historical Tables, Budget of the United States Government: Fiscal Year 2018* (Washington, DC: U.S. Government Printing Office, 2018), Table 8.5; Medicaid: Centers for Medicare and Medicaid Services, *2016 Actuarial Report on Financial Outlook for Medicaid* (Washington, DC: Department of Health and Human Services, 2016).

treatment and to focus more attention within the Health and Human Services Department on mental health and drug addiction. Lawmakers created a new sub-Cabinet-level position of assistant secretary for mental health and substance use disorders. Many of the discussions that led to this legislation sprang from a realization of the connection between mental health and gun violence, and to win these limited measures, lawmakers had to fold them into other legislation. Yet amid public and congressional outrage over mass shootings at a school in Newtown, Connecticut, an office park in San Bernardino, California, and a nightclub in Orlando, Florida, Congress could not agree on gun control measures. Proponents of stricter gun laws met unyielding opposition from the National Rifle Association, sportsmen, and lawmakers who said restrictions would step on Second Amendment rights of law-abiding citizens.

In an area with broader agreement, Congress was able to pass legislation to better regulate compounding pharmacies, or companies that compound pharmaceutical substances in small batches for select groups of patients. The push for passage in 2013 of the Drug Quality and Security Act (HR 3204—PL 113–54) followed a 2012 outbreak of fungal meningitis linked to a contaminated

HEALTH AND HUMAN SERVICES LEADERSHIP

The nearly ceaseless concerns and complaints from congressional Republicans about the Patient Protection and Affordable Care Act (ACA) made it virtually inevitable that Senate Republicans would have tough questions for officials nominated for powerful health care positions in the Obama administration. Yet Sylvia Mathews Burwell sailed through her confirmation as Health and Human Services Secretary in just two months, while Viveck Murthy faced a thirteen-month delay before winning confirmation as surgeon general.

Health and Human Services Secretary

Obama nominated Burwell on April 11, 2014, for Health and Human Services Secretary. Burwell, the director of the White House Office of Management and Budget, would replace Kathleen Sebelius, who resigned after the ACA's first open enrollment period. Burwell, a West Virginia native, had come to the White House from the Wal-Mart Foundation, where she was president, and had been president of the Bill & Melinda Gates Foundation's Global Development Program before that. In a reflection of high regard for her executive skills, the Senate in 2013 had confirmed Burwell 96–0 to be White House budget chief.

The main questions that senators asked during Burwell's confirmation to take over HHS therefore focused largely on how she would deal with the new health law, not whether she had the skills to run the agency. Responding to the announcement of her nomination, Republican Sen. John McCain of Arizona tweeted that she was "an excellent choice," while West Virginia Democratic Sen. Joe Manchin issued a statement saying her leadership could help assure "commonsense fixes" to the health law. Introducing Burwell at a Senate Finance Committee hearing on May 14, 2014, Republican Tom Coburn of Oklahoma, a physician, praised Burwell's competence, character, listening skills, and common sense.

The confirmation vote, on June 5, 2014, was 78–17, with every Democrat supporting Burwell. Several Republican opponents said that any leadership would be insufficient short of a commitment to overhaul the ACA. But twenty-four Republicans voted for confirmation.

During Burwell's tenure, she repeatedly defended the ACA against Republican criticism. When she left her position at the end of the Obama administration, she announced that she would be getting health insurance through the ACA, saying it would be helpful for her family because her husband had a preexisting medical condition that would be covered under the law.

Surgeon General

Confirmation for Murthy, a prominent Boston physician, was nowhere near as rapid or smooth. Nominated by Obama for the position of surgeon general on November 14, 2013, Murthy finally won confirmation on December 15, 2014, shortly before Democrats lost their majority.

Murthy, just thirty-seven when he assumed the office of surgeon general, was the son of immigrants from India. He had been a physician and instructor at Brigham and Women's Hospital in Boston, an affiliate of Harvard Medical School. He was previously a member of the Advisory Group on Prevention, Health Promotion and Integrative and Public Health, a federal advisory panel formed under the 2010 Affordable Care Act to bring perspectives from outside of government on improving the nation's health. The Harvard- and Yale-educated doctor also had been cofounder and president of Doctors for America, a group of physicians and medical students that advocated for the Affordable Care Act. His work for the ACA as well as past support for gun control drew considerable Republican opposition.

The Senate Health, Education, Labor, and Pensions Committee on February 27, 2014, approved Murthy's nomination in a 13–9 vote, with Republican Mark S. Kirk of Illinois crossing party lines to support him. But with the National Rifle Association opposed to Murthy, the White House decided to slow its confirmation push. The NRA said in a February 26 letter to Senate leaders that it would oppose Murthy because of what it called his record of political activism in support of gun control.

But there was another consideration for the White House in its decision to delay its push: the way the Senate on March 5 had blocked a different confirmation, of Debo Adegbile, to head the Justice Department's Civil Rights Division. Obama had nominated Adegbile at the same time as Murthy. But seven Democrats had joined with Republicans to block Adegbile's confirmation on a simple majority vote on a cloture motion, a procedural move to end debate. Adegbile's confirmation was problematic to them and law enforcement groups because as an attorney, he had worked to overturn the death penalty imposed on Mumia Abu-Jamal, an inmate in Pennsylvania convicted of murdering Philadelphia police officer Daniel Faulkner in 1981.

This had nothing to do with Murthy. But the Senate's 47–52 vote on Adegbile was the first time Democrats had lost a simple majority on cloture since they changed Senate rules to shut off debate on confirmations with a simple majority rather than the sixty votes previously needed under a cloture rule in place since 1975. The White House failure on Adegbile's confirmation signaled risk for other controversial nominees.

After Senate Democrats lost their majority in the 2014 midterm elections, they faced new pressure to confirm Murthy before Republicans took control in January. Democratic supporters argued that the Ebola outbreak in West Africa and subsequent cases in the United States had underscored the need for a surgeon general to be in place.

Despite the continuing opposition of the NRA and concerns by conservatives that Murthy lacked experience and had limited knowledge of public health, he was confirmed on December 15, 2014, on a 51–43 vote. Three Democrats opposed him: Indiana's Joe Donnelly, North Dakota's Heidi Heitkamp, and West Virginia's Joe Manchin. Kirk was the only Republican who voted for confirmation.

Murthy served through the rest of Obama's term.

---

injectable steroid distributed by the New England Compounding Center in Massachusetts. The bill expanded the FDA's oversight and created a system to trace drugs through the supply chain.

Another area for consensus was the 21st Century Cures Act, intended to streamline the U.S. Food and Drug Administration's drug-approval process. While a small number of lawmakers said they worried speed might trump safety, most said the new process was long overdue, since it could take 15 years to take a drug from discovery to approval (HR 34—PL 114–255).

Lawmakers responded in 2016 to the Zika virus, by then having infected thousands of Americans, by providing $1.1 billion for such things as mosquito control and surveillance of the disease, vaccine research, and patient treatment. Like many other issues, partisan differences—and issues such as contraception, abortion, and Planned Parenthood's role as a care provider—slowed congressional action. This even spilled into the presidential campaigns, with Senate Majority Leader Mitch McConnell telling the Republican National Convention that "Clinton Democrats" were to blame for the slow speed of action and Democratic presidential candidate Hillary Clinton telling a Florida audience that Republican intransigence was to blame. The funding measure was included in a military construction and Veterans Affairs spending bill (HR 5325—PL 114–223).

Chronology of Action on Health and Human Services

2013–2014

If measured in words and time, Congress's main accomplishment at the start of President Barack Obama's second term might be length of speech and effort on two major topics: the Patient Protection and Affordable Care Act and abortion rights. House and Senate Republicans tried numerous ways to roll back or repeal the former and restrict the latter.

The efforts failed, but the issues were important to the GOP—the health law because Republicans said it represented a huge intrusion of government into personal choice and markets; abortion because many Republicans had seen a need to stop the practice as a moral imperative ever since the Supreme Court's 1973 *Roe v. Wade* decision. Abortion efforts centered on attempts to ban terminating pregnancies after twenty weeks, a point at which abortion opponents said a fetus was viable and was capable of feeling pain. But the legislation languished in the end.

On health care, Democrats stymied try after try by Republicans to change the parameters of the 2010 law, to delay its implementation, to withhold federal money necessary to carry out the law's requirements, and to repeal the law outright. The health law had symbolic and practical implications for both parties, and the unending battles made that crystal clear.

Health and human services legislation in other areas showed more promise of becoming law in the 113th Congress, although some would have to wait until the 114th Congress to make it through. Attempts to deal with mental health, for example, wound up paired with measures tied to gun violence or criminal justice, derailing the efforts for a time.

Similarly, a long-term "doc fix" to change Medicare's method of payments—and the constant threat of fee cuts to health care providers—would have to wait, with the 113th Congress passing and then extending only a temporary fix: its seventeenth to date.

But the House and Senate in the 113th Congress passed a bill, the HIV Organ Policy Equity Act, to end the long-term ban on organ transplants from patients with HIV (S 330—PL 113–51). Prompted by a fungal meningitis outbreak linked to a

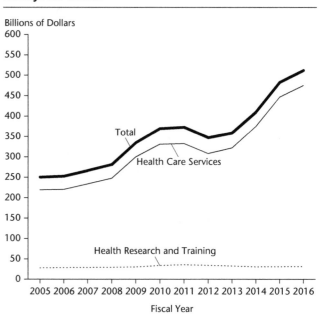

Outlays for Health

Billions of Dollars

Total

Health Care Services

Health Research and Training

2005 2006 2007 2008 2009 2010 2011 2012 2013 2014 2015 2016

Fiscal Year

SOURCE: Office of Management and Budget, *Historical Tables, Budget of the United States Government: Fiscal Year 2018* (Washington, DC: U.S. Government Printing Office, 2018), Table 3.2.

NOTE: Total line includes expenditures not shown separately.

compounding center that lawmakers said had lax oversight, Congress passed the Drug Quality and Security Act (HR 3204—PL 113–54) to expand the Food and Drug Administration's oversight and created a system to trace drugs through the supply chain.

And in the final days of the 113th Congress, before Senate control would shift to Republicans as a result of the November 2014 elections, the Senate confirmed Dr. Vivek Murthy as surgeon general. Murthy's nomination had languished more than a year while Republicans criticized his embrace of the Affordable Care Act and past support for gun control.

Organ Transplant Bill

Congress moved with rare bipartisan spirit in 2013 to enact a bill removing a 25-year-old ban on the transplantation of organs from people infected with HIV to others with the same disease.

Sponsored in the Senate by liberal Democrat Barbara Boxer of California, with conservative Republican Tom Coburn of Oklahoma as a prime cosponsor, the HIV Organ Policy Equity Act, or HOPE Act (S 330—PL 113–51), was designed to lift a 1988 ban on HIV-infected transplants (PL 100–607) so that doctors could study whether organs donated from infected people might be safely transplanted to others who already carried the same virus.

The 1988 law prohibited the Organ Procurement Transplantation Network, which maintained the national organ matching system, from acquiring organs from HIV-positive individuals. The ban also applied to organ donations for research purposes (AIDS law, *1988 CQ Almanac*, p. 296).

The bill directed the Health and Human Services Department (HHS) to set up guidelines for researching organ transplantation from HIV donors. Within four years of enactment and annually after that, HHS was to review research results to decide whether a change in rules on organ donations from HIV-positive donors was warranted. If the department decided that a change was warranted, the transplant network would need to revise its standards without diminishing safety, and transplants could be allowed among HIV-positive individuals.

Senate supporters came from across the political spectrum, with Democrats Tammy Baldwin of Wisconsin and Elizabeth Warren of Massachusetts and Republicans Michael B. Enzi of Wyoming and Rand Paul of Kentucky signed on as cosponsors. Rep. Lois Capps, D-Calif., introduced a companion House measure, with Democrat Elijah E. Cummings and Republican Andy Harris, both of Maryland, as initial cosponsors.

More than forty organizations, from AIDS groups to the Human Rights Campaign, which champions LGBT rights, pushed for the legislation, maintaining that the existing ban was medically outdated. In a January 18 letter to lawmakers, they noted that many people infected with HIV—while able to live longer due to medical treatment advances—had a greater risk of organ failure and required transplants sooner than those without HIV, causing many to die while waiting.

Coburn, a physician, echoed those sentiments and said there were many cases of people infected with the virus who needed new kidneys and livers.

Beyond the possible benefits for patients, supporters said permitting transplants might save money for Medicare because patients receiving kidney transplants might not need dialysis.

Congressional Action

The Senate Health, Education, Labor, and Pensions Committee approved S 330 by voice vote on March 20, 2013. Before acting, the panel added language that could allow for the transplant of HIV-infected organs into individuals participating in clinical research if the Health and Human Services Department determined in reviews of research that it was safe and effective.

With little opposition—and vigorous bipartisan support—the bill was expedited for floor action. And with essentially no debate on the floor, the Senate passed the bill by voice vote June 17.

The companion House measure (HR 698—H Rept 113–181, Part 1) also easily won voice vote approval on July 17, 2013, from the Energy and Commerce Committee.

As in the Senate, the decision to move the bill was made long before it came to a vote. Andy Harris, R-Md., a physician, told House colleagues the process had already been validated in other countries and the United States was behind.

By voice vote on November 12, the full House cleared S 330, with no lawmaker speaking in opposition. Energy and Commerce Chair Fred Upton, R-Mich., said during floor debate that he and Capps had opted to accept the Senate's version of the bill to move quickly and avoid the need for a conference.

President Obama signed S 330 November 21, 2013 (PL 113–51).

Affordable Care Act Repeal

From the Affordable Care Act's passage in 2010 through the 2012 elections, talk of repeal was incessant. The Supreme Court had upheld the law's constitutionality, but GOP presidential nominee Mitt Romney went so far as to promise repeal of the statute on his first day in office. It was, after all, one of the most sweeping social policy initiatives since Lyndon Johnson's Great Society programs.

But Obama cruised to reelection, and Democrats gained seats in the House and Senate. House Speaker John A. Boehner, R-Ohio, had declared in an interview with *ABC News* on November 8, 2012, after the election, that "Obamacare is the law of the land."

Boehner's seeming declaration of a truce, however, did not last long as the 113th Congress convened.

Driven by Tea Party–backed lawmakers and conservative interest groups, the House Republican majority and the GOP minority in the Senate continued their crusade against the health care law (PL 111–148, PL 111–152), whose provisions to extend private-sector health insurance coverage and Medicaid to millions of uninsured Americans were taking full effect over a several-year phase-in (Health care law, *2010 Almanac*, p. 9–3).

Congressional opponents of the law ultimately focused their efforts on cutting off funding that was supposed to be used by federal departments and agencies to implement the health law. This was money for operating online insurance "exchanges" or marketplaces, for tax credits that would help consumers cut their out-of-pocket premium costs, for enforcement of numerous requirements (notably the individual and employer mandates to buy coverage or face penalties), and for financing the expansion of Medicaid. Medicaid, a program for low-income Americans, typically split costs with states—the average federal portion was 57 percent—but the Affordable Care Act expanded enrollment eligibility and picked up all the costs initially, with a planned rollback to 90 percent by the year 2020 and beyond.

House Republicans pursued legislation to repeal or delay coverage requirements, and they pushed language in spending bills to withhold money for implementation. None of those came even close to becoming law. Democrats suffered some defections along the way in both chambers, but the Democrat-led Senate in the 113th Congress spared Obama the need to exercise his veto power.

When 2013 and 2014 came to an end, Obamacare remained the law of the land, although it had been tarnished by startup difficulties that initially made it difficult for many Americans to sign up for new insurance policies. By then, however, no greater symbol existed to display the differences between Republicans and Democrats in Congress than the health law.

FULL REPEAL

A time-honored practice in Congress is to try to starve a program of money if other efforts to kill the program fail. And so the House Republicans' fiscal 2014 budget resolution (H Con Res 25), drafted by Budget Chair Paul D. Ryan of Wisconsin and adopted by a 221–207 vote on March 21, 2013, had an assumption written into it: The health care law would end. All but ten Republicans voted for the resolution, and every Democrat voted no.

This was a nonbinding measure, however, and on May 16, 2013, the House passed a bill, HR 45, with more force, assuming it could ever clear both chambers. Introduced by Michele Bachmann, R-Minn., at the start of the 113th Congress, HR 45 would have specifically repealed the Affordable Care Act. Unlike some bills with catchy names, HR 45's title was straightforward: "To repeal the Patient Protection and Affordable Care Act and health care-related provisions in the Health Care and Education Reconciliation Act of 2010."

The 229–195 vote—all 227 Republicans and two Democrats, Jim Matheson of Utah and Mike McIntyre of North Carolina—marked the third time that the Republican-led chamber had voted for full repeal, although it had attempted scores of more limited measures aimed at delaying, altering, or blocking implementation of the law. The Senate, however, was under Democratic control and never considered HR 45.

This attempt at a full repeal stood in contrast to a narrower bill (HR 1549) introduced in April by some Republicans. They wanted to put more money into the risk pools—temporary state-based programs to cover people with preexisting conditions and higher risk of needing medical care—that had been created by the Affordable Care Act and served as a temporary step to help high-risk patients before the ACA's full implementation in 2014. They named their bill the Helping Sick Americans Now Act.

Backers of the risk pool expansion, led by Joseph Pitts, R-Penn., saw that effort as a more targeted method of extending coverage than the broad mandates in other parts of the Affordable Care Act. But conservative lawmakers and allied groups, including Heritage Action for America and the Club for Growth, decried the House bill as an attempt to fix the health care law, one that could undermine efforts to scrap it.

The Energy and Commerce Committee approved the risk pool measure 27–20 on April 17, 2013, and it was scheduled for floor action later that month. But a vote never occurred, to the delight of its critics.

"I can't imagine going back and explaining to my constituents how that vote is consistent with . . . opposing Obamacare," Tim Huelskamp, R-Kan., told *CQ Roll Call* in an April 24 interview.

Republican leaders pulled the risk-pool measure in favor of HR 45, the full repeal bill.

NARROWLY TARGETED REPEAL BILLS

In the months that followed, the GOP shifted to more narrowly drawn attacks on elements of the Affordable Care Act, a way to attract more support from wavering Democrats.

On July 17, 2013, the House voted 264–161 to pass a bill (HR 2667) that would have delayed the effective date of the requirement that employers of fifty or more full-time workers provide health insurance coverage or pay a tax penalty of $2,000 per worker. The so-called employer mandate was supposed to begin in 2014, but the bill would have delayed it for a year.

The bill to delay the employer mandate drew support from thirty-five House Democrats, perhaps in part because the Obama administration had announced two weeks earlier that it was using its administrative authority to implement such a delay anyway. Obama's action had provoked criticism from Republicans, not because of the delay itself—which businesses wanted—but rather because they said the president did not have the right to pick and choose which parts of legislation to enforce or delay.

The 2010 health law had another mandate, called the individual mandate, that required individuals not covered by employers to obtain health coverage of their own, with or without a federal subsidy, or to pay a fine. The individual mandate was to begin in 2014, too, and the president had not delayed it when he pushed back the large-employer mandate.

But when the House voted on July 17 to delay the large-employer mandate, it also voted 251–174 on a bill (HR 2668) that would delay the individual mandate for a year, too. On that measure, twenty-two Democrats voted with the GOP majority, and one Republican, Morgan Griffith, R-Va., voted no.

Taken together, these would amount to a temporary repeal of the Affordable Care Act's major provisions if the

Senate would go along. Obama threatened a veto of both bills, with the White House saying the employer one was unnecessary and redundant, and the individual delay could disrupt insurance markets getting ready for 2014 open enrollment, drive up costs, and harm individuals who needed coverage the most.

A veto was unnecessary, however, because the Senate did not take up either of these bills.

Then, on August 2, 2013, the House voted 232–185 to pass a bill (HR 2009, the Keep the IRS Off Your Health Care Act) that would have barred the Treasury Department and IRS from enforcing any health care law provisions. The bill was sponsored by Tom Price of Georgia—he would later be tapped by President Donald Trump to head the Department of Health and Human Services—and only four Democrats supported that legislation.

The Senate did not take up that bill, either.

GRANDFATHERING HEALTH PLANS

Of all the years leading up to individual enrollment under the Affordable Care Act, 2013 was to be key simply because of the calendar: For health coverage to kick in on January 1, 2014, people would have to enroll before the end of 2013.

To facilitate this enrollment, the Affordable Care Act established a new method for health insurance shopping, setting up an online national health care marketplace or "exchange" that was called HealthCare.gov. States could establish their own exchanges or simply piggyback off the federal exchange, managed and overseen by the Health and Human Services Department and its Centers for Medicare and Medicaid Services.

Glitches arose, however, and HHS and several states stumbled with the rollout of the online marketplaces. Some problems were a result of technology, creating delays when customers tried to enroll. A separate concern arose when the exchanges opened for business and people discovered that many policies previously sold to individuals—bought directly through insurers or brokers before the exchanges existed—did not meet the health care law's minimum requirements. The Affordable Care Act required that policies cover emergency care, hospitalization, maternity and newborn care, and mental health treatment. Previous coverage could be more limited and was often dictated by the breadth or narrowness of the features customers wanted and the premiums they were willing to pay.

As a result of the health law's more expansive coverage requirements, some people learned as they prepared for 2014 enrollment that their existing health policies would have to be canceled because they did not comport with the new law. This contradicted repeated pledges by Obama that people who liked their existing policies could keep them.

In response, the House passed a bill, the Keep Your Health Plan Act of 2013 (HR 3350), on November 15 that would have allowed individuals to keep their existing policies through 2014, even if those plans did not meet the health law's minimum requirements. Thirty-nine

Democrats voted with all but four Republicans to pass the bill by a 261–157 vote.

The White House threatened a veto, however, and the Senate did not take up the measure.

REPEAL THROUGH APPROPRIATIONS AND SHUTDOWN

Still hoping to repeal the Affordable Care Act, delay its implementation, or nix provisions, conservatives tried one more tactic: They tried to turn off the funding spigot, using the appropriations process.

Timing was central to these efforts. House Republicans earlier had wanted to use the regular Labor-HHS-Education and Financial Services spending bills to delay the effective dates of health care law provisions. They wanted to block implementation by prohibiting agencies and departments from using money for that purpose. But lawmakers had made very little progress in finishing any regular spending bills as the start of the new fiscal year approached.

So Congress members seized on the timing when they reconvened from their August break after Labor Day in 2013. The new start of the fiscal year and the start of open enrollment shared the same date, October 1. This meant Republicans had to be willing to play a game of chicken—to risk shutting down parts of government for lack of funding—if they truly hoped to starve the health law.

This triggered the year's most heated confrontation—and the sixteen-day shutdown of nonessential government activities.

Sen. Ted Cruz, R-Texas, played a central role. For months he had stressed the importance of the date, warning that if the health care law was not derailed before October 1, it would probably never be undone. "We either stand for principle now or, I believe, we surrender to Obamacare permanently," Cruz told reporters in the capitol on July 30, 2013.

House Action

The post–Labor Day spending bill showdown began in the House, first with an attempted narrow assault on the health law through an appropriations-linked measure (HR 2775) that would have barred subsidies for individual purchasers of insurance until the Health and Human Services inspector general certified that a system was in place to verify that subsidy recipients were eligible under the health law's financial guidelines. Subsidies in the form of advance tax credits were available for purchasers with incomes up to 400 percent of the poverty level, varying by premium costs and family size and scaling down as incomes approached the top threshold. Republicans said they worried that states operating their own health insurance marketplaces, rather than the federal government's, might not adequately verify applicants' incomes when applicants said they were eligible for income-based subsidies.

The bill passed in a 235–191 vote on September 12, 2013, with five Democrats in favor. They were Jack Barrow of Georgia, Daniel Lipinski of Illinois, Jim Matheson of

Utah, Mike McIntyre of North Carolina, and Collin Peterson of Minnesota. But the Senate still needed to act, and lawmakers were still divided on other spending priorities. The House turned its attention to a continuing resolution—a budgetary placeholder to keep spending at current levels until a broader agreement could be reached. On September 20, the House passed, on a 230–189 vote, a continuing resolution (H J Res 59) to maintain appropriations at the fiscal 2013 postsequester level through December 15, 2013. The measure would have allowed

- no spending on health care law implementation,
- no collections by the IRS of new taxes under the health care law,
- no subsidies for lower-income individuals to buy insurance, and
- no federal funding to cover states' costs for expansion of the Medicaid rolls.

Senate Action

In the Senate, some moderate Republicans such as Susan Collins of Maine were antagonistic toward the House conservative insistence on getting rid of the health law by any means, even if it meant shutting down the government. She suggested her colleagues pursue alternative means of repealing or defunding Obamacare that did not involve a potential government shutdown.

The Senate's consideration of the House-passed continuing resolution was dramatic, even though the outcome was a foregone conclusion. On September 24, 2013, Cruz and seven allies began a twenty-two-hour talkathon against the health care law. Although it was popularly referred to as a filibuster, it was in reality a faux filibuster, because agreement had already been reached to vote the following afternoon on a cloture motion, or a motion to proceed with H J Res 59, the House-passed continuing resolution.

Cruz gave a rambling talk, filled with cultural references and a mention of the White Castle hamburger chain, which had claimed the costs of providing insurance under the health law would hamper growth. "I like their little burgers," Cruz said. He credited his father with inventing green eggs and ham—you can use spinach or food coloring, he said. *Green Eggs and Ham* happens to be the title of a Dr. Seuss story that Cruz also read, as well as King Solomon's Wise Words from Proverbs, speaking to his children at their bedtime. They were watching on CSPAN, he explained.

Cruz's tales were not persuasive, and once cloture was invoked, Majority Leader Harry Reid, D-Nev., was able to strip out the House's health care law curtailment on a 54–44 vote on September 27. By the same tally, the Senate returned the amended measure to the House. This put the House and Senate versions in conflict with one another.

Final Days of Fiscal Year

In the early-morning hours of September 29, a government shutdown loomed because the 2013 fiscal year was ending soon and Congress still had not authorized new or continuing spending for the fiscal year starting October 1. The House volleyed the continuing resolution, H J Res 59, back to the Senate after amending it at 12:16 a.m. by a 231–192 vote, almost entirely along party lines, to include a one-year delay in health care law provisions and to give companies and insurers until 2015 to opt out of providing coverage for birth control expenses. By a 248–174 vote, a repeal of the health care law's 2.3 percent tax on medical devices was added. This tax was never universally liked by Democrats, some with device manufacturers or dealers in their districts, and seventeen Democrats joined every House Republican on this provision.

On the busy final day of fiscal 2013, the Democrat-led Senate rejected the House amendments by a 54–46 vote, entirely along party lines. The House almost immediately sent back yet another version, passed by a 228–201 vote, that called for a one-year delay in the individual mandate and incorporated language sought by Sen. David Vitter, R-La., prohibiting the government from paying the employer's share of health insurance purchased by the president, vice president, members of Congress, congressional aides, and political appointees. Twelve Republicans crossed lines to vote with Democrats on this measure, which was largely symbolic since the health care law already required them to buy insurance through the exchanges. Those amendments were in turn rejected along party lines by the Senate, 54–46, and the government shutdown began.

The Shutdown

As the shutdown entered its first week, some House Republicans began to have second thoughts about the party's strategy. Some blamed Cruz and other hard-line conservatives for creating unrealistic expectations about the likelihood of blocking implementation of the health law.

Rep. Dennis A. Ross, R-Fla., said on October 5, 2013, that in reality, Congress had control of only 30 percent of the Affordable Care Act's funding through discretionary spending bills. That meant 70 percent of the funding was for mandatory spending that took effect already on October 1, he said, so "while we're in the fifth day of the shutdown, we're in our fifth day of Obamacare" (*CQ Almanac 2013*).

Other Republicans continued to view the appropriations process as a way to block implementation of the law. A different kind of political realization was also seeping into the picture, connected with the 2014 midterm elections. If Republicans could win the Senate and keep the House in those elections, a unified Congress would stand a much better chance of repealing the health law. Yet those elections were more than a year away, and some Republicans worried that a government shutdown that their party had forced would not play well to 2014 voters.

The Government Reopens

On October 16, 2013, Senate leaders of both parties announced an agreement to reopen the government through January 15, 2014. The only health care law provision in that revised continuing appropriations bill (HR 2775) was language accepted by the Obama administration requiring the Health and Human Services Department to certify that insurance exchanges had verified individuals' eligibility for subsidies and ordering reports on verification procedures. Similar language had been in the original House version of HR 2775.

The shutdown cost the government and the economy money, although estimates of how much varied because of different economic assumptions. Federal environmental permits and export licenses sought by businesses were not issued when agency offices were closed. Admission fees for national parks and museums were not collected because the facilities were not open. Lost productivity of furloughed workers cost $2 billion, the White House Office of Management and Budget said in an analysis on November 7, 2013. The Congressional Research Service ultimately said, in a report issued on September 11, 2015, that the effect on the national economy "was significant for the duration of the shutdown" but relatively small in the long term.

The Senate passed the amended version of HR 2775 by an 81–18 vote that evening, October 16, 2013. Those voting no were all Republicans, including conservatives such as Cruz, Tom Coburn of Oklahoma, and Richard Shelby of Alabama. The House cleared it (PL 113–46) by a vote of 285–144 the same night, a result of eighty-seven Republicans supporting it along with every Democrat voting.

The government now was back open. But since the bill held spending at 2013 levels until new sums could be agreed upon—or, failing that, until another shutdown—there was still a possibility of cutting off money for the health care law. Some House Republicans hoped to use the regular appropriations bills for that purpose. They did not succeed.

In fact, by the time appropriators began assembling the omnibus package to cover all twelve regular spending bills for fiscal 2014, the 2013 battle over the health care law was essentially over. The omnibus package was attached to an unrelated commercial space launch measure (HR 3547—PL 113–67), which was passed by the House 359–67 on January 15, 2014, cleared by the Senate 72–26 on January 16, and signed into law on January 17. As enacted, the omnibus did not include any of the Republicans' significant efforts to scrap the health law, delay its provisions, or deny money for its implementation.

The omnibus did rescind $10 million from the Independent Payment Advisory Board, which had been created through the health care law to make cost-cutting recommendations if Medicare spending exceeded target growth rates. But President Obama had not nominated anyone to serve on the board.

The omnibus also reallocated a portion of $1 billion in spending from the Prevention and Public Health Fund that had been created by the health care law to finance a variety of health-related programs. Critics said the spending adjustment was intended to prevent the administration from using the fund to implement the health care law.

The omnibus included no language barring the IRS from spending money to implement the health law, although Congress in the end kept the IRS from receiving any additional money for fiscal 2014 for that purpose.

Defining Full-Time Employees

When a new calendar year began, House Republicans turned again to a narrower approach and what to some appeared to be a newly discovered problem with the health law. The law defined full-time work as thirty hours a week and required businesses with fifty or more full-time employees—those working at least thirty hours a week—to offer health coverage or pay a penalty.

Retailers and restaurants with inconsistent work schedules, local governments with seasonal employees, fire departments whose part-time crews worked uneven or unpredictable hours, and universities with adjunct faculty said the thirty-hour definition would force them to classify semi–part-time workers as full-time—and force them to provide health benefits. Some said that to make sure they complied with the law, they would simply categorize all such workers as full-time and provide health benefits. But others said they could not afford the cost of providing health insurance and would have to cut workers' hours to be safe. For some workers, that would mean pay cuts.

"In my hometown of Richmond, many school districts have begun to limit part-time workers to less than 30 hours a week to avoid added costs imposed by the advent of this health care law," House Majority Leader Eric Cantor, R-Va., said on the House floor on April 2, 2014. Why, he asked, "is the government punishing those who are looking to earn an honest wage?"

The White House ordered a delay in this provision in response to complaints, but by then, the House Ways and Means Committee was already trying to change the definition of full-time entirely rather than simply delay implementation.

House Committee Action

The House Ways and Means Committee, controlled by Republicans, approved a bill (HR 2575) 23–14 in a party-line vote on February 4, 2014, to raise the threshold for full-time work from thirty hours to forty hours.

The bill also would shield more businesses from the coverage requirement by increasing the standard under which the number of full-time equivalent employees was calculated, from the law's 120 hours a month to 174 hours.

The Congressional Budget Office and the Joint Committee on Taxation reported that the GOP bill would cost $73.7 billion and would cause 1 million people to lose their employer-based health insurance. The measure, the analysis said, would reduce federal revenues by lowering the number of employers that would be penalized and lowering the penalties owed—$63.4 billion less over ten years than under existing law. That would be partially offset by a $12.4 billion tax revenue increase because fewer people would be receiving employer-based coverage, which is not subject to taxes, so a greater share of compensation would be taxable.

While the number of people with employer-provided health insurance would drop under the proposed bill, some would be able to pick up coverage in other ways, the CBO said. It said the bill would increase the number of uninsured by less than 500,000 people and increase the number of people receiving coverage through Medicaid, the Children's Health Insurance Program, or the exchanges by between 500,000 and 1 million.

But the CBO report also noted that most employers still would have an incentive to offer health coverage. "All told, CBO and JCT expect that a small percentage of employers would either reassign or reduce hours of employees who work 40 hours per week or slightly more," the CBO said in its February 25, 2014, report.

House Floor Action

The House passed the Ways and Means Committee's bill, 248–179, on April 3, 2014, with eighteen Democrats joining every Republican in supporting the bill. Republicans built their case on an argument that they were protecting workers. Dave Camp, R-Mich., chair of the Ways and Means Committee, said in an April 2 House floor speech that people nationwide were "having their hours cut at work and seeing smaller paychecks" as a direct result of the thirty-hour rule. He said the bill would restore the traditional definition of full-time employment as forty hours a week.

"Today we're voting to restore hours and wages and give businesses and their workers some relief from the burdens of Obamacare," Camp said.

Sandy Levin of Michigan, the top-ranking Democrat on the tax-writing committee, disagreed and said Republican claims about the law were myths. "Essentially, what you are doing here today is saying to many, many people who are working hard and who need insurance that this bill will knock you off your employer-based insurance and increase the number of uninsured by half a million, while increasing the deficit by $74 billion," Levin said on April 2 on the House floor.

Senate Action

In the Senate, Maine Republican Susan Collins introduced legislation (S 1188) on June 19 to move the threshold to forty hours. She counted two Democrats among the bill's thirteen cosponsors—Joe Donnelly of Indiana and Joe Manchin III of West Virginia. Her bill never made it out of the Finance Committee, however.

White House Action

The White House was already working to appease employers before the full House voted on its forty-hour measure, although Republicans questioned its motivation. On February 10, 2014, six days after the Ways and Means Committee passed its bill, the administration delayed enforcement of the thirty-hour standard until 2015. Under an Internal Revenue Service final rule, employers would need to cover 70 percent of their full-time employees in 2015 and 95 percent in 2016 or later.

Administration officials said the change was a response to complaints about the law's definition of a full-time worker. But as the House nearly two months later persisted in trying to make legislative changes, the White House made clear that while it would allow employers time to adapt, it would not kill the standard.

On April 1, 2014, the White House issued a Statement of Administration Policy saying Obama would veto the House bill if it ever reached him.

"While the administration welcomes ideas to improve the law," the statement said, "HR 2575 would undermine it by shifting costs to taxpayers and causing employers either to drop or to not expand health insurance coverage."

The legislation by summer was essentially dead for the year. But Congress would return to it in 2015.

Congress Gives FDA New Authority over Compounding

Drug compounding is a process in which laboratories and pharmacies combine, mix, or alter ingredients to create a custom-made medication, prescribed by a doctor or health care facility when a more readily available drug is not appropriate for a patient. Made in limited quantities, compounded drugs were regulated by state boards of pharmacies, and while the U.S. Food and Drug Administration had oversight capability, the FDA did not scrutinize their approval and manufacture in the same manner as more broadly prescribed medications.

But in 2012, an outbreak of fungal meningitis was linked to a contaminated injectable steroid distributed by the New England Compounding Center in Massachusetts. The tainted drugs led to at least 750 cases of fungal meningitis and sixty-four deaths, according to the Centers for Disease Control and Prevention. Six years earlier, the FDA had sent the New England Compounding Center a warning letter, on December 4, 2006, after an inspection found what the FDA described as potentially serious health risks associated with the misuse of compounded local anesthetic products. But it was unclear to what extent the FDA followed up.

So Congress in 2013 responded with the Drug Quality and Security Act (HR 3204—PL 113-54), expanding the FDA's oversight and creating a system of tracing drugs through the supply chain. It gave the FDA authority to oversee large compounding pharmacies. Pharmacies that chose to be overseen were supposed to register with the FDA as "outsourcing facilities," to tell the agency what products they made, and to share reports about problems that patients experienced after taking their drugs. Facilities that chose to remain traditional compounding pharmacies—generally catering to individual patients—were to continue being regulated primarily by state boards of pharmacy but could be subject to FDA inspection as well.

Senate Action

The fungal meningitis outbreak traced to the New England Compounding Center sparked lawmakers to demand greater federal accountability. On May 22, 2013, the Senate Health, Education, Labor, and Pensions Committee gave voice-vote approval to a bill (S 959) to clarify the FDA's authority over large compounding pharmacies. S 959 also would require the FDA to investigate compounding manufacturers on a risk-based schedule, focusing most heavily on those that produced vaccines, gene therapies, and drugs with complex manufacturing processes. The bill also would allow traditional pharmacies to compound drugs without a prescription if the work was done in limited quantities and if the compounding was based on a history of receiving prescription orders for that drug.

Before the vote, HELP Chair Tom Harkin, D-Iowa, incorporated into the bill language to implement an electronic prescription drug tracking system.

The same day as the markup, May 22, 2013, the committee released a report showing that FDA or state regulators had identified at least forty-eight compounding companies during the previous eight months that were producing or selling drugs that were contaminated or made in unsafe conditions. In that same period, ten drug compounders had issued national recalls because of contamination concerns, and eleven had been ordered to stop producing some or all of their drugs, the report said.

"This report confirms that the tragic meningitis outbreak came on the heels of many reports about dangerous practices at poorly regulated large-scale compounders, and will happen again if we do not clarify oversight," Lamar Alexander of Tennessee, the committee's top-ranking Republican, said in a written statement, according to *CQ News*.

Harkin and Alexander began pressing for Senate floor action in June, calling attention to a new disease outbreak that had been linked to a compounded drug made in Tennessee and might have caused twenty illnesses in three states.

On July 25, 2013, the HELP Committee released a substitute amendment to S 959 that proposed mostly technical changes to the bill, clarifying that oversight of traditional compounding pharmacies would be left up to the states, while the FDA would regulate pharmacies that compounded sterile products without a prescription and sold them across state lines.

In addition, the substitute would have banned compounding of some types of drugs, including marketed drugs and drugs that had been removed from the market for safety and efficacy concerns.

House Action

While the Senate was moving ahead on S 959, the House Energy and Commerce Committee was holding a series of hearings on the subject. Although House Democrats had called for legislation similar to the Senate bill to expand the FDA's oversight role, many House Republicans said they were not convinced that giving the FDA more authority was the best way to respond.

Republicans argued that the FDA could already have used its existing authority to more aggressively respond to problems at the New England Compounding Center. House Oversight and Investigations Subcommittee Chair Tim Murphy, R-Pa., said at an April hearing that because the FDA had inspected almost fifty compounding facilities over six months, it clearly had the authority to oversee the companies.

And Michael Burgess, R-Texas, said at a May 23, 2013, hearing of the Energy and Commerce Committee's health subcommittee that if the FDA could conduct that many inspections, "you have to ask yourself, by what authority did these 50 inspections occur? If the FDA has the authority today, they had it 6 months ago."

House supporters of stepped-up oversight from both parties pressed their case by introducing a bill on September 12 that was in many respects similar to the Senate committee–approved measure. Introduced by Morgan Griffith, R-Va., and cosponsored initially by Diana DeGette, D-Colo., and Gene Green, D-Texas, the bill (HR 3089) would have created a new category for pharmacies that compounded sterile medications for interstate use, subject to FDA supervision. State boards of pharmacy would have continued to oversee traditional compounding pharmacies.

The FDA under this bill would be given authority to oversee "outsourcing facilities"—pharmacies that shipped sterile compounded drugs across state lines in cases where those drugs accounted for more than 5 percent of the products they produced. The facilities would have had to register annually with the FDA, report and list the drugs they compounded, report adverse events to the FDA, and label their products. They also would have been subject to inspections on a risk-based schedule and paid annual fees for registration and inspections.

The bill would have allowed the FDA to create lists of drug ingredients that were not to be compounded due to safety or efficacy concerns. It would have banned the compounding of products that were essentially copies of marketed and approved drugs.

Compromise Emerges

Once the House bill was introduced, negotiators moved quickly to produce a bicameral compromise that could be enacted. House and Senate committee leaders announced on September 25, 2013, that they had an agreement, and a bill incorporating the deal (HR 3204) was introduced two days later. The compromise blended provisions from the refined version of S 959, which never came to a floor vote, and HR 3089. The provisions were as follows:

- The FDA's oversight would be expanded, with a new system of tracing drugs through the supply chain. The bill gave the FDA authority to oversee large compounding pharmacies—entities that made specialty drugs, often in bulk, tailored to meet needs not satisfied by drugs that were mass produced and already regulated.

- Pharmacies that chose to be overseen were supposed to register with the FDA as "outsourcing facilities," to tell the agency what products they made, and to share reports about problems that patients experienced after taking their drugs. Facilities that chose to remain traditional compounding pharmacies—generally catering to individual patients—were to continue being regulated primarily by state boards of pharmacy.

- The FDA was to conduct risk-based inspections of compounding pharmacies, focusing most heavily on those that produced vaccines, gene therapies, and drugs with complex manufacturing processes. The law also required detailed labeling of compounded drugs and collection of fees to pay for the oversight.

- It also required detailed labeling of compounded drugs and collection of fees to pay for the oversight.

- The measure established a national system for tracking and tracing pharmaceuticals, under which all members of the pharmaceutical distribution supply chain—including manufacturers, wholesale distributors, pharmacies, and repackagers—were to keep detailed records of transactions when drugs changed hands.

The House passed HR 3204 by voice vote September 28, 2013. Prime sponsor Fred Upton, R-Mich., chair of the Energy and Commerce Committee, said on the House floor that the measure was an "important step in helping to prevent any such tragedy from occurring again."

Some Democrats, including Rep. Rosa DeLauro of Connecticut, objected that the bill only required large compounding pharmacies to voluntarily register for FDA oversight. DeLauro said in a House floor speech before the vote that the bill was "not strong enough to ensure the public safety" and lacked "meaningful enough penalties for failure to comply."

FDA Commissioner Margaret A. Hamburg called the compromise approach "a step" toward solving a regulatory problem. "I don't think that it's going to be as comprehensive as maybe we initially had hoped," she said at a Bloomberg Government health care summit, according to *CQ News* on November 5, 2013.

The Senate cleared the bill by voice vote November 18, following a delay in which Sen. David Vitter, R-La., tried unsuccessfully to get a vote on an unrelated amendment that would have required lawmakers to disclose any aides they exempted from enrolling in Affordable Care Act insurance exchanges. Senate Majority Leader Harry Reid would not allow it.

President Obama signed HR 3204 on November 27, 2013 (PL 113–54).

Attempt to Limit Abortions

The fight over abortion rights has been waged legislatively for decades, and House conservatives in the 113th Congress had no intention of letting up. Although the U.S. Supreme Court's landmark *Roe v. Wade* decision in 1973 affirmed a woman's right to obtain an abortion up to the point of fetal viability, which is generally considered to be about twenty-three or twenty-four weeks after fertilization, critics of that decision have pushed to test the legal extent of reproductive rights ever since. The question in 2013: Could Congress pass a law banning a woman from getting an abortion after the twentieth week of pregnancy? Two events in 2013 coincided with annual lobbying from anti-abortion activists to do so.

One occurred on May 21, when the 9th Circuit Court of Appeals ruled unconstitutional an Arizona law that banned abortions twenty weeks after fertilization, one of the twelve so-called pain-based laws that states had enacted. Proponents of the Arizona law said a fetus is capable of feeling pain at that point of a pregnancy, a claim unsupported by scientific evidence. A three-judge 9th Circuit panel cited in its ruling "a long line of invariant Supreme Court precedents" that began with the *Roe* decision. The Supreme Court would later decline to accept the 9th Circuit ruling for review, allowing it to stand.

The other event was the first-degree murder conviction on May 13 of Kermit Gosnell, a Philadelphia abortion doctor. Gosnell provided abortions late in pregnancies and was arrested in 2011 and convicted in 2013 of killing three infants that prosecutors said had been delivered alive. Antiabortion groups used Gosnell's trial to press for legislative constraints on late-term abortions.

House Action

Arizona Republican Rep. Trent Franks introduced the twenty-week-limit bill (HR 1797) on April 26 with ninety-three original cosponsors, all but one of them Republicans. Daniel Lipinski of Illinois was the lone Democrat. Three other Democrats—Nick Rahall of West Virginia, Mike McIntyre of North Carolina, and Collin Peterson of Minnesota—subsequently signed on, making the cosponsor roster 180 Republicans and four Democrats.

As introduced, the bill was to apply to the District of Columbia, banning abortions after twenty weeks of pregnancy unless the woman's life was in danger. But on June 4, the House Judiciary Subcommittee on the Constitution and Civil Justice voted 6–4 along party lines to approve HR 1797 for full committee action after broadening it to apply nationwide. In advocating for the expansion of the bill's reach, Subcommittee Chair Franks cited the Gosnell case. The bill said that "it is the purpose of the Congress to assert a compelling governmental interest in protecting the lives of unborn children from the stage at which substantial medical evidence indicates that they are capable of feeling pain."

Franks had sponsored a similar, D.C.-specific abortion-limiting bill in 2012, which did not pass. The earlier measure fell short on a 220–154 vote on the House floor, where it was brought up under suspension of the rules, an expedited process that required a two-thirds majority for passage (*2012 Almanac*, p. H-186).

The subcommittee removed language from the bill that would have allowed a woman receiving an abortion after twenty weeks—or the father or maternal grandparent of the unborn child—to sue the abortion provider for damages.

The House Judiciary Committee approved HR 1797 (H Rept 113–109) by a 20–12 party-line vote on June 12. As approved in committee, the measure required abortion providers to determine when fertilization occurred and barred procedures leading to an abortion twenty weeks after that date or later.

Physicians performing abortions in violation of the ban would have been subject to fines and imprisonment for up to five years. The committee-approved measure included an exception for pregnant women whose lives were endangered "by a physical disorder, physical illness, or physical injury, including a life-endangering physical condition caused by or arising from the pregnancy itself." But the bill specifically barred exceptions for rape or incest, and for "psychological or emotional conditions."

During the full committee markup, Republicans blocked Democratic efforts to add rape and incest exemptions. Franks justified the lack of those exceptions by saying that such pregnancies were rare—an assertion that drew strong criticism from Democrats. Louise M. Slaughter of New York and Diana DeGette of Colorado, the Democratic cochairwomen of the House Pro-Choice Caucus, accused the House majority of reigniting "its war on women," *CQ News* reported on June 12, 2013.

Before the bill reached the House floor, House GOP leaders took two steps intended to mollify criticisms. First, they added exceptions for rape and for incest involving a minor in specific situations. Rapes would have had to have been reported to "an appropriate law enforcement agency" before the abortion was performed, and incest would have had to be reported prior to the abortion to a law enforcement agency or to a government agency legally authorized to act on reports of child abuse or neglect.

Also, Republican leaders removed Franks as floor manager for the bill, giving the role to Marsha Blackburn, R-Tenn. They gave other women prominent roles during debate even though none of them were on the Judiciary Committee.

Democrats derided the latter maneuver, with Slaughter calling it a public relations move and noting that all Republicans on the Judiciary Committee were men. Susan A. Davis, D-Calif., said the requirements for reporting a rape to law enforcement before an abortion could be performed ignored the trauma a rape survivor endures.

But John Fleming, R-La., a physician, said the bill was about protecting life and preventing "torture to that young life" (*CQ Weekly*, June 24, 2013).

The House voted 228–196 on June 18 to pass HR 1797. Six Republicans voted against the bill: Paul C. Broun of Georgia, Charles Dent of Pennsylvania, Rodney P. Frelinghuysen of New Jersey, Richard L. Hanna of New York, John Runyan of New Jersey, and Rob Woodall of Georgia.

Six Democrats voted in favor: Henry Cuellar of Texas, Daniel Lipinski of Illinois, Jim Matheson of Utah, Mike McIntyre of North Carolina, Collin Peterson of Minnesota, and Nick Rahall of West Virginia.

Senate Action

Although Senate Democrats had indicated that they had no intention of considering the House-passed bill, Sen. Lindsey Graham, R-S.C., introduced a similar companion measure (S 1670) on November 7 in the hope of eventually securing a vote. Graham garnered forty Republican cosponsors for the measure, but Democrats appeared united in opposition.

At the time of introduction, Graham acknowledged support fell short of the fifty votes needed for passage but said he thought support would grow and the debate itself was worthwhile.

Antiabortion groups pressed for a Senate vote on the legislation, arguing that public opinion was on their side. But abortion rights groups lashed out against the measure in statements, calling it dangerous.

Democratic opponents of the legislation derided Graham's action as blatantly political during a Senate floor appearance and said it would leave women who needed abortions for health reasons after twenty weeks with no options. They also said the bill was destined to fail.

"We are here today to make one thing abundantly clear, and that is that this extreme, unconstitutional abortion ban is an absolute non-starter," Patty Murray, D-Wash., said in a floor speech on November 7. "It is going nowhere in the Senate and those Republicans know it."

She was correct. Senate leaders did not schedule it for a vote.

Back to the House for a New Attempt

House Republicans did not give up. They began early in the next year, 2014, with an effort to bar federal funding in the Affordable Care Act from supporting abortion coverage and to exclude the procedure from some federal tax benefits.

The House Judiciary Committee approved a bill on January 15, 2014, sponsored by Christopher H. Smith, R-N.J. (HR 7), that would have prohibited use of federal funds to pay for abortions or health insurance plans that cover abortions. Cases of rape, incest, or situations in which the woman is in danger of death would be exempt.

Under the measure, individuals could not have gotten tax credits established under the 2010 health care law (PL 111–148, PL 111–153) that help low- and moderate-income people pay for insurance through the health care exchanges if the plans covered abortion. However, individuals could still buy separate out-of-pocket insurance coverage for abortion.

Eight amendments—all by Democrats—were offered during the Judiciary Committee markup. One concerned patient communications and the right of a woman to make informed, private decisions, which Republicans pushed back on as too vague. Another amendment would have freed the District of Columbia from the restrictions if it used its own locally raised funds. The panel's ranking Democrat, John

Conyers Jr., said this was necessary because the bill's language otherwise was on par with blocking a state from making decisions on how to spend its own money.

Each of the amendments was rebuffed, however, either by roll-call vote or through a ruling that they were outside of the panel's jurisdiction or not germane. Committee chair Robert W. Goodlatte, R-Va., opposed Conyers's District of Columbia proposal, arguing that the Constitution gives Congress legislative authority over the district. Since Congress is constitutionally responsible for the use of the district's funds, Goodlatte said, Congress is responsible for protecting unborn children in the nation's capital.

Another objection came from the White House, which said in a statement of administration policy on January 27, 2014, that federal policy already barred using federal funds for abortions except in certain circumstances and that this prohibition was maintained in the 2010 health care law and reinforced through a 2010 executive order. "HR 7 would go well beyond these safeguards by interfering with consumers' private health care choices," the statement said.

But on January 28, the House passed the measure 227–188. Only one Republican, Richard Hanna of New York, voted no on the bill, while six Democrats who often parted company with the majority of their party on social issues, such as Jim Matheson of Utah and Mike McIntyre of North Carolina, voted for the bill.

The final version of the House bill dropped earlier provisions that would have prevented individuals from claiming medical expense tax deductions for abortion costs and using flexible spending accounts and health savings accounts, which get special tax treatment, to pay for the procedure.

Senate Action

The Senate let the bill languish, taking no action on it. But the Senate Judiciary Committee debated a different abortion-related proposal: Connecticut Democrat Richard Blumenthal's bill (S 1696) that would overturn state laws deemed restrictive enough that they interfered with access to abortion.

The past several years had seen the emergence of hundreds of state laws affecting abortion providers, some of which required waiting periods and mandated that an ultrasound be performed and shown to the woman so she could see the fetus in her womb. Other state laws required that abortion clinics have medical capabilities similar to those of hospitals or surgical clinics.

Blumenthal's legislation would have essentially invalidated such laws unless they could be shown to substantially protect or enhance women's health. The Connecticut Democrat said at a July 15, 2014, Judiciary Committee hearing that his measure was a response to a "cascading avalanche of restrictions on reproductive health" and was aimed at "regulations that do nothing to help a woman's health or safety and in fact are more likely to harm it."

Despite Blumenthal's insistence that his bill would target only "bogus" state legislation, Republicans at the hearing said it would affect a broad swath of statutes, including those that allow doctors to refuse to provide abortions or other care if it runs contrary to their consciences.

Judiciary ranking Republican Charles E. Grassley of Iowa said the Blumenthal bill would allow abortion providers to operate without state-level oversight. Such a move, he said, would unconstitutionally interfere with states' rights to regulate abortion under the 10th Amendment, which reserved powers to states unless delegated by the Constitution.

Grassley called mandatory ultrasound and twenty-four-hour waiting period laws helpful to women's health, and he raised the specter of Gosnell, the Pennsylvania abortion provider convicted of murder, involuntary manslaughter, and other charges related to his illegal operations and the dismal sanitary conditions of his facilities. Grassley acknowledged that Gosnell was in violation of several laws already on the books, but he said new legal restrictions created after his arrest would help make it harder for someone like him to operate.

"If the bill we are discussing today, the so-called Women's Health Promotion Act, were to become law, Pennsylvania's laws would be invalidated," Grassley said at a June 15, 2014, Judiciary Committee hearing. "The laws that helped convict Kermit Gosnell would be wiped away."

Blumenthal's bill did not get a committee vote in 2014.

"Doc Fix"

For years, doctors, hospital administrators, and members of their trade groups made an annual trek from their hometowns to Capitol Hill with a warning: Pay us what we need to treat seniors in the Medicare program, or we might have to stop accepting new Medicare patients. Medicare is the federal health insurance program for people sixty-five and older.

This was not a matter of greed, they said. Rather, the payment-for-treatment formula set under the Balanced Budget Act of 1997 (PL 105–33) failed to keep up with medical costs and put physicians in a bind. They said they wanted to be paid fairly and keep accepting new Medicare patients. But they said the increasingly stringent payment reductions required under the 1997 law made that difficult *(1997 Almanac, p. 6–3)*.

The 1997 law established a sustainable growth rate formula, or SGR, under which doctors were reimbursed for treating patients covered by Medicare Part B, which pays for medically necessary outpatient and preventive services. The SGR formula took into account overall Medicare patient enrollment, the U.S. economy's annual growth rate, and the efficiency of health care providers in delivering service. But it was a flawed formula, physicians said, because it tied government payments for medical services to general economic growth and encouraged holding down medical costs while ignoring the increasingly complex medical environment and actual costs for treating patients.

Beginning in 2002, this misalignment—higher medical costs than the SGR formula allowed for—resulted in what could have been annual reductions in fee rates (PL 105–33, *Congress and the Nation Vol. X*, p. 432). The cut was 4.8 percent that year, and that was the last time Congress allowed such a reduction to take place. Instead, Congress routinely overrode the law for short periods at a time. This had a cumulative cost on paper, because the SGR was still in the law, and it built on year-to-year changes. Each delay pushed the mounting cuts higher, and they reached double digits eventually.

But 2013 was different from most previous years, because Congress got closer than ever before to enacting a permanent "doc fix" that would end the annual threatened cuts.

Three committees in the two chambers—House Energy and Commerce, House Ways and Means, and Senate Finance—shared jurisdiction over Medicare and in 2013 approved largely similar bills (HR 2810, S 1871) to revise the reimbursement regime. Changing the system was going to be an expensive proposition, because it involved giving up billions of dollars in anticipated savings from payment cutbacks. And none of the committee-approved bills addressed the crucial question of how to offset that cost.

As the year ended, the press of other weighty budget matters interceded, and lawmakers punted the issue into 2014 with a three-month extension of existing law as part of a broader continuing spending resolution and with the hope that they might solve the long-vexing problem in the new year (H J Res 59—PL 113–67). Then in 2014, lawmakers bogged down over other matters again. But they used another budget deal to avert cuts to physicians through March 31, 2015, by which time they finally arrived at a long-term solution.

LEGISLATIVE ACTION

Work on the doc fix for 2013 had actually started under the previous Congress, with lawmakers incorporating a short-term patch in the "fiscal cliff" spending law (PL 112–240), which prevented tax increases for most Americans and delayed for two months the spending sequester that was to have taken effect at the beginning of the year. Although the fiscal cliff measure, which cleared on January 1, 2013, just before the official end of the 112th Congress, was largely unrelated to Medicare, it froze Medicare payment rates to doctors for one year, through December 31, 2013, averting a scheduled 27 percent reduction in reimbursements *(2012 Almanac, p. 9–4)*.

This still left the long-term problem unresolved, and despite the 2013 reprieve, doctors were facing a threatened cut of 24 percent at the start of 2014.

So each of the three committees with jurisdiction approved its own bill to permanently replace the SGR during 2013. All three measures would have created a period of stable payments, and all three proposed changes in the Medicare reimbursement program aimed to improve the existing fee-for-service system and to reward physicians who participated in alternative payment models.

The committees worked closely with one another during the year. House Energy and Commerce acted first, and Senate Finance and House Ways and Means released a joint proposal at the end of October. As they went through the process, the committees solicited input from a variety of affected industries and trade associations.

House Energy and Commerce Bill

The Energy and Commerce panel approved its version of HR 2810 (H Rept 113–257, Part 1) by a 51–0 vote on July 31. The Energy and Commerce version called for an enhanced fee-for-service system, as well as alternative payment models, to replace the existing Medicare fee-for-service regime and the SGR repayment formula. The measure did not address the potential cost.

Lawmakers knew that they would have to find ways to replace the lost savings, at the time estimated at $139.1 billion over ten years. "Today's vote is an important milestone, but we are all resolved to achieve reform in a fiscally responsible manner," Energy and Commerce Chair Fred Upton, R-Mich., said in a statement on July 31, 2013.

Despite uncertainty about offsetting the cost, many medical professionals and lawmakers supported the underlying structure of the Energy and Commerce bill. It would have established a five-year transition period away from the existing payment system and provided annual payment increases of 0.5 percent to give providers time to test new quality-of-care measurements and improvement activities associated with the new payment structure.

Physicians would have been allowed to enter into alternative payment models. The new models were meant to encourage cost savings and improved quality of care through collaboration among medical providers and to move away from the fee-for-service system that many providers and health care experts criticized for rewarding volume of services over value. Physicians would have been allowed to continue operating in a revised fee-for-service system if they did not participate in alternative care delivery models.

One model that some providers favored was known as the patient-centered medical home, which organized primary care services and encouraged collaboration among several providers. The team of providers in the medical home was to be responsible for meeting the majority of the patient's physical- and mental-health needs and was to focus on the patient's needs, culture, and preferences.

The Department of Health and Human Services was to follow two tracks for approving the alternative payment models—one for models whose effectiveness data had been gathered and another for models that might be developed and tested for up to three years.

House Ways and Means and Senate Finance Bills

The House Ways and Means and Senate Finance committees worked closely during the year to refine the payment system, a sign that lawmakers were determined to find bipartisan agreement on the issue. The Finance panel met the same day that the House Energy and Commerce panel approved its version of the bill to announce that it would produce an alternative later in the year.

"Obviously, fixing the SGR is the main objective here," Sen. John Thune, R-S.D., said on July 31, 2013, after the Finance Committee meeting. "But we also want to look at what we can do in terms of policy to create a new system that actually works better and rewards value." And there was still the question of how to pay for it, he acknowledged.

Ways and Means and Finance released their joint draft framework for a bill on October 31. Lawmakers and aides said the framework was intended to be a less expensive alternative to the version approved by the House Energy and Commerce Committee.

Because of the way the Energy and Commerce bill had been drafted—including small annual increases in payment rates—the Congressional Budget Office said it would cost $175.5 billion over ten years, much more than the cost of a straight repeal of the SGR. The annual increases alone were estimated by the CBO to cost $63.5 billion over a decade. The Ways and Means and Finance framework called instead for a freeze in payments, along with other changes.

In many respects, the joint framework shared the goals and approach of the Energy and Commerce bill: repealing the SGR, moving to a system that rewarded value of care over volume of services, and encouraging physicians to participate in alternative payment models.

Committee leaders called for comments on the draft by November 12 in an effort to allow time to act before the end of the year. Initial reactions were positive from lawmakers and provider groups.

Less than six weeks after the legislative framework was released, the two committees held markup sessions on the same day, December 12, 2013, and easily approved largely similar bills. The Ways and Means Committee markup went briskly. Although several panel members cited concerns they had with the legislation and noted changes they wanted to make, they held off on offering amendments. Republican Tom Price of Georgia, for example, said the expansion of authority of the Centers for Medicare and Medicaid Services troubled him, as did the interference with Medicare's fee-for-service system, but "this day is a real opportunity," he said on December 12, and he voted for the bill. The panel's vote was 39–0 to approve its version of HR 2810 on December 12 (H Rept 113–257, Part 2).

The Senate Finance markup on its version, S 1871, proceeded less quickly, but by voice vote and with little difficulty, the panel approved the proposal (S Rept 113–135) on January 16, 2014.

Panel members either did not offer or withdrew most of the 140 amendments they had filed. But by voice vote, the panel adopted an amendment to create a demonstration-project version of bipartisan mental health legislation (S 264) sponsored by Debbie Stabenow, D-Mich. The demonstration project would have allowed community behavioral health providers in up to ten states that gave a higher level of service, such as twenty-four-hour crisis services, to receive Medicaid reimbursement based on the system for qualified health centers. S 264 was one of the mental health bills considered in 2013 in response to concerns over rising gun violence.

Neither the Energy and Commerce bill nor the Finance bill addressed the question of lost savings from a repeal of the SGR physician payment formula. By the time of the markups, the CBO had reestimated the cost of a straight repeal to be $116.5 billion over ten years. Coupled with other changes proposed in the two bills, the cost was expected to be as high as $150 billion.

Lawmakers insisted they would find a way to offset the cost but said that issue would not be resolved until floor debate. "Let me say it in no uncertain terms: This bill will be offset. Period," said Senate Finance ranking Republican Orrin G. Hatch of Utah at the January 16, 2014, markup.

But in late January 2014, the CBO announced even higher cost estimates. The Ways and Means version was estimated to cost $121.1 billion over ten years, while the Finance version was estimated to cost $148.6 billion. The CBO reestimated the cost of the Energy and Commerce version, with its annual payment increases, at $153.2 billion.

Then on February 6, 2014, Baucus resigned from the Senate, having been confirmed to serve as ambassador to China. Although Ron Wyden, D-Ore., took over as chair of the Finance Committee, efforts to find a bipartisan solution appeared stalled. The House, however, on March 14 passed a revised version of the Energy and Commerce and Ways and Means committee bills (HR 4015) by a near-party-line vote of 238–181.

Only twelve Democrats voted for the measure, while 181 were opposed, a result of a rule (H Res 515) that provided for floor consideration but automatically added an amendment that Democrats considered untenable. The amendment by Ways and Means Chair Dave Camp, R-Mich., would offset the bill's $138 billion cost with a five-year delay of the 2010 health care law's (PL 111–148, PL 111–152) individual mandate penalty.

Democrats declared the amendment a nonstarter, and the White House said it would veto this bill if it was sent to the president.

Back in the Senate, Wyden introduced a revised version of the Finance Committee bill (S 2157) on March 25, 2014, but no immediate action was scheduled on that bill.

More Temporary Fixes

The three committees showed signs of making progress. Yet the year-long extension worked out in the January 1, 2013, fiscal cliff measure was expiring. Congressional leaders saw some hope that a permanent fix might be attainable, but more time was needed, as was new authorizing legislation. Patient and industry groups asked lawmakers not to enact another yearlong patch, fearing that work on the overhaul bills would fall by the wayside in early 2014 without the pressure of a deadline.

In response, Congress attached a three-month Medicare payment extension to the broad fiscal-year 2014 budget deal (H J Res 59—PL 113-67) that cleared on December 18, 2013. It provided physicians with a 0.5 percent increase on top of existing payment rates through March 31, 2014.

A portion of the cost of the three-month extension was offset by cuts in payments to long-term-care hospitals and to "disproportionate share" hospitals, which treated a high number of uninsured or underinsured patients. They normally were paid extra by the government to compensate for potential monetary losses for treating these patients. The cost was further offset by a two-year extension of the automatic 2 percent cuts for Medicare providers that was required as part of the spending sequester created by the 2011 debt limit law (PL 112-25) (Sequester, p. 3-4; 2011 debt limit law, 2011 Almanac, p. 3-11).

Congress still wanted to find a permanent SGR overhaul. But in late March 2014, the three-month extension passed in December was expiring, and there was no sign that a bipartisan, House-and-Senate agreement was near. So Congress extended the three-month "doc fix" for a full year (HR 4302—PL 113-93). The House passed HR 4302 by voice vote March 27, 2014, and the Senate cleared the bill by a vote of 64-35 on March 31.

This was the seventeenth measure since 2003 to temporarily protect Medicare doctors from cuts. Some members said they were disappointed Congress had put off a permanent solution yet again.

The measure preserved the 0.5 percent payment increase through 2014, followed by flat payments through March 2015. The law also extended increased inpatient payments for certain low-volume hospitals and specialized Medicare Advantage plans for individuals with special needs. Unlike traditional Medicare, in which patients pick a health care provider and the provider bills the government, Medicare Advantage plans are run or coordinated by insurers in partnership with networks of doctors and hospitals, in much the way that private insurance and health network plans operate.

To offset the cost of the one-year extension, the measure modified the timing of scheduled Medicare sequester cuts for fiscal 2024 so that they were contained within a ten-year budget scorekeeping window. The cuts were to be 4 percent in the first six months of the fiscal year and zero percent in the second six months. A similar timing adjustment had been used for the three-month "doc fix" in December 2013.

President Obama signed the bill into law on April 1, 2014, the day after 24 percent cuts were scheduled to occur.

Mental Health and Guns

The deadly shootings of twenty students and six educators at Sandy Hook Elementary School in Newtown, Conn., in December 2012 brought renewed attention to federal mental health policy. That was because the shooter, twenty-year-old Adam Lanza, had a history of psychiatric ailments that had gone untreated. In response, President Obama proposed a variety of legislative measures in January 2013 as part of his strategy to reduce gun violence, and he identified a handful of policy actions that his administration planned to take on its own.

Lawmakers also introduced several bipartisan mental health bills in the wake of the Sandy Hook shootings. But they struggled to move them after an agreement on expanded background checks for gun purchases (S 649) stalled on the Senate floor in April. This was not the only sticking point. Nearly every aspect of firearms-related legislation got caught up in disagreement involving passionate, deeply held beliefs. Sportsmen and recreational shooters said a few acts by a tiny number of troubled people should not be cause to impede Second Amendment rights. Gun control advocates countered that the right to bear arms had limits.

Even on the issue of mental health, the divide could not be bridged, with some authorities noting that unlike Lanza, who had access to weapons and was reportedly preoccupied with violence, most people with mental health issues were not mass killers. Mental health advocacy groups cautioned against labeling all people being treated for disorders as potential killers.

As 2013 ended, Congress had taken no action to increase access to mental health treatment services, to bolster training, to support research, or to address privacy concerns—all of which were covered by various legislative proposals.

In November, however, the Obama administration fulfilled the president's commitment to issue long-awaited final regulations requiring parity for mental health treatment in health insurance coverage, based on a 2008 law (PL 110-343). That law, enacted after more than a decade of effort, required insurers that offered mental health benefits to make them equal in cost and scope to traditional medical benefits (Mental-health parity, 2008 Almanac, p. 9-5).

LEGISLATIVE ACTION

Senate Bills

Most of the legislative effort took place in the Senate, where the Health, Education, Labor, and Pensions Committee advanced legislation (S 689) in April 2013 that incorporated ideas from mental health measures introduced by several senators.

The bill, sponsored by HELP Chair Tom Harkin, D-Iowa, would have reauthorized until 2018 various mental health programs run by the Department of Health and Human Services and the Department of Education. It was approved by voice vote on April 10 and had bipartisan support, with five Democratic and six Republican cosponsors on the date it was approved.

The measure would have reauthorized the Mental Health and Substance Use Disorder Services on Campuses grant program. But it would also have updated the program to allow the use of money for students, families, faculty, and staff to increase awareness and training to respond to students with mental health and substance use disorders. It also would have reauthorized programs related to suicide prevention and spending to support a national network of child trauma centers. Provisions that were similar to those in two other bills—one dealing with suicide and substance abuse (S 116), by Jack Reed, D-R.I., and one to help train teachers to recognize symptoms of mental illnesses (S 153), by Mark Begich, D-Alaska—were also included.

The HELP committee bill was seen as a necessary element complementing S 649, the Safe Communities, Safe Schools Act of 2013, which was a broader gun control bill that was headed to the Senate floor the same week. Harkin sponsored a floor amendment to S 649 that included language from S 689. It was adopted on a 95–2 vote.

That was the last vote on the gun measure, however, before it was pulled from the floor.

Lawmakers could not agree on many of its more controversial provisions, including a proposed crackdown to close loopholes on "straw" purchasers—people who buy guns and give them to others who are ineligible for a purchase because of a felony conviction—and proposed background checks on people who buy guns from unlicensed sellers at gun shows, flea markets, or on the Internet.

Consideration of another mental health bill (S 264), introduced by Michigan Democrat Debbie Stabenow, had been expected as part of the Senate's gun control measure. But Stabenow's bill, which would have increased access to community mental health services, fell into limbo when the broader gun package stalled.

On December 12, however, Stabenow offered a demonstration-project version of her bill as an amendment during Finance Committee consideration of legislation (S 1871) to overhaul the Medicare physician payment system. The demonstration project would have allowed community behavioral health providers in up to ten states that gave a higher level of service, such as twenty-four-hour crisis services, to receive Medicaid reimbursement based on the system for qualified health centers. The committee adopted Stabenow's amendment and approved the bill by voice vote. But work on the Medicare bill, a long-sought effort to find a permanent "doc fix," stalled for other reasons and did not see floor action in 2013.

A third bill (S 162), sponsored by Al Franken, D-Minn., which addressed mental health issues in the criminal justice system, was approved by the Judiciary Committee by voice vote on June 20 but was not considered by the Senate.

The Franken measure would have reauthorized and expanded a 2004 law (PL 108–414) that set up grants to support mental health courts and other collaborative programs between the criminal justice and mental health systems. It would have authorized spending for the program through fiscal 2019 and made some alterations, including provisions to help veterans with mental illnesses or substance use disorders. Franken eventually had thirty-eight cosponsors, including

fourteen Republicans. Calling it the right thing to do, Franken noted that it had support from authorities in law enforcement, corrections, and mental health.

The measure was so uncontroversial that it had been expected to be "hotlined," or approved by the full Senate by voice vote, with no need for a roll call. But two senators, Mike Lee, R-Utah, and Tom Coburn, R-Okla., held it up. Coburn said he supported the bill's ideals and agreed that "incarcerated offenders suffering from mental illness should have access to treatment." But he said he had concerns about the federal government taking on responsibilities for inmates in state and local jails. Lee said he had questions and just needed to clear up some issues. Franken's bill never made it to the Senate floor.

House Bill

In the House, Energy and Commerce Committee leaders announced at the start of the year that the Oversight and Investigations Subcommittee would examine mental health policies in the wake of the Newtown tragedy. The subcommittee, chaired by Pennsylvania Republican Tim Murphy, a child psychologist, held a forum in March on violence and severe mental illness and followed up with two hearings related to mental health issues.

Murphy introduced legislation (HR 3717) on December 12, 2013, the last day the House took roll call votes before adjourning for the year. His bill was designed to address a broad range of mental health issues including access, treatment, and privacy.

"Bottom line: If we want to change these trends in victimization of the mentally ill and the persistently mentally ill, if we want to reduce the high number of suicides, homicides and assaults . . . if we want to prevent the Newtowns, Tucsons, Auroras, Pittsburghs and Columbines, we have to do something comprehensive, research-based, and we have to do it now," Murphy said on the House floor the day he introduced the bill.

The measure included provisions to address access to acute-care psychiatric beds, alternatives to long-term inpatient care, health information technology, mental health courts, telepsychiatry, and programs at the Substance Abuse and Mental Health Services Administration. Republicans Bill Cassidy of Louisiana and Leonard Lance of New Jersey and Democrat Eddie Bernice Johnson of Texas were original cosponsors.

The bill also would have ended programs under the auspices of the Substance Abuse and Mental Health Services Administration that were "not explicitly authorized or required by statute" and prohibited the agency from providing financial assistance to mental health or substance use diagnosis or treatment programs unless they relied on "evidence-based practices." Those proposed changes in existing practice drew criticism from some mental health advocates.

But this bill, too, saw no further action.

2015–2016

After the 2014 midterm elections, House and Senate Republicans finally had the majorities for a major bill repealing many of the policy, tax, and revenue features of the Affordable Care Act. But they ran into a presidential veto.

The unceasing tussles between Obama and Republicans over the health law known as Obamacare may well be what history remembers. But those spats and vitriol did not define the entire two years in health care legislation. After seventeen temporary fixes since 2003, Congress finally passed and the president signed a permanent "doc fix," ending the annual plea by health care providers not to cut Medicare payments for their services. Had this not occurred, health care providers might have had a 21 percent fee cut when they billed Medicare, the federal health insurer for seniors, although a short-term fix from Congress—the eighteenth—might have been more likely.

Congress and the president also agreed on legislation to speed up the government's process for approving new drugs, approving a bill called the 21st Century Cures Act. Before this, scientists and pharmaceutical companies could spend up to fifteen years to get approval and sell a new medicine or treatment after its discovery. The Food and Drug Administration had justified a slow approach as necessary for thorough, cautious, and scientifically sound testing and analysis, and no one disputed that it was better to be safe than to release a drug with untested and potentially catastrophic results. But lawmakers who wanted a better, albeit safe, process said that 95 percent of rare diseases currently had no known cures—and the system in place hampered the development of cures.

The 21st Century Cures Act would authorize $4.8 billion in funding to the National Institutes of Health over ten years, specifically for programs including Obama's cancer "moonshot" initiative, so named because the White House wished to summon for a cure for cancer the same level of national resolve and resources that helped put a man on the moon in 1969. The Cures Act also provided $500 million over nine years to the Food and Drug Administration and $1 billion to states over two years to help fight prescription drug abuse. This was a time of a growing, deadly crisis of improper and illegal opioid use and abuse. Although the cost was fully offset upon House passage, some of the offsets were later used in other year-end legislation, which forced the Senate to find new funding sources.

The 114th Congress also passed legislation, after a months-long battle, to provide $1.1 billion for fighting the then-spreading Zika virus.

Other issues, however, resisted solution. The abortion debate continued in these two years, impassioned and unresolved. So too did discussions over what to do on the intersection of mental health and gun violence. Nearly everyone agreed on a need to address the role mental health played, particularly when it came to high-profile mass shootings such as those at Sandy Hook, Columbine, and Virginia Tech. Yet discussions broke down over possible restrictions of gun rights—how keeping guns out of the hands of unstable young people could also keep them away from law-abiding sportsmen and -women exercising their Second Amendment rights. Some mental health provisions were folded into the 21st Century Cures Act as a way to get them passed and funded, independent of measures to control firearms, which failed.

A Final "Doc Fix"

In mid-April 2015, Congress finally ended the long-running routine of temporarily blocking scheduled fee cuts to doctors who treated Medicare patients. Lawmakers did so by replacing the oft-criticized Medicare payment formula. The urgency of the moment played a role: The measure passed with strong bipartisan support just hours before 21 percent reimbursement reductions were scheduled to take effect (HR 2—PL 114–10).

This would be the last of the periodic, temporary bills to delay the fee cuts that had come to be known as the "doc fix." The Sustainable Growth Rate, or SGR, formula was designed to limit growth in Medicare spending to growth in the economy, a way to incentivize medical efficiency. Physicians treating seniors in Medicare got bigger payments when growth in Medicare spending was lower than the economy's growth rate, a form of rewarding doctors for cost containment.

But the SGR formula cut medical providers' fees if Medicare spending outpaced the growth of the gross domestic product—even though this did not always correlate to things a doctor could directly control. Because this was a national formula, it affected doctors everywhere, and

REFERENCES

Discussion of human services policy for the years 1945–1964 may be found in *Congress and the Nation Vol. I*, pp. 1225–1331; for the years 1965–1968, *Congress and the Nation Vol. II*, pp. 745–778; for the years 1969–1972, *Congress and the Nation Vol. III*, pp. 605–633; for the years 1973–1976, *Congress and the Nation Vol. IV*, pp. 403–432; for the years 1977–1980, *Congress and the Nation Vol. V*, pp. 679–712; for the years 1981–1984, *Congress and the Nation Vol. VI*, pp. 581–612; for the years 1985–1988, *Congress and the Nation Vol. VII*, p. 607–632; for the years 1989–1992, *Congress and the Nation Vol. VIII*, pp. 611–624; for the years 1993–1996, *Congress and the Nation Vol. IX*, pp. 571–596; for the years 1997–2000, *Congress and the Nation Vol. X*, pp. 486–496; for the years 2001–2004, *Congress and the Nation Vol. XI*, pp. 520–529; for the years 2005–2008, *Congress and the Nation Vol. XII*, pp. 579–588; for the years 2009–2012, *Congress and the Nation Vol. XIII*, pp. 465–470.

Outlays for Income Security

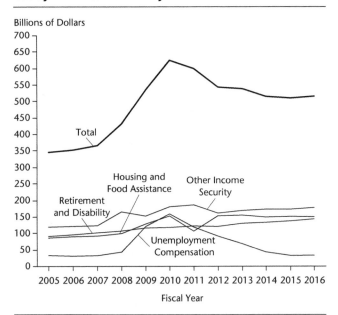

Billions of Dollars

SOURCE: Office of Management and Budget, Historical Tables, *Budget of the United States Government: Fiscal Year 2018* (Washington, DC: U.S. Government Printing Office, 2018), Table 3.2.

in many years they were scheduled to get a fee cut, which they said was unfair. So Congress had stepped in, starting in 2003, with a "doc fix" to block the reductions in payments to physicians. This had become an annual ritual, but like a debt temporally ignored, the cumulative balance—the sum of debts ultimately owed—grew to double digits.

House Action

There had been seventeen "doc fixes" already. Would there be an eighteenth?

The House convened in early 2015 hoping that if there was, it would be the last one. The bill number, HR 2, signaled this as a high priority, and it was negotiated by Speaker John A. Boehner, R-Ohio, and Minority Leader Nancy Pelosi, D-Calif.

Time was short, since the last doc fix was set to expire March 31, 2015, potentially forcing doctors who treated the elderly to take a 21 percent fee cut. And the bill text was not released until March 24. It did not help that lawmakers had a spring recess scheduled to start at the end of that week. This gave the House two days to review and pass the roughly $200 billion bill.

HR 2 would

- repeal the SGR and provide Medicare doctors with 0.5 percent annual updates from July 2015 through 2019
- freeze automatic updates after that, through 2025, and
- allow adjustments after 2019 through a program intended to reward quality rather than quantity.

These provisions were similar to the previous year's compromise proposal. But whereas the previous proposals did not have offsets, about a third of the cost of HR 2 was expected to be offset—an improvement, but still a potential concern to conservatives. Wealthier Medicare patients were to help pay by shouldering a bigger share of premiums, although the final threshold agreed to by lawmakers—individuals with incomes of $133,500 or more—would only affect about 2 percent of beneficiaries, according to the Kaiser Family Foundation.

The bill also faced potential trouble over abortion restrictions, funding for community health centers, and loan repayment and training for health professionals, the latter two needing extensions or else facing mandatory funding stream cutoffs. The House Pro-Choice Caucus supported the deal. Planned Parenthood and NARAL Pro-Choice America opposed it.

Similarly, hospitals were lukewarm over the small initial fee increases and then the freezes but resigned in accepting that the package could end their annual worries. The Federation of American Hospitals and the American Hospital Association both offered their support.

Lawmakers did not like the time pressure, but it had taken time to write such a complex bill. The CBO issued its score, or cost estimate, of HR 2 a day after its language was released and said it would increase the federal deficit by $141 billion over eleven years. The CBO said the bill would increase basic monthly premiums for Medicare coverage of doctor and outpatient services by $10 in 2025, compared to $7.50 if physician payment rates were frozen.

The House Rules Committee, the same day, March 25, 2015, passed by voice vote a rule barring amendments on the bill when it got to the House floor and allowing for only one hour of floor debate. This was in recognition that the bill was likely to pass the House with bipartisan support, and it did so on March 26 with a 392–37 vote.

Senate Action

Senators were displeased with the speed with which they had to take up and pass the doc fix measure, a major bill with fiscal and social policy ramifications that some said deserved more time. So they waited, assured that the speed with which the Centers for Medicare and Medicaid Services pays bills—fourteen days after they were received—would buy them just enough time to take a spring break and return without physicians seeing an actual cut.

Finally, the Senate cleared HR 2 on a 92–8 vote on April 14, 2015, after first dealing with a series of amendments on issues including how to pay for it; abortion restrictions on community health center funding; and a proposed four-year extension, rather than two, of funding for the Children's Health Insurance Program, which gives health coverage to low-income children if their families lack insurance.

The previous doc fix had expired on March 31. Without a vote by the end of the night on April 14, cuts of 21 percent could not be avoided, Senate Majority Leader Mitch McConnell, R-Ky., warned his chamber that evening.

Eight Republican senators voted against the measure: Ted Cruz of Texas, Mike Lee of Utah, David Perdue of Georgia, Marco Rubio of Florida, Ben Sasse of Nebraska, Tim Scott of South Carolina, and Jeff Sessions and Richard C. Shelby, both of Alabama. The conservatives wanted the Senate to pay for the entire cost of the package, which the Congressional Budget Office estimated would add $141 billion to the deficit through fiscal 2025.

Before the final vote, the Senate agreed, 71–29, to waive a budget point of order raised by Sessions in hopes of having the bill fully paid for. The Senate also rejected an amendment from Lee, 42–58, that would have eliminated an exemption to the budget rules included in the bill. Lee's language was one of two amendments that required a simple majority rather than 60 votes.

The Senate turned back a Democratic amendment that would have removed language in the bill to apply abortion restrictions to community health center funding. The proposal, offered by Patty Murray of Washington, would have also provided money for the health centers for an additional two years and renewed for two more years and expanded a funding boost that expired the previous year for Medicaid primary care doctors. It had the backing of both NARAL Pro-Choice America and Planned Parenthood. Senators rejected a motion, 43–57, to waive a budget point of order against the Murray amendment.

Senators also voted down

- an amendment by Colorado Democrat Michael Bennet that would have extended funding for the Children's Health Insurance Program for four years rather than the two years included in the bill. They did so by rejecting a budget point of order, with a 50–50 vote, on the proposal.
- a proposal to scrap limits on Medicare spending for therapy services, which had the support of the AARP. The amendment, by Maryland Democrat Benjamin L. Cardin, was defeated in a 58–42 tally, falling two votes short of the 60-vote threshold.
- an amendment from Texas Republican John Cornyn, 54–45, that would have repealed the requirement under the 2010 health law (PL 111–148, PL 111–152) that most individuals maintain health coverage or pay a penalty.
- an amendment from Tom Cotton, R-Ark., to scrap the new system laid out in the bill to pay Medicare doctors and replace it with 0.5 percent annual updates indefinitely. Cotton noted before the 11–89 vote that the Centers for Medicare and Medicaid Services chief actuary predicted the new system would require future fixes.

In addition to replacing the SGR, the bill required wealthier seniors to pay more for their Medicare outpatient and prescription drug coverage starting in 2018 to help offset the cost. The measure had broad support among physician groups.

Presidential Action

President Obama signed the bill April 16, 2015, holding an outdoor signing ceremony in the Rose Garden at which he congratulated Boehner and Pelosi. In a statement when the Senate cleared the measure, Obama said the package would strengthen the nation's health care system in the long run by encouraging physicians to participate in new payment models that could slow Medicare spending growth while preserving access to care (PL 114–10).

Abortion

The perennial abortion debate in Congress started early in 2015, as is typical because of the annual scheduling in January of the antiabortion March for Life, a large gathering in Washington around the anniversary of *Roe v. Wade*. But the issue's intensity was rekindled by the release in July 2015 of controversial sting videos on fetal tissue donation practices at Planned Parenthood.

The videos, taken and distributed by a group that called itself the Center for Medical Progress, showed Planned Parenthood employees candidly discussing the process of extracting aborted fetal tissue for medical research. Abortion foes argued that Planned Parenthood profited from selling fetal tissue. Officials of the organization said they only received compensation for reasonable costs such as storage and transportation, which was legal. Angered by what they said were purposeful distortions, abortion advocates questioned the ethical and legal tactics used by the group behind the videos.

In Congress, abortion foes and advocates remained divided, largely along party lines, over whether the family planning organization had violated any laws and whether it should continue to receive federal funding. Republicans contended that Planned Parenthood was profiting from the sale of fetal body parts, while Democrats panned the videos as an attack on women's health.

House Minority Leader Nancy Pelosi, D-Calif., said Republicans were creating a false controversy. White House Press Secretary Josh Earnest said the videos appeared to be selectively edited to distort the words of the individual speaking as well as the position of Planned Parenthood.

The difficult and emotional debate over reproductive rights has long been a dividing line in Congress but tends to energize voters, and it can present a political minefield for candidates. The years 2015 and 2016 were no different. Bills differed along several themes:

- an attempt to ban most abortions after twenty weeks of pregnancy
- an attempt to cut off federal funds for Planned Parenthood, and
- a "born alive" bill concerning infants born alive during failed abortions.

TWENTY-WEEK BILLS AND GOVERNMENT
FUNDING

GOP leaders in January 2015 briefly considered a new
twenty-week abortion ban bill (HR 36), the latest attempt
in an ongoing try to limit abortion rights. This was to be a
largely symbolic vote, coinciding with the annual antiabortion rally in Washington on the anniversary of the Supreme
Court's *Roe v. Wade* decision.

But they pulled the bill after a group of Republican
women and moderates objected to language that would
have allowed exceptions in cases of rape and incest only if
the woman seeking the abortion had reported the attack to
law enforcement agencies. The bill's allowance for abortion
in the case of incest would have applied only if the incest
had been committed against a minor.

Republican Reps. Renee Ellmers of North Carolina and
Jackie Walorski of Indiana withdrew their cosponsorship of
the measure, although Walorski wrote in a Facebook post
that she still intended to vote for the ban, as she had in 2013.

The ban was viewed as a long shot in the Senate anyway,
since its Senate supporters appeared to lack the votes to overcome a filibuster. The White House also threatened to veto
the measure, saying in a statement on January 20, 2015, that
the bill's basis was not only "scientifically disputed" but also
that its reporting requirement in instances of rape "demonstrates a complete disregard for the women who experience
sexual assault and the barriers they may face in reporting."

Holding off on the twenty-week abortion ban, the House
instead took up HR 7, a bill to permanently ban the use of
federal funds to pay for abortions and ensure that insurance
plans purchased on Affordable Care Act exchanges would not
use federal funds for abortion services.

HR 7 also would have required all qualified health
plans that provide abortion coverage to prominently disclose that fact to enrollees at the time of enrollment and
to prominently display such information in any marketing or advertising materials, plan comparison tools, or
summaries of benefits and coverage. Christopher H.
Smith, R-N.J., sponsor of HR 7, said on the House floor
on January 22, 2015, the day of the vote, that this kind of
disclosure was needed because consumers "have no idea
when they are buying a plan that it is paying for abortion
on demand." The bill was named the No Taxpayer
Funding for Abortion and Abortion Insurance Full
Disclosure Act of 2015.

The measure would have prohibited federal medical
facilities and health professionals from providing abortion
services, and it would have prohibited individuals and small
businesses from receiving federal subsidies and tax credits
under the 2010 health care overhaul (PL 111–148, PL 111–
152) to purchase health care plans that cover abortions. The
measure would have provided an exception for abortions in
cases of rape or incest and for saving the life of the mother.

Just before the vote, dozens of Democrats lined up to ask
unanimous consent to submit near-identical statements
in the record expressing "that this House should be voting

for bigger paychecks and better infrastructure instead of
these relentless attacks on women's access to health care."

The revised HR 7 passed 242–179 on January 22, largely
along party lines. Only one Republican, Richard Hanna of
New York, voted against passage, while three Democrats—
Henry Cuellar of Texas, Dan Lipinski of Illinois, and Collin
Peterson of Minnesota—voted for it.

But this never came up for a vote in the Senate, where a
filibuster was likely to block passage anyway.

NEXT ATTEMPT

The House next passed a revamped version of the
twenty-week abortion ban it took up briefly in January
(HR 36). This time, it passed the measure by a vote of
242–184 on May 13, 2015.

The bill included exceptions for rape, incest committed
against a minor, and when the mother's life was in danger.
In the revised version of the bill, rape would not have to be
reported to authorities for the exception to be valid, but
incest or rape against a minor would have to be reported.
Also, abortion doctors would have to ensure that rape victims received medical treatment or counseling at least
forty-eight hours prior to the procedure.

Other changes to the measure included protections for
infants born alive and a requirement that women receiving an
abortion under an exception must sign a consent form that
included the age of the unborn child and a description of the
law, among other items. The legislation also would impose
criminal penalties for physicians who violated the ban.

The Senate, however, never cleared the twenty-week
abortion ban. On September 22, Senate Democrats blocked
it with a 54–42 vote on a procedural measure called "cloture" to end debate so the underlying matter could get an
up-or-down vote on the floor. With failure to get the requisite 60 votes required under Senate rules for cloture on a
bill, this effectively ended consideration of the measure.

Three Democrats—Bob Casey of Pennsylvania, Joe
Donnelly of Indiana, and Joe Manchin III of West
Virginia—voted to invoke cloture on the bill. Two
Republicans—Mark S. Kirk of Illinois and Susan Collins of
Maine—voted against cloture.

Democrats admonished the GOP for using the tight legislative calendar to debate abortion instead of considering legislation to keep the government running into the new fiscal
year, on October 1, little more than a week later. "Here we are,
just days away from another reckless government shutdown,
and Republican leadership thinks the best use of our time is
to vote on a bill to give the government the power to intrude
on the most wrenching, private medical decision a woman
will ever make," Sen. Elizabeth Warren of Massachusetts said
on the Senate floor on September 21, 2015.

PLANNED PARENTHOOD

Republican leaders in the House and Senate wanted to
give their members a chance to vote on legislation to cut
off federal funding for Planned Parenthood, as they had

tried to do in years past, but they did not want the issue to delay or defeat vital year-end budget and spending bills.

The White House had made it clear that the president would veto any legislation that denied funding to Planned Parenthood.

In late July, with Congress approaching its summer recess, a working group of Republican senators reached a deal on a bill to stop funding Planned Parenthood that would be voted on before the break. Republican Joni Ernst of Iowa unveiled the legislation (S 1881) that would have deprived Planned Parenthood of its federal funding. She had the backing of at least thirty-four Republican cosponsors, including Majority Leader Mitch McConnell of Kentucky, who began shifting the procedural gears to bring the bill directly to the floor.

The bill would have diverted funds from Planned Parenthood to other women's health organizations that do not provide abortions in order to ensure women receive family planning services, prenatal and postpartum care, and sexually transmitted disease testing, among other services. Bill supporters hoped the added provision would quell concerns that slashing funding for Planned Parenthood would diminish women's access to health care, and they said other health centers were capable of absorbing the extra patients and new funds.

"This legislation would ensure taxpayer dollars for women's health are actually spent on women's health—not a scandal-plagued political lobbying giant," McConnell said in a joint statement in support of the measure, released on July 28, 2015.

The bill's supporters did not have the 60 votes necessary to limit debate, though. The vote to invoke cloture on August 3, 2015, was 53–46, largely along party lines.

SYMBOLIC ATTEMPT

When Congress returned in September, it was clear that Democrats had enough votes in the Senate to block any fresh attempt to deny money to Planned Parenthood. Republican leaders worried that if their caucus tried to force the issue again, this time so late in the fiscal year, by tying it to government funding, they could risk a government shutdown.

Yet the forty-some conservative Republicans in the House Freedom Caucus vowed to vote against any spending bill in their chamber that included money for Planned Parenthood. Constituents known as "values voters," who supported or rejected candidates based on conservative values, would be "outraged," Tim Huelskamp, R-Kan., told CQ Roll Call on September 8, 2015, if Republicans who campaigned on a prolife majority did not demonstrate their commitment.

The solution Republican leaders chose was to investigate Planned Parenthood and hope for a new president who agreed with their views.

"We just don't have the votes to get the outcome that we'd like," McConnell told an eastern Kentucky TV station, WYMT, on August 31, 2015. "The president has made it very clear he's not going to sign any bill that includes defunding of Planned Parenthood, so that's another issue that awaits a new president hopefully with a different point of view about Planned Parenthood."

House Republican leaders began moving a stand-alone bill (HR 3134) by Rep. Diane Black, R-Tenn., that would have given conservatives the chance to go on record against Planned Parenthood without tying the politically toxic issue to a continuing resolution, which Congress needed to pass before the end of September, or the federal government would shut down.

Black's bill, called the Defund Planned Parenthood Act of 2015, would have put a one-year moratorium on federal funding for Planned Parenthood, including mandatory revenue streams, unless the group certified it would not perform abortions during that period or provide funds to other abortion providers.

Conservatives supported Black's bill. Yet they also made clear that a vote on stand-alone legislation was not sufficient because such a measure would almost certainly lose in the Senate. They would have rather tied defunding language to a continuing spending resolution and forced Senate Democrats to block, or President Barack Obama to veto, a measure that would keep the government lights on.

The House, on September 18, 2015, passed Black's bill (HR 3134) to freeze funding for Planned Parenthood for one year while Congress investigated the organization. The vote was 241–187, with one member, Steve King, R-Iowa, voting "present." A vote of "present" is neither a yes nor a no, but the lawmaker's presence is noted for purposes of assuring a minimum threshold for taking a vote. King was an abortion opponent but disliked the process for this vote, saying in a statement that "innocent, unborn babies deserve more than just a show vote," or a vote for political purposes that lawmakers knew was unlikely to become law and therefore, to some, accomplished nothing.

It was unclear if passage would dissuade enough Republicans from tying the issue to critical government funding efforts in the following two weeks, as the end of the 2015 fiscal year approached.

Speaker John A. Boehner's leadership team had touted the bill as its chief response to the Planned Parenthood uproar, but many Republicans thought it nothing more than a show vote because the bill was unlikely to pass the Senate. Diehard abortion foes preferred to attach defunding language to must-pass spending legislation.

The expectations proved realistic all around. After House passage, the Defund Planned Parenthood Act was quickly sent to the Senate—where it got no further action.

BORN-ALIVE BILL

On the same day as it passed HR 3134, the bill to freeze Planned Parenthood funding for a year, the House passed legislation (HR 3504) to strengthen protection for infants born alive during failed abortions.

On a 248–177 vote, with one Democrat, John Garamendi of California, voting "present," the House backed the bill that would require health care providers to immediately take infants who survive an attempted abortion to a hospital and administer the same degree of medical care as they would give any child born at the same gestational age. Anyone who violated such requirements would have faced criminal fines and penalties, while anyone who intentionally killed a baby born alive after an abortion would have been charged with murder.

Democrat Daniel Lipinski of Illinois and four other Democrats—Matt Cartwright of Pennsylvania, Henry Cuellar of Texas, Jim Langevin of Rhode Island, and Collin Peterson of Minnesota—broke with their party to support the measure. But this bill, too, went nowhere in the Senate.

OTHER ABORTION MEASURES

On September 29, 2015, the House took still another action against Planned Parenthood, voting 236–193 to pass a bill (HR 3495) that would have allowed states to exclude providers such as Planned Parenthood that perform abortions from state Medicaid contracts. The legislation by Rep. Sean P. Duffy, R-Wis., contained exceptions for rape, incest, and saving the life of the mother.

Legal questions had arisen over whether Congress could actually restrict Medicaid dollars to Planned Parenthood because that would deny beneficiaries access to a qualified provider of their choice, which is illegal.

But this bill, too, was destined to go nowhere in the Senate, which referred HR 3495 to the Finance Committee without further action.

Republican leaders adopted a new strategy at the beginning of October, drawing up a budget reconciliation bill that would have cut off hundreds of millions of dollars in federal funding to Planned Parenthood and repealed major portions of the landmark Affordable Care Act.

A reconciliation bill allows Congress to change tax and spending laws so they conform to the overall fiscal policy laid out in an annual joint budget resolution. Both the House and Senate must adopt such a joint resolution for reconciliation to be possible, and Congress had done so on May 5, 2015, for the first time in six years. Reconciliation bills also move through the Senate with a simple majority, sidestepping the usual sixty-vote requirement for consideration that doomed so many other abortion-related measures that had House support. The president may veto reconciliation bills, however.

GOP leaders had already been planning since early in the year to use reconciliation to undo the 2010 health law (PL 111–148, PL 111–152). They added Planned Parenthood to the mix as leaders struggled to find a way to unite a deeply fractured GOP conference. The language in the 2015 reconciliation bill would have redirected to community health centers the $235 million in projected savings from defunding Planned Parenthood for one year.

As Republicans on House committees hurried to approve the reconciliation instructions to deny money to Planned Parenthood, Democrats rebuked them. Ranking

Democrat Frank Pallone Jr. of New Jersey said the move was nothing but a political farce. California Democrat Lois Capps said the attempts to cut off Planned Parenthood appeared to be bordering on obsession.

Meanwhile, the House Rules Committee on October 6, 2015, approved a privileged resolution (H Res 461) to establish an Energy and Commerce subcommittee to investigate fetal tissue procurement and abortion practices at medical providers such as Planned Parenthood. Only the chair of the newly created panel would have to sit on Energy and Commerce, and the investigative subcommittee would have subpoena powers and be required to submit a final report on its findings. Then it would disband days after filing the report.

The Rules Committee's intent was to centralize the investigations that already had been launched by the House Judiciary, Oversight and Government and Reform, and Energy and Commerce committees. The House voted 242–184 on October 7 to adopt the resolution and form the committee.

Two days later, the House Budget Committee approved by a party-line vote of 21–11 the reconciliation bill that would have denied money to Planned Parenthood for a year.

Planned Parenthood, in an effort to blunt the Republican attacks, announced on October 13 that it would no longer accept reimbursements for donating aborted fetal tissue to scientific research. In a letter to the National Institutes of Health, the Planned Parenthood Federation of America said it would immediately stop taking payments for covering the costs of procuring fetal tissue from abortions. Officials said that only two of its affiliates were involved in fetal tissue research and a third was involved in placenta research.

Planned Parenthood president Cecile Richards said the decision to stop receiving reimbursements would prove the GOP was targeting her group based on political motivations, as opposed to genuine concerns about fetal tissue. Thus far, congressional investigations had not turned up any concrete evidence of wrongdoing, while six states had cleared Planned Parenthood of illegal activity.

LATE-YEAR ACTION

The House passed the reconciliation measure (HR 3762) on October 23, 2015, by a 240–189 vote, despite objections from the conservative group Heritage Action for America, which said the measure was not strong enough because it would not fully repeal the health law (PL 111–148, PL 111–152). Seven Republicans voted against the measure while one Democrat, Collin Peterson of Minnesota, voted for it.

The Senate passed the reconciliation bill, 52–47, on December 3 with a substitute amendment from McConnell that dramatically expanded the scope of the repeal of the health care law from the version the House passed in October. The substitute included provisions that would have scrapped in 2018 the overhaul's Medicaid expansion, as well as subsidies to help individuals buy coverage through the insurance exchanges.

The Senate also rejected more than a dozen amendments to the package during a nearly seven-hour vote-a-rama, or a day with multiple votes, sometimes dozens, in a compressed timeframe. These included a proposal that would have stripped out the language cutting federal funding for Planned Parenthood, proposals to toughen firearms sales and, separately, to ensure better reporting in the National Instant Criminal Background Check System.

During the vote-a-rama, senators rejected, 48–52, an amendment by Collins, Kirk, and Republican Lisa Murkowski of Alaska to strike the language in the bill that would have defunded Planned Parenthood for a year. Collins argued the funding cutoff would likely result in the closure of several hundred clinics across the country and deprive millions of women of options for care.

Oklahoma Republican James Lankford urged colleagues to oppose the amendment, highlighting another provision in the package that would have boosted funding for community health centers—a point other Republicans had made as well throughout the year. They said they wanted to show they were not out to take care options away from women but, rather, wanted to restrict Planned Parenthood

specifically because of its abortion services. But Democrats and public health allies said that some counties lacked alternatives to Planned Parenthood, so women would be deprived of other health services.

The House concurred with the Senate amendment to the reconciliation bill on January 6, 2016, by a vote of 240–181. President Obama vetoed it. The House on February 2 voted 241–186 on whether to override the veto, failing to reach the two-thirds majority necessary.

Mental Health and Shootings

Democrats and Republicans could agree on one thing about gun violence: Mental health issues deserved to be considered.

"Consider" is not the same as passing legislation, however, as had been seen in the 113th Congress. The 114th Congress saw talk but no ultimate action on a stand-alone bill. Portions of a mental health bill that grew out of these discussions, however, ultimately were incorporated into an unrelated late-session bill, the 21st Century Cures Act, that passed and became law in 2016—albeit without gun provisions (see p. 316, "Streamlining Drug Approval.")

ELECTRONIC HEALTH RECORDS

The federal government had pushed the medical profession for several years to better coordinate medical records through computerization—a way to track patients' histories, diagnoses, treatments, and prescriptions across providers. But the going was slow and bumpy, despite nearly $30 billion in funding from the American Recovery and Reinvestment Act of 2009 (PL 111–5), part of a hoped-for stimulus approach to modernizing the nation's infrastructure.

Doctors and groups such as the Alliance of Specialty Medicine, the American Medical Association, and the American Hospital Association maintained the efforts were being implemented in an unworkable fashion. They said they supported the broad goals but said the rules for what had to be digitized or computerized were confusing and required too much time at a computer, which they said took time away from patient care.

That's why this was still an issue in the 114th Congress. Making it all the more timely, the initial law establishing the electronic records regimen had a staged set of incentives for compliance, and the harshest noncompliance penalties from the Centers for Medicare and Medicaid Services, or CMS, were about to kick in for providers who had failed in 2015. Some doctors were so fed up with the rules they

considered cumbersome that they said they were willing to face penalties or stop taking new patients whose care was covered by CMS.

Days before taking office in 2009, Barack Obama set a goal of moving to electronic health records for all Americans within five years "to save lives by reducing the deadly but preventable medical errors that pervade our health care system." Next came the Recovery Act's passage and the first stage of compliance rules from CMS in late 2010. CMS, a division within the Health and Human Services Department, said that through a phased approach, electronic medical records could help providers reduce disparities in care, better control chronic diseases, and promote a more accountable health care system for the good of communities and the country.

The priority of the project rose again in 2014, when Democrats and Republicans were hoping to overhaul Medicare's payment system for doctors and hospitals, which to that point had been tied to the volume of medical services provided, the rate of the nation's economic growth, and a formula factoring in whether the cost of health care grew at, above, or below the nation's economic growth. Congress wanted to change the system and pay Medicare providers for quality, not quantity (See "A Final 'Doc Fix,'" p. 307). But

(Continued)

ELECTRONIC HEALTH RECORDS (Continued)

to do so, it needed better data—the kind it could glean from information in electronic medical records.

Medical providers, however, said the CMS definitions required for the records—the so-called meaningful use standards to show electronic records improved quality and safety, engaged patients, and led to improved care—were imprecise. Adding to the pressure and doctors' frustration, the final set of CMS meaningful use standards was scheduled for release in 2015. The first two had been in 2010 and 2012. But CMS was tardy, failing to release the final rule until October 16, 2015.

This created a new challenge for health care providers because in order to show they were following electronic-records rules and could therefore avoid penalties from CMS, they had to attest to compliance for any ninety-day period in the calendar year. Yet they now had fewer than ninety days left in 2015. Providers could seek waivers from noncompliance on a case-by-case basis, and CMS said it granted about 85 percent of those requests to this point, but medical providers were not appeased, and lawmakers were sympathetic to their side.

It did not hurt the medical industry's cause that groups such as the Alliance of Specialty Medicine said the measures were not relevant to their unique patient populations, and the American Medical Association said doctors found the requirements hampered their productivity and required extra hours of work.

"The interface is so 1990," Sen. Bill Cassidy, R-La., a doctor, said at a HELP Committee hearing on September 17, 2015. "I'm sitting there typing into a screen as opposed to looking into someone's eyes."

So lawmakers worked in a bipartisan fashion in 2015 to make it easier for providers to avoid penalties. Moving with unaccustomed speed and urgency on the last legislative day of the year, lawmakers—working with the Obama administration—introduced a small package of Medicare policy changes (S 2425) on December 18 and cleared it in hours without a single objection in either the House or Senate.

The legislation gave CMS broader authority to exempt more doctors from penalties for not meeting targets on practices preferred by consumers, such as email communication and electronic transmittal of prescriptions to pharmacies. The law was expected to allow CMS to handle exceptions with a swifter batch process rather than on a case-by-case basis.

"This much-needed relief will make the hardship application process much easier for doctors to avoid penalties," Rep. Tom Price, R-Ga., an orthopedic surgeon, said in a statement on December 18.

Price spearheaded the bipartisan, behind-the-scenes work. He had introduced a bill (HR 3940) in November that sought to give CMS the power to make blanket exemptions and got a dozen Democrats among ninety-five cosponsors.

Much of that measure was folded into a package of small Medicare policy changes slated for action in the last week of December as part of the House's fast track for noncontroversial bills, known as the suspension calendar. This is reserved for measures expected to get the support of at least two-thirds of voting members.

When that House effort got overburdened by unrelated items, Sens. Rob Portman, R-Ohio, and Bob Casey, D-Penn., pulled together a very narrow package of Medicare policy adjustments, including a provision on the records. Introduced on the morning of December 18, the Patient Access and Medicare Protection Act, S 2425, cleared Congress several hours later, with a nearly empty Senate chamber approving it by voice vote just before noon and the House agreeing without objection at 1:01 p.m.

Obama signed the bill into law on December 28, 2015 (PL 114–115).

The legislation to overhaul the mental health system was first approved by a House Energy and Commerce subcommittee on November 4, 2015. It so happened that less than a month later, on December 2, forty-nine people were killed and twenty-two others injured at an office park in San Bernardino, Calif. The FBI was investigating the rampage by Syed Rizwan Farook and his wife, Tashfeen Malik, as an act of terrorism, but some Republican leaders said that the legislation could form the basis for a congressional response to mass shootings in general. Such discussions had also taken place after the deaths of twenty-six people, including twenty children, at an elementary school in Newtown, Conn., in December 2012. In the case of Newtown, the shooter, twenty-year-old Adam Lanza, had a history of psychiatric ailments.

But Congress was divided over how much and even whether new laws or regulations were needed.

A leading figure in the debate was Rep. Tim Murphy, a Republican from the Pittsburgh suburbs who drew from his experience as a psychologist to become his party's point man on overhauling the mental health care system. From his post as chair of the Energy and Commerce subcommittee on oversight and investigations, Murphy had examined the mental health issues raised by the Newtown massacre and then introduced broad, bipartisan legislation (HR 1717) in December 2013.

Some of the provisions in the bill had proved controversial, and a group of Democrats introduced a competing bill in May 2014, stalling progress on Murphy's measure. But in June 2015, he introduced a revised measure (HR 2646) that received a much warmer response.

The bill was crafted to avoid specific restrictions on firearms. Then, during the bill's consideration, a gunman killed forty-nine people and wounded fifty-three more at a nightclub in Orlando, Florida. But lawmakers again rebuffed an effort to insert gun restrictions into Murphy's legislation.

House Action

Murphy's 2015 legislation, the Helping Families in Mental Health Crisis Act, included provisions to change medical privacy rules; create an assistant secretary at the Health and Human Services Department for mental health and substance use disorders; and encourage assisted outpatient treatment programs, under which some people with serious mental illness could receive court-ordered treatment while living in a community setting. It would have redirected federal funds from the Substance Abuse and Mental Health Services Administration, or SAMHSA, to programs that focused on serious mental illness.

After a marathon markup with votes on nearly thirty amendments on November 3 and 4, 2015, the Energy and Commerce subcommittee on health backed the measure, 18–12, mostly along party lines. Murphy's bill was largely endorsed by mental health advocacy groups such as the American Psychiatric Association, the National Association of Psychiatric Health Systems, and the Behavioral Health Information Technology Coalition.

Yet the panel's Democrats said they felt shut out of the legislative process and said their concerns over patient privacy, assisted outpatient treatment laws, and funding were not assuaged. A flashpoint in the debate was a provision that would adjust privacy rules under the Health Insurance Portability and Accountability Act, or HIPAA (PL 104–191), to allow some patient health information about serious mental illness to be disclosed under certain conditions.

Republicans maintained it would help family members better assist in treating loved ones with serious mental illness. Democrats argued it would hinder patients' privacy and deter them from seeking care, even with a manager's amendment clarifying when health providers could share such information.

During the markup, the subcommittee rebuffed, in a 12–16 party-line vote, a Democratic substitute amendment that they said would have strengthened behavioral health, suicide prevention, and trauma programs; tweaked the HIPAA language; and invested resources back into SAMHSA, among other things. Lawmakers rejected a spate of other Democratic amendments, ranging from provisions to replace assisted outpatient treatment language with grants for community treatment programs to language aimed at addressing the opioid abuse epidemic.

But the panel agreed by voice vote to an amendment by the top-ranking Democratic committee member, Frank Pallone, D-N.J., that would encourage more psychiatrists to accept health insurance. The panel also narrowly backed, 14–13, an amendment to ensure states did not kick juveniles off Medicaid if they were jailed.

HR 2646 next moved to the full Energy and Commerce Committee, whose schedule for considering the matter on June 15, 2016, happened to come just three days after the deaths of forty-nine people in a mass shooting at the Pulse nightclub in Orlando, Florida.

Tony Cárdenas, D-Calif., offered an amendment to end a decades-long ban on gun violence research at the Centers for Disease Control and Prevention. President Obama had already issued an executive order in 2013, soon after the Sandy Hook shootings, to resume such research, but appropriators blocked its implementation with a long-standing legislative rider to spending bills that funded the CDC and limited money for gun control. Policy riders are amendments to spending bills that add conditions or restrictions for how an agency's money may be used, and lawmakers sometimes use riders to set government policy without passing freestanding bills. The committee rejected the Cárdenas amendment, 23–29, along party lines.

Cárdenas also introduced but then withdrew an amendment that would have identified how improved diets can affect mental health treatment.

Bobby L. Rush, D-Ill., offered an amendment to require HHS to study the relation between posttraumatic stress and drug abuse among residents in areas with chronic violence, an issue he said needed to be better understood. But he withdrew it before a vote. Rush represented part of Chicago, a city that had seen a large uptick in gun-related violence.

The committee approved HR 2646 53–0, after resolving the parties' differences over HIPAA. Rather than take a prescriptive approach to the privacy rules, the bill directed HHS to issue rules clarifying federal privacy protections for patients.

The committee's updated draft also restored a provision from earlier versions of Murphy's bill to replace the head of the SAMHSA with an assistant secretary for mental health and substance use at HHS.

Several Democrats offered, then withdrew, amendments, including those by:

- Paul Tonko, D-N.Y., who would have added occupational therapists to the National Health Service Corps, an HHS program that provides loan-repayment assistance to licensed medical providers
- Lois Capps, D-Calif., who would have allowed the director of the National Institutes of Health to intensify research to both better understand the underlying causes of chronic pain and inform the development of nonopioid pain medications
- Joseph P. Kennedy III, D-Mass., who would have added additional reporting requirements to ensure compliance with the federal parity law that requires insurers to provide mental health benefits that equal coverage for physical health care
- Ben Ray Luján, D-N.M., who would have authorized $30 million to allow states to establish offices of behavioral health assistance and identify problems

encountered by individuals when seeking mental health care and educating individuals on their rights to access treatment.

On July 6, 2016, the full House considered HR 2646 and passed it 422–2, with Republicans Justin Amash of Michigan and Thomas Massie of Kentucky voting no. Massie issued a statement saying that Republicans, who campaigned on reducing the federal government's role in health care, should keep that pledge.

Senate Action

A bipartisan Senate version of HR 2646 was offered but stalled over gun-related provisions. That was because a provision in the Senate's bill, S 2680, would have allowed individuals who were previously institutionalized but had since been deemed mentally competent by a judge to regain their right to own firearms.

Majority Whip John Cornyn, R-Texas, had wanted that provision but stepped back after the bill appeared to stall. Lawmakers and mental health groups were trying to find a way to pass a clean mental health bill. Paul Gionfriddo, president of Mental Health America, told *CQ* that Democrats and Republicans alike hoped to avoid a debate over gun control and that neither side wanted to offer controversial amendments that could consume significant Senate floor time.

Yet S 2680, introduced by Lamar Alexander, R-Tenn., chair of the Health, Education, Labor and Pensions Committee, on March 15, 2016, faced other problems.

Senate Republican Conference Vice Chair Roy Blunt of Missouri and Democratic Sen. Debbie Stabenow of Michigan wanted to add language from other legislation (S 2525) that would expand a pilot program underway in twenty-four states that was designed to improve the way Medicaid reimburses for mental health care. Expansion would cost billions, a reason for some Republican resistance.

This was not the Senate's only approach for dealing with mental health issues. In late December 2015, the sponsors of three mental health bills were considering combining forces to try to forge a consensus plan they could promote in 2016. The same issue that doomed other approaches, however—including the sensitive issue of background checks for gun purchases—complicated the effort.

- One of the bills was S 1893, the Mental Health Awareness and Improvement Act, pursued by the HELP committee's ranking Democrat, Patty Murray of Washington. It would reauthorize suicide prevention and mental health awareness programs. It passed the Senate by unanimous consent on December 18, 2015, but got nowhere as a freestanding bill in the House.
- Another Senate measure, S 2002, sponsored by Cornyn, focused on mental health within the criminal justice system. It would authorize the Justice Department to award grants to better coordinate mental health programs between law enforcement

and corrections agencies. But it would also allow someone who had once been adjudicated mentally incompetent to eventually regain his firearms rights with court approval if he were declared competent.
- Louisiana Republican Bill Cassidy and Connecticut Democrat Christopher S. Murphy had a wide-reaching third measure, the Mental Health Reform Act (S 1945), that centered on the health care side of the issue. Like Rep. Murphy's House bill, it would have created the position of Assistant Secretary for Mental Health and Substance Use Disorders to oversee SAMHSA.

None of these bills passed, separately or combined. But provisions were incorporated into the 21st Century Cures Act, focusing on biomedical research and drug approval, which passed and became law in late 2016—without gun provisions.

Streamlining Drug Approval

It could take fifteen years for a new drug to go from discovery to the marketplace. The Food and Drug Administration had justified this slow approach as necessary for thorough, scientifically sound testing and analysis, and no one disputed that it was better to be safe than to release a drug with untested and potentially catastrophic results. Pharmaceutical history had enough incidents of that happening when rigor had not been demanded.

Yet drug companies and developers said the process was unnecessarily slow. And lawmakers who wanted a better, albeit safe, process said that 95 percent of rare diseases currently had no known cures—and the system in place hampered the development of cures.

The 1,000-page 21st Century Cures Act (HR 34—PL 114–255), which gained final passage in the waning days of the Obama presidency, was designed to change that. It required the Food and Drug Administration to develop a framework to allow for greater consideration of the patient perspective in new drugs under review. It changed the leadership structure at the Substance Abuse and Mental Health Services Administration, which would now be under an assistant Cabinet secretary at the Health and HHS. It imposed several new transparency requirements on the National Institutes of Health, which grant research funds to universities and laboratories across the country. And it included a few provisions from mental health bills that had stalled in other forms.

But to win final passage and find the money to fund the Cures Act, Congress had to spend much of its 114th session working, massaging, and reworking the legislation.

House Action

House Energy and Commerce Chair Fred Upton, R-Mich., and a senior Democrat on the committee, Diana DeGette of Colorado, spearheaded the initial bipartisan congressional effort to streamline the drug approval process at the FDA. The panel's subcommittee on health approved draft legislation on May 14, 2015, by voice vote, but a full committee markup scheduled a week later was delayed amid debate over how to pay for a package that could cost as much as $13 billion.

Gene Green of Texas, one of the leading Democrats supporting the bill, said his party had been caught off guard by a last-minute proposal to cover the costs. The proposal called for drawing down and selling from the Strategic Petroleum Reserve, the government's stockpile of emergency crude oil, to generate about $5.2 billion in savings. The payment proposal also called for adjusting the timing of Medicare prepayments to Medicare Advantage Part D prescription drug sponsors—private health plans that cared for seniors—so that the government would keep the interest revenue instead of the insurers, a step that would save $5 billion to $7 billion.

The payment plan also would have limited the rates paid for durable medical equipment—wheelchairs, oxygen supplies, and other physical equipment—in Medicaid (a program for low-income Americans) to levels paid by Medicare (the program for seniors). Medicare required equipment sellers to submit bids so the government could pick lower-priced vendors and save money, a requirement Medicaid lacked. Extending the lower prices to Medicaid could generate another $2.8 billion. Additional savings were to come from limiting federal payments for X-ray imaging services that use film, an effort that would also incentivize a transition toward digital imaging.

But despite any reservations, the full Energy and Commerce Committee approved the bill, 51–0, on May 21, 2015, and the full House passed it on July 10 with a strong bipartisan vote of 344–77—with 7 Democrats joining 70 Republicans in opposition. Fiscal conservatives were displeased with the bill's mandatory funding for biomedical research, setting up a funding process that House Budget Chair Tom Price, R-Ga., said was troubling and unnecessary since spending is generally approved through an annual, discretionary process. California Republican Darrell Issa complained the mandatory funding would add to the national debt.

The handful of Democrats were upset over abortion restrictions and other policy riders that would apply to the funding stream.

Yet the roughly 350-page House bill (which would later grow to more than triple that size) had 230 cosponsors and the support of the Obama administration and House Republican leaders. Patient advocacy groups, research communities, and the pharmaceutical and biotechnology industries praised the bill for its potential to unlock cures and treatments for conditions such as Alzheimer's disease.

Bill supporters had worried that an amendment by Virginia Republican Dave Brat to make the money discretionary would derail the measure. But Brat's amendment language to do just that was rebuffed, 141–281.

The House also defeated, 176–245, a Democratic amendment to remove language that would make policy riders in annual Labor-HHS-Education appropriations bills—including those prohibiting federal dollars for abortion—applicable to the Cures Act's funding.

Democrats were generally united in their support for the bill, although they criticized the fact that the final draft trimmed the mandatory pot of money for the National Institutes of Health (NIH) by $1.25 billion, to $8.75 billion. There were also some concerns over whether granting extended exclusivity periods for certain drugs would increase their cost and whether streamlining the drug approval process would jeopardize patient safety.

After the bill's mid-2015 House passage, it still had to get to the Senate. As the year dragged on and as the Cures bill sat, Congress turned its attention to other measures, many needing sources of payment, too. Suddenly the Cures offsets started getting snapped up for other priorities. Both the surface transportation law and multiyear budget deal had already tapped revenue from selling portions of the Strategic Petroleum Reserve earlier in the year. The Cures Act sponsors would now have to find money somewhere else.

Senate Action

Leaders of the Senate Health, Education, Labor, and Pensions Committee in mid-January 2016 released the first of several measures that would ultimately become their template for the Cures Act. But the committee took a broader approach than the House, with a focus that extended beyond speeding the development of new drugs.

Chair Lamar Alexander, R-Tenn., and top Democrat Patty Murray of Washington wanted to include provisions to ease the documentation required of providers that participate in federal electronic health records programs. Among the proposed changes was a provision to allow nonphysician members of health care teams, such as nurses, to document information instead.

The bipartisan Senate bill, using a tsunami research measure, HR 34, as a legislative vehicle, also established a rating system for health information technology to help doctors and hospitals choose the best products. And the measure established a set of common elements and formats for certain health care data, such as birthdates of patients, to help facilitate information sharing between providers.

The Department of Health and Human Services inspector general gained authority to investigate health care providers and any health IT developers who appeared to be blocking the sharing of electronic health information. The bill also aimed to support the certification and development of technology so that patients could tap into secure software.

Alexander held three markups in February, March, and April and approved dozens of targeted measures designed to adjust the FDA's and NIH's approval and research processes. But the overall package was delayed by disagreement similar to that voiced in the House by conservatives:

the mandatory funding for the NIH. Alexander backed a dedicated stream of money. Republicans and Democrats disagreed, however, on the amount and on potential offsetting cuts elsewhere in the federal budget.

In September, after more problems developed in areas of the legislation, House and Senate Republican leaders decided to delay any final action on a Cures package until the lame-duck session following the November election.

The maneuvering and changes continued into the post-election session.

For instance, a controversial proposal to change requirements that doctors disclose any payments they get from drug and device companies was dropped from the biomedical innovation legislation just before a House vote on the final agreement in late November. The provision would have exempted some compensation, including medical textbooks and some payments to physicians for public speaking, from the reporting requirements under federal law. Senate Judiciary Chair Charles E. Grassley, R-Iowa, had threatened to block an expected request for unanimous consent in the Senate if the provision stayed in the legislation.

The Senate added some new provisions, however. One was for Obama's cancer "moonshot" initiative, headed by Vice President Joe Biden, to provide more money and better coordinate cancer research efforts across the country. The Cures legislation under the Senate also directed $500 million over nine years to the FDA and $1 billion to states over two years to help fight prescription drug abuse, in recognition of the growing opioid-addiction crisis in the country.

Final Action

The final deal was struck around Thanksgiving 2016. The recent election of President-elect Donald Trump was seen as a motivating force for Democrats to get the best deal that they could on funding for NIH and opioids. The bill also included a variety of changes to Medicare, and it became the vehicle for language based off the mental health bill (HR 2646) that passed the House 422–2 in July.

The House on November 30, 2016, passed, 392–26, the sweeping final Cures package (HR 34) of biomedical innovation bills intended to spur the development of new drugs and medical devices. The legislation also included changes to the U.S. mental health care system, including creation, reauthorization, or expansion of numerous mental health care grant and treatment programs. It did not specifically change medical privacy law as it pertained to mental health, but it directed HHS to clarify the HIPAA rules on when and whether protected information can be shared with family members and caregivers and to advise on whether changes were needed.

Unlike the previous House version (HR 6), the new legislation contained no drug exclusivity provisions protecting drug makers' patents for longer periods.

While the previous bill would have provided $8.75 billion in funding for the NIH over five years, updated language provided $4.8 billion over a decade for specified projects within the agency, including Obama's Precision Medicine Initiative and cancer "moonshot" program.

The new legislation provided $500 million over nine years for the FDA. It also provided $1 billion to the states to help fight the opioid epidemic.

The package as a whole made several changes to the FDA's drug and device approval pathway. It required the agency to develop a framework to allow for greater consideration of the patient perspective in new drugs under review. It also gave the FDA greater flexibility in how it hires new scientists. It created an accelerated approval pathway at the agency for stem cell therapies, a controversial provision that drew criticism from Elizabeth Warren, D-Mass., on the Senate floor, because she said it benefited an unnamed major Republican donor.

The bill also made changes to the leadership structure at the Substance Abuse and Mental Health Services Administration, placing it under a newly created position of assistant secretary for mental health and substance use, and required the NIH to be more transparent about how it funds specific programs and grants. It created and reauthorized grants for state and community mental health care and encouraged greater participation in clinical trials from certain underrepresented populations.

It required the federal government to issue a voluntary model framework on the sharing of health information. The legislation also included several measures related to Medicare payments to hospitals.

The Senate cleared it 94–5 on December 7. Most Democrats supported the bill despite what they saw as its shortcomings. But Warren said it was a bad deal, echoing concerns of consumer watchdog groups, such as Public Citizen, and a few other Senate Democrats who said they feared it portended an erosion of FDA safety standards.

On the Republican side, Mike Lee, R-Utah, voted no because leadership refused to hold votes on a pair of amendments: one related to legal barriers for generic pharmaceutical companies obtaining samples of the products they are copying and another on a measure that would give dying patients a chance to obtain experimental drugs that are not yet approved.

Others voiced concerns about how the bill was paid for. About $1.5 billion came from sales of the nation's strategic petroleum reserves, down from the much higher sum the House had considered in 2015. Lisa Murkowski, R-Alaska, came to the floor as a "no," objecting to the sale of energy stockpiles as shortsighted. She nevertheless switched to a "yes" before the vote concluded.

Another $3.5 billion was taken from a fund established as part of the 2010 Affordable Care Act (PL 111–148, PL 111–152) that promoted preventive health care. Some health care advocates found it ironic that money originally slated for prevention would instead go toward developing costly treatments.

President Obama signed HR 34 into law on December 13, 2016 (PL 114–255).

Zika Virus Response

The spread of the Zika virus in Central and South America, Africa, and Asia prompted the Obama administration in February 2016 to ask Congress for $1.9 billion for a U.S. response. But it took the House and Senate eight months of wrangling over such issues as contraception and budget offsets before they agreed to provide $1.1 billion in emergency spending as part of a stopgap appropriations package, or a bill to keep the government operating in the short term without a shutdown while Congress tried to resolve issues that kept it from passing full-year funding (HR 5325).

U.S. health officials had warned for months that resources were urgently needed to develop vaccines and combat mosquitoes capable of transmitting the disease, especially before the summer months when the insects come out in droves. The Zika virus is known to cause microcephaly in infants, described by the Mayo Clinic as a rare neurological condition in which an infant's head is significantly smaller than the heads of other children of the same age and sex.

The Obama administration's initial request was met with skepticism from most Republicans in Congress, prompting heavy criticism from Democrats over the lack of a response as summer arrived. Republicans meantime were concerned that the public health crisis could be used to change reproductive health policies as a result of requests by Democrats that the U.S. response to the virus include expanded access to contraception and family planning services for women in countries affected by Zika.

House Appropriations Chair Harold Rogers, R-Ky., for instance, let it be known that he did not support new or expanded emergency spending for contraception or family planning services. But Democrats and the Planned Parenthood Federation of America said that since Zika can be sexually transmitted and can cause birth and developmental defects, it was shortsighted and dangerous to restrict Zika-related funding from family planning clinics that focus on contraception.

The initial response from Republican leaders to Obama's request was that the government should use money left over from the Ebola response in 2014 to deal with the threat of Zika in the United States. Though administration officials said the leftover money was already committed and could not be used to fight Zika, the GOP persisted for several months. Shaun Donovan, director of the Office of Management and Budget, ultimately announced in April that the administration had identified $589 million in existing funds that could be immediately redirected to target the virus.

Democrats tried to find more money. But in mid-April, the House Appropriations Committee approved a fiscal 2017 Military Construction–VA spending bill after rejecting an attempt by Democrats to attach emergency supplemental funding to combat the Zika virus.

While Congress that month did add Zika to a different bill (S 2512) intended to create incentives for drug makers to speed work on disease treatments, White House Press Secretary Josh Earnest said at an April 13, 2016, press briefing that it was like "passing out umbrellas in the event of a hurricane," saying Congress was frittering away a chance to protect Americans, particularly pregnant women. The bill added potential Zika treatments to the list of other treatments (for diseases such as cholera, dengue, and malaria) eligible for expedited Food and Drug Administration review.

House Energy and Commerce Committee Chair Fred Upton, R-Mich., said that with much more to be learned about Zika, research and development of treatments was essential. He accused the White House of being vague on how it would spend the requested $1.9 billion, saying that without defined parameters, the money could wind up being used for any purpose.

Obama signed the drug-incentive bill (PL114-146) on April 19, 2016, after the Senate had passed it by unanimous consent on March 17 and the House cleared it with a voice vote on April 12, but pressed for money as more months passed. He finally got agreement on a pure Zika response bill in September, although with a lower sum of $1.1 billion.

Legislative Action

The House and Senate passed separate, competing Zika-response funding packages in May—the Senate's providing $1.1 billion through a combined Military Construction–VA and HUD-Transportation spending bill (HR 2577), the House's providing $622 million through a stand-alone supplemental spending bill (HR 5243).

When it came time in late June to work out the chambers' differences, the gulf was equally wide, not over money, since Republican conferees agreed on $1.1 billion, but on policy differences. In fact, when Republican negotiators unveiled their $1.1 billion compromise measure, using HR 2577, around 11 p.m. on June 22, 2016, it was without the support of Democratic conferees.

That was partly because the $1.1 billion had $750 million in offsets: $107 million in unspent Ebola funds, $100 million in unspent Health and Human Services funds, and $543 million for health exchanges in the territories under the 2010 health care law (PL 111–148, PL 111–152) that Rogers said were never set up. The White House said in a statement that night that the proposal "steals funding from other health priorities."

Democrats also said the proposal would limit birth control services for women and included a policy rider to allow pesticides for mosquito control that Sen. Barbara Mikulski, D-Md., said endangered clean water protections.

As for the $1.1 billion,

- $476 million was for the Centers for Disease Control and Prevention for mosquito control, surveillance of the disease, laboratory activities, and public education efforts;
- $230 million was for the National Institutes of Health for vaccine research and development;

- $85 million was for the Biomedical Advanced Research and Development Authority for new rapid diagnostic tests;
- $40 million was for community health centers in Puerto Rico and U.S. territories;
- $95 million was for the Social Services Block Grant to be used in U.S. territories by public health departments, hospitals, and Medicaid managed-care clinics but not family planning clinics that focus on contraception; and
- $175 million was for the State Department and U.S. Agency for International Development to combat Zika for the remaining three months of fiscal 2016.

The House passed the measure 239–171, mostly on party lines, around 3:12 a.m. the next morning, then swiftly broke for a Fourth of July recess. The Senate was not yet scheduled for its break, but it nevertheless faced uncertainty over whether it could meet the sixty-vote procedural threshold to end debate on the Zika bill.

The matter was put to the test on June 28, 2016, and the Senate failed, with a 52–48 vote to block advancement of the appropriations package. All Democrats except Joe Donnelly of Indiana voted against cloture, and two Republicans, James Lankford of Oklahoma and Mike Lee of Utah, voted with Democrats against ending debate.

The vote coincided with confirmation from the Florida Department of Public Health of the first Zika-related case of microcephaly, a birth defect, in a child born in Florida. The mother, from Haiti, delivered the baby in Florida.

Following the Independence Day recess, Republicans and Democrats appeared no closer to agreement. Their time for consideration was short, since a summer break would start on July 15 for the presidential nominating conventions and an August recess. On July 14, 2016, they took another vote on cloture, or ending debate so they could move to a final vote, which only needed a simple majority of fifty-one to pass. But the cloture vote was 52–44, short of the 60 votes needed.

Debate, posturing, and disagreement continued through the summer and Labor Day and included rhetorical jabs by one party at the other over their respective refusal to compromise. It spilled into the Republican National Convention in Cleveland, where Senate Majority Leader Mitch McConnell, R-Ky., blamed Democrats in a July 19, 2016, speech. "As we sit here tonight, a terrifying mosquito-borne illness threatens expectant mothers and their babies along our Southern coast," McConnell said. He faulted "Clinton Democrats." Democratic presidential candidate Hillary Clinton had a rejoinder when campaigning in Florida on September 6, saying Republicans "can't help themselves from playing games, even when lives are on the line."

The same day, September 6, 2016, Congress returned from the recess. The Senate took another cloture vote, its third to date, on the summer spending package with money for Zika. It failed again, 52–46.

But by now, as the virus was spreading—there were 2,686 travel-related cases in states by that point, and 13,971

cases in Puerto Rico—a compromise appeared possible. It took until late in the month, when the Senate amended and passed HR 5325 by 72–26 on September 28, 2016, and the House concurred the same day with a 342–85 vote.

The funding remained the same, at $1.1 billion, and was passed as part of a stopgap appropriations package. Negotiators were able to resolve partisan disputes over controversial provisions related to contraceptives funding and pesticide spraying.

The Zika response included $933 million for mostly domestic efforts through the Department of Health and Human Services. The funds included

- $394 million for the Centers for Disease Control and Prevention to combat mosquito populations and more;
- $397 million to develop vaccines and diagnostic tests at the National Institutes of Health and the Biomedical Advanced Research and Development Authority;
- $75 million to reimburse health care provided to those without private health insurance in states and territories with active Zika transmission.

The legislation also provided $175 million for international efforts through the State Department and U.S. Agency for International Development.

A provision in a previous House-passed Zika response (HR 2577) related to environmental permits for pesticide spraying, seen as a "poison pill" by Democrats, was dropped from the final measure.

Negotiators also reached a compromise on funding for contraceptive services in Puerto Rico. Instead of allocating money through a social services block grant, as in previous versions, the package made $75 million available to reimburse Zika-related health care. This helped qualify Profamilias, an affiliate of Planned Parenthood, to seek reimbursement for Zika-related services. The final legislation included $400 million in offsets.

Obama signed the bill into law on September 29, 2016 (PL 114-223).

Obamacare Repeal, and a Veto

Six years after passage of the Patient Protection and Affordable Care Act, Republicans finally achieved their goal of repealing the sweeping 2010 health insurance law, which they considered the biggest government overreach in a generation. But Obama vetoed the repeal bill in short order.

Nearly every step of this came as no surprise, given the fact that Republicans knew they lacked a big enough majority for a veto override. But symbolically, the vote was important in an election year, serving as a symbol of what might ultimately be done if a Republican could win the White House and persuade Americans they would be better off without the ACA.

House Republicans had already voted more than sixty times to repeal parts or all of the law, which many considered to require the most far-reaching changes to health coverage since the creation of Medicare and Medicaid in 1965, as part of President Lyndon Johnson's "Great Society" agenda to end inequality. Opponents nicknamed the 2010 health law "Obamacare" before it was even enacted, much as they had derided Bill Clinton's failed 1993 health care plan as "Hillarycare" because then–First Lady Hillary Clinton led the task force that devised it. But the White House and Democratic allies started appropriating the name from the critics, some using "Obamacare" as a phrase of ironic honor.

Polls at the time showed that the 2010 law did not enjoy widespread popularity. Problems implementing the law's requirements further weakened support, especially when the federal website Healthcare.gov—the portal through which Americans could sign up for coverage if they lacked health insurance—did not work well from its opening in October 2013 until about two months later. The law also had faced numerous legal challenges. The most high-profile judicial decision occurred in 2012 when the Supreme Court upheld the constitutionality of the law's so-called individual mandate, or the requirement for most individuals to have at least an essential minimum level of health coverage or pay a penalty.

The high court upheld the law again in June 2015 in *King v. Burwell*. The justices, in a 6–3 decision, said that Congress intended for federal tax credits—to help individuals defray the cost of premiums—to be available in every state, regardless of whether the state created its own marketplace, or "exchange," for selling health insurance or simply used the one operated by the federal government. The decision was important because it supported one of the health law's cornerstones, the availability of subsidies to reduce individuals' costs.

House Action

Congress started its then-latest repeal action in late 2015, using a budget reconciliation bill, HR 3762. Reconciliation bills must only contain provisions that affect revenue, spending, and the debt limit, but they can pass with a simple majority of votes in the House and Senate, which means backers can avoid Senate difficulty over cloture, or the requirement on other legislation to first get 60 votes to end debate. While technically a procedural requirement, cloture can be used in a closely divided Senate to block a final vote on passage.

Because of narrow rules for budget reconciliation, HR 3762 could not be used to repeal the entire Affordable Care Act. But the House bill contained repeal of major provisions that underpinned the health law. As presented for a vote, it would

- eliminate the mandates on individuals to buy health coverage and on employers to offer it to workers or face penalties
- strike the law's 2.3 percent tax on the sale of medical devices

- eliminate the tax on "Cadillac" employer-sponsored plans, or health plans with the most generous coverage benefits
- eliminate the law's fund for prevention and public health activities and a still-unenforced requirement for large employers to automatically enroll new full-time employees in coverage
- defund Planned Parenthood for one year while providing more money to community health centers. Planned Parenthood received about $450 million a year in federal payments, mostly through Medicaid reimbursements for medical services. Federal law already prohibited using federal funds for abortions.

The bill originally included a provision to repeal the health law's Independent Payment Advisory Board, which did not yet have appointees but was supposed to eventually recommend cuts to constrain Medicare spending if it rose beyond certain targets. Republicans said the board would have too much independent authority over matters typically decided by Congress.

But the provision striking the board was removed when the Senate parliamentarian was consulted on which provisions would be allowable under budget reconciliation. Removal of the board was considered policy related but not a fiscal matter, and the House excised this provision when adopting the rule governing floor debate (H Res 483).

The House passed HR 3762 on October 23, 2015, with a 240–189 vote, nearly along party lines. Only one Democrat, Collin Peterson of Minnesota, voted yes. Peterson had voted against the law in 2010 because he said he did not think his constituents wanted the government to tell them what to do, and he thought the law was unworkable.

With some conservatives grumbling that this was not a full repeal bill, seven Republicans voted against the repeal measure: Ken Buck of Colorado; Robert Dold of Illinois; Richard Hanna of New York; Matt Salmon of Arizona; and Walter Jones, Mark Meadows, and Mark Walker of North Carolina. Heritage Action, a conservative group, had said the bill failed to address the health law's expansion of Medicaid, its insurance regulations, and its subsidies to help low- and middle-income Americans buy coverage on the insurance exchanges.

Senate Action

As the bill moved to the Senate, potential parliamentary problems arose. They related to long-term budgetary implications of elements Republicans wished to repeal. Although budget reconciliation allowed for repeal of items related specifically to revenue, expenses, and debt, the so-called Byrd rule in the Senate said these budgetary impacts had to fall within a ten-year window. A senator could use the Byrd rule to strike provisions he or she disliked if the provisions were extraneous to the budgetary effects or did not comport with the ten-year timeline.

The Byrd rule presented problems for repeal of the health law's Cadillac tax because eliminating the tax would increase the deficit after 2025, outside the ten-year window.

Also problematic was the proposed repeal of a requirement that large employers automatically enroll their workers in a health insurance plan or else pay a penalty. The provision had already been adopted as part of a recent two-year budget deal (PL 114–74), so the budgetary impact had already been accounted for. Its inclusion in the health care repeal bill therefore could have made it extraneous.

Republican Senate leaders dealt with this by preparing a substitute amendment to HR 3762 with ways to comply with the Byrd rule. For example, the Cadillac tax on employer health plans would be scrapped only from its planned start in 2018 through 2024. Realistically, many Republicans expected most of the Affordable Care Act to implode before then anyway, with help from this repeal effort.

But beyond these changes, Republicans added an array of other provisions that won support from conservative members who had worried the bill would not go far enough. The Senate measure had a provision to scrap in 2018 the Affordable Care Act's Medicaid expansion scheduled for that year. Another would end subsidies to help individuals buy health coverage through the insurance exchanges. The language called for ending the subsidies in 2018, providing time, Republicans said, to devise an alternative for people who needed insurance.

The bill also would effectively end the requirements that most individuals get health insurance or face tax penalties and that employers with more than fifty employees provide health insurance. It did this not by actually ending the requirements but by setting the penalties for violations at $0.

Republicans Lisa Murkowski of Alaska, Mark Kirk of Illinois, and Susan Collins of Maine tried to strike the language to defund Planned Parenthood for a year, saying millions of women might not have access to care if that happened. But James Lankford, R-Okla., said alternatives for women would exist at community health centers getting more money. The amendment to continue Planned Parenthood funding was rejected 48–52.

Also rejected was an amendment from West Virginia Democrat Joe Manchin III and Pennsylvania Republican Patrick J. Toomey to expand the federal background checks of firearms sold at gun shows and over the Internet. The provision fell outside the parameters of budget reconciliation, but the rule could be waived if senators wanted. But on the gun measure, the Senate rejected, 48–50, the motion to waive the Congressional Budget Act rule.

The Senate voted 52–47 on December 3, 2015, to pass the substitute version of the House bill. Republicans Collins and Kirk joined the entire Democratic caucus in voting no, although Vermont Independent Bernie Sanders was not there to vote.

Final Action

This set things up for 2016, since the House had to adopt the Senate amendments. House Republicans were intent on following through on their promise to send a repeal measure to Obama, with House Majority Leader Kevin McCarthy saying the vote would set a tone and demonstrate to Americans the path Republicans planned for the country.

Democrats said it would demonstrate heartlessness, since under the GOP package, at least 22 million people would lose health coverage starting in 2018, according to a December 2015 estimate by the Congressional Budget Office and the Joint Committee on Taxation.

The House cleared the bill, 240–181, on January 6, 2016, in a vote that again fell almost entirely along party lines. Peterson again broke with Democrats to support the measure, and Republicans Dold, Hanna, and John Katko of New York were the only ones in their party to oppose it.

With little public fanfare, Obama vetoed the bill on January 8, 2016. He said in a veto message that the health care law was working, and the Republican measure would "reverse the significant progress we have made in improving health care in America."

That vote on the House Republican attempt to override Obama's veto occurred on February 2, 2016. But the vote, 241–186, fell well short of the two-thirds majority needed. Peterson again was the lone Democrat to side with Republicans, and Republicans Dold, Hanna, and Katko voted in support of the president's veto. A vote had been scheduled for January 26 but was delayed after a blizzard prompted the House to cancel legislative action.

CHAPTER 10

Education Policy

Education Policy

As President Barack Obama began his second term, Congress and the White House were far more consumed with issues such as health care and the economy than with education. Yet policies related to schools played out in a broader context in Washington. The big-picture question that hovered over congressional Republicans and Democrats: What role, exactly, should the federal government play when it came to K–12 and college education?

This question helped determine the outcome of the few substantial education bills that made it through Congress from 2013 through 2016. One new law redefined the role of federally mandated performance standards and proficiency testing in elementary and high school education under the much-debated Bush-era No Child Left Behind program. Another ended with President Obama and Congress making some changes to student loans to curb interest rates and ease monthly payments. But Congress and the White House were unable to resolve the overall issue of mounting cumulative student debt—the total amount of money that students owed on their loans.

MORE FLEXIBLE PERFORMANCE STANDARDS

One of the major education issues during the second Obama administration concerned K–12 testing. A state-based testing regimen had been championed by President George W. Bush and passed by Congress in a show of bipartisan unity as part of the 2002 reauthorization of the Elementary and Secondary Education Act (ESEA), better known as the No Child Left Behind Act (PL 107-110). No Child Left Behind tied federal K–12 school aid to student proficiency on math and reading tests, so schools that failed to demonstrate an acceptable standard risked losing federal money over time. The penalties were scheduled to begin in 2014, giving schools years to prepare, try out their tests, and adjust their teaching methods.

Yet criticism built among states, teachers, parents, and eventually lawmakers as the target date neared. They complained that despite the lofty goal of demanding accountability in education, No Child wasted classroom time in pursuit of unrealistic or ill-considered ideals. Critics also said that in preparing for No Child, school districts and teachers geared too much of the school curriculum toward "teaching to the test" rather than delivering meaningful education.

It took time to reach a compromise on No Child. At the end of the 113th Congress (2013–2014), lawmakers had made no changes despite months of trying. Finally, at the end of 2015, the House, Senate, and White House agreed on a compromise: No Child Left Behind would end, although some related requirements would remain in place.

The new law, known as the Every Child Succeeds Act, would still require states to measure school performance, but the states would get considerably more leeway and flexibility in how they designed their performance standards and tests. Obama, who signed the bill in December 2015, hailed the compromise as a "Christmas miracle" after the substantial policy disagreements between the administration and Congress.

REFERENCES

Discussion of education policy for the years 1945–1964 may be found in *Congress and the Nation Vol. I*, pp. 1195–1215; for the years 1965–1968, *Congress and the Nation Vol. II*, 709–733; for the years 1969–1972, *Congress and the Nation Vol. III*, pp. 581–604; for the years 1973–1976, *Congress and the Nation Vol. IV*, pp. 377–402; for the years 1977–1980, *Congress and the Nation Vol. V*, 655–677; for the years 1981–1984, *Congress and the Nation Vol. VI*, pp. 555–580; for the years 1985–1988, *Congress and the Nation Vol. VII*, pp. 647–663; for the years 1989–1992, *Congress and the Nation Vol. VIII*, pp. 641–660; for the years 1993–1996, *Congress and the Nation Vol. IX*, pp. 607–634; for the years 1997–2001, *Congress and the Nation Vol. X*, pp. 507–549; for the years 2001–2004, *Congress and the Nation Vol. XI*, pp. 537–552; for the years 2005–2008, *Congress and the Nation Vol. XII*, pp. 599–618; for the years 2009–2012, *Congress and the Nation Vol. XIII*, pp. 473–494.

Outlays for Education

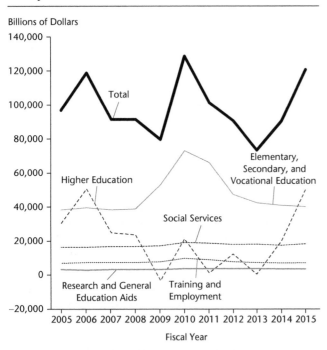

Billions of Dollars

Total

Higher Education

Elementary, Secondary, and Vocational Education

Social Services

Research and General Education Aids

Training and Employment

Fiscal Year

SOURCE: Office of Management and Budget, *Historical Tables, Outlays by Function and Subfunction: 1962–2021* (Washington, DC: U.S. Government Printing Office, 2018), Table 3.2.

NOTE: Total line includes expenditures not shown separately.

THE GOVERNMENT'S ROLE IN COLLEGE LOANS

As students took out more and more loans to pay for college and postgraduate education, policy experts squared off over the issue of student debt. Throughout this period, as previously, some Republicans questioned why the federal government stayed so heavily involved in student loans, since the basic terms of consumer finance were otherwise established by private markets. Pushing against that viewpoint were education advocates and White House officials who worried about total student indebtedness that exceeded $1 trillion. The Education Department warned that student-loan debt could squeeze graduates' ability to buy houses, build bank accounts, and save for the future. In addition, they noted, the federal government already played a role in helping students get these very loans.

For decades, the federal government had subsidized major postsecondary loan programs and guaranteed that lenders would get repaid if borrowers defaulted on their loans. Congress staked a statutory obligation dating to the Higher Education Act of 1965, establishing what became known as the Federal Family Education Loan (FFEL) program. By 2013, the government had a nearly fifty-year history of involvement in regulating several kinds of student loans and setting their interest rates.

Congress ultimately failed to pass major legislation addressing cumulative student debt. Obama instead acted on his own, signing an executive order that tied the maximum monthly loan repayments to graduates' incomes so the loans wouldn't consume so much of their disposable pay. Separately, Congress used its authority, with the president's blessing, in 2013 to set new annual interest rates for the loan program used most widely by college students, known as the Stafford Direct Student Loan program. The legislation kept Stafford interest rates from rising sharply.

"It's a very good thing for students, and it's a very good thing for taxpayers, and it's a sign that we can get things done," John Kline of Minnesota, the chair of the House Education and the Workforce Committee, told a reporter from *MinnPost*. The Republican congressman had flown back to Washington from Minneapolis for the Friday bill-signing ceremony. Lawmakers also extended the Perkins college loan program, but only for three years.

Perkins loans were supposed to fill gaps in financial aid for students with exceptional financial need. With interest rates of 5 percent on Perkins loans, however, Republicans such as Sen. Lamar Alexander, a former university president and former U.S. education secretary, said they added redundancy to the broader federal student loan program, and at a higher cost to students.

Perkins loans would have ended in September 2014 under a prior Higher Education Act authorization. Congress extended the program through September 30, 2017, thereby covering the 2017–2018 school year for undergraduates.

Chronology of Action on Education Policy

2013-2014

Debate on education in the 113th Congress focused on two distinct areas and education levels, a reflection of lawmakers' broad education-policy portfolio. One area pertained to loan interest rates for college and graduate school students and, somewhat separately, the cumulative debt that graduates carried. Congress was able to agree on a new structure for setting the interest rates. The House and Senate differed, however, on what to do about overall debt, and Obama ultimately acted on his own to keep monthly loan payments from becoming too onerous. The other area pertained to K-12 education. The 113th Congress tried but failed to replace the No Child Left Behind program and its requirements for performance standards and testing.

Federal Student Loans

College students were coming back from their winter breaks as Congress convened the first session in 2013. Interest rates on new undergraduate student loans were 3.4 percent at the time, but the rates were scheduled to rise to 6.8 percent in the coming 2013-2014 academic year. Before that doubling could occur, Congress passed HR 1911, signed by Obama on August 9, 2013. The new rate would be 3.86 percent, tied to a formula based on Treasury note yields but building in an additional margin, albeit with caps. The formula under HR 1911 set interest rates on loans for graduate and professional students at 5.4 percent for the next academic year.

BACKGROUND

The battle over the college loans extended back to the Clinton administration, and Democrats and Republicans rewaged it every few years. They debated over such issues as what interest rates to charge and whether to keep funneling federally backed loans through private lenders. Under the old system, private banks including student loan specialists such as Sallie Mae dominated the student loan market for what were known as Stafford Loans. Depending on family income and financial need, a Stafford Loan recipient could get favorable interest rates and the government protected the lender against student loan defaults and other losses. The program was named after Sen. Robert T. Stafford, a Vermont Republican who championed education.

While some Democrats said the government could save money if it cut out the private middlemen from these loan transactions, congressional leaders including House Speaker John Boehner had maintained that the private sector operated more efficiently. Not all student loans were handled this way, and a minority of colleges and universities already administered their own campus-based but government-backed and -funded loans under the William D. Ford Direct Loan Program, as well as another program, called the Perkins Loan program, designed for lower-income families. (Congress would later end the Perkins program; see *Chronology of Action on Education Policy*, 2015-2016, pp. 334-339.)

The split system for subsidized loans, with some issued by lenders, others directly by universities, ended when a portion of the 2010 health care overhaul bill (PL 111-152) moved authority for issuance of subsidized student loans to colleges and universities. This made direct, campus-based lending the standard delivery mechanism, although private lenders still maintained a portion of the business by contracting to handle collections and by issuing their own unsubsidized and parent loans (*2010 Almanac*, pp. 9-16).

This switch to much more direct lending, however, still didn't end the periodic need for Congress to determine interest rates. Throughout the decade of the 2000s, rates on Stafford loans had generally been set by statute but were tied to private lenders' cost of money, or the interest rates, fees, administrative costs, and other obligations they incurred to get the money in the first place. Democrats asserted the rates were too high, saying if the nation wanted to encourage higher education, it should do more to make college affordable. In the early 2000s, the annual interest rate for all Stafford loans (today generally referred to simply as Direct Loans because of the new way they are administered) was 6.8 percent.

DUNCAN STEPS DOWN, KING GETS GRUDGING CONFIRMATION

Education Secretary Arne Duncan, who had served in the Obama administration since 2009, announced in October 2015 that he would leave at the end of the year and return to Chicago, were he once was CEO of the city's public school system. President Obama, with just a year left in his term at the time of the departure, picked John B. King Jr. as the acting education secretary.

But Obama decided to drop "acting" in early February 2016 and nominated King to be the education secretary for the duration of the term. King had come to the Education Department in January 2015 as a principle senior advisor, overseeing preschool-to-12th-grade programs as well as serving as Education's liaison to the president's My Brother's Keeper initiative, which worked on closing opportunity gaps for boys and young men of color. Before that, King was New York's state education commissioner, the first African American and Puerto Rican to serve in that position. A Harvard graduate with several advanced degrees, including a law degree from Yale, he once led a charter school in Boston and was a managing director of a nonprofit management organization operating charter schools in New York, New Jersey, and Massachusetts.

King's Senate confirmation was quick, but it was not enthusiastic. On March 14, 2016, he got only 49 votes for confirmation. While shy of the typical 51-vote majority in the 100-member Senate, he won confirmation because 11 senators did not vote—8 of them Republicans, 2 Democrats, and Independent Bernie Sanders of Vermont—leaving only 40 to vote against him. The votes in support of his confirmation were the fewest for a successful Cabinet appointment since at least the beginning of Jimmy Carter's presidency.

Republicans questioned whether King was the right person to implement the Every Child Succeeds Act, which replaced No Child Left Behind. They wondered whether King would give states freedom from federal restrictions, as they intended when they wrote the law. They also noted that King, as New York state's education commissioner in 2011, had overseen a bumpy rollout of the controversial Common Core standards, a joint effort of the states to adopt like curricula. King defended the program even as test scores fell and the state's largest teachers union called for his resignation. New York Sen. Kirsten Gillibrand was the lone Democrat to oppose his confirmation. Only seven Republicans voted to confirm him.

As part of an overhaul of the system pushed by Democrats in 2007 (PL 110–84), the rate charged for subsidized undergraduate loans was reduced to 3.4 percent (*2007 Almanac*, p. 8–3). For subsidized loans, the 2007 law also relieved students of having to pay accrued interest while they were in school. The federal government paid it instead. For unsubsidized loans (those going to students with higher family incomes), students were responsible for the interest accrued while they were still enrolled.

As favorable for students as this seemed, the lower rate for subsidized loans enacted in 2007 was to have expired in 2012, and rates were to rise to 6.8 percent. Democrats forced a one-year extension (PL 112–141). That extension set up what would happen next.

House Bill

House Republicans were determined to gain the upper hand in the student loan debate in 2013 by acting quickly. The previous year, in the midst of the presidential campaign, GOP presidential nominee Mitt Romney had undermined the position of congressional Republicans by urging them to go along with the administration's drive to extend for a year the 3.4 percent interest rate on subsidized loans. While some Democratic lawmakers wanted to freeze the low, fixed rate in place in 2013, Republicans insisted on making student loan interest rates variable and tied to the market yield on Treasury notes, a position that in broad

terms Obama had also embraced—but with limits—in his fiscal 2014 budget request.

The House Education and the Workforce Committee approved Bill HR 1911 (H Rept 113–82) on May 16 by a 24–13 vote. As approved, it would have tied interest rates on newly issued student loans to the ten-year Treasury note yield, plus 2.5 percentage points for undergraduate loans and plus 4.5 percentage points for graduate loans. Those rates would have been capped at 8.5 percent and 10.5 percent, respectively, but rates charged on loans would have been adjusted annually to account for market changes.

Two Democrats, Jared Polis of Colorado and John Yarmuth of Kentucky, voted for the measure, sponsored by committee Chair John Kline, R-Minn. Kline estimated that the interest rate on undergraduate loans for the 2013–14 school year would have been 4.4 percent under the bill.

Democratic amendments to reduce rates below those called for by the bill were rejected. The full House then passed HR 1911 by a 221–198 vote. Four Democrats voted in favor of the measure, while eight Republicans voted against it. President Obama threatened to veto the House bill in part because it would have allowed interest rates on outstanding loans to fluctuate from year to year. The president proposed to lock in the rate at the time the loan was issued until it was paid off. Otherwise, according to the Congressional Budget Office, the Republican plan would establish the subsidized Stafford rate at 5 percent in 2014 but allow it to eventually rise much higher than the 6.8 percent scheduled to take effect if Congress did nothing.

The administration also took issue with House committee leaders saying the bill would reduce the deficit by $3.7 billion over ten years, a characterization based on a CBO estimate of the bill's $3.7 billion reduction in direct spending. Democrats on the Education and the Workforce Committee contended that this would be a burden of $3.7 billion in more debt for students.

Senate Bills

The debate then moved to the Senate, which voted down several competing proposals, mostly along party lines. On June 6, 2013, the Senate rejected, on a 40–57 vote, a motion to invoke cloture, or end debate, on a bill (S 1003) sponsored by Oklahoma Republican Tom Coburn that would have tied student loan interest rates to the ten-year Treasury note yield. It takes 60 votes in the 100-member Senate to invoke cloture, creating a tougher threshold than required once a bill gets past that point and can pass with a simple majority. The underlying bill seemed consistent with the House-passed version, but Coburn's version would have locked in a loan's rate until it was paid off, while the House bill would have allowed the rates to fluctuate yearly on the outstanding loan (Senate vote 142, p. S 30).

The same day, the chamber also rejected, on a 51–46 vote, a cloture motion to proceed to a bill (S 953) sponsored by Rhode Island Democrat Jack Reed that would have preserved the expiring 3.4 percent fixed interest rate on subsidized Stafford undergraduate loans for two years. Both Coburn's and Reed's motions required 60 votes to be approved because of Senate filibuster rules (Senate vote 143).

Reed, with a new bill (S 1238) to preserve the lower rate for one year, and Minority Leader Mitch McConnell, R-Ky., with an alternative bill (S 1241) to set adjustable rates, tried again on June 27. Neither received unanimous consent to immediately bring up his bill. On July 10, after the July 1 deadline on interest hikes had passed and rates on Stafford subsidized loans were to double to 6.8 percent, Senate Democrats tried one more time, but a cloture vote on S 1238 was rejected 51–49.

Compromise

Behind the scenes, negotiations continued among a small bipartisan Senate group—Joe Manchin III, D-W.Va.; Angus King, I-Maine; Jack Reed, D-R.I.; Tom Harkin, D-Iowa; Thomas R. Carper, D-Del.; Lamar Alexander, R-Tenn.; and Richard M. Burr, R-N.C. The main sticking point in their talks was the insistence by Democrats that, if interest rates were to be tied to Treasury yields, they should be capped to protect student borrowers. Republicans, for their part, strived to make the proposal deficit neutral. The group finally announced an accord after Obama prodded them during a White House session to quickly settle on a solution. The members agreed to include caps assuring interest rates would not reach 10 percent, the threshold

insisted upon by Democrats, but to otherwise link rates to the market, as Republicans wished.

The Congressional Budget Office, however, prompted a new concern, saying on July 11 the tentative deal would have cost $22 billion over ten years, mostly due to the rate cap on the front end of the deal. This sent negotiators back to work and led to a solution announced on July 17: By slightly increasing the margin amounts added to the ten-year Treasury yields, they produced a deficit-neutral bill. Both Senate Majority Leader Harry Reid, D-Nev., and House Speaker John A. Boehner, R-Ohio, indicated their support.

Senators voted 81–18 for this amended version of HR 1911 on July 24. A small band of Democratic dissenters, however, grumbled that the interest rate margins and the caps were still too high. They vowed to reopen the issue during the next reauthorization of the Higher Education Act, which sets the terms for higher education financial aid and policy. The act had last been reauthorized in 2008 and then extended after its expiration in 2013. (Talks over legislation to reauthorize the bill began in 2017.)

The House cleared HR 1911, the student loan bill, 392–31 on July 31, 2013 (House vote 426). The chamber's Republican leaders pronounced it a win and pointedly noted that the compromise was very similar to the market-based interest rate proposals that they and the president had proposed in the first place. Obama signed the bill on August 9, 2013, making it retroactive to July 1 so it covered the coming academic year.

No Child Left Behind

No Child Left Behind was the name of a 2002 law that updated the Elementary and Secondary Education Act, authorizing federal policy and funding guidelines. But it also was the name of a specific policy within that act, promoted as a way to demand that all students, no matter their circumstances, get a good education. Through testing, No Child Left Behind held schools accountable for results. Many lawmakers and school officials, however, chafed at the law's methods, which they said were flawed. Both the House and Senate advanced proposals to overhaul the law, but the 113th Congress ended without passing comprehensive legislation.

BACKGROUND

The George W. Bush–era No Child Left Behind Act, passed in 2001 and signed by the president in 2002, required elementary and high school proficiency in math and reading. Unwinding it during the second Obama administration would take two sessions of Congress. Some of the pressure on schools had been relieved toward the end of the Bush presidency, simply by letting the No Child law's authorizations for federal education assistance programs expire in 2007, although Congress continued appropriating money for education assistance anyway.

The Obama administration started offering waivers from No Child to states as early as 2011 in exchange for their instituting new accountability standards and enacting other education policy changes. In 2013, the Education Department granted waivers to forty-three states and the District of Columbia, freeing them from the disliked Adequate Yearly Progress accountability system, which set specific academic attainment goals for math and reading. In return, states had to promise to restructure specific parts of their education systems to the administration's liking by, for example, adopting more rigorous academic standards and overhauling their teacher evaluations to include students' test scores.

Still, lawmakers in the House and Senate wanted a more definitive resolution rather than continuing a piecemeal approach. It took several years before Congress found agreement, at least in part because so many states had obtained waivers, which in turn reduced political pressure.

Senate Bill

The Senate started in late spring of 2013, when the Senate Health, Education, Labor and Pensions (HELP) Committee approved a reauthorization bill (S 1094—S Rept 113–113) that would have given school districts more flexibility in creating student accountability systems. Committee Chair Tom Harkin, D-Iowa, sponsored the bill, which exceeded 1,000 pages. Despite the flexibility, the bill also would have required evaluation systems for teachers and principals and interventions to improve failing schools.

During two days of debate prior to the June 12, 2013, vote, the committee considered two dozen amendments to the bill, rejecting twelve of thirteen offered by Republicans and adopting nine of eleven offered by Democrats. One amendment offered by Al Franken, D-Minn., promoted dual high school–college enrollment programs. It was adopted by voice vote. Kay Hagan, D-N.C., and Elizabeth Warren, D-Mass., won support by voice vote on an amendment to increase learning time for schools getting School Improvement Grants, which go to districts demonstrating the greatest need and commitment to raise achievement in low-performing schools.

But the panel rejected on a 12–10 vote an amendment from Mike Enzi, R-Wyo., that would have eliminated federal guidelines that state and local officials use to identify and improve low-performing schools. Similarly, it voted 9–13 against an amendment by Richard Burr, R-N.C., to eliminate a number of education programs including Race to the Top, a program that rewards schools with grants for innovation, and Promise Neighborhoods, which provides funding for partnerships of schools and nonprofit organizations to promote education in impoverished neighborhoods.

The committee approved the underlying bill, S 1094, on a party-line vote of 12–10. Republicans opposed it because they said the legislation would maintain too strong a federal role in the affairs of local schools.

The committee's bill would have eliminated the No Child law's accountability system and required states to replace it with new systems that tracked student academic achievement and growth, English-language proficiency and, for high schools, graduation rates for all students. States with Education Department waivers that had already adopted new accountability systems with higher standards than those in existing law would have been allowed to retain them.

The bill would have retained the No Child law's emphasis on data collection, requiring states to continue separating student achievement data across subgroups to highlight disparities, and would have expanded the categories to include gender and English-language proficiency. And it would have required states and local school districts to develop their own teacher evaluation systems, based in part on student test scores and third-person evaluations.

S 1094 also would have specifically authorized the Race to the Top, which had been created with $5 billion from the 2009 economic stimulus law (PL 111–5) and financed through appropriations bills since then. However, it had not been explicitly authorized by law. In addition, S 1094 would have required states to expand early-childhood-education initiatives, such as writing guidelines for what children should know and be able to do prior to beginning kindergarten, in an effort to reduce gaps in school readiness.

Harkin and the committee's ranking Republican, Lamar Alexander of Tennessee, had worked together in 2011 to produce a bipartisan bill that the committee had approved with support from both sides of the aisle, although both had reservations about the final product. But this time, Harkin and Alexander abandoned the bipartisan approach, agreeing to let the Democratic majority in the committee produce a bill that would be fully open to amendment on the floor.

"Our goal is to move forward with competing discussions, move the bill to the floor in whatever form it comes out of committee," Alexander said. "If we can then bring it up on the floor and have the same kind of debate with amendments, I would be in favor of moving ahead to see what kind of bill we can get there."

But such a bill never got that far. The Senate had spent much of the prior months dealing with federal student loan policy and interest rates, and unlike the student loans facing steeply rising rates, the No Child program faced no immediate, must-fix deadlines, thanks in large part to Duncan's waivers. Senators put the measure aside.

House Bill

Republicans in the House made more progress than senators, pushing their overhaul bill, HR 5, the Student Success Act, to floor passage. But the House bill, sponsored by Kline, the chair of the education committee, differed so dramatically from the Senate bill, drafted by Democrats, that reconciling the two would have been difficult. In fact, the GOP majority in the House took an almost diametrically opposite position from that of the Senate Democratic majority, with a bill that would have greatly diminished the federal role in the public education system.

The House Education and the Workforce Committee met a week after the Senate panel acted, approving its 500-plus-page measure by a party-line vote of 23–16 on June 19, 2013. The House bill would have eliminated the existing accountability system and instead allowed states to develop their own academic standards in reading, math, and science and in other subjects if they chose to do so. The bill also would have allowed states to identify their poorest-performing schools and permitted local school districts to develop strategies for improving those schools.

Several K–12 programs would have been consolidated into a new Local Academic Flexible Grant to let states and local school districts support their own priorities. The House bill would have required states and school districts to create teacher and principal evaluation systems based on several parameters, including student achievement and multiple measures of teacher performance.

Before approving the bill, the committee adopted by voice vote an amendment by Todd Rokita, R-Ind., that would have allowed states to use teacher development grants to meet the needs of students with different learning styles, particularly nonnative English speakers, gifted students,

and students with disabilities. But so much else about HR 5 was seen as so partisan that Democrats offered only one amendment, a 610-page comprehensive substitute by ranking Democrat George Miller of California that would have retained a strong federal role in public education. The committee rejected it by a party-line vote of 16–23.

A similar fate awaited when HR 5 got a full House vote after two days of floor debate. It had gained even more language scorned by Democrats, especially an amendment successfully added by Majority Leader Eric Cantor, R-Va., to allow Title I money for economically disadvantaged schools to follow students from school to school. For congressional Democrats, as well as teachers in a number of districts with low-income families, this equated to taking money to improve poorly performing schools and sending it to schools elsewhere—deservedly so, said Republicans, but unfairly so, said Democrats.

A second amendment, by Steve Scalise, R-La., struck language from the bill that would have required states to overhaul their teacher evaluation systems to include student test scores. Kline, who disagreed with many Republicans on the issue, had included that language in the bill.

Put to a vote on July 19, 2013, HR 5 passed by a near-party-line vote of 221–207. No Democrats voted for the measure, but 12 Republicans voted "nay" (House vote 374, p. H-140).

The bill then got put on hold, the subject iced for two more years. Thanks to the Education Department waivers, there was little pressure to pursue a No Child legislative fix. The White House had issued a veto threat to the House bill, anyway.

BUDGET PRESSURES

As with other areas of the federal government, education spending was affected by partisan differences over budget priorities. Congress was stuck in an ongoing deadlock over spending levels, under pressure from the nearly governmentwide budget caps known as the "sequester" that lawmakers had passed during the first Obama administration to limit spending.

In the FY 2014 omnibus spending bill (HR 83, PL 113-76), the Education Department received $70.6 billion, $603 million less than enacted for fiscal 2013 and $3.9 billion less than the president's budget request. Similarly, the FY 2015 omnibus appropriations bill—signed on December 16, 2014, two and a half months into the fiscal year—provided $70.5 billion for the Education Department, about $100 million less than in fiscal 2014 (HR 83, PL 113-236).

Then Congress furnished a spending increase. FY 2016 appropriations provided $71.7 billion for education programs, more than the previous year but less than the $74.1 billion Obama requested (HR 2029—PL 114-113). Title 1 grants, for school districts with a large number of

economically disadvantaged students, totaled $5.2 billion, up from $4.7 billion the year before. Grants for states to support children with special needs were raised to $11.9 billion, but appropriators declined to create an account for preschool grants, for which the Obama administration requested $750 million.

One of the major funding priorities of Senate Democrats and the Obama administration was to beef up Head Start, the preschool program for low-income households. Its programming and funding fell under the Department of Health and Human Services rather than the Education Department, and it got $8.6 billion in fiscal year 2014. That was $702 million more than enacted for 2013. Congress held Head Start spending steady in fiscal year 2015 at $8.6 billion before climbing to $9.2 billion in the following fiscal year.

In its final year, the 114th Congress couldn't agree on how much to spend for the year ahead. It continued current-year funding and pushed off decisions for a new Congress to make in 2017.

HR 5, Education Secretary Arne Duncan said in a statement, marked "a retreat from high standards for all students and would virtually eliminate accountability for the learning of historically underserved students—a huge step backward for efforts to improve academic achievement."

Student Loan Debt

With college debt becoming an increasing concern, Congress considered several bills to help graduates. It failed, however, to advance major legislation, and the administration instead took some steps on its own.

BACKGROUND

Lots of people talked about student loan debt in 2014, and not just about rising interest rates, as addressed in Congress the previous year. They also complained about the financial burden the accumulated debt placed on college graduates, putting a squeeze on their personal budgets and abilities to save for a home or put aside money in a bank account. Average total costs for the 2014–2015 academic year for in-state tuition at public four-year schools were $18,943 and at private schools, $42,419, according to the College Board.

After adjustment for inflation, prices rose 40 percent between the 2001–2002 school year and 2011–2012 at public schools and 28 percent at private schools, according to the National Center for Education Statistics, a branch of the Education Department. Many students received grants or scholarships and did not pay the total amount. But total student accumulated debt nevertheless exceeded $1 trillion.

Congress and the president talked about this, too. There were dueling views, one being that the debt was extraordinary. A White House fact sheet noted that 71 percent of those earning a bachelor's degree graduate with debt that averages $29,400. At a White House ceremony in June 2014, Obama recognized recent college graduates who were "feeling pretty good." But once "the glow" of graduation wore off, he said, they'd be "asking themselves, 'How on Earth am I going to pay off all these student loans?'" Some Republicans argued that because college graduates earn so much more money over the course of their lifetimes—$1 million, according to the College Board—the increased debt and payments early in a career were worth it in the long run. They also argued that truly large loans—those more than $100,000—were generally used to pay for graduate school and represent a small fraction of overall loans.

Sen. Lamar Alexander, R-Tenn., at the time the top-ranking Republican on the Health, Education, Labor and Pensions (HELP) Committee, compared the average graduate's debt with the price of a car, according to the *Washington Post*, saying, "It's the best investment that a person's ever likely to make. They don't think twice about it when they buy a car and the car depreciates the day you drive it off the dealership."

Republicans were among those offering bills to address the issue, however, especially in the House. Theirs largely focused on better informing students before they borrowed, emphasizing a know-before-you-owe approach rather than seeking loan forgiveness or repayment deferral. But none of the House bills were taken up by the Senate. President Obama wound up taking steps on his own.

House Action

The House moved three bills pertaining to student-loan debt.

HR 4983, the Strengthening Transparency in Higher Education Act. Introduced by Virginia Foxx, R-N.C., on June 26, 204, HR 4983 called for a redesign of existing higher education data collection and dissemination. It would have ended the requirement that the secretary of education make publicly available on the College Navigator website information on college affordability, state higher education spending, and a multiyear tuition calculator.

Instead, the bill would have created a new requirement to develop a public College Dashboard website that listed the percentage of degree- or certificate-seeking undergraduate students who obtained their certificates within the normal time, 150 percent of that time, and 200 percent of that time. The dashboard also was to list the institution's average net prices for undergraduates getting financial aid, their average debt, and a link to the Bureau of Labor Statistics on starting salaries in all major occupations.

HR 4983 passed the House on a voice vote (based on calls of yea or nay, without individual tallies) on July 23, 2014.

HR 3136, the Advancing Competency-Based Education Demonstration Project Act. Introduced on September 19, 2013, but seeing no action until 2014, the bill by Matt Salmon, R-Az., called for waiving some federal financial aid rules for thirty voluntary pilot projects in competency-based education. Unlike traditional higher-education classes, these are programs that would measure students' knowledge, skills, and experience through assessments instead of or in addition to measuring their credit or clock hours.

It passed unanimously, 414–0, in a roll-call vote on July 23, 2014.

HR 4984, the Empowering Students Through Enhanced Financial Counseling Act. Introduced by Brett Guthrie, R-Ky., on June 26, 2014, the bill would have required colleges to counsel recipients getting federal student loans and Pell Grants, in a simple and understandable manner, on the terms and repayment requirements. The counseling also would have included

- an explanation of how the student could budget for typical educational expenses based on the cost of attendance;
- an explanation of the borrower's right to request a consumer credit report annually;
- estimates comparing the average incomes and employment rates in the applicable state for people with a high school diploma, those with some postsecondary education without completion, and those with a bachelor's degree.

The House approved the bill overwhelmingly, 405–11, on July 24, 2014.

Senate Action

Despite their easy House passage, none of these bills got a vote in the Senate. They arrived just before the hyper-partisan months that preceded the midterm elections.

Senate Democrats offered a bill in June 2014 that would allow borrowers with older student loans to refinance at current lower interest rates. Sponsor Elizabeth Warren, D-Mass., proposed paying for it by imposing a Fair Share Tax on adjusted gross incomes more than $1 million. The Congressional Budget Office and staff of the Joint Committee on Taxation wrote that the Senate Democrats' 2014 bill would increase deficits over the short term, because the government would receive less interest income once loans were refinanced at lower rates. But the bill would reduce deficits in the long run as a result of the measure's offset—Warren's proposed tax on higher-income individuals, the CBO said.

Senate Republicans rejected the proposed higher taxes. With a 56–38 vote, the Warren bill fell short of the 60 votes needed for cloture. Democratic leaders vowed to try to bring it to a vote again in the fall, but it fell victim to other priorities.

Executive Action

President Obama, meanwhile, signed an executive order on June 9, 2014, expanding an existing loan-forgiveness program known as Pay As You Earn. It capped student loan payments at 10 percent of borrowers' incomes, with any remaining balance forgiven after twenty years of payments, or ten years for those in public-service jobs.

Obama's order built on legislation that Congress had passed and he had signed in 2010 and on regulations adopted by the administration in 2012. The program to this point was limited to borrowers who took on student debt during a specific period: They had obtained their first loan after September 30, 2007, and got at least one more loan disbursement after September 30, 2011. Many were graduating from college at a time of unusually high unemployment, and the White House had promoted Pay As You Earn as helping teachers, nurses, first responders, and others in lower-paying public-service careers.

Already in place was a different program, Income-Based Repayment, for federal student loans since 2009, and it capped payments to 15 percent of a graduate's discretionary income. Obama's executive order in 2014 expanded the lower cap under his Pay As You Earn program to older federal Direct Loans.

The White House had estimated when the original program launched that it would assist nearly 1.6 million Americans with student loan debt. With the expansion, the White House said 5 million more borrowers would get help.

"This is commencement season, a time for graduates and their families to celebrate one of the greatest achievements of a young person's life," Obama said in his weekly White House address on June 7, 2014. "But for many graduates, it also means feeling trapped by a whole lot of student loan debt. And we've got to do more to lift that burden."

2015–2016

With Republicans in control of both chambers, Congress replaced No Child Left Behind with a law that allowed for a more limited federal role, although Washington kept some oversight. Congress also phased out Perkins loans, geared toward the most financially needy college students but criticized as more expensive than, and redundant to, other financial aid tools.

No Child Left Behind

BACKGROUND

Newly appointed to chair the HELP Committee, Lamar Alexander, R-Tenn., made good on his vow to replace No Child Left Behind and return authority to states in many areas of elementary and secondary education. And he did so early, releasing a draft reauthorization bill on January 13, 2015. Although the legislation ultimately won bipartisan support in Congress and was signed into law by the president, some Republicans remained disappointed that Washington still would have a say over state plan approval or disapproval.

Senate Action

Alexander's draft reauthorization bill proposed giving states the authority to determine their own school accountability systems and interventions in failing schools. The bill would in many ways have limited the areas in which the U.S. Education Department could dictate state education practices and would have allowed states to set their own testing requirements if they wanted.

States would have had to submit plans detailing their "challenging academic standards" and their testing and school accountability models. Peers would have had to review and judge the plans "in deference to state and local jurisdictions, with the goal of supporting state- and local-led innovation."

The Education Department would have had to approve the plans, yet it would have been prohibited from requiring states to adopt or remove academic standards, curricula, or teacher evaluation systems. Arguably the most controversial feature from a social-policy standpoint was Alexander's provision to help students move from one school to another within their districts, with priority for moves given to students from the lowest-performing schools. The provision would have allowed states to create programs that would permit Title I funding for low-income children, the biggest source of federal K–12 education dollars, to follow students from school to school.

Proponents said this would reward higher-performing schools, create a new system of accountability for schools, and give students better options. Critics, including Democrats and teacher unions, said it would deprive some of the neediest schools of money.

House Action

Kline, the House committee chair, on February 3, 2015, introduced his own draft bill, largely tracking the House measure from 2013. Like Alexander's bill, Kline's proposal would have eliminated many specific program funding streams and given states a greater say in how federal money is used. Kline's bill would have consolidated all the money, besides Title I funding, into what he called a local academic flexible grant that would have let states and schools support initiatives "based on their priorities," according to a committee fact sheet.

Kline's bill would have maintained the requirement that states test students annually in grades three through eight and once in high school in reading and math and three times throughout their school careers in science. But it would have allowed states to set their own accountability standards and interventions in failing schools. And it would have allowed Title I funding for low-income students to follow those students as they moved among public schools.

House Democrats criticized both the substance of the legislation and the process by which it was handled. The bill would dismantle federal accountability, "shortchange students and their achievement, and rob our most disadvantaged children of vital resources," Robert C. Scott of Virginia, the top-ranking Democrat on the Education and the Workforce Committee, said. In a letter, Scott also expressed displeasure that the markup would occur without the committee having held any hearings.

The House Education and the Workforce Committee approved the bill (HR 5) on February 11 by a vote of 21–16. The committee rejected more than a dozen Democratic amendments that would have authorized new or continued federal roles in an array of education programs. One pertained to grants for states to improve student literacy, and another called for state-based, K–12 college and career readiness standards so graduates did not enter college needing remedial courses.

"For the last 50 years, Washington has assumed more programs, more spending and more top-down mandates will cure an ailing education system," Kline said in a statement when the committee considered the bill. "We have doubled down on this approach time and time again, and it isn't working."

The White House had a far different take, criticizing the House committee bill for its attempted spending cuts. "This bill attempts to cut our way to better schools,"

AN EDUCATION VETERAN TAKES THE GAVEL

Even before assuming the chairmanship of the Senate Health, Education, Labor and Pensions (HELP) Committee in 2015, Lamar Alexander, R-Tenn., had extensive experience in education leadership. The three-term senator had been president of the University of Tennessee and then secretary of education under President George H. W. Bush. A pragmatist who sometimes worked across the aisle, Alexander wanted to end the controversial No Child Left Behind program, which tied federal dollars to elementary and high school achievement testing. He also wanted to simplify the process for applying for college aid, and he wanted fewer federal regulations.

But Democrats had their own priorities. While the White House agreed in principle on aspects of No Child Left Behind, for example, and President Obama wanted to amp up spending on community colleges, Obama and Alexander disagreed more broadly on the extent of state leeway for policy and spending.

With Republicans lacking a filibuster-proof majority, Alexander said he believed progress would be possible if the legislative process were given a chance to play out. This meant that senators from both parties should be heard and get to offer amendments on legislation, he said. "A bipartisan process is not when two senators go in a back room and come up with their own proposal and tell everybody else that's the way it's got to be," he said in an interview with *CQ Roll Call*.

Bipartisanship was hardly in vogue during the 114th Congress. But Alexander worked with Patty Murray of Washington, the HELP Committee's ranking Democrat, on compromise legislation to replace No Child Left Behind. The resulting law, the Every Student Succeeds Act, won the support of key members of both parties in revamping the testing procedures that had drawn considerable criticism from educators and policy makers.

Bipartisan support, however, proved insufficient in achieving another goal of Alexander's: restoring year-round Pell grants. The need-based college grants, designed in 1972 (and called Basic Education Opportunity grants at the time), had originally been issued for fall and spring enrollment. The program was subsequently expanded to allow for year-round eligibility, helping students who wanted to accelerate their educations. In 2011, Pell grants were cut back to fall and summer, a result of federal cost-savings measures. Alexander pressed for year-round restoration of the grants in 2016. But House appropriators balked over concerns about future funding—a sign of the fiscal obstacles that beset even comparatively popular programs during Obama's second term. (Appropriators would eventually relent in 2017, restoring Pell grants to year-round eligibility.)

White House Domestic Policy Adviser Cecilia Muñoz told reporters. "This approach is backwards, and our teachers and kids deserve much, much better."

This debate, like the broader reauthorization bills, was about much more than just No Child Left Behind. Congress was attempting to deal with numerous education provisions in the reauthorization. As HR 5 was teeing up for House floor debate, the conservative groups Club for Growth and Heritage Action for America wanted deeper cuts than the House was considering, arguing the federal government had too big a role in what should be state decisions in education. Still, HR 5 made it to the House floor for a day of debate—and then debate came to a halt the next day, February 27, as a number of conservatives balked.

This could have left No Child Left Behind in place, a point Kline tried to impress upon the Republican caucus when he delivered a speech to the Council of Chief State School Officers, a group of public officials who head state school departments, at its annual legislative conference on March 24, 2015, in Washington, D.C.: "The most important thing all my colleagues need to understand is No Child Left Behind is the law and it stays the law until

Congress changes it. I'm embarrassed to tell you that some of my colleagues who said they couldn't vote for HR 5 didn't understand that."

Back to the Senate, Then the House

Alexander and Patty Murray of Washington, the ranking Democrat on the Senate HELP Committee, tried to find a way forward by working on a compromise. Their draft education bill won approval by the HELP Committee on a 22–0 vote on April 16. It called for states to continue testing students annually but would leave it up to states to decide what weight those scores would have when rating schools. Yet despite the bipartisan committee votes, Senate Democrats held qualms, saying the bill did not do enough to ensure students in all states would receive an equal education. "I am not sure this bill measures up as a civil rights law," said Sen. Christopher S. Murphy, D-Conn.

The bill moved back to the House again, with the original House version passing 218–213 on July 8, more than four months after suspending floor debate in February, but with some changes. For example, the House adopted, by 251–178, a Republican amendment that would have allowed parents to opt their students out of testing requirements.

Ten groups, including the Council of Chief State School Officials and the U.S. Chamber of Commerce, sent lawmakers in both chambers a letter opposing any proposals that would weaken test participation requirements. Their concern, shared by Democrats, was that struggling students could be excluded from data, masking the real performance of schools.

"America's students deserve a strong education bill that builds on the tremendous progress of the last decade and supports opportunity for every American child," Duncan, the education secretary, said in a statement after the House vote. "Instead, House Republicans have chosen to take a bad bill and make it even worse."

Testing proponents were nevertheless able to push back on some proposed changes. The House rejected, 195–235, an amendment by Republican Mark Walker of North Carolina that would have allowed states to opt out of as many as eighty federal programs for up to five years and still receive federal funding. "Just like No Child Left Behind erred too far in the direction of not enough flexibility, so too we must be careful not to err in the direction of too much flexibility without accountability," said Rep. Jared Polis, D-Colo., a member of the Education and Workforce Committee.

In addition, the House adopted Republican amendments to shorten the length of the authorization from six years to four, through 2019; to prohibit federal actions against a state that withdraws from Common Core standards or any other specific standards; and to express a sense of Congress that the Education secretary should review regulations addressing issues of student privacy. Common Core is the name of a set of math and English standards adopted voluntarily by multiple states and the District of Columbia. Created with input from the National Governors Association and Council of Chief State School Officers, they outline what students should learn by the end of each grade. Supporters say they eliminate a patchwork of uneven academic standards while leaving the curriculum up to states. Critics say Common Core is a proxy for a national standard and uses methods that have confused some parents.

Now that the House had approved the bill, it moved back to the Senate, which had been working on a parallel track with its Alexander-Murray compromise. The Senate version, S 1177, would have kept federal tests already required but would have made states responsible for creating accountability systems and determining the weight of test results in assessing school performance.

It would also have prohibited the Education Department from mandating certain educational standards, such as Common Core. The bill passed 81–17 on July 16, but the White House maintained its objections. Education Secretary Duncan said S 1177 "still falls short" because it would not identify problematic schools, require interventions, or ensure those most in need of additional resources get them.

"We cannot tolerate continued indifference to the lowest performing schools, achievement gaps that let some students fall behind, or high schools where huge numbers of students never make it to graduation," Duncan said in a statement. "This bill should also do more to maintain focus on what matters most—whether students are actually learning and graduating, and whether those that need the greatest help receive the resources and support they need."

Final Action

These objections notwithstanding, each chamber of Congress had now signed off on its respective No Child reform legislation. A House–Senate conference committee reached agreement on a final bill on November 19, paving the way to an overhaul of federal K–12 authority. The House passed it on December 2 by a 359–63 vote and the Senate by 85–12 on December 9. Obama signed the bill, called the Every Child Succeeds Act, on December 10, 2015 (S 1177, PL 114–95).

The bill eliminated No Child's federal school accountability system and goals. In its place, states and local school districts would have to establish their own accountability systems and goals, to be approved by the Education Department. These would include how to use test scores to determine a school's performance and how to hold schools accountable and improve poorly performing schools. Despite its role in some oversight, the Education Department would be barred from requiring particular academic standards.

As for proficiency testing, a core complaint of No Child Left Behind, the bill maintained the requirement for regular testing of students to assess their proficiency in math, reading, and science. It said the results of those student assessments should be disaggregated by race, income, English proficiency, and other specified categories in order to determine whether any particular subgroup of students was lagging academically.

The measure required states to develop plans to help the lowest-performing 5 percent of all public schools that receive Title I funding, all public high schools that fail to graduate one-third or more of their students, as well as schools where any subgroup of students consistently underperforms. It prohibited the Education Department from setting national academic standards or otherwise imposing conditions on states and school districts in exchange for federal grants or waivers from ESEA (Elementary and Secondary Education Act) requirements, and it required the department to downsize to reflect the elimination of forty-nine federal education programs. Notably, the final bill did not include the controversial "portability" provisions that would have allowed Title I money to follow children to the school of their choice.

The conference agreement reauthorized the Elementary and Secondary Education Act for four years, through fiscal 2020, and modified programs and policies throughout the law with the overall goal of giving states, school districts, schools, teachers, and parents greater control over all aspects of elementary and secondary education. Total authorizations in the measure equaled $24.5 billion for fiscal 2017, or $1.2 billion more than the fiscal 2015 appropriation, and increased to $26.1 billion in fiscal 2020. The measure eliminated or consolidated forty-nine elementary and secondary education programs, including many from Title I. The final bill maintained formula calculations used to allocate Title I funds to states, as well as "maintenance of effort" requirements under which state and local school district education funding must be maintained at 90 percent or more of the previous year's funding in order to receive a full allotment of federal dollars. The measure modified the education plans that states and local school districts must develop and submit to the Education Department in order to receive Title I funding. Among the new provisions, states must describe how they will intervene in schools that are "low performing," and the department must assemble peer-review teams to review state plans.

Like both the House and the Senate bills, the conference agreement eliminated the term *highly qualified teacher* created under No Child and prohibited the Education Department from prescribing standards for the evaluation of teachers. It significantly rewrote Title II of ESEA, which deals with teacher training and evaluations, setting the goals of the program as increasing student achievement, improving teacher and school leader effectiveness, increasing the number of teachers and school leaders who are effective in improving student academic achievement, and providing low-income and minority students greater access to effective teachers and school leaders. The measure authorized $2.3 billion annually for teaching grants through fiscal 2020, as well as $469 million each year through fiscal 2019 and $489 million for fiscal 2020 for other national activities.

Other provisions included:

English learners. $756 million authorized in fiscal 2017 increasing to $885 million in fiscal 2020 and redefined goals to increase expectations and standards.

Student support and academic enrichment grants. $1.7 billion authorized in fiscal 2017 and $1.6 billion each subsequent year for a new program aimed at increasing the capacity of states, local educational agencies, schools, and communities to provide students with a well-rounded education, improve school conditions for learning, and enhance the use of technology for academic achievement.

Preschool development grants. $250 million authorized per year for a new preschool development program administered by the Health and Human Services Department in conjunction with the Education Department. The provision aimed to coordinate preschool programs to provide better access to early childhood education for low-income and disadvantaged children, with a goal of preparing them for kindergarten.

Impact aid. $1.3 billion authorized each year for the Impact Aid program, which provides direct funding to school districts affected by the presence of the federal government.

Homeless children. $85 million authorized each year for the Education for Homeless Children and Youths program of the McKinney-Vento Homeless Assistance Act, the primary federal law that provides funding to states and school districts to educate homeless children and youth.

Native populations education. Reauthorized the American Indian, Alaska Native Education, and the Native Hawaiian Education programs. The measure also modified the programs to promote greater academic achievement in those populations and to emphasize the preservation of their cultures, particularly their native languages.

Perkins Loans

In the array of financing options for a college education, Perkins Loans were hailed as a financial bridge for low-income students, yet they were also criticized as redundant and more expensive than other loan programs. The 114th Congress voted to phase them out.

BACKGROUND

Perkins loans were direct, low-interest loans geared toward students with exceptional financial need attending one of the 1,700 postsecondary schools that participated in the program. They were named in 1986 for Rep. Carl D. Perkins, a Kentucky Democrat and long-time chair of the House Education and Labor Committee who had died two years before. The $1 billion annual program had previously been known as National Direct Student Loans, and when it was first created in 1958, the loans were called National Defense Student Loans—part of the effort to improve technical and science education in the post-*Sputnik* competition with the Soviet Union.

Perkins loans were made by schools, a model adopted later for all federally subsidized loans. Interest was at 5 percent. With the broader Direct Loan program now providing a more competitive rate, some Congress members

FOR-PROFIT COLLEGES

Dropout rates at for-profit, career-training colleges tend to be higher than at traditional universities. So do the student-loan default rates. To members of Congress and policy makers, this raised a basic question: Did some career colleges prey on students, as the Obama administration said, by luring them in with aggressive recruiting tactics, easy loans, and misleading claims of job preparation? Or did the schools give nontraditional students—older ones, poorer ones, some military veterans, people whose educational trajectory was anything but linear—a fresh chance at success even though that could lead to higher dropout rates?

The question spilled over into the 113th and 114th Congresses from late 2010 and 2011, when the administration first issued new rules on *gainful employment*. The rules, revised in 2014 and challenged in courts and in Congress, sought to link the availability of federally backed student aid with graduation rates and job-placement rates. Education Secretary Arne Duncan said the rules were reasonable and necessary. For-profit, career-oriented colleges as a group had disproportionate default and dropout rates, documented in several studies.

Yet Republicans in Congress, like the proprietary schools themselves, contended the Obama rules were unfair and even elitist. Ivy League and other four-year universities recruit and accept students selectively while enrolling relatively few low-income or nontraditional students, they said. Career colleges and other proprietary institutions filled the void and took chances on students, they said. Their willingness to do so should not result in punishment, said some of the 90,000 public comments submitted to the Education Department when the rules were proposed.

As first released, the Gainful Employment rules set guidelines and penalties based on three criteria:

- a loan repayment rate designed to measure how effectively students repaid the loans they borrowed to attend the program. A program would have failed in this category if more than 35 percent of graduates were in default.
- an earnings rate for program graduates requiring that annual loan repayments not exceed 30 percent of their discretionary income.
- a discretionary income rate for the graduates requiring that repayments not exceed 12 percent of their total earnings.

A program failing to pass at least one of the three performance measures in a year would have to take corrective steps. If it failed all three performance metrics for any three out of the most recently completed four fiscal years, the school could lose eligibility to participate in federal aid programs.

The Association of Private Sector Colleges and Universities, representing for-profit colleges, sued in the U.S. District Court for the District of Columbia in advance of the rules' enforcement, criticizing not only the requirements but also what colleges said would be an unfair cost for them to collect and report the data necessary to comply. On June 30, 2012, the association won a decision that vacated most of the provisions, keeping only the provision requiring public disclosure of the graduation and loan data. The court said that while the Education Department had a right to regulate gainful employment programs, it failed to provide a sound rationale for the 35 percent repayment rate threshold. The Education Department started working to revise the rules, unveiling a new version in 2014, but Republicans in Congress introduced legislation and held hearings aimed at eliminating the rules entirely.

A bill, the Supporting Academic Freedom Through Regulatory Relief Act (HR 2637), introduced by Rep. Virginia Foxx, R-North Carolina, passed 22–13 in the House Education

including Alexander, the new Senate HELP Committee chair, said it was time to end the Perkins program and simplify students' financial aid options.

Paring down the number of loan programs was already the plan, in fact, since Congress in its 2008 reauthorization of the Higher Education Act provided authority for Perkins loans only until the end of September 2014. But through a congressional mechanism in 2014 linked to the authorization of appropriations, the Perkins program got a one-year extension to September 30, 2015.

Perkins loans were only used by 5 percent of student borrowers, Alexander said, and represented "a little more than 0.5 percent of all the outstanding student loans we have in the country today." Democrats led by HELP

Committee member Tammy Baldwin, D-Wisc., disputed the notion that Perkins loans should end, saying with other Perkins supporters that lower-income students rely on the loans to cover the gap between other funding sources and the cost of college, including supplies, housing and transportation, or urgent circumstances.

Congressional Action

The House passed a voice vote in September 2015 for a one-year Perkins program extension under a bill sponsored by Mike Bishop, R-Mich. (HR 3594). Alexander blocked the bill, saying he wanted to handle the issue in a broader reauthorization of the Higher Education Act, and in his view that reauthorization would not include the and the Workforce Committee on July 24, 2013. Committee Chair John Kline, R-Minn., said to committee members as they met that day to consider the measure that "postsecondary institutions—and career colleges in particular—have been unfairly targeted by punitive federal mandates that drag down the entire higher education system in the name of weeding out a few bad actors."

George Miller of California, the committee's ranking Democrat, disputed the premise, saying the federal role in financing education for so many students at for-profit institutions cried out for heightened scrutiny and accountability. "At a time when the higher education market is in so much flux with new kinds of programs popping up around the country and online, this is the wrong time to reopen loopholes for manipulating student aid dollars," Miller said at the July 24 committee meeting. "For-profit colleges enroll about 10 percent of all students but take in about 25 percent of all federal aid and are responsible for almost half of all defaults in the federal loan program."

HR 2637 failed to advance after it left the committee, but the debate did not end. The Education Department announced new rules in October 2014, with new criteria: Loan payments for a typical graduate could not exceed 20 percent of discretionary income, or 8 percent of total earnings, without triggering a warning. If the loan payments exceeded 30 percent of discretionary income, or 12 percent of annual earnings, the institution would be considered failing—and failure in two of three consecutive three-year periods would result in aid ineligibility.

The department said that had such a requirement been in place already, 1,400 programs serving 840,000 students would have been at risk of losing federal student aid eligibility.

"Career colleges must be a stepping stone to the middle class," Duncan said in a press release on October 30,

2014, when announcing the revised rules. "But too many hard-working students find themselves buried in debt with little to show for it. That is simply unacceptable."

Soon after this, news media reports and investigations by state and federal authorities turned up allegations of career colleges spending heavily on marketing and recruiting of students while giving short shrift to instructional budgets. Corinthian Colleges, fined $30 million by the Education Department and accused of misleading students about job placement rates, closed on April 27, 2015, mostly affecting students at its Western United States campuses.

Public pressure was building on the propriety college industry. Trade groups representing the colleges countered that it was unfair to tarnish the reputation of all such schools with selective examples. But by the end of the 114th Congress, lawmakers were unable to muster support for killing the gainful employment rules, whose new start for reporting debt-to-earnings rates to the department was to be July 1, 2015.

Implementation issues forced the Education Department to delay publicly disseminating the information the colleges provided, but on January 9, 2017, less than two weeks before Obama left office, the department announced some findings. They were not favorable for the proprietary school industry. The department said in a statement announcing the career schools' debt-to-earnings rates that "over 800 programs serving hundreds of thousands of students fail the Department's accountability standards with an annual loan payment that is at least greater than 30 percent of discretionary income and greater than 12 percent of total earnings." Ninety percent of the programs failing the regulations, the department said, were at for-profit institutions.

With the issue continuing to divide policy makers, the Trump administration was expected to hew more closely to the position of for-profit colleges.

Perkins program. Alexander said his committee was considering ways to simplify student aid "so there is one grant and one loan." For the grant, he referred to the Pell grant program.

By December 2015, though, Alexander agreed to a compromise with Baldwin and others who wanted to keep the Perkins loans going. Baldwin had said, "One of the things I hear the most about these days from my constituents is their frustration that Congress isn't doing enough to make higher education more affordable and more accessible. Yet, today, the fact that we just saw a single senator stand up and reject a bipartisan and commonsense measure to do just that is, frankly, a perfect example of why my constituents and the American people are so upset with Washington."

On December 16, the Senate by unanimous consent took up the House bill from September (HR 3594), added a year to the authorization for undergraduates, and passed it by voice vote. The next day, the House concurred in the amendment by unanimous consent. With the president's signature on December 18, this continued the Perkins loan program until September 30, 2017, for undergraduate students, covering the 2017–18 school year. Graduate students who had previously received Perkins loans could get new ones through September 30, 2016 (PL 114–105).

The revised bill required that students first use other financial aid before being offered a Perkins loan. Schools also had to disclose information about the differences between the Perkins loan program and other loan programs.

CHAPTER 11

Housing and Urban Aid

Housing and Urban Aid

The changes in the housing market since the government's interventions in 2008–2009 greatly influenced congressional views of priorities in housing, the real estate market, and home loans. The clearing of the "rubble," as President Barack Obama put it in his 2013 State of the Union address, helps explain why Congress wanted to do more yet stopped short of achieving lawmakers' goals. Republicans wanted to peel back the government's newly expanded role in mortgage lending. Democrats wanted to keep it but make private markets absorb future losses. Congress wound up doing neither. The House and Senate took incremental steps instead, and some of those steps had broad support from Democrats, Republicans, borrowers, lenders, renters, realtors, and builders alike. But more generally, the years 2013 through 2016 were not filled with expansive action.

This made a certain amount of sense. By 2013, the housing market was stabilizing, and much of the nation's financial crisis was in the rear-view mirror. "Our housing market is healing, our stock market is rebounding, and consumers, patients and homeowners enjoy stronger protections than ever before," President Obama said in his State of the Union address on February 12, 2013.

The causes of the crisis that prompted so many earlier interventions were still debated. They included the recession of the early 2000s, accelerated by the terrorist attacks on New York and Washington in 2001; policies from President George W. Bush and Congress to promote homeownership and encourage more lending; relaxed lending standards that enabled banks and mortgage brokers to promote home loans to borrowers with lower incomes, lower credit scores, and higher risk of being unable to make their payments, and Wall Street egging on this behavior while bundling risky mortgages into securities that could be sold to investors. Each component fed on the others, for a time offloading each side's risks.

Then came the implosion. Mortgage delinquencies, or loans on which borrowers were thirty or more days late in making payments, jumped dramatically, reaching 10 percent in the first quarter of 2010, according to surveys of the Mortgage Bankers Association's members. Using a slightly different measure—loans from commercial banks—the Federal Reserve Bank of St. Louis said 11.53 percent of all

mortgages were delinquent in the first quarter of 2010. The rates were substantially higher for subprime mortgages, or home loans given to borrowers with weaker credit histories and higher risk of default, said a report from the Federal Reserve Bank of Richmond.

Fast-forward to 2013. Foreclosures and underwater mortgages (home loans in which the amounts owed to the bank exceeded the homes' value) remained problematic in the industrial Midwest and California. But more broadly, the financial and mortgage crises that had rocked the American economy were subsiding rapidly. By the time members of the 113th Congress were sworn in in 2013, the traditional mortgage-financing system that provided the backbone for the nation's housing market was functioning largely as designed. This was partly a result of the government's $188 billion rescue and conservatorship in the fall of 2008 of the Federal National Mortgage Association, or Fannie Mae, and the Federal Home Loan Mortgage Corporation, or Freddie Mac. (Fannie Mae and Freddie Mac are the nation's biggest providers of cash and liquidity for the mortgage market, buying or guaranteeing about 60 percent of the nation's home loans.) Their rescue was just one action taken in Washington around that time. For struggling homeowners, Congress had also approved the Hope for Homeowners program (PL 110–289) in 2008 and the related Helping Families Save Their Homes Act of 2009 (PL 111–22). Both measures helped borrowers modify or refinance their mortgages. And in 2012, the Treasury Department amended terms of the bailout and required Fannie and Freddie to pay all future profits as a dividend to the Treasury, providing what the administration said was greater market certainty.

This heavily influenced action on housing in the 113th Congress. Some House Republicans said in 2013 that it was time to unwind the financial entanglements with Fannie and Freddie and let the private sector take over. The Republican-based Protecting American Taxpayers and Homeowners Act (HR 2767), for example, would have wound down Fannie and Freddie over five years and led to the creation of the National Mortgage Market Utility to facilitate private-market mortgage securitization—one without a government guarantee. House Democrats were opposed, however, and even some Republicans expressed qualms when the housing and lending industries said that without a federal backstop for mortgage-market liquidity, home buyers could find it harder to get loans. The measure died after committee passage.

The Senate tried a different approach with the Housing Finance Reform and Taxpayer Protection Act (S 1217), which called for creation of an entity called the Federal Mortgage Insurance Corporation. This would be an independent agency with an explicit full-faith-and-credit federal government guarantee, but the government would only have to cover losses after the private sector absorbed some of them first. But this, too, stalled after committee passage, with Democrats saying it might make home loans harder to get or more expensive for buyers.

Legislation aside, the Senate confirmed a new housing secretary, former San Antonio Mayor Julian Castro, in 2014, and he and President Obama pledged an ongoing active government role in housing. "I look forward to being part of a department that will help ensure that millions of Americans all across the country have the chance to get good, safe, affordable housing and to reach their American dreams," Castro said at a White House ceremony on May 23, 2014, when nominated.

But lawmakers in the 114th Congress stepped back substantially from postcrisis, housing-related lawmaking. For the most part, Congress handled housing policy in a piecemeal fashion, mostly through provisions in omnibus spending bills. The one exception was the Housing Opportunity through Modernization Act (HR 3700, PL 114-201), which garnered unanimous support in the House in 2015 and the Senate in 2016. The bill made it tougher for households with substantial assets to qualify for HUD subsidies that help low-income families pay rent, and it assured that people living in subsidized housing would not be able to stay very long if their incomes had grown too high. It also made it possible for low-income families to buy relatively inexpensive modular homes with government support and made it easier for buyers to finance condominiums using mortgages insured by the Federal Housing Administration (FHA), which could allow for lower down payments.

"I will be the first to point out that this legislation won't necessarily change the world," Rep. Blaine Luetkemeyer, R-Mo., the sponsor of HR 3700, said at a hearing on October 21, 2015. "It won't end homelessness overnight, or meet the overwhelming need for affordable housing, but it is a first step in a long journey to reforming our housing system. We have to take a first step before we can get a second step."

Striving to shrug off the spending limits imposed in 2013 and beyond by sequestration, or spending cuts imposed as a result of the Budget Control Act of 2011, Congress slowly but unevenly increased spending for the Department of Housing and Urban Development (HUD) programs that subsidize rent for very low-income families. Rising rents and a limited supply of affordable rental apartments and homes, however, made it hard for HUD and its congressionally mandated budget to match the need or demand from families eligible to get federally funded rent vouchers. Due to sequestration, the availability of some subsidies even took a dip.

In 2012, for example, HUD data show that 2.168 million households used Section 8 tenant-based rental assistance, or vouchers, toward rent in private apartments or homes.

REFERENCES

Discussion of housing and urban aid action for the years 1945–1964 may be found in *Congress and the Nation Vol. I,* pp. 459–515; for the years 1965–1968, *Congress and the Nation Vol. II,* 183–226; for the years 1969–1972, *Congress and the Nation Vol. III,* pp. 635–657; for the years 1973–1976, *Congress and the Nation Vol. IV,* pp. 471–502; for the years 1977–1980, *Congress and the Nation Vol. V,* 429–448; for the years 1981–1984, *Congress and the Nation Vol. VI,* pp. 629–639; for the years 1985–1988, *Congress and the Nation Vol. VII,* pp. 667–684; for the years 1989–1992, *Congress and the Nation Vol. VIII,* pp. 663–700; for the years 1993–1996, *Congress and the Nation Vol. IX,* pp. 637–650; for the years 1997–2001, *Congress and the Nation Vol. X,* pp. 553–567; for the years 2001–2004, *Congress and the Nation Vol. XI,* pp. 555–560; for the years 2005–2008, *Congress and the Nation Vol. XII,* pp. 621–648; for the years 2009–2012, *Congress and the Nation Vol. XIII,* pp. 497–512.

Congressional Appropriations for Section 8 Tenant-Based Rental Assistance

HUD tenant-based assistance provides vouchers that very-low-income families can apply toward rent. These serve the most economically vulnerable families in the country, HUD says, and represent the biggest share of HUD's budget.

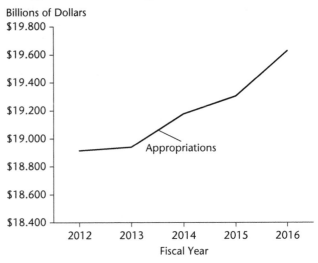

SOURCE: U.S. Department of Housing and Urban Development, https://www.hud.gov/budget/additional.

In 2013, the number of households using those vouchers went up to 2.386 million. But in 2014, the number dropped to 2.166 million. Increases over a longer time frame "lagged far behind growth in the number of renters with very low incomes, the group typically eligible for subsidies," said a report from the Joint Center for Housing Studies of Harvard University. "Between 1987 and 2015, the number of very low-income renters grew by 6 million while the number assisted rose only 950,000, reducing the share with assistance from 29 percent to 25 percent."

Congress used an omnibus spending bill in late 2015 to infuse $2 billion into a different housing-related program. Called the Hardest Hit Fund, this program provided grants from the Treasury Department to state and local housing-finance and counseling agencies. The agencies then extended the money as loans or used it for counseling, advice, and refinancing guidance for residents staving off foreclosure. The Hardest Hit Fund grew out of the 2008

Troubled Asset Relief Program, or TARP, created under the Bush administration to help banks and auto manufacturers during the financial crisis. The Obama administration expanded TARP in 2010 to help homeowners. The omnibus spending bill in 2015 then extended TARP's Hardest Hit Fund to cover more home demolitions in areas with high rates of abandoned housing.

The idea of bulldozing homes may have sounded like an odd way to help homeowners. But housing groups and lawmakers from Michigan and Ohio, leading the push, said that by demolishing abandoned, blighted buildings and creating green space and plots for redevelopment, they could prevent further drops in home values. Falling home values had been a factor during the crisis, when owners found themselves "underwater," owing more on their mortgages than their homes were worth. This heightened the temptation for some to just walk away. Demolition of abandoned homes could stop the cycle, proponents said.

Chronology of Action on Housing and Urban Aid

2013–2014

With no immediate housing crisis to deal with, Congress found little urgency to push for new or expanded housing programs. It wasn't that the legislative climate for housing and urban development at the start of the 113th Congress was totally conducive to lethargy. But partisan political differences and discomfort within the housing and mortgage industries made it difficult to advance bills sponsored by Republicans who wanted to end or dramatically pare back the government's role in supporting Fannie Mae and Freddie Mac. Obama supported a bipartisan plan to keep a government backstop in the mortgage-financing industry while forcing greater liability on mortgage-finance investors, but some Democrats said they worried lower-income households would find it harder to buy houses. The bills never advanced to the full chambers of the House or Senate. In the end, instead of passing major housing legislation, lawmakers in the 113th Congress used the appropriations process to make relatively minor adjustments in funding for housing programs that help lower-income residents.

Housing Finance

BACKGROUND

The Federal National Mortgage Association (Fannie Mae) and the Federal Home Loan Mortgage Corporation (Freddie Mac) serve to provide cash and liquidity for the mortgage market. They assure that banks and mortgage companies have money to lend to people who want to buy homes. Their origin dates to the Great Depression, when Congress and the Franklin D. Roosevelt administration responded to a wave of foreclosures by establishing the Federal Housing Administration (FHA) to insure mortgages and Fannie Mae (then the National Mortgage Association of Washington, now the Federal National Mortgage Association) to stimulate lending by buying mortgages from lenders.

The FHA transformed the mortgage industry and made financing available and affordable for more people by requiring relatively long terms and fixed rates for the loans it covered. Fannie Mae, which became a shareholder-owned company in the late 1960s, provided lenders with the cash they needed to originate more mortgages. Congress in 1970 created Freddie Mac, as a private corporation, to provide additional liquidity and stability to the market. Congress's intent seemed to pay off, with home-ownership among families reaching 69.2 percent by 2004.

Fannie Mae and Freddie Mac did not directly give loans to home buyers. But they assured that banks and mortgage companies had the money to issue mortgages by agreeing to purchase or hold some of the lenders' obligations, guaranteeing payment to the lenders in case of losses, and selling some mortgages in batches to subsequent investors. As long as mortgage delinquencies stayed low, each party generally benefitted. Fannie Mae and Freddie Mac typically have required higher creditworthiness thresholds for borrowers than those in the packagers of subprime-backed securities pushed by investment houses. Yet they, too, were affected by the housing crisis because as subprime lending spread, Fannie and Freddie took on more risk, too, and suffered losses before their rescue.

At the time of the housing crisis, Fannie Mae and Freddie Mac were holding billions of dollars' worth of problematic mortgages. To stave off a collapse, the federal government created a new regulator, the Federal Housing Finance Agency, and put Fannie and Freddie under a conservatorship, a method of taking authority over the companies in order to assure they survived. The companies and their officers gave up certain control and autonomy in the interest of preserving and conserving their operations and missions. As part of the arrangement, the government loaned them money, to be paid back with interest. By 2013, Fannie and Freddie had repaid their $187.5 billion bailout and were pouring additional billions of dollars into the Treasury through dividends. But while they seemingly were flush with cash, Fannie and Freddie could build no capital to weather future problems because of the way the bailout had been structured.

JULIAN CASTRO CONFIRMED AS HOUSING SECRETARY

The brothers heard the joke a lot and sometimes told it themselves. Identical twins Julian and Joaquin Castro were so hard to tell apart they could fool people at political events. Both were in politics and public life. Once when Julian was on the city council of San Antonio, Texas, but running for mayor, he had a scheduling conflict, so his brother, then a Texas state representative, walked in a parade and waved. Onlookers assumed it was Julian, although the then-mayoral hopeful and eventual HUD secretary told the Associated Press that he and his brother weren't trying to fool anyone.

Joaquin, born one minute after Julian, got to Washington first, elected as a congressman in 2012. Julian was San Antonio mayor by then, winning the office in 2009. When President Obama made a multistep change in the White House, naming then-housing secretary Shaun Donovan to budget director after moving then-budget director Sylvia Mathews Burwell to head the Department of Health and Human Services, he tapped Julian, then 39, to be the nation's sixteenth housing secretary.

The president made the announcement of his new housing secretary on May 23, 2014. The Senate confirmed Castro, 71–26, on July 9.

Julian Castro had been a rising star with a compelling story, heard for the first time by a national audience when he addressed the Democratic National Convention in Charlotte, N.C., two years earlier. He had an undergraduate degree from Stanford University and a J.D. from Harvard Law School, and as he told the audience at the convention, he credited his grandmother, an orphan who left her home in Mexico and moved in with relatives in San Antonio. Her schooling never went beyond fourth grade because she dropped out to work. "My grandmother spent her whole life working as a maid, a cook and a babysitter, barely scraping by, but still working hard to give my mother, her only child, a chance in life, so that my mother could give my brother and me an even better one," he told the convention.

The president recalled that speech when publicly naming Castro as his HUD pick, saying Castro was a young guy and a pretty good speaker who had talked about how America was the only place where his story would be possible. The people of San Antonio, the president said, already knew about Julian Castro's focus "on revitalizing one of our most wonderful cities—planning thousands of housing units downtown, attracting hundreds of millions of dollars of investment." He went on to say that Castro had built relationships with mayors across the country and had become a leader in housing and economic development.

This was not Obama's first attempt to lure the San Antonio mayor to Washington. The *New York Times* reported that the president had approached Castro about becoming transportation secretary in 2012, but the mayor preferred to stay in his position at the time.

Twenty-six Senate Republicans voted against his confirmation to HUD in 2014, a sign of tensions between the political parties over approaches to government. Yet at Castro's June 17 confirmation hearing, the only public criticism came from Republican Patrick J. Toomey of Pennsylvania, who expressed displeasure when Castro declined to formally oppose efforts by officials in Richmond, California, and other cities to use eminent domain authority to seize some delinquent home mortgages.

Toomey urged Castro to ban the Federal Housing Administration from participating in refinancing mortgages seized by municipalities. Using eminent domain was an approach some cities had considered as they coped with the financial crisis of 2008 and the recession that left homeowners with mortgages that exceeded the value of their homes. Castro said he needed more time to get further details on the issue and understand it better. A fellow Texan, Sen. Ted Cruz, R-Texas, summed up why he, like the other Republicans voting no when the confirmation was on the floor, opposed Castro: He wanted the government to wind down its heavy role in housing and believed Castro would continue what he considered to be Obama's overly active approach.

Disagreements over the White House approach would continue through the remainder of Obama's, and thus Castro's, tenure. HUD in 2015 issued a rule, which had been two years in the making, to mandate that cities and states "affirmatively further fair housing" when using federal housing and development money. This required them to use a new data and mapping tool that could pinpoint local disparities in income, race, education, access to transportation, and other potential segregation points or barriers. With the use of this data, applicants for HUD-funded projects then were supposed to incorporate their explanations of how their plans could help eliminate racial and economic disparities.

The White House said this could help achieve the goals of the 1968 Fair Housing Act. "A ZIP code should never prevent any person from reaching their aspirations," Castro said on a conference call with reporters after announcing the rule.

Conservative groups such as Americans for Limited Government said this represented an incursion by Washington into local affairs. Some commentators said it could lead to government-driven social engineering, forcing changes in housing patterns they said had been largely dictated by nothing but free will. Republicans including Rep. Paul Gosar of Arizona tried to block the regulation through

(Continued)

The rescue of Fannie and Freddie was just one action that had been taken in Washington during the housing crisis. For struggling homeowners, Congress had also approved the Hope for Homeowners program (PL 110–289) in 2008 and the related Helping Families Save Their Homes Act of 2009 (PL 111–22). Both measures helped borrowers modify or refinance their mortgages. And in 2012, the Treasury Department amended terms of the bailout and required Fannie and Freddie to pay all future profits as a dividend to the Treasury, providing what the administration said was greater market certainty.

These actions set the stage for congressional debates in the 113th Congress. Some House Republicans said in 2013 that it was time to unwind the financial entanglements with Fannie and Freddie and let the private sector take over. House Democrats, however, were opposed. The Senate discussed relaxing the federal ties to minimize future government risk with Fannie and Freddie while maintaining some form of federal oversight. For his part, Obama laid out a set of principles for legislation during a speech in Phoenix on August 6, 2013. He wanted a limited government backstop and protection of the thirty-year fixed-rate mortgage. "I believe that our housing system should operate where there's a limited government role and private lending should be the backbone of the housing market," the president said at the speech at Desert Vista High School. Phoenix was where Obama had laid out his ideas for helping homeowners after first taking office, and on this return trip, he mentioned how far the country had come. "The storm hit harder here in Phoenix than almost anywhere," he said.

House Action

House Financial Services Chair Jeb Hensarling, R-Texas, and other Republicans on his committee wanted the government mostly out of the mortgage market, although members differed on the best way to do that. Hensarling

was a proponent of free markets, saying the federal role distorted the economy and risked future bailouts. The existing system, he said at a Financial Services Committee markup on July 23, 2013, to discuss housing finance, let "Washington elites decide who can qualify for a mortgage" and forced "hardworking taxpayers who struggle to pay their own mortgages" to subsidize "somebody else's while they are continually on the hook for $5 trillion in mortgage guarantees."

Financial Services Committee member Scott Garrett, R-N.J., introduced the housing finance legislation, the Protecting American Taxpayers and Homeowners Act (HR 2767), the previous day, July 22, 2013, proposing to wind down Fannie and Freddie over five years. The bill would have removed Fannie's and Freddie's federal charters, placed certain assets and liabilities into a receivership entity, and created a National Mortgage Market Utility to facilitate private market mortgage securitization but without a government guarantee. The Financial Services Committee approved the legislation two days later, 30–27, on a mostly party-line vote. All ten amendments offered by Democrats, mostly to keep the government active in housing finance and assure mortgage availability for affordable housing initiatives, were rejected. This included an amendment by Gary Peters, D.-Mich., that would have kept the Fannie and Freddie federal charters alive unless federal officials could certify that the private market had enough liquidity to assure that low-income buyers still could get thirty-year, fixed-income mortgages. It was rejected, 26–31.

Despite its committee passage, the bill faced concerns from the housing and lending industries. They worried that without a federal backstop for mortgage-market liquidity, home buyers could find it harder to get a loan, particularly one that allowed repayment over thirty years. Thirty-year, fixed-interest-rate mortgages are the most commonly used form of home loans that borrowers take out, and they are also the least risky from the borrowers' perspective, according to the U.S. Bureau of Labor Statistics. Tom Cole, R-Okla., said he and other GOP lawmakers wanted to defer to Hensarling's leadership position on removing the government as guarantor of mortgage debt, but they were hearing concerns from the real estate industry. "If I have constituents in the home-building industry, in the real estate industry that are worried, he's got to educate me to a point where I can deal with that," Cole said in an article in *Congressional Quarterly* (*CQ Weekly*) on September 9, 2013.

The House took no further action on HR 2767, although the bill amassed fifty-five cosponsors by the end of 2014. Ultimately, Democrats and even some Republicans worried Hensarling's idea would curb access to homeownership. Their concerns weren't only about helping home buyers. The risks of tampering with the housing market, which accounts for about 17 percent of the roughly $17 trillion U.S. economy, were too great.

Senate Action

At the same time that the House Financial Services Committee was discussing Hensarling's approach, the Senate took a more bipartisan approach. Two members of the Committee on Banking, Housing, and Urban Affairs—Republican Bob Corker of Tennessee and Democrat Mark Warner of Virginia—said they wanted to phase out Fannie and Freddie but establish a government mortgage reinsurance system in their place, with the private sector assuming more responsibility and risk. On June 25, 2013, they introduced S 1217, the Housing Finance Reform and Taxpayer Protection Act, which would create an entity called the Federal Mortgage Insurance Corporation. This would be an independent agency with an explicit full-faith-and-credit federal government guarantee, but it would only pay out on its guarantee on mortgages after a significant amount of private capital absorbed the first losses.

The chair and ranking minority member of the Senate Banking, Housing and Urban Affairs Committee, Tim Johnson, D-S.D., and Michael D. Crapo, R-Idaho, focused on a different bill, the FHA Solvency Act (S 1376). Its goal was to ensure that FHA's single-family programs were financially sound. The bill, introduced on the same day as the Corker-Warner measure, did not focus on limiting FHA's market role or extensively shifting risk to the private sector. But after a series of hearings, Johnson and Crapo on March 16, 2014, unveiled a new, substitute version of the Corker-Warner bill as the legislative vehicle for any further Senate debate and action, thereby uniting the four senators behind a single bill.

The new Johnson-Crapo plan would have eventually eliminated Fannie and Freddie and established a new Federal Mortgage Insurance Corp. It was part of an effort, supporters said, to entice private capital back to the mortgage market. "Our housing finance system is badly in need of reform," Johnson said when announcing the substitute bill. "This proposal includes an explicit government guarantee in order to add stability to the economy, keep costs reasonable for borrowers and renters, and ensure fair access to the secondary market for all lenders."

The senators' plan would have established a type of mortgage-backed security with an explicit government backstop, but investors would be on the line first to put up capital equivalent to 10 percent of the value of the mortgages included in the securities. The proposed Federal Mortgage Insurance Corp. would provide liquidity in the mortgage market and would provide insurance on mortgage-backed securities that met its standards. The company would have been run by a bipartisan board of directors, headed by a chairperson named by the president and subject to Senate confirmation. The company's underwriting standards would have echoed those guiding the Consumer Financial Protection Bureau's qualified mortgage rules. First-time homebuyers would have needed at least a 3.5 percent down payment, while other borrowers would have had to pony up 5 percent.

On May 15, 2014, the Senate Banking committee approved the Johnson-Crapo legislation, 13–9, with some support from members of both parties but too narrow a majority to persuade skeptical Senate Democratic leaders to devote floor time to a 600-page tome that did not readily boil down to campaign-trail talking points—except that it might have made it tougher or pricier to get a home loan. Several of the Democrats who voted "no," including Charles Schumer of New York, Elizabeth Warren of Massachusetts, and Sherrod Brown of Ohio, said they worried about the impact of the bill on the future of homeownership for lower-income borrowers. Some disliked the bill's provisions to scrap Fannie and Freddie's affordable housing goals in favor of a market-based incentive system to encourage lenders to offer mortgages to people with smaller down payments or imperfect credit scores.

Economists and housing advocates also said the bill might increase the costs of home loans, though many argued it was a small price to pay for more certainty in the housing system. The Obama administration supported the bill, however, and press secretary Jay Carney said on May 15, 2014, in a White House statement on housing policy reform that the committee vote was "an important step toward achieving a more sustainable housing finance system that helps protect the American dream of homeownership." The vote, the statement added, "marks important progress toward completing one of the biggest remaining pieces of post-Recession reform of the financial system."

Final Proposals

House members still were not done considering the matter. On March 27, 2014, barely a week after Johnson and Crapo unveiled their revised Senate bill, Maxine Waters, the ranking Democrat on the House Financial

MEASURING POSTCRISIS IMPROVEMENT

The foreclosure crisis drove numerous changes in the nation's housing policy, including new laws and regulations over mortgage finance and new ways of dealing with foreclosed properties. The Hardest Hit Fund's creation and extension was one example, as was the government conservatorship over Fannie Mae and Freddie Mac. Another was a rule from the Consumer Financial Protection Bureau, using its authority under the 2010 Dodd-Frank financial reform act to require that lenders make reasonable, good-faith efforts to determine a borrower's ability to repay a mortgage loan. This became effective January 10, 2014.

Whether because of these changes or for other reasons related to the overall economic recovery, the housing market strengthened significantly during the 113th and 114th Congresses.

Delinquencies and Foreclosures

In the first quarter of 2007, the national rate of delinquent mortgages, or home loans in which no payment had been made for thirty days or more, was 4.84 percent, according to surveys of lenders by the Mortgage Bankers Association, a group that represents the mortgage industry. Three years later, in the first quarter of 2010, the rate more than doubled, reaching 10.06 percent.

Not every home with late payments went into foreclosure, or an attempt by the lender to claim title to the home, evict the occupants, and recover its investment or halt its losses. But in the same quarter that delinquencies hit 10.06 percent, lenders reported that homes in foreclosure represented 4.63 percent of their mortgage inventories, the association said.

Looking at raw numbers rather than percentages, this meant that lenders filed notices of foreclosure on 2.87 million properties across the nation in 2010, according to data from Attom Data Solutions, a firm that tracks extensive real estate transaction information. Not every one of those homes wound up in a bank's foreclosure inventory. Some borrowers were able to make their mortgage payments, albeit late, and some sold their homes or found other arrangements, but

lenders actually repossessed 1.05 million homes in 2010, Attom data show.

By the first quarter of 2013, the start of the 113th Congress, the delinquency rate had come down to 7.25 percent and the foreclosure inventory was at 3.55 percent, the mortgage bankers' group said. And by the end of the 114th Congress, in the final quarter of 2016, the delinquency rate had dropped to 4.80, and the share of foreclosed homes among lenders was 1.53 percent.

In raw numbers, lenders repossessed 379,437 homes in 2016, Attom Data Solutions said. That was a drop of 64 percent from the peak.

The improvement continued into the following years. TransUnion, a credit monitoring company, projected that by the end of 2018, the share of "serious borrower-level delinquency," or those with payments sixty or more days past due, would fall to 1.65 percent. That's a 61.7 percent drop from the 2013 level.

As for "underwater" mortgages, or those in which the borrowers owe more than their home is worth, Harvard University's Joint Center for Housing Studies cited data from CoreLogic showing the number of owners underwater shrank from more than 12.1 million in 2011 to 2.5 million in 2017.

Housing Starts

The economic and mortgage crises were closely intertwined, affecting nearly all facets of housing. One key indicator of change was housing starts, or construction of new privately owned housing units.

In 2005, 2.06 million housing units started construction, most of them single-family homes, according to the U.S. Census Bureau. The number dropped dramatically by 2007 to 1.355 million. By 2009, the number nose-dived to 554,000, and it was 586,900 in 2010.

By 2016, the number of housing starts was up, at 1.17 million. While not back to pre-recession levels, that was close to the number of housing starts in 1992, at the end of a previous, though less deep, recession.

Services Committee, laid down a marker in her chamber with a draft bill, the Housing Opportunities Move the Economy (HOME) Forward Act. She described it in a press release on March 27, 2014, as emphasizing certain principles, including "maintaining the thirty-year fixed rate mortgage, protecting taxpayers, ensuring transparency, stability and liquidity within a new market, and preventing disruptions to the U.S. housing market during a transition to a new finance system." The bill proposed

establishing a lender-owned cooperative to issue government-guaranteed mortgage-backed securities. The framework, intended to ensure that home loans were widely available and affordable, reflected ideas from white papers from the Federal Reserve Bank of New York and the liberal Center for Responsible Lending.

But a trio of other Democrats offered a different House measure. HR 5055, introduced by Jim Himes of Connecticut, John Delaney of Maryland, and John Carney of Delaware on July 10, 2014, proposed to wind down Fannie and Freddie within five years. Unlike the proposal backed by Hensarling, the Republican House financial services chair, their measure would have set up a government guarantee through another entity, Ginnie Mae (the Government National Mortgage Association). Ginnie Mae, an arm of the Department of Housing and Urban Development, already served as the primary financing mechanism for government-guaranteed mortgage loans, such as those issued through the Federal Housing Administration (FHA) and the Department of Veterans Affairs (VA).

The Himes-Delaney-Carney bill would have expanded Ginnie Mae's authority in the private sector. It would have required a 5 percent capital buffer, or first-loss cushion, that private banks, insurance companies, or other investors would have to pay before taxpayers would be on the hook. Ginnie Mae and private reinsurers would then share the remaining 95 percent risk. "To ensure a stable housing finance system, we must move past the current state to a new system that engages more private sector capital and private sector pricing of risk in partnership with an explicit government role in the provision of stabilizing liquidity to the market," Delaney said in a January 16, 2014, press announcement on the legislation.

Neither of the measures received a committee vote. The fact that reform stalled was no surprise. As recorded in *CQ Almanac 2014*, even Himes predicted it when unveiling the Democratic trio's House proposal. "Candidly, I don't imagine that GSE [government sponsored enterprise] reform gets done this year," Himes said. He added, however, that it was important that proposals get a thorough vetting before the next crisis.

MONEY FOR LOW-INCOME HOUSING

The House and Senate appropriations committees cleared fiscal year 2014 spending for the departments of Transportation and HUD in freestanding bills (HR 2610, S 1243) on the same day, June 27, 2013. Yet neither the full House nor Senate moved those bills. Instead, both chambers packed all fiscal year 2014 spending into omnibus bills passed in January 2014, making some comparatively small adjustments to spending for low-income housing programs.

Annual spending bills are particularly important for housing policies because they include funding for multiple HUD programs. The most closely watched top-line appropriations items pertain to the Section 8 housing assistance programs and the Community Development Block Grant (CDBG) program, directly affecting state and local agencies and residents. Section 8 rental vouchers provide rental assistance subsidies for low-income families who live in private units (tenant-based assistance) or in public housing developments (project-based assistance) owned by or in connection with local housing agencies. The CDBG program awards money to communities for neighborhood

Number of Households Getting Any Form of HUD Assistance / Number Specifically Getting Tenant-Based Assistance

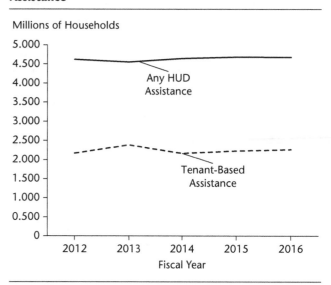

SOURCE: U.S. Department of Housing and Urban Development, Assisted Housing annual datasets, https://www.huduser.gov/portal/datasets/assthsg .html.

improvements, housing, and nonprofit center projects and antiblight efforts.

For HUD, the omnibus (HR 3547, PL 113–76), signed by the president on January 17, 2014, produced a cut of $687 million, for a total of $32.8 billion in new discretionary spending authority. Though less than President Obama's request of $34.9 billion and the Senate spending panel's recommended $35 billion, the omnibus appropriation was higher than the $28.5 billion in discretionary spending for HUD that House appropriators had approved in June. The omnibus cut money for community planning and development by $145 million, to $6.6 billion. But the CDBG program, providing popular grants to state and local governments, got an $82 million boost, to just over $3 billion. The House passed the omnibus 359–67 on January 15, 2014, and the Senate cleared it 72–26 on January 16.

For fiscal year 2015, the House passed a freestanding Transportation-HUD spending bill on June 10, 2014 (HR 4745), that called for $769 million in housing-program cuts. House appropriators said this was necessary because of projections that mortgage insurance premiums paid by borrowers to the Federal Housing Administration were insufficient to cover costs for home mortgage defaults in the aftermath of the 2008 financial meltdown. Reduced HUD spending elsewhere would have to compensate. Senate appropriators offered an alternative, S 2438, making up for the revenue shortfall by cutting nonhousing programs or finding other ways to fund them while still meeting overall discretionary spending caps. Both bills then got caught up in larger disagreements between party leaders over amendments, and the appropriations process stalled. With midterm elections approaching, lawmakers agreed to a continuing resolution, returning later in a lame-duck session to agree on an omnibus, HR 83 (PL 113–235).

The omnibus kept money for Obama's priorities and averted most of the cuts the House had wanted for housing programs. The total discretionary allocation for HUD for fiscal year 2015 was $35.6 billion. Included in that total was a very small increase of about $126 million, or less than 1 percent, for tenant-based rental assistance. Housing advocates said the money would not cover inflation or make up for many, if any, of the estimated 100,000 vouchers lost under sequestration. The omnibus also cut $100 million, or 1 percent, from the HOME investment partnership program, which helps to finance construction of low-income owner-occupied and rental housing.

The House passed HR 83 in a 219–206 vote on December 11, 2014, and the Senate cleared it 56–40 on December 13. The president signed it December 16.

2015–2016

Action on housing in the 114th Congress lacked vigor not only because the mortgage crisis had largely faded. There were also political headwinds as the parties geared up for the final two years of the Obama presidency and a charged 2016 presidential election. Republicans had gained a Senate majority in the 2014 midterm elections and therefore controlled both chambers in 2015 and 2016, but their Senate majority was too slim to overcome Democratic procedural objections. Yet there were notable bipartisan accomplishments.

One was passage of the Housing Opportunity through Modernization Act, which added more home-purchasing options for buyers with low incomes or small down payments. It also clamped down on reported abuses of the Section 8 program by families whose incomes were higher than allowed under guidelines for housing assistance.

Through a spending bill, Congress also extended funding to help the nation's hardest-hit communities deal with stubbornly lingering remnants of the housing and economic crises. This included more money for tearing down already foreclosed, abandoned houses—a blight-fighting effort that housing advocates and industrial state lawmakers said would stabilize neighborhoods and, therefore, stop the slide in home values and underwater mortgages.

Housing Opportunity through Modernization Act

In the last two years of the Obama presidency, the House and Senate found common ground on a measure that low-income-housing groups, lenders, and the real estate industry all cheered. The various sides said the Housing Opportunities through Modernization Act (HR 3700—PL 114–201) would fix a number of problems for home and condo buyers, renters, mobile home occupants, and sellers. "This important, widely supported legislation will expand housing opportunities for first-time homebuyers and low-income rental housing residents, ease restrictions on existing homeowners and landlords, streamline rural housing programs, and save taxpayers money," the National Association of Realtors said in a letter to senators on March 7, 2016.

Both the House and Senate passed the measure without opposition.

BACKGROUND

Blane Luetkemeyer, R-Mo., chair of the Housing and Insurance Subcommittee of the House Financial Services Committee, introduced the measure on October 7, 2015, to modify the United States Housing Act of 1937 and other housing laws governing HUD's Section 8 voucher and public housing programs. The bill also made changes to the Federal Housing Administration's (FHA's) requirements for condominium mortgage insurance and the Department of Agriculture's (USDA's) single-family housing guaranteed loan program. Within weeks of the introduction, Luetkemeyer gained several cosponsors including Democrats Emanuel Cleaver of Missouri and Brad Sherman of California.

The bill's goals weren't all new. The proposed Affordable Housing and Self-Sufficiency Improvement Act of 2012 had attempted to expand renters' self-sufficiency and streamline HUD rules, but that measure failed to win support in Congress.

One of the main objectives of the bill was to ensure that HUD aid flowed to those families with greatest need. Eligibility for HUD programs is generally based on household income. The rules generally vary by program, from 50 percent to 80 percent of a local area's median income, but for the Section 8 Housing Choice program, the family's income in general may not exceed 50 percent of the median income for the county or metropolitan area in which the family chooses to live, according to HUD. Restricting this even further, HUD guidelines state that a public housing agency by law "must provide 75 percent of its vouchers to applicants whose incomes do not exceed 30 percent of the area median income." Subsidies are then set and adjusted based on the cost of area rents.

A problem arose with these guidelines, however, because the law that established them was silent on ongoing eligibility even when annual reviews showed a sharp rise in income. Instead, HUD gave local housing agencies discretion on how to deal with rising incomes. A HUD inspector general's audit, released July 21, 2015, found as many as 25,226 families whose income exceeded HUD's 2014 eligibility income limits—and most of those families had earned more than the qualifying amount for more than a year. As a result, "HUD did not assist as many low-income families in need of housing as it could have," the audit report said. "We estimate that HUD will pay $104.4 million over the next year for public housing units occupied by over-income families that otherwise could have been used to house low-income families."

To remedy this situation, the bill would require housing agencies either to end assistance to families that have earned too much income to qualify for two consecutive years or to impose certain charges. But it also included provisions to safeguard tenants from being penalized in the event of a sudden or temporary wage hike.

Another goal of the bill was to make it easier for condominium buyers to get FHA mortgages. "Condominiums are often the most affordable homeownership option for first-time buyers, small families, single people, urban residents, and older Americans," National Association of Realtors President Chris Polychron told the Financial Services Committee's Subcommittee on Housing and Insurance in prepared testimony on October 21, 2015. "Unfortunately, current FHA regulations prevent buyers from purchasing condominiums, harm homeowners who need to sell their condominiums, and limit the ability of condominium projects to attract resident buyers."

House and Senate Action

The Housing Opportunity through Modernization Act moved swiftly. After being discussed at a hearing of the House Financial Services Committee's Subcommittee on Housing and Insurance on October 21, 2015, the bill was approved 44–10 at a Financial Services Committee markup on December 9, 2015.

"My legislation doesn't include everything I want," Luetkemeyer said at the hearing. "I recognize that it doesn't include everything the minority wants, or that housing advocates want. But it does represent an opportunity to show that despite rhetoric and what goes on around here daily, Congress can work together, and in collaboration with a diverse group of stakeholders, to foster a positive change." The committee approved an amendment by Peter Welch, D-Vt., to change the way low-income families could get subsidies when paying for manufactured homes. Housing-choice vouchers had been limited in the case of manufactured homes to rent of the unit, tenant-paid utilities, and rent for the land the home was on. The amendment, which had the support of committee chair Jeb Hensarling and ranking Democrat Maxine Waters, extended the definition of "rent" to include monthly payments for the purchase of a manufactured home itself and the property taxes, as well as rent for the land. Advocates said the measure could ease the tight supply for HUD housing programs and provide parity between low-income apartment renters with housing-choice vouchers and low-income residents whose decision to live in a manufactured home could save them and the government money.

On February 2, 2016, the House passed the bill in a unanimous roll-call vote. A bipartisan group of senators—Tim Scott, R-S.C., chair of the Senate Banking Subcommittee on Housing, Transportation, and Community Development; Bob Menendez, D-N.J., the top-ranking Democrat on the panel; Chris Coons, D-Del.; and Roy Blunt, R-Mo.—had introduced a companion bill, S 3083, on June 22, 2016. The Senate Banking Committee adopted the House measure on July 14, 2016, and approved it the same day by unanimous consent.

The full Senate then passed it by unanimous consent that day. The president signed the bill, which became PL 113–201, on July 29, 2016.

HIGHLIGHTS

The new law gave more leeway for families to move into subsidized housing units that do not pass an initial health and safety inspection, as long as violations were not life threatening and deficiencies were fixed within thirty days. Conversely, it let housing agencies take money they were withholding from landlords in rent if a property had uncorrected, serious defects and use it to help the family move.

The Housing Opportunity through Modernization Act added a protection for families who might lose their rent vouchers or lose some of their vouchers' value if their family's adjusted annual incomes suddenly rose above allowable thresholds. The same provision, however, would also assure those families could not keep getting subsidies for years on end.

The new law required housing agencies to terminate assistance to families that have been over-income for two consecutive years or charge them the greater of the local fair market rent or an amount equivalent to the public housing subsidy being paid. But prior-year incomes would be measured, not current-year, except in the case of new tenants, so a sudden or temporary wage hike would not prompt an immediate penalty.

Another provision, intended to keep people from gaming the rental-subsidy system, stated that someone with family assets exceeding $100,000 could not get assistance, with exceptions such as one for victims of domestic violence.

The new law allowed for an expansion of Section 8 vouchers for use in buildings specifically owned or controlled by local public housing agencies, with more liberal allotment of these vouchers for homeless families, veterans, supportive housing for persons with disabilities or elderly persons, or in areas where vouchers were difficult to use. HUD policy, law, and annual spending bills had otherwise prioritized tenant-based vouchers, which allow families to use them in any house or apartment with a landlord willing to accept them. With demand for both kinds of vouchers outstripping supply, this provision gave housing agencies more flexibility to help specific tenants.

The law also made it easier for condominium buyers to get an FHA mortgage, often allowing for lower down payments and a federal guarantee against foreclosure loss for lenders. Previous law had imposed a series of restrictions, and not just on the condo buyer. The entire condo complex had to meet certain requirements, including one that said if a condo complex had more than 50 percent renters as opposed to owner-occupiers, a buyer of a unit could not get an FHA loan. Another restriction concerned the amount of allowable commercial space in the complex. These constraints were intended to ensure "that FHA insures mortgages on condominiums only in buildings that are well-managed and financially viable, since broader problems in a condominium building could lead to individual homeowners in the building defaulting on their mortgages," the Congressional Research Service said in a March 3, 2016, report.

The law relaxed some of those standards. It reduced FHA's owner-occupancy threshold to 35 percent unless the FHA ruled otherwise. On October 26, 2016, HUD issued a letter to all FHA-approved mortgagees saying the owner-occupied threshold would drop as low as 35 percent for existing complexes, as long as the complex had adequate reserves for capital and deferred maintenance expenses and

---

HARDEST HIT FUND

Tucked into the year-end omnibus that funded the government through fiscal 2016 was $2 billion extra for a program designed to help keep troubled homeowners from losing their houses through foreclosure. Since its start in 2010, the Treasury Department–run program, called the Hardest Hit Fund®, had provided money to eighteen states and the District of Columbia for temporary loans, mortgage payments, and homeowner counseling. Started by the Obama administration, the Hardest Hit Fund® grew out of the recession-era Troubled Asset Relief Program, or TARP, which provided loans, guarantees, and other supports to financial institutions and the auto industry. TARP was created by the Emergency Economic Stabilization Act, signed into law under President George W. Bush in late 2008 to stabilize the financial system and auto industry during their crisis.

The fund was strictly for states hardest hit in the foreclosure crisis: Alabama, Arizona, California, Florida, Georgia, Illinois, Indiana, Kentucky, Michigan, Nevada, New Jersey, North Carolina, Ohio, Oregon, Rhode Island, South Carolina, and Tennessee, plus Washington, D.C. But the $2 billion addition, approved in the late-year omnibus that passed in 2015, came with a twist. Local and state housing interests would be able to use a large share of the proceeds to buy already abandoned homes, tear them down, and use the cleared property for park-like green space or as land for new homes.

The logic was that once a home is abandoned, it can become a visual eyesore and attract vandals, drug crime, or squatters. This creates blight, and blight brings down the values of neighboring properties. If property values fall because of blight, nearby homeowners may see little reason to make up late payments if they are delinquent and facing foreclosure, since their lower home values can put them "under water," or reduce their values so deeply that they owe more money than they could get even if they tried to sell. Abandoned properties are like dominoes that can fall on entire blocks, advocates in cities such as Cleveland and Detroit said.

Sen. Sherrod Brown, D-Ohio, noted that when a home is foreclosed on or abandoned, it has a ripple effect that lowers the value of neighboring homes. She added that eliminating abandoned properties helps strengthen neighborhoods and reduce crime.

Treasury since 2013 had already allowed some TARP money to go to antiblight demolition. It gave Michigan permission to divert $100 million of its TARP allotment for such a use, and Ohio had gotten $79.5 million. But by 2015, local officials in Michigan and Ohio, and congressional allies such as Brown and Sen. Debbie Stabenow, D-Mich., and Rob Portman, an Ohio Republican, were trying to get more. The foreclosure crisis had subsided in much of the country, but additional remedies were still needed, not only in Ohio and Michigan but also in California, Illinois, North Carolina, and Florida, they said.

As for where to get the money, the Midwesterners said a source existed already: a program within TARP called the Home Affordable Modification Program, or HAMP. HAMP encouraged banks to modify loans for borrowers in arrears. Even with lower payments, however, about a third of borrowers with modified mortgages fell back into default. As criticism of HAMP grew, some in Congress wanted to end the program and use its money for road building and bridge repair. Senate Republicans tried and failed to make that happen earlier in 2015. By the end of the year, they were discussing closing HAMP and using the money for deficit reduction.

Instead, the omnibus that passed in late 2015 transferred the HAMP money to the Hardest Hit Fund®. It required that the funds be used by the end of 2020.

This was not an easy sell. Brown, Stabenow, and fellow Democrats Rep. Dan Kildee of Michigan and Detroit Mayor Mike Duggan talked it up to Democratic members of Congress, and Portman and Rep. Dave Joyce, R-Ohio, lobbied Senate Majority Leader Mitch McConnell and incoming House Speaker Paul Ryan. Dan Gilbert, founder and chair of Detroit-based Quicken Loans, owner of the Cleveland Cavaliers, and a donor to Republican campaigns, worked the phones as well. His business interests included urban real estate and revitalization, particularly in Detroit.

The spending bill passed December 18. Treasury announced it would make awards in two installments, allocating the money among state housing finance agencies and taking into account a state's population, its past use of TARP housing money, its housing market needs, and its success in acquiring titles and razing properties to date. The money would go for demolition and land acquisition or help for struggling borrowers, depending on each state's application and Treasury's acceptance or rejection of its justification.

could provide at least three years of acceptable financial documents. HUD said the minimum owner-occupancy threshold would be 30 percent for proposed complexes or those under construction.

SPENDING BATTLES

In the year-end omnibus spending bill for fiscal year 2016 (HR 2029—PL 114–113), Congress cleared and the president signed a measure providing HUD with a boost, from $35.6 billion to $38.3 billion in discretionary spending. While that was a 7.5 percent hike over fiscal year 2015 levels, it was below the $40.6 billion Obama had requested.

One area in which the administration and Congress were largely in accord was the Community Development Block Grant (CDBG) program. The CDBG program received $3.1 billion, about $200 million more than the administration requested and in line with fiscal 2015 funding. The program is popular among lawmakers, many of whom are former state and local officials and see the grants as a way to make more funding available to communities and states.

Housing programs, including rental assistance programs for the elderly disabled and veterans, got $11.3 billion, or $930 million above the previous year's spending but $202 million below the White House request. Additionally, public and Indian housing in the bill received a total of $26.9 billion, which allowed federal housing assistance to continue without reductions. It was, however, $1.9 billion less than Obama had sought. The omnibus also contained a provision barring the administration from making any changes to the federal conservatorship of Fannie Mae and Freddie Mac for the next two years unless Congress first acted on an overhaul.

Appropriators the following year were initially concerned by a preliminary Congressional Budget Office estimate that Federal Housing Administration receipts to HUD would be down more than $2 billion in fiscal 2017. Those receipts include up-front fees and monthly premiums that borrowers with FHA-backed mortgages pay to the agency for insurance against default. If a homeowner defaults on an FHA-backed loan, HUD in turn must pay the lender. While such payments are expenses, not receipts, factors that can reduce receipts include lower interest rates, which can tempt some new homebuyers to forgo FHA loans and can prompt those with existing FHA loans to refinance with lower mortgage rates elsewhere. Either way, that means fewer up-front payments and monthly premiums to FHA. At the same time, rising rents threatened to affect the 5.5 million households receiving rental assistance. But a revised CBO estimate in March found that FHA's Mutual Mortgage Insurance Program and the Government National Mortgage Association's mortgage-backed securities program had higher receipts than estimated. "Higher CBO projections from an appropriations perspective are helpful. They make it easier to

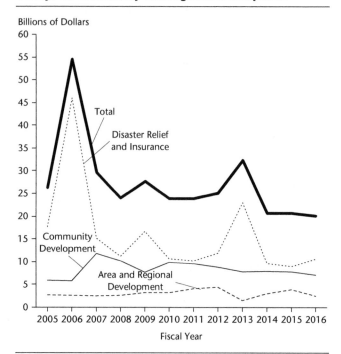

Outlays for Community and Regional Development

SOURCE: Office of Management and Budget, *Historical Tables, Budget of the United States Government: Fiscal Year 2018* (Washington, DC: U.S. Government Printing Office, 2018), Table 3.2.

spend money," said Ethan Handelman, vice president for policy and advocacy at the National Housing Conference, a housing advocacy group.

On April 21, the Senate Appropriations Committee, 30–0, approved the $56.5 billion transportation-housing bill, with $39.2 billion specifically for HUD. On May 19, the full Senate passed the bill (S 2844), 89–8, after packaging it with a Military Construction–VA spending measure that also had $1.1 billion in emergency funding to combat the mosquito-borne Zika virus.

One day before the Senate vote, appropriators on the House Transportation–HUD subcommittee gave voice vote approval to a $58.2 billion transportation-housing bill. The subcommittee included $38.7 billion for HUD, $500 million less than Senate appropriators allocated but $384 million more than the fiscal 2016 enacted level. Mario Diaz-Balart, R-Fla., chair of the subcommittee, said there would be enough funding for "providing a HUD housing option to all current assisted families," *CQ News* reported on May 18, 2016. The subcommittee's ranking Democrat, David E. Price of North Carolina, said HUD's Homeless Assistance Grants program would receive $237 million more than the previous year's enacted level, which would provide a "significant boost to local anti-homelessness efforts across the country," *CQ News* said.

The House Appropriations Committee approved the bill (HR 5394) on May 24 by voice vote. But unlike the Senate version, the House measure never got a floor vote. The appropriations process ground to a halt in the summer amid partisan differences as well as battles between different factions of the Republican caucus. The coming presidential election in the fall only heightened tensions.

Congress in 2016 wound up passing two continuing resolutions, keeping government departments and agencies operating at existing levels. The first ran from October 1 (the start of fiscal 2017) through the end of December 2016, and the second extended funding until April 28, 2017, when a new Congress would have responsibility. The latter bill allowed flexible apportionment for the HUD tenant-based rental assistance to renew grants for rental assistance and to cover certain administrative costs.

CHAPTER 12

Labor and Pensions

Labor and Pensions

As the 113th Congress prepared to open at the start of President Barack Obama's second term, the nation's economy showed hints of recovery from the long recession that had started in December 2007. The nation's leaders hoped economic improvement would continue but initially sought ways to expedite that recovery for U.S. workers and businesses. However, partisan differences blocked progress on many of Obama's priorities.

The unemployment rate, which had peaked at 10.1 percent in October 2009, was 7.9 percent in January 2013. But that rate had not budged since September 2012, and President Obama pointed to the 4.7 million long-term unemployed workers who he said needed further financial assistance, improved benefits, and job retraining opportunities.

Democrats could achieve only limited, if any, success on such priorities in the face of Republican control of the House in the 113th Congress. Their prospects dimmed further with the GOP takeover of the Senate following the 2014 midterm elections and the looming 2016 presidential election.

Congress in early 2013 agreed to a one-year extension of long-term unemployment benefits, but Republicans blocked any further extensions. An improving employment picture—with unemployment dropping to 6.7 percent by February 2014—ultimately sapped any momentum among Democrats. Meanwhile, members had turned their attention to debates on job training, income inequality, the minimum wage, faltering worker pension plans, and other unrelated matters.

Both parties had long called for a rewrite of federal workforce training programs. Each chamber advanced its own bill in 2013 and in 2014 passed a bill overhauling and reauthorizing federal workforce training programs.

But Republicans and Democrats could not come to terms on proposals to boost the federal minimum wage, strengthen a law barring wage discrimination, boost overtime pay and sick leave, and address several other worker benefits. Congressional debate highlighted stark political views on how to expedite the economic recovery and serve business interests while protecting workers.

Objecting to Democratic priorities, Republicans blocked confirmation for several of Obama's executive branch nominees. Nominees for the National Labor Relations Board, which oversaw union elections and evaluated charges of unfair labor practices, were among those blocked by Republican filibuster, leading to a drawn-out fight in Congress and the courts. A bipartisan agreement ultimately allowed nominations to move forward, but ultimately Senate Democratic leaders changed a Senate rule to make it easier for senators in the future to end such filibusters on nominations.

Meanwhile, the House and Senate during the 113th Congress separately made progress on measures to revamp the visa programs for temporary foreign workers, aiming to address concerns of employers looking for seasonal or high-tech employees. But the two chambers

REFERENCES

Discussion of labor and pension policy for the years 1945–1964 may be found in *Congress and the Nation Vol. I,* pp. 565–657, 1220–1272, 1289–1320; for the years 1965–1968, *Congress and the Nation Vol. II,* pp. 601–622, 734–743, 745–778; for the years 1969–1972, *Congress and the Nation Vol. III,* pp. 605–621, 703–742; for the years 1973–1976, *Congress and the Nation Vol. IV,* pp. 403–432, 681–713; for the years 1977–1980, *Congress and the Nation Vol. V,* pp. 231–251, 399–425; for the years 1981–1984, *Congress and the Nation Vol. VI,* pp. 643–672; for the years 1985–1988, *Congress and the Nation Vol. VII,* pp. 687–709; for the years 1989–1992, *Congress and the Nation Vol. VIII,* pp. 703–738; for the years 1993–1996, *Congress and the Nation Vol. IX,* pp. 653–675; for the years 1997–2000, *Congress and the Nation Vol. X,* pp. 571–585; for the years 2001–2004, *Congress and the Nation Vol. XI,* pp. 563–578; for the years 2005–2008, *Congress and the Nation Vol. XII,* pp. 651–671; for the years 2009–2012, *Congress and the Nation Vol. XIII,* pp. 515–544.

Outlays for Social Security

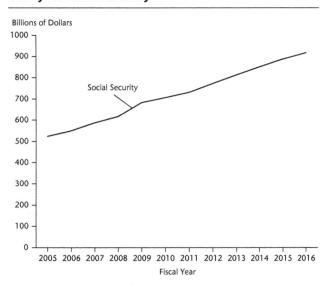

Billions of Dollars

Social Security

Fiscal Year

SOURCE: Office of Management and Budget, *Historical Tables, Budget of the United States Government: Fiscal Year 2018* (Washington, DC: U.S. Government Printing Office, 2018), Table 3.2.

NOTE: Total line includes expenditures not shown separately.

were unable to move a final bill. In the following Congress, Republicans temporarily expanded the cap for some nonagricultural guest worker visas and made it easier for employers to use the H-2B seasonal worker visa program.

On another front, the House and Senate in 2014 passed a measure that aimed to protect faltering multiemployer pension plans and bolster the Pension Benefit Guarantee Corporation, which was supposed to protect employer-provided retirement accounts but was expected to see a high deficit in the coming decade. The new law allowed some plans to reduce participants' benefits if necessary to remain solvent and increased the premiums that companies paid to the PBGC.

In 2016, Congress provided funding to provide a four-month extension on coalminers' health care plans, as the fund that financed their pensions and health care had run out of money.

Chronology of Action on Labor and Pensions

2013–2014

At the start of 2013, the unemployment rate remained stagnant at 7.9 percent, and lawmakers moved swiftly to grant a one-year extension of benefits for long-term unemployed workers—even before the new session of Congress began. Democrats wanted to further those extensions, but Republicans felt workers had been provided enough assistance and feared the benefits were discouraging many from even trying to return to work. By August, the rate had dropped slightly to 7.3 percent and continued to gradually decline. The improved figures forced Democrats to drop the issue and turn to other legislative priorities.

Republicans were more agreeable to renewing federal job training programs, which had not been reauthorized for a decade. Congress in 2014 passed a bipartisan renewal of the program that consolidated some duplicative programs, overhauled Job Corps, and heightened the level of job training for certain workers.

But during the 113th Congress, Republicans blocked Democratic measures to boost the minimum wage and strengthen the federal prohibition on gender-based wage discrimination.

Senate Majority Leader Harry Reid, D-Nev., failed to muster the sixty votes necessary to overcome GOP filibusters of those bills and others. The House, meanwhile, passed a measure that would allow workers to offer compensatory time off rather than overtime pay, but the Senate never considered the bill.

The Senate passed a comprehensive immigration overhaul measure that included several provisions aimed at easing restrictions on visas for foreign high-tech workers and agricultural and seasonal workers. The House never drafted an immigration reform bill, but the Judiciary committee passed separate measures that included visa provisions similar to those in the Senate's immigration bill but which were never considered on the House floor.

Throughout the session, fierce partisan debate and procedural maneuvering also slowed the confirmation of several of Obama's executive-branch nominees, particularly those for the National Labor Relations Board. Republicans had long criticized the board as too biased in favor of labor unions and refused to act on the nominees. President Obama chose to place his nominees on the board while the Senate was in recess, further fueling the partisan debate. Republicans and Democrats ultimately compromised on the nominations. Shortly afterward, the Supreme Court ruled that the president did not have constitutional authority to make appointments while the Senate was in recess.

The 113th session also saw quick passage of a law that aimed to allow certain employer pension plans—many of which were threatening to falter as a result of the economic recession—to reduce benefits for retirees in order to keep their plans solvent.

Unemployment Compensation

Congress in January 2013 provided a one-year extension of a federal benefits program for long-term unemployed workers who were still struggling to find jobs as the Great Recession that began in 2007 subsided. But lawmakers allowed the long-term assistance programs, mostly initiated in 2008, to lapse after 2013 as Republicans pointed to dropping unemployment numbers and increasingly criticized such programs for not incentivizing the unemployed to return to work.

In January 2013, 4.7 million long-term unemployed workers accounted for 38.1 percent of the unemployed. Democrats called for an extension of long-term unemployment assistance that was set to expire after January 2. They focused on two programs: the Emergency Unemployment Compensation program and the Extended Benefits Program.

The Emergency Unemployment Compensation program (PL 110–252), created by Congress at the start of the recession in 2008, provided benefits for workers who had been unemployed for more than the twenty-six weeks covered by state-based unemployment programs. After exhausting the six months of state benefits, workers who were still unemployed could receive up to forty-seven weeks of assistance from the federal program, depending on the state's unemployment rate.

Congress had renewed the program several times over the previous five years, but during the 113th Congress,

SECRETARY OF LABOR

President Obama's second secretary of Labor, Thomas E. Perez, maintained a tense relationship with Republicans, who believed he too strongly favored labor unions and immigrants and, as an assistant U.S. attorney general, had too vigorously and improperly enforced civil rights laws. Republicans fought against a series of new Labor Department rules and regulations addressing workers' wages, sick leave and overtime pay, union activity, and prosecution of worker safety violations.

Announcing Perez's nomination to replace Hilda Solis, who had resigned on January 22, President Barack Obama said March 17, 2013, "Like so many Americans, Tom knows what it's like to climb the ladder of opportunity . . . He's the son of Dominican immigrants. He helped pay his way through college as a garbage collector and working at a warehouse. He went on to become the first lawyer in his family. So his story reminds us of this country's promise."

Perez's parents had emigrated to the United States from the Dominican Republic and settled in Buffalo, New York, where he was born. He earned degrees in international relations and political science at Brown University then a law degree and master's in public policy from Harvard University.

In the late 1990s, he served as special counsel to the late Sen. Edward M. Kennedy, D-Mass. He later served as director of the Office for Civil Rights at the Health and Human Services Department under President Bill Clinton. He was the first Latino elected to the Montgomery County Council, and he served as secretary of Maryland's Department of Labor, Licensing and Regulation, where he crafted an overhaul of lending practices that addressed the state's foreclosure crisis.

Many Republicans opposed the nomination of Perez, who at the time was serving as assistant attorney general for civil rights in the Justice Department. Sen. Charles E. Grassley, R-Iowa, ranking member of the Senate Judiciary Committee, had been heading a GOP investigation into an alleged deal between the Justice Department and the city of

St. Paul, Minn., that led the city to withdraw from a lending discrimination case before the Supreme Court. The investigation also led the federal government to agree not to join a pair of housing-related False Claims Act lawsuits against the city.

"It's hard to believe that the president would nominate somebody at the heart of a congressional investigation and so deeply involved in a controversial decision to make a shady deal with the city of St. Paul, Minnesota," Grassley said in a statement on March 10, 2013. "Not to mention the fact that he'd be handed the keys to the whistleblower kingdom at the Labor Department. I shudder to think how whistleblowers will be treated in the Labor Department if this quid pro quo with St. Paul is any indication of Mr. Perez's approach to this important area of law."

While working at the Justice Department, Perez had raised Republican ire for his prosecution of several cases.

Perez was the first Democrat since passage of the 1965 Voting Rights Act to oversee the state redistricting process, and he worked to crack down on police misconduct in many cities. His division charged Joe Arpaio, Republican sheriff of Maricopa County, Ariz., with racial profiling.

Many Democrats, unions, and Hispanic advocacy organizations supported Perez's nomination. Perez also was known to advocate for rights for illegal immigrants and to support laws mandating higher wages for U.S. workers.

Sen. Jeff Sessions, R-Ala., criticized Perez for his advocacy of illegal immigrants as past president of the board of Casa de Maryland. He said during a press briefing on March 18 that the president, by nominating Perez as Labor secretary, "has placed his drive to promote his flawed immigration policies over the needs of the millions of unemployed Americans."

In 2012, Perez had helped challenge voter identification laws in Florida, South Carolina, Texas, and other states. Many Democrats said those laws could restrict minority voting rights, but Republicans said they would protect elections from fraud.

Republicans increasingly argued the extra assistance only incentivized workers to stay home rather than seek a job, and Republicans wanted to end the program.

The Extended Benefits program (PL 91–373), which Congress created in 1970, offered additional weeks of benefits for unemployed workers if they lived in a state with an unemployment rate higher than certain thresholds.

On January 1, before the start of the 113th Congress, the House and Senate renewed long-term unemployment assistance for one year as part of a measure (HR 8) that

aimed to avert a so-called fiscal cliff, or economic decline, caused by rising taxes and declining spending. The Senate passed the bill on January 1 by a vote of 89–8, and the House cleared the bill, by a 257–167 vote, on the same day. The president signed the bill into law (PL 112–240) on January 2.

The law extended benefits through December 31 and maintained the same structure and requirements as approved in an extension passed the previous February (PL 112–96). That law imposed job-search requirements on beneficiaries

Sen. David Vitter, R-La., vowed to block Perez's nomination until Attorney General Eric H. Holder Jr. responded to a letter Vitter sent him in November 2011 requesting information about the department's enforcement of the National Voter Registration Act of 1993. Vitter said news reports indicated Perez's division in the Justice Department aggressively enforced a provision in the law that aimed to encourage welfare recipients to register to vote but neglected to enforce a provision that sought to prevent the registration of individuals—such as convicted felons—who were ineligible to vote. The Justice Department responded to Vitter with a letter that pointed to a March 12 Office of Inspector General report that refuted the allegations.

During a tense confirmation hearing April 16, 2013, Republicans on the Senate Health, Education, Labor and Pensions Committee further questioned Perez about his work at the Justice Department.

But Democrats defended Perez. "You can make all kinds of allegations . . . but they have no professional conduct rule, no court decision, no bar ethics opinion, no secondary authority that supports their allegations," committee chair Tom Harkin, D-Iowa, said during the hearing.

The committee's vote on the confirmation was repeatedly delayed, while Senate Majority Leader Harry Reid, D-Nev., vowed to bring the nomination to the floor. The committee ultimately approved the nomination, 12–10, in a party-line vote on May 16, 2013. But the nomination still faced a potential filibuster on the floor.

A bipartisan deal on a handful of nominations, including that of Perez and two nominees for the National Labor Relations Board, paved the way for a floor vote. The Senate on July 18, 2013, confirmed Perez's nomination by a vote of 54–46.

Over the next four years, Perez issued a series of Labor Department rules and regulations addressing wages, sick days, overtime pay, and union activity. In 2015, the administration also increased by 78 percent the maximum penalties for violations of Occupational Safety and Health Administration standards. Republicans opposed most of the regulations, saying they would harm businesses and ultimately workers.

Perez faced heavy GOP criticism for a 2015 rule on overtime pay, which would expand overtime protection and pay to workers making up to $47,892, almost double the existing level of $23,660.

In March 2016, House Republicans warned Perez they were closely watching his department's actions as it formulated new rules affecting businesses and the workplace.

"The department's my-way-or-the-highway approach will not deliver the lasting positive change working families and job creators need to move this country forward," said Rep. John Kline, R-Minn., chair of the labor committee. Republicans also questioned Perez about the Labor Department's proposed rule to expand the types of retirement investment advice covered by regulations.

The rule, finalized in April 2016, aimed to close a loophole in existing law in which broker-dealers were not held to a fiduciary standard of serving their client's interest. Instead, they were held to a lesser standard of recommending investments that may be appropriate but not necessarily the best option for the client. The rule applied to plans such as 401(k) plans that offered tax advantages. The administration estimated investors were losing about $17 billion a year in fees when they shifted from company-sponsored retirement plans to individual retirement accounts with higher fees.

Perez said the rule aimed to address current circumstances in which individuals were more in charge of managing their retirement funds. But Republicans such as Rep. Phil Roe, R-Tenn., warned the rules could increase the cost of doing business with financial advisers, making their services too expensive for lower- and middle-income workers. Several efforts in Congress to block or overturn the rule failed.

Perez served during Obama's entire second term and in 2016 was an active campaigner for Democratic presidential candidate Hillary Clinton and was one of her potential vice presidential picks. After Clinton chose Sen. Tim Kaine, D-Va., as her running mate, Perez turned his sights to the chairmanship of the Democratic National Committee.

and authorized states to mandate drug tests for beneficiaries whose employment had been terminated for unlawful drug use. The law also extended unemployment benefits for railroad workers through December 31.

LONG-TERM UNEMPLOYMENT BENEFITS LAPSE

Through 2013, the unemployment rate fell almost another full percentage point. Republicans increasingly argued long-term unemployment benefits were no longer

necessary, but Democrats pointed to statistics indicating that 4 million of the 11 million unemployed workers in November that year had been out of work for at least twenty-six weeks. That December, Republicans worked to block Democratic attempts to add another one-year benefits extension to a deal being negotiated to raise discretionary spending caps and limit the effects of the budget sequester.

The federal program for extended benefits for the jobless ended on December 28, 2013, stopping aid for 1.3 million long-term unemployed people.

In January 2014, the Senate took up a bill (S 1845), introduced by Democrat Jack Reed of Rhode Island and cosponsored by Republican Dean Heller of Nevada, which would have restored for three months the lapsed unemployment benefits.

Senate Republicans tried to block the bill until Democrats proposed spending cuts elsewhere to offset the bill's cost. But Majority Leader Harry Reid, D-Nev., rejected that request. He also refused to bring for a vote a proposal by Minority Leader Mitch McConnell of Kentucky for a longer-term extension of broader aid that would be paid for by eliminating the individual coverage mandate under the 2010 health care law (PL 111–148). Reid also refused to allow votes on several other Republican proposals to offset the measure's cost.

With the support of six senators, Democrats overcame a Republican filibuster on Reed's benefits extension bill, voting 60–37 on January 7 to end debate and proceed to the bill. Further partisan conflict on the bill, however, led to another vote to end debate on February 6. That vote, 55–42, failed to achieve the necessary 60 votes to end debate and allow the Senate to vote on the bill.

In mid-March, a bipartisan group of senators negotiated a proposal to retroactively extend payments under the Emergency Unemployment Compensation program and the Extended Program for five months, from January through May 2014. The deal proposed to offset the estimated $9.7 billion cost in part through an extension of customs user fees.

On April 7, the Senate passed the extension of unemployment benefits (HR 3979—originally a House-passed bill that would have addressed emergency service volunteers in the Internal Revenue Code, and a bill that the Senate ultimately used as a vehicle for the defense authorization bill). The vote was 59 to 38. Six Republicans supported the measure.

In the House, Republicans said extending unemployment benefits would further encourage unemployment. "It's supposed to be a temporary program," said James Lankford, R-Okla., chair of the Republican Policy Committee. "How long do we carry this out?" GOP House Speaker John A. Boehner of Ohio would not take up a one-year extension (HR 3545) offered by Democrats, and he refused to allow a vote on the Senate deal, saying it did not meet his test of creating jobs and being fiscally responsible.

The bill languished for months. Near the end of 2014, the jobless rate had again fallen, from 6.7 percent at the start of the year to 5.8 percent in October, and Congress's attention was focused on wage inequality, the minimum wage, and several noneconomic matters.

Workforce Training

One area in which Republicans and Democrats resolved their ideological conflict was in job training, ultimately passing in July 2014 a reauthorization of federal job training programs (PL 113–128) that had expired a decade before.

Both parties had long wanted to rewrite a law that created a series of federal workforce training programs that provided One-Stop Career Centers where job seekers could obtain services and that established state and local workforce investment boards to direct funding and oversee the centers. The law had expired in 2003, but funding had continued.

Both parties wanted to address problems that had been identified with the programs and respond to changes in employment needs in the wake of the recession. But they had difficulty agreeing on how to update the law.

In 2013, the House passed a partisan bill (HR 803) to overhaul worker training activities, and a Senate committee approved a more bipartisan version (S 1356). But the two versions were vastly different, and lawmakers made no effort to reconcile differences between the two before the end of the year.

In 2014, however, the two parties in both chambers negotiated a compromise on the reauthorization, which Obama signed into law on July 22.

House Partisan Measure

House Republicans in 2013 pushed a reauthorization (HR 803) of the 1998 Workforce Investment Act (PL 105–220) that would have consolidated thirty-five of the forty-seven federally administered job-training programs, operated across nine agencies, and merge funding into block grants to states. It also would have required that two-thirds of the members of each state and local workforce board be employers. Workforce boards were where people sought job leads and learned new job skills and where employers sought new hires with specific skills.

Republicans said the bill (HR 803), introduced by Virginia Foxx, R-N.C., on February 25, 2013, would fulfill Obama's request in his 2012 State of the Union address that there be "one program" to replace a "maze of confusing training programs." The Government Accountability Office had found in 2011 that forty-four of the programs overlapped and should be consolidated to increase efficiency. Many lawmakers said the mass of available programs had confused applicants and cost the government money.

Committee Republicans rejected Democratic requests to negotiate a more bipartisan measure and approved the bill in a 23–0 vote after committee Democrats walked out of the markup in protest.

"We viewed boycotting this proceeding as our only alternative after many months of repeatedly requesting bipartisan negotiations and being rebuffed by committee Republicans," panel Democrats said in a March 6, 2013, written statement.

But the Obama administration opposed the bill, which was similar to a job-training measure the House Education and the Workforce Committee had approved the previous year. In a March 13, 2013, statement, the White House said, "The bill would eliminate, or allow the consolidation of, many targeted programs, without providing the critical assistance needed by vulnerable populations."

In its March 13 statement, the White House had said it strongly opposed the bill because it would eliminate many programs that help vulnerable populations. Democrats agreed, saying that by consolidating funding into a single block grant program, the bill would decrease funding for job training efforts that target the homeless, veterans, and workers with disabilities. Democrats also objected to increasing business representation on local workforce boards, saying it would push out union representatives and community college officials.

"This bill is a political product. It puts ideology over practical solutions and evidence-based reforms," George Miller of California, ranking Democrat on the Education and the Workforce Committee, said in a prepared statement March 15 before passage of the bill.

During floor debate on the bill on March 15, 2013, the House adopted an amendment by Foxx to authorize a process for the local or regional boards to be designated as local workforce investment areas within states. Foxx said the amendment would empower local leaders who are "much better enforced and equipped to serve the needs of local job seekers."

The House rejected, 192–227, a Democratic alternative to the bill that would have made it easier for local governments to contract with community colleges to train workers. The amendment mirrored a reauthorization bill (HR 798) introduced by John F. Tierney, D-Mass., on February 15.

The House then voted 215–202 to pass the bill. Only two Democrats—John Barrow of Georgia and Jim Matheson of Utah—voted for the measure, while 14 Republicans voted against it.

Senate Bipartisan Action

Senators Patty Murray, D-Wash., and Johnny Isakson, R-Ga., for months negotiated a more bipartisan measure, which the Senate Health, Education, Labor and Pensions (HELP) Committee approved in July. The bill (S 1356), which the committee approved in an 18–3 vote, would have reauthorized the 1998 worker training law, keeping the structure largely intact but allowing states to submit to the Labor Department a single plan detailing their workforce training efforts and use a single set of performance indicators to evaluate their programs' success. The bill also would have required that business interests hold a majority of the seats on each state and local workforce board to ensure training met businesses' needs.

Before adopting the bill, the panel adopted by voice vote an amendment by Bob Casey, D-Pa., that would have required further reporting by the inspector general and Department of Labor secretary on Job Corps, a program that aimed to prepare students for careers or postsecondary education.

But Senate leaders did not bring the bill to the floor before the end of 2013. The following year, House Majority Leader Eric Cantor, R-Va., called for the Senate to act on the House-passed job training reauthorization bill (HR 803), while the Obama administration took executive action to boost investments in job training programs. In April, the White House announced the Labor Department would sponsor a nearly $500 million job training competition as part of the existing Trade Adjustment Assistance and Community College and Career Training grant program. The White House also announced new apprenticeship programs, including an American Apprenticeship Grant competition funded with $100 million from H-1B visa fees for highly skilled workers. The program would fund apprenticeship models in high-growth job sectors.

Republicans balked, saying Congress and the administration should be consolidating existing programs rather than creating new ones. They increased pressure on the Senate to pass the House bill.

Compromise Reached

In May 2014, members of the House workforce committee and the Senate HELP committee unveiled a bipartisan compromise that would eliminate fifteen of the forty-seven existing programs, including fourteen workforce training programs and one higher education program. It also sought to reduce the size of the workforce advisory boards from forty-three to twenty-two members at the state level and from twenty-three to nineteen at the local level and maintained a requirement that a majority of members represent the business community. The bill also would

- overhaul Job Corps by limiting renewal for chronically underperforming program operators;
- eliminate a "sequence of services" provision that permitted job seekers to obtain more intensive levels of training only after trying and failing to find employment after having received less intensive training;
- allow job seekers to receive the highest level of training for a specific career at an educational institution if the One-Stop Center believed the jobseeker would benefit; and
- specify annual authorized appropriations for each program through fiscal 2020.

The Senate passed, by a 95–3 vote, the new version of the bill (HR 803) on June 25, 2014, after rebuffing two Republican amendments. The House agreed to the compromise on July 9 by a 415–6 vote. The president signed the bill into law (PL 113–128) on July 22.

Job Training Funding

In 2013, the Senate Appropriations Committee on July 11 approved a $783.4 billion funding bill for the Labor, Health and Human Services and Education department (S 1284). It included an increase of $86 million in spending for Labor Department training and employment services grants to states and matched the fiscal 2013 appropriation of $1.7 billion for the Job Corps. But the bill did not make it to the Senate floor, and the House did not mark up its spending bill. As in the previous three years, Congress maintained funding for the department in a continuing resolution that permitted few changes to existing law.

In his fiscal 2015 request, Obama proposed setting aside $2 billion in mandatory funding for new Bridge to Work programs that would allow people to keep their unemployment benefits while accepting short-term work contracts to ease them back into the workforce. He proposed another $4 billion in mandatory funding to create grants to help businesses hire long-term unemployed workers and a $1.5 billion program to create summer and year-round jobs for young workers.

In 2014, House appropriators did not introduce a fiscal 2015 measure, though Democrats offered their own version. Funding was included in the fiscal 2015 omnibus measure (PL 113–235) providing the Labor Department $13.3 billion, less than the previous year.

Minimum Wage

President Obama and congressional Democrats in 2013 renewed their effort to boost the federal minimum wage, hoping that momentum in the states would carry over in Washington. But they were unsuccessful. Democrats were divided on how much the hourly wage should be increased, while Republicans said states should be left to make their own adjustments and raised concerns that increasing costs on employers would stifle job recovery.

The issue also lost some traction when the Labor Department reported in October 2014 that the unemployment rate had fallen to 5.8 percent, the lowest level since July 2008. The Department also reported slight wage growth of 0.1 percent month to month.

Congress had last cleared legislation boosting the minimum wage in 2007, providing increases over three consecutive years and leaving it at $7.25 an hour in 2009. By early 2013, eighteen states had set minimum wages higher than the national minimum wage, and ten states had required cost-of-living adjustments: Arizona, Colorado, Florida, Missouri, Montana, Nevada, Ohio, Oregon, Vermont, and Washington. "States are ahead of us," Iowa Sen. Tom Harkin, chair of the House, Education, Labor and Pensions Committee, said in June, adding that he feared the issue would languish in Congress until the 2014 campaign season began, according to *Roll Call*, a newspaper on Capitol Hill.

In the State of the Union address on February 12, 2013, Obama called for an increase in the hourly minimum wage to $9 an hour. In his fiscal 2014 budget request, he also proposed raising the minimum wage in two steps and mandated annual indexing for inflation. "We have to get wages and incomes rising," Obama said. He said annual increases would boost the wage scale for all workers.

Republicans said such an increase would burden small businesses and other employers and ultimately hurt the economy. House Speaker Boehner pointed to the limited economic growth and the 7.6 percent unemployment rate

at that time. He said increasing the minimum wage would discourage employers from hiring, particularly when added to their cost of employer premiums, beginning in 2014, as mandated under the 2010 health care overhaul (PL 111–148, 111–152). Republicans instead advocated business tax breaks and streamlined job-training programs.

Most Democrats supported a minimum wage increase, although some advocated a higher raise than Obama proposed. Rep. Miller and Sen. Harkin introduced companion bills (HR 1010, S 1737) that aimed to increase the minimum wage to $10.10 in three steps over two years, before annual inflation adjustments began. Their measures also would have raised the hourly minimum wage of those who received tips from 29 percent of the minimum wage (or $2.13 per hour) to 70 percent of the federal minimum wage.

On March 25, 2013, in a 184–233 vote, House Republicans, with six centrist Democrats, defeated a Democratic procedural motion aimed at raising the minimum wage. Republicans also rejected a Democratic attempt to attach a minimum wage increase to the bill aimed at streamlining job training programs (HR 803). Miller's bill (HR 1010) languished in the House in 2013.

Senate Majority Leader Harry Reid of Nevada pledged to bring a Democratic leadership-backed version of Harkin's bill to the floor, bypassing committee, but he did not do so in 2013. On April 30, 2014, Reid pushed Harkin's proposal, but then fell 6 votes short of the 60 votes he needed to end debate and thereby quash a filibuster. Sen. Bob Corker of Tennessee was the only Republican to support the motion to end debate.

In the House, Rep. Chris Van Hollen, Jr., D-Md., on April 9 unsuccessfully pushed an alternative fiscal 2015 budget resolution (H Con Res 96) that would have assumed an increase of the minimum wage to $10.10 per hour. Rep. Gwenn Moore, D-Wis., offered a similar substitute, which also was rejected.

House Democrats in 2014 also pressed—unsuccessfully—for passage of the minimum wage bill in a package with Van Hollen's draft bill to end corporate tax breaks for executive compensation packages that exceed $1 million a year if companies do not raise workers' pay.

The 113th Congress ended without action on the minimum wage, but Democrats vowed to continue to press the issue in the next session.

FEDERAL CONTRACTORS

On February 12, 2014, the White House issued a directive (Executive Order 13658) raising the minimum wage for federal contractors to $10.10 an hour, beginning January 1, 2015. The directive also increased the wage for tip workers to a minimum of $4.90 an hour or 70 percent of the minimum wage for contractors. The executive order said, "Raising the pay of low-wage workers increases their morale and the productivity and quality of their work, lowers turnover and its accompanying costs, and reduces supervisory costs."

COMPENSATORY TIME/OVERTIME PAY

The House on May 8, 2013, passed a measure (HR 1406) that would have allowed employers to offer workers compensatory time off with pay rather than overtime pay. The Senate, however, never followed suit.

The 1938 Fair Labor Standards Act required employers to pay workers for overtime, but the public sector and certain exempt private-sector companies had the option to provide compensatory time off instead.

Rep. Martha Roby, R-Ala., member of the House Education and the Workforce Committee, said current law was "hypocritical" and "unfair" because employers in the private sector had to follow different rules. "Why should government workers have more freedom in the workplace than everybody else?" she asked during consideration of the bill by the House Education and Workforce Committee on April 17, 2013.

Under Roby's bill (HR 1406), introduced on April 9, employers could have offered their employees time off at the rate of 1.5 hours per hour of overtime work. Private-sector workers such as clerical, maintenance, or inside sales workers, could have accrued up to 160 hours of compensatory time (or comp time) a year, and employers would have had to pay cash wages for any unused time at year's end.

But Democrats said the bill provided only employers, not workers, more flexibility. During committee debate on the measure April 17, Miller said the bill would not provide protections for "workers who are fired or see their schedules cut because they refuse to take comp time in lieu of overtime pay."

The president threatened to veto the measure if it reached the White House. "This legislation undermines the existing right to hard-earned overtime pay, on which many working families rely to make ends meet," the Office of Management and Budget said in a May 6, 2013, statement.

The Education and the Workforce Committee approved the bill in a 23–14 vote on April 17. The House passed the bill by a vote of 223 to 204.

The Senate did not act on the measure.

WORKWEEK

The House in 2014 also passed a measure (HR 2575) to increase the work week from thirty hours to forty hours for full-time employees to be eligible for employer-mandated coverage under the 2010 Affordable Care Act. This was one of a number of measures that Republicans pursued to weaken the controversial health care law.

The House Ways and Means Committee had approved the bill on March 26, 2014. The House passed the bill in a mostly party-line 248–179 vote on April 3. The Senate did not act on it.

Wage Discrimination

Wage differences between men and women continued to be a growing political debate among voters and lawmakers as several reports indicated that pay for women continued to lag behind that for their male counterparts in equivalent jobs. But Republicans and Democrats could not agree on whether new legislation was necessary or how to address current law. Democrats could not overcome a Republican filibuster on a Senate measure and ultimately left the issue languishing into the next Congress.

Republicans said the Lilly Ledbetter Fair Pay Act (PL 111–2), signed by Obama in 2009, had fully addressed the issue of pay equity, but Sen. Barbara A. Mikulski, D-Md., and other Democrats said women continued to be discriminated against, earning on average 77 cents for every dollar that a man makes. "This is a disgrace," Mikulski said.

Mikulski, chair of the Appropriations Committee, on April 1, 2014, introduced a bill (S 2199) that would have made it easier to sue employers over allegations of wage discrimination. The bill would have changed the 2009 law so that employers could defend different salaries for a male and female worker only if they could prove the difference was based on job duties and not based on gender differences. Employers who violated pay discrimination rules would have faced lawsuits that could result in compensatory or punitive damages. The bill also would have required the Equal Employment Opportunity Commission to collect companies' data on pay related to workers' gender, race, and national origin. A similar bill had failed on a test vote in 2012.

On April 9, the Senate voted 53–44 against a motion to end debate and proceed to the bill. Without the required 60 votes for cloture—to end debate—the bill could not advance.

Republicans had promised to support the vote for cloture if Senate Majority Leader Reid permitted the Senate to vote on their amendments that they said would create jobs. Their amendments included proposals to repeal parts of the 2010 health care law, approve construction of the Keystone XL pipeline, and bar certain EPA regulations. Reid rejected the offer, and Democrats warned the GOP that inaction on the issue of wage discrimination would influence voters in the midterm elections that November.

Sen. Angus King, I-Maine, said when he voted against cloture that he believed the plan "fails to address the real causes that are driving the wage gap" and that it "could impose substantial burdens on businesses in justifying pay differentials," according to *CQ Roll Call*.

On September 15, the Senate again failed to reach the required 60 votes to end debate and proceed to the bill. The vote was a 52–40 vote, largely along party lines.

Presidential Action

On April 8, 2014, just before the Senate took up the pay equity bill, Obama signed executive actions aimed at making women's pay more equitable to that for men. One executive order required that federal contractors no longer forbid employees from discussing their pay. An executive memorandum directed the Department of Labor to collect aggregate pay information from federal contractors to be broken down by gender and race.

Foreign Worker Visas

Congress during the 113th Congress looked at ways to reform visa programs for temporary foreign workers to balance U.S. employers' needs for a reliable and flexible workforce in agriculture and high-tech fields. They also sought to provide protections for foreign workers and U.S. workers.

The Senate in June 2013 passed an immigration reform measure (S 744) that included provisions that would have eased visa restrictions for high-tech workers. The House, however, never completed a comprehensive bill, and leaders backed away from efforts to move smaller, stand-alone measures to address guest worker visas for both agricultural and nonagricultural workers seeking to fill temporary jobs in the United States.

Some lawmakers had wanted to add protections to ensure the visa programs were not abused while others wanted to ensure employers did not seek visas so they could hire foreign workers for lower pay than they offered U.S. workers.

The focus was on the H-2 temporary worker program, designed for foreign workers filling temporary or seasonal jobs in the United States. The program had been authorized by the Immigration and Nationality Act in 1952 (PL 82–414) and later amended by the Immigration Reform and Control Act of 1986 (PL 99–603) to divide the program into two: the H-2A program for agricultural workers to receive visas no longer than twelve months and the H-2B program for nonagricultural workers to receive work visas for no longer than ten months.

According to the Brookings Institution, about 600,000 visas were given to temporary workers and their families. Particularly during the Great Recession, some lawmakers and other observers had raised concerns that employers were abusing the program to obtain low-wage labor among foreign workers and thereby leaving many U.S. workers unemployed. But many lawmakers, particularly those from agricultural states or districts with high-tech companies, said the visa program was critical to providing much-needed labor that could not be filled by U.S. workers.

Senate-Passed Immigration Reform

The Senate Judiciary Committee approved an immigration overhaul bill (S 744) on May 21, 2013, that would have eased restrictions for H-1B visas for high-tech workers. Provisions regarding the visa, authored by Republican Orrin G. Hatch of Utah and Democrat Charles E. Schumer of New York, would have eased existing requirements that called on companies to recruit Americans for jobs before hiring foreign workers. That compromise, introduced as a substitute amendment to the underlying bill, called on all employers to make "good-faith efforts" to find U.S. workers first but would have imposed higher standards on firms where at least 15 percent of the workers were on visas. Those employers would have had to seek qualified U.S. workers first.

The panel agreed to insert the new language by a 6–2 vote before approving the underlying measure by a vote of 13–5.

The bill would have set a series of annual caps on H-1B visas for high-skilled workers, beginning at 115,000 and gradually increasing to 180,000. The cap would have increased annually only if each previous year's limit had been reached but would not have increased if the unemployment rate in those professions reached 4.5 percent. The provision also would have let visa workers change jobs once their sponsoring employers filed green cards on their behalf.

The committee rejected, 5–13, an amendment by Sen. Grassley that would have accelerated the implementation of a new employment verification system, modeled off the existing E-Verify system permanently authorized under the bill. E-Verify, administered by the U.S. Citizens and Immigration Services in the Department of Homeland Security, allowed employers to check the Social Security Administration and relevant Homeland Security databases for potential employees' employment authorization.

E-Verify was optional for employers to use. Under the bill, employers would be required to use the new system. That mandate would have been phased in over five years.

The full Senate passed the bill on June 27, 2013.

Hours after the Senate approved its bill, Obama urged voters to pressure the House to follow suit. The House did not act on the Senate bill because Republicans said they did not like the Senate strategy.

House Bills

In the House, negotiators from both parties failed to produce a draft immigration reform bill, but the Judiciary Committee took up several related measures that were similar to some provisions of an immigration reform bill moving through the Senate.

The committee on June 18, 2013, approved, in a vote of 20–16, a measure (HR 1773), introduced by Chair Robert W. Goodlatte, R-Va. Goodlatte's bill would have created a new program for agricultural guest workers, called an H-2C visa program, to replace the existing H-2A program and would not have been limited to temporary agricultural work. The bill would have required employers to first attempt to recruit U.S. workers, then file a petition with the U.S. Department of Agriculture explaining their recruitment efforts and worker benefits and wages. To hire a foreign worker, the employer would have had to pay either the prevailing wage rate or the applicable minimum wage, whichever was higher. The measure would have allowed up to 500,000 temporary workers annually.

Under the bill, people residing in the United States illegally and working in agriculture would have been eligible to apply for legal status as temporary guest workers for two years. Those workers then would have had to leave the country for about three months before reentering on an H-2C visa.

Goodlatte said in a written statement released by the Judiciary Committee on June 19, 2013, that the program would "help deter illegal immigration, protect the jobs of

U.S. workers, discourage the exploitation of authorized workers and stabilize industries."

Democrats, however, said several provisions would have decreased wages for foreign workers and would have eliminated requirements that employers grant work guarantees, transportation, and housing, as provided in the Senate-passed bill. They also objected to a provision that would have required employers to place 10 percent of workers' wages in a trust fund, with the wages to be repaid if the worker applied at a consulate or embassy within 120 days of their last day of work.

Democrats said low-paid farmworkers could not afford to have pay withheld. The committee's ranking Democrat, John Conyers Jr. of Michigan, said withholding the workers' pay was cold-blooded. Democrats also objected that the bill did not include a pathway to citizenship for agricultural workers.

Also on June 18, 2013, the committee voted 20–14 to approve a measure (HR 2131), introduced by Darrell Issa, R-Calif., that would have increased to 55,000 the number of visas for immigrants who had graduated from U.S. universities in science and technology fields. Issa's bill also would have added 10,000 visas for foreign entrepreneurs and up to 155,000 for skilled workers in the H-1B program. The bill would have balanced the increase by cutting 65,000 visas available annually for siblings of U.S. citizens and 56,000 available annually under a so-called diversity visa program. Issa said he aimed to make the bill as neutral as possible relative to existing quotas.

Also on June 18, the committee approved, 22–9, a bill (HR 1772) that would have mandated more employers to use a new employment verification system modeled off E-Verify. Under the House bill, mandated use of the system would have been phased in over two years. The bill was similar to provisions included in the Senate immigration measure.

Bill sponsor Lamar Smith, R-Texas, said the expanded use of an employment verification system such as E-Verify would end "the jobs magnet that attracts so many illegal immigrants to the United States." But Democrats said the measure would not provide any recourse for workers whom the system improperly flagged as ineligible to work. Those workers' only recourse would be to file a complaint under the Federal Tort Claims Act (PL 79–601), which would be costly and time consuming.

None of the immigration bills made it to the House floor.

National Labor Relations Board

A decade-long partisan conflict over the role of the National Labor Relations Board (NLRB) during the previous Congress led to a dispute over the confirmation of presidential nominees to the board that, in the 113th Congress, in part led to a change to the Senate's application of the filibuster rule on presidential nominees, as well as a Supreme Court ruling related to presidential appointments. It also resulted in a full board for the first time in several years.

BACKGROUND

The five-member NLRB, created during the New Deal era to oversee union elections and adjudicate charges of unfair labor practices, had for years been the subject of partisan debates that eventually led each party to block the other party's presidential nominees. Between January 2008 and April 2010, only two members were serving on the board, because Democrats refused to confirm GOP President George W. Bush's nominees and Republicans would not confirm President Obama's nominees.

In June 2010, the Supreme Court had ruled that the board's decisions made without a quorum—three members—present were invalid, heightening partisan tensions to find a solution. Those tensions only worsened in 2011 when Republicans opposed an NLRB decision to delay a plan by Boeing Company—which had employed more than half of its global workforce in Washington State—to build an aircraft factory in South Carolina, where lawmakers are less welcoming of labor unions.

The NLRB had filed a complaint that alleged that Boeing had planned to open a nonunion plant in South Carolina to retaliate against the International Association of Machinists and Aerospace Workers in Washington State for previous strikes. Republicans, along with business groups, said the complaint was politically motivated and interfered with the company's ability to do business. Sen. Lindsey Graham, R-S.C., vowed in a written statement released December 9, 2011, that he would block any NLRB nominee "until we get satisfactory answers regarding [the agency's] role in the entire saga." After Boeing promised to build a retooled version of its 737 jet at a union plant in Renton, Washington, the NLRB withdrew its complaint.

In January 2012, while the Senate was on break, Obama granted recess appointments to three nominees, all of whom were employment law attorneys whose nominations had been pending: Democrats Sharon Block and Richard F. Griffin Jr. and Republican Terence F. Flynn. Block and Flynn had worked for the NLRB in other positions, and Griffin was a union lawyer. Flynn's nomination had been pending through 2011, while the other two nominations had been pending for a few weeks.

Republicans objected to Obama's appointments, saying they had been made when the Senate was in "pro forma session," meaning a brief session of the chamber when no votes are held. At the time, the Senate had been holding pro forma sessions every three days—a tactic both Republicans and Democrats had employed to prevent presidents from making recess appointments.

Soon after, three federal courts—the U.S. Court of Appeals for the District of Columbia, the 3rd Circuit Court of Appeals, and the 4th Circuit Court of Appeals—ruled that the NLRB nominations were unconstitutional because they were made without a Senate confirmation vote. The Justice Department appealed, arguing that the D.C. appeals court ruling was contrary to established legal precedent and would severely curtail the scope of the president's authority. The Supreme Court in June 2013 said it would consider the question in its fall term.

Senate Action in 2013

Obama in February 2013 resent to the Senate the nominations of Block and Griffin. At that point, the board had three members, because the term of one member had expired in December 2012, and the other recess appointee—Flynn—had been forced to resign the previous May when the board's inspector general discovered he had leaked documents to Republican political allies.

In April, Obama nominated three more people to the board, including Mark Gaston Pearce, a Democrat who had served as NLRB chair since March 2010 and whose term was due to expire in August. The other two were Republican employment law attorneys: Harry I. Johnson II, who had represented unions, and Philip A. Miscimarra, who had represented businesses.

On May 22, the Health, Education, Labor and Pensions (HELP) Committee approved all five nominees. The nomination of Pearce was approved 18–5 and the nominations of Johnson and Miscimarra were each approved in separate 20–0 votes. The committee approved the nominations of Block and Griffin in 13–9 votes.

But Senate floor action was uncertain, as many Republicans opposed the nominations of Block and Griffin, who had continued to sit on the board after the appeals courts' rulings. Several senators threatened to filibuster the nominations. Senate Majority Leader Harry Reid, D-Nev., said in July that if Republicans blocked votes on any of seven pending presidential nominees (which included those to the NLRB), he would move to change the Senate rules on the filibuster of executive branch nominees so that only a simple majority of 51 votes—rather than two-thirds of the Senate, or 60 votes—would be needed to end debate and move to a vote.

"I am not going to wait another month, another few weeks, another year, for Congress to take action on the things we have been doing for almost 240 years," Reid said July 11, 2013, when scheduling cloture votes on seven executive branch nominees, according to *CQ Roll Call.*

Republicans objected. Sen. Orrin Hatch, R-Utah, said that same day in response to Reid (according to *CQ Roll Call*): "It's going around the time-honored precepts of the Senate, and it's going to cause total warfare around here."

In a bipartisan negotiation led by Sen. John McCain, R-Ariz., Republicans agreed to confirm two NLRB nominees in place of Block and Griffin. The nominees were presumed to be favored by labor unions: Nancy Schiffer, a former AFL-CIO attorney, and Kent Hirozawa, chief counsel to sitting NLRB Chair Pearce. The HELP Committee approved each nomination, in separate 13–9 votes, on July 24, 2013.

On July 30, the Senate approved the nominations of Schiffer and Hirozawa by separate votes of 54–44, and the nomination of Pearce—who would continue as chair—by a 59–38 vote. The chamber approved the two Republican nominees, Johnson and Miscimarra, by voice vote.

The deal temporarily averted Reid's threat to change the Senate filibuster rule, the so-called nuclear option. (However, Reid did follow through on his threat on November 21, 2013, when Republicans continued to block several judicial nominees.)

After Obama withdrew Griffin's nomination to the board, the president nominated him to a four-year term as the agency's general counsel, prompting renewed partisan debate about the board's role in labor union–employer disputes. Sen. Lamar Alexander, R-Tenn., ranking member of the HELP committee, said the board behaved as an advocate more than as an umpire.

Nevertheless, the committee approved Griffin's nomination in a 13–9 vote on September 18, 2013. The Senate then confirmed the nomination in a 55–44 vote on October 29. Labor committee chair Tom Harkin, D-Iowa, said he hoped the general counsel would provide some confidence in the board, as it deals with 20,000 to 30,000 complaints per year from employees, unions, and employers.

Senate Action in 2014

Meanwhile, the Supreme Court had agreed to consider *NLRB v. Noel Canning*, a case in which a small bottling company in Washington State had challenged the board's authority to rule that the company had engaged in unfair labor practices. The company alleged the board had no authority to act with recess-appointed members and therefore did not have an established quorum, meaning it did not have the required minimum number of members present to take official action.

The case was argued before the high court in January 2014. On June 26, the justices ruled unanimously that President Obama had overstepped his constitutional authority by making the three recess appointments of Block, Griffin, and Flynn in January 2012.

On July 14, Obama renominated Block—one of his three 2012 recess appointments—to replace Schiffer, whose term was due to expire December 16. Republicans vowed to block the nomination. In November, Obama instead nominated Lauren McFerran, the labor counsel at the Senate HELP Committee since 2005. The Senate on December 8 confirmed McFerran's nomination, 54–40.

NLRB AUTHORITY

Early in 2013, House Republicans responded to the refusal of Obama's 2012 appointees to step down by passing legislation (HR 1120) to limit the NLRB's authority. Under the bill, the board would have been barred from voting, enforcing decisions, and appointing personnel until the Supreme Court ruled on the appointments or the Senate had confirmed a full quorum of members.

Republicans said the recess appointments were in violation of the Constitution's separation of powers doctrine, which grants the Senate authority to confirm nominees to executive branch positions. Rep. Todd Rokita, R-Ind., said "we are trying to stop the president from abusing the power granted by the people of this country and trampling over the checks and balances that our Constitution very clearly lays out."

Rep. George Mill of California, ranking Democrat of the Education and Workforce Committee, said Republicans caused the recess appointments by filibustering the nominations.

On March 20, the Education and Workforce Committee approved the bill, introduced by Phil Roe, R-Tenn., by a party-line vote of 23–15. On April 12, the House passed the bill in a 219–209 vote. Ten Republicans joined all Democrats in opposing the measure.

The Senate did not consider the bill—which the White House said it would veto—and moved instead to approve the five nominees under the bipartisan deal.

Republicans continued to complain about the direction of the NLRB. Rep. John Kline, R-Minn., chair of the House Education and Workforce Committee, said he wanted to update the 1935 National Labor Relations Act, which created the NLRB and regulated employer–employee relationships.

The House GOP made one other move to limit NLRB's authority by including a provision in the full-year omnibus spending bill for fiscal 2014 (HR 3547, PL 113–76), cleared on January 16, 2014. The provision blocked the board from setting up union votes over the Internet.

NLRB OVERHAUL

Republicans in 2014 initiated an attempt to overhaul the NLRB. Lamar Alexander of Tennessee, ranking Republican of the Senate HELP committee, and Minority Leader Mitch McConnell of Kentucky circulated a draft bill that would have increased the size of the board from five to six members, including three Democrats and three Republicans. Four members would have had to agree to decisions, which Alexander said would encourage some consensus.

"I would rather have a balanced NLRB that is an umpire rather than an advocate," Alexander said in a phone call with reporters on September 16, 2014, according to *CQ Roll Call*.

The bill also would have permitted litigants to take cases to federal court if the board did not take action within a year and would have reduced the NLRB's funding by 20 percent if the board did not act on 90 percent of its cases in a year.

The Senate did not act on the bill before the close of the 113th Congress, but Alexander said the measure would be a priority in 2015 if the GOP regained control of the Senate following the 2014 midterm elections. (The Republicans did win control of the Senate.)

UNION ELECTION RULES

On April 9, 2014, the House Education and the Workforce Committee approved two bills that would establish timelines and appeals processes for union elections and require disclosure of employee information to unions before elections are held. Neither bill was considered on the House floor.

The bills were a response to the NLRB's proposed rule, announced that February and later finalized, to expedite the timeline of union elections and limit the appeals available to employers before an election. The board had voted to implement the rule in 2011 but dropped it after a federal court said the agency did not have a full quorum and therefore its decision was nonbinding.

Labor unions and Democrats said the rule was necessary to halt the practice of employers filing lawsuits before union elections to delay the process. But Republicans said the rule would deprive business owners of their legal right to make their case before elections were held.

The panel approved, 21–14, a bill (HR 4320) that would have required NLRB to hold hearings on disputed elections at least fourteen days after a petition for unionization is filed and would have required union elections to occur at least thirty-five days after filing. It also would have required the board to resolve disputes before certifying election results. The approved measure included an amendment by Tom Price, R-Ga., adopted 21–13, to prohibit "microunions" that are not part of a broader union organization.

The committee also approved, 21–17, a measure (HR 4321) that would have required employers to make available to unions all employees' names and contact information.

NLRB ACTION

The NLRB approved new union election regulations on December 12, 2014, by a party-line 3–2 vote. The new rules required employers to provide union organizers with employees' phone numbers and emails as well as mailing addresses and set new timelines for pre- and postelection hearings; allowed parties to file documents electronically; and eliminated automatic delays of elections for NLRB reviews of regional directors' decisions.

AFL-CIO President Richard Trumka said the new rules would reduce delays in deciding cases, but Republicans and business groups said they were "ambush election" rules.

In the fiscal 2015 omnibus spending measure (PL 113–235), appropriators gave the National Labor Relations Board $274.2 million and continued a policy rider from past years that barred the board from conducting union elections online.

Pension Benefits

Before the end of the 113th Congress, the House and Senate quickly moved to help protect faltering employer-provided pension plans by allowing them to cut participants' benefits.

Lawmakers included provisions in the fiscal 2015 omnibus spending measure (HR 83, PL 113–235) just before it cleared Congress.

The recession had threatened the solvency of many pension plans, as well as the Pension Benefit Guaranty Corporation (PBGC), which had been created by the Employment Retirement Income Security Act of 1974 (PL 93–406) to guarantee workers' employer-sponsored retirement accounts. The PBGC was funded solely by premiums, and because of the economic downturn, its potential liabilities had become greater than its assets as many pension plans threatened to falter.

In 2013, President Obama proposed allowing the PBGC to adjust the premiums it charged companies and take risk into account when setting premiums.

On December 10, 2014, Rep. John Kline, R-Minn., and George Miller, D-Calif., the chair and ranking Democrat on the House Committee on Education and the Workforce, introduced the Multiemployer Pension Reform Act of 2014 as part of the omnibus spending bill for fiscal 2015 (HR 83). Their measure addressed pension-benefit plans that were created by collective bargaining agreements between a labor union and two more employers within an industry.

Many such plans were running out of money as a result of the recent economic recession. The PBGC reported on November 14, 2014, that 200 of the 1,400 multiemployer plans that covered 1 million participants could fail within the next decade. The Teamsters Central States plan, for instance, was nearly $18 million short of what it needed to pay benefits for 400,000 members, the Labor Department reported. Meanwhile, the PBGC itself projected a $42.2 billion deficit for fiscal 2014, compared to the $8.3 billion deficit predicted one year earlier.

The Kline-Miller measure increased the premiums that sponsors of multiemployer plans paid to PBGC to $26 per participant in 2015—up from a flat rate of $12 per participant in 2014 and $13, in 2015. Their measure also required the premiums be indexed to changes in the average national wage, starting in 2016, and changed the PBGC's authority over mergers and divisions of multiemployer pension plans.

The measure also included provisions that allowed multiemployer pension plans—with approval by the Treasury Department secretary and a majority of plan participants—to reduce benefits for existing retirees to keep the pension plans solvent. Trustees of plans near insolvency also could suspend benefits, but not for retirees age eighty or older or those who were disabled. Plan trustees, however, would have to prove to the Treasury Department that the proposed reductions were necessary to keep their plan from running out of money.

Kline and Miller said the measure would help prevent the collapse of failing pension plans and better protect retirees' pensions. But not everyone supported the proposal.

Sen. Ron Wyden, D-Ore., chair of the Senate Finance Committee, said in a written statement released December 11, 2014, that the "last-minute scheme worked out largely in private" produced a "lopsided solution" that would result in reversing "a major tenet enshrined in pension law—never take away money a pensioner has already earned."

Karen Friedman, executive vice president of the Pension Rights Center, said in a written statement released December 17, 2014, "We are furious that without debate Congress has placed the burden of rescuing underfunded plans on the people who can least afford it—retirees and surviving spouses who rely on their pensions for food, medication, and other necessities." The Brotherhood of Teamsters also criticized the last-minute action.

In the House on December 10, 2014, the Rules committee included Kline and Miller's measure as an amendment to the fiscal 2015 omnibus spending bill (HR 83) to be considered on the floor. On December 11, the House automatically folded the amendment into the bill when it approved the rule limiting floor debate by a vote of 214–212. The House then approved the bill, 219–206. The Senate cleared the bill on December 13 in a 56–40 vote.

2015–2016

In the 114th Congress, Democrats continued to press labor-related issues heading into the presidential election. But Republicans again blocked Democratic proposals to increase the minimum wage as well as to give workers more paid sick days and grant employees more control over their work schedules. The Republicans argued such proposals would only stifle job creation, while Democrats argued the GOP was more interested in granting more tax cuts to the wealthiest Americans and rolling back regulations on corporations and ultimately hurting workers.

Republicans, meanwhile, tried to block a new Labor Department rule that would raise the salary limit under which employers would have to pay workers overtime, while several business groups filed a lawsuit to stop the rule. Just before the rule was to take effect in December 2016, a federal district court judge in Texas issued a temporary injunction on the rule.

Meanwhile, Sen. Deb Fischer, R-Neb., made another effort to push legislation focused on eliminating wage discrimination based on gender. The Senate GOP in 2015 backed a budget resolution amendment by Fischer to allow legislation to make it illegal for employers to retaliate against employees who talk about or compare compensation. She then introduced a bill (S 875), but the Senate Health, Education, Labor, and Pensions (HELP) Committee never took it up amid opposition from Republicans, who continued to state that current law already prohibited wage discrimination.

But Congress did make it easier to use the H-2B immigration visa program for seasonal workers and expanded the number of visas for nonagricultural workers. And lawmakers funded a four-month extension for retired coalminers' health care plans that were due to lapse because a benefits fund was depleted. But they postponed discussions on how to provide a long-term fix for the fund that was expected to pay for pensions and health care for retired coalminers and their families.

Minimum Wage

Democrats in the 114th Congress again pushed for a boost in the federal minimum wage, which they had emphasized in the lead-up to the 2014 midterm elections. They hoped that state action over the previous year would help spur movement, as twenty states had raised their minimum wages, effective January 1, 2015, and two more states were preparing to raise their standards later in the year. Overall, twenty-nine states by then had minimum standards higher than the federal standard. But they were unsuccessful because they could not unify behind one plan, and conservative Republicans fought against an increase.

Obama again pushed for an increase in the minimum wage in his State of the Union speeches in 2015 and 2016. "To everyone in this Congress who still refuses to raise the minimum wage, I say this: If you truly believe you could work full-time and support a family on less than $15,000 a year, go try it," he said in his 2015 speech.

Sen. Patty Murray, D-Wash., ranking member on the Senate HELP committee, introduced a measure (S 1150) that would have increased the minimum wage in stages to $12 an hour by 2020. Rep. Robert C. Scott, D-Va., pressed the case from his position as ranking member of the House Committee on Education and Labor. But Democrats largely disagreed over how much to raise the wage.

Conservatives rallied early against the Democratic plot. Sen. Lamar Alexander of Tennessee, the new HELP Committee chair, continued to oppose an increase, saying he preferred to let states set their own minimum wage standards, and many Republicans warned a wage increase could slow job creation. He and other Republicans said they preferred to help low-earning workers through such measures as an expanded earned income tax credit and a broad income tax overhaul. In the House, Education, and the Workforce Chair John Kline, R-Minn., continued to lead opposition to a hike in the federal minimum wage.

Sen. Susan Collins, R-Maine, in early 2015 tried to pick up support for a draft proposal that would raise the hourly minimum from $7.25 to $9 over several years—matching the proposal Obama made at the start of the previous Congress. But GOP leaders said states should set their own standards, and many Democratic leaders wanted to stick with their previous proposal to target $10.10 an hour.

In February 2015, Wal-Mart Stores Inc., the nation's largest private employer, announced it would raise its minimum wage close to $10 by February 2016—matching steps taken by such other major employers as Gap Inc., Costco Wholesale Corp., and Starbucks Corp. Many thought that would propel Congress to act on the federal standard.

In March, Minority Leader Harry Reid tried to rally support for a new proposal by Sen. Murray to raise the minimum wage to $12 an hour by 2020—a plan that drew support from liberal Democrats, such as Barbara Boxer of California, but received mixed reaction. Centrists such as Angus King, I-Maine, and Joe Manchin III, D-W.Va., wanted a more modest increase that GOP members might stomach. Reid tried, unsuccessfully, to have Murray's proposal considered as an amendment to the budget resolution (S Con Res 11).

The Senate did take up a nonbinding budget amendment by Sen. Bernie Sanders, I-Vt., that would increase the minimum wage but rejected it in a 52–48 vote.

AMERICAN SAMOA

President Obama on October 7, 2015, signed into law a measure (HR 2617, PL 114–61) that postponed the planned increase in the minimum wage in American Samoa until December 31, 2016. The minimum level would increase 50 cents every third year after that increase, until it reached the federal minimum wage. Congress had repeatedly delayed a wage increase for American Samoa since 2010.

The House passed its measure by voice vote on September 28, 2015. On September 30, the Senate passed, by unanimous consent, an amended version, which the House subsequently cleared.

PUERTO RICO

On June 30, 2015, President Obama signed into law (PL 114–187) a bill aimed at helping Puerto Rico cope with a $72 billion debt, in part by lowering the minimum wage for some workers.

Under the measure (S 2328), the governor of Puerto Rico was authorized to lower the minimum wage for some young workers and exempt some employers from the Labor Department's new overtime rule. Democrats had vowed to strip the minimum wage and overtime provisions, but Obama signaled he would sign the bill as it was written.

The House passed a version of the bill (HR 5278) by a vote of 297 to 127 on June 9. The Senate passed the measure, 68–30, on June 29, 2015. Obama signed the bill into law (PL 114–187) on June 30, one day before the territory was set to default on a $2 billion debt payment.

HOME HEALTH CARE WORKERS

On August 21, 2015, the U.S. Court of Appeals for the D.C. Circuit approved the Labor Department's 2013 regulations that extended federal minimum-wage and overtime provisions to employees who provide home health care through a third-party agency. The panel said the regulations were a reasonable interpretation of the Fair Labor Standards Act (PL 93–259).

The rules, issued in 2013, removed third-party-agency health care workers from an exemption in labor law. The appeals court ruling overturned a district court decision in December 2014 that said the Labor Department had overstepped its authority.

SENATE FOOD WORKERS

Food workers in the Senate held strikes for more than a year, beginning in November 2014, for higher wages and union representation before winning a new seven-year contract in December 2015 that granted them a nearly $3-per-hour raise. The seven-year extension of their contract lifted the minimum wage from $10.50 per hour to $13.30 per hour.

Employment Discrimination

Congress in 2015 included a provision in its fiscal 2016 budget resolution (S Con Res 11)—a spending blueprint for appropriators—aimed at barring employment discrimination against pregnant workers.

The Senate passed, 100–0, a nonbinding amendment to the budget resolution (S Con Res 11) by Sen. Bob Casey, D-Pa., that barred employment discrimination against pregnant workers and granted them a right to workplace accommodations. The provision was included in the final budget resolution cleared by both chambers.

The issue had come into the public light when a Supreme Court ruling on March 25, 2015, allowed a woman, Peggy Young, to pursue a workplace pregnancy discrimination claim against the United Parcel Service of America (UPS). She sued the company after she was denied a light-duty assignment on her doctor's orders to restrict lifting during pregnancy in 2006. Lower courts had thrown out her suit, but the Supreme Court upheld her right to pursue the claim in a 6–3 decision.

Sick Leave

Several senators sought to require businesses to provide their employees paid sick leave, but a measure introduced by Sen. Patty Murray, D-Wash., never saw action. Obama had pushed for such legislation, and the Labor Department in 2016 issued a rule requiring sick pay for federal contract workers.

On February 12, 2015, Murray introduced her bill (S 497), which would have required businesses with more than fifteen employees to allow their workers to earn up to seven paid sick days a year. The Senate did not act on the bill, but that March, senators did adopt, in a 61–39 vote, similar language in a nonbinding amendment by Murray to the Senate budget resolution.

The vote came on the heels of Obama's call on Congress to provide up to seven paid sick days for American workers. Three states and seventeen cities, including Philadelphia and Washington, D.C., also had passed laws guaranteeing the rights of workers to earn paid sick days.

The Labor Department subsequently issued a rule, on September 29, 2016, that allowed federal contract workers to earn up to seven paid days of sick leave. "Not only is access to paid sick leave imperative, it is also important for public health," Labor Secretary Thomas E. Perez wrote in a September 30, 2016, column on CNN.com.

The rule, scheduled to take effect the following January 1, was estimated to cover about 1.15 million workers and to cost employers about $27.3 million annually for each of the next ten years. Murray vowed to continue to push her legislation, but neither chamber acted on it before the end of the session.

Overtime Pay

House and Senate Republicans scrambled to try to halt implementation of a new Labor Department rule, set to take effect December 1, 2016, that would increase the salary limit under which employees would have to be paid overtime. The urgency subsided when a federal district court judge in Texas imposed a temporary injunction against the rule, leaving the issue to carry over into the next session of Congress and the new administration.

President Obama had told the Labor Department in 2014 to review the salary limit under which salaried employees must be paid overtime for working more than forty hours per week. The White House said the existing limit of $455 per week, set in 2004, was by 2014 below the poverty line for a family of four people. Rep. Mark Takano, D-Calif., said that cap covered about 11 percent of salaried workers in 2014.

In June 2015, the Labor Department proposed rules to increase the pay ceiling from $23,600 to $50,440. Many Democrats supported the increased cap. Sen. Murray supported the proposal in a written statement released June 30: "Without updated overtime protections, big corporations can exploit the rules to avoid paying workers the time-and-a-half pay they've earned, robbing them of money they could put toward groceries, the mortgage, or college tuition."

But many businesses said the changes could hurt their industries. Several Republicans, along with two moderate Democrats—Colin C. Peterson of Minnesota and Brad Ashford of Nebraska—in February 2017 sent a letter to the Labor Department opposing the proposal. They said the rule might encourage employers to move salaried workers to hourly wages or to reduce their fringe benefits.

Republicans also proposed bills in the House (HR 4773) and the Senate (S 2707) to block the rule before the final regulation was issued, but Congress never acted on either bill.

The Labor Department issued the final rule, published in the *Federal Register* on May 23, 2016, which set the limit slightly lower than it had proposed, at $47,476, to embrace an estimated 4.2 million workers. The rule, scheduled to take effect that December 1, would automatically update the salary threshold every three years to remain at the fortieth percentile of full-time salaried workers in the lowest-income region of the nation. Democrats applauded the rule, saying it would boost fair wages for workers, but opponents said it would hurt business and potentially increase unemployment.

Republican Sens. Lamar Alexander of Tennessee and Ron Johnson of Wisconsin on June 7 introduced a resolution (SJ Res 34) to overturn the rule, but their measure was not put to a vote. In the House, Rep. Virginia Foxx, R-N.C., introduced a similar resolution (HJ Res 59), which likewise did not come to a vote.

Rep. Martha Roby, R-Ala., pushed her own measure (HR 465), which was similar to a measure she introduced during the 113th Congress and would have authorized employers to provide compensatory time off to employees at a rate of 1.5 hours per hour of overtime work. But the bill did not see action. Senate Republicans in September started pushing legislation (S 3464) to implement the overtime pay rule incrementally through 2020, but the bill did not move.

Meanwhile, a coalition of twenty-one states, the U.S. Chamber of Commerce, and several other business groups filed a lawsuit, arguing the administration had exceeded its authority in mandating such a significant increase so quickly. They said that the increase would lead to layoffs and reduced hours for workers and higher college tuition and that it would hurt nonprofits.

In November, days before the rule was to take effect, U.S. District Court Judge Amos L. Mazzant III in Texas temporarily halted its implementation, ruling that the Obama administration had exceeded its authority by boosting the overtime salary limit so much. The judge's ruling suggested that the administration lacked the authority even to establish such a salary limit. The judge imposed the injunction until he could rule on the merits of the regulation. By that time, however, many large employers had already raised the pay for some workers above the new $47,476 limit, concluding that would be more cost effective than paying overtime.

The Labor Department said in a statement that the rule was the result of a comprehensive, inclusive rule-making process and on December 1 appealed to the 5th Circuit. Sen. Murray vowed to continue to fight for the rule. She also appealed to President-elect Donald Trump to support it, although Trump had said during the campaign that he was in favor of repealing it.

Secret Service Agents

Congress in 2016 passed and sent to the White House for the president's signature a measure to ensure Secret Service agents received overtime pay for work they did in 2016. The House Oversight and Government Reform Committee approved, by voice vote, on November 16 a bill (HR 6302) to accomplish this goal by increasing the amount an agent could earn in total compensation in one year. The committee had held a hearing the day before in the wake of news reports that 1,000 agents had maxed out their annual overtime pay allowance that year.

The full House passed the measure on November 30, 2016, by voice vote. On December 10, the Senate passed a slightly amended version of the bill by unanimous consent, which the House cleared on December 14. The president signed the measure into law (PL 114–331) on December 16, 2016.

H-2B Immigrant Visas

The omnibus spending bill (PL 114–113) that Congress cleared on December 18, 2015, included provisions to make it easier for employers to use the H-2B seasonal worker visa program and expanded the number of nonagricultural guest workers permitted. The provisions sought to temporarily relieve a years-long debate over Labor Department rules governing the program.

The bill temporarily—through September 2016—expanded the number of visas for foreign guest workers for nonagricultural, seasonal jobs such as landscaping, hotel, and restaurant services. Republicans opposing the bill said the domestic job market was weak and pointed to statistics showing many Americans had dropped out of the workforce. Obama, however, said the 5 percent unemployment rate and steady job gains over recent months had been positive news.

The House passed the measure on December 18 by a vote of 316–113, and the Senate cleared it the same day on a 65–33 vote. The president signed it into law that same day.

Labor Department Rules

Rules governing the H-2B guest worker program had been embroiled in partisan wrangling for several years. In 2011, the Labor Department issued a set of rules aimed at setting stricter pay standards and overwriting Bush administration regulations that worker rights groups opposed. The new rules required businesses to do more job advertising and give American workers longer to apply. But businesses said that the rules were overly burdensome and that the department did not have authority to write them.

Several lawmakers from both sides of the aisle sought to block the rules. And the U.S. Chamber of Commerce and other business groups sued the Labor Department over the regulations. A Florida court ruled in the businesses' favor, which then left in place Labor Department rules from 2008. Then Gabriel Perez, a server and busboy in Palm Beach County, Florida, filed a lawsuit, contending he was paid less than foreign workers whose wages are set by the Labor Department. He also said he had difficulty finding work because such job openings typically were not advertised.

In March 2015, federal district court Judge M. Casey Rodgers in Florida ruled that Labor regulations on the H-2B seasonal visa program were invalid because Congress never gave the department authority to write them. Subsequently, the Labor Department, along with the Homeland Security Department, which processes the visas, suspended the program, causing many lawmakers to fear that employers in their districts would not be able to find enough workers in the upcoming fishing and agricultural seasons.

In a March 16, 2015, letter to Perez and Homeland Secretary Jeh Johnson, a bipartisan group of senators led by Mikulski and Benjamin L. Cardin of Maryland said, "the H-2B program is a necessity for businesses across the country, such as seafood, hospitality, tourism, forestry and other seasonal industries."

On March 18, 2015, Judge Rodgers issued a stay of his ruling, allowing the government to process visas through April 15 while the Labor and Homeland Security departments drafted a new set of rules.

The departments' new interim rules, issued on April 27, 2015, required that employers first seek American workers nationwide, not just in their immediate area, and pay wages comparable to those offered by other regional employers for similar work.

Sen. Thad Cochran, R-Miss., chair of the Senate Appropriations Committee, said the rules were too similar to those the court had just shot down. According to *CQ Roll Call*, Robert W. Goodlatte, R-Va., chair of the House Judiciary Committee, immediately released a statement saying the new interim rules "are overly burdensome for the small and seasonal businesses that play by the rules and use this guest worker program to hire a legal workforce."

OMNIBUS BILL

Seeking to soften the impact of the rules, both chambers approved the provision in the omnibus spending bill that made it easier for employers to hire foreign guest workers. The provision exempted from the Labor Department rule's annual cap of 66,000 visas any returning foreign workers who had held H-2B visas in the previous three years. The provision also allowed employers to conduct their own wage surveys to set the foreign workers' pay and provided employers in the seafood industry who had approved H-2B petitions more time to bring in workers under those petitions.

House Speaker Paul D. Ryan of Wisconsin shepherded the provision through the chamber, raising criticisms from the conservative Breitbart news website. Immigration opponents and Tea Party activists noted the conflict between the Republicans' defense of the visa program and the party's overall positive assessment of the labor market during discussions of the minimum wage and other issues.

Democrats were divided. Sen. Barbara A. Mikulski, D-Md., for example, applauded the visa provision in the omnibus spending bill, saying it would help her state's seafood industry, while other Democrats and independent Sen. Bernie Sanders of Vermont opposed it.

In March 2016, House appropriators questioned Perez on why there were growing delays in approval or denial of the visas. Perez said that was due to the expanded number of visas for foreign guest workers and new rules governing reviews of applications. But Rep. Andy Harris, R-Md., accused department officials of "dragging their feet" and said delays beyond April 1 could hurt the seafood processing industry in Maryland or induce employers to hire undocumented immigrants.

That spring, lawmakers in both parties and both sides of the Capitol moved to expand the visa program in the government funding bills—essentially renewing provisions from the previous year regarding returning workers that potentially quadrupled the number of visas that could be issued.

"Many businesses will be severely impacted, and some may be unable to operate, without this cap relief," said a letter dated April 26, 2016, by nine House lawmakers, led by Rep. Billy Long, R-Mo., to appropriators. More than 1,000 organizations that composed the H-2B Workforce Coalition wrote to House and Senate appropriators urging them to keep the provision in the next spending bills.

The expansion of the visa numbers upset conservatives as well as many unions and liberal lawmakers. With the presidential elections looming, several conservatives also were driven by the rhetoric of GOP presidential candidate Donald Trump, who took a hard stance on immigration.

The spending bills never made it to the House or Senate floors, and funding for the government was maintained through a continuing resolution, which did not renew the provision. The exemption to the cap on H-2B visas expired September 30, 2016.

NLRB Rule and Employer Liability

Several Republicans were unsuccessful in their efforts to overturn a National Labor Relations Board ruling that altered how so-called joint employers were identified for purposes of union negotiations and employment actions.

The House Education and Workforce Committee on October 28, 2015, adopted a bill (HR 3459) that would have invalidated the NLRB's decision of the previous August that redefined the board's standard for determining joint employer status. Under joint employer status, companies that work together must both participate in union negotiations and potentially be liable for subcontractor employment actions, including worker-safety violations.

Under the panel's bill, the National Labor Relations Act would have been modified to state that two or more employers can be considered joint employers only if each organization shares and exercises "actual, direct and immediate control" over workers and their employment.

John Kline, R-Minn., chair of the committee, said the board's August decision had made large contractors and franchisors wary of working with subcontractors. Democrats countered that the legislation aimed to protect from liability large employers that exert indirect control over subcontractors' work conditions.

The committee voted 21–15, along party lines, to adopt the bill. The bill was not considered on the House floor.

Coalminers' Benefits

As part of the continuing resolution (HR 2028, PL 114–254) to keep the government funded, Congress in December 2016 authorized $45 million to fund a four-month extension of protections for coalminers' health care benefits after rejecting efforts by several coal-state senators for more expansive, long-term protections for former coalminers and their families. The fund that financed pensions and health care had been depleted, and without a fix, retired coalminers' benefits were scheduled to end at the end of 2016.

On December 8, 2016, just before departing for recess, the House passed, 329–96, the continuing resolution that funded most federal agencies through April 29. The bill included a provision directing $45 million to be transferred from a fund used to clean up abandoned mines to the United Mine Workers Association's benefit plans to ensure continued federal health care coverage for former coalminers and their families through April 2017.

Sen. Joseph Manchin III, D-W.Va., threatened to hold up the short-term spending bill on the Senate floor until senators agreed to more protection for coalminers' benefits. He said the House measure's provision for coalminers was inadequate because it could still leave many families at risk of losing their health benefits after the end of the year, and it did not address worker pensions or provide a permanent fix for the fund.

Manchin and Shelley Moore Capitol, R-W.Va., had been pushing separate legislation (S 3470), introduced by Sen. Orrin G. Hatch on November 16, 2016, and approved by the Senate Finance Committee in an 18–8 vote in September. That bill would have rescued the fund with about $3.5 billion, about $3 billion of which would have come from an extension of customs user fees from September 30, 2025, to April 29, 2026.

Without the fix, Manchin said more than 12,000 retired coalminers and their families were at risk of losing benefits by the end of the year, while another 10,000 were at risk of losing benefits in the next year.

The full Senate never considered Hatch's bill. Manchin wanted the bill's provisions included in the continuing resolution, but he faced resistance to the last-ditch appeal. Several Republican senators opposed the financial rescue for the fund for union workers. Sen. John Barrasso, R-Wyo., said the health care fund should be fixed by boosting coal mining in the country rather than bailing out the healthcare plan.

"The solution ought to be to let coal miners mine coal again. Let them go back to what they know how to do, mine coal. That's a way they can take care of themselves and take care of their own," Barrasso said on the Senate floor December 9, 2016, according to *CQ Roll Call*. He blamed Obama's "war on coal" for the health care and pension problems.

Ultimately, Manchin and other Democrats decided to hold the fight until the next session of Congress and allow the continuing funding resolution to move forward rather than risk a government shutdown.

"When we return in January, we're going to be looking at every way we can to make sure the miners receive full funding," incoming Minority Leader Charles E. Schumer, D-N.Y., pledged December 9 as senators announced they would allow a vote on a continuing funding resolution to move forward. Senate Majority Leader Mitch McConnell, R-Ky., promised to seek a permanent fix for the coalminers' health care fund.

The Senate cleared the continuing resolution, which included the original provision for coalminers' health care, on December 9 in a 63–36 vote. The president signed the bill into law on December 10, 2016.

Many lawmakers, worried about lapsing health care for former coalminers, had been responding in part to reports indicating a record number of current and former miners diagnosed with black lung disease at clinics around the country. The disease had caused about 78,000 deaths since 1968, according to the Federal Mine Safety and Health Administration.

Under the fiscal 2015 omnibus measure, funding for the Black Lung Disability Trust Fund for former miners increased from $4.9 million to $30.4 million. In 1969, Congress had passed a law (PL 91–173) aimed at eradicating the disease by setting a limit on miners' exposure to a breathable dust called silica. In April 2014, the Labor Department issued a new rule lowering that limit, requiring new technology to allow more continuous monitoring of dust levels in mines and closing several loopholes that would have allowed companies to put workers at risk.

CHAPTER 13

Law and Justice

Law and Justice

LAW AND LAW ENFORCEMENT

President Barack Obama suffered some of the most painful setbacks of his second term in the areas of law and justice. After his 2012 reelection was secured, in part, by overwhelming support by Latino voters, he put a priority on overhauling the nation's immigration system. But Congress could not reach an agreement, and the courts subsequently blocked his executive orders on immigration. After a mass shooting claimed the lives of twenty children and six adults at the end of 2012, he urged lawmakers to pass restrictions on firearms. But conservatives in both chambers of Congress rejected his appeals, even as subsequent mass shootings claimed more lives. After Supreme Court Justice Antonin Scalia died in February 2016, Obama nominated an experienced judge to succeed him. Senate Republicans, in a historic rebuke of the president, said it should be up to the next administration to fill the seat.

Even proposals that drew bipartisan support fell by the wayside. An effort to change criminal sentencing laws, backed by both conservatives and liberals, failed to get a floor vote in either chamber as lawmakers battled over key details. Similarly, lawmakers failed to advance legislation to salvage a key provision of the 1965 Voting Rights Act that the Supreme Court threw out, although there was some Republican interest in working with Democrats on the issue.

Obama and his Democratic allies in Congress did have more modest successes. In the first months of the 113th Congress, lawmakers cleared legislation to renew the Violence Against Women Act. They foiled GOP efforts to restrict abortions. And Senate Democrats successfully confirmed a series of controversial Obama nominees to powerful judgeships and positions in the executive branch—but only after weakening the filibuster.

The legislative battles over law and justice issues took place against a backdrop of cultural and racial changes and tensions. Gay rights activities celebrated victories that would have been unimaginable a generation earlier, culminating in a 2015 Supreme Court decision legalizing gay marriage in all fifty states. However, a new LGBT battle broke out over the use of bathrooms by transgender people. For African Americans, the issue of police violence took center stage after a black teen was fatally shot by a white police officer in the St. Louis suburb of Ferguson, Missouri, in 2014, touching off months of protests and sometimes violent demonstrations and spawning a national movement, Black Lives Matter. Congress did not take action on the issue, but the Justice Department in 2016 sued the city of Ferguson over police misconduct. It subsequently reached an agreement to overhaul Ferguson's police department and municipal court system.

PRESIDENTIAL SETBACKS

After Latinos voted overwhelmingly for Obama in 2012, Democrats and Republicans alike called for an overhaul of the immigration system, which was a top priority of many Latinos and other recent immigrants. The Senate passed a comprehensive bill on a strong bipartisan vote in June 2013. It would have tightened border security, updated visa programs and—most controversially—provided a path to citizenship for many of the estimated 11 million illegal

REFERENCES

Discussion of law enforcement policy for the years 1945–1964 may be found in *Congress and the Nation Vol. I*, pp. 1671–1676; for the years 1965–1968, *Congress and the Nation Vol. II*, pp. 309–334; for the years 1969–1972, *Congress and the Nation Vol. III*, pp. 255–286; for the years 1973–1976, *Congress and the Nation Vol. IV*, pp. 559–618; for the years 1977–1980, *Congress and the Nation Vol. V*, pp. 715–753; for the years 1981–1984, *Congress and the Nation Vol. VI*, pp. 675–709; for the years 1985–1988, *Congress and the Nation Vol. VII*, pp. 713–784; for the years 1989–1992, *Congress and the Nation Vol. VIII*, pp. 741–799; for the years 1993–1996, *Congress and the Nation Vol. IX*, pp. 679–758; for the years 1997–2000, *Congress and the Nation Vol. X*, pp. 589–683; for the years 2001–2004, *Congress and the Nation Vol. XI*, pp. 581–629; for the years 2005–2008, *Congress and the Nation Vol. XII*, pp. 675–726; for the years 2009–2012, *Congress and the Nation Vol. XIII*, pp. 547–583.

Outlays for Law Enforcement

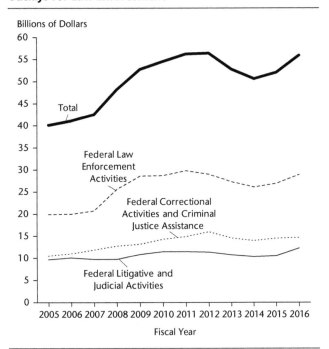

Billions of Dollars

SOURCE: Office of Management and Budget, *Historical Tables, Budget of the United States Government: Fiscal Year 2018* (Washington, DC: U.S. Government Printing Office, 2018), Table 3.2.

immigrants currently living in the country. It was that final piece that proved too much for House conservatives to swallow. They likened such a plan to an amnesty program that would effectively reward illegal behavior. When the House refused to act, Obama took matters into his own hands, issuing executive orders to protect millions of undocumented immigrants from deportation. Republican lawmakers denounced the actions as executive overreach. But before they could make much headway on attempts to stop Obama, the courts blocked the executive orders.

Obama had even less success when it came to the charged issue of gun control. For conservatives in both parties, any attempt to impose additional regulations on guns was a nonstarter, because they viewed it as both violating the constitutional right to bear arms and preventing people from defending themselves. Despite the long odds, Obama urged Congress to expand the system of background checks and renew bans on some military-style assault weapons. Although senators attempted to reach a bipartisan agreement on the issue, a series of floor votes fell short in the face of concerted opposition by gun rights advocates and the influential National Rifle Association. Subsequent mass shootings, highlighted in the media, provoked additional calls for gun control measures and even a sit-in by House Democrats on the floor of the House in 2016. But Congress did not advance legislation on the issue except a relatively noncontroversial measure to renew a prohibition on firearms made entirely of plastic.

Although congressional resistance to major immigration and gun legislation was hardly new, the decision by Senate Republicans against filling the vacant Supreme Court seat was highly unusual. Merrick Garland, a federal appeals judge nominated by Obama in March 2016, did not even get a hearing, let alone a committee or floor vote. Republicans justified this by saying that, with Obama in his final year, the winner of the election should get to decide the next justice. Without Scalia, the Supreme Court was divided 4–4 between liberals and conservatives, so the new justice would have uncommon sway. Democrats bitterly protested, but they were powerless to force a vote.

Obama had some success with lower-court judgeships after Senate Democrats weakened the filibuster in late 2013 to allow judges, as well as executive branch nominees, to be confirmed by a simple majority instead of needing a 60-vote supermajority. This enabled the president to place four judges on the influential U.S. Court of Appeals for the District of Columbia Circuit. However, that victory came with a considerable price, as it meant that Republicans could have a largely free hand in confirming judges when they controlled both the White House and the Senate.

DEMOCRATIC VICTORIES

Republicans, however, also faced some significant defeats. As the 113th Congress began, Democrats won a five-year renewal of the Violence Against Women Act, which was designed to prevent domestic and sexual violence and to help victims. Although the underlying bill enjoyed bipartisan support, many Republicans opposed new provisions related to violence against gays and lesbians, illegal immigrants, and American Indians. After the Senate passed it on a strong bipartisan vote, House Speaker John A. Boehner allowed it to clear the House even though a majority of his own caucus opposed it.

Republicans fell short on a top conservative priority: banning most abortions performed at twenty weeks or more after fertilization. A dozen states had passed such legislation, although they faced court challenges. The House passed the abortion measure in 2013, but Obama issued a veto threat, and the Senate did not take it up. A House bill that would have barred federal funding for abortions similarly did not go anywhere in the Senate during the 113th Congress.

Even when both parties worked together, major legislation proved elusive. The Obama administration and leading liberals and conservatives had high hopes in the 114th Congress for legislation to change criminal sentencing requirements. Fueling the efforts were the mounting costs and social toll of strict sentencing laws and long imprisonments. But legislative efforts sputtered amid opposition by tough-on-crime conservatives and a controversial proposal to change some prosecutorial standards. As the heated presidential campaign moved into high gear, lawmakers gave up their efforts without either chamber passing a bill.

JUSTICE LEADERSHIP

Attorney General Eric H. Holder Jr. stepped down in 2014 after a controversial tenure, and a closely divided Senate approved Loretta Lynch to succeed him. Both Lynch and the new director of the Federal Bureau of Investigation, James B. Comey, came under fire in 2016 for what some saw as interference during the presidential campaign in a closely watched investigation of Democratic nominee Hillary Clinton's handling of classified information. The new director of the Bureau of Alcohol, Tobacco and Firearms, B. Todd Jones, left office after attempting to restrict sales of certain bullets.

Attorney General

Lynch, a former federal prosecutor, was confirmed as Attorney General on April 23, 2015, more than five months after President Barack Obama nominated her to succeed Holder. The first black woman to head the Justice Department, she had waited longer than almost any other attorney general nominee vote and had one of the closest confirmation votes in decades for a cabinet position: 56–43.

Ten Republicans joined all the Democrats to confirm Lynch. The biggest surprise was the "aye" of Majority Leader Mitch McConnell, who had tied Lynch's confirmation vote to an unrelated human trafficking bill, further delaying it.

As U.S. attorney in the Eastern District of New York, Lynch was widely considered to have the experience and qualifications to be the nation's top law enforcement official. But her nomination first became a proxy for Republican ire at President Barack Obama's immigration executive actions, then a political bargaining chip in an unrelated legislative battle, and finally an emblem of increased congressional polarization. Republicans raised concerns that her positions aligned her with a politicized Justice Department, although Democrats hoped she would establish better congressional relations than Holder, who had openly contentious exchanges with lawmakers.

Lynch, in her confirmation hearing's opening statement, told senators she looked forward "to fostering a new and improved" relationship "based on mutual respect and constitutional balance." But she drew the ire of Republicans for supporting the Justice Department's conclusion that the president had legal authority to take broad immigration executive actions announced in late 2014 that would extend legal status to an estimated 4 million illegal immigrants.

Still, Republicans said they welcomed a change after Holder. The House in 2012 had voted to find Holder in contempt of Congress in a dispute over records sought as part of an oversight investigation—the first time for a sitting attorney general. Senate and House Republicans repeatedly called for his resignation. Holder finally obliged them in September 2014, although he went out on a comparatively high note after helping calm residents in Ferguson, Missouri, after racially charged protests—and before he would have to try to shepherd confirmations through a Republican-led Senate.

Confirmation Battle

Lynch rose from humble beginnings in North Carolina to Harvard Law School and on to a career as a lawyer and federal prosecutor overseeing major terrorism, gang, and civil rights cases. When Obama announced her nomination in November 2014, he had praised Lynch's tough-on-crime thirty-year career in the Eastern District of New York, where she took on mob bosses and corrupt public officials. "I could not be more confident that Loretta will bring her signature intelligence and passion and commitment to our key priorities, including important reforms in our criminal justice system," Obama said.

The Senate Judiciary Committee confirmed her on February 26, 2015, by a vote of 12–8. Three Republicans—Jeff Flake of Arizona, Lindsay Graham of South Carolina, and Orrin Hatch of Utah—joined the committee's nine Democrats in advancing the nomination. Supporters praised her experience; opponents said her support of the president's executive orders on immigration should disqualify her.

Her confirmation then bogged down because Republicans linked it to an unrelated dispute over abortion-related language in the human trafficking bill (S 178). McConnell said the Senate would move on the Lynch nomination only after a vote on the otherwise bipartisan bill, and a deal on rewording the law took weeks of negotiations. Obama and Senate Democrats denounced Republicans for moving so slowly, but Republicans said Democrats bore some responsibility for the difference over S 178.

Criticism of a Private Meeting

Although Lynch's tenure was less contentious than Holder's, she drew widespread criticism for a private meeting on June 27, 2016, with former president Bill Clinton aboard the Justice Department jet when it was parked on the tarmac during a trip to Phoenix. The Justice Department at the time was looking into the former president's wife and presumptive Democratic presidential nominee, Hillary

(Continued)

Clinton, for her use of a private email service for official communications while she had been Secretary of State. The meeting raised questions about the impartiality of the Justice Department in handling a sensitive inquiry during a heated presidential contest.

Lynch characterized the meeting as primarily social, focusing on such topics as grandchildren and golf. She conceded, however, that it had raised concerns and said she certainly would not do it again. Several Democrats said the meeting was a mistake, but they believed Lynch's characterization of it and did not think she would interfere with the investigation. Republicans, however, sharply criticized the meeting, saying it showed the need for a special prosecutor to take over the investigation.

In early July, Lynch accepted an FBI recommendation to close the investigation against Clinton without charges. At a July 12 hearing of the House Judiciary Committee, she frustrated Republicans by declining to answer questions about the email probe. It would be "inappropriate for me to comment further on the underlying facts of the investigation or the legal basis for the team's recommendation," she said at the beginning of her testimony. Instead, she referred questions to Comey, who she said was more directly involved in the investigation.

FBI Director

Comey, the former deputy attorney general under George W. Bush, won widespread bipartisan praise after Obama nominated him in June 2013 to succeed Robert S. Mueller III as FBI director. The Senate Judiciary Committee approved his nomination on an 18–0 vote on July 18, and the full Senate confirmed him on July 28 by a vote of 93–1. The only Senate opposition came from Rand Paul, R-Ky., who briefly placed a hold on the nomination because of concerns over the FBI's use of drones to conduct surveillance operations.

But Comey subsequently faced harsh criticism from Republicans and Democrats alike over his handling of the FBI's investigation into Clinton's use of a private email server while she was Secretary of State.

Just three days after FBI agents interviewed Clinton, Comey on July 5, 2016, announced that he recommended no criminal charges against her. The FBI had found no evidence that Clinton had intentionally transmitted or mishandled classified information, and therefore Comey said, "our judgment is that no reasonable prosecutor would bring such a case." In his fifteen-minute announcement at FBI headquarters, however, Comey sharply scolded Clinton, calling her "extremely careless" for using a private email address and server that was less secure than her State Department email.

Although Democrats welcomed the FBI decision, they were stunned by his criticism of Clinton. It was rare, if not unprecedented, for the FBI to publicly disclose its recommendations to the Justice Department about whether to pursue charges in a high-profile case. Comey, however, wanted to make the FBI's position public before referring the case to the Justice Department. He said he wanted to assure Americans that the investigation was being handled thoroughly and impartially.

Republicans were also critical, albeit for different reasons. They questioned the decision not to pursue charges and called upon the FBI to release more details about the investigation. "If it wants to avoid giving the impression that the FBI was pulling punches," said Senate Judiciary Chair Charles E. Grassley of Iowa in a statement hours after Comey's announcement, "the agency must now be more transparent than ever in releasing information."

Less than two weeks before the closely contested election, Comey again found himself in the middle of a firestorm. He informed lawmakers on October 28, 2016, that the FBI had found emails in an unrelated investigation that could have bearing on the probe into Clinton's handling of classified information. However, he did not know if the additional emails were significant or how long it would take the FBI to review them. Multiple reports indicated the new emails were discovered during an investigation into Democratic former Rep. Anthony Weiner, the estranged husband of Clinton aide Huma Abedin.

The announcement roiled the presidential election. Lawmakers demanded more details. "Without additional context, your disclosure is not fair to Congress, the American people, or Secretary Clinton," Grassley wrote to Comey. Democrats were especially incensed. Some questioned whether Comey was trying to sink Clinton's election prospects. Senate Minority Leader Harry Reid, D-Nev., said Comey might have broken the law, and he accused the FBI of treating the nominees with a double standard.

On Sunday, November 6, 2016—just two days before Election Day, but after millions of early votes had already been cast—Comey announced that the FBI had finished its review and again was not recommending criminal charges. "Based on our review, we have not changed our conclusions that we expressed in our July recommendation," Comey wrote to leaders of eight congressional committees.

Democrats, however, remained infuriated. They felt that Comey, by again bringing up the issue of Clinton's emails, might have contributed to her narrow defeat. But Comey felt he had no choice. If he had kept the decision to reopen the investigation a secret, he could have faced criticism for suppressing information in order to get Clinton elected. Instead, he decided to err on the side of going public.

ATF Director

As part of his gun control agenda, Obama announced his intention in January 2013 to name B. Todd Jones to be the director of the Bureau of Alcohol, Tobacco, Firearms and Explosives. Jones had been the acting director since 2011 while also holding a position as a U.S. attorney. The bureau, which frequently found itself facing criticism from conservatives over its role as a firearms regulator, had been operating with an acting director for more than six years.

Influential gun rights groups such as the National Rifle Association did not oppose Jones. Even so, his confirmation vote was delayed as part of a generalized battle in 2013 over Obama's nominations.

The Senate Judiciary Committee advanced the nomination on a 10–8 party-line vote on July 11. With the NRA remaining neutral, six Republicans and conservative Democrats helped provide the minimum number of votes on the Senate floor needed to invoke cloture and limit debate on the nomination. The 60–40 roll call vote on the cloture motion was held open for a record five hours. The Senate then confirmed Jones by a 53–42 vote on July 31, making him the agency's first Senate-confirmed director.

Jones stepped down in March 2015 after the agency came under sharp criticism by Republicans over an attempt to restrict sales of M855 "green tip" bullets for the AR-15 rifle. The agency said it was concerned that the bullets could put law enforcement officers at risk, but gun rights advocates said it amounted to a type of gun ban. Thomas E. Brandon, the deputy director, served as acting director for the remainder of the Obama administration.

However, liberals worked across the aisle to score an unexpected win in the 114th Congress when Congress added a rider to the fiscal 2016 appropriations bill directing the Justice Department to take no action against states where marijuana use for medical purposes is legal. The provision was also included in fiscal 2017 appropriations language. Lawmakers also backed appropriations language to allowing certain research on industrial hemp. Such provisions were a sign of growing political support for marijuana, which had been legalized by a majority of states for medical purposes and, beginning in 2012, by a few states for recreational use.

Chronology of Action on Law and Law Enforcement

2013–2014

The 113th Congress began with a significant legislative achievement, as Congress cleared legislation to renew the Violence Against Women Act. But that proved to be the high point of legislative consensus. Congress subsequently failed to come to agreement on a comprehensive overhaul of immigration policy, even after a bipartisan group of eight senators assembled a bill that passed the Senate by a wide margin. Lawmakers sparred over whether to give illegal immigrants a path to citizenship, which was a priority of Obama, as well as policies related to border security and visa programs. House committees focused on several narrower measures, but these never advanced to the floor.

Lawmakers also debated gun regulations in the wake of a mass shooting at a Connecticut elementary school that left twenty children dead. The Senate rejected a bipartisan proposal to expand some gun regulations in the face of strong opposition by conservatives, leaving Democrats with such minor victories as increased funding for background checks. On another hot-button issue, Republicans pressed unsuccessfully for legislation banning most abortions twenty weeks or more after fertilization. The House passed the measure, but Obama issued a veto threat, and the Senate did not take it up.

Simmering partisan tensions over the Senate confirmation of judicial nominations boiled over in late 2013. Frustrated at the success of Republicans in blocking several of Obama's nominees, Senate Democrats took the controversial step of weakening the filibuster to enable both judicial and executive branch nominees to be confirmed by a simple majority vote rather than a 60-vote supermajority. This change allowed Democrats to move forward on several of Obama's nominees. But it further exacerbated partisan tensions and threatened to weaken Democratic influence over nominations in the event that they lost their Senate majority at a time when a Republican occupied the White House. *(See box, pp. 395–396, and discussion of filibuster, Chapter 15, pp. 477–478.)*

Immigration

The contentious issue of immigration became a central focus of the 113th Congress. Legislation to overhaul the immigration system passed the Senate in 2013, but the House never took it up, focusing instead on narrower, partisan measures. President Obama then took matters into his own hands after the midterm elections, issuing an executive order to lift the threat of deportation for 5 million illegal immigrants who had entered the country as children. The action enraged congressional Republicans and sparked court battles.

Efforts to revamp immigration policy had simmered for years since a major initiative during the second administration of President George W. Bush collapsed in 2007. They gained momentum after Latino voters helped reelect President Barack Obama in 2012, increasing public awareness of immigration. The challenge, however, was to find a way forward on such charged issues as tightening security, updating visa programs, and—above all—determining whether many of the estimated 11 million undocumented immigrants living in the United States should be allowed to remain in the country and have a path to citizenship.

Bipartisan groups in both the House and Senate began meeting in early 2013 to write legislation, hoping to resolve such contentious issues in private before releasing fully formed bills. In April, a "gang of eight" Democratic and Republican senators unveiled, with much fanfare, a comprehensive immigration bill designed to set in motion a process to grant citizenship to those in the United States illegally. The measure (S 744—S Rept 113–40) survived five days of markup in the Judiciary Committee in May largely without change. It picked up support from national Republican leaders as well as several additional GOP senators. Advocates lobbied heavily on behalf of the Senate bill and appeared to help neutralize the anti-immigration groups that had been influential in past debates.

The Senate in June passed the measure largely intact. Senate Democratic leaders worked successfully to achieve a bipartisan floor vote, which they thought would increase pressure on the House to act. To that end, they agreed to a floor amendment by Republican Sens. John Hoeven of North Dakota and Bob Corker of Tennessee intended to significantly beef up border security by requiring the government to double the number of guards on the Southwest border, build 700 miles of fencing, and spend billions of dollars on new patrol technology.

In spite of the bipartisan support in the Senate, the House proved to be a far more difficult venue. A bipartisan group of House members spent much of the year working on a bill, but they divided over such issues as health insurance for illegal immigrants and never released a draft bill. House Republican leaders stepped into the vacuum and deputized committee chairs to write a series of incremental bills in the spring of 2013 as a piecemeal alternative to the Senate measure. The House Homeland Security Committee in May marked up a border security bill (HR 1417—H Rept 113–87) that won bipartisan support. In June, the majority of Republicans on the House Judiciary Committee approved four partisan bills dealing with agricultural guest workers (HR 1773), employment verification (HR 1772), state and local immigration enforcement (HR 2278), and visas for highly skilled workers (HR 2131).

But House GOP leaders were reluctant to move any further, at least in part because of wariness among conservatives that passage of immigration legislation in the House might lead to conference negotiations that would favor the Senate approach. With conservatives deriding the Senate bill as an "amnesty" measure that did little to shore up the nation's borders while granting citizenship to millions of people, House leaders grew increasingly hostile to it.

Immigration advocates, fearing that momentum was faltering, turned up the pressure during the August recess in 2013 and launched a series of sit-ins, rallies, and hunger strikes in the fall, but to no avail. House Republican leaders, unable to navigate the factions within their caucus, declined to bring any of the immigration measures to the floor. But they denounced Obama's executive orders on immigration after the 2014 elections, setting the stage for more immigration battles in the 114th Congress.

BACKGROUND

At the start of the 113th Congress, the stars seemed to be aligning for comprehensive immigration legislation. One of the primary reasons had to do with demographics: there were more than 50 million Latinos in the United States, or about 17 percent of the total population. The fast-growing minority had accounted for about half of the nation's population growth since 2000. This translated into influence at the polls. Although Latino voter turnout tended to lag that of whites and African Americans, they still exerted enormous influence—and, increasingly, they voted Democratic. Obama had picked up about 70 percent of the nation's Latino vote in the 2012 election, which was critical to his electoral victory over the Republican nominee, Mitt Romney.

Asked why the moment seemed to be right for immigration legislation, Sen. John McCain, R-Ariz., provided a two-word answer at a January 28, 2013, bipartisan press conference: "Elections, elections." He added, "The Republican Party is losing the support of our Hispanic voters."

Exercising their political clout, leading Hispanic lawmakers met with Obama in January to press him on immigration legislation. Obama subsequently used his State of the Union address on February 12, 2013, to call for a comprehensive immigration overhaul that would include tighter border security, a path to citizenship for illegal immigrants already in the United States, and revised policies to make it easier for high-skilled workers to remain in the country. GOP leaders such as House Speaker John A. Boehner, R-Ohio, expressed support for immigration legislation, although they differed with the president on key details. Leading business groups such as the U.S. Chamber of Commerce joined with liberal groups such as the AFL-CIO on the issue.

But, foreshadowing the political battles to come, many Republicans expressed skepticism, or even outright hostility, toward the notion of granting citizenship to immigrants who had broken the law by living in the United States. They wanted to focus on border security instead. Lamar Smith, R-Texas, issued a statement after Obama's State of the Union address that assailed his immigration plan. "If the president was serious about creating jobs and spurring economic growth, amnesty for illegal immigrants would not be on his agenda," said Smith, a former House Judiciary Committee chair. "The president's plan to legalize all those in the U.S. illegally will make it easier for 11 million illegal immigrants to compete with hard-pressed American workers."

Efforts at immigration legislation had long bedeviled members of both parties. The number of illegal immigrants had more than tripled since 1990, even though illegal immigration had been expected to slow down after Congress passed the Immigration Reform and Control Act (PL 99–603) in 1986. That law granted amnesty to 2.7 million people living in the country illegally while imposing tough sanctions on employers who hired undocumented workers. But the law had not been strictly enforced. (1986 act, *Congress and the Nation, Vol. VII*, p. 717).

The unspoken fact was that there were many beneficiaries of the status quo, including businesses and families that employed illegal labor, as well as the immigrants themselves, who wanted any job they could get. Consumers also benefited from the lower-priced goods and services that resulted from immigrant labor. However, immigration became an increasingly deadly fact of life in isolated sections of Arizona, as smugglers sought to evade the stepped-up border enforcement and some immigrants could not survive the heat of the Sonoran Desert. The border enforcement also increased the number of undocumented immigrants who stayed in the United States instead of going back and forth to their home countries.

The larger impacts on the U.S. economy were mixed and uncertain. Although immigration advocates said the new arrivals filled the types of jobs that Americans did not want, some studies suggested that illegal immigration suppressed the wages of the least-skilled Americans. The effect on jobs became a larger concern after 2008 as displaced workers during the Great Recession, trying to support themselves and their families, faced an increasingly competitive job market. Another complicating factor was the effect of immigration on government spending. The federal government benefited by collecting income and payroll taxes from the 50 to 60 percent of illegal immigrants whose work was reported by businesses and individuals. But state and local governments struggled to foot the bill for health care, education, and other services.

In his second term, President George W. Bush made a concerted push for a new immigration policy, favoring an approach that would crack down on illegal immigrants while also allowing aliens to enter the country temporarily to work. But he could not overcome deep divisions among Republicans and Democrats, particularly on the treatment of illegal immigrants. With the Republicans in charge of both chambers in 2005–6, the Senate followed Bush's lead and passed a comprehensive immigration bill that aimed to both crack down on illegal immigration and create a guest worker program. But the House passed legislation focusing on border security and tough enforcement of immigration laws, especially in the workplace, and it would have punished those found aiding illegal immigrants. After Democrats took charge of both chambers in 2007, the push to overhaul immigration laws again foundered. Many moderate and conservative Democrats, like their Republican counterparts, believed that a path to citizenship sounded like amnesty and were willing to defy their leaders and oppose such legislation. An attempt to pass a narrower bill that would have provided a path to citizenship to some children of illegal immigrants also fell short. In the end, the only significant immigration bill to emerge during Bush's second term authorized 700 miles of fencing along the southwestern border with Mexico, as well as advanced surveillance technology along the entire U.S.–Mexico border.

Immigration advocates hoped the election of Obama would provide fresh impetus for legislation. But lawmakers put a greater focus on economic recovery and health care. When it came to immigration, their main action was to clear a $600 million border security bill. Similarly, Congress did not advance comprehensive immigration legislation in 2011–12, although the House passed a bipartisan measure, which the Senate did not take up, that aimed to help U.S. businesses hire highly skilled immigrants.

As Congress convened in 2013, it remained highly uncertain whether lawmakers could finally get a comprehensive bill across the finish line. At the House Judiciary Committee's first hearing on the issue on January 30, Republicans indicated that their views had not substantially changed. While they supported granting more visas to high-tech foreign workers, they would hesitate to grant citizenship to people who had broken the law in moving to the country. "What we cannot become," said Rep. Trey Gowdy, R-S.C., the immigration subcommittee's new chair, "is a country where the laws apply to some of the people some of the time."

Senate Committee

The bipartisan gang of eight introduced S 744 on April 16, 2013. Charles E. Schumer, D-N.Y., was the lead sponsor, with the seven co-sponsors consisting of Democrats Michael Bennet of Colorado, Richard J. Durbin of Illinois, and Robert Menendez of New Jersey and Republicans Jeff Flake and John McCain of Arizona, Lindsey Graham of South Carolina, and Marco Rubio of Florida. The Judiciary Committee on May 21 approved the measure, 13–5, after extensive deliberations.

As drafted, the 844-page bill would have granted provisional legal status and issued Social Security cards to most of the estimated 11 million immigrants then illegally in the United States. After ten years in provisional status, they would have been allowed to apply for green cards and ultimately citizenship, provided that they met specified requirements.

The bill would have authorized $4.5 billion to hire additional Border Patrol agents, launch drones to watch for illegal crossings, and strengthen a fence that was to be two or even three layers thick in places. It would have increased the number of new permanent residents permitted in the United States, enhanced programs for highly skilled temporary workers, and created new visas for less-skilled temporary workers and agriculture workers.

During five long days of debate on scores of amendments, the committee fended off most Republican efforts to pare back the provisions that critics most disliked or to make the bill's granting of provisional legal status contingent on beefed-up border security. The eight authors met before each day of the markup to discuss upcoming amendments, determining which ones would be deal-breakers.

In the end, Republican Orrin G. Hatch of Utah, plus two gang-of-eight Republicans on the panel, Graham and Flake, joined all the Democrats in voting for the bill. Hatch's support was cemented on the last night of the markup, when the panel agreed to a compromise amendment to boost visas for highly skilled workers. Hatch's amendment, which the Judiciary Committee adopted 16–2 on May 21, 2013— the final day of the markup—would have relaxed the bill's requirement that companies recruit Americans for jobs before hiring immigrants through special visas. The amendment would have required employers to make "good-faith efforts" to find U.S. workers first and would have imposed a higher standard on companies where 15 percent of skilled workers were visa recipients. That category of employers would have been required to first offer the job to a citizen.

The amendment would have placed a series of caps on H-1B visas for highly skilled workers, beginning with

115,000 and maxing out at 180,000 a year. The annual cap was to rise incrementally if each limit was reached over time.

At the outset of deliberations, the committee adopted, 14–4, a comprehensive substitute that incorporated some negotiated changes, most of which were minor. One significant element of the substitute would have increased fees on visa applications in order to give the Homeland Security Department an additional $900 million to implement the bill.

During the five-day markup, the committee also adopted the following amendments:

- By voice vote, an amendment from the chair, Democrat Patrick J. Leahy of Vermont, and Republican John Cornyn of Texas designed to give Homeland Security greater flexibility in spending the $1.5 billion allocated for fence building. The amendment would have allowed the department to use some of the money for other infrastructure and technology to deter unlawful crossings, but $1 billion would still have to go toward fencing.
- By voice votes, two amendments from Richard Blumenthal, D-Conn., regarding immigration enforcement procedures. One amendment would have in most cases blocked immigration officials from taking enforcement actions at sensitive locations such as schools, hospitals, and places of worship. The second amendment would have put limits on circumstances in which immigrant detainees could be held in solitary confinement.
- 13–5, a Republican amendment that would have expanded the use of biometrics technology to keep track of foreigners in the United States, helping to identify those in the United States on expired visas.

Conservatives were largely unsuccessful in limiting the measure. On the opening day, the panel rejected on a 5–13 vote a broad amendment from Texas Republican Ted Cruz that would have blocked the granting of provisional legal status until a lengthy list of security goals had been met. The amendment called for tripling the number of U.S. Border Patrol agents along the boundary with Mexico, installing additional fencing, and buying more equipment such as drones and surveillance cameras.

But Flake balked, saying it would cost too much and add to the delays of changing the status of illegal immigrants. Flake, Graham, and Hatch sided with all Democrats against the amendment.

The committee also rejected

- 6–12, an amendment from committee ranking Republican Charles E. Grassley of Iowa to block the provisional legal status until Homeland Security showed it had maintained effective control of the Southern border for six months.
- 5–13, an amendment by Grassley to accelerate the implementation of the E-Verify employment verification system for all U.S. employers. As drafted, the bill would have phased in over five years a requirement that all employers use the electronic verification system, which helps determine whether prospective employees are in the United States legally and are eligible to work.
- 6–12, an amendment by Republican Mike Lee of Utah to require Congress to sign off on the implementation of border security strategies before provisional status could be offered.
- 5–13, during the final day of the markup, an amendment by Cruz to remove all "path to citizenship" language from the bill. Cruz would have allowed legal status but not full citizenship. He said a pathway to citizenship was unfair to legal immigrants and would encourage more illegal immigration. Schumer, however, said that allowing full citizenship was the heart of the bill, and he argued that Cruz's proposal would create "two classes of Americans."

Senate Floor

As Majority Leader Harry Reid, D-Nev., prepared to bring S 744 to the Senate floor in June, the gang of eight held together to defend it, pledging they would keep the core of the bill intact even if they did not vote the same way on amendments. That core, they said, consisted of the conditional pathway to citizenship, the crackdown on illegal hiring, the guest worker program, and improved border security.

Floor debate on S 744 began in earnest during the second week of June. More than 200 amendments were filed against the bill, most of which were divisive. The first test of the measure's strength came June 13, on an amendment by Iowa Republican Charles E. Grassley that would have required the government to have "effective control over the entire Southern border" for six months before any illegal immigrants would have been allowed to apply for legal status. This was one of the more hard-edged of several GOP attempts to make tighter border enforcement a prerequisite for any path to citizenship for undocumented immigrants.

The Senate, 57–43, voted to table, or kill, the amendment. All four GOP members of the gang of eight voted to table Grassley's amendment, as did Alaska Republican Lisa Murkowski. Two Democrats sided with Grassley: Joe Manchin III of West Virginia and Mark Pryor of Arkansas.

A border security amendment negotiated by GOP Sens. Hoeven and Corker with Democratic sponsors helped solidify the support of wavering Republicans. It would have doubled the number of armed officers patrolling the border to about 40,000 and supported them with a $3.2 billion investment in technology such as cameras, helicopters, or drones. It also would have mandated the completion of 700 miles of fencing along the border and changed entry and exit systems in an effort to improve tracking of those who overstayed their visas. Once those conditions were met, immigrants illegally in the United States were to be allowed to move toward legal permanent residence.

The Hoeven-Corker amendment was offered by Leahy and adopted June 26, 2013, on a 69–29 vote, with 15 Republicans voting in favor. Democrats such as Durbin felt the added security was unnecessary, but it met the conditions of Republicans who wanted to ensure enhanced security before supporting the overall bill. The border language did not win over such vocal conservative critics as Cornyn, who said he did not think the promises made in the legislation would be kept. Sessions complained that the language was weaker than that in a border security provision that had been defeated during the Senate's 2007 immigration debate. Minority Leader Mitch McConnell, R-Ky., also was unswayed, saying the border language fell short of a "very firm, results-based security trigger."

Such a trigger had been proposed in an earlier amendment by Cornyn. It would have required Homeland Security to meet specific targets, including the apprehension of 90 percent of illegal border crossers, before illegal immigrants could be granted permanent legal status. But senators voted to table it, 54–43. They similarly tabled, 61–37, a Rand Paul, R-Ky., amendment that would have required Congress to confirm that the border was secure in order for provisional legal status applications to be processed. The defeat of those amendments paved the way for the ensuing border security compromise.

A few noncontroversial amendments were adopted by voice vote, including one by Mary L. Landrieu, D-La., that would have granted citizenship to foreign children adopted by U.S. citizens before a 2000 adoption law (PL 106–395) was enacted. In the end, the chamber took roll call votes on eleven amendments, most of which were rejected.

Prospects for passage further improved on June 18, 2013, when the Congressional Budget Office released an analysis showing that the legislation would reduce the federal deficit by about $197 billion over a decade and would cost about $22 billion to implement, leading to a net deficit reduction of $175 billion. The CBO released a separate report concluding that the bill would expand economic growth by 3.3 percent by 2023 and 5.4 percent by 2033. Supporters of the bill pointed to the CBO reports to contend that it would benefit the government's bottom line and the economy.

However, opponents seized on another finding: that the measure would reduce unauthorized immigration into the country by only 25 percent compared to existing projections. The CBO predicted that some of the millions of guest workers to be added would stay beyond the end of their visas, adding to the undocumented population. Grassley said the finding argued for a tougher crackdown on undocumented immigrants to ensure that policy makers in the future would not be saddled with the problem.

On June 27, 2013, after five months of private negotiations and almost two months of public deliberations in committee and on the floor, the Senate passed S 744 with a solid bipartisan majority, 68–42. With Vice President Joseph R. Biden Jr. presiding, senators voted from their desks in the Senate chamber—a practice reserved for high-profile legislation. All of the chamber's Democrats and fourteen Republicans voted in support.

House Action

Overhaul supporters had hoped the bipartisan vote in the Senate was strong enough to bring aboard enough House Republicans to persuade Boehner to bring an immigration bill to the floor. But the House, despite fitful efforts in the fall, never took up a major immigration overhaul.

A bipartisan group of House members who repeatedly met to discuss the issue failed to reach consensus. The eight representatives—Republicans John Carter and Sam Johnson of Texas, Mario Díaz-Balart of Florida, and Raúl R. Labrador of Idaho and Democrats Xavier Becerra and Zoe Lofgren of California, Luis V. Gutierrez of Illinois, and John Yarmuth of Kentucky—emerged from a closed-door session on May 16, 2013, to say their bipartisan group had reached an agreement in principle and would begin drafting a bill. But that agreement was achieved largely because the group set aside the more controversial issues they had been negotiating, such as a guest worker program. The group began coming apart in June, when Labrador walked away after objecting to how illegal immigrants would receive health insurance. In September, Carter and Johnson abandoned the group, leaving only Díaz-Balart to negotiate with Democrats.

Even before that, there had been signs that differences over immigration policy were too great to bridge in the House. Boehner was noncommittal after the Senate vote, saying he would wait until a July 10 House Republican Conference meeting on immigration to roll out his legislative strategy. But after that closed-door meeting, he and other House leaders were more determined than ever to reject the Senate's comprehensive bill even though they had no unified response to the question of how to address the immigration issue. House Republicans, many from districts with few Latino voters, said they did not see an overriding political need to pass a broad immigration measure. Instead, they were interested in moving narrower bills that focused on such issues as border security.

Some Republicans, led by Majority Leader Eric Cantor of Virginia, worked on a bill—tentatively called the KIDS Act—that would have granted legal status to young people brought to the United States illegally as children. That effort never jelled, however.

Instead, two House committees with jurisdiction over immigration matters worked on their own incremental bills in 2013. The Homeland Security Committee passed a bill to strengthen border security, and the Judiciary Committee passed four bills in ten days to help state and local officials with immigration enforcement and make changes to guest worker and visa programs. The bills, none of which made it to the House floor, focused on:

- **Border control strategy.** The Homeland Security Committee approved a bill (HR 1417) by voice vote that would require a strategy for gaining and maintaining situational awareness and operational control of high-traffic areas of the border within two years.

The approval came after the committee, by voice vote, adopted a substitute amendment from panel Chair Michael McCaul, R-Texas, to extend the deadlines for the completion of strategies and the submission of reports required by the measure. The committee also adopted by voice vote an amendment by Lamar Smith, R-Texas, to require a plan to gain operational control of the entire Southwest border within five years.

The panel considered more than two dozen amendments during the four-hour markup, rejecting one. That amendment, offered by ranking Democrat Bennie Thompson of Mississippi, would have authorized $3 billion over five years to carry out the bill's provisions. It was defeated on a 14–15 party-line vote. McCaul agreed that money would be needed but said it should be authorized only after Homeland Security had completed its plan and an estimate of how much would be needed.

- **State and local enforcement authority.** The Judiciary Committee approved a bill, HR 2278, on June 18, 2013, to empower state and local law enforcement agencies to implement federal immigration laws. Prior to the 20–15 party-line vote, the panel rejected a series of Democratic amendments to limit the measure. These included an amendment by ranking Democrat John Conyers Jr. of Michigan, rejected 12–18, that would have stripped out the bill's core provisions.

The committee rejected, 16–20, an amendment by Judy Chu, D-Calif., that sought to end the 287(g) program, which allows states and localities to help enforce immigration law through cooperative agreements with the Homeland Security Department. The panel also rejected, 16–19, an amendment by Melvin Watt, D-N.C., to block localities under investigation for civil rights violations from entering into 287(g) agreements and to require certification that participating jurisdictions have adequate policies to eliminate racial profiling.

The panel adopted, 19–17, an amendment by Iowa Republican Steve King to block the administration from offering a reprieve from deportation to young immigrants, referred to as "dreamers," brought to the United States illegally as children. The House had earlier voted to add a similar King amendment to the fiscal 2014 Homeland Security appropriations bill (HR 2217).

- **Agricultural workers.** On June 19, 2013, the Judiciary Committee approved a bill (HR 1773) by a 20–16 party-line vote to create a new program for agricultural guest workers. The bill would have replaced the existing H-2A visa program with a new program, dubbed H-2C, which would have allowed up to 500,000 temporary agricultural workers each year.

It would have allowed people in the United States illegally to apply for legal status as a temporary guest worker for two years until the proposed H-2C program went into effect. A manager's amendment, adopted on a 17–15 party-line vote, specified that only illegal immigrants employed in agriculture were to be eligible to apply for legal status as temporary guest workers. They would have had to leave the country for three months or one-sixth of their total work period, whichever was less, before reentering on an H-2C visa.

Committee Chair Robert W. Goodlatte, R-Va., said a successful guest worker program would help deter illegal immigration, protect U.S. workers' jobs, and stabilize industries.

Democrats criticized several elements of the bill, including provisions that they said would have decreased wages for farm workers and provisions that would have eliminated requirements that employers provide work guarantees, transportation, and housing. They said the committee should have used as the basis for the bill a compromise negotiated by the United Farm Workers and American Farm Bureau, which had been included in S 744, the Senate immigration overhaul.

- **Employment verification.** The Judiciary Committee on June 26, 2013, approved a bill (HR 1772) that would have expanded the use of the E-Verify employment verification system. Under the bill, passed by a party-line vote of 22–9, employers would have had to review new employees' identification and work authorization documents and then request confirmation from the electronic system. The system would have been required to provide a confirmation or tentative nonconfirmation within three business days.

The increased use of E-Verify would shut off "the jobs magnet that attracts so many illegal immigrants to the United States," said bill sponsor Lamar Smith, R-Texas, during the markup.

Goodlatte endorsed a provision in the bill that would have allowed states to investigate and enforce violations. He said the measure would empower states to help enforce the law and prevent the president from unilaterally shutting down federal enforcement efforts.

Gutierrez offered but then withdrew an amendment to prohibit the bill's implementation until the Homeland Security Department certified that there were sufficient lawful methods for immigrants in the United States illegally on the date of enactment to adjust their status to that of lawful permanent resident.

Democrats also criticized the bill for providing virtually no recourse for employees who were improperly flagged as ineligible to work, apart from filing an administrative claim under the Federal Tort Claims Act (PL 79–601). They said it might take months for such claims to reach a federal court, that such cases were costly, and that attorneys' fees were capped, making it difficult to find legal representation.

Under the bill, the use of the system was to be phased in beginning six months after enactment for employers with more than 10,000 employees and was to be fully in effect in two years for employers with fewer than twenty employees. Employers would have had to reverify the work authorization for certain employees, including federal, state, and local government employees, certain federal contractors, and employees who hold security clearances.

- **High-tech visas.** Hours after the Senate passed its comprehensive immigration overhaul on June 27, the House Judiciary Committee approved its fourth immigration overhaul bill, HR 2131, by a 20–14 vote.

    The bill would have made available 55,000 visas for foreign graduates of U.S. universities in the fields of science, technology, engineering, and mathematics. It also would have added 10,000 visas for foreign entrepreneurs and up to 155,000 visas for skilled workers in the H-1B program. It would have eliminated the 65,000 visas available annually for siblings of U.S. citizens and the 56,000 visas available annually under the diversity visa program.

    Sponsor Darrell Issa, R-Calif., said the bill was designed to be as neutral as possible in regard to existing quotas.

    A manager's amendment, offered by Goodlatte and adopted by voice vote, would have provided that applicants for sibling green cards pending as of September 30, 2013, would be eligible for a visa if the application were approved within ten years.

    Democrats, however, said the amendment would prevent 850,000 people with pending sibling visa applications from receiving one. The committee rejected, 11–22, an amendment by Chu that would have allowed everyone with a pending sibling visa application to receive one under the existing process.

Obama Executive Orders

When President Obama announced a policy in 2012 to defer deportation of immigrants who came to the United States as children, most Republicans were opposed. They roundly criticized the administration, both for that policy (known as Deferred Action for Childhood Arrivals, or DACA) and for what they viewed as overall lax enforcement of immigration laws. Nevertheless, the president went further, announcing executive orders on November 20, 2014, that lifted the threat of deportation for an estimated 5 million illegal immigrants.

In his prime-time speech from the White House to unveil the new policy, Obama defended himself about charges of presidential overreach. "To those members of Congress who question my authority to make our immigration system work better, or question the wisdom of me acting where Congress has failed, I have one answer: Pass a bill," he said in his fifteen-minute address. "I want to work with both parties to pass a more permanent legislative solution. And the day I sign that bill into law, the actions I take will no longer be necessary."

Republicans, however, said the president's orders were unconstitutional and would sink any bipartisan efforts to pass comprehensive legislation.

Tensions between congressional Republicans and the administration over immigration policy had come to the fore months earlier. Republicans on the House Judiciary Committee directed a fusillade of criticism at Homeland Security Secretary Jeh Johnson in his first oversight hearing before the panel in May 2014, taking aim at what they saw as the administration's lax enforcement of immigration laws.

"The Obama administration has taken unprecedented, and most likely unconstitutional, steps in order to shut down the enforcement of our immigration laws for millions of unlawful and criminal aliens not considered high enough priorities," Goodlatte, R-Va., said in an opening statement that set the tone for the hearing.

Johnson defended the administration's approach and disagreed with Republicans' assessment that it amounted to amnesty for illegal immigrants. He also echoed the White House's calls for the GOP to take up and pass a comprehensive overhaul of the immigration system.

In August 2014, after passing a $694 million supplemental spending bill to beef up border security and make it easier to deport unaccompanied children apprehended in the Southwest, the House passed a separate bill (HR 5272) intended to block federal money from being used to continue or expand the DACA program.

Supporters of the measure contended that DACA was a major reason for the influx of migrants at the border. Goodlatte said it acted like a beacon that encouraged unlawful immigrants to cross into the United States illegally. But Obama issued a veto threat against HR 5272 and vowed to act on his own to manage deportations and enforcement.

True to his word, two weeks after the November elections, Obama issued his executive order to lift the threat of deportation for millions of illegal immigrants who were living in the United States and had not broken the law. Republicans were infuriated, threatening to take the issue to court and accusing the president of acting unilaterally instead of working with Congress to fix the immigration system. Sen. Marco Rubio, R-Fla., a member of the gang of eight senators who drafted the bipartisan immigration measure that passed the Senate in 2013, said the scope of Obama's action made legislating on the issue that much harder.

In early December, the House responded to Obama's November 20 action by passing a bill, 219–197, which would have prohibited the executive branch from exempting or deferring from removal certain categories of undocumented immigrants. The bill (HR 5759) by Rep. Ted Yoho, R-Fla., won support from three Democrats, John Barrow of Georgia, Mike McIntyre of North Carolina, and Collin C. Peterson of Minnesota. Barrow had been defeated in the November 4 election and McIntyre had chosen to retire, but Peterson had just won his thirteenth term in the House.

Seven Republicans, including some from districts with large Latino populations such as David Valadao and Jeff Denham of California, voted against Yoho's bill.

SENATE DEMOCRATS CONFIRM JUDGES AFTER WEAKENING FILIBUSTER

Long-simmering tensions over the Senate's process for approving judicial nominees came to a head in 2013. Senate Democrats won the confirmation of four of President Barack Obama's nominees to the U.S. Court of Appeals for the District of Columbia Circuit, shifting the balance of power on this powerful court to judges named by Democratic presidents. But the victory came at a significant cost: Democrats had to weaken the filibuster in order to get the nominees through, potentially leaving them vulnerable to Republicans responding in kind and seating conservative judges if they captured both the White House and the Senate majority.

The year began with Obama signaling his intention to make judicial nominations a priority in the 113th Congress by renominating thirty-three people to the federal bench who did not receive up-or-down votes in the previous Congress. The president noted that several of the people had been waiting for a vote for more than six months, even though they had bipartisan support. One of those renominated—Caitlin J. Halligan for the D.C. Circuit—had first been named more than two years earlier. Three of the court's eleven seats were empty at the beginning of the year, and its chief judge took senior status in February, creating a fourth vacancy. Republicans contended that the D.C. circuit was not overburdened by its vacancies.

The Senate had not confirmed any circuit court nominee since June 2012. Delays in confirming judicial nominees had become increasingly common in presidential election years, as the opposition party sought to hold vacancies open in the event that their party's nominee won the White House.

But some legal experts worried that the vacancies affected the effectiveness of the courts. In his annual end-of-year report on the federal judiciary, Chief Justice John G. Roberts Jr. had noted that twenty-seven vacancies in federal courts were designated as "judicial emergencies" that should be filled as quickly as possible.

Battle over Halligan

Judicial nominations had become increasingly contentious in recent decades. Judges were asked to weigh in on some of the most divisive issues in the country, including abortion, gun rights, and the reach of federal regulations. Their lifetime appointments meant they could influence such issues for decades.

Although the largest judicial battles were reserved for Supreme Court vacancies, both parties also battled over district and circuit judicial nominations. They were particularly focused on the D.C. Circuit, which was widely considered second only to the Supreme Court because of the important regulatory cases assigned to it. The D.C. court was frequently at the center of national debates over health care, the environment, and national security.

Republicans did not object to all appellate court nominees who came before the chamber in early 2013. On February 13, the Senate confirmed William J. Kayatta Jr. for a seat on the 1st Circuit Court of Appeals by a vote of 88–12. And on February 25, the Senate confirmed Robert E. Bacharach for a seat on the 10th Circuit Court of Appeals by a vote of 93–0. Both had been blocked in 2012, but in neither case was a cloture vote held to break a filibuster in 2013.

Republicans strongly objected to Halligan, complaining that the former solicitor general of New York had an activist record and did not show sufficient respect for the Second Amendment right to keep and bear arms. Senate Republicans had blocked her confirmation with a filibuster in December 2011 and were determined to do so again. Only one Republican, Lisa Murkowski of Alaska, had voted with Democrats to invoke cloture and cut off debate in 2011, and the cloture motion received only 54 "yea" votes, six short of the 60 needed.

When the Judiciary Committee considered Halligan's nomination on February 14, 2013, no Republican supported her, and the committee sent her nomination to the floor on a 10–7 vote. Majority Leader Harry Reid, D-Nev., brought Halligan's nomination to the floor on March 6, but the motion to invoke cloture and cut off debate was rejected 51–41, well short of the 60 votes needed. Shortly afterward, Obama withdrew her nomination.

Other administration nominees also faced obstacles in the Senate. The same day as the Halligan vote, Sen. Rand Paul, R-Ky., began a talking filibuster against the nomination of John O. Brennan to be director of the CIA. Paul pledged to talk as long as possible to express opposition to the Obama administration's policy regarding targeted killing of American citizens using drones. And earlier in February, Republicans had blocked an up-or-down vote on the nomination of Chuck Hagel, a former Republican senator from Nebraska, to be Defense secretary.

Hagel was confirmed two weeks after his unsuccessful cloture vote, and Brennan was confirmed the day after Paul began his filibuster. Nonetheless, those actions and the rejected Halligan cloture vote stirred up complaints from outside liberal groups who were furious with Reid and other Democrats for declining to force a rules change to allow a simple majority vote to invoke cloture. On the day of the Halligan vote, Majority Whip Richard J. Durbin, D-Ill., said the Democrats might need to consider limiting the filibuster. Senate leaders in both parties had made such

(Continued)

SENATE DEMOCRATS CONFIRM JUDGES AFTER WEAKENING FILIBUSTER (Continued)

threats from time to time, but they had always stepped back from the brink.

Invoking the Nuclear Option

In the two months after the Halligan vote, the Senate confirmed three more appellate court judges, without incident and without cloture votes. Then, in a further bipartisan flourish on May 23, the Senate overwhelmingly backed Sri Srinivasan, the principal deputy solicitor general in the Justice Department, for a seat on the D.C. Circuit. The vote was 97–0.

But in confirming Srinivasan—the D.C. Circuit's first new judge since 2006—both parties appeared to be looking past the nominee and toward a bigger, looming fight over the D.C. Circuit bench. With Srinivasan's arrival, the court was evenly split, 4–4, between Democratic and Republican appointees, and Obama's moves to fill the remaining three vacancies set off a political firestorm.

In a Rose Garden ceremony in June, Obama nominated Patricia Ann Millett, a veteran appellate attorney; Cornelia "Nina" Pillard, a Georgetown University law professor; and Robert L. Wilkins, a federal district judge. It was the first time the president had personally appeared alongside judicial nominees for a court other than the Supreme Court.

Republicans characterized the White House strategy as overly aggressive and immediately questioned whether the court's workload warranted three more judges. In October and early November, Republicans used filibusters to block confirmation votes for all three D.C. Circuit nominees on the Senate floor.

Those filibusters—on top of a protracted fight over National Labor Relations Board nominees earlier in the year and other nomination battles—led Democrats on November 21 to carry out their threat. Reid invoked a parliamentary maneuver called the "nuclear option" to change the interpretation of Senate rules to require only a simple majority—51 votes, if all senators participated—rather than a flat 60 votes to overcome filibusters on executive branch and judicial nominees other than those to the Supreme Court.

The result was a series of confirmation votes for seven judges and nine executive-branch officials before the

year ended. Two of the three D.C. Circuit judges were confirmed—Millett, by 56–38 on December 10, and Pillard, by 51–44 on December 12—as were five district court judges. In the case of the sixteen nominees confirmed in December, all were subject to cloture votes and in no case did more than fifty-eight senators vote to cut off debate.

Two more pending nominees were confirmed in early January. Janet L. Yellen was confirmed to be chair of the Federal Reserve Board of Governors by a 56–26 vote on January 6, 2014. And Wilkins was confirmed for the D.C. Circuit by a 55–43 vote on January 13. With Wilkins's confirmation, Democratic appointees had a 7–4 advantage on the court.

Aftermath

Republicans responded to the filibuster change with a series of tactics to slow action, such as refusing to yield back postcloture debate time and using Senate rules to block committees from meeting. As the session came to a close, Leahy said Republicans, for the first time ever, refused to allow any pending judicial nominees to be held over for the second session of the 113th Congress so they could be ready for immediate action in 2014. Under Senate rules, any nomination not acted upon would have to be returned to the White House. If resubmitted, the process for that nominee would begin anew.

All told, in the first session of the 113th Congress, the Senate confirmed eleven circuit court judges, all by roll-call votes, and thirty-two district court judges, according to the committee. In the first session of the 112th Congress, the Senate had confirmed nine circuit court judges and fifty-five district court judges.

The rules change had less relevance for the 114th Congress because Republicans enjoyed a Senate majority and could block Obama nominees without resorting to a filibuster. But it loomed large after the 2016 presidential election. By controlling both the White House and the Senate, Republicans were well positioned to overcome Democratic objections and win confirmation of judicial and executive branch nominees. *(See discussion of filibuster and the nuclear option, Chapter 15, pp. 477–478.)*

The Obama administration strongly opposed the measure, saying it would make the immigration system worse. The Senate did not take it up.

Conservatives also sought to stop Obama's immigration actions by including restrictions in spending bills. That spending battle, along with the court battles, would stretch into 2015.

Domestic Violence

Capping a rare moment of bipartisan agreement, Obama in early March 2013 signed a five-year renewal of the Violence Against Women Act, a 1994 law designed to prevent domestic and sexual violence and to provide a range of assistance programs to those who were victims of such violence.

Quick passage of the reauthorization measure (S 47—PL 113-4) in the first two months of the 113th Congress belied a bitter partisan debate that derailed action the previous year. The underlying law had always enjoyed broad bipartisan support in Congress, but Democrats and Republicans had sparred in 2012 over a handful of contentious additions to the law and did not reach a compromise that year.

Enacted in 1994 as part of an omnibus crime bill (PL 103–322), the law operated primarily through awarding federal grants to state and local authorities, nonprofit organizations, and universities for services such as transitional housing and legal assistance. It promoted a coordinated response by creating the Office of Violence Against Women in the Justice Department to bring together victim advocates, law enforcement, courts, health care professionals, and faith leaders.

Senate Democrats had sought to expand the law's coverage to domestic-violence victims who were gay and lesbian, grant a larger number of visas to illegal immigrants who were victims of domestic violence, and give American Indian authorities the power to prosecute non-Indians accused of abusing Indian women on tribal lands. Republicans said those provisions were unnecessary and politically motivated. The House also balked because the 2012 Senate-passed bill contained a $30 visa fee increase that GOP leaders said violated the Constitution's requirement that revenue measures originate in the House.

For their part, Senate Democratic leaders refused to accept the House-passed counterpart, which omitted the proposed additions to the law. When Congress did not act, the law's previous reauthorization (PL 109–162) expired in September 2012.

Senate Democrats started fresh in early 2013 with a new version of the 2012 bill that did not include the constitutionally questionable fee increase but preserved the expanded coverage for gay and lesbian victims, illegal immigrants, and American Indians. The bill passed the Senate with significant Republican support.

Even though a majority of House Republicans opposed the Senate bill, Speaker John A. Boehner, R-Ohio, decided to bring the politically popular measure to the House floor. House Republicans offered a substitute to pare back the expanded language, but the tide had turned, and the substitute was rejected when more than a fourth of the GOP caucus voted against it. The chamber then cleared the Senate measure without amendment.

The House vote to send the bill to the president marked a notable instance in which Boehner broke the so-called Hastert rule, named for former Republican Speaker J. Dennis Hastert of Illinois, who as an informal practice declined to bring legislation to the floor unless it had the support of a majority of the Republican Conference.

Senate Floor

A bipartisan majority of the Senate voted, 78–22, on February 12 to pass the five-year reauthorization of the Violence Against Women Act. All Democrats and 23 Republicans voted for the bill, compared with 15 Republican "yes" votes for the 2012 version.

Senators twice rejected GOP attempts to excise language that would have given American Indian tribes greater authority over non-Indian domestic-violence offenders, the main remaining sticking point. The provision was designed to counter high rates of violence against American Indian women, but opponents said it would undermine constitutional protections for accused offenders.

An amendment by Sen. Tom Coburn, R-Okla., to strike the tribal court language was rejected, 31–59, the day before passage. Four days earlier, the Senate rejected, 34–65, a broad Republican substitute offered by Charles E. Grassley of Iowa that was aimed at the tribal court provisions and other elements of the Senate bill.

Before passage, the Senate adopted, 93–5, an amendment by Patrick J. Leahy, D-Vt., to extend through 2017 the Trafficking Victims Protection Act (PL 106–386). The act aimed to expand law enforcement grants for prosecuting human-trafficking crimes and to criminalize the confiscation of passports or other immigration documents by human traffickers.

Coburn, who blocked a similar proposal in 2012, called Leahy's amendment well intended but duplicative and costly. Four other GOP senators joined Coburn to vote against the amendment. Renewal of the antitrafficking law, which expired in 2012, had also been the subject of a partisan battle over a Health and Human Services Department decision not to renew a contract with the U.S. Conference of Catholic Bishops for trafficking victims' services because the bishops did not include abortion and contraceptive services in their program. By attaching the antitrafficking language to the domestic and sexual-violence bill, Leahy avoided a replay of that fight in 2013.

Senators also unanimously supported a related amendment by Rob Portman, R-Ohio, to include sex-trafficking victims in a grant program designed to help children exposed to violence.

The Senate-passed measure included a grant proposal designed to reduce the backlog of untested DNA evidence, including rape kits. But senators rejected two Coburn amendments that he said would also help rape victims. One amendment, rejected 46–53, would have required the Justice Department to streamline programs and use the resulting savings to reduce the DNA evidence backlog. The second amendment, rejected 43–57, would have taken 20 percent of criminal-justice-related grants from recipients who did not test accused rapists for sexually transmitted diseases.

House Floor

The House vote on February 28, 2013, to clear S 47 as passed by the Senate came somewhat as a surprise. But Republicans said it was necessary to reauthorize the expired law and conceded they did not have the votes to force concessions from Senate Democratic sponsors.

The 286–138 vote to clear the measure included 87 Republicans who joined a united Democratic caucus in the "yea" column; 138 Republicans voted "nay." Just before passage, the House rejected, 166–257, a GOP substitute that would have required tribal courts to be certified by the Justice Department to handle domestic- and sexual-violence cases involving nontribe defendants and to prove they gave defendants their constitutional rights.

Democrats opposed the alternative because it did not include the Senate's expanded language on gays, lesbians, and illegal immigrants. But many Republicans were also opposed, mostly because they wanted further changes in the tribal provisions. Sixty Republicans voted against the substitute, and only two Democrats—Daniel Lipinski of Illinois and Mike McIntyre of North Carolina—voted for it.

Gun Control

The long-divisive issue of gun control emerged as a major political flash point in the 113th Congress. Despite entrenched opposition to restrictions on guns, President Obama and gun control advocacy groups were emboldened to make a new push for tougher laws after mass shootings in schools, a theater, an Army base in Texas, and a U.S. Navy office building not far from the Capitol—not to mention the 2011 shooting of a House member and others during a constituent event in Arizona. In particular, the fatal shootings of twenty children at Sandy Hook Elementary School in Newtown, Connecticut, on December 14, 2012, galvanized the administration.

Virtually all of the gun control efforts fell short. Advocates won minor victories, such as the renewal of a ban on plastic guns and additional funding for background checks. But in the face of unyielding opposition by most conservatives, they failed to gain traction on proposals for expanded background checks or a ban on assault weapons.

Long before the 2013 gun control debate, the political reality surrounding the issue in Congress was firmly established. Politicians, especially in rural areas, had become well aware during the two decades that followed the enactment of an assault weapons ban in 1994 that their constituents would not tolerate new restrictions on guns. For voters who viewed guns as critical for sporting activities and as a means to protect themselves and their families, the right to bear arms was a defining political issue. Gun rights groups, led by the National Rifle Association, kept voters informed of any lawmakers who voted for restrictions on guns. Republicans and Democrats from much of the West, South, Midwest, and rural portions of the East could be expected to oppose almost any attempt to restrict gun ownership or impose new regulations for the sake of reducing violence.

The Supreme Court's 2008 ruling in *District of Columbia v. Heller*—that the Constitution granted individuals a right to have guns in their homes—hardened public opposition to gun control. A series of tragic events involving guns in the hands of mentally unstable killers was not enough to change the political equation.

Many gun control advocates attributed the outbreak of shootings to the ready availability of firearms—particularly semiautomatic rifles—after the expiration of bans on some semiautomatic long guns in 2004 that had been enacted ten years earlier. That ban had included military-style assault weapons and large-capacity ammunition magazines. Gun rights proponents, however, were determined not to give an inch, reasoning that any concession might open the floodgates to new restrictions that would deprive law-abiding gun owners without affecting persons with criminal intentions or improving public safety.

The issues in play in 2013 included whether to require background checks of all gun purchasers and whether the expired ban on assault weapons ought to be reinstated. For gun control proponents, the best hope for a breakthrough was a compromise amendment on background checks sponsored by Democrat Joe Manchin III of West Virginia and Republican Patrick J. Toomey of Pennsylvania. But it fell five votes short of being adopted on the Senate floor in April, with only a handful of defections from each party's caucus.

The renewal of an expiring twenty-five-year-old federal ban on plastic firearms was signed into law in December 2013, but that was seen as only a minor victory by gun control advocates. It was accomplished only after gun control opponents thwarted attempts to strengthen the ban so it would reflect twenty-first-century technology. The only other success claimed by the Obama administration and Democrats in 2013 was Senate confirmation in late July, after some controversy and a lengthy delay, of B. Todd Jones to be the director of the Bureau of Alcohol, Tobacco, Firearms and Explosives, which enforced gun regulations.

The following year, both gun control and gun rights advocates claimed comparatively minor victories in the appropriations process.

The NRA emerged from the showdown with a reinforced reputation as an effective and aggressive lobbying organization. Obama, despite his convincing 2012 reelection victory, was left weakened after failing to win over key lawmakers. Pro–gun control votes proved to be too much to ask of some Democratic senators facing reelection campaigns in conservative states where gun rights were certain to be major issues for their opponents.

The deadlock on Capitol Hill left gun control policy to state capitals, where results were mixed. Some legislatures tightened state gun laws while others relaxed restrictions, particularly those related to carrying concealed weapons. The result deepened the divide between Republican- and Democratic-leaning states.

SHOOTINGS SET THE STAGE

Constraints on gun ownership date from the 1934 National Firearms Act (PL 73–474), which regulated the manufacture and sale of weapons and required the registration of owners of machine guns and other firearms that were especially lethal and used by criminals. The Gun Control Act of 1968 (PL 90–618) established the basic federal law governing commerce in firearms, requiring licenses for retail dealers and the keeping of sales records by licensed dealers, prohibiting interstate sales of handguns and interstate mail-order sales of other firearms, and specifying the types of people to whom sales of firearms were prohibited. A ban on the ownership of newly manufactured machine guns was included in a 1986 law (PL 99–308) that was otherwise broadly intended to assert the rights of gun owners (*1968 Almanac*, p. 549; *1986 Almanac*, p. 82).

Two important measures enacted in the 1990s were the last major efforts at gun control until 2013. The Brady Handgun Violence Prevention Act of 1993 (PL 103–159) required background checks on all firearm purchases from licensed retailers. The law, debated for seven years before enactment, was named for former White House Press Secretary James S. Brady, who was permanently disabled during the 1981 assassination attempt on President Ronald Reagan (*1993 Almanac*, p. 300).

Subsequently, a broad 1994 anticrime law (PL 103–322) established a ten-year ban on the manufacture and import of specific semiautomatic, military-style assault weapons and large-capacity ammunition magazines. It also increased penalties for the criminal use of firearms. The legislation was strongly criticized by many gun rights advocates, and it played a role in the Democrats subsequently losing their majorities in both chambers in the 1994 midterm elections. The Senate voted to extend the partial ban on assault weapons in March 2004, but the House refused to go along. After the ban expired, on September 13, 2004, there was no serious proposal to renew it (*1994 Almanac*, p. 273; *2004 Almanac*, p. C-5).

Gun control was barely evident as an issue during Obama's first four years in the White House, and it was not a significant part of his second-term agenda until the December 2012 fatal shootings of twenty students and six staff members at Sandy Hook Elementary School in Newtown, Conn. The shooter, Adam Lanza, a twenty-year-old man with a history of mental illness, also killed himself and his mother, who was the legal owner of the guns he had used.

Obama told the nation that such horrific incidents should not be tolerated, and he swiftly appointed a Cabinet-level task force on gun violence, headed by Vice President Joseph R. Biden Jr. On January 16, days before his second inauguration, Obama announced a package of legislative proposals and twenty-three executive actions designed to curtail gun use. He promised a national lobbying campaign to advance his agenda on Capitol Hill. Obama's legislative proposals included

- expanding the criminal and mental-health background checks already required for purchases from licensed retail stores to include purchases at gun shows and private transactions.
- renewing bans on the sale and manufacture of some military-style assault weapons and of magazines that hold more than ten rounds of ammunition.
- expanding an existing ban on the manufacture and import of armor-piercing bullets to also prohibit their possession and transfer.
- strengthening existing penalties for "straw purchasers" who buy guns for people ineligible to own firearms.
- providing more money for police, mental health services, and school security.

The proposed background check expansion and the renewed partial ban of semiautomatic weapons were the top priorities for gun control groups, and they generated the most controversy.

Trying to minimize opposition, Obama repeatedly maintained he was not trying to take on gun ownership, and he emphasized his belief that the Second Amendment guarantees an individual right to bear arms. Nevertheless, it was wishful thinking on Obama's part that he could mobilize a grass-roots uprising against gun violence that would persuade lawmakers to place new requirements on gun purchases and limit the ownership of certain kinds of weapons. In addition to the political opposition, it was not immediately apparent that the steps the administration proposed would have prevented the mass shootings.

The initial response from gun rights advocates was indicative of what was to come. House Judiciary Chair Robert W. Goodlatte, R-Va., said that any legislation must be meaningful in reducing shooting deaths and not interfere with the rights of Americans. NRA Executive Vice President Wayne LaPierre rallied his organization's membership for what he predicted would be "the fight of the century."

Senate Committee

The Newtown shootings prompted the introduction of a flurry of gun-related bills in both chambers, including efforts to make it easier to carry concealed weapons. But House Republican leaders made clear after Obama articulated his proposals that their chamber would not address the gun control issue unless it received legislation from the Democratic-controlled Senate.

In the first two weeks of March, the Senate Judiciary Committee approved four gun-related bills, beginning with one (S 54—S Rept 113–9) to toughen laws against gun purchases that were made for people not legally allowed to have them. The measure was approved by an 11–7 vote on March 7, 2013, with Iowa's Charles E. Grassley the only Republican in support. It would have imposed prison terms of up to twenty-five years for buyers of "straw purchases" of firearms who passed the weapons on to persons not legally permitted to own them, including felons, fugitives, drug abusers, illegal immigrants, domestic abusers, or persons suffering from mental illness. The legislation was considered the gun control proposal most likely to enjoy bipartisan support, but Republicans such as John Cornyn of Texas called it unnecessary.

The committee on March 12 approved, 14–4, a second bill (S 146), which would have authorized increased spending for such school safety measures as tip lines, surveillance equipment, and metal detectors. The measure would have authorized $40 million in grants annually for ten years.

By a 10–8 party-line vote on March 14, the panel approved a third bill (S 374), which would have required buyer background checks for all private gun sales and expanded the National Instant Criminal Background Check System (NICS) used to conduct such screenings. Sponsor Charles E. Schumer, D-N.Y., described the measure as a placeholder while efforts continued to negotiate a bipartisan approach to expanding background checks. Grassley argued that criminals could hardly be expected to comply with background check requirements and would rely on straw purchases and theft to obtain weapons.

The committee by a 10–8 party-line vote on March 14 approved a bill (S 150), sponsored by California Democrat Dianne Feinstein, to reinstate and expand the expired federal ban on assault weapons that had been enacted in 1994. But that proposal was seen by most observers as the gun control bill least likely to succeed. Opponents insisted that any ban on semiautomatic weapons infringed on constitutional rights and the self-defense needs of law-abiding citizens, although Feinstein dismissed the argument that such weapons were needed for self-defense.

The bill would have blocked the future sale, transfer, manufacture, and import of 157 semiautomatic guns and of ammunition magazines holding more than ten bullets. It also would have banned rifles, handguns, and shotguns that accepted detachable magazines and included pistol grips or folding stocks. The bill would have required background checks for the sale or transfer of grandfathered semiautomatic guns.

The committee rejected, on 8–10 party-line votes, amendments offered by Cornyn to exempt from the ban individuals living in rural areas or near the Southern U.S. border, those who had obtained a protective court order, and victims of sexual assault, domestic violence, dating violence, or stalking.

Senate Floor

Signifying the significance of the legislative effort, Senate Majority Leader Harry Reid, D-Nev., took responsibility for introducing a new bill (S 649) on March 21, 2013, which drew on the earlier work of the Judiciary Committee and incorporated elements of three of the bills it considered.

The highlight of S 649 was language from S 374 that would have expanded the requirement for background checks of gun purchasers. Reid's bill also included language from S 54 on straw purchases and from S 146 on school safety. Notably, Reid omitted language on the assault weapon ban from S 150, deeming it too controversial for Democrats to unite behind. An unhappy Feinstein was told she would have to offer her plan as an amendment during floor debate and try to muster sufficient support.

Reid called up the combined bill on April 8, with a cloture vote to break a filibuster on the motion to proceed scheduled for April 11. A bipartisan agreement on background checks emerged the day before the cloture vote, and the motion was approved, 68–31, suggesting that the compromise might survive the NRA's opposition. Sixteen Republicans supported the cloture motion and 29 were opposed. Two Democrats voted against it—Mark Begich of Alaska and Mark Pryor of Arkansas.

With Biden presiding and Newtown families watching from the visitors' gallery, the Senate voted on nine amendments to the bill over two days, April 17 and 18. Seven amendments were rejected; two were adopted. Five of the rejected amendments were supported by a majority of those voting, but as an alternative to time-consuming cloture proceedings, senators operated under an agreement requiring at least 60 votes for adoption.

The debate began with a pivotal amendment: a bipartisan plan offered by Manchin and Toomey on behalf of themselves, Schumer, and Mark S. Kirk, R-Ill., that would have required background checks of buyers in all commercial gun sales. In an effort to draw needed support, the amendment stopped short of the background check requirement approved by the Judiciary Committee, which called for screenings for most private sales as well. It would have exempted transactions between family members and friends. And it included language prohibiting the creation of a national registry of gun owners, something not proposed during the 2013 debate but feared by gun rights advocates.

In a critical blow to any significant progress on gun control, senators rejected the amendment, 54–46, on April 17. It drew the backing of only four Republicans: Toomey, Kirk, Susan Collins of Maine, and John McCain of Arizona. Democrats Begich, Max Baucus of Montana, Heidi Heitkamp of North Dakota, and Mark Pryor of Arkansas broke Democratic Party ranks to oppose the amendment. (Reid changed his vote to "nay" when the outcome was apparent in order to preserve his prerogative to reconsider the vote later.)

The Senate next rejected, 52–48, a Republican substitute amendment to the bill offered by Grassley and Ted Cruz of Texas that left out broader background check language while including the prohibition on straw purchases and language expanding the definitions of mental illnesses that disqualified individuals from owning guns. It would have authorized grants for school security, mental health services, and crime prevention; provided money to help states use the background check database; required federal courts to submit records to the database; and called for a study of the causes of mass shootings, including the impact of violent video games.

The third amendment considered—and defeated—was one by Collins and Judiciary Chair Patrick J. Leahy, D-Vt. It would have exempted firearms purchased as gifts, prizes, commemorative awards, employee bonuses, or gratuities for hunting guides from the legislation's prohibition on straw purchases. It was rejected 58–42.

A Republican amendment by Cornyn, rejected 57–43, sought to make it easier for individuals authorized by their own state to carry concealed and loaded handguns to carry their weapons while traveling in other states regardless of the restrictions in those places.

Banning assault weapons—the issue that Feinstein championed and that was the focus of many liberals—was dismissed easily with the defeat of one of two amendments that did not get even 50 votes in favor. The Senate rejected, by a vote of 40–60, Feinstein's amendment to outlaw ammunition clips that held more than ten rounds and the future manufacture, sale, possession, or import of 157 semiautomatic assault-style weapons. The amendment designated 2,258 other guns used for activities including hunting as legal.

A related amendment by Sen. Richard Blumenthal, which would have prohibited large-capacity ammunition magazines but did not address assault weapons, also failed to get even a simple majority. It was rejected, 46–54.

The Senate rejected, 56–44, an amendment by Republican Richard M. Burr of North Carolina to prevent veterans who were mentally incapacitated, deemed mentally incompetent, or experiencing an extended loss of consciousness from being classified as "mentally defective," and thus barred from owning guns, unless a court found that the veteran posed a danger.

The first of two amendments adopted April 18 was offered by Republican John Barrasso of Wyoming. It would have permitted the withholding of 5 percent of Community Oriented Policing Services grant money from states and local governments that released information on individual gun owners or identified firearms license holders. The amendment allowed exceptions for information sought in a criminal probe or legal proceeding. The goal, Barrasso said, was to protect the privacy of lawful gun owners and prevent information about them from being shared with the public. Senators adopted it, 67–30.

The second adopted amendment called for the expansion of mental health and substance abuse programs. Offered by Iowa Democrat Tom Harkin, the chair of the Health, Education, Labor and Pensions Committee, the amendment would have reauthorized programs run by the Health and Human Services and Education departments, including grants for college mental health services to educate students, families, faculty, and staff on how to respond to students with mental health and substance use disorders. It also would have renewed programs on suicide prevention and grants for child trauma centers. It was adopted on a 95–2 vote.

After the high-profile setbacks, particularly the vote on background checks, Reid pulled the bill off the Senate floor. Obama and gun control advocates promised to rally public support to continue the fight, and Reid said senators would face the background check issue again, perhaps before year's end. But there was no indication during the following months that any of the opponents were prepared to change their votes, and the majority leader made no move to resume consideration of the package.

Among the issues left unresolved was a Senate effort to update definitions of mental illness as they relate to gun ownership. Begich, Pryor, and Republicans Lindsey Graham of South Carolina and Jeff Flake of Arizona had the backing of gun rights supporters for a bill (S 480) that would change the designation of people "adjudicated as a mental defective" or committed to a mental institution as ineligible for gun ownership.

The bill's sponsors, who called the existing language outdated and offensive, would have added individuals to the national database if they were adjudicated to be an imminent danger to themselves or others; if they had been found guilty but mentally ill in a criminal case, found not guilty by reason of insanity, or found incompetent to stand trial; or if they had been voluntarily committed to a psychiatric hospital.

To advance, however, the legislation would almost certainly have had to be linked to an expansion of background checks—and all four authors of the bill had voted against the Manchin-Toomey compromise during consideration of S 649.

PLASTIC GUNS BANNED

Gun control made a brief return to the legislative agenda in December 2013, as a twenty-five-year-old law banning firearms made entirely of plastic was about to expire.

The 1988 Undetectable Firearms Act (PL 100–649) required firearms to contain at least 3.7 ounces of metal and to be shaped like guns in order to ensure that they could be spotted by X-ray machines, metal detectors, and other security devices. Although there were no all-plastic guns in circulation, there was bipartisan backing for renewing the prohibition (1988 Almanac, p. 82).

Democrats, led by Schumer, wanted to expand the law's reach to cover plastic guns with removable metal parts and undetectable ammunition magazines. In an alternative, Schumer proposed a straight one-year extension of existing law to give Congress an opportunity to consider whether new technology, such as three-dimensional printers, should be taken into account by the law. Republicans and gun rights groups resisted, however, and pushed for a long-term extension of existing law.

The House passed a ten-year "clean" extension (HR 3626—PL 113–57) by voice vote December 3, and the Senate cleared the bill by voice vote six days later. Obama signed it into law the same day to keep the existing prohibition from expiring.

FUNDING FOR BACKGROUND CHECKS

The debate over gun control also made its way into the fiscal 2014 appropriations process. The omnibus spending bill (HR 3547—PL 113–76), signed into law on January 17, 2014, required the FBI to free up $60 million to handle an increased number of gun buyer background checks. The extra money for the National Instant Criminal Background Check System was a victory for gun control groups, including Mayors Against Illegal Guns.

In response to school shootings, including Newtown, appropriators also included $75 million for a Comprehensive School Safety Initiative by the National Institute of Justice, the department's research arm, to investigate causes of school violence, to develop technologies and strategies for increasing school safety, and to provide grants to test innovative approaches.

For their part, Republicans touted provisions they said would protect Second Amendment rights, including prohibitions of various firearms import and export restrictions.

Abortion Restrictions

The politically divisive issue of abortion remained in the spotlight in the 113th Congress, with Republicans advancing a pair of bills that would have restricted abortions or largely eliminated federal support for them. Democrats, for their part, proposed legislation to target certain antiabortion measures passed in state houses. Neither side was able to get legislation through Congress.

Abortion opponents won a victory in 2013 when the Republican-led House, following the lead of a dozen states but also in the face of an adverse federal appeals court ruling, voted to ban most abortions performed at twenty weeks or more after fertilization. However, Obama issued a veto threat against the bill, and the Democratic-led Senate did not take up a companion measure. The following year, the House passed legislation to bar federal funding for abortions and exclude the procedure from some federal tax benefits. That proposal also failed to gain traction in the Senate. For their part, Senate Democrats discussed—but never voted on—a measure that would have overturned state laws that were deemed to have reduced access to abortion.

TWENTY-WEEK LIMIT

Republicans opposed to abortion initially focused their efforts on the twenty-week limit. Sponsors in both chambers justified such a nationwide limit with their claim—unproved by scientific research—that a fetus could feel pain beginning at the twenty-week point in a pregnancy. Starting with Nebraska in 2010, twelve states had enacted similar bans, but they were under challenge in the courts. Limiting abortions based on the presumption of fetal pain ran counter to the standard set by the Supreme Court in its 1992 decision, *Casey v. Planned Parenthood,* that abortions were permissible up to the point of fetal viability, which is generally considered to be about twenty-three or twenty-four weeks after fertilization.

With Congress divided on the issue, the federal courts did not show an inclination to revise the viability standard. In May 2013, the 9th Circuit Court of Appeals ruled unconstitutional an Arizona law that banned abortions twenty weeks after fertilization. The three-judge 9th Circuit panel cited in its ruling "a long line of invariant Supreme Court precedents" that began with the Court's 1973 decision in the landmark abortion case *Roe v. Wade.* The Supreme Court in 2014 declined to accept the 9th Circuit ruling for review, allowing it to stand. Challenges to twenty-week bans in other states continued to work their way through the courts.

In addition to the circuit court ruling, another event in May 2013 focused national attention on abortion: the first-degree murder conviction of Kermit Gosnell, a Philadelphia abortion doctor. Gosnell provided abortions late in pregnancies and was convicted of killing three infants that prosecutors said had been delivered alive. Antiabortion groups had used Gosnell's trial to press for legislative constraints on late-term abortions.

Arizona Republican Rep. Trent Franks introduced a limited twenty-week-limit bill (HR 1797) in April with ninety-three original cosponsors, all but one of them Republicans. The bill as introduced would have applied solely to abortions performed in the District of Columbia. A similar bill that Franks had sponsored in 2012 had fallen short that year on a 220–154 vote on the House floor, where it was brought up under suspension of the rules, an expedited process that required a two-thirds majority for passage.

House Committee Action

The House Judiciary Subcommittee on the Constitution and Civil Justice on June 4 voted 6–4 along party lines to approve HR 1797 after broadening it to apply nationwide. In advocating for the expansion of the bill's reach, subcommittee Chair Franks cited the Gosnell case. The subcommittee removed language from the bill that would have allowed a woman receiving an abortion after twenty weeks—or the father or maternal grandparent of the unborn child—to sue the abortion provider for damages.

The full Judiciary Committee approved HR 1797 (H Rept 113–109) by a 20–12 party-line vote on June 12. The measure would have required abortion providers to determine when fertilization occurred and barred procedures leading to an abortion twenty weeks after that date or later. Physicians performing abortions in violation of the ban would have been subject to fines and imprisonment for up to five years. The committee-approved measure included an exception for pregnant women whose lives were endangered "by a physical disorder, physical illness, or physical injury, including a life-endangering physical condition caused by or arising from the pregnancy itself."

But the bill specifically barred exceptions for rape or incest and for "psychological or emotional conditions." During the full committee markup, Republicans blocked Democratic efforts to add rape and incest exemptions. Franks justified the lack of those exceptions by saying that such pregnancies were rare—an assertion that drew strong criticism from Democrats.

House Floor

The House voted 228–196 on June 18 to pass HR 1797. Six Republicans voted against the bill; six Democrats voted in favor.

Supporters said the bill was not just about abortion but pain to young lives. Opponents, however, took issue with the underlying assertion that fetuses could feel pain at twenty weeks, saying the belief was a minority opinion in the medical community and that it was not the business of Congress to legislate based on unproven findings.

Before the bill reached the floor, House GOP leaders took two steps that were intended to mollify criticisms. First, they added exceptions for rape and for incest involving a minor in specific situations. Rapes would have had to have been reported to an appropriate law enforcement agency before the abortion was performed, and incest would likewise have had to have been reported to law enforcement or an appropriate government agency. Also, Republican leaders removed Franks as floor manager for the bill, giving the role to Marsha Blackburn, R-Tenn. They gave other women prominent roles during debate even though none of them were on the Judiciary Committee.

Democrats derided such maneuvers as a public-relations stunt, noting that all the Republicans on the Judiciary Committee were men. They also criticized the bill's language requiring rape and incest to be reported. "Do the sponsors of this legislation understand the trauma that a rape survivor endures?" said Susan A. Davis, D-Calif., during the floor debate. "And do they understand what a cruel message that is to send to a woman in her time of greatest need?"

Senate Version

Although Senate Democrats had no intention of taking up the House-passed bill, Sen. Lindsey Graham, R-S.C., introduced a companion measure (S 1670) on November 7 in the hope of eventually securing a vote. Graham garnered forty Republican cosponsors for the measure, but Democrats appeared united in opposition. Graham said there was an informal debate among his Senate colleagues about how to impose a ban in a way that would not be ruled unconstitutional in the courts, but in the end he decided to move ahead in order to benefit unborn babies.

Antiabortion groups pressed for a Senate vote on the legislation, arguing that public opinion was on their side. But abortion rights groups lashed out against the measure, and Democratic senators said that it would leave women who needed abortions for health reasons after twenty weeks with no options.

FEDERAL FUNDING FOR ABORTIONS

The House in 2014 passed legislation to bar federal funding for abortions in most cases and exclude the procedure from some federal tax benefits. The Senate took no action on the measure.

The House Judiciary Committee approved a bill (HR 7), sponsored by Christopher H. Smith, R-N.J., that would have prohibited use of federal funds to pay for abortions or health insurance plans that cover abortions. Cases of rape, incest, or situations in which the woman is in danger of death would be exempt.

Under the measure, individuals could not have gotten tax credits established under the 2010 health care law (PL 111–148, PL 111–153) that help low- and moderate-income people pay for insurance through the health care exchanges if the plans cover abortion. However, individuals could still buy separate out-of-pocket insurance coverage for abortion.

Eight amendments—all by Democrats—were offered during the Judiciary Committee markup. Each was rebuffed, either by roll call vote or because of rulings that they were outside of the panel's jurisdiction or not germane to the bill.

A few weeks later, the House passed the measure 227–188. Only one Republican, Richard Hanna of New York, voted "no" on the bill, while six Democrats who often parted company with the majority of their party on social issues, such as Jim Matheson of Utah and Mike McIntyre of North Carolina, voted for it.

The final version of the House bill dropped earlier provisions that would have prevented individuals from claiming medical expense tax deductions for abortion costs and using flexible spending accounts and health savings accounts, which get special tax treatment, to pay for the procedure.

Those changes failed to win over the White House, which issued a statement on January 22, 2015, saying that federal policy had long barred using federal funds for abortions, except for certain circumstances, and that this prohibition was maintained in the 2010 health care law and reinforced through a 2010 executive order. "HR 7 would go well beyond these safeguards by interfering with consumers' private health care choices," the statement said.

As with much legislation the House passed in 2014, the Senate took no action on the measure.

OVERRIDING STATE LAWS

The Senate Judiciary Committee debated a bill (S 1696) by Connecticut Democrat Richard Blumenthal that would have overturned state laws deemed restrictive enough that they interfered with access to abortion. The past several years had seen the emergence of hundreds of state laws affecting abortion providers, including requirements for waiting periods and ultrasounds, as well as rules that abortion clinics have capabilities similar to those of hospitals or surgical clinics.

Blumenthal's legislation would have essentially invalidated such laws unless they were shown to substantially protect or enhance women's health. The Connecticut Democrat said he was concerned over the proliferation of state abortion restrictions that, in his view, could harm rather than help a woman's health or safety.

But Republicans at the hearing warned the measure would affect a broad swath of statutes, including those that allow doctors to refuse to provide abortions or other care if it runs contrary to their consciences. Judiciary ranking Republican Charles E. Grassley of Iowa said the Blumenthal bill would allow abortion providers to operate without state-level oversight. Such a move, he said, would unconstitutionally interfere with states' rights to regulate abortion under the tenth amendment. Furthermore, he said that mandatory ultrasound and twenty-four-hour waiting period laws were helpful to women's health.

Blumenthal's bill never got a committee vote.

SPENDING PACKAGE

At year's end, House Republican leaders praised the abortion-related provisions they had insisted be included in the fiscal 2015 spending package. But instead of being in the bill itself, the provisions were in the report language released with the bill text that does not have the same force of law.

Pennsylvania Republican Joe Pitts, co-chair of the House Values Action Team, said he thought that was all conservatives could get, although he would have preferred the provisions to be stronger. "It would be better if it were . . . in the language of the bill, but when you're negotiating with Harry Reid and the White House, you know, you've got to negotiate," he said. "That's all we could get from them."

Marijuana

Federal marijuana policy faced a period of uncertainty during the 113th Congress. Colorado and Washington legalized marijuana use through ballot initiatives in 2012, and President Obama pledged to respect the initiatives and not enforce the federal ban on the drug in those states.

In 2014, members of Congress, divided on the issue, arrived at a somewhat muddled consensus. They ended the year by agreeing to language in the omnibus spending bill (HR 83) that gave a slap on the wrist to the District of Columbia for moving to legalize marijuana possession, but they did nothing to bring clarity to federal marijuana policy.

House Republicans were split between the libertarian, states' rights faction, which included members such as Rep. Dana Rohrabacher of California, Ted Yoho of Florida, and Thomas Massie of Kentucky, and the far larger group of more traditional, law-and-order members who made up about three-quarters of the Republican caucus. The libertarians were inclined to defer to state wishes on marijuana, while the law-and-order members wanted to crack down on the drug.

But Republicans and many Democrats were largely united in criticizing the administration's inconsistencies on marijuana. In 2013, the Justice Department decided not to intervene in cases in Colorado and Washington, although it continued to classify marijuana as highly dangerous. Pointing out this contradiction, seventeen House Democrats and a Republican (Rohrabacher) sent a letter to Obama on February 12, 2014, asking that he "instruct" Attorney General Eric H. Holder Jr. "to delist or classify marijuana in a more appropriate way, at the very least eliminating it from Schedule I or II." They argued that Schedule I or II—the two most extreme tiers of federal classification of the drug—disregarded its medicinal value and overstated the extent to which it was harmful. They said the classification also perpetuated a criminal justice system in which certain groups were disproportionately targeted and arrested on charges that would haunt them for life.

The letter, led by Rep. Earl Blumenauer, D-Ore., also chided Obama for allowing administration officials to send conflicting and potentially misleading messages to the public. Specifically, it cited James L. Capra, the chief of operations at the U.S. Drug Enforcement Administration (DEA), who appeared to break with Obama by referring to the legalization of marijuana at the state level as "reckless and irresponsible."

Although the letter highlighted concerns that the administration was too strict in enforcing marijuana laws, many conservatives worried that it was too lax. In March 2014, the House passed a bill to make it easier for Congress to sue the Obama administration for failing to enforce certain laws. In addition to wanting the administration to more fully enforce the federal marijuana ban, Republicans criticized the White House for granting reprieves from deportation to some young illegal immigrants and delaying parts of the 2010 Affordable Care Act (PL 111–148, PL 111–152). The legislation (HR 4138) passed in a 233–181 vote. Five Democrats—John Barrow of Georgia, Henry Cuellar and Pete Gallego of Texas, Collin C. Peterson of Minnesota, and Nick J. Rahall II of West Virginia—joined Republicans in support of the bill.

At an April 29, 2014, hearing, House Republican appropriators sparred with Treasury Secretary Jacob J. Lew over the administration's green light for banking transactions related to legalized marijuana in Colorado and Washington.

Appropriations Chair Harold Rogers of Kentucky told Lew that Treasury's Financial Crimes Enforcement Network (FinCEN) might have opened the door to broader drug trafficking by saying it would not impose extra enforcement scrutiny of bank transactions with state-sanctioned marijuana vendors. Rogers charged that joint Treasury and Justice advisories had blurred the line on tough enforcement of banking restrictions aimed at drug traffickers and other criminals. "This is still an illegal product in practically every state," Rogers said at the hearing. "Is it wise to offer regulatory guidance of the federal government on illegal activity?"

Lew defended a Treasury memorandum that made clear FinCEN would not target banking transactions with legitimate marijuana-related businesses when scanning banks' suspicious activity reports (SARs) that are filed under the bank secrecy law. Without the guidance, Lew said, there would be a proliferation of cash-only businesses, and it would be impossible to know when there were violations of federal and state law.

But two Florida Republicans in the House, Ander Crenshaw, the chair of the Financial Services Appropriations Subcommittee, and Mario Díaz-Balart, said the guidance could be confusing and appear as though the federal government was advising people on how to deal with an illegal activity. They said they would scrutinize Treasury's handling of banking transactions involving marijuana-related businesses.

The appropriators' push for tougher marijuana enforcement ran counter to an initiative by other House members such as Ed Perlmutter, D-Colo., to assuage concerns of banks that deal with state-authorized marijuana vendors. Perlmutter offered a proposal (HR 2652) that would have barred prosecutions, probes, or penalties such as the suspension of federal deposit insurance for banks that provided services to "a marijuana-related legitimate business."

Senators also raised alarms over the administration's marijuana policies. Iowa Republican Charles E. Grassley, siding with Rogers, said the administration's decision to issue guidelines aimed at letting banks work with state-sanctioned marijuana providers was contrary to the mission of a Treasury Department unit that enforces financial laws. Grassley and Sen. Dianne E. Feinstein, D-Calif., who headed the Senate Caucus on International Narcotics Control, sent a letter on April 2, 2014, to FinCEN director Jennifer Shasky Calvery asking how the agency's mission—"to safeguard the nation's financial system from illicit use and to combat money laundering"—was being advanced by the administration's guidelines.

The two senators asked Calvery whether she believed that the guidelines overrode federal law, which has long banned marijuana. Calvery responded that the guidelines did not replace federal law and that marijuana remains illegal, but she said the regulations "enhance financial transparency," which she called a key part of FinCEN's mission. She acknowledged that banks still faced risks by providing financial services to state-sanctioned marijuana businesses in Colorado and Washington.

MEDICAL MARIJUANA

The House in May 2014 backed a measure that advocates of marijuana legalization hoped would be a watershed moment for drug policy. It passed a $51.2 billion Commerce-Justice-Science spending measure (HR 4660) that included a medical marijuana amendment. The key marijuana vote was on a proposal by Rohrabacher to block the Justice Department from prosecuting medical marijuana users and providers who were abiding by state laws that had legalized the substance.

The Rohrabacher amendment was adopted in a 219–189 vote, with 49 Republicans joining 170 Democrats to lift it to victory. Its backers saw the vote as a step toward the inevitable loosening of federal marijuana restrictions.

Medical marijuana advocates then scrambled to get a member of the Senate Appropriations Committee to offer the same language during either the subcommittee or full committee markup of the Commerce-Justice-Science (C-J-S) spending bill. But when Senate appropriators advanced their bill in June, they ignored the House decision to adopt the Rohrabacher language on medical marijuana. No senators offered a version of Rohrabacher's amendment.

However, the panel adopted, 22–8, an amendment by Jeff Merkley, D-Ore., to the C-J-S bill to allow for industrial hemp research by blocking the Justice Department from spending money in contravention of research provisions in the 2014 farm bill (PL 113–79). Those provisions, similar to language in the House version, let academic institutions or state agriculture departments grow hemp for research purposes, as long as it was legal under the relevant state law. Merkley said his proposal was aimed at countering efforts to obstruct research, noting a federal ban on industrial hemp production had fueled a U.S. reliance on expensive imports from overseas.

Federal agents had seized hemp seeds intended for Kentucky's agriculture department, prompting congressional concern. Minority Leader Mitch McConnell, a Kentucky Republican, was a cosponsor of Merkley's proposal.

LEGALIZATION IN WASHINGTON, D.C.

Underscoring concerns about marijuana legalization, the House Appropriations Committee in June approved an anti-marijuana amendment to the fiscal 2015 Financial Services spending bill. The amendment by Rep. Andy Harris, R-Md., a medical doctor, would have prohibited federal and local funds in the District of Columbia from going toward the legalization or decriminalization of marijuana. The District government had been implementing a law decriminalizing possession of a small amount of the drug.

In the November 2014 election, voters in Washington, D.C., approved a ballot initiative on recreational marijuana. Nearly 65 percent of voters supported the initiative legalizing the possession of up to two ounces of marijuana for personal use and the growing of no more than six cannabis plants within a person's residence.

One month later, House and Senate appropriators unveiled a $1.1 trillion spending package that struck a compromise on marijuana legalization in the District of Columbia. While it did not undo the District's decriminalization or medical use laws, it did bar federal and local funding from being used to implement the November referendum.

Media Shield

Lawmakers from both parties joined forces in 2013 to try to advance media shield bills that were intended to protect journalists engaged in newsgathering from government demands for the identity of sources and other information in court, except in specific and extraordinary circumstances. But the legislation stalled after winning approval in the Senate Judiciary Committee.

After decades of trying, supporters of the measure were heartened when members of the Judiciary Committee reached a bipartisan agreement about which journalists were to be covered by the legislation. Despite that agreement and White House support for the effort, the bill (S 987) failed to reach the Senate floor. A similar measure (HR 1962), also bipartisan, languished in a House Judiciary subcommittee.

The legislative push had gained temporary momentum after the revelation in May 2013 that the Justice Department had seized home and office telephone records from Associated Press reporters and editors during a 2012 investigation into a failed al-Qaida plot. The resulting scandal—the AP was not notified of the records request—led to an unusual administration listening tour in which Attorney General Eric H. Holder Jr. met with media organizations. The Justice Department issued new guidelines in July to govern requests for information involving journalists. But Holder also called on Congress to enact shield legislation to provide further protections for reporters by creating a judicial process to ensure that they were not compelled to identify their sources unless specific conditions were met.

The proposed federal shield law was intended to match statutes or case law precedents on the books in every state except Wyoming. But not everyone supported the idea of establishing special statutory protections for the press that the Supreme Court had never found within the Constitution.

Many journalists and free-speech advocates also warned that language in the House and Senate bills would still give the government wide latitude to pursue reporters. The bills would have allowed the government to compel reporters to disclose their sources under a range of conditions, including situations that would help in "preventing or mitigating" harm to national security. David Pozen, an information law expert at Columbia Law School, said the judicial process that would have been created by the bills was not guaranteed to be preferable for journalists to the existing law that had allowed for the secret seizure of the AP's phone records. On balance, Pozen said, journalists had done quite well without a federal shield law.

Republican lawmakers also questioned Democratic motives in seeking the shield law, saying that the Obama administration had been more aggressive than any other in seeking to prosecute those who leaked sensitive information to the press.

Another key obstacle, which had stymied past attempts to pass a media shield law, was how to define who was a journalist—and who was not.

When Congress had last focused on the issue in 2009, the Senate Judiciary Committee approved a bipartisan bill that would have set a high threshold for circumstances in which the government could force a reporter to identify sources. Subsequently, the website WikiLeaks ignited an intense controversy by publishing reams of sensitive documents obtained from Army Pfc. Bradley Manning. The flood of embarrassing information quickly killed the shield bill, amid fears that an organization such as WikiLeaks might have been protected. Manning was sentenced in August 2013 to thirty-five years in prison for the largest national security leak in U.S. history.

Senate Legislative Action

The Senate Judiciary Committee approved S 987 (S Rept 113–118) on a 13–5 vote on September 12, with Republicans Charles E. Grassley of Iowa, Orrin G. Hatch of Utah, and Lindsey Graham of South Carolina joining all Democrats in favor.

The committee began deliberations on S 987 with bill sponsor Charles E. Schumer, D-N.Y., immediately calling for revising the measure to incorporate the new Justice Department guidelines on how journalists were treated in federal investigations. Those changes included stricter standards on how quickly journalists had to be notified when the government sought access to their records. Under the revisions, the Justice Department was to be allowed to ask a federal judge to delay notifying journalists for a maximum of ninety days. As introduced, the bill had a more open-ended standard, which would have allowed forty-five-day extensions each time a judge found that giving notice would have undermined a criminal investigation or posed national security or other risks.

Schumer also called for expanding the scope of records addressed by the bill to include not only those from communications companies but also those from other holders of business records, such as credit card companies.

After agreeing to Schumer's changes, the committee turned to the thorny issue of who was to be identified as a journalist and protected under the bill. Members adopted an amendment by Dianne Feinstein, D-Calif., to narrow its definition of journalists to cover only individuals actively or previously affiliated with a news entity, including student journalists and those with substantial freelance experience. Feinstein's amendment included a mechanism for a judge to grant protections on a case-by-case basis to those who did not fit the definition.

In an acknowledgment of the fallout from the Manning-WikiLeaks case, Feinstein's amendment denied protection to anyone whose purpose was "to publish primary source documents that have been disclosed to such person or entity without authorization." The amendment reflected a compromise negotiated with Schumer and Richard J. Durbin, D-Ill.

Democrats defended the narrow definition as a necessary guard against virtually anyone claiming legal protections under the bill. But Republicans other than those supporting the bill took issue with the narrowed definition. Ted Cruz, R-Texas, complained that the measure unjustly excluded citizen bloggers. John Cornyn, R-Texas, worried about "government licensing of legitimate media." The committee rejected, 4–13, a Cornyn amendment to expand coverage to anyone addressed by the free-press clause of the First Amendment.

Under the committee-approved measure, the government would have had to show that it had exhausted all other avenues to obtain information before seeking information from a protected journalist. That standard, however, would not have applied in cases in which the journalist engaged in criminal conduct to get the information or if government access would have prevented terrorist activity or other harm to national security.

House Bill

HR 1962 was introduced with bipartisan support on May 13, 2013, the same day that the seizure of the AP telephone records was revealed. Sponsors Ted Poe, R-Texas, and John Conyers Jr., D-Mich., appeared with a group of lawmakers from both parties to announce growing House support for media shield legislation.

As introduced, the House bill contained a much broader definition of who was protected than the Senate committee-approved bill. It would have defined protected journalism as the "gathering, preparing, collecting, photographing, recording, writing, editing, reporting or publishing of news or information that concerns local, national or international events or other matters of public interest for dissemination in the public."

The bill, however, was not considered in committee.

Nondiscrimination

After years of trying, the Senate in 2013 passed a bill that would have prohibited most employers from discriminating against gay, lesbian, bisexual, and transgender workers. The House did not take it up.

The passage came almost twenty years after similar legislation was first introduced. The 2013 action was the first movement on the issue on Capitol Hill since 2007, when the Democratic-controlled House had passed a measure that would have protected gay, lesbian, and bisexual workers.

Gay rights activists had been buoyed in the early part of 2013 by an increasing number of Republicans announcing their support for gay marriage, as well as by the Supreme Court's June 26 decision to strike down the federal Defense of Marriage Act (PL 104–199). The activists focused their attention on the Senate version of a bill (S 815) titled the Employment Non-Discrimination Act, or ENDA. They organized a grassroots campaign during the August congressional recess to pressure a handful of Democratic senators who had not cosponsored the bill and several Republicans who were regarded as likely to back it.

By the fall, sponsors said they were close to collecting the sixty Senate supporters they needed to overcome a filibuster. After Majority Leader Harry Reid, D-Nev., announced he would bring the bill to the floor in early November, several targeted senators signaled that they would vote for it.

Reid's home-state Republican colleague, Dean Heller, was the sixtieth senator to announce his support, doing so on the morning of November 4, 2013, the date on which Reid had scheduled a cloture vote to allow action on the measure to proceed. With Heller's public endorsement, the measure's eventual success in the Senate was assured.

The Senate action—and, in particular, the votes of ten Senate Republicans for passage—was taken as a sign that Congress was warming to the idea of barring discrimination in the workplace on the basis of sexual orientation or gender identity and that the measure had a chance of becoming law. However, leaders of the GOP-controlled House pushed back and said enacting such a ban would be likely to create more lawsuits. The House did not take any action on either the Senate-passed bill or a companion House version (HR 1755).

Senate Committee Action

The Senate Health, Education, Labor, and Pensions Committee approved S 815 by a 15–7 vote on July 10, 2013, with three Republicans—Mark S. Kirk of Illinois, Orrin G. Hatch of Utah, and Lisa Murkowski of Alaska—voting with all of the panel's Democrats in favor.

The bill would have prohibited employers from firing, refusing to hire, or discriminating against those employed or seeking employment on the basis of their perceived or actual sexual orientation or gender identity. Such federal protections were already in law based on race, religion, gender, national origin, age, and disability. In addition, seventeen states and the District of Columbia had workplace nondiscrimination laws that covered members of the lesbian, gay, bisexual, and transgender (LGBT) community, according to the Human Rights Campaign. But the LGBT individuals were not explicitly protected from workplace discrimination under federal law.

The bill would have exempted employers that were otherwise not subject to workplace discrimination laws concerning employees' religions—primarily churches and religious schools. Courts had defined such employers as those whose "purpose and character are primarily religious."

The HELP committee by unanimous consent adopted a substitute amendment offered by chair Tom Harkin, D-Iowa, that made several changes in the bill as drafted. In particular, Harkin's amendment inserted language to require plaintiffs to demonstrate that sexual orientation or gender identity was a "motivating factor" for an adverse employment action in cases in which several reasons for the action were involved.

The committee vote came amid increasing public concern about discrimination against the LGBT community and two weeks after a Supreme Court ruling overturned a central part of the Defense of Marriage Act, which had defined marriage under federal law as only between a man and a woman. In a June 13, 2013, poll by the Pew Research Center, 21 percent of LGBT adults said they had been treated unfairly by an employer in hiring or promotions. In addition to workplace discrimination, LGBT employees said they faced wage disparities. And a joint study by the National Gay and Lesbian Task Force and the National Center for Transgender Equality found that 26 percent of transgender people said they had lost a job because of their gender identification, and 50 percent said they had been harassed.

Bill advocates were also buoyed by a survey from Republican pollster Alex Lundry, which found that 68 percent of voters, including 56 percent of Republicans, supported the Senate bill. They also cited endorsements from dozens of major corporations, including Nike, Pfizer, and Bank of America.

Senate Floor

Reid called for a vote on November 4, 2013, to invoke cloture and cut off debate on the motion to proceed to the bill. The motion was agreed to by a vote of 61–30, with 7 GOP senators voting in favor and no Democrats opposed. Three Republicans—Kelly Ayotte of New Hampshire, Rob Portman of Ohio, and Patrick J. Toomey of Pennsylvania—agreed to support the motion after negotiating a deal during the roll call to secure votes on amendments.

Three days later, the chamber voted 64–32 to pass S 815. Two Republicans who had missed the initial cloture vote—John McCain of Arizona and Murkowski of Alaska—voted "yes." So did Jeff Flake of Arizona, who had opposed cloture.

Throughout floor consideration, Senate opponents largely left it up to advocacy groups such as the Family Research Council and Heritage Action, an arm of the Heritage Foundation, to make the case against the bill in comments away from the chamber. Only Dan Coats, R-Ind., spoke against the measure on the Senate floor, saying its religious exemptions were too narrow. He also contended that workers who did not support homosexuality might be silenced by their supervisors because the bill would have allowed lawsuits against employers if they permitted the existence of a workplace hostile to gay and transgender employees.

Two Republican amendments offered on the Senate floor were designed to assuage concerns expressed by religious groups about the bill's limited exemptions.

One amendment, by Ayotte and Portman, was designed to bar retaliation against religious groups by local, state, or federal government agencies in granting federal contracts, licenses, or other business dealings. Senators adopted the amendment, which applied to employers already protected under the bill, by voice vote.

The other GOP amendment, offered by Toomey, would have broadened the definition of religious employers exempted under the measure. It was rejected by a vote of 43–55 on November 7, 2013.

House Bill

On April 25, 2013, the same day the Senate bill was introduced, Reps. Jared Polis, D-Colo., and Ileana Ros-Lehtinen, R-Fla., introduced a companion measure, HR 1755. But they knew it would be a hard sell in the more conservative House. Indeed, groups that opposed the legislation stepped up their lobbying after Senate committee approval. Hoping to hold the line in the House and worried that the measure ran counter to traditional Christian values, opponents such as the Family Research Council said the legislation could undermine religious freedom and result in discrimination in the workplace against people who opposed homosexuality. They also warned it would interfere in the free market and with company personnel decisions.

Following Senate passage of S 815, the White House and Senate Democratic leaders called on Speaker John A. Boehner, R-Ohio, to bring the bill to a vote, saying it could pass the House with broad support from Democrats and a minority of Republicans. By December 2013, the House measure had 200 cosponsors, including almost the entire Democratic Caucus. But only a handful of Republicans cosponsored it, and Boehner did not bring it up.

Patent Litigation

A large bipartisan majority of the House voted late in 2013 to crack down on frivolous patent infringement lawsuits. But disagreements over the scope of the problem and the proper solution prevented Senate action on several competing measures, even though the White House lent support for elements of both the House-passed measure and the Senate bills.

The 2013 fight focused on "patent assertion entities," which were companies often disparaged as patent "trolls" that did not make products or provide services but instead acquired patents solely for the purpose of obtaining licensing fees for their use. These companies often enforced their patents with lawsuits claiming patent infringement. Such lawsuits tended to be costly to litigate and often ended in expensive settlements. However, opponents of changing the patent system pointed to the complaints of independent inventors, who said their ideas were often stolen and whom patent assertion entities claimed to represent.

The push to protect intellectual property from lawsuits brought by patent trolls arose just two years after Congress passed a long-sought overhaul of federal patent law (PL 112–29). Lawmakers had debated that measure for six years, navigating difficult disputes between industry groups and large and small companies. The resulting law gave the Patent and Trademark Office additional resources to assess the quality of patents—defective or overly broad patents were viewed as one reason for the proliferation of lawsuits—and courts had raised the standard for plaintiffs to bring suit. But the proposed legislation in 2013 was a sign that the earlier effort had produced an incomplete result.

Some of the world's biggest corporations sought to influence the debate in the 113th Congress. These included such high-tech enterprises as Google Inc. and Microsoft Corp., whose business interests positioned them as potential defendants in infringement cases, and such pharmaceutical giants as AstraZeneca and Eli Lilly & Co., whose interests positioned them as plaintiffs.

Representatives of a group calling itself the Big Tent Coalition made the rounds on Capitol Hill in July 2013, urging members to make lawsuits by patent trolls more difficult. The coalition, which included big technology companies, retailers, and advertising agencies, said that the practice of occasional lawsuits in the past had mushroomed into a booming industry of wholesale litigation. In a July letter to House and Senate leaders and to the leaders of each chamber's Judiciary committee, the coalition wrote that nuisance suits had quadrupled since 2005 and that companies had paid $29 billion to settle them.

The coalition said companies filing infringement suits were targeting smaller and medium-sized businesses, which were less capable of mounting a defense. Another lobbying group, Stop Patent Abuse Now, said retailers had been hit with lawsuits for using store locators on their websites and for transmitting Web links in text messages. Companies, especially smaller ones, were willing to settle, the group said, just to make the suits go away.

The issue attracted the attention of lawmakers from both parties. In the Senate, Democrat Charles E. Schumer of New York and Republican John Cornyn of Texas were principal players trying to prevent patent litigation from increasing. In the House, the push came from Republicans Darrell Issa of California and Jason Chaffetz of Utah and from Democrats Peter A. DeFazio of Oregon and Judy Chu of California.

Their legislative proposals included forcing plaintiffs to pay attorneys' fees if they lost and further tightening the standards for issuing patents.

The executive branch also weighed in. The Obama administration in mid-2013 gave district court judges additional discretion to award attorneys' fees to defendants when patent suits were judged to be frivolous. And the Federal Trade Commission (FTC) began investigating the seriousness of patent trolls as a problem.

House Legislative Action

House Judiciary Committee Chair Robert W. Goodlatte, R-Va., introduced a broad patent litigation overhaul (HR 3309) in late October and pushed it through his committee and the full House within six weeks. Despite that pace, the path to passage was not simple. Widespread agreement among Obama administration officials and influential lawmakers from both parties that Congress needed to crack down on abusive lawsuits gave way to a contentious Judiciary panel markup that exposed fault lines over how best to overhaul the system of protecting the rights of inventors.

The committee approved HR 3309 by a vote of 33–5 on November 20 after making changes in legal-fee provisions and removing controversial language regarding business method patents. All Republicans and twelve Democrats backed Goodlatte's revised bill. Democrats John Conyers Jr. of Michigan, Robert C. Scott of Virginia, Melvin Watt of North Carolina, Sheila Jackson Lee of Texas, and Hank Johnson of Georgia were opposed.

As approved by the committee, the measure would have required patent holders filing lawsuits to provide basic details about their products and more specificity about how their intellectual property rights were allegedly being violated, as a way of ensuring that their legal claims were valid. It also would have given courts the ability to limit the discovery process as a way to mitigate the costs for companies being sued. This addressed a concern of Goodlatte, who said legal discovery was out of balance and put defendants of infringement claims at a disadvantage. In addition, the bill included a provision requiring the losing party in an infringement suit to pay the winning side's costs unless the loser's claims were judged to be "reasonably justified," a step designed to reduce the economic incentive for patent trolls.

Goodlatte said the bill would help address abusive practices that were damaging the patent system and harming the nation's economy. "The patent system was never intended to be a playground for litigation extortion and frivolous claims," he said at the markup.

But Conyers, the committee's ranking Democrat, objected that although the issue merited congressional attention, the committee-approved bill went too far. He said it could undermine innovation and also encroach on the independence of the judicial branch. Watt, the ranking Democrat on the Courts, Intellectual Property and the Internet Subcommittee, also raised objections, saying the committee-approved bill

was written entirely from the point of view of those defending claims from an abusive, nonpracticing patent acquirer.

The panel rejected, 14–19, a substitute amendment offered by Conyers that would have taken a narrower approach and provided additional money for the Patent and Trademark Office to implement the 2011 law. All voting Republicans opposed the substitute, and three Democrats—Suzan DelBene of Washington, Zoe Lofgren of California, and Pedro R. Pierluisi of Puerto Rico—broke from their party and voted in opposition.

The full House on December 5 passed HR 3309 by a wide margin, 325–91, with majorities of both Republicans and Democrats voting in favor. Before passage, the House rejected, 157–258, a Conyers substitute amendment that would have removed a number of provisions from the bill, including language dealing with the payment of attorneys' fees and with discovery limits. It also would have modified provisions requiring the disclosure of information about how a patent was to be used by the plaintiff when filing an infringement lawsuit.

The chamber adopted, 341–73, a manager's amendment by Goodlatte to exempt from the bill's discovery limits actions dealing with competitive products, to allow for parties to a lawsuit to volunteer to not have those limits apply, and to delay deadlines for reports required by the bill.

The House also gave voice-vote approval to an amendment by Jared Polis, D-Colo., that added to provisions already in the bill aimed at vague "demand letters" that charged infringement and threatened lawsuits if recipients did not pay restitution. The bill would have required such letters to include information about the patent at issue and how the person receiving the letter was allegedly willfully infringing on it—a means to increasing restitution payments.

While the House rejected several amendments aimed at narrowing the bill's scope, lawmakers adopted, 260–156, an amendment by Dana Rohrabacher, R-Calif., leaving intact a provision in existing law that enabled patent applicants to appeal decisions by the Patent and Trademark Office in district court, where they could introduce new information rather than in federal circuit court. The committee-approved version of the bill would have removed that provision from existing law.

Senate Bills

The Senate Judiciary Committee, which had several competing bills, proved to be a tougher legislative battleground than the House for those seeking to change patent law. Senate bills included Republican-sponsored measures that would have taken many of the same steps as the House-passed measure and Democrat-sponsored alternatives that would have made narrower changes. In the end, the committee took no action.

Judiciary Chair Patrick J. Leahy, D-Vt., and Mike Lee, R-Utah, introduced a leading alternative (S 1720) in November that won White House support. Similar to the rejected Conyers substitute amendment in the House, S 1720 was designed to curtail demand letters. The measure would have allowed the FTC to crack down on such letters if they were found to be misleading, and it would have created legal protections for consumers who were targeted for infringement actions simply because they used patented products or services.

Orrin G. Hatch, R-Utah, sponsored a competing bill (S 1612), similar to the House-passed measure, that was focused on shifting legal costs to the losers in patent infringement suits. However, trial lawyers had long opposed such measures, and some senators also said it could penalize small inventors who tried to protect their own patents. Another bill (S 1013), sponsored by Cornyn, was also similar to the House measure but would have imposed requirements on plaintiffs to show more clearly how they were harmed by the alleged infringement.

Schumer sponsored a bill (S 866) that focused on improving the patents. He contended that patent trolls had been able to acquire poor-quality patents that should never have been granted. His bill would have allowed the Patent and Trademark Office to review decisions as an alternative to litigation.

In May 2014, Leahy announced that he was setting the issue aside. He said that competing companies on different sides of the issue could not come to an agreement, meaning he could not muster broad bipartisan support on the committee behind any of the proposals.

Voting Rights

When a closely divided Supreme Court in June 2013 invalidated a central provision of the 1965 Voting Rights Act, the justices suggested that Congress could revisit the issue with an approach that would pass constitutional muster. Leading lawmakers responded with proposed legislation the following year, but it did not advance in either chamber.

The Voting Rights Act was an iconic legislative achievement of the civil rights era. It aimed to end a century of discrimination that made it virtually impossible for most black residents to vote in many states, particularly those in the South. The law eliminated such barriers to voting as poll taxes and literacy tests, and it installed additional scrutiny in states where discrimination had been most pronounced.

The Supreme Court's controversial 2013 decision, *Shelby County v. Holder*, struck down the "coverage formula" of the Voting Rights Act, which had subjected all or parts of sixteen mainly Southern states to federal approval of their voting laws as a way to ensure that election changes would not impose burdens on minority voters. The majority of justices said the provision was based on decades-old data and did not accurately reflect conditions in those states.

In its 5–4 decision, the high court in effect told Congress to write a new formula to replace the one it had invalidated. "Congress may draft another formula based on current conditions," the court majority wrote. That would have meant Congress devising a new way to determine which parts of the country would be required to undergo special Justice Department scrutiny—called "pre-clearance" in legal parlance—of their voting procedures, election districts, and other aspects of their voting systems.

But congressional leaders in the 113th Congress did not take up the issue. It was not a priority for House GOP leaders, although House Majority Leader Eric Cantor of Virginia expressed an interest in finding a way for Congress to respond to the high court ruling. In a statement that his office issued hours after the Supreme Court decision on June 25, 2013, he said he hoped Congress could produce legislation ensuring that "the sacred obligation of voting in this country remains protected." But any realistic prospect of the House updating the law vanished in June 2014 when Cantor unexpectedly lost his primary election and subsequently departed from Congress.

PROPOSED LEGISLATION

In January 2014, Senate Judiciary Chair Patrick J. Leahy, D-Vt., and Reps. Jim Sensenbrenner, R-Wis., and John Conyers Jr., D-Mich., respectively House Judiciary's No. 2 Republican and top Democrat, introduced legislation to respond to the Court's decision and update the Voting Rights Act.

The coverage formula invalidated by the high court had applied to nine states and parts of seven others. It required federal approval of state voting laws if those states had a discriminatory "test or device" that limited residents' access to the polls at the time the law was passed and if they had less than 50 percent participation by voters in the 1964 presidential election. The law was later updated to include the 1968 and 1972 presidential elections.

The new formula in the Leahy-Sensenbrenner-Conyers bill would have subjected only four states to federal oversight in the short term: Georgia, Louisiana, Mississippi, and Texas. Other states, however, could have been added based on changes in voting conditions for minority groups, and the bill contained other language that would have made it easier to challenge state voting laws in the courts.

State requirements that voters provide photo identification in order to vote—favored by many Republicans but opposed by Democrats and minority groups—would not be considered a voting rights violation under the terms of the Leahy-Sensenbrenner-Conyers bill.

The proposal also would have addressed late election changes that might impede voters' access to the polls. For example, it would have required states and localities to provide public notice of changes in their voting procedures at least 180 days before federal elections, as well as to notify residents of changes in polling resources and redistricting.

In a statement, Leahy said the bipartisan legislation was designed to ensure that no American would be denied the constitutional right to vote because of discrimination based on race or color. Sensenbrenner urged lawmakers to revise the Voting Rights Act before the next election.

But few Republicans saw a pressing need to rewrite the Voting Rights Act. They noted that the Supreme Court's ruling had not touched other sections of the act, which remained available as tools for the Justice Department to prosecute states and localities that discriminated at the polls. The lack of Republican interest appeared to be another sign of the growing partisan rifts in Congress. As recently as 2006, lawmakers in both parties had voted overwhelmingly to renew the Voting Rights Act, even as some questioned whether the law was still necessary.

Appropriations

Lawmakers clashed repeatedly over annual appropriations bills in both fiscal year 2013 and fiscal year 2014. As a result, the Commerce-Justice-Science bill was combined with other appropriations measures into omnibus packages that were not passed until months into the new fiscal years. The C-J-S bills enabled lawmakers to prioritize certain law enforcement functions and to weigh in on guns and other hot-button issues.

FISCAL 2014

Several federal law enforcement agencies received sizable budget increases in the omnibus appropriations package for fiscal year 2014. Lawmakers said they wanted to boost antiterrorism and cybersecurity efforts. Gun control proponents were pleased with additional spending to speed up background checks of firearms purchasers. But opponents of firearms restrictions pointed to provisions they viewed as victories for their side.

These increases were included in the Commerce-Justice-Science bill, one of twelve regular appropriations measures. Overcoming partisan differences, lawmakers wrapped all twelve appropriations measures into the omnibus (HR 3547—PL 113–76) that the Senate cleared on January 15, 2014. The C-J-S measure was $51.6 billion, almost 3 percent greater than the previous year's enacted level. It was structured such that lawmakers from both parties were able to claim at least small victories.

The omnibus bill ended a protracted appropriations process that had extended more than three months beyond the October 1 start of the fiscal year and included a sixteen-day government shutdown. House and Senate appropriators assembled it under the terms of a bipartisan, two-year budget agreement (H J Res 59—PL 113–67) negotiated in December 2013 that pared back cuts imposed by the sequester and raised the caps on discretionary spending first set in the 2011 debt limit law (PL 112–25).

The House and Senate Appropriations committees were roughly $5 billion apart as they approved very different versions of the regular, stand-alone fiscal 2014 Commerce-Justice-Science spending bill in mid-July. Neither chamber considered its C-J-S bill on the floor.

Freestanding Bill

The House Appropriations committee approved its C-J-S bill (HR 2787—H Rept 113–171) by voice vote on July 17, proposing $26.7 billion for the Justice Department, a reduction of about $722 million from the previous year. House Republican appropriators added policy restrictions to their bill, including two related to immigration. One would have barred the government from challenging state immigration laws, while the other would have blocked states and cities receiving some Justice Department grants from prohibiting the maintenance of information about the immigration status of individuals or the exchange of that data with other federal, state, or local agencies. A third policy restriction in the House committee bill would have prevented the Justice Department from requiring gun dealers to report on sales of multiple rifles or shotguns to a single buyer.

The Senate Appropriations panel approved its C-J-S bill (S 1329—S Rept 113–78) on July 18 by a 21–9 vote, with most Republicans opposed. It included $28.5 billion for the Justice Department, a $1.1 billion boost over the presequester 2013 appropriation. State and local law enforcement grants would have received roughly $2.5 billion, compared with $1.9 billion in the House committee bill.

Omnibus Highlights

As enacted, the omnibus included $27.7 billion for the Justice Department, an increase of $357 million. FBI spending was set at $8.3 billion, or $222 million more than the enacted fiscal 2013 level. Within the FBI's budget, the spending law prioritized counterterrorism and cybersecurity, and it required the agency to free up $60 million to handle an increased number of gun buyer background checks. The extra money for the National Instant Criminal Background Check System was a victory for gun control groups, including Mayors Against Illegal Guns.

The Drug Enforcement Agency was given an essentially unchanged budget of $2 billion. The Bureau of Alcohol, Tobacco, Firearms and Explosives received $1.18 billion, a $47 million increase. The Bureau of Prisons, which managed a steadily rising federal inmate population, received $6.9 billion for salaries and expenses, an increase of $79 million.

The omnibus provided $2.3 billion for grants to state and local law enforcement agencies, an increase of $51 million.

In response to school shootings, including the killing of twenty elementary school students in Newtown, Conn., in December 2012, appropriators included $75 million for a Comprehensive School Safety Initiative by the National Institute of Justice, the department's research arm, to investigate causes of school violence, to develop technologies and strategies for increasing school safety, and to provide grants to test innovative approaches.

The measure also included $1 million to create a task force to study successful strategies to reduce incarceration that might be replicated at the federal level. Frank R. Wolf, R-Va., chair of the House C-J-S Appropriations Subcommittee, had long raised concerns about the rise in the federal prison population.

The omnibus provided $1 million for a second Wolf priority—an independent review of operation and management of the Department of Justice's Civil Rights Division. A 2013 report by the department's inspector general found widespread political polarization within the division, and the assessment was intended to recommend changes.

Both sides of the gun control issue pointed to language they favored. House Republicans touted provisions they said would protect Second Amendment rights, including prohibitions of various firearms import and export restrictions. House Democrats praised the omission of several firearms-related proposals, including one that would have blocked a reporting requirement for multiple sales of rifles or shotguns to a single purchaser.

Democrats hailed the additional money for background checks, the school security initiative, and the ATF's increase. The omnibus also included $58.5 million to help states submit records to the federal background check database and $15 million to train local police to respond to shootings.

Republicans preserved some other policy riders. The measure extended a prohibition on the transfer or release into the United States of detainees at the Guantánamo Bay prison in Cuba and a prohibition of construction or acquisition of facilities in the United States for detention or imprisonment of Guantánamo detainees.

FISCAL 2015

In 2014, for the fifth year in a row, Congress was unable to complete a single one of its twelve regular appropriations bills. Instead, lawmakers assembled an omnibus measure (HR 83—PL 113-235) that finally reached Obama's desk nine days before Christmas.

The C-J-S title was perhaps most notable for including a legislative rider preventing the Justice Department from cracking down on the medical use of marijuana in those states that had legalized medical marijuana.

Freestanding Bill

The House Appropriations Committee on May 8, 2014, approved the fiscal 2015 C-J-S bill (HR 4660) by voice vote after endorsing a GOP gun proposal and beating back a number of Democratic firearm policy amendments.

Overall, the bill would have provided $51.2 billion in discretionary funds, including $27.8 billion for the Justice Department, a $383 million increase from current funding. But it would cut funding for DOJ grant programs, including a sharp reduction for Community Oriented Policing Services hiring grants used to hire or retain local police officers.

Panel members, 29–18, voted to add a proposal from Texas Republican John Carter to withhold funding for efforts to make gun dealers inform the Justice Department when they sold multiple rifles or shotguns to the same person. The proposal aimed to stymie an Obama administration requirement that gun dealers in Arizona, California, New Mexico, and Texas notify the Bureau of Alcohol, Tobacco, Firearms, and Explosives when they sell two or more of certain high-powered long guns to the same buyer within five days. The administration said the policy is designed to counter violence along the Southwestern border, but many gun rights advocates viewed it as a veiled form of government gun registration that amounted to discrimination against those living in the region.

The panel rejected, 18–29, an amendment by Mike Quigley, D-Ill., to repeal language in a fiscal 2013 appropriations law (PL 113-6) that would permanently block funds for any federal rule requiring gun dealers to conduct physical inventories. The existing funding ban prevented the ATF from effectively identifying lost or stolen guns, Quigley said. But Carter argued the proposal would burden small businesses.

Appropriators also rejected, 18–29, an amendment by James P. Moran, D-Va., to require gun dealers to conduct background checks on their prospective employees.

Committee members also rejected, 20–26, a Barbara Lee, D-Calif., amendment to reverse much of the bill's proposed cut to community policing grants. And it rejected, by voice vote, a Moran amendment to strike language that withholds funds for transferring Guantánamo Bay detainees to the United States.

The House May 30 passed the bill on a strong bipartisan vote, 321–87, after a free-wheeling floor debate that loosened some restrictions on medical marijuana. California Republican Dana Rohrabacher offered the amendment to block the Justice Department from prosecuting medical marijuana users and providers who were abiding by state legalization laws, which passed on a vote of 219–189. Backers hailed the vote as a step toward the inevitable loosening of federal marijuana restrictions.

The Senate Appropriations Committee easily passed its version of the fiscal 2015 C-J-S bill by a vote of 30–0 on June 5, 2014. Members ignored the House language on medical marijuana. But members approved an amendment by Jeff Merkley, D-Ore., to allow for industrial hemp research by blocking the Justice Department from spending money in contravention of research provisions in the 2014 farm bill (PL 113-79). Those provisions let academic institutions or state agriculture departments grow hemp for research purposes, as long as it is legal under the relevant state law.

Omnibus Highlights

Overall, the C-J-S title of the omnibus bill provided $50.1 billion for C-J-S programs, a decrease of $1.5 billion compared to the previous year. The Justice Department got $27 billion, a decrease of $706 million.

Among law enforcement agencies, the Federal Bureau of Investigation would receive $8.4 billion, or $93 million more than the 2014 enacted level, with priority placed on counterterrorism activities and investigating human trafficking, the House summary states.

The Drug Enforcement Administration would receive $2.4 billion, or an increase of $21 million. The Bureau of Prisons would get $6.9 billion, an increase of $62 million to maintain staffing levels at facilities.

Grants to state and local enforcement would be funded at $2.3 billion under the bill, an increase of $65 million. The bill would increase the funding for the Executive Office for Immigration Review from $315 million to $351 million. That includes funding for thirty-five new Immigration Judge Teams allowing EOIR to adjudicate up to 39,000 more cases annually.

The measure included the policy rider blocking funds for any Justice Department effort to intervene in states that had legalized medical marijuana. It also had language that would bar funds for supporting or justifying the use of torture by U.S. government officials or contract employees. Despite the concerns of some Democrats, it included a new gun-related prohibition that would block funds to implement an international arms trade treaty unless the Senate ratifies the proposal.

2015-2016

Although they controlled both chambers of Congress, Republicans did not pass major legislation. Instead they largely settled on opposing Obama priorities related to immigration and gun regulations and preventing the president in the final months of his administration from filling a Supreme Court vacancy. *(See box, pp. 429–431.)*

Lawmakers again found themselves divided over immigration. They failed to advance measures to tighten border security or to punish so-called sanctuary cities that did not cooperate with the federal government on enforcing immigration laws. They also fell short in efforts to block Obama's executive orders related to immigration, but they got an assist from federal judges who put them on hold.

Republicans were more successful in parrying Democratic attempts to expand background checks of gun purchases and other firearms regulations. A series of mass shootings highlighted such issues, but Democrats could not overcome the GOP commitment to upholding the constitutional rights of gun owners. Congress also failed to reach consensus on overhauling criminal sentencing laws or on the hot-button issue of transgender rights. However, lawmakers did agree on protecting medical marijuana in states that had legalized it.

Immigration Policy

Consensus on immigration policy continued to elude Congress in the 114th, even as sanctuary cities and Donald Trump's promise of a border wall became hot topics in the 2016 presidential campaign. Lawmakers sparred over proposals to countermand Obama's executive orders on treatment of illegal immigrants, tighten border security, and punish sanctuary cities. But they failed to advance major legislation on any of those issues.

The stalemate extended Congress's inability to pass an overhaul of the nation's immigration laws. Many business leaders supported such an overhaul as a way of boosting the economy, which needed more labor to offset the generation of Baby Boomers who are retiring. Democrats continued to press for comprehensive legislation, and some GOP leaders worried their party had lost standing with Hispanic voters.

But there was disagreement over whether the estimated 11.3 million immigrants who came to the United States illegally should eventually be granted citizenship or another kind of earned legal status. Conservatives derided such a path as "amnesty" and said it would reward illegal behavior. These differences stymied efforts in the 113th Congress to change immigration laws, even after the Senate passed a bipartisan immigration bill in 2013.

Frustration with Congress's inability to revamp immigration law led Obama in November 2014 to issue executive orders intended to shield millions of undocumented immigrants from deportation and allow them to work legally in the United States. But his decision further antagonized Republicans, sinking hopes of comprehensive legislation in the 114th Congress.

BACKGROUND

No comprehensive immigration law had been enacted since the Reagan administration, when the Immigration Reform and Control Act of 1986 legalized nearly 3 million undocumented immigrants living in the United States—although Congress in 1996 during the Clinton administration did enact an enforcement-focused immigration law. President George W. Bush advocated for but failed to achieve a major immigration overhaul, largely because of deep philosophical differences over how to address the growing illegal immigrant population in the country.

By the latter part of Bush's administration, there was growing concern about the situation of "Dreamers," young adult immigrants brought to the United States as children and educated in the United States, who were now seeking legal status to remain. However, neither President Obama once he came into office nor the then-Democratic Congress made any major efforts on immigration during the 111th Congress, focusing instead on responding to the economic recession and financial crisis and on health care overhaul legislation. When Congress did try to take up the DREAM Act (Development, Relief, and Education for Alien Minors), it wasn't until late in 2010 after House Democrats had lost their majority in the midterm elections.

In 2011, with House Republicans showing no interest in taking up the DREAM Act, the Obama administration began trying to meet the needs of certain classes of immigrants in other ways. A series of memos written by Immigration and Customs Enforcement (ICE) Director John Morton in 2011 and 2012 outlined groups of immigrants who should have the highest priority for deportation, such as violent criminals, national security threats, and recent border crossers. The memos provided that "prosecutorial discretion" (essentially more relaxed enforcement) could be applied to other groups of illegal immigrants that the administration did not consider a national security or public safety threat, such as students or relatives of legal residents. The memos also limited the use of some immigration enforcement tools such as detainers, which allow ICE to remove an illegal immigrant who is being held in local or state custody.

In 2012, President Obama used executive actions to create the Deferred Action for Childhood Arrivals (DACA) program. Patterned after the proposed DREAM Act, DACA provided temporary, two-year protection from deportation to illegal immigrants who had been brought to the United States by their parents before June 15, 2007, who were under the age of sixteen at that time and had lived in the United States since then. DACA applicants also had to meet other standards, such as a clean criminal record and completion of high school or military service.

After Republican presidential candidate Mitt Romney lost two-thirds of the Latino vote in the 2012 election, many national GOP leaders were eager to improve the party's image with that group. But after House Republicans refused to take up any immigration legislation, Obama announced in a Rose Garden speech on June 29, 2014, that he would seek "to fix as much of our immigration system as I can on my own" through executive actions.

EXECUTIVE ORDERS

On November 20, 2014, after Republicans had won control of the Senate in the midterm elections, the president announced actions that the White House said would prevent nearly 5 million illegal immigrants from being deported.

Under this initiative (Deferred Action for Parents of Americans and Lawful Permanent Residents, or DAPA), the government's immigration enforcement activities would be focused on national security threats, serious criminals, and recent border crossers. A new deferred action category would be created for illegal immigrants who had been in the country for more than five years and were parents of children who are U.S. citizens or lawful permanent residents. Those people would have the opportunity to request temporary relief from deportation and obtain a work authorization for three years at a time if they registered with the government, submitted biometric data, passed background checks, and paid back taxes.

The initiative also expanded DACA to apply to children who entered the United States before January 1, 2010, regardless of how old they were. It increased the work authorization to three years instead of two.

However, Obama's orders were soon put on hold after twenty-six states filed a lawsuit in December 2014. U.S. District Court Judge Andrew Hanen, a George W. Bush appointee who sat in Texas, found that one of the states, Texas, had the legal right to file a lawsuit challenging the actions because of potential costs to the state. The government appealed that ruling.

In a further setback to the administration, Senate Majority Leader Mitch McConnell, R-Ky., effectively killed chances for a comprehensive immigration bill in the 114th Congress when he declared during an August 6, 2015, news conference that Obama's executive actions the year before had "made it impossible for us to go forward."

Just three months later, a three-judge panel of the U.S. Court of Appeals for the 5th Circuit ruled, 2–1, that Texas and the other states had a legal right to challenge the federal government because the states could face millions of dollars in costs if the immigrants got drivers' licenses and other benefits.

As the case made its way to the Supreme Court, House and Senate Republicans in April 2016 filed separate briefs to support Texas and the other states challenging Obama's actions on immigration. The briefs argued that Obama had overstepped his authority with actions that would give federal benefits to millions of undocumented immigrants that are not in the law.

The House, in its brief, argued that "neither any immigration law now on the books nor the Constitution empowers the Executive to authorize—let alone facilitate—the prospective violation of those laws on a massive class-wide scale." And the Senate Republicans argued that the administration's actions were "part of an explicit effort to circumvent the legislative process." "Congress has never given the executive unchecked discretion to rewrite federal immigration policy or to fashion its own immigration code," the brief stated.

In June 2016, the shorthanded Supreme Court deadlocked 4–4 on the legal challenge to the Obama executive actions. This left in place the appeals court decision blocking the DAPA program and leaving the administration powerless to do much more on immigration.

IMMIGRATION RIDERS

Obama's executive orders on immigration set the stage for a remarkably bruising legislative fight at the beginning of the 114th Congress. Many House conservatives, looking for a vehicle to roll back the orders, eyed the Homeland Security appropriations bill (HR 240) to roll back Obama's orders because the Department of Homeland Security (DHS) includes agencies that enforce immigration laws.

Senate Democrats resisted that plan, and Republicans were worried about being blamed for another government shutdown if the two sides reached an impasse. The result was that Congress in March 2015 eventually passed a "clean" bill to fund DHS through the end of fiscal 2015, without any immigration riders. President Obama signed it into law (PL 114–4).

LEGISLATIVE ACTION

Soon after President Obama issued his new immigration orders in November 2014, many Republicans called the actions unconstitutional and pushed for legislative action to block them, favoring the use of the pending FY 2015 Homeland Security appropriations bill to deny funding for the president's initiatives. House and Senate appropriators at that time were negotiating an omnibus spending measure to wrap up the FY 2015 appropriations process during the postelection lame duck session.

To appease those conservatives while at the same time avoiding a year-end government shutdown that likely would occur if the House tried to include such defunding language in the omnibus, GOP leaders adopted a plan under which the omnibus spending measure would include full-year appropriations for all spending bills except Homeland Security. That department would be funded only through February 27, 2015. This would provide House conservatives a chance to address Obama's immigration actions as part of a Homeland Security bill early in the new Congress, when Republicans would have majorities in both chambers.

In returning to the Capitol to convene the new Congress, however, GOP leaders faced the conundrum of how to enact a full-year Homeland Security spending bill in the face of White House opposition to any language that would limit the president's new immigration initiative while also satisfying the demands of GOP conservatives.

If GOP House leaders started with a "clean" Homeland Security funding bill without defunding language, a large contingent of Republicans would likely vote against the legislation. Alternatively, they knew that voting early on a plan favored by the House's staunchest critics of the immigration actions might give Republican leaders enough time to return to the issue if it failed in the Senate or was vetoed by the president.

House Action

The House Appropriations Committee unveiled a fiscal 2015 Homeland Security spending bill (HR 240) on January 9, 2015, that would have beefed up funding for immigration enforcement and border protection agencies while paring funding for other domestic priorities. The committee-approved bill did not include provisions to nullify the president's executive actions on immigration, as those were expected to be added as amendments on the House floor.

More than half the budget increase for Customs and Border Protection (CBP) and Immigration and Customs Enforcement (ICE) went toward immigration detention programs in order to sustain 34,000 detention beds and to increase family detention by more than 3,700 beds. Republicans had butted heads with the White House on detention bed levels for years. In 2014, for example, the administration had requested that the mandate be brought down to fewer than 31,000 beds, which cost $119 per day to maintain.

The House passed the Homeland Security bill on January 14 by a 236–191 vote after adopting five hotly contested GOP amendments intended to block Obama's immigration orders and require the use of certain immigration enforcement methods. These included

- An amendment by Robert B. Aderholt, R-Ala., to bar the use of any funds to implement various administrations' immigration policies or to grant any federal benefit to any illegal immigrant as a result of those policies. The prohibition would have applied to deferred action against those classes of illegal immigrants included in the executive actions announced by the president in November 2014. It also would have applied to four memos written by Immigration and Customs Enforcement (ICE) Director John Morton in 2011 and 2012 that focused on prosecutorial discretion and changes to immigration enforcement priorities, as well as any substantially similar policies issued after January 9, 2015. The amendment declared that such immigration policies had no statutory or constitutional basis. It did not, however, restrict the president's original 2012 Deferred Action for Childhood Arrivals (DACA) program. The amendment was adopted 237–190.
- A DACA amendment by Marsha Blackburn, R-Tenn., to bar the use of any funds after January 9, 2015, to consider new, renewal, or previously denied applications under the president's 2012 DACA program or under any other succeeding executive policy. Under the amendment, the prohibition applied to any funds or fees collected or otherwise made available to the Homeland Security Department or to any other federal agency by any bill for any fiscal year. The amendment was adopted 218–209, the closest margin of the five.
- A "treatment of criminals" amendment by Ron DeSantis, R-Fla., would have required Homeland Security to prioritize immigration enforcement actions against illegal immigrants convicted of any offense involving domestic violence, sexual abuse, child molestation, or child exploitation. Specifically, it would have barred the use of funds for any department policy relating to the apprehension, detention, or removal of immigrants who failed to treat any alien convicted of those offenses as being within the highest-priority categories for taking immigration enforcement actions. The amendment was adopted 278–149.
- A "disadvantaged workers" amendment by Matt Salmon, R-Ariz., that expressed the sense of Congress that the administration should not pursue policies that disadvantage the hiring of U.S. citizens and those lawfully present in the United States by making it economically advantageous to hire workers who came to the country illegally, such as granting deferred action and work authorization to illegal immigrants. It stated that because immigrants who are granted deferred action are exempt from being counted toward the employer mandate under the 2010 health care overhaul (which requires employers with fifty or more employees to offer health insurance or pay a penalty), it creates an incentive to hire illegal immigrants over lawfully present workers. The amendment was adopted 253–171.
- A "fairness to legal immigrants" amendment by Aaron Schock, R-Ill., that expressed the sense of Congress that the administration should stop putting the interest of immigrants who worked within the legal framework to enter the United States behind those who came here illegally. It stated that such policies create a backlog for legal immigrants applying for immigration benefits and that it was "unfair to use the fees paid by other aliens to cover the costs of adjudicating petitions and applications for aliens unlawfully present." It also expressed the sense of Congress that ICE should use available funds to improve services and increase the efficiency of the immigration benefits application process for immigrants abroad or who are lawfully present in the United States.

Senate Action

Prospects for the bill were not as favorable in the Senate, where the Democratic leader, Harry Reid of Nevada, accused Republicans of picking a political fight and indicated that Democrats would band together to oppose the immigration provisions.

Republicans were banking on the public to blame Democrats for risking a shutdown of the Homeland Security Department at the end of February if they blocked passage of the appropriations bill containing the GOP's immigration amendments. But Democrats held firm against the $39.7 billion House-passed bill (HR 240), blocking Senate consideration in a series of votes in which they cited opposition to the five GOP amendments that would effectively have reversed the president's immigration executive actions.

On the first procedural vote on February 3, 2015, Democrats prevented the Senate from moving ahead on the measure, with all forty-six members of the Democratic caucus voting against cloture on the motion to proceed to the House-passed bill. Republican Dean Heller of Nevada also voted against cloture. On each of the two following days, Democrats similarly blocked action. The Senate voted 53–47 and 52–47 to move ahead, remaining well short of the 60 votes needed.

This left GOP leaders scrambling to find another path forward to challenge the president over immigration. In the days following the Senate votes, House GOP leaders continued to hold firm, maintaining that it was up to Senate Republicans to find a way to pass the measure. Trying to break the impasse, two former House members, Sens. Shelley Moore Capito of West Virginia and Cory Gardner of Colorado, talked to their former House colleagues on February 11 about what was politically possible in the Senate, where GOP leaders needed the support of six Democrats to move anything through the chamber. But many House conservatives continued to express outrage at Senate Republicans for what they saw as a lack of leadership on immigration and the Senate's inability to pass the House bill.

The political calculus changed on February 16, 2015, however, when U.S. District Judge Andrew Hanen granted a temporary injunction against Obama's orders. Hanen did not immediately rule on the legal issues raised in the case, such as whether the administration had overstepped its legal authority to implement a new deferred deportation program that would offer temporary legal status to at least 4 million immigrants. But the injunction reduced the congressional imperative to stop Obama.

Final Maneuvers

With the court having blocked the program and time running out to enact a Homeland Security spending bill, Majority Leader McConnell early in the final week of February offered a dual-track process. This consisted of a clean spending bill without immigration language as well as separate GOP legislation (S 534) that would block spending on Obama's November action but not affect the president's earlier immigration initiatives. After some hesitation, Reid agreed to this approach.

That set off an extraordinary sequence of events in which the Senate did its best to wrap up its spending debate despite GOP opposition, while House Republicans marched off in another direction.

On the morning of the 27th, the Senate voted 68–31 to close debate on the appropriations bill. Democrats were united in seeking the "clean" funding bill, but Republicans fractured, with most voting to filibuster the plan put forward by their leader to break the impasse. The Senate then voted 66–33 to swap in McConnell's clean substitute before voting 68–31 to pass HR 240.

The motion to proceed to the separate immigration bill (S 534), meanwhile, was blocked by Democrats on a 57–42 vote where 60 votes were needed.

House Republicans remained opposed to a "clean" funding bill. Conservatives in particular urged GOP leaders to continue blocking funding for Obama's immigration actions, pointing out that the judge's decision could be overturned.

Consequently, House GOP leaders brought to the House floor on February 27, 2015, a three-week continuing resolution (H J Res 35) for the Homeland Security Department. They said this would give the House and Senate time to set up a conference committee to negotiate their respective versions of the spending bill and immigration provisions.

But that effort to pass stopgap funding for the department collapsed in the face of Republican division and almost unified Democratic opposition. The measure was defeated 203–224 as 52 Republicans and nearly all Democrats voted against it, despite GOP leaders keeping the vote open for almost an hour in an attempt to twist Republicans' arms to support it.

The bulk of the GOP opponents were hard-line conservatives who were angered that the continuing resolution (CR) did not block funding for the president's immigration actions. The result left a number of Republicans fuming, with some criticizing party leaders for their tactical decisions.

With mere hours to go until Homeland Security funding expired and House Republicans in disarray, the Senate passed a more modest one-week CR for the department (HR 33) that the House quickly passed, 357–60, with 55 Republicans and 5 Democrats voting no. The stopgap, which extended spending authority through March 6, 2015, was a political parachute of sorts for House GOP leaders who had been holed up in Boehner's office through the evening searching for a way out of an embarrassing turn of events.

The following Monday, March 2, Senate Democrats blocked an attempt to go to conference with the House on the full-year Homeland Security bill (HR 240), after which the chamber voted to return the Senate-modified bill to the House. That put the burden back on the House to find a solution to the funding standoff.

House GOP leaders, recognizing that they would be unable to force the Senate to pass a spending bill that defunded the president's immigration actions, the next day allowed the House to vote on and pass the Senate-modified "clean" bill providing full funding for the Homeland

Security Department without any immigration provisions. While the vote on the clean bill infuriated GOP conservatives, House Democrats implied to reporters that Boehner had promised them a vote on a clean bill in exchange for their support the previous Friday on the week-long CR.

The 257–167 House vote to clear the $39.7 billion fiscal 2015 bill for President Obama ended a funding showdown that had embarrassed Republican leaders and consumed the first two months of the congressional agenda. And while averting a potentially politically damaging shutdown of the Homeland Security Department, it also exacerbated a deep rift between mainstream GOP leaders and the most conservative Republicans.

Sanctuary Cities

After a Mexican immigrant living in the country illegally was accused of murdering a young woman in San Francisco, congressional Republicans in 2015 focused on efforts to crack down on the more than 300 communities, including San Francisco, that declined to cooperate with the federal government in enforcing immigration laws. One appropriations rider would have deprived such "sanctuary cities" of homeland security grants. The measure, which Democrats fiercely opposed, was ultimately dropped from the omnibus appropriations bill. Republicans returned to the issue in 2016 but again were unable to get legislation passed.

The July 2015 fatal shooting of Kathryn Steinle in San Francisco crystallized conservative concerns about sanctuary cities. Police charged a Mexican immigrant, Jose Ines Garcia Zarate (also known by the alias of Juan Francisco Lopez Sanchez), who had been deported five times. The shooting drew the attention of presidential candidates, with former Florida Gov. Jeb Bush and former Secretary of State Hillary Rodham Clinton weighing in and Sen. Rand Paul of Kentucky introducing a bill to cut federal funding to cities that did not comply with requests by U.S. Immigration and Customs Enforcement, or ICE, to detain undocumented immigrants.

Republicans in the House such as Lou Barletta of Pennsylvania, Marsha Blackburn of Tennessee, and Matt Salmon of Arizona introduced stand-alone bills that sought to force cities with such sanctuary policies and ordinances to comply with federal immigration law. In the Senate, Arizona Republicans John McCain and Jeff Flake introduced a bill to ensure the deportation of certain undocumented immigrants who committed crimes. Tom Cotton, R-Ark., offered an amendment to an education bill (S 1177) to render cities ineligible for federal grants if they refused to cooperate with immigration agencies.

Many Democrats, however, said such bills did not promote public safety or offer comprehensive solutions to the issue of immigration. Rep. Luis V. Gutiérrez, D-Ill., a member of the Judiciary Subcommittee for Immigration and Border Security, said the focus on sanctuary cities was misplaced. He criticized the Judiciary Committee for focusing on the few immigrants who were criminals instead of the millions who never committed crimes.

This was not the first time bills addressing sanctuary cities had been introduced, although the flurry of legislation in the 114th Congress exceeded previous efforts. For six years, Rep. Duncan Hunter, R-Calif., had sponsored legislation (most recently HR 3009) to deny federal funding for cities that did not comply with immigration laws.

Cities varied in cooperating—or not cooperating—with federal agencies in enforcing immigration laws. Some of the friction arose over conflicting political attitudes toward illegal immigrants. In addition, many communities were leery of having their local police viewed as an extension of federal law enforcement.

House Judiciary Chair Robert W. Goodlatte, R-Va., contended that sanctuary issues had been made worse by the Obama administration's decision in 2014 to end the Secure Communities program, which checked fingerprints of all arrested individuals against immigration records. Although a similar program had been put in place, Goodlatte said it was not as strict as its predecessor and allowed more undocumented immigrants to remain in the United States.

ICE Assistant Director Pedro Ribeiro countered that officials had become more selective through the replacement for Secure Communities—the Priority Enforcement Program, which focused more on deporting individuals who posed a danger to the community.

2015 LEGISLATIVE ACTION

Republicans raised concerns about sanctuary cities even before the shooting of Steinle. In March 2015, the House Judiciary Committee approved a bill (HR 1148) by Trey Gowdy, R-S.C., to require all localities and states to comply with ICE's request to detain an individual or lose federal grants. The bill also would have defunded President Barack Obama's executive order on immigration and allowed states and localities to enact and enforce their own immigration laws, as long as they were consistent with federal laws.

The bill did not advance any further. Instead, sanctuary cities became a major point of contention on the 2016 homeland security appropriations bill.

The House Appropriations Committee on July 14 adopted three amendments prompted by the San Francisco shooting. One, adopted by a 28–21 party-line vote, would have blocked sanctuary cities from receiving certain Homeland Security grants, including Federal Emergency Management Agency–related funds. Democrats warned against denying FEMA preparedness funds to a community exercising its lawful discretion on immigration policy. But DHS Subcommittee Chair John Carter, R-Texas, said at the markup, "A state or local government that opts to ignore the homeland security [implications] of this policy does not warrant Homeland Security grant funding."

The committee also approved an amendment by Texas Republican John Culberson to bar funding for federal agencies to release from custody any immigrant who fell into DHS's

Priority 1 or 2 categories of migrants until the immigrant is deported. Culberson said the provision was meant to target immigrants such as felons, gang members, and people with repeated arrests, as DHS outlined in a November 2014 memo.

The House on July 23, 2015, by a vote of 241–179, passed Hunter's legislation (HR 3009) to deny some federal grants for cities, counties, and states that restricted how their law enforcement officials cooperated with federal authorities and prohibited their police and sheriffs from asking about an individual's legal status. Hunter said the legislation sought to enforce what was required by law. But Democrats called the legislation a reckless response to a tragedy that missed the bigger picture.

Later that day, the White House issued a statement on the bill warning that the measure "would threaten the civil rights of all Americans, lead to mistrust between communities and state and local law enforcement agencies, and impede efforts to safely, fairly and effectively enforce" existing immigration laws. It instead called for comprehensive immigration legislation.

While Republicans said the bill was focused on ensuring that laws were obeyed, angry Democrats nicknamed the legislation the "Donald Trump" bill. They invoked the controversial Republican presidential candidate who had made heated statements about unauthorized immigrants, including saying that many Mexicans who came to the United States were criminals, drug dealers, and rapists.

Senate Republicans also pressed the issue. Louisiana Republican David Vitter introduced legislation (S 2146) to deny funding for cities and states with sanctuary policies that bar local law enforcement from fully cooperating with federal immigration authorities. Vitter's bill would have increased the maximum penalty from two years to five years for unauthorized immigrants who reenter the country illegally. It also would have created a maximum penalty of ten years for unauthorized immigrants who reenter the country illegally and have been deported three or more times.

But Republicans could not muster the needed sixty votes to prevent a Democratic filibuster. Democrats in October blocked S 2146 on a 54–45 vote. Their opposition also kept any sanctuary city legislation from being included in the year-end omnibus (HR 2029; PL 114–113).

2016 LEGISLATIVE ACTION

Senate Democrats, in July 2016, blocked progress on two immigration enforcement bills—one aimed at punishing local jurisdictions that decline to comply with federal immigration laws and another that would have increased prison sentences for undocumented criminals who reentered the United States multiple times.

Republicans fell short of the needed sixty votes to invoke cloture on the bill (S 3100), sponsored by Sen. Patrick J. Toomey, R-Pa., that would have punished sanctuary cities by denying them federal funding. It failed on a 53–44 vote, with Sen. Mark S. Kirk, R-Ill., joining most Democrats against the procedural motion, while two

Democrats—Joe Donnelly of Indiana and Joe Manchin III of West Virginia—sided with Republicans.

The second bill (S 2193), sponsored by Sen. Ted Cruz, R-Texas, was rejected by a 55–42 vote, short of the 60-vote requirement. Donnelly and Manchin again sided with Republicans and were joined by Sen. Heidi Heitkamp, D-N.D. Cruz's bill would have set a five-year mandatory minimum sentence for immigrants with felony convictions or caught illegally crossing the border two or more times and a ten-year maximum sentence on immigrants caught reentering the U.S. three times.

McConnell scheduled the bills on the anniversary of Steinle's shooting. The GOP cited her death in the effort to push tough-on-immigration legislation, and Cruz's bill was dubbed Kate's Law.

Although lawmakers could not agree on sanctuary cities, the issue remained a political flashpoint. After Trump won the Republican presidential nomination, he mentioned Steinle in his acceptance speech at the Republican National Convention.

Border Security

Congressional Republicans in 2015 planned to focus on border security as a first step toward dealing with broader immigration issues. But legislation to ensure that the U.S. border was secure fell victim to opposition on both sides of the aisle, with a GOP-drafted border security bill (HR 399) being pulled from House floor consideration in the first month of the year.

After the failure of comprehensive immigration legislation in the 113th Congress, House Republicans in the 114th Congress planned to address immigration issues, including strengthened enforcement of U.S. immigration laws, through a step-by-step process. They generally maintained that any major overhaul of the U.S. immigration system could not occur until the nation's borders were secure and immigrants could no longer illegally enter the United States, so they viewed border security legislation as the logical first step.

Despite increases in manpower and funding, it was difficult to assess how much progress had been made in securing the U.S.–Mexico border. One commonly used proxy measure was the number of people caught by the U.S. Border Patrol trying to cross the southwest border. That had gradually increased over the prior four years. However, levels were far below those of the 1990s and early 2000s, when apprehensions peaked at 1.6 million in 2000, according to the U.S. Border Patrol.

In 2011, there were 328,000 apprehensions at the southwest border, the lowest since 1972. But the number rose to 479,000 in 2014 after a surge of women and children from Central America were caught trying to cross the border. Part of the overall dip in apprehensions was attributed to fewer people from Mexico entering the country illegally. In 2014, for the first time, more non-Mexicans than Mexicans were apprehended at the border.

Border legislation in 2015 was developed at the same time that congressional Republicans were challenging President Obama's November 2014 executive actions to defer the deportation of several million illegal immigrants whose children were U.S. citizens or lawful permanent residents. The conflicts over that issue proved fatal for the border bill.

BORDER BILL MARKUP

Although the House Homeland Security Committee had approved a bipartisan border security bill in the previous Congress, Chair Michael McCaul of Texas drafted an alternative that he introduced on January 16, 2015. It was optimistically named Secure Our Borders First Act of 2015. The committee marked up the measure on January 21, and House floor action was scheduled for the following week. Senate Republicans introduced a matching bill.

McCaul's bill required the Homeland Security Department to take actions to gain and maintain situational awareness and operational control of "high-traffic" areas of the northern and southern U.S. land borders within two years and to effectively lock down the U.S.–Mexico border within five years. Unlike the prior bipartisan bill, it also required the department to deploy certain surveillance and detection resources to specified sectors along the southern and northern borders, such as drones and surveillance towers. In addition, it required the department to build new border fencing, access roads, and forward operating bases for the Border Patrol.

Democrats considered the bill overly prescriptive and said it would set an unattainable goal for border security. They also criticized Republicans for drafting the bill without Democratic input. In an effort to slow down the process, Democrats called for roll-call votes on routine procedural motions and demanded the reading of all seventy-two pages of the legislation.

Although McCaul ended up allowing debate and votes on five amendments proposed by Democrats, he threatened to call a vote on approving the bill without considering their amendments if they continued their delaying tactics. After an eight-hour markup, the panel ultimately approved the bill on an 18–12 party-line vote.

CONSERVATIVE OPPOSITION

While much of the initial focus was on Democratic opposition to the bill, conservatives became increasingly concerned that the measure could be used to advance other legislation measures that they opposed. Many Republicans warned that the legislation could be modified in the Senate as part of a broader immigration push that would include a pathway to legalization for undocumented immigrants. In addition, some Republicans, including Sen. Jeff Sessions of Alabama, argued that any legislation should include provisions to strengthen enforcement actions against undocumented immigrants already in the United States.

Hard-line conservatives also expressed concern that McCaul's border security bill would simply provide cover for members to eventually clear a fiscal year 2015 Homeland Security appropriations bill without immigration provisions favored by Republicans. The Homeland Security Department at that time was operating under stopgap funding that expired February 27, 2015, and the House the week before had passed a year-long spending bill that also included provisions to block President Obama's various executive actions to defer the deportation of certain illegal aliens, including the president's recent November 2014 initiative. Conservatives wanted to force the Senate to pass that measure with those immigration provisions intact, despite opposition from the president and Senate Democrats.

McCaul insisted that his bill was meant to focus on border security, not the broader issue of immigration. But he was learning that even narrowly drawn legislation would touch off the same overarching arguments that had long blocked any congressional overhaul of the nation's immigration system.

In the last week of January 2015, with wintry weather grounding planes across the country, House Republican leaders dropped McCaul's border security bill from the announced floor schedule for the week. They blamed the weather and an already shortened week because of the Democrats' annual retreat.

Though the weather quickly improved, the bill's forecast did not. Speaker John A. Boehner, R-Ohio, would not commit to a timeline for resurrecting the legislation. He said there would continue to be conversations with members about the issues.

Those conversations, however, never got resolved in a way that would enable the bill to move forward. Rep. Raúl R. Labrador said that some of the credit for holding up the border security bill belonged to the new group of hardline House conservatives that had just been formed in the beginning of 2015, the House Freedom Caucus. At the group's first meeting, he said much of the discussion centered on immigration and the border security bill.

Acknowledging the fractured nature of the GOP caucus, Labrador told reporters on January 26, 2015, "We have 40 conservatives with 40 different ideas. And we're less successful because we're taking 40 different ideas to the leadership. It's better to have 40 conservatives working together to take one idea to the leadership."

Criminal Sentencing

Few issues in the 114th Congress were more widely anticipated than the revision of criminal sentencing laws. Concern about the social and financial toll of strict sentencing laws and long imprisonments had generated support across the political spectrum for change, even putting the Obama administration and conservative industrialists Charles and David Koch on the same side. Budget constraints helped fuel momentum: the White House requested $7.3 billion for the Bureau of Prisons in fiscal 2016, a sum that would double the cost of housing federal prisoners since 1998.

But legislative efforts fell far short in the midst of a super-heated presidential campaign. Tough-on-crime Republicans warned against loosening sentencing laws too much, lawmakers differed over the scope of proposed legislation, and some conservatives pressed to change certain prosecutorial standards. In the end, neither chamber passed a bill.

Once a political third rail, the crime-and-punishment debate had shifted noticeably. During the Reagan era, mandatory minimum prison sentences enacted with the Anti-Drug Abuse Act of 1986 were seen as a cure-all for the crack cocaine epidemic. In recent years, though, those same minimum sentences were roundly blamed for a mass incarceration mess. Prisons were overcrowded; a disproportionate number of African-Americans and Latinos were behind bars; and government budgets were tapped out.

Having spent decades putting nonviolent criminals and drug offenders behind bars under increasingly rigid sentences, the nation was staring the costs in the face. Those included the economic toll of incarcerating 2.4 million people at $80 billion a year and the social costs of disrupted families, untreated addictions, and punitive laws that barred felons from work, voting, and housing. The swirl of fiscal, civil liberties, and social justice crises had galvanized activists on the far left and the far right, creating an unusual opening for action.

Yet overturning mandatory minimums proved to be a heavy political lift. In the first months of the new Congress, more than a dozen bills were introduced that would have ended strict criminal sentencing requirements, adjusted them, and given judges more flexibility to make the punishment fit the crime. But the chair of the Senate Judiciary Committee, Iowa Republican Charles E. Grassley, warned that changing sentencing minimums could be lenient and dangerous if not handled carefully.

It then took months for House and Senate committees to analyze and negotiate the various proposals into legislative packages that might pass. Lawmakers ran into a series of hurdles, including a major dispute over making it more difficult to prosecute certain federal crimes. Momentum for the legislation collapsed in late 2016, with advocates pledging to revisit the issue in the following year.

2015

Senate Legislative Action

Grassley used his considerable leverage to shape a compromise measure (S 2123) after several months of bipartisan backroom negotiations on several bills. His committee voted 15–5 on October 22 to approve the measure and send it to the floor. All Democrats supported the bill, along with four Republicans.

The bill contained three parts the White House had said it would need to see in any sentencing legislation. Those were "front-end" changes to reduce the number of inmates entering federal prisons; "back-end" changes for prisoners to take classes and reduce the chance they might return to prison; and changes to juvenile offender laws.

The bill would have reduced some mandatory minimum prison sentences, given judges more discretion to impose sentences shorter than those minimums, and made some criminals eligible for early release in exchange for participating in programs aimed at reducing recidivism, or relapse into criminal behavior. It would have applied the Fair Sentencing Act of 2010 (PL 111–220), which reduced the disparity between sentences for cocaine and crack possession that largely fell along racial lines, to defendants who were sentenced before the bill was passed. Thousands of defendants could have qualified, and the White House had been giving relief to them through the clemency process since 2014.

The legislation was backed by a diverse coalition that included both civil liberties and conservative activists. Grassley had been long resistant to an overhaul but recently joined senators from both parties to unveil the bill.

Several Judiciary Republicans expressed concern that the bill went too far, warning that reducing mandatory minimum sentences retroactively would release thousands of criminals from behind bars. The bill's defenders, however, said the legislation would not automatically relax minimums for those already in prison but instead would give judges discretion to release them on a case-by-case basis.

Sen. Ted Cruz, R-Texas, worried that the scope of the bill would extend beyond nonviolent drug offenders and include violent criminals. Republican Mike Lee of Utah, a supporter of the bill, rejected the suggestion that it would result in an uptick in violent crime or release a number of violent criminals. He noted that the legislation would strengthen some existing mandatory minimum sentences and set out only to reduce from fifteen to ten years the terms imposed on some offenders possessing firearms.

In a series of 15–5 votes, the panel rejected amendments by Cruz, David Perdue, R-Ga., and Jeff Sessions, R-Ala., intended to ensure that the more-relaxed sentencing minimums would not apply retroactively or to firearms offenders.

House Legislative Action

The House Judiciary Committee on November 18 approved, by voice vote, a sentencing measure (HR 3713) that mirrored part of the Senate legislation but contained only front-end changes to the system. Among other provisions, the bill would have given federal judges more leeway to sentence fewer defendants to long mandatory minimum prison terms. It also would have reduced some of the toughest mandatory minimum sentences for drug offenders. Like the Senate version, it would have applied the Fair Sentencing Act to defendants who had been previously sentenced.

Judiciary Chair Robert W. Goodlatte, R-Va., said the bipartisan bill proposed "targeted, responsible sentencing reforms" and balanced shorter prison sentences with public safety. He said it would help keep violent offenders behind bars while saving taxpayer money. Ranking Democrat John Conyers Jr. of Michigan praised provisions in the bill as long overdue but hoped to make further efforts to overhaul sentencing laws in future legislation.

The committee adopted by voice vote an amendment by Jim Sensenbrenner, R-Wis., that required the Justice Department and the U.S. Sentencing Commission to report on the use of mandatory minimum sentences in prosecutions, such as how often they were used as part of plea agreements and what charges were dropped in those agreements. The amendment also expressed the sense of Congress that further overhaul of the nation's criminal justice system would require a component that would include mental health care, amid concerns that prisons and jails had effectively become America's mental health facilities.

2016

In the midst of a contentious presidential campaign, lawmakers failed to make additional progress on the criminal justice issue.

In an ominous sign for the bill, Goodlatte said in January 2016 that an overhaul of sentencing laws would not pass the House unless it included a controversial provision related to criminal intent. The provision he favored would have required a *mens rea* ("guilty mind") standard for some federal crimes, particularly activities criminalized by agency regulations. Under the standard, federal prosecutors would have to prove that the accused knew they were breaking the law.

But the Justice Department, along with civil rights, environmental, and food safety groups, had raised concerns about a mens rea bill (HR 4002) that the House Judiciary Committee passed in November. They said that such a bill could harm the ability to prosecute for environmental or food safety violations. Conyers had supported the mens rea bill in committee, although he also noted the concerns that had been raised over the issue.

It was clear before the end of January that the "guilty mind" issue was crucial. The Senate's version of a sentencing overhaul bill did not include a mens rea requirement, but Sen. Orrin G. Hatch, R-Utah, was pushing for the language to be added.

Grassley, however, worried that the mens rea provisions would harm prosecutions of activities criminalized by agency regulations, potentially jeopardizing public health and safety. "No one ever tells me that it is too easy to send corporate executives to jail for fraud or selling poisonous food or polluting the environment," he said at a Judiciary Committee hearing on January 20, 2016. "Just the opposite."

With prospects uncertain for an all-encompassing bill, a group of Senate Republicans launched a campaign in early 2016 to rally opponents. Republicans Orrin G. Hatch of Utah, Jeff Sessions of Alabama, Tom Cotton of Arkansas, and David Perdue of Georgia simultaneously published opinion pieces that criticized the key provisions of S 2123 and took to the floor to denounce it. They and other Republicans focused on how mandatory minimum sentence laws helped reverse high crime rates of the 1980s and said the drug traffickers who would benefit from the bill were inherently violent.

Cotton pointed out that sentencing laws had contributed to a significant drop in crime in recent decades and that the U.S. Sentencing Commission had already reduced sentences for drug offenders. "This is badly misguided," Cotton said in a floor speech on February 9, 2016. "The Senate would be launching a massive social experiment in criminal leniency. . . . This experiment threatens to undo the historic drops in crime we have seen over the past 25 years."

The split among Republicans sparked a flurry of Capitol Hill events, letters from interest groups to Senate leaders, opinion pieces from lawmakers, backroom negotiations, and lobbying efforts. But such frayed support among Republicans was enough to convince Senate leaders—who had already cast doubt on the bill's future—that it was not worth floor time in an election year to advance a measure that cropped up on many Democratic wish lists.

By April, the sentencing bill had stalled.

Speaker Paul D. Ryan of Wisconsin had said he would bring criminal justice measures to the floor in September, but lawmakers faced numerous policy and political hurdles. In the wake of the presidential election, enthusiasm waned and the bill stalled. Instead, some Republican senators said in December they would push an overhaul of the nation's criminal justice system in the next Congress. But it remained unclear how such a measure could win sufficient bipartisan support amid the ongoing controversy over the "guilty mind" provision. Moreover, one of the most vocal critics of changing the sentencing law was Republican Sen. Jeff Sessions of Alabama, who would become the new president's attorney general.

Gun Regulations

Legislation to regulate guns or gun sales in any form remained well out of reach of the Obama administration and its Democratic allies on Capitol Hill during the 114th Congress despite heightened concerns about violence related to firearms. Against a backdrop of continued mass shootings, Obama implored lawmakers to increase regulation of guns, and House Democrats waged a sit-in on the floor of the House to draw attention to the issue. But Republicans adamantly rejected proposals for expanded regulations as an infringement on the Second Amendment rights of Americans to own guns. The Senate voted down amendments in 2015 and 2016 to impose some regulations; the House did not take up the issue at all. For those lawmakers who wanted some measure of control over who could buy guns in the country, the session was one long frustration. If gun control advocates could find any consolation during the 114th Congress, it was that the issue was generating increased discussion, even though the obstacles to any legislative action continued to appear insurmountable.

Gun violence, along with associated events such as school lockdowns and tightened security at many buildings and public events, was a fact of life for the nation. More than 30,000 Americans were shot to death each year,

FORMER VIRGINIA GOVERNOR'S CONVICTION OVERTURNED BY SUPREME COURT

In one of the more prominent political corruption cases in recent years, former Virginia Gov. Bob McDonnell was convicted in 2014 for taking money and other items of value in exchange for helping a businessman. Two years later, however, a unanimous Supreme Court wiped out the conviction, and McDonnell was spared a prison term.

McDonnell, a once-rising Republican star, was convicted in 2014 on corruption charges that he accepted more than $175,000 in money, luxury goods, and trips in exchange for helping Virginia businessman Jonnie Williams and his dietary supplement business. Federal prosecutors said McDonnell's moves were an "official act" under the federal bribery and honest-services fraud laws, which make it a felony to agree to take "official action" in exchange for money, campaign contributions, or anything of value.

But the Supreme Court found that the jury was not properly instructed on the meaning of "official act" and clarified those laws for elected officials—including members of Congress. The court said a more limited interpretation of the term "official act" leaves room for prosecuting corruption while not subjecting officials to prosecution—without fair notice—for the most commonplace interactions with constituents.

"There is no doubt that this case is distasteful; it may be worse than that," Chief Justice John G. Roberts Jr. wrote for the court. "But our concern is not with tawdry tales of Ferraris, Rolexes, and ball gowns. It is instead with the broader legal implications of the government's boundless interpretation of the federal bribery statute."

Conscientious public officials arrange meetings for constituents and contact other public officials on their behalf all the time, the Supreme Court found—such as a union official worried about a plant closure or homeowners who wonder why it took five days to restore power to their neighborhood after a storm.

"The Government's position could cast a pall of potential prosecution over these relationships if the union had given a campaign contribution in the past or the homeowners invited the official to join them on their annual outing to the ballgame," the opinion states. "Officials might wonder whether they could respond to even the most commonplace requests for assistance, and citizens with legitimate concerns might shrink from participating in democratic discourse."

During the sometimes-sensational trial, it was revealed that McDonnell and his wife, Maureen, received $20,000 for a New York shopping spree, a monogrammed Rolex worth more than $5,000, and use of a convertible Ferrari. McDonnell was sentenced to two years in prison, and his wife, also convicted in the corruption scheme, was sentenced to one year. Her appeal was put on hold while the court determined her husband's fate. The McDonnells stayed out of prison during the appeals process.

In wiping out McDonnell's conviction, the Supreme Court sent the case back to a lower court for a retrial. Federal prosecutors, however, decided not to pursue the case further. That included dropping corruption charges against McDonnell's wife.

Lobbyists and campaign finance experts said that although the Supreme Court's decision in the McDonnell case could give big donors a sense of relief, the narrow decision might not have far-reaching implications. Sheila Krumholz, who ran the nonprofit Center for Responsive Politics, which tracks campaign money and lobbying, said the legal issue had to do with bad jury instructions. However, she added that it may be an additional sign of a relaxation of rules regarding lobbyists and donors, potentially making prosecutors less likely to pursue future corruption cases.

---

including those who killed themselves, and more than 70,000 were injured. In 2015 alone, which the *PBS Newshour* called "the year of mass shootings," headlines told of killings at a church in downtown Charleston, S.C., a community college campus near Roseburg, Ore., a Planned Parenthood clinic in Colorado Springs, Colo., and a rented banquet room in San Bernardino, Calif. The following year, the nation suffered its worst death toll since the September 11, 2001, terrorist attacks when a mass shooter killed forty-nine people and wounded fifty-eight others inside a gay nightclub.

Obama repeatedly called on Congress to increase regulations of guns, such as expanded background checks of gun purchasers. Although federally licensed gun dealers were required to check the backgrounds of purchasers,

individuals who might sell a gun from time to time, including at a gun show, did not have to be licensed. "At some point, we, as a country, will have to reckon with the fact that this type of mass violence does not happen in other advanced countries," he said after nine people were killed at the historically black church in Charleston in June 2015. "It doesn't happen in other places with this kind of frequency. And it is in our power to do something about it."

Congressional Republicans, however, continued to oppose any restrictions on gun sales or ownership, including enhanced background checks. Such restrictions, they said, would infringe on the right to bear arms and interfere with the right of Americans to hunt and to defend themselves while failing to curb gun violence. Lawmakers also continued a policy dating back to the 1990s that banned the Centers for Disease Control and Prevention from using any federal funds for research into gun deaths and injuries.

2015

The political power of gun owners and the National Rifle Association was clearly evident in March 2015 after the Bureau of Alcohol, Tobacco, Firearms and Explosives proposed to restrict sales of M855 "green tip" ammunition for the AR-15 rifle. The ATF proposed rescinding a 1986 exception granted for the bullets from a ban on "armor-piercing ammunition." The agency said it was worried that law enforcement officers could be at risk from M855 rounds fired by a handgun.

The NRA, however, called the rule "a gun ban by another name." ATF Director B. Todd Jones was barraged with complaints from Congress about the proposed rule, including a letter from the two most senior Republicans on the House Judiciary Committee, Chair Robert W. Goodlatte of Virginia and Jim Sensenbrenner of Wisconsin, which was signed by 237 other members. Two Louisiana Republicans, Sen. David Vitter and House Majority Whip Steve Scalise, wrote Jones on March 5, 2015, that the proposed rule was "nothing more than an overreaching attempt at expanding gun control."

Not only did the ATF quickly shelve the rule, but within weeks, Jones had resigned as the agency's director "to pursue other opportunities in the private sector," as the official announcement put it.

That left gun regulations on the legislative back burner until a December 2 shooting rampage that killed fourteen people in San Bernardino. Senate Democrats decided to use a far-reaching budget bill pending on the floor to press for measures to tighten gun control laws. The move was largely symbolic, because adding such controversial provisions would require more than a few Republicans and because Obama had already vowed to veto the underlying measure, which was designed to gut his 2010 health care law.

The first attempt by Democrats was a proposal by Dianne Feinstein of California to enable the attorney general to deny gun sales or licenses to anyone suspected of terrorism. It fell fifteen votes short of the sixty required to overcome procedural obstacles. Then Democrat Joe Manchin III from the gun-friendly state of West Virginia tried to revive a 2013 proposal designed with Pennsylvania Republican Patrick J. Toomey that would have expanded the federal background-check system to include firearms purchased at gun shows and over the Internet. In 2013, they had gotten fifty-four of the sixty votes they needed to advance their proposal. This time, they only got forty-eight votes.

Only four Republicans backed the amendment: Susan Collins of Maine, Mark S. Kirk of Illinois, John McCain of Arizona, and Toomey. They were the same four who had supported the 2013 amendment, and the latter three faced tough 2016 reelection bids. Among Democrats, only Heidi Heitkamp of North Dakota voted against the plan, as she had in 2013.

The votes illustrated that the political dynamic surrounding the issue had not changed since late 2012, when the mass shooting of children at an elementary school in Newtown, Conn., spurred renewed calls for gun control measures.

2016

Despite the recent legislative setbacks, Obama announced in early January that he would seek to tighten federal gun laws, including gun sales "loopholes," and put more resources into hiring federal agents and upgrading the background-check system for gun purchases. Gun rights groups and their supporters in Congress promptly promised they would allow no such things, setting the agenda for the rest of the year and the remainder of Obama's term. Though there was a great deal of debate, there was no further substantive action.

Rep. John Culberson, R-Texas, chair of the House Appropriations subcommittee that oversees funding for the Justice Department, set the tone in January 2016, sending a letter to Attorney General Loretta Lynch warning that his committee would not provide money to implement the president's proposals. He said he would do everything possible to restrict funding if the Justice Department took any steps to restrict the rights of gun owners.

GOP presidential candidates and congressional leaders, including House Speaker Paul D. Ryan, R-Wis., and Senate Majority Leader Mitch McConnell, R-Ky., also blasted Obama's gun plans. Democratic leaders lined up behind Obama but lacked the power to do much about the issue except highlight the continuing inaction on Capitol Hill.

Further fueling the debate, a twenty-nine-year-old security guard walked into a gay nightclub in Orlando, Fla., on June 12, killing forty-nine people and wounding fifty-eight others. Three days later, after a nearly fifteen-hour talking filibuster led by Connecticut Democrat Christopher S. Murphy, Senate Majority Leader Mitch McConnell, R-Ky., agreed to allow votes on amendments to a Commerce-Justice-Science appropriations bill (HR 2578) then on the floor—one Democratic amendment to bar terror suspects from purchasing firearms and another provision to extend background checks to gun show and online sales. Two Democratic and two Republican gun proposals were subsequently rejected on procedural motions.

On June 23, the Senate gave a bipartisan show of support to a proposal by Maine Republican Susan Collins that would ban gun sales to people on the FBI's no-fly list, but the underlying spending bill she was trying to amend was left on hold.

Collins's amendment survived a tabling motion by McConnell that would have effectively killed the measure. His motion to table was blocked with a 46–52 vote, leaving the amendment still pending on the Senate floor but short of the 60 votes it would need to be adopted. The Senate did not take further action on the bill.

In the House, meanwhile, a group of about sixty House Democrats led by civil rights veterans John Lewis of Georgia and Katherine Clark of Massachusetts began a sit-in on the

House floor on June 22, saying they would stay there until Speaker Paul Ryan, R-Wis., allowed votes on gun control legislation. Republican leaders responded by ordering a recess and having the C-SPAN cameras turned off. The Democrats responded by live-streaming their protest with cell phones. After the House adjourned for the July 4th holiday, the Democrats relinquished the floor on June 23.

With Democrats highlighting concerns about terrorists taking advantage of the availability of guns, House Republicans on July 1 unveiled a bill (HR 5611) that would curb gun sales to those suspected of having ties to terrorist organizations. Sponsored by House Majority Leader Kevin McCarthy, R-Calif., the bill would set up a new office in the Department of Homeland Security to identify risk factors contributing to "radical Islamist terrorism," identify Americans being targeted, manage outreach, conduct research into methods employed by militants, and come up with countermessages to push back on the recruitment tactics employed by militant groups.

The new measure included provisions already rejected by the Senate that would allow the attorney general to delay by three days the sale of guns to those on terrorism watch lists. The provision would then allow the top law enforcement official to block the sale if there was probable cause to do so.

As the summer ebbed away, the chances of House action on HR 5611 faded. The measure was opposed by Democrats as well as some Republicans, including the roughly forty hard-line conservatives in the House Freedom Caucus.

In mid-September, House Democrats renewed their quest of push gun safety legislation, along with a demand for a vote on a bill expanding background checks. The lawmakers also asked for a "no-fly, no-buy" bill that would prevent individuals on terrorist watch lists from obtaining firearms.

One by one, Democrats approached the podium holding photos of victims of gun violence and asked for unanimous consent to bring up a bill that would expand background checks. Their requests were ruled out of order because the time that had been yielded to Democrats related to debate on a different measure.

Transgender Rights

The Obama administration, Congress, and the courts were drawn into a debate over laws restricting the restroom use of transgender people after the Justice Department in March 2016 told North Carolina officials that their new "bathroom law" violated the 1964 Civil Rights Act. The state government was engaged in a "pattern or practice of discrimination" against transgender state employees by implementing the Republican-backed law, since it treated them differently than nontransgender employees, the Justice Department wrote. Two months later, the administration directed public schools to allow transgender students to use the bathroom consistent with their gender identity (their own internal sense of gender, which can be different from the sex they were assigned at birth).

The North Carolina bathroom law sparked a debate in the presidential race and among civil rights groups, as the nation considered just how to define a person's gender or sex when it came to the use of restrooms or locker rooms.

Other states and local governments were considering bathroom laws even as North Carolina ran into a backlash. Companies such as PayPal and Deutsche Bank either canceled or scaled back plans for expansion in the state, and the National Basketball Association threatened to move its 2017 All-Star Game out of Charlotte if changes to the law were not made. Conservatives, however, kept up the pressure on organizations over their restroom policies. In Texas, Attorney General Ken Paxton sent a letter to Target as a warning over the retailer's policy of allowing transgender people to use the restroom of their choice.

The Justice and Education departments gave guidance on schools' obligations under Title IX of the Education Amendments of 1972 as they related to transgender students and restroom use, participation in athletics, single-sex classes, and housing and overnight accommodations. The federal action implied that schools could lose federal funds if they ran afoul of Title IX.

Questions had arisen from school districts, colleges, and universities about transgender students, the Justice Department said. Its letters to school districts even defined basic terminology when it comes to transgender issues, describing how a person's gender identity may differ from their assigned gender at birth. Attorney General Loretta Lynch said the guidance was intended to help administrators, teachers, and parents protect transgender students from being harassed by their peers and to identify school policies that failed to take into account their needs.

A FEDERAL OR A LOCAL ISSUE?

The chair of the Senate Health, Education, Labor and Pensions Committee, Tennessee Republican Lamar Alexander, said the administration lacked authority to issue the directive and that such choices should be made at the local level. "This is the kind of issue that parents, school boards, communities, students, and teachers should be allowed to work out in a practical way with a maximum amount of respect for the individual rights of all students," said Alexander.

Experts disagreed over the Education Department's legal authority under Title IX.

Roger Severino, the director of the DeVos Center for Religion and Civil Society at the conservative Heritage Foundation, called on states to follow the example of North Carolina in using the courts to challenge the Obama administration. He said the administration's guidance was outside the scope of Title IX, which focused on sex discrimination, not gender identity.

But that was not the conclusion implied by the 1988 Supreme Court case, *Price Waterhouse v. Hopkins*, which found gender stereotyping was a form of sex discrimination, said Robin Wilson, director of the Family Law and Policy Program at the University of Illinois College of Law.

While gender stereotyping and gender identity are different, Wilson said there is enough of a connection for the Education Department to make its case.

STATE LAWSUITS

In late May, officials in Texas and ten other states filed a lawsuit challenging the administration's guidance on transgender students, including the use of bathrooms and other facilities at public schools.

Texas, along with Alabama, Wisconsin, West Virginia, Tennessee, Oklahoma, Louisiana, Utah, and Georgia, asked a federal judge in Texas to put a stop to the guidance from the Justice and Education departments and declare it unlawful. The Arizona Department of Education, an Arizona school district, and Maine Gov. Paul R. LePage also joined the suit.

A dozen states and the District of Columbia that summer filed an amicus brief supporting federal guidance on how public schools should treat transgender students, including allowing students to use the bathroom of the gender with which they identify.

On Capitol Hill, meanwhile, amendments on LGBT discrimination and transgender issues helped defeat an energy-water appropriations bill (HR 5055) in the House and caused chaos on a military construction–VA spending bill (HR 4974).

The inclusion of a Democratic amendment by Rep. Sean Patrick Maloney, D-N.Y., to prohibit discrimination on the basis of sexual orientation or gender identity in federal contracts drew strong opposition from conservatives. A Twitter hashtag campaign, #StopMaloney, emerged before the vote, and the conservative group Heritage Action for America issued a key vote alert to defeat the bill, citing the Maloney amendment among its reasons.

In August, the issue of transgender rights reached the Supreme Court, with an appeal from school district officials in Virginia. In its petition to the Court, the Gloucester County School Board asked the justices to stop a lower court's injunction that required schools to allow a seventeen-year-old transgender boy, identified in court documents as G.G. (his full name was Gavin Grimm), to use the boys' restroom at his high school.

The school district argued that a 4th Circuit Court ruling turned "upside down" the longstanding expectation under Title IX of a 1972 federal law that schools could have separate facilities and programs on the basis of sex for certain intimate settings—toilets, locker rooms, and shower areas.

"The court reasoned that the term 'sex' in the applicable Title IX regulation does not simply mean biological males and females, which is what Congress and the Department of Education (and everyone else) thought the term meant when the regulation was promulgated," the school district's August 29 petition stated. "To the contrary, the Fourth Circuit now tells us that 'sex' is ambiguous as applied to persons whose 'gender identity' diverges from their biological sex."

In late October, the Supreme Court agreed to step into the debate by deciding the case of *G.G. vs. Gloucester County School Board*. The move stopped a lower-court order that sided with Grimm, the transgender boy.

"I never thought that my restroom use would ever turn into any kind of national debate," Grimm said in a written statement on October 28, 2016, released via the American Civil Liberties Union, which was representing him. "The only thing I ever asked for was the right to be treated like everyone else."

Appropriations

The 114th Congress continued the recent practice of combining the Commerce-Justice-Science (C-J-S) appropriations bill and other spending measures into an omnibus bill instead of passing them individually. The House and Senate appropriations committees in 2015 passed separate versions of the C-J-S bill before lawmakers added the measure to an omnibus appropriations bill that they cleared at the end of the year. In 2016, the committees again passed their versions of the bill amid debates over gun riders. Congress did not finalize action on C-J-S and other appropriations bills but instead passed a continuing resolution that delayed final action until 2017.

2015

The omnibus appropriations bill (PL 114–113) set discretionary spending for Commerce-Justice-Science programs in fiscal 2016 at $55.7 billion, an increase of $5.6 billion over fiscal 2015. House and Senate appropriators marked up and moved their bills relatively quickly, but the process stalled during the summer, and the C-J-S measure was wrapped into the omnibus.

The omnibus did not include some of the more controversial policy riders from the House and Senate versions of the fiscal 2016 bill, such as a provision to defund Obama's legal defense of his executive action on immigration. However, it did include language to prevent the administration from spending funds to transfer Guantanamo Bay detainees to the United States. Another rider directed the Justice Department to take no action against states where marijuana use for medical purposes is legal.

Freestanding Bills

The House Commerce-Justice-Science Appropriations subcommittee approved a draft bill on May 14 that increased total discretionary spending levels, continuing to expand on recent increases for law enforcement. The bill totaled $51.4 billion in discretionary funding, including $27.5 billion for the Justice Department, an $852 million increase from the comparable fiscal 2015 level. The measure, however, would have reduced funds to the Justice Department for state and local law enforcement and crime prevention grant programs, including the Community Oriented Policing Services program.

The full committee approved the bill on May 20 after adopting an amendment by Rep. Betty McCollum, D-Minn., to require the Justice Department to report on efforts and resources used to prevent the recruitment of youth by foreign terrorist organizations. But the committee rejected an amendment from Rep. Sam Farr, D-Calif., to remove a provision that ensured that any export to Cuba did not get funneled through the island nation's military and security services. It also rejected an amendment that would prevent people on a terrorist watch list from purchasing firearms.

On June 3, the House passed the bill, 242–183, after two days of debate that included the adoption of several amendments to ensure states could engage in lawful activities involving hemp and marijuana. The House also adopted several GOP amendments barring regulation of firearms sales and certain ammunition. It also added immigration-related amendments, including one by Rep. Steve King, R-Iowa, to prevent the use of funds for the government to defend itself in the current court case where states are challenging President Obama's immigration executive order.

Much of the floor debate involved efforts to shift funding, with amendments being adopted to boost popular law enforcement assistance programs.

In addition, the House voted to block the administration from temporarily detailing, or transferring, employees to the Office of the Pardon Attorney to screen clemency applications. The chamber also voted to block the administration from using funds to compel a journalist or reporter to testify about information or sources that he or she regarded as confidential. In addition, the bill would prevent the administration from using "disparate impact" legal theory in housing discrimination cases, which focuses on the impact of actions rather than the intent.

Senate Action

The Senate Appropriations Committee approved its version of the C-J-S bill on June 11. The overall bill had $51.1 billion in discretionary funding, including $27.8 billion for the Justice Department. It included a provision directing the Justice Department to take no action against states where marijuana use for medical purposes is legal and to allow universities to conduct research authorized by the 2014 farm bill on industrial hemp.

An amendment by the ranking Democrat on Appropriations, Barbara Mikulski of Maryland, would have added $2.78 billion to the bill, with a majority of additional money going to programs fostering innovation and improving community and public safety. It was rejected by a 14–16 vote.

The bill was not taken up on the Senate floor.

Omnibus Highlights

The final version of the legislation provided the Justice Department with $29.1 billion for fiscal 2016. That spending level was an increase of $2.1 billion, or 8 percent, from regular fiscal 2015 appropriations.

Among law enforcement agencies, the FBI received $8.8 billion, or $362 million more than the fiscal 2015 level, with priority placed on investigating human and sex trafficking. The Drug Enforcement Administration received a net $2.1 billion, or an increase of $47 million, and the U.S. Marshals Service received $2.7 billion. The Bureau of Prisons was provided $7.5 billion, an increase of $558 million to maintain staffing levels at facilities.

Grants to state and local law enforcement were funded at $2.2 billion under the omnibus, a decrease of $133 million. This amount included $212 million for Community Oriented Policing Services, a $4 million increase from the fiscal 2015 level. The measure also included funding for fifty-five new Immigration Judge Teams to adjudicate more cases annually and oversee removal proceedings.

For the second year in a row, the C-J-S appropriations title offered a boost for backers of medical marijuana—a policy rider that blocked funds for the Justice Department to intervene in states that have legalized medical marijuana. The measure also continued a prohibition on funds to implement an international arms trade treaty unless the Senate ratified the proposal, one of several gun-related provisions opposed by Democrats.

Fiscal 2017

Much of the congressional debate over the fiscal 2017 spending bill focused on the Obama administration's plan to crack down on gun sales. The administration requested funding for an additional 200 agents for the Bureau of Alcohol, Tobacco, Firearms, and Explosives as well as 230 more FBI agents to review background checks on firearms purchases. Republicans criticized the move, though, and what they considered the potential for harassing law-abiding gun owners.

The Senate Commerce-Justice-Science Appropriations Subcommittee approved a draft fiscal 2017 spending bill with no new money for the administration's gun initiative. The bill contained $56.3 billion in discretionary spending, of which $29.2 billion was for the Justice Department, including money for new efforts to combat heroin use.

The Federal Bureau of Investigation would get a $652 million increase under the bill, which included $646 million toward the construction of a new FBI headquarters.

Senate Committee

The Senate Appropriations Committee unanimously approved the bill on April 21, 2016, by a 30–0 vote. The bill kept language preventing the administration from spending money to transfer Guantanamo Bay detainees to the United States or to find places to house them here. Obama was reported to be close to announcing a plan to do so as part of closing that center.

The bill would provide a total of $132 million to address the growing abuse of heroin and prescription drugs.

The committee approved on a voice vote an amendment from Sen. Jon Tester, D-Mont., that would dedicate 5 percent of the money in the DOJ's Crime Victims Fund for grants to tribal governments to improve services. The money would help combat the reported higher rates of sexual assault and other crimes on tribal lands, Tester said.

The committee also approved an amendment from Sen. Barbara Mikulski, D-Md., to prohibit the DOJ's Drug Enforcement Administration from prosecuting legal medical marijuana sales in states where medical marijuana legislation has been approved.

Another amendment from Sen. Jeff Merkley, D-Ore., would prohibit the DOJ from preventing a state from implementing its own state laws about the use, distribution, possession, or cultivation of industrial hemp. It was approved on a voice vote.

The committee rejected 4–26 an amendment from Sen. James Lankford, R-Okla., that would set a permanent cap on spending from the Crime Victims Fund so it could not be used to offset other spending.

Subcommittee Chair Richard C. Shelby, R-Ala., said he understood the concern the amendment tried to address but that he and others were already in discussions with the Senate Judiciary Committee about changes to the fund. Lankford's amendment would have undermined those discussions, Shelby said.

House Subcommittee

The bill that the House Commerce-Justice-Science Appropriations Subcommittee approved by voice vote on May 18 would provide $56 billion in discretionary funding. It would allocate $29 billion for the Justice Department.

The bill included $103 million for programs to help address the rising abuse of opioids. That amount would fully fund a recently passed House bill (HR 5046) that would establish Justice Department grants to help state and local governments expand programs for the prevention and treatment of drug abuse and train first responders to administer overdose-reversal drugs, among other things.

House Committee

The House Appropriations Committee approved an amended fiscal 2017 Commerce-Justice-Science spending bill on May 24, but without changes Democrats sought on firearms and the Justice Department's civil settlements.

The committee defeated an amendment from Nita Lowey, D-N.Y., that she said would have blocked firearm purchases by individuals on the federal government's terrorist watch list. The vote was 17–29.

Another amendment, from Rep. Marcy Kaptur, D-Ohio, sought to strike three provisions from the bill, including Republican-backed language that would stop the Justice Department from using settlement agreements to require defendants to donate money to outside groups. It was defeated in a voice vote.

Congress took no further action on the standalone bills. Instead it passed short-term funding extensions in September and December, leaving it to the 116th Congress to finish the work on fiscal 2017 appropriations.

The Supreme Court, 2013–2016

The Supreme Court steered a generally conservative course during President Barack Obama's second four-year term in the White House despite some significant liberal victories, including a decision guaranteeing same-sex couples the right to marry nationwide. The Roberts Court's conservative majority held sway in most of the closely divided decisions even as Obama's two justices, Sonia Sotomayor and Elena Kagan, settled in comfortably as part of a bloc of four generally liberal Democratic appointees.

The conservative bloc consisted of five Republican-appointed justices, including two appointed by President George W. Bush: Chief Justice John G. Roberts Jr. and Samuel A. Alito Jr. Two others provided ideological heft as committed supporters of originalist and textualist interpretation of constitutional and statutory provisions: Antonin Scalia and Clarence Thomas, appointed by presidents Ronald Reagan and George H. W. Bush, respectively. The fifth of the Republican appointees, Anthony M. Kennedy, Reagan's fourth and final justice, had a generally conservative record, but he also helped form five-vote majorities with the liberal justices in several major rulings, including the same-sex marriage decision.

The liberal bloc included, along with Sotomayor and Kagan, President Bill Clinton's two appointees to the Court: Ruth Bader Ginsburg and Stephen G. Breyer. Ginsburg was the oldest of the justices: she marked her eightieth birthday in 2013; Breyer was seventy-eight as Obama neared the end of his presidency in 2016.

Obama appeared to have the opportunity to transform the Court's ideological balance of power after Scalia's unexpected death at age seventy-nine on February 13, 2016, with nearly a full year remaining in his presidential term. As successor to the veteran conservative jurist, Obama nominated Merrick Garland, a well-regarded judge on the U.S. Court of Appeals for the District of Columbia Circuit with a record as a moderate liberal.

Even before Obama's March 16 announcement, however, the Senate's majority leader, Republican Mitch McConnell of Kentucky, announced that the Senate would not hold hearings or allow a floor vote on any Obama nominee. His rationale was that such an important vacancy not be filled until voters had an opportunity to weigh in by choosing the next president. As a result, the seat remained vacant for more than a year until the Senate confirmed President Donald J. Trump's nomination of the solidly conservative jurist Neil M. Gorsuch in April 2017.

The administration had a mixed record at the Court as Obama's signature domestic policy achievement, the Affordable Care Act, faced two more challenges after the Court's 5–4 decision in 2012 largely sustaining the omnibus health care reform. In the first of the new cases, the Court in 2014 allowed employers with religious objections to some forms of contraception a partial exemption from the regulation requiring cost-free coverage of contraception in employee health benefit plans. In a second decision, however, the Court in 2015 ruled against a conservative-backed challenge to the administration's decision to extend tax credits to low- to moderate-income customers of newly created health insurance exchanges in all states, whether established by the state or the federal government.

Obama continued to comment on the Court's decisions on occasion despite the backlash he received for using his State of

REFERENCES

Discussion of the Supreme Court for the years 1945–1964 may be found in *Congress and the Nation Vol. I*, pp. 1141–1454; for the years 1965–1968, *Congress and the Nation Vol. II*, pp. 335–340; for the years 1969–1972, *Congress and the Nation Vol. III*, pp. 289–327; for the years 1973–1976, *Congress and the Nation Vol. IV*, pp. 619–659; for the years 1977–1980, *Congress and the Nation Vol. V*, pp. 755–791; for the years 1981–1984, *Congress and the Nation Vol. VI*, pp. 711–768; for the years 1985–1988, *Congress and the Nation Vol. VII*, pp. 785–840; for the years 1989–1992, *Congress and the Nation Vol. VIII*, pp. 801–851; for the years 1993–1996, *Congress and the Nation Vol. IX*, pp. 759–799; for the years 1997–2001, *Congress and the Nation Vol. X*, pp. 684–729; for the years 2001–2005, *Congress and the Nation Vol. XI*, pp. 630–680; for the years 2005–2008, *Congress and the Nation Vol. XII*, pp. 727–737; for the years 2009–2012, *Congress and the Nation Vol. XIII*, pp. 584–594.

SENATE THWARTS OBAMA ON SCALIA VACANCY

The Republican-controlled Senate in 2016 made the momentous decision to block President Barack Obama from filling the Supreme Court vacancy left by the unexpected death of Justice Antonin Scalia. Senators refused to give Obama's nominee a hearing or allow a Senate floor vote on the nomination. As a result, Obama was stymied in his effort to move the Court to the left, and his Republican successor, Donald J. Trump, instead named a conservative judge to the Court.

Although the Senate on occasion has rejected presidential nominees to the Supreme Court, it was exceedingly rare for the chamber to refuse to even take a vote. What made it even more unusual in this case was that Obama's nominee, Merrick Garland, was a veteran judge on the U.S. Court of Appeals for the District of Columbia Circuit with an impeccable résumé and a reputation as a moderate liberal.

The showdown over Scalia's seat marked a dramatic escalation in the partisan battles over Supreme Court judgeships. Although qualified Supreme Court nominees once received strong bipartisan approval—Scalia had won Senate approval in 1986 by a vote of 98–0—recent nominees now routinely failed to win much support from the opposition party.

Almost as soon as news spread on February 13, 2016, of Scalia's overnight death, Senate Majority Leader Mitch McConnell made it clear that he would not consider any nominee by Obama. "The American people should have a voice in the selection of their next Supreme Court justice," McConnell, a veteran Republican from Kentucky, declared at a hastily arranged press opportunity in the Capitol. "Therefore, this vacancy should not be filled until we have a new president."

His unyielding opposition left White House officials stunned.

Scalia's Enduring Legacy

Scalia, 79, was found dead of natural causes at a West Texas hunting lodge at which he was an invited guest of the owner, businessman John Poindexter.

Since being elevated to the high court by President Ronald Reagan, Scalia's sharp wit, writing, and opinions generated controversy and sparked plenty of partisan opinions of him over thirty years on the court. Not only did he dissent from liberal opinions, but he used increasingly colorful terms, such as "pure applesauce" when criticizing a decision upholding the Affordable Care Act or "legal argle-bargle" when characterizing majority opinions protecting gay men and lesbians from discrimination.

Beyond such memorable phrases, however, he left an enduring conservative legacy. Obama, who once taught constitutional law, praised Scalia after he died for a "brilliant legal mind with an energetic style, incisive wit and colorful opinions." In his statement after Scalia's death, the president added, "He influenced a generation of judges and lawyers and students and profoundly shaped the legal landscape."

Scalia drew the ire of liberals and the praise of conservatives for his originalist approach to interpreting the Constitution. He was a fierce defender of the death penalty and opponent of abortion. He was hostile to affirmative action policies at colleges. But he sided with the Court's liberals when upholding the constitutional right of flag burning.

Scalia was notoriously unwilling to defer to legislative intent. "The Constitution gives legal effect to the 'laws' Congress enacts not the objectives its members aimed to achieve in voting for them," Scalia wrote in a 2010 concurring opinion in which he also called it "utterly irrelevant" whether the members of Congress intended something other than what was written in the law. "Anyway, it is utterly impossible to discern what the members of Congress intended except to the extent that intent is manifested in the only remnant of 'history' that bears the unanimous endorsement of the majority in each House: the text of the enrolled bill that became law."

In one of Scalia 's most notable statements, he delivered the majority opinion in a landmark 2008 decision in *District of Columbia v. Heller* that struck down a handgun ban, interpreting the Second Amendment to include a right to possess a handgun for self-defense in the home. That opinion broke with previous Supreme Court precedent, evoking strong praise from gun rights advocates and criticism from those who favored gun restrictions.

"Undoubtedly some think that the Second Amendment is outmoded in a society where our standing army is the pride of our nation, where well-trained police forces provide personal security, and where gun violence is a serious problem," Scalia wrote. "That is perhaps debatable, but what is not debatable is that it is not the role of this court to pronounce the Second Amendment extinct."

Garland Seen as Moderate

Obama announced his nomination of Merrick Garland on March 16, 2016. The president praised Garland for what he called his "spirit of decency, modesty, integrity, even-handedness and excellence." He answered McConnell's challenge by calling the threatened refusal to consider the nomination "an abdication of the Senate's constitutional duty."

(Continued)

SENATE THWARTS OBAMA ON SCALIA VACANCY (Continued)

Speaking briefly after Obama, Garland declared that "fidelity to the Constitution and the law have been the cornerstone of my professional life." He promised to "continue on that course" if confirmed to the Supreme Court.

The nomination was, in some respects, a concession to political reality. Legal experts generally viewed Garland as more moderate than Obama's first two Supreme Court picks: Sonia Sotomayor and Elena Kagan. Nevertheless, Garland's appointment would have shifted the ideological balance on the Court by giving it a Democratic-appointed majority for the first time since 1968.

Garland, age sixty-three at the time, was serving as chief judge of the D.C. Circuit after his appointment to the court in 1997 by the Democratic president Bill Clinton. He earned degrees from Harvard College and Harvard Law School and went on to prestigious clerkships with the federal appeals court judge Henry J. Friendly and Supreme Court Justice William J. Brennan Jr. and two stints with the Justice Department.

Garland began making courtesy calls on Democratic senators, but Republican senators generally declined meetings. Four Republican senators stated their support in the succeeding weeks for proceeding with hearings, but two of them—Jerry Moran of Kansas and Lisa Murkowski of Alaska—reversed their positions. The other two were Mark Kirk of Illinois and Susan Collins of Maine. Facing a 54-vote Republican majority, Democrats had no parliamentary opening to force a hearing or floor vote.

Republicans and political and legal conservatives defended the decision to deny Garland a hearing on the basis of what McConnell and others described as a historical tradition of declining to confirm a Supreme Court nominee in a president's final year in office. McConnell and other GOP senators also invoked what they called the "Biden rule," based on a speech by Obama's future vice president Joe Biden when he was chair of the Senate Judiciary Committee in 1992 with the Republican George H. W. Bush in the White House. Biden, who had presided in fall 1991 over the contentious confirmation hearing for Bush's second Supreme Court nominee, Clarence Thomas, had stated that Bush should wait until the election to nominate a replacement if a Supreme Court seat were to become vacant during the summer or should appoint a moderate acceptable to what was then the Democratic-majority Senate.

Democrats answered the Republicans' arguments by pointing out that no vacancy had actually arisen in 1992. They also noted that several Supreme Court nominees had been confirmed in the final year of a president's term—most recently, Anthony M. Kennedy in President Ronald Reagan's last year in office in 1988.

Evenly Divided Decisions

The failure to fill the vacancy left the eight-justice Court with four evenly divided 4–4 decisions at the end of the 2015 term, three of them argued before Scalia's death and the other argued two months afterward. Under Supreme Court procedure, the lower court decisions in the four cases were listed as "affirmed by an equally divided Court," but without establishing a legal precedent. The Court does not specify the justices' individual votes in such cases.

In the most prominent of the cases, the Court in *United States v. Texas* (2016) rejected the Obama administration's effort to reinstitute its so-called Deferred Action for Parents of Americans policy, known as DAPA, aimed at protecting unauthorized immigrants from deportation if they had U.S. citizen children. Lower federal courts in Texas had ruled that the administration had exceeded its lawful authority in adopting the policy. The case was argued in April, with the eight justices evidently divided along conservative–liberal lines.

In a second important case, the Court in *Friedrichs v. California Teachers Association* (2016) turned aside a free-speech plea by dissident teachers in California seeking to eliminate the requirement that nonunion members pay a prorated "agency fee" to cover the union's costs in representing them in collective bargaining and grievances. The Court had upheld agency fee arrangements by public employee unions four decades earlier in *Abood v. Detroit Board of Education* (1977). The Court was to overturn that precedent in a 5–4 decision in *Janus v. American Federation of State, County, and Municipal Employees* (2018) after Justice Neil M. Gorsuch took office as Scalia's successor.

The two other 4–4 decisions came in less significant cases. The ruling in *Dollar General Corporation v. Mississippi Band of Choctaw Indians* (2016) slightly enlarged tribal courts' jurisdiction over civil suits against a non-Indian defendant for a tort committed against an Indian on tribal land. The ruling in *Hawkins v. Community Bank of Raymore* (2016) allowed banks to hold spouses who guarantee a spouse's loan responsible after a default without violating the federal law against discrimination in credit terms based on marital status.

The unfilled Supreme Court vacancy may have had a more consequential effect by helping the Republican Trump win the November 2016 election as president. Trump repeatedly emphasized the issue in his campaign. Exit polling by CNN indicated that 26 percent of Trump's voters considered the president's power to nominate Supreme Court justices to be the "most important" factor in their vote; only 18 percent of Hillary Clinton's voters considered the issue to be the most important factor for their votes.

Trump lost the nationwide popular vote by approximately 2.9 million votes. But he won the presidency with 304 electoral votes thanks in part by narrowly taking three states normally carried by Democrats in presidential contests: Pennsylvania, Michigan, and Wisconsin.

Garland's nomination formally expired with the convening of a new Congress on January 3, 2017. Trump nominated Gorsuch, a veteran federal appeals court judge, as Scalia's successor in his first month in office at the end of the month. Gorsuch took office in April 2017 after the Republican-majority Senate confirmed him on a 54–45 vote with three Democrats joining 51 Republicans in supporting the nomination. The vote came after the Republican majority adopted a change in Senate rules to allow a simple majority, instead of a 60-vote supermajority, to close debate on Supreme Court nominations.

the Union address in January 2010 to denounce the controversial *Citizens United* campaign finance decision, with the justices seated just below him. Among major decisions in Obama's second term, for example, the president said that he was "deeply disappointed" with the Court's 5–4 ruling in June 2013 that effectively nullified the Voting Rights Act's provision requiring states or localities with a history of discrimination to obtain preclearance for any changes in voting procedures.

On the other hand, Obama praised the Court's decision on June 26, 2015, to guarantee marriage equality for same-sex couples. The ruling, Obama told the lead plaintiff James Obergefell in a telephone call broadcast live on cable news channels, "affirms what millions of Americans already believe in their hearts." Representing the administration, Solicitor General Donald Verrilli Jr. had made a strong and effective argument supporting the same-sex couples when the justices heard the case two months earlier.

The administration joined liberal and progressive groups in counting several other victories in the Court's 2015 and 2016 terms despite the conservative bloc's overall dominance. Kennedy, who wrote and provided the critical fifth vote for the marriage equality decision, also provided critical votes for other closely divided liberal rulings. These included a 2015 decision that strengthened the federal Fair Housing Act and a pair of 2016 decisions that upheld limited use of racial preferences in university admissions and that struck down a restrictive Texas law regulating abortion clinics.

On the other hand, the administration suffered a significant loss when the eight-justice Court divided 4–4 in 2016 in upholding a lower-court injunction against the administration's Deferred Action for Parents of Americans and Lawful Permanent Residents (DAPA) policy granting lawful status to illegal immigrants with U.S. citizen children. The tie vote affirmance in *United States v. Texas* was one of the term's four 4–4 rulings that ended with no resolution of the legal issues presented because of the unfilled vacancy after Scalia's death. Such tie votes left the rulings by lower courts in place.

Health Care

The Obama administration suffered setbacks in two successive challenges to a regulation issued under the Affordable Care Act to require employers to include cost-free coverage of contraception in employee health benefit plans. In the first of the decisions, the Court in 2014 held on a 5–4 vote divided along conservative–liberal lines that employers could be exempted from the requirement based on religious objections to some forms of contraception. The Court skirted a definitive ruling in the second case two years later by urging the administration to work on finding an accommodation with religious schools and charities that had similar objections to including contraceptives in student or employee health plans.

Two family-owned companies challenged the birth-control mandate on religious freedom grounds in separate cases in two federal circuits. The Oklahoma City–based Hobby Lobby Stores and the Pennsylvania-based Conestoga Wood Specialties both contended that the mandate violated provisions of the federal Religious Freedom Restoration Act (RFRA) that prohibited the federal government from substantially burdening a person's free exercise of religion unless the burden was narrowly tailored to further a "compelling interest." The Tenth U.S. Circuit Court of Appeals upheld Hobby Lobby's claim, while the Third Circuit ruled for the government in the Conestoga case.

The Supreme Court's decision to resolve the conflict by hearing the government's appeal in what was eventually called *Burwell v. Hobby Lobby Stores, Inc.* (2014) set the stage for a major showdown between the administration and women's health groups, among others, on one side and political conservatives and religious organizations on the other. In his opinion for the majority, Alito began by concluding that a closely held corporation qualified as a "person" under RFRA because the law "protects the religious liberty of the humans who own and control those companies." On the merits, Alito said that the mandate imposed a substantial and unnecessarily restrictive burden on the owners' religious exercise by forcing them to choose between their religious beliefs and conducting business as a corporation. Ginsburg led the four liberal justices in dissenting on the ground that the link between the birth-control mandate and the owners' religious belief was "attenuated." She also rejected Alito's argument that the government could further its goal by direct subsidies for contraceptives.

GAY RIGHTS

The Supreme Court awarded gay rights advocates their greatest legal victory in U.S. history in 2015 with a bitterly divided 5–4 decision to guarantee marriage rights to same-sex couples nationwide.

The ruling in *Obergefell v. Hodges* (2015) was the Court's fourth decision over a twenty-year period to extend constitutional protections to gay men and lesbians. Justice Anthony M. Kennedy led the four liberal justices in the majority as Chief Justice John G. Roberts Jr. and his three conservative colleagues each answered with sharply written dissents.

Kennedy had led narrow majorities in each of the preceding gay rights decisions. In the first of the decisions, Kennedy led a 6–3 majority in *Romer v. Evans* (1996) to strike down a Colorado ballot measure that prohibited enactment of any state or local laws to protect gays, lesbians, or bisexuals from discrimination in employment or public accommodations. Seven years later, Kennedy led the same six-justice majority in a decision, *Lawrence v. Texas* (2003), to strike down state antisodomy laws: criminal provisions used, though infrequently, to prosecute gay men for consensual sex.

The legal drive to win marriage rights for same-sex couples began in the early 1990s with a landmark state court case in Hawaii. Congress responded in 1996 by enacting a law, the Defense of Marriage Act (DOMA), to prohibit the federal government from extending marriage-based benefits, such as tax breaks, to same-sex couples even in legally recognized marriages.

Gay rights advocates continued efforts to win marriage rights in state and federal court cases. Massachusetts' highest state court applied the state's constitution in becoming the first U.S. court to grant marriage equality to same-sex couples; the ruling in November 2003 cited *Lawrence* as a persuasive precedent and gave the state legislature six months to enact legislation to comply with the ruling.

Five years after the Massachusetts court's ruling, the California Supreme Court in May 2008 followed that example in recognizing same-sex marriages under its state constitution. California voters nullified the decision in November 2008, however, by approving a ballot measure known as Proposition 8 that defined marriage as the union of "one man and one woman." Gay rights advocates succeeded over the next five years in gaining recognition for same-sex marriages in several states by legislation or state court rulings.

The first of the marriage cases to reach the Court was an effort by sponsors of California's Proposition 8 to reinstate the same-sex marriage ban after it had been ruled unconstitutional by the Ninth U.S. Circuit Court of Appeals. The Prop 8 sponsors, led by former state senator Dennis Hollingsworth, filed the appeal after the state's Democratic governor and attorney general declined to appeal the Ninth Circuit's decision.

Gay rights advocates hoped that the case could be the vehicle for the Court to rule on the merits in favor of marriage equality for same-sex couples. Instead, however, the Court declined in *Hollingsworth v. Perry* (2013) to rule on the merits on the ground that the Prop 8 sponsors had no legal standing to appeal the lower court decision.

Writing for the 5–4 majority, Roberts explained that the Prop 8 sponsors' "generalized grievance" was "insufficient to confer standing." Justice Antonin Scalia and three liberal justices—Ruth Bader Ginsburg, Stephen G. Breyer, and Elena Kagan—concurred. Writing for the four dissenters, Kennedy emphasized that the California Supreme Court had ruled as a matter of state law that the ballot measure's supporters did have standing in the case. The other dissenters were two conservatives, Clarence Thomas and Samuel A. Alito Jr., and one liberal justice, Sonia Sotomayor.

The Court on the same day issued a 5–4 ruling to strike down the Defense of Marriage Act as a violation of due process rights for same-sex couples. The ruling in *United States v. Windsor* (2013) came in a case filed by a New York City woman, Edith Windsor, who challenged the $363,000 tax bill on her late wife's estate. Under DOMA, Windsor could not claim the tax benefit available to surviving spouses of opposite-sex marriages. The Obama administration joined Windsor in arguing that DOMA was unconstitutional, but Republican members of Congress formed the so-called Bipartisan Legal Advisory Group (BLAG) to defend the law in the Supreme Court case.

On a preliminary issue, the justices divided 6–3 in ruling that they had jurisdiction to hear the appeal despite what Kennedy called in his opinion for the Court the "friendly, non-adversary proceeding." The House group's "sharp adversarial presentation of the issues satisfies the prudential concerns" against ruling in the case, Kennedy reasoned.

In the second case, more than two dozen religious schools and charities challenged the procedure for obtaining an exemption from the birth-control mandate. Under the government's plan, the exemption required the school or organization's health insurer to provide birth-control coverage itself for students or employees. The religious nonprofits in what eventually became *Zubik v. Burwell* (2016) contended that the process of requesting the exemption burdened their religious exercise by implicating them in providing contraceptives such as the so-called "morning after" pill, which they

On the merits, Kennedy noted that family law, including marriage, had traditionally been left to state law and found that DOMA had no purpose other than to "place same-sex couples . . . in a second-tier marriage." On that basis, Kennedy concluded that the law was "unconstitutional as a deprivation of the liberty of the person protected by the Fifth Amendment of the Constitution."

In a dissent on the merits for three of the four conservatives, Scalia argued that the differential treatment for same-sex marriages could be upheld as constitutional under the permissive "rational basis" test. "[T]he Constitution neither requires nor forbids our society to approve of same-sex marriage," Scalia wrote.

Scalia also sharply attacked the majority's decision to recognize jurisdiction in the case. Roberts and Thomas joined that part of the opinion, but not Alito. In his separate opinion, Roberts argued for upholding the law as promoting "interests in uniformity and stability" but without joining Scalia's more expansive discussion of the merits. Thomas joined Scalia's opinion in full and wrote a separate dissent. Alito joined Scalia's discussion of the merits but joined with the majority in finding jurisdiction to hear the case.

Over the next year, three federal appeals courts issued decisions that found state bans on same-sex marriages to be unconstitutional. States in the affected circuits asked the Supreme Court to review the decisions, but the justices unexpectedly denied review in all three as they opened the 2014 term on the traditional first Monday in October. One month later, the Sixth U.S. Circuit Court of Appeals issued a decision on November 6, 2014, upholding same-sex marriage bans in the four states within the circuit: Kentucky, Michigan, Ohio, and Tennessee.

Plaintiffs in all four states asked the Court to review the decision. The Court agreed on January 16, 2015, to review the case under the name of the lead plaintiff in the Ohio case, James Obergefell, versus Richard Hodges, director of the state's Department of Health. Obergefell had married his longtime partner John Arthur in Maryland in 2013, a few months before Arthur's death in October from amyotrophic lateral sclerosis, the neurogenerative disease known alternately as ALS or Lou Gehrig's disease. Obergefell filed a federal court suit after the state's Health Department applied Ohio law in refusing to list him as Arthur's husband on Arthur's death certificate.

The Court heard arguments in the consolidated cases in an extended ninety-minute session on April 28, 2015, and issued the sharply divided 5–4 decision two months later on June 26, the final decision day for the term. Writing for the majority, Kennedy began by noting prior decisions that defined the right to marriage as fundamental. "[T]he reasons marriage is fundamental under the Constitution apply with equal force to same-sex couples," Kennedy wrote.

Kennedy went on to base the decision on due process and equal protection principles. "The right of same-sex couples to marry that is part of the liberty promised by the Fourteenth Amendment is derived, too, from that Amendment's guarantee of the equal protection of the laws," he wrote. The four liberal justices—Ginsburg, Breyer, Sotomayor, and Kagan—joined Kennedy's opinion without writing separately.

In the longest of the dissenting opinions, Roberts criticized Kennedy's due process rationale and, for the first time in his tenure, emphasized his disagreement by reading portions from the bench. Roberts criticized what he called Kennedy's "aggressive application of substantive due process" and also faulted the equal protection analysis as "hard to follow." He argued for upholding the state bans on same-sex marriages as "rationally related to the States' 'legitimate state interest' in 'preserving the traditional institution of marriage.'"

The three other conservatives joined Roberts's dissent, and each wrote separate dissenting opinions. In his opinion, Scalia criticized what he called "a judicial Putsch" and mocked Kennedy's style as "pretentious . . . and egotistic." Thomas joined Scalia's opinion and wrote a longer dissent joined by Scalia to reiterate his criticism of substantive due process. Alito used his dissent, joined by Scalia and Thomas, to criticize the majority's decision as "contrary to long-established tradition."

Most states moved promptly to comply with the decision, but officials in some states resisted. Alabama's chief justice instructed court clerks not to comply for a period of time, and court clerks in at least two other states, Kentucky and Tennessee, declined to issue marriage licenses to same-sex couples. Public opinion polls had found majority support for recognizing same-sex marriage as early as 2011. Resistance to the Court's decision dissipated over time as polls registered increasing public support.

believed operated by inducing an abortion. Federal appeals courts divided on the issue. The Court heard arguments in the case in March 2016, one month after Scalia's death. Two months later, the eight-justice Court issued a unanimous, unsigned opinion that avoided a direct ruling by remanding all four cases under review to federal circuit courts to allow the respective parties "sufficient time to resolve any outstanding issues between them."

Before that ruling, the administration had prevailed in a major challenge to the Affordable Care Act's system of government-operated health insurance marketplaces—so-called exchanges to be operated either by individual states or the federal government.

Critics of the law argued that, contrary to a ruling by the Internal Revenue Service (IRS), the tax credits provided under the law were available only to customers of exchanges "established by the State," not to customers of federal exchanges in states that had declined to set up such market-places. The Court's 6–3 decision in *King v. Burwell* (2015) held that the subsidies were available on federal as well as state exchanges. Writing for a majority that also included Kennedy and the four liberal justices, Roberts reasoned that the operative statutory provision was ambiguous and was best interpreted to treat state and federal exchanges the same for purposes of the tax credits. In a sharply written dissent, Scalia, coauthor of a widely noticed book on statutory construction, called the reasoning "quite absurd."

First Amendment

The Roberts Court burnished its reputation somewhat as a pro–free speech tribunal with a miscellany of favorable decisions on relatively narrow First Amendment claims. The prospeech rulings included a decision that somewhat strengthened rights for antiabortion demonstrators to protest near women's health clinics and another that protected social media users from criminal prosecution for inflammatory language short of actual threats. Among two lesser setbacks for free-speech claimants, the Court upheld states' authority to censor objectionable language proposed by private groups for vanity vehicle license plates.

In religious freedom cases, a closely divided Court in 2014 upheld the common practice of opening legislative sessions with prayers even if the invocations are explicitly sectarian and predominantly from a single faith: Christianity. The five conservative justices voted in that case to support religious expression against an Establishment Clause claim brought by nonbelievers just as they had supported the religiously motivated employer in the Hobby Lobby case.

The ruling in the abortion-protest case, *McCullen v. Coakley* (2014), struck down a Massachusetts law that established a thirty-five-foot "buffer zone" around clinics that provided abortion services. A lower federal court had upheld the law by pointing to the Supreme Court's decision in *Hill v. Colorado* (2000) that upheld a "floating" eight-foot buffer zone to protect employees or patients entering or leaving abortion clinics. Roberts led five justices in finding that the Massachusetts law imposed more limits on antiabortion protesters than necessary to further the state's legitimate interests in protecting access to the clinics. Four conservative justices concurred separately in opinions that would have given states less room to limit abortion clinic protests.

The Court's decision in the social media case *Elonis v. United States* (2015) overturned a Pennsylvania man's federal conviction for a series of violent rants on Facebook aimed at his estranged wife. Anthony Elonis had been convicted

under a federal criminal code provision that prohibits transmitting in interstate commerce "any communication containing any threat . . . to injure the person of another." Writing for seven justices, Roberts explained that a conviction required some evidence of the speaker's state of mind beyond evidence that a "reasonable" observer would regard the language as a threat. In separate opinions, Alito agreed on setting aside the conviction but argued in favor of upholding a conviction based on recklessness; Thomas said he would have sustained the conviction.

The Court considered First Amendment claims in a number of election-related disputes and sided in most of the decisions with parties challenging the laws at issue: local, state, or federal. In the most important of those decisions, the Court in *McCutcheon v. Federal Election Commission* (2014) struck down the provision in federal campaign finance law that limited an individual's aggregate contributions to federal candidates during a single election cycle. In another campaign finance case, however, the Court in *Williams-Yulee v. Florida Bar* (2015) upheld a state bar rule prohibiting candidates for judicial office from directly soliciting campaign contributions.

Among other decisions, the Court in *Susan B. Anthony List v. Driehaus* (2014) cleared the way for political advocacy groups to bring a First Amendment challenge to an Ohio law prohibiting "false" speech during political campaigns even though no formal enforcement actions had been initiated. The unanimous decision sent the case back to the Sixth U.S. Circuit Court of Appeals, which ruled the Ohio law unconstitutional in 2016.

The Court in *Reed v. Town of Gilbert* (2015) struck down an ordinance enacted by a midsized town near Phoenix, Arizona, that set different rules for the size, placement, and time of outdoor signs based on their subject matter. The ordinance favored political or ideological signs over so-called "directional" signs advertising the time and location of one-time events, which were strictly limited as to size and as to the length of time they could be posted. Writing for six justices, Thomas applied strict scrutiny in finding the content-based law invalid because it was not narrowly tailored to further a compelling government interest. In an opinion for three liberal justices, Kagan agreed that the ordinance was unconstitutional but disagreed with applying strict scrutiny to local sign ordinances.

In addition to *McCutcheon*, the Court issued one other decision striking down a federal law as a violation of First Amendment free-speech rights. The 6–2 decision in *Agency for International Development v. Alliance for Open Society International, Inc.* (2013) struck down a provision of the United States Leadership Against HIV/AIDS, Tuberculosis, and Malaria Act of 2003 that required organizations seeking funding from a federal program designed to combat global pandemics to publicly oppose prostitution and sex trafficking. Writing for the majority, Roberts acknowledged that the government can refrain from funding speech that promotes sex trafficking or prostitution but concluded that it cannot use a spending program to unduly restrict speech outside the scope of the particular program. Scalia and Thomas dissented; Kagan was recused because of her involvement with the case while U.S. solicitor general.

In a setback for free-speech rights, the Court in *Walker v. Sons of Confederate Veterans* (2015) held that states can reject privately proposed messages for specialty license plates without offending the First Amendment on the ground that those messages convey government speech. Breyer led a 5–4 majority in upholding a decision by a Texas state agency to reject a license plate containing a depiction of a Confederate battle flag that some members of the public had objected to as racially offensive. He reasoned that the messages convey government, instead of private, speech. Thomas provided the liberal bloc the critical fifth vote; Alito led four conservatives in a dissent; he argued the license plates would be private, instead of government, speech.

In a second setback for free speech, the Court in *Clapper v. Amnesty International USA* (2013) rejected a suit by a coalition of lawyers, human rights activists, journalists, and others to block any government surveillance of their conversations with foreign parties. Alito led a five-justice majority in finding that the plaintiffs' fear of foreign intelligence surveillance without proof of any actual eavesdropping did not create legal standing for the suit. Breyer led four liberal justices in dissent.

The legislative prayer case, *Town of Greece v. Galloway* (2014), relied heavily on historical tradition dating to the eighteenth century in refusing to set strict limits on such invocations. Two non-Christians in the small upstate New York town had argued that the town council violated the prohibition against establishment of religion by use of sectarian, predominantly Christian, prayers at the opening of public sessions. Writing for the 5–4 majority, Kennedy hinted at possible constitutional violations only if government bodies "directed the public to participate in the prayers, singled out dissidents for opprobrium, or indicated that [the legislators'] decisions might be influenced by a person's acquiescence in the prayer opportunity." In a dissent for the four liberal justices, Kagan said that she would have found the town's practice in violation of "the constitutional requirement of neutrality" on religious matters.

In a second religious freedom case, the Court in *Holt v. Hobbs* (2015) unanimously ruled that the state of Arkansas violated a Muslim inmate's rights under the federal Religious Land Use and Institutionalized Persons Act (RLUIPA) by a policy prohibiting prisoners from growing beards—a practice that many devout Muslims view as part of their faith. Alito cited the *Hobby Lobby* decision as a precedent in finding that the state could have achieved its stated goal of prison security in other ways without infringing on the inmate's religious freedom.

Election Law

The Court's election law decisions over the four-year period returned to contentious disputes in such areas as voting rights, campaign finance, and redistricting. Conservatives flexed their muscles in two 5–4 decisions, both written by Roberts, that ruled unconstitutional important voting rights and campaign finance provisions in federal laws. Liberal justices picked up Kennedy's vote, however, to form 5–4 majorities in two significant redistricting cases, including a decision to uphold reformers' proposals to create independent redistricting commissions to combat partisan gerrymandering.

Roberts's opinion in the voting rights case, *Shelby County v. Holder* (2013), gutted the most important enforcement tool in the federal Voting Rights Act: the requirement that some states or localities obtain preclearance for any changes in voting procedures. Roberts faulted Congress for failing to significantly update the formula enacted in 1965 as the basis for imposing the preclearance requirement. Despite previous decisions upholding the law, Roberts called the act "extraordinary legislation" that departed from what he called a constitutional principle of "equal sovereignty" for individual states.

The ruling left the other parts of the law intact, including the general prohibition in section 2 against any election laws or practices that resulted in racial discrimination. Writing for the four liberal dissenters, however, Ginsburg argued that the preclearance requirement had proven to be effective in protecting voting rights and that the loss of that enforcement mechanism would leave voting rights advocates powerless to combat what she called "second-generation barriers" to voting rights. The ruling left it up to Congress to revise the formula, but lawmakers declined to take up the issue during the remainder of the Obama administration.

Voting rights advocates prevailed in two other decisions, however. The 7–2 decision in *Arizona v. Inter-tribal Council of Arizona, Inc.* (2013) blocked the state of Arizona from requiring persons registered to vote in federal elections to present proof of citizenship beyond the sworn statement included in federal voting registration forms. Scalia wrote for the majority; Thomas and Alito dissented. In a second decision, the Court upheld the traditional practice of implementing the "one person, one vote" requirement in redistricting cases on the basis of districts' total population instead of voter-eligible population. The 8–0 ruling in *Evenwel v. Abbott* (2016) rejected an effort by some Texas voters to require districts based on voter-eligible population. "Total population apportionment," Ginsburg wrote in the main opinion, "promotes equitable and effective representation."

The Court continued to look askance at federal campaign finance laws in a 5–4 decision that struck down part of the 1970s-era law that set an overall limit on the amount an individual could donate to candidates for federal office.

Writing for a four-justice plurality in *McCutcheon v. Federal Election Commission* (2014), Roberts said that the aggregate limit—set at $48,600 per election cycle at the time of the decision—was not closely tied to preventing corruption or the appearance of corruption as required to be constitutional. Thomas provided the fifth vote in an opinion that argued for ruling all contribution limits unconstitutional. Breyer led the four liberal justices in dissent.

The ruling in support of independent redistricting commissions rejected an effort by Arizona's Republican-majority legislature to nullify a voter initiative that stripped the legislature of any role in drawing legislative or congressional districts. The lawmakers argued that the Constitution's Election Clause specified that the "times, places, and manners" of federal elections were to be "prescribed in each state by the legislature thereof." Writing for the 5–4 majority in *Arizona State Legislature v. Arizona Independent Redistricting Commission* (2015), Ginsburg found "no constitutional barrier" to a state's use of voter initiatives as a form of lawmaking. Kennedy joined the liberal bloc in the decision; Roberts led four conservative justices in dissent.

In another victory for the liberal bloc, the Court reaffirmed that plaintiffs can challenge race-based redistricting on an individual district basis without contending that race was the predominant factor in an overall state districting plan. Breyer wrote the 5–4 opinion in *Alabama Legislative Black Caucus v. Alabama* (2015); Scalia led four conservatives in dissent.

Business Law

Business interests generally fared well in Supreme Court cases pitting employers and companies against workers, customers, other plaintiffs, or government regulators. Overall, however, business-related decisions were somewhat mixed, and business groups were disappointed with their failure to win decisive victories in some important areas.

Among perennial issues, business interests prevailed in two decisions strengthening enforcement of mandatory arbitration clauses in consumer or other contracts and won two federal preemption decisions limiting state court remedies for disaffected customers. On class actions, however, the Court's rulings included two somewhat favorable to plaintiffs, including one that eased plaintiffs' burdens in proving classwide damage claims.

Business groups scored one important victory in an area outside their usual bread-and-butter issues: separation of powers between Congress and the president. Business interests succeeded in challenging President Obama's attempt late in his first term to fill three vacancies on the National Labor Relations Board (NLRB) through recess appointments while the Senate was technically not in recess.

The ruling in *National Labor Relations Board v. Noel Canning* (2014) represented the Court's first interpretation of the Constitution's Recess Appointments Clause, which gives the president the power to "fill up all Vacancies that may happen during the recess of the Senate" by making temporary appointments to positions requiring Senate confirmation. Obama resorted to recess appointments after Republican opposition to his nominees left the NLRB with only two members, short of the quorum needed to conduct business.

A Washington-state based bottler, Noel Canning Corporation, forced the issue by contesting a labor law violation finding upheld by the NLRB with the recess appointees. Major business groups backed the company's challenge. The justices unanimously agreed that Obama had no authority to make recess appointments while the Senate was conducting *pro forma* sessions, though without conducting any business. Breyer wrote an opinion for five justices, while four conservative justices argued in a partial concurrence for a more restrictive reading that the president could make recess appointments not during intrasession breaks but only during the recess between Senate sessions.

The Court continued to favor business groups seeking to uphold, under the Federal Arbitration Act (FAA), mandatory arbitration clauses that prohibited any collective or classwide dispute proceedings. The 5–3 decision in *American Express Co. v. Italian Colors Restaurant* (2013) blocked an Oakland, California, restaurant from bringing other merchants into its antitrust claim against American Express for allegedly using its monopoly power to force merchants into accepting its high-cost consumer cards. Writing for the conservative majority, Scalia rejected the restaurant's claim that pursuing its claim on an individual basis would be prohibitively expensive. Kagan wrote a strong dissent for three liberal justices; Sotomayor was recused because she had participated in the case while on the Second Circuit.

In a second decision, the Court admonished a California court for a seeming attempt to circumvent its line of decisions enforcing mandatory arbitration clauses in the face of state laws protecting access to courts to resolve disputes. The 6–3 decision in *DIRECTV, Inc. v. Imburgia* (2016) allowed the satellite television service DIRECTV to force two customers dissatisfied with early termination fees into individual arbitration. In his opinion for the majority, Breyer said that California courts were wrong to block arbitration on the basis of a state law that banned mandatory arbitration clauses as unconscionable but that had been held preempted under a prior decision. Breyer pointedly said that state courts have "an undisputed obligation" to follow Supreme Court decisions on the issue. Ginsburg and Sotomayor dissented on the same grounds that liberal justices had cited in prior arbitration decisions; Thomas dissented separately by repeating his view that the FAA does not apply to state court proceedings.

In federal preemption decisions, the Court in *Mutual Pharmaceutical Co. v. Bartlett* (2013) blocked state court suits against drug manufacturers for allegedly inadequate warning labels. Alito wrote the 5–4 decision with four liberal justices in dissent. The Court in *Northwest, Inc. v. Ginsberg* (2014) similarly spared airlines from state court suits claiming false advertising in their frequent-flyer programs. The decision, by Alito, was unanimous.

In class action cases, the Court gave business groups a victory in *Comcast Corp. v. Behrend* (2013) by requiring plaintiffs to prove a method of calculating class damages before certification of the class action. Scalia wrote the 5–4 decision with liberal justices in dissent. Three years later, however, Kennedy led a 6–2 majority in *Tyson Foods, Inc. v. Bouaphakeo* (2016) to allow plaintiffs in an overtime-pay class action to use a statistical average to estimate classwide damages. In the same term, the Court in *Campbell-Ewald v. Gomez* (2016) held that class action defendants cannot moot a case by settling with the named plaintiff or plaintiffs; Ginsburg wrote the 6–3 decision with Roberts, Scalia, and Alito in dissent.

In another important litigation area, the Court in *Halliburton Co. v. Erica P. John Fund, Inc.* (2014) significantly reaffirmed the so-called fraud on the market theory for securities fraud suits that dated from a 1988 precedent known as *Basic*. The ruling favored defendants somewhat by allowing them to defend such suits by showing that the alleged misstatements had no impact on stock prices. All nine justices agreed on that point, but three conservatives—Scalia, Thomas, and Alito—argued in a partial concurrence for overruling *Basic*.

One term later, the Court opened the door somewhat to securities fraud suits against new stock issuers for opinions contained in registration statements. The unanimous ruling in *Omnicare, Inc. v. Laborers District Council Construction Industry Pension Fund* (2015) held that an issuer could be liable for omitting material facts about its knowledge concerning the opinions challenged as fraudulent. The Court had helped plaintiffs in an earlier decision, *Amgen Inc. v. Connecticut Retirement Plans and Trust Funds* (2013), that allowed certification of a securities fraud class action without a preliminary showing of materiality as to the alleged misstatements at issue. The Court dealt business groups another setback with its 8–0 decision in *Merrill Lynch, Pierce, Fenner & Smith Inc. v. Manning* (2016) that state courts can hear stock manipulation suits if filed under state law instead of under a parallel federal law.

Despite the conservative justices' general skepticism of antitrust remedies, the Court favored the Federal Trade Commission (FTC) in two separate cases in the 2012 term. The 5–3 ruling in *Federal Trade Commission v. Actavis, Inc.* (2013) allowed the agency to pursue antitrust charges against a common practice in the drug industry: brand-name pharmaceutical companies paying generic manufacturers to keep low-cost versions of patent-protected medications off the market. Breyer wrote the opinion;

Roberts, Thomas, and Scalia dissented, with Alito recused. Earlier in the term, Sotomayor led a unanimous Court in *Federal Trade Commission v. Phoebe Putney Health System, Inc.* (2013) in holding that a municipal hospital authority does not enjoy the immunity from antitrust suits ordinarily extended to government entities in the acquisition of a competing hospital.

Employers had a mostly favorable record in labor law cases apart from the more mixed record in job discrimination cases under civil rights laws. The Court backed employers in a pair of unanimous decisions in the 2013 term in enforcing contract terms unfavorable to employees. The ruling in *Heimeshoff v. Hartford Life & Accident Ins. Co.* (2013) enforced the two-year statute of limitations in the company's health insurance plan on bringing disability benefits claims. Thomas noted that the applicable federal law, the Employee Retirement Income Security Act (ERISA), established no deadline for disability claims. The ruling in *Sandifer v. United States Steel Corp.* (2014) enforced a provision of the company's collective bargaining agreement that it interpreted to deny pay for time spent putting on or taking off protective gear. Scalia noted that the Fair Labor Standards Act had been amended to exclude pay for "changing clothes" and that employees at the plant typically put on the required protective glasses during the workday itself.

Business groups won significantly in three decisions blocking suits in U.S. courts against U.S. or multinational companies based on conduct overseas. The 9–0 ruling in *Kiobel v. Royal Dutch Petroleum* (2013) blocked an effort by Nigerian nationals to use the Alien Tort Statute to sue Royal Dutch and its British partner, Shell Transport and Trading Co., for complicity in human rights violations by the Nigerian government in putting down protests of oil drilling in their homelands. Roberts reasoned in the main opinion that the presumption against extraterritorial application of U.S. laws applied to the 1791 statute. Breyer led four liberal justices in a separate opinion, however, for leaving the door open to some suits if "important" U.S. interests were implicated.

One term later, the Court in *Daimler AG v. Bauman* (2014) blocked state courts from exercising jurisdiction over foreign companies for human rights abuses abroad based solely on their affiliation with a U.S. subsidiary based in the state. The ruling was unanimous. Two terms later, the Court in *RJR Nabisco v. European Community* (2016) blocked the European Community and its member states from using the federal antiracketeering law, known as RICO, to sue U.S. tobacco manufacturers in U.S. courts for alleged money-laundering schemes abroad. Alito wrote the 4–3 decision, with Ginsburg, Breyer, and Kagan in dissent and Sotomayor recused.

The Court continued to take a special interest in patent cases, often in disagreement with the Federal Circuit Court of Appeals, the specialized court created by Congress with exclusive jurisdiction over appeals in patent cases, and often ruling against patent holders or patent litigators. In one case closely watched by the biotech industry, the Court in *Association for Molecular Pathology v. Myriad Genetics, Inc.* (2013) blocked patents for human genes but allowed patents for synthetic DNA created in the laboratory. The 9–0 ruling by Thomas reversed one prong of the Federal Circuit's decision that had held human genes to be patent eligible.

One term later, the Court sided with the Federal Circuit in a unanimous opinion by Thomas in *Alice Corporation Pty. Ltd. v. CLS Bank International* (2014) by limiting patent eligibility for computerized business methods. In other rulings in the same term, the Court reversed Federal Circuit decisions by limiting liability somewhat for patent infringement (*Limelight Networks, Inc. v. Akami Technologies, Inc.*) and making it easier for companies to be awarded attorney fees for successfully defending against patent infringement claims (*Highmark Inc. v. Allcare Health Management System, Inc.*; *Octane Fitness, LLC v. ICON Health & Fitness, Inc.*). The Court also established a slightly tighter standard for specifying patent claims than the Federal Circuit had adopted (*Nautilus, Inc. v. Biosig Instruments, Inc.*).

Two terms later, the Court gave patent holders a victory by rejecting a Federal Circuit decision that had limited judges' authority to award treble damages—triple the amount of "actual" damages proved—for "egregious" patent infringement in some cases. The 8–0 ruling by Roberts in *Halo Electronics v. Pulse Electronics* (2016) held that the Federal Circuit was wrong to disallow treble damages if the accused infringer had a "reasonable" defense.

In another intellectual property area, the Court issued two decisions that favored copyright holders in infringement cases. The ruling in *American Broadcasting Companies, Inc. v. Aereo, Inc.* (2014) found that a start-up company providing online access to broadcast television programs was subject to copyright liability for "public performance" of the material. Breyer wrote the 6–3 decision with Scalia, Thomas, and Alito in dissent. In the same term, the Court held on a 6–3 vote in *Petrella v. Metro-Goldwyn-Mayer, Inc.* (2014) that copyright holders can bring an infringement claim within the three-year statute of limitations even if the claim could have been brought earlier. Ginsburg wrote the opinion, with Breyer writing in dissent for himself, Roberts, and Kennedy.

Environmental Law

Environmental advocacy groups suffered setbacks along with the federal Environmental Protection Agency (EPA) in several Supreme Court decisions issued in the final years of Obama's generally environment-friendly presidency.

In the most important of those decisions, the Court forced the EPA to reconsider an Obama-era regulation setting limits on emissions of mercury and other hazardous pollutants from fossil-fueled power plants. The 5–4 ruling in *Utility Air Regulatory Group v. Environmental Protection Agency* (2015), divided along conservative–liberal lines, found that the EPA had acted unreasonably in failing to consider costs before adopting the so-called Mercury and Air Toxics Standards in 2011 after a fifteen-year rulemaking proceeding.

Scalia led the majority in concluding that "some attention to cost" was necessary to comply with the Clean Air Act's directive that EPA regulations governing power plants be "appropriate and necessary." In a dissent for the four liberal justices, Kagan argued that the EPA had adopted the standards with the intention of considering costs in later rulemaking stages. On remand, the EPA reissued the rule a year later. Power companies complied with the rule but continued to criticize it as imposing greater costs than the health benefits claimed from reducing emission of hazardous pollutants.

In an earlier decision, the Court issued a mixed decision in 2014 that somewhat limited the EPA's ability to regulate carbon dioxide and other greenhouse gas emissions. As in the later decision, Scalia led a conservative 5–4 majority in *Utility Air Regulatory Group v. Environmental Protection Agency* (2014) in striking down an EPA rule as beyond its statutory authority despite leading a 7–2 majority to give the agency a partial victory on a second issue. On the main issue, the Court said that the EPA was wrong to impose two of its major pollution control programs on industrial and power plants solely to prevent increases in greenhouse gas emissions. On the second point, however, the Court upheld the EPA's authority to develop rules requiring so-called stationary sources to adopt "best available control technology"—BACT in EPA jargon—to control greenhouse gas emissions. Thomas and Alito dissented on that issue.

The EPA prevailed in a separate, narrower decision, *Environmental Protection Agency v. EME Homer City Generation, L.P.* (2014), that dealt with the agency's rules on cross-state pollution. With liberal justices in the majority, the 6–2 ruling upheld the EPA's decision to allocate mandated emission reductions among upwind states by requiring proportionately greater reductions in states that could achieve the reductions with lesser costs.

Environmentalists suffered setbacks in other, less significant decisions. The 8–0 ruling in *United States Army Corps of Engineers v. Hawkes Co.* (2016) allowed landowners to obtain preenforcement judicial review of the Corps' determination that their property was subject to antipollution restrictions under the Clean Water Act because of wetlands regulable as "waters of the United States." In a second decision, the Court in *CTS Corporation v. Waldburger* (2014) refused on a 7–2 vote to apply a federal law to override state law provisions setting fixed time limits for plaintiffs to bring environmental contamination suits in state courts. Kennedy wrote the opinion; Ginsburg and Breyer dissented.

Criminal Law and Procedure

The Court split the difference somewhat evenly between prosecutors and criminal defendants and suspects during the final four years of the Obama presidency. Overall, an unofficial count showed that the Court ruled in favor of defendants, suspects, or prison inmates in thirty-nine out of seventy-four signed decisions in criminal or habeas corpus cases.

Among major rulings, the Court cleared the way for the most common method of lethal injection executions in death penalty cases but also gave defendants two significant victories in regard to sentencing hearings in capital cases. In Fourth Amendment cases, the Court generally gave police somewhat broader discretion, but it also struck a blow for digital privacy by requiring a warrant before a search of a suspect's cell phone.

In the most important of the death penalty cases, the Court divided 5–4 along conservative-liberal lines in *Glossip v. Gross* (2015) in rejecting an Eighth Amendment challenge to the three-drug protocol widely used by states in lethal injection executions. Richard Glossip was one of four Oklahoma death row inmates who argued that the sedative used at the start of the procedure, midazolam, failed to render the inmate unconscious and left the inmate awake and writhing in pain as the next two drugs paralyzed and then stopped the inmate's heart.

The Court had upheld the three-drug protocol in an earlier case, *Baze v. Rees* (2008), but states were using a more powerful sedative, sodium thiopental, at the time. When European manufacturers blocked the use of sodium thiopental, states had to turn to midazolam instead. In rejecting the inmates' challenge, Alito concluded that they had failed to show the executions would likely violate the Eighth Amendment's prohibition against cruel or unusual punishment and had also failed to show the risk of the procedure to be "substantial when compared to known and available methods of execution."

In her dissenting opinion for the four liberal justices, Sotomayor argued that the state's procedure left the inmates "exposed to what may well be the chemical equivalent of being burned at the stake." In a separate and longer dissent, Breyer, joined by Ginsburg, called for a broad reexamination of capital punishment and signaled he would likely vote to find it unconstitutional.

In two other decisions, the Court strengthened procedural rights for defendants in capital sentencing hearings. Kennedy joined with the liberal bloc in the 5–4 decision in *Hall v. Florida* (2014) to bar states from using a fixed IQ of 70 or below as the threshold for intellectual disability in determining eligibility for the death penalty. Kennedy reasoned that what he called Florida's "rigid rule" created "an unacceptable risk that persons with intellectual disability will be executed." Alito led four conservative justices in dissent.

The Court gave capital defendants another procedural victory in an 8–1 ruling in *Hurst v. Florida* (2016) that overturned a provision of Florida's capital murder law that allowed judges, rather than juries, to find aggravating factors needed to impose the death penalty. The ruling, in an opinion by Sotomayor with Alito dissenting, extended the earlier decision in *Ring v. Arizona* (2008) that also required factual findings by a jury, instead of a judge, to impose the death penalty. One week after *Hurst*, the Court held in an 8–1 decision in *Kansas v. Carr* (2016) that judges in capital cases do not need to instruct jurors that a defendant does not have to prove mitigating factors beyond a reasonable doubt. The ruling, with Sotomayor dissenting, was Scalia's last majority opinion before his death three weeks later.

In a significant noncapital case, the Court extended an earlier ruling that eased penalties for defendants convicted of murder as juveniles. The Court had prohibited capital punishment for juvenile offenders in 2005 and further limited punishment for juvenile murderers with its 5–4 decision in *Miller v. Alabama* (2012) to nullify state laws that required life imprisonment without parole in such cases. The 6–3 ruling in the new case, *Montgomery v. Louisiana* (2016), applied *Miller* retroactively by holding that prisoners sentenced to life without parole for murders committed as juveniles before 2012 must be given the opportunity to show that sentence to have been unwarranted. Kennedy wrote for a majority that included the four liberal justices along with Roberts, a dissenter in the earlier decision. Scalia wrote the main dissent, joined by Thomas and Alito.

Despite close divisions in several police search cases, Roberts led a virtually unanimous Court in holding that police generally must obtain a warrant before searching a suspect's cell phone. The 9–0 ruling in *Riley v. California* (2014) settled a conflict between lower state and federal appellate courts on the issue. Roberts acknowledged prior decisions allowing warrantless searches of items found on a suspect's person but refused to extend those precedents to cell phones because of the amount of private information commonly stored on the devices. Roberts left open the possibility of searching a cell phone without a warrant under some exigent circumstances. Seven justices, all but Alito, joined Roberts's opinion in full. Alito concurred in part but said he would reconsider the issue if Congress or state legislatures enacted laws to allow warrantless searches for specific categories of information.

In other cases, the Court upheld police searches even after legally dubious investigative stops. The 8–1 ruling in *Heien v. North Carolina* (2014) allows police to search an automobile after a traffic stop even if it is based on what the Court described as a "reasonable mistake of law"—specifically, a nonexistent violation. The suspects in the case had been arrested on drug charges based on cocaine found after police had stopped the car because of a faulty brake light. The officers mistakenly thought that North Carolina law required two functioning brake lights, but the Court refused to suppress the evidence found as a result. "[T]he Fourth Amendment allows for some mistakes on the part of government officials," Roberts wrote. Sotomayor was the lone dissenter.

The Court divided 5–3 in a second decision, *Utah v. Strieff* (2016), that allowed the use of evidence found after an illegal on-the-street investigation, based on the after-the-fact discovery of an outstanding arrest warrant against the suspect. Thomas led a majority that included Breyer along with his three conservative colleagues in holding that the discovery of the warrant "attenuated" the connection between the illegal stop and discovery of the evidence. Sotomayor argued in a strong dissent that the ruling opened the door to police abuse. "This case allows the police to stop you on the street, demand your identification, and check it for outstanding traffic warrants—even if you are doing nothing wrong," she wrote. Ginsburg joined most of Sotomayor's opinion; Kagan wrote a separate dissent.

In other Fourth Amendment cases, the Court's 5–4 decision in *Maryland v. King* (2013) allowed police to take DNA samples from suspects arrested and detained for serious offenses. Kennedy wrote the opinion over a strong dissent by Scalia joined by liberal justices Ginsburg, Sotomayor, and Kagan. Earlier in the term, however, the Court had ruled 5–4 in *Missouri v. McNeely* (2013) that police ordinarily need a warrant for a nonconsensual blood draw in a DUI investigation. Sotomayor wrote the opinion. As in *Strieff*, Breyer joined conservatives Roberts, Thomas, and Alito in voting, this time in dissent, to give police broad discretion for investigatory searches. The Court's subsequent 6–2 decision in *Birchfield v. North Dakota* (2016) clarified that police do not need a warrant to administer a breath test in a roadside DUI investigation. Alito wrote the opinion, with Ginsburg and Sotomayor in dissent.

The Court significantly narrowed the basis for federal antigraft prosecutions of government officials in a decision, *McDonnell v. United States* (2016), that overturned the conviction of former Virginia governor Robert McDonnell.

Roberts led the unanimous decision in holding that public officials can be convicted under the federal bribery statute only if they agreed to take action or make a decision in return for accepting something of value, not—as in McDonnell's case—if they set up meetings or attended public events in exchange for gifts. *(See box, p. 422.)*

In another decision narrowing federal criminal statutes, the Court in *Johnson v. United States* (2015) struck down on an 8–1 vote a provision of the Armed Career Criminals Act (ACCA) that provided increased sentences for federal firearm offenders with three prior convictions for "violent" offenses. Scalia led the majority in concluding that the so-called residual clause was unconstitutionally vague.

In the same term, the Court in *Elonis v. United States* (2015) made it somewhat harder to convict a defendant under the federal threat statute by requiring proof that the defendant understood his communications—in the instant case, Facebook-posted rants against the suspect's estranged wife—as a threat. The Court in *Yates v. United States* (2015) also somewhat narrowed the destruction of evidence provisions in the Sarbanes-Oxley financial fraud by construing the law in effect to apply only to financial records.

Among other decisions, the Court held on a 5–4 vote in *Alleyne v. United States* (2013) that the Sixth Amendment requires a jury, not a judge, to make any factual finding necessary to increase a mandatory minimum sentence. The decision overruled an earlier decision, *Harris v. United States* (2002), that allowed judges to make such findings. In an unrelated sentencing case, the Court in *Betterman v. Montana* (2016) narrowed the Sixth Amendment somewhat by ruling that the right to a speedy trial does not apply to delays in sentencing after a verdict or guilty plea. The Court also continued to be generally unreceptive to federal habeas corpus cases challenging convictions or sentences in state courts with several decisions that faulted lower federal courts for failing to show deference to state court rulings in challenges to convictions or sentences filed by state prison inmates.

CHAPTER 14

General Government

General Government

President Barack Obama's second term was marked by attempts by congressional Republicans to subvert the power of some of his landmark achievements, namely the Patient Protection and Affordable Care Act (ACA) and the Dodd-Frank Wall Street Reform and Consumer Protection Act. Both pieces of legislation were passed in 2010 with the support of a Democratic-controlled House and Senate but drew fierce Republican opposition over what they considered examples of government overreach. The four years were also consumed by anger over an Internal Revenue Service (IRS) directive that improperly applied additional regulatory scrutiny and slowed the tax-exempt applications of conservative groups. Divided control of the House and Senate in 2013 and 2014 made it difficult for overtly partisan legislation to pass, and even when Republicans took back control of the Senate in the 2014 midterms, Congress remained gridlocked on a variety of issues.

IRS REPORT ON IDEOLOGICAL TARGETING OF CONSERVATIVE GROUPS

As part of the regular activities of the IRS, it is responsible for reviewing applications for groups seeking 501(c)(4) tax-exempt status. To be eligible, groups must meet a range of criteria, the most important of which is that the group engage in some type of social welfare activity. In March 2013, the Treasury Inspector General released a report finding that the IRS had improperly applied extra regulatory scrutiny to conservative groups. The activity was directly linked to a 2010 IRS directive that required additional review of applications for 501(c)(4) status bearing words such as *tea party*.

In response, Republicans sought to undermine the IRS in a variety of ways. They specifically attempted to limit the agency's ability to implement the provisions of the ACA for which it was responsible, namely penalties linked to the individual and employer mandates. The proposals included in a number of funding measures never garnered enough support to make it past the House and Senate, but members were successful in including some policy riders attached to funding bills that prevented the IRS from using federal funds to target Americans exercising their First Amendment rights or groups based on their ideologies. In 2015, the House and Senate approved language attached to the Consolidated Appropriations Act for fiscal 2016 (HR 2029), signed by the president on December 18, to allow for fast termination of IRS employees who take politically motivated action against taxpayers, require IRS employees to respect the taxpayer bill of rights, prohibit IRS officers or employees from using a personal email account to conduct official business, and require the creation of an appeals process for groups denied tax-exempt status.

Additionally, in the spring of 2014, the House approved a symbolic motion that would declare Lois Lerner, the former director of the IRS unit responsible for determining tax-exempt status, in contempt of Congress over her refusal to testify at two Congressional hearings. Congress then turned its focus to IRS Commissioner John Koskinen. Republicans claimed that the commissioner had lied under oath about the tax-exempt reviews and had overseen the destruction of records that would have provided important information to

REFERENCES

Discussion of general government action for the years 1945–1964 may be found in *Congress and the Nation Vol. I*, pp. 1455–1516; for the years 1965–1968, *Congress and the Nation Vol. II*, 655–660; for the years 1969–1972, *Congress and the Nation Vol. III*, pp. 435–468; for the years 1973–1976, *Congress and the Nation Vol. IV*, pp. 795–826; for the years 1977–1980, *Congress and the Nation Vol. V*, 817–870; for the years 1981–1984, *Congress and the Nation Vol. VI*, pp. 771–793; for the years 1985–1988, *Congress and the Nation Vol. VII*, pp. 843–867; for the years 1989–1992, *Congress and the Nation Vol. VIII*, pp. 855–909; for the years 1993–1996, *Congress and the Nation Vol. IX*, pp. 803–858; for the years 1997–2001, *Congress and the Nation Vol. X*, pp. 733–754; for the years 2001–2004, *Congress and the Nation Vol. XI*, pp. 683–701; for the years 2005–2008, *Congress and the Nation Vol. XII*, pp. 781–806; for the years 2009–2012, *Congress and the Nation Vol. XIII*, pp. 597–636.

Outlays for Science, Space, and General Government

Billions of Dollars

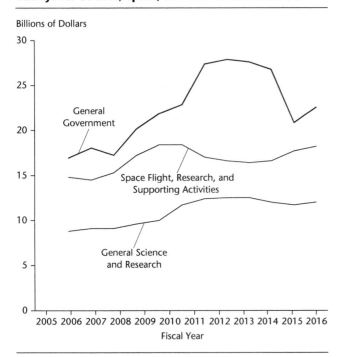

SOURCE: Office of Management and Budget, *Historical Tables, Budget of the United States Government: Fiscal Year 2018* (Washington, DC: U.S. Government Printing Office, 2018), Table 3.2.

NOTE: Total line includes some expenditures not shown separately.

investigators looking into the matter. House Republicans moved to impeach Koskinen but never gained enough traction for passage. In 2015, the Justice Department would announce that its investigation resulted in no findings that any IRS official had acted in such a politically biased manner to support criminal prosecution and that no IRS official had attempted to obstruct justice. The Justice Department did, however, note that it found evidence of mismanagement and poor judgment that should be corrected.

DODD-FRANK DRAWS SCRUTINY

In the wake of a recession that resulted in multiple bank bailouts, in 2010 Congress passed the Dodd-Frank Wall Street Reform and Consumer Protection Act to reorganize financial oversight organizations to better protect the U.S. economy. The act included the creation of two new oversight bodies, the Consumer Financial Protection Bureau (CFPB) and the Financial Services Oversight Council, both of which would be housed within the Federal Reserve. The CFPB was specifically dedicated to educating and enforcing certain financial regulations to protect the American consumer. Republicans and financial industry groups were vocal in their opposition to CFPB from the start, arguing that the body was given sweeping powers that lacked appropriate federal oversight. Years of contentious debate

prevented Congress from confirming a director to lead the CFPB until 2013, thus preventing it from carrying out many of its duties in its first few years of existence. In its existence, CFPB has handed out massive fines against banks, targeted payday lenders, and worked to protect students and members of the military from unfair lending practices.

Throughout the 113th and 114th Congress, Republicans worked to limit the power of Dodd-Frank, specifically by targeting the CFPB. However, because CFPB is an independent bureau of the Federal Reserve, and the Federal Reserve does not fall under the purview of the congressional appropriations process, it was difficult to control the group's activities. Absent a proposal eliminating the CFPB outright, Republicans instead inserted policy riders into funding bills that would move CFPB under the normal appropriations process. The measures never gained enough traction to be included in any final funding bills. However, Republicans were successful in adding provisions to legislation that would require additional reporting on both Dodd-Frank and CFPB activities. *(See Dodd-Frank discussion in Chapter 2.)*

FCC ISSUES NET NEUTRALITY RULES

Another target of Republicans during Obama's second term was the Federal Communications Commission (FCC), which in May 2014 issued a Notice of Proposed Rule Making (NPRM) seeking comment from the public on its intent to institute net neutrality regulations on broadband providers. The rule was intended to prohibit internet service providers from throttling consumer access to certain websites, regardless of whether that access slowed down the network. In February 2015, the FCC issued a new Open Internet Order that established stronger regulations than what was proposed in the NPRM. The order reclassified broadband internet as a telecommunications service under Title II of the Communications Act, giving the FCC greater regulatory power. Republicans argued that the regulations were unnecessary and burdensome and that they have the potential to stifle innovation and investment in technology. Through the Financial Services and General Government appropriations process, Republicans sought to both cut the FCC's budget and prevent it from implementing the net neutrality regulations, at least until existing court cases targeting the regulations were complete. The highly charged partisan debates to keep the government open and funded meant that most of the FCC policy riders were never included in final legislation.

POSTAL SERVICE IN CRISIS

Due to the 2007–2009 recession, coupled with an ongoing shift among Americans to communicate and complete transactions electronically, the United States Postal Service (USPS), a quasi-government agency, faced a significant financial crisis. The situation was in part driven by a 2006 requirement approved by Congress that USPS prefund the anticipated health care expenses of future retirees in an effort to protect U.S. taxpayers from bearing the brunt of any future unfunded liability. Under the law, the postal service makes annual payments to the Treasury of approximately $5 billion to cover these benefits, and it was able to do so until December 2011. At that time, Congress agreed to postpone the regular payment until the following year, and it would approve additional delays in September 2012 and September 2013.

The postal service attempted to alleviate some of its financial woes on its own, in 2012 proposing the closure of 3,600 low-revenue locations that served fewer than five customers per day. Congress did not approve the move and in fact regularly included in spending measures language requiring USPS to keep these rural locations open. In February 2013, Postmaster General Patrick Donahoe suggested that ending Saturday delivery would save $2 billion annually. Congress blocked the move by including in spending legislation a provision that would require mail to continue being delivered six days per week. In September 2013, the postal service resorted to increasing some mail prices, including that of first-class stamps.

In July 2013, the House Oversight and Government Reform Committee considered a measure that would make a number of changes to postal service operations to shore up its budget. The bill would have allowed USPS to cut service back to five days per week for first-class mail but prohibited two consecutive days without mail delivery and still required that packages be delivered six days per week. The bill would also phase out doorstep delivery, eliminate the prohibition on closing post offices based on revenue, and restructure payments to the retiree health fund. The Senate introduced a similar measure in 2013 (although markup did not take place until 2014) that would also change the retiree health care formula to require the postal service to only prefund 80 percent of its projected liability. The 2013 House version, and a revival of the bill in 2015, never saw floor action, nor did the Senate's legislation.

Chronology of Action
on General Government Issues

2013–2014

Federal Workforce Training Bill

Despite efforts in both chambers in 2013 to pass an overhaul to the 1998 Workforce Investment Act (WIA) that expired in fiscal 2003, the House and Senate failed to reach a compromise. Democrats considered the House version too partisan and believed that it would reduce workforce training opportunities for vulnerable populations, especially veterans and the homeless, while instilling too much power in businesses to determine how best to structure and fund local training programs. The Senate bill was less contentious, written following months of behind-the-scenes negotiations, but it never came to a floor vote. No further action was taken in 2013 to amend federal workforce programs. The House and Senate would eventually pass a WIA replacement in June 2014, known as the Workforce Innovation and Opportunity Act (WIOA), which was largely based on the House-passed measure. It became law on July 22, 2014 (PL 113-128).

BACKGROUND

There have long been competing opinions at the federal level about the best way to build an American workforce that not only meets the needs of domestic employers but also allows those companies to compete in the global marketplace. There are two primary schools of thought: one based on skills building and the other on work-first training. The former focuses on providing Americans the training they need based on the assumption that building their skills and knowledge provides a long-term benefit economically to the individual as well as to the employer, who can engage a more productive workforce. The latter is focused on the idea that it is economically beneficial to get Americans to work as quickly as possible.

Congress first passed the Workforce Investment Act (WIA) in 1998 with the intent of creating a national program that would prepare Americans to enter the workforce, help them advance their careers, and meet the needs of the nation's employers. The WIA sought to consolidate existing training and vocational rehabilitation programs by creating one-stop shop centers for employment-related training. The WIA was written with a work-first approach during a time of economic expansion when studies were suggesting that it was more cost effective for the employee, employer, and federal government to focus on the job itself above skills and training. The original law was structured to first help an individual find a job, and, if that proved unsuccessful, then provide training and skill building. Subsequent regulations added to the WIA removed the tiered structure and allowed job seekers to access services in the way that best fit their needs.

In 2003, the year WIA authorization expired, and again in 2011, the Government Accountability Office authored reports outlining the duplication in forty-four of the forty-seven different federal employment and training programs. The 2011 report stated that "little is known about the effectiveness of most programs" despite the federal government spending approximately $18 billion in fiscal year 2009 to facilitate these programs. That report admits that combining the overlapping programs to eliminate duplication is not necessarily a simple prospect. Due to the location of services, client base served, and the specific services required by individuals, simply consolidating services into fewer locations may be unfeasible. Republicans, however, seized on the reports as an example of government waste. But their efforts to root out the duplication and cut spending were, until 2013, largely unsuccessful.

House Action

In February 2013 in the Postsecondary Education and Workforce Training Subcommittee, Rep. Virginia Foxx, R-N.C., introduced the Supporting Knowledge and Investing in Lifelong Skills (SKILLS) Act (HR 803), a bill that would reauthorize federal workforce-development programs first authorized under WIA and overhaul their structure. The measure was similar to what the House Higher Education and Workforce Committee had passed a year before. The 2013 bill consolidated thirty-five federal employment and training programs into one state block grant, known as the Workforce Investment Fund, and gave state governors the authority to consolidate similar state-level training programs for additional efficiency. To enhance accountability, the SKILLS Act required that a consistent set of performance measures be utilized to evaluate program effectiveness. The bill also called for two-thirds of the local workforce boards responsible for running job training programs and allocating federal funds to represent the interests of employers. This, Republicans argued, was vital to ensure that the training programs being offered meet the needs of local companies. Democrats disagreed, noting that involving more business representatives pushes out unions and community colleges.

Democrats strongly opposed the bill based on their belief that it failed to protect vulnerable populations and their group-specific training needs. Republicans, however, felt that the bill aligned with President Obama's desire to streamline training by simplifying the myriad existing training programs and make them more accessible to a wider range of Americans. The old way of doing business, Republicans said, had resulted in unnecessarily high costs and few successes. A heated exchange took place in the subcommittee, with Democrats accusing Republicans of trying to push through a measure that had not been properly vetted and for which they were unwilling to seek compromise.

When the bill reached the Higher Education and Workforce Committee for markup, Democrats read a statement objecting to the way the bill had been handled and then walked out. "We viewed boycotting this proceeding as our only alternative after many months of repeatedly requesting bipartisan negotiations and being rebuffed by committee Republicans. . . . Democrats can only come to the conclusion that this bill is being advanced for political reasons, not to make the workforce investment system work better," the March 6, 2013, statement read. Democrats went on to state that every effort to date to provide workforce training and development has been bipartisan, while this effort was not. Republicans proceeded with the markup, passing an amendment to require the Office of Management and Budget (OMB) to report on the number of federal employees impacted by the programs that would be consolidated and then unanimously approved the measure for floor consideration.

HR 803 passed the full House on March 15, 2013, by a vote of 215–202, with 14 Republicans joining Democrats in opposition and 2 Democrats voting in favor. The bill included two amendments, one that would add training in advanced manufacturing for veterans and another that would guarantee that 1 percent of authorized spending be set aside for American Indian, Alaska Native, and Native Hawaiian employment and training grants. One amendment, rejected along party lines, would have reauthorized existing job-training programs and allowed local governments to partner with community colleges to train workers in high-demand skills.

Upon passage, Rep. Foxx said the bill creates a more efficient and accountable workforce development system that closely reflects the needs of American workplaces. She added that the legislation removes unnecessary bureaucracy and meets the president's goal of streamlining the nation's exiting programs.

According to the Congressional Budget Office, the final bill would cost an estimated $26 billion to implement from fiscal 2014 through fiscal 2018. The White House issued a Statement of Administration Policy on March 13, 2013, expressing its opposition to the bill, noting that it "would eliminate, or allow the consolidation of, many targeted programs, without providing the critical assistance needed by vulnerable populations such as veterans, low-income adults, youth, adults with literacy and English language needs, people with disabilities, ex-offenders, and others with significant barriers to employment."

Senate Action

The Senate Health, Education, Labor, and Pensions (HELP) Committee passed its own version of WIA replacement legislation (S 1356), although it maintained most of the structure of the existing program but increased assessment requirements to ensure success of the programs being funded. The Senate committee bill required that each state submit a single plan detailing its workforce and development training efforts and rely on a single set of performance metrics to evaluate success. The committee did include a provision that a majority of local board members should represent business interests but stopped short of asking for two-thirds as the House had done. The HELP committee approved the bill 18–3 on July 31, with three Republicans voting against the measure and one abstaining. The committee did not report the measure to the floor until November, and although a motion to proceed was made on the floor, the full Senate never voted on the legislation in 2013.

United States Postal Service Financial Crisis

Congress revived its consideration of reforms to the United States Postal Service (USPS) in 2013 amid the agency's ongoing financial struggles. USPS had lost more than $40 billion since 2007 and defaulted on three consecutive payments owed to its retiree health benefits fund in 2012 and 2013. The agency was also projecting a net loss of $5 billion for fiscal year 2013. Lawmakers have generally agreed that drastic changes are needed to keep the postal service financially solvent, but disagreement over what those changes should be prevented Congress from passing legislation addressing the crisis in 2011 and 2012.

BACKGROUND

USPS was once a federal government agency, the Post Office Department, but became a private, self-supporting enterprise with an independent board of governors, budget authority, and a non–civil service workforce in 1971.

However, USPS continues to operate under a congressional charter, which constrains the postal service in ways a truly private company would not be (e.g., the law limits the closure of post offices and other USPS facilities). To some degree, these constraints have exacerbated, if not directly contributed to, the postal service's financial troubles.

A central issue in the debate surrounding postal service reform is the requirement Congress approved in 2006 that USPS prefund future health care expenses for retirees. Federal law divides responsibility for postal retirees' premium payments among USPS, the federal government, and retirees. USPS used to make its required payments through a pay-as-you-go system, in which payments are made as health costs are incurred. However, since passage of the Postal Accountability and Enhancement Act (PL 109–435), the postal service has been obligated to make fixed, annual payments ranging from $5.4 billion to $5.8 billion into the Postal Service Retiree Health Benefits Fund, housed within the U.S. Treasury Department, from fiscal year 2007 to fiscal year 2016. Any estimated health benefit liability that remained unfunded once those payments were complete was to be paid over a forty-year period starting in 2017. The Office of Personnel Management was set to begin drawing from the fund in fiscal year 2017 to cover USPS's share of premiums for future retiree health benefits. This system was designed to help reduce the risk to taxpayers of USPS not being able to afford the benefits it promised to employees.

Initially, USPS was able to make payments to the new benefits fund without issue but began to struggle following the 2008 recession. Congress deferred $4 billion of the $5.4 billion USPS owed to the fund in 2009 but declined to make a similar deferral in 2010. In December 2011, Congress agreed to postpone that year's $5.5 billion payment to the retirement fund until August 2012. However, the postal service defaulted on that payment, as well as payments due in September 2012 and September 2013. By the end of fiscal year 2012, the USPS retiree health fund held $46 billion—roughly half of its total estimated liability of $94 billion.

USPS officials and postal unions argue that the prefund obligation is a major reason for the postal service's financial struggles. According to the USPS Office of the Inspector General, the $15 billion in debt held by the postal service was caused by the requirement that it prefund its retiree health program. Doing so, the Inspector General's office said, prevents the postal service from investing in new research and projects.

Others have claimed that the 2006 law requires USPS to prefund retirement benefits for potential future employees. House Oversight and Government Reform Committee Chair Darrell Issa, R-Calif., refuted these claims, explaining that the intent of the law is to ensure retiree health care for existing employees is covered, because these are the benefits USPS employees negotiated for and were promised. The Oversight Committee further noted that if USPS stopped making prefund payments, it would have an unfunded health care liability of nearly $100 billion by 2017. According

to the committee, this would be a burden USPS could not afford, one that might require a taxpayer-funded bailout.

Some efforts by the postal service to reduce its costs have been blocked by Congress. In 2012, for example, USPS sought to close 3,600 post offices that were among the lowest-revenue-generating locations and served fewer than five customers per day, but Congress did not provide the required approval for the closures to take place. Lawmakers have also routinely included measures in spending bills that require USPS to continue delivering mail six days per week and keep small, rural post offices open.

However, it has been widely noted that the postal service would be facing financial challenges with or without congressional action. Advances in technology have led Americans to send emails and text messages or communicate via social networks or other online platforms rather than mailing cards or letters. They also increasingly pay bills and conduct other transactions online instead of by mail, and businesses are responding to this demand by invoicing electronically and enabling automatic bill pay. According to USPS data, the volume of first-class mail dropped 30 percent from 2007 to 2013.

House Action

On July 19, Issa introduced the Postal Reform Act of 2013 (HR 2748). The bill would have allowed USPS to cut back to five days of delivery per week for letters, though there could not be more than two consecutive days without mail delivery in a week, and six-day-per-week delivery of packages was still required. The bill would also have phased out doorstep delivery by September 2022, with USPS instead delivering to cluster and curbside mailboxes. Customers would have received the option to pay a fee to continue doorstep delivery, and waivers would be granted for those with physical hardships.

Another measure would have eliminated the prohibition on closing post offices based solely on revenue, although it did require USPS to ensure customers in affected areas would still have access to postal services. Additionally, the bill would have eliminated USPS's fiscal year 2013 and fiscal year 2014 payments to the retiree health fund, allowed the postal service to skip its past-due payments, and enabled it to make remaining payments to the fund over a forty-year period. A new oversight body, the Financial Responsibility and Management Assistance Authority, would have been created to take over USPS management from its board of governors until the postal service was able to meet its financial targets.

Issa included several provisions from separate bills in his proposed legislation. From HR 2690, sponsored by Rep. Elijah Cummings, D-Md., Issa incorporated measures allowing USPS to use more specific demographic assumptions to calculate its payments to federal retirement systems, creating a new chief innovation officer charged with identifying opportunities to generate revenue, and raising price caps on experimental products. From HR 2615, proposed by Rep. Adrian Smith, R-Neb., Issa included a provision requiring USPS to consider available cell phone service, penetration of broadband access, and the distance to the nearest postal facility before closing rural post offices.

Markup took place on July 24, and several amendments were considered. The committee approved by voice vote an amendment from Rep. Patrick Meehan, R-Penn., requiring USPS to consider input from property owners and local and state governments before making any changes to a community's delivery method. It rejected amendments from Cummings and Rep. Stephen Lynch, D-Mass., by votes of 17 to 22. Cummings sought to remove the five-day delivery provision while adding a measure that would have allowed USPS to deliver alcoholic beverages as another source of revenue. Lynch wanted to strike the proposed transition from doorstep delivery, arguing that in some urban areas, there was not sufficient room to build cluster mailboxes.

The amended bill was approved by the committee in a party-line vote of 22 to 17 on July 24, 2013. No further action was taken by the full House before the end of the year. The bill was later revived in 2015; however, it did not see floor action.

Senate Action

Senators Tom Carper, D-Del., and Tom Coburn, R-Wy., introduced the Senate's reform bill (S 1486) on August 1, 2013. The bill was referred to the Senate Homeland Security and Governmental Affairs Committee, which held two related hearings in September. However, bill markup did not occur until the end of January and early February 2014.

The draft bill would have allowed the USPS to shift to five-day delivery, as did the House bill, but prevented the postal service from making this change before October 2017. It also called for a transition to more centralized delivery points but required USPS to obtain a customer's permission before switching from doorstep delivery to curbside delivery. The bill would have altered the formula for calculating USPS's obligations to the retiree health care fund to use demographic data and revised economic assumptions of wage and salary growth. Additionally, the bill would have reduced the prefunding requirement for retiree health benefits to 80 percent of the postal service's projected liability rather than the existing 100 percent requirement. Other measures would have imposed a two-year moratorium on processing center closures, required USPS to consider alternative options before closing post office locations (e.g., reducing hours of operation), authorized it to deliver alcoholic beverages, allowed the postal service to negotiate new retirement benefits for newly hired workers, and created a chief information officer position.

The committee approved the bill by a vote of 9 to 1 on February 6, 2014. However, it never saw floor action.

Postal Service Action

USPS leadership attempted to take action on their own ahead of congressional deliberations. In February 2013, Postmaster General Patrick Donahoe announced an end to Saturday delivery, projecting it would save USPS $2 billion

annually. He asserted this change was allowed because the continuing resolution keeping the government open at that point did not specifically mandate Saturday delivery for first-class mail. This plan was withdrawn in March, however, after the Government Accountability Office stated that USPS had incorrectly interpreted the legislation to mean that the statute mandating Saturday delivery had expired. Later that month, Congress passed a spending bill that explicitly restated USPS's obligation to maintain six-day delivery.

In September 2013, USPS increased the price of several mail categories, including a 3-cent increase that brought the cost of first-class mail stamps to 49 cents. The increases took effect on January 1, 2014, and were expected to generate an additional $2 billion in annual revenue. Postal Service Board of Governors Chairman Mickey Barnett said in a letter to customers dated September 25, 2013, that the primary reasons for the price increases were the "precarious financial condition" of the service and the "uncertain path toward enactment of postal reform legislation."

Financial Services and General Government Appropriations for 2014

The fiscal 2014 Financial Services and General Government Appropriation bill was a lightning rod for House and Senate Republicans, who attempted to utilize the bill to punish the Internal Revenue Service (IRS) for allegedly targeting conservative-leaning organizations applying for tax-exempt status and to strip the body of its ability to implement the taxation portions of the 2010 Patient Protection and Affordable Care Act (ACA). Although appropriators in both the House and Senate created Financial Services and General Government appropriations measures that were approved in committee, they were not brought to the floor. After a protracted negotiation that lasted into the new fiscal year and resulted in a sixteen-day government shutdown, the bill was one of twelve regular appropriations measures that was wrapped into an omnibus spending package (HR 3547—PL 113–76). The omnibus was signed by President Obama on January 17, 2014, three months after the start of the federal fiscal year. *(See discussion of fiscal year 2014 omnibus in Chapter 2.)*

House Action

The House Appropriations Committee was the first to pass a fiscal 2014 stand-alone Financial Services and General Government Appropriations Act (HR 2786). Their $17 billion measure represented funding to the Treasury Department, Executive Office of the President, Judiciary, District of Columbia, Small Business Administration, Securities and Exchange Commission, General Services Administration, and several other independent agencies at a level $4.3 billion below the fiscal 2013 enacted level. The House Appropriations Committee bill would have increased the allocation to the Securities and Exchange

Commission (SEC) to $1.4 billion, $50 million more than the enacted fiscal 2013 budget but less than President Obama's request. An amendment by Democrats in the committee to increase SEC funding to the president's requested level was rejected along party lines. The bill also included a ban on the SEC spending any money from its reserve fund, which the committee described as a slush fund for SEC programs that Congress had not approved. According to the committee, the budget increase would offset reserve fund spending.

The House committee version also took aim at the Consumer Financial Protection Bureau (CFPB), an independent bureau within the Federal Reserve that was created under the 2010 Dodd-Frank Wall Street Reform and Consumer Protection Act. Republicans have been highly critical of the law since its passage and have sought to gut what they saw as a massive government overreach that lacked adequate oversight. In the fiscal 2014 appropriation process, Republicans added to the bill a measure that would require CFPB to become subject to the regular appropriation process beginning in fiscal 2015 rather than having their budget controlled by the Federal Reserve. The Federal Reserve does not receive Congressional appropriations because it is primarily funded through earned interest, therefore making it difficult for Congress to control CFPB activity.

Perhaps the biggest point of contention in House negotiations was the IRS. The House committee version of the bill would have reduced the allocation to the Department of the Treasury, of which the IRS is the largest bureau, by 26 percent. In doing so, Republicans were seeking to address two of their top concerns. First, the bill would have withheld 10 percent of IRS enforcement spending and 25 percent of its salary budget for top officials until it implemented strategies to ensure groups seeking tax-exempt status would not be targeted based on their ideological leanings. This followed a May 2013 report by the Treasury Inspector General that found the IRS was slowing the process for conservative groups applying for tax-exempt status by making their review more rigorous. Second, Republicans on the committee wanted to hamper the ability of the IRS to collect penalties enforced on individuals and businesses as a result of the ACA. Under the health care law, the IRS is responsible for collecting annual fees from individuals who do not have health insurance coverage as well as from large employers that fail to offer health insurance to their employees. Republicans argued that the decision to seek or offer health insurance coverage was an individual liberty that should not be subject to enforcement by the federal government. The House appropriations bill, which was reported out of committee on July 23, 2013, barred the IRS from spending any of its funds on implementation of its portions of the ACA. *(See discussion of ACA in Chapter 9, pp. 290–291.)*

The financial services bill was not considered by the full House.

Senate Action

The Senate Appropriations Committee cleared its own Financial Services and General Government Appropriations Act (S 1371) on July 25, 2103, by a party-line vote of 16–14. No Republican supported the bill, arguing that it differed too much from the House version, which would make it difficult to seek compromise on a final piece of legislation that could clear both houses of Congress. The Democratic-controlled committee provided $23 billion in discretionary appropriations for the agencies covered under the bill, up $1.6 billion from the enacted fiscal 2013 budget. Unlike the House, the Senate increased spending for the IRS to $12.1 billion, $253 million over fiscal 2013, and included a rider dictating that the IRS could not use federal funds against Americans exercising their First Amendment rights. The Senate rejected a Republican amendment that would have withheld enforcement funds from the IRS until it implemented policies that would prevent targeting of political groups seeking tax-exempt status, with Sen. Richard Durbin, D-Ill., admitting that the IRS had acted inappropriately but that the committee should not stop the body from doing its other essential work. The committee also rejected two Republican amendments that would have stopped the IRS from enforcing the individual mandate and employer ACA tax penalties.

The full Senate did not take up the committee's financial services appropriation measure.

Final Omnibus

Funding for the federal government ran out on October 1, 2013, forcing a sixteen-day government shutdown before a continuing resolution was passed to keep the government funded through the end of the year and allow budget negotiations to continue. It was not until January 15 when the House passed an omnibus spending package that included nearly $21.9 billion in discretionary funding for the Treasury, IRS, Executive Office of the President, federal judiciary, various regulatory agencies, Office of Personnel Management, and the federal contribution to the District of Columbia. The Senate passed the bill one day later, and the president signed the omnibus measure into law on January 17, 2014. The negotiations resulted in a bipartisan agreement to reduce the automatic cuts to federal spending imposed by the 2011 debt limit law while also raising discretionary spending caps.

Of the $21.9 billion for financial services, the omnibus measure allocated $11.3 billion for the IRS, $526 million less than the previous fiscal year and less than what the Senate and White House had requested but $2.3 billion above what the House proposed. No additional money was included in the allocation for the implementation of the ACA, but the IRS was also not barred from collecting penalties. The IRS was, however, banned from using the funds to target groups or individuals based on their beliefs, and it required that all employees receive training on taxpayer rights. The omnibus also took aim at spending on employee bonuses and training videos after it was discovered that the IRS had used federal funds to create parody videos for its conferences. The IRS was asked to submit a number of new reports to Congress, including one on employee bonuses; one on training; and another on the organization, its missions and functions, and activities to the House and Senate appropriations committees within forty-five days of the end of each calendar quarter.

Other funding for agencies covered by the Financial Services and General Government appropriations included in the omnibus were

- $1.35 billion for the SEC, an increase from the fiscal 2013 budget, and in line with the House committee-passed measure
- $339.8 million for the Federal Communications Commission (FCC); the omnibus also included a provision directing the FCC to consult with the Federal Bureau of Investigation (FBI), as well as the Secretaries of Transportation and Homeland Security,

before issuing a rule on whether airline passengers would be allowed to use their mobile devices in flight and asked that the FCC report to the appropriations committees any developments on this topic

- $673 million for the District of Columbia, lower than fiscal 2013; the package included a prohibition on the use of these federal funds for abortions, except in instances of rape, incest, or when a mother's life is endangered if the fetus is carried to term, and also banned D.C. from using the federal appropriation toward legalization of marijuana or a reduction of penalties associated with marijuana possession, use, or distribution

In addition to the funds provided to the agencies covered under the financial services appropriation, the omnibus froze the salaries of the vice president and senior political appointees at 2013 levels through 2014 and also kept intact a freeze on Congressional salaries. However, the freeze on federal civilian employee pay was allowed to

---

ATTEMPTS TO REPEAL OR CHANGE THE AFFORDABLE CARE ACT

The debate over the Patient Protection and Affordable Care Act (ACA), a law that would mark the first major overhaul of the nation's health care system in a century, consumed a majority of President Obama's first year in office. Republicans strongly opposed the bill as it made its way through committee and onto the floor, arguing that it would devastate the American health care system and drive up costs for individuals seeking care. Charged rhetoric in Congress spilled over into chaotic townhall meetings at which Republicans and Democrats squared off with sometimes hostile constituents. No Republican in the House voted to support the final measure that the president signed into law in March 2010 (the Senate vote was slightly less partisan at 60–39), but Obama said the bill was "not a victory for any one party—it's a victory for them, it's a victory for the American people. And it's a victory for common sense."

Congressional efforts to dismantle the landmark health care law began in earnest in January 2011, on the heels of a Republican takeover of the House during the 2010 midterm election. By the bill's fourth anniversary in March 2014, the House had voted fifty-four times to either repeal or make changes to the law. Democratic control of the Senate through 2014 made it unlikely that any Republican attempt to repeal the law would pass; however, the two parties did reach consensus on making minor adjustments to the legislation. The White House also codified changes in the law that delayed implementation of some provisions and altered how the law works in practice due to technical difficulties with the HealthCare.

gov federal health insurance marketplace and industry complaints. *(See discussion of ACA in Chapter 9, pp. 290–291.)*

At the start of the 113th Congress in January 2013, Rep. Michele Bachmann, R-Minn., introduced HR 45, an ACA repeal bill. Republicans seized on the scandal plaguing the IRS—a Treasury Inspector General report finding that the IRS had improperly targeted conservative groups applying for tax-exempt status for additional regulatory scrutiny—to call for passage of the bill. The IRS is responsible for enacting a number of the bill's provisions, including the controversial individual mandate that requires all Americans to have health insurance or pay a penalty. Bachmann's bill passed the House on May 16, 2013, by a party-line vote of 229–195, but was never considered by the Democratic-controlled Senate. The House Appropriations Committee also included in its Financial Services and General Government appropriations bill a provision banning the IRS from spending the appropriated funds on implementing the ACA. That measure did not make it to the final omnibus spending package.

In July 2013, the White House announced that it was delaying for one year the requirement that businesses with more than fifty employees provide affordable health insurance to their staff. Democrats argued that the change indicated that the White House was listening to concerns from Republicans and the American public, while Republicans said the delay was indicative of a law that still had serious problems. By October, Republicans in the House refused to pass a funding measure to keep the federal government open if it did not include a

(Continued)

ATTEMPTS TO REPEAL OR CHANGE THE AFFORDABLE CARE ACT (Continued)

---

repeal of the ACA. Democrats in the Senate, however, said they would only pass a clean funding bill, and the impasse led to a sixteen-day government shutdown. The bill that reopened the government did not include any stipulations preventing the ACA from taking effect. Republicans would try again during budget negotiations in 2014 to stop the implementation of the ACA, but those efforts proved unsuccessful.

In February 2015, the House voted again to repeal the ACA. This marked their sixty-seventh attempt to defund, repeal, or change the law. The president promised to veto the legislation if it made it to his desk, but it never did. The Republican-controlled Senate failed to pass an ACA repeal effort in July, 49–43. In October, the House passed the Restoring Americans' Healthcare Freedom Reconciliation Act of 2015 (HR 3762). The bill would not repeal the ACA but would make a number of significant changes to the law including the elimination of the individual and employer mandates, a phaseout of subsidies that help lower-income Americans afford care, a phaseout of the Medicaid expansion, and a ban on the federal government operating a health care exchange. The Senate made some changes to the bill to avoid a filibuster, and the House passed the revised measure on January 6, 2016. The president vetoed it two days later, and the House failed to garner enough votes to override the veto.

While HR 3762 was making its way through the House and Senate, Republicans and the White House did find compromise on the medical device tax provision of the ACA that requires a 2.3 percent sales tax on certain medical devices. Republicans, some Democrats, and those in the medical community argued that the tax impeded technological innovation. Republicans had long sought a repeal of the tax and

viewed it as an easy way to chip away at the ACA because of Democratic support; however, Republicans faced opposition in their own party from those who refused to back any ACA bill that did not fully repeal the law. Included in the Consolidated Appropriations Act of 2016 (HR 2029) was a two-year delay on the implementation of the tax. Without further legislation, the medical device tax would go into effect on January 1, 2018.

Notably, the ACA did not face attacks solely in Congress. There were several court filings against provisions of the law, including two cases that made it to the Supreme Court. In *National Federation of Independent Businesses v. Sebelius*, twenty-six states sued the federal government, arguing that portions of the law, specifically the individual mandate and the expansion of the Medicaid program, were unconstitutional. The court upheld the law 5–4 on June 28, 2012. In March 2015, the Supreme Court heard oral arguments in *King v. Burwell*, a case challenging the Treasury's ability to provide tax subsidies to those who cannot afford health insurance. On June 25, 2015, the court ruled 6–3 that if a state did not establish its own health care exchange through which to offer insurance and subsidies, the federal government could step in to distribute subsidies through the federal exchange.

The election of Donald Trump as president in November 2016, paired with a Republican House and Senate, virtually guaranteed that the ACA would face additional challenges. In an interview on November 20, 2016, Vice President–elect Mike Pence told Fox News that Trump "wants to focus out of the gate on repealing Obamacare and beginning the process of replacing Obamacare with the kind of free-market solutions that he campaigned on."

---

expire at the end of 2013, and President Obama used that as an opportunity to issue an executive order raising civilian and military pay by 1 percent effective January 1, 2014.

Federal Worker Pay Increase and Pension Cut (2013)

A three-year-long pay freeze for federal civilian workers came to an end in December 2013, when Congress declined to reauthorize it in its final action of the year. The freeze was popular among many Republicans, who saw it as a means to cut back federal spending, especially in light of the 2011 debt limit bill and its automatic spending cuts, while Democrats argued that it hampered the government's ability to attract and retain the best workers for federal jobs. The end of the pay freeze opened the door for President Obama to issue an executive order on December 23, 2013, to provide a 1 percent pay raise to all federal civilian and military employees beginning January 1, 2014. Typically,

Congress would have the opportunity to block the president's measure, as it did with a similar executive order in 2012. However, having already passed its final piece of legislation on December 18—a budget deal to avoid a federal government shutdown—Congress took no further action for the year, and the president's pay increase took effect by default. Sen. Barbara Mikulski, D-Md., who represents tens of thousands of federal workers, called the increase a step toward recognizing the value of federal workers. Democrats were less pleased with a December 2013 decision to increase the amount new federal workers are asked to contribute to their retirement plans, but the move garnered tempered support from the White House due to the tradeoff for higher discretionary spending caps.

BACKGROUND

Regular increases in federal employee pay have traditionally been supported by members of both parties. In 1990, President George H.W. Bush supported passage of the

Federal Employees Pay Comparability Act (FEPCA). The Act would, over a number of years, provide annual pay increases for federal employees to bring them in line with comparable positions in the private sector based on locality. At the time, federal employees were paid around 20 percent less than those outside of government. Bush's successor, President Bill Clinton, felt that FEPCA provided raises that were overly generous and requested a review of total federal civilian employee compensation packages against private-sector wages, arguing that health care and retirement benefits are traditionally more lucrative in the public sector. President Clinton further proposed a 0 percent wage increase in the first year of his presidency, but congressional Democrats, especially those representing tens of thousands of federal workers in Maryland and Virginia, pushed back and passed a pay increase. That instance set off a cycle of the president proposing below-FEPCA pay raises, while Congress would ultimately provide something more substantial.

This began to change in the fiscal 2011 budget, when President Obama requested a 1.4 percent raise for federal civilian employees. Congress took no action on his request, so to protect federal workers from the larger cuts suggested by Republicans, the president instead sought to freeze their pay. The president said the decision was necessary to bring the budget deficit under control, which required broad sacrifices that must be shared by federal workers. Congress agreed to the freeze, which would extend from January 1, 2011, through December 31, 2012, in its December 2010 omnibus spending measure. Due to ongoing budgetary concerns, the pay freeze was extended through December 31, 2013. Over the course of the three-year freeze, federal spending on employee pay fell by an estimated $99 billion. Federal civilian employees were still eligible for performance-based financial awards and salary increases gained through promotion during the pay freeze, and because of this, according to the Office of Personnel Management (OPM), federal civilian worker pay actually increased an average of 1.4 percent in 2012.

Notably, military pay is handled somewhat differently, and members of the military have often received pay increases larger than those of their civilian counterparts. Indeed, while civilian employees had their pay frozen from 2010 through 2013, members of the military received an increase each year.

Civilian Worker Pay Freeze

On January 1, 2013, the last day of session for the outgoing 112th Congress, the House passed the Congressional Pay Freeze and Fiscal Responsibility Act (HR 6726) by a vote of 287–129 to extend the federal civilian worker pay freeze through 2013. Although that vote was primarily symbolic because a new Congress was about to take office, the 113th Congress quickly voted on February 15 to pass HR 273, a pay freeze bill, 261–154. Republicans defended the freeze, pointing to a 2012 report by the Congressional Budget Office (CBO) indicating that federal workers make, on average,

16 percent more than those in equivalent private-sector positions in total compensation (pay plus benefits). House Oversight and Government Reform Chair Darrell Issa, R-Calif., called the ongoing freeze necessary, arguing that pay increases only waste taxpayer money. He added that federal employees had already been receiving pay increases within their pay grades and that the number of workers leaving the federal government voluntarily was nearing an all-time low. Although the president, along with Congressional Democrats, opposed the bill, he did not threaten to veto it.

The Senate never considered the House-passed measure because it was focused on passing a spending bill to avoid a government shutdown. At the time, the government had been operating under a continuing resolution passed on October 1, 2012. Shortly before the continuing resolution expired, both houses passed a full-year spending measure (HR 933—PL 113–6) that preserved the pay freeze for federal civilian employees through the end of 2013. When budget negotiations began anew for fiscal 2014, Congress considered but did not include in the final budget agreement (H J Res 59—PL 113–67) an extension of the pay freeze.

Civilian Worker Pensions

Federal civilian workers faced other cuts throughout 2013 with the implementation of furloughs and hiring freezes, both of which were forced by the 2011 debt limit law that instituted sequestration. Congress also took action in 2013 to decrease the government's contribution to federal retiree pensions. Their action arose during year-end budget talks, with the idea that by reducing the contribution the government makes to the pensions for new hires, it could use that savings against the spending limits set by the sequester to allow for increased budgets in other areas. Compared to the private sector, where only a minority even receive a pension, federal workers enjoy generous contributions toward their retirement plans. A majority of workers hired before 1984 are covered by the Civil Service Retirement System (CSRS). These workers contribute 7 percent of their pay toward their own pension in return for a 19 percent contribution from the federal government. These workers are not covered by Social Security and therefore do not pay Social Security taxes. Those workers hired in 1984 and later fall into the Federal Employees' Retirement System. These workers contribute 0.8 percent of their pay in return for an 11.9 percent contribution from the federal government, but unlike workers in CSRS, they are subject to Social Security payroll taxes. Starting in 2012, new workers were asked to contribute 3.1 percent of their pay.

The proposal to ask federal workers to contribute more to their pension plans was backed by both House Republicans and the president, but they differed in their suggested decreases. Republicans called for new federal employees to increase their pension contributions by 5.5 percentage points, for a savings of $132 billion over the next decade. The president called for a far more modest increase of 1.2 percentage points, equating to a savings of $20 billion during the next decade. Congressional Democrats did not throw their support behind either proposal, and the Senate's fiscal 2014 budget resolution (S Con Res 8) did not call for any change in new-hire pensions. Unions representing federal employees strongly opposed the measure, arguing that civilian employees had already been hit by the pay freeze and furloughs and that imposing a larger pension contribution from employees was essentially a further pay cut.

In the end, the House and Senate struck a deal with the White House to decrease federal contributions to pension plans, asking any federal worker hired after January 1, 2014, to contribute 4.4 percent of their pay to the pension fund. This was coupled with a 1 percent reduction in the cost-of-living adjustment provided to military retirees under age sixty-two. Together, these were expected to save the federal government $12 billion during the next ten years. In return, the president received his desired increase in discretionary spending measures.

Financial Services and General Government Appropriations for 2015

The IRS was again the target of funding cuts in the fiscal 2015 Financial Services and General Government appropriations process. As it had done when negotiating the fiscal 2014 appropriation, ultimately passed in an omnibus package in January 2014, House Republicans pushed for cuts to the agency's budget because the IRS had targeted conservative political groups seeking tax-exempt status for additional regulatory scrutiny. Republicans were also seeking to further impede the implementation of the 2010 Patient Protection and Affordable Care Act (ACA) by removing the ability of the IRS to collect penalties assessed on individuals and businesses that failed to comply with the law's requirements. For the first time since 2009, the full House passed a stand-alone Financial Services and General Government Appropriations Act (HR 5016); however, the Senate version was never reported out of committee, and funding for the covered agencies was ultimately rolled into an omnibus spending package (HR 83—PL 113–235) passed in December 2014, just hours before the deadline to avoid a government shutdown.

Legislative Action

As they had in fiscal 2014 budget negotiations, House Republicans continued to target the IRS for cuts over both the ACA and its handling of tax-exempt status applications from conservative groups. In the $21.3 billion financial services bill passed by the House Appropriations Financial Services Subcommittee and reported out to the House Appropriations Committee on June 18, the IRS was allocated $10.95 billion, or $341 million less than fiscal 2014 and 12 percent below the president's request. The committee's

ranking member, Rep. Nita M. Lowey, D-N.Y., said the cuts would decrease services to citizens while making it easier for those skirting tax law to go undetected.

Democrats were also unhappy with a policy rider included in the bill that would prohibit the IRS from implementing its portions of the ACA, specifically, the tax penalties assessed on individuals who chose to go without health insurance coverage and large businesses that do not offer insurance. Other IRS provisions included in the bill were

- a prohibition on funds for IRS employee bonuses and awards that do not consider the conduct and tax compliance of the employee
- a prohibition on funds for targeting groups for regulatory scrutiny based on their ideological beliefs or citizens exercising their First Amendment rights
- a prohibition on using funds for the creation of videos that have not been reviewed and certified as appropriate
- a requirement that the IRS submit a report on the amount of official time used by IRS employees
- a prohibition on the White House ordering the IRS to determine the tax-exempt status of an organization
- additional extensive reporting on IRS spending

The House Appropriations Committee also took aim at funding for the District of Columbia. Republicans and Democrats argued at length about subjecting the District's funds to federally dictated policies regarding abortion and marijuana. Along party lines, the committee adopted an amendment that would prohibit federal and local funds in Washington, D.C., from being used toward legalization or decriminalization of marijuana. And, despite strong Democratic opposition, Republicans added to the appropriation a ban on the District utilizing federal funds to cover abortion services. A separate amendment also prohibited the District from using funds in the bill to cover abortion services under the multistate federal health care exchange established under the ACA, except in the case of rape, incest, or if the mother's life is in danger.

The full House took up the spending bill in July and further cut the IRS enforcement budget by nearly 25 percent and the total IRS budget by 13 percent to $9.8 billion. The White House issued a statement on July 14, 2014, strongly opposing HR 5016, saying that "The bill impedes implementation of the Affordable Care Act, undermines critical components of Wall Street reform, and fails to provide the resources necessary to provide robust taxpayer services and improve tax enforcement. Further, the legislation includes ideological and political provisions that are beyond the scope of funding legislation." Republicans ignored the president's request for additional funding in the bill, and the $20.2 billion measure passed 228–195 on a party-line vote on July 16, 2014. The White House threatened a veto if the bill made it to the president's desk.

The Senate Financial Services Subcommittee passed a $22.7 billion financial services appropriation bill in June, but it never received full committee markup or floor consideration. Unlike the House version, the Senate subcommittee included budget increases for both the IRS and the Securities and Exchange Commission (SEC), the latter of which was given 26 percent more than the enacted fiscal 2014 budget. The Senate subcommittee version avoided many of the controversial policy riders that had forced a White House veto threat and instead recommended that the IRS establish and maintain effective internal controls and strong management oversight to ensure that applications for tax-exempt status are approved or denied quickly using objective criteria. Reflecting the president's priorities, the Senate subcommittee included an increase in funding for the Commodity Futures Trading Commission (CFTC) to $280 million. The CFTC was essential to enforcement of Dodd-Frank provisions.

Final Omnibus

House and Senate negotiators came to an agreement in mid-December 2014 on a $1 trillion omnibus spending package (PL 113–235) that included funding for the agencies covered under the Financial Services and General Government appropriations. The massive spending bill's passage was uncertain until just hours before the deadline to avoid a government shutdown due to strong disagreement between the two parties over a number of provisions.

Among the financial services sticking points were provisions on the Dodd-Frank Wall Street Reform and Consumer Protection Act and the District of Columbia. Republicans wanted to eliminate the portion of the financial regulatory law that requires banks to remove some derivatives trading operations from the portion of the institution that is federally insured. The intent of that Dodd-Frank provision was to instill greater financial security in banks to avoid another recession and federal government bailout of major financial institutions. Democrats fought against the measure but eventually agreed with its inclusion in return for increased funding for the Securities and Exchange Commission (SEC), the body responsible for the implementation of portions of Dodd-Frank. Funding for the District of Columbia also threatened to derail passage, with Republicans holding firm on a policy rider similar to what was passed in the House regarding marijuana decriminalization and legalization. Ultimately, negotiators reached a consensus that would only prohibit the District from using federal funds to implement a referendum legalizing recreational marijuana but left alone the issue of decriminalization.

On December 11, the House failed to pass what became known as the cromnibus, a combination of traditional full-year omnibus spending with a continuing resolution for the Department of Homeland Security, but late in the evening would vote 219–206 for passage; the Senate voted in favor on December 13, 56–40, and the president signed the measure on December 16.

A total of $21.8 billion was allocated to the financial services and general government agencies in the final bill, down 1 percent from the enacted fiscal 2014 budget and $2 billion lower than President Obama's requested total. Of this, the IRS received $10.9 billion, $345.6 million below fiscal 2014 and lower than the $12.5 billion requested by the president. The fiscal 2015 IRS budget was lower than what the agency received in fiscal 2009. Approximately $4.8 billion was provided for tax enforcement, up from the $3.8 billion allocated in the House measure. The IRS had requested additional funds for enforcement activities, arguing that every dollar spent on enforcement yields $6 in additional IRS revenue. Another policy rider targeting the IRS prohibited the agency from using its funds to target citizens exercising their First Amendment rights or groups based on ideological beliefs and a requirement that the IRS provide detailed information on how it makes decisions on allocating bonuses following a report that some tax-delinquent employees had received financial performance awards.

The omnibus package included new reporting requirements for the executive branch, extended the pay freeze for the vice president's office, and required that all executive orders issued in fiscal 2015 include budgetary impact statements. The final bill also prohibited a requirement that companies bidding on federal contracts disclose their campaign contributions and banned federal funds allocated under the law to be utilized to paint portraits of federal officials, including the president. Additional financial services funding included in the omnibus were

- $1.5 billion for the SEC, up from $1.35 billion in fiscal 2014
- $680 million for the District of Columbia
- $6.7 billion for the federal courts, up nearly 3 percent from fiscal 2014

House Holds IRS Official in Contempt

IRS practices for determining organizations' tax-exempt status were the subject of ongoing congressional investigation and legislative action in 2014, following revelations in 2013 that the agency may have improperly applied extra scrutiny to conservative groups. Lois Lerner, the director for the IRS's Exempt Organization Unit, which determines tax-exempt status, was a particular focus of lawmakers' attention. In the spring, the House approved a motion put forward by Oversight Committee leadership to declare Lerner in contempt of Congress for declining to testify at two hearings. The House also approved several measures that sought to limit the IRS's ability to change the rules for determining tax-exempt status and implement other agency reforms.

BACKGROUND

Under Section 501(c)(4) of the U.S. tax code, organizations may apply for and obtain tax-exempt status if they primarily operate to promote social welfare in the community. These groups are permitted to advocate for legislation and endorse political candidates and can spend up to 50 percent of their time participating in political activities, as long as politics were not their "primary purpose."

Congress began scrutinizing IRS practices for determining organizations' 501(c)(4) tax-exempt status in 2012 after hearing from several conservative groups that their applications were delayed in processing and that they had been asked to provide additional information such as the names of their donors. Increasing congressional inquiries prompted the Treasury Department's Inspector General for Tax Administration (TIGTA) to launch an investigation into the matter.

On May 14, 2013, TIGTA released the findings of its investigation, concluding that the IRS had created a "be on the lookout" list for employees to use when screening applications for tax-exempt status. This list included terms such as *tea party* and *patriots*, in addition to advising employees to look for groups mentioning government spending, taxes, or debt as a focus issue; criticizing the current government; or seeking to educate Americans about the Constitution or Bill of Rights. If a group's application included any of these words or phrases, it was flagged for extra scrutiny, and a request was sent for additional information. This practice was reportedly implemented in 2010 and was discontinued in 2012. The report further revealed that IRS leadership was informed about the practice as early as May 2012 yet did not share the information with Republican lawmakers who had inquired about potential targeting. Sen. Orrin Hatch, R-Utah, said he had written to the IRS three times expressing a concern that conservative groups had been improperly targeted but that in response to the first letter, the acting IRS Commissioner assured Hatch that no such activity was taking place.

A few days before the report's release, Lerner publicly apologized for "absolutely inappropriate" actions. She denied that the determination process was politically motivated, instead citing poor management and misguided efforts to streamline application review. Lerner claimed that the practice was only used by a few "front-line people" in the IRS Cincinnati office. However, the TIGTA report revealed that employees in other locations—including two California offices and the agency's headquarters in Washington, D.C.—had also sent conservative groups additional queries.

The TIGTA report caused an uproar on Capitol Hill, with Republicans claiming the Obama administration was purposefully singling out conservative groups for greater scrutiny. White House Press Secretary Jay Carney told reporters that IRS employees' actions were "of concern" and "inappropriate" but reinforced that the IRS "is an independent enforcement agency." President Obama called the report findings "outrageous" and fired acting IRS Commissioner Steven Miller shortly after the report's release. Investigations were launched and hearings held by the Senate Finance Committee and Permanent Subcommittee on Investigations,

as well as the House Ways and Means Committee and Oversight and Government Reform Committee. The FBI also investigated the matter, concluding in January 2014 that there was no evidence to support criminal charges, though the investigation was ongoing.

The House Oversight Committee's investigation focused on Lerner's role in the scandal, and she was twice invited to offer testimony. At a hearing in May 2013, Lerner briefly asserted her innocence before invoking her Fifth Amendment right to decline to answer questions. "I have not done anything wrong. I have not broken any laws," she said. "I have not violated any I.R.S. rules and regulations, and I have not provided false information to this or any other Congressional committee." Committee Chair Darrell Issa, R-Calif., dismissed Lerner and her lawyer but said he reserved the right to call her back for another hearing. Lerner was summoned for another hearing, the committee's sixth on the issue, in March 2014 but once again invoked her Fifth Amendment right. Republican committee members sought to pressure Lerner into testifying by suggesting she could be held in contempt of Congress. They claimed that by making a statement before invoking the Fifth Amendment during the 2013 hearing, Lerner had waived her constitutional right to remain silent. Democrats on the committee countered that Lerner had maintained her rights throughout the investigation process. In a letter to Issa dated March 25, 2014, the House Office of the General Counsel provided its opinion that the House had legal standing to pursue contempt charges against Lerner.

The committee also repeatedly requested the IRS provide emails sent by Lerner, demanding on March 26 that it share *all* emails for the committee to review and determine which were relevant. IRS Commissioner John Koskinen replied that the agency was working to hand over any emails related to determinations, appeals, exams, and rule making, per guidance received from House Ways and Means Committee staff. He also noted that redacting confidential taxpayer information, which committee members did not have clearance to see, was very time consuming and part of the reason why the IRS was only providing emails related to certain categories. Then in June, Koskinen testified that Lerner's computer had crashed in mid-2011, meaning that the IRS was unable to recover external messages sent to or from her email address, and that her hard drive had likely been recycled and destroyed, along with the hard drives of other officials involved in the scandal. It was later revealed that Koskinen knew about the email issue as early as April but waited to tell Congress until the summer. TIGTA later recovered approximately 30,000 of the emails Koskinen said had been lost.

While the committees pursued their investigations, lawmakers also debated a proposal put forward by Treasury Department and IRS officials in November 2013 to revise the rules for tax-exempt status qualifications. Specifically, officials proposed to define "candidate-related political activity" as including campaign contributions, campaign endorsements, and voter-registration activities, among others, and to make it clear that these activities do not constitute the promotion of social welfare. Officials stated the proposed changes would reduce the need for the IRS to apply its existing "facts and circumstances" test, which involves "fact-intensive inquiries" into issues such as whether the group's communications are neutral and unbiased, to determine whether an organization is engaged in political campaign activities that do not promote social welfare.

Republicans claimed the proposed changes were further evidence that the IRS was targeting conservative groups because the updated rule would not apply to labor unions or other tax-exempt groups. House Ways and Means Committee Chair David Camp, R-Mich., claimed the rule was "drafted in a manner, in my view, intended to shut down tea party groups." Republicans also argued the proposal would restrict organizations' First Amendment rights. Issa and Rep. Jim Jordan, R-Ohio, asked Koskinen to withdraw the proposed rule. Supporters of the rule denied it was politically motivated and said it would be helpful in managing the major influx of applications for tax-exempt status that had followed the Supreme Court's 2010 ruling in *Citizens United v. Federal Election Commission.* They also argued that taxpayers should not be asked to subsidize political activity. Democrats accused Republicans of trying to protect "dark money"—funds received by certain political groups from undisclosed sources and spent to influence elections—and seeking to energize their voter base by spreading conspiracy theories.

House Action

Lawmakers in the House approved several measures in response to the IRS scandal and proposed rule change. On February 11, the House Ways and Means Committee voted 23 to 13 to approve a bill (HR 3865) sponsored by Camp that would have prohibited the IRS from modifying the standards for social welfare groups to receive tax-exempt status, thereby blocking the proposed rule change. This bill was approved by the full House on February 26, with a vote of 243 to 176.

On February 25, the House approved, by voice vote, two bills that were initially introduced by Rep. Peter Roskam, R-Ill., in June 2013. One bill (HR 2531) would prohibit the IRS from asking taxpayers about their personal religious, political, or social beliefs. Republicans said the bill would help prevent the IRS from targeting certain political groups; Democrats generally agreed that no American should be targeted for their personal views but said the IRS should not be prohibited from asking about political activities. The other (HR 2530) would require the IRS to provide a "substantive written response" within thirty days of receiving written correspondence from a taxpayer. The agency would also have to provide a written explanation if it did not complete an audit of an individual's tax return within a year of its receipt.

The House Ways and Means Committee held an unusual two-hour, closed-door executive session on April 9, during which members debated sending a letter to Attorney General Eric Holder to ask that he pursue charges against Lerner based on findings from the committee's investigation. These findings included that Lerner improperly influenced IRS actions against conservative organizations, impeded investigations into the matter by making misleading statements, and may have disclosed confidential taxpayer information by using her personal email to conduct official business. The committee ultimately voted 23 to 14—along party lines—to send the letter. Democrats argued it was unnecessary to do so because the Justice Department was already investigating the incident, including Lerner's role.

The next day, the House Oversight Committee voted to hold Lerner in contempt of Congress for refusing to testify before the committee as required by congressional subpoena. The committee split along party lines in the 21 to 12 vote. On May 7, Issa introduced to the full House a motion (H Res 574) holding Lerner in contempt and calling on the Justice Department to explore criminal charges. Rep. Elijah Cummings, D-Md., the ranking member on the House Oversight Committee, moved to refer the resolution back to the committee for further consideration, but the motion failed by a vote of 191 to 224. Issa's resolution was approved later that day in a 231 to 187 vote. Just a few days earlier, the House passed a resolution (H Res 565) calling on Holder to appoint a special prosecutor to determine whether Lerner should face criminal charges. That resolution, introduced by Jordan, passed by a vote of 250 to 168.

The contempt citation was mostly symbolic; Lerner had been placed on administrative leave in May 2013 and retired from the IRS in September 2013. The Justice Department declined to comment on whether it would pursue prosecution.

Senate Action

Action in the Senate was relatively limited compared to that of the House. Senate Majority Leader Mitch McConnell, R-Ky., Senate Finance Committee Chair Orrin Hatch, R-Utah, Sen. Jeff Flake, R-Ariz., and Sen. Pat Roberts, R-Kan., introduced the Senate's companion bill (S 2011) to HR 3865—prohibiting the IRS tax-exempt status rule change—on February 11, 2014. "The fact of the matter is these proposed regulations demonstrate that the IRS is willing and able to carry the president's political water, even when the agency is, by law, supposed to be independent and non-partisan," said Hatch during a speech on the Senate floor. "We need to send a message to the administration that it can't tamper with the rules of free speech just because it doesn't like what's being said." The bill was referred to the Senate Finance Committee, but no further action was taken.

The Senate did not act to introduce companion legislation to HR 2530 or HR 2531.

2015–2016

Secret Service Investigation and Reform Legislation

In 2015, the United States Secret Service was the subject of both an investigation by the House Oversight and Government Reform Committee and proposed reform legislation. The House committee's investigation began after an incident on September 19, 2014, in which a man breached five rings of the Secret Service's protective perimeter around the White House. The committee subsequently called a hearing on security and protocol breaches, technological issues, training reductions, and a culture in the Secret Service that discouraged whistle-blowing. During the investigation that followed, Secret Service employees accessed and circulated House Oversight Committee Chair Jason Chaffetz's, R-Utah, 2003 application for a position with the agency. The breach was confirmed by the Secret Service's inspector general. Chaffetz claimed agency staff did so to embarrass and intimidate him. Another hearing, this time led jointly by the House and Senate Homeland Security Committees, was called to examine the Chaffetz matter, which Rep. Scott Perry, R-Penn., called just one example of poor judgment shown by Secret Service employees. Forty-one Secret Service agents were ultimately disciplined for the leak of Chaffetz's personnel file.

The House Oversight and Government Reform Committee released its report in December 2015, describing the Secret Service as an organization "in crisis" and finding that the agency suffered from severely weakened morale due to a reduced workforce, drastic budget cuts, and a slew of embarrassing scandals. The report included details of agency employees' misconduct and focused on four recent security breaches that threatened the agency's protective mission: a November 2011 shooting outside the White House; the soliciting of prostitutes in April 2012 by Secret Service personnel who also engaged in other security and protocol breaches during a presidential visit to Cartagena, Colombia; security failures during a presidential visit at the Centers for Disease Control and Prevention in Atlanta, Georgia, in September 2014; and the March 2015 interference of two intoxicated senior agency officials with a bomb threat crime scene near the White House.

The report stated that perhaps the greatest threat to the agency was the staffing crisis caused by shrinking budgets that were reduced annually, chronic mismanagement, and depleted employee morale. A net decline in operational personnel, including the number of agents in the Uniformed Division tasked with protecting the White House, since 2011 led to remaining staff being overworked.

The committee's ranking member, Rep. Elijah Cummings, D-Md., said it would be unreasonable for Congress to believe that the budget cuts would have no repercussions.

Although cuts to the agency's budget predated the decline in staff, the investigation found they contributed to hiring freezes and an inefficient hiring process that brought in low-quality applicants and left the agency vulnerable to risks in regard to approving security clearances. The report also disclosed remarks by agency whistleblowers that employees had little to no confidence in their leadership due to a lack of accountability for supervisors and managers as well as widespread fear of retaliation.

Additionally, the investigation found the Secret Service had strayed from its primary mission to protect the president and other elected leaders and foreign dignitaries to keep up with investigative demands, which the committee deemed a resource-intensive distraction. The report recommended the agency reconsider this "dual mission."

Of equal importance, the report said, was the need for fresh leadership from outside the agency who would be willing to implement drastic reforms to help the Secret Service overcome its resistance to change. The report also prodded lawmakers to ensure sufficient funding and support the president's fiscal year 2016 Secret Service appropriations request to assist in rebuilding the agency's ranks. Further, the report noted that an independent Protective Mission Panel had assessed the Secret Service and provided recommendations for correcting internal issues at the agency and tightening security around the White House compound in 2014 but that serious deficiencies remained.

House Action

While the House Oversight Committee conducted its investigation, the House Judiciary Committee weighed a legislative solution to enact change within the agency. On March 26, 2015, Chair Bob Goodlatte, R-Va., introduced a bipartisan bill (HR 1656) cosponsored by Reps. Jim Sensenbrenner, R-Wisc., John Conyers Jr., D-Wisc., and Sheila Jackson Lee, D-Texas. The bill's proposed provisions sought to address concerns highlighted during the 2014 hearing, as well as recommendations provided by Protective Mission Panel to correct deficiencies within the Secret Service.

The bill included a controversial requirement that the Senate be consulted on and approve any nominations for the presidentially appointed position of Secret Service director. The bill also authorized the hiring of new personnel, including eighty-five additional agents for the president's protective detail and at least 200 new Uniformed Division officers. Additionally, to help address recent security lapses, the bill prohibited any object—such as the drone that landed on the White House's lawn in January of

2015—from entering a restricted area that "disrupts the orderly conduct of government business."

Following its introduction, the bill was referred to the Subcommittee on Crime, Terrorism, Homeland Security, and Investigations at the end of April. The subcommittee's investigations were discharged on July 14, and the bill returned to the full committee for consideration and markup the next day. After adopting an amendment, proposed by Jackson Lee, that called for the creation of an Ethics Program Office within the Secret Service, the committee approved the bill by unanimous voice vote.

On July 27, 2015, the bill passed the House by a vote of 365 to 16 after forty minutes of debate and without further amendment.

Senate Action

The House bill was received in the Senate on July 28 and referred to the Committee on Homeland Security and Governmental Affairs, but the committee did not act until the following year.

The committee took up the bill on February 10, 2016, at which time Chair Ron Johnson, R-Wisc., put forward a modified amendment that more clearly extended Secret Service protection to the immediate families of former vice presidents, removed the House clause ordering the Senate be consulted and provide consent for any presidential nominee for director of the Secret Service, and required the Government Accountability Office to report on the implementation of both HR 1656 and recommendations by the Protective Mission Panel no later than two years after the bill's enactment.

The committee adopted the amendment and ordered the act be reported (S Rept 114–302) to the full Senate by voice vote on July 13, 2016. No further action was taken by the Senate.

House Seeks Impeachment of IRS Commissioner

Still outraged by the IRS's handling of tax-exempt status determinations for conservative organizations, House Republicans shifted their anger from Lois Lerner, the former IRS official held in contempt of Congress in 2014, to IRS Commissioner John Koskinen. While Koskinen became commissioner in December 2013, after the incidents in question occurred, Republicans claimed that he lied while testifying about the matter before Congress—while under oath—and that he oversaw the destruction of key records that could have provided important findings. House Republicans pursued Koskinen's impeachment in 2015. The Senate Finance Committee and the Justice Department both concluded their respective investigations of the IRS scandal in 2015. House and Senate lawmakers also succeeded in passing several IRS reforms at the end of the year. (*See "IRS Commissioner Spared Impeachment," p. 464.*)

DEPARTMENT OF JUSTICE INVESTIGATION

On October 23, 2015, Assistant Attorney General Peter Kadzik informed congressional committees that the Justice Department was closing its investigation after interviewing more than 100 people, reading more than one million pages of IRS documents, and reviewing nearly 500 applications for tax-exempt status. In his letter to the committees, Kadzik wrote, "We found no evidence that any IRS official acted based on political, discriminatory, corrupt, or other inappropriate motives that would support a criminal prosecution. We also found no evidence that any official involved in the handling of tax-exempt applications or IRS leadership attempted to obstruct justice." Kadzik acknowledged the department did find substantial evidence of mismanagement and poor judgment that "may necessitate corrective action" but did "not warrant criminal prosecution."

Committee leaders responded critically. House Ways and Means Committee Chair Paul Ryan, R-Wisc., said the department's determination was predictable but disappointing, adding that the investigating committees found that Lerner took action that amounted to depriving the targeted organizations of their constitutional rights. Former House Oversight Committee Chair Darrell Issa, R-Calif., called the decision a low point that ignored the evidence against the IRS.

House Action

On July 27, 2015, twenty-one Republicans from the House Oversight Committee sent a letter to President Obama stating that Koskinen had obstructed congressional investigations. "His obstruction takes the form of failure to comply with a congressional subpoena, failure to testify truthfully, and a failure to preserve and produce up to 24,000 emails relevant to the investigation," they wrote. "Commissioner Koskinen bears responsibility for a number of actions that may have permanently deprived the American people of a complete understanding of the IRS scandal. In the course of doing so, he misled Congress and acted with complete disregard for Congress's efforts to find out the truth."

Three months later, House Oversight Committee Chair Jason Chaffetz, R-Utah, introduced a motion (H Res 494) to impeach Koskinen for "high crimes and misdemeanors." The articles of impeachment included in the measure stated that Koskinen had failed to comply with a congressional subpoena for certain IRS documents and that he provided false and misleading information to Congress about employee emails—including those sent and received by Lerner—that he claimed were missing. Treasury Department officials were later able to retrieve the emails in question. The bill was cosponsored by eighteen of the Oversight Committee's twenty-four Republican members and some Republicans who were not on the committee. It was referred to the Judiciary Committee, which declined to give the measure further consideration. As a result, the motion was not taken up by the full House.

Senate Action

While House members pursued Koskinen's impeachment, the Senate Finance Committee concluded its investigation into IRS screening of political groups' applications for tax-exempt status. The investigation was launched in May 2013 and conducted mostly in private, except for one public hearing. The committee reviewed roughly 1.5 million pages of documents and interviewed thirty-two people during a two-year period.

In a report of its findings released on August 5, 2015, the committee concluded that IRS managers failed to provide effective direction to agents on how to process political groups' applications and failed to provide adequate oversight of the process. The committee also found that Lerner had led several efforts to speed up application processing, but none of these measures were successful, and Lerner failed to seek counsel on the legal implications of her efforts. Lerner, along with former IRS Commissioners Doug Shulman and Steve Miller, also made misleading written or oral statements to Congress in 2012 and 2013 about the IRS's handling of conservative groups and concealed information about the processing of those groups' applications for tax-exempt status.

The report was written by the committee's Republican staff, but both Republican and Democratic staff issued supplemental views along with the report. The Republicans continued to claim that political biases underlay the IRS's management issues. "The IRS systemically selected tea party and other conservative organizations for heightened scrutiny, in a manner wholly different from how the IRS processed applications submitted by left-leaning and non-partisan organizations," they wrote. For their part, the Democrats argued that Republicans' claims of political bias were "based purely on speculation" and an assumption that the IRS received an equal number of applications for tax-exempt status from conservative and liberal groups, when it was possible that the influx of applications that began in 2010 came mostly from conservative groups.

Joint Action

On December 16, 2015, Senate Finance Committee Chair Orrin Hatch, R-Utah, House Ways and Means Committee Chair Kevin Brady, R-Texas, and Senate Finance Committee Ranking Member Ron Wyden, D-Ore., announced a bipartisan tax cut extenders deal that included several IRS reforms related to the 2013 scandal. Called the Protecting Americans from Tax Hikes Act of 2015, or PATH Act, the deal provided for the quick termination of IRS employees who take politically motivated actions against taxpayers, required IRS employees to respect the taxpayer bill of rights, prohibited IRS officers or employees from using a personal email account to conduct any official U.S. government business, and required the IRS to establish an appeal process for organizations that apply for and are denied 501(c) status. The PATH Act

was attached to the Consolidated Appropriations Act for fiscal year 2016 (HR 2029) as an amendment on December 18, 2015. The appropriations bill was approved by Congress and signed by the president the same day (PL 114–113).

Campaign Financial Disclosure

The influence of money in electoral politics was a prominent issue in 2016 due to the ongoing presidential campaign, but despite Republican and Democratic candidates' criticism of existing campaign finance law, reform in this area was not a priority for Congress. A package of campaign finance reforms proposed by a group of Democratic senators and Sen. Angus King, I-Maine, was ignored by Senate leadership, while one measure loosening disclosure rules passed the House.

PRESIDENTIAL CANDIDATES COMMENT ON CAMPAIGN FINANCE RULES

Candidates from both sides of the aisle lamented the outsized influence over the election system that existing campaign finance regulations gave wealthy people, corporations, and super PACs. Former Secretary of State Hillary Clinton and Sen. Bernie Sanders, I-Vt., both said that as president, they would nominate justices to the U.S. Supreme Court who would overturn the Court's 2010 ruling in *Citizens United v. Federal Election Commission*. That decision has allowed corporations, unions, and wealthy individuals to spend unlimited amounts of money on ads and other political tools calling for the election or defeat of a specific candidate. Clinton and Sanders also promised to push for greater public transparency of donations, public matching funds for small donors, and a new Securities and Exchange Commission (SEC) rule that would require more disclosures of public companies' political spending.

Among the Republican candidates, Donald Trump was the most vocal in criticizing campaign finance laws, describing them as "broken" and declaring that, as a billionaire and campaign donor, he knew he had greater access to politicians. Trump also boasted that his campaign was self-financed and criticized his rivals for raising and spending huge amounts of money on their presidential bids. Sen. Ted Cruz, R-Texas, noted that he had introduced legislation during the 113th Congress that would have required campaigns to report contributions over $200 to the Federal Election Commission (FEC) within 24 hours of their receipt and would have eliminated individual donor contribution limits. However, most candidates did not offer specific details about how they would change campaign finance laws if elected president.

House Committee Action

On April 26, Rep. Peter Roskam, R-Ill., introduced the Preventing IRS Abuse and Protecting Free Speech Act (HR 5053). The bill was in part a campaign finance measure, but it also sought to address lingering Republican concerns about alleged IRS targeting of conservative groups applying for tax-exempt status. It would amend the Internal Revenue Code to prohibit the IRS from requiring tax-exempt organizations, including 501(c)(3)s and 501(c)(4)s, to include the name of, address of, or other identifying information about contributors in their annual tax returns. Exceptions to this rule were provided for required disclosures about prohibited tax shelter transactions and contributions from the organization's officers, directors, or five highest compensated employees, including those paid by related organizations.

The House Ways and Means Committee approved the bill on April 28 by a vote of 23 to 15. Committee Chair Kevin Brady, R-Texas, said the legislation would remove reporting requirements and lead to better protection for groups to ensure they are not improperly targeted by the IRS. Rep. Sander Levin, D-Mich., the committee's ranking member, countered that the bill opened the door for excessive secret money to flow into U.S. elections.

House Action

Roskam's bill was brought before the full House on June 14, 2015. Rep. John Sarbanes, D-Md., made a motion for the committee to amend the bill so that it did not apply to 501(c) groups that directly or indirectly provide support to a political campaign on behalf of or in opposition to any candidate. Before offering his motion, Sarbanes sharply criticized the bill, saying it did little to address accountability issues in political donations and that it in fact decreased transparency. Sarbanes's motion failed by a vote of 180 to 238. The bill was approved 240 to 182 later that day. It was received in the Senate on June 15 and referred to the Senate Finance Committee, but no further action was taken.

Senate Action

Two days after Roskam's bill passed the House, Sen. Tom Udall, D-N.M., and twenty-four Democratic cosponsors introduced a package of campaign finance measures (S 6) known as the We the People Act of 2016. Udall said his bill was meant to address concerns of Americans regarding the amount of money flowing into political campaigns, and he vowed to fight to ensure greater accountability in U.S. elections by bringing to light campaign donors who have been able to remain anonymous.

The bill included a proposed constitutional amendment that would have repealed the *Citizens United* decision and given states and Congress authority to enact campaign finance reforms that limited independent expenditures, including those made by corporations and super political action committees (PACs). It also called for the creation of a new independent agency called the Federal Election Administration (FEA) to replace the Federal Election Commission (FEC). The FEA was envisioned to consist of five presidentially appointed and Senate-confirmed commissioners and to have greater enforcement and investigation powers than the FEC.

Another provision would prohibit former members of Congress from ever lobbying a current lawmaker. Existing law prohibits outgoing senators from engaging in such lobbying activity for two years after leaving Congress; a one-year limit is in place for outgoing House members. Lawmakers further sought to tighten lobbying restrictions by requiring consultants to register as federal lobbyists if they made two or more lobbying contacts for a client over a two-year period, regardless of the total amount of time they spend lobbying and their lobbying-related income. (Currently, lobbyists must meet three income, time, and contact criteria before they are required to register.)

Additionally, the bill would require all organizations that spend money on elections, including super PACs and 501(c)(4)s, to promptly disclose donors who gave $10,000 or more during an election cycle. Other provisions sought to shut down super PACs for individual candidates, require all candidates for federal office to report campaign contributions over $1,000 to the FEC within forty-eight hours, and prohibit private sector financial services companies from offering bonuses to employees who leave the company to take a position in government. This last provision was included out of concern that some employees were receiving a payout from a company they would be regulating.

The bill was referred to the Senate Committee on Rules and Administration the day it was introduced. No further action was taken by the Senate.

Financial Services and General Government Appropriations for 2016

With majority control of both the House and Senate, Republicans were better positioned in 2015 to take aim at agencies and regulations they disagreed with. This was evident in the debate over the fiscal 2016 Financial Services and General Government appropriations bill, which covers agencies responsible for overseeing provisions in the Dodd-Frank Wall Street Reform and Consumer Protection Act and the Patient Protection and Affordable Care Act (ACA), as well as funding for the Internal Revenue Service (IRS) and the District of Columbia. Republicans had been keen on cutting funding from the IRS since 2013 when it was discovered that the agency inappropriately targeted conservative groups applying for tax-exempt status with additional regulatory scrutiny. Both the House and Senate Appropriations Committees reported out measures for financial services to their full bodies; however, neither bill was taken up for consideration. Funding for the agencies covered was instead included in the fiscal 2016 omnibus legislation (HR 2029—PL 114–113) signed by President Obama on December 18, 2015. In an effort to ensure omnibus passage, Republicans and Democrats negotiated out many of the funding cuts and regulations Republicans had proposed in committee, and many of the covered agencies saw their budgets increase.

CAMPAIGN FINANCE IN FEDERAL SPENDING MEASURES

Following the Supreme Court's *Citizens United* ruling in 2010, Democrats and public-interest groups began pushing the Securities and Exchange Commission (SEC) to implement a rule that would require public companies to disclose their political contributions. Supporters of such a rule argued that it would bring much-needed transparency and accountability to companies' political activities in the wake of the Court's decision to loosen campaign finance regulations while also providing information of interest to company shareholders. They also highlighted the Court's own acknowledgment of the value of disclosures. In the majority opinion, Justice Anthony Kennedy wrote, "Prompt disclosure of expenditures can provide shareholders and citizens with the information needed to hold corporations and elected officials accountable for their positions and supporters." He added, "Shareholders can determine whether their corporation's political speech advances the corporation's interest in making profits, and citizens can see whether elected officials are 'in the pocket' of so-called moneyed interests."

When the SEC released its regulatory agenda for 2013, the list included consideration of a petition from the Committee on Disclosure of Corporate Political Spending, a group of ten professors specializing in corporate and securities law, that called for the SEC to develop political disclosure rules. Soon after taking office as SEC chair on April 10 of that year, Mary Jo White faced pressure from Republicans in Congress to abandon the petition, as they claimed that it was highly partisan. Some drew a link between a potential SEC rule and a highly controversial Internal Revenue Service directive that slowed the tax-exempt applications of conservative groups. House Financial Services Committee Chair Jeb Hensarling, R-Texas, asked White during a May 16, 2013, hearing if the White House had communicated with the SEC about the disclosure issue. White told lawmakers that she was not aware of any such contact while seeking to assure them that she was an "apolitical" and "very independent" person. She also stated that "no one is working on a proposed rule now." The SEC ultimately dropped the petition and disclosure rules from its regulatory agenda.

In 2015, Republicans leveraged their majority in Congress to add a policy rider to the FY 2016 omnibus (PL 114–113) that prohibited the SEC from issuing or implementing "any rule, regulation or order regarding the disclosure of political contributions, contributions to tax exempt organizations, or dues paid to trade associations." Despite this legislative development, disclosure rule advocates continued to show their support. More than 1.2 million people submitted comments to the SEC in support of corporate political spending disclosures. Forty-four senators, seventy investing endowed foundations, five state treasurers, and a group of former SEC chairs and members were also among those calling for a disclosure rule.

Democrats also kept up the pressure in Congress, including at a confirmation hearing for two SEC officials in March 2016, during which Sen. Charles Schumer, D-N.Y., warned the nominees that he might vote against their confirmation if they did not strongly state their support for corporate disclosure of political contributions. Sen. Elizabeth Warren, D-Mass., wrote a letter to President Obama on October 14, 2016, urging him to replace White as head of the SEC. "Chair White's refusal to move forward on a political spending disclosure rule serves the narrow interests of powerful executives who would prefer to hide their expenditures of company money to advance their own personal ideologies," she argued. Democrats also threatened to withhold their agreement to a continuing resolution keeping the government open past October 1 unless the 2015 policy rider was removed from spending legislation. This effort proved unsuccessful: The language was preserved in two continuing resolutions passed by Congress late in the year, including one that funded the government through April 2017. Schumer accused House Majority Leader Paul Ryan, R-Wisc., and Senate Majority Leader Mitch McConnell, R-Ky., of trying to leverage the federal budget to stop transparency in campaign donations.

It was generally understood that Democrats' resistance to the SEC policy rider was primarily symbolic, since it was highly unlikely that the SEC would have produced a disclosure rule before President Obama left office, and even if it had, President-elect Trump was not expected to promote such a rule. Furthermore, Republicans had expressed their desire to loosen campaign finance regulations in 2017 now that their party controlled the White House and both chambers of Congress.

House Action

The House Appropriations Committee approved its Financial Services and General Government bill (HR 2995) in July 2015. It included a total of $20.2 billion in spending, or 6 percent below fiscal 2015 enacted spending levels, and provided $4.8 billion less than the White House had requested. The largest funding cut targeted the IRS, whose annual appropriation would be slashed by $838 million. As they had in years past, House Republicans also included in the bill a measure that would make the Consumer Financial Protection Bureau (CFPB) subject to annual appropriations rather than receiving its budget from the Federal Reserve, which is funded through interest instead of Congressional appropriations. This would give Republicans greater control over the activities of a body they saw as a government over-reach. Another Treasury bureau, the Office of Financial Research, created under Dodd-Frank to research the U.S. financial system and analyze risks in order to promote financial stability in the markets, was also moved to regular appropriations. The intent of appropriators was to provide Congress more influence over monitoring the stability of the nation's markets and decisions on whether some financial institutions warranted increased federal oversight. As a final 2015 blow to Dodd-Frank, the House committee added to the bill a requirement for the administration to report to Congress the cost and regulatory burdens of the act.

The Federal Communications Commission (FCC), which had recently approved net neutrality regulations intended to provide an open and fair internet by preventing internet service providers from throttling access to content created by certain companies, also saw its budget cut, but only by $25 million. The House appropriations bill also barred the agency from spending money to implement its net neutrality regulations until legal challenges against the measure had been resolved.

Additional measures included in the House committee bill prohibited the Securities and Exchange Commission (SEC) from requiring the disclosure of political donations in regular filings and barred the organization from spending money in its reserve fund, which House Republicans felt lacked the necessary oversight. The District of Columbia was also subject to a prohibition on using federal or local funds to stop local employers from discriminating against employees for their reproductive health choices. Republicans explained that this was intended to allow private businesses to hire staff that align with their ideological views.

The bill was never brought for a floor vote.

Senate Action

The Senate Appropriations Committee worked on its own Financial Services and General Government appropriations bill that allocated $4 billion below the president's request and $1.3 billion less than fiscal 2015. The IRS was also a target of Senate appropriators, although the cut to their budget was smaller than what had been proposed in the House at $10.5 billion, or $470 million less than the prior fiscal year. IRS taxpayer services would have received a boost of $90 million, and the bill called for the IRS to spend $2.3 billion of its funds responding to taxpayer phone inquiries, assisting with identity theft cases, and providing other taxpayer services. As was included in appropriations measures over the past few fiscal years, the IRS was prohibited from targeting groups based on their ideological views or individuals expressing their First Amendment rights.

The Senate appropriations bill included many of the House provisions, such as moving the Consumer Financial Protection Bureau (CFPB) under the annual appropriations process, requiring new reports regarding Dodd-Frank, and relaxing some campaign finance rules governing the coordination between political parties and outside groups. The Senate also reduced funding to the FCC by $20 million, prohibited the body from regulating rates under its net neutrality regulations, and nullified a rule change on joint sales agreements in broadcast television markets. The Senate also included some provisions on U.S. relations with Cuba, which the White House and the State Department were in the process of attempting to normalize. Specifically, the Senate bill included a lifting of the ban on travel to Cuba, allowed U.S. banks to offer credit for agricultural exports to Cuba, and ended the licensing requirement for U.S. ships to load and unload in Cuba.

Perhaps the most controversial of the policy riders added to the appropriations measure was the inclusion of the Financial Regulatory Improvement Act of 2015 (S 1484), a bill reported by the Senate Banking, Housing, and Urban Affairs Committee on June 2. The bill would overhaul banking rules by reducing some of the regulatory burden on banks with the tradeoff that it would expand consumer access to credit. Democrats argued that such a measure would remove consumer protections and risk sending the United States back into recession. The White House threatened to veto the spending measure if language from S 1484 was included in the final bill that made it to the president's desk.

The bill never received a floor vote.

Omnibus Measure

As had occurred many times in recent years, the Financial Services and General Government appropriations were wrapped into a larger, $1.15 trillion omnibus measure. Financial services agencies would receive $23.2 billion for fiscal 2016, an increase from fiscal 2015, and the policy riders that had divided Democrats and Republicans on the House and Senate Appropriations Committees were largely dropped. The IRS received $11.2 billion, 3 percent higher than the allocation in the enacted fiscal 2015 budget but less than what the president had requested. Congress directed that the additional funds be utilized for customer service, fraud detection and prevention, and cybersecurity. The ban on targeting individuals or groups over First Amendment and ideological expressions was maintained, as was a requirement that federal tax compliance be considered as a factor in hiring and awarding bonuses.

Dodd-Frank escaped some of the harsher requirements included in the House and Senate appropriations bills. However, the final omnibus still required the Office of Management and Budget (OMB) to report on the costs of implementing the law. CFPB was not folded into the regular appropriations process, but Congress required that the bureau make annual reports to Congress on its spending plans and publicly disclose the requests for funding it makes to the Federal Reserve.

The Federal Communications Commission (FCC) was spared a provision included in both the House and Senate versions that would limit its ability to implement its net neutrality rules. However, the omnibus did include a policy rider regarding an FCC rule change intended to increase diversity in television station ownership. The FCC had voted in March 2014 to ban joint sales agreements that allow a television station to sell advertising for a competing station located in the same market, which effectively allows larger broadcast companies to control more than one television station in a given market. Under the omnibus, through 2025, all existing contracts would be grandfathered in to the current FCC joint sales agreements rules.

Other financial services provisions included in the omnibus were

- a ban on the use of federal funds for abortions within employee health plans, except in cases of rape, incest, or if the mother's life is in danger
- a requirement that federal prescription drug coverage include contraceptive coverage, except if a health care plan objects on the basis of religion
- ten years of credit monitoring to be provided by the Office of Personnel Management (OPM) for those impacted by recent data breaches
- a requirement that OMB submit to Congress a financial impact statement for any executive order issued in fiscal 2016 that was expected to have a regulatory cost greater than $100 million
- $729 million for the District of Columbia, up $50 million from the previous fiscal year, with a prohibition on using federal funds toward legalizing recreational marijuana or for a needle-exchange program; a ban was also maintained on the use of federal or local government funds to pay for abortions in Washington, D.C., except in the case of rape, incest, or if the mother's life is in danger
- a $105 million boost for the SEC, but $25 million was rescinded from the reserve fund, and the body was prohibited from requiring corporations to disclose campaign finance activities.

To avoid a presidential veto, the final omnibus package did not include S 1484, which the White House said would threaten the financial security of middle-income Americans by allowing risky lending practices to continue. The omnibus package passed the House and Senate on December 18, 2015, by a vote of 316–113 and 65–33, respectively. It was signed by President Obama the same day. *(See discussion of fiscal year 2015 omnibus, Chapter 2.)*

IRS Commissioner Spared Impeachment

More than three years after reports surfaced that the IRS may have singled conservative groups out for additional scrutiny when making tax-exempt status determinations, some House Republicans continued to call for punitive measures against the agency's leadership. Specifically, lawmakers revived a push to impeach IRS Commissioner John Koskinen for allegedly obstructing congressional investigations of the matter.

House Action

In 2016, the House Judiciary Committee held three hearings about the articles of impeachment that had been filed against Koskinen in 2015. The commissioner was invited to testify at the first hearing, on May 24, but declined to participate due to scheduling issues. Committee members refused to enter Koskinen's written statement denying the charges against him into the record. House Oversight Committee Chair Jason Chaffetz, R-Utah, and Rep. Ron DeSantis, R-Fla., an Oversight Committee member, were the only witnesses at the hearing. A second hearing was conducted on June 22 and featured several lawyers and law professors as witnesses. The third and final hearing took place on September 21; Koskinen was the sole witness.

In prepared testimony, Koskinen acknowledged the "level of suspicion and distrust caused by the IRS's failure to properly handle" tax-exempt status applications. "I took this job in large part to help restore confidence in the IRS and to ensure that the agency never returned to the unacceptable practices that had occurred before I arrived," he said. "I believe we have made real progress during my tenure in ending the practices that gave rise to concerns, addressing operational weaknesses, creating a culture of risk management, and working to reassure taxpayers that our tax system treats taxpayers fairly." Koskinen's testimony noted that the IRS had accepted all the recommendations made by the Treasury Inspector General for Tax Administration (TIGTA) in its May 2013 report and had taken action to implement all but one. These actions included eliminating the use of inappropriate criteria, retraining employees, expediting application processing, and instituting a quality-review process. Koskinen added that the IRS also eliminated the use of "be on the lookout" lists, similar to the one that led to the additional and improper scrutiny of some groups' applications. The commissioner declared that he had always directed IRS staff to cooperate fully with Congress and provided testimony that he believed to be correct. "But the truth is that we did not succeed in preserving all of the information requested and some of my testimony later proved mistaken. I regret both of those failings," he said. However, he concluded, "impeachment would be improper."

Shortly before Congress adjourned for the year, Rep. Jim Jordan, R-Ohio, chairman of the House Freedom Caucus, offered a resolution to impeach Koskinen (H Res 828) as a privileged resolution. Per House rules, privileged business takes precedence over the regular order of business, meaning that if a privileged motion is proposed, it may supersede or interrupt other matters before the House. The resolution had been introduced by Rep. John Fleming, R-La., on July 13, but stalled in the Judiciary Committee. As in 2015, the measure sought Koskinen's impeachment for "high crimes and misdemeanors." The articles of impeachment included in the resolution alleged that Koskinen had destroyed evidence related to the IRS's handling of applications from groups seeking tax-exempt status, failed to comply with a congressional subpoena to turn over evidence, and made false statements to Congress under oath.

House Minority Leader Nancy Pelosi, D-Calif., moved to table the measure, but her motion was rejected by a vote of 180–235. House Judiciary Committee Chair Bob Goodlatte, R-Va., proposed the resolution be referred to his committee for further consideration, in part to allow Congress to finish the rest of its work before the session ended. House members approved Goodlatte's motion by a vote of 342–72.

Koskinen's lawyers maintained the commissioner's actions did not meet the standard for high crimes and misdemeanors set forth by the Constitution. Impeachment authority, said attorney Reginald Brown, is reserved for only the most serious instances.

No further action was taken on the impeachment measure before the end of the year. Many lawmakers acknowledged that even if the bill passed the House, it would have encountered strong resistance in the Senate. Additionally, incoming House Freedom Caucus Chair Mark Meadows, R-N.C., said Koskinen's impeachment would not be a priority for the group moving forward.

NASA Authorization

In 2016, a bipartisan group of lawmakers sought a new authorization for the National Aeronautics and Space Administration (NASA) that set funding levels and long-term goals for the agency. Congress last passed a NASA authorization bill in 2010 (PL 111–267); however, lawmakers continued to provide year-to-year funding that allowed the agency to maintain operations.

A major provision of the proposed authorization codified NASA's plan to conduct a manned mission to Mars in the 2030s by making this target an official part of the agency's goals and objectives. This provision built on language from the prior authorization that allowed NASA to make investments "that enable human missions beyond low-Earth orbit ultimately leading to Mars." Sending astronauts to Mars has been a long-held goal for NASA and for many lawmakers, due both to the scientific value of such missions and to the economic benefits continued investments in space exploration have generated for some states, particularly Texas and Florida, which are home to the Johnson Space Center and Kennedy Space Center, respectively.

Senate Action

On July 13, 2016, Senate Commerce Subcommittee on Space, Science, and Competitiveness Chair Ted Cruz, R-Texas, convened a hearing on the policies needed to provide stability for NASA during the upcoming presidential transition and to ensure the United States would remain the global leader in space exploration. Witnesses included William Gerstenmaier, associate administrator of human exploration and operations for NASA; Dr. Mary Lynne Dittmar, executive director of the Coalition for Deep Space Exploration; Mike Gold, vice president of Washington operations for SSL, a commercial satellite and spacecraft developer; Mark Sirangelo, vice president of Sierra Nevada

Corporation's space systems group; and Dan Dumbacher, professor of engineering practice at Purdue University.

Subcommittee members and witnesses discussed the importance of continuing NASA's existing Mars programs, noting the "dire" effect President Obama's decision to cancel the Constellation program (a return-to-the-moon initiative announced by President George W. Bush) had on agency staff and momentum, as well as the potential negative consequences program cancellations would have for commercial partners. Dittmar noted in prepared testimony that "the supply chain for human space exploration alone . . . is distributed across all 50 states and is made up of hundreds of companies, ranging from large contractors with thousands of employees to hundreds of small, privately owned businesses." Gerstenmaier, Gold, and Sirangelo also spoke favorably about public-private partnerships in space exploration. "I think what we really learned is that the private sector, if we give them the right incentives and we have the contracting structures set up, they can deliver the capabilities that we, at NASA, need in a very effective manner," said Gerstenmaier. Gold added that the future of low–Earth orbit spaceflight "remains squarely on the shoulders of the private sector, which presents both an extraordinary challenge and an equally extraordinary opportunity."

Cruz introduced the draft NASA authorization bill (S 3346) on September 15. It was co-sponsored by the committee's ranking member, Sen. Bill Nelson, D-Fla., as well as Senators Marco Rubio, R-Fla., Gary Peters, D-Mich., Roger Wicker, R-Miss., and Tom Udall, D-N.M.

The bill would have authorized $19.5 billion in funding for NASA for fiscal year 2017—an increase from the $19.3 billion provided for fiscal year 2016. It called for the United States to "extend humanity's reach into deep space, including cis-lunar space, the Moon, the surface and moons of Mars, and beyond." It would have amended existing law to add "human exploration of Mars and beyond" to the agency's key objectives and required NASA to develop and submit a plan to Congress for achieving "the long-term goal of human missions near or on the surface of Mars in the 2030s." It also would have added the expansion of a "permanent human presence beyond low-Earth orbit" and the "capability to extend human presence, including potential habitation on another celestial body and a thriving space economy in the 21st Century" to NASA's long-term goals. To support future missions to Mars and deep space, the bill would have directed NASA to continue developing its new Orion spacecraft and Space Launch System (a new rocket designed to launch the Orion capsule), with the goal of achieving an unmanned launch of both in 2018, followed by a manned mission in 2021.

Other provisions called for the United States to support the full use of the International Space Station (ISS) through at least 2024 and to explore if it could be used through 2028. The ISS is widely viewed as a crucial testing ground for the science and technology needed for astronauts to reach Mars. To help facilitate the station's continued use, NASA should maintain its ongoing collaboration with the private sector, including transporting crew and supplies to the ISS and exploring the possibility of transferring the ISS to the private sector. The bill also called on NASA to develop and submit a plan to Congress for the "commercialization and economic development" of low–Earth orbit activities.

NASA's efforts to work with the private sector included the 2006 launch of its Commercial Orbital Transportation Services Program, which sought to develop commercially operated, automated cargo spacecraft that could be used for ISS resupply missions. In 2011, the agency announced the Commercial Crew Program and began working with private companies to develop launch systems and spacecraft capable of bringing astronauts to the ISS. The program also seeks to return human spaceflight launches to U.S. soil. NASA has relied on Russia to transport astronauts to and from the ISS since the agency's space shuttle program ended in 2011. Together, these programs have enabled NASA to focus its budget and resources on developing the technology and spacecraft needed for missions to Mars and beyond while giving rise to a burgeoning commercial spaceflight industry that includes companies such as SpaceX, Boeing, and Orbital Sciences Corporation.

Additionally, the authorization bill included the TREAT Astronauts Act, which would have allowed the government to provide health care coverage to astronauts who spent extended periods of time in space. It also provided for long-term medical monitoring of those astronauts following their return to Earth.

Cruz said the NASA reauthorization bill would help reassert America's leadership in space by providing the agency what it needs to grow. He added that in states like Texas, the bill would foster continuing growth in jobs and activity related to space exploration.

Rubio further highlighted the space industry's economic impact, declaring that his home state is a leader in the aerospace industry, where there are dozens of companies focused on commercial spaceflight, engineering, and manufacturing for the space industry. He also spoke to the bill's national security implications, claiming that it would help ensure the United States maintains its access to space, which is strategically important for national defense.

The measure was reported out of committee favorably on December 5 and passed the full Senate with unanimous consent on December 10. It was too late in the year for the House to take action, but the 115th Congress took up the authorization in early 2017.

Financial Services and General Government Appropriations for 2017

As in previous years, the fiscal 2017 Financial Services and General Government appropriations bill was a point of contention among Democrats and Republicans in Congress. The bill provides funding for the agencies responsible for regulating the financial services industry but also sets the

rules for the industry. The bill is popular among lobbyists, especially those in the finance, insurance, and real estate (FIRE) sectors, who are among the largest contributors to federal political candidates and parties. These lobbyists also spend a significant amount of time and money trying to influence the work of House and Senate appropriators. The total spent by FIRE lobbyists used to be evenly divided between Republicans and Democrats, but the money began skewing toward Republicans in 2010 with the passage of the Dodd-Frank Wall Street Reform and Consumer Protection Act. This is primarily because those lobbying on behalf of the financial services bill support a rollback in the Dodd-Frank provisions, much like Republicans, while Democrats back an increase in regulations and oversight for the financial services industry. According to the Center for Responsive Politics, during the 2008 election cycle, FIRE lobbyists made 51 percent of their contributions to Democrats and 48 percent to Republicans. By 2012, Democrats received only 32 percent to the Republicans' 67 percent. Given the partisan squabbling over funding for the agencies included under the bill, since 2009, the House had only passed one stand-alone Financial Services and General Government appropriations bill, and the Senate had not passed any since that time.

The House managed in 2016 to pass a stand-alone bill (HR 5485); however, it included so many policy riders that targeted President Obama's legacy legislation, such as Dodd-Frank and the Patient Protection and Affordable Care Act (ACA), that the president threatened to veto the bill if it made it to his desk. The Senate Appropriations Committee passed a cleaner version that did not include as many of the policy riders, and it actually maintained funding levels for many covered agencies where the House had sought drastic cuts. That bill never saw a floor vote. The House and Senate never came to a consensus on the bill, nor on an omnibus package that would include financial services, and were forced to pass a continuing resolution in December to keep the government funded through April 28, 2017, and prevent a shutdown. That bill maintained funding at 2016 levels for federal agencies.

House Action

The House Financial Services Appropriations Subcommittee adopted its version of a Financial Services and General Government appropriations bill by voice vote on May 25, 2016. The bill targeted for cuts and new regulations the Consumer Financial Protection Bureau (CFPB), Securities and Exchange Commission (SEC), and the General Services Administration (GSA). The largest budget cut singled out the Internal Revenue Service (IRS). Subcommittee Chair Ander Crenshaw, R-Fla., said the cut was brought on by a recent history of inappropriate behavior tied to the 2013 discovery that the IRS had targeted for additional regulatory scrutiny conservative groups applying for tax-exempt status. Democrats on the subcommittee worried that the significant decrease in funding for the IRS, coupled with a slew of policy riders, would make compromise between the two parties—and ultimately between the two houses of Congress—nearly impossible.

When the House Appropriations Committee took up the bill, it added even more policy riders. Its $21.7 billion funding package was passed on June 9, by a vote of 30–17. The president threatened to veto the measure if it made it to his desk, and the committee's ranking member, Rep. Nita M. Lowey, D-N.Y., said that the amendments approved by Republicans could jeopardize the success of the overall appropriations process. Republicans, however, argued that their bill, which cut $1.5 billion in spending from the fiscal 2016 enacted level, prioritized spending on agencies that provide critical services to Americans while reining in the spending of agencies that have underperformed expectations.

There were several party-line votes on policy riders. Amendments supported by Republicans included a denial of funding to CFPB to implement its proposed payday lending rule, shielding churches from losing tax-exempt status for political activities unless the IRS believed the church intervened in a political campaign, reversing a change made by Dodd-Frank in the Truth in Lending Act related to manufactured homes, denying funding to implement Executive Order 13673 that sought to protect employees from wage theft and unsafe working conditions, barring the IRS from changing the standards it uses to review tax-exemption applications, and halting a rule to stop payday lenders from lending to borrowers who cannot repay. As it had in past years, the bill also brought the CFPB and Office of Financial Research into the regular appropriations process.

When the full House took up the financial services appropriation, they considered additional amendments, adding those that would bar the SEC from implementing rules on executive compensation and conflict minerals—raw materials sourced from areas of the world where an ongoing conflict impacts their mining and trading; barring the Financial Stability Oversight Council from adding any large financial institutions to its "too big to fail" list; preventing CFPB from enforcing guidance on indirect auto lending; and prohibiting the use of funds to change the Selective Service System registration requirements by delaying until 2017 a requirement for women to register. The House rejected two proposed amendments, one that would eliminate the IRS commissioner's salary and another that would make a 1 percent spending cut to all agencies covered by the bill. The final House measure, passed on July 7, 2016, 239–185, reduced the overall financial services budget by 6.5 percent below the enacted fiscal 2016 level. It brought the IRS budget to $11 billion, its lowest funding level since 2008, although $290 million was allocated specifically for consumer services

after complaints surfaced that due to staffing cuts, phone wait times had risen above twenty minutes. The final bill also cut the Federal Communications Commission (FCC) budget by $69 million to $315 million, prevented the enactment of net neutrality regulations until all court cases involving the issue were resolved, and reduced the SEC budget by $50 million to $1.56 billion. In total, twelve agencies received funding cuts.

Senate Action

The Senate Financial Services Appropriations Subcommittee passed a $22.6 billion fiscal 2017 bill that included few of the policy riders attached to the House version. Democrats praised Republicans for their restraint and for the funding levels that had been maintained. The riders that were included primarily impacted the IRS, including a ban on the use of funds to target groups for additional regulatory scrutiny based on ideology. Another rider required the FCC to complete an impact study of its set-top box proposal, and another prohibited the use of funds for painting portraits of federal employees, including the president. Republicans said that the policies included in the bill were intended to focus the financial services agencies on their most critical duties rather than on politically charged ancillary work.

The Senate Appropriations Committee approved a $22.4 billion measure, $842 million lower than fiscal 2016. Unlike the House version, it held IRS funding at the enacted 2016 level of $11.2 billion and also left the SEC budget intact at $1.61 billion. The Senate proposed a smaller reduction of the FCC budget of only 11 percent, as opposed to the House-proposed 18 percent. Amendments adopted by the committee included defunding any effort to keep financial institutions from providing financial services to those involved in the business of making and selling marijuana where the drug is legal. And, as it had in its fiscal 2016 bill, the Senate Appropriations Committee also included language on Cuba, lifting the travel ban to the country, allowing U.S. banks to extend credit to Cuban buyers of U.S. agricultural products, and allowing aircraft to refuel in the United States and obtain other airport services on flights to and from Cuba. Rejected amendments included two related to the FCC budget, with Democrats arguing that reduced funding for the agency would lead to a hiring freeze and furloughs and would prevent the FCC from meeting its moving costs and making necessary technology upgrades. The Senate committee also rejected an amendment that would bar the SEC from adopting a rule requiring that corporations disclose their political contributions, similar to an amendment it had adopted in fiscal 2016. The Senate version passed out of committee on June 16, 2016.

CHAPTER 15

Inside Congress

Inside Congress

Partisanship reached extraordinary levels during President Barack Obama's second term, making it increasingly difficult to find majorities even for high-priority appropriations bills and thwarting Senate action on presidential nominees. The polarization prompted a highly contentious decision by Senate Democrats in 2013 to hasten the confirmation of judges and other administration nominees by limiting filibusters. In addition to partisan battles, ideological divisions widened among Republicans: a weakened House Speaker John A. Boehner of Ohio resigned midterm in 2015, while the man once seen as his likely successor, Eric Cantor of Virginia, was knocked out of office by a little-known primary challenger. In contrast, House minority leader Nancy Pelosi of California retained a firm grip on her caucus, as did Senate Democratic leader Harry Reid of Nevada and Senate Republican leader Mitch McConnell of Kentucky. McConnell gained new power after Republicans captured control of the Senate in the 2014 elections, enabling him to block Obama's pick to fill an empty Supreme Court seat.

The increasingly rancorous atmosphere in Congress stymied efforts to pass gun control legislation despite deadly mass shootings. It also sank proposals to overhaul immigration policy, although senior officials in both parties favored action on illegal immigration. Lawmakers, however, cleared several significant measures, including funding recovery efforts after Superstorm Sandy, a five-year highway bill, and a five-year farm bill. They also agreed to keep their salaries frozen as a way of highlighting their concern for fiscal austerity.

INCREASED POLARIZATION

In the 113th Congress, the majorities of the two parties in the House and Senate differed with each other on 7 out of every 10 roll-call votes. It was the first time in more than six decades of analysis of voting patterns by *Congressional Quarterly* that the percentage of partisan votes was so high in both chambers. In a corollary pattern, the majority party in each chamber—Republicans in the House and Democrats in the Senate—set records in 2013 by voting as a bloc on measures that divided the parties. Edward G. Carmines, the research director of the Center on Congress at Indiana University, said the productivity reached a historic low for the previous half-century, whether measured in the number of bills enacted, the substance of what got done, or the important issues that never got hearings.

Partisanship remained high in the 114th Congress as focus began turning to the upcoming presidential election. In the House, a majority of Republicans confronted a majority of Democrats 75.1 percent of the time in 2015 and 75.7 percent in 2016. That just missed the record mark of 75.8 percent in 2011, the highest since *Congressional Quarterly* began studying votes in 1953. In the Senate, which has a far more bipartisan tradition, majorities squared off 69.3 percent of the time in 2015 for the fourth-highest mark on record.

The antagonism between a Republican House and a Democratic Senate during the 113th Congress prevented consensus on spending bills, leading to a sixteen-day government shutdown in October 2013. Even after reopening, it took until mid-January 2014 for Congress to approve an

REFERENCES

Discussion of congressional action for the years 1945–1964 may be found in *Congress and the Nation Vol. I*, pp. 1407–1431; for the years 1965–1968, *Congress and the Nation Vol. II*, pp. 893–924; for the years 1969–1972, *Congress and the Nation Vol. III*, pp. 353–433; for the years 1973–1976, *Congress and the Nation Vol. IV*, pp. 743–794; for the years 1977–1980, *Congress and the Nation Vol. V*, pp. 873–953; for the years 1981–1984, *Congress and the Nation Vol. VI*, pp. 797–840; for the years 1985–1988, *Congress and the Nation Vol. VII*, pp. 871–910; for the years 1989–1992, *Congress and the Nation Vol. VIII*, pp. 913–988; for the years 1993–1996, *Congress and the Nation Vol. IX*, pp. 861–925; for the years 1997–2001, *Congress and the Nation Vol. X*, pp. 757–794; for the years 2001–2004, *Congress and the Nation Vol. XI*, pp. 705–742; for the years 2005–2008, *Congress and the Nation Vol. XII*, pp. 809–850; for the years 2009–2012, *Congress and the Nation Vol. XIII*, pp. 639–685.

omnibus appropriations bill for the rest of the fiscal year. Lawmakers found themselves deadlocked again during 2014, unable to complete any individual appropriations bills and shoveling annual spending instead into a midwinter omnibus that finally reached the president nine days before Christmas. The regular appropriations process broke down again in the summer of 2015 when Senate Democrats vowed to block consideration of any spending bills that adhered to discretionary spending limits set in 2011. Congress approved a series of short-term spending extensions before completing work December 18 with a deal that raised discretionary spending caps evenly between defense and nondefense accounts while lifting the debt limit through early 2017. In 2016, despite commitments of Republican leaders to pass all twelve appropriations bills under "regular order," none was approved. A continuing resolution kept the government operating through March 2017 so the next Congress could resolve spending disputes.

The usually bipartisan annual spending bill for the legislative branch also got caught up in the fray. Lawmakers each year added it to the other spending measures in the annual omnibus appropriations bills. The legislative spending measure set off relatively few sparks during the 113th Congress, but Democrats in the 114th Congress objected to language instructing the Library of Congress to continue use of the term *illegal alien* for undocumented immigrants and to continue tight funding levels.

WEAKENED FILIBUSTER

Senators of whichever party held the White House had complained for years that the other side dragged its feet in confirming nominees. Republicans in 2005 even threatened to change the rules in a way that would weaken filibusters of confirmation votes. By 2013, Senate Democrats became so frustrated with GOP tactics to block some of Obama's executive-branch and judicial nominees that they made the fateful decision to limit debate on nominees other than for the Supreme Court. The highly contentious rules change, which infuriated Republicans, opened the door to confirmation of numerous nominees whom conservatives had previously blocked.

Reid was able to change the filibuster by turning to an arcane parliamentary maneuver that had become known as the "nuclear option." The result meant that fifty-one senators could vote to limit debate rather than the sixty-vote threshold that had been required since filibuster rules had last been changed in 1975. Lawmakers would still need sixty votes to invoke cloture, or cut off debate, on most pieces of legislation. Fully aware that their own hand would be weakened once Republicans regained the majority, Democrats made the change with great reluctance, and several of them voted against it. Republicans, for their part, tried twice unsuccessfully to reverse the new precedent. After that, they often declined to yield back postcloture debate time on legislation or nominations, slowing the pace of action. But they did not go nuclear in response by employing every opportunity to obstruct the Senate, as some had predicted.

Some traditionalists worried that the change would further undermine the Senate's traditional bipartisan approach to policy. Although most senators continued to support the right to filibuster other measures, it remained uncertain whether filibusters of Supreme Court nominees or most pieces of legislation might someday be eroded as well. Such a change would mean the upper chamber would more closely resemble the House, where the minority party has little leverage to prevent the majority from ramming through even highly controversial pieces of legislation.

NEW CONGRESSIONAL LEADERSHIP

House leadership got a rare midyear shakeup in 2014 when Eric Cantor, R-Va., became the first majority leader in history to lose a primary. Dave Brat, an economics professor and tea party favorite, slammed Cantor over immigration policy while taking an anti-government approach to policy. After his defeat in the June primary, Cantor resigned August 18, allowing a special election for Brat to gain extra seniority during the lame-duck session. Cantor's exit elevated Kevin McCarthy of California to majority leader and opened the door to Steve Scalise of Louisiana to become majority whip.

The divisions roiling House Republicans over national strategy and legislative tactics continued the following year, highlighted by the creation of a new, highly conservative faction called the House Freedom Caucus. This faction, associated with the tea party, could prevent Republicans from mustering a majority to pass legislation on the floor. On the other flank of the Republican Party, a group of moderates known as the Tuesday Group often objected to highly conservative legislation, although they tended to be more compromising than the Freedom Caucus. The intractable splits among Republicans left Boehner sometimes needing votes from Democrats to pass legislation. Increasingly frustrated, Boehner resigned in October 2015. He was succeeded by Ways and Means Chair Paul D. Ryan, R-Wis., the one House member who appeared to be able to bring together the disparate wings of his party, at least to some degree.

The Senate flipped decisively from Democratic to Republican majority in the 2014 election after eight years of Democratic control. Democrats had held fifty-three seats, plus two independents who caucused with them, during the 113th Congress. But Republicans picked up nine seats, giving them a solid 54–46 majority. Now that McConnell was majority leader, he could block Obama nominations regardless of filibuster rules. This would prove to have historical consequences when McConnell refused to take up Obama's nomination of Merrick Garland to a vacancy on the Supreme Court in March 2016, saying that voters should essentially decide on Election Day by casting their ballots for a Republican or Democrat. The election of

Donald Trump ensured that conservatives would be able to fill the vacancy.

MAJOR LEGISLATION

The Senate mounted a significant debate in 2013 over gun control after the shooting deaths of twenty-six people at a Connecticut school in December but was unable to reach agreement. The Senate fared slightly better on an immigration overhaul, sending the House a comprehensive package of legislation, which the House ignored. Congress approved a five-year renewal of the Violence Against Women Act and overhauled the system for federally backed student loans.

Congress cleared a five-year farm bill in 2014, more than a year after the previous law expired, with significant changes in how farmers were paid when crops did not meet specified targets. In February 2014, Congress extended the debt limit to $17.3 trillion, which was projected to last until March 2015, rather than fight another budget battle months after a shutdown. Republicans opposed in near unanimity the Dodd-Frank financial overhaul that won some long-sought changes as part of an omnibus spending bill. The Terrorism Risk Insurance Act, which was approved in 2002 to stabilize the insurance market after the 9/11 attacks, was extended the first week of 2015 after an unrelated fight involving the retiring Sen. Tom Coburn, R-Okla.

In foreign affairs, a coalition of Republicans joined a small band of protrade Democrats to deliver the Obama administration a rare bipartisan victory in June 2015 by granting fast-track authority for trade agreements called Trade Promotion Authority. The Senate voted three times in September 2015 to block President Barack Obama's agreement with Iran to disable the country's nuclear program in exchange for the removal of sanctions. Each time, the result was the same: Republicans failed to persuade enough Democrats to cut off debate. The Obama administration announced November 6, 2015, that it had rejected the proposed Keystone XL pipeline from Canada. Congressional Republicans tried to force the administration to approve the project but couldn't override Obama's veto. The only time Congress voted to override Obama's veto was September 28, 2016, to approve a law (S 2040) that allowed U.S. citizens to sue foreign nations for state sponsorship of terrorism.

Domestically, the latest highway bill received rare bipartisan support to close out 2015, when Congress approved a five-year, $305 billion authorization for road and transit programs. Senate Democrats were unable to obtain majority support for restrictions on gun sales, as a few Democrats joined most Republicans in opposing tighter standards, despite the shooting deaths of forty-nine patrons at an Orlando nightclub. Congress agreed to spend $1.1 billion in response to the Zika virus, an infection spread primarily by mosquitoes that spread north from South America and reached Florida and other states in 2015. And Congress threw a lifeline to storm-ravaged Puerto Rico by clearing a bill to rescue the U.S. territory from $72 billion debt just days before an anticipated default.

Chronology of Action on Congress: Members and Procedures

2013–2014

The 113th Congress opened with a vacancy in the Illinois delegation, after Jesse L. Jackson Jr. resigned in November 2012—two weeks after winning a ninth term. He was under investigation for misuse of campaign funds and pleaded guilty to fraud charges in February 2013. He was succeeded by Democrat Robin Kelly in a special election April 9, 2013. Rep. Trey Radel, R-Fla., resigned in January 2014, halfway through his first term, after he was charged with cocaine possession in Washington, D.C. He was succeeded by Republican Curt Clawson in a June special election. Rep. Robert E. Andrews, D-N.J., resigned in February 2014 while under investigation by the Ethics Committee for using campaign money for a family trip to Scotland. He was succeeded by Democrat Donald Norcross, who declared his candidacy the same day Andrews announced he was leaving.

Organization: 113th Congress

The 113th Congress convened at noon January 3, 2013. No major changes were made in the leadership of either chamber because Republicans maintained control of the House and Democrats kept the Senate.

Senate leadership for both parties remained relatively stable for the 113th Congress, other than routine changes atop campaign committees.

SENATE

Majority Leadership

Senate Democrats reelected Majority Leader Harry Reid of Nevada, Majority Whip Richard J. Durbin of Illinois, Caucus Vice Chair Charles E. Schumer of New York, Caucus Secretary Patty Murray of Washington, and Policy Committee Chair Charles E. Schumer of New York.

Michael Bennet of Colorado succeeded Patty Murray of Washington as chair of the Democratic Senatorial Campaign Committee. Patrick J. Leahy, D-Vt., began the Congress as the longest-serving member of the majority party, with the title President Pro Tempore, after the death of Daniel Inouye of Hawaii on December 17, 2012.

Minority Leadership

On November 14, 2012, Republicans reelected Minority Leader Mitch McConnell of Kentucky, Minority Whip John Cornyn of Texas, and Conference Chair John Thune of South Dakota. Jerry Moran of Kansas ran unopposed to succeed John Cornyn of Texas as chair of the National Republican Senatorial Committee. John Barrasso of Wyoming was reelected chair of the Policy Committee.

Committees

Democrats retained control of the Senate, but death and retirements led to changes atop the Appropriations, Budget, Energy and Natural Resources, Foreign Relations, Homeland Security and Government Affairs, Indian Affairs, Special Aging, and Veterans' Affairs committees.

Retaining their chairs were Debbie Stabenow of Michigan at Agriculture; Carl Levin of Michigan at Armed Services; Tim Johnson of South Dakota at Banking, Housing, and Urban Affairs; Jay Rockefeller of West Virginia at Commerce, Science, and Transportation; Barbara Boxer of California at Environment and Public Works; Max Baucus of Montana at Finance; Tom Harkin of Iowa at Health, Education, Labor, and Pensions; Patrick J. Leahy of Vermont at Judiciary; Charles E. Schumer of New York at Rules; Boxer at Select Ethics; Dianne Feinstein of California at Select Intelligence; Mary L. Landrieu of Louisiana at Small Business and Entrepreneurship; and Bob Casey of Pennsylvania at Joint Economic.

Barbara A. Mikulski of Maryland became chair of the Appropriations Committee after the death of Daniel K. Inouye of Hawaii on December 17, 2012. Patty Murray of Washington became chair of the Budget Committee after the retirement of Kent Conrad of North Dakota. Ron Wyden of Oregon became chair of the Energy and Natural Resources Committee after the retirement of Jeff Bingaman of New

Mexico. Robert Menendez of New Jersey became chair of the Foreign Relations Committee after the departure of John Kerry of Massachusetts to become secretary of State.

Thomas R. Carper of Delaware became chair of the Homeland Security and Government Affairs Committee after the retirement of Joseph I. Lieberman of Connecticut, an independent who caucused with Democrats. The change marked the first time since the creation of the Department of Homeland Security in the aftermath of the terrorist hijackings September 11, 2001, that neither Lieberman nor Republican Susan Collins of Maine was heading the panel.

Maria Cantwell of Washington became chair of the Indian Affairs Committee after the retirement of Daniel K. Akaka of Hawaii. She was fifth in line for the gavel, but others either retired or took other chairmanships.

Bill Nelson of Florida became chair of Special Aging, succeeding Herb Kohl of Wisconsin. Bernard Sanders of Vermont, an independent who caucused with Democrats, became chair of the Veterans' Affairs Committee after Murray took the Budget gavel. Many Republicans kept their ranking-member status, with six-year term limits forcing musical chairs among a number of committees. Remaining as the top GOP committee members were Jeff Sessions of Alabama at Budget; Orrin G. Hatch of Utah at Finance; John Barrasso of Wyoming at Indian Affairs; Charles E. Grassley of Iowa at Judiciary; Johnny Isakson of Georgia at Ethics; Saxby Chambliss of Georgia at Select Intelligence; Richard Burr of North Carolina at Veterans' Affairs; and Dan Coats of Indiana at Joint Economic.

Thad Cochran of Mississippi became ranking member of Agriculture after surrendering the post at Appropriations because of term limits. Richard C. Shelby of Alabama became ranking member of Appropriations after Cochran moved to Agriculture. James M. Inhofe of Oklahoma became ranking member of Armed Services after John McCain gave up the post because of term limits. Michael D. Crapo of Idaho became ranking member of Banking, Housing, and Urban Affairs after Shelby took the post at Appropriations. John Thune of South Dakota became ranking member of Commerce, Science, and Transportation after the retirement of Kay Bailey Hutchison of Texas.

David Vitter of Louisiana became ranking member of Environment and Public Works after Inhofe moved to Armed Services because of term limits. Bob Corker of Tennessee became ranking member of Foreign Relations after Richard G. Lugar of Indiana was defeated in his Republican primary. Lamar Alexander of Tennessee became ranking member of Health, Education, Labor, and Pensions after Michael B. Enzi of Wyoming gave up the slot because of term limits. Tom Coburn of Oklahoma became ranking member of Homeland Security and Government Affairs after Susan Collins of Maine moved to Special Aging because of term limits. Pat Roberts of Kansas became ranking member of Rules after Alexander moved to HELP. Jim Risch of Idaho became ranking member of Small Business and Entrepreneurship after the retirement

of Olympia J. Snowe of Maine. Susan Collins of Maine became ranking member of Special Aging after Corker moved to Foreign Relations and Hatch stayed at Finance.

HOUSE

Republicans reelected John A. Boehner of Ohio as Speaker on January 3 by a vote of 220–192. At a meeting November 14, 2014, Republicans reelected Eric Cantor of Virginia as majority leader and Kevin McCarthy of California as majority whip.

Cathy McMorris Rodgers of Washington was elected conference chair, succeeding Jeb Hensarling of Texas, by fending off an upstart challenge from Tom Price of Georgia. Lynn Jenkins of Kansas succeeded McMorris Rodgers as conference vice chair by defeating Martha Roby of Alabama.

James Lankford of Oklahoma was unopposed to succeed Price as Republican Policy Committee chair. Greg Walden of Oregon succeeded Pete Sessions of Texas as chair of the National Republican Congressional Committee. After Cantor's primary defeat, Republicans elevated McCarthy to majority leader on July 31, 2014, and Steve Scalise of Louisiana succeeded him as majority whip.

Minority Leadership

Democrats stayed with Nancy Pelosi of California as minority leader, Steny H. Hoyer of Maryland as minority whip, and James E. Clyburn of South Carolina as assistant leader.

Xavier Becerra of California remained caucus chair, Joseph Crowley of New York remained caucus vice chair, and John Lewis of Georgia remained senior chief deputy whip. Ben Ray Lujan of New Mexico succeeded Steve Israel of New York as chair of the Democratic Congressional Campaign Committee.

Committees

Republicans continued to hold the gavels, which saw little turnover from the previous Congress.

Continuing their chairmanships were Frank D. Lucas of Oklahoma at Agriculture; Harold Rogers of Kentucky at Appropriations; Howard "Buck" McKeon of California at Armed Services; Paul D. Ryan of Wisconsin at Budget; John Kline of Minnesota at Education and the Workforce; Fred Upton of Michigan at Energy and Commerce; Doc Hastings of Washington at Natural Resources; Darrell Issa of California at Oversight and Government Reform; Sam Graves of Missouri at Small Business; Jeff Miller of Florida at Veterans' Affairs; Dave Camp of Michigan at Ways and Means; and Mike Rogers of Michigan at Intelligence.

K. Michael Conaway of Texas became chair of Ethics after Jo Bonner of Alabama left the job, which members viewed as thankless. Jeb Hensarling of Texas became chair of Financial Services after Spencer Bachus of Alabama gave up the gavel because of term limits.

Ed Royce of California beat out Christopher H. Smith of New Jersey to become chair of Foreign Affairs after Ileana Ros-Lehtinen of Florida gave up the gavel because of term limits.

Michael McCaul of Texas became chair of Homeland Security after Peter T. King of New York gave up the gavel because of term limits. McCaul won a hotly contested, three-way race in the Republican Steering Committee against Candice S. Miller of Michigan and Mike D. Rogers of Alabama.

Candice S. Miller of Michigan became chair of Administration after the retirement of Dan Lungren of California. The committee eliminated two subcommittees on February 5, one on oversight and the other on elections, with the stated purpose of streamlining operations.

Robert W. Goodlatte of Virginia became chair of Judiciary, which Lamar M. Smith of Texas had to vacate because of term limits. Pete Sessions of Texas became chair of Rules after the retirement of David Dreier of California.

Lamar M. Smith of Texas became chair of Science, Space, and Technology because Ralph Hall of Texas faced term limits. Smith moved after facing his own term limits atop Judiciary. Bill Shuster of Pennsylvania, whose father had chaired Transportation and Infrastructure, became chair of the panel after John L. Mica of Florida gave up the gavel because of term limits.

Minority Leadership

While most ranking members stayed at their posts, Democrats made changes on several committees.

The ranking member carryovers were Collin C. Peterson of Minnesota at Agriculture; Adam Smith of Washington at Armed Services; Chris Van Hollen of Maryland at Budget; George Miller of California at Education and the Workforce; Henry A. Waxman of California at Energy and Commerce; Linda T. Sanchez of California at Ethics; Bennie Thompson of Mississippi at Homeland Security; Robert A. Brady of Pennsylvania at Administration; John Conyers Jr. of Michigan at Judiciary; Edward J. Markey of Massachusetts at Natural Resources; Elijah E. Cummings of Maryland at Oversight and Government Reform; Louise M. Slaughter of New York at Rules; Eddie Bernice Johnson of Texas at Science, Space, and Technology; Nydia M. Velazquez of New York at Small Business; Nick J. Rahall II of West Virginia at Transportation and Infrastructure; Sander M. Levin of Michigan at Ways and Means; and C. A. Dutch Ruppersberger of Maryland at Intelligence.

Nita M. Lowey of New York beat out Marcy Kaptur of Ohio to become ranking member of Appropriations after the retirement of Norm Dicks of Washington. Maxine Waters of California became ranking member of Financial Services after Barney Frank of Massachusetts retired.

Eliot L. Engel of New York became ranking member of Foreign Affairs after Howard L. Berman of California lost his primary to Brad Sherman of California. Peter A. DeFazio of Oregon became ranking member of Natural Resources in June 2013, after Edward J. Markey of Massachusetts won election to the Senate to succeed John F. Kerry. Michael H. Michaud of Maine became ranking member of Veterans' Affairs after Bob Filner of California left to run for mayor of San Diego.

Rules Changes

The House rules package (H Res 5) for the 113th Congress adopted January 3 by a vote of 228–196 included several changes, in addition to extending the rules from the 112th Congress. Among the changes were greater authority for the Speaker and chair of the Committee of the Whole to reduce voting times, an expanded rule against nepotism, and greater latitude for members to use private aircraft.

Other provisions in the package authorized the House to continue its legal efforts to defend the Defense of Marriage Act and to force Attorney General Eric H. Holder to comply with subpoenas related to the Fast and Furious gun-tracking operation. It deactivated provisions of the 2010 health care overhaul that required congressional consideration of recommendations by the Independent Payment Advisory Board and required the annual budget resolution to include details on means-tested and non–means-tested mandatory spending programs.

The package also authorized consideration of legislation the next day, under suspension of the rules, that aimed to boost borrowing authority for the National Flood Insurance Program, in response to the damage done in New Jersey and New York by Superstorm Sandy.

Floor Votes

The resolution modified clause 6 of rule XVIII to authorize the chair of the Committee of the Whole to reduce from five minutes to no less than two minutes the time for votes in a series of votes that occur immediately after a quorum call—similar to the Speaker's authority in the House to shorten such votes following a quorum call. A quorum of the House is 218 members when all 435 seats are filled, and a quorum call is when a series of bells is rung in the Capitol and House office buildings to summon lawmakers to the chamber. The resolution allowed the chair to shorten votes to two minutes for postponed votes on amendments after the Committee of the Whole had temporarily risen for other business—if the chair believed that "Members would be afforded an adequate opportunity to vote." Under the previous rule, votes on postponed amendments could be shortened to two minutes only if the postponed vote immediately followed another electronic vote "without intervening business."

The resolution provided similar authority in Rule XX, clause 8(c) for the Speaker to shorten votes to two minutes in the House following a report from the Committee of the Whole, as long as the Speaker believed members would be afforded an adequate opportunity to vote. The provision modified Rule XX, clause 9 to authorize the Speaker to shorten to five minutes any initial vote held in the House immediately after the Committee of the Whole had risen, as well as for a motion to instruct.

The measure also modified clause 12(a)(2) of Rule XXII to eliminate the requirement that a recorded vote be held on any motion to close a House-Senate conference committee, thereby allowing a conference to be closed by voice vote.

Committee-Related Rules. The resolution reduced the frequency with which committees must submit committee activity reports from four times a Congress (every six months) to just two times per Congress (once per year)—with those reports to be submitted by January 2 of each following year. Those reports outline the legislative and oversight actions taken by the committees during the Congress and are required by clause 1 of Rule XI.

The measure modified Rule X, clause 1(j) regarding the jurisdiction of the Homeland Security Committee, to include "general management" of the department as well as organization and administration. The measure modified Rule XI, clause 2(l) to clarify that if one member of a committee notices his or her intent to file supplemental, minority, or additional "views" to a committee report on legislation reported by the committee, then all the committee members would be allowed to file views. The measure modified Rule XIII clause 3(e)(1)(B) to allow additional statutory text to be displayed in the "Ramseyer" portion of a committee report if "useful to enable the intent and effect of the amendment to be clearly understood." The measure also modified Rule XV, clause 2 to clarify that floor motions to discharge committees of legislation, which are in order on the second and fourth Mondays of each month, apply to all House committees and not just standing committees.

The resolution made several changes to the House's Code of Conduct and authorities of the House Ethics Committee. The measure expanded Rule XXIII, clause 8(c) against nepotism by expanding the ban on hiring spouses for pay to include committees on which the member sits. The measure also expanded the prohibition against hiring spouses to ban any "relative" out to first cousins and down to grandchildren.

The measure modified restrictions included in Rule XXIII, clause 13 regarding the use of private aircraft by members, which were established to prevent conflicts under which members could accept favors from lobbyists. The goal was for the rules to generally conform with the Senate, with waivers for extraordinary circumstances such as the aftermath of a natural disaster. In addition to the current exception for flying on aircraft owned by family members or personal friends, the resolution added exceptions for aircraft owned by other members of Congress and allowed members to take charter flights as long as they paid a share of the fair market value of the flight. The chair and ranking member of the Ethics Committee could jointly issue a waiver of aircraft restrictions.

The measure allowed the chair and ranking member of the Ethics Committee to jointly extend the time allotted for consideration of recommendations from the Office of Congressional Ethics to dismiss a possible case. The measure also extended the authority of the office and directed the committee to empanel investigative subcommittees within thirty days of a member's indictment.

Ethics Investigations

REP. JESSE JACKSON

Rep. Jesse L. Jackson Jr., D-Ill., pleaded guilty in February 2013 to fraud charges relating to misuse of campaign funds and was sentenced in August to thirty months in prison. Jackson had resigned in November 2012, just weeks after winning a ninth term. He had missed several months of work while being treated for bipolar disorder, but his arrest and imprisonment derailed a once-meteoric rise in politics. Jackson had been seen as a potential U.S. senator or Chicago mayor. Jackson was succeeded by Democrat Robin Kelly in a special election April 9, 2013.

REP. TREY RADEL

Rep. Trey Radel, R-Fla., was arrested in October 2013 by D.C. police for allegedly buying cocaine. Radel was having dinner with an acquaintance and an undercover police officer, who offered to sell him 3.5 grams of cocaine. Radel was arrested outside the restaurant when he bought the cocaine from the officer. He kept the arrest confidential until just before his arraignment. Radel, a former radio host and television anchor, initially refused to step down, invoking a history of alcohol addiction and taking a leave of absence for treatment. But he pleaded guilty November 20 to a misdemeanor and was sentenced to one year of probation. He stated that he was disappointed in himself and prepared to face the consequences of his actions. The Ethics Committee established an investigative subcommittee in December, but the case ended with his resignation on January 27, 2014, midway through his first term. He was succeeded by Republican Curt Clawson, a wealthy retired businessman, who won a June 24 special election for the Fort Myers–area seat.

ROBERT ANDREWS

Rep. Robert E. Andrews, D-N.J., resigned February 18, 2014, while under investigation by the Ethics Committee for using campaign money for a family trip to Scotland. The investigation began in April 2012 when the Office of Congressional Ethics recommended the committee investigate the allegations. The committee voted unanimously in February 2013 to empanel a subcommittee to investigate whether Andrews had improperly used funds from his campaign committee and PAC for personal purposes or made false statements to federal officials. The committee ended its investigation with Andrews's resignation. He was succeeded by Democrat Donald Norcross, an electrician, who won the November 4 special election.

Weakening the Filibuster

By far the most momentous change to Senate rules in the 113th Congress occurred when Democrats forced through a measure in November 2013 to make it easier for the president to obtain an up-or-down vote on nominees to judgeships and executive-branch offices. Over strenuous

Republican objections, they voted to enable a simple Senate majority to end filibusters of nominees, erasing the previous requirement that a three-fifths majority would be necessary. However, they retained the rule requiring a three-fifths majority to end filibusters of most pieces of legislation.

The change came eight years after Senate Republicans threatened—but in the end did not pursue—a rules change to allow a simple majority to end filibusters of judicial nominees. The decision by Democratic leaders to invoke what had long been known as the "nuclear option" came at the end of a year in which they were repeatedly frustrated by Republican roadblocks to confirmation votes on Obama's nominees to Cabinet positions, regulatory agencies, and courts.

Democrats were especially rankled by filibusters of Obama's nominees to the National Labor Relations Board (which had been a target of GOP obstruction for several years), the Labor Department, the Consumer Financial Protection Board (which was created by the 2010 Dodd-Frank law and which the GOP wanted to change significantly), the Federal Housing Finance Agency, the EPA, and the Court of Appeals for the District of Columbia Circuit (which had several vacancies and was considered second only to the Supreme Court in importance). Republicans also mounted filibusters against former Sen. Chuck Hagel, a Nebraska Republican, to be secretary of Defense, and John O. Brennan, a career CIA officer who served in the White House under President George W. Bush, to be director of Central Intelligence.

As the year began, Senate Majority Leader Harry Reid, D-Nev., was already threatening to use the nuclear option—a procedural move that drew upon an interpretation of the Constitution that a simple majority of the chamber was entitled to pass judgment on its rules. Under Rule XXII of the standing rules of the Senate, a majority of sixty senators (three-fifths of the sworn membership) was needed to invoke cloture to end any filibuster and move to a vote on the pending business, including confirmations. A two-thirds majority of those voting (sixty-seven, if all senators participated) was required to end a filibuster of a formal change in the standing rules.

The idea of the nuclear option was that the rules could be reinterpreted by a simple majority. However, that brought with it the political danger that the minority might retaliate with an escalation of procedural delays and obstructions to the majority's agenda and the electoral reality that the party invoking such an interpretation of the rules might one day find itself in the minority.

Judicial nominees who could be characterized as overly ideological had long been the target of attacks from both parties because the Constitution provided most judges with lifetime appointments. Chafing under Democratic filibusters of several of Bush's judicial nominees, Senate Republicans openly considered using the nuclear option in 2005, but they rejected the idea. At the time, it was unclear that a sufficient number of GOP senators were willing to take the political risk.

Some experts warned that using the nuclear option would have long-term consequences. Robert B. Dove, a professor at George Washington University and former Senate parliamentarian under the Republicans, said that the filibuster was an important tool for forcing compromise, and weakening it would risk putting the chamber on a slippery slope to greater dysfunction. Dove said in the heat of the filibuster debate in 2013 that if the maneuver happened repeatedly, the Senate would become a majoritarian—and partisan—institution like the House. Increasing acrimony between Democrats and Republicans during the Obama presidency—and particularly following his reelection in November 2012—appeared to override concerns by most Senate Democrats about changing the Senate's filibuster rule.

Weakening Minority Rights

Prior to 2013, the Senate had not made a substantive change in minority rights since 1975. That year, in the midst of other changes to congressional procedure that followed from the election of the so-called Watergate class in 1974, the Senate forced a formal change in Rule XXII, the cloture rule, to limit the number of senators required to invoke cloture and cut off debate in the chamber. Whereas the rule previously required a two-thirds majority to invoke cloture; the chamber after a contentious debate approved a change that three-fifths of sworn membership (usually sixty) would need to support cloture for debate to be ended. The two-thirds majority was retained for cutting off debate on proposals to change the rules themselves.

In 2003 and 2004, the Democratic minority used filibusters to block Bush's efforts to alter the ideological cast of the federal courts, halting confirmation of ten of Bush's appellate court nominees and threatening to filibuster several others. At the beginning of the 109th Congress in 2005, Majority Leader Bill Frist, R-Tenn., warned that he would not hesitate to employ what was by then known as the nuclear option if Democrats persisted. In February, Bush renominated seven of ten previously filibustered candidates, along with several others whom Democrats had threatened to block.

For several months, lawmakers seemed headed toward a climactic confrontation, but in May, seven Republicans and seven Democrats—who became known as the Gang of 14—seized control of the process, striking a deal on judicial nominees that averted the showdown. The seven Democrats in the group agreed to vote to invoke cloture on three previously filibustered nominations but made no specific commitments on four others. The Democrats also agreed that judicial nominees should be filibustered only under "extraordinary circumstances," though the definition of that term was left to each senator to decide. In return, the seven Republicans agreed to oppose any change in Senate rules or procedures that would eliminate filibusters of judicial nominees—unless Democrats mounted a filibuster in what Republicans considered less than "extraordinary circumstances." The pact, however fragile, was never put to the test because no one tried to force another filibuster of an appellate court nominee before Democrats won a Senate majority in the 2006 elections.

After Obama won the election in 2008, two newly elected Democratic senators—Jeff Merkley of Oregon and Tom Udall of New Mexico—began agitating for changes in the filibuster rule. Among their proposals was to require "talking" filibusters, in which senators would actually have to hold the floor in debate to prevent moving on to votes, rather than the majority leader being forced to shelve legislation if sixty votes were not available for cloture.

Democratic leaders resisted the Merkley and Udall proposals, instead bringing two small rules changes to the floor at the outset of the 113th Congress. Both were adopted January 24, as the first Senate business of the new Congress.

The temporary change (S Res 15), which was in force only for the 113th Congress, allowed Reid to avoid a filibuster on motions to proceed on bills so long as he guaranteed votes on two Republican and two Democratic amendments to the legislation. Debate on motions to proceed, under those circumstances, was limited to four hours. It also allowed for expedited votes on some nominations after cloture was invoked. Postcloture debate was limited to eight hours on many nominations, excluding the nominations of Cabinet members, circuit court judges, and Supreme Court justices. Post-cloture debate on district court judge nominations was limited to two hours. The Senate adopted the temporary rules change on a 78–16 vote, with 15 Republicans and Vermont independent Bernard Sanders voting against it.

A second, permanent change to Rule XXII and to Rule XXVIII, which governed conference committees, was designed to expedite some Senate floor proceedings. That rule change (S Res 16) was adopted 86–9, with Sanders and eight Republicans voting against it.

The permanent change permitted next-day consideration of a cloture petition if it was signed by the majority leader, the minority leader, and seven other senators from each side. Previously, the rules required an intervening day between a cloture motion and the vote. Also, if cloture was invoked, senators could then vote immediately on the motion to proceed, eliminating the thirty hours of debate time typically required postcloture. However, sixty votes were still required to invoke cloture.

The rule change also reduced the time needed to consider a conference committee report by requiring only one motion instead of the three under previous rules. Debate time on conference report motions was limited to two hours.

In a colloquy inserted into the *Congressional Record* the day the Senate approved the changes, Reid promised that any other rules changes would be considered under regular order requiring a two-thirds vote for adoption, and Minority Leader Mitch McConnell, R-Ky., promised to allow nominations to move consistent with the norms and traditions of the Senate.

MOUNTING FRUSTRATION

The rule changes, however, could not mollify many Democrats at a time of paralyzing partisanship. Some congressional scholars said the Senate had never been more polarized, dysfunctional, and prone to petty differences.

Filibusters had become so routine that the chamber could hardly do any business unless sixty senators were willing to go along. In 2012, for example, some 45 percent of all recorded votes required at least sixty "yeas" to succeed. This meant that almost half of all votes that year were decided by a supermajority of the chamber.

By midsummer, battles over a succession of nominees led Reid to complain that Republicans had not lived up to the earlier agreement to move nominations along and that fifteen executive-branch nominees had been waiting about 260 days for confirmation votes. Reid said he would not wait another month or another year for Congress to take action that had been happening for nearly 240 years. For his part, McConnell for several weeks went to the Senate floor each morning to call on Reid to keep his word about not changing the rules.

In the deteriorating climate, and following a meeting of the Democratic caucus over how to proceed, Reid on July 11 filed cloture motions on nominations that Republicans had opposed: three Democratic nominees for the National Labor Relations Board (NLRB), Richard Cordray to continue as director of the Consumer Financial Protection Bureau (FPB), Thomas E. Perez to head the Department of Labor, Gina McCarthy to head the EPA, and Fred P. Hochberg to be president of the Export-Import Bank. The NLRB nominees and Cordray had been given contested recess appointments by Obama in 2012, and the Supreme Court in May had agreed to consider an appeals court ruling that the NLRB appointments were invalid, which also had bearing for Cordray's service.

In complaining that Republicans were not living up to their promise, Democrats also cited the nomination of Hagel for Defense, which had been initially blocked in February, and a filibuster of Caitlin J. Halligan of New York to be a judge on the D.C. Circuit Court of Appeals that had forced her name to be withdrawn. But the rules-change threat was defused in July by another deal struck behind closed doors, with significant help from John McCain, R-Ariz. In an extraordinary meeting, all senators met in the Old Senate Chamber to discuss the issue and air their differences. That resulted in a bipartisan deal announced July 16 under which a sufficient number of Republicans voted to advance to a confirmation vote eight contested nominees—three NLRB Democrats, Cordray, Hochberg, McCarthy, Perez, and B. Todd Jones for the Bureau of Alcohol, Tobacco, Firearms, and Explosives.

Reid praised his longtime antagonist from Arizona for helping to broker the compromise and said both sides would benefit from it. The rules change threat was shelved for a few more months.

PULLING THE TRIGGER

It was only a matter of time before Republican unwillingness to let nominations advance again caused tensions to flare. In June, Obama had nominated Patricia Ann Millett, Cornelia "Nina" Pillard, and Robert Wilkins to vacancies on the D.C. Circuit, which Republicans did not want to fill. GOP senators also continued to block the nomination of Rep. Melvin Watt, a North Carolina Democrat, to head the Federal Housing Finance Agency, which regulated the mortgage giants Fannie Mae and Freddie Mac. GOP objections to Watt centered on their view that he would promote the administration's affordable housing agenda rather than wind down operations of the two finance companies that had been caught in the 2008 financial crisis and put under government conservatorship.

These filibusters resulted in four rejected cloture motions in late October and early November, even though there were sufficient "yea" votes to confirm the nominees. At that point, Democratic frustration peaked.

Reid acted on November 21, when he moved to reconsider the vote by which cloture failed on Millett's nomination to the D.C. Circuit. When the presiding officer ruled that sixty votes were required to invoke cloture and end debate, Reid appealed the ruling of the chair, which was put to a vote of the membership.

Fifty-one other Democrats voted with Reid, and the ruling of the chair was rejected, 48–52. The chair then held that a majority vote was all that was required to invoke cloture on nominations, except those for the Supreme Court (a condition stipulated by Reid). The Senate voted 52–48 to sustain the second ruling of the chair, and the reinterpretation of the rules was established. Voting against the rules interpretation were all forty-five Republicans and three Democrats—Levin, Joe Manchin III of West Virginia, and Mark Pryor of Arkansas.

Cloture was immediately invoked on Millett's nomination, just before the Senate left for its Thanksgiving recess. Reid moved on December 10 to confirm Millett and then to confirm Watt for the FHFA. McConnell tried again that day to reverse the rules interpretation, but Democrats held together, with the same three exceptions. Once again, the chair's ruling that a simple majority was all that was required to invoke cloture on most nominations was sustained, 52–48.

That opened the floodgates, and sixteen executive-branch and judicial nominees were confirmed before year's end. Two more nominees who had been held up were confirmed in the first days of January 2014.

Special Elections

2013

Tim Scott

South Carolina Gov. Nikki Haley appointed Rep. Tim Scott in January 2013 to succeed Sen. Jim DeMint, who resigned to run the Heritage Foundation. Scott, the first African American Republican to represent South Carolina in Congress in a century, is a strong conservative and perhaps the state's brightest Republican star. Scott was unopposed in the Republican primary and then defeated Democrat Joyce Dickerson, a city councilwoman, in the November 2014 special election. Scott then defeated Democrat Thomas Dixon in the 2016 general election for a full term.

Robin Kelly

Democrat Robin Kelly handily defeated Republican Paul McKinley in the April 9 special House election in Illinois. Democratic Rep. Jesse L. Jackson Jr. vacated the seat in November 2012, two weeks after he won a ninth term and before he pleaded guilty to fraud charges for misuse of campaign funds in February 2013. Kelly's real test on Chicago's South Side came in the Democratic primary in February, when rivals included former Rep. Debbie Halvorson. Kelly favored gun control, while Halvorson had an "A" rating from the National Rifle Association in previous elections.

Mark Sanford

Mark Sanford, a Republican former House member and governor of South Carolina, completed a remarkable comeback in winning a May 7 special election to reclaim his old seat when Rep. Tim Scott was appointed to the Senate. Sanford defeated Democrat Elizabeth Colbert Busch, a Clemson University official who was also the sister of political satirist Stephen Colbert. Sanford began the race in the heavily Republican district as the favorite, despite negative reaction to his extramarital affair while he was governor. The affair led to his divorce and public humiliation. During the special-election campaign, news broke that he had trespassed at his ex-wife's home, but Sanford survived a sixteen-person GOP primary on March 19 and then beat Curtis Bostic, a former Charleston County councilman, in an April 2 runoff.

Jason Smith

Republican Jason Smith, a fiscally and socially conservative state legislator, won a June 4 special House election in southeast Missouri by easily defeating Democratic state Rep. Steve Hodges. Smith succeeded Jo Ann Emerson, a Republican who resigned on January 23 to become president of the National Rural Electric Cooperative Association. Smith, a lawyer and farm owner, was endorsed by such well-known GOP conservatives as former Alaska Gov. Sarah Palin, former Arkansas Gov. Mike Huckabee, and former Sen. Rick Santorum of Pennsylvania, as well as by groups including the Tea Party Express and the National Rifle Association.

Edward J. Markey

Edward J. Markey left the House after more than thirty-six years to win a Senate seat in a June 25 special election to succeed John F. Kerry, who resigned February 1 to become secretary of State. Gov. Deval Patrick appointed Democrat William "Mo" Cowan, a political novice who did not seek election, to hold the seat in the interval. When Markey was sworn in, he had more experience in Congress than all but five of his new colleagues. Markey defeated fellow Rep. Stephen F. Lynch in the Democratic primary April 30. Markey then beat Republican Gabriel Gomez, a private-equity investor and former Navy SEAL, in the general election. Markey won reelection to a full term in November 2014 against Republican Brian Herr, a town selectman.

Cory Booker

Newark Mayor Cory Booker, a media-savvy Democrat, won the October 16 special election to succeed Frank R. Lautenberg to represent New Jersey in the Senate. GOP Gov. Chris Christie appointed Republican Jeffrey S. Chiesa, the state's former attorney general, after Lautenberg died June 3 of viral pneumonia. Booker had announced his candidacy before Lautenberg, who was first elected in 1982, fell ill. Booker topped three fellow Democrats in the August 13 primary, including Reps. Frank Pallone Jr. and Rush D. Holt. Booker then defeated Republican activist Steve Lonegan, a legally blind former mayor of a Bergen County borough, in the special election on October 16. Booker later beat Republican Jeff Bell in November 2014 to win reelection to a full term.

Vance McAllister

Vance McAllister, a Republican business owner and self-financed political novice, stunned the Louisiana political establishment by soundly beating the favored candidate in a November 16 special House election. The race decided the successor to Rodney Alexander, who resigned on September 27 to become Gov. Bobby Jindal's secretary of Veterans' Affairs. McAllister parlayed help from the reality show Duck Dynasty, which was filmed in the district, in beating GOP state Sen. Neil Riser by more than 17,000 votes. Riser had been considered a shoo-in, and he captured 32 percent of the vote to McAllister's 18 percent in the October 16 open primary. McAllister grew up in the northeastern corner of the state and joined the Army when he finished high school. He later worked his way up through positions in the oil industry. McAllister, a social conservative who defended gun owners' rights and opposed abortion, did not differentiate his politics much from Riser's during the campaign.

Katherine M. Clark

Democratic state Sen. Katherine M. Clark got two-thirds of the vote against Republican attorney Frank Addivinola in a December 10 special election in Massachusetts to succeed fellow Democrat Edward J. Markey. Markey resigned July 15 after winning his own special election to the Senate. Clark beat six other Democrats in the October primary. Clark had served on her hometown school board in Melrose. She later worked in the state child care services office as general counsel and was the policy director for Massachusetts Attorney General Martha Coakley.

Bradley Byrne

Republican Bradley Byrne, a lawyer and former state education official, cruised to an easy victory in Alabama's special House election December 17 to succeed GOP Rep. Jo Bonner. Byrne beat Democrat Burton LeFlore for the seat that Bonner vacated August 2 to become vice chancellor for government affairs at the University of Alabama. Byrne had been elected to the state Board of Education and had served as chancellor of the Alabama Community College System. Byrne survived a nine-way Republican primary on September 24 with not quite 35 percent of the vote. He defeated Dean Young, a socially conservative, anti-establishment candidate, in the runoff. Bonner and the National Rifle Association each endorsed Byrne.

2014

Max Baucus

Sen. Max Baucus, D-Mont., resigned his seat February 6, 2014, to become President Obama's ambassador to China. His successor, Democrat John Walsh, was appointed February 9. Walsh did not seek election and departed January 3, 2015. Walsh was succeeded by Republican Steve Daines, a one-term House member, who helped tip control of the Senate to the GOP by defeating Democrat Amanda Curtis.

Alma Adams

Alma Adams was a twenty-year veteran of the North Carolina legislature when she easily won the House seat of fellow Democrat Melvin Watt, who resigned in January 6, 2014, to become director of the Federal Housing Finance Agency. His departure sparked a crowded primary for the seat he had held for twenty-one years. A half-dozen Democrats qualified to run for the "I-85 District," whose population centers of Charlotte in the south and Winston-Salem and Greensboro in the north are separated by about ninety miles of territory, roughly along Interstate 85. Adams avoided a runoff by claiming 44 percent of the vote in the seven-way March primary. She also won the special election in November to serve the final months of Watt's unexpired term, which gave her a slight edge in seniority. When Adams was sworn in November 12, Congress for the first time had 100 voting women members.

Donald Norcross

Donald Norcross declared his candidacy for a New Jersey House seat the same day in February 2014 that Democratic Rep. Robert E. Andrews announced he would resign. Andrews was under investigation by the Ethics Committee for using campaign money for a family trip to Scotland. Norcross's ambition was no secret as the electrician rose through the political ranks at breakneck speed. After defeating the poorly funded Republican candidate, former Philadelphia Eagles linebacker Gary W. Cobb, Norcross was sworn in in November to serve out the rest of Andrews's term, giving him seniority over other members of the class of 2014 who would start in January.

David Jolly

Republican David Jolly won the high-stakes Florida special election in March 2014 to succeed the late GOP Rep. C. W. Bill Young, who had chaired the Appropriations Committee and was the longest-serving Republican in the House. Jolly spent twelve years on Young's staff and earned a law degree before leaving to become a lobbyist.

When Young was hospitalized in fall 2013 after breaking his hip, he urged Jolly to seek the seat representing the St. Petersburg area. Young died October 18, 2013.

Jolly was a relative unknown to voters and faced Rep. Kathleen Peters and Mark Bircher, an Iraq War veteran, in the Republican primary in January. Jolly won with a plurality. The general election March 11, 2014, in a district that supported President Obama in 2012, pitted Jolly against Alex Sink, a Democratic nominee for governor in 2010. Despite gossip columns carrying news of Jolly's divorce becoming final two days after the primary, Jolly won the general election with about 48.5 percent of the vote.

Eric Cantor

House Majority Leader Eric Cantor's unexpected defeat in the Virginia primary in June put a face to the conflicts within the Republican Conference. Dave Brat, an economics professor from Randolph-Macon College, made history by knocking off the first House majority leader in an election. Cantor then resigned August 18, allowing Gov. Terry McAuliffe to call a special election for November, giving the winner extra seniority in the lame-duck session. Brat criticized Cantor on immigration and took an antigovernment approach to policy and politics, arguing to remove the federal government from all but the narrowest of activities. Brat beat Cantor by 11 points and then a Randolph-Macon colleague, John K. Trammell, in the special election by 24 points. Brat also won the general election.

There had been tension between Cantor and Boehner when Cantor pushed the interests of the conservative wing of the party such as the Republican Study Committee. In early 2011, he resisted a plan devised by Boehner and President Barack Obama for pairing spending cuts with increases in revenue. In January 2013, he voted against the "fiscal cliff" deal that allowed higher tax rates on income over $400,000 while permanently extending lower rates under that threshold. Boehner voted for it.

But Cantor made it clear after tough 2012 elections that he would not challenge Boehner, calling him a mentor in a real partnership to deliver results. Cantor said he stood with Boehner in an effort to rise above dysfunction and to do the right thing for our country, for economic growth, entitlement reform, and resolving the spending crisis.

Cantor, a former member of the Ways and Means Committee, developed GOP strategy on business-related themes. He is a lawyer with a master's degree in real estate development from Columbia University.

Curt Clawson

Curt Clawson, a wealthy retired businessman, easily won the June special House election in Florida's Fort Myers area. Republican Trey Radel resigned January 27, 2014, after he was charged in Washington, D.C., and convicted of cocaine possession. Clawson had been a star basketball player at Purdue University in the 1980s and a Harvard MBA. As former CEO of an automotive wheel manufacturer, Clawson loaned his campaign more than $3.6 million. He also had

the backing of the Tea Party Express in the primary and seven months later gave the tea party response to President Barack Obama's State of the Union address in January 2015. In a four-way Republican primary, Clawson won with 38 percent of the vote. In the heavily Republican district, Clawson easily beat his Democratic opponent April Freeman in the June 24, 2014, special election. A rematch in November yielded the same result.

Brian Schatz

Hawaii Gov. Neal Abercrombie appointed Lt. Gov. Brian Schatz to succeed Daniel Inouye, who had just died, as a Democratic senator representing the state on December 26, 2012. Schatz won the seat in a special election primary in August 2014, when he defeated Rep. Colleen Hanabusa, Inouye's preferred successor, with a margin of 1,769 votes out of more than 233,000 cast. Schatz then beat Republican former state Rep. Campbell Cavasso in a general-election landslide. Schatz won a full reelection to a full term in 2016 against Republican John Carroll, Libertarian Michael Kokoski, and Constitution Party candidate Joy Allison.

James Lankford

With only four years in the House under his belt, Rep. James Lankford, R-Okla., jumped into the race to succeed Sen. Tom Coburn, who announced his plans to retire at the end of the 113th Congress. His eventual primary opponent was state House Speaker T. W. Shannon, who was backed by tea party leaders including former Alaska Gov. Sarah Palin and Sen. Mike Lee, R-Utah and endorsed by Sen. Ted Cruz of Texas. But Lankford got a boost when Coburn condemned ads from outside groups and added some flattering words for the candidate. Lankford beat Shannon easily to avoid a runoff and then defeated Democratic state Sen. Connie Johnson in the general election. He won reelection in 2016 to a full term against Democrat Mike Workman.

Presidential Nominations

Despite the change to the Senate's filibuster rules, several Obama nominees still faced difficult paths to confirmation in the 113th Congress. Among the most controversial of Obama's nominations was that of Chuck Hagel for secretary of defense. An Army veteran who served in Vietnam, Hagel weathered a stormy confirmation battle to become the twenty-fourth secretary of Defense despite being a former Republican senator from Nebraska. The treatment, especially needling by Ted Cruz, R-Texas, incensed Reid and stiffened his resolve to end filibusters of executive-branch nominees in late 2013.

The fight began before President Obama announced Hagel's nomination January 7, when questions arose about some of Hagel's past pronouncements on Israel, Iran, the Iraq War surge, and the nation's nuclear deterrent. Criticism intensified after Hagel's shaky testimony at a January 31 Senate Armed Services Committee confirmation hearing, after which Arizona Republican John McCain called the nominee the least impressive witness he had seen in twenty-six years. Hagel backtracked on a series of policy positions he had taken as a senator. After the committee approved the nomination in a party-line vote, Reid could not muster the sixty votes then required to cut off debate when the nomination arrived on the floor, as Republicans demanded more time to discuss Hagel's qualifications. Critics called attention to statements attributed to Hagel including 2010 remarks that Israel was on its way to becoming an apartheid state and that Israeli Prime Minister Benjamin Netanyahu was a radical. After a 71–27 vote to cut off debate February 26, Hagel was confirmed 58–41.

Antonio Weiss, who was nominated to become undersecretary of the Treasury for domestic finance, was blocked by liberal Democrats, led by populist Sen. Elizabeth Warren of Massachusetts. She criticized his ties to Wall Street and his involvement in corporate "inversions," when U.S. corporations merge with foreign companies and move their headquarters offshore to reduce their U.S. taxes.

Former NAACP Legal Defense Fund attorney Debo P. Adegbile was nominated to head the Justice Department's Civil Rights Division. He ran into opposition from law enforcement groups because of his legal representation of Mumia Abu-Jamal, the convicted killer of a Philadelphia police officer, more than three decades earlier.

The fight over Obama's nominees became so contentious that approval for economist Janet L. Yellen to become the first female chair of the Federal Reserve Board of Governors in its 100-year history was stretched across the 2013 holidays. The Senate invoked cloture on December 20 and voted to confirm her January 6. Yellen, who was Fed vice chairwoman when Obama tapped her October 9, 2013, to succeed Ben S. Bernanke, had strong credentials, including having been president of the Federal Reserve Bank of San Francisco and chairwoman of the White House Council of Economic Advisers under President Bill Clinton.

Senate Democrats and Wall Street supported her as architect of the Fed's unprecedented and controversial stimulus program called quantitative easing, which used hundreds of billions of dollars for monthly purchases to government bonds to hold down interest rates, intended to revive the economy from late 2007 through mid-2009. Many Republicans strongly criticized the Fed's actions. Michael D. Crapo of Idaho, the ranking Republican on the Senate Banking Committee, opposed her nomination and said the long-term costs of the policies were unclear and worrisome.

Other appointments were less contentious as Obama assembled his second-term Cabinet in 2013. John Kerry was confirmed January 29 as secretary of State. Sarah Jewell was confirmed April 10 as Interior secretary. Ernest Moniz was confirmed May 16 as secretary of Energy. Penny Pritzker was confirmed June 25 as secretary of Commerce. Anthony Foxx was confirmed June 27 as secretary of Transportation. Fred P. Hochberg was confirmed July 17 as president of the Export-Import Bank. Regina McCarthy was confirmed July 18 as administrator of the Environmental Protection Agency. Thomas E. Perez was confirmed July 19 to be secretary of Labor. Samantha Power was confirmed August 1 as ambassador to the United Nations. Jeh Johnson was confirmed December 16 as secretary of Homeland Security. John Koskinen was confirmed December 20, 2013, to be commissioner of the Internal Revenue Service. Julian Castro was confirmed July 9, 2014, as secretary of Housing and Urban Development. Robert McDonald was confirmed July 29, 2014, as secretary of Veterans Affairs.

LOIS LERNER

The House voted to hold former IRS official Lois Lerner in contempt of Congress in May 2014, a year after the disclosure that tax officials had targeted tea party and other groups for special scrutiny when they applied for tax exemptions as social welfare organizations. The contempt citation against Lerner, who had retired from the IRS the previous September, was mostly symbolic. Republican leaders had argued for months that the administration had been using the IRS to target conservative groups. The investigation had begun after an inspector general's report in May 2013 revealed that, starting in 2010, IRS agents assessing applications for tax exemptions searched for phrases such as "tea party," "patriots," or "9/12" when singling out groups for extra scrutiny. Republicans were furious when the Justice Department said in January 2014 that it had found no evidence to warrant criminal charges.

Major Legislation

The intense partisan divisions in Congress torpedoed efforts to reach consensus on high-profile and contentious issues such as gun control. Congressional leaders even struggled over must-pass bills with support on both sides of the aisle, such as surface transportation legislation. The appropriations process became increasingly difficult as well, with lawmakers needing extra time after the October 1 start of the new fiscal year before agreeing on spending levels. In some cases, they passed continuing resolutions to keep the government running, but a lack of consensus led to a temporary government shutdown in 2013. In contrast, the annual spending bill to fund the legislative branch enjoyed bipartisan support.

2013

Gun Control

The December 2012 shooting deaths of twenty students and six staff members at Sandy Hook Elementary School in Newtown, Conn., following a series of other mass shootings, sparked a gun-control effort at the start of the 113th Congress. Five days before his inauguration to a second term in January, Obama announced a package of legislation and executive orders designed to curtail gun use, but the measures ended with Senate rejection or impasse in both chambers. The exception was the December renewal of an expiring twenty-five-year-old federal ban on plastic firearms.

THE HASTERT RULE

The Hastert Rule is an informal understanding among Republicans controlling the House that they should agree among themselves on legislation before bringing it to the floor. The rule, named after former Speaker Dennis Hastert, R-Ill., held that leadership should not move legislation unless a majority of the majority supported it.

But the rule aimed at enforcing unity also exposed dissension within the Republican conference. Conservatives could potentially block a bill, even if it could win a majority with Democrats on the House floor.

The rule bedeviled Hastert's Republican successors, John A. Boehner of Ohio and Paul D. Ryan of Wisconsin,

on a variety of subjects. Boehner agreed not to bring immigration measures to the floor under the rule in 2013. Candidates jockeying for leadership of the Republican Study Committee in 2014 proposed codifying the informal policy as a rule. Ryan was repeatedly hindered in moving spending bills during 2016 because of the rule.

The disputes pushed spending decisions into early 2017 for a new Congress and president to resolve.

Rep. Jeff Fortenberry, R-Neb., a House Appropriations Committee member, said lawmakers were living with a new set of realities amid the volatile presidential race, so that regular order in Congress had become irregular order.

Violence Against Women Act

In March 2013, Obama signed a five-year renewal of the Violence Against Women Act (S 47—PL 113-4), a law dating to 1994 that was designed to prevent domestic and sexual violence and to provide assistance to victims of such violence. Although the bill generally enjoyed bipartisan support, a bitter partisan debate had derailed the effort the previous year over such issues as whether to expand coverage to domestic-violence victims who were gay and lesbian, to grant more visas to illegal immigrants who were victims, and to give American Indian authorities the power to prosecute non-Indians accused of abusing Indian women on tribal lands. House passage of the bill on a 286–138 vote was notable in part because Boehner broke the so-called Hastert rule, named for former Republican Speaker J. Dennis Hastert of Illinois, who as an informal practice declined to bring legislation to the floor unless it had the support of a majority of the Republican Conference.

Immigration Enforcement

The House and Senate each separately took a stab at changing federal immigration, but strong feelings on both sides prevented action. The Senate passed a comprehensive measure (S 744) 68–32 on June 27, 2013, that included sections to ease visa restrictions for high-tech workers, strengthen border security and interior enforcement, set up a guest-worker program, and establish a thirteen-year process for immigrants in the country illegally to earn citizenship. In the House, however, a bipartisan group of seven House members splintered after trying for months to develop an overhaul plan, leaving that chamber with a series of narrow bills advanced by the House Judiciary Committee that addressed topics such as agricultural guest workers and border enforcement.

Student Loans

After lengthy negotiations, Congress overhauled the system of interest on federally backed loans for college

students, shifting from fixed rates to variable rates pegged to financial-market trading. The legislation locked the rate on student loans for the life of the debt and eliminated the distinction between undergraduate loans with higher rates for families with higher income. The final version represented a victory for congressional Republicans who favored variable rates over Democrats (particularly in the Senate) who wanted to keep rates fixed. However, Obama had also called for market-based rates.

Compounding Pharmacies

More than a year after an outbreak of fungal meningitis blamed for sixty-four deaths that resulted from tainted drugs, President Barack Obama signed into law November 27 a measure overhauling the regulation of specialty pharmacies that combine, mix, or alter drugs under a process called *compounding*. The measure established a national pharmaceutical tracking system for compounded drugs at the Food and Drug Administration. House Republican leaders initially resisted the legislation, but supporters produced a bipartisan compromise (HR 3204—PL 113-54) that the House passed by voice vote September 28. The Senate cleared the measure by voice vote November 18.

Government Shutdown

An appropriations train wreck resulted in a sixteen-day shutdown of non-essential functions of government for the start of the fiscal year in October 2013. House Republicans and Senate Democrats fundamentally disagreed over spending levels: the House aimed for the $967 billion spending level that had been set by the sequestration agreement of 2011, but the Senate panel wanted an additional $91 billion. Further aggravating partisan differences, the House repeatedly passed continuing resolutions to clamp down on implementation of the 2010 Affordable Care Act, or Obamacare (PL 111-148, PL 111-152), and Sen. Ted Cruz, R-Texas, staged a twenty-one-hour talkathon in late September to urge defunding it. But the House proposals drew an Obama veto threat, and Senate Democrats refused to go along. After lengthy negotiations and a three-month spending plan that included an increase in the debt limit, legislative leaders agreed to $1.012 trillion in spending, roughly splitting the difference between the two chambers. Despite objections by conservatives about too much spending, the agreement also reduced the scope of automatic sequester cuts for two years by $63 billion. The resulting bill (HR 3547—PL 113-76), passed with substantial bipartisan majorities and signed by Obama on January 17, 2014, did not include GOP-backed provisions to roll back the 2010 health care law.

Legislative Branch Spending Bill

With Congress focused on cutting costs, lawmakers tightened funding for the legislative branch. This continued a longer-term trend: the Legislative Branch spending bill was the smallest of the twelve annual appropriations measures, and its size had declined each year since fiscal 2010 as lawmakers sought to demonstrate to voters that they were committed to thrift in their own institution.

The Legislative Branch bill finances the activities of Congress and other legislative agencies, including the Library of Congress, the Government Accountability Office, and the Capitol Police. It is often one of the first measures out of the gate and is generally less controversial than other bills. It is also unique: unlike the other twelve annual spending bills, its line items are requested by the agencies it funds rather than by the president.

For fiscal year 2014, the Legislative Branch measure—like the other regular spending bills—was wrapped into the omnibus appropriations measure in December 2013 and ultimately passed in January 2014 as part of the final omnibus bill. It provided an almost unchanged level of appropriations for lawmakers' expenses, short of the increased amounts initially envisioned for agencies that served Congress. The $4.26 billion in discretionary budget authority provided by the omnibus was about $19 million less than the amount enacted for fiscal 2013, about $19 million more than the postsequester spending level, and $250 million below the figure lawmakers initially requested for all congressional offices, plus the Capitol Police, the Architect of the Capitol, the Government Accountability Office, the Government Printing Office, the Congressional Budget Office, and the Library of Congress.

The Senate Appropriations Committee approved its version (S 1283—S Rept 113-70) by a 16–14 party-line vote on July 11 (acting en bloc with the Labor-HHS-Education measure). The bill would have provided almost $3 billion in discretionary spending for the Senate and congressional agencies, including $872 million for the Senate itself. (By tradition, House and Senate bills for the Legislative Branch did not initially include money for the other chamber. The individual chamber proposals were combined before enactment.)

A week later, the House Appropriations Committee approved its bill (HR 2792—H Rept 113-173) by voice vote. It would have provided more than $3.2 billion, including $1.17 billion for the House. Its spending levels for almost every jointly controlled legislative agency were less than those in the Senate version. Neither the full House nor Senate took up the bill.

When the legislative branch spending bill was rolled into the omnibus, the largest line item was $1.18 billion for the operations of the House, which was $45 million less than fiscal 2013 and $52 million less than first proposed for fiscal 2014. The House appropriation included $22 million for party leadership offices, caucuses, and committees, a 23 percent reduction from the 2013 enacted level. The measure provided $554 million for members' representational allowances, a 3 percent reduction. Committee salaries and expenses took a 4 percent cut, to $147 million. House Legislative Branch Appropriations Subcommittee Chair Tom Cole, R-Okla., said staff at the committee and individual member level had "stepped up to the plate" to accept cuts, but he indicated that the effort at austerity had probably reached its limit.

The agreement included $859 million for Senate operations, about $8 million less than the fiscal 2013 enacted amount. The total included $390 million for senators' office expenses and staffing, along with $176 million for the salaries of Senate officers and other employees, $132 million for inquiries and investigations, and $128 million for the Office of the Sergeant at Arms and Senate Doorkeeper. All those figures represented reductions of 2 percent or less.

The Architect of the Capitol received $602 million. The omnibus included $61 million for the Capitol building, including $16 million for the next phase of the dome-repair project, as well as $71 million for operation and maintenance of the House office buildings, $73 million for the Senate's buildings, $53 million for Library of Congress buildings and grounds, $21 million for the Capitol Visitor Center, and $14 million to maintain the Capitol grounds.

The measure included language allowing commercial activities including filming in Union Square, an 11-acre parcel on the west front of the Capitol containing the Grant Memorial and reflecting pool. Filming was not otherwise permitted on the Capitol grounds. The Union Square land had been under the jurisdiction of the National Park Service, which permitted filming, before being transferred to the Architect of the Capitol in 2011.

The omnibus package included $338.5 million for the Capitol Police, a number that matched the Senate committee's figure and the enacted fiscal 2013 level but fell almost $25 million below the amount requested by the House. Appropriators said they were providing enough money for a force of 1,775 officers. During an April 2013 hearing on the agency's fiscal 2014 budget, Capitol Police Chief Kim Dine requested more money for training, radio modernization, and overtime pay.

For the Library of Congress, the omnibus provided $579 million, about $10 million less than the 2013 enacted figure and about halfway between the amounts proposed by the House and Senate Appropriations panels. The

Government Accountability Office received $505 million, about $1 million less than was appropriated for the previous year. Spending by the Government Printing Office was held at the 2013 level of $119 million. The omnibus imposed a prohibition on the printing of paper copies of bills or the *Congressional Record* for House offices.

2014

Farm Bill

More than a year after the previous law expired, Congress cleared a five-year farm bill in 2014. The final bill eliminated direct and "countercyclical" payments to farmers in favor of new forms of crop insurance. Countercyclical payments are made to farmers when designated crops fail to meet targeted prices. The bill also cut spending on food stamps after an intense partisan battle, reduced subsidies for cotton producers, set new limits on how much federal assistance individual farmers may receive each year, and changed the method of subsidizing dairy farmers. The House adopted the conference report 251–166 on January 29, the Senate cleared it by a vote of 68–32 on February 4, and President Barack Obama signed the legislation (HR 2642—PL 113–79) on February 7.

Debt Limit

Republicans had a smorgasbord of demands for concessions in exchange for increasing the debt limit. Repealing the 2.3 percent excise tax on medical devices, limiting Internal Revenue Service investigations of nonprofit groups, or increasing congressional authority to block regulations were each considered at a party retreat in January. But after the government shutdown the previous October, the Republicans did not have enough votes to resist Obama's demand for a clean debt ceiling bill. Over the nay votes of most Republicans, Congress agreed in February to increase the debt limit to $17.3 trillion, which was projected to last until March 15, 2015.

Terrorism Risk Insurance Act

Congress had created the program with the Terrorism Risk Insurance Act (PL 107–297) in 2002 in order to stabilize the insurance market following the September 11, 2001, attacks. Real estate, insurance, and tourism groups spent all year urging lawmakers to extend the program set to expire December 31, 2014. But it took until the first week of 2015 for Congress to clear the legislation because of concerns by retiring Sen. Tom Coburn, R-Okla., over a provision to create a fee-supported body to allow for licensing of insurance brokers in states beyond their home jurisdiction.

Dodd-Frank

Republicans who voted in near unanimity against the Dodd-Frank financial overhaul (PL 111–203)—only three GOP members in either chamber voted for the bill in 2010—won changes in December 2014. The biggest change, endorsed by the Federal Reserve but strongly opposed by the Treasury Department, repealed a provision in Dodd-Frank that had required banks to spin off their business operations on swaps—a type of derivative in which parties exchange cash flows—from the part of the institution that was federally insured.

It was included in the omnibus spending bill (PL 113–235). Another change to Dodd-Frank allowed regulators to exempt large insurers from bank capital requirements. The Senate had passed the legislation (S 2270) by unanimous consent in June, and the House cleared it December 10 for Obama to sign December 18.

Surface Transportation

Congress failed to pass a long-term reauthorization of surface transportation legislation because of the difficulty of boosting the stream of funding for the Highway Trust Fund, which was projected to run dry by August 1. After giving up on ambitions for a multiyear bill, lawmakers agreed on July 31 to a nine-month extension until May 31, 2015. Obama had sketched out a four-year, $302 billion surface transportation plan that would have boosted transit funding, combined rail programs into the Highway Trust Fund, and put $87 billion more into repairing aging bridges, transit systems, and other facilities. But lawmakers balked at how to replenish the Highway Trust Fund after years of stagnant revenue from fuel taxes, the result of more efficient vehicles and less driving. The short-term compromise featured a $10.8 billion transfer from other federal funds to the Highway Trust Fund.

Immigration

The Senate approved legislation in June 2013 that included a path to citizenship for illegal immigrants, but House Republicans refused to take it up. After the 2014 midterm elections, Obama announced he would use his authority to prevent the deportation of nearly 5 million illegal immigrants. The initiative, called the Deferred Action for Parents of Americans and Lawful Permanent Residents (DAPA), focused enforcement activities on national-security threats, criminals, and recent border crossers. A new deferred-action category was created for illegal immigrants who had been in the country for five years and were the parents of children who were U.S. citizens or lawful permanent residents. Those actions were put on hold in federal court by a lawsuit filed by twenty-six states in December 2014 because of the potential costs to the states.

Appropriations

In 2014, for the fifth year in a row, Congress was unable to complete a single one of its twelve regular appropriations bills and had to shovel everything into an omnibus that finally reached Obama nine days before Christmas. After the August recess, House and Senate leaders put together a $1.012 trillion continuing resolution (HJ Res 124) to carry the government past the October 1 start of the new fiscal year and into December. The bill that Congress subsequently passed in December (HR 83—PL 113–236) was nicknamed the cromnibus because it combined omnibus appropriations for most government agencies through the rest of fiscal 2015 (with a short-term continuing resolution for the Homeland Security Department), when Republican leaders hoped to force a showdown with the White House over immigration policy. But Obama dug in on immigration, and Congress ultimately passed the full-year appropriations bill on March 3 after dropping provisions to roll back Obama's controversial DAPA initiative.

Legislative Branch Spending Bill

Lawmakers in 2014 followed a similar pattern as in the previous year: they advanced standalone versions of the legislative branch spending bill, only to see their work rolled into an omnibus appropriations package. The omnibus continued funding for both chambers of Congress and related Capitol Hill agencies was slightly above the previous year's enacted levels, while extending a freeze on lawmakers pay and slightly trimming funds for the Architect of the Capitol.

The House version would have kept funding essentially unchanged from fiscal 2014, while the Senate version would have provided a small funding bump. When they rolled the legislative branch bill into the omnibus, appropriators agreed to an overall funding level that was close to a 1 percent increase above fiscal 2014 but $200 million less than the administration's $4.5 billion request. The measure provided about $1.2 billion for House operations, nearly $1 billion for Senate operations, and $2.1 billion for legislative branch agencies and offices. It maintained the freeze on salaries for members of Congress that began in 2010.

One spending area that had split House and Senate appropriators during earlier debates was the funding level for the Architect of the Capitol, which is responsible for maintaining the Capitol complex and its grounds. The House had proposed $489 million, while the Senate asked for $600 million. Negotiators settled on the Senate's proposal, which was slightly less than the fiscal 2014 enacted level of $602 million. Meanwhile, the Capitol Dome restoration project received $21 million under the bill, which was expected to fully fund the final phase of the project.

The Government Accountability Office received $522 million under the bill, a $17 million increase over the fiscal 2014 enacted level, while funding levels for the Congressional Budget Office would be set at $46 million, slightly down from $46.4 million. The measure provided $348 million for the Capitol Police, a $9.5 million increase from the fiscal 2014 enacted level, and $591 million for the Library of Congress, an increase of $11 million.

One area of concern for some lawmakers due to Russian aggression in Ukraine had been overfunding for the Open World Leadership Center, which brings Russian and other Eurasian leaders together to "experience American democracy and civil society in action." Appropriators set aside $5.7 million for the center but included a provision that would require any funding for Russian participants to be used only on those who engage in free-market development and civic engagement and humanitarian activities and explicitly bars funds from being used on central Russian government officials.

2015–2016

Rather than heal the rifts during the 114th Congress, the divisions remained almost intractable, despite Republicans winning control of the Senate in addition to the House. But lawmakers reached compromises on a highway bill and an education overhaul.

Organization: 114th Congress

SENATE

The Senate flipped decisively from a Democratic to Republican majority after the 2014 election, after eight years of Democratic control. In the 113th Congress, Democrats held fifty-three seats, plus two independents who caucused with them, to Republicans holding forty-five seats. (The majority temporarily narrowed by one seat between June and October 2013 because a Republican appointee in New Jersey succeeded the late Frank Lautenberg, but a special election returned the seat to Democrats.) For the 114th Congress, Republicans held fifty-four seats and the Democrats forty-six seats, including two independents who caucused with them. Despite the rank-and-file changes, faces among Senate leadership stayed the same.

Majority Leadership

Mitch McConnell of Kentucky had been Republican leader since 2007 but was unanimously reelected to the post for the first time to lead the majority on November 13, 2014. John Cornyn of Texas was reelected as whip, and John Thune of South Dakota was reelected conference chair.

Roger Wicker of Mississippi succeeded Jerry Moran of Kansas as chair of the National Republican Senatorial Committee. Wicker beat Dean Heller of Nevada in the closed-door conference meeting.

Orrin G. Hatch of Utah became president pro tempore as the longest-serving Republican. He succeeded Patrick J. Leahy of Vermont, the longest-serving Democrat.

Minority Leadership

Harry Reid of Nevada had led the Democrats since 2005, but he had to survive a four-hour conference meeting November 13, 2014, that featured several members voting against him remaining leader of the minority. Richard J. Durbin of Illinois was reelected whip, Charles E. Schumer of New York was reelected caucus vice chair, Patty Murray of Washington was reelected as caucus secretary, and Schumer remained chair of the policy committee.

Jon Tester of Montana succeeded Michael Bennet of Colorado as chair of the Democratic Senatorial Campaign Committee. Amy Klobuchar of Minnesota succeeded Mark Begich, who lost his election, as chair of the Democratic Steering and Outreach Committee. Democrats created a new leadership position for Elizabeth Warren of Massachusetts as strategic adviser to the policy committee, as a bridge to progressives.

Committees

The change from Democratic to Republican majority meant every committee was getting a new chair, but in some cases the leadership changed names in addition to titles.

Majority. Pat Roberts of Kansas became chair of Agriculture, Nutrition and Forestry, taking the gavel from Debbie Stabenow of Michigan. Thad Cochran of Mississippi became chair of Appropriations, taking the gavel from Barbara A. Mikulski of Maryland. Cochran exerted his seniority over the panel, despite Richard Shelby of Alabama serving as ranking member during the 113th Congress.

John McCain of Arizona became chair of Armed Services, succeeding Democrat Carl Levin of Michigan. Richard Shelby of Alabama became chair of Banking, Housing and Urban Affairs, succeeding Democrat Tim Johnson of South Dakota. Michael D. Crapo of Idaho had been ranking member, but Shelby had more seniority and claimed the gavel. Michael B. Enzi of Wyoming became chair of Budget, succeeding Democrat Patty Murray. Jeff Sessions of Alabama had been ranking member, but Enzi had more seniority. John Thune of South Dakota became chair of Commerce, Science and Transportation, succeeding retiring Democrat Jay Rockefeller of West Virginia. Lisa Murkowski of Alaska became chair of Energy and Natural Resources, succeeding Democrat Ron Wyden of Oregon.

James Inhofe of Oklahoma became chair of Environment and Public Works, succeeding Democrat Barbara Boxer of California, who remained as ranking member. Johnny Isakson of Georgia became chair of Ethics, succeeding Democrat Barbara Boxer of California, who remained as ranking member. Orrin G. Hatch of Utah became chair of Finance, succeeding Democrat Max Baucus of Montana. Bob Corker of Tennessee became chair of Foreign Relations, succeeding Democrat Robert Menendez of New Jersey. Lamar Alexander of Tennessee became chair of Health, Education, Labor and Pensions, succeeding retiring Democrat Tom Harkin of Iowa.

Ron Johnson of Wisconsin became chair of Homeland Security and Government Affairs, succeeding Democrat Thomas R. Carper of Delaware. The former ranking member, Tom Coburn, R-Okla., retired. John Barrasso of Wyoming became chair of Indian Affairs, succeeding Democrat Maria Cantwell of Washington. He had been the ranking member. Charles E. Grassley of Iowa became chair of Judiciary, succeeding Democrat Patrick J. Leahy of Vermont, who remained as ranking member.

Roy Blunt of Missouri became chair of Rules and Administration, succeeding Democrat Charles E. Schumer of New York, who remained as ranking member. Richard Burr of North Carolina became chair of Select Intelligence, succeeding Dianne Feinstein of California, who remained as ranking member. Saxby Chambliss of Georgia had been ranking member but retired. David Vitter of Louisiana became chair of Small Business and Entrepreneurship, succeeding Democrat Mary L. Landrieu of Louisiana. Susan Collins of Maine became chair of Special Aging, succeeding Democrat Bill Nelson of Florida. Johnny Isakson became chair of Veterans' Affairs, succeeding Bernard Sanders of Vermont.

Minority. Democrats mostly remained atop the committees they had led, with some movement as colleagues retired or lost elections. Debbie Stabenow of Michigan remained ranking member of Agriculture after giving the gavel to Pat Roberts of Kansas. Barbara A. Mikulski of Maryland remained ranking member of Appropriations after giving the gavel to Thad Cochran of Mississippi. Jack Reed of Rhode Island became ranking member of Armed Services after the retirement of Carl Levin of Michigan. Sherrod Brown of Ohio became ranking member of Banking after the retirement of Tim Johnson of South Dakota. Barbara Boxer of California remained ranking member of Ethics after handing the gavel to Johnny Isakson of Georgia.

Bernard Sanders of Vermont, an independent who caucused with Democrats, became the ranking member of Budget after Patty Murray of Washington became ranking member of Health, Education, Labor and Pensions. Bill Nelson of Florida became ranking member of Commerce after the retirement of Jay Rockefeller of West Virginia. Nelson got the post despite the greater seniority of Barbara Boxer of California because she wanted to remain atop Environment and Public Works. Maria Cantwell of Washington became ranking member of Energy after Ron Wyden of Oregon became ranking member of Finance after Max Baucus of Montana became ambassador to China. Barbara Boxer of California remained ranking member of Environment and Public Works after handing the gavel to James Inhofe of Oklahoma. Robert Menendez of New Jersey remained ranking member of Foreign Relations after handing the gavel to Bob Corker of Tennessee. But Menendez voluntarily gave up the ranking slot in April 2015 while facing federal corruption charges and was succeeded by Benjamin L. Cardin of Maryland.

Patty Murray of Washington became the ranking member of HELP after the retirement of Tom Harkin of Iowa. Thomas R. Carper of Delaware remained ranking member of Homeland Security after giving the gavel to Ron Johnson of Wisconsin. Jon Tester of Montana became ranking member of Indian Affairs after the former chair, Maria Cantwell of Washington, moved to Energy. Patrick J. Leahy of Vermont remained ranking member of Judiciary after handing the gavel to Charles E. Grassley of Iowa. Charles E. Schumer of New York remained ranking member of Rules after handing the gavel to Roy Blunt of Missouri.

Dianne Feinstein of California remained ranking member of Select Intelligence after handing the gavel to Richard Burr of North Carolina. Jeanne Shaheen of New Hampshire became ranking member of Small Business and Entrepreneurship after the former chair, Mary L. Landrieu of Louisiana, lost her election. Claire McCaskill of Missouri became ranking member of Special Aging after Bill Nelson of Florida moved to Commerce. Richard Blumenthal of Connecticut became ranking member of Veterans' Affairs after Bernard Sanders of Vermont, an independent who caucused with Democrats, moved to Budget.

HOUSE

After the mid-year turbulence of GOP Majority Leader Eric Cantor's primary loss, the 114th Congress began with the leadership of both parties in the House largely unchanged. However, the divisions roiling House leadership ultimately toppled Speaker John A. Boehner of Ohio, who stepped down in October 2015. Paul D. Ryan, Wis., became speaker atop a nearly unchanged leadership team. After James Lankford, Okla., was elected to the Senate, Luke Messer, Ind., became chair of the Policy Committee. The Chief Deputy Whip changed from Peter Roskam, Ill., to Patrick McHenry, N.C.

Majority Leadership

The House reelected John A. Boehner, R-Ohio, as Speaker on January 6 by a vote of 216–164. More seeds of discontent were sown, however, as a dozen other Republicans got votes, including Daniel Webster, Fla., with 12.

House Republicans on November 13, 2014, voted to keep Kevin McCarthy of California as majority leader and Steve Scalise of Louisiana as majority whip. Cathy McMorris Rodgers of Washington was reelected as conference chair, with Lynn Jenkins of Kansas as vice chair. Luke Messer of Indiana became chair of the Policy Committee after James Lankford of Oklahoma was elected to the Senate. Patrick McHenry of North Carolina succeeded Peter Roskam of Illinois as chief deputy whip. Greg Walden of Oregon continued as chair of the National Republican Congressional Committee. After Boehner's resignation in October 2015, Republican Paul D. Ryan of Wisconsin was elected Speaker on October 29 by a vote of 236–184.

Minority Leadership

Democrats stayed with Nancy Pelosi of California as minority leader, Steny H. Hoyer of Maryland as minority whip, and James E. Clyburn of South Carolina as assistant leader. Xavier Becerra of California remained caucus chair, Joseph Crowley of New York remained caucus vice chair, and John Lewis of Georgia remained senior chief deputy whip. Ben Ray Lujan of New Mexico remained chair of the Democratic Congressional Campaign Committee.

Committees

Republicans continued to hold the gavels, which saw little turnover from the previous Congress.

Majority. Continuing their chairmanships were Candice S. Miller of Michigan at Administration; Harold Rogers of Kentucky at Appropriations; John Kline of Minnesota at Education and the Workforce; Fred Upton of Michigan at Energy and Commerce; Jeb Hensarling of Texas at Financial Services; Ed Royce of California at Foreign Affairs; Michael McCaul of Texas at Homeland Security; Robert W. Goodlatte of Virginia at Judiciary; Pete Sessions of Texas at Rules; Lamar M. Smith of Texas at Science, Space, and Technology; Bill Shuster of Pennsylvania at Transportation and Infrastructure; and Jeff Miller of Florida at Veterans' Affairs.

K. Michael Conaway of Texas became chair of Agriculture, succeeding Frank D. Lucas of Oklahoma, who had to give up the gavel because of term limits. Mac Thornberry of Texas became chair of Armed Services after the retirement of Howard "Buck" McKeon of California. Tom Price of Georgia became Budget chair after Paul D. Ryan of Wisconsin moved to Ways and Means. Charlie Dent of Pennsylvania became chair of Ethics after K. Michael Conaway moved to Agriculture. Rob Bishop of Utah became chair of Natural Resources after the retirement of Doc Hastings of Washington.

Jason Chaffetz of Utah became chair of Oversight and Government Reform, succeeding Darrel Issa of California, who was term limited. Chaffetz won the gavel in a four-way battle against Michael R. Turner of Ohio, Jim Jordan of Ohio, and John L. Mica of Florida. Steve Chabot of Ohio became chair of Small Business, succeeding Sam Graves of Missouri, who was term limited. Paul D. Ryan of Wisconsin became chair of Ways and Means after the retirement of Dave Camp of Michigan. Kevin Brady of Pennsylvania later picked up the gavel after Ryan became Speaker. Devin Nunes of California became chair of Intelligence after the retirement of Mike Rogers of Michigan.

Minority. While most ranking members stayed at their posts, Democrats made changes on several committees. The ranking member carryovers were Robert A. Brady of Pennsylvania at Administration; Collin C. Peterson of Minnesota at Agriculture; Nita M. Lowey of New York at Appropriations; Adam Smith of Washington at Armed Services; Chris Van Hollen of Maryland at Budget; Linda T. Sanchez of California at Ethics; Maxine Waters of California at Financial Services; Eliot L. Engel of New York at Foreign Affairs; Bennie Thompson of Mississippi at Homeland Security; John Conyers Jr. of Michigan at Judiciary; Edward J. Markey of Massachusetts at Natural Resources; Elijah E. Cummings of Maryland at Oversight and Government Reform; Louise M. Slaughter of New York at Rules; Eddie Bernice Johnson of Texas at Science, Space, and Technology; Nydia M. Velazquez of New York at Small Business; Nick J. Rahall II of West Virginia at Transportation and Infrastructure; and Sander M. Levin of Michigan at Ways and Means.

Bobby Scott of Virginia became ranking member of Education and Workforce after the retirement of George Miller of California. Frank Pallone Jr. of New Jersey became ranking member of Energy and Commerce after the retirement of Henry A. Waxman of California. Minority Leader Nancy Pelosi roiled her caucus by supporting fellow Californian Anna G. Eshoo against Pallone in the contest, despite his seniority on the panel.

Raul M. Grijalva of Arizona became ranking member of Natural Resources after Peter A. DeFazio of Oregon moved to Transportation and Infrastructure. Peter A. DeFazio of Oregon became ranking member of Transportation and Infrastructure after the retirement of Nick J. Rahall II of West Virginia. Corrine Brown of Florida became ranking member of Veterans' Affairs after Michael H. Michaud of Maine left to run for governor. Adam B. Schiff of California became ranking member of Intelligence after Minority Leader Nancy Pelosi chose him to succeed C. A. "Dutch" Ruppersberger of Maryland.

Rules

The House adopted a rules package (H Res 5) for the 114th Congress on January 6 by a vote of 234–172. The most controversial rule change required that the official budget "scores" of tax and direct spending bills incorporate so-called dynamic scoring, which factors in the broader macroeconomic impact of the legislation. The measure also required all new House members to receive mandatory ethics training within sixty days; required nongovernmental witnesses scheduled to testify before House committees to disclose any contracts or payments that they or the organization they represent have received from foreign governments; and created a point of order against any legislation that would reduce the actuarial balance of Social Security's Old-Age and Survivors Insurance Trust Fund, in an effort to prevent diversions from shoring up Social Security's Disability Insurance trust fund. The resolution also continued the House's Select Committee on Benghazi, as well as the House's ability to continue pursuing certain legal activities—including the lawsuit against the president for allegedly exceeding his legal authority when implementing the 2010 health care overhaul and the lawsuit against the attorney general with respect to the 2009 Operation Fast and Furious gun-tracking program.

Since 2003, House rules (Rule XIII, Clause 3(h)(2)) generally required tax bills reported by the Ways and Means Committee be accompanied by a macroeconomic impact analysis prepared by the Joint Committee on Taxation, but those estimates were not incorporated into the official budget score prepared by the Congressional Budget Office and used for budget enforcement. The resolution modified Rule XIII to require CBO and JCT to incorporate where practicable the macroeconomic effects of "major legislation" covering taxes and direct spending but not appropriations.

The resolution included numerous provisions dealing with committee operations by:

- modifying Rule XI, Clause 2(g)(5) to require that nongovernmental witnesses who are scheduled to testify before House committees disclose any contracts or payments that they or the organization they represent have received from foreign governments during the current calendar year and previous two years. The previous rule required only such disclosure with regard to the receipt of federal grants or contracts.

- reducing the frequency under Rule XI, Clause 1 that committees must submit activity reports from annually to just one for each two-year Congress. The change effectively returned the pace to what existed before the 112th Congress.
- recognizing "dissenting" views in committee reports, which essentially codified the current practice, and required that the Ramseyer portion of a committee report show the entire text of existing law that would be amended or repealed, along with changes proposed. To illustrate changes to current statute, the Ramseyer rule provides that whenever a committee reports a bill or joint resolution, the text shows the omissions and insertions by stricken-through type, italics, parallel columns, or other typographical devices.
- increasing the size under Rule X, Clause 11(a)(1) of the Permanent Select Committee on Intelligence by two members, from twenty to twenty-two, and stipulating that no more than thirteen may be from the majority party. The effect was to give each party one more seat.
- clarifying under Rule X the jurisdiction of the Judiciary Committee to ensure that legislation criminalizing conduct is referred to the panel, and the jurisdiction of the Appropriations Committee to ensure that legislation providing loan obligations and guarantees is referred to that panel. The measure also clarified the House Administration Committee's jurisdiction over the chief administrative officer and explicitly prohibited the Ethics Committee and the Office of Congressional Ethics from denying any right or protection under the Constitution.
- eliminating a point of order on the House floor under Rule XIII, Clause 4 against the consideration of an appropriations bill unless the Appropriations Committee has published printed hearing transcripts for the measure. The point of order was routinely waived as part of floor rules.

The resolution also included "separate orders" for committees, which are not formally incorporated into House rules. During the 2015 session, staffers from four committees—Energy and Commerce; Financial Services; Science, Space, and Technology; and Ways and Means—could take depositions from witnesses, subject to regulations issued by the Rules Committee chair that must be printed in the *Congressional Record.*

Four committees got more subcommittees under the resolution. Armed Services and Foreign Affairs were each authorized seven subcommittees. Agriculture and Transportation and Infrastructure were each authorized six subcommittees. Rule X, Clause 5(d) generally barred panels from having more than five subcommittees, although Appropriations had thirteen subcommittees and Oversight and Government Reform had seven.

The resolution also required all new House members to receive mandatory ethics training within sixteen days. Under Rule XI, Clause 3(a)(6), the Ethics Committee must offer training to members and staffers, but only new workers were required to receive it.

The measure modified Rule I, Clause 12 to allow the Speaker in consultation with the minority leader to reconvene earlier than previously scheduled if in the public interest. The provision also lengthened the time before members could offer unlimited motions to instruct conferees on legislation pending before a House–Senate conference committee. Under Rule XXII, Clause 7(c)(1), members could offer privileged motions to instruct conferees any time after a House-Senate conference committee on a bill had been appointed for twenty calendar days and ten legislative days but had failed to issue a conference report. Floor consideration of the motion occurs the day after the member announces his or her intention to offer the motion. The resolution lengthens the period before such motions may be offered to forty-five calendar days and twenty-five legislative days after a House–Senate conference is appointed.

The measure explicitly authorized the Bipartisan Legal Advisory Group, which includes the speaker, the majority, and minority leaders as well as the majority and minority whips, and directs under Rule II, Clause 8 the House Office of General Counsel to take legal actions on behalf of the House.

The resolution also authorized continued legal efforts:

- extending the authority to pursue legal efforts alleging that President Obama exceeded his legal authority while implementing the 2010 health care overhaul (the Affordable Care Act; PL 111–148 and PL 111–152). The House on July 30, 2014, voted 225–201 to authorize the Speaker of the House to file a lawsuit in federal court on behalf of the House against the president and other administration officials for failing "to act in a manner consistent with that official's duties under the Constitution and laws of the United States" to implement provisions of the 2010 health care law "or any other related provision of law."
- continuing efforts to enforce a subpoena against Attorney General Eric H. Holder Jr. with respect to the Oversight and Government Reform Committee's investigation of the Operation Fast and Furious gun-tracking program. The House on June 28, 2012, voted 255–67 to hold Holder in contempt for refusing to comply with a subpoena to provide certain documents to the committee regarding the failed gun-tracking program.
- authorizing Michael W. Sheehy, who previously worked for the House Intelligence Committee, to provide testimony in the federal criminal trial of Jeffrey Sterling, a former CIA employee who was

charged with violating the Espionage Act. The government had subpoenaed Sheehy to describe a meeting he had with Sterling in August 2000.

- continuing the House's Select Committee on Benghazi, which was created in May 2014 by a 232–186 vote to investigate all actions related to the September 11, 2012, attack on U.S. facilities in Benghazi, Libya, that resulted in the death of U.S. Ambassador to Libya J. Christopher Stevens and three other Americans.

The resolution included several separate orders dealing with the budget, several of which continued from the 113th Congress:

- providing budget enforcement of the fiscal year 2014 budget resolution (H Con Res 25) until a fiscal year 2015 budget resolution is adopted. The measure approved budget allocations pursuant to the December 2013 Bipartisan Budget Act (PL 113–67), but the provision allows the House Budget chair to revise allocations to maintain the solvency of the Highway Trust Fund.
- creating a point of order against any legislation that would reduce the actuarial balance of Social Security's Old-Age and Survivors Insurance (OASI) Trust Fund by 0.01 percent or more. The point of order is intended to protect the OASI trust fund from possible diversions of trust fund resources to shore up Social Security's Disability Insurance trust fund, which is projected to become insolvent in 2016.
- continuing a provision that House appropriations bills include a "spending reduction account" in the last section that can be used to "wall off" amounts cut from other parts of a bill. Previously, cutting funding by amendment allowed the money to shift to other programs in the bill.
- barring consideration of an annual budget resolution unless it includes a dedicated section regarding direct spending. This portion of the budget resolution must display totals for means-tested direct spending and non–means-tested direct spending—with details on the average rate of growth for each category in the prior ten-year period, estimates for the rate of growth during the budget resolution's budget window (normally ten years), and information on proposed reforms for such spending.
- The resolution provided that provisions of the 2010 health care overhaul (PL 111–148; PL 111–152) requiring congressional consideration of recommendations by the Independent Payment Advisory Board will not apply. The health care law charged IPAB with drafting recommendations to slow the growth rate in Medicare spending if spending exceeds a certain target rate, and those recommendations would be binding and would be automatically implemented absent congressional action to change them.

Change in House Leadership

The deepening chasm among Republican factions in the House over national strategy and legislative tactics eventually led to an overhaul of leadership. Majority Leader Eric Cantor of Virginia lost his Republican primary in June 2014. House Speaker John A. Boehner of Ohio resigned in October 2015. Majority Leader Kevin McCarthy of California could not marshal enough votes to succeed Boehner. Eventually the conference elected Paul D. Ryan of Wisconsin—chair of the Ways and Means Committee and Mitt Romney's vice presidential running mate in 2012—as Speaker.

The opposition to leadership eventually birthed the House Freedom Caucus, which grew to about thirty to forty members who effectively challenged Boehner by preventing him from bringing legislation to the floor without Democratic support. The caucus in some ways challenged the 170-member Republican Study Committee, which many conservatives thought had become too large and too cozy with leadership.

Republican success at the polls proved a two-edged sword. The conservative tea-party movement vehemently opposed to President Barack Obama allowed Republicans to regain the House majority in 2011 after four years of Democratic control, but those more doctrinaire newcomers clashed with Boehner almost from the start. A frustrated Boehner disciplined several party members by denying them coveted committee assignments at the end of 2012. Amid the outrage that followed, nine Republicans denied him their votes for Speaker in January 2013. The post was so untenable that nobody wanted it. Ron Bonjean, who had been communications director for Speaker J. Dennis Hastert, R-Ill., said in 2013 that House Republican leadership likely faced a difficult two years because of the lack of consensus within the conference.

By January 2015, resistance to Boehner had doubled, with twenty-five Republicans denying him votes for Speaker. Boehner said after retaking the gavel that all he asked was that lawmakers disagree without being disagreeable, to prove the skeptics wrong. On January 25, however, nine of the most insistent conservatives announced the formation of the House Freedom Caucus, with an agenda for a "limited, constitutional government in Congress." The initial caucus included Scott Garrett of New Jersey, Jim Jordan of Ohio, John Fleming of Louisiana, Matt Salmon of Arizona, Justin Amash of Michigan, Raúl R. Labrador of Idaho, Mick Mulvaney of South Carolina, Ron DeSantis of Florida, and Mark Meadows of North Carolina.

A flashpoint for conservatives was a spending bill for the Department of Homeland Security. The lack of immigration provisions in the spending compromise left conservatives furious, but leaders forced a vote on the bill over objections by conservatives by exercising a procedural tool on the House floor that bypassed the Rules Committee to agree to a Senate-passed version of the bill. Rep. Mick Mulvaney, R-S.C., called the spending agreement a fool's bargain that Republicans should not have gotten into in the first place. The homeland-security bill was adopted primarily with Democratic votes, as two-thirds of Republicans opposed it, but Boehner said the result was the right one for this team.

Another conflict arose in June, during a fight over whether to provide President Obama "fast track" Trade Promotion Authority (TPA) to speed up consideration of trade agreements. GOP leaders removed three members of the Freedom Caucus from their whip team—those in charge of rounding up votes—as punishment for voting against the rule to bring TPA to the floor. Days later, the chair of the House Oversight and Government Reform Committee, Jason Chaffetz of Utah, took away the gavel of Government Operations Subcommittee Chair Mark Meadows for voting "no" on the Trade Promotion Authority rule and for not paying dues to the National Republican Congressional Committee. Chaffetz reversed course, but it was too late.

On July 28, during a series of votes before the August recess, Meadows filed with the House a signed resolution he had written to "vacate the chair," a motion to force a vote on whether Boehner should continue as speaker. The 260-word resolution read as a blistering indictment of Boehner from a member of his own party, saying he caused the power of Congress to atrophy, punished members who voted their conscience, and limited straightforward debate. The motion was referred to committee and not brought before the House for an immediate vote. The message, however, was clear.

On September 25, the day after Pope Francis addressed Congress, Boehner told a closed-door meeting of House members that he would step down from his office at the end of October. A Boehner aide said later that the Speaker had originally planned to leave office at the end of 2014 but that the surprise primary defeat of Cantor had changed that calculation.

"The first job of any Speaker is to protect this institution that we all love. It was my plan to only serve as Speaker until the end of last year, but I stayed on to provide continuity to the Republican Conference and the House," Boehner said in a statement. "It is my view, however, that prolonged leadership turmoil would do irreparable damage to the institution."

Majority Leader Kevin McCarthy, R-Calif., was the leading candidate to succeed Boehner. But tea party organizers rejected McCarthy out of hand, saying that the next speaker should be someone from the Freedom Caucus. On October 4, Chaffetz announced he would run for Speaker and said McCarthy could not count on 218 votes on the floor. McCarthy acknowledged as much in a closed-door meeting of the Republican conference on October 8 by taking himself out of the race. As others promoted Ryan, he initially said he would not run but relented on October 20.

Ryan was elected the fifty-fourth speaker of the House on October 29, and he asked colleagues to help him fix a broken chamber. Ryan got 236 votes, and Minority Leader Nancy Pelosi, D-Calif., got 184 votes. Even at that point, Rep. Daniel Webster of Florida, a Freedom Caucus stalwart, got nine Republican votes. Ryan said he was not interested in laying blame or settling scores but rather in wiping the slate clean. GOP Conference Chairwoman Cathy McMorris Rodgers, R-Wash., who had formally nominated Ryan before the vote, said the House was eager for a fresh start.

Ethics Investigations

MICHAEL G. GRIMM

Rep. Michael G. Grimm, the tough-talking State Island Republican, resigned effective January 5, 2015. He had been investigated for his campaign finances and tax records of a health-food restaurant he owned before his election to Congress. Grimm, a former Marine and FBI agent, had steadfastly maintained his innocence. In January 2014, he threatened to throw a New York television reporter off a balcony in the House for asking about the case during an interview.

Grimm had been indicted in April 2014 on twenty federal tax charges. He won reelection that November by dismissing the charges as a "political witch hunt" and "character assassination." Grimm initially refused to relinquish his House seat, even after pleading guilty in December 2014 to a single count of felony tax fraud and acknowledging he committed perjury, hired illegal immigrants, and committed wire fraud. Loretta Lynch, the U.S. Attorney for the Eastern District of New York who soon succeeded Eric Holder as President Barack Obama's Attorney General, described Grimm's efforts to cover up his activities as breathtaking. Grimm quietly announced he would give up the seat January 5, 2015, a day before the new Congress was sworn in. The following summer, a federal judge sentenced Grimm to eight months in prison for tax evasion.

AARON SCHOCK

Rep. Aaron Schock of Illinois, an ambitious, thirty-three-year-old Republican just starting his fourth term, resigned on March 17 after the Office of Congressional Ethics began a review of his official spending, including concert tickets, charter planes, overseas trips, and, most remarkably, a $40,000 tab to decorate his office in the opulent style of *Downton Abbey*. At the annual Gridiron Club dinner held a few days before Schock's resignation announcement, the emcee joked that the event was the only place in Washington with a white tie dress code, besides Congressman Aaron Schock's office. A fitness buff who once showed off his abs on the cover of *Men's Health* magazine, Schock was a gregarious, social media–savvy up-and-comer with prodigious fundraising skills, and he was mentioned as a potential future chair of the National Republican Congressional Committee.

But Schock's ethics had been questioned before. In May 2012, the semiautonomous Office of Congressional Ethics, which can make recommendations to the House Ethics Committee, found substantial reason to believe that Schock had solicited a donation above the legal limit for a political action committee. The Ethics Committee never said a word about the matter, though, and it faded from view. The recent complaints focused on the interior designer offering services for free, which prompted liberal watchdog groups to allege that it was an inappropriate gift. Schock subsequently paid $40,000 from his personal finances to cover the cost. That incident prompted a flurry of stories about his use of private charter planes he said were needed to get around his district, concert ticket purchases, trips overseas, and other forms of travel, including mileage for his car. After several weeks of news coverage, Schock announced on March 17 that the questions had proven to be a great distraction from his work and that he would quit the House at the end of the month.

ROBERT MENENDEZ

Months of rumor and speculation culminated in April 2015 with an indictment against Sen. Robert Menendez, D-N.J., on federal corruption charges for alleged favors he did for Florida ophthalmologist Salomon Melgen and gifts he received from Melgen that allegedly included campaign donations and private aircraft flights. Menendez pleaded not guilty and kept his Senate seat and committee assignments, although he temporarily stepped aside as ranking Democrat on the Foreign Relations Committee. Menendez eventually outlasted a three-year saga when a hung jury in his federal trial in November 2017 and prosecutors agreed to drop charges in January 2018.

On April 14, 2015, Melgen was indicted for defrauding Medicare of as much as $190 million. A Justice Department spokesman discussing the corruption case said Melgen and Menendez were indicted for a scheme in which "Menendez allegedly accepted gifts from Melgen in exchange for using the power of his Senate office to benefit Melgen's financial and personal interests." *Roll Call* had reported that Melgen used many avenues in recent decades to contribute more than $800,000 to Menendez, both directly and indirectly. Menendez and Melgen were each indicted on one count of conspiracy, one count of violating the travel act, eight counts of bribery, and three counts of honest services fraud. Menendez also was charged with one count of making false statements. On September 28, six months after the indictment, a federal judge in New Jersey struck down four of the bribery counts against Menendez and Melgen, citing key campaign finance decisions, but other charges were left standing.

The legal opinions struck a blow to Congress's ability to shield its work from prosecutors under the Constitution's Speech or Debate Clause. According to the original indictment, Menendez allegedly used his position as a senator to influence visa proceedings for Melgen's foreign girlfriends and advocated for Melgen's financial interests related to Medicare billing and shipping disputes. The judge rejected Menendez's argument that those actions were protected, stating that some official acts, particularly those related to oversight of the executive branch, "fall into a 'middle category' of activities that are not 'clearly protected.'"

Menendez's eleven-week trial in Newark, N.J., ended with a hung jury in November 2017. Federal prosecutors dropped the charges on January 31, 2018. Menendez, who said he never wavered in his innocence and his confidence that justice would prevail, reclaimed his position as ranking member on Foreign Relations in February 2018.

J. DENNIS HASTERT

The highest-profile criminal case dealing with Congress involved former House speaker J. Dennis Hastert, who was charged in May 2015 with evading federal bank reporting requirements and lying to the FBI. The charges stemmed from his paying $1.7 million in hush money linked to possible sexual misconduct that occurred when he was a high school wrestling coach. Hastert had served twenty years in Congress, including eight as the longest-serving Republican Speaker in history, after succeeding Newt Gingrich in 1999. Hastert pleaded guilty in October 2015 to evading federal bank reporting requirements and eventually served thirteen months of a fifteen-month prison sentence before his release in 2017.

CHAKA FATTAH

Chaka Fattah, D-Pa., a twenty-year veteran of the House, was indicted July 29 with several associates on federal charges for alleged racketeering and influence peddling. Prosecutors charged Fattah in a twenty-nine-count indictment with racketeering conspiracy, bribery, and wire fraud as part of a probe launched by the FBI and IRS in March 2013. Fattah responded that he had done nothing wrong and would run for a twelfth term in 2016. He said he had never been involved in any illegal activity or misappropriation of funds. He did, however, relinquish his position as ranking Democrat on the Commerce, Justice, Science Appropriations Subcommittee and stepped down as board chair of the Congressional Black Caucus Foundation. His reelection chances dimmed in November when state Rep. Dwight Evans, a longtime Philadelphia politician with considerable clout, announced he would challenge Fattah in the primary the following April. Evans won the primary. A federal jury convicted Fattah on June 21, 2016, of conspiracy, money laundering, and other charges, including that he had arranged to get an illegal $1 million loan to finance his mayoral bid in 2007. Fattah was sentenced to ten years in prison in December 2016 and was ordered to pay $600,000 in restitution and to forfeit $14,500.

"As a former congressman, Fattah conspired with his co-defendants in a series of schemes to use his position for personal gain at the expense of the public good," U.S. Attorney Zane David Memeger said. According to evidence at trial, Fattah borrowed $1 million from a wealthy supporter for his failed 2007 campaign for mayor of Philadelphia and disguised the money as a loan to a consulting company. After he lost, Fattah returned $400,000 to the donor and arranged for a nonprofit entity he controlled to repay the remainder using charitable funds and federal grants. To conceal the scheme, Fattah and others created sham contracts and made false entries in accounting records, tax returns, and campaign-finance disclosure records.

After his election defeat, Fattah also sought to retire $130,000 in campaign debt to a political consultant by agreeing to arrange a $15 million federal grant for the consultant. The consultant did not receive the grant.

Fattah also misappropriated funds from his mayoral and congressional campaigns to repay approximately $23,000 of his son's student loan debt. Beginning in 2008, Fattah communicated with individuals in the legislative and executive branches in an effort to secure for sixty-nine-year-old lobbyist Herbert Vederman an ambassadorship or an appointment to the U.S. Trade Commission in exchange for an $18,000 bribe. Vederman, of Palm Beach, Fla., was also charged in the indictment.

On August 3, 2015, just five days after the indictment, the House Ethics Committee announced it had formed an investigative subcommittee to look into possible misconduct by Fattah. But the committee made no further announcements—in keeping with precedent—and Fattah was defeated before the criminal case ran its course.

MICHAEL M. HONDA

The House Ethics Committee announced September 3, 2015, that it was extending a year-long investigation of Rep. Michael M. Honda, D-Calif., by the panel and the Office of Congressional Ethics into internal emails that appeared to show the California Democrat's staff mixing official duties with campaign considerations. The panel stopped short, however, of opening a full probe.

According to documents the ethics office released in September, Honda's 2014 campaign manager, Doug Greven, attended a district office staff retreat and presented a strategy in which district office events would be used to raise political donations. When Honda was shown notes from the meeting, he allegedly acknowledged to ethics investigators that what he was seeing was open to a lot of interpretation but that it did not look good.

OCE's wide-ranging investigation included internal emails exposed in a September 2014 report by the Silicon Valley publication *San Jose Inside* that showed Honda's longtime chief of staff, Jennifer Van der Heide, and his then-campaign coordinator, Lamar Heystek, strategizing to invite campaign contributors to an official State Department round table. Staff members researched the campaign contribution histories of a list of potential invitees to cull names for an invite list, according to email records included in the report.

In a July 2015 letter released by the ethics office, lawyers representing Van der Heide and former District Director Meri Maben argued the actions did not violate applicable ethics rules or "at worst, present narrow concerns." To the extent that his staff's conduct could be construed to fall too close to crossing the line, Honda had already imposed "stringent remedial measures," they stated.

BLAKE FARENTHOLD

A sexual harassment suit against Rep. Blake Farenthold, R-Texas, was halted on November 18, 2015, after a sealed and mediated agreement was reached in federal court by the two parties, details of which were not disclosed. The Texas Republican's former communications director, Lauren Greene, had filed the suit in District of Columbia court in December 2014, alleging that Farenthold had sexually harassed her, discriminated against her because she is a woman, and retaliated against her for complaining about the harassment. On November 18, 2015, lawyers for Greene and the House Employment Counsel, representing Farenthold, filed a joint one-sentence document stating that "pursuant to the agreement of the parties," the case should be dismissed.

Congress's Office of Compliance had already paid $84,000 to settle claims of harassment that were tied to Farenthold's office. The lawmaker later said he would pay the money back to the government, but he didn't before leaving Congress. CNN reported December 13, 2017, that a male former senior staff member had approached the Ethics Committee with reports of Farenthold being verbally abusive and sexually demeaning when he worked in the office in 2015.

Farenthold had earlier blamed his problems on his own inexperience. "I'd never served in public office before," Farenthold said in a video posted on his campaign's Facebook page on December 14, 2017. "I had no idea how to run a congressional office, and as a result I allowed a workplace culture to take root in my office that was too permissive and decidedly unprofessional."

Farenthold abruptly resigned from office on April 6, 2018. "While I planned on serving out the remainder of my term in Congress, I know in my heart it's time for me to move along and look for new ways to serve," he said in a statement explaining his sudden departure.

ROBERT PITTENGER

The House Ethics Committee voted on November 19, 2015, to form an investigative subcommittee to look into allegations that Rep. Robert Pittenger, R-N.C., "received compensation for his involvement with a fiduciary business, a real estate investment firm known as Pittenger Land Investments, Inc." while in Congress. At the request of the Justice Department, however, the committee recommended the subcommittee defer its investigation. Federal authorities announced in May 2017 they would not file charges. Pittenger lost a Republican primary for his seat in May 2018.

Pittenger had requested the Ethics Committee investigate the allegations amid reports the FBI and IRS were looking into whether he transferred money from the company to his campaign. Pittenger had said in August that

FBI agents had asked questions several months earlier about a real estate company he founded in 1985.

Pittenger said his objective was to address these issues directly and confirm that he always acted properly and in full respect for the law and House Ethics rules.

As a House freshman in 2013, Pittenger had paid a $31,000 fine for a campaign finance disclosure violation in his first federal election. His campaign committee had failed to file a forty-eight-hour contribution notice prior to his May 8 primary election in 2012—a preelection notice that would have disclosed Pittenger's own $309,000 contribution to his campaign on April 26, 2012. The fine was a relatively small amount for Pittenger, the thirteenth-richest member of Congress.

Special Elections and Resignations

Two House Democrats lost their seats in 2016 primaries after they were indicted for federal crimes, and a third who was under investigation by the House Ethics Committee lost his reelection after serving sixteen years.

Florida Rep. Corrine Brown lost a Democratic primary in August after she was indicted on fraud charges in July. She was first elected to a north Florida district in 1992 but got only 39 percent of the vote against former state Sen. Al Lawson. She and her chief of staff, Elias "Ronnie" Simmons, were charged with twenty-four counts, among them mail and wire fraud, theft of government property, and filing false tax returns, related to their connection to a group that billed itself as a charity but was not registered as a nonprofit. Brown was eventually convicted of eighteen charges in May 2017, and she asked for a new trial.

Pennsylvania Rep. Chaka Fattah of Pennsylvania lost a Democratic primary in April, nine months after he and four associates were indicted on federal corruption charges stemming from his 2007 Philadelphia mayoral bid. It would have been his twelfth term in Congress. Fattah was convicted in June 2016 on all counts and resigned his seat at that point. He was sentenced to ten years in federal prison in December.

California Rep. Michael Honda lost to fellow Democrat Ro Khanna on November 8, 2016, no doubt in part because of a lingering ethics investigation into allegations that his House staff had been improperly involved in his 2014 reelection campaign. The Office of Congressional Ethics investigated for more than a year whether Honda's staff had crossed congressional duties with campaign activities. The case was referred to the House Committee on Ethics, which indicated it would take up the review indefinitely. Khanna, who lost to Honda by 3.6 percent in the 2014 primary before the allegations arose, freely used the ethics allegation in his campaign.

Some cases pending a decision by the committee were older than that of Honda, including those in which an indefinite pending review was issued in early 2014. That meant Honda could be waiting for a final decision well past the election.

WARREN DAVIDSON

Warren Davidson, a former Army Ranger and manufacturing executive, won the June 7 special House election in Ohio to serve out the final seven months of former Speaker John A. Boehner's term. Republican Davidson got three-quarters of the vote against Democrat Corey Foister and Green Party candidate James Condit.

OUTSIDERS

Congress became a familiar punching bag during the 2016 Republican presidential campaign. Billionaire real estate developer Donald Trump called lawmakers a bunch of "babies." Sen. Ted Cruz of Texas said fellow Republicans are just part of the "Washington cartel." And neurosurgeon Ben Carson said Congress "stands in the way," demanding "pensions and perks."

The complaints were nothing new, but voters in New Hampshire and other early primary states increasingly told pollsters of frustrations at representatives failing to deliver on the conservative agenda. More than three-quarters of GOP voters preferred an outsider over someone with Washington experience, an Associated Press-GfK poll found in October 2015.

Barbara Perry, presidential studies director at the University of Virginia's Miller Center, said there had never been anyone like the outsiders who were getting as close to the presidency as polls suggested.

Veteran lawmakers warned of the risks of electing someone without governing experience.

Former GOP Senate Majority Leader Trent Lott said it was not realistic to expect someone who was not in politics or government to take over. Lott said candidates needed to know how to get things done in Washington in order to succeed.

Despite such concerns, voters—especially Republicans—demonstrated a growing comfort with entrusting political decisions to outsiders. In one of the more surprising upsets in recent years, primary voters in 2014 ousted House Majority Leader Eric Cantor, R-Va., in favor of an economics professor, Dave Brat. And in the 2016 presidential election, they nominated Trump, despite—or because of—his lack of political experience. Although Democratic nominee Hillary Clinton touted her many years in government as first lady, senator, and secretary of state, Trump's image as an outsider ultimately helped him win the election.

The hard-line conservatives of the House Freedom Caucus, who pushed Boehner into an early retirement in 2015, helped propel Davidson past fourteen opponents in the March 15 primary. Like many Republicans, Davidson was frustrated that GOP majorities in the House and Senate had not blocked what Republicans saw as President Barack Obama's abuse of executive power, such as suspending the deportation of millions of undocumented immigrants.

DAN DONOVAN

Staten Island, New York, District Attorney Dan Donovan, a Republican, easily won a May 5 special election to succeed Michael G. Grimm, who resigned in January after pleading guilty to tax evasion. Donovan defeated Democrat Vincent Gentile, a City Council member from Brooklyn. The district, which includes Staten Island and part of Brooklyn, had been in Republican hands for most of the past thirty-five years, with just one two-year hiatus when Democrat Michael E. McMahon won it in the 2008 election, losing to Grimm. Donovan agreed with his party's rhetorical attacks on President Obama's Iran negotiations. But Donovan seemed willing to make some accommodations with Democrats on illegal immigration.

TRENT KELLY

District Attorney Trent Kelly rolled to victory in a June 2 special-election runoff in Mississippi to succeed Rep. Alan Nunnelee, who had died on February 6 from brain cancer. Thirteen candidates had run in the May 12 special election, and when no candidate garnered the necessary 50 percent to win outright, the race went to a runoff between Republican Kelly and Democrat Walter Zinn. Kelly won the runoff in the deeply conservative district with 70 percent of the vote. A colonel in the Army National Guard and an Iraq War veteran, Kelly fit the template of Republicans who advocate a robust national defense while looking for ways to curb other spending and opposing tax increases. Kelly had the support of Nunnelee's widow and a base of voters from his role as prosecutor.

DARIN LAHOOD

Republican state Sen. Darin LaHood, the son of former longtime House member and Transportation secretary Ray LaHood, won the September 10 special House election in Illinois to succeed Rep. Aaron Schock, who resigned in March amid a federal investigation of whether he misused funds to travel and decorate his office. LaHood, a former state and federal prosecutor, won the July 7 Republican primary, which was tantamount to the overall victory in the deeply conservative district, by defeating Breitbart editor Mike Flynn by about 69 percent to 29 percent. LaHood scored high-profile endorsements and raised at least $1.2 million for the campaign, compared to about $20,000 for his Democratic challenger, high school history teacher and Army Reserve officer Rob Mellon. LaHood was already familiar with the House, having worked as an intern and legislative assistant from 1990 to 1994 for California Republican and Appropriations Committee member Jerry Lewis.

MARK TAKAI

Rep. Mark Takai, 49, died July 20, 2016. The Hawaii Democrat was first elected in 2014. Colleen Hanabusa, another Democrat, won the special House election November 8, 2016, which allowed her to gain seniority over new members and to serve during the lame-duck session.

EDWARD WHITFIELD

Rep. Edward Whitfield, R-Ky., resigned effective September 6, 2016, nearly a year after he announced he would retire because of an ethics investigation. He had not sought reelection that year, but his leaving before the end of the term allowed his successor greater seniority in the next Congress. The Ethics Committee concluded unanimously in July 2016 that Whitfield failed to prohibit lobbying contacts between his staff and his wife Constance Harriman from 2011 through at least 2015. But the committee also found that the eleven-term lawmaker had not broken the rules by corrupt or willful intent. The committee found that Whitfield violated House Rule XXV, clause 7, which prohibited staffers from making any lobbying contact with a lawmaker's spouse; House Rule XXIII, which required lawmakers to behave creditably at all times; and the Code of Ethics of Government Service section 5, which said lawmakers must never dispense special favors or privileges to anyone for remuneration or not. The committee found that Whitfield had not familiarized himself with applicable rules and standards of conduct, which warranted reproval by the committee. Whitfield acknowledged that his oversights had led to unintentional violations of House rules. His departure allowed Republican James Comer, who won a special election November 8, 2016, to gain seniority over new members and to serve during the lame-duck session.

JANICE HAHN

Rep. Janice Hahn, D-Calif., resigned December 4, 2016, to become a member of the Los Angeles County Board of Supervisors. The seat remained vacant until the next Congress.

CANDICE S. MILLER

Rep. Candice S. Miller, R-Mich., resigned December 31, 2016, to become Macomb County Public Works Commissioner. Her seat remained vacant until the next Congress.

Administration Nominations

ASHTON B. CARTER

Ashton B. Carter was easily confirmed in February 2015 as Obama's fourth Defense secretary, the most turnover since the post was created during the Truman administration. The Senate voted 93–5 to confirm Carter barely two months after his nomination, and his recovery from back surgery prompted part of the delay.

LORETTA LYNCH

Loretta Lynch, a former federal prosecutor, was confirmed as Attorney General on April 23, 2015. She succeeded Eric H. Holder Jr. The first black woman to head the Justice Department, Lynch had waited longer than almost any other attorney general nominee, was the first to require a cloture vote, and had one of the closest confirmation votes in decades for a cabinet position: 56–43. She served as a proxy for Republican criticism of President Barack Obama's executive actions on immigration.

JOHN B. KING JR.

President Barack Obama's nominee to become secretary of Education, John B. King Jr., received the fewest votes on March 14, 2016, of any successful Cabinet appointment since the beginning of Jimmy Carter's presidency nearly forty years earlier. King squeaked by, 49–40.

Republicans' objections centered on whether King was the right person to implement the law they had enacted in 2015 to revise the landmark 2002 No Child Left Behind Act. The 2015 update scaled back federal authority over state education that the 2002 law had granted, and Republicans questioned whether King would give states the level of jurisdiction they intended.

When King was New York State's education commissioner in 2011, he had overseen a bumpy rollout of the controversial Common Core standards, a joint effort of the states to adopt like curricula. The program was not popular among conservatives. King defended the program even as test scores fell and the state's largest teachers' union called for his resignation. New York Sen. Kirsten Gillibrand was the lone Democrat to oppose his confirmation.

MERRICK GARLAND

In their boldest response to an Obama nomination, Senate Republicans refused to consider the president's choice to fill a Supreme Court vacancy. The February 13, 2016 death of Supreme Court Justice Antonin Scalia—a revered and influential conservative—gave the Democratic president a rare opportunity to move the Court to the left. In March, Obama nominated U.S. Circuit Judge Merrick Garland, an experienced jurist who won high marks in the legal community for his generally moderate if left-leaning opinions.

Senate Majority Leader Mitch McConnell, R-Ky., however, said that the vacancy should go unfilled until after the election. He refused to allow a hearing on the nominee or even to meet with Garland. This was a highly unusual and controversial stand: senators since the mid-1800s had invariably agreed to at least consider Supreme Court nominations even if they ultimately voted them down. Democrats heatedly denounced McConnell's position, but the majority leader's remarkable gamble paid off when

Donald Trump won election in November, ensuring that the vacancy would be filled by a Republican president.

Major Legislation

2015

Trade Promotion Authority

A coalition of Republicans joined a small band of pro-trade Democrats to deliver the Obama administration a rare bipartisan victory in June by granting fast-track authority for trade agreements, known as Trade Promotion Authority. The Senate passed fast-track legislation on May 22 as part of an unrelated bill (HR 1314) that included Trade Promotion Authority despite concerns by Sen. Bernie Sanders, I-Vt., and others about potential impacts on jobs. House Democrats, however, disregarded an eleventh-hour plea from Obama and essentially voted down the trade package on June 12 by joining Republicans in rejecting a key element, Trade Adjustment Assistance, on a vote of 126–302.

Republican leaders in both chambers then pursued two pieces of legislation, with Obama only signing Trade Promotion Authority if he also received the trade adjustment extension. The House approved Trade Promotion Authority 218–208 on June 18. The House trade preferences bill also contained a fix for the contentious $700 million cut to Medicare spending in 2024 that had been used as an offset for reauthorizing trade assistance. Senate Majority Leader Mitch McConnell, R-Ky., then filed cloture on a motion to concur with a House bill after receiving unanimous consent to amend it with Trade Adjustment Assistance provisions. The Senate approved the measure June 24 by voice vote and cleared fast-track authority for the president 60–38. Rep. Rosa DeLauro, D-Conn., conceded defeat, and Minority Leader Nancy Pelosi, D-Calif., said she would back the bill. AFL-CIO President Richard Trumka said members would not be punished for voting their conscience. The House voted the next day 286–138 to send trade assistance to the president. Resistance faded quickly.

Patriot Act

In June, Congress reauthorized the counterterrorism law known as the Patriot Act through 2019 while curtailing the National Security Agency's authority to collect bulk phone records of Americans' telephone calls. The approval culminated in a bruising fight in which the House supported language that set limits on the National Security Agency's ability to review phone records. McConnell proposed a series of amendments that he said were crucial to preserving national security. But in the June 2 voting, more than a dozen Republicans voted against at least one of the amendments. Then the Senate voted 67–32 to clear the bill (HR 2048). The new legislation would require the agency to go to the phone companies with a warrant when it wanted to review those records in the future.

Iran Nuclear Pact

The Senate voted three times in September 2015 to block President Obama's agreement with Iran to disable that country's nuclear program in exchange for the removal of sanctions. Each time, the result was the same, however: Republicans could gain the support of no more than four Democrats, thereby failing to cut off debate. The highest level of support was recorded September 10, with a 58–42 vote, but 60 votes were required to cut off debate. The Republicans' failure marked a major foreign policy achievement for Obama, who had championed the deal despite the objections of Israeli Prime Minister Benjamin Netanyahu and American pro-Israel activists.

Export-Import Bank

The first successful House discharge petition in thirteen years helped revive the Export-Import Bank. The debate exemplified the biggest policy showdown of ideological camps in the Republican Conference, with traditional pro-business mainstreamers besting insurgent small-government purists. The bank had helped American businesses since the New Deal sell their goods and services abroad by providing loans and financing guarantees to overseas customers. Critics argued that the bank represented crony capitalism, and the GOP tea party wing engineered a legislative impasse that prevented the bank from engaging in new business after June, when its authorization expired.

In October, Republicans sympathetic to the entreaties of big corporations, such as Boeing and General Electric, fought back. After Speaker John A. Boehner's resignation announcement, Republicans circulated a discharge petition, a process that rarely works because majority party members fear reprisal for signing on. This time, however, forty-one GOP members joined most Democrats in adding their names. It was the first successful discharge petition since the 2002 enactment of a campaign-finance law. The House voted 246–177 on a motion to discharge a rule to bring the bank measure (HR 597) to the floor. The language reauthorizing the bank until 2019 was ultimately added to the highway bill cleared in December.

Keystone Pipeline

With the proposed Keystone XL pipeline from Canada becoming a potent political symbol for supporters and opponents with respect to North American energy security versus global climate change, Republicans and some Democrats tried to force the administration to approve the project. Within days of Republicans taking control of the Senate, the Energy and Natural Resources committee approved the Keystone bill January 8 on the same day that the House approved its own version (HR 3) by 266–153 despite a White House veto threat. The full Senate approved the bill 62–36 with nine Democrats supporting it on January 29. The House cleared the Senate version 270–152 on February 11, but Obama vetoed it on February 24. On March 4, the Senate mustered sixty-two votes to try to override the veto but needed sixty-seven votes. The administration subsequently used its executive authority to reject the pipeline.

Surface Transportation

Even in the most acrimonious times, a highway bill can unite Republicans and Democrats as few other pieces of legislation can. In December, Congress approved a five-year, $305 billion authorization for road and transit programs. The House voted 359–65 on December 3 to agree to the conference report on the surface transportation authorization (HR 22), and the Senate cleared the measure, 83–16, later the same day. With lawmakers at odds over how to bolster spending, conferees transferred $70 billion from the General Fund to the Highway Trust Fund.

Elementary and Secondary Education Act

Broad frustration with the George W. Bush administration's No Child Left Behind education law (PL 107–110) led to passage of an overhaul bill that Obama signed on December 10. One of the major achievements of the 114th Congress, the Elementary and Secondary Education Act (S 1177—PL 114–95) ended many federal accountability mandates over schools, resulting in less testing, and gave states significantly more say in education policy. The overhaul won bipartisan support for rolling back federal involvement in education, although some Republicans opposed the measure for not going far enough to reduce the Education Department's influence. Supporters of the bill, though, pointed out that it prohibited the education secretary from setting national academic standards, such as Common Core, or imposing conditions on states and school districts in exchange for grants or waivers.

Foreign Terrorism

The only time Congress voted to override President Barack Obama's veto was September 28, 2016. The House and Senate each voted to enact a law (S 2040) that allowed U.S. citizens to sue foreign nations for state sponsorship of terrorism. The Obama White House said the law called into question sovereign immunity and would jeopardize relations with Saudi Arabia and other countries. But supporters of the legislation argued it was narrowly written, and if foreign governments were to pass reciprocal laws, there would be little to fear because the United States does not sponsor terrorist attacks. The impetus for the legislation was that fifteen of the nineteen terrorists who hijacked planes on September 11, 2001, came from Saudi Arabia. Some believed Saudi officials knew about the attack and may have supported it. The Senate approved the legislation by voice vote in May, and the House passed it in September. Obama vetoed it September 23. The House voted 348–77 and the Senate voted 97–1 to override the veto.

Flint, Michigan

Despite concerns by conservatives, Congress authorized $170 million to help Flint, Mich., repair its lead-tainted drinking water system during its postelection lame-duck session. Congress also approved a stopgap spending bill that provided $120 million. Republicans from House Speaker Paul D. Ryan on down argued that the problem with Flint's water was a state and local responsibility and that helping the city would set a precedent for other water systems across the country. But Democrats led by Michigan Sens. Debbie Stabenow and Gary Peters insisted that the situation in Flint, where thousands of children were dealing with lead poisoning, required emergency action in Washington.

State Department

The State Department got its first authorization bill since 2002, after two years of persistent work by the House Foreign Affairs and Senate Foreign Relations committees. The authorization bill was narrowly written and did not set specific aid levels for Israel, Egypt, or other nations. Instead, it primarily authorized funding for department programs; embassy security enhancements; multilateral aid, such as international peacekeeping funds; and U.S. educational and cultural programs. Passage of the bill came the night before lawmakers closed up shop for the year. The House approved the amended package (S 1635) 374–16 on December 5. The Senate concurred by unanimous consent on December 10. President Obama signed it (PL 114–323) December 16.

Appropriations for 2016

The regular appropriations process for fiscal 2016 broke down early in the summer when Senate Democrats vowed to block consideration of any spending bills that adhered to discretionary spending limits set by the 2011 Budget Control Act (PL 112–25). To avoid a government shutdown when fiscal 2015 appropriations expired on September 30, Congress passed a ten-week continuing resolution (PL 114–53) on the last day of the fiscal year to keep the government open through December 11. On October 26, congressional leaders and the White House reached an agreement to raise discretionary spending caps by $80 billion over two years and suspend the debt limit until March 2017. The increases in spending limits—$50 billion in fiscal 2016 and $30 billion in fiscal 2017—were split evenly between defense and nondefense accounts, a victory for Democrats who had long maintained that any boost in defense spending should be accompanied by an equal increase in domestic spending. Congress passed two short-term continuing resolutions (HR 2250, H J Res 78) to fund the government for a combined eleven days after the initial December 11 deadline, giving negotiators extra time to finish the wrap-up fiscal legislation.

The spending legislation was tied to a package of tax-break extensions and included provisions reauthorizing the 9/11 first responders health care program and lifting a decades-old ban on crude oil exports. The increases in spending limits set by the budget deal were offset by a variety of spending cuts and revenue increases, including selling crude oil from the Strategic Petroleum Reserve at the rate of 5 million barrels a year starting in fiscal 2018, rising to 10 million barrels from 2023 through 2025. The plan also would raise revenue through auctioning off government-controlled electromagnetic spectrum, and it included tax-compliance provisions to raise revenue without an actual tax increase. Another provision in the legislation repealed a requirement in the 2010 health care law (PL 111–148, PL 111–152) for large employers to automatically enroll their employees in health care plans, saving them billions of dollars. The package further included a series of changes aimed at preventing the exhaustion of the Social Security disability insurance trust fund late in 2016, including a reallocation of payroll tax revenue between the main fund and the disability fund and various measures aimed at encouraging work and cracking down on fraud and abuse. In addition, the package provided relief to Medicare beneficiaries who otherwise would be hit by steeply rising Medicare premiums. The talks resulted in a $1.15 trillion omnibus appropriations bill (HR 2029), which was passed by both chambers on December 18 and signed into law by the president the same day.

Legislative Branch Spending Bill

The legislative branch spending plan was one of the first appropriations bills to move on the House side, passing in May 2015. The draft Senate proposal was backed by the Appropriations Committee but was never considered on the floor. Facing a December 11 deadline to keep the government open, the House bill was used as a sort of shell for a five-day continuing resolution (H J Res 75) to fund government operations until the omnibus appropriations bill was ready. The omnibus bill (HR 2029) passed the House, 316–113, on December 18 and the Senate, 65–33, on the same day, with Obama signing it into law hours later.

Overall, HR 2029 provided about $1.2 billion for House operations, equal to the fiscal 2015 enacted level. The Senate received $870.2 million, $5.9 million above the fiscal 2015 enacted level, with the additional funding marked for upgrades to the Senate financial management system and data network security. Once again, lawmakers wrote themselves out of a pay raise and maintained a freeze on salaries for members of Congress that began in 2010. Rank-and-file members and senators earned $174,000 a year, while the top elected leaders in both parties earned more.

With terrorist attacks in Paris and San Bernardino fresh in the minds of lawmakers, the omnibus provided $375 million for the Capitol Police, a $27 million increase from the fiscal 2015 enacted level. The agency's budget had more than quadrupled in the fifteen years since the September 11, 2001, attacks. The funding increase also took into account Capitol Police security provided to congressional leaders attending the 2016 Republican and Democratic presidential nominating conventions in Cleveland and Philadelphia, respectively.

The Architect of the Capitol's office, which is responsible for maintaining the Capitol complex and its grounds, received

$528.7 million under the measure—a $73 million decrease from the fiscal 2015 enacted level. With the four-year, $60 million Capitol Dome restoration fully paid for and on schedule for completion in 2017, the focus shifted to the modernization of the 108-year-old Cannon House Office Building. That project was expected to take a decade and cost nearly $800 million, with $62 million provided for fiscal 2016.

The bill also provided $600 million for the Library of Congress, an increase of $9.1 million above fiscal 2015; $531 million for the Government Accountability Office, an increase of $9 million; and $46.5 million for the Congressional Budget Office, a slight increase above the $46 million in fiscal 2015. The bill included a provision that urged the Capitol Police Board to allow sledding on Capitol Hill. Children in the surrounding neighborhood had drawn national headlines in the previous year for defying a ban on the pastime that was implemented after the 9/11 attacks.

2016

EPA Water Rules

The House voted 253–166 on January 13 to rescind an Obama-era regulation that allowed the Environmental Protection Agency to regulate small streams and wetlands to check pollution under the Clean Water Act. The Senate had earlier passed the resolution (J Res 22) 53–44 in November, but President Barack Obama vetoed the measure six days after the House vote.

Conservatives, farm groups, and others blasted the rule known as Waters of the United States from the EPA and the U.S. Army Corps of Engineers as a costly and invasive example of executive overreach. The rule's enforcement was stayed by a federal appeals court, but under the Congressional Review Act, Republicans could vote to nullify it within sixty days of finalization.

LGBT Discrimination

Amid the national debate over LGBT rights and religious liberty, the House voted 223–195 on May 25 to bar federal contractors from discriminating against LGBT employees. The vote on an Energy–Water appropriations bill (HR 5055) came after North Carolina enacted a law requiring individuals in public schools and government buildings to use bathrooms and other facilities that correspond to the sex on their birth certificates. Rep. Sean Patrick Maloney, D-N.Y., an openly gay, married father, tried to add the provision a week before the energy vote to a bill funding military construction and the Department of Veterans Affairs. But Republican leaders held the vote open and defeated the amendment 212–213 as Democrats shouted, "Shame!"

Gun Control

After the shooting deaths of forty-nine patrons of an Orlando nightclub June 12, Democrats urged for more restrictions on gun sales. The killings blamed on either an act of Islamic terrorism or a hate crime against gays were the deadliest mass shooting in American history at the time. Neither of two Senate amendments were adopted. Democratic Sen. Christopher S. Murphy of Connecticut, a longtime proponent of stricter gun laws, spoke for fifteen hours on the Senate floor just three days after the killings, holding up debate of the Commerce-Justice-Science appropriations bill. The move won him votes on two gun-control amendments. One from Dianne Feinstein, D-Calif., aimed to bar gun sales to known or suspected terrorists. The other from Murphy would have closed a loophole that allowed gun dealers to sell firearms at gun shows without subjecting buyers to background checks required at shops. The Feinstein amendment was blocked on a procedural vote 47–53. The Murphy amendment, similar to a proposal voted down in 2013 after the mass shooting at Sandy Hook Elementary School, was rejected 44–56.

Zika Funding

Congress agreed to spend $1.1 billion in response to the Zika virus, an infection spread primarily by mosquitoes that spread north from South America and reached Florida and other states in 2015. President Obama sought $1.9 billion for the effort, but House Republicans agreed to $1.1 billion as part of the Military Construction–VA appropriations bill (HR 2577) with a 239–171 vote on the conference report June 23. Although that bill never became law, the Zika provision became part of a stopgap spending measure approved in September.

Puerto Rico Debt

Congress threw a lifeline to storm-ravaged Puerto Rico on June 29 when the Senate cleared a bill (S 2328) 68–30 to rescue the U.S. territory from its crippling $72 billion debt. The legislation would halt creditor lawsuits while providing a path for debt restructuring and establishing a seven-member oversight board to manage the island's finances. Despite its passage, the measure provoked opposition from all sides. Democrats favored Chapter 9 bankruptcy protection for Puerto Rico, similar to what was afforded Detroit and other governmental authorities. Opponents, including bondholders and Republicans, argued that such a move would reward bad behavior and only solve about 30 percent of the island's debt problems. Lawmakers also worried that states would seek bankruptcy protection. Liberals deplored provisions that lowered the island's minimum wage for young workers, while others said that instituting an unelected fiscal control board to run much of the country's finances amounted to neocolonialism.

Appropriations for 2017

Republican leaders of the House and Senate promised a return to "regular order" for appropriations in which they would pass all twelve individual spending bills for the first time since 1994. But House Speaker Ryan and

Senate Majority Leader McConnell were unable to pass even a year-end omnibus appropriations bill as they had in 2015. The most they could manage were continuing resolutions—one that would keep the government operating through the end of the fiscal year in September and another to extend spending through March 2017.

On September 28, with two days to spare before a partial government shutdown, the Senate passed a ten-week continuing resolution to fund the government through December 9 (PL 114–223). After the election of Trump as president, Republican leaders settled on a plan to punt final fiscal 2017 funding decisions into the spring of 2017, giving the new administration a chance to weigh in. The continuing resolution would fund the government until April 28 at the fiscal 2017 cap of $1.07 trillion.

Legislative Branch Spending Bill

The House passed a fiscal 2017 legislative branch appropriations bill in June 2016. It skipped a pay raise for the eighth consecutive year, but there was no conference with the Senate, where a bill had been hastily marked up in May but went no further. Instead, the House bill (HR 5325) in September became the vehicle for a ten-week continuing resolution that kept the government operating until December.

The House Legislative Branch Appropriations Subcommittee approved a $3.5 billion draft bill on April 20 by voice vote. The spending level would be about $73 million above the fiscal 2016 enacted level and $152 million below the request from the Obama administration. The bill contained $1.2 billion to fund the operations of the House, the same level as fiscal 2016.

Political differences overshadowed the House bill. The ranking Democrat on the subcommittee, Debbie Wasserman Schultz of Florida, complained of last-minute changes, such as instructing the Library of Congress to continue use of the term *illegal alien* for undocumented immigrants. Subcommittee Chair Tom Graves, R-Ga., said that he did not consider the term controversial and that it represented an attempt to use the references that are found in U.S. code.

The Library of Congress would have a $629 million budget for fiscal 2017, an increase of $29 million above the previous year. The increase would be used to migrate the library's primary computing facility to a new location, which would provide improved reliability to support the library's operations. Graves had expressed concerns the year before about technological weaknesses at the library.

The bill would provide $391.3 million for the Capitol Police, an increase of $16.3 million. The Architect of the Capitol's office would be funded at $560 million, $31 million above the fiscal 2016 enacted level. Its major expenditures for fiscal 2017 would include $62 million for the restoration and renovation of the Cannon House Office Building and $30.8 million for the Rayburn House Office Building garage rehabilitation project.

The House Appropriations Committee approved the $3.5 billion bill by voice vote on May 17 after adopting a proposal from Rep. Sam Farr, D-Calif., that would provide an additional $8.3 million for the Members Representational Allowance account. The 1.5 percent increase, which would come out of the Architect of the Capitol's construction and operations fund, would amount to $18,821 of additional funding per office. Lawmakers who backed the proposal lamented the constant turnover of personnel leaving for better-paying opportunities. They said their staffs—but not the members—deserved a raise. Wasserman Schultz read aloud housing costs in Washington to illustrate how hard she said it was to survive when just starting out.

Lawmakers rejected, 24–25, Wasserman Schultz's amendment removing report language instructing the Library of Congress to continue using *illegal alien* to describe undocumented immigrants. The library had announced it would be changing the term *aliens* to *noncitizens* and *illegal immigration* to *unauthorized immigration*. The committee also rejected Democratic amendments to increase public access to reports by the Congressional Research Service and to defund the Select Investigative Panel on Infant Lives, which was established in October 2015 to investigate fetal tissue procurement and abortion practices.

CHAPTER 16

The Obama Presidency

The Presidency of Barack Obama: The Second Term

Despite a clear electoral victory over Republican presidential nominee Mitt Romney in 2012, President Barack Obama's second term was beset from the beginning by intractable Republican opposition, fueled in part by continued hostility to the Affordable Care Act. Obama began 2013 staring at a fiscal cliff of difficult choices about government spending that culminated with a temporary government shutdown, as the fundamental disputes about priorities remained unresolved. As he assembled his second Cabinet, several of his nominees faced unexpected opposition. Sluggishness on a variety of nominees prompted Senate Democrats to change the filibuster rule to reduce the threshold needed to approve executive-branch and judicial nominees other than for the Supreme Court. Deepening Obama's challenges, Republicans took control of the Senate in the 2014 elections. He spent most of his final year unable to fill a vacancy on the high court—one of the biggest defeats of his presidency, with an impact that could potentially last decades.

Legislative priorities fared little better. Even the strongest spurs couldn't budge Obama's proposals for gun control and an immigration overhaul. The shooting deaths of twenty children and six staffers at an elementary school on the eve of his second term was not enough to persuade the Senate to adopt restrictions on buying guns or ammunition. Yet gun violence echoed repeatedly across the country during his second term, sending him to eulogize the victims at a South Carolina church, meet with survivors at an Oregon community college, speak more broadly about terrorism at a California workplace, and meet with survivors of a Florida nightclub shooting. An immigration overhaul made only slightly more progress. A Senate compromise on comprehensive immigration changes was ignored in the House, where Republicans instead approved stricter enforcement measures. The opposition also killed measures large and small. Obama proposed to provide free tuition for students to attend community college, but the effort died amid Republican reluctance to create another federal program. During the 113th Congress, he had to thread the needle for legislation between a Republican House and Democratic Senate that differed on seven out of every ten roll-call votes—the highest partisanship in six decades of *Congressional Quarterly* analysis. The challenge became more pronounced for the final two years of his term, when Republicans gained control of the Senate, too.

Aware of the partisan challenges he faced, Obama announced what became known as his pen-and-phone strategy for 2014 and beyond. He would focus on initiatives he could accomplish through executive action, such as raising the minimum wage for federal contractors. And when legislation was needed, he would work the phones to recruit supporters. "We are not just going to be waiting for legislation in order to make sure that we are providing Americans the kind of help that they need," Obama said at a Cabinet meeting January 14, 2014. "I've got a pen and I've got a phone. I can use that pen to sign executive orders and take executive actions and administrative actions to move the ball forward."

Results of the executive action were mixed. The Environmental Protection Agency released long-awaited climate-change rules in 2014 for power plants to reduce carbon emissions by about one-third by 2030. The rules never went into effect, however, because of court challenges. Meanwhile, he temporarily blocked the proposed Keystone XL Pipeline, first by vetoing congressional authorization and then by rejecting the application outright. Obama recognized the rights of lesbian, gay, bisexual, and transgender individuals through an executive order expanding workplace protections to prevent discrimination against LGBT employees of federal contractors.

Obama avoided the pitfalls of second terms of his two predecessors: Democrat Bill Clinton having been impeached in the House and Republican George W. Bush having faced the worst economic collapse since the Great Depression. Obama took office during the downturn, and he left with the highest level of household income ever recorded, according to an analysis by FactCheck.org. The economy added 11.6 million jobs, according to the Bureau of Labor Statistics. The unemployment rate declined from 7.8 percent to 4.8 percent during his tenure. The Standard and Poor's 500 stock index more than doubled, rising by 166 percent while Obama was in office.

Whatever the domestic friction, Obama achieved some of his grandest accomplishments through foreign affairs.

In a landmark opening to Cuba, he reopened diplomatic relations with the island neighbor that had been severed before he was born. Years of secret negotiations with Iran led to a historic agreement that aimed to freeze the adversary's nuclear-weapons program. Such initiatives could be reversed, however, by a subsequent administration's own executive orders because Obama did not win legislative approval for them.

Proving that the pen was mightier than the sword was difficult in military action. In his 2009 acceptance speech for the Nobel Peace Prize, Obama had said, "War is sometimes necessary, and war at some level is an expression of human folly." While he significantly reduced the number of U.S. troops serving in Afghanistan, he did not reach his goal of completely withdrawing them. Congressional Republicans criticized his plans to withdraw from Afghanistan entirely, warning that setting a deadline would allow enemies in the Taliban and elsewhere to run out the clock on the U.S. military and then regain control of the country. In one of a series of coordinated speeches June 19, 2014, Minority Leader Mitch McConnell, R-Ky., said Obama was leaving America weaker and would leave his successor with daunting problems. Sen. Lindsey Graham, R-S.C., said as U.S. defenses erode around the world, enemies would be emboldened, and another attack like 9/11 could hit the United States.

Obama made little headway in curbing the civil war in Syria even after the use of chemical weapons by Damascus, with a Congress and American public weary of long-running conflicts in Afghanistan and Iraq. After Obama asked Congress in 2013 for authorization to use military force against Syria for the use of chemical weapons, congressional Republicans were divided. The chair of the Senate Foreign Relations Committee, Sen. Bob Corker, R-Tenn., said he supported air strikes but not sending troops into Syria. Sens. John McCain, R-Ariz., and Lindsey Graham, R-S.C., said military strikes should be part of an overall strategy to change momentum on the battlefield. The chair of the House Armed Services Committee, Rep. Mac Thornberry, R-Texas, said military action might be necessary in the future but not at that point. House Speaker Paul D. Ryan, R-Wis., said Obama's proposal would not achieve its stated objectives. Senate Republican Leader Mitch McConnell of Kentucky said a vital security risk was clearly not at play. Obama's dismissive attitude toward the Islamic State was met with dramatic expansion of militant territory in Iraq and Syria under his watch. Obama was unable to reverse Russia's seizure of Crimea through sanctions. And while Obama reduced the number of detainees in Guantanamo, he was unable to close the military prison that had been the subject of one of his first executive orders in taking office.

Obama did succeed in promoting a message of peace and reconciliation through unique travels. He visited Vietnam and lifted an arms embargo that had stood for fifty years. He visited Hiroshima, one of two cities in Japan where the United States dropped atomic bombs to end World War II. "We are not bound by genetic code to repeat the mistakes of the past," Obama said in a speech in Hiroshima on May 27, 2016. "We can learn. We can choose. We can tell our children a different story, one that describes a common humanity, one that makes war less likely and cruelty less easily accepted."

During the final weeks of the 2016 presidential campaign, Obama tried to cement his legacy by campaigning for Democrat Hillary Clinton to succeed him rather than Republican Donald Trump. Obama planned to devote one or two days each week during October to campaign with rallies, targeted radio and television ads, and fundraising as a referendum on his agenda. Obama told a Congressional Black Caucus Foundation dinner September 18, 2016, that he would work as hard as he could to protect his legacy. Typical household incomes rose about $2,800 and 3.5 million people were lifted out of poverty, he said. Tolerance, justice, good schools, and ending mass incarceration were all on the ballot, he said.

"We've still got so much work to do, and we are sprinting all the way through the tape," Obama said at the dinner. "My name may not be on the ballot, but our progress is on the ballot."

Obama also needed a Democrat to succeed him or risk reversal of executive actions as varied as setting power-plant emissions standards, restoring diplomatic ties with Cuba, blocking the Keystone XL Pipeline, or setting rules governing the military use of drones. Trump's victory and continued Republican control of Congress threatened those policies. It also meant that Obama's signature legislative achievements during this two-term presidency, such as the Affordable Care Act, could be greatly scaled back or even terminated.

Obama had his highest approval rating—67 percent—the week he took office in 2009, according to the Gallup daily national survey of about 1,500 adults. He entered his second term with a 54 percent approval rating and it ebbed to its lowest at 40 percent several times during 2014, when criticism of the health-care overhaul was fiercest. Obama left office at a second-term peak of 59 percent approval rating, but he had the most polarized approval ratings of any president dating to Dwight D. Eisenhower in the 1950s, according to Gallup. Obama averaged 83 percent job approval among Democrats and only 13 percent among Republicans during his administration. That 70-point gap eclipsed the previous high of 61 points for George W. Bush. Other presidents had gaps of 55 points or less, according to Gallup. Obama sparked strong feelings on both sides. While those on the left continued to support him, Republicans were almost uniformly hostile. At times, their opposition took the form of racist remarks. The mayor of the small West Virginia town of Clay, for example, generated a national uproar and subsequently resigned after approving comments by another official that compared First Lady Michelle Obama to an ape. For his part, Obama said America was imperfect but always striving for improvement.

"If I had told you eight years ago that America would reverse a great recession, reboot our auto industry, and unleash the longest stretch of job creation in our history, if I had told you that we would open up a new chapter with the Cuban people, shut down Iran's nuclear weapons program without firing a shot, and take out the mastermind of 9/11, if I had told you that we would win marriage equality, and secure the right to health insurance for another 20 million of our fellow citizens—you might have said our sights were set a little too high," Obama said in his farewell address January 10, 2017. "But that's what we did. That's what you did."

Domestic Policy

Obama made proposals on some of the most contentious issues facing the country, including gun control, immigration policy, and climate change. But Congress thwarted these initiatives. Instead, disputes over federal spending often dominated the domestic agenda during Obama's second term, leading to a government shutdown in 2013 and punting final decisions in 2016 into the lap of his successor.

BUDGET BATTLES

The 2013 term opened with Congress standing on the edge of a so-called fiscal cliff of potential spending cuts and tax increases that both parties feared could send the economy into recession. A compromise negotiated during the closing days of 2012 raced through both chambers on January 1, despite grumbling primarily among House Republicans about tax hikes without big enough spending cuts.

The respite was temporary. The antagonism between the Republican House and a Democratic Senate prevented consensus even on spending bills, leading to a sixteen-day government shutdown in October 2013. Looming behind the fight was the Republican effort to repeal Obama's signature Affordable Care Act. But Obama refused to budge on spending cuts or Obamacare, and Republicans surrendered to reopen the government and raise the debt ceiling. He told reporters on October 8 that corporate CEOs and economists had warned that failing to raise the debt limit, as Republicans had flirted with two years earlier, would be "insane, catastrophic, chaos."

The debt limit had been raised $305 billion in May 2013 to nearly $16.7 trillion. The deal to reopen the government led to another $512 billion increase in February 2014 to more than $17.2 trillion.

The regular appropriations process for fiscal 2016 broke down early in the summer when Senate Democrats vowed to block consideration of any spending bills that adhered to discretionary spending limits set by the 2011 Budget Control Act. Democrats argued for negotiations toward a bipartisan budget deal similar to the one struck in 2013 to provide more money for both defense and nondefense programs. Eventually, after a ten-week continuing resolution into the new fiscal year, congressional leaders and the White House then reached a compromise in December 2015 to raise discretionary spending caps by $80 billion over two years and suspend the debt limit until March 2017. The fight would resume with a new president.

"I'm not wild about everything in it—I'm sure that's true for everybody—but it is a budget that, as I insisted, invests in our military and our middle class, without ideological provisions that would have weakened Wall Street reform or rules on big polluters," Obama told reporters at the White House on December 18, 2015.

GUN CONTROL

Spasms of gun violence echoed repeatedly throughout Obama's second term. He met with relatives of victims. He urged more effective gun control repeatedly, but his legislative proposals were ignored in the House and died in the Senate. The only success came in an extension of a twenty-five-year-old ban on plastic guns.

The shooting deaths of twenty students and six staff members at Sandy Hook Elementary School in Newtown, Conn., put gun control at the top of Obama's agenda in December 2012. The gunman, Adam Lanza, who had a history of mental illness, had also killed his mother, who was the legal owner of the guns, and himself. Obama appointed a Cabinet-level task force headed by Vice President Joseph R. Biden Jr. On January 16, 2013—days before his second inauguration—Obama announced a package of legislative proposals and twenty-three executive actions designed to curtail gun use.

The legislative proposals included expanding criminal and mental-health background checks required for buying from licensed retail stores to include purchases at gun shows and private sales; renewing the bans on sale and manufacture of military-style assault weapons and magazines that hold more than ten rounds of ammunition; expanding a ban on manufacture and import of armor-piercing bullets to also prohibit their possession and transfer; strengthening penalties for "straw purchases" in which purchasers buy guns for people ineligible to own firearms; and providing more money for police, mental-health services, and school security. Republican House leaders refused to take up any measures until the Democratic-led Senate approved something. After a series of high-profile setbacks, Majority Leader Harry Reid, D-Nev., pulled the bill from the floor.

The defeat left Obama largely empty-handed as he mourned more shooting deaths with the relatives of victims. He gave a eulogy June 26, 2015, for the victims of a racially motivated church shooting in Charleston, S.C. He met October 9, 2015, with survivors of a shooting at Umpqua Community College in Oregon. He gave a broader speech on terrorism after the San Bernardino shootings on December 8, 2015. And he met with the survivors of the June 16, 2016, shooting in a gay Orlando nightclub.

One exception to the legislative defeats was the extension in December 2013 of the 1988 Undetectable Firearms

Act (PL 100–649). The law against plastic weapons required firearms to contain at least 3.7 ounces of metal and to be shaped like guns so they could be spotted in X-ray machines and by metal detectors.

IMMIGRATION

Immigration was another long-debated issue for which Obama urged action repeatedly but without legislative success. On January 29, 2013, one of the first speeches of his second term fleshed out his proposal for a path to citizenship for 11 million illegal immigrants. "I'm here because most Americans agree that it's time to fix a system that's been broken for way too long," Obama said at Del Sol High School in Las Vegas. "I'm here because business leaders, faith leaders, labor leaders, law enforcement, and leaders from both parties are coming together to say now is the time to find a better way to welcome the striving, hopeful immigrants who still see America as the land of opportunity." He called attention to the issue repeatedly, with speeches on June 11, October 24, and November 25, but the ambitious legislation stalled in Congress. Even when Obama relied on executive action to defer the deportation of as many as 4 million immigrants, lawmakers challenged him and tried to block him.

The Senate Judiciary Committee supported a comprehensive, bipartisan bill after five days of markup in May. The bill was designed to set in motion a thirteen-year process to grant citizenship to illegal immigrants, with an expedited process for those who arrived as children. Other provisions aimed to ease visa restrictions for high-tech workers, strengthen border security and interior enforcement, set up an agriculture worker program, and reduce the backlog of applicants for permanent-residency visas. A floor amendment from Republican Sens. John Hoeven of North Dakota and Bob Corker of Tennessee would have doubled the number of border guards in the Southwest and built 700 miles of fencing. On June 27, the Senate approved the bill on a 68–32 vote, with fourteen Republicans joining all Democrats.

The House refused to consider a comprehensive package of legislation, amid concerns that more conservative provisions would be weakened in conference. Instead, House committees developed a series of narrower bills for subjects such as employment verification and farm workers, most of which were not considered on the floor. House Speaker John A. Boehner, R-Ohio, became more noncommittal as the year progressed.

The 114th Congress opened in January 2015 with another bruising fight over Obama's executive action aimed at preventing the deportation of nearly 5 million illegal immigrants. The goal of the initiative called Deferred Action for Parents of Americans and Lawful Permanent Residents (DAPA) was to focus enforcement actions on national-security threats, serious criminals, and recent border crossers. The program allowed immigrants to obtain work authorization for three years at a time if they registered with

the government, submitted biometric data, passed background checks, and paid back taxes. House conservatives tried and failed to block the initiative through legislation. Opponents won in court what they could not block through legislation. Some twenty-six states brought a lawsuit in December 2014 against Obama's latest executive actions. U.S. District Court Judge Andrew Hanen, a George W. Bush appointee who sits in Texas, found that one of the states, Texas, had the legal right to file a lawsuit challenging the actions because of potential costs to the state. On February 16, 2015, Hanen blocked implementation of Obama's actions until the conclusion of the case. The lawsuit's success was what gave the Republican-controlled Congress the confidence to pass a Homeland Security spending bill without immigration riders. The administration appealed that ruling, but a panel of the U.S. Court of Appeals for the 5th Circuit upheld the lower court's decision in a 2–1 ruling handed down on November 9, 2015.

MINIMUM WAGE

The minimum wage for businesses with federal contracts rose from $7.25 per hour to $10.10 in 2015 under an executive order Obama signed February 12, 2014. The order covered contracts that provide the federal government with concessions, services, and construction but not that provide goods such as supplies. Workers who benefitted were concession workers in national parks, nursing assistants caring for veterans, and people who maintain the grounds on military bases, according to the White House. "Not only is it good for the economy, it's the right thing to do," Obama told a gathering in the East Room of the White House on February 12, 2014. "If you work full-time, you shouldn't be living in poverty."

The last time Congress had raised the minimum wage was in 2007, which phased in the higher rate from $6.55 per hour to $7.25 in July 2009. States increased the challenge. Voters approved ballot initiatives to raise the minimum wage in New Jersey in 2013; in Alaska, Arkansas, Illinois, Nebraska, and South Dakota in 2014; and in Arizona, California, Colorado, Maine, and Washington state in 2016.

CLIMATE CHANGE

The Environmental Protection Agency released long-awaited climate-change rules in 2014 for power plants to reduce carbon emissions by about one-third by 2030. The rules never went into effect because of court challenges. Meanwhile, Obama temporarily blocked the proposed Keystone XL Pipeline, first by vetoing congressional authorization and then by rejecting the application outright.

In a June 25, 2013, speech at Georgetown University, Obama directed the EPA to move ahead with strict limits on carbon emissions and instructed the State Department to reject the Keystone pipeline if it would significantly boost greenhouse-gas emissions. "We don't have time for a meeting of the Flat Earth Society," he told the Georgetown audience after 97 percent of scientists agreed that the planet is warming and human activity is contributing to it.

Obama said the question is whether the country will have the courage to act before it is too late. "As a President, as a father, and as an American, I'm here to say we need to act," Obama told the Georgetown University audience June 25, 2013.

Congressional Republicans and fossil-fuel industries immediately criticized the action plan, calling it a war on coal. Senate Minority Leader Mitch McConnell, R-Ky., said declaring a war on coal was tantamount to declaring a war on jobs.

The Supreme Court blocked the plan from taking effect in early 2016, pending the outcome of a lawsuit by two dozen states, coal, and utility companies. The lawsuit, which accused the EPA of exceeding its authority, was not resolved during Obama's administration.

On another climate-related issue, Obama on February 24, 2015, vetoed legislation authorizing the Keystone pipeline. The Senate vote of 62–36 to override the veto fell short of the 66 needed. Obama formally rejected TransCanada's application for the pipeline on November 6, 2015. "It became a symbol too often used as a campaign cudgel by both parties rather than a serious policy matter," Obama told reporters that day in the Roosevelt Room of the White House, flanked by Secretary of State John Kerry and Vice President Joseph R. Biden Jr.

COMMUNITY COLLEGE

Another example where a lofty proposal from Obama died amid congressional opposition dealt with his proposal to provide free tuition for community college. If all fifty states participated, the White House estimated 9 million students each year could save an average of $3,800 in tuition while earning half a bachelor's degree or technical skills needed in the workforce. The proposal was estimated to cost $61 billion over a decade.

The proposal envisioned the federal government paying three-quarters of the costs if each participating state contributed the remainder. Students who participated would have been required to attend at least half time and maintain a 2.5 grade point average. Community colleges were required to offer academic programs accepted at four-year colleges and universities or occupational training with high graduation rates.

"Forty percent of our college students choose community college," Obama said in his 2015 State of the Union speech. "Some are young and starting out. Some are older and looking for a better job. Some are veterans and single parents trying to transition back into the job market. Whoever you are, this plan is your chance to graduate ready for the new economy, without a load of debt."

Congressional Democrats introduced legislation in July mirroring Obama's proposal, but the bills stalled without votes. Congressional Republicans were reluctant to start

another government program, and none cosponsored the bills. "I've gotten a little resistance from members of Congress—that will shock you," Obama said September 9, 2015, at Macomb Community College outside Detroit. A former U.S. Education secretary, Sen. Lamar Alexander, R-Tenn., who chaired the panel overseeing education policy, suggested simplifying the 108-question application for student aid, which would encourage more applications for Pell grants that students do not have to repay. Pell grants average $3,300, while the average tuition for community college averaged $3,800, he said. Nationally, sixteen states had community-college tuition that could be covered by Pell grants, he said.

LGBT RIGHTS

With the public increasingly supportive of gay rights, Obama enjoyed success in extending protections to the lesbian, gay, bisexual, and transgender community without legislation. He signed an executive order July 21, 2014, expanding workplace protections to prevent discrimination against LGBT employees of federal contractors. The move came as a Senate-passed bill to extend workplace protections for all Americans languished without a vote in the House. At the time, eighteen states and the District of Columbia prohibited workplace discrimination based on sexual orientation or gender identity, and another three prohibited workplace discrimination based only on sexual orientation, according to the Human Rights Campaign.

On June 24, 2015, the Supreme Court struck down the Defense of Marriage Act and legalized gay marriage in the case called *Obergefell v. Hodges*. A year later, Obama designated the Stonewall National Monument for Christopher Park in New York City to recognize the significance of a 1969 uprising that galvanized the LGBT movement. The park was a popular destination during the 1960s for youths who had run away from home or been kicked out. Early on June 28, 1969, a riot broke out in response to a police raid on the Stonewall Inn, at the time one of the city's best-known LGBT bars. "The Stonewall Uprising is considered by many to be the catalyst that launched the modern LGBT civil rights movement," Obama said in a statement accompanying the declaration.

PUERTO RICO

Puerto Rico's economic crisis prompted Obama to propose a package of legislation in November 2015 in an effort to spur growth, enhance the labor force, and increase Medicaid coverage. At the time, Puerto Rico's $70 billion of debt and $45 billion in unfunded pension liabilities dwarfed the commonwealth's stagnant economy, and servicing the debt consumed one-third of government revenues.

In June 2016, Congress threw Puerto Rico a lifeline two days before the territory said it would default on a $2 billion debt payment. The legislation put a halt to creditor lawsuits against the island and established a seven-member oversight board to manage the island's finances. Sen. Robert Menendez, D-N.J., criticized the bill for treating the people of Puerto Rico "like subjects, not citizens." Treasury Secretary Jacob J. Lew made several trips to Capitol Hill lobbying for the bill and warning of chaos if it was not passed. "This bill is not perfect," Obama said after the Senate cleared the bill, "but it is a critical first step toward economic recovery and restored hope for millions of Americans who call Puerto Rico home."

Foreign Policy

Military challenges around the globe defied easy answers for Obama, as they had for his predecessors. Militants in Afghanistan prevented the United States from withdrawing entirely, as he had proposed. The Islamic State significantly expanded its territory in the Middle East. The military prison in Guantanamo Bay remained open despite being one of Obama's earliest goals to close. And he was unable to reverse Russia's annexation of Crimea through sanctions.

Obama enjoyed some of his biggest successes in foreign affairs, however, through landmark initiatives with fierce adversaries. He reopened diplomatic relations with Cuba after a half-century hiatus by arguing that the previous policy of isolation had not worked. He also negotiated a deal with Iran to halt its nuclear-weapons program in exchange for an easing of sanctions. Congressional Republicans harshly criticized each of his military and diplomatic initiatives as naïve and potentially weakening U.S. national security.

AFGHANISTAN

Withdrawing troops from Afghanistan was a priority during Obama's second term, with the aspiration of having Afghan troops defend their own country. Defense Secretary Leon Panetta had announced in November 2012 that U.S. troops would no longer be involved in combat operations by the end of 2014. In the State of the Union speech February 12, 2013, Obama announced the goal of cutting the U.S. troop level in half, from 68,000 to 34,000 during the next year. "This drawdown will continue and by the end of next year, our war in Afghanistan will be over," Obama said.

However, the persistent threat that the Taliban would reclaim ground forced a lingering obligation for U.S. troops to remain a presence in their longest conflict beyond the end of Obama's term. The United States attacked Afghanistan for harboring al Qaeda terrorists less than a month after the September 11 attacks, in October 2001. The number of troops swelled from thousands to 20,300 by April 2004 in an effort to provide security along the border with Pakistan and for reconstruction projects, but the war in Iraq shifted attention and resources there. As fighting in Afghanistan intensified, Obama ordered in December 2009 another 33,000 troops to join the 67,000 already there. The number of troops peaked at 100,000 in August 2010, and the number was the same when Osama bin Laden was found and killed in neighboring Pakistan in May 2011. Obama announced a troop-reduction plan the next month. With 34,000 troops in Afghanistan in March 2014, Obama asked the Pentagon for options to completely withdraw because Afghan President Hamid Karzai refused to sign a security agreement with the United States. Obama's goal was to remove nearly all troops by the end of 2016. But with threats from terrorism lingering, his revised plan in October 2015 was to leave 5,500 troops by the end of 2016. By July 2016, however, Afghanistan's security remained precarious enough that Obama kept the troop level at 8,400 for his successor to determine the next move.

HUMOR

President Barack Obama lightened up during his second term, wielding a wicked comic streak in an attempt to expand his political audience.

He appeared on a webcast titled *Between Two Ferns* with actor Zach Galifianakis on March 11, 2014, to promote his health care overhaul. After bantering about the *Hangover* movies and trash-talking about basketball, Obama got to promote the site healthcare.gov.

On *Jimmy Kimmel Live!* on October 24, 2016, Obama read mean tweets that had been written about him. "Is there any way we could fly Obama to some golf course halfway around the world and just leave him there?" one tweet asked.

"Well, RWSurferGirl, I think that's a great idea," Obama said.

On *The Late Show with Stephen Colbert* on October 18, 2016, he got some tips for finding another job because Colbert noted the difficulty in finding new work at fifty-five years old.

When asked to list his accomplishments, Obama lists reopening relations with Cuba, saving the auto industry, providing health care to tens of millions of people and receiving a Nobel Peace Prize. What did he do to win the prize? "To be honest, I still don't know," Obama said.

On *The Tonight Show Starring Jimmy Fallon* on June 9, 2016, Obama wrote thank-you notes with the host.

"Thank you, Congress, for spending eight years wishing you could replace me with a Republican," Obama said as a picture of Donald Trump appeared on the screen. "Or, to put it another way, how do you like me now?"

"As you are well aware, I do not support the idea of endless war," Obama said in the Roosevelt Room of the White House on October 15, 2015, but he was firmly convinced the country should make an extra effort to prevent the emergence of future threats.

Congressional Republicans welcomed the reversal but said it might not be enough to keep the peace. Senate Armed Services Chair John McCain of Arizona said Obama's goal of eventually reducing to 5,500 troops would be adequate for counterterrorism or training Afghans but not both. House Armed Services Chair Mac Thornberry of Texas said the plan avoided disaster but was not a plan for success.

Obama visited Bagram Air Base on May 25, 2014, to express thanks for the half-million troops who served in Afghanistan and the approximately 2,200 killed. Amid Afghan elections to choose a new government, Obama said the country was sending more girls to school and making dramatic improvements in public health and life expectancy and literacy. "Al Qaeda is on its heels in this part of the world, and that's because of you," Obama told the troops. "Even with all the challenges, more Afghans have hope for their future. And so much of that is because of you."

BOWE BERGDAHL

Obama announced a prisoner swap with the Taliban on May 31, 2014, days after his visit to Bagram Air Base, to secure the release of Sgt. Bowe Bergdahl after five years as a prisoner of war. Bergdahl was released in exchange for five Taliban detainees held at Guantanamo Bay, Cuba. Bergdahl "wasn't forgotten by his country because the United States of America does not ever leave our men and women in uniform behind," Obama told reporters May 31, 2014, in the Rose Garden at the White House while flanked by the soldier's parents, Bob and Jani Bergdahl.

The move became controversial almost immediately because of concerns the Taliban detainees could return to fighting. Bergdahl was also later revealed to have deserted his post, which endangered the troops who had searched for him. The Taliban detainees included two senior commanders said to be linked to operations that killed Americans. "I believe this decision will threaten the lives of American soldiers for years to come," said Rep. Mike Rogers, R-Mich., chair of the House Intelligence Committee.

Bergdahl was scheduled to face trial by court-martial after the end of Obama's term for desertion and misbehavior that endangered other soldiers. He had left his outpost in Afghanistan without permission in 2009 and was captured by militants, which prompted a fruitless search. His lawyers asked Obama in December 2016 to pardon Bergdahl because President-elect Donald Trump had called him "a no-good traitor who should have been executed." Obama did not pardon Bergdahl before leaving office.

ISLAMIC STATE

The Islamic State proved an expanding and difficult challenge during Obama's second term after he initially derided the stateless threat as a junior-varsity team in school. Obama had voted as a senator against the war in Iraq that began in 2003. After he was elected president in 2008, he withdrew all U.S. troops from Iraq by 2011. In a January 27, 2014, profile in *The New Yorker* magazine, Obama said al Qaeda had been decimated and Osama bin Laden had been killed. But in their wake, the Islamic State's flag was flying over Fallujah in Iraq and parts of Syria. "The analogy we use around here sometimes, and I think is accurate, is if a jayvee team puts on Lakers uniforms that doesn't make them Kobe Bryant," Obama said.

He later said he was not singling out the Islamic State but referring to various militant groups in the region. Even so, the group, also called the Islamic State of Iraq and the Levant or the Islamic State of Iraq and al-Sham, declared its caliphate on June 29, 2014. By midyear, it controlled hundreds of thousands of square miles of territory and was inspiring terrorist acts in the United States and other nations. In November, Obama authorized an additional 1,500 U.S. troops to Iraq, doubling the number of Americans meant to train Iraqi and Kurdish forces. In his 2016 State of the Union address, Obama acknowledged that conflict would continue to roil the Middle East for years. "The Middle East is going through a transformation that will play out for a generation, rooted in conflicts that date back millennia," he said.

GUANTANAMO BAY

One of the first actions Obama took in office was an executive order he signed January 22, 2009, to close the prison base for captured terrorists in Guantanamo Bay, Cuba. Proposals included prosecuting the detainees in U.S. courts, but the prospect of moving the detainees to U.S. prisons proved consistently controversial. While Obama reduced the number of detainees during his eight years, disputes about where to move dozens of detainees remained intractable and kept the prison open after his term ended.

Obama's initial order noted about 800 people had been detained during seven years at the base as enemy combatants. More than 500 had been returned to their home country or transferred to a third country. Obama sought "prompt and appropriate" action as to where to place the remaining individuals and closure of the facilities because of significant concerns raised in the United States and the international community about the detentions. By September 2015, Deputy Defense Secretary Robert Work said the administration had only developed a list of facilities where detainees could potentially be moved, with the costs associated with each option. Senate Armed Services Chair John McCain, R-Ariz., who had been pushing the administration for a more detailed roadmap, called the plan a wish or a hope.

Congressional Republicans warned that transfers from detention could jeopardize U.S. security. Sen. Kelly Ayotte, R-N.H., a member of the Armed Services Committee, said the safety of Americans, rather than the fulfillment of a misguided campaign promise, should guide national-security decisions. McCain threatened legislation that would suspend transfers of medium- and high-risk detainees from the prison and prohibit any transfers to Yemen for two years. McCain said in six years the administration never gave Congress a concrete plan for resolving the detainee issue. Obama threatened to veto legislation if it reached him.

The base held 242 detainees when Obama took office, and his administration repatriated or resettled 197, according to the group Human Rights First.

SYRIA

Obama said in 2012 that if Syria used chemical weapons against its own people, that would represent a red line that could draw international action. A revolt against Syrian President Bashar al-Assad had sunk into civil war. After a chemical attack in August 2013 in a Damascus suburb killed more than 1,500 people, Obama said the United States should act, but only after Congress authorized military action. "Our intelligence shows the Assad regime and its forces preparing to use chemical weapons, launching rockets in the highly populated suburbs of Damascus, and acknowledging that a chemical weapons attack took place," Obama said standing next to Vice President Joseph R. Biden Jr. in the White House Rose Garden on August 31, 2013. Obama gave a nationally televised speech September 10 reminding the country that the U.S. Senate had overwhelmingly agreed to join an international agreement in 1997, which now includes 189 governments, to prohibit the use of chemical weapons. "When dictators commit atrocities, they depend upon the world to look the other way until those horrifying pictures fade from memory. But these things happened. The facts cannot be denied," Obama said.

Despite horrific images of hundreds of children killed in the attack, there was little appetite in Congress to add to long-running military action in Afghanistan and Iraq. The United States endorsed a Russian-backed plan to remove 1,300 tons of chemical stocks from Syria, but chlorine that makes a potent weapon was not included because it is commonly used for water treatment and other industrial purposes. By October 2015, the administration announced it was sending a small number of special-operations forces to advise Syrian opposition fighters against the Islamic State. But that decision came weeks after the Pentagon walked away from a proposal to train and equip the rebels. Assad remained firmly in power. Leon Panetta, who served as secretary of Defense from 2011 to 2013, after a stint as Obama's CIA director, said that as time went on, uncertainty and ambivalence began to sneak in.

MILITARY DRONES

Obama defended the use of military drones as a necessary option in fighting the war against terrorists, despite the risk of unintended civilian casualties and moral concerns about targeting individuals for assassination. Despite his strong preference for detaining, interrogating, and prosecuting terrorists, Obama said in a May 23, 2013, speech at National Defense University that approach is sometimes unrealistic in distant tribal regions, empty deserts, and rugged mountains where they train.

Drone strikes are legal under domestic and international law because Congress authorized military force—a just war with proportional response—against al Qaeda, the Taliban, and associated forces a week after the attacks of September 11, 2001, according to Obama. Drone strikes are effective, having removed dozens of highly skilled al Qaeda commanders, trainers, and bomb makers from the battlefield, Obama said. "Simply put, these strikes have saved lives," he said.

In several cases, American citizens were targeted and killed. The highest-profile case was Anwar Awlaki, chief of external operations for al Qaeda in the Arabian Peninsula. Obama said it would not be constitutional to deploy armed drones over U.S. soil or kill just any citizen—with a drone or a shotgun—without due process. But Awlaki tried to kill people for years, including overseeing a cargo-bomb plot in 2010 and hosting attempted underwear bomber Farouk Abdulmutallab in 2009. Obama compared targeting him to having a SWAT team shoot a sniper firing on an innocent crowd. "As president, I would have been derelict in my duty had I not authorized the strike that took him out," Obama said in a speech May 23, 2013, at National Defense University at Fort McNair in Washington, D.C.

In July 2016, as the Obama administration neared its end, it released a report that between 64 and 116 civilians died from 2009 to 2015 from U.S. drone strikes outside of Iraq and Afghanistan. The strikes eliminated 2,372 to 2,581 militants during that period, according to the report, which was released to provide more transparency about the use of drones. Human rights groups, however, estimated that the figures undercounted civilians. Groups such as the Bureau of Investigative Journalism, the *Long War Journal*, and the New America Foundation estimated 200 to 1,000 civilians were killed. The identifications are sometimes murky. An easy case was a 2014 strike on a wedding in Yemen that killed twelve, but other cases were less clear. Hina Shamsi, director of the American Civil Liberties Union's National Security Project, said the government continued to conceal the identities of people it had killed, the specific definitions used to determine who could be targeted legitimately, and the investigations into credibly alleged wrongful killings.

IRAN

The Obama administration negotiated what officials called a groundbreaking freeze to Iran's nuclear program in exchange for relief from sanctions on that country. The deal provoked relentless opposition from congressional Republicans—and a key Senate Democrat—who tried to overturn it.

Hostilities between the countries dated to the 1979 Iranian revolution, when fifty-two U.S. officials were held hostage at the embassy for more than a year. Beginning in 1995, Congress passed a series of laws authorizing sanctions against Iran that gave the president wide discretion in how to put them into place. Presidents Bill Clinton, George W. Bush, and Obama all signed executive orders ramping up those sanctions, which Obama aides credit with bringing Iran to the table for negotiations.

The initial deal was announced November 24, 2013, for Iran to freeze its nuclear program for six months in exchange for limited sanctions relief. Negotiations then reached a longer-term deal between Iran and the United States, the United Kingdom, Russia, France, China, Germany, and the European Union. The Joint Comprehensive Plan of Action was announced July 14, 2015, for Iran to convert and reduce its nuclear facilities and allow for international inspections in exchange for access to tens of billions of dollars in oil revenue and frozen assets overseas. But details were disputed as Iran and the United States released separate summaries of the agreement. Iran agreed to give inspectors from the International Atomic Energy Agency access to all declared facilities and supply chains to ensure they were not being used to manufacture weapons. In exchange, the United States agreed to lift sanctions against companies that do business with Iran. The EU agreed to remove energy and banking sanctions. And the UN agreed to annul all resolutions sanctioning Iran.

Senate Republicans criticized the agreement, saying the administration was swindled and bamboozled. At a July 2015 hearing, a day after a classified briefing on the deal, Senate Foreign Relations Chair Bob Corker, R-Tenn., faulted the lack of access to the agreement between Iran and IAEA for resolving questions about nuclear-related military research. "With every detail of the deal that was laid out, our witnesses successfully batted them away with the hyperbole that it is either this deal or war," Corker said. Republicans tried to reject the deal with a Senate resolution. Sen. Charles E. Schumer, D-N.Y., joined the fight against the deal, saying basically that he did not think the United States was better off with the deal than without it. He specifically cited the twenty-four-hour notice for inspections, which he said would allow Iranians to hide key equipment, and the inability of the United States to demand inspections on its own. Schumer said the first ten years of the agreement had serious weaknesses. A September vote fell short of the sixty votes needed to overcome a Democratic filibuster, allowing the deal to go into effect.

Obama signed an executive order in January 2016 lifting some sanctions against Iran because of the nuclear agreement while leaving others in place. The most significant aspect freed Iran assets held in the international financial system, which the administration estimated to be worth $56 billion. The Treasury Department granted waivers for Americans to import goods such as carpets from Iran and removed 400 Iranians from its blocked persons list, unfreezing their assets. House Speaker Paul D. Ryan, R-Wisc., said Obama lifted sanctions on the world's leading state sponsor of terrorism and noted that it came weeks after an Iranian missile test and just days after Iran held ten U.S. sailors who had found themselves in Iranian waters.

UKRAINE

After Russia seized the Crimea region of Ukraine in March 2014, Obama signed a series of executive orders placing sanctions on individuals close to Russian President Vladimir Putin. Obama's efforts failed to reverse the biggest clash with Russia since the end of the Cold War, and Ukraine's fate remained unresolved as Obama left office.

Crimea was long important to Russia as a strategic port for its navy, but the region fell under Ukraine in the 1990s during the breakup of the Soviet Union. The March 6 sanctions imposed travel restrictions on people and organizations that violated the territorial integrity of Ukraine and stole that people's assets, according to the Treasury Department. The March 17 order found that the Russian government's deployment of military in Crimea undermined democracy in Ukraine and threatened its peace and security. The March 20 sanctions expanded the scope of the emergency under the purported annexation of Crimea. Among the people targeted by the sanctions were Sergei Ivanov, Putin's chief of staff; Gennady Timchenko, a billionaire investor; and Yuri Kovalchuk, who was described as a personal banker for Russian leaders including Putin. On December 19, 2014, another Obama executive order increased the sanctions to cover fourteen defense companies and individuals in Putin's inner circle, six of Russia's largest banks, and four energy companies. The order prohibited the provision or exportation of goods, services, and technology to support Russia's offshore oil exploration.

Despite a ceasefire in 2015, an impasse remained between the Ukrainian government and rebels the United States contends are backed by Russia. Obama signed an executive order extending sanctions in March 2016 saying Russia's actions continued to pose an unusual and extraordinary threat. Russia insisted the sanctions were unjustified, with Putin spokesman Dmitry Peskov saying the Kremlin regretted the extension.

EBOLA

Ebola, a rare but painful disease that usually kills its victims, usually remains a threat overseas. In the fall of 2014, however, Ebola arrived in the United States, sparking widespread concern and fear about international travel. Obama mobilized several arms of the federal government to combat the disease in the United States and help contain it in the West African countries of Liberia, Sierra Leone, and Guinea, where an estimated 15,000 people became ill and more than 5,000 died during the outbreak.

Ebola is a fearsome disease because those infected typically develop a fever, with vomiting and diarrhea, before bleeding internally and externally. Caring for victims is difficult and dangerous. Thomas Eric Duncan, a Liberian national, was diagnosed with Ebola during a trip to Dallas in September 2014, the Centers for Disease Control and Prevention announced. He died October 8. Two nurses who treated Duncan were diagnosed days later with the disease, but they were treated and survived. A doctor who returned from Guinea, where he worked with the group Doctors Without Borders, was diagnosed in New York City later that month but was treated and survived. Martin Salia, a doctor who contracted the disease while treating patients in Sierra Leone, died November 17, 2014, at Nebraska Medical Center.

Some lawmakers called for a travel ban for people from West Africa, where there would be no direct flights to the United States. Obama said that would discourage health and military workers from helping treat and contain the disease there. Instead, officials in the three outbreak countries measured the temperatures for travelers at their airports and stopped anyone above 100.4 degrees. In the United States, Customs and Border Protection and the Centers for Disease Control and Prevention began similar screening at five major airports that handled 94 percent of the daily arrivals from the three countries. By February 2015, with a lack of new cases in the United States and the outbreak contained in West Africa, Obama was recalling troops that had been deployed. "America in the end is not defined by fear. That's not who we are. America is defined by possibility," Obama told reporters on the South Lawn of the White House on October 28, 2014. "And when we see a problem and we see a challenge, then we fix it."

CUBA

In a landmark initiative, Obama proposed to restore diplomatic relations with Cuba after a fifty-year hiatus. Some congressional Republicans opposed the overture to the Communist government long headed by Fidel Castro, while others pledged to study it. Obama noted that the United States had long had diplomatic relations with other Communist countries, including China and Vietnam. In March 2016, Obama became the first sitting president to visit the island since Calvin Coolidge in 1928.

The 1959 Cuban revolution isolated the island ninety miles from Florida with travel restrictions and a trade embargo. The United States tried repeatedly to overthrow the Castro government, including with the unsuccessful covert military action at the Bay of Pigs. Soviet missiles on the island created one of the biggest crises of the Cold War in October 1962, until the United States forced their removal. Obama argued that decades of isolation had not worked and it was time for a new approach.

The harshest criticism came from Cuban exiles in the United States who fled the Communist government. Sen. Marco Rubio, R-Fla., whose parents are from Cuba, called Obama naïve for engaging with Cuba and said the United States conceded everything and gained very little by not securing free elections or an uncensored internet.

The normalization agreement announced by Obama and Cuban President Raúl Castro, the brother of Fidel, resulted from months of secret talks assisted by Pope Francis and Canada. The first result of the thaw on the day the agreement was announced was the release of Alan Gross, a U.S. Agency for International Development subcontractor who had been wrongfully imprisoned for five years, and an intelligence agent who had been detained for two decades. In exchange, three Cuban agents were released after being jailed in the United States for more than fifteen years. Another early result was the lifting of some travel restrictions and the resumption of commercial flights. On April 14, 2015, the Obama administration removed Cuba from its list of state sponsors of terrorism. Congress had forty-five days to vote against removing Cuba from the terror list, but no legislation was even introduced. On the other hand, Congress also did not vote to end the trade embargo against Cuba as Obama had proposed. The agreement led to the reopening of embassies in Washington and Havana on July 20, 2015, after both had closed in 1961 because of Cuba's alliance with the Soviet Union. "I have come here to bury the last remnant of the Cold War in the Americas," Obama said during his visit March 22, 2016.

Fidel Castro died at ninety on November 26, 2016. "During my presidency, we have worked hard to put the past behind us, pursuing a future in which the relationship between our two countries is defined not by our differences but by the many things that we share as neighbors and friends," Obama said in offering condolences to Castro's family and the Cuban people.

On January 12, 2017, in one of his last actions as president, Obama rescinded the 1995 wet-foot-dry-foot policy that allowed Cubans attempting to enter the United States illegally to remain and seek residency if they reached land, while those intercepted at sea would be returned. The change meant that all undocumented Cuban immigrants would be returned, to conform with broader immigration policy under the Department of Homeland Security.

VIETNAM

During a visit to Vietnam in May 2016, President Barack Obama announced an end to an arms embargo with the country that had been in place for fifty years since the two countries were at war. The move was an effort toward having a fully normalized relationship with Vietnam, two decades after the resumption of relations and forty-one years after the end of war between the former adversaries. "It's clear from this visit that both our peoples are eager for an even closer relationship, a deeper relationship," Obama said at a news conference in Hanoi with Vietnamese President Tran Dai Quang.

Since Obama took office, U.S. exports to Vietnam increased 150 percent, he said. Vietnam became one of the top countries with students in the United States, reaching nearly 19,000 that year. The countries reached deals involving trade, health care, humanitarian assistance, education, and law enforcement, according to Quang. The United States would continue helping to remove unexploded landmines and bombs from the country, Obama said. With efforts nearly complete to remove dioxin from the defoliant Agent Orange from Danang Airport, Obama said the United States would assist in the cleanup at Bien Hoa Air Base. "We believe the people of this region should live in security, prosperity, and dignity," Obama said May 23, 2016, during a joint news conference in Hanoi with Quang.

HIROSHIMA

President Barack Obama became the first sitting president to visit Hiroshima, one of two cities in Japan where the United States dropped atomic bombs to end World War II. His visit May 27, 2016, was another of his efforts toward reconciliation as the end of his term approached. He noted the deaths of 100,000 Japanese men, women, and children, along with thousands of Koreans and a dozen American prisoners.

Rather than focus on the bombing nearly seventy-one years earlier, Obama emphasized the future. Although technology that allows ever-more-sophisticated weaponry could doom humanity, he said that people have an obligation to curb future suffering. "We may not be able to eliminate man's capacity to do evil, so nations and the alliances that we form must possess the means to defend ourselves," Obama said. "But among those nations like my own that hold nuclear stockpiles, we must have the courage to escape the logic of fear and pursue a world without them."

Appointments

FILIBUSTER

Tensions over stalled confirmation votes boiled over in the summer amid disputes over tactics and positions of the nominees. Republicans blocked five nominees to the National Labor Relations Board because Obama had used recess appointments to install two of them in January 2012. A court challenge made its way to the Supreme Court. Republicans held up another recess appointee, Consumer Financial Protection Bureau Director Richard Cordray, as part of a fight over the Dodd-Frank financial regulatory overhaul law (PL 111–203). Labor nominee Thomas E. Perez ran into a wall of Republican opposition because of what they considered his liberal positions as head of the Justice Department's Civil Rights Division. Fred P. Hochberg's nomination to a second term as president of the Export-Import Bank was held up by opposition from some Republicans to federal financial support for the bank. And the post of director of the Bureau of Alcohol, Tobacco, Firearms and Explosives, to which B. Todd Jones had been named, had not been permanently filled since the job became a Senate-confirmed position in 2006.

The delays led to threats to change the filibuster rule requiring sixty votes to support a nominee. Sen. John McCain, R-Ariz., defused the threat July 16, 2013, with a White House deal to withdraw the two nominees to the NLRB who were recess appointees and Republicans agreeing to confirm two replacements for the first five-member board in a decade. The deal also allowed quick confirmation of Cordray, Hochberg, Jones, and Gina McCarthy to lead the EPA and Perez as secretary of the Labor Department.

Nominations piled up again in the fall. The disputes included a sitting House member, Democrat Melvin Watt of North Carolina, to lead the Federal Housing Finance Agency, which regulated mortgage giants Fannie Mae and Freddie Mac. Republicans argued that Watt lacked experience despite serving for two decades on the Financial Services Committee and its predecessor. On November 21, 2013, Senate Democrats deployed the so-called nuclear option to change rules to require a simple majority rather than sixty votes to overcome filibusters on executive-branch and judicial nominees other than those for the Supreme Court.

In December, nine backlogged executive branch nominees were confirmed, including Watt and Jeh Johnson as secretary of Homeland Security. Seven judicial nominees were also confirmed that month. Republicans retaliated against the rules change by slow-walking nominations when they could and blocking numerous committee meetings. All sixteen confirmations in December required cloture votes, and none received the sixty votes they would have needed under the previous rule. Republicans often refused to yield back allowed debate time on the Senate floor after cloture was invoked. That meant the vote to confirm Janet L. Yellen as chair of the Federal Reserve Board of Governors was pushed back until January 6, 2014.

SENATE FLIPS

Obama's difficulties with Congress grew worse after the 2014 election, when the Senate flipped decisively from a Democratic to Republican majority after eight years of Democratic control. In the 113th Congress, Democrats held fifty-three seats, plus two independents who caucused with them, to Republicans holding fifty-five seats. (The majority narrowed by one seat because of a Republican appointee in New Jersey after the June 2013 death of Frank Lautenberg, but the seat returned to Democrats on October 31.) For the 114th Congress, Republicans held fifty-four seats and the Democrats forty-six seats, including two independents who caucused with them. Despite the rank-and-file changes, faces among Senate leadership stayed the same.

VETOES

Despite Obama's contentious relationship with Republican lawmakers during his second term, which included numerous attempts to overturn his signature health care overhaul, Congress overrode only one of his dozen vetoes.

The override came in the waning days of his term on September 23, 2016. The decisive votes were 348–77 in the House and 97–1 in the Senate supporting the legislation (PL 114–222) that allowed lawsuits against nations accused of supporting terrorism.

Obama objected to the bill by saying it would hurt relations with other countries by stripping them of immunity from lawsuits. Different courts could reach different decisions about whether a country was behind an attack. Moreover, other countries might begin allowing lawsuits against U.S. armed forces in tempestuous regions, Obama said in his veto statement.

Supporters of the bill argued that Saudi Arabia, for example, could be held accountable through lawsuits for the hijackings of September 11, 2001. "If the Saudi government had no involvement in 9/11, it has nothing to fear, but if it was culpable it should be held accountable," said Sen. Richard Blumenthal, D-Conn.

Obama vetoed seven bills with an explanation of his opposition and pocket vetoed five others without stating his objections by refusing to sign the bills after Congress adjourned. He vetoed a bill to authorize the Keystone XL Pipeline, which he rejected February 24, 2015. On January 8, 2016, he vetoed a bill (HR 3762), that aimed to rescind

PRESIDENT BARACK OBAMA'S CABINET

Following is a list of cabinet officers who served in the administration of President Barack Obama during his two terms in office between January 20, 2009, and January 20, 2017. Dates given are for actual service in office, beginning with the cabinet officers' swearing-in date, which often varies from date of confirmation by the Senate. Some cabinet members remained in office into Obama's second term. Only heads of the major departments are listed; offices that have not been designated as cabinet level are not included.

Department Head	Dates of Service
Secretary of State	
Hillary Rodham Clinton	January 21, 2009–February 1, 2013
John Kerry	February 1, 2013–January 20, 2017
Secretary of the Treasury	
Timothy Geithner	January 26, 2009–January 25, 2013
Jack Lew	February 28, 2013–January 20, 2017
Secretary of Defense	
Robert M. Gates	December 18, 2006–July 1, 2011[1]
Leon Panetta	July 1, 2011–February 26, 2013
Chuck Hagel	February 27, 2013–February 17, 2015
Ash Carter	February 17, 2015–January 20, 2017
Attorney General	
Eric Holder Jr.	February 3, 2009–April 27, 2015
Loretta Lynch	April 27, 2015–January 20, 2017
Secretary of the Interior	
Ken S. Salazar	January 20, 2009–April 12, 2013
Sally Jewell	April 12, 2013–January 20, 2017
Secretary of Agriculture	
Thomas J. Vilsack	January 21, 2009–January 20, 2017
Secretary of Commerce	
Gary Locke	March 26, 2009–August 1, 2011
Rebecca Blank (Acting)	August 1, 2011–October 21, 2011
John Bryson	October 21, 2011–June 11, 2012
Rebecca Blank (Acting)	June 11, 2012–June 1, 2013
Penny Pritzker	June 26, 2013–January 20, 2017

Department Head	Dates of Service
Secretary of Labor	
Hilda L. Solis	February 24, 2009–January 22, 2013
Thomas Perez	July 23, 2013–January 20, 2017
Secretary of Health and Human Services	
Kathleen Sebelius	April 28, 2009–June 9, 2014
Sylvia Mathews Burwell	June 9, 2014–January 20, 2017
Secretary of Education	
Arne Duncan	January 21, 2009–December 31, 2015
John King Jr.	January 1, 2016–January 20, 2017
Secretary of Housing and Urban Development	
Shaun Donovan	January 26, 2009–July 28, 2014
Julian Castro	July 28, 2014–January 20, 2017
Secretary of Transportation	
Ray LaHood	January 23, 2009–July 2, 2013
Anthony Foxx	July 2, 2013–January 20, 2017
Secretary of Energy	
Steven Chu	January 21, 2009–April 22, 2013
Ernest Moniz	May 21, 2013–January 20, 2017
Secretary of Veterans Affairs	
Eric K. Shinseki	January 21, 2009–May 30, 2014
Bob McDonald	July 30, 2014–January 20, 2017
Secretary of Homeland Security	
Michael Chertoff	February 15, 2005–January 21, 2009[2]
Janet Napolitano	January 21, 2009–September 6, 2013
Jeh Johnson	December 23, 2013–January 20, 2017

[1] Robert M. Gates served as defense secretary in the administration of George W. Bush, President Obama's predecessor. Obama retained him as defense secretary when his administration began in January 2009. Gates did not require reconfirmation by the Senate.

[2] Michael Chertoff, who held the post in President Bush's administration, remained in office until the day after Obama was inaugurated to expedite transition to the new administration.

parts of the Affordable Care Act, nicknamed Obamacare, in a way the Congressional Budget Office said would increase the number of uninsured Americans.

Obama turned over much of his Cabinet for fresh faces for the second term. But several nominees ran into delays, and fewer than half of Obama's executive nominations in 2013 were confirmed by the Senate, a rate much lower than experienced in preceding years. The delays prompted Senate Democrats to change the filibuster rule in November to allow a simple majority to approve executive nominees and judges below the level of the Supreme Court. Republicans warned that Democrats would regret the move.

Despite the friction, Obama made a number of notable appointments, including another Republican in the Cabinet and the first woman to head the Federal Reserve. Chuck Hagel, a Republican former senator from Nebraska, became secretary of Defense during the second term. Robert Gates had remained as secretary of Defense when Obama succeeded Republican President George W. Bush, and Ray LaHood, a Republican former House member from Illinois, served as secretary of Transportation during Obama's first term. Obama also suffered one of his worst defeats by failing to win confirmation of a Supreme Court nominee after the death of Justice Antonin Scalia in February 2016. The nearly year-long vacancy allowed his successor an enviable opportunity.

STATE DEPARTMENT

President Barack Obama's reshaping of his cabinet for his second term began with the national-security team, kicking off with the easy confirmation of Massachusetts Sen. John Kerry as secretary of State. The Democratic nominee for president in 2004, Kerry was confirmed January 29, 2013, on a vote of 94–3. Kerry, a Vietnam veteran turned antiwar protester, had led the Foreign Relations Committee for four years and served as an emissary for the administration on diplomatic missions to such global hot spots as Afghanistan and Pakistan. The top Republican on the Foreign Relations Committee, Bob Corker of Tennessee, hailed Kerry for being open to listening to opposing points of view, even when they disagreed. At his confirmation hearing, Kerry voiced support for scaled-back plans for the U.S. diplomatic presence and assistance levels in Afghanistan after 2014, when all NATO combat troops were scheduled to depart. Kerry backed Obama's cautious approach in Syria, advocating a political solution to the conflict there that would ease President Bashar al-Assad from power without plunging the country further into sectarian violence. Kerry also assured lawmakers that the administration's policy on countering a nuclear Iran "is not containment" but prevention.

His confirmation was a foregone conclusion after Susan E. Rice withdrew from consideration. Republicans John Cornyn and Ted Cruz of Texas and James M. Inhofe of Oklahoma cast the only no votes. Inhofe, the ranking member of the Armed Services Committee, doubted that Kerry would be a strong advocate of U.S. sovereignty and worried that Kerry favored expanding United Nations powers at the expense of the United States.

DEPARTMENT OF DEFENSE

The path to confirmation was stormier for former Sen. Chuck Hagel, a Nebraska Republican, who faced delays and stiff opposition from his former colleagues before succeeding Leon Panetta to become the twenty-fourth secretary of Defense. The criticism revealed the extent to which Hagel, a one-time presidential contender, had become anathema to his party. Even before President Barack Obama nominated Hagel January 7, questions arose about Hagel's past pronouncements on Israel, Iran, the Iraq War surge, and the nation's nuclear deterrent. The former two-term senator called the Iran regime, a core subject at his January 31 Armed Services Committee confirmation hearing, "an elected legitimate government, whether we agree or not." The testiest exchange dealt with a troop surge credited with turning the tide in the Iraq war. Fellow Vietnam veteran John McCain, R-Ariz., asked his "old friend" whether Hagel was correct in characterizing the troop increase as "the most dangerous foreign policy blunder in this country since Vietnam." Hagel refused to give a yes-or-no answer, saying history would judge.

Senate Republicans delayed voting on Hagel and demanded more information. Lindsey Graham of South Carolina threatened to hold up confirmation unless the White House released more information about the September 11, 2012, attack on the U.S. consulate in Benghazi, Libya. Twenty-six senators asked for more financial details about Hagel's speaking engagements, a request that Armed Services Chair Carl Levin, D-Mich., dismissed out of hand. Cruz said the lack of detail about fees meant there was something he did not want made public. The nomination was voted out of committee February 12, 2013, on a vote of 14–11. The Senate agreed February 26, 2013, to cut off debate on a vote of 71–27. And Hagel was eventually confirmed February 26, 2013, on a vote of 58–41, with support from all Democrats but only four Republicans.

TREASURY DEPARTMENT

Despite Republican complaints about the country's finances, Jacob J. Lew was confirmed as Treasury secretary February 27, 2013, on a vote of 71–26. Republicans vocally criticized the former White House chief of staff and director of the Office of Management and Budget but did not slow the process. The top Republican on the Budget Committee, Alabama Sen. Jeff Sessions, complained that a budget Lew had prepared was a complete fabrication and the greatest financial misrepresentation in the country's history. GOP Whip John Cornyn of Texas called Lew one of the principal architects of President Barack Obama's refusal to deal with the country's fiscal problems. And Iowa Republican Charles E. Grassley complained after the September 13, 2013, confirmation hearing that Lew would not answer questions there about offshore investments and bonuses he received while working for the bailed-out Citigroup.

The criticism was not entirely partisan. Vermont independent Bernard Sanders, who caucuses with Democrats, said it was unpatriotic for Lew to run to the Cayman Islands, where Lew had an investment in a venture-capital fund from 2007 to 2010, to avoid paying taxes. Lew told the panel he was not initially aware where the investment was located and that he sold it when he became OMB director. Sanders also said Lew was too closely aligned with Wall Street. But the top Republican on the Finance Committee, Utah's Orrin G. Hatch, said that despite his reservations, he voted for Lew in deference to the president's prerogative. Lew said overhauling the tax code was an extremely important priority and that he hoped to broaden the tax base while reducing rates, something many Republicans have said is crucial to U.S. global economic competitiveness. Finance Chair Max Baucus, D-Mont., said Lew would help make tax reform a reality.

CENTRAL INTELLIGENCE AGENCY

John O. Brennan was confirmed to head the Central Intelligence Agency after fielding questions about the administration's drone-strike policy and a nearly thirteen-hour Senate filibuster led by Kentucky Republican Rand Paul. Brennan, a twenty-five-year CIA veteran who had been President Barack Obama's chief counterterrorism adviser for four years, was confirmed March 7, 2013, by a 63–34 vote. Brennan staunchly defended the administration's drone-strike policy and his own record on the subjects of harsh interrogation techniques and leaks. On the eve of his February 7, 2013, confirmation hearing, the White House said it would provide classified Office of Legal Counsel documents to the House and Senate intelligence panels about targeted killings of U.S. citizens suspected of terrorism. In addition, a white paper provided the previous year that summarized the legal thinking on such operations was leaked to the media. Intelligence Committee Chair Dianne Feinstein, D-Calif., suggested the possibility of creating a new court to review drone strikes. Brennan said the judicial tradition of determining guilt or innocence is very different from decisions made on the battlefield against terrorists.

Paul wanted answers from the Obama administration about its drone program. He held the Senate floor—with a little help from his friends—from 11:47 a.m. on March 6 until 12:39 a.m. on March 7, when he yielded to procedural reality, and nature. Attorney General Eric H. Holder Jr. sent Paul a letter that day that said the president does not have the authority to use a weaponized drone to kill an American not engaged in combat on American soil. Paul said he was happy with the answer but disappointed it took a root canal to get it. Saxby Chambliss of Georgia, the

ranking Republican on the Intelligence Committee, asked whether Brennan had any role in creating or implementing the harsh interrogation program under the George W. Bush administration as deputy CIA director and head of the National Counterterrorism Center. Brennan was categorical that he did not play a role, despite the claims of a former supervisor and his name appearing approximately fifty times in email traffic included in a 6,000-page committee report on the program.

DEPARTMENT OF THE INTERIOR

The nomination of Sally Jewell to succeed Ken Salazar as secretary of the Department of the Interior rekindled the federal debate about how to balance land conservation efforts with economic development. Jewell, a former engineer in the oil and gas industry who was then CEO of outdoor-sporting-goods company Recreational Equipment Inc., was confirmed April 10, 2013, by a vote of 87–11. Energy and Natural Resources Chair Ron Wyden, D-Ore., said she got a resounding vote because she was the right person to oversee the department's 500 million acres of federal land, as well as the outer continental shelf, recreational activities, oil and gas development, and water reclamation efforts.

But Republicans voiced a variety of concerns. Sen. John Barrasso of Wyoming tried to get Jewell to recuse herself from development of regulations governing hydraulic fracturing to extract oil and gas on public lands because she served for a decade on the board of the National Parks Conservation Association (NPCA), which sued the department nearly sixty times. She declined, saying she would consult ethics officials about steps to take if NPCA issues arose. Lisa Murkowski of Alaska, where nearly two-thirds of the land is federal, secured Jewell's commitment to consult with a Native Alaskan community before deciding whether to build a road through a remote wildlife refuge. Before allowing a Senate floor vote on the nomination, Sen. James E. Risch of Idaho got a commitment from Jewell to collaborate with the Idaho governor's office on a science-based solution to manage the sage grouse because of his concern that the Fish and Wildlife Service could list the bird as an endangered species.

DEPARTMENT OF ENERGY

Ernest J. Moniz, a physicist nominated as secretary of the Energy Department, personified President Barack Obama's "all of the above" energy policy that included an expansion of domestic fossil fuel production. Moniz, who had served as undersecretary of Energy during the Clinton administration, was confirmed May 16, 2013, by a vote of 97–0 despite concerns from some environmentalists. Moniz directed MIT's Energy Initiative, which was funded largely by oil and gas companies and electric utilities. But when an MIT analysis showed that natural gas would play a key role in weaning the United States off more carbon-intensive resources, Moniz told a Senate panel in 2011 that gas was no substitute for zero-emission power. Moniz advocated for nuclear power, including small modular reactors that proponents said held great promise with fewer risks than large-scale reactors.

Moniz worried some environmentalists as he listed past or current ties to BP, the Electric Power Research Institute, and the King Abdullah Petroleum Studies and Research Center of Saudi Arabia. Bill Snape, senior counsel with the Center for Biological Diversity, raised concerns that Moniz would delay research into dangers of fracking and divert resources from solar, geothermal, and other renewable sources. The advocacy group Food and Water Watch organized an online petition to oppose the nomination. But Obama insisted that the drive to develop domestic energy resources is not inconsistent with protecting the environment. "Ernie knows that we can produce more energy and grow our economy, while still taking care of our air, our water and our climate," Obama said March 4, 2013, at the White House while announcing his nomination of Moniz.

DEPARTMENT OF COMMERCE

In contrast to other nominees who had to face the hurdles placed in front of them, Chicago businesswoman Penny Pritzker sailed to confirmation easily as secretary of the Commerce Department on June 25, on a 97–1 vote. Sen. Richard Blumenthal, D-Conn., summed up her support by saying she had the experience and acumen to build strong partnerships between the federal government and the business community. Pritzker founded and led the PSP Capital Partners private investment firm and Pritzker Realty Group before her confirmation. She served as President Barack Obama's national finance director during his 2008 campaign and then served on the President's Council on Jobs and Competitiveness and the Economic Recovery Advisory Board. The ranking Republican on the Commerce panel, John Thune of South Dakota, said Pritzker's skills would facilitate job creation and economic recovery. Pritzker understood the cost of regulations and the impact of taxes, Thune said.

Pritzker's membership on the board of Hyatt Hotels, the chain cofounded by her father, prompted the only vote against her. Sen. Bernard Sanders, a Vermont independent, argued that the secretary of commerce should represent the interests of working Americans rather than CEOs and large corporations. Workers at Hyatt were unjustly fired for trying to form a union and Pritzker did not defend them, Sanders said.

DEPARTMENT OF TRANSPORTATION

Anthony Foxx, the former mayor of Charlotte, N.C., was confirmed as secretary of the Department of Transportation on June 27 in a vote of 100–0 as Congress prepared to develop a multiyear highway bill. Transportation Chair Jay Rockefeller, D-W.Va., called Foxx aggressive and skilled at getting things done. Foxx secured approval of an interstate highway expansion through Charlotte, a light-rail extension,

and the addition of a third runway at the Charlotte Douglas International Airport. Foxx, who is African American, also helped address criticism of a lack of diversity in Obama's second-term Cabinet.

The ranking Republican on the panel, John Thune of South Dakota, asked how Foxx would deal with budget cuts mandated by the sequester. The Federal Aviation Administration had furloughed air-traffic controllers that year before Congress enacted legislation to transfer up to $253 million in unspent airport improvement grant funds. Foxx said he had experience making do with less, noting that the recession caused tax revenue to fall by $200 million in his first year as mayor. But Foxx sidestepped questions before his confirmation about how to fill revenue shortfalls in the Highway Trust Fund, saying he would bring together a wide variety of stakeholders. His predecessor, former GOP Rep. Ray LaHood, earned a White House rebuke for endorsing consideration of a new vehicle mileage tax early in Obama's first term.

DEPARTMENT OF HOUSING AND URBAN DEVELOPMENT

As the country recovered from the Great Recession, Julian Castro's biggest challenge when he was nominated as secretary of Housing and Urban Development (HUD) was the Federal Housing Administration. The agency that insures home loans took a beating with the massive defaults in 2008 and needed a $1.7 billion infusion the year before Castro's nomination to bail out its Mutual Mortgage Insurance Fund. Castro was confirmed July 9, 2014, in a vote of 71–26 to succeed Shaun Donovan, who became director of the Office of Management and Budget.

Before joining the administration, Castro was mayor of San Antonio, where he launched an initiative called Decade of Downtown in 2010 to develop 2,400 housing units by 2014 in older neighborhoods and downtown. "He's become a leader in housing and economic development," Obama said at the White House in announcing Castro's nomination May 23, 2014. Housing industry groups were comfortable with Castro. David H. Stevens, CEO of the Mortgage Bankers Association, called Castro a brilliant academic who brought HUD practical experience as mayor of a major city with diverse housing needs. Sen. Charles E. Grassley, R-Iowa, said the administration should make larger changes because too many housing authority executives use tax dollars to feather their own nests.

DEPARTMENT OF LABOR

Thomas E. Perez was confirmed as secretary of the Labor Department as part of a July 2013 deal that Republicans negotiated for the approval of four nominees to prevent Democrats from changing procedural rules to make it easier to approve nominees. The compromise allowed Perez, the head of the Justice Department's Civil Rights Division, to be confirmed July 18, 2013, by a vote of 54–46 without any Republican support. The vote came only after Republicans used up some of the thirty hours of postcloture debate by renewing criticism of Perez that portrayed him as a left-wing ideologue who presided over a highly polarized and partisan atmosphere in the Civil Rights Division.

For example, Sen. Lamar Alexander of Tennessee and other Republicans alleged that Perez improperly asked the city of St. Paul, Minn., to withdraw from a Supreme Court case about lending discrimination, in exchange for the federal government agreeing not to join housing-related False Claims Act lawsuits against the city that were instigated by a whistleblower. Democrats defended Perez by saying he acted properly and consulted with ethics experts at the Justice Department before taking action.

ENVIRONMENTAL PROTECTION ADMINISTRATION

Despite objections to the Obama administration's efforts to limit greenhouse gas emissions from power plants and criticism from Republicans, who accused the administration of pursuing a "war on coal," Gina McCarthy was confirmed head of the Environmental Protection Agency on July 18 in a vote of 59–40. She was confirmed as part of the same compromise and on the same day as Thomas E. Perez was confirmed to head the Labor Department. Republicans Lamar Alexander and Bob Corker of Tennessee, Kelly Ayotte of New Hampshire, Susan Collins of Maine, and Jeff Flake and John McCain of Arizona supported her confirmation. Joe Manchin III of West Virginia was the only Democrat to vote no.

McCarthy at the time was assistant administrator of the EPA's Office of Air and Radiation. Before that, she had been commissioner of the Connecticut Department of Environmental Protection. Under her tenure at the EPA, the agency moved to limit greenhouse gas emissions from power plants—standards that would effectively end future construction of coal-fired facilities without carbon capture and storage technology if finalized. She also oversaw tighter standards for mercury and soot pollution and stricter fuel economy standards for cars and trucks. Opposition was grounded in Republicans' concern about how the EPA administrator would implement the Obama administration's pollution-prevention policies.

DEPARTMENT OF VETERANS AFFAIRS

To overhaul the troubled Department of Veterans Affairs, President Barack Obama sought fresh leadership outside the military from the former chief executive of the world's largest consumer-goods company, Robert McDonald. McDonald, the former CEO of Procter & Gamble, succeeded Army Gen. Eric Shinseki, who resigned from the embattled department after a scandal beneath him focused on long wait times for medical care and misconduct. McDonald graduated from West Point and served in the 82nd Airborne Division before leaving the Army at the rank of captain. Making him more palatable among Republicans, McDonald had contributed to the campaigns of House

Speaker John A. Boehner and Sen. Rob Portman of Ohio and presidential nominee Mitt Romney. McDonald was confirmed July 29, 2014, in a vote of 97–0.

Taming a 300,000-employee bureaucracy with the nation's largest integrated health care system posed different challenges than selling Crest toothpaste, Tide detergent, and Bounty paper towels. At Procter & Gamble, McDonald championed the use of technology to analyze data and customer feedback to increase productivity, cut costs, and grow brands. A report in 2014 by Deputy White House Chief of Staff Rob Nabors cited "cumbersome and outdated" technology, including a software system largely unchanged since 1985 as a major shortcoming for the Department of Veterans Affairs. McDonald also has emphasized promotion, recruitment, and training as the tools that a successful organization uses to promote renewal and create a high-performance culture. McDonald said he always focused on the customer, and at the department, veterans would be the customers.

DEPARTMENT OF HOMELAND SECURITY

The Obama administration's immigration policies were what dominated the debate when Jeh Johnson was confirmed December 16, 2013, by a vote of 76–13 to become the fourth secretary of the Department of Homeland Security. Johnson was respected as a former general counsel at the Defense Department. Homeland Security Chair Thomas R. Carper, D-Del., called Johnson a strong leader ready for the challenge facing him. The top Republican on the panel, Tom Coburn of Oklahoma, said he found Johnson open and honest, even if they did not share the same views on everything. Johnson said his first priority would be to address the large number of senior-level vacancies at the department, which was at 40 percent when he took office.

Criticism focused on immigration policies. Six members of the Senate Judiciary Committee sent a letter asking for his views on border-patrol screening, whistleblowers, and criminal procedures for undocumented immigrants. Sen. John McCain, R-Ariz., pressed Johnson on a reported rise in Border Patrol apprehensions. The reported 20 percent increase contradicted statements made by former Secretary Janet Napolitano, who had left the post in September. McCain said he admired and appreciated Johnson but could not support his confirmation until he got more information.

ANTONIO WEISS

Despite the filibuster change, some of Obama's nominees ran into delays in 2014—from fellow Democrats. Antonio Weiss was nominated to be undersecretary of the Treasury for Domestic Finance. He had been the global head of investment banking for Lazard, one of the world's premier asset management firms. He was widely respected in the world of finance and had ties to the Democratic establishment, serving as a member of the Center for

American Progress's economic advisory council. Two days after Weiss's nomination was received by the Senate, populist Democrat Elizabeth Warren of Massachusetts said she would vote against him because of his ties to Wall Street. Warren said that as long as the revolving door keeps spinning, government policies would favor Wall Street rather than Main Street. Other Democratic opposition emerged in the following days. Senate Finance Chair Ron Wyden, D-Ore., had opted not to begin the confirmation process for Weiss during the lame-duck session, which ensured that Republicans would control the process in the new year. On January 12, 2015, Weiss asked the White House to withdraw his nomination. He would instead be named counselor to Treasury Secretary Jacob J. Lew, a post that did not require Senate confirmation.

DEBO P. ADEGBILE

The failure to confirm Debo P. Adegbile to lead the Department of Justice's Civil Rights Division demonstrated that the Democratic deployment of the so-called nuclear option did not guarantee approval of all nominees. Adegbile's nomination needed a simple majority to cut off debate, but the Senate voted 47–52 against him on March 5, 2014. Seven Democrats—Bob Casey of Pennsylvania, Chris Coons of Delaware, Joe Donnelly of Indiana, Heidi Heitkamp of North Dakota, Joe Manchin III of West Virginia, Mark Pryor of Arkansas, and John Walsh of Montana—joined Republicans in opposing Adegbile amid a controversy over his legal defense of Mumia Abu-Jamal, who had been convicted of killing a Philadelphia police officer three decades earlier. Majority Leader Harry Reid, D-Nev., also voted no to preserve his right to reconsider the vote. President Barack Obama called the vote a travesty based on wildly unfair character attacks against a good and qualified public servant.

Tough questions had been expected. Adegbile had spent a dozen years at the NAACP's Legal Defense and Educational Fund, where he served in numerous roles including as special counsel and acting president. What derailed the nomination was Adegbile's past legal representation of Abu-Jamal. Sen. Charles E. Grassley of Iowa, the ranking Republican on the Judiciary Committee, introduced a strongly worded

letter from the Fraternal Order of Police, a group that expressed its vehement opposition to Adegbile and his work on behalf of Abu-Jamal. "This nomination can be interpreted in only one way: it is a thumb in the eye of our nation's law enforcement officers," read the January 6, 2014, letter from the 330,000-member police organization to Obama.

SUPREME COURT

In 2016, Supreme Court Justice Antonin Scalia's death on February 13 set up a battle over the court vacancy between Democratic Obama and the Republicans who controlled the Senate. Majority Leader Mitch McConnell, R-Ky., made it clear from the start that he would not consider any nominee Obama might put forward and that the seat should be filled by the next president. "The American people should have a voice in the selection of their next Supreme Court Justice," McConnell said in a statement February 13. "Therefore, this vacancy should not be filled until we have a new President." After Obama nominated U.S. Circuit Judge Merrick Garland in March, McConnell refused to allow a hearing on the nominee or even to meet with Garland. His gamble that a Republican would succeed Obama proved successful.

Senate Judiciary Committee Chair Charles E. Grassley, R-Iowa, said it had been standard practice not to choose a Supreme Court justice in a presidential election year. Democrats, however, noted that the Senate approved the nomination of Anthony Kennedy to the Supreme Court in 1988, the final year of Ronald Reagan's presidency. Even as Democrats pressed Republicans not to prevent a confirmation, they had to deal with their own statements on the issue in the past. Vice President Joseph R. Biden Jr. had given a speech in June 1992 when he was a senator from Delaware and chair of the Judiciary Committee, in which he said President George H. W. Bush should consider following the practice of the majority of his predecessors and not name a nominee until after the November election was completed. Though polls showed a majority of Americans thought Congress should consider the Garland nomination, and Democrats pressed for action, Republicans would not budge.

Appendix

Glossary of Congressional Terms

AA—*(See Administrative Assistant.)*

Absence of a Quorum—Absence of the required number of members to conduct business in a house or a committee. When a quorum call or roll-call vote in a house establishes that a quorum is not present, no debate or other business is permitted except a motion to adjourn or motions to request or compel the attendance of absent members, if necessary by arresting them.

Absolute Majority—A vote requiring approval by a majority of all members of a chamber rather than a majority of members present and voting. Also referred to as constitutional majority.

Account—Organizational units used in the federal budget primarily for recording spending and revenue transactions.

Act—(1) A bill passed in identical form by the House and Senate and signed into law by the president or enacted over the president's veto. A bill also becomes an act without the president's signature if it is unsigned but not returned to Congress within ten days (Sundays excepted) and if Congress has not adjourned within that period. (2) Also, the technical term for a bill passed by at least one house and engrossed.

Ad Hoc Select Committee—A temporary committee formed for a special purpose or to deal with a specific subject. Conference committees are ad hoc joint committees. A House rule adopted in 1975 authorizes the Speaker to refer measures to special ad hoc committees, appointed by the Speaker with the approval of the House. *(See also and compare Select or Special Committee.)*

Adjourn—A motion to adjourn is a formal motion to end a day's session or meeting of a house or a committee. A motion to adjourn usually has no conditions attached to it, but it sometimes may specify the day or time for reconvening or make reconvening subject to the call of the chamber's presiding officer or the committee's chair. In both houses, a motion to adjourn is of the highest privilege, takes precedence over all other motions, is not debatable, and must be put to an immediate vote. Adjournment of a chamber ends its legislative day. For this reason, the House or Senate sometimes adjourns for only a brief period of time, during the course of a day's session. The House does not permit a motion to adjourn after it has resolved into the Committee of the Whole or when the previous question has been ordered on a measure to final passage without an intervening motion.

Adjourn for More Than Three Days—Under Article I, Section 5, of the Constitution, neither house may adjourn for more than three days without the approval of the other. The necessary approval is given in a concurrent resolution to which both houses have agreed.

Adjournment *Sine Die*—Final adjournment of an annual or two-year session of Congress; literally, adjournment without a day. The two houses must agree to a privileged concurrent resolution for such an adjournment. A *sine die* adjournment precludes Congress from meeting again until the next constitutionally fixed date of a session (January 3 of the following year) unless Congress determines otherwise by law or the president calls it into special session. Article II, Section 3, of the Constitution authorizes the president to adjourn both houses until such time as the president thinks proper when the two houses cannot agree to a time of adjournment. No president, however, has ever exercised this authority.

Adjournment to a Day (and Time) Certain—An adjournment that fixes the next date and time of meeting for one or both houses. It does not end an annual session of Congress.

Administration Bill—A bill drafted in the executive office of the president or in an executive department or agency to implement part of the president's program. An administration bill is introduced in Congress by a member who supports it or as a courtesy to the administration.

Administrative Assistant (AA)—The title formerly given to a member's chief aide, political advisor, and head of office staff. Today, the title most commonly used for such an individual is chief of staff. The administrative assistant often represents the member at meetings with visitors or officials when the member is unable (or unwilling) to attend.

Adoption—The usual parliamentary term for approval of a conference report. It is also commonly applied to amendments.

Advance Appropriation—In an appropriation act for a particular fiscal year, an appropriation that does not become available for spending or obligation until a subsequent fiscal year. The amount of the advance appropriation is counted as part of the budget for the fiscal year in which it becomes available for obligation.

Advance Funding—A mechanism whereby statutory language may allow budget authority for a fiscal year to be increased, and obligations to be incurred, with an offsetting decrease in the budget authority available in the succeeding fiscal year. If not used, the budget authority remains available for obligation in the succeeding fiscal year. Advance funding is sometimes used to provide contingency funding of a few benefit programs.

Adverse Report—A committee report recommending against approval of a measure or some other matter. Committees usually pigeonhole measures they oppose instead of reporting them adversely, but they may be required to report them by a statutory rule, chamber rule, or an instruction from their parent body.

Advice and Consent—The Senate's constitutional role in consenting to or rejecting the president's nominations to executive-branch and judicial offices and treaties with other nations. Confirmation of nominees requires a simple majority vote of senators present and voting. Treaties must be approved by a two-thirds majority of those present and voting.

Aisle—The center aisle of each chamber. When facing the presiding officer, Republicans usually sit to the right of the aisle, Democrats to the left. When members speak of "my side of the aisle" or "this side," either literally or metaphorically, they are referring to their party.

Amendment—A formal proposal to alter the text of a bill, resolution, amendment, motion, treaty, or some other text. Technically, it is a motion. An amendment may strike out (eliminate) part of a text, insert new text, or strike out and insert—that is, replace all or part of the text with new text. The texts of amendments considered on the floor are printed in full in the *Congressional Record.*

Amendment in the Nature of a Substitute—Usually an amendment to replace the entire text of a measure. It strikes out everything after the enacting clause of a bill or resolving clause of a resolution and inserts a version that may be somewhat, substantially, or entirely different. When a committee adopts extensive amendments to a measure, the panel often incorporates them into such an amendment. Occasionally, the term is applied to an amendment that replaces a major portion of a measure's text.

Amendment Tree—A diagram showing the number and types of amendments that the rules and practices of a house permit to be offered to a measure before any of the amendments is voted on. It shows the relationship of one amendment to the others, and it may also indicate the degree of each amendment, whether it is a perfecting or substitute amendment, the order in which amendments may be offered, and the order in which they are put to a vote. The same type of diagram can be used to display an actual amendment situation.

Amendments between the Houses—This is a method for reconciling differences between the House and Senate versions of a measure by passing the measure with successive amendments back and forth between the two chambers until both chambers have agreed to identical language.

Annual Authorization—Legislation that authorizes appropriations for a single fiscal year and usually for a specific amount. Under the rules of the authorization-appropriation process, an annually authorized agency or program must be reauthorized each year if it is to receive appropriations for that year. Sometimes Congress fails to enact the reauthorization (or authorization) but nevertheless provides appropriations to continue (or fund) the program, circumventing the rules by one means or another. *(See also Authorization.)*

Appeal—A member's formal challenge of a ruling or decision by the presiding officer or committee or subcommittee chair. On appeal, a house or a committee or subcommittee may overturn the ruling by majority vote. The right of appeal ensures the body against arbitrary control by the chair. Appeals are rarely made in the House and are even more rarely successful. Rulings are more frequently appealed in the Senate and occasionally overturned, in part because its presiding officer may not be of the same party or disposition as the Senate majority.

Apportionment—The action, after each decennial census, of allocating the number of seats in the House of Representatives to each state. By law, the total number of House members (not counting delegates and a resident commissioner) is fixed at 435. The number allotted to each state is based approximately on its proportion of the nation's total population. Because the Constitution guarantees each state one representative no matter how small its population, exact proportional distribution is virtually impossible. The mathematical formula currently used to determine the apportionment is called the Method of Equal Proportions. *(See also Method of Equal Proportions.)*

Appropriated Entitlement—An entitlement program, such as veterans' pensions, that is funded through annual appropriations rather than by a permanent appropriation. Because such an entitlement law requires the government to provide eligible recipients the benefits to which they are entitled, whatever the cost, Congress must appropriate the necessary funds.

Appropriation—(1) Legislative language that permits a federal agency to incur obligations and make payments from the Treasury for specified purposes, usually during a specified period of time. (2) The specific amount of money made available by such language. The Constitution prohibits payments from the Treasury except "in Consequence of Appropriations made by Law." With some exceptions, the rules of both houses forbid consideration of appropriations for purposes that are unauthorized in law or of appropriation amounts larger than those authorized in law. The House of Representatives claims the exclusive right to originate appropriation bills—a claim the Senate denies in theory but accepts in practice. *(See also General Appropriation Bill.)*

At-Large—Elected by and representing an entire state instead of a district within a state. The term usually refers to a representative rather than to a senator. *(See also Apportionment; Congressional District; Redistricting.)*

August Adjournment—A congressional adjournment during the month of August in odd-numbered years, required by the Legislative Reorganization Act of 1970. (In practice, Congress typically adjourns as well during August in even-numbered years.) The law instructs the two houses to adjourn for a period of at least thirty days before the second day after Labor Day, unless Congress provides otherwise, or if, on July 31, a state of war exists by congressional declaration.

Authorization—(1) A statutory provision that establishes or continues a federal agency, activity, or program for a fixed or indefinite period of time. It may also establish policies and restrictions and deal with organizational and administrative matters. (2) A statutory provision, as described in (1), may also, explicitly or implicitly, authorize congressional action to provide appropriations for an agency, activity, or program. The appropriations may be authorized for one year, several years, or an indefinite period of time, and the authorization may be for a specific amount of money or an indefinite amount ("such sums as may be necessary"). Authorizations of specific amounts are construed as ceilings on the amounts that subsequently may be appropriated in an appropriation bill, but not as minimums; either house may appropriate lesser amounts or nothing at all.

Authorization-Appropriation Process—The two-stage procedural system that the rules of each house require for establishing and funding federal agencies and programs: first, enactment of authorizing legislation that creates or continues an agency or program; second, enactment of appropriations legislation that provides funds for the authorized agency or program. *(See also Appropriation; Authorization.)*

Automatic Roll Call—Under a House rule, the automatic ordering of the yeas and nays when a quorum is not present on a voice or division vote and a member objects to the vote on that ground. It is not permitted in the Committee of the Whole.

Backdoor Spending Authority—Authority to incur obligations that evades the normal congressional appropriations process because it is provided in legislation other than appropriation acts. The most common forms are borrowing authority, contract authority, and entitlement authority. *(See also Borrowing Authority; Contract Authority; Entitlement Program; Spending Authority.)*

Baseline—A projection of the levels of federal spending, revenues, and the resulting budgetary surpluses or deficits for the upcoming and subsequent fiscal years, taking into account laws enacted to date and assuming no new policy decisions. It provides a benchmark for measuring the budgetary effects of proposed changes in federal revenues or spending, assuming certain economic conditions.

Bells—A system of electric signals and lights that informs members of activities in each chamber. The type of activity taking place is indicated by the number of signals and the interval between them. When the signals are sounded, a corresponding number of lights are lit around the perimeter of many clocks in House or Senate offices and corridors.

Bicameral—Consisting of two houses or chambers. Congress is a bicameral legislature whose two houses have an equal role in enacting legislation. In other national bicameral legislatures, one house may be significantly more powerful than the other. Most state legislatures are bicameral.

Bigger Bite Amendment—An amendment that substantively changes a portion of a text including language that had previously been amended. Normally, language that has been amended may not be amended again. However, a part of a sentence that has been changed by amendment, for example, may be changed again by an amendment that amends a "bigger bite" of the text—that is, by an amendment that also substantively changes the unamended parts of the sentence or the entire section or title in which the previously amended language appears. The biggest possible bite is an amendment in the nature of a substitute that amends the entire text of a measure. Once adopted, therefore, such an amendment ends the amending process. *(See also Amendment in the Nature of a Substitute.)*

Bill—The term for the chief vehicle Congress uses for enacting laws. Bills that originate in the House of Representatives are designated as "H.R." and are followed by a number assigned in the order in which the bills are introduced during a two-year

Congress. Bills in the Senate are similarly designated except they begin with an "S." Any bill that has not passed both houses of Congress in identical form at the end of a two-year Congress dies; its proponents must introduce a bill again in the next Congress to seek its consideration. A bill becomes a law if passed in identical language by both houses and signed by the president or passed over the president's veto or if the president fails to sign it within ten days after receiving it while Congress is in session.

Bill of Attainder—An act of a legislature finding a person guilty of treason or a felony. The Constitution prohibits the passage of such a bill by the U.S. Congress or any state legislature.

Bills and Resolutions Introduced—Members formally present measures to their respective houses by delivering them to a clerk in the chamber when their house is in session. Both houses permit any number of members to join in introducing a bill or resolution. The first member listed on the measure is the sponsor; the other members listed are its cosponsors. *(See also Hopper.)*

Bills and Resolutions Referred—After a bill or resolution is introduced, it is normally sent to one or more committees that have jurisdiction over its subject, as defined by House and Senate rules and precedents. A Senate measure is usually referred to the committee with jurisdiction over the predominant subject of its text, but it may be sent to two or more committees by unanimous consent or on a motion offered jointly by the majority and minority leaders. In the House, a rule requires the Speaker to refer a measure to the committee that has primary jurisdiction. The Speaker is also authorized to refer measures to additional committees with subject jurisdiction over one or more of a bill's provisions under House rules and to impose time limits on such referrals.

Bipartisan Committee—A committee with an equal number of members from each political party. The House Committee on Ethics and the Senate Select Committee on Ethics are the only bipartisan permanent full committees.

Borrowing Authority—Statutory authority permitting a federal agency, such as the Export-Import Bank, to borrow money from the public or the Treasury to finance its operations. It is a form of backdoor spending. To bring such spending under the control of the congressional appropriation process, the Congressional Budget Act requires that new borrowing authority is effective only to the extent and in such amounts as are provided in appropriations acts. *(See also Backdoor Spending Authority.)*

Budget—A detailed statement of actual or anticipated revenues and expenditures during an accounting period. For the national government, the period is the federal fiscal year (October 1 to September 30). The budget usually refers to the president's budget submission to Congress early each calendar year. The president's budget estimates federal government income and spending for the upcoming fiscal year and contains detailed recommendations for appropriation, revenue, and other legislation. Congress is not required to accept or even vote directly on the president's proposals, and it often revises the president's budget extensively. *(See also Fiscal Year.)*

Budget Act—Common name for the Congressional Budget and Impoundment Control Act of 1974, which established the basic procedures of the current congressional budget process; created the House and Senate Budget Committees; and enacted procedures for reconciliation, deferrals, and rescissions. *(See also Congressional Budget and Impoundment Control Act of 1974; Deferral; Gramm-Rudman-Hollings Act of 1985; Impoundment; Reconciliation; Rescission.)*

Budget and Accounting Act of 1921—The law that, for the first time, authorized the president to submit to Congress an annual budget for the entire federal government. Before passage of the act, most federal agencies sent their budget requests to the appropriate congressional committees without review by the president. Also established the Bureau of the Budget, forerunner of today's Office of Management and Budget. *(See also Budget; Office of Management and Budget.)*

Budget Authority—Generally, the amount of money that may be spent or obligated by a government agency or for a government program or activity. Technically, it is statutory authority to enter into obligations that normally result in outlays. The main forms of budget authority are appropriations, borrowing authority, and contract authority. It also includes authority to obligate and expend the proceeds of offsetting receipts and collections (that is, proceeds treated not as revenue but as negative budget authority). Congress may make budget authority available for only one year, several years, or an indefinite period, and it may specify definite or indefinite amounts. *(See also Appropriation; Borrowing Authority; Contract Authority; Obligation; Outlays.)*

Budget Control Act—PL 112-25, legislation enacted in the 112th Congress to provide for an increase in the statutory limit on the public debt in conjunction with other measures to reduce the budget deficit, including the creation of a Joint Select Committee on Deficit Reduction. The committee failed to report recommendations, thereby triggering automatic spending reductions.

Budget Enforcement Act of 1990—An act that revised the sequestration process established by the Gramm-Rudman-Hollings Act of 1985, replaced the earlier act's fixed deficit targets with adjustable ones, established discretionary spending limits for fiscal years 1991 through 1995, instituted pay-as-you-go rules to enforce deficit neutrality on revenue and mandatory spending legislation, and reformed the budget and accounting rules for federal credit activities. Unlike the Gramm-Rudman-Hollings Act, the 1990 act emphasized restraints on legislated changes in taxes and spending instead of fixed deficit limits. *(See also Gramm-Rudman-Hollings Act of 1985.)*

Budget Enforcement Act of 1997—An act that revised and updated the provisions of the Budget Enforcement Act of 1990, including by extending the discretionary spending caps and pay-as-you-go rules through 2002. *(See also Budget Enforcement Act of 1990.)*

Budget Process—(1) In Congress, the procedural system it uses to approve an annual concurrent resolution on the budget that sets goals for aggregate and functional categories of federal expenditures, revenues, and the surplus or deficit for an upcoming fiscal year; and to implement those goals in spending, revenue, and, if necessary, reconciliation and debt-limit legislation. (2) In the executive branch, the process of formulating the president's annual budget, submitting it to Congress, defending it before congressional committees, implementing subsequent budget-related legislation, impounding or sequestering expenditures as permitted by law, auditing and evaluating programs, and compiling final budget data. The Budget and Accounting Act of 1921 and the Congressional Budget and Impoundment Control Act of 1974 established the basic elements of the current budget process. Major revisions were enacted in the Gramm-Rudman-Hollings Act of 1985, the Budget Enforcement Act of 1990, and the Budget Enforcement Act of 1997. *(See also individual entries for the laws named in this entry.)*

Budget Resolution—A concurrent resolution in which Congress establishes or revises its version of the federal budget's broad financial features for the upcoming fiscal year and several additional fiscal years. As with other concurrent resolutions, it does not have the force of law, but it provides the framework within which Congress subsequently considers revenue, spending, and other budget-implementing legislation. The framework consists of two basic elements: (1) aggregate budget amounts (total revenues, new budget authority, outlays, loan obligations and loan guarantee commitments, deficit or surplus, and debt limit); and (2) subdivisions of the relevant aggregate amounts among the functional categories of the budget. Although it does not allocate funds to specific programs or accounts, the Budget Committees' reports accompanying the resolution often discuss the major program assumptions underlying the functional amounts. These assumptions are not binding. *(See also Budget Authority; Debt Limit; Federal Debt; Function or Functional Category; Outlays.)*

By Request—A designation indicating that a member has introduced a measure on behalf of the president, an executive agency, or a private individual or organization. Members introduce such measures as a courtesy because neither the president nor any person other than a member of Congress may introduce legislation. The term, which appears next to the sponsor's name, implies that the member who introduced the measure does not necessarily endorse it. A House rule dealing with by-request introductions dates from 1888, but the practice goes back to the earliest history of Congress.

Byrd Rule—The popular name of an amendment to the Congressional Budget Act that bars the inclusion of extraneous matter in any reconciliation legislation considered in the Senate. The ban is enforced by points of order sustained by the presiding officer. The provision defines different categories of extraneous matter, but it also permits certain exceptions. Its chief sponsor was Sen. Robert C. Byrd, D-W.Va.

Calendar—A list of measures or other matters (most of them favorably reported by committees) that are eligible for floor consideration. The House has four calendars; the Senate has two. A place on a calendar does not guarantee consideration. Each house decides which measures and matters it will take up, when, and in what order, in accordance with political considerations, rules, and practices.

Call Up—To bring a measure or report to the floor for immediate consideration.

Casework—Assistance to constituents who seek help in dealing with federal and local government agencies. Constituent service is a high priority in most members' offices.

Caucus—(1) A common term for the official organization of each party in each house. (2) The official title of the organization of House Democrats. House and Senate Republicans and Senate Democrats call their organizations "conferences." (3) A term for an informal group of members who share legislative interests, such as the Black Caucus, Hispanic Caucus, and Children's Caucus. These groups in the House are formally called Congressional Member Organizations and were formerly called Legislative Service Organizations. *(See also Party Caucus.)*

Censure—The strongest formal condemnation of a member for misconduct short of expulsion. A house usually adopts a resolution of censure to express its condemnation, after which the presiding officer reads its rebuke aloud to the member in the presence of his or her colleagues.

Chairman—The presiding officer of a committee, a subcommittee, or a task force. Increasingly, the term chairwoman is used, reflecting the growing number of women in Congress who have gained seniority, or simply "chair." At meetings, the chair preserves order, enforces the rules, recognizes members to speak or offer motions, and puts questions to a vote. The chair of a committee or subcommittee usually appoints its staff and sets its agenda, subject to the panel's veto. The presiding officer in the House or Senate may be referred to as the chair.

Chamber—The Capitol room in which a house of Congress normally holds its sessions. The chamber of the House of Representatives, officially called the Hall of the House, is considerably larger than that of the Senate because it must accommodate 435 representatives, five delegates, and one resident commissioner. Unlike the Senate chamber, members have no desks or assigned seats. In both chambers, the floor slopes downward to the well in front of the presiding officer's raised desk. A chamber is often referred to as "the floor," as when members are said to be on or going to the floor. Those expressions usually imply that the member's house is in session. *(See also Floor.)*

Christmas Tree Bill—Jargon for a bill adorned with amendments, many of them unrelated to the bill's subject, that provide benefits for interest groups, specific states, congressional districts, companies, and individuals.

Classes of Senators—A class under the Constitution consists of the thirty-three or thirty-four senators elected to a six-year term in the same general election. Because the terms of approximately one-third of the senators expire every two years, there are three classes.

Clean Bill—After a House committee extensively amends a bill, it often assembles its amendments and what is left of the bill into a new measure that one or more of its members introduce as a "clean bill." The revised measure is assigned a new number, reported to the House, and placed on the appropriate calendar.

Clerk of the House—An officer of the House of Representatives responsible principally for administrative support of the legislative process in the House. The clerk is invariably the choice of the majority party.

Cloakrooms—Two rooms with access to the rear of each chamber's floor, one for each party's members, where members may confer privately, sit quietly, or have a snack. The presiding officer sometimes urges members who are conversing too loudly on the floor to retire to their cloakrooms. *(See also Chamber.)*

Closed Hearing—A hearing closed to the public and the media; a hearing conducted "in executive session" is a closed hearing. A House committee may close a hearing only if it determines that disclosure of the testimony to be taken would endanger national security, violate any law, or tend to defame, degrade, or incriminate any person. The Senate has a similar rule. Both houses require roll-call votes in open session to close a hearing.

Closed Rule—A special rule reported from the House Rules Committee that prohibits amendments to a measure or that only permits amendments offered by the reporting committee. *(See also Rule.)*

Cloture—A Senate procedure that limits further consideration of a pending proposal to thirty hours to end a filibuster. Sixteen senators must first sign and submit a cloture petition to the presiding officer. One hour after the Senate meets on the second calendar day thereafter, the chair puts the motion to a yea-and-nay vote following a live quorum call. If three-fifths of all senators (sixty if there are no vacancies) vote for the motion to invoke cloture, the Senate must take final action on the cloture proposal by the end of the thirty hours of consideration and may consider no other business until it takes that action. Cloture on a proposal to amend the Senate's standing rules requires approval by two-thirds of the senators present and voting. *(See also Nuclear Option.)*

Code of Official Conduct—A House rule that bans certain actions by House members, officers, and employees; requires them to conduct themselves in ways that "reflect creditably" on the House; and orders them to adhere to the spirit and the letter of House rules and those of its committees. The code's provisions govern the receipt of outside compensation, gifts, and honoraria, and the use of campaign funds; prohibit members from using their clerk-hire allowance to pay anyone who does not perform duties commensurate with that pay; forbid discrimination in members' hiring or treatment of employees on the grounds of race, color, religion, sex, disability, age, or national origin; restrict members convicted of a crime who might be punished by imprisonment of two or more years from participating in committee business or voting on the floor until exonerated or reelected; and restrict employees' contact with federal agencies on matters in which they have a significant financial interest. The Senate's rules contain some similar prohibitions.

College of Cardinals—A popular term for the subcommittee chairs of the appropriations committees, reflecting their influence over appropriation measures.

Colloquy—A discussion between members to put a mutual understanding about the intent of a measure or amendment on the record. The discussion may be scripted in advance.

Comity—The practice of maintaining mutual courtesy and civility between the two houses in their dealings with each other and in members' speeches on the floor. Although the practice is largely governed by long-established customs, a House rule explicitly cautions its members not to characterize any Senate action or inaction, refer to individual senators except under certain circumstances, or quote from Senate proceedings except to make legislative history on a measure. The Senate has no rule on the subject, but references to the House have been held out of order on several occasions. Generally the houses do not interfere with each other's appropriations in the legislative-branch appropriations bill, although minor conflicts sometimes occur. A refusal to receive a message from the other house has also been held to violate the practice of comity.

Committee—A panel of members elected or appointed to perform some service or function for its parent body. Congress has four types of committees: standing, special or select, joint, and, in the House, a Committee of the Whole. Committees conduct investigations, make studies, issue reports and recommendations, and, in the case of standing committees, review and prepare measures on their assigned subjects for action by their respective houses. Most committees divide their work among several subcommittees. With rare exceptions, the majority party in a house holds a majority of the seats on its committees, and their chairs are also from that party. *(See also Committee of the Whole.)*

Committee Jurisdiction—The legislative subjects and other functions assigned to a committee by rule, precedent, resolution, or statute. A committee's title usually indicates the general scope of its jurisdiction but often fails to mention other significant subjects assigned to it.

Committee of the Whole—Common name of the Committee of the Whole House on the State of the Union, a committee consisting of all members of the House of Representatives. Measures from the Union Calendar must be considered in the Committee of the Whole before the House completes action on them; the committee often considers other major bills as well. A quorum of the committee is 100, and it meets in the House chamber under a chair appointed by the Speaker. Procedures in the Committee of the Whole expedite consideration of legislation because of its smaller quorum requirement, its ban on certain motions, and its five-minute rule for debate on amendments. The Senate does not use a Committee of the Whole.

Committee Ratios—The ratios of majority to minority party members on committees. By custom, the ratios of most committees reflect party strength in their respective houses.

Committee Report on a Measure—A document submitted by a committee to report a measure to its parent chamber. Customarily, the report explains the measure's purpose, describes provisions and any amendments recommended by the committee, and presents arguments for its approval. House and Senate rules prescribe the content of their committees' reports. The House requires its committees to write a report on legislation reported to the House; the Senate does not. *(See also Cordon Rule; Ramseyer Rule.)*

Committee Staff—Employees who assist the majority or minority party members of a committee. Most committees hire separate majority and minority party staffs, but they instead may hire nonpartisan staff, either professional and administrative staff or only administrative staff. Senate rules state that a committee's staff must reflect the relative number of its majority and minority party committee members, and the rules guarantee the minority at least one-third of the funds available for hiring partisan staff. In the House, each committee is authorized for thirty professional staff, and the minority members of most committees may select up to ten of these staff (subject to full committee approval). Under House rules, the minority party is to be "treated fairly" in the apportionment of any additional staff resources. Each House committee determines the portion of its additional staff that it allocates to the minority; some committees allocate one-third, and others allot less. *(See also Staff Director.)*

Committee Veto—A procedure that requires an executive department or agency to submit certain proposed policies, programs, or action to designated committees for review before implementing them. Before 1983, when the Supreme Court declared that a legislative veto was unconstitutional, these provisions permitted committees to veto the proposals. Language is still included in committee reports requiring agencies to seek committee approval before taking a specified action or type of action. Agencies usually take the pragmatic approach of trying to reach a consensus with a committee before carrying out an action, especially when an appropriations committee is involved. *(See also Legislative Veto.)*

Concur—To agree to an amendment of the other house by adopting either a motion to concur in that amendment or a motion to concur with an amendment to that amendment. After both houses have agreed to the same version of an amendment, neither house may amend it further, nor may any subsequent conference change it or delete it from the measure. Concurrence by one house in all amendments of the other house completes action on the measure; no vote is then necessary on the measure as a whole because both houses previously passed it.

Concurrent Resolution—A resolution that requires approval by both houses but does not need the president's signature and therefore cannot have the force of law. Concurrent resolutions deal with the prerogatives or internal affairs of Congress as a whole. Designated "H. Con. Res." in the House and "S. Con. Res." in the Senate, they are numbered consecutively in each house in their order of introduction during a two-year Congress. *(See also, for example, Budget Resolution.)*

Conferees—A common title for managers, the members from each house appointed to a conference committee. The Senate usually authorizes its presiding officer to appoint its conferees. The Speaker appoints House conferees, and under a rule adopted in 1993, can remove conferees "at any time after an original appointment" and also appoint additional conferees at any time. Conferees are expected to support the positions of their houses despite their personal views, but in practice this is not always the case. The party ratios of conferees generally reflect the ratios in their houses. Each house may appoint as many conferees as it pleases. House conferees often outnumber their Senate colleagues; however, each house has only one vote in a conference, so the size of its delegation is immaterial. *(See also Conference; Conference Committee; Conference Report.)*

Conference—(1) A formal meeting or series of meetings between members representing each house to reconcile House and Senate differences on a measure (occasionally several measures). Because one house cannot require the other to agree to its proposals, the conference usually reaches agreement by compromise. When a conference completes action on a measure, or as much action as appears possible, it sends its recommendations to both houses in the form of a conference report, accompanied by an explanatory statement. (2) The official title of the organization of all Democrats or Republicans in the Senate and of all Republicans in the House of Representatives. *(See also Conferees; Conference Committee; Conference Report; Party Caucus.)*

Conference Committee—A temporary joint committee formed for the purpose of resolving differences between the houses on a measure. Major and controversial legislation may require conference committee action. Voting in a conference committee is not by individuals but within the House and Senate delegations. Consequently, a conference committee report requires the support of a majority of the conferees from each house. Both houses require that conference committees open their meetings to the public. The Senate's rule permits the committee to close its meetings if a majority of conferees in each delegation agree by a roll-call vote. The House rule permits closed meetings only if the House authorizes them to do so on a roll-call vote. Otherwise, there are no congressional rules governing the organization of or procedure in a conference committee. The committee chooses its chair, but on measures that go to conference regularly, such as general appropriation bills, the chairmanship traditionally rotates between the houses. *(See also Conferees; Conference; Conference Report.)*

Conference Report—A document submitted to both houses that contains a conference committee's agreements for resolving their differences on a measure. It must be signed by a majority of the conferees from each house separately and must be accompanied by an explanatory statement. Both houses prohibit amendments to a conference report and require it to be accepted or rejected in its entirety, although specific disagreements may be presented to a chamber in a manner allowing the chamber to agree to its conferees' recommendation. *(See also Conferees; Conference; Conference Committee; Recommit a Conference Report.)*

Congress—(1) The national legislature of the United States, consisting of the House of Representatives and the Senate. (2) The national legislature in office during a two-year period. Congresses are numbered sequentially; thus, the 1st Congress of 1789–1791 and the 113th Congress of 2013–2015. Before implementation of the Twentieth Amendment in 1935, the two-year period began on the first Monday in December of odd-numbered years. Since then it has extended from January of an odd-numbered year through noon on January 3 of the next odd-numbered year. A Congress usually holds two annual sessions, but some have had three sessions and the pre-1935 67th Congress had four. When a Congress expires, measures die if they have not yet been enacted.

Congressional Accountability Act of 1995 (CAA)—An act applying eleven labor, workplace, and civil rights laws to the legislative branch and establishing procedures and remedies for legislative-branch employees with grievances in violation of these laws. The following laws are covered by the CAA: Fair Labor Standards Act of 1938; Title VII of the Civil Rights Act of 1964; Americans with Disabilities Act of 1990; Age Discrimination in Employment Act of 1967; Family and Medical Leave Act of 1993; Occupational Safety and Health Act of 1970; Chapter 71 of Title 5, *U.S. Code* (relating to federal service labor–management relations); Employee Polygraph Protection Act of 1988; Worker Adjustment and Retraining Notification Act; Rehabilitation Act of 1973; and Chapter 43 of Title 38, *U.S. Code* (relating to veterans' employment and reemployment).

Congressional Budget and Impoundment Control Act of 1974—The law that established the basic elements of the congressional budget process, the House and Senate Budget Committees, the Congressional Budget Office, and the procedures for congressional review of impoundments in the form of rescissions and deferrals proposed by the president. The budget process consists of procedures for coordinating congressional revenue and spending decisions made in separate tax, appropriations, and legislative measures. The impoundment provisions were intended to give Congress greater control over executive-branch actions that delay or prevent the spending of funds provided by Congress. *(See also Budget Process; Budget Resolution; Congressional Budget Office; Deferral; Impoundment; Rescission.)*

Congressional Budget Office (CBO)—A congressional support agency created by the Congressional Budget and Impoundment Control Act of 1974 to provide nonpartisan budgetary information and analysis to Congress and its committees. CBO acts as a scorekeeper when Congress is voting on the federal budget, tracking bills' compliance with overall budget goals. The agency also estimates what proposed legislation would cost over a five-year period. CBO works most closely with the House and Senate Budget Committees.

Congressional Directory—The official who's who of Congress, usually published during the first session of a two-year Congress. Contains statistical and other information on past Congresses and the current one as well as rosters of executive-branch officials, foreign ambassadors, and other individuals.

Congressional District—The geographical area represented by a single member of the House of Representatives. For states with only one representative, the entire state is a congressional district. After the reapportionment from the 2010 census, seven states had only one representative each: Alaska, Delaware, Montana, North Dakota, South Dakota, Vermont, and Wyoming. *(See also Apportionment; Gerrymandering; Redistricting.)*

Congressional Record—The daily, printed, and substantially verbatim account of proceedings in both the House and Senate chambers. Extraneous materials submitted by members appear in a section titled "Extensions of Remarks." A "Daily Digest" appendix contains highlights of the day's floor and committee action plus a list of committee meetings and floor agendas for the next day's session.

Although the official reporters of each house take down every word spoken during the proceedings, members are permitted to edit and "revise and extend" their remarks before they are printed. In the Senate section, all speeches, articles, and other material submitted by senators but not actually spoken or read on the floor are set off by large black dots, called bullets. However, bullets do not appear when a senator reads part of a speech and inserts the rest. In the House section, undelivered speeches and materials are printed in a distinctive typeface. The term "permanent *Record*" refers to the bound volumes of the daily *Records* of an entire session of Congress, which are repaginated so that page numbers run consecutively through a whole session of Congress. *(See also* Journal.*)*

Congressional Research Service (CRS)—Established in 1914, a department of the Library of Congress whose staff provide nonpartisan, objective analysis and information on virtually any subject to committees, members, and staff of Congress. Originally the Legislative Reference Service, it is the oldest congressional support agency, except for the Library of Congress.

Congressional Support Agencies—A term often applied to three agencies in the legislative branch that provide nonpartisan information and analysis to committees and members of Congress: the Congressional Budget Office (CBO), the Congressional Research Service (CRS) of the Library of Congress, and the Government Accountability Office (GAO)—previously called the General Accounting Office. The Library of Congress also supports Congress in many ways but provides numerous services to the public and to specialized users, including copyright and book cataloguing. *(See also Congressional Budget Office; Congressional Research Service; Government Accountability Office.)*

Congressional Terms of Office—A term normally begins on January 3 of the year following a general election and runs two years for representatives and six years for senators. A representative chosen in a special election to fill a vacancy is sworn in for the remainder of the predecessor's term. An individual appointed or elected to fill a Senate vacancy usually serves until the next general election or until the end of the predecessor's term, whichever comes first.

Constitutional Option—*(See Nuclear Option.)*

Constitutional Rules—Constitutional provisions that prescribe procedures for Congress. In addition to certain types of votes required in particular situations, these provisions include the following: (1) the House chooses its Speaker, the Senate its president pro tempore, and both houses their officers; (2) each house requires a majority quorum to conduct business; (3) less than a majority may adjourn from day to day and compel the attendance of absent members; (4) neither house may adjourn for more than three days without the consent of the other; (5) each house must keep a journal; (6) the yeas and nays are ordered when supported by one-fifth of the members present; (7) all revenue-raising bills must originate in the House, but the Senate may propose amendments to them. The Constitution also sets out the procedure in the House for electing a president, the procedure in the Senate for electing a vice president, the procedure for filling a vacancy in the office of vice president, and the procedure for overriding a presidential veto.

Constitutional Votes—Constitutional provisions that require certain votes or voting methods in specific situations. They include (1) the yeas and nays at the desire of one-fifth of the members present; (2) a two-thirds vote by the yeas and nays to override a veto; (3) a two-thirds vote by one house to expel one of its members and by both houses to propose a constitutional amendment; (4) a two-thirds vote of senators present to convict someone whom the House has impeached and to consent to ratification of treaties; (5) a two-thirds vote in each house to remove political disabilities from persons who have engaged in insurrection or rebellion or given aid or comfort to the enemies of the United States; (6) a majority vote in each house to fill a vacancy in the office of vice president; (7) a majority vote of all states to elect a president in the House of Representatives when no candidate receives a majority of the electoral votes; (8) a majority vote of all senators when the Senate elects a vice president under the same circumstances; and (9) the casting vote of the vice president in case of tie votes in the Senate.

Contempt of Congress—Willful obstruction of the proper functions of Congress. Most frequently, it is a refusal to obey a subpoena to appear and testify before a committee or to produce documents demanded by it. Such obstruction is a misdemeanor, and persons cited for contempt are subject to prosecution in federal courts. A house cites an individual for contempt by agreeing to a privileged resolution to that effect reported by a committee. The presiding officer then refers the matter to a U.S. attorney for prosecution.

Continuing Body—A characterization of the Senate on the theory that it continues from Congress to Congress and has existed continuously since it first convened in 1789. The rationale for the theory is that under the system of staggered six-year terms for senators, the terms of only about one-third of them expire after each Congress and, therefore, a quorum of the Senate is always in office. Consequently, under this theory, the Senate, unlike the House, has not adopted its rules at the beginning of each Congress because those rules continue from one Congress to the next. Under Senate rules, a two-thirds vote of the senators present and voting is needed to invoke cloture against a filibuster of a proposed rules change.

Continuing Resolution (CR)—A joint resolution that provides funds to continue the operation of federal agencies and programs at the beginning of a new fiscal year if their annual appropriation bills have not yet been enacted; also called continuing appropriations. Continuing resolutions are enacted shortly before or after the new fiscal year begins and usually make funds available for a specified period. Additional resolutions may be needed after the first expires. Some continuing resolutions have provided appropriations for an entire fiscal year. Continuing resolutions for specific periods customarily fix a rate at which agencies may incur obligations based either on the previous year's appropriations, the president's budget request, or the amount as specified in the agency's regular annual appropriation bill if that bill has already been passed by one or both houses. In the House, continuing resolutions are privileged after September 15. *(See also Appropriation; Privilege.)*

Contract Authority—Statutory authority permitting an agency to enter into contracts or incur other obligations even though it has not received an appropriation to pay for them. Congress must eventually fund them because the government is legally liable for such payments. The Congressional Budget Act of 1974 requires, with a few exceptions, that new contract authority may not be used unless provided for in advance by an appropriation act. *(See also Backdoor Spending Authority.)*

Cordon Rule—A Senate rule that requires a committee report to show changes the reported measure would make in current law. The rule was named after its sponsor, Sen. Guy Cordon, R-Ore. The House's analogous rule is called the Ramseyer Rule. *(See also Committee Report on a Measure; Ramseyer Rule.)*

Correcting Recorded Votes—The rules of both houses prohibit members from changing their votes after a vote result has been announced. Nevertheless, the Senate permits its members to withdraw or change their votes, by unanimous consent, immediately after the announcement. In rare instances, senators have been granted unanimous consent to change their votes several days or weeks after the announcement. Votes tallied by the electronic voting system in the House may not be changed. But when a vote actually given is not recorded during an oral call of the roll, a member may demand a correction as a matter of right. On all other alleged errors in a recorded vote, the Speaker determines whether the circumstances justify a change. Occasionally, members merely announce that they were incorrectly recorded; announcements can occur hours, days, or even months after the vote and appear in the *Congressional Record.*

Cosponsor—A member who has joined one or more other members to sponsor a measure. Joining on the day of introduction qualifies the member as an original sponsor.

Credit Authority—Authority granted to an agency to incur direct loan obligations or to make loan guarantee commitments. The Congressional Budget Act of 1974 bans congressional consideration of credit authority legislation unless the extent of that authority is made subject to provisions in appropriation acts.

C-SPAN—Cable-Satellite Public Affairs Network, which provides live, gavel-to-gavel coverage of Senate floor proceedings on one cable television channel and coverage of House floor proceedings on another channel. C-SPAN also televises selected committee hearings of both houses. Each house also transmits its televised proceedings directly to congressional offices.

Current Services Estimates—Executive-branch estimates of the anticipated costs of federal programs and operations for the next and future fiscal years at existing levels of service and assuming no new initiatives or changes in existing law. The president submits these estimates to Congress with the annual budget and includes an explanation of the underlying economic and policy assumptions on which they are based, such as anticipated rates of inflation, real economic growth, and unemployment, plus program caseloads and pay increases.

Custody of the Papers—Possession of an engrossed measure and certain related basic documents that the two houses produce as they pass and then try to resolve their differences over the measure.

Dean—Within a state's delegation in the House of Representatives, the member with the longest continuous service; also the longest-serving member of the House.

Debate—In congressional parlance, speeches delivered during consideration of a measure, motion, or other matter, as distinguished from speeches in other parliamentary situations, such as one-minute and special-order speeches when no business is pending. Virtually all debate in the House of Representatives is under some kind of time limitation. Most debate in the Senate is unlimited; that is, a senator, once recognized, may speak for as long as he or she chooses, unless the Senate invokes cloture or agrees by unanimous consent to limit debate time.

Debt Limit—The maximum amount of outstanding federal public debt permitted by law. The limit (or ceiling) covers virtually all debt incurred by the government except agency debt. A congressional budget resolution sets forth the new debt limit that may be required under its provisions. *(See also Budget Resolution; Federal Debt; Public Debt.)*

Deferral—An impoundment of funds for a specific period of time that may not extend beyond the fiscal year in which it is proposed. Under the Impoundment Control Act of 1974, the president must notify Congress that he is deferring the spending or obligation of funds provided by law for a project or activity. Congress can disapprove the deferral by legislation. *(See also Congressional Budget and Impoundment Control Act of 1974.)*

Deficit—The amount by which the government's outlays exceed its budget receipts for a given fiscal year. Both the president's budget and congressional budget resolutions provide estimates of the deficit or surplus for the upcoming and several future fiscal years. *(See also Budget Resolution.)*

Degrees of Amendment—Designations that indicate the relationships of amendments to the text of a measure and to each other. In general, an amendment offered directly to the text of a measure is an amendment in the first degree, and an amendment to that amendment is an amendment in the second degree. Both houses normally prohibit amendments in the third degree—that is, an amendment to an amendment to an amendment. *(See also Amendment; Amendment Tree.)*

Delegate—A nonvoting member of the House of Representatives elected to a two-year term from the District of Columbia, the territory of Guam, the territory of the Virgin Islands, the territory of American Samoa, or the territory of the Northern Marianas. By law, delegates may not vote in the full House, but they may participate in debate, offer motions (except to reconsider), and serve and vote on standing and select committees. On their committees, delegates possess the same powers and privileges as other members, and the Speaker may appoint them to appropriate conference committees and select committees. Delegates are given an office budget according to the same formulas as representatives. *(See also Resident Commissioner from Puerto Rico.)*

Denounce—A formal action that condemns a member for misbehavior; considered by some experts to be equivalent to censure. *(See also Censure.)*

Dilatory Tactics—Procedural actions intended to delay or prevent action by a house or a committee. They include, among others, offering numerous motions, demanding quorum calls and recorded votes at every opportunity, making numerous points of order and parliamentary inquiries, and speaking as long as the applicable rules permit. The Senate rules permit a battery of dilatory tactics, especially lengthy speeches, except under cloture or a unanimous consent agreement. In the House, possible dilatory tactics are more limited. Speeches are always subject to time limits and debate-ending motions. Moreover, a House rule instructs the Speaker not to entertain dilatory motions and lets the Speaker decide whether a motion is dilatory. However, the Speaker may not override the constitutional right of a member to demand the yeas and nays and in practice usually waits for a point of order before exercising that authority. *(See also Cloture.)*

Discharge a Committee—Remove a measure from a committee to which it has been referred in order to make it available for floor consideration. Noncontroversial measures are often discharged by unanimous consent. However, because congressional committees have no obligation to report measures referred to them, each house has procedures to extract measures from committees.

District and State Offices—Representatives maintain one or more offices in their districts for the purpose of assisting and communicating with constituents. The costs of maintaining these offices are paid from members' official allowances. Senators can use the official expense allowance to rent offices in their home state, subject to a funding formula based on their state's population and other factors.

District Work Period—The House term for a congressional recess during which members may visit their districts and conduct constituency business.

Division Vote—A vote in which the chair first counts those in favor of a proposition and then those opposed to it, with no record made of how each member voted. In the Senate, the chair may count raised hands or ask senators to stand, whereas the House requires members to stand; hence, often called a standing vote. Committees in both houses ordinarily use a show of hands. A division usually occurs after a voice vote and may be demanded by any member or ordered by the chair if there is any doubt about the outcome of the voice vote. The demand for a division can also come before a voice vote. In the Senate, the demand must come before the result of a voice vote is announced. It may be made after a voice vote announcement in the House, but only if no intervening business has transpired and only if the member was standing and seeking recognition at the time of the announcement. A demand for the yeas and nays or, in the House, for a recorded vote takes precedence over a demand for a division vote.

Earmark—A set-aside within a measure, committee report, or conference report for a specific purpose. *(See also Pork or Pork Barrel Legislation.)*

Effective Dates—Provisions of an act that specify when the entire act or individual provisions in it become effective as law. Most acts become effective on the date of enactment, but it is sometimes necessary or desirable to delay the effective dates of some provisions or to make them effective retroactively.

Electronic Voting—Since 1973, the House has used an electronic voting system to record the yeas and nays and to conduct recorded votes. Members vote by inserting their voting cards in one of the boxes at several locations in the chamber. They are given at least fifteen minutes to vote. However, when several votes occur immediately after each other, the Speaker or chair of the Committee of the Whole may reduce the voting time to five minutes (or less in some circumstances) on the second and subsequent votes. The Speaker or chair routinely allows additional time on each vote but may close a vote at any time after the minimum time has expired. Members can change their votes at any time before the Speaker announces the result. The House also uses the electronic system for quorum calls. While a vote is in progress, a large panel above the Speaker's desk displays how each member has voted. Smaller panels on either side of the chamber display running totals of the votes and the time remaining. The Senate does not have electronic voting.

Enacting Clause—The opening language of each bill, stating "Be it enacted by the Senate and House of Representatives of the United States of America in Congress assembled. . . . " This language gives legal force to measures approved by Congress and signed by the president or enacted over the president's veto. A successful motion to strike it from a bill kills the entire measure.

Engrossed Bill—The official copy of a bill or joint resolution as passed by one chamber, including the text as amended by floor action, and certified by the clerk of the House or the secretary of the Senate (as appropriate). Amendments by one house to a measure or amendments of the other also are engrossed. House engrossed documents are printed on blue paper; the Senate's are printed on white paper.

Enrolled Bill—The final official copy of a bill or joint resolution passed in identical form by both houses. An enrolled bill usually is printed on parchment. After it is certified by the chief officer of the house in which it originated and signed by the House Speaker and the Senate president pro tempore, the measure is sent to the White House for the president's signature.

Entitlement Program—A federal program under which individuals, businesses, or units of government that meet the requirements or qualifications established by law are entitled to receive certain payments if they seek such payments. Major examples include Social Security, Medicare, Medicaid, unemployment insurance, and military and federal civilian pensions. Congress cannot control their expenditures by refusing to appropriate the sums necessary to fund them because the government is legally obligated to pay eligible recipients the amounts to which the law entitles them. *(See also Backdoor Spending Authority.)*

Equality of the Houses—A component of the Constitution's emphasis on checks and balances under which each house is given essentially equal status in the enactment of legislation and in the relations and negotiations between the two houses. Although the House of Representatives initiates revenue and appropriation measures, the Senate has the right to amend them. Either house may initiate any other type of legislation, and neither can force the other to agree to, or even act on, its measures. Moreover, each house has a potential veto over the other because legislation requires agreement by both. Similarly, in a conference to resolve their differences on a measure, each house casts one vote, as determined by a majority of its conferees. In other national bicameral legislatures, the powers of one house may be markedly greater than those of the other.

Ethics Rules—Several rules or standing orders in each house that mandate certain standards of conduct for members and congressional employees in finance, employment, franking, and other areas. The Senate Select Committee on Ethics and the House Committee on Ethics investigate alleged violations of conduct and recommend appropriate actions to their respective houses.

Exclusive Committee—(1) Under the rules of the Republican Conference and House Democratic Caucus, a standing committee whose members usually cannot serve on any other standing committee. As of 2013, the Appropriations, Energy and Commerce (for Democrats beginning service in the 105th Congress), Financial Services (for Democrats beginning in the 109th Congress), Ways and Means, and Rules committees were designated as exclusive committees. The parties may choose to ignore or waive their rule for specific members. (2) Under the rules of the two-party conferences in the Senate, a standing committee whose members may not simultaneously serve on any other exclusive committee.

Executive Calendar—The Senate's calendar for executive business, that is, treaties and nominations. The calendar numbers indicate the order in which items were referred to the calendar but have no bearing on when or if the Senate will consider them. The Senate, by motion or unanimous consent, resolves itself into executive session to consider items on the executive calendar. The Senate's legislative calendar is the Calendar of General Orders and is referred to colloquially as the Senate Calendar. *(See also Executive Session; Nomination; Resolution of Ratification.)*

Executive Document—A document, usually a treaty, sent by the president to the Senate for approval. It is referred to a committee in the same manner as other measures. Resolutions to ratify treaties have their own "treaty document" numbers. For example, the first treaty submitted in the 113th Congress was "Treaty Document 113-1," a treaty on fishery resources in the South Pacific Ocean. *(See also Ratification; Resolution of Ratification; Treaty.)*

Executive Order—A document signed by the president that has a policy-making or legislative impact on the management of the federal government's operations. Members of Congress have challenged some executive orders on the grounds that they usurped the authority of the legislative branch. Although the Supreme Court has ruled that a particular order exceeded the president's authority, it has upheld others as falling within the president's general constitutional powers. An executive order might also be explicitly or implicitly authorized by law.

Executive Privilege—The assertion that presidents have the right to withhold certain information from Congress. Presidents have based their claim on (1) the constitutional separation of powers; (2) the need for secrecy in military and diplomatic affairs; (3) the need to protect individuals from unfavorable publicity; (4) the need to safeguard the confidential exchange of ideas in the executive branch; and (5) the need to protect individuals who provide confidential advice to the president.

Executive Session—(1) A Senate meeting devoted to the consideration of treaties or nominations. Normally, the Senate meets in legislative session; it resolves itself into executive session, by motion or by unanimous consent, to deal with its executive business. It also keeps a separate *Journal* for executive sessions. Executive sessions are usually open to the public, but the Senate may choose to close them. (Closed committee meetings in the House and Senate are also referred to as executive sessions.) *(See also Executive Calendar.)*

Expulsion—A member's removal from office by a two-thirds vote of his or her chamber; the supermajority is required by the Constitution. It is the most severe and most rarely used sanction a house can invoke against a member. Although the Constitution provides no explicit grounds for expulsion, the courts have ruled that it may be applied only for misconduct during a member's term of office, not for conduct before the member's election. Generally, neither house will consider expulsion of a member convicted of a crime until the judicial processes have been exhausted. At that stage, members sometimes resign rather than face expulsion. In 1977, the House adopted a rule urging members convicted of certain crimes to voluntarily abstain from voting or participating in other legislative business.

Extensions of Remarks—An appendix to the daily *Congressional Record* that consists primarily of miscellaneous material submitted by members. It often includes members' statements not delivered on the floor, newspaper articles and editorials, praise for a member's constituents, and noteworthy letters received by a member, among other material. Representatives supply the bulk of this material; senators submit little. "Extensions of Remarks" pages are separately numbered, and each number is preceded by the letter "E." Materials may be placed in the Extensions of Remarks section only by unanimous consent. *(See also Congressional Record.)*

Fast Track—Also called expedited procedures, this refers to any set of procedures applicable to a specific piece or specific subject of legislation. A fast track set of procedures circumvents or speeds up all or part of the legislative process to ensure or better ensure that a congressional decision is reached. Rulemaking statutes may prescribe expedited procedures for designated measures, such as statutes granting trade promotion authority to the president.

Federal Debt—The total amount of monies borrowed and not yet repaid by the federal government. Federal debt consists of public debt and agency debt. Public debt is the portion of the federal debt borrowed by the Treasury or the Federal Financing Bank directly from the public or from another federal fund or account. For example, the Treasury regularly borrows money from the Social Security trust fund. Public debt accounts for about 99 percent of the federal debt. Agency debt refers to the debt incurred by federal agencies such as the Export-Import Bank but excluding the Treasury and the Federal Financing Bank, which are authorized by law to borrow funds from the public or from another government fund or account. *(See also Debt Limit; Public Debt.)*

Filibuster—The use of time-consuming debate and parliamentary tactics by one member or a group of members to delay, modify, or defeat proposed legislation or rules changes. Filibusters are also sometimes used to delay urgently needed measures to force the body to consider other legislation. The Senate's rules permitting unlimited debate and the extraordinary majority it requires to invoke cloture make filibustering particularly effective in that chamber. Under the restrictive debate and other rules of the House, filibusters in that body are short-lived and infrequently attempted. *(See also Cloture.)*

Fiscal Year—The federal government's annual accounting period. It begins October 1 and ends on the following September 30. A fiscal year is designated by the calendar year in which it ends and is often referred to as FY. Thus, fiscal year 2014 began October 1, 2013, ended September 30, 2014, and is called FY14. In theory, Congress is supposed to complete action on all budgetary measures applying to a fiscal year before that year begins. It rarely does so. *(See also Budget.)*

Five-Minute Rule—A House rule that limits debate on an amendment offered in the Committee of the Whole to five minutes for its sponsor and five minutes for an opponent. In practice, the committee routinely permits longer debate by three devices: offering pro forma amendments, each debatable for five minutes; unanimous consent for a member to speak longer than five minutes; and special rule. Consequently, debate on an amendment could continue for hours or, more commonly today, be limited to ten or twenty minutes, with the amendment's proponent and an opponent each controlling half the time and yielding parcels of it to colleagues. In the absence of a special rule or unanimous consent, however, at any time after the first ten minutes, the committee may shut off debate immediately or by a specified time, either by unanimous consent or by majority vote on a nondebatable motion. *(See also Committee of the Whole; Pro Forma Amendment; Rule.)*

Floor—The level of the House or Senate chamber where members sit and the houses conduct their business. When members are attending a meeting of their house, they are said to be on the floor. Floor action refers to the procedural actions taken during floor consideration such as deciding on motions, taking up measures, amending them, and voting. *(See also Chamber.)*

Floor Manager—A majority party member responsible for guiding a measure through its floor consideration in a house and for devising the political and procedural strategies that might be required to get it passed. The presiding officer gives the floor manager priority recognition to debate, offer amendments, oppose amendments, and make crucial procedural motions. The minority party member is referred to as the minority floor manager.

Frank—Informally, members' legal right to send official mail postage free under their signatures; often called the franking privilege. Technically, it is the autographic or facsimile signature used on envelopes instead of stamps that permits members and certain congressional officers to send their official mail free of charge. The franking privilege has been authorized by law since the first Congress, except for a few months in 1873. Congress reimburses the U.S. Postal Service for the franked mail it handles.

Function *or* Functional Category—A broad category of national need and spending of budgetary significance. A category provides an accounting method for allocating and keeping track of budgetary resources and expenditures for that function because it includes all budget accounts related to the function's subject or purpose such as agriculture, administration of justice, commerce and housing, and energy. Functions do not necessarily correspond with appropriations acts or with the budgets of individual agencies. As of 2013, there were twenty functional categories, each divided into a number of subfunctions. *(See also Budget Resolution.)*

Gag Rule—A pejorative term for any type of special rule reported by the House Rules Committee that proposes to prohibit amendments to a measure or only permits amendments offered by the reporting committee.

Galleries—The balconies overlooking each chamber from which the public, news media, staff, and others may observe floor proceedings.

General Appropriation Bill—A term applied to each of the annual bills that provide funds for most federal agencies and programs and also to the supplemental appropriation bills that contain appropriations for more than one agency or program. *(See also Appropriation.)*

Germaneness—The requirement that an amendment be closely related—in terms of subject or purpose, for example—to the text it proposes to amend. A House rule requires that all amendments be germane. In the Senate, only amendments offered to general appropriation bills and budget measures or proposed under cloture must be germane. Germaneness rules can be waived by suspension of the rules in both houses, by unanimous consent agreements in the Senate, and by special rules from the Rules Committee in the House. Moreover, presiding officers usually do not enforce germaneness rules on their own initiative; therefore, a nongermane amendment can be adopted if no member raises a point of order against it. Under cloture in the Senate, however, the chair may take the initiative to rule amendments out of order as not being germane, without a point of order being made. All House debate must be germane except during general debate in the Committee of the Whole, but special rules invariably require that such debate be "confined to the bill." The Senate requires germane debate only during the first three hours of each daily session. Under the precedents of both houses, an amendment can be relevant but not necessarily germane. A crucial factor in determining germaneness in the House is how the subject of a measure or matter is defined. For example, the subject of a measure authorizing construction of a naval vessel is defined as being the construction of a single vessel; therefore, an amendment to authorize an additional vessel is not germane.

Gerrymandering—The manipulation of legislative district boundaries to benefit a particular party, politician, or minority group. The term originated in 1812 when the Massachusetts legislature redrew the lines of state legislative districts to favor the party of Gov. Elbridge Gerry, and some critics said one district resembled a salamander. *(See also Congressional District; Redistricting.)*

Government Accountability Office (GAO)—A congressional support agency, often referred to as the investigative arm of Congress. It evaluates and audits federal agencies and programs in the United States and abroad on its initiative or at the request of congressional committees or members. The office, created in 1921, was called the General Accounting Office until 2004.

Gramm-Rudman-Hollings Act of 1985—Common name for the Balanced Budget and Emergency Deficit Control Act of 1985, which established new budget procedures intended to balance the federal budget by fiscal year 1991. (The timetable subsequently was extended and then deleted.) The act's chief sponsors were senators Phil Gramm, R-Texas, Warren Rudman, R-N.H., and Ernest Hollings, D-S.C.

Grandfather Clause—A provision in a measure, law, or rule that exempts an individual, entity, or a defined category of individuals or entities from complying with a new policy or restriction. For example, a bill that would raise taxes on persons who reach the age of sixty-five after a certain date inherently grandfathers out those who are sixty-five before that date. Similarly, a Senate rule limiting senators to two major committee assignments also grandfathers some senators who were sitting on a third major committee before a specified date.

Grants-in-Aid—Payments by the federal government to state and local governments to help provide for assistance programs or public services.

Hearing—Committee or subcommittee meetings to receive testimony on proposed legislation or for oversight purposes. Relatively few bills are important enough to justify formal hearings. Witnesses often include experts, government officials, spokespersons for interested groups, officials of the Government Accountability Office, and members of Congress.

Hold—A senator's request that his or her party leaders delay or halt floor consideration of certain legislation or presidential nominations. The majority leader usually honors a hold for a reasonable period of time, especially if its purpose is to assure the senator that the matter will not be called up during his or her absence or to give the senator time to gather necessary information.

Hold (or Have) the Floor—A member's right to speak without interruption, unless he or she violates a rule, after recognition by the presiding officer. At the member's discretion, he or she may yield to another member for a question in the Senate or for a question or statement in the House but may reclaim the floor at any time.

Hold-Harmless Clause—In legislation providing a new formula for allocating federal funds, a clause to ensure that recipients of those funds do not receive less in a future year than they did in the current year if the new formula would result in a reduction for them. Similar to a grandfather clause, it has been used most frequently to soften the impact of sudden reductions in federal grants. *(See also Grandfather Clause.)*

Hopper—A box on the clerk's desk in the House chamber into which members deposit bills and resolutions to introduce them. In House jargon, to drop a bill in the hopper is to introduce it.

Hour Rule—A House rule that permits members, when recognized, to hold the floor in debate for no more than one hour each. A member recognized for one hour typically yields one-half of the time to an opposing member. In the instance of debate on a special rule, the majority party member customarily yields one-half the time to a minority member. Although the hour rule also applies to general debate in the Committee of the Whole, special rules routinely vary the length of time for such debate and its control to fit the circumstances of particular measures. *(See also Rule, second definition.)*

House as in Committee of the Whole—A hybrid combination of procedures from the general rules of the House and from the rules of the Committee of the Whole, seen infrequently today and most often only when the House considers a private bill. *(See also Private Bill.)*

House Calendar—The calendar reserved for all public bills and resolutions that do not raise revenue or directly or indirectly appropriate money or property when they are favorably reported by House committees.

House Manual—A commonly used title for the compilation of the rules of the House of Representatives, the Constitution, *Jefferson's Manual,* and rulemaking statutes, published in each Congress. Its official title is *Constitution, Jefferson's Manual, and Rules of the House of Representatives.*

House of Representatives—The house of Congress in which states are represented roughly in proportion to their populations, but every state is guaranteed at least one representative. By law, the number of voting representatives is fixed at 435. Five delegates and one resident commissioner also serve in the House; they may vote in their committees but not on the House floor. Although the House and Senate have equal legislative power, the Constitution gives the House sole authority to originate revenue measures. The House also claims the right to originate appropriation measures, a claim the Senate disputes in theory but concedes in practice. The House has the sole power to impeach (only the

Senate convicts, however) and elects the president when no candidate has received a majority of the electoral votes. The House is sometimes referred to as the lower body. *(See also Delegate; Lower Body; Representative; Resident Commissioner from Puerto Rico; Senate.)*

Immunity—(1) Members' constitutional protection from lawsuits and arrest in connection with their legislative duties. They may not be tried for libel or slander for anything they say on the floor of a house or in committee. Nor may they be arrested while attending sessions of their houses or when traveling to or from sessions of Congress, except when charged with treason, a felony, or a breach of the peace. (2) In the case of a witness before a committee, a grant of protection from prosecution based on that person's testimony to the committee. It is used to compel witnesses to testify who would otherwise refuse to do so on the constitutional ground of possible self-incrimination. Under such a grant, none of a witness's testimony may be used against him or her in a court proceeding except in a prosecution for perjury or for giving a false statement to Congress. *(See also Contempt of Congress.)*

Impeachment—The first step to remove the president, the vice president, Supreme Court justices, or other federal civil officers from office and possibly to disqualify them from any future federal office "of honor, Trust or Profit." An impeachment is a formal charge of treason, bribery, or "other high Crimes and Misdemeanors." The House has the sole power of impeachment and the Senate the sole power of trying the charges and convicting. The House impeaches by a simple majority vote; conviction requires a two-thirds vote of all senators present.

Impeachment Trial, Removal, and Disqualification—The Senate conducts an impeachment trial under a separate set of twenty-six rules that appears in the *Senate Manual.* Under the Constitution, the chief justice of the Supreme Court presides over the impeachment trial of the president, but the vice president, the president pro tempore, or any other senator may preside over the impeachment trial of another official.

The Constitution requires senators to take an oath for an impeachment trial. During the trial, senators may not engage in colloquies or participate in arguments, but they may submit questions in writing to House managers or defense counsel. After the trial concludes, the Senate votes separately on each article of impeachment without debate unless the Senate orders the doors closed for private discussions. During deliberations, senators may speak no more than once on a question, not for more than ten minutes on an interlocutory question, and not more than fifteen minutes on the final question. These rules may be set aside by unanimous consent or suspended on motion by a two-thirds vote.

The Senate's impeachment trial of President Bill Clinton in 1999 was only the second such trial involving a president (the first being the impeachment trial of President Andrew Johnson in 1868). It continued for five weeks, with the Senate voting not to convict on the two impeachment articles.

Senate impeachment rules allow the Senate, at its discretion, to name a committee to hear evidence and conduct the trial, with all senators thereafter voting on the charges. The impeachment trials of three federal judges were conducted this way, and the Supreme Court upheld the validity of these rules in *Nixon v. United States* (506 U.S. 224, 1993).

An official convicted on impeachment charges is removed from office immediately. However, the convicted official is not barred from holding a federal office in the future unless the Senate, after its conviction vote, also approves a resolution disqualifying the convicted official from future office. For example, federal judge Alcee L. Hastings was impeached and convicted in 1989, but the Senate did not vote to bar him from office in the future. In 1992, Hastings was elected to the House of Representatives, and no challenge was raised against seating him when he took the oath of office in 1993.

Impoundment—An executive-branch action or inaction that delays or withholds the expenditure or obligation of budget authority provided by law. The Impoundment Control Act of 1974 classifies impoundments as either deferrals or rescissions, requires the president to notify Congress about all such actions, and gives Congress authority to approve or reject them. *(See also Congressional Budget and Impoundment Control Act of 1974; Deferral; Rescission.)*

Inspector General in the House of Representatives—A position established with the passage of the House Administrative Reform Resolution of 1992. The duties of the office have been revised several times and are now contained in House Rule II. The inspector general (IG), who is subject to the policy direction and oversight of the Committee on House Administration, is appointed for a Congress jointly by the Speaker and the majority and minority leaders of the House. The IG communicates the results of audits to the House officers or officials who were the subjects of the audits and suggests appropriate corrective measures. The IG submits a report of each audit to the Speaker, the majority and minority leaders, and the chair and ranking minority member of the House Administration Committee; notifies these five members in the case of any financial irregularity discovered; and reports to the Committee on Ethics on possible violations of House rules or any applicable law by any House member, officer, or employee. The IG's office also has certain duties to audit various financial operations of the House that had previously been performed by the Government Accountability Office.

Instruct Conferees—A formal action by a house urging its conferees to uphold a particular position on a measure in conference. The instruction may be to insist on certain provisions in the measure as passed by that house or to accept a provision in the version passed by the other house. Instructions to conferees are not binding because the primary responsibility of conferees is to reach agreement on a measure, and neither house can compel the other to accept particular provisions or positions.

Investigative Power—The authority of Congress and its committees to pursue investigations, upheld by the Supreme Court but limited to matters related to, and in furtherance of, a legitimate task of the Congress. Standing committees in both houses are permanently authorized to investigate matters within their jurisdictions. Major investigations are sometimes conducted by temporary select, special, or joint committees established by resolutions for that purpose.

Some rules of the House provide certain safeguards for witnesses and others during investigative hearings. These permit counsel to accompany witnesses, require that each witness receive a copy of the committee's rules, and order the committee to go into closed session if it believes the testimony to be heard might defame, degrade, or incriminate any person. The committee may subsequently decide to hear such testimony in open session. There are no Senate rules of this kind.

Item Veto—Item veto authority, which is available in some form to most state governors, allows governors to eliminate or reduce items in legislative measures presented for their signature without vetoing the entire measure, and sign the rest into law. A similar authority was briefly granted to the U.S. president under the Line Item Veto Act of 1996. According to the majority opinion of the Supreme Court in its 1998 decision *Clinton v. City of New York* (524 U.S. 417) overturning that law, a constitutional amendment would be necessary to give the president such veto authority. *(See also Line Item; Line Item Veto Act of 1996.)*

Jefferson's Manual—Short title of *Jefferson's Manual of Parliamentary Practice,* prepared by Thomas Jefferson for his guidance when he was president of the Senate from 1797 to 1801. Although it reflects English parliamentary practice in his day, many procedures in both houses of Congress are still rooted in its precepts. Under a House rule adopted in 1837, the manual's provisions govern House procedures when applicable and when they are not inconsistent with its standing rules and orders. The Senate, however, has never officially acknowledged it as a direct authority for its legislative procedure.

Johnson Rule—A policy instituted in 1953 under which all Democratic senators are assigned to one major committee before any Democrat is assigned to two. The Johnson Rule is named after its author, Sen. Lyndon B. Johnson, D-Texas, then the Senate's Democratic leader. Senate Republicans adopted a similar policy soon thereafter.

Joint Committee—A committee composed of members selected from each house. The functions of contemporary joint committees involve investigation, research, or oversight of agencies or activities closely related to congressional work, although they might have regulatory authority over a legislative-branch agency or function. Permanent joint committees, created by statute, are sometimes called standing joint committees. Only four joint committees existed as of 2013: Joint Economic, Joint Taxation, Joint Library, and Joint Printing. None has authority to report legislation.

Joint Explanatory Statement—This is a statement appended to a conference report that explains in plain English the conference agreement and the intent of the conferees.

Joint Resolution—A legislative measure that Congress uses for special purposes based on tradition. Similar to a bill, a joint resolution has the force of law when passed by both houses and either approved by the president or passed over the president's veto. Unlike a bill, a joint resolution enacted into law is not called an act; it retains its original title. Most often, joint resolutions deal with such relatively limited matters as the correction of errors in existing law, a single appropriation, or the establishment of permanent joint committees. They are also used for important matters such as declaring war or providing continuing appropriations and to carry out fast-track procedures included by Congress

in some statutes. Joint resolutions, in addition, are used to propose constitutional amendments, which are submitted to the states for ratification when approved by a two-thirds vote in each house of Congress; these joint resolutions do not require the president's signature and become effective only when ratified by three-fourths of the states. The House designates joint resolutions as "H. J. Res." and the Senate as "S. J. Res." Each house numbers its joint resolutions consecutively in the order of introduction during a two-year Congress. Unless passed by both chambers in identical form before the end of a two-year Congress, joint resolutions die with the Congress's *sine die* adjournment. *(See also Bill; Continuing Resolution; Fast Track.)*

Joint Session—Informally, any combined meeting of the Senate and the House. Technically, a joint session is a combined meeting to count the electoral votes for president and vice president or to hear a presidential address, such as the State of the Union message; any other formal combined gathering of both houses is a joint meeting. Joint sessions are authorized by concurrent resolutions and are held in the House chamber, because of its larger seating capacity. Although the president of the Senate and the Speaker sit side by side at the Speaker's desk during combined meetings, the former presides over the electoral count and the latter presides on all other occasions and introduces the president or other guest speaker. The president and other guests may address a joint session or meeting only by invitation.

Joint Sponsorship—Two or more members sponsoring the same measure.

Journal—The official record of House or Senate actions, including every motion offered, every vote cast, amendments agreed to, quorum calls, and so forth. Unlike the *Congressional Record,* it does not provide reports of speeches, debates, statements, and other items. The Constitution requires each house to maintain a *Journal* and to publish it periodically. *(See also Congressional Record.)*

Junket—A derisive term for a member's trip at government expense, especially abroad, on official business but, it is often alleged, for pleasure.

Killer Amendment—An amendment that, if agreed to, might lead to the defeat of the measure it amends, either in the house in which the amendment is offered or at some later stage of the legislative process. Also called a poison-pill amendment. Members sometimes deliberately offer or vote for such an amendment in the expectation that it will undermine support for the measure in Congress or increase the likelihood that the president will veto it.

King of the Mountain (or Hill Rule)—*(See Queen of the Hill Rule.)*

LA—*(See Legislative Assistant.)*

Lame Duck—Jargon for a member who has not been reelected, or did not seek reelection, and is serving the balance of his or her term.

Lame Duck Session—A session of a Congress held after the election for the succeeding Congress, so-called after the lame duck members still serving.

Last Train Out—Colloquial name for last must-pass bill of a session of Congress.

Law—An act of Congress (in the form of a bill or joint resolution, the latter of which is not a constitutional amendment) that has been signed by the president, passed over the president's veto, or allowed by the president to become law without his signature.

Lay on the Table—A motion to dispose of a pending proposition immediately, finally, and adversely; that is, to kill it without a direct vote on its substance. Often simply called a motion to table, it is not debatable and is adopted by majority vote or without objection. It is a highly privileged motion, taking precedence over all others except the motion to adjourn in the House and all but three additional motions in the Senate. It can kill a bill or resolution, an amendment, another motion, an appeal, or virtually any other matter.

Tabling an amendment also tables the measure to which the amendment is pending in the House but not in the Senate. The House does not allow the motion against the motion to recommit, in the Committee of the Whole, and in some other situations. In the Senate, it is the only permissible motion that immediately ends debate on a proposition, but only to kill it.

(The) Leadership—Usually, a reference to the majority and minority leaders of the Senate or to the Speaker and minority leader of the House. The term sometimes includes the majority leader in the House and the majority and minority whips in each house and, at other times, other party officials as well.

Legislation—(1) A synonym for legislative measures: bills and joint resolutions. (2) Provisions in such measures or in substantive amendments offered to them. (3) In some contexts, provisions that change existing substantive or authorizing law rather than provisions that make appropriations.

Legislation on an Appropriation Bill—A common reference to provisions changing existing law that appear in or are offered as amendments to a general appropriation bill. A House rule prohibits the inclusion of such provisions in general appropriation bills unless they retrench expenditures. An analogous Senate rule permits points of order against amendments to a general appropriation bill that propose general legislation. In both chambers, such prohibitions may be waived by procedures such as special rules in the House, by failure of any member to make a point of order against such a provision, or by other means. *(See also Authorization-Appropriation Process.)*

Legislative Assistant (LA)—A member's staff person responsible for monitoring and preparing legislation on particular subjects and for advising the member on them; commonly referred to as an LA. Today, members' offices typically employ a legislative director (LD) to oversee an office's LAs.

Legislative Day—The day that begins when a house meets after an adjournment and ends when it next adjourns. Because the House of Representatives normally adjourns at the end of a daily session, its legislative and calendar days usually coincide. The Senate, however, might recess at the end of a daily session, and its legislative day may extend over several calendar days or longer. Among other uses, this technicality permits the Senate to continue for procedural purposes on the same day or to save time by circumventing its morning hour, a procedure required at the beginning of every legislative day.

Legislative History—(1) A chronological list of actions taken on a measure during its progress through the legislative process. (2) The official documents relating to a measure, the entries in the *Journals* of the two houses on that measure, and the *Congressional Record* text of its consideration in both houses. The documents include all committee reports and the conference report and joint explanatory statement, if any. Courts and affected federal agencies might study a measure's legislative history for congressional intent about its purpose and interpretation.

Legislative Process—(1) Narrowly, the stages in the enactment of a law from introduction to final disposition. An introduced measure that becomes law typically travels through reference to committee; committee and subcommittee consideration; committee report to the chamber; floor consideration and amendment; passage; engrossment; messaging to the other house; similar steps in that house, including floor amendment of the measure; return of the measure to the first house; consideration of amendments between the houses or a conference to resolve their differences; approval of the conference report by both houses; enrollment; approval by the president or override of the president's veto; and deposit with the Archivist of the United States. (2) Broadly, the political, lobbying, and other factors that affect or influence the process of enacting laws.

Legislative Veto—A procedure, declared unconstitutional in 1983, that allowed Congress or one of its houses to nullify certain actions of the president, executive-branch agencies, or independent agencies. Sometimes called congressional vetoes or congressional disapprovals. Following the Supreme Court's 1983 decision in *Immigration and Naturalization Service v. Chadha* (462 U.S. 919), Congress amended several legislative veto statutes to require enactment of joint resolutions, which are subject to presidential veto, for nullifying executive-branch actions. Alternately, Congress may include in a statute a provision requiring congressional approval of a proposed executive action before its implementation. *(See also Committee Veto.)*

Limitation on a General Appropriation Bill—Language that prohibits expenditures for part of an authorized purpose from funds provided in a general appropriation bill. Precedents require that the language be phrased in the negative: that none of the funds provided in a pending appropriation bill shall be used for a specified authorized activity. Limitations in general appropriation bills are permitted on the grounds that Congress can refuse to fund authorized programs and, therefore, can refuse to fund any part of them as long as the prohibition does not change existing law. House precedents have established that a limitation does not change existing law if it does not impose additional duties or burdens on executive-branch officials, interfere with their discretionary authority, or require them to make judgments or determinations not required by existing law.

The proliferation of limitation amendments in the 1970s and early 1980s prompted the House to adopt a rule in 1983 making it more difficult for members to offer them. The rule bans such amendments during the reading of an appropriation bill for amendment, unless they are specifically authorized in existing law. Other limitations may be offered after the reading, but the Committee of the Whole can foreclose them by adopting a motion to rise and report the bill back to the House. In 1995, the rule was amended to allow the motion to rise and report to be made only by the majority leader or his or her designee. The House Appropriations Committee, however, can include limitation provisions in the bills it reports.

Line Item—An amount in an appropriation measure. It can refer to a single appropriation account or to separate amounts within the account. In the congressional budget process, the term usually refers to assumptions about the funding of particular programs or accounts that underlie the broad functional amounts in a budget resolution. These assumptions are discussed in the reports accompanying each resolution and are not binding.

Line-Item Veto—*(See Item Veto; Line Item Veto Act of 1996.)*

Line Item Veto Act of 1996—A law, in effect only from January 1997 until June 1998, that granted the president authority intended to be functionally equivalent to an item veto by amending the Impoundment Control Act to incorporate an approach known as enhanced rescission. Key provisions established a new procedure that permitted the president to cancel amounts of new discretionary appropriations (budget authority), new items of direct spending (entitlements), or certain limited tax benefits. It also required the president to notify Congress of the cancellation in a special message within five calendar days after signing the measure. The cancellation would become permanent unless legislation disapproving it was enacted within thirty days. On June 25, 1998, in *Clinton v. City of New York* (524 U.S. 417), the Supreme Court held the Line Item Veto Act unconstitutional, on the grounds that its cancellation provisions violated the presentment clause in Article I, clause 7, of the Constitution. *(See also Item Veto; Line Item.)*

Live Pair—A voluntary and informal agreement between two members on opposite sides of an issue, one of whom is absent for a recorded vote, under which the member who is present withholds or withdraws his or her vote to offset the failure to vote by the member who is absent. Usually the member in attendance announces that he or she has a live pair, states how each would have voted, and votes "present." In the House, under a rules change enacted in the 106th Congress, a live pair is only permitted on the rare occasions when electronic voting is not used.

Live Quorum—In the Senate, a quorum call to which senators are expected to respond. Senators usually suggest the absence of a quorum, not to force a quorum to appear but to provide a pause in the proceedings during which senators can engage in private discussions or wait for a senator to come to the floor (a "dead quorum"). A senator desiring a live quorum usually announces his or her intention, giving fair warning that there will be an objection to any unanimous-consent request that the quorum call be dispensed with before it is completed.

Loan Guarantee—A statutory commitment by the federal government to pay part or all of a loan's principal or interest or both to a lender or the holder of a security in case the borrower defaults.

Lobby—To try to persuade members of Congress to propose, pass, modify, or defeat proposed legislation or to change or repeal existing laws. Lobbyists attempt to promote their preferences or those of a group, organization, or industry. Originally the term referred to persons frequenting the lobbies or corridors of legislative chambers in order to speak to lawmakers. In a general sense, lobbying includes not only direct contact with members but also indirect attempts to influence them, such as writing to them or persuading others to write or visit them, attempting to mold public opinion toward a desired legislative goal by various means, and contributing or arranging for contributions to members' election campaigns. The right to lobby stems from the First Amendment to the Constitution, which bans laws that abridge the right of the people to petition the government for a redress of grievances.

Lobbying Disclosure Act of 1995—The principal statute requiring disclosure of—and also, to a degree, circumscribing—the activities of lobbyists. In general, it requires lobbyists who spend more than 20 percent of their time on lobbying activities to register and make semiannual reports of their activities to the clerk of the House and the secretary of the Senate, although the law provides for a number of exemptions. Among the statute's prohibitions, lobbyists are not allowed to make contributions to the legal defense fund of a member or high government official or to reimburse for official travel. Civil penalties for failure to comply may include fines. The act does not include grassroots lobbying in its definition of lobbying activities.

The act amended several other lobby laws, notably the Foreign Agents Registration Act (FARA), so that lobbyists can submit a single filing. The 1995 act repealed the 1946 Federal Regulation of Lobbying Act.

Logrolling—Jargon for a legislative tactic or bargaining strategy in which members try to build support for their legislation by promising to support legislation desired by other members or by accepting amendments they hope will induce their colleagues to vote for their bill.

Lower Body—A way to refer to the House of Representatives, which is sometimes considered pejorative by House members. One source of this designation is the design of the capitol in colonial Williamsburg. The House of Burgesses met in a chamber on the ground floor of the capitol; the Council met in a chamber on the second floor above the Burgesses's chamber.

Mace—The symbol of the authority of the House and entrusted to the office of the House sergeant at arms. Under the direction of the Speaker, the sergeant at arms is responsible for preserving order on the House floor by holding up the mace in front of an unruly member or by carrying the mace up and down the aisles to quell boisterous behavior. When the House is in session, the mace sits on a pedestal at the Speaker's right; when the House is in Committee of the Whole, it is moved to a lower pedestal. The mace is forty-six inches high and consists of thirteen ebony rods bound in silver and topped by a silver globe with a silver eagle, wings outstretched, perched on it.

Majority Leader—The majority party's chief floor strategist, elected by that party's caucus, sometimes called floor leader. In the Senate, the majority leader develops the party's political and procedural strategy, usually in collaboration with other party officials and committee chairs, and serves as his or her party's principal spokesperson. The majority leader negotiates the Senate's agenda and committee ratios with the minority leader and usually calls up measures for floor action. The chamber traditionally concedes to the majority leader the right to determine the days on which it will meet and the hours at which it will convene and adjourn. In the House, the majority leader is the Speaker's deputy and possibly heir apparent, helps plan the floor agenda, leads the party's legislative strategy, and often speaks for the party leadership in debate. *(See also (The) Leadership.)*

Majority Staff—*(See Committee Staff.)*

Managers—(1) The official title of members appointed to a conference committee, commonly called conferees. The ranking majority and minority managers for each house also manage floor consideration of the committee's conference report. (2) The members who manage the initial floor consideration of a measure. (3) The official title of House members appointed to present impeachment articles to the Senate and to act as prosecutors on behalf of the House during the Senate trial of the impeached person. *(See also Conferees; Floor Manager; Impeachment Trial, Removal, and Disqualification.)*

Mandatory Appropriations—Amounts that Congress must appropriate annually because it has no discretion over them unless it first amends existing substantive law. Certain entitlement programs, for example, require annual appropriations. *(See also Appropriated Entitlement.)*

Markup—A meeting or series of meetings by a committee or subcommittee during which members mark up a measure by offering, debating, and voting on amendments to it.

Means-Tested Programs—Programs that provide benefits or services to low-income individuals who meet a test of need. Most are entitlement programs, such as Medicaid, food stamps, and Supplementary Security Income. A few—for example, subsidized housing and various social services—are funded through discretionary appropriations.

Members' Allowances—Official expenses that are paid for or for which members are reimbursed by their houses. Among these are the costs of office space in their home states or districts; office equipment and supplies; postage-free mailings (the franking privilege); a set number of trips to and from home states or districts, as well as travel elsewhere on official business; telephone and other telecommunications services; and staff salaries. Other cost items are not allocated to individual members, such as the cost of offices in the congressional office buildings in Washington, D.C., or staff overhead such as health insurance, life insurance, and retirement.

Member's Staff—The personal staff to which a member is entitled. The House sets a maximum number of staff and a monetary allowance equal for each representative. The Senate does not set a maximum staff level, but it does set a monetary allowance for each senator based on the population of a senator's state. In each house, the staff allowance is included with office expense allowances and other allowances such as travel and mail in a consolidated allowance. Representatives and senators can generally spend as much money in their consolidated allowances for staff, office expenses, or other allowable expenses, as long as they do not exceed the monetary value of the consolidated allowance. This provides members with flexibility in operating their offices.

Method of Equal Proportions—The mathematical formula used since 1950 to determine how the 435 seats in the House of Representatives should be distributed among the fifty states in the apportionment following each decennial census. It minimizes as much as possible the proportional difference between the average district population in any two states. Because the Constitution guarantees each state at least one representative, fifty seats are automatically apportioned. The formula calculates priority numbers for each state, assigns the first of the 385 remaining seats to the state with the highest priority number, the second to the state with the next-highest number, and so on until all seats are distributed. *(See also Apportionment.)*

Midterm Elections—The general elections for members of Congress that occur in November of the second year in a presidential term.

Minority Leader—The minority party's leader and chief, strategist and spokesperson, elected by the party caucus; sometimes called minority floor leader. With the assistance of other party officials and the ranking minority members of committees, the minority leader devises the party's political and procedural strategy. *(See also (The) Leadership.)*

Minority Staff—*(See Committee Staff.)*

Modified Rule—A special rule from the House Rules Committee that permits only certain amendments to be offered to a measure during its floor consideration or that bans certain specified amendments or amendments on certain subjects. Also referred to as a structured rule or a restrictive rule. *(See also Rule, second definition.)*

Morning Business—In the Senate, routine business that is to be transacted at the beginning of the morning hour. The business consists, first, of laying before the Senate and referring to committees matters such as messages from the president and the House, federal agency reports, and unreferred petitions, memorials, bills, and joint resolutions. Next, senators may present additional petitions and memorials. Then committees may present their reports, after which senators may introduce bills and resolutions. Finally, resolutions coming over from a previous day are taken up for consideration. In practice, the Senate adopts standing orders that permit senators to introduce measures and file reports at any time, but only if there has been a morning business period on that day. Because the Senate often remains in the same legislative day for several days, it orders a morning business period almost every calendar day for the convenience of senators who wish to introduce measures or make reports. *(See also Legislative Day; Morning Hour.)*

Morning Hour—A two-hour period at the beginning of a new legislative day during which the Senate is supposed to conduct routine business, call the calendar on Mondays, and deal with other matters described in a Senate rule. In practice, the morning hour rarely, if ever, occurs, because the Senate today typically agrees to a period for morning business for its next meeting in a unanimous-consent agreement at the end of a daily session. If the Senate recesses at the end of day rather than adjourns, the rule requiring morning hour does not apply when the Senate next meets. The Senate's rules reserve the first hour of the morning for morning business. After the completion of morning business, or at the end of the first hour, the rules permit a motion to proceed to the consideration of a measure on the calendar out of its regular order (except on Mondays). Because that normally debatable motion is not debatable if offered during the morning hour, the majority leader may but rarely does use this procedure in anticipating a filibuster on the motion to proceed. If the Senate agrees to the motion, it can consider the measure until the end of the morning hour, and if there is no unfinished business from the previous day, the Senate can continue considering it after the morning hour. But if there is unfinished business, a motion to continue consideration is necessary, and that motion is debatable. *(See Legislative Day; Morning Business.)*

Motion—A formal proposal for a procedural action, such as to consider, to amend, to lay on the table, to reconsider, to recess, or to adjourn. It has been estimated that at least eighty-five motions are possible under various circumstances in the House of Representatives, somewhat fewer in the Senate. Not all motions are created equal; some are privileged or preferential and enjoy priority over others. Some motions are debatable, amendable, or divisible, while others are not.

Multiple and Sequential Referrals—The practice of referring a measure to two or more committees for joint consideration (multiple referral) or successively to several committees in sequence (sequential referral). A measure may also be divided into several parts, with each referred to a different committee or to several committees sequentially (split referral). In theory, this gives all committees that have jurisdiction over parts of a measure the opportunity to consider and report on them.

Before 1975, House precedents banned such referrals. A 1975 rule required the Speaker to make concurrent and sequential referrals "to the maximum extent feasible." On sequential referrals, the Speaker could set deadlines for reporting the measure. The Speaker ruled that this provision authorized him to discharge a committee from further consideration of a measure and place it on the appropriate calendar of the House if the committee failed to meet the Speaker's deadline. In 1995, joint referrals were prohibited. Measures are referred to a primary committee and also may be referred, either additionally or sequentially, to one or more other committees, but usually only for consideration of portions of the measure that fall within the jurisdiction of each of those other committees. In 2003, the Speaker was authorized to not designate a primary committee under "extraordinary circumstances."

In the Senate, before 1977, joint and sequential referrals were permitted only by unanimous consent. In that year, a rule authorized a privileged motion for such a referral if offered jointly by the majority and minority leaders. Debate on the motion and all amendments to it is limited to two hours. The motion may set deadlines for reporting and provide for discharging the committees involved if they fail to meet the deadlines. To date, this procedure has never been invoked; multiple referrals in the Senate, if made, continue to be made by unanimous consent.

Multiyear Appropriation—An appropriation that remains available for spending or obligation for more than one fiscal year; the exact period of time is specified in the act making the appropriation. *(See also Appropriation.)*

Multiyear Authorization—(1) Legislation that authorizes the existence or continuation of an agency, program, or activity for more than one fiscal year. (2) Legislation that authorizes appropriations for an agency, program, or activity for more than one fiscal year. *(See also Authorization.)*

Nomination—A proposed presidential appointment to a federal office submitted to the Senate for confirmation. Approval is by majority vote. The Constitution explicitly requires Senate confirmation for ambassadors, consuls, "public Ministers" (department heads), and Supreme Court justices. By law, other federal judges, all military promotions of officers, and many high-level civilian officials must be confirmed by the Senate. *(See also Executive Calendar.)*

Nuclear Option—A popular name for a parliamentary maneuver to interpret Senate rules to allow the Senate to limit debate on most nominations by a simple majority rather than the sixty votes that had previously been required. The Senate invoked this option in 2013. Also referred to as the constitutional option.

Oath of Office—On taking office, members of Congress must swear or affirm that they will "support and defend the Constitution . . . against all enemies, foreign and domestic," that they will "bear true faith and allegiance" to the Constitution, that they take the obligation "freely, without any mental reservation or purpose of evasion," and that they will "well and faithfully discharge the duties" of their office. The oath is required by the Constitution, and the wording is prescribed by a statute. All House members must take the oath at the beginning of each new Congress. Usually, the member with the longest continuous service in the House swears in the Speaker, who then swears in the other members. The president of the Senate (the vice president of the United States) or a surrogate administers the oath to newly elected or reelected senators.

Obligation—A binding agreement by a government agency to pay for goods, products, services, studies, and so on, either immediately or in the future. When an agency enters into such an agreement, it incurs an obligation. As the agency makes the required payments, it liquidates the obligation. Appropriation laws usually make funds available for obligation for one or more fiscal years but do not require agencies to spend their funds during those specific years. The actual outlays can occur years after the appropriation is obligated, as with a contract for construction of a submarine that may provide for payment to be made when it is delivered in the future. Such obligated funds are often said to be "in the pipeline." Under these circumstances, an agency's outlays in a particular year can come from appropriations obligated in previous years as well as from its current-year appropriation. Consequently, the money Congress appropriates for a fiscal year does not equal the total amount of appropriated money the government will actually spend in that year. *(See also Budget Authority; Outlays.)*

Off-Budget Entities—Specific federal entities whose budget authority, outlays, and receipts are excluded by law from the calculation of budget totals, although they are part of government spending and income. As of 2005, these included the Social Security trust funds (Federal Old-Age and Survivors Insurance Fund and the Federal Disability Insurance Trust Fund) and the Postal Service. Government-sponsored enterprises are also excluded from the budget because they are considered private rather than public organizations.

Office of Management and Budget (OMB)—A unit in the Executive Office of the President, reconstituted in 1990 from the former Bureau of the Budget. The Office of Management and Budget (OMB) assists the president in preparing the budget and in formulating the government's fiscal program. The OMB also plays a central role in supervising and controlling implementation of the budget, pursuant to provisions in appropriations laws and other statutes. In addition to these budgetary functions, the OMB has various management duties, including those performed through its three statutory offices: Federal Financial Management, Federal Procurement Policy, and Information and Regulatory Affairs.

Officers of Congress—The Constitution refers to the Speaker of the House and the president of the Senate as officers and declares that each house "shall chuse" its "other Officers," but it does not name them or indicate how they should be selected. A House rule refers to its clerk, sergeant at arms, and chaplain as officers. Officers are not named in the Senate's rules, but *Riddick's Senate Procedure* lists the president pro tempore, secretary of the Senate, sergeant at arms, chaplain, and the secretaries for the majority and minority parties as officers. A few appointed officials are sometimes referred to as officers, including the parliamentarians and the legislative counsels. The House elects its officers by resolution at the beginning of each Congress. The Senate also elects its officers, but once elected, Senate officers serve from Congress to Congress until their successors are chosen, following a change in party control or an individual officer's death or retirement. *(See also Clerk of the House; Parliamentarian; President Pro Tempore; Secretary of the Senate; Sergeant at Arms; Speaker.)*

Official Objectors—House members who screen measures on the Private Calendar and decide whether or not to object to the consideration of any one or more of them. *(See also Private Bill.)*

Omnibus Bill—A measure that combines the provisions of several disparate subjects into a single and often lengthy bill. Omnibus appropriations bills have become commonplace in recent years.

One-Minute Speeches—Addresses by House members that can be on any subject but are limited to one minute. They are usually permitted at the beginning of a daily session after the chaplain's prayer, the Pledge of Allegiance, and approval of the *Journal,* although they may be permitted at other times, such as at the conclusion of legislative business. They are a customary practice, not a right granted by rule. Consequently, recognition for one-minute speeches requires unanimous consent and is entirely within the Speaker's discretion. The Speaker sometimes does not permit them when the House has a heavy legislative schedule, or he or she limits or postpones them until a later time of the day.

Open Rule—A special rule from the House Rules Committee that permits members to offer as many floor amendments as they wish as long as the amendments are germane and do not violate other House rules. *(See also Rule, second definition.)*

Order of Business (House)—The sequence of events prescribed by a House rule during the meeting of the House on a new legislative day, also called the general order of business. The sequence consists of (1) the chaplain's prayer; (2) reading and approval of the *Journal;* (3) the Pledge of Allegiance; (4) correction of the reference of public bills to committee; (5) disposal of business on the Speaker's table; (6) unfinished business; (7) the morning hour call of committees and consideration of their bills; (8) motions to go into Committee of the Whole; and (9) orders of the day. In practice, the House never fully complies with this rule. Instead, the items of business that follow the Pledge of Allegiance are supplanted by any special orders of business that are in order on that day (for example, conference reports; the discharge or private calendars; or motions to suspend the rules) and by other privileged business (for example, general appropriation bills and special rules) or measures made in order by special rules or unanimous consent. The regular order of business is also modified by unanimous consent practices and orders that govern recognition for one-minute speeches (which date from 1937) and for morning-hour debates, begun in 1994. By this combination of an order of business with privileged interruptions, the House gives precedence to certain categories of important legislation, brings to the floor other major legislation from its calendars in any order it chooses, and provides expeditious processing for minor and noncontroversial measures.

Order of Business (Senate)—The sequence of events at the beginning of a new legislative day, as prescribed by Senate rules and standing orders. The sequence consists of (1) the chaplain's prayer; (2) the Pledge of Allegiance; (3) the designation of a temporary presiding officer if any; (4) *Journal* reading and approval; (5) recognition of the majority and minority leaders or their designees under the standing order adopted by unanimous consent at the beginning of each Congress; (6) morning business in the morning hour; (7) call of the calendar during the morning hour (largely obsolete); and (8) unfinished business from the previous session day.

Organization of Congress—The actions each house takes at the beginning of a Congress that are necessary to its operations. These include swearing in newly elected members, notifying the president that a quorum of each house is present, making committee assignments, and fixing the hour for daily meetings.

Because the House of Representatives is not a continuing body, it must also elect its Speaker and other officers and adopt its rules.

Original Bill—(1) A measure drafted by a committee and introduced by its chair or another designated member when the committee reports the measure to its house. Unlike a clean bill, it is not referred back to the committee after introduction. The Senate permits all its legislative committees to report original bills. In the House, this authority is referred to in the rules as the "right to report at any time," and five committees (Appropriations, Budget, House Administration, Rules, and Ethics) have such authority under circumstances specified in House Rule XIII, clause 5.

(2) In the House, special rules reported by the Rules Committee often propose that an amendment in the nature of a substitute be considered as an original bill for purposes of amendment, meaning that the substitute, as with a bill, may be amended in two degrees. Without that requirement, the substitute may only be amended in one further degree. In the Senate, an amendment in the nature of a substitute automatically is open to two degrees of amendment, as is the original text of the bill, if the substitute is offered when no other amendment is pending.

Original Jurisdiction—The authority of certain committees to originate a measure and report it to the chamber. For example, general appropriation bills reported by the House Appropriations Committee are original bills, and special rules reported by the House Rules Committee are original resolutions.

Other Body—A commonly used reference to a chamber by a member of the other chamber. Congressional comity discourages members from directly naming the other chamber during debate.

Outlays—Amounts of government spending. They consist of payments, usually by check or in cash, to liquidate obligations incurred in prior fiscal years as well as in the current year, including the net lending of funds under budget authority. In federal budget accounting, net outlays are calculated by subtracting the amounts of refunds and various kinds of reimbursements to the government from actual spending. *(See also Budget Authority; Obligation.)*

Override a Veto—Congressional enactment of a measure over the president's veto. A veto override requires a recorded two-thirds vote of those voting in each house, a quorum being present. Because the president must return the vetoed measure to its house of origin, that house votes first, but neither house is required to attempt an override, whether immediately or at all. If an override attempt fails in the house of origin, the veto stands and the measure dies.

Oversight—Congressional review of the way in which federal agencies implement laws to ensure that they are carrying out the intent of Congress and to inquire into the efficiency of the implementation and the effectiveness of the law. The Legislative Reorganization Act of 1946 defined oversight as the function of exercising continuous watchfulness over the execution of the laws by the executive branch.

Parliamentarian—The official advisor to the presiding officer in each house on questions of procedure. The parliamentarian and his or her assistants also answer procedural questions from members and congressional staff, refer measures to committees on behalf of the presiding officer, and maintain compilations of the precedents. The House parliamentarian revises the House Manual at the beginning of every Congress and usually reviews special rules before the Rules Committee reports them to the House. Either a parliamentarian or an assistant is always present and near the podium during sessions of each house.

Party Caucus—Generic term for each party's official organization in each house. Only House Democrats officially call their organization a caucus. House and Senate Republicans and Senate Democrats call their organizations conferences. The party caucuses elect their leaders, approve committee assignments and chairmanships (or ranking minority members if the party is in the minority), establish party committees and study groups, and discuss party and legislative policies. On rare occasions, they have stripped members of committee seniority or expelled them from the caucus for party disloyalty. *(See also Caucus.)*

Pay-as-You-Go (PAYGO)—A provision first instituted under the Budget Enforcement Act of 1990 that applies to legislation enacted before October 1, 2002. It requires that the cumulative effect of legislation concerning either revenues or direct spending should not result in a net negative impact on the budget. If legislation does provide for an increase in spending or decrease in revenues, that effect is supposed to be offset by legislated spending reductions or revenue increases. If Congress fails to enact the appropriate offsets, the act requires presidential sequestration of sufficient offsetting amounts in specific direct spending accounts. Congress and the president can circumvent this requirement if both agree that an emergency requires a particular action or if a law is enacted declaring that deteriorated economic circumstances make it necessary to suspend the requirement.

Permanent Appropriation—An appropriation that remains continuously available, without current action or renewal by Congress, under the terms of a previously enacted authorization or appropriation law. One such appropriation provides for payment of interest on the public debt and another the salaries of members of Congress. *(See also Appropriation.)*

Permanent Authorization—An authorization without a time limit. It usually does not specify any limit on the funds that may be appropriated for the agency, program, or activity that it authorizes, leaving such amounts to the discretion of the appropriations committees and the two houses. *(See also Authorization.)*

Personally Obnoxious (or Objectionable)—A characterization a senator sometimes applies to a president's nominee for a federal office in that senator's state to justify his or her opposition to the nomination.

Pocket Veto—The indirect veto of a bill as a result of the president withholding approval of it until after Congress has adjourned *sine die*. A bill the president does not sign but does not formally veto while Congress is in session automatically becomes a law ten days (excluding Sundays) after it is received. But if Congress adjourns its annual session during that ten-day period, the measure dies even if the president does not formally veto it.

Point of Order—A parliamentary term used in committee and on the floor to object to an alleged violation of a rule and to demand that the chair enforce the rule. The point of order immediately halts the proceedings until the chair decides whether the contention is valid. In some instances, a member may be able to reserve a point of order, hear the proponent's argument, and then insist on or withdraw the point of order. If the point of order is insisted on, the chair must rule.

Pork or Pork Barrel Legislation—Pejorative terms for federal appropriations, bills, or policies that provide funds to benefit a legislator's district or state, with the implication that the legislator presses for enactment of such benefits to ingratiate himself or herself with constituents rather than on the basis of an impartial, objective assessment of need or merit. The terms are often applied to such benefits as new parks, federal office buildings, dams, canals, bridges, roads, water projects, sewage treatment plants, and public works of any kind, as well as demonstration projects, research grants, and relocation of government facilities. Funds released by the president for various kinds of benefits or government contracts approved by him allegedly for political purposes are also sometimes referred to as pork. *(See also Earmark.)*

Postcloture Filibuster—A filibuster conducted after the Senate invokes cloture. It employs an array of procedural tactics rather than lengthy speeches to delay final action. The Senate curtailed the postcloture filibuster's effectiveness by closing a variety of loopholes in the cloture rule in 1979 and 1986. *(See also Cloture.)*

Power of the Purse—A reference to the constitutional power Congress has over legislation to raise revenue and appropriate monies from the Treasury. Article I, Section 8, states that Congress "shall have Power To lay and collect Taxes, Duties, Imposts and Excises, [and] to pay the Debts." Section 9 declares: "No Money shall be drawn from the Treasury, but in Consequence of Appropriations made by Law."

Preamble—Introductory language describing the reasons for and intent of a measure, sometimes called a whereas clause. It occasionally appears in joint, concurrent, and simple resolutions but rarely in bills.

Precedent—A previous ruling on a parliamentary matter or a long-standing practice or custom of a house. Precedents serve to control arbitrary rulings and serve as the common law of a house.

President of the Senate—One constitutional role of the vice president is serving as the president of the Senate, its presiding officer. The Constitution permits the vice president to cast a vote in the Senate only to break a tie, but the vice president is not required to do so.

President Pro Tempore—Under the Constitution, an officer elected by the Senate to preside over it during the absence of the vice president of the United States. Often referred to as the "pro tem," this senator is usually the member of the majority party with the longest continuous service in the chamber and may also be, by virtue of seniority, a committee chair. When attending to committee and other duties, the president pro tempore appoints other, usually junior, senators to preside.

Presiding Officer—In a formal meeting, the individual authorized to maintain order and decorum, recognize members to speak or offer motions, and apply and interpret the chamber's rules, precedents, and practices. The Speaker of the House and the president of the Senate are the chief presiding officers in their respective houses.

Previous Question—A nondebatable motion that, when agreed to by majority vote, cuts off further debate, prevents the offering of additional amendments, and brings the pending matter to an immediate vote. A decision to order the previous question is a decision saying that the debate and amending process are completed and the body is ready to move to a final vote on the main proposition. A special rule in the House may by its provisions allow some specified business despite a provision in the special rule ordering the previous question. It is a major debate-limiting device in the House; it is not permitted in the Committee of the Whole in the House or in the Senate.

Private Bill—A bill that applies to one or more specified persons, corporations, institutions, or other entities, usually to grant relief when no other legal remedy is available to them. Many private bills deal with claims against the federal government, immigration and naturalization cases, and land titles.

Private Calendar—The title for a calendar in the House reserved for private bills and resolutions favorably reported by committees.

Private Law—A private bill enacted into law. Private laws are numbered separately but in the same fashion as public laws. *(See also Public Law.)*

Privilege—An attribute of a motion, measure, report, question, or proposition that gives it priority status for consideration. Privileged motions and motions to bring up privileged questions are not debatable.

Privilege of the Floor—In addition to the members of a house, certain individuals are admitted to its floor while it is in session. The rules of the two houses differ somewhat, but both extend the privilege to the president and vice president, Supreme Court justices, cabinet members, state governors, former members of that house, members of the other house, certain officers and officials of Congress, certain staff of that house in the discharge of official duties, and the chamber's former parliamentarians. They also allow access to a limited number of committee and members' staff when their presence is necessary.

Pro Forma Amendment—In the House, an amendment that ostensibly proposes to change a measure or another amendment by moving "to strike the last word" or "to strike the requisite number of words." A member offers it not to make any actual change in the measure or amendment but only to obtain time for debate. *(See also Five-Minute Rule.)*

Pro Tem—A common reference to the president pro tempore of the Senate or, occasionally, to a Speaker pro tempore. *(See also President Pro Tempore; Speaker Pro Tempore.)*

Procedures—The methods of conducting business in a deliberative body. The procedures of each house are governed first by applicable provisions of the Constitution and then by its standing rules and orders, precedents, traditional practices, and any statutory rules that apply to it. The authority of the houses to adopt rules in addition to those specified in the Constitution is derived from Article I, Section 5, clause 2 of the Constitution, which states: "Each House may determine the Rules of its Proceedings...." By rule, the House of Representatives also follows the procedures in *Jefferson's Manual* that are not inconsistent with its standing rules and orders. Many Senate procedures also conform with Jefferson's provisions but by practice rather than by rule. At the beginning of each Congress, the House uses procedures in general parliamentary law until it adopts its standing rules. *(See also Rule, first definition.)*

Proxy Voting—The practice of permitting a member to cast the vote of an absent colleague in addition to his or her own vote. Proxy voting is prohibited on the floors of the House and Senate, but the Senate permits its committees to authorize proxy voting, and most do. In 1995, House rules were changed to prohibit proxy voting in committee.

Public Bill—A bill dealing with general legislative matters having national applicability or applying to the federal government or to a class of persons, groups, or organizations.

Public Debt—Federal government debt incurred by the Treasury or the Federal Financing Bank by the sale of securities to the public or borrowings from a federal fund or account. *(See also Debt Limit; Federal Debt.)*

Public Law—A public bill or joint resolution enacted into law. It is cited by the letters "PL" followed by a hyphenated number. The digits before the hyphen indicate the number of the Congress in which it was enacted; the digits after the hyphen indicate its position in the numerical sequence of public measures that became law during that Congress. For example, the Budget Enforcement Act of 1990 became PL 101-508 because it was the 508th measure in that sequence for the 101st Congress. This system of numbering began in the late 1950s; before that, the number of the Congress in which a law was enacted was not part of the law's numerical designation. *(See also Private Law.)*

Qualification (of Members)—The Constitution requires members of the House of Representatives to be twenty-five years of age at the time their terms begin. They must have been citizens of the United States for seven years before that date and, when elected, must be "Inhabitant[s]" of the state from which they were elected. There is no constitutional requirement that they reside in the districts they represent. Senators are required to be thirty years of age at the time their terms begin. They must have been citizens of the United States for nine years before that date and, when elected, must be "Inhabitant[s]" of the states in which they were elected. The "Inhabitant" qualification is broadly interpreted, and in modern times, a candidate's declaration of state residence has generally been accepted as meeting the constitutional requirement.

Queen of the Hill Rule—A special rule from the House Rules Committee that permits votes on a series of amendments, especially complete substitutes for a measure, in a specified order but directs that the amendment receiving the greatest number of votes shall be the winning one. This kind of rule permits the House to vote directly on a variety of alternatives to a measure. In doing so, it sets aside the precedent that once an amendment has been adopted, no further amendments may be offered to the text it has amended. Under an earlier practice that took root in the 1970s, the Rules Committee reported "king of the hill" rules under which there also could be votes on a series of amendments, again in a specified order. If more than one of the amendments was adopted under this kind of rule, it was the last amendment to receive a majority vote that was considered as having been finally adopted, whether or not it had received the greatest number of votes. *(See also Rule, second definition.)*

Quorum—The minimum number of members required to be present for the transaction of business. Under the Constitution, a quorum in each house is a majority of its members: 218 in the House and 51 in the Senate when there are no vacancies. By House rule, a quorum in the Committee of the Whole is 100. In practice, both houses usually assume a quorum is present even if it is not, unless a member makes a point of no quorum in the House or a live quorum or vote exposes the absence of a quorum in the Senate. Consequently, each house transacts much of its business, and even passes bills, when only a few members are present. For House and Senate committees, chamber rules allow a minimum quorum of one-third of a committee's members to conduct many types of business. *(See also Live Quorum.)*

Quorum Call—A procedure for determining whether a quorum is present in a chamber. In the Senate, a clerk calls the roll (roster) of senators. The House usually employs its electronic voting system. *(See also Quorum.)*

Ramseyer Rule—A House rule that requires a committee's report on a bill or joint resolution to show the changes the measure, and any committee amendments to it, would make in existing law. The rule requires the report to present the text of any statutory provision that would be repealed and a comparative print, showing, through typographical devices such as stricken-through type or italics, other changes that would be made in existing law. The rule, adopted in 1929, was named after its sponsor, Rep. Christian W. Ramseyer, R-Iowa. The Senate's analogous rule is called the Cordon Rule. *(See also Committee Report on a Measure; Cordon Rule.)*

Rank or Ranking—A member's position on the list of his or her party's members on a committee or subcommittee. When first assigned to a committee, a member is usually placed at the bottom of the list, then moves up as those above leave the committee. On subcommittees, however, a member's rank may not have anything to do with the length of his or her service on it.

Ranking Member—(1) A reference to the minority member with the highest ranking on a committee or subcommittee. (2) A reference to the majority member next in rank to the chair or to the highest-ranking majority member present at a committee or subcommittee meeting.

Ratification—(1) The president's formal act of promulgating a treaty after the Senate has approved it. The resolution of ratification agreed to by the Senate is the procedural vehicle by which the Senate gives its consent to ratification. (2) A state legislature's (or state convention's) act in approving a proposed constitutional amendment. Such an amendment becomes effective when ratified by three-fourths of the states. *(See also Executive Document; Ratification; Resolution of Ratification; Treaty.)*

Reapportionment—*(See Apportionment.)*

Recess—(1) A temporary interruption or suspension of a meeting of a chamber or committee. Unlike an adjournment, a recess does not end a legislative day. Because the Senate might recess from one calendar day to another, its legislative day may extend over several calendar days or longer. (2) A period of adjournment for more than three days to a day certain.

Recess Appointment—A presidential appointment to a vacant federal position made after the Senate has adjourned *sine die*. Presidents have also argued that a recess appointment is possible when the Senate has adjourned or recessed for more than thirty days and for shorter periods, including times of recess when the Senate is conducting pro forma sessions. If the president submits the recess appointee's nomination during the next session of the Senate, that individual can continue to serve until the end of the session even though the Senate might have rejected the nomination.

Recommit—To send a measure back to the committee that reported it; sometimes called a straight motion to recommit to distinguish it from a motion to recommit with instructions. A successful motion to recommit kills the measure. A motion to recommit with instructions is normally an attempt to amend a measure. In the House, the rules provide that the minority will have a motion to commit or recommit a measure with or without instructions before a vote on final passage of the measure. The motion to recommit in the Senate may be offered during the amending process. *(See also Recommit with Instructions.)*

Recommit a Conference Report—To return a conference report to the conference committee for renegotiation of some or all of its agreements. A motion to recommit may be offered with or without instructions. Once one chamber has approved a conference report, a motion to recommit is no longer possible since that vote dissolved the conference. *(See also Conference Report.)*

Recommit with Instructions—To send a measure back to a committee with instructions to take some action on it, usually to amend it as provided in the instructions. In the House, the instructions must be written so that the measure remains on the House floor and does not literally return to committee. *(See also Recommit.)*

Reconciliation—A procedure for changing existing revenue and spending laws to bring total federal revenues and spending within the limits established in a budget resolution. This procedure is triggered by the inclusion of reconciliation instructions directed at specific committees in a budget resolution. Congress has applied reconciliation chiefly to revenues and mandatory spending programs, especially entitlements. Discretionary spending is controlled through annual appropriation bills. *(See also Budget Process; Budget Resolution.)*

Reconsider—A practice that gives a chamber an opportunity to review its action on any proposition. Any member who voted on the prevailing side can ask to reconsider the vote, creating, in effect, the opportunity for another vote on the same proposition. In practice, a proposition's proponents typically engage in a scripted dialogue where one member moves that the vote be reconsidered and a second member moves to lay that motion on the table, and the presiding officer then states that the motion to table has been agreed to. Invoking this procedure may create the anomalous situation of an opponent of a measure changing his or her "no" vote to a "yea" vote (or a proponent changing a "yea" vote to a "no" vote) to force a new vote. Not all votes on propositions may be reconsidered.

Recorded Vote—(1) Generally, any vote in which members are recorded by name for or against a measure; also called a record vote or roll-call vote. The only recorded vote in the Senate is a vote by the yeas and nays and is commonly called a roll-call vote. (2) Technically, a recorded vote is one demanded in the House of Representatives and supported by at least one-fifth of a quorum (forty-four members) in the House sitting as the House or at least twenty-five members in the Committee of the Whole.

Redistricting—The redrawing of congressional district boundaries within a state after a decennial census. Redistricting may be required to equalize district populations or to accommodate an increase or decrease in the number of a state's House seats that might have resulted from the decennial apportionment. While redistricting was traditionally a responsibility of state legislatures, and still is in most states, some states use commissions instead of or as a complement to the role of their state legislatures, and courts have become active players, sometimes imposing their own district maps on a state. *(See also Apportionment; Congressional District; Gerrymandering.)*

Referral—The assignment of a measure to one or more committees for consideration; also called reference in the Senate. *(See also Multiple and Sequential Referrals.)*

Report—(1) As a verb, a committee is said to report when it submits a measure or other document to its parent chamber. (2) A clerk is said to report when he or she reads a measure's title, text, or the text of an amendment to the body at the direction of the chair. (3) As a noun, a committee document that accompanies a reported measure. It describes the measure, the committee's views on it, its costs, and the changes it proposes to make in existing law; it also includes certain impact statements. (4) A committee document submitted to its parent chamber that describes the results of an investigation or other study or provides information it is required to provide by rule or law. *(See also Committee Report.)*

Representative—An elected and duly sworn member of the House of Representatives who is entitled to vote in the chamber. The Constitution requires that a representative be at least twenty-five years old, a citizen of the United States for at least seven years, and an inhabitant of the state from which he or she is elected. Customarily, members reside in the districts they represent. Representatives are elected in even-numbered years to two-year terms that begin the following January. Representatives may also be elected in special elections to fill a vacancy created by a death or resignation; they then serve until the next general election.

Reprimand—A formal condemnation of a member for misbehavior, considered a milder reproof than censure. The House of Representatives first used it in 1976. The Senate first used it in 1991. *(See also Censure.)*

Rescission—A provision of law that repeals previously enacted budget authority in whole or in part. Under the Impoundment Control Act of 1974, the president can impound such funds by sending a message to Congress requesting one or more rescissions and the reasons for doing so. If Congress does not pass a rescission bill for the programs requested by the president within forty-five days of continuous session after receiving the message, the president must make the funds available for obligation and expenditure. If the president does not, the comptroller general of the United States is authorized to bring suit to compel the release of those funds. A rescission bill may rescind all, part, or none of an amount proposed by the president and may rescind funds the president has not impounded. *(See also Congressional Budget and Impoundment Control Act of 1974; Deferral; Impoundment.)*

Reserve the Right to Object—A member's declaration that the member may object to a unanimous consent request. It provides an alternative to silence (acquiescence to the request) or to objecting, instead allowing the member making the reservation to clarify the requester's purpose, suggest an amendment to the request, express views, or undertake another purpose. The member reserving the right to object must ultimately withdraw the reservation, allowing the unanimous consent request to take effect, or object. *(See also Unanimous Consent.)*

Resident Commissioner from Puerto Rico—A nonvoting member of the House of Representatives, elected to a four-year term. The resident commissioner has the same status and privileges as delegates. As with the delegates, the resident commissioner may not vote in the House but may do so in committee. *(See also Delegate.)*

Resolution—(1) A simple resolution; that is, a nonlegislative measure effective only in the house in which it is proposed and not requiring concurrence by the other chamber or approval by the president. Simple resolutions are designated "H. Res." in the House and "S. Res." in the Senate. Simple resolutions express nonbinding opinions on policies or issues or deal with the internal affairs or prerogatives of a house. (2) Any type of resolution: simple, concurrent, or joint. *(See also Concurrent Resolution; Joint Resolution.)*

Resolution of Inquiry—A resolution usually simple rather than concurrent calling on the president or the head of an executive agency to provide specific information or papers to one or both houses.

Resolution of Ratification—The Senate vehicle for consenting to ratification of a treaty. The constitutionally mandated vote of two-thirds of the senators present and voting applies to the adoption of this resolution. However, it may also contain amendments, reservations, declarations, or understandings that the Senate had previously added to it by majority vote. *(See also Executive Document; Ratification; Treaty.)*

Revenue Legislation—Measures that levy new taxes or tariffs or change existing ones. Under Article I, Section 7, clause 1 of the Constitution, the House of Representatives originates federal revenue measures, but the Senate can propose amendments to them. The House Ways and Means Committee and the Senate Finance Committee have jurisdiction over such measures, with a few minor exceptions. *(See also Budget Resolution.)*

Revise and Extend One's Remarks—A unanimous consent request to publish in the *Congressional Record* a statement a member did not deliver on the floor, a longer statement than the one made on the floor, or miscellaneous extraneous material. *(See also Congressional Record.)*

Revolving Fund—A trust fund or account, the income of which remains available to finance its continuing operations without any fiscal-year limitation.

Rider—Congressional slang for an amendment unrelated or extraneous to the subject matter of the measure to which it is attached. Riders may contain proposals that are less likely to become law on their own merits as separate bills, either because of opposition in the committee of jurisdiction, resistance in the other house, or the probability of a presidential veto.

Roll Call—A call of the roll to determine whether a quorum is present, to establish a quorum, or to vote on a question. Usually, the House uses its electronic voting system for a roll call. The Senate does not have an electronic voting system; its roll is always called by a clerk.

Rule—(1) A permanent regulation that a house adopts to govern its conduct of business, its procedures, its internal organization, behavior of its members, regulation of its facilities, duties of an officer, or some other subject it chooses to govern in that form. (2) In the House, a privileged simple resolution reported by the Rules Committee that provides methods and conditions for floor consideration of a measure or several measures.

Rule Twenty-Two—A common reference to the Senate's cloture rule, which is contained in Senate Rule Twenty-Two. *(See also Cloture.)*

Second-Degree Amendment—An amendment to an amendment in the first degree. *(See also Degrees of Amendment.)*

Secretary of the Senate—The chief financial, administrative, and legislative officer of the Senate. Elected by resolution or order of the Senate, the secretary is invariably the candidate of the majority party and usually chosen by the majority leader. In the absence of the vice president and pending the election of a president pro tempore, the secretary presides over the Senate. The secretary is subject to policy direction and oversight by the Senate Committee on Rules and Administration. The secretary manages a wide range of functions that support the administrative operations of the Senate as an organization as well as those functions necessary to its legislative process, including record keeping, document management, certifications, housekeeping services, administration of oaths, and lobbyist registrations. The secretary is responsible for accounting for all funds appropriated to the Senate and conducts audits of Senate financial activities.

Section—A subdivision of a bill or statute. By law, a section must be numbered and, as nearly as possible, contain "a single proposition of enactment."

Select or Special Committee—A committee established by a resolution in either house for a special purpose and, usually, for a limited time. Most select and special committees are assigned specific investigations or studies but are not authorized to report measures to their chambers. A select or special committee might, however, be given legislative authority in the resolution establishing it. Legislative authority allows legislation to be referred to the select or special committee and provides the committee with authority to report measures to its parent chamber. *(See also Ad Hoc Select Committee.)*

Senate—The house of Congress in which each state is represented by two senators; each senator has one vote. Article V of the Constitution declares that "No State, without its Consent, shall be deprived of its equal Suffrage in the Senate." The Constitution also gives the Senate equal legislative power with the House of Representatives. Although the Senate is prohibited from originating revenue measures, and as a matter of practice it does not originate appropriation measures, it can amend both. Only the Senate can give or withhold consent to treaties and nominations from the president. It also acts as a court to try impeachments by the House and elects the vice president when no candidate receives a majority of the electoral votes. It is often referred to as "the upper body" but not by members of the House. *(See also House of Representatives; Lower Body.)*

Senate Manual—The compilation of the Senate's standing rules and orders and the laws and other regulations that apply to the Senate.

Senator—A duly sworn elected or appointed member of the Senate. The Constitution requires that a senator be at least thirty years old, a citizen of the United States for at least nine years, and an inhabitant of the state from which he or she is elected. Senators are usually elected in even-numbered years to six-year terms that begin the following January; one-third of the Senate—known as a class—is subject to election every two years. When a vacancy occurs before the end of a term, the state governor follows state law on appointing a replacement or calling a special election to fill the position until a successor is chosen at the state's next general election to serve the remainder of the term. Until the Seventeenth Amendment was ratified in 1913, senators were chosen by their state legislatures.

Senatorial Courtesy—The Senate's practice of declining to confirm a presidential nominee for an office in the state of a senator of the president's party unless that senator approves.

Seniority—The priority, precedence, or status accorded members according to the length of their continuous service in a house or on a committee.

Seniority Loss—A type of punishment that reduces a member's seniority on his or her committees, including the loss of chairmanships. Party caucuses in both houses have occasionally imposed such punishment on their members, for example, for publicly supporting candidates of the other party.

Seniority Rule—The customary practice, rather than a rule, of assigning the chairmanship of a committee to the majority party member who has served on the committee for the longest continuous period of time.

Seniority System—A collection of long-standing customary practices under which members with longer continuous service than their colleagues in their house or on their committees receive various kinds of preferential treatment. Although some of the practices are no longer as rigidly observed as in the past, they still pervade the organization and procedures of Congress.

Sequestration—A procedure for canceling budgetary resources—that is, money available for obligation or spending—to enforce budget limitations established in law. Sequestered funds are no longer available for obligation or expenditure.

Sergeant at Arms—The officer in each house responsible for maintaining order, security, and decorum in its wing of the Capitol, including the chamber and its galleries. Although elected by their respective houses, both sergeants at arms are invariably the candidates of the majority party.

Session—(1) The annual series of meetings of a Congress. Under the Constitution, Congress must assemble at least once a year at noon on January 3 unless it appoints a different day by law. (2) The special meetings of Congress or of one house convened by the president, called a special session. (3) A house is said to be in session during the period of a day when it is meeting.

Severability (or Separability) Clause—Language stating that if any particular provisions of a measure are declared invalid by the courts, the remaining provisions shall remain in effect.

Sine Die—Without fixing a day for a future meeting. An adjournment *sine die* signifies the end of an annual or special session of Congress.

Slip Law—The first official publication of a measure that has become law. It is published separately in unbound, single-sheet form or pamphlet form. A slip law usually is available two or three days after the date of the law's enactment. *(See also Statutes at Large; U.S. Code.)*

Speaker—The presiding officer of the House of Representatives and the leader of its majority party. The Speaker is selected by the majority party and formally elected by the House at the beginning of each Congress. Although the Constitution does not require the Speaker to be a member of the House, in fact, all Speakers have been members.

Speaker Pro Tempore—A member of the House who is designated as the temporary presiding officer by the Speaker or elected by the House to that position during the Speaker's absence.

Speaker's Vote—The Speaker is not required to vote, and the Speaker's name is not called on a roll-call vote unless so requested.

The Speaker might vote either to create a tie vote, and thereby defeat a proposal, or to break a tie in favor of a proposal. Occasionally, the Speaker votes to emphasize the importance of a matter.

Special Rule—*(See Rule, second definition.)*

Special Session—A session of Congress convened by the president, under his constitutional authority, after Congress has adjourned *sine die* at the end of a regular session. *(See also Adjournment Sine Die; Session.)*

Spending Authority—The technical term for backdoor spending. The Congressional Budget Act of 1974 defines it as borrowing authority, contract authority, and entitlement authority for which appropriation acts do not provide budget authority in advance. Under the Budget Act, legislation that provides new spending authority may not be considered unless it provides that the authority shall be effective only to the extent or in such amounts as provided in an appropriation act. *(See Backdoor Spending Authority; Borrowing Authority; Contract Authority; Entitlement Program.)*

Spending Cap—The statutory limit for a fiscal year on the amount of new budget authority and outlays allowed for discretionary spending. The Budget Enforcement Act of 1997 required a sequester if the cap was exceeded. *(See also Sequestration.)*

Split Referral—A measure divided into two or more parts, with each part referred to a different committee. *(See also Multiple and Sequential Referrals; Referral.)*

Sponsor—The principal proponent and introducer of a measure or an amendment.

Staff Director—The most frequently used title for the head of staff of a committee or subcommittee. On some committees, that person is called chief of staff, clerk, chief clerk, chief counsel, general counsel, or executive director. The head of a committee's minority staff is usually called minority staff director. *(See also Committee Staff.)*

Standing Committee—A permanent committee established by a House or Senate standing rule or standing order. The rule also describes the subject areas on which the committee may report bills and resolutions and conduct oversight. Most introduced measures are referred to one or more standing committees according to their jurisdictions.

Standing Order—A continuing regulation or directive that has the force and effect of a rule but is not incorporated into the standing rules. The Senate's numerous standing orders, such as its standing rules, continue from Congress to Congress unless changed or the order states otherwise. The House uses relatively few standing orders, and those it adopts expire at the end of a session of Congress.

Standing Rules—The rules of the Senate that continue from one Congress to the next and the rules of the House of Representatives that it adopts at the beginning of each new Congress.

Standing Vote—An alternative and informal term for a division vote, during which members in favor of a proposal and then members opposed stand and are counted by the chair. *(See also Division Vote.)*

Star Print—A reprint of a bill, resolution, amendment, or committee report correcting technical or substantive errors in a previous printing; so called because of the small black star that appears on the front page or cover.

State of the Union Message—A presidential message to Congress under the constitutional directive that the president shall "from time to time give to the Congress Information of the State of the Union, and recommend to their Consideration such Measures as he shall judge necessary and expedient." Customarily, the president sends an annual State of the Union message to Congress, usually late in January, presenting it in person in an address to a joint session.

Statutes at Large—A chronological arrangement of the laws enacted in each session of Congress. Though indexed, the laws are not arranged by subject matter, nor is there an indication of how they affect or change previously enacted laws. The volumes are numbered by Congress, and the laws are cited by their volume and page number. The Gramm-Rudman-Hollings Act, for example, appears as 99 Stat. 1037. *(See also Slip Law; U.S. Code.)*

Straw Vote Prohibition—Under a House precedent, a member who has the floor during debate may not conduct a straw vote or otherwise ask for a show of support for a proposition. Only the chair may put a question to a vote.

Strike from the *Record*—Expunge objectionable remarks from the *Congressional Record,* after a member's words have been taken down on a point of order.

Strike the Last Word—*(See Pro Forma Amendment.)*

Subcommittee—A panel of committee members assigned a portion of the committee's jurisdiction or other functions. On legislative committees, subcommittees hold hearings, mark up legislation, and report measures to their full committee for further action; they cannot report directly to the chamber. A subcommittee's party composition usually reflects the ratio on its parent committee.

Subpoena Power—The authority granted to committees by the rules of their respective houses to issue legal orders requiring individuals to appear and testify or to produce documents pertinent to the committee's functions or both. Persons who do not comply with subpoenas can be cited for contempt of Congress and prosecuted.

Subsidy—Generally, a payment or benefit made by the federal government for which no current repayment is required. Subsidy payments may be designed to support the conduct of an economic enterprise or activity, such as ship operations, or to support certain market prices, as in the case of farm subsidies.

Sunset Legislation—A term sometimes applied to laws authorizing the existence of agencies or programs that expire annually or at the end of some other specified period of time. One of the purposes of setting specific expiration dates for agencies and programs is to encourage the committees with jurisdiction over them to determine whether they should be continued or terminated. *(See also Authorization.)*

Sunshine Rules—Rules requiring open committee hearings and business meetings, including markup sessions, in both houses, and also open conference committee meetings. However, all may be closed under certain circumstances and using certain procedures required by the rules. *(See also Closed Hearing.)*

Supermajority—A term sometimes used for a vote on a matter that requires approval by more than a simple majority of those members present and voting; also referred to as extraordinary majority. *(See also Constitutional Votes; Suspension of the Rules (House).)*

Supplemental Appropriation Bill—A measure providing appropriations for use in the current fiscal year, in addition to those already provided in annual general appropriation bills. Supplemental appropriations are often for unforeseen emergencies. *(See also Appropriation.)*

Suspension of the Rules (House)—An expeditious procedure for passing relatively noncontroversial or emergency measures by a two-thirds vote of those members voting, a quorum being present.

Suspension of the Rules (Senate)—A procedure to set aside one or more of the Senate's rules; it is used infrequently.

Task Force—A title sometimes given to a panel of members assigned to a special project, study, or investigation. A task force might be convened by leadership, a party caucus or conference, or a committee. Ordinarily, these groups do not have authority to report measures to their respective houses.

Tax Expenditure—Loosely, a tax exemption or advantage, sometimes called an incentive or loophole; technically, a loss of governmental tax revenue attributable to some provision of federal tax laws that allows a special exclusion, exemption, or deduction from gross income or that provides a special credit, preferential tax rate, or deferral of tax liability.

Televised Proceedings—Television and radio coverage of the floor proceedings of the House of Representatives have been available since 1979 and of the Senate since 1986. They are broadcast over a coaxial cable system to all congressional offices and to some congressional agencies on channels reserved for that purpose. Coverage is also available free of charge to commercial and public television and radio broadcasters. C-SPAN carries gavel-to-gavel coverage of both houses. *(See also C-SPAN.)*

Third Reading—A required reading to a chamber of a bill or joint resolution by title only before the vote on passage. In modern practice, it has merely become a pro forma step.

Third-Degree Amendment—An amendment to a second-degree amendment. Both houses prohibit such amendments. *(See also Degrees of Amendment.)*

Three-Day Rule—(1) In the House, a measure cannot be considered until the third calendar day on which the committee report has been available. (2) In the House, a conference report cannot be considered until the third calendar day on which its text has been available in the *Congressional Record.* (3) In the House, a general appropriation bill cannot be considered until the third calendar day on which printed hearings on the bill have been available. (4) In the Senate, when a committee votes to report a measure, a committee member is entitled to three calendar days within which to submit separate views for inclusion in the committee report. (In House committees, a member is entitled to two calendar days for this purpose, after the day on which the committee votes to report.) (5) In both houses, a majority of a committee's members may call a special meeting of the committee if its chair fails to do so within three calendar days after three or more of the members, acting jointly, formally request such a meeting. In calculating such periods, the House omits holiday and weekend days on which it does not meet. The Senate makes no such exclusion.

Tie Vote—When the votes for and against a proposition are equal, it loses. The president of the Senate—the constitutional role of the vice president—may cast a vote only to break a tie. Because the Speaker is invariably a member of the House, the Speaker is entitled to vote but usually does not. The Speaker may choose to do so to break or create a tie vote.

Title—(1) A major subdivision of a bill or act, designated by a roman numeral and usually containing legislative provisions on the same general subject. Titles are sometimes divided into subtitles as well as sections. (2) The official name of a bill or act, also called a caption or long title. (3) Some bills also have short titles that appear in the sentence immediately following the enacting clause. (4) Popular titles are the unofficial names given to some bills or acts by common usage. For example, the Balanced Budget and Emergency Deficit Control Act of 1985 (short title) is almost invariably referred to as Gramm-Rudman (popular title). In other cases, significant legislation is popularly referred to by its title number *(see definition (1) above).* For example, the federal legislation that requires equality of funding for women's and men's sports in educational institutions that receive federal funds is popularly called Title IX.

Track System—An occasional Senate practice that expedites legislation by dividing a day's session into two or more specific time periods, commonly called tracks, each reserved for consideration of a different measure.

Transfer Payment—A federal government payment to which individuals or organizations are entitled under law and for which no goods or services are required in return. Payments include welfare and Social Security benefits, unemployment insurance, government pensions, and veterans benefits.

Treaty—A formal document containing an agreement between two or more sovereign nations. The Constitution authorizes the president to make treaties, but the president must submit them to the Senate for its approval by a two-thirds vote of the senators present. Under the Senate's rules, that vote actually occurs on a resolution of ratification. Although the Constitution does not give the House a direct role in approving treaties, that body has sometimes insisted that a revenue treaty is an invasion of its prerogatives. In any case, the House may significantly affect the application of a treaty by its equal role in enacting legislation to implement the treaty. *(See also Executive Document; Ratification; Resolution of Ratification.)*

Trust Funds—Special accounts in the Treasury that receive earmarked taxes or other kinds of revenue collections, such as user fees, and from which payments are made for special purposes or to recipients who meet the requirements of the trust funds as established by law. Of the more than 150 federal government trust funds, several finance major entitlement programs, such as Social Security, Medicare, and retired federal employees' pensions. Others fund infrastructure construction and improvements, such as highways and airports.

Unanimous Consent—Without an objection by any member. A unanimous consent request asks permission, explicitly or implicitly, to set aside one or more rules. Both houses and their committees frequently use such requests to expedite their proceedings. If all members are silent, consent is given. If any member objects, unanimous consent is denied. *(See also Reserve the Right to Object.)*

Uncontrollable Expenditures—A frequently used term for federal expenditures that are mandatory under existing law and therefore cannot be controlled by the president or Congress without a change in the existing law. Uncontrollable expenditures include spending required under entitlement programs and also fixed costs, such as interest on the public debt and outlays to pay for prior-year obligations. In recent years, uncontrollables have accounted for approximately three-quarters of federal spending in each fiscal year.

Unfunded Mandate—Generally, any provision in federal law or regulation that imposes a duty or obligation on a state or local government or private-sector entity without providing the necessary funds to comply. The Unfunded Mandates Reform Act of 1995 amended the Congressional Budget Act of 1974 to provide a mechanism for the control of new unfunded mandates.

Union Calendar—A calendar of the House of Representatives for bills and resolutions favorably reported by committees that raise revenue or directly or indirectly appropriate money or property. In addition to appropriation bills, measures that authorize expenditures are also placed on this calendar. The calendar's full title is the Calendar of the Committee of the Whole House on the State of the Union.

Upper Body—A common reference to the Senate but not used by members of the House. *(See also Lower Body.)*

U.S. Code—Popular title for the *United States Code: Containing the General and Permanent Laws of the United States in Force on . . . .* It is a consolidation and partial codification of the general and permanent laws of the United States arranged by subject under fifty titles. The first six titles deal with general or political subjects, the other forty-four with subjects ranging from agriculture to war, alphabetically arranged. A supplement is published after each session of Congress, and the entire *Code* is revised every six years. *(See also Slip Law; Statutes at Large.)*

User Fee—A fee charged to users of goods or services provided by the federal government. When Congress levies or authorizes such fees, it determines whether the revenues should go into the general collections of the Treasury or be available for expenditure by the agency that provides the goods or services.

Veto—The president's disapproval of a legislative measure passed by Congress. The president returns the measure to the house in which it originated without his signature but with a veto message stating his objections to it. When Congress is in session, the president must veto a bill within ten days, excluding Sundays, after the president has received it; otherwise it becomes law without his signature. The ten-day clock begins to run at midnight following his receipt of the bill. *(See also Override a Veto; Pocket Veto.)*

Voice Vote—A method of voting in which members who favor a question answer "aye" in chorus, after which those opposed answer "no" in chorus, and the chair decides which position prevails.

Voting—Members vote in three ways on the floor: (1) by shouting "aye" or "no" on voice votes in the House; (2) by standing for or against on division votes; and (3) on recorded votes (including the yeas and nays), by answering "aye" or "no" when their names are called or, in the House, by recording their votes through the electronic voting system. In the Senate, members do not shout their position on voice votes; rather, the majority's position is presumed to prevail unless there is a request for a roll-call vote.

War Powers Resolution of 1973—An act that requires the president "in every possible instance" to consult Congress before committing U.S. forces to ongoing or imminent hostilities. If the president commits forces to a combat situation without congressional consultation, the president must notify Congress within forty-eight hours. Unless Congress declares war or otherwise authorizes the operation to continue, the forces must be withdrawn within sixty or ninety days, depending on certain conditions. No president has ever acknowledged the constitutionality of the resolution.

Well—The sunken, level, open space between members' seats and the podium at the front of each chamber. House members usually address their chamber from their party's lectern in the well on its side of the aisle or from their party's two tables among the House seats. Senators usually speak at their assigned desks.

Whip—The majority or minority party member in each house who acts as assistant leader, helps plan and marshal support for party strategies, encourages party discipline, and advises his or her leader on how colleagues intend to vote on the floor.

Yeas and Nays—A vote in which members usually respond "aye" or "no" (despite the official title of the vote) on a question when their names are called in alphabetical order. In the House, such votes are conducted by electronic device. The Constitution requires the yeas and nays when a demand for it is supported by one-fifth of the members present, and it also requires an automatic yea-and-nay vote on overriding a veto. Senate precedents assume the presence of a quorum and therefore require the support of at least one-fifth of a quorum, a minimum of eleven members with the present membership of 100. If a live quorum or vote has exposed the absence of a quorum, the yeas and nays will be ordered with the support of one-fifth of those present.

The Legislative Process in Brief

Note: *Parliamentary terms used below are defined in the glossary.*

INTRODUCTION OF BILLS

A House member (including the resident commissioner of Puerto Rico and nonvoting delegates of the District of Columbia, Guam, the Virgin Islands, and American Samoa) may introduce any one of several types of bills and resolutions at any time the House is in session by handing it to the clerk of the House or placing it in a box called the hopper. A senator usually introduces a measure by presenting it, along with a formal statement, to a clerk at the presiding officer's desk.

As the usual next step in either the House or the Senate, the bill is numbered, referred to the appropriate committee (or, in the House, committees), labeled with the sponsor's name and sent to the Government Printing Office so that copies can be made for subsequent study and action. House and Senate bills may be jointly sponsored and carry several lawmakers' names. Print and electronic versions of the bill are available to the public. A bill written in the executive branch and proposed as an administration measure usually is introduced by the chair of the congressional committee that has jurisdiction, as a courtesy to the White House.

Bills—Prefixed with "HR" in the House, "S" in the Senate, followed by a number. Used as the form for most legislation, whether general or special, public or private.

Joint Resolutions—Designated "H J Res" or "S J Res." Subject to the same procedure as bills, with the exception of a joint resolution proposing an amendment to the Constitution. The latter must be approved by two-thirds of both houses and is thereupon sent directly to the archivist of the United States at the National Archives and Records Administration for submission to the states for ratification instead of being presented to the president for his approval.

Concurrent Resolutions—Designated "H Con Res" or "S Con Res." Used for matters affecting the operations of both houses. These resolutions do not become law.

Resolutions—Designated "H Res" or "S Res." Used for a matter concerning the operation of either house alone and adopted only by the chamber in which it originates.

COMMITTEE ACTION

With few exceptions, bills are referred to the appropriate standing committees. The job of referral formally is the responsibility of the Speaker of the House and the presiding officer of the Senate, but this task usually is carried out on their behalf by the parliamentarians of the House and Senate. Precedent, statute, and the jurisdictional mandates of the committees as set forth in the rules of the House and Senate determine which committees receive what kinds of bills. Bills are technically considered "read for the first time" when referred to House committees. Bills are read twice before being referred to Senate committees.

When a bill reaches a committee it is placed on the committee's calendar. Failure of a committee to act on a bill is equivalent to killing it and most fall by the legislative roadside. The measure can be withdrawn from the committee's purview by a discharge petition signed by a majority of the House membership on House bills. Both the House and Senate discharge bills from committees by unanimous consent, with the cooperation of committees. Other discharge options are available in both chambers.

The first committee action taken on a bill may be a request for comment on it by interested agencies of the government. The committee chair may assign the bill to a subcommittee for study and hearings, or it may be considered by the full committee. Hearings may be public, closed (executive session) or both. A subcommittee, after marking up a bill (considering amendments to it), reports to the full committee its recommendations for action and any proposed amendments.

The full committee then marks up and votes on its recommendation to the House or Senate. This procedure is called "ordering a bill reported." Occasionally a committee may order a bill reported unfavorably, especially if it must report a measure pursuant to a rule, rulemaking law, or chamber order. Most of the time a report, submitted by the chair of the committee to the House or Senate, calls for favorable action on the measure since the committee can effectively "kill" a bill by simply failing to take any action.

When the bill is reported, the committee chair instructs the staff to prepare a written report. The report describes the purposes and scope of the bill, explains the committee revisions, notes proposed changes in existing law and, usually, includes the views of the executive branch agencies consulted. Often committee members opposing a measure issue dissenting minority statements that are included in the report.

Usually, the committee "marks up" or proposes amendments to the bill. If they are substantial and the measure is complicated, the committee may order a "clean bill" introduced, which will embody the proposed amendments. The original bill then is put aside and the clean bill, with a new number, is reported to the floor.

The chamber must approve, alter, or reject the committee amendments before the bill itself can be put to a vote.

FLOOR ACTION

After a bill is reported back to the house where it originated, it is placed on the calendar.

There are four legislative calendars in the House, issued in one cumulative document titled *Calendars of the United States House of Representatives and History of Legislation.* The House calendars are:

The Union Calendar to which are referred bills raising revenues, general appropriations bills, and any measures directly or indirectly appropriating money or property. It is the Calendar of the Committee of the Whole House on the state of the Union.

The House Calendar to which are referred bills of public character not raising revenue or appropriating money.

The Private Calendar to which are referred bills for relief in the nature of claims against the United States or private immigration bills that may be passed without debate when the Private Calendar is called the first and third Tuesdays of each month.

The Discharge Calendar to which are referred motions to discharge committees when the necessary signatures are signed to a discharge petition.

There is only one legislative calendar in the Senate and one "executive calendar" for treaties and nominations submitted to the Senate.

Debate

A bill is brought to debate by varying procedures. In the Senate the majority leader, often in consultation with the minority leader and others, schedules the bills that will be taken up for debate. If it is widely supported by senators, it can be taken up in the Senate either by unanimous consent or by a motion agreed to by majority vote.

Senate debate is unlimited unless it is limited by unanimous consent, rule, rulemaking law, or supermajority vote. Typically, the Senate attempts to invoke cloture to limit debate, which requires a three-fifths vote of all senators. If invoked, debate may continue for only another thirty hours. To invoke cloture on a proposed change to Senate rules, a two-thirds vote of all senators is required.

In the House, precedence is granted to a bill if a special rule is obtained from the Rules Committee. A request for a special rule usually is made by the chair of the committee that favorably reported the bill, after consultation with the majority party leadership. The request is considered by the Rules Committee in the same fashion that other committees consider legislative measures. The committee proposes a simple resolution (H. Res.) providing for the consideration of the bill. The Rules Committee reports the resolution to the House, where it is debated and voted on in the same fashion as regular bills.

The resolutions providing special rules are important because they specify how long the bill may be debated and whether it may be amended from the floor. If floor amendments are banned, the bill is considered under a "closed rule."

When a bill is debated under an "open rule," germane amendments may be offered from the floor. A "structured rule" has become the most commonly used form of rule. In the resolution reported by the Rules Committee, those amendments that may be offered are listed and the duration of debate on each prescribed. Committee amendments always are taken up first but may be changed, as may all amendments up to the second degree, if permitted by the rule; that is, an amendment to an amendment to an amendment is not in order.

Duration of debate in the House depends on whether the bill is under discussion by the House proper or before the House when it is sitting as the Committee of the Whole House on the state of the Union. In the former, the amount of time for debate occurs under the one-hour rule, which allows members to hold the floor for one hour each. In practice, the member first recognized to speak moves the previous question after an hour, which the House almost always approves and which ends further debate. In the Committee of the Whole, the amount of time specified in the special rule for general debate is equally divided between proponents and opponents. At the end of general debate, the bill is often read section by section for amendment if it is considered under an open rule. Debate on an amendment is limited to five minutes for each side; this is called the "five-minute rule." In practice, amendments under an open rule are regularly debated more than ten minutes, with members gaining the floor by offering pro forma amendments or obtaining unanimous consent to speak longer than five minutes.

The House considers almost all important bills within a parliamentary framework known as the Committee of the Whole. It is not a committee as the word usually is understood; it is the full House meeting under another name for the purpose of speeding action on legislation. Technically, the House sits as the Committee of the Whole when it considers any tax measure or bill dealing with public appropriations or authorizations. Upon adoption of a special rule, the Speaker declares the House resolved into the Committee of the Whole and appoints a member of the majority party to serve as the chair. Instead of the required quorum of 218 for the House, the rules of that chamber permit the Committee of the Whole to meet when a quorum of 100 members is present on the floor and to amend and act on bills. When the Committee of the Whole has concluded consideration of a bill for amendment, it "rises," the Speaker returns as the presiding officer of the House, and the member appointed chair of the Committee of the Whole reports the action of the committee and its recommendations.

The Committee of the Whole cannot pass a bill; instead it reports the measure to the full House with whatever amendments it has adopted. Before the vote on final passage, the minority under House rules is guaranteed one attempt to kill or change the bill. This attempt is called the motion to recommit. A motion to recommit with no additional language is an attempt to get a majority to vote to kill the bill. A motion to recommit with instructions is an attempt to get a majority to adopt the amendatory language that comprises the instructions. These motions rarely succeed. After this vote, the House votes to pass or reject the bill. Amendments adopted in the Committee of the Whole may be put to a second vote in the full House.

Votes

Voting on bills may occur repeatedly before they are finally approved or rejected. The House votes on the rule for the bill and on various amendments to the bill. Voting on amendments often is a more illuminating test of a bill's support than is the final tally. Sometimes members approve final passage of bills after vigorously supporting amendments that, if adopted, would have scuttled the legislation.

The Senate has three different methods of voting: an untabulated voice vote, a standing vote (called a division), and a recorded roll call to which members answer "yea" or "nay" when their names are called. The House also employs voice and standing votes, but since January 1973, yeas and nays have been recorded by an electronic voting device, eliminating the need for time-consuming roll calls.

After amendments to a bill have been voted upon and, in the House, the motion to recommit disposed of, it is "read for the third time." The final vote is taken and is followed by a pro forma motion to reconsider, which is laid on the table. With that, the bill has been formally passed by the chamber.

ACTION IN SECOND CHAMBER

After a bill is passed, it is sent to the other chamber. This body may then take one of several steps. It may pass the bill as is—accepting the other chamber's language. It may send the bill to committee for scrutiny or alteration or reject the entire bill, advising the other house of its actions. Or it simply may ignore the bill submitted while it continues work on its version of the proposed legislation. Frequently, one chamber may approve a version of a bill that is greatly at variance with the version already passed by the other house and then substitute its contents for the language of the other, retaining only the latter's bill number.

Often the second chamber makes only minor changes. If these are readily agreed to by the other house, the bill then is routed to the president. Large or small differences between each chamber's version of a bill are commonly dealt with today by amendments between the houses, whereby the first chamber considers the changes of the second chamber and may accept those changes, clearing the bill for the president, or respond with additional changes. The second chamber then considers the first chamber's additional changes and may accept them, clearing the bill for the president, or respond with additional changes. This exchange of amendments may continue until differences are resolved. If the opposite chamber significantly alters the bill submitted to it or the houses are not able to reach agreement through an exchange of amendments, the measure may be "sent to conference." The chamber that has possession of the "papers" (engrossed bill, engrossed amendments, messages of transmittal) requests a conference, and the other chamber may agree to it. If the second chamber does not agree, the bill dies unless subsequent parliamentary actions take place.

How a Bill Becomes Law

This graphic shows the most typical way in which proposed legislation is enacted into law. There are more complicated, as well as simpler, routes, and most bills never become law. The process is illustrated with two hypothetical bills, House bill No. 1 (HR 1) and

Senate bill No. 2 (S 2). Bills must be passed by both houses in identical form before they can be sent to the president. The path of HR 1 is traced by a black line, that of S 2 by a gray line. In practice, most bills begin as similar proposals in both houses.

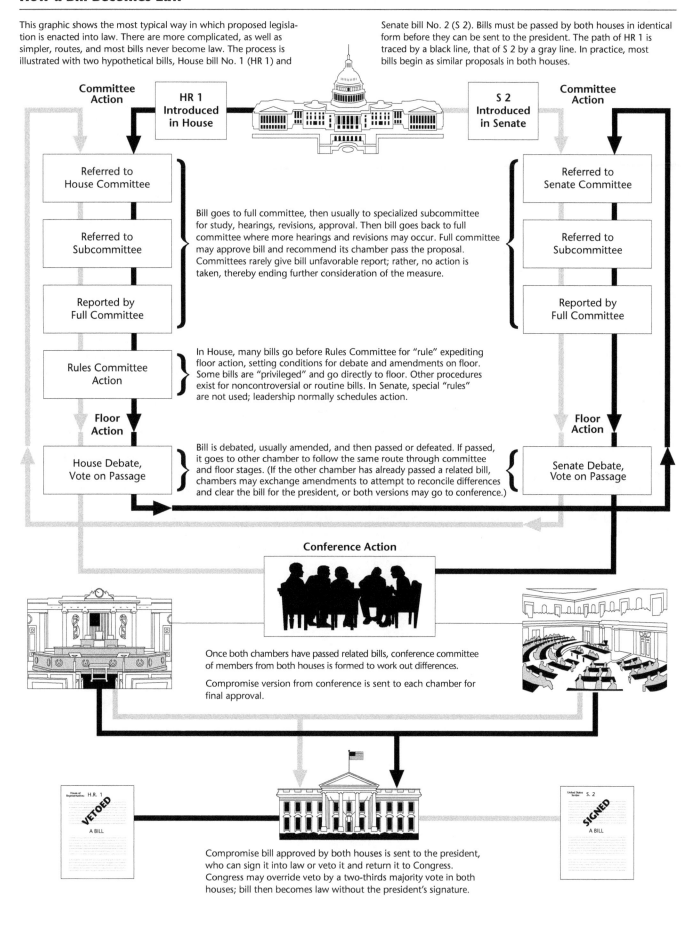

Committee Action

HR 1 Introduced in House

S 2 Introduced in Senate

Committee Action

Referred to House Committee

Referred to Subcommittee

Reported by Full Committee

Bill goes to full committee, then usually to specialized subcommittee for study, hearings, revisions, approval. Then bill goes back to full committee where more hearings and revisions may occur. Full committee may approve bill and recommend its chamber pass the proposal. Committees rarely give bill unfavorable report; rather, no action is taken, thereby ending further consideration of the measure.

Referred to Senate Committee

Referred to Subcommittee

Reported by Full Committee

Rules Committee Action

In House, many bills go before Rules Committee for "rule" expediting floor action, setting conditions for debate and amendments on floor. Some bills are "privileged" and go directly to floor. Other procedures exist for noncontroversial or routine bills. In Senate, special "rules" are not used; leadership normally schedules action.

Floor Action

House Debate, Vote on Passage

Bill is debated, usually amended, and then passed or defeated. If passed, it goes to other chamber to follow the same route through committee and floor stages. (If the other chamber has already passed a related bill, chambers may exchange amendments to attempt to reconcile differences and clear the bill for the president, or both versions may go to conference.)

Floor Action

Senate Debate, Vote on Passage

Conference Action

Once both chambers have passed related bills, conference committee of members from both houses is formed to work out differences.

Compromise version from conference is sent to each chamber for final approval.

H.R. 1 VETOED — A BILL

S. 2 SIGNED — A BILL

Compromise bill approved by both houses is sent to the president, who can sign it into law or veto it and return it to Congress. Congress may override veto by a two-thirds majority vote in both houses; bill then becomes law without the president's signature.

CONFERENCE ACTION

A conference works out conflicting House and Senate versions of a legislative bill. The conferees include senior members from the committees that managed the legislation who are appointed by the presiding officers of the two houses. Under this arrangement, the conferees of one house have the duty of trying to maintain their chamber's position in the face of amending actions by the conferees (also referred to as "managers") of the other house.

The number of conferees from each chamber may vary from single to double or even triple digits depending on the length or complexity of the bill and the number of committees involved. But a majority vote controls the action of each group so that a large representation does not give one chamber a voting advantage over the other chamber's conferees.

Theoretically, conferees are not allowed to write new legislation in some parliamentary circumstances in reconciling the two versions before them, but this curb sometimes is bypassed. Many bills have been put into acceptable compromise form only after new language was provided by the conferees. Frequently the ironing out of difficulties takes days or even weeks. Conferences on complex and controversial bills sometimes are particularly drawn out.

As a conference proceeds, conferees reconcile differences between the versions, but generally they grant concessions only insofar as they remain sure that the chamber they represent will accept the compromises. Occasionally, uncertainty over how either house will react or the positive refusal of a chamber to back down on a disputed amendment results in an impasse, and the bill dies in conference even though each version was approved by its sponsoring chamber.

When the conferees have reached agreement, they prepare a conference report embodying their recommendations (compromises in the form of legislative text) and a joint explanatory statement. The report, in document form, must be submitted to each house. The conference report must be approved by each house. Consequently, approval of the report is approval of the compromise bill. In the order of voting on conference reports, the chamber that asked for a conference yields to the other chamber the opportunity to vote first.

FINAL ACTION

After a bill has been passed by both the House and Senate in identical form, all of the original papers are sent to the enrolling clerk of the chamber in which the bill originated. The clerk then prepares an enrolled bill, which is printed on parchment paper.

When this bill has been certified as correct by the secretary of the Senate or the clerk of the House, depending on which chamber originated the bill, it is signed first (no matter whether it originated in the Senate or House) by the Speaker of the House and then by the president of the Senate. It is next sent to the White House to await action.

If the president approves the bill, he signs it, dates it, and usually writes the word "approved" on the document. If he does not sign it within ten days (Sundays excepted) and Congress is in session, the bill becomes law without his signature, an extremely rare event.

If Congress adjourns *sine die* at the end of the second session, the president can pocket veto a bill, and it dies without Congress having the opportunity to override. While presidents have sought to pocket veto bills after the adjournment of the first session of a Congress, they and Congress have engaged in additional procedures surrounding these vetoes that have left it unclear whether or not constitutional authority for pocket vetoes exists in an intersession adjournment.

A president vetoes a bill by refusing to sign it and, before the ten-day period expires, returning it to Congress with a message stating his reasons. The message is sent to the chamber that originated the bill. If no action is taken on the message, the bill dies. Congress, however, can attempt to override the president's veto and enact the bill, "the objections of the president to the contrary notwithstanding." Overriding a veto requires a two-thirds vote of those present in each chamber, who must number a quorum and vote by roll call.

If the president's veto is overridden by a two-thirds vote in both houses, the bill becomes law. Otherwise it is dead.

When bills are passed finally and signed or passed over a veto, they are given law numbers in numerical order as they become law. There are two series of numbers, one for public and one for private laws, starting at the number "1" for each two-year term of Congress. They are then identified by law number and by Congress—for example, Private Law 1, 112th Congress (or Private Law 112-1); Public Law 75, 113th Congress (or PL 113-75).

Congress and Its Members

Senate Membership in the 113th Congress

Membership at the beginning of Congress in January 2013: Democrats 51; Republicans 47; Independents 2. Changes during the 2013–2014 period are noted.

Alabama
Jeff Sessions (R)
Richard Shelby (R)

Alaska
Mark Begich (D)
Lisa Murkowski (R)

Arizona
Jeff Flake (R)
John McCain (R)

Arkansas
Mark Pryor (D)
John Boozman (R)

California
Dianne Feinstein (D)
Barbara Boxer (D)

Colorado
Mark Udall (D)
Michael Bennet (D)

Connecticut
Chris Murphy (D)
Richard Blumenthal (D)

Delaware
Tom Carper (D)
Chris Coons (D)

Florida
Bill Nelson (D)
Marco Rubio (R)

Georgia
Saxby Chambliss (R)
Johnny Isakson (R)

Hawaii
Mazie Hirono (D)
Brian Schatz (D)

Idaho
Jim Risch (R)
Mike Crapo (R)

Illinois
Dick Durbin (D)
Mark Kirk (R)

Indiana
Joe Donnelly (D)
Dan Coats (R)

Iowa
Tom Harkin (D)
Chuck Grassley (R)

Kansas
Pat Roberts (R)
Jerry Moran (R)

Kentucky
Mitch McConnell (R)
Rand Paul (R)

Louisiana
Mary Landrieu (D)
David Vitter (R)

Maine
Angus King (I)
Susan Collins (R)

Maryland
Ben Cardin (D)
Barbara Mikulski (D)

Massachusetts
Elizabeth Warren (D)
John Kerry (D)[1]
Mo Cowan (D)
Ed Markey (D)

Michigan
Debbie Stabenow (D)
Carl Levin (D)

Minnesota
Amy Klobuchar (D)
Al Franken (D)

Mississippi
Roger Wicker (R)
Thad Cochran (R)

Missouri
Claire McCaskill (D)
Roy Blunt (R)

Montana
Jon Tester (D)
Max Baucus (D)[2]
John Walsh (D)

Nebraska
Deb Fischer (R)
Mike Johanns (R)

Nevada
Dean Heller (R)
Harry Reid (D)

New Hampshire
Jeanne Shaheen (D)
Kelly Ayotte (R)

New Jersey
Bob Menendez (D)
Frank Lautenberg (D)[3]
Jeffrey Chiesa (D)
Cory Booker (D)

New Mexico
Martin Heinrich (D)
Tom Udall (D)

New York
Kirsten Gillibrand (D)
Chuck Schumer (D)

North Carolina
Kay Hagan (D)
Richard Burr (R)

North Dakota
Heidi Heitkamp (D)
John Hoeven (R)

Ohio
Sherrod Brown (D)
Rob Portman (R)

Oklahoma
Jim Inhofe (R)
Tom Coburn (R)

Oregon
Jeff Merkley (D)
Ron Wyden (D)

Pennsylvania
Bob Casey Jr. (D)
Pat Toomey (R)

Rhode Island
Sheldon Whitehouse (D)
Jack Reed (D)

South Carolina
Lindsey Graham (R)
Tim Scott (R)

South Dakota
Tim Johnson (D)
John Thune (R)

Tennessee
Bob Corker (R)
Lamar Alexander (R)

Texas
Ted Cruz (R)
John Cornyn (R)

Utah
Orrin Hatch (R)
Mike Lee (R)

Vermont
Bernie Sanders (I)
Patrick Leahy (D)

Virginia
Tim Kaine (D)
Mark Warner (D)

Washington
Maria Cantwell (D)
Patty Murray (D)

West Virginia
Joe Manchin (D)
Jay Rockefeller (D)

Wisconsin
Tammy Baldwin (D)
Ron Johnson (R)

Wyoming
John Barrasso (R)
Mike Enzi (R)

[1]Kerry resigned from the Senate February 1, 2013, to serve as Secretary of State; Cowan was appointed in his place during a special election. When his term ended, he did not seek reelection and Markey was sworn in July 16, 2013.

[2]Baucus retired from the Senate on February 6, 2014. Walsh, as an incumbent in the race, was sworn in February 11, 2014.

[3]Lautenberg passed away on June 3, 2013, and was succeeded by Chiesa until October 31, 2013, who declined to run for reelection in the 2013 special election. Booker was sworn into the Senate October 31, 2013.

House Membership in the 113th Congress

Membership at the beginning of the Congress in January 2013: Republicans, 240; Democrats, 191. Changes during the 2013–2014 period are noted.

Alabama

1. Jo Bonner (R)
   (resigned August 2, 2013)
   Bradley Byrne (R)
   (sworn in December 17, 2013)
2. Martha Roby (R)
3. Mike Rogers (R)
4. Robert Aderholt (R)
5. Mo Brooks (R)
6. Spencer Bachus (R)
7. Terri Sewell (D)

Alaska

AL Don Young (R)

Arizona

1. Ann Kirkpatrick (D)
2. Ron Barber (D)
3. Raúl Grijalva (D)
4. Paul Gosar (R)
5. Matt Salmon (R)
6. David Schweikert (R)
7. Ed Pastor (D)
8. Trent Franks (R)
9. Kyrsten Sinema (D)

Arkansas

1. Rick Crawford (R)
2. Timothy Griffin (R)
3. Steve Womack (R)
4. Tom Cotton (R)

California

1. Doug LaMalfa (R)
2. Jared Huffman (D)
3. John Garamendi (D)
4. Tom McClintock (R)
5. Mike Thompson (D)
6. Doris Matsui (D)
7. Ami Bera (D)
8. Paul Cook (R)
9. Jerry McNerney (D)
10. Jeff Denham (R)
11. George Miller (D)
12. Nancy Pelosi (D)
13. Barbara Lee (D)
14. Jackie Speier (D)
15. Eric Swalwell (D)
16. Jim Costa (D)
17. Mike Honda (D)
18. Anna Eshoo (D)
19. Zoe Lofgren (D)
20. Sam Farr (D)
21. David Valadao (R)
22. Devin Nunes (R)
23. Kevin McCarthy (R)
24. Lois Capps (D)
25. Buck McKeon (R)
26. Julia Brownley (D)
27. Judy Chu (D)
28. Adam Schiff (D)
29. Tony Cardenas (D)
30. Brad Sherman (D)
31. Gary Miller (R)
32. Grace Napolitano (D)
33. Henry Waxman (D)
34. Xavier Becerra (D)
35. Gloria Negrete McLeod (D)
36. Raul Ruiz (D)
37. Karen Bass (D)
38. Linda Sanchez (D)
39. Ed Royce (R)
40. Lucille Roybal-Allard (D)
41. Mark Takano (D)
42. Ken Calvert (R)
43. Maxine Waters (D)
44. Janice Hahn (D)
45. John Campbell (R)
46. Loretta Sanchez (D)
47. Alan Lowenthal (D)
48. Dana Rohrabacher (R)
49. Darrell Issa (R)
50. Duncan D. Hunter (R)
51. Juan Vargas (D)
52. Scott Peters (D)
53. Susan Davis (D)

Colorado

1. Diana DeGette (D)
2. Jared Polis (D)
3. Scott Tipton (R)
4. Cory Gardner (R)
5. Doug Lamborn (R)
6. Mike Coffman (R)
7. Ed Perlmutter (D)

Connecticut

1. John Larson (D)
2. Joe Courtney (D)
3. Rosa DeLauro (D)
4. Jim Himes (D)
5. Elizabeth Esty (D)

Delaware

AL John Carney (D)

Florida

1. Jeff Miller (R)
2. Steve Southerland (R)
3. Ted Yoho (R)
4. Ander Crenshaw (R)
5. Corrine Brown (D)
6. Ron DeSantis (R)
7. John Mica (R)
8. Bill Posey (R)
9. Alan Grayson (D)
10. Daniel Webster (R)
11. Rich Nugent (R)
12. Gus Bilirakis (R)
13. Bill Young (R)
    (resigned October 18, 2013)
    David Jolly (R)
    (sworn in March 11, 2014)
14. Kathy Castor (D)
15. Dennis Ross (R)
16. Vern Buchanan (R)
17. Tom Rooney (R)
18. Patrick Murphy (D)
19. Trey Radel (R)
    (resigned January 27, 2014)
    Curt Clawson (R)
    (sworn in June 25, 2014)
20. Alcee Hastings (D)
21. Ted Deutch (D)
22. Lois Frankel (D)
23. Debbie Wasserman Schultz (D)
24. Frederica Wilson (D)
25. Mario Diaz-Balart (R)
26. Joe Garcia (D)
27. Ileana Ros-Lehtinen (R)

Georgia

1. Jack Kingston (R)
2. Sanford Bishop (D)
3. Lynn Westmoreland (R)
4. Hank Johnson (D)
5. John Lewis (D)
6. Tom Price (R)
7. Rob Woodall (R)
8. Austin Scott (R)
9. Doug Collins (R)
10. Paul Broun (R)
11. Phil Gingrey (R)
12. John Barrow (D)
13. David Scott (D)
14. Tom Graves (R)

Hawaii

1. Colleen Hanabusa (D)
2. Tulsi Gabbard (D)

Idaho

1. Raul Labrador (R)
2. Mike Simpson (R)

Illinois

1. Bobby Rush (D)
2. Robin Kelly (D)
   (sworn in April 11, 2013)
3. Dan Lipinski (D)
4. Luis Gutiérrez (D)
5. Mike Quigley (D)
6. Peter Roskam (R)
7. Danny K. Davis (D)
8. Tammy Duckworth (D)
9. Jan Schakowsky (D)
10. Brad Schneider (D)
11. Bill Foster (D)
12. William Enyart (D)
13. Rodney L. Davis (R)
14. Randy Hultgren (R)
15. John Shimkus (R)
16. Adam Kinzinger (R)
17. Cheri Bustos (D)
18. Aaron Schock (R)

Indiana

1. Pete Visclosky (D)
2. Jackie Walorski (R)
3. Marlin Stutzman (R)
4. Todd Rokita (R)
5. Susan Brooks (R)
6. Luke Messer (R)
7. André Carson (D)
8. Larry Bucshon (R)
9. Todd Young (R)

Iowa

1. Bruce Braley (D)
2. David Loebsack (D)
3. Tom Latham (R)
4. Steve King (R)

Kansas

1. Tim Huelskamp (R)
2. Lynn Jenkins (R)
3. Kevin Yoder (R)
4. Mike Pompeo (R)

Kentucky

1. Ed Whitfield (R)
2. Brett Guthrie (R)
3. John Yarmuth (D)
4. Thomas Massie (R)
5. Hal Rogers (R)
6. Andy Barr (R)

Louisiana

1. Steve Scalise (R)
2. Cedric Richmond (D)
3. Charles Boustany (R)
4. John Fleming (R)
5. Rodney Alexander (R)
   (resigned September 26, 2013)
   Vance McAllister (R)
   (sworn in November 16, 2013)
6. Bill Cassidy (R)

Maine

1. Chellie Pingree (D)
2. Mike Michaud (D)

Maryland

1. Andrew Harris (R)
2. Dutch Ruppersberger (D)
3. John Sarbanes (D)
4. Donna Edwards (D)
5. Steny Hoyer (D)
6. John Delaney (D)
7. Elijah Cummings (D)
8. Chris Van Hollen (D)

Massachusetts

1. Richard Neal (D)
2. Jim McGovern (D)
3. Niki Tsongas (D)
4. Joseph P. Kennedy III (D)
5. Ed Markey (D)
   (resigned July 15, 2013, to join the Senate)
   Katherine Clark (D)
   (sworn in December 12, 2013)

6. John Tierney (D)
7. Mike Capuano (D)
8. Stephen Lynch (D)
9. Bill Keating (D)

Michigan
1. Dan Benishek (R)
2. Bill Huizenga (R)
3. Justin Amash (R)
4. Dave Camp (R)
5. Dan Kildee (D)
6. Fred Upton (R)
7. Tim Walberg (R)
8. Mike Rogers (R)
9. Sander Levin (D)
10. Candice Miller (R)
11. Kerry Bentivolio (R)
12. John Dingell (D)
13. John Conyers (D)
14. Gary Peters (D)

Minnesota
1. Tim Walz (D)
2. John Kline (R)
3. Erik Paulsen (R)
4. Betty McCollum (D)
5. Keith Ellison (D)
6. Michele Bachmann (R)
7. Collin Peterson (D)
8. Rick Nolan (D)

Mississippi
1. Alan Nunnelee (R)
2. Bennie Thompson (D)
3. Gregg Harper (R)
4. Steven Palazzo (R)

Missouri
1. Lacy Clay (D)
2. Ann Wagner (R)
3. Blaine Luetkemeyer (R)
4. Vicky Hartzler (R)
5. Emanuel Cleaver (D)
6. Sam Graves (R)
7. Billy Long (R)
8. Jo Ann Emerson (R)
   (resigned January 22, 2013)
   Jason T. Smith (R)
   (sworn in June 4, 2013)

Montana
AL Steve Daines (R)

Nebraska
1. Jeff Fortenberry (R)
2. Lee Terry (R)
3. Adrian M. Smith (R)

Nevada
1. Dina Titus (D)
2. Mark Amodei (R)
3. Joe Heck (R)
4. Steven Horsford (D)

New Hampshire
1. Carol Shea-Porter (D)
2. Ann McLane Kuster (D)

New Jersey
1. Rob Andrews (D)
   (resigned February 18, 2014)
   Donald Norcross (D)
   (sworn in November 12, 2014)
2. Frank LoBiondo (R)
3. Jon Runyan (R)
4. Chris Smith (R)
5. Scott Garrett (R)
6. Frank Pallone (D)
7. Leonard Lance (R)
8. Albio Sires (D)
9. Bill Pascrell (D)
10. Donald Payne Jr. (D)
11. Rodney Frelinghuysen (R)
12. Rush Holt Jr. (D)

New Mexico
1. Michelle Lujan Grisham (D)
2. Steve Pearce (R)
3. Ben Ray Lujan (D)

New York
1. Timothy Bishop (D)
2. Peter King (R)
3. Steve Israel (D)
4. Carolyn McCarthy (D)
5. Gregory Meeks (D)
6. Grace Meng (D)
7. Nydia Velazquez (D)
8. Hakeem Jeffries (D)
9. Yvette Clarke (D)
10. Jerrold Nadler (D)
11. Michael Grimm (R)
12. Carolyn Maloney (D)
13. Charles Rangel (D)
14. Joe Crowley (D)
15. Jose E. Serrano (D)
16. Eliot Engel (D)
17. Nita Lowey (D)
18. Sean Patrick Maloney (D)
19. Chris Gibson (R)
20. Paul Tonko (D)
21. Bill Owens (D)
22. Richard Hanna (R)
23. Thomas Reed (R)
24. Daniel Maffei (D)
25. Louise Slaughter (D)
26. Brian Higgins (D)
27. Chris Collins (R)

North Carolina
1. G. K. Butterfield (D)
2. Renee Ellmers (R)
3. Walter Jones Jr. (R)
4. David Price (D)
5. Virginia Foxx (R)
6. Howard Coble (R)
7. Mike McIntyre (D)
8. Richard Hudson (R)
9. Robert Pittenger (R)
10. Patrick McHenry (R)
11. Mark Meadows (R)
12. Mel Watt (D)
    (resigned January 6, 2014)

Alma Adams (D)
   (sworn in November 4, 2014)
13. George Holding (R)

North Dakota
AL Kevin Cramer (R)

Ohio
1. Steve Chabot (R)
2. Brad Wenstrup (R)
3. Joyce Beatty (D)
4. Jim Jordan (R)
5. Bob Latta (R)
6. Bill Johnson (R)
7. Bob Gibbs (R)
8. John Boehner (R)
9. Marcy Kaptur (D)
10. Mike Turner (R)
11. Marcia Fudge (D)
12. Pat Tiberi (R)
13. Tim Ryan (D)
14. David Joyce (R)
15. Steve Stivers (R)
16. Jim Renacci (R)

Oklahoma
1. Jim Bridenstine (R)
2. Markwayne Mullin (R)
3. Frank Lucas (R)
4. Tom Cole (R)
5. James Lankford (R)

Oregon
1. Suzanne Bonamici (D)
2. Greg Walden (R)
3. Earl Blumenauer (D)
4. Peter DeFazio (D)
5. Kurt Schrader (D)

Pennsylvania
1. Bob Brady (D)
2. Chaka Fattah (D)
3. Mike Kelly (R)
4. Scott Perry (R)
5. Glenn Thompson (R)
6. Jim Gerlach (R)
7. Pat Meehan (R)
8. Mike Fitzpatrick (R)
9. Bill Shuster (R)
10. Tom Marino (R)
11. Lou Barletta (R)
12. Keith Rothfus (R)
13. Allyson Schwartz (D)
14. Michael F. Doyle (D)
15. Charles Dent (R)
16. Joseph R. Pitts (R)
17. Matt Cartwright (D)
18. Timothy F. Murphy (R)

Rhode Island
1. David Cicilline (D)
2. James Langevin (D)

South Carolina
1. Mark Sanford (R)
   (sworn in May 15, 2013)
2. Joe Wilson (R)

3. Jeff Duncan (R)
4. Trey Gowdy (R)
5. Mick Mulvaney (R)
6. Jim Clyburn (D)
7. Tom Rice (R)

South Dakota
AL Kristi Noem (R)

Tennessee
1. Phil Roe (R)
2. Jimmy Duncan (R)
3. Chuck Fleischmann (R)
4. Scott DesJarlais (R)
5. Jim Cooper (D)
6. Diane Black (R)
7. Marsha Blackburn (R)
8. Stephen Fincher (R)
9. Steve Cohen (D)

Texas
1. Louie Gohmert (R)
2. Ted Poe (R)
3. Sam Johnson (R)
4. Ralph Hall (R)
5. Jeb Hensarling (R)
6. Joe Barton (R)
7. John Culberson (R)
8. Kevin Brady (R)
9. Al Green (D)
10. Michael McCaul (R)
11. Mike Conaway (R)
12. Kay Granger (R)
13. Mac Thornberry (R)
14. Randy Weber (R)
15. Ruben Hinojosa (D)
16. Beto O'Rourke (D)
17. Bill Flores (R)
18. Sheila Jackson Lee (D)
19. Randy Neugebauer (R)
20. Joaquin Castro (D)
21. Lamar S. Smith (R)
22. Pete Olson (R)
23. Pete Gallego (D)
24. Kenny Marchant (R)
25. Roger Williams (R)
26. Michael C. Burgess (R)
27. Blake Farenthold (R)
28. Henry Cuellar (D)
29. Gene Green (D)
30. Eddie Bernice Johnson (D)
31. John Carter (R)
32. Pete Sessions (R)
33. Marc Veasey (D)
34. Filemon Vela Jr. (D)
35. Lloyd Doggett (D)
36. Steve Stockman (R)

Utah
1. Rob Bishop (R)
2. Chris Stewart (R)
3. Jason Chaffetz (R)
4. Jim Matheson (D)

Vermont
AL Peter Welch (D)

Virginia
1. Rob Wittman (R)
2. Scott Rigell (R)
3. Bobby Scott (D)
4. Randy Forbes (R)
5. Robert Hurt (R)
6. Bob Goodlatte (R)
7. Eric Cantor (R)
   (resigned August 18, 2014)
   Dave Brat (R)
   (sworn in November 4, 2014)

8. Jim Moran (D)
9. Morgan Griffith (R)
10. Frank Wolf (R)
11. Gerry Connolly (D)

Washington
1. Suzan DelBene (D)
2. Rick Larsen (D)
3. Jaime Herrera Beutler (R)
4. Doc Hastings (R)
5. Cathy McMorris Rodgers (R)
6. Derek Kilmer (D)

7. Jim McDermott (D)
8. Dave Reichert (R)
9. Adam Smith (D)
10. Dennis Heck (D)

West Virginia
1. David McKinley (R)
2. Shelley Moore Capito (R)
3. Nick Rahall (D)

Wisconsin
1. Paul Ryan (R)
2. Mark Pocan (D)

3. Ron Kind (D)
4. Gwen Moore (D)
5. Jim Sensenbrenner (R)
6. Tom Petri (R)
7. Sean Duffy (R)
8. Reid Ribble (R)

Wyoming
AL Cynthia Lummis (R)

NOTE: Changes that occurred during 2013 and 2014 are noted following the names of individuals who did not serve their full terms. Members of the 113th Congress also included delegates Eni F. H. Faleomavaega, D–American Samoa; Eleanor Holmes Norton, D–District of Columbia; Madeleine Z. Bordallo, D–Guam; Gregorio Kilili Camacho Sablan, I–Northern Mariana Islands; Donna M. Christensen, D–Virgin Islands; and resident commissioner Pedro Pierluisi, D–Puerto Rico. AL–At Large.

Membership Changes, 113th and 114th Congresses

113th Congress

Member/Party	Died	Resigned	Successor	Appointed	Elected	Sworn In
Senate						
John Kerry, D-Ma.[1]		2/1/2013	Mo Cowan, D	1/30/2013		2/1/2013
Frank Lautenberg , D-N.J.	6/3/2013		Jeffrey Chiesa, R		6/6/2013	6/10/2013
Mo Cowan, D-Ma.[2]		7/16/2013	Ed Markey, D		4/30/2013	7/16/2013
Jeffrey Chiesa, R-N.J.[3]		10/31/2013	Cory Booker, D		10/16/2013	10/31/2013
Max Baucus, D-Mont.[4]		2/6/2014	John Walsh, D	2/9/2014		11/2/2014
House						
Jo Ann Emerson, R-Mo.[5]		1/22/2013	Jason Smith, R		6/4/2013	6/5/2013
Ed Markey, D-Ma.[6]		7/15/2013	Katherine Clark, D		12/10/2013	12/12/2013
Jo Bonner, R-Ala.[7]		8/2/2013	Bradley Byrne, R		12/17/2013	12/17/2013
Rodney Alexander, R-La.[8]		9/27/2013	Vance McAllister, R		11/16/2013	11/16/2013
Bill Young, R-Fl.	10/18/2013		David Jolly, R		3/11/2014	3/13/2014
Mel Watt, D-N.C.[9]		1/6/2014	Alma Adams, D		11/4/2014	11/12/2014
Trey Radel, R-Fl.[10]		1/27/2014	Curt Clawson, R		6/24/2014	6/25/2014
Rob Andrews, D-N.J.[11]		2/18/2014	Donald Norcross, D		11/4/2014	11/12/2014
Eric Cantor, R-Va.[12]		8/18/2014	Dave Brat, R		11/4/2014	11/12/2014

114th Congress

Member/Party	Died	Resigned	Successor	Appointed	Elected	Sworn In
Senate						
There were no changes in Senate membership.						
House						
Michael Grimm, R-N.Y.[13]		1/5/2015	Dan Donovan, R		5/5/2015	5/12/2015
Alan Nunnelee, R-Miss.	2/6/2015		Trent Kelly, R		6/2/2015	6/9/2015
Aaron Schock, R-Ill.[14]		3/31/2015	Darin LaHood, R		9/10/2015	9/17/2015
John Boehner, R-Ohio[15]		10/31/2015	Warren Davidson, R		6/7/2016	6/9/2016
Chaka Fattah, D-Penn.[16]		6/23/2016	Dwight Evans, D		11/8/2016	11/14/2016
Mark Takai, D-Hawaii	7/20/2016		Colleen Hanabusa, D		11/8/2016	11/14/2016
Ed Whitfield, R-Ky.[17]		9/6/2016	James Comer, R		11/8/2016	11/14/2016
Janice Hahn, D-Calif.[18]		12/5/2016	(Vacant)			
Candice Miller, R-Mich.[19]		12/31/2016	(Vacant)			

[1]Kerry was appointed by President Obama to the position of Secretary of State. He was confirmed and assumed office on February 1, 2013.

[2]Cowan served as legal counsel and chief of staff to Governor Deval Patrick, until Patrick appointed him to the Senate seat vacated by John Kerry, who was appointed Secretary of State. Cowan declined to run in the special election to fulfill the remainder of the term, and the seat was subsequently won by Ed Markey.

[3]Chiesa served as New Jersey Attorney General until Governor Chris Christie appointed him to the Senate seat vacated by Frank Lautenberg upon his death. Chiesa declined to run in the special election to fulfill the remainder of the term, and the seat was subsequently won by Cory Booker.

[4]Baucus was appointed by President Obama to the position of U.S. Ambassador to China.

[5]Emerson resigned to become president of the National Rural Electric Cooperative Association.

[6]Markey resigned his seat in the House to fill the remainder of John Kerry's term in the Senate, following Kerry's appointment as Secretary of State by President Obama.

[7]Bonner resigned to become president of the University of Alabama.

[8]Alexander announced his early resignation due to frustration with congressional gridlock. Shortly after, he accepted the position of secretary of Louisiana Veterans Affairs.

[9]Watt was appointed by President Obama to the position of director of the Federal Housing Finance Agency. He was confirmed on December 10, 2013, and resigned from the Senate shortly thereafter.

[10]Radel resigned following his arrest for possession of cocaine and was sentenced to one year of supervised probation.

[11]Andrews resigned to take a position with a Philadelphia law firm.

[12]Cantor announced his early resignation after losing the primary for his seat to Dave Brat.

[13]Grimm resigned following fraud, federal tax evasion, and perjury charges. He was sentenced to eight months of prison on July 17, 2015.

[14]Schock resigned amidst a scandal concerning misuse of public and campaign funds. A congressional ethics investigation showed improper use of taxpayer money, and a federal grand jury indicted him on November 10, 2016.

[15]Boehner resigned following opposition and discord from within the Republican caucus demanding Planned Parenthood be defunded or the government would face a shutdown.

[16]Fattah resigned after he was convicted of racketeering, fraud, and corruption. He was sentenced to ten years in prison.

[17]Whitfield resigned in the midst of a lobbying ethics probe.

[18]Hahn resigned to run for the Los Angeles County Board of Supervisors. Her seat remained vacant for the rest of the term.

[19]Miller resigned to become Macomb County Public Works Commissioner. Her seat remained vacant for the rest of the term.

Senate Membership in the 114th Congress

Membership at the beginning of Congress in 2015: Democrats 53; Republicans 45; Independents 2. Changes that occurred during the two-year period are noted.

Alabama
Jeff Sessions (R)
Richard Shelby (R)

Alaska
Dan Sullivan (R)
Lisa Murkowski (R)

Arizona
Jeff Flake (R)
John McCain (R)

Arkansas
Tom Cotton (R)
John Boozman (R)

California
Dianne Feinstein (D)
Barbara Boxer (D)

Colorado
Cory Gardner (R)
Michael Bennet (D)

Connecticut
Chris Murphy (D)
Richard Blumenthal (D)

Delaware
Tom Carper (D)
Chris Coons (D)

Florida
Bill Nelson (D)
Marco Rubio (R)

Georgia
David Perdue (R)
Johnny Isakson (R)

Hawaii
Mazie Hirono (D)
Brian Schatz (D)

Idaho
Jim Risch (R)
Mike Crapo (R)

Illinois
Dick Durbin (D)
Mark Kirk (R)

Indiana
Joe Donnelly (D)
Dan Coats (R)

Iowa
Joni Ernst (R)
Chuck Grassley (R)

Kansas
Pat Roberts (R)
Jerry Moran (R)

Kentucky
Mitch McConnell (R)
Rand Paul (R)

Louisiana
Bill Cassidy (R)
David Vitter (R)

Maine
Angus King (I)
Susan Collins (R)

Maryland
Ben Cardin (D)
Barbara Mikulski (D)

Massachusetts
Elizabeth Warren (D)
Ed Markey (D)

Michigan
Debbie Stabenow (D)
Gary Peters (D)

Minnesota
Amy Klobuchar (D)
Al Franken (D)

Mississippi
Roger Wicker (R)
Thad Cochran (R)

Missouri
Claire McCaskill (D)
Roy Blunt (R)

Montana
Jon Tester (D)
Steve Daines (R)

Nebraska
Deb Fischer (R)
Ben Sasse (R)

Nevada
Dean Heller (R)
Harry Reid (D)

New Hampshire
Jeanne Shaheen (D)
Kelly Ayotte (R)

New Jersey
Bob Menendez (D)
Cory Booker (D)

New Mexico
Martin Heinrich (D)
Tom Udall (D)

New York
Kirsten Gillibrand (D)
Chuck Schumer (D)

North Carolina
Thom Tillis (R)
Richard Burr (R)

North Dakota
Heidi Heitkamp (D)
John Hoeven (R)

Ohio
Sherrod Brown (D)
Rob Portman (R)

Oklahoma
Jim Inhofe (R)
James Lankford (R)

Oregon
Jeff Merkley (D)
Ron Wyden (D)

Pennsylvania
Bob Casey Jr. (D)
Pat Toomey (R)

Rhode Island
Sheldon Whitehouse (D)
Jack Reed (D)

South Carolina
Lindsey Graham (R)
Tim Scott (R)

South Dakota
Mike Rounds (R)
John Thune (R)

Tennessee
Bob Corker (R)
Lamar Alexander (R)

Texas
Ted Cruz (R)
John Cornyn (R)

Utah
Orrin Hatch (R)
Mike Lee (R)

Vermont
Bernie Sanders (I)
Patrick Leahy (D)

Virginia
Tim Kaine (D)
Mark Warner (D)

Washington
Maria Cantwell (D)
Patty Murray (D)

West Virginia
Joe Manchin (D)
Shelley Moore Capito (R)

Wisconsin
Tammy Baldwin (D)
Ron Johnson (R)

Wyoming
John Barrasso (R)
Mike Enzi (R)

House Membership in the 114th Congress

Membership at the beginning of Congress in January 2015: Republicans, 234; Democrats, 201. Changes during the 2015–2016 period are noted.

Alabama
1. Bradley Byrne (R)
2. Martha Roby (R)
3. Mike Rogers (R)
4. Robert Aderholt (R)
5. Mo Brooks (R)
6. Gary Palmer (R)
7. Terri Sewell (D)

Alaska
AL Don Young (R)

Arizona
1. Ann Kirkpatrick (D)
2. Martha McSally (R)
3. Raúl Grijalva (D)
4. Paul Gosar (R)
5. Matt Salmon (R)
6. David Schweikert (R)
7. Ruben Gallego (D)
8. Trent Franks (R)
9. Kyrsten Sinema (D)

Arkansas
1. Rick Crawford (R)
2. French Hill (R)
3. Steve Womack (R)
4. Bruce Westerman (R)

California
1. Doug LaMalfa (R)
2. Jared Huffman (D)
3. John Garamendi (D)
4. Tom McClintock (R)
5. Mike Thompson (D)
6. Doris Matsui (D)
7. Ami Bera (D)
8. Paul Cook (R)
9. Jerry McNerney (D)
10. Jeff Denham (R)
11. Mark DeSaulnier (D)
12. Nancy Pelosi (D)
13. Barbara Lee (D)
14. Jackie Speier (D)
15. Eric Swalwell (D)
16. Jim Costa (D)
17. Mike Honda (D)
18. Anna Eshoo (D)
19. Zoe Lofgren (D)
20. Sam Farr (D)
21. David Valadao (R)
22. Devin Nunes (R)
23. Kevin McCarthy (R)
24. Lois Capps (D)
25. Steve Knight (R)
26. Julia Brownley (D)
27. Judy Chu (D)
28. Adam Schiff (D)
29. Tony Cardenas (D)
30. Brad Sherman (D)
31. Pete Aguilar (D)
32. Grace Napolitano (D)
33. Ted Lieu (D)
34. Xavier Becerra (D)
35. Norma Torres (D)
36. Raul Ruiz (D)
37. Karen Bass (D)
38. Linda Sánchez (D)
39. Ed Royce (R)
40. Lucille Roybal-Allard (D)
41. Mark Takano (D)
42. Ken Calvert (R)
43. Maxine Waters (D)
44. Janice Hahn (D)
    (resigned December 5, 2016)[1]
45. Mimi Walters (R)
46. Loretta Sanchez (D)
47. Alan Lowenthal (D)
48. Dana Rohrabacher (R)
49. Darrell Issa (R)
50. Duncan D. Hunter (R)
51. Juan Vargas (D)
52. Scott Peters (D)
53. Susan Davis (D)

Colorado
1. Diana DeGette (D)
2. Jared Polis (D)
3. Scott Tipton (R)
4. Ken Buck (R)
5. Doug Lamborn (R)
6. Mike Coffman (R)
7. Ed Perlmutter (D)

Connecticut
1. John Larson (D)
2. Joe Courtney (D)
3. Rosa DeLauro (D)
4. Jim Himes (D)
5. Elizabeth Esty (D)

Delaware
AL John Carney (D)

Florida
1. Jeff Miller (R)
2. Gwen Graham (D)
3. Ted Yoho (R)
4. Ander Crenshaw (R)
5. Corrine Brown (D)
6. Ron DeSantis (R)
7. John Mica (R)
8. Bill Posey (R)
9. Alan Grayson (D)
10. Daniel Webster (R)
11. Rich Nugent (R)
12. Gus Bilirakis (R)
13. David Jolly (R)
14. Kathy Castor (D)
15. Dennis Ross (R)
16. Vern Buchanan (R)
17. Tom Rooney (R)
18. Patrick Murphy (D)
19. Curt Clawson (R)
20. Alcee Hastings (D)
21. Ted Deutch (D)
22. Lois Frankel (D)
23. Debbie Wasserman Schultz (D)
24. Frederica Wilson (D)
25. Mario Diaz-Balart (R)
26. Carlos Curbelo (R)
27. Ileana Ros-Lehtinen (R)

Georgia
1. Buddy Carter (R)
2. Sanford Bishop (D)
3. Drew Ferguson (R)
4. Hank Johnson (D)
5. John Lewis (D)
6. Tom Price (R)
7. Rob Woodall (R)
8. Austin Scott (R)
9. Doug Collins (R)
10. Jody Hice (R)
11. Barry Loudermilk (R)
12. Rick Allen (R)
13. David Scott (D)
14. Tom Graves (R)

Hawaii
1. Mark Takai (D)
   (died July 20, 2016)
   Colleen Hanabusa (D)
   (sworn in November 14, 2016)
2. Tulsi Gabbard (D)

Idaho
1. Raul Labrador (R)
2. Mike Simpson (R)

Illinois
1. Bobby Rush (D)
2. Robin Kelly (D)
3. Dan Lipinski (D)
4. Luis Gutiérrez (D)
5. Mike Quigley (D)
6. Peter Roskam (R)
7. Danny Davis (D)
8. Tammy Duckworth (D)
9. Jan Schakowsky (D)
10. Bob Dold (R)
11. Bill Foster (D)
12. Mike Bost (R)
13. Rodney Davis (R)
14. Randy Hultgren (R)
15. John Shimkus (R)
16. Adam Kinzinger (R)
17. Cheri Bustos (D)
18. Aaron Schock (R)
    (resigned March 31, 2015)
    Darin LaHood (R)
    (sworn in September 17, 2015)

Indiana
1. Pete Visclosky (D)
2. Jackie Walorski (R)
3. Marlin Stutzman (R)
4. Todd Rokita (R)
5. Susan Brooks (R)
6. Luke Messer (R)
7. André Carson (D)
8. Larry Bucshon (R)
9. Todd Young (R)

Iowa
1. Rod Blum (R)
2. David Loebsack (D)
3. David Young (R)
4. Steve King (R)

Kansas
1. Tim Huelskamp (R)
2. Lynn Jenkins (R)
3. Kevin Yoder (R)
4. Mike Pompeo (R)

Kentucky
1. Ed Whitfield (R)
   (resigned September 6, 2016)
   James Comer (R)
   (sworn in November 14, 2016)
2. Brett Guthrie (R)
3. John Yarmuth (D)
4. Thomas Massie (R)
5. Hal Rogers (R)
6. Andy Barr (R)

Louisiana
1. Steve Scalise (R)
2. Cedric Richmond (D)
3. Charles Boustany (R)
4. John Fleming (R)
5. Ralph Abraham (R)
6. Garret Graves (R)

Maine
1. Chellie Pingree (D)
2. Bruce Poliquin (R)

Maryland
1. Andy Harris (R)
2. Dutch Ruppersberger (D)
3. John Sarbanes (D)
4. Donna Edwards (D)
5. Steny Hoyer (D)
6. John Delaney (D)
7. Elijah Cummings (D)
8. Chris Van Hollen (D)

Massachusetts
1. Richard Neal (D)
2. Jim McGovern (D)
3. Niki Tsongas (D)
4. Joe Kennedy (D)
5. Katherine Clark (D)

6. Seth Moulton (D)
7. Mike Capuano (D)
8. Stephen Lynch (D)
9. Bill Keating (D)

Michigan
1. Dan Benishek (R)
2. Bill Huizenga (R)
3. Justin Amash (R)
4. John Moolenaar (R)
5. Dan Kildee (D)
6. Fred Upton (R)
7. Tim Walberg (R)
8. Mike Bishop (R)
9. Sander Levin (D)
10. Candice Miller (R)
    (resigned December 31, 2016)[1]
11. Dave Trott (R)
12. Debbie Dingell (D)
13. John Conyers (D)
14. Brenda Lawrence (D)

Missouri
1. Lacy Clay (D)
2. Ann Wagner (R)
3. Blaine Luetkemeyer (R)
4. Vicky Hartzler (R)
5. Emanuel Cleaver (D)
6. Sam Graves (R)
7. Billy Long (R)
8. Jason Smith (R)

Montana
AL Ryan Zinke (R)

Nebraska
1. Jeff Fortenberry (R)
2. Brad Ashford (D)
3. Adrian Smith (R)

Nevada
1. Dina Titus (D)
2. Mark Amodei (R)
3. Joe Heck (R)
4. Cresent Hardy (R)

New Hampshire
1. Frank Guinta (R)
2. Ann McLane Kuster (D)

New Jersey
1. Donald Norcross (D)
2. Frank LoBiondo (R)
3. Tom MacArthur (R)
4. Chris Smith (R)
5. Josh Gottheimer (D)
6. Frank Pallone (D)
7. Leonard Lance (R)
8. Albio Sires (D)
9. Bill Pascrell (D)
10. Donald Payne Jr. (D)
11. Rodney Frelinghuysen (R)
12. Bonnie Watson Coleman (D)

New Mexico
1. Michelle Lujan Grisham (D)
2. Steve Pearce (R)
3. Ben Ray Luján (D)

New York
1. Lee Zeldin (R)
2. Peter King (R)
3. Steve Israel (D)
4. Kathleen Rice (D)
5. Gregory Meeks (D)
6. Grace Meng (D)
7. Nydia Velázquez (D)
8. Hakeem Jeffries (D)
9. Yvette Clarke (D)
10. Jerrold Nadler (D)
11. Michael Grimm (R)
    (resigned January 5, 2015)
    Dan Donovan (R)
    (sworn in May 12, 2015)
12. Carolyn Maloney (D)
13. Charles Rangel (D)
14. Joseph Crowley (D)
15. José E. Serrano (D)
16. Eliot Engel (D)
17. Nita Lowey (D)
18. Sean Patrick Maloney (D)
19. Chris Gibson (R)
20. Paul Tonko (D)
21. Elise Stefanik (R)
22. Richard Hanna (R)
23. Thomas Reed (R)
24. John Katko (R)
25. Louise Slaughter (D)
26. Brian Higgins (D)
27. Chris Collins (R)

North Carolina
1. G. K. Butterfield (D)
2. Renee Ellmers (R)
3. Walter B. Jones Jr. (R)
4. David Price (D)
5. Virginia Foxx (R)
6. Mark Walker (R)
7. David Rouzer (R)
8. Richard Hudson (R)
9. Robert Pittenger (R)
10. Patrick McHenry (R)
11. Mark Meadows (R)
12. Alma Adams (D)
13. George Holding (R)

North Dakota
AL. Kevin Cramer (R)

Ohio
1. Steve Chabot (R)
2. Brad Wenstrup (R)
3. Joyce Beatty (D)
4. Jim Jordan (R)
5. Bob Latta (R)
6. Bill Johnson (R)
7. Bob Gibbs (R)
8. John Boehner (R)
    (resigned October 31, 2015)

Warren Davidson (R)
    (sworn in June 9, 2016)
9. Marcy Kaptur (D)
10. Mike Turner (R)
11. Marcia Fudge (D)
12. Pat Tiberi (R)
13. Tim Ryan (D)
14. David Joyce (R)
15. Steve Stivers (R)
16. Jim Renacci (R)

Oklahoma
1. Jim Bridenstine (R)
2. Markwayne Mullin (R)
3. Frank Lucas (R)
4. Tom Cole (R)
5. Steve Russell (R)

Oregon
1. Suzanne Bonamici (D)
2. Greg Walden (R)
3. Earl Blumenauer (D)
4. Peter DeFazio (D)
5. Kurt Schrader (D)

Pennsylvania
1. Bob Brady (D)
2. Chaka Fattah (D)
    (resigned June 23, 2016)
    Dwight Evans (D)
    (sworn in November 14, 2016)
3. Mike Kelly (R)
4. Scott Perry (R)
5. Glenn Thompson (R)
6. Ryan Costello (R)
7. Pat Meehan (R)
8. Mike Fitzpatrick (R)
9. Bill Shuster (R)
10. Tom Marino (R)
11. Lou Barletta (R)
12. Keith Rothfus (R)
13. Brendan Boyle (D)
14. Michael Doyle (D)
15. Charles Dent (R)
16. Joe Pitts (R)
17. Matt Cartwright (D)
18. Tim Murphy (R)

Rhode Island
1. David Cicilline (D)
2. James Langevin (D)

South Carolina
1. Mark Sanford (R)
2. Joe Wilson (R)
3. Jeff Duncan (R)
4. Trey Gowdy (R)
5. Mick Mulvaney (R)
6. Jim Clyburn (D)
7. Tom Rice (R)

South Dakota
AL Kristi Noem (R)

Tennessee
1. Phil Roe (R)

2. Jimmy Duncan (R)
3. Chuck Fleischmann (R)
4. Scott DesJarlais (R)
5. Jim Cooper (D)
6. Diane Black (R)
7. Marsha Blackburn (R)
8. Stephen Fincher (R)
9. Steve Cohen (D)

Texas
1. Louie Gohmert (R)
2. Ted Poe (R)
3. Sam Johnson (R)
4. John Ratcliffe (R)
5. Jeb Hensarling (R)
6. Joe Barton (R)
7. John Culberson (R)
8. Kevin Brady (R)
9. Al Green (D)
10. Michael McCaul (R)
11. Mike Conaway (R)
12. Kay Granger (R)
13. Mac Thornberry (R)
14. Randy Weber (R)
15. Ruben Hinojosa (D)
16. Beto O'Rourke (D)
17. Bill Flores (R)
18. Sheila Jackson Lee (D)
19. Randy Neugebauer (R)
20. Joaquin Castro (D)
21. Lamar Smith (R)
22. Pete Olson (R)
23. Will Hurd (R)
24. Kenny Marchant (R)
25. Roger Williams (R)
26. Michael Burgess (R)
27. Blake Farenthold (R)
28. Henry Cuellar (D)
29. Gene Green (D)
30. Eddie Bernice Johnson (D)
31. John Carter (R)
32. Pete Sessions (R)
33. Marc Veasey (D)
34. Filemon Vela Jr. (D)
35. Lloyd Doggett (D)
36. Brian Babin (R)

Utah
1. Rob Bishop (R)
2. Chris Stewart (R)
3. Jason Chaffetz (R)
4. Mia Love (R)

Vermont
AL Peter Welch (D)

Virginia
1. Rob Wittman (R)
2. Scott Rigell (R)
3. Bobby Scott (D)
4. Randy Forbes (R)
5. Robert Hurt (R)
6. Bob Goodlatte (R)
7. Dave Brat (R)
8. Don Beyer (D)

9. Morgan Griffith (R)
10. Barbara Comstock (R)
11. Gerry Connolly (D)

Washington

1. Suzan DelBene (D)
2. Rick Larsen (D)
3. Jaime Herrera Beutler (R)
4. Dan Newhouse (R)
5. Cathy McMorris Rodgers (R)
6. Derek Kilmer (D)
7. Jim McDermott (D)
8. Dave Reichert (R)
9. Adam Smith (D)
10. Dennis Heck (D)

West Virginia

1. David McKinley (R)
2. Alex Mooney (R)
3. Evan Jenkins (R)

Wisconsin

1. Paul Ryan (R)
2. Mark Pocan (D)
3. Ron Kind (D)
4. Gwen Moore (D)
5. Jim Sensenbrenner (R)
6. Glenn Grothman (R)
7. Sean Duffy (R)
8. Reid Ribble (R)

Wyoming

AL Cynthia Lummis (R)

NOTE: Changes that occurred during 2013 and 2014 are noted following the names of individuals who did not serve their full terms. Members of the 113th Congress also included delegates Eni F. H. Faleomavaega, D–American Samoa; Eleanor Holmes Norton, D–District of Columbia; Madeleine Z. Bordallo, D–Guam; Gregorio Kilili Camacho Sablan, I–Northern Mariana Islands; Donna M. Christensen, D–Virgin Islands; and resident commissioner Pedro Pierluisi, D–Puerto Rico. AL–At Large.

[1]Seat left vacant for the remainder of the term.

Congressional Leadership and Committees, 113th and 114th Congresses

Senate Leadership

President Pro Tempore, 113th Congress: Joe Biden, Del.; Patrick Leahy, Vt.

President Pro Tempore, 114th Congress: Joe Biden, Del.; Orrin Hatch, Utah

Democratic Leaders, 113th Congress

Majority Floor Leader 113th Congress: Harry M. Reid, Nev.

Assistant Floor Leader 113th Congress: Richard J. Durbin, Ill.

Chief Deputy Whip 113th Congress: Barbara Boxer, Calif.

Republican Leaders, 113th Congress

Minority Floor Leader 113th Congress: Mitch McConnell, Ky.

Minority Whip 113th Congress: John Cornyn, Texas

Democratic Leaders, 114th Congress

Minority Floor Leader 114th Congress: Harry M. Reid, Nev.

Minority Whip 114th Congress: Richard J. Durbin, Ill.

Republican Leaders, 114th Congress

Majority Floor Leader 114th Congress: Mitch McConnell, Ky.

Assistant Floor Leader 114th Congress: John Cornyn, Texas

Chief Deputy Whip 114th Congress: Mike Crapo, Idaho

Senate Political Committees

Democratic Policy Committee—Charles Schumer, N.Y., Chair (113th Congress and 114th Congress).

Democratic Senatorial Campaign Committee—Michael Bennet, Colo., Chair (113th Congress); Jon Tester, Mont., Chair (114th Congress).

Democratic Steering and Outreach Committee—Mark Begich, Ark., Chair (113th Congress); Amy Klobuchar, Minn., Chair (114th Congress).

Democratic Communications Center—Charles Schumer, N.Y., Chair (113th Congress and 114th Congress).

National Republican Senatorial Committee—Jerry Moran, Kan., Chair (113th Congress); Roger Wicker, Miss., Chair (114th Congress).

Republican Conference—John Thune, S.D., Chair (113th Congress and 114th Congress).

Republican Policy Committee—John Barrasso, Wyo., Chair (113th Congress and 114th Congress).

House Leadership

Speaker of the House:

John Boehner, R, Ohio (113th Congress and 114th Congress; *until October 29, 2015*)

Paul Ryan, R, Mass. (114th Congress)

Republican Leaders 113th Congress

Eric Cantor, Va.; Kevin McCarthy, Calif., Majority Leader

Kevin McCarthy, Calif.; Steve Scalise, La., Majority Whip

Peter Roskam, Ill.; Patrick McHenry, N.C., Chief Deputy Majority Whip

Republican Leaders 114th Congress

Kevin McCarthy, Calif., Majority Leader

Steve Scalise, La., Majority Whip

Patrick McHenry, N.C., Majority Chief Deputy Whip

Democratic Leaders 113th Congress

Nancy Pelosi, Calif., Minority Leader

Steny H. Hoyer, Md., Minority Whip

James E. Clyburn, S.C., Assistant Leader

Democratic Leaders 114th Congress

Nancy Pelosi, Calif., Minority Leader

Steny H. Hoyer, Md., Minority Whip

James E. Clyburn, S.C., Assistant Leader

Political Committees

Democratic Congressional Campaign Committee—Steve Israel, N.Y., Chair (113th Congress); Ben Ray Luján, N.M., Chair (114th Congress)

Democratic Steering and Policy Committees—Rosa DeLauro, Conn., Co-Chair (Steering, 113th and 114th Congress); Rob Andrews, N.J., Co-Chair (Policy, 113th Congress); George Miller, Calif., Co-Chair (Policy, 113th Congress); Donna Edwards, Md., Co-Chair (Policy, 114th Congress).

Democratic Caucus—Xavier Becerra, Calif., Chair (113th and 114th Congress).

National Republican Congressional Committee—Greg Walden, Ore., Chair (113th and 114th Congress).

Republican Conference—Cathy McMorris Rodgers, Wash., Chair (113th and 114th Congress).

Republican Policy Committee—James Lankford, Okla., Chair (113th Congress); Luke Messer, Ind., Chair (114th Congress).

Republican Steering Committee—John A. Boehner, Ohio, Chair (113th and 114th Congress).

Congressional Committees

Following is a list of House and Senate leaders and congressional committees and subcommittees for the 113th and 114th Congresses. The committee listings are as of the beginning of both Congresses. Some changes, usually because of resignations or death, occurred later.

Committee jurisdictions, party ratios, committee chairs and the dates of their service in that capacity, ranking minority members (in italics), and subcommittee chairs are included. Political and joint committees also are listed.

Senate Committees

AGRICULTURE, NUTRITION AND FORESTRY

Agriculture in general; animal industry and diseases; crop insurance and soil conservation; farm credit and farm security; food from fresh waters; food stamp programs; forestry in general; home economics; human nutrition; inspection of livestock, meat, and agricultural products; pests and pesticides; plant industry, soils, and agricultural engineering; rural development, rural electrification, and watersheds; school nutrition programs.

D 11–R 9 (113th Congress)

Debbie Stabenow, Mich.
Thad Cochran, Miss.

Commodities, Risk Management and Trade—Joe Donnelly, Ind.
Rural Development and Energy—Heidi Heitkamp, N.D.
Conservation, Forestry and Natural Resources—Michael Bennet, Colo.
Nutrition, Specialty Crops and Agricultural Research—Mo Cowan, Mass.
Livestock, Marketing and Agriculture Security—Kirsten Gillibrand, N.Y.

R 11–D 9 (114th Congress)

Debbie Stabenow, Mich.
Pat Roberts, Kan.

Commodities, Risk Management and Trade—John Boozman, Ark.
Rural Development and Energy—Joni Ernst, Iowa
Conservation, Forestry and Natural Resources—David Perdue, Ga.
Nutrition, Specialty Crops and Agricultural Research—John Hoeven, N.D.
Livestock, Marketing and Agriculture Security—Ben Sasse, Neb.

APPROPRIATIONS

Appropriation of revenue; rescission of appropriations; new spending authority under the Congressional Budget Act.

D 16–R 14 (113th Congress)

Barbara A. Mikulski, Md.
Richard C. Shelby, Ala.

Agriculture, Rural Development, Food and Drug Administration—Mark Pryor, Ark.
Commerce, Justice, Science—Barbara Mikulski, Md.
Defense—Dick Durbin, Ill.
Energy and Water Development—Dianne Feinstein, Calif.
Financial Services and General Government—Tom Udall, N.M.
Homeland Security—Mary Landrieu, La.
Interior and Environment—Jack Reed, R.I.
Labor, Health and Human Services, Education—Tom Harkin, Iowa
Legislative Branch—Jeanne Shaheen, N.H.
Military Construction, Veterans Affairs—Tim Johnson, N.D.
State, Foreign Operations, and Related Programs—Patrick Leahy, Vt.
Transportation, Housing, and Urban Development—Patty Murray, Wash.

R 16–D 14 (114th Congress)

Thad Cochran, Mo.
Barbara A. Mikulski, Md.

Agriculture, Rural Development, Food and Drug Administration—Jerry Moran, Kan.

Commerce, Justice, Science—Richard Shelby, Ala.
Defense—Thad Cochran, Miss.
Energy and Water Development—Lamar Alexander, Tenn.
Financial Services and General Government—John Boozman, Ark.
Homeland Security—John Hoever, N.D.
Interior and Environment—Lisa Murkowski, Ark.
Labor, Health and Human Services, Education—Roy Blunt, Mo.
Legislative Branch—Shelley Moore Capito, W.Va.
Military Construction, Veterans Affairs—Mark Kirk, Ill.
State, Foreign Operations, and Related Programs—Lindsey Graham, S.C.
Transportation, Housing, and Urban Development—Susan Collins, Maine

ARMED SERVICES

Defense and defense policy generally; aeronautical and space activities peculiar to or primarily associated with the development of weapons systems or military operations; maintenance and operation of the Panama Canal, including the Canal Zone; military research and development; national security aspects of nuclear energy; naval petroleum reserves (except Alaska); armed forces generally; Selective Service System; strategic and critical materials.

D 14–R 12 (113th Congress)

Carl Levin, Mich.
James M. Inhofe, Okla.

Airland Forces—Joe Manchin, W.Va.
Emerging Threats and Capabilities—Kay Hagan, N.C.
Personnel—Kirsten Gillibrand, N.Y.
Readiness and Management Support—Jeanne Shaheen, N.H.
Seapower—Jack Reed, R.I.
Strategic Forces—Mark Udall, Colo.

R 14–D 12 (114th Congress)

John McCain, Ariz.
Jack Reed, R.I.

Airland Forces—Tom Cotton, Ariz.
Emerging Threats and Capabilities—Deb Fischer, Neb.
Personnel—Lindsey Graham, S.C.
Readiness and Management Support—Kelly Ayotte, N.H.
Seapower—Roger Wicker, Miss.
Strategic Forces—Jeff Sessions, Ala.

BANKING, HOUSING, AND URBAN AFFAIRS

Banks, banking, and financial institutions; price controls; deposit insurance; economic stabilization and growth; defense production; export and foreign trade promotion; export controls; federal monetary policy, including Federal Reserve System; financial aid to commerce and industry; issuance and redemption of notes; money and credit, including currency and coinage; nursing home construction; public and private housing, including veterans' housing; renegotiation of government contracts; urban development and mass transit; international economic policy.

D 12–R 10 *(113th Congress)*

Tim Johnson, S.D.
Michael Crapo, Idaho

Economic Policy—Jeff Merkley, Ore.
Financial Institutions—Sherrod Brown, Ohio
Housing, Transportation, and Community Development—Robert Menendez, N.J.
Security and International Trade and Finance—Evan Bayh, Ind.
Securities, Insurance, and Investment—Jon Tester, Mont.

R 12–D 10 *(114th Congress)*

Richard Shelby, Ala.
Sherrod Brown, Ohio

Economic Policy—Dean Heller, Nev.
Financial Institutions and Consumer Protection—Patrick Toomey, Pa.
Housing, Transportation, and Community Development—Tim Scott, S.C.
Security and International Trade and Finance—Mark Kirk, Ore.
Securities, Insurance, and Investment—Mike Crapo, Idaho

BUDGET

Federal budget generally; concurrent budget resolutions; Congressional Budget Office.

D 12–R 10 *(113th Congress)*

Patty Murray, Wash.
Jeff Sessions, Ala.

R 12–D 10 *(114th Congress)*

Michael B. Enzi, Wyo.
Bernie Sanders, Vt.

No standing subcommittees.

COMMERCE, SCIENCE, AND TRANSPORTATION

Interstate commerce and transportation generally; Coast Guard; coastal zone management; communications; highway safety; inland waterways, except construction; marine fisheries; Merchant Marine and navigation; nonmilitary aeronautical and space sciences; oceans, weather, and atmospheric activities; interoceanic canals generally; regulation of consumer products and services; science, engineering, and technology research, development and policy; sports; standards and measurement; transportation and commerce aspects of outer continental shelf lands.

D 13–R 11 *(113th Congress)*

John D. Rockefeller IV, W.Va.
John Thune, S.D.

Aviation Operations, Safety, and Security—Maria Cantwell, Wash.
Communications, Technology, and the Internet—Mark L. Pryor, Ark.

Consumer Protection, Product Safety and Insurance—Claire McCaskill, Mo.
Oceans, Atmosphere, Fisheries, and Coast Guard—Mark Begich, Ark.
Science and Space—Bill Nelson, Fla.
Surface Transportation and Merchant Marine—Mark Warner, Va.

R 13–D 11 *(114th Congress)*

John Thune, S.D.
Bill Nelson, Fla.

Aviation Operations, Safety, and Security—Kelly Ayotte, N.H.
Communications, Technology, and the Internet—Roger Wicker, Miss.
Consumer Protection, Product Safety, and Insurance—Jerry Moran, Kan.
Oceans, Atmosphere, Fisheries, and Coast Guard—Marco Rubio, Fla.
Science and Space—Ted Cruz, Texas
Surface Transportation and Merchant Marine—Deb Fischer, Neb.

ENERGY AND NATURAL RESOURCES

Energy policy, regulation, conservation, research, and development; coal; energy-related aspects of deep-water ports; hydroelectric power, irrigation, and reclamation; mines, mining, and minerals generally; national parks, recreation areas, wilderness areas, wild and scenic rivers, historic sites, military parks, and battlefields; naval petroleum reserves in Alaska; nonmilitary development of nuclear energy; oil and gas production and distribution; public lands and forests; solar energy systems; territorial possessions of the United States.

D 12–R 10 *(113th Congress)*

Mary Landrieu, La.
Lisa Murkowski, Alaska

Energy—Al Franken, Minn.
Public Lands and Forests—Joe Manchin, W.Va.
National Parks—Mark Udall, Colo.
Water and Power—Brian Schatz, Hawaii

R 12–D 10 *(114th Congress)*

Lisa Murkowski, Alaska
Maria Cantwell, Wash.

Energy—James Risch, Idaho
Public Lands and Forests—John Barrasso, Wyo.
National Parks—Mark Udall, Colo.
Water and Power—Mike Lee, Utah

ENVIRONMENT AND PUBLIC WORKS

Environmental policy, research, and development; air, water, and noise pollution; construction and maintenance of highways; environmental aspects of outer continental shelf lands; environmental effects of toxic substances other than pesticides; fisheries and wildlife; flood control and improvements of rivers and harbors; nonmilitary environmental regulation and control of nuclear energy; ocean dumping; public buildings and grounds; public works, bridges, and dams; regional economic development; solid waste disposal and recycling; water resources.

D 10–R 8 (113th Congress)

Barbara Boxer, Calif.
David Vitter, La.

Clean Air and Nuclear Safety—Thomas R. Carper, Del.
Fisheries, Water, and Wildlife—Benjamin L. Cardin, Md.
Superfund, Waste Management, and Regulatory Oversight—Tom Udall, N.M.
Transportation and Infrastructure—Max Baucus, Mont.

R 11–D 9 (114th Congress)

James M. Inhofe. Okla.
Barbara Boxer, Calif.

Clean Air and Nuclear Safety—Shelley Moore Capito, W.Va.
Fisheries, Water, and Wildlife—Dan Sullivan, Ark.
Superfund, Waste Management, and Regulatory Oversight—Mike Rounds, S.D.
Transportation and Infrastructure—David Vitter, La.

FINANCE

Revenue measures generally; taxes; tariffs and import quotas; reciprocal trade agreements; customs; revenue sharing; federal debt limit; Social Security; health programs financed by taxes or trust funds.

D 13–R 11 (113th Congress)

Ron Wyden, Ore.
Orrin Hatch, Utah

Energy, Natural Resources, and Infrastructure—Debbie Stabenow, Mich.
Health Care—John D. Rockefeller IV, W.Va.
International Trade, Customs, and Global Competitiveness—Ron Wyden, Ore.
Social Security, Pensions, and Family Policy—Sherrod Brown, Ohio
Taxation and IRS Oversight—Michael Bennet, Colo.
Fiscal Responsibility and Economic Growth—Robert Casey, Pa.

R 14–D 12 (114th Congress)

Orrin G. Hatch, Utah
Ron Wyden, Ore.

Energy, Natural Resources, and Infrastructure—Daniel Coats, Ind.
Health Care—Patrick Toomey, Pa.
International Trade, Customs, and Global Competitiveness—John Cornyn, Texas
Social Security, Pensions, and Family Policy—Dean Heller, Nev.
Taxation and IRS Oversight—Mike Crapo, Idaho
Fiscal Responsibility and Economic Growth—Rob Portman, Ohio

FOREIGN RELATIONS

Relations of the United States with foreign nations generally; treaties; foreign economic, military, technical, and humanitarian assistance; foreign loans; diplomatic service; International Red Cross; international aspects of nuclear energy; International Monetary Fund; intervention abroad and declarations of war; foreign trade; national security; oceans and international environmental and scientific affairs; protection of U.S. citizens abroad; United Nations; World Bank and other development assistance organizations.

D 10–R 8 (113th Congress)

Robert Menendez, N.J.
Bob Corker, Tenn.

Africa and Global Health Policy—Christopher A. Coons, Del.
East Asian and Pacific Affairs—Ben Cardin, Md.
Europe and Regional Security Cooperation—Christopher Murphy, Conn.
Multilateral International Development, Multilateral Institutions, and International Economic, Energy, and Environmental Policy—Ed Markey, Mass.
State Department and USAID Management, International Operations, and Bilateral International Development—Barbara Boxer, Calif.
Near East, South Asia, Central Asia, and Counterterrorism—Tom Udall, N.M.
Western Hemisphere, Transnational Crime, Civilian Security, Democracy, Human Rights and Global Women's Issues—Christopher J. Dodd, Conn.

R 10–D 9 (114th Congress)

Bob Corker, Tenn.
Ben Cardin, Md.

Africa and Global Health Policy—Jeff Flake, Ariz.
East Asian and Pacific Affairs—Cory Gardner, Colo.
Europe and Regional Security Cooperation—Ron Johnson, Wisc.
Multilateral International Development, Multilateral Institutions, and International Economic, Energy, and Environmental Policy—John Barrasso, Wyo.
State Department and USAID Management, International Operations, and Bilateral International Development—David Perdue, Ga.
Near East, South Asia, Central Asia, and Counterterrorism—James Risch, Idaho
Western Hemisphere, Transnational Crime, Civilian Security, Democracy, Human Rights and Global Women's Issues—Marco Rubio, Fla.

HEALTH, EDUCATION, LABOR, AND PENSIONS

Education, labor, health, and public welfare in general; aging; arts and humanities; biomedical research and development; child labor; convict labor; domestic activities of the Red Cross; equal employment opportunity; handicapped people; labor standards and statistics; mediation and arbitration of labor disputes; occupational safety and health; private pensions; public health;

railway labor and retirement; regulation of foreign laborers; student loans; wages and hours; agricultural colleges; Gallaudet University; Howard University; St. Elizabeth's Hospital in Washington, D.C.

D 12–R 10 *(113th Congress)*

Tom Harkin, Iowa
Lamar Alexander, Tenn.

Children and Families—Kay Hagan, N.C.
Employment and Workplace Safety—Robert Casey, Pa.
Primary Health and Retirement Security—Bernard Sanders, Vt.

R 12–D 10 *(114th Congress)*

Lamar Alexander, Tenn.
Patty Murray, Wash.

Children and Families—Rand Paul, Ky.
Employment and Workplace Safety—Johnny Isakson, Ga.
Primary Health and Retirement Security—Mike Enzi, Wyo.

HOMELAND SECURITY AND GOVERNMENTAL AFFAIRS

Homeland Security Department except the Coast Guard, Transportation Security Administration, Federal Law Enforcement Training Center, Secret Service, Citizenship and Immigration Service, immigration and commercial functions of Customs and Border Protection and Immigration and Customs Enforcement, and customs revenue functions; Archives of the United States; budget and accounting measures; census and statistics; federal civil service; congressional organization; intergovernmental relations; government information; District of Columbia; organization and management of nuclear export policy; executive branch organization and reorganization; Postal Service; efficiency, economy, and effectiveness of government.

D 9–R 7 *(113th Congress)*

Thomas R. Carper, Del.
Tom Coburn, Okla.

Permanent Subcommittee on Investigations—Carl Levin, Mich.
Federal Spending Oversight and Emergency Management—Rand Paul, Ky.
Regulatory Affairs and Federal Management—James Lankford, Ohio

R 9–D 7 *(114th Congress)*

Ron Johnson, Wisc.
Thomas R. Carper, Del.

Permanent Subcommittee on Investigations—Rob Portman, Ohio
Federal Spending Oversight and Emergency Management—Rand Paul, Ky.
Regulatory Affairs and Federal Management—James Lankford, Ohio

INDIAN AFFAIRS

Problems and opportunities of Native Americans, including Native American land management and trust responsibilities, education, health, special services, loan programs, and claims against the United States.

D 8–R 6 *(113th Congress)*

Jon Tester, Mont.
John Barrasso, Wyo.

R 8–D 6 *(114th Congress)*

John Barrasso, Wyo.
Jon Tester, Mont.

No standing subcommittees.

JUDICIARY

Civil and criminal judicial proceedings in general; national penitentiaries; bankruptcy, mutiny, espionage, and counterfeiting; civil liberties; constitutional amendments; apportionment of representatives; government information; immigration and naturalization; interstate compacts in general; claims against the United States; patents, copyrights, and trademarks; monopolies and unlawful restraints of trade; holidays and celebrations; revision and codification of the statutes of the United States; state and territorial boundary lines.

D 10–R 8 *(113th Congress)*

Patrick J. Leahy, Vt.
Charles Grassley, Iowa

Antitrust, Competition Policy, Consumer Rights—Amy Klobuchar, Minn.
Crime and Terrorism—Sheldon Whitehouse, R.I.
The Constitution—Dick Durbin, Ill.
Immigration and the National Interest—Chuck Schumer, N.Y.
Oversight, Federal Rights and Agency Action—Richard Blumenthal, Conn.
Privacy, Technology and the Law—Al Franken, Minn.

R 10–D 9 *(114th Congress)*

Charles Grassley, Iowa
Patrick J. Leahy, Vt.

Antitrust, Competition Policy, Consumer Rights—Mike Lee, Utah
Crime and Terrorism—Lindsey Graham, S.C.
The Constitution—John Cornyn, Texas
Immigration and the National Interest—Jeff Sessions, Ala.
Oversight, Federal Rights and Agency Action—Ted Cruz, Texas
Privacy, Technology and the Law—Jeff Flake, Ariz.

RULES AND ADMINISTRATION

Senate rules and regulations; Senate administration in general; corrupt practices; qualifications of senators; contested elections; federal elections in general; Government Printing Office; *Congressional Record*; meetings of Congress and attendance of members; presidential succession; the Capitol, congressional office buildings, the Library of Congress, the Smithsonian Institution, and the Botanic Garden; purchase of books and manuscripts and erection of monuments to the memory of individuals.

D 10–R 8 *(113th Congress)*

Charles E. Schumer N.Y.
Pat Roberts, Kan.

R 10–D 8 *(114th Congress)*

Roy Blunt, Miss.
Charles E. Schumer, N.Y.

No standing subcommittees.

SELECT ETHICS

Studies and investigates standards and conduct of Senate members and employees and may recommend remedial action.

D 3–R 3 *(113th Congress)*

Barbara Boxer, Calif.
Johnny Isakson, Ga.

D 3–R 3 *(114th Congress)*

Barbara Boxer, Calif.
Johnny Isakson, Ga.

No standing subcommittees.

SELECT INTELLIGENCE

Legislative and budgetary authority over the Central Intelligence Agency, the Defense Intelligence Agency, the National Security Agency, and intelligence activities of the Federal Bureau of Investigation, and other components of the federal intelligence community.

D 10–R 9 *(113th Congress)*

Dianne Feinstein, Calif.
Saxby Chambliss, Ga.

R 8–D 7 *(114th Congress)*

Richard Burr, N.C.
Dianne Feinstein, Calif.

No standing subcommittees.

SMALL BUSINESS AND ENTREPRENEURSHIP

Problems of small business; Small Business Administration.

D 10–R 8 *(113th Congress)*

Maria Cantwell, Wash.
James Risch, Idaho

R 10–D 9 *(114th Congress)*

David Vitter, La.
Jeanne Shaheen, N.H.

No standing subcommittees.

SPECIAL AGING

Problems and opportunities of older people including health, income, employment, housing, and care and assistance. Reports findings and makes recommendations to the Senate but cannot report legislation.

D 13–R 8 *(111th Congress)*

Bill Nelson, Fla.
Claire McCaskill, Mo.

D 11–R 10 *(112th Congress)*

Susan Collins, Maine
Bob Casey, Pa.

No standing subcommittees.

VETERANS' AFFAIRS

Veterans' measures in general; compensation; life insurance issued by the government on account of service in the armed forces; national cemeteries; pensions; readjustment benefits; veterans' hospitals, medical care and treatment; vocational rehabilitation and education; soldiers' and sailors' civil relief.

D 8–R 6 *(113th Congress)*

Bernard Sanders, Vt.
Richard Burr, N.C.

R 8–D 7 *(114th Congress)*

Johnny Isakson, Ga.
Richard Blumenthal, Conn.

No standing subcommittees.

House Committees

AGRICULTURE

Agriculture generally; forestry in general, and forest reserves other than those created from the public domain; adulteration of seeds, insect pests, and protection of birds and animals in forest reserves; agricultural and industrial chemistry; agricultural colleges and experiment stations; agricultural economics and research; agricultural education extension services; agricultural production and marketing and stabilization of prices of agricultural products, and commodities (not including distribution outside the United States); animal industry and diseases of animals; commodities exchanges; crop insurance and soil conservation; dairy industry; entomology and plant quarantine; extension of farm credit and farm security; inspection of livestock, poultry, meat products, seafood and seafood products; human nutrition and home economics; plant industry, soils, and agricultural engineering; rural electrification; rural development; water conservation related to activities of the Department of Agriculture.

R 25–D 21 *(113th Congress)*

Frank D. Lucas, Okla.
Collin C. Peterson, Minn.

Conservation and Forestry—Glenn Thompson, Pa.
Nutrition—Steve King, Ind.
General Farm Commodities and Risk Management—Michael Conaway, Texas
Biotechnology, Horticulture, and Research—Austin Scott, Ga.
Livestock and Foreign Agriculture—Rick Crawford, Ariz.

R 26–D 19 *(114th Congress)*

Michael Conaway, Texas
Collin C. Peterson, Minn.

Commodity Exchanges, Energy, and Credit—Austin Scott, Ga.
Conservation and Forestry—Glenn Thompson, Pa.
Nutrition—Jackie Walorski, Iowa
General Farm Commodities and Risk Management—Rick Crawford, Ariz.
Biotechnology, Horticulture, and Research—Rodney Davis, Ill.
Livestock and Foreign Agriculture—David Rouzer, N.C.

APPROPRIATIONS

Appropriation of the revenue for the support of the government; rescissions of appropriations contained in appropriation acts; transfers of unexpended balances; new spending authority under the Congressional Budget Act.

R 29–D 22 *(113th Congress)*

Harold Rogers, Ky.
Nita Lowey, N.Y.

Agriculture, Rural Development, Food and Drug Administration—Robert Aderholt, Ala.
Commerce, Justice, Science and Related Agencies—Frank Wolf, Va.
Defense—Rodney Frelinghuysen, N.J.
Energy and Water Development—Michael K. Simpson, Idaho
Financial Services and General Government—Ander Crenshaw, Fla.
Homeland Security—John Carter, Texas
Interior, Environment, and Related Agencies—Ken Calvert, Calif.
Labor, Health and Human Services, Education and Related Agencies—Jack Kingston, Ga.
Legislative Branch—Tom Cole, Okla.
Military Construction, Veterans Affairs, and Related Agencies—John Abney Culberson, Texas

State, Foreign Operations, and Related Agencies—Kay Granger, Texas
Transportation, Housing and Urban Development, and Related Agencies—Tom Latham, Iowa

R 30–D 21 *(114th Congress)*

Harold Rogers, Ky.
Nita Lowey, N.Y.

Agriculture, Rural Development, Food and Drug Administration and Related Agencies—Robert Aderholt, Ala.
Commerce, Justice, Science and Related Agencies—John Culberson, Texas
Defense—Rodney Frelinghuysen, N.J.
Energy and Water Development and Related Agencies—Michael K. Simpson, Idaho
Financial Services and General Government—Ander Crenshaw, Fla.
Homeland Security—John Carter, Texas
Interior, Environment, and Related Agencies—Ken Calvert, Calif.
Labor, Health and Human Services, Education, and Related Agencies—Tom Cole, Okla.
Legislative Branch—Tom Graves, Ga.
Military Construction, Veterans Affairs, and Related Agencies—Charlie Dent, Pa.
State, Foreign Operations, and Related Agencies—Kay Granger, Texas
Transportation, Housing and Urban Development, and Related Agencies—Mario Diaz-Balart, Fla.

ARMED SERVICES

Ammunition depots; forts; arsenals; Army, Navy, and Air Force reservations and establishments; common defense generally; conservation, development, and use of naval petroleum and oil shale reserves; Department of Defense generally, including the Departments of the Army, Navy, and Air Force generally; interoceanic canals generally; including measures relating to the maintenance, operation, and administration of interoceanic canals; Merchant Marine Academy, and state maritime academies; military applications of nuclear energy; tactical intelligence and intelligence related activities of the Department of Defense; national security aspects of merchant marine, including financial assistance for the construction and operation of vessels, the maintenance of the U.S. shipbuilding and ship repair industrial base, cabotage, cargo preference, and merchant marine officers and seamen as these matters relate to the national security; pay, promotion, retirement, and other benefits and privileges of members of the armed forces; scientific research and development in support of the armed services; selective service; size and composition of the Army, Navy, Marine Corps, and Air Force; soldiers' and sailors' homes; strategic and critical materials necessary for the common defense.

R 34–D 27 *(113th Congress)*

Howard P. "Buck" McKeon, Calif.
Adam Smith, Wash.

Tactical Air and Land Forces—Michael Turner, Ohio
Readiness—Rob Wittman, Va.
Emerging Threats and Capabilities—Mac Thornberry, Texas
Military Personnel—Joe Wilson, S.C.
Strategic Forces—Mike Rogers, Ala.
Seapower and Expeditionary Forces—J. Randy Forbes, Va.
Oversight and Investigations—Joe Heck, Nev.

R 36–D 27 *(114th Congress)*

Mack Thornberry, Texas
Adam Smith, Wash.

Tactical Air and Land Forces—Michael Turner, Ohio
Readiness—Rob Wittman, Va.
Emerging Threats and Capabilities—Joe Wilson, S.C.
Military Personnel—Joseph Heck, Nev.
Strategic Forces—Mike Rogers, Ala.
Seapower and Expeditionary Forces—J. Randy Forbes, Va.
Oversight and Investigations—Vicky Hartzler, Miss.

BUDGET

Congressional budget process generally; concurrent budget resolutions; measures relating to special controls over the federal budget; Congressional Budget Office.

R 22–D 15 *(113th Congress)*

Paul Ryan, Wisc.
Chris Van Hollen, Md.

R 22–D 16 *(114th Congress)*

Tom Price, Ga.
Chris Van Hollen, Md.

No standing subcommittees.

EDUCATION AND THE WORKFORCE

Measures relating to education or labor generally; child labor; Columbia Institution for the Deaf, Dumb, and Blind; Howard University; Freedmen's Hospital; convict labor and the entry of goods made by convicts into interstate commerce; food programs for children in schools; labor standards and statistics; mediation and arbitration of labor disputes; regulation or prevention of importation of foreign laborers under contract; U.S. Employees' Compensation Commission; vocational rehabilitation; wages and hours of labor; welfare of miners; work incentive programs.

R 22–D 17 *(113th Congress)*

John Kline, Minn.
George Miller, Calif.

Early Childhood, Elementary and Secondary Education—Todd Rokita, Ind.
Higher Education and Workforce Training—Virginia Foxx, N.C.
Workforce Protections—Tim Walberg, Mich.
Health, Employment, Labor and Pensions—Phil Roe, Tenn.

R 22–D 16 *(114th Congress)*

John Kline, Minn.
Bobby Scott, Calif.

Early Childhood, Elementary and Secondary Education—Todd Rokita, Ind.
Higher Education and Workforce Training—Virginia Foxx, N.C.
Workforce Protections—Tim Walberg, Mich.
Health, Employment, Labor and Pensions—Phil Roe, Tenn.

ENERGY AND COMMERCE

Interstate and foreign commerce generally; biomedical research and development; consumer affairs and consumer protection; health and health facilities, except health care supported by payroll deductions; interstate energy compacts; measures relating to the exploration, production, storage, supply, marketing, pricing, and regulation of energy resources, including all fossil fuels, solar energy, and other unconventional or renewable energy resources; measures relating to the conservation of energy resources; measures relating to energy information generally; measures relating to (1) the generation and marketing of power (except by federally chartered or federal regional power marketing authorities), (2) the reliability and interstate transmission of, and ratemaking for, all power, and (3) the siting of generation facilities, except the installation of interconnections between government water power projects; measures relating to general management of the Department of Energy, and the management and all functions of the Federal Energy Regulatory Commission; national energy policy generally; public health and quarantine; regulation of the domestic nuclear energy industry, including regulation of research and development reactors and nuclear regulatory research; regulation of interstate and foreign communications; travel and tourism; nuclear and other energy.

R 30–D 24 *(113th Congress)*

Fred Upton, Mich.
Henry A. Waxman, Calif.

Digital Commerce and Consumer Protection—Lee Terry, Neb.
Energy and Power—Ed Whitfield, Ky.
Environment—John Shimkus, Ill.
Health—Joseph R. Pitts, Pa.
Oversight and Investigations—Tim Murphy, Pa.
Communications and Technology—Greg Walden, Ore.

R 31–D 23 *(114th Congress)*

Fred Upton, Mich.
Frank Pallone Jr., N.J.

Digital Commerce and Consumer Protection—Michael Burgess, Texas
Energy and Power—Ed Whitfield, Ky.
Environment—John Shimkus, Ill.
Health—Joseph R. Pitts, Pa.
Oversight and Investigations—Tim Murphy, Pa.
Communications and Technology—Greg Walden, Ore.

ETHICS

R 5–D 5 *(113th Congress)*

K. Michael Conaway, Texas
Linda T. Sánchez, Calif.

R 5–D 5 *(114th Congress)*

Charles Dent, Pa.
Linda T. Sánchez, Calif.

No standing subcommittees.

FINANCIAL SERVICES

Banks and banking, including deposit insurance and federal monetary policy; economic stabilization, defense production, renegotiation, and control of the price of commodities, rents, and services; financial aid to commerce and industry (other than transportation); insurance generally; international finance; international financial and monetary organizations; money and credit, including currency and the issuance of notes and redemption thereof; gold and silver, including the coinage thereof; valuation and revaluation of the dollar; public and private housing; securities and exchanges; and urban development.

R 33–D 27 *(113th Congress)*

Jeb Hensarling, Texas
Maxine Waters, Calif.

Capital Markets and Government-Sponsored Enterprises— Scott Garrett, N.J.
Financial Institutions and Consumer Credit—Shelley Moore Capito, W.Va.
Housing and Insurance—Randy Neugebauer, Texas
Monetary Policy and Trade—John Campbell, Calif.
Oversight and Investigations—Patrick McHenry, N.C.

R 34–D 26 *(114th Congress)*

Jeb Hensarling, Texas
Maxine Waters, Calif.

Capital Markets and Government-Sponsored Enterprises— Scott Garrett, N.J.
Financial Institutions and Consumer Credit—Randy Neugebauer, Texas
Housing and Insurance—Blaine Luetkemeyer, Mo.
Monetary Policy and Trade—Bill Huizenga, Mich.
Oversight and Investigations—Sean Duffy, Wisc.
Terrorism and Illicit Finance—Michael G. Fitzpatrick, Pa.

FOREIGN AFFAIRS

Relations of the United States with foreign nations generally; acquisition of land and buildings for embassies and legations in foreign countries; establishment of boundary lines between the United States and foreign nations; export controls, including nonproliferation of nuclear technology and nuclear hardware; foreign loans; international commodity agreements (other than those involving sugar), including all agreements for cooperation in the export of nuclear technology and nuclear hardware; international conferences and congresses; international education; intervention abroad and declarations of war; measures relating to the diplomatic service; measures to foster commercial intercourse with foreign nations and to safeguard American business interests abroad; measures relating to international economic policy; neutrality; protection of American citizens abroad and expatriation; American National Red Cross; trading with the enemy; U.N. organizations.

R 24–D 21 *(112th Congress)*

Edward R. Royce, Calif.
Eliot L. Engel, N.Y.

Africa, Global Health, Global Human Rights, and International Organizations—Chris Smith, N.J.
Asia and the Pacific—Steve Chabot, Ohio
Europe, Eurasia, and Emerging Threats—Dana Rohrabacher, Calif.
The Middle East and North Africa—Ileana Ros-Lehtinen, Fla.
Terrorism, Nonproliferation, and Trade—Ted Poe, Texas
Western Hemisphere—Matt Salmon, Ariz.

R 25–D 19 *(114th Congress)*

Edward R. Royce, Calif.
Eliot L. Engel, N.Y.

Africa, Global Health, Global Human Rights, and International Organizations—Chris Smith, N.J.
Asia and the Pacific—Matt Salmon, Ariz.
Europe, Eurasia, and Emerging Threats—Dana Rohrabacher, Calif.
The Middle East and North Africa—Ileana Ros-Lehtinen, Fla.
Terrorism, Nonproliferation, and Trade—Ted Poe, Texas
Western Hemisphere—Jeff Duncan, S.C.

HOMELAND SECURITY

Overall homeland security policy; organization and administration of the Department of Homeland Security; functions of the Department of Homeland Security; border and port security (except immigration policy and non-border enforcement); customs (except customs revenue); integration, analysis, and dissemination of homeland security information; domestic preparedness for and collective response to terrorism; research and development; transportation security.

R 17–D 14 *(113th Congress)*

Michael McCaul, Texas
Bennie G. Thompson, Miss.

Border and Maritime Security—Candice S. Miller, Mich.
Counterterrorism and Intelligence—Pete King, N.Y.
Cybersecurity and Infrastructure Protection—Patrick Meehan, Pa.

Emergency Preparedness, Response, and Communications— Susan Brooks, Ind.
Oversight and Management Efficiency—Jeff Duncan, S.C.
Transportation Security—Richard Hudson, N.C.

R 18–D 12 *(114th Congress)*

Michael McCaul, Texas
Bennie G. Thompson, Miss.

Border and Maritime Security—Candice S. Miller, Mich.
Counterterrorism and Intelligence—Pete King, N.Y.
Cybersecurity and Infrastructure Protection—John Ratcliffe, Texas
Emergency Preparedness, Response, and Communications— Martha McSally, Ariz.
Oversight and Management Efficiency—Scott Perry, Pa.
Transportation Security—John Katko, N.Y.

HOUSE ADMINISTRATION

Accounts of the House generally; assignment of office space for members and committees; disposition of useless executive papers; matters relating to the election of the president, vice president, or members of Congress; corrupt practices; contested elections; credentials and qualifications; federal elections generally; appropriations from accounts for committee salaries and expenses (except for the Committee on Appropriations), House Information Systems, and allowances and expenses of members, House officers, and administrative offices of the House; auditing and settling of all such accounts; expenditure of such accounts; employment of persons by the House, including clerks for members and committees, and reporters of debates; Library of Congress and the House Library; statuary and pictures; acceptance or purchase of works of art for the Capitol; the Botanic Garden; management of the Library of Congress; purchase of books and manuscripts; Smithsonian Institution and the incorporation of similar institutions; Franking Commission; printing and correction of the *Congressional Record*; services to the House, including the House restaurant, parking facilities, and administration of the House office buildings and of the House wing of the Capitol; travel of members of the House; raising, reporting, and use of campaign contributions for candidates for office of representative in the House of Representatives, of delegate, and of resident commissioner to the United States from Puerto Rico; compensation, retirement and other benefits of the members, officers, and employees of the Congress.

R 6–D 3 *(113th Congress)*

Candice Miller, Mich.
Robert A. Brady, Pa.

R 6–D 3 *(114th Congress)*

Candice Miller, Mich.
Robert A. Brady, Pa.

No standing subcommittees.

JUDICIARY

The judiciary and judicial proceedings, civil and criminal; administrative practice and procedure; apportionment of representatives; bankruptcy, mutiny, espionage, and counterfeiting; civil liberties; constitutional amendments; federal courts and judges, and local courts in the territories and possessions; immigration and naturalization; interstate compacts, generally; measures relating to claims against the United States; meetings of Congress, attendance of members and their acceptance of incompatible offices; national penitentiaries; patents, the Patent Office, copyrights, and trademarks; presidential succession; protection of trade and commerce against unlawful restraints and monopolies; revision and codification of the Statutes of the United States; state and territorial boundaries; subversive activities affecting the internal security of the United States.

R 22–D 17 *(113th Congress)*

Bob Goodlatte, Va.
John Conyers Jr., Mich.

Regulatory Reform, Commercial, and Antitrust Law—Tom Marino, Pa.
Constitution and Civil Justice—Trent Franks, Ariz.
Courts, Intellectual Property, and the Internet—Darrell Issa, Calif.
Crime, Terrorism, Homeland Security, and Investigations— Jim Sensenbrenner, Wisc.
Immigration and Border Security—Trey Gowdy, S.C.

R 23–D 16 *(114th Congress)*

Bob Goodlatte, Va.
John Conyers Jr., Mich.

Regulatory Reform, Commercial, and Antitrust Law—Tom Marino, Pa.
Constitution and Civil Justice—Trent Franks, Ariz.
Courts, Intellectual Property, and the Internet—Darrell Issa, Calif.
Crime, Terrorism, Homeland Security, and Investigations— Jim Sensenbrenner, Wisc.
Immigration and Border Security—Trey Gowdy, S.C.

NATURAL RESOURCES

Public lands generally, including entry, easements, and grazing; mining interests generally; fisheries and wildlife, including research, restoration, refuges, and conservation; forest reserves and national parks created from the public domain; forfeiture of land grants and alien ownership, including alien ownership of mineral lands; Geological Survey; international fishing agreements; interstate compacts relating to apportionment of waters for irrigation purposes; irrigation and reclamation, including water supply for reclamation projects, and easements of public lands for irrigation projects, and acquisition of private lands when necessary to complete irrigation projects; measures relating to the care and management of Indians, including the care and allotment of Native American lands and general and special measures relating to claims that are paid out of Native American funds; measures relating generally to the insular possessions of the United States, except those affecting the revenue and appropriations; military parks and battlefields, national cemeteries administered by the secretary of the interior, parks within the District of Columbia, and the erection of monuments to the memory of individuals; mineral land laws and claims and entries thereunder; mineral resources of the public lands; mining schools and experimental stations; marine affairs (including coastal zone management), except for measures relating to oil and other pollution of navigable waters; oceanography; petroleum conservation on the public lands and conservation of the radium supply in the United States; preservation of prehistoric ruins and objects of interest on the public domain; relations of the United States with the Native Americans and the Native American tribes; disposition of oil transported by the Trans-Alaska Oil Pipeline.

R 26–D 21 (113th Congress)

Doc Hastings, Wash.
Peter DeFazio, Ore.

Federal Lands—Rob Bishop, Utah
Indian, Insular, and Alaska Native Affairs—Don Young, Alaska.
Energy and Mineral Resources—Doug Lamborn, Colo.
Water, Power, and Oceans—John Fleming, La.

R 26–D 18 (114th Congress)

Rob Bishop, Utah
Raúl M. Grijalva, Ariz.

Federal Lands—Tom McClintock, Calif.
Indian, Insular, and Alaska Native Affairs—Don Young, Alaska.
Energy and Mineral Resources—Doug Lamborn, Colo.
Water, Power, and Oceans—John Fleming, La.
Oversight and Investigations—Louie Gohmert, Texas

OVERSIGHT AND GOVERNMENT REFORM

Civil service, including intergovernmental personnel; the status of officers and employees of the United States, including their compensation, classification, and retirement; measures relating to the municipal affairs of the District of Columbia in general, other than appropriations; federal paperwork reduction; budget and accounting measures, generally; holidays and celebrations; overall economy, efficiency, and management of government operations and activities, including federal procurement; National Archives; population and demography generally, including the census; Postal Service generally, including the transportation of mail; public information and records; relationship of the federal government to the states and municipalities generally; reorganizations in the executive branch of the government.

R 23–D 12 (113th Congress)

Darrell Issa, Calif.
Elijah Cummings, Md.

National Security—Jason Chaffetz, Utah
Government Operations—John Mica, Fla.

R 25–D 18 (114th Congress)

Jason Chaffetz, Utah
Elijah J. Cummings, Md.

National Security—Ron DeSantis, Fla.
Government Operations—Mark Meadows, N.C.
Health Care, Benefits, and Administrative Rules—Jim Jordan, Ohio
Information Technology—Will Hurd, Texas
Interior, Energy, & Environment—Cynthia Lummis, Wyo.

RULES

Rules and joint rules (other than rules or joint rules relating to the Code of Official Conduct), and order of business of the House; recesses and final adjournments of Congress.

R 9–D 4 (113th Congress)

Pete Sessions, Texas
Louise M. Slaughter, N.Y.

Legislative and Budget Process—Rob Woodall, Ga.
Rules and Organization of the House—Richard B. Nugent, Fla.

R 9–D 4 (114th Congress)

Pete Sessions, Texas
Louise M. Slaughter, N.Y.

Legislative and Budget Process—Rob Woodall, Ga.
Rules and Organization of the House—Steve Stivers, Ohio

SCIENCE, SPACE, AND TECHNOLOGY

All energy research, development, and demonstration, and projects thereof, and all federally owned or operated nonmilitary energy laboratories; astronautical research and development, including resources, personnel, equipment, and facilities; civil aviation research and development; environmental research and development; marine research; measures relating to the commercial application of energy technology; National Institute of Standards and Technology, standardization of weights and measures and the metric system; National Aeronautics and Space Administration; National Space Council; National Science Foundation; National Weather Service; outer space, including exploration and control thereof; science scholarships; scientific research, development, and demonstration, and projects thereof.

R 21–D 18 (113th Congress)

Lamar Smith, Texas
Eddie Bernice Johnson, Texas

Space—Steven Palazzo, Miss.
Environment—David Schweikert, Ariz.
Energy—Cynthia Lummis, Wyo.
Research and Science Education—Larry Bucshon, Ind.
Oversight—Paul Broun, Ga.

R 21–D 16 *(114th Congress)*

Lamar Smith, Texas
Eddie Bernice Johnson, Texas

Space—Brian Babin, Texas
Environment—Jim Bridenstine, Okla.
Energy—Randy Weber, Texas
Research and Science Education—Barbara Comstock, Va.
Oversight—Barry Loudermilk, Ga.

PERMANENT SELECT INTELLIGENCE

Legislative and budgetary authority over the National Security Agency and the director of central intelligence, the Defense Intelligence Agency, the National Security Agency, intelligence activities of the Federal Bureau of Investigation, and other components of the federal intelligence community.

(Committee did not exist in the 113th Congress)

R 13–D 9 *(114th Congress)*

Devin Nunes, Calif.
Adam Schiff, Calif.

CIA—Frank LoBiondo, N.J.
Department of Defense Intelligence and Overhead Architecture—Joe Heck, Nev.
Emerging Threats—Tom Rooney, Fla.
NSA and Cybersecurity—Lynn Westmoreland, Ga.

SMALL BUSINESS

Assistance to and protection of small business, including financial aid, regulatory flexibility, and paperwork reduction; participation of small business enterprises in federal procurement and government contracts.

R 14–D 11 *(113th Congress)*

Sam Graves, Mo.
Nydia M. Velazquez, N.Y.

Agriculture, Energy and Trade—Scott Tipton, Colo.
Health and Technology—Chris Collins, N.Y.
Economic Growth, Tax and Capital Access—Tom Rice, S.C.
Investigations, Oversight and Regulations—Vacant
Contracting and Workforce—Richard Hanna, N.Y.

R 12–D 10 *(114th Congress)*

Steve Chabot, Ohio
Nydia M. Velazquez, N.Y.

Agriculture, Energy and Trade—Carlos Curbelo, Fla.
Health and Technology—Aumua Amata Coleman Radewagen, Am. Samoa
Economic Growth, Tax and Capital Access—Tim Huelskamp, Kan.
Investigations, Oversight and Regulations—Cresent Hardy, Nev.
Contracting and Workforce—Richard Hanna, N.Y.

TRANSPORTATION AND INFRASTRUCTURE

Transportation, including civil aviation, railroads, water transportation, transportation safety (except automobile safety), transportation infrastructure, transportation labor, and railroad retirement and unemployment (except revenue measures); water power; the Coast Guard; federal management of emergencies and natural disasters; flood control and improvement of waterways; inspection of merchant marine vessels; navigation and related laws; rules and international arrangements to prevent collisions at sea; measures, other than appropriations, that relate to construction, maintenance and safety of roads; buildings and grounds of the Botanic Gardens, the Library of Congress, and the Smithsonian Institution and other government buildings within the District of Columbia; post offices, customhouses, federal courthouses, and merchant marine, except for national security aspects; pollution of navigable waters; and bridges and dams and related transportation regulatory agencies.

R 33–D 27 *(113th Congress)*

Bill Shuster, Pa.
Nick J. Rahall II, W.Va.

Aviation—Frank LoBiondo, N.J.
Coast Guard and Maritime Transportation—Duncan Hunter, Calif.
Economic Development, Public Buildings, and Emergency Management—Lou Barletta, Pa.
Highways and Transit—Tom Petri, Wisc.
Railroads, Pipelines, and Hazardous Materials—Jeff Denham, Calif.
Water Resources and Environment—Bob Gibbs, Ohio

R 34–D 25 *(114th Congress)*

Bill Shuster, Pa.
Peter A. DeFazio, Ore.

Aviation—Frank LoBiondo, N.J.
Coast Guard and Maritime Transportation—Duncan Hunter, Calif.
Economic Development, Public Buildings, and Emergency Management—Lou Barletta, Pa.
Highways and Transit—Sam Graves, Mo.
Railroads, Pipelines, and Hazardous Materials—Jeff Denham, Calif.
Water Resources and Environment—Bob Gibbs, Ohio

VETERANS' AFFAIRS

Veterans' measures generally; cemeteries of the United States in which veterans of any war or conflict are or may be buried, whether in the United States or abroad, except cemeteries administered by the secretary of the Interior; compensation, vocational rehabilitation, and education of veterans; life insurance issued by the government on account of service in the armed forces; pensions of all the wars of the United States, readjustment of service personnel to civil life; soldiers' and sailors' civil relief; veterans' hospitals, medical care, and treatment of veterans.

R 14–D 11 *(113th Congress)*

Jeff Miller, Fla.
Michael H. Michaud, Maine

Disability Benefits and Memorial Affairs—Jon Runyan, N.J.
Economic Opportunity—Bill Flores, Texas
Health—Dan Benishek, Mich.
Oversight and Investigations—Mike Coffman, Colo.

R 14–D 10 *(114th Congress)*

Jeff Miller, Fla.
Corrine Brown, Fla.

Disability Benefits and Memorial Affairs—Ralph Abraham, La.
Economic Opportunity—Brad Wenstrup, Ohio
Health—Dan Benishek, Mich.
Oversight and Investigations—Mike Coffman, Colo.

WAYS AND MEANS

Revenue measures generally; reciprocal trade agreements; customs, collection districts, and ports of entry and delivery; revenue measures relating to the insular possessions; bonded debt of the United States; deposit of public moneys; transportation of dutiable goods; tax-exempt foundations and charitable trusts; national Social Security, except (1) health care and facilities programs that are supported from general revenues as opposed to payroll deductions and (2) work incentive programs.

R 23–D 16 *(113th Congress)*

Dave Camp, Mich.
Sander M. Levin, Mich.

Trade—Devin Nunes, Calif.
Oversight—Charles Boustany, La.
Health—Kevin Brady, Texas
Human Resources—Dave Reichert, Wash.
Tax Policy—Pat Tiberi, Ohio
Social Security—Sam Johnson, Texas

R 24–D 15 *(114th Congress)*

Kevin Brady, Texas
Sander M. Levin, Mich.

Trade—Devin Nunes, Calif.
Oversight—Peter Roskam, Ill.
Health—Pat Tiberi, Ohio
Human Resources—Vern Buchanan, Fla.
Tax Policy—Charles Boustany Jr., La.
Social Security—Sam Johnson, Texas

Joint Committees

Joint committees are set up to examine specific questions and are established by public law. Membership is drawn from both chambers and both parties. When a senator serves as chairman, the vice chairman usually is a representative, and vice versa. The chairmanship traditionally rotates from one chamber to the other at the beginning of each Congress. However, the Committee on Taxation chairmanship rotates at the start of each session with the House having the chair in the first session and the Senate in the second session. In the alternate sessions the House and Senate members have the vice chair.

ECONOMIC

Studies and investigates all recommendations in the president's annual Economic Report to Congress. Reports findings and recommendations to the House and Senate.

Rep. Kevin Brady, R-Texas, Chair (113th Congress)

Sen. Amy Klobuchar, D-Minn., Vice Chair (113th Congress)

Sen. Dan Coats, R-Ind., Chair (114th Congress)

Rep. Carolyn Maloney, D-N.Y., Vice Chair (114th Congress)

LIBRARY

Management and expansion of the Library of Congress; receipt of gifts for the benefit of the library; development and maintenance of the Botanic Garden; placement of statues and other works of art in the Capitol.

Vacant, Chair (113th Congress)

Sen. Charles E. Schumer, D-N.Y., Vice Chair (113th Congress)

Sen. Roy Blunt, R-Mo., Chair (114th Congress)

Rep. Gregg Harper, R-Miss., Vice Chair (114th Congress)

PRINTING

Probes inefficiency and waste in the printing, binding, and distribution of federal government publications. Oversees arrangement and style of the *Congressional Record*.

Sen. Charles E. Schumer, D-N.Y., Chair (113th Congress)

Vacant, Vice Chair (113th Congress)

Rep. Gregg Harper, R-Miss., Chair (114th Congress)

Sen. Roy Blunt, R-Mo., Vice Chair (114th Congress)

TAXATION

Operation, effects, and administration of the federal system of internal revenue taxes; measures and methods for simplification of taxation.

Vacant, Chair (113th Congress)

Rep. Dave Camp, R-Mich., Vice Chair (113th Congress)

Sen. Orrin Hatch, R-Utah, Chair (114th Congress)

Rep. Kevin Brady, R-Wisc., Vice Chair (114th Congress)

Postelection Sessions

A postelection session of Congress often is labeled a lame duck session. It takes place after an election for the next Congress but before the official end of the current Congress. As a result, members who participate in the lame duck session are from the existing, or current, Congress, not from the Congress that will convene as a result of the just-held elections.

Lame duck sessions in the modern sense began in 1935 after the Twentieth Amendment to the Constitution was ratified in 1933. This amendment specified that regular congressional sessions would begin on January 3 of each year unless Congress passed a law designating a different date. Also, terms of members of Congress begin and end on January 3 of odd-numbered years, regardless of the date that a Congress officially ends its session. Originally, the Constitution specified much later starting dates in recognition of the difficulty of travel in the early years of the nation, but those dates meant that lame duck sessions occurred in the second session of every Congress. In the modern sense, post-1935, a lame duck session is any meeting of Congress after election day in even-numbered years but before the following January 3.

Between 1935 and 2017, Congress held twenty-one lame-duck sessions.

1941. The 76th Congress actually had adjourned in 1939 but President Franklin D. Roosevelt called the legislators into special session—technically, the third session of that Congress—to deal with the threat of war in Europe. However, little of substance was accomplished during the lame duck session.

1942. By this year, the United States was at war with Germany, Japan, and Italy but little was done during the period as legislators decided to leave many major decisions to the next Congress. Congress did approve bills on overtime pay for government workers and to provide for the military draft of eighteen- and nineteen-year-old men.

1944. World War II was well along by this time, which meant Congress faced a host of exceptionally important issues including postwar universal military training, continuing the war effort, Social Security taxes, a rivers and harbors bill, and various postwar reconstruction matters. But, like the previous several lame duck sessions, legislators decided to postpone most actions until the new Congress convened in 1945.

1948. The 1948 postelection session of the 80th Congress lasted only two hours. Both chambers swore in new members, approved several minor resolutions, and received last-minute reports from committees. In addition to final floor action, several committees resumed work. The most active was the House Un-American Activities Committee, which continued its investigation of alleged communist espionage in the federal government.

1950. After the 1950 elections, President Harry S. Truman sent a "must" agenda to the lame duck session of the 81st Congress. The president's list included supplemental defense appropriations, an excess profits tax, aid to Yugoslavia, a three-month extension of federal rent controls, and statehood for Hawaii and Alaska. During a marathon session that lasted until only a few hours before its successor took over, the 81st Congress acted on all of the president's legislative items except the statehood bills, which were blocked by a Senate filibuster.

1954. Only one chamber of the 83rd Congress convened after the 1954 elections. The Senate returned November 8 to hold what has been called a "censure session," a continuing investigation

Congressional Lame Duck Sessions

Year	Congress	Dates
1941	76th	Adjourned January 3, 1941*
1942	77th	Adjourned December 16, 1942*
1944	78th	November 14, 1944–December 19, 1944
1948	80th	December 31, 1948 (two-hour session)
1950	81st	November 27, 1950–January 2, 1951
1954	83rd	November 8, 1954–December 2, 1954
1970	91st	November 16, 1970–January 2, 1971 (Senate)
1974	93rd	November 18, 1974–December 20, 1974
1980	96th	November 12, 1980–December 16, 1980
1982	97th	November 29, 1982–December 23, 1982 (Senate)
		November 29, 1982–December 21, 1982 (House)
1994	103rd	November 29, 1994 (House)
		November 30, 1994–December 1, 1994 (Senate)
1998	105th	December 17, 1998–December 19, 1998 (House)
2000	106th	November 13, 2000–December 15, 2000 (House)
		November 14, 2000–December 15, 2000
2002	107th	Adjourned November 20, 2002 (Senate)*
		Adjourned November 22, 2002 (House)*
2004	108th	November 16, 2004–December 7, 2004 (House)
		November 16, 2004–December 8, 2004 (Senate)
2006	109th	November 13, 2006–December 8, 2006 (House)
		November 13, 2006–December 8, 2006 (Senate)
2008	110th	November 19, 2008–December 10, 2008 (House)
		November 17, 2008–December 11, 2008 (Senate)
2010	111th	November 15, 2010–December 22, 2010 (House)
		November 15, 2010–December 22, 2010 (Senate)
2012	112th	November 13, 2012–January 3, 2013 (House)
		November 13, 2012–January 2, 2013 (Senate)**
2014	113th	November 12, 2014–January 2, 2015 (House)
		November 12, 2014–December 16, 2014 (Senate)
2016	114th	November 14, 2016–January 2, 2017

* Congress stayed in session.

** The Senate did not adjourn *sine die*.

into the conduct of Sen. Joseph R. McCarthy, R-Wisc. (1947–1957). By a 67–22 roll call, the Senate on December 2 voted to "condemn" McCarthy for his behavior. In other postelection floor action, the Senate passed a series of miscellaneous and administrative resolutions and swore in new members.

1970. President Richard Nixon criticized the lame duck Congress as one that had "seemingly lost the capacity to decide and the will to act." Filibusters and intense controversy contributed to inaction on the president's request for trade legislation and welfare reform. Congress nevertheless claimed some substantive results during the session, which ended January 2, 1971. Several major appropriations bills were cleared for presidential signature. Congress also approved foreign aid to Cambodia, provided interim funding for the supersonic transport (SST) plane, and repealed the Tonkin Gulf Resolution that had been used as a basis for American military involvement in Vietnam.

1974. In a session that ran from November 18 to December 20, 1974, the 93rd Congress cleared several important bills for presidential signature, including a mass transit bill, a Labor–Health, Education and Welfare appropriations bill, and a foreign assistance package. A House–Senate conference committee reached agreement on a major strip-mining bill, but President Gerald R. Ford vetoed it. Congress approved the nomination of Nelson A. Rockefeller as vice president. It also overrode presidential vetoes of two bills: one broadening the Freedom of

Information Act, a second authorizing educational benefits for Korean War– and Vietnam-era veterans.

1980. The lame duck session of the 96th Congress was productive, at least until December 5, the original adjournment date set by congressional leaders. By that date, a budget had been approved, along with a budget reconciliation measure. Ten regular appropriations bills had cleared, though one subsequently was vetoed. Congress had approved two major environmental measures—an Alaskan lands bill and toxic waste "superfund" legislation—as well as a three-year extension of general revenue sharing.

After December 5, however, the legislative pace slowed noticeably. Action on a continuing appropriations resolution for those departments and agencies whose regular funding had not been cleared was delayed, first by a filibuster on a fair housing bill and later by more than 100 "Christmas tree" amendments, including a $10,000-a-year pay raise for members. After the conference report failed in the Senate and twice was rewritten, the bill was shorn of virtually all its "ornaments" and finally cleared by both chambers on December 16.

1982. Despite the reluctance of congressional leaders, President Ronald Reagan urged the convening of a postelection session at the end of the 97th Congress, principally to pass remaining appropriations bills. Rising unemployment—and Democratic election gains in the House—made job-creation efforts the focus of the lame duck Congress, however. Overriding the objections of Republican conservatives, Congress passed Reagan-backed legislation raising the federal gasoline tax from 4 cents to 9 cents a gallon to pay for highway repairs and mass transit. Supporters said the legislation would help alleviate unemployment by creating 300,000 jobs.

Congress eventually cleared four additional appropriations bills, packaging the remaining six in a continuing appropriations resolution that also included a pay raise for House members. Conferees dropped funding for emergency jobs programs to avert a threatened veto of the resolution. The lame duck session also was highlighted by Congress's refusal to fund production and procurement of the first five MX intercontinental missiles. This was the first time in recent history that either house of Congress had denied a president's request to fund production of a strategic weapon.

1994. Congress reconvened to reconsider, and ultimately approve, the Uruguay Round pact strengthening the General Agreement on Tariffs and Trade (GATT). The bill had been submitted September 27, 1994, by President Bill Clinton under fast-track rules for trade legislation, which allowed each chamber only an up-or-down vote on the bill without amendments. But the rules also allowed every chairman with jurisdiction to take up to forty-five days to review the bill. Sen. Ernest F. Hollings, D-S.C., demanded his forty-five days, forcing the Senate leadership to schedule a two-day lame duck session. Clinton asked the House to approve the bill before the October adjournment, but the Democratic leadership delayed consideration. The House reconvened for a one-day session November 29 and passed the GATT bill by a wide margin. Following a twenty-hour debate November 30 and December 1, the Senate gave overwhelming approval to the bill.

1998. The House reconvened in December for a remarkable and historic event: to vote on the impeachment of a president. After a tumultuous political year, House Republicans pushed through articles of impeachment for what they believed was President Clinton's lying under oath. The event was characterized by a year-long political chasm between House Republicans, who led the effort for impeachment, and Democrats in both chambers. It also was characterized by charges of sexual misconduct involving Clinton and release of a controversial and in places graphic report about sexual conduct of the president that Republicans defended as necessary to prove their case. The report was prepared by an independent prosecutor. In the short time the House was in session, it voted—largely along party lines—in favor of impeachment charges, which would be tried and rejected by the Senate early in the following year.

2000. Congress returned after the 2000 elections largely to complete action on appropriations measures that had remained unfinished as President Clinton continued to wrestle with his Republican adversaries in Congress over spending priorities. Partisan fighting over spending and taxes had been one of the principal matters that divided the White House and Capitol Hill during the latter years of Clinton's presidency. The year 2000 was no exception, as Congress was unable to avert its annual pileup of appropriations bills at the end of the session. The pileup was exacerbated in 2000 because of the controversial presidential elections that were not decided until a Supreme Court decision in December awarding contested Florida electoral votes to Republican George W. Bush. With the GOP about to reclaim the White House, party members in Congress suddenly had new leverage in the final bargaining over appropriations. The lame duck session lumbered into mid-December when an omnibus package was used to close the books on four spending bills and move other unrelated legislation.

2004. Congress came back after Republicans scored impressive gains in the fall elections that returned Bush to the White House and increased GOP control of both chambers of Congress. The additional votes meant the GOP was strongly positioned to push Bush's legislative program in the 109th Congress. But before they could get there, important legislative matters remained for the 108th Congress. The most important was a sweeping overhaul of the U.S. intelligence community, Congress's last major act of the year. It came only at the prodding of the independent, bipartisan National Commission on Terrorist Attacks Upon the United States—better known as the 9/11 Commission—and the powerful lobbying of some of the victims' families of those attacks. In addition, all but four of the appropriations bills had been left hanging when Congress went out of the elections break. Congress bundled the other nine into an omnibus bill during the lame duck session and cleared it on November 20.

2006. Legislators returned after the 2006 midterm elections to a wholly new playing field, because Democrats had recaptured control of both chambers, although the Senate by only a one-vote margin. The principal agenda for the postelection session was completion of appropriations bills, only two of which (defense and homeland security) had been completed. A continuing resolution keeping the government operating was set to expire November 17. Dealing with several expiring tax benefits also was on the list of actions needed. But much of the plan never got going, as Democrats decided to fund the government until February 15, 2007, through additional continuing resolutions, thereby leaving all the other regular appropriation bills to die. But some work was done. A package of tax benefits was completed in connection with a trade package. Perhaps most significantly, Congress approved a bill allowing President Bush to negotiate a nuclear power agreement with India, one of the president's most significant foreign policy accomplishments. The Senate also confirmed Robert M. Gates as defense secretary to replace Donald Rumsfeld.

2008. The main focus of attention in the postelection session was the continuing financial crisis in the United States and worldwide, but the elections, like those two years earlier, had put a new cast on events. In the elections, Democrats had improved their margin in the House and significantly increased it in the Senate and had won the presidential contest when Barack Obama defeated John McCain by a comfortable 53–47 percentage margin. This meant that governmental activity to stave off an economic collapse that many economists thought would rival the Great Depression of the 1930s was left to coordination of action between the outgoing Bush administration and the new Obama administration. Congress, which had passed a $700 billion package of aid for the financial services industry before the election, was left with little to do. One major effort failed: with the nation's three principal auto manufacturers facing bankruptcy, Congress considered providing $14 billion in loans to the companies from an existing program. The House passed the bill, but the Senate did not go along. As a result, Bush later provided $13.4 billion in loans to the automakers from the funds previously approved to save the financial services industry.

2010. The 111th Congress turned out to be one of the odder two-year periods because of the amount of significant and highly controversial legislation that became law. Earlier in the year, Democrats forced through a far-reaching health care reform bill; later in the summer, they passed a financial regulation overhaul that grew from the vast economic collapse that started in 2008. These actions alone would have made the 111th Congress exceptionally notable and hardly required a lame duck session.

But one was to occur anyway, and it too turned out to be significant. The postelection session was unusual because it came after an election in which Democrats, previously riding high with their successes, took a beating when Republicans surged back to recapture the House majority. Even President Obama acknowledged his party had taken a "shellacking" in the election. Although little was expected in the session after the voting, Congress extended income and estate taxes, approved a conditional repeal of the ban on gays in the military, and approved ratification of a nuclear arms treaty with Russia. The tax legislation also included a year-long extension of extra benefits for long-term unemployed persons. Congress also approved a food safety bill and worked out funding to keep the government operating into 2012.

2012. For the eighth time in a row, going back to the 105th Congress in 1998, legislators in 2012 returned after the national elections—in which the political divisions in Washington were largely repeated—to deal with tangled issues that the divisions had blocked from resolution before the voting took place. But unlike the lame duck session two years earlier, only the most pressing issues were addressed, and then only—as many observers noted—by kicking cans down the road.

The issues, mainly taxes and spending, were so intractable that the 112th Congress went past New Year's Eve right up to the January 3 deadline, when the Constitution decreed it had to end. It was the first time in forty-two years that Congress slid past the turn of the calendar and evening celebrations.

In fact, there was little to celebrate in legislative terms. The legislators struck a deal on the looming deadline that had come to be called the fiscal cliff, which at the end of 2012 would have sent tax rates for all Americans back to levels last seen more than a decade earlier. The "cliff" described not only the expiration of an array of earlier tax cuts that were put in place as temporary but also an existing law that would force across-the-board spending cuts of some $109 billion, starting January 2, 2013.

The deal that emerged permanently extended the existing reduced tax rates for most taxpayers while allowing rates on higher earners (above $400,000 for individuals and $450,000 for couples) to rise. A long-standing fight over federal estate taxes was settled, and a permanent "patch" was included for the alternative minimum tax to limit that levy from reaching into middle-class incomes. The bill also extended long-term unemployment benefits for another year.

On the other hand, the across-the-board cuts, known as a sequester, were only delayed until March 1, 2013. Backers of the extension said it would give Congress time to work out a compromise. But Congress did not, and the forced cuts began then.

The 112th Congress did end, with the House adjourning a few minutes before the required session's end and the Senate merely allowing the clock to run out. Traditionally, at the end of a Congress, leaders make a ceremonial telephone call to the president and then hold news conferences about their accomplishments. None of that occurred for the 112th.

2014. The 113th Congress returned after the midterm elections to finalize a cromnibus spending bill, which combined omnibus appropriations for most agencies with a short-term continuing resolution for the Department of Homeland Security. The legislation, which passed the House narrowly before being cleared by the Senate, included a number of controversial measures such as a ban on funding to implement a referendum decriminalizing marijuana in the District of Columbia. It also extended the moratorium on state and local internet access taxes until October 1, 2015.

In addition, lawmakers also scaled back some financial regulations in the Dodd-Frank Act, and they agreed to a one-year extension of popular tax credits. They also gave overwhelming bipartisan approval to a fiscal 2015 defense authorization bill.

Lawmakers debated but failed to pass several politically contentious proposals. These included bills that would have granted the president fast-track trade authority and that would have approved the Keystone XL pipeline.

2016. With Republicans poised for control of both the White House and Congress after the 2016 elections, lawmakers returned to town to wrap up business on several significant pieces of legislation. They agreed to a continuing resolution to extend fiscal 2017 funding through April 28, 2017. The legislation included provisions to address the drinking water in Flint, Michigan, which contained high amounts of lead.

Lawmakers passed the 21st Century Cures Act, authorizing funding for medical research and an accelerated review process for new drugs and medical devices. They also overwhelmingly passed a fiscal 2017 defense authorization bill, and they voted for legislation, which Obama allowed to become law without his signature, that extended sanctions on Iran.

Senate Cloture Votes, 1917–2016

The filibuster, identified by the public primarily as nonstop speech, has been an enshrined Senate tradition throughout the chamber's history but became a focus of increasing criticism in the twentieth century as a device to thwart majority decisions. It was not until 1917 that the Senate adopted a rule, known as cloture, that allowed a majority—albeit a supermajority—to end a filibuster and bring a measure to a vote. The number of votes required to invoke cloture has varied over the years, standing at sixty in 2012 if there are no Senate vacancies. (The actual rules required a three-fifths majority of members to invoke cloture; the Senate has 100 members.)

Even with the rule in place, however, the number of filibusters and attempts to invoke cloture were limited until the 92nd Congress in 1971–1973. From that time on, and especially after 2000, cloture attempts expanded greatly as the character of the Senate changed from what one scholar called "communitarian" and deliberative to individualistic, increasingly partisan, and media driven. This pattern was seen during the 1990s also. In both decades, deep-seated partisan divisions in Congress led both parties to try whatever tools worked to block the initiatives or judicial or executive appointments of the other.

In the ten Congresses during the twenty years from 1971 to 1991, cloture was attempted no fewer than thirteen times in each two-year period, and on the average twenty-five times each Congress. As dramatic as that growth was, it paled against the expansion in the following eleven Congresses from 1991 through 2012. During those eleven Congresses from the 102nd through the 112th, cloture votes were taken an average of nearly sixty-three times for each two-year period.

During this two-decade period, cloture was typically used more for political and legislative maneuvering than to consider far-reaching national issues. For example, senators might start or threaten a filibuster to gain leverage for a matter completely unrelated to the legislation before the Senate. In one instance during President Barack Obama's first term, his nomination to head a new consumer protection bureau was blocked by a filibuster even though most senators agreed the nominee was qualified. The opposition to him centered, rather, on Republican demands that the bureau as enacted in a previous Congress be restricted in ways that reflected their unhappiness with the agency's powers.

The filibuster also was used increasingly in this period to thwart the choices of both Republican and Democratic presidents for positions in the federal judiciary, as each party saw control of the courts as core, nonnegotiable interests of their political bases.

CHANGES IN THE RULE

The Senate's ultimate check on the filibuster is the provision for cloture, or limitation of debate, contained in Rule 22 of its Standing Rules. The original Rule 22 was adopted in 1917 following a furor over the "talking to death" of a proposal by President Woodrow Wilson for arming American merchant ships before the United States entered World War I. The new cloture rule required the votes of two-thirds of all the senators present and voting to invoke cloture. In 1949, during a parliamentary skirmish preceding scheduled consideration of a Fair Employment Practices Commission bill, the requirement was raised to two-thirds of the entire Senate membership.

A revision of the rule in 1959 provided for limitation of debate by a vote of two-thirds of the senators present and voting, two days after a cloture petition was submitted by sixteen senators. If cloture was adopted by the Senate, further debate was limited to one hour for each senator on the bill itself and on all amendments affecting it. No new amendments could be offered except by unanimous consent. Amendments that were not germane to the pending business and dilatory motions were out of order. The rule applied both to regular legislation and to motions to change the Standing Rules.

Rule 22 was revised significantly in 1975 by lowering the vote needed for cloture to three-fifths of the Senate membership (sixty if there were no vacancies). That revision applied to any matter except proposed rules changes, for which the old requirement of a two-thirds majority of senators present and voting still applied.

In a further revision of the rule, the Senate in 1979 limited postcloture delaying tactics by providing that once cloture was invoked, a final vote had to be taken after no more than 100 hours of debate. All time spent on quorum calls, roll-call votes, and other parliamentary procedures was to be included in the 100-hour limit.

When the Senate decided to televise its floor proceedings in 1986, it further tightened up the time on postcloture debate. Rule 22 was revised to reduce to 30 hours, from 100, the time allowed for debate, procedural moves and roll-call votes after the Senate had invoked cloture to end a filibuster.

Following is a list of the 1,386 cloture votes taken between 1917, when Senate Rule 22 was adopted, and the end of 2016. Those in **bold type**, 676, were successful; 710 votes, 51.2 percent, were not.

Cloture Votes between 2013–2016

Issue	Date	Vote	Yeas needed
Versailles Treaty	November 15, 1919	78–16	63
Emergency tariff	February 2, 1921	36–35	48
Tariff bill	July 7, 1922	45–35	54
World Court	January 25, 1926	68–26	63
Migratory birds	June 1, 1926	46–33	53
Branch banking	February 15, 1927	65–18	56
Colorado River	February 26, 1927	32–59	61
Disabled officers	February 26, 1927	51–36	58
D.C. buildings	February 28, 1927	52–31	56

Issue	Date	Vote	Yeas needed
Prohibition Bureau	February 28, 1927	55–27	55
Banking Act	January 19, 1933	58–30	59
Anti-lynching	January 27, 1938	37–51	59
Anti-lynching	February 16, 1938	42–46	59
Anti-poll tax	November 23, 1942	37–41	52
Anti-poll tax	May 15, 1944	36–44	54
Fair Employment Practices Commission	February 9, 1946	48–36	56
British loan	May 7, 1946	41–41	55

Issue	Date	Vote	Yeas needed	Issue	Date	Vote	Yeas needed
Labor disputes	May 25, 1946	63–77	54	**Government pay raise**	March 6, 1974	67–31	66
Anti-poll tax	July 31, 1946	39–33	48	Public campaign financing	April 4, 1974	60–36	64
Fair Employment	May 19, 1950	52–32	64	**Public campaign financing**	April 9, 1974	64–30	63
Fair Employment	July 12, 1950	55–33	64	Public debt ceiling	June 19, 1974	45–48	62
Atomic energy Act	July 26, 1954	44–42	64	Public debt ceiling	June 19, 1974	50–43	62
Civil Rights Act	March 10, 1960	42–53	64	Public debt ceiling	June 26, 1974	48–50	66
Amend Rule 22	September 19, 1961	37–43	54	Consumer Agency	July 30, 1974	56–42	66
Literacy tests	May 9, 1962	43–53	64	Consumer Agency	August 1, 1974	59–39	66
Literacy tests	May 14, 1962	42–52	63	Consumer Agency	August 20, 1974	59–35	63
Comsat Act	August 14, 1962	63–27	60	Consumer Agency	September 19, 1974	64–34	66
Amend Rule 22	February 7, 1963	54–42	64	Export-Import Bank	December 3, 1974	51–39	60
Civil Rights Act	June 10, 1964	71–29	67	Export-Import Bank	December 4, 1974	48–44	62
Legislative reapportionment	September 10, 1964	30–63	62	**Trade reform**	December 13, 1974	71–19	60
Voting Rights Act	May 25, 1965	70–30	67	Export-Import Bank	December 14, 1974	49–35	56
Right-to-work repeal	October 11, 1965	45–47	62	**Fiscal 1975 supplemental funds**	December 14, 1974	56–27	56
Right-to-work repeal	February 8, 1966	51–48	66	Export-Import Bank	December 16, 1974	54–34	59
Right-to-work repeal	February 10, 1966	50–49	66	**Tax law changes**	December 17, 1974	67–25	62
Civil Rights Act	September 14, 1966	54–42	64	**Social services programs**	December 17, 1974	70–23	62
Civil Rights Act	September 19, 1966	52–41	62	**Rail Reorganization Act**	February 26, 1975	86–8	63
D.C. Home Rule	October 10, 1966	41–37	52	**Amend Rule 22**	March 5, 1975	73–21	63
Amend Rule 22	January 24, 1967	53–46	66	**Amend Rule 22**	March 7, 1975	73–21	63
Open Housing	February 20, 1968	55–37	62	Tax reduction	March 20, 1975	59–38	60
Open Housing	February 26, 1968	56–36	62	**Tax reduction**	March 21, 1975	83–13	60
Open Housing	March 1, 1968	59–35	63	**Consumer Advocacy Agency**	May 13, 1975	71–27	60
Open Housing	March 4, 1968	65–32	65	**Senate staffing**	June 11, 1975	77–19	64
Fortas nomination	October 1, 1968	45–43	59	New Hampshire Senate seat	June 24, 1975	57–39	60
Amend Rule 22	January 16, 1969	51–47	66	New Hampshire Senate seat	June 25, 1975	56–41	60
Amend Rule 22	January 28, 1969	50–42	62	New Hampshire Senate seat	June 26, 1975	54–40	60
Electoral College	September 17, 1970	54–36	60	New Hampshire Senate seat	July 8, 1975	57–38	60
Electoral College	September 29, 1970	53–34	58	New Hampshire Senate seat	July 9, 1975	57–38	60
Supersonic transport	December 19, 1970	43–48	61	New Hampshire Senate seat	July 10, 1975	54–38	60
Supersonic transport	December 22, 1970	42–44	58	**Voting Rights Act**	July 21, 1975	72–19	60
Amend Rule 22	February 18, 1971	48–37	57	**Voting Rights Act**	July 23, 1975	76–20	60
Amend Rule 22	February 23, 1971	50–36	58	Oil price decontrol	July 30, 1975	54–38	60
Amend Rule 22	March 2, 1971	48–36	56	Anti-school busing amendments	September 23, 1975	46–48	60
Amend Rule 22	March 9, 1971	55–39	63	**Anti-school busing amendments**	September 24, 1975	64–33	60
Military Draft	June 23, 1971	65–27	62	**Common-site picketing**	November 11, 1975	66–30	60
Lockheed loan	July 26, 1971	42–47	60	Common-site picketing	November 14, 1975	58–31	60
Lockheed loan	July 28, 1971	59–39	66	**Common-site picketing**	November 18, 1975	62–37	60
Lockheed loan	July 30, 1971	53–37	60	**Rail reorganization**	December 4, 1975	61–27	60
Military Draft	September 21, 1971	61–30	61	**New York City aid**	December 5, 1975	70–27	60
Rehnquist nomination	December 10, 1971	52–42	63	**Rice Production Act**	February 3, 1976	70–19	60
Equal job opportunity	February 1, 1972	48–37	57	**Antitrust amendments**	June 3, 1976	67–22	60
Equal job opportunity	February 3, 1972	53–35	59	**Antitrust amendments**	August 31, 1976	63–27	60
Equal job opportunity	February 22, 1972	71–23	63	**Civil rights attorneys' fees**	September 23, 1976	63–26	60
U.S.–Soviet arms pact	September 14, 1972	76–15	61	Draft resisters pardons	January 24, 1977	53–43	60
Consumer Agency	September 29, 1972	47–29	51	Campaign financing	July 29, 1977	49–45	60
Consumer Agency	October 3, 1972	55–32	58	Campaign financing	August 1, 1977	47–46	60
Consumer Agency	October 5, 1972	52–30	55	Campaign financing	August 2, 1977	52–46	60
School busing	October 10, 1972	45–37	55	**Natural gas pricing**	September 26, 1977	77–17	60
School busing	October 11, 1972	49–39	59	Labor Law revision	June 7, 1978	42–47	60
School busing	October 12, 1972	49–38	58	Labor Law revision	June 8, 1978	49–41	60
Voter registration	April 30, 1973	56–31	58	Labor Law revision	June 13, 1978	54–43	60
Voter registration	May 3, 1973	60–34	63	Labor Law revision	June 14, 1978	58–41	60
Voter registration	May 9, 1973	67–32	66	Labor Law revision	June 15, 1978	58–39	60
Public campaign financing	December 2, 1973	47–33	54	Labor Law revision	June 22, 1978	53–45	60
Public campaign financing	December 3, 1973	49–39	59	**Revenue Act of 1978**	October 9, 1978	62–28	60
Rhodesian chrome ore	December 11, 1973	59–35	63	**Energy taxes**	October 14, 1978	71–13	60
Legal services program	December 13, 1973	60–36	64	Windfall profits tax	December 12, 1979	53–46	60
Rhodesian chrome ore	December 13, 1973	62–33	64	Windfall profits tax	December 13, 1979	56–40	60
Legal services program	December 14, 1973	56–29	57	Windfall profits tax	December 14, 1979	56–39	60
Rhodesian chrome ore	December 18, 1973	63–26	60	**Windfall profits tax**	December 17, 1979	84–14	60
Legal services program	January 30, 1974	68–29	65	Lubbers nomination	April 21, 1980	46–60	60
Genocide Treaty	February 5, 1974	55–36	61	**Lubbers nomination**	April 22, 1980	62–34	60
Genocide Treaty	February 6, 1974	55–38	62	Rights of institutionalized	April 28, 1980	44–39	60

Issue	Date	Vote	Yeas needed	Issue	Date	Vote	Yeas needed
Rights of institutionalized	April 29, 1980	56–34	60	Broadcasting of Senate proceedings	September 21, 1984	37–44	60
Rights of institutionalized	April 30, 1980	53–35	60	**Surface Transportation Act**	September 24, 1984	70–12	60
Rights of institutionalized	May 1, 1980	60–34	60	**Continuing funds**	September 29, 1984	92–4	60
Bottlers' antitrust immunity	May 15, 1980	86–6	60	**Anti-apartheid**	July 10, 1985	88–8	60
Draft registration funding	June 10, 1980	62–32	60	Line-item veto	July 18, 1985	57–42	60
Zimmerman nomination	August 1, 1980	51–35	60	Line-item veto	July 23, 1985	57–41	60
Zimmerman nomination	August 4, 1980	45–31	60	Line-item veto	July 24, 1985	58–40	60
Zimmerman nomination	August 5, 1980	63–31	60	Anti-apartheid	September 9, 1985	53–34	60
Alaska lands	August 18, 1980	63–25	60	Anti-apartheid	September 11, 1985	57–41	60
Vessel tonnage/strip mining	August 21, 1980	61–32	60	Anti-apartheid	September 12, 1985	11–88	60
Fair Housing amendments	December 3, 1980	51–39	60	Debt limit/balanced budget	October 6, 1985	57–38	64
Fair Housing amendments	December 4, 1980	62–32	60	Debt limit/balanced budget	October 9, 1985 [1]	53–39	62
Fair Housing amendments	December 9, 1980	54–43	60	**Conrail sale**	January 23, 1986	90–7	60
Breyer nomination	December 9, 1980	68–28	60	**Conrail sale**	January 30, 1986	70–27	60
Justice Department authorization	July 10, 1981	38–48	60	**Fitzwater nomination**	March 18, 1986	64–33	60
Justice Department authorization	July 13, 1981	54–32	60	Washington airports transfer	March 21, 1986	50–39	60
Justice Department authorization	July 29, 1981	59–37	60	**Washington airports transfer**	March 25, 1986	66–32	60
Justice Department authorization	September 10, 1981	57–33	60	Hobbs Act amendments	April 16, 1986	44–54	60
Justice Department authorization	September 16, 1981	61–36	60	Defense authorization, fiscal 1987	August 6, 1986	53–46	60
Justice Department authorization	December 10, 1981	64–35	60	Aid to Nicaraguan contras	August 13, 1986	59–40	60
State, Justice, Commerce, Judiciary funds	December 11, 1981	59–35	60	**Aid to Nicaraguan contras**	August 13, 1986	62–37	60
Justice Department authorization	February 9, 1982	63–33	60	**South Africa sanctions**	August 13, 1986	89–11	60
Broadcast Senate proceedings	April 20, 1982	47–51	60	**Rehnquist nomination**	September 17, 1986	68–31	60
Criminal Code Reform Act	April 27, 1982	45–46	60	**Product liability reform**	September 25, 1986	97–1	60
1982 supplemental funds	May 27, 1982	95–2	60	Omnibus drug bill	October 15, 1986	58–38	60
Voting Rights Act	June 15, 1982	86–8	60	**Immigration reform**	October 17, 1986	69–21	60
Debt limit increase	September 9, 1982	41–47	60	Contra aid moratorium	March 23, 1987	46–45	60
Debt limit increase	September 13, 1982	45–35	60	Contra aid moratorium	March 24, 1987	50–50	60
Debt limit increase	September 15, 1982	50–44	60	Contra aid moratorium	March 25, 1987	54–46	60
Debt limit increase	September 20, 1982	50–39	60	**Relief for the homeless**	April 9, 1987	68–29	60
Debt limit increase	September 21, 1982	53–47	60	Defense authorization, fiscal 1988	May 15, 1987	52–36	60
Debt limit increase	September 22, 1982	54–46	60	Defense authorization, fiscal 1988	May 19, 1987	58–41	60
Debt limit increase	September 23, 1982	53–45	60	Defense authorization, fiscal 1988	May 20, 1987	59–39	60
Antitrust Equal Enforcement Act	December 2, 1982	38–58	60	Campaign finance	June 9, 1987	52–47	60
Antitrust Equal Enforcement Act	December 2, 1982	44–51	60	Campaign finance	June 16, 1987	49–46	60
Transportation Assistance Act	December 13, 1982	75–13	60	Campaign finance	June 17, 1987	51–47	60
Transportation Assistance Act	December 16, 1982	48–50	60	Campaign finance	June 18, 1987	50–47	60
Transportation Assistance Act	December 16, 1982	5–93	60	Campaign finance	June 19, 1987	45–43	60
Transportation Assistance Act	December 19, 1982	89–5	60	Kuwaiti tanker reflagging	July 9, 1987	57–42	60
Transportation Assistance Act	December 20, 1982	87–8	60	Kuwaiti tanker reflagging	July 14, 1987	53–40	60
Transportation Assistance Act	December 23, 1982	81–5	60	Kuwaiti tanker reflagging	July 15, 1987	54–44	60
Jobs funding/interest withholding	March 16, 1983	50–48	60	**Wells nomination**	September 9, 1987	65–24	60
Jobs funding/interest withholding	March 16, 1983	59–39	60	Campaign finance	September 10, 1987	53–42	60
International trade/interest withholding	April 19, 1983	34–53	60	Campaign finance	September 15, 1987	51–44	60
International trade /interest withholding	April 19, 1983	39–59	60	Defense authorization, fiscal 1988	October 1, 1987	41–58	60
Defense authorizations, 1984	July 21, 1983	55–41	60	Kuwaiti tanker escort	October 1, 1987	54–45	60
Radio broadcasting to Cuba	August 3, 1983	62–33	60	**Verity nomination**	October 13, 1987	85–8	60
National Gas Policy Act	November 3, 1983	86–7	60	**War powers compliance**	October 20, 1987	67–28	60
Capital punishment	February 9, 1984	65–26	60	**Nuclear waste depository**	November 10, 1987	87–0	60
Hydroelectric power plants	July 30, 1984	60–28	60	Campaign finance	February 26, 1988	53–41	60
Wilkinson nomination	July 31, 1984	57–39	60	**Polygraph protection**	March 3, 1988	77–19	60
Agriculture funds, fiscal 1985	August 6, 1984	54–31	60	**Intelligence oversight**	March 15, 1988	73–18	60
Agriculture funds, fiscal 1985	August 8, 1984	68–30	60	Risk notification	March 23, 1988	33–59	60
Wilkinson nomination	August 9, 1984	65–32	60	Risk notification	March 24, 1988	2–93	60
Financial Services Act	September 10, 1984	89–3	60	Risk notification	March 28, 1988	41–44	60
Financial Services Act	September 13, 1984	92–6	60	Risk notification	March 29, 1988	42–52	60
Broadcasting of Senate proceedings	September 18, 1984	73–26	60	Campaign spending limitations	April 21, 1988	52–42	60
				Campaign spending limitations	April 22, 1988	53–37	60
				Immigration legalization program extension	April 28, 1988	40–56	60

Issue	Date	Vote	Yeas needed	Issue	Date	Vote	Yeas needed
Drug-related killings death penalty	June 9, 1988	70–26	60	**Federal Facility Compliance Act**	October 17, 1991	85–14	60
Great Smoky Mountain Wilderness Act	June 20, 1988	49–35	60	**Civil Rights Act**	October 22, 1991	93–4	60
Great Smoky Mountain Wilderness Act	June 21, 1988	54–42	60	National energy policy	November 1, 1991	50–44	60
Plant-closing notification	June 29, 1988	58–39	60	**Banking reform**	November 13, 1991	76–19	60
Plant-closing notification	July 6, 1988	88–5	60	Iranian hostage release investigation	November 22, 1991	51–43	60
Textile import quotas	September 7, 1988	68–29	60	Crime conference report	November 27, 1991	49–38	60
Minimum wage restoration	September 22, 1988	53–43	60	**School improvement bill**	January 21, 1992	93–0	60
Minimum wage restoration	September 23, 1988	56–35	60	**National energy strategy**	February 4, 1992	90–5	60
Parental and medical leave	October 3, 1988	85–6	60	**Joint ventures antitrust**	February 25, 1992	98–0	60
Parental and medical leave	October 7, 1988	50–46	60	Lumbee Tribe recognition	February 27, 1992	58–39	60
Defense authorization, fiscal 1990	August 2, 1989	84–13	60	**Public Broadcasting Corp.**	March 3, 1992	87–7	60
Airline smoking ban	September 14, 1989	77–21	60	Crime bill	March 19, 1992	54–43	60
Eastern Airlines strike commission	October 3, 1989	61–36	60	Defense/domestic spending walls	March 26, 1992	50–48	60
Nicaraguan election aid	October 13, 1989	52–42	60	**Fetal tissue research**	March 31, 1992	98–2	60
Nicaraguan election aid	October 17, 1989	74–25	60	**Motor-voter registration**	May 7, 1992	61–38	60
Eastern Airlines strike commission	October 26, 1989	62–38	60	Motor-voter registration	May 12, 1992	58–40	60
Capital gains tax cut	November 14, 1989	51–47	60	**Drug abuse mental health**	June 9, 1992	84–9	60
Capital gains tax cut	November 15, 1989	51–47	60	Striker replacement	June 11, 1992	55–41	60
Government pay-and-ethics package	November 17, 1989	90–9	60	Striker replacement	June 16, 1992	57–42	60
Armenian genocide day	February 22, 1990	49–49	60	Balanced budget amendment	June 30, 1992	56–39	60
Armenian genocide day	February 27, 1990	48–51	60	Balanced budget amendment	July 1, 1992	56–39	60
Hatch Act revisions	May 1, 1990	70–28	60	National energy strategy	July 23, 1992	58–33	60
AIDS emergency relief	May 15, 1990	95–3	60	**National energy strategy**	July 28, 1992	93–3	60
Chemical weapons sanctions	May 17, 1990	87–4	60	**Carnes nomination**	September 9, 1992	66–30	60
Omnibus crime package	June 5, 1990	54–37	60	Product liability	September 10, 1992	57–39	60
Omnibus crime package	June 7, 1990	57–37	60	Product liability	September 10, 1992	58–38	60
Air travel rights for the blind	June 12, 1990	56–44	60	**School improvement bill**	September 15, 1992	85–6	60
Civil Rights Act of 1990	July 17, 1990	62–38	60	Labor, HHS, education funds	September 16, 1992	56–38	60
Defense authorization, fiscal1991	August 3, 1990	58–41	60	**START treaty**	September 29, 1992	87–6	60
Motor Vehicle Fuel Efficiency Act	September 14, 1990	68–28	60	Crime bill	October 2, 1992	55–43	60
Motor Vehicle Fuel Efficiency Act	September 25, 1990	57–42	60	School improvement bill	October 2, 1992	59–40	60
Title X family planning amendments	September 26, 1990	50–46	60	**Fetal tissue research**	October 2, 1992	85–12	60
National motor-voter registration	September 26, 1990	55–42	60	**Tax bill**	October 8, 1992	80–10	60
Foreign operations funds, fiscal 1991	October 12, 1990	51–38	60	**National energy strategy**	October 8, 1992	84–8	60
Vertical price fixing	May 7, 1991	61–37	60	Motor-voter registration	March 5, 1993	52–36	60
Vertical price fixing	May 8, 1991	63–35	60	**Motor-voter registration**	March 9, 1993	62–38	60
Crime bill	June 28, 1991	41–58	60	Motor-voter registration	March 16, 1993	59–41	60
Crime bill	July 10, 1991	56–43	60	Stimulus package	April 2, 1993	55–43	60
Crime bill	July 10, 1991	71–27	60	Stimulus package	April 3, 1993	52–37	60
VA-HUD funds, fiscal 1992	July 18, 1991	57–40	60	Stimulus package	April 5, 1993	49–29	60
National motor-voter registration	July 18, 1991	57–41	60	Stimulus package	April 21, 1993	56–43	60
National motor-voter registration	July 18, 1991	59–40	60	**Motor-voter registration**	May 11, 1993	63–37	60
Foreign aid authorization	July 24, 1991	87–10	60	Campaign finance	June 10, 1993	53–41	60
Foreign aid authorization	July 25, 1991	52–44	60	Campaign finance	June 15, 1993	52–45	60
Foreign aid authorization	July 25, 1991	63–33	60	**Campaign finance**	June 16, 1993	62–37	60
Extended unemployment benefits	July 29, 1991	96–1	60	National service	July 29, 1993	59–41	60
Defense authorization, fiscal 1992	August 2, 1991	58–40	60	Dellinger nomination	October 7, 1993	59–39	60
Interior funds, fiscal 1992	September 19, 1991	55–41	60	Interior funds	October 21, 1993	53–41	60
				Interior funds	October 26, 1993	51–45	60
				Interior funds	October 28, 1993	54–44	60
				State Department nominations	November 3, 1993	58–42	60
				Brady bill (gun controls)	November 19, 1993	57–41	60
				Brady bill (gun controls)	November 19, 1993	57–42	60
				Napolitano nomination	November 19, 1993	72–26	60
				Competitiveness bill	March 15, 1994	56–42	60
				Federal worker retirement buyout	March 24, 1994	58–41	60
				Federal worker retirement buyout	March 24, 1994	63–36	60
				Education goals 2000	March 26, 1994	62–23	60
				Brown nomination	May 24, 1994	54–44	60
				Shearer nomination	May 24, 1994	63–35	60

Issue	Date	Vote	Yeas needed
Brown nomination	May 25, 1994	56–42	60
Product liability	June 28, 1994	54–44	60
Product liability	June 29, 1994	57–41	60
Striker replacement	July 12, 1994	53–47	60
Striker replacement	July 13, 1994	53–46	60
Crime bill	August 25, 1994	61–38	60
Campaign finance	September 22, 1994	96–2	60
California desert protection	September 23, 1994	73–20	60
Campaign finance	September 27, 1994	57–43	60
Campaign finance	September 30, 1994	52–46	66[2]
Tigert nomination	October 3, 1994	63–32	65[3]
Sarokin nomination	October 4, 1994	85–12	60
Elementary and secondary education	October 5, 1994	75–24	60
Lobbying disclosure/gift ban	October 6, 1994	52–46	60
Lobbying disclosure/gift ban	October 7, 1994	55–42	60
California desert protection	October 8, 1994	68–23	60
Unfunded mandates	January 19, 1995	54–44	60
Balanced-budget amendment	February 16, 1995	57–42	60
Striker replacement	March 15, 1995	58–39	60
Health insurance tax deduction	April 3, 1995	83–0	60
Supplemental funds and rescissions	April 6, 1995	56–44	60
Product liability	May 4, 1995	46–53	60
Product liability	May 4, 1995	47–52	60
Product liability	May 8, 1995	43–49	60
Product liability	May 9, 1995	60–38	60
Interstate waste	May 12, 1995	50–47	60
Telecommunications	June 14, 1995	89–11	60
Foster nomination	June 21, 1995	57–43	60
Foster nomination	June 22, 1995	57–43	60
Regulatory overhaul	July 17, 1995	48–46	60
Regulatory overhaul	July 18, 1995	53–47	60
Regulatory overhaul	July 20, 1995	58–40	60
State Department authorization	August 1, 1995	55–45	60
State Department authorization	August 1, 1995	55–45	60
Cuba sanctions	October 12, 1995	56–37	60
Cuba sanctions	October 17, 1995	59–36	60
Cuba sanctions	October 18, 1995	98–0	60
Farm bill	February 1, 1996	53–45	60
Farm bill	February 6, 1996	59–34	60
District of Columbia funds	February 27, 1996	54–44	60
District of Columbia funds	February 29, 1996	52–42	60
District of Columbia funds	March 5, 1996	53–43	60
Whitewater committee extension	March 12, 1996	53–47	60
District of Columbia funds	March 12, 1996	56–44	60
Whitewater committee extension	March 13, 1996	53–47	60
Whitewater committee extension	March 14, 1996	51–46	60
Whitewater committee extension	March 20, 1996	53–47	60
Product liability	March 20, 1996	60–40	60
Whitewater committee extension	March 21, 1996	52–46	60
Presidio Park management	March 27, 1996	51–49	60
Presidio Park management	March 28, 1996	55–45	60
Whitewater committee extension	April 16, 1996	51–46	60
Term limits constitutional amendment	April 23, 1996	58–42	60
Immigration revision	April 29, 1996	91–0	60
Immigration revision	May 2, 1996	100–0	60

Issue	Date	Vote	Yeas needed
White House Travel Office reimbursement	May 7, 1996	52–44	60
White House Travel Office reimbursement	May 8, 1996	53–45	60
White House Travel Office reimbursement	May 9, 1996	52–44	60
White House Travel Office reimbursement	May 14, 1996	54–43	60
Missile defense	June 4, 1996	53–46	60
Campaign finance overhaul	June 25, 1996	54–46	60
Defense authorization	June 26, 1996	52–46	60
Defense authorization	June 28, 1996	53–43	60
Right-to-work legislation	July 10, 1996	31–68	60
Nuclear waste storage	July 16, 1996	65–34	60
FAA reauthorization	October 3, 1996	6–31	60
Volunteer liability limitation	April 29, 1997	53–46	60
Volunteer liability limitation	April 30, 1997	55–44	60
Supplemental funds	May 7, 1997	100–0	60
Compensatory time, flexible credit	May 15, 1997	53–47	60
Compensatory time, flexible credit	June 4, 1997	51–47	60
Defense authorization, fiscal 1998	July 8, 1997	46–45	60
Klein nomination	July 14, 1997	78–11	60
FDA overhaul	September 5, 1997	89–5	60
FDA overhaul	September 16, 1997	94–4	60
District of Columbia funds, fiscal 1998	September 30, 1997	58–41	60
Campaign finance reform	October 7, 1997	52–48	60
Campaign finance reform	October 7, 1997	53–47	60
District of Columbia funds	October 7, 1997	99–1	60
Campaign finance reform	October 8, 1997	52–47	60
Campaign finance reform	October 9, 1997	51–48	60
Campaign finance reform	October 9, 1997	52–47	60
Highway and Transit reauthorization	October 23, 1997	48–50	60
Highway and Transit reauthorization	October 23, 1997	48–52	60
Highway and Transit reauthorization	October 24, 1997	43–49	60
Highway and Transit reauthorization	October 28, 1997	52–48	60
Education savings accounts	October 31, 1997	56–41	60
Defense authorization, fiscal 1998	October 31, 1997	93–2	60
Education savings accounts	November 4, 1997	56–44	60
Fast track trade procedures	November 4, 1997	69–31	60
Satcher confirmation	February 10, 1998	75–23	60
Human cloning research ban	February 11, 1998	42–54	60
Restrict political use of union dues	February 26, 1998	45–54	60
Restrict political use of union dues	February 26, 1998	51–48	60
Highway and mass transit programs	March 11, 1998	96–3	60
Education savings accounts	March 17, 1998	74–24	60
Expand education savings accounts	March 19, 1998	55–44	60
Expand education savings accounts	March 26, 1998	58–42	60
U.S. anti-missile defense policy	May 13, 1998	59–41	60
Create nuclear waste storage in Nevada	June 2, 1998	56–39	60

Issue	Date	Vote	Yeas needed
Set federal policies to curb smoking	June 9, 1998	42–56	62
Set federal policies to curb smoking	June 10, 1998	43–55	60
Set federal policies to curb smoking	June 11, 1998	43–56	60
Set federal policies to curb smoking	June 17, 1998	57–42	60
Limit product liability suits	July 7, 1998	71–24	60
Limit product liability punitive damages	July 9, 1998	51–47	60
U.S. court review, local zoning decisions	July 13, 1998	52–42	60
Legislative branch funds, fiscal 1999	July 21, 1998	83–16	60
U.S. missile defense policy	September 9, 1998	59–41	60
Consumer bankruptcy laws	September 9, 1998	99–1	60
Campaign finance reform	September 10, 1998	52–48	60
Parental consent abortion bill	September 11, 1998	97–0	60
Limit union organizing	September 14, 1998	52–42	60
Evading parental consent abortion laws	September 22, 1998	54–45	60
Limit presidential appointment powers	September 24, 1998	96–1	60
Limit presidential appointment powers	September 28, 1998	53–38	60
Internet sales taxes	September 29, 1998	89–6	60
Banking regulation revision	October 5, 1998	93–0	60
Ban Internet sales taxes for two years	October 7, 1998	94–4	60
Waive federal education spending rules	March 8, 1999	54–41	60
Waive federal education spending rules	March 9, 1999	55–39	60
Authorize $11.4 billion for new teachers	March 10, 1999	44–55	60
Special education funding	March 10, 1999	55–44	60
U.S. troops in Kosovo	March 23, 1999	55–44	60
Social Security "lockbox," debt limit	April 22, 1999	54–45	60
Y2K liability limits	April 26, 1999	94–0	60
Y2K liability limits	April 29, 1999	52–47	60
Social Security "lockbox," debt limit	April 30, 1999	49–44	60
Y2K liability limits	May 18, 1999	53–45	60
Social Security "lockbox" debt limit	June 15, 1999	53–46	60
Steel, oil, gas loan guarantee	June 15, 1999	70–29	60
Social Security "lockbox"	June 16, 1999	55–44	60
Steel import quotas	June 22, 1999	42–57	60
Commerce, State, Justice funds, fiscal 2000	June 28, 1999	49–39	60
Transportation funds, fiscal 2000	June 28, 1999	49–40	60
Foreign operations funds, fiscal 2000	June 28, 1999	49–41	60
Agriculture funds, fiscal 2000	June 28, 1999	50–37	60
Budget procedures	July 1, 1999	99–1	60
Social Security "lockbox," debt limit	July 16, 1999	52–43	60
Intelligence authorization, fiscal 2000	July 20, 1999	99–0	60
Juvenile justice programs	July 28, 1999	77–22	60
Agriculture funds/milk marketing	August 4, 1999	53–47	60

Issue	Date	Vote	Yeas needed
Transportation funds, fiscal 2000	September 9, 1999	49–49	60
Oil royalty valuation system	September 13, 1999	54–40	60
Puerto Rican nationalists clemency	September 13, 1999	93–0	60
Bankruptcy law revision	September 21, 1999	53–45	60
Stewart nomination	September 21, 1999	55–44	60
Oil royalty valuation system	September 23, 1999	62–39	60
Agriculture funds, fiscal 2000	October 12, 1999	79–20	60
Campaign finance soft money ban	October 19, 1999	52–48	60
Campaign finance soft money, union dues	October 19, 1999	53–47	60
Trade with Sub-Saharan Africa	October 26, 1999	91–8	60
Sub-Saharan African, Caribbean trade	October 29, 1999	45–46	60
Sub-Saharan African, Caribbean trade	November 2, 1999	74–23	60
Omnibus funds, fiscal 2000	November 19, 1999	87–9	60
Nuclear waste storage	February 2, 2000	94–3	60
Paez nomination	March 8, 2000	85–14	60
Berzon nomination	March 8, 2000	86–13	60
Flag desecration amendment	March 29, 2000	100–0	60
Federal gas tax suspension	March 30, 2000	86–11	60
Federal gas tax suspension	April 11, 2000	43–56	60
Marriage penalty tax	April 13, 2000	53–45	60
Marriage penalty tax	April 13, 2000	53–45	60
Victims rights	April 25, 2000	82–12	60
Marriage penalty tax	April 27, 2000	51–44	60
African trade agreement	May 11, 2000	76–18	60
Estate tax repeal	July 11, 2000	99–1	60
Intelligence authorization, fiscal 2001	July 26, 2000	96–1	60
Treasury funds, fiscal 2001	July 26, 2000	97–0	60
Energy, water funds, fiscal 2001	July 27, 2000	100–0	60
Trade with China	July 27, 2000	86–12	60
High technology visas	September 19, 2000	97–1	60
High technology visas	September 26, 2000	94–3	60
High technology visas	September 28, 2000	92–3	60
Interior funds, fiscal 2001	October 5, 2000	89–8	60
Bankruptcy law revision	November 1, 2000	53–30	60
Bankruptcy law revision	December 5, 2000	67–31	60
Bankruptcy law revision	March 14, 2001	80–19	60
ESEA reauthorization	May 1, 2001	96–3	60
Bankruptcy law revision	July 12, 2001	88–10	60
Bankruptcy law revision	July 17, 2001	88–10	60
Mexican trucks access to U.S.	July 26, 2001	70–30	60
Mexican trucks in U.S.	July 27, 2001	57–27	60
Supplemental farm funds	July 30, 2001	95–2	60
Transportation/Mexican trucks in U.S.	August 2, 2001	100–0	60
Supplemental farm funds	August 3, 2001	49–48	60
Defense/energy funds authorization	October 2, 2001	100–0	60
Federal airport security	October 9, 2001	97–0	60
Aviation workers assistance	October 11, 2001	56–44	60
Foreign operations funds	October 15, 2001	50–46	60
Foreign operations funds	October 23, 2001	50–47	60
Safety officers collective bargaining rights	November 6, 2001	56–44	60
Pension contribution limits	November 29, 2001	96–4	60
Energy policies/human cloning	December 3, 2001	1–94	60
Railroad retirement pension board	December 3, 2001	81–15	60

Issue	Date	Vote	Yeas needed	Issue	Date	Vote	Yeas needed
Farm policy revisions	December 5, 2001	73–26	60	Estrada appeals court nomination	March 18, 2003	55–45	60
Farm policy revisions	December 13, 2001	53–45	60	Estrada appeals court nomination	April 2, 2003	55–44	60
Farm policy revisions	December 18, 2001	54–43	60	Owen appeals court nomination	May 1, 2003	52–44	60
Farm policy revisions	December 19, 2001	54–43	60	Estrada appeals court nomination	May 5, 2003	52–39	60
Business tax cut/unemployment benefits	February 6, 2002	48–47	60	Owen appeals court nomination	May 8, 2003	52–45	60
Tax bill/unemployment benefits	February 6, 2002	56–39	60	Estrada appeals court nomination	May 8, 2003	54–43	60
Election procedures requirements	March 1, 2002	49–39	60	Medical malpractice award caps	July 9, 2003	49–48	60
Election procedures requirements	March 4, 2002	51–44	60	Owen appeals court nomination	July 29, 2003	53–43	60
Campaign finance revisions	March 20, 2002	68–32	60	Estrada appeals court nomination	July 30, 2003	55–43	60
Energy policy bill	April 10, 2002	48–50	60	Pryor appeals court nomination	July 31, 2003	53–44	60
Energy bill/ANWR drilling	April 18, 2002	36–64	60	Class action lawsuits	October 22, 2003	59–39	60
Energy bill/ANWR drilling	April 18, 2002	46–54	60	Pickering appeals court nomination	October 30, 2003	54–43	60
Energy policy bill	April 23, 2002	86–13	60	Pryor appeals court nomination	November 6, 2003	51–43	60
Andean duty-free trade	April 29, 2002	69–21	60	Owen appeals court nomination	November 14, 2003	53–42	60
Andean trade/steelworkers health insurance	May 21, 2002	56–40	60	Kuhl appeals court nomination	November 14, 2003	53–43	60
Andean duty-free trade	May 22, 2002	68–29	60	Brown appeals court nomination	November 14, 2003	53–43	60
Supplemental funds, fiscal 2002	June 6, 2002	87–10	60	FAA authorization	November 17, 2003	45–43	60
Hate crimes definitions	June 11, 2002	54–43	60	Dorr agriculture undersecretary nomination	November 18, 2003	57–39	60
Terrorism insurance	June 18, 2002	65–31	60	Dorr Commodity Credit Corp. nomination	November 18, 2003	57–39	60
Defense authorization, fiscal 2003	June 26, 2002	98–0	60	Energy policy bill conference report	November 21, 2003	57–40	60
Accounting industry reform	July 12, 2002	91–2	60	**Medicare prescription drug bill**	November 24, 2003	70–29	60
Smith appeals court nomination	July 15, 2002	94–3	60	Omnibus appropriations, fiscal 2004	January 20, 2004	48–45	60
Drug patents	July 17, 2002	99–0	60	**Omnibus appropriations, fiscal 2004**	January 22, 2004	61–32	60
Clifton appeals court nomination	July 18, 2002	97–1	60	**Highway funding**	February 2, 2004	75–11	60
Carmona surgeon general nomination	July 23, 2002	98–0	60	**Highway funding**	February 12, 2004	86–11	60
Gibbons appeals court nomination	July 26, 2002	89–0	60	Medical malpractice lawsuit caps	February 24, 2004	48–45	60
Drug patents	July 31, 2002	66–33	60	**Gun liability lawsuits**	February 25, 2004	75–22	60
Trade promotion authority	August 1, 2002	64–32	60	Corporate tax changes	March 24, 2004	51–47	60
Interior funds, fiscal 2002/farm disaster aid	September 17, 2002	50–49	60	Welfare reauthorization	April 1, 2004	51–47	60
Homeland security department	September 19, 2002	50–49	60	Medical malpractice lawsuit caps	April 7, 2004	49–48	60
Interior funds, fiscal 2002/farm disaster aid	September 23, 2002	49–46	60	Corporate tax changes	April 7, 2004	50–47	60
Homeland security department	September 25, 2002	49–49	60	Asbestos claims fund	April 22, 2004	50–47	60
Interior funds, fiscal 2002/farm disaster aid	September 25, 2002	51–47	60	**Internet tax moratorium**	April 26, 2004	74–11	60
Homeland security/worker union rights	September 26, 2002	44–53	60	Internet tax/ethanol	April 29, 2004	40–59	60
Homeland security department	September 26, 2002	50–49	60	Internet tax/energy policy	April 29, 2004	55–43	60
Homeland security/worker union rights	October 1, 2002	45–52	60	**Internet tax moratorium**	April 29, 2004	64–34	60
Justice department reauthorization	October 3, 2002	93–5	60	**Corporate tax changes**	May 11, 2004	90–8	60
Use of force against Iraq	October 3, 2002	95–1	60	Class action lawsuits	July 8, 2004	44–43	60
Use of force against Iraq	October 10, 2002	75–25	60	Same-sex marriage amendment	July 14, 2004	48–50	60
Homeland security/worker union rights	November 13, 2002	89–8	60	Myers appeals court nomination	July 20, 2004	53–44	60
Homeland security department	November 15, 2002	65–29	60	Saad appeals court nomination	July 22, 2004	52–46	60
Homeland security department	November 19, 2002	83–16	60	McKeague appeals court nomination	July 22, 2004	53–44	60
Terrorism insurance	November 19, 2002	85–12	60	Griffin appeals court nomination	July 22, 2004	54–44	60
Estrada appeals court nomination	March 6, 2003	55–44	60	**Intelligence operations overhaul**	October 5, 2004	85–10	60
Estrada appeals court nomination	March 13, 2003	55–42	60	**Senate intelligence oversight**	October 8, 2004	88–3	60
				Corporate tax changes	October 10, 2004	66–14	60
				Tariffs and trade bill	November 19, 2004	88–5	60
				Bankruptcy overhaul	March 8, 2005	69–31	60

Issue	Date	Vote	Yeas needed	Issue	Date	Vote	Yeas needed
Iraq, Afghanistan war funding	April 19, 2005	100–0	60	**Port security overhaul**	September 14, 2006	98–0	60
Foreign workers temporary U.S. status	April 19, 2005	21–77	60	**U.S.–Mexican border fence**	September 20, 2006	94–0	60
Agricultural workers in U.S. illegally	April 19, 2005	53–45	60	**U.S.–Mexican border fence**	September 28, 2006	71–28	60
Seasonal workers exemption	April 19, 2005	83–17	60	Abortion parental notification	September 29, 2006	57–42	60
Surface transportation reauthorization	April 26, 2005	94–6	60	**FDA commissioner nomination**	December 7, 2006	89–6	60
Johnson EPA administrator nomination	April 28, 2005	61–37	60	**Jordan appeals court nomination**	December 8, 2006	93–0	60
Surface transportation reauthorization	May 12, 2005	92–7	60	**Tax and trade package**	December 9, 2006	78–10	60
Owen appeals court nomination	May 24, 2005	81–18	60	**Ethics and lobbying overhaul**	January 16, 2007	95–2	60
Bolton United Nations nomination	May 26, 2005	56–42	60	Ethics and lobbying overhaul	January 17, 2007	51–46	60
Brown appeals court nomination	June 7, 2005	65–32	60	Minimum wage increase	January 24, 2007	49–48	60
Pryor appeals court nomination	June 8, 2005	67–32	60	Minimum wage increase	January 24, 2007	54–43	60
Bolton United Nations nomination	June 20, 2005	54–38	60	**Minimum wage increase**	January 30, 2007	87–10	60
Energy policy overhaul	June 23, 2005	92–4	60	**Minimum wage increase**	January 31, 2007	88–8	60
Defense authorization	July 26, 2005	50–48	60	U.S. troop levels in Iraq	February 1, 2007	0–97	60
Gun liability limitations	July 26, 2005	66–32	60	U.S. troop levels in Iraq	February 5, 2007	49–47	60
Defense appropriations	October 5, 2005	95–4	60	**Continuing appropriations fiscal 2007**	February 13, 2007	71–26	60
Labor-HHS-Education appropriations	October 27, 2005	97–0	60	Iraq war troop surge	February 17, 2007	56–34	60
Patriot Act reauthorization	December 16, 2005	52–47	60	**September 11 commission recommendations**	February 27, 2007	97–0	60
Defense appropriations	December 21, 2005	56–44	60	September 11 commission recommendations	March 9, 2007	46–49	60
Alito Supreme Court nomination	January 30, 2006	72–25	60	**September 11 commission recommendations**	March 9, 2007	69–26	60
Asbestos trust fund	February 7, 2006	98–1	60	**Iraq mission**	March 14, 2007	89–9	60
Patriot Act reauthorization	February 16, 2006	96–3	60	**Supplemental appropriations fiscal 2007**	March 28, 2007	97–0	60
Patriot Act reauthorization	February 28, 2006	69–30	60	**Intelligence authorization fiscal 2007**	April 12, 2007	94–3	60
Patriot Act reauthorization	March 1, 2006	84–15	60	Intelligence authorization fiscal 2007	April 16, 2007	41–40	60
Low income home energy assistance	March 7, 2006	75–25	60	Intelligence authorization fiscal 2007	April 17, 2007	50–45	60
Lobbying overhaul	March 9, 2006	51–47	60	Medicare prescription drug negotiations	April 18, 2007	55–42	60
Lobbying overhaul	March 28, 2006	81–16	60	**Court security**	April 18, 2007	93–3	60
Immigration overhaul	April 6, 2006	38–60	60	**FDA overhaul**	May 3, 2007	63–28	60
Immigration overhaul	April 6, 2006	39–60	60	**FDA overhaul**	May 7, 2007	82–8	60
Immigration overhaul	April 7, 2006	36–62	60	**Water projects authorization**	May 10, 2007	89–7	60
Flory Defense Department nomination	April 7, 2006	52–41	60	Iraq troop withdrawal by March 31, 2008	May 16, 2007	29–67	60
Iraq, Afghanistan war funding	May 2, 2006	92–4	60	Withholding Iraq economic aid	May 16, 2007	52–44	60
Medical malpractice	May 8, 2006	48–42	60	**Sense of Senate on Iraq funding**	May 16, 2007	87–9	60
Medical malpractice	May 8, 2006	49–44	60	**Sense of Senate on Iraq mission**	May 17, 2007	94–1	60
Small business health plans	May 9, 2006	96–2	60	**Immigration overhaul**	May 21, 2007	69–23	60
Small business health plans	May 11, 2006	55–43	60	Immigration overhaul	June 7, 2007	33–63	60
Immigration overhaul	May 24, 2006	73–25	60	Immigration overhaul	June 7, 2007	34–61	60
Kavanaugh appeals court nomination	May 25, 2006	67–30	60	Immigration overhaul	June 7, 2007	45–50	60
Interior secretary nomination	May 26, 2006	85–8	60	No confidence: Attorney General Gonzales	June 11, 2007	53–38	60
Same-sex marriage ban amendment	June 7, 2006	49–48	60	**Energy policy**	June 11, 2007	91–0	60
Native Hawaiians policy	June 8, 2006	56–41	60	Energy policy	June 21, 2007	57–36	60
Estate tax repeal	June 8, 2006	57–41	60	**Energy policy**	June 21, 2007	61–32	60
Defense authorization	June 22, 2006	98–1	60	**Energy policy**	June 21, 2007	62–32	60
Gulf of Mexico offshore drilling	July 26, 2006	86–12	60	Employee union formation	June 26, 2007	51–48	60
Gulf of Mexico offshore drilling	July 31, 2006	72–23	60	**Immigration overhaul**	June 26, 2007	64–35	60
Tax package and minimum wage	August 3, 2006	56–42	60	Immigration overhaul	June 28, 2007	46–53	60
				Defense authorization fiscal 2008	July 11, 2007	56–41	60
				Defense authorization fiscal 2008	July 17, 2007	52–47	60

Issue	Date	Vote	Yeas needed	Issue	Date	Vote	Yeas needed
Small business tax breaks	July 30, 2007	80–0	60	Foreign intelligence surveillance	June 25, 2008	80–15	60
Ethics and lobbying overhaul	August 2, 2007	80–17	60	Medicare physician payments	June 26, 2008	58–40	60
District of Columbia voting rights	September 18, 2007	57–42	60	Mortgage relief	July 7, 2008	76–10	60
Defense authorization fiscal 2008	September 19, 2007	56–43	60	Medicare physician payments	July 9, 2008	69–30	60
Defense authorization fiscal 2008	September 27, 2007	60–39	60	Foreign intelligence surveillance	July 9, 2008	72–26	60
Children's Health Insurance	September 27, 2007	69–30	60	Mortgage relief	July 10, 2008	84–12	60
Defense authorization fiscal 2008	September 27, 2007	89–6	60	HIV/AIDS program reauthorization	July 11, 2008	65–3	60
Immigrant education	October 24, 2007	52–44	60	Energy futures speculation	July 22, 2008	94–0	60
Southwick appeals court nomination	October 24, 2007	62–35	60	Energy futures speculation	July 25, 2008	50–43	60
Amtrak reauthorization	October 30, 2007	79–13	60	Mortgage relief	July 25, 2008	80–13	60
Children's health insurance	October 31, 2007	62–33	60	Low-income energy assistance	July 26, 2008	50–35	60
Children's health insurance	November 1, 2007	65–30	60	Omnibus domestic and foreign policy bills	July 28, 2008	52–40	60
Iraq war appropriations	November 16, 2007	45–53	60	Tax cuts extensions	July 29, 2008	53–43	60
Iraq war appropriations/troop withdrawal	November 16, 2007	53–45	60	Media shield	July 30, 2008	51–43	60
Farm bill reauthorization	November 16, 2007	55–42	60	Tax reduction extensions	July 30, 2008	51–43	60
Alternative minimum tax	December 6, 2007	46–48	60	Defense authorization fiscal 2009	July 31, 2008	51–39	60
Energy policy	December 7, 2007	53–42	60	Defense authorization fiscal 2009	September 8, 2008	83–0	60
Energy policy/CAFE standards	December 13, 2007	59–40	60	Defense authorization fiscal 2009	September 16, 2008	61–32	60
Farm bill reauthorization	December 13, 2007	78–12	60	Continuing appropriations	September 27, 2008	83–12	60
Foreign intelligence surveillance	December 17, 2007	76–10	60	Railroad safety/Amtrak authorization	September 29, 2008	69–17	60
Omnibus appropriations fiscal 2008	December 18, 2007	44–51	60	Unemployment benefits extension	November 20, 2008	89–6	60
Foreign intelligence surveillance	January 28, 2008	48–45	60	Automobile industry loans	December 11, 2008	52–35	60
Foreign intelligence surveillance	January 28, 2008	48–45	60	Public lands designations	January 11, 2009	66–12	60
Economic stimulus	February 4, 2008	80–4	60	Public lands designations	January 14, 2009	68–24	60
Economic stimulus	February 6, 2008	58–41	60	Wage discrimination/Lilly Ledbetter	January 15, 2009	72–23	60
Foreign intelligence surveillance	February 12, 2008	69–29	60	Economic stimulus legislation	February 9, 2009	61–36	60
Intelligence authorization fiscal 2008	February 13, 2008	92–4	60	District of Columbia House membership	February 24, 2009	62–34	60
Indian health care reauthorization	February 25, 2008	85–2	60	Omnibus appropriations fiscal 2009	March 10, 2009	62–35	60
U.S. troop deployments in Iraq	February 26, 2008	70–24	60	Public lands historic sites	March 16, 2009	73–21	60
Report on al Qaeda	February 27, 2008	89–3	60	National Service Programs authorization	March 23, 2009	74–14	60
Renewable energy	February 28, 2008	48–46	60	Hill nomination as Iraq ambassador	April 20, 2009	73–17	60
Consumer Product Safety Commission	March 3, 2008	86–1	60	Expand federal fraud laws	April 27, 2009	84–4	60
Renewable energy	April 1, 2008	94–1	60	Hayes nomination as Interior secretary	May 13, 2009	57–39	60
Renewable energy/mortgage relief	April 8, 2008	92–6	60	Credit card company regulation	May 19, 2009	92–2	60
Surface Transportation law corrections	April 14, 2008	93–1	60	Supplemental appropriations fiscal 2009	May 21, 2009	94–1	60
Surface transportation corrections	April 17, 2008	90–2	60	Tobacco regulation by FDA	June 2, 2009	84–11	60
Veterans benefits expansion	April 22, 2008	94–0	60	Tobacco regulation by FDA	June 8, 2009	61–30	60
Wage discrimination	April 23, 2008	56–42	60	Tobacco regulation by FDA	June 10, 2009	67–30	60
FAA reauthorization	April 28, 2008	88–0	60	Foreign tourism promotion office	June 16, 2009	53–34	60
FAA reauthorization	May 6, 2008	49–42	60	Foreign tourism promotion office	June 16, 2009	90–3	60
National flood insurance	May 6, 2008	90–1	60	Koh State Department nomination	June 24, 2009	65–31	60
Public safety workers organizing rights	May 13, 2008	69–29	60	Groves nomination as Census director	July 13, 2009	76–15	60
Climate change trading system	June 2, 2008	74–14	60	Expanding federal hate crime laws	July 16, 2009	63–28	60
Climate change trading system	June 6, 2008	48–36	60				
Tax reduction extensions	June 10, 2008	50–44	60				
Energy and oil company taxes	June 10, 2008	51–43	60				
Medicare physician payments	June 12, 2008	54–39	60				
Tax reduction extensions	June 17, 2008	52–44	60				
Mortgage relief	June 24, 2008	83–9	60				

Issue	Date	Vote	Yeas needed	Issue	Date	Vote	Yeas needed
Agriculture appropriations fiscal 2010	August 3, 2009	83–11	60	Tax cut extension, unemployment benefits	June 17, 2010	56–40	60
Foreign tourism promotion office	September 8, 2009	80–19	60	Tax cut extension, unemployment benefits	June 24, 2010	57–41	60
Sunstein nomination to OMB office	September 9, 2009	63–35	60	**Small business taxes and lending fund**	June 29, 2010	66–33	60
State, Justice, Commerce appropriations fiscal 2010	October 13, 2009	56–38	60	Tax extension and unemployment benefits	June 30, 2010	58–38	60
Energy, water appropriations fiscal 2010	October 14, 2009	79–17	60	**Financial regulatory overhaul**	July 15, 2010	60–38	60
Medicare doctor reimbursements	October 21, 2009	47–53	60	**Unemployment benefits extension**	July 20, 2010	60–40	60
Defense funding authorization fiscal 2010	October 22, 2009	64–35	60	Supplemental appropriations fiscal 2010	July 22, 2010	46–51	60
Unemployment benefits extension	October 27, 2009	87–13	60	**Small business lending fund**	July 22, 2010	60–37	60
Unemployment benefits extension	November 2, 2009	85–2	60	Campaign finance disclosure	July 27, 2010	57–41	60
Unemployment benefits extension	November 4, 2009	97–1	60	Small business taxes and lending fund	July 29, 2010	58–42	60
State, Justice, Commerce appropriations fiscal 2010	November 5, 2009	60–39	60	**Medicaid and education assistance**	August 4, 2010	61–38	60
Hamilton circuit court nomination	November 17, 2009	70–29	60	Health care overhaul law amendments	September 14, 2010	46–52	60
Health care overhaul, homeowners tax	November 21, 2009	60–39	60	Health care overhaul law amendments	September 14, 2010	56–42	60
Omnibus appropriations fiscal 2010	December 12, 2009	60–34	60	**Small business taxes and lending fund**	September 14, 2010	61–37	60
Defense appropriations fiscal 2010	December 18, 2009	63–33	60	**Small business taxes and lending fund**	September 16, 2010	61–38	60
Health care overhaul	December 21, 2009	60–40	60	"Don't ask, don't tell" policy	September 21, 2010	56–43	60
Health care overhaul	December 22, 2009	60–39	60	Campaign finance disclosure	September 23, 2010	59–39	60
Health care overhaul	December 23, 2009	60–39	60	Social Security tax cut for corporations	September 28, 2010	53–45	60
Bernanke Federal Reserve nomination	January 28, 2010	77–23	60	**Continuing appropriations fiscal 2010 and 2011**	September 28, 2010	84–14	60
Smith Labor Dept. solicitor nomination	February 1, 2010	60–32	60	Wage discrimination	November 17, 2010	58–4	60
Johnson GSA administrator nomination	February 4, 2010	82–16	60	**Food safety overhaul, FDA enforcement**	November 17, 2010	74–25	60
Becker nomination Labor Relations Board	February 9, 2010	52–33	60	**Food safety overhaul, FDA enforcement**	November 29, 2010	69–26	60
Jobs package; payroll tax holiday	February 22, 2010	62–30	60	Tax rate extensions	December 4, 2010	53–36	60
Travel Promotion, Capitol Police	February 25, 2010	76–20	60	Tax rate extensions	December 4, 2010	53–37	60
Keenan appeals court nomination	March 2, 2010	99–0	60	Social Security single payment	December 8, 2010	53–45	60
Extend tax cut, unemployment benefits	March 9, 2010	66–34	60	Public safety workers collective bargaining	December 8, 2010	55–43	60
Extend tax cuts, unemployment benefits	March 10, 2010	66–33	60	"Don't ask, don't tell" policy	December 9, 2010	57–40	60
Business taxes, highway extension	March 15, 2010	61–30	60	Health, compensation fund first-responders	December 9, 2010	57–42	60
Short-term program extension	April 12, 2010	60–34	60	**Tax rate extensions**	December 13, 2010	83–15	60
Short-term program extensions	April 15, 2010	60–38	60	Immigration policy revisions	December 18, 2010	55–41	60
Brainard Treasury nomination	April 19, 2010	84–10	60	**"Don't ask, don't tell" policy repeal**	December 18, 2010	63–33	60
Financial regulatory overhaul	April 26, 2010	57–41	60	**New START agreement with Russia**	December 21, 2010	67–28	60
Financial regulatory overhaul	April 27, 2010	57–41	60	**Continuing appropriations fiscal 2011**	December 21, 2010	82–14	60
Financial regulatory overhaul	April 28, 2010	56–42	60	**FAA reauthorization**	February 17, 2011	96–2	60
Financial regulatory overhaul	May 19, 2010	57–42	60	**Patent law overhaul**	March 7, 2011	87–3	60
Financial regulatory overhaul	May 20, 2010	60–40	60	**Small business research**	March 14, 2011	84–12	60
Supplemental appropriations fiscal 2010	May 27, 2010	69–29	60	Small business research	May 4, 2011	52–44	60
				McConnell judicial nomination	May 4, 2011	63–33	60
				Cole Justice Department nomination	May 9, 2011	50–40	60
				Liu judicial nomination	May 19, 2011	52–43	60
				Patriot Act extension	May 23, 2011	74–8	60
				Patriot Act extension	May 26, 2011	79–18	60

Issue	Date	Vote	Yeas needed
Ethanol tax provisions	June 14, 2011	40–59	60
Economic development reauthorization	June 21, 2011	49–51	60
Millionaires' taxes sense of Senate	July 7, 2011	74–22	60
Millionaires' taxes sense of Senate	July 13, 2011	51–49	60
Military constructions, VA funding	July 13, 2011	89–11	60
Military constructions, VA funding	July 14, 2011	71–26	60
Debt limit increase	July 31, 2011	50–49	60
Patent law overhaul	September 6, 2011	93–5	60
Myanmar sanctions	September 12, 2011	53–33	60
Myanmar sanctions	September 13, 2011	61–38	60
Trade preferences	September 19, 2011	84–8	60
Short-term continuing appropriations	September 26, 2011	54–35	60
Currency misalignment/China	October 3, 2011	79–19	60
Currency misalignment/China	October 6, 2011	62–38	60
Job creation	October 11, 2011	50–49	60
Public employee jobs funding	October 20, 2011	50–50	60
Tax withholding payments repeal	October 20, 2011	57–43	60
Agriculture, CJS, housing appropriations	October 20, 2011	82–16	60
Tax withholding payments repeal	November 7, 2011	94–1	60
Energy, State, Treasury appropriations	November 10, 2011	81–14	60
Defense funding authorization	November 30, 2011	88–12	60
Halligan judicial nomination	December 6, 2011	54–45	60
Cordray consumer agency nomination	December 8, 2011	53–45	60
Aponte ambassador nomination	December 12, 2011	49–37	60
Eisen ambassador nomination	December 12, 2011	70–16	60
Congressional insider-trading ban	January 30, 2012	93–2	60
Surface transportation reauthorization	February 9, 2012	85–11	60
Jordan judicial nomination	February 13, 2012	89–5	60
Surface transportation reauthorization	February 17, 2012	54–42	60
Surface transportation reauthorization	March 6, 2012	52–44	60
Small business auditing, SEC oversight	March 20, 2012	54–45	60
Small business auditing, SEC oversight	March 20, 2012	55–44	60
Small business auditing, SEC oversight	March 21, 2012	76–22	60
Congressional insider-trading ban	March 22, 2012	96–3	60
Oil and gas tax breaks repeal	March 26, 2012	92–4	60
Postal Service overhaul	March 27, 2012	51–46	60
Oil and gas tax breaks repeal	March 29, 2012	51–47	60
Millionaires minimum tax	April 16, 2012	51–45	60
Postal Service overhaul	April 17, 2012	74–22	60
Student loan interest rate extension	May 8, 2012	52–45	60
Outlaw wage discrimination by gender	June 5, 2012	52–47	60
Farm, food, nutrition reauthorizations	June 7, 2012	90–8	60
Hurwitz judicial nomination	June 11, 2012	60–31	60

Issue	Date	Vote	Yeas needed
Aponte ambassador nomination	June 14, 2012	62–37	60
Flood insurance reauthorization	June 21, 2012	96–2	60
FDA user fees reauthorization	June 25, 2012	89–3	60
Small business tax cuts	July 10, 2012	80–14	60
Small business tax cuts	July 12, 2012	53–44	60
Small business tax cuts	July 12, 2012	57–41	60
Campaign finance disclosure	July 16, 2012	51–44	60
Campaign finance disclosure	July 17, 2012	53–45	60
U.S. jobs outsourcing tax credits	July 19, 2012	56–42	60
Cybersecurity standards	July 26, 2012	84–11	60
Bacharach judicial nomination	July 30, 2012	56–34	60
Cybersecurity standards	August 2, 2012	52–46	60
Veterans job trainings	September 11, 2012	95–1	60
Continuing appropriations fiscal 2013	September 19, 2012	76–22	60
Continuing appropriations fiscal 2013	September 21, 2012	62–30	60
Hunting access on U.S. lands	September 21, 2012	84–7	60
Cybersecurity standards	November 14, 2012	51–47	60
Hunting access on U.S. lands	November 15, 2012	84–12	60
Defense authorization fiscal 2013	December 3, 2012	93–0	60
Extend FDIC insurance	December 11, 2012	76–20	60
Disaster supplement, Superstorm Sandy	December 21, 2012	91–1	60
Nominee Charles Timothy Hagel	February 14, 2013	58–40	60
Nominee Charles Timothy Hagel Vote No. 21 reconsidered	February 26, 2013	71–27	60
A bill to provide for a sequester replacement	February 28, 2013	38–62	60
Sequestration legislation	February 28, 2013	51–49	60
Judicial nominee Caitlin Joan Halligan	March 6, 2013	51–41	60
Nominee John Owen Brennan	March 7, 2013	81–16	60
Department of Defense, Military Construction and Veterans Affairs, and Full-Year Continuing Appropriations	March 13, 2013	UC	60
Department of Defense, Military Construction and Veterans Affairs, and Full-Year Continuing Appropriations	March 18, 2013	63–35	60
Department of Defense, Military Construction and Veterans Affairs, and Full-Year Continuing Appropriations	March 20, 2013	63–36	60
Safe Communities, Safe Schools Act of 2013	April 11, 2013	68–31	60
Bill to Restore States' Sovereign Rights to Enforce State and Local Sales and Use Tax Laws and for Other Purposes	April 22, 2013	74–20	60
Bill to Restore States' Sovereign Rights to Enforce State and Local Sales and Use Tax Laws and for Other Purposes	April 25, 2013	63–30	60

Issue	Date	Vote	Yeas needed		Issue	Date	Vote	Yeas needed
Water Resources Development Act of 2013	May 6, 2013	UC	60		Judicial nominee Patricia Ann Millett	October 31, 2013	55–38	60
Water Resources Development Act of 2013	May 15, 2013	UC	60		Nominee Melvin L. Watt	October 31, 2013	56–42	60
Judicial nominee Srikanth Srinivasan	May 23, 2013	UC	60		**Employment Non-Discrimination Act of 2013**	November 4, 2013	61–30	60
Comprehensive Student Loan Protection Act	June 6, 2013	40–57	60		**Employment Non-Discrimination Act of 2013**	November 7, 2013	64–34	60
Student Loan Affordability Act	June 6, 2013	51–46	60		Judicial nominee Cornelia T. L. Pillard	November 12, 2013	56–41	60
Agriculture Reform, Food, and Jobs Act of 2013	June 6, 2013	75–22	60		**Drug Quality and Security Act**	November 12, 2013	97–1	60
Border Security, Economic Opportunity, and Immigration Modernization Act	June 11, 2013	82–15	60		Judicial nominee Robert Leon Wilkins	November 18, 2013	53–38	60
Border Security, Economic Opportunity, and Immigration Modernization Act	June 24, 2013	67–27	60		**National Defense Authorization Act for Fiscal Year 2014**	November 18, 2013	91–0	60
Border Security, Economic Opportunity, and Immigration Modernization Act	June 26, 2013	67–31	60		**Drug Quality and Security Act**	November 18, 2013	UC	60
Border Security, Economic Opportunity, and Immigration Modernization Act	June 27, 2013	68–32	60		National Defense Authorization Act for Fiscal Year 2014	November 21, 2013	51–44	60
Keep Student Loans Affordable Act of 2013	July 10, 2013	51–49	60		Judicial nominee Patricia Ann Millett Vote No. 227 reconsidered	November 21, 2013	55–43	60
Nominee Richard Cordray	July 16, 2013	71–29	60		Judicial nominee Cornelia T. L. Pillard Vote No. 233 reconsidered	December 10, 2013	56–42	60
Nominee Richard F. Gri	July 16, 2013	UC	60		Nominee Melvin L. Watt Vote No. 226 reconsidered	December 10, 2013	57–40	60
Nominee Sharon Block	July 16, 2013	UC	60		Judicial nominee Elizabeth A. Wolford	December 12, 2013	55–41	60
Nominee Mark Gaston Pearce	July 16, 2013	UC	60		Nominee Chai Rachel Feldblum Reid	December 12, 2013	57–39	60
Nominee Thomas Edward Perez	July 17, 2013	60–40	60		Judicial nominee Brian Morris	December 12, 2013	57–40	60
Nominee Fred P. Hochberg	July 17, 2013	82–18	60		Nominee Patricia M. Wald	December 12, 2013	57–41	60
Nominee Regina McCarthy	July 18, 2013	69–31	60		Judicial nominee Susan P. Watters	December 12, 2013	58–39	60
Transportation, Housing and Urban Development, and Related Agencies Appropriations	July 23, 2013	73–26	60		Nominee Deborah Lee James	December 12, 2013	58–39	60
Nominee James B. Comey Jr.	July 29, 2013	UC	60		Judicial nominee Landya B. McCafferty	December 12, 2013	58–40	60
Nominee Kent Yoshiho Hirozawa	July 30, 2013	64–34	60		Nominee Heather Anne Higginbottom	December 13, 2013	51–34	60
Nominee Nancy Jean Schiffer	July 30, 2013	65–33	60		Nominee Anne W. Patterson	December 13, 2013	54–36	60
Nominee Mark Gaston Pearce	July 30, 2013	69–29	60		Nominee Jeh Charles Johnson	December 16, 2013	57–37	60
Nominee Samantha Power	July 30, 2013	UC	60		**Bipartisan Budget Act**	December 17, 2013	67–33	60
Nominee Byron Todd Jones	July 31, 2013	60–40	60		**Department of Defense Authorization Act, FY2014**	December 18, 2013	71–29	60
Transportation, Housing and Urban Development, and Related Agencies Appropriations	August 1, 2013	54–43	60		Nominee Alejandro Nicholas Mayorkas	December 19, 2013	55–45	60
Continuing Appropriations Resolution, 2014	September 25, 2013	100–0	60		Judicial nominee Brian J. Davis	December 20, 2013	56–36	60
Continuing Appropriations Resolution, 2014	September 27, 2013	79–19	60		Nominee John Andrew Koskinen	December 20, 2013	56–39	60
Debt Limit bill	October 12, 2013	53–45	60		Nominee Janet L. Yellen	December 20, 2013	59–34	60
Continuing Appropriations Resolution, 2014	October 16, 2013	83–16	60		**Nominee Sloan D. Gibson**	December 20, 2013	UC	60
Nominee Richard F. Griffin	October 29, 2013	62–37	60		**Nominee Sarah Sewall**	December 20, 2013	UC	60
Nominee Thomas Edgar Wheeler	October 29, 2013	no vote	60		**Nominee Michael L. Connor**	December 20, 2013	UC	60
Nominee Katherine Archuleta	October 30, 2013	81–18	60		**Nominee Sarah Bloom Raskin**	December 20, 2013	UC	60
Nominee Alan F. Estevez	October 30, 2013	91–8	60		**Nominee Jessica Garfola Wright**	December 20, 2013	UC	60
Nominee Jacob J. Lew	October 30, 2013	UC	60		**Nominee Richard J. Engler**	December 20, 2013	UC	60
					Emergency Unemployment Compensation Extension Act	January 7, 2014	60–37	60
					Judicial nominee Robert Leon Wilkins Vote No. 235 reconsidered	January 9, 2014	55–38	60
					Emergency Unemployment Compensation Extension Act	January 14, 2014	52–48	60

Issue	Date	Vote	Yeas needed	Issue	Date	Vote	Yeas needed
Emergency Unemployment Compensation Extension Act	January 14, 2014	55–45	60	Judicial nominee M. Douglas Harpool	March 26, 2014	56–43	60
Consolidated Appropriations Act, 2014	January 16, 2014	72–26	60	Judicial nominee Gerald Austin McHugh Jr.	March 26, 2014	56–43	60
Homeowner Flood Insurance Affordability Act	January 27, 2014	86–13	60	**Judicial nominee Edward G. Smith**	March 26, 2014	75–23	60
Farm Bill	February 3, 2014	72–22	60	Judicial nominee John B. Owens	March 27, 2014	54–44	60
Emergency Unemployment Compensation Extension Act	February 6, 2014	55–43	60	**Legislative vehicle for the unemployment insurance extension**	March 27, 2014	65–34	60
Emergency Unemployment Compensation Extension Act	February 6, 2014	58–40	60	**Legislative vehicle for the unemployment insurance extension**	April 2, 2014	61–38	60
Bill to Repeal Section 403 of the Bipartisan Budget Act of 2013	February 10, 2014	94–0	60	**Legislative vehicle for the unemployment insurance extension**	April 3, 2014	61–35	60
Temporary Debt Limit Extension Act	February 12, 2014	67–31	60	Paycheck Fairness Act	April 9, 2014	53–44	60
Judicial nominee Jeffrey Alker Meyer	February 24, 2014	55–37	60	Judicial nominee Michelle T. Friedland	April 10, 2014	56–41	60
Judicial nominee James Maxwell Moody Jr.	February 24, 2014	58–34	60	Nominee David Weil	April 28, 2014	51–42	60
Judicial nominee James Donato	February 25, 2014	55–42	60	Judicial nominee Stanley Allen Bastian	April 29, 2014	55–41	60
Judicial nominee Beth Labson Freeman	February 25, 2014	56–42	60	Judicial nominee Cynthia Ann Bashant	April 29, 2014	56–41	60
Comprehensive Veterans Health and Benefits and Military Retirement Pay Restoration Act of 2014	February 25, 2014	99–0	60	Judicial nominee Daniel D. Crabtree	April 29, 2014	57–39	60
Comprehensive Veterans Health and Benefits and Military Retirement Pay Restoration Act of 2014	February 27, 2014	no vote	60	Judicial nominee Manish S. Shah	April 29, 2014	57–40	60
Comprehensive Veterans Health and Benefits and Military Retirement Pay Restoration Act of 2014	February 27, 2014	no vote	60	Judicial nominee Sheryl H. Lipman	April 29, 2014	58–39	60
Judicial nominee Debo P. Adegbile	March 5, 2014	47–52	60	**Judicial nominee Jon David Levy**	April 29, 2014	63–34	60
Nominee Rose Eilene Gottemoeller	March 5, 2014	55–45	60	Minimum Wage Fairness Act	April 30, 2014	54–32	60
Judicial nominee Pedro A. Delgado Hernandez	March 5, 2014	57–41	60	Judicial nominee Theodore David Chuang	May 1, 2014	54–43	60
Judicial nominee Vince Girdhari	March 5, 2014	57–43	60	Judicial nominee George Jarrod Hazel	May 1, 2014	55–42	60
Judicial nominee Timothy L. Brooks	March 5, 2014	59–41	60	**Judicial nominee Nancy L. Moritz**	May 1, 2014	60–38	60
Judicial nominee Pamela L. Reeves	March 5, 2014	62–37	60	**Energy Savings and Industrial Competitiveness Act of 2014**	May 6, 2014	79–20	60
Child Care and Development Block Grant Act of 2013	March 5, 2014	UC	60	Judicial nominee Nancy J. Rosenstengel	May 8, 2014	54–42	60
Victims Protection Act of 2014	March 6, 2014	100–0	60	Judicial nominee Indira Talwani	May 8, 2014	55–41	60
Military Justice Improvement Act of 2013	March 6, 2014	55–45	60	Judicial nominee James D. Peterson	May 8, 2014	56–40	60
Judicial nominee Carolyn B. McHugh	March 10, 2014	62–34	60	Judicial nominee Robin S. Rosenbaum	May 8, 2014	57–37	60
Judicial nominee Matthew Frederick Leitman	March 11, 2014	55–43	60	Energy Savings and Industrial Competitiveness Act of 2014	May 12, 2014	55–36	60
Judicial nominee Judith Ellen Levy	March 11, 2014	56–42	60	**Legislative vehicle for the tax extenders**	May 13, 2014	96–3	60
Judicial nominee Linda Vivienne Parker	March 11, 2014	56–42	60	Judicial nominee Steven Paul Logan	May 14, 2014	58–37	60
Judicial nominee Laurie J. Michelson	March 11, 2014	56–43	60	**Judicial nominee John Joseph Tuchi**	May 14, 2014	62–35	60
Sovereignty and Democracy in Ukraine Act	March 24, 2014	78–17	60	**Judicial nominee Diane J. Humetewa**	May 14, 2014	64–34	60
Judicial nominee Christopher Reid Cooper	March 26, 2014	56–43	60	Legislative vehicle for the tax extenders	May 15, 2014	53–40	60
				Judicial nominee Rosemary Marquez	May 15, 2014	58–35	60
				Judicial nominee Gregg Jeffrey Costa	May 15, 2014	58–36	60

Issue	Date	Vote	Yeas needed
Judicial nominee Douglas L. Rayes	May 15, 2014	59–35	60
Judicial nominee James Alan Soto	May 15, 2014	61–35	60
Legislative vehicle for the tax extenders	May 15, 2014	UC	60
Nominee Stanley Fischer	May 20, 2014	62–35	60
Judicial nominee David Jeremiah Barron	May 21, 2014	52–43	60
Nominee Keith M. Harper	June 2, 2014	51–37	60
Nominee Sharon Y. Bowen	June 3, 2014	50–44	60
Judicial nominee Tanya S. Chutkan	June 3, 2014	54–40	60
Judicial nominee Mark G. Mastroianni	June 3, 2014	56–39	60
Judicial nominee Bruce Howe Hendricks	June 3, 2014	59–35	60
Nominee Sylvia Mathews Burwell	June 4, 2014	67–28	60
Judicial nominee M. Hannah Lauck	June 9, 2014	52–32	60
Judicial nominee Leo T. Sorokin	June 9, 2014	52–33	60
Judicial nominee Richard Franklin Boulware II	June 9, 2014	53–34	60
Nominee Stanley Fischer	June 10, 2014	56–38	60
Nominee Jerome H. Powell	June 10, 2014	58–36	60
Nominee Lael Brainard	June 10, 2014	59–35	60
Refinancing Federal student loans	June 11, 2014	56–38	60
Judicial nominee Salvador Mendoza Jr.	June 16, 2014	55–37	60
Judicial nominee Staci Michelle Yandle	June 16, 2014	55–37	60
Judicial nominee Darrin P. Gayles	June 16, 2014	55–37	60
Judicial nominee Peter Joseph Kadzik	June 17, 2014	54–43	60
Commerce, Justice, Science, and Related Agencies Appropriations Act, 2015	June 17, 2014	95–3	60
Judicial nominee Geoffrey W. Crawford	June 23, 2014	52–32	60
Judicial nominee Paul G. Byron	June 23, 2014	53–30	60
Judicial nominee Carlos Eduardo Mendoza	June 23, 2014	53–31	60
Judicial nominee Beth Bloom	June 23, 2014	53–31	60
Nominee Leon Rodriguez	June 24, 2014	52–44	60
Judicial nominee Cheryl Ann Krause	June 26, 2014	57–39	60
Bipartisan Sportsmen's Act	July 7, 2014	82–12	60
Bipartisan Sportsmen's Act	July 10, 2014	41–56	60
Nominee Norman C. Bay	July 15, 2014	51–45	60
Nominee Cheryl A. LaFleur	July 15, 2014	85–10	60
Judicial nominee Ronnie L. White	July 16, 2014	54–43	60
Protect Women's Health From Corporate Interference	July 16, 2014	56–43	60
Judicial nominee Julie E. Carnes	July 17, 2014	68–23	60
Judicial nominee Andre Birotte Jr.	July 22, 2014	56–43	60
Judicial nominee John W. deGravelles	July 22, 2014	57–39	60
Judicial nominee Robin L. Rosenberg	July 22, 2014	58–42	60

Issue	Date	Vote	Yeas needed
Bring Jobs Home Act	July 23, 2014	93–7	60
Judicial nominee Pamela Harris	July 24, 2014	54–41	60
Bring Jobs Home Act	July 30, 2014	54–42	60
Emergency Supplemental Appropriations Act, 2014	July 30, 2014	63–33	60
Judicial nominee Jill A. Pryor	July 31, 2014	58–33	60
Emergency Supplemental Appropriations Act, 2014	July 31, 2014	no vote	60
Proposing an amendment to the Constitution of the United States relating to contributions and expenditures intended to affect elections	September 8, 2014	79–18	60
Paycheck Fairness Act	September 10, 2014	73–25	60
Proposing an amendment to the Constitution of the United States relating to contributions and expenditures intended to affect elections	September 11, 2014	54–42	60
Nominee Jeffery Martin Baran	September 15, 2014	52–39	60
Paycheck Fairness Act	September 15, 2014	52–40	60
Nominee Stephen G. Burns	September 15, 2014	54–37	60
Continuing Appropriations Resolution, 2015	September 18, 2014	73–27	60
Judicial nominee Randolph D. Moss	November 12, 2014	53–45	60
Judicial nominee Leigh Martin May	November 12, 2014	67–30	60
Child Care and Development Block Grant	November 13, 2014	96–1	60
Judicial nominee Eleanor Louise Ross	November 17, 2014	66–29	60
Judicial nominee Mark Howard Cohen	November 17, 2014	67–29	60
Judicial nominee Leslie Joyce Abrams	November 17, 2014	68–28	60
Surveillance Overhaul bill	November 18, 2014	58–42	60
Judicial nominee Victor Allen Bolden	November 19, 2014	51–44	60
Judicial nominee Brenda K. Sannes	November 19, 2014	55–42	60
Judicial nominee Madeline Cox Arleo	November 19, 2014	56–40	60
Judicial nominee Wendy Beetlestone	November 19, 2014	58–38	60
Judicial nominee Pamela Pepper	November 19, 2014	58–39	60
Nominee Noah Bryson Mamet	December 1, 2014	50–36	60
Nominee Colleen Bradley Bell	December 1, 2014	50–36	60
Nominee Robert S. Adler	December 2, 2014	52–40	60
Nominee P. David Lopez	December 2, 2014	54–43	60
Nominee Charlotte A. Burrows	December 2, 2014	57–39	60
Nominee Nani A. Coloretti	December 2, 2014	59–34	60
Judicial nominee Mark A. Kearney	December 3, 2014	60–36	60
Judicial nominee David J. Hale	December 3, 2014	65–31	60
Judicial nominee Gerald J. Pappert	December 3, 2014	67–28	60
Nominee Joseph S. Hezir	December 3, 2014	68–27	60
Nominee Franklin M. Orr Jr.	December 3, 2014	71–35	60
Nominee Lauren McGarity McFerran	December 4, 2014	51–42	60

Issue	Date	Vote	Yeas needed	Issue	Date	Vote	Yeas needed
Judicial nominee Lydia Kay Griggsby	December 4, 2014	53–36	60	Department of Homeland Security Appropriations, FY2015	February 4, 2015	53–47	60
Nominee Jeffery Martin Baran	December 4, 2014	53–40	60	Department of Homeland Security Appropriations, FY2015	February 5, 2015	52–47	60
Nominee Ellen Dudley Williams	December 4, 2014	57–34	60				
Judicial nominee Joseph F. Leeson Jr.	December 4, 2014	66–26	60	Department of Homeland Security Appropriations, FY2015	February 23, 2015	47–46	60
Judicial nominee Gregory N. Stivers	December 4, 2014	69–24	60	**Department of Homeland Security Appropriations, FY2015**	February 25, 2015	98–2	60
Nominee Virginia Tyler Lodge	December 9, 2014	63–32	60	Immigration Rule of Law Act	February 27, 2015	57–42	60
Nominee Ronald Anderson Walter	December 9, 2014	65–31	60	**Department of Homeland Security Appropriations, FY2015**	February 27, 2015	68–31	60
National Defense Authorization Act for Fiscal Year 2015	December 12, 2014	89–11	60	Department of Homeland Security Appropriations, FY2015	March 2, 2015	47–43	60
Consolidated and Further Continuing Appropriations Act, 2015	December 13, 2014	77–19	60	**Keystone Pipeline**	March 4, 2015	UC	60
Nominee Carolyn Watts Colvin	December 13, 2014	UC	60	**Iran Nuclear Agreement Review Act of 2015**	March 9, 2015	UC	60
Nominee Frank A. Rose	December 15, 2014	54–39	60	Justice for Victims of Trafficking Act 2015	March 17, 2015	55–43	60
Nominee Daniel J. Santos	December 15, 2014	54–39	60	Justice for Victims of Trafficking Act 2015	March 17, 2015	55–43	60
Judicial nominee Stephen R. Bough	December 16, 2014	51–38	60	Justice for Victims of Trafficking Act 2015	March 18, 2015	57–41	60
Nominee Vivek Hallegere Murthy	December 16, 2014	51–43	60	Justice for Victims of Trafficking Act 2015	March 19, 2015	56–42	60
Nominee Antony Blinken	December 16, 2014	53–40	60	Justice for Victims of Trafficking Act 2015	March 19, 2015	56–42	60
Nominee Sarah R. Saldana	December 16, 2014	53–41	60				
Nominee Colette Dodson Honorable	December 16, 2014	65–28	60	**Justice for Victims of Trafficking Act 2015**	April 16, 2015	UC	60
Nominee Estevan R. Lopez	December 16, 2014	UC	60	**Nominee Loretta E. Lynch**	April 23, 2015	66–34	60
Nominee Marcus Dwayne Jadotte	December 16, 2014	UC	60	**Iran Nuclear Agreement Review Act of 2015**	May 7, 2015	93–6	60
Nominee Jonathan Nicholas Stivers	December 16, 2014	UC	60	**Iran Nuclear Agreement Review Act of 2015**	May 7, 2015	UC	60
Nominee John Charles Cruden	December 16, 2014	UC	60	Legislative vehicle for trade promotion authority	May 12, 2015	52–45	60
Nominee Christopher Smith	December 16, 2014	UC	60	**Legislative vehicle for trade promotion authority**	May 14, 2015	65–33	60
Judicial nominee Jorge Luis Alonso	December 16, 2014	UC	60	**Legislative vehicle for trade promotion authority**	May 21, 2015	62–38	60
Judicial nominee Haywood Stirling Gilliam Jr.	December 16, 2014	UC	60	**Legislative vehicle for trade promotion authority**	May 22, 2015	61–38	60
Judicial nominee Amit Priyavadan Mehta	December 16, 2014	UC	60	Two month FISA extension	May 23, 2015	45–54	60
Judicial nominee Allison Dale Burroughs	December 16, 2014	UC	60	USA Freedom Act of 2015	May 23, 2015	57–42	60
Judicial nominee John Robert Blakey	December 16, 2014	UC	60	**USA Freedom Act of 2015**	May 31, 2015	77–17	60
Judicial nominee Amos L. Mazzant III	December 16, 2014	UC	60	**USA Freedom Act of 2015**	June 2, 2015	83–14	60
Judicial nominee Robert Lee Pitman	December 16, 2014	UC	60	**National Defense Authorization, FY2016**	June 2, 2015	UC	60
Judicial nominee Robert William Schroeder III	December 16, 2014	UC	60	National Defense Authorization, FY2016	June 11, 2015	56–40	60
Judicial nominee Joan Marie Azrack	December 16, 2014	UC	60	**National Defense Authorization, FY2016**	June 16, 2015	83–15	60
Judicial nominee Elizabeth K. Dillon	December 16, 2014	UC	60	**National Defense Authorization, FY2016**	June 17, 2015	84–14	60
Judicial nominee Loretta Copeland Biggs	December 16, 2014	UC	60	Department of Defense Appropriations, FY2016	June 18, 2015	50–45	60
Keystone Pipeline	January 12, 2015	63–32	60	**Legislative vehicle for trade promotion authority**	June 23, 2015	60–37	60
Keystone Pipeline	January 26, 2015	53–39	60				
Keystone Pipeline	January 26, 2015	53–39	60	**Trade Preferences Extension Act of 2015**	June 24, 2015	76–22	60
Keystone Pipeline	January 29, 2015	62–35	60				
Department of Homeland Security Appropriations, FY2015	February 3, 2015	51–48	60				

Issue	Date	Vote	Yeas needed
Trade Facilitation and Trade Enforcement Act of 2015	June 24, 2015	UC	60
National Defense Authorization, FY2016	July 9, 2015	81–15	60
Every Child Achieves Act of 2015	July 15, 2015	86–12	60
Every Child Achieves Act of 2015	July 16, 2015	79–18	60
Legislative vehicle for highway funding act	July 21, 2015	41–56	60
Legislative vehicle for highway funding act	July 22, 2015	62–36	60
Legislative vehicle for highway funding act	July 26, 2015	49–43	60
Legislative vehicle for highway funding act	July 26, 2015	67–26	60
Legislative vehicle for highway funding act	July 27, 2015	62–32	60
Legislative vehicle for highway funding act	July 29, 2015	65–35	60
A bill to prohibit Federal funding of Planned Parenthood Federation of America	August 3, 2015	53–46	60
Cybersecurity Information Sharing Act	August 5, 2015	UC	60
Legislative vehicle for Iran nuclear agreement resolution of disapproval	September 10, 2015	58–42	60
Legislative vehicle for Iran nuclear agreement resolution of disapproval	September 10, 2015	UC	60
Legislative vehicle for Iran nuclear agreement resolution of disapproval	September 15, 2015	56–42	60
Legislative vehicle for Iran nuclear agreement resolution of disapproval	September 15, 2015	UC	60
Legislative vehicle for Iran nuclear agreement resolution of disapproval	September 17, 2015	53–45	60
Legislative vehicle for Iran nuclear agreement resolution of disapproval	September 17, 2015	56–42	60
Legislative vehicle for Iran nuclear agreement resolution of disapproval	September 17, 2015	UC	60
Pain-Capable Unborn Child Protection Act	September 22, 2015	54–42	60
Department of Defense Appropriations, FY2016	September 22, 2015	54–42	60
Legislative vehicle for the continuing resolution, FY 2016	September 24, 2015	47–52	60
TSA Offce of Inspection Accountability Act of 2015	September 28, 2015	77–19	60
Military Construction and Veterans Affairs amd Related Agencies Appropriations Act	October 1, 2015	50–44	60
National Defense Authorization, FY2016	October 6, 2015	73–26	60
Energy and Water Appropriations Act	October 8, 2015	49–47	60
Sanctuary Jurisdictions	October 20, 2015	54–45	60
Cybersecurity Information Sharing Act	October 22, 2015	83–14	60
Cybersecurity Information Sharing Act	October 27, 2015	UC	60

Issue	Date	Vote	Yeas needed
Bipartisan Budget Act of 2015	October 30, 2015	63–35	60
Federal Water Quality Protection Act	November 3, 2015	57–41	60
Department of Defense Appropriations Act	November 5, 2015	51–44	60
Legislative vehicle for highway funding act	November 10, 2015	82–7	60
Departments of Transportation, Housing and Urban Development, and Related Agencies Appropriations	November 17, 2015	UC	60
Every Child Achieves Act of 2015	November 18, 2015	91–6	60
Departments of Transportation, Housing and Urban Development, and Related Agencies Appropriations	November 19, 2015	UC	60
Departments of Transportation, Housing and Urban Development, and Related Agencies Appropriations	November 19, 2015	UC	60
Every Child Achieves Act of 2015	December 8, 2015	84–12	60
Military Construction and Veterans Affairs and Related Agencies Appropriations Act	December 18, 2015	72–26	60
Federal Reserve Transparency Act of 2015	January 12, 2016	53–44	60
American Security Against Foreign Enemies Act	January 20, 2016	55–43	60
Veto message to accompany S.J.Res.22, the WOTUS rule resolution of disapproval	January 21, 2016	52–40	60
Energy Policy Modernization Act	February 4, 2016	43–54	60
Energy Policy Modernization Act	February 4, 2016	46–50	60
Trade Facilitation and Trade Enforcement Act	February 11, 2016	73–22	60
Nominee Robert McKinnon Cali	February 22, 2016	80–6	60
Comprehensive Addiction and Recovery Act	February 29, 2016	89–0	60
Comprehensive Addiction and Recovery Act	March 7, 2016	86–3	60
Comprehensive Addiction and Recovery Act	March 9, 2016	93–3	60
Defund Planned Parenthood Act	March 16, 2016	48–49	60
Legislative vehicle for FAA Reauthorization Act	April 6, 2016	98–0	60
Legislative vehicle for FAA Reauthorization Act	April 14, 2016	94–4	60
Legislative vehicle for FAA Reauthorization Act	April 18, 2016	89–5	60
Energy and Water Appropriations Act	April 20, 2016	UC	60
Further Continuing Appropriations	April 27, 2016	50–46	60
Departments of Transportation, Housing and Urban Development, and Related Agencies Appropriations	April 27, 2016	UC	60
Further Continuing Appropriations	April 28, 2016	52–43	60
Further Continuing Appropriations	May 9, 2016	50–42	60

Issue	Date	Vote	Yeas needed
Further Continuing Appropriations	May 11, 2016	57–42	60
Further Continuing Appropriations	May 11, 2016	97–2	60
Further Continuing Appropriations	May 12, 2016	UC	60
Departments of Transportation, Housing and Urban Development, and Related Agencies Appropriations	May 17, 2016	50–47	60
Departments of Transportation, Housing and Urban Development, and Related Agencies Appropriations	May 17, 2016	52–45	60
Departments of Transportation, Housing and Urban Development, and Related Agencies Appropriations	May 17, 2016	68–29	60
Departments of Transportation, Housing and Urban Development, and Related Agencies Appropriations	May 19, 2016	88–10	60
Departments of Transportation, Housing and Urban Development, and Related Agencies Appropriations	May 19, 2016	UC	60
National Defense Authorization, FY2017	May 25, 2016	98–0	60
Military Construction, Veterans Affairs, and Related Agencies Appropriations FY2017 and Zika Response	June 8, 2016	93–2	60
National Defense Authorization, FY2017	June 9, 2016	43–55	60
National Defense Authorization, FY2017	June 9, 2016	56–42	60
National Defense Authorization, FY2017	June 10, 2016	68–23	60
Commerce, Justice, Science, and Related Agencies Appropriations, FY2016	June 14, 2016	94–3	60
Comprehensive Addiction and Recovery Act	June 16, 2016	95–1	60
Commerce, Justice, Science, and Related Agencies Appropriations, FY2016	June 20, 2016	44–56	60
Commerce, Justice, Science, and Related Agencies Appropriations, FY2016	June 20, 2016	47–53	60
Commerce, Justice, Science, and Related Agencies Appropriations, FY2016	June 20, 2016	53–47	60
Commerce, Justice, Science, and Related Agencies Appropriations, FY2016	June 20, 2016	53–47	60
Commerce, Justice, Science, and Related Agencies Appropriations, FY2016	June 22, 2016	58–38	60
Military Construction, Veterans Affairs, and Related Agencies Appropriations FY2017 and Zika Response	June 28, 2016	58–48	60
Legislative vehicle for PROMESA	June 29, 2016	68–32	60
Sanctuary cities	July 6, 2016	53–44	60
Kate's Law	July 6, 2016	55–42	60
Legislative vehicle for GMO food labeling	July 6, 2016	65–32	60
Department of Defense Appropriations, FY2017	July 7, 2016	50–44	60
Energy Policy Modernization Act	July 12, 2016	84–3	60
Comprehensive Addiction and Recovery Act	July 13, 2016	90–2	60
Military Construction, Veterans Affairs, and Related Agencies Appropriations FY2017 and Zika Response	July 14, 2016	52–44	60
Department of Defense Appropriations, FY2017	July 14, 2016	55–42	60
National Defense Authorization, FY2017	July 14, 2016	90–7	60
Military Construction, Veterans Affairs, and Related Agencies Appropriations FY2017 and Zika Response	September 6, 2016	52–46	60
Department of Defense Appropriations, FY2017	September 6, 2016	55–43	60
Water Resources Development Act	September 12, 2016	90–1	60
Water Resources Development Act	September 14, 2016	94–3	60
Military Construction, Veterans Affairs, and Related Agencies Appropriations FY2017 and Zika Response	September 20, 2016	89–7	60
Military Construction, Veterans Affairs, and Related Agencies Appropriations FY2017 and Zika Response	September 27, 2016	40–59	60
Military Construction, Veterans Affairs, and Related Agencies Appropriations FY2017 and Zika Response	September 27, 2016	45–55	60
Military Construction, Veterans Affairs, and Related Agencies Appropriations FY2017 and Zika Response	September 28, 2016	77–21	60
Military Construction, Veterans Affairs, and Related Agencies Appropriations FY2017 and Zika Response	September 28, 2016	77–21	60
American Energy and Conservation	November 17, 2016	51–47	60
21st Century Cures Act	December 5, 2016	85–13	60
National Defense Authorization, FY2017	December 7, 2016	92–7	60
Further Continuing Appropriations	December 9, 2016	61–38	60
WINN Act	December 10, 2016	69–30	60

NOTE: UC—Unanimous Consent

[1]Vote was taken after midnight in the session that began October 8, 1985.

[2]Because the bill would have changed Senate rules, two-thirds of those present and voting were required to invoke cloture: sixty-six in this case instead of the usual sixty.

[3]Because the bill would have changed Senate rules, two-thirds of those present and voting were required to invoke cloture: sixty-five in this case instead of the usual sixty.

Attempted and Successful Cloture Votes, 1919–2017

	Congress	First Session		Second Session		Total	
		Attempted	*Successful*	*Attempted*	*Successful*	*Attempted*	*Successful*
66th	(1919–1921)	2	1	0	0	2	1
67th	(1921–1923)	1	0	0	0	1	0
68th	(1923–1925)	0	0	0	0	0	0
69th	(1925–1927)	2	1	5	2	7	3
70th	(1927–1929)	0	0	0	0	0	0
71st	(1929–1931)	0	0	0	0	0	0
72nd	(1931–1933)	1	0	0	0	1	0
73rd	(1933–1935)	0	0	0	0	0	0
74th	(1935–1937)	0	0	0	0	0	0
75th	(1937–1939)	0	0	2	0	2	0
76th	(1939–1941)	0	0	0	0	0	0
77th	(1941–1943)	0	0	1	0	1	0
78th	(1943–1945)	0	0	1	0	1	0
79th	(1945–1947)	0	0	4	0	4	0
80th	(1947–1949)	0	0	0	0	0	0
81st	(1949–1951)	0	0	2	0	2	0
82nd	(1951–1953)	0	0	0	0	0	0
83rd	(1953–1955)	0	0	1	0	1	0
84th	(1955–1957)	0	0	0	0	0	0
85th	(1957–1959)	0	0	0	0	0	0
86th	(1959–1961)	0	0	1	0	1	0
87th	(1961–1963)	1	0	3	1	4	1
88th	(1963–1965)	1	0	2	1	3	1
89th	(1965–1967)	2	1	5	0	7	1
90th	(1967–1969)	1	0	5	1	6	1
91st	(1969–1971)	2	0	4	0	6	0
92nd	(1971–1973)	10	2	10	2	20	4
93rd	(1973–1975)	10	2	21	7	31	9
94th	(1975–1977)	23	13	4	4	27	17
95th	(1977–1979)	5	1	8	2	13	3
96th	(1979–1981)	4	1	17	9	21	10
97th	(1981–1983)	7	2	20	7	27	9
98th	(1983–1985)	7	2	12	9	19	11
99th	(1985–1987)	9	1	14	9	23	10
100th	(1987–1989)	23	5	20	6	43	11[1]
101st	(1989–1991)	9	6	15	5	24	11
102nd	(1991–1993)	20	9	28	14	48	23
103rd	(1993–1995)	20	4	22	10	42	14[2]
104th	(1995–1997)	21	4	29	5	50	9
105th	(1997–1999)	24	7	29	11	53	18
106th	(1999–2001)	36	11	22	17	58	28
107th	(2001–2003)	22	12	39	22	61	34
108th	(2003–2005)	23	1	26	11	49	12
109th	(2005–2007)	21	13	33	21	54	34
110th	(2007–2009)	62	31	50	30	112	61
111th	(2009–2011)	39	35	52	28	91	63
112th	(2011–2013)	34	19	39	22	73	41
113th	(2013–2015)	64	50	154	137	218	187
114th	(2015–2017)	64	31	60	30	124	61
Totals		570	265	760	423	1,330	688

SOURCES: "Indicators of Congressional Workload and Activity," Congressional Research Service; U.S. Senate (www.senate.gov/pagelayout/reference/cloture_motions/clotureCounts.htm); *Congress and the Nation*, selected volumes (Washington, DC: CQ Press, selected years); *CQ Almanac*, selected volumes (Washington, DC: Congressional Quarterly, selected years); Richard S. Beth, Congressional Research Service, Library of Congress; www.senate.gov/reference.

NOTE: The number of votes required to invoke cloture was changed March 7, 1975, from two-thirds of those present and voting, to three-fifths of the total Senate membership, as Rule XXII of the standing rules of the Senate was amended.

[1]The Senate Historical Office records twelve successful votes. One of the twelve, taken on July 16, 1987, and related to Kuwaiti tanker flagging, is recorded by the Office as having been by unanimous consent. For this table, the eleven votes were all by roll call.

[2]The Senate Historical Office records forty-six attempted cloture votes for the 100th Congress. However, five of those votes, all on nominations, were taken together with one roll call. For this table, CQ Press treats the five as a single vote, giving a total of forty-two.

House Discharge Petitions since 1931

The discharge petition is a little-used but dramatic House device that enables a majority of representatives to bring to the floor legislation blocked in committee. The following table shows the frequency with which the discharge petition has been used since the present discharge procedure was adopted in 1931 through 2017.

Although the procedure is rarely used and even more rarely successful, it may on occasion indirectly succeed by prompting a legislative committee, the Rules Committee, or the leadership to act on a measure and thereby avoid the discharge.

Congress		Discharge Petitions	Discharge Motion		Committee Discharged	Underlying Measure[3]	
			Entered[1]	Called Up[2]		Passed House	Received Final Approval[4]
72nd	(1931–1933)	12	5	5	1	1	–
73rd	(1933–1935)	31	6	1	1	1	–
74th	(1935–1937)	33	3	2	2	–	–
75th	(1937–1939)	43	4	4	3[5]	2	1
76th	(1939–1941)	37[5]	2	2	2	2	–
77th	(1941–1943)	15	1	1	1	1	–
78th	(1943–1945)	21	3	3	3	3	1[6]
79th	(1945–1947)	35	3	1	1	1	–
80th	(1947–1949)	20	1	1	1	1	–
81st	(1949–1951)	34	3[7]	1	1	1	–
82nd	(1951–1953)	14	–	–	–	–	–
83rd	(1953–1955)	10	1	1	1	1	–
84th	(1955–1957)	6	–	–	–	–	–
85th	(1957–1959)	7	1	1	1	1	–
86th	(1959–1961)	7	1	1	1	1	1
87th	(1961–1963)	6	–	–	–	–	–
88th	(1963–1965)	5	–	–	–	–	–
89th	(1965–1967)	6	1	1	1	1	–
90th	(1967–1969)	4	–	–	–	–	–
91st	(1969–1971)	12	1	1	1	1	–
92nd	(1971–1973)	15	1	1	1	–	–
93rd	(1973–1975)	10	–	–	–	–	–
94th	(1975–1977)	15	–	–	–	–	–
95th	(1977–1979)	11	–	–	–	–	–
96th	(1979–1981)	14	2	1	1	–	–
97th	(1981–1983)	24	1	–	–	–	–
98th	(1983–1985)	13	1	–	–	–	–
99th	(1985–1987)	10	1	–	–	–	–
100th	(1987–1989)	5[8]	–	–	–	–	–
101st	(1989–1991)	8	1	–	–	–	–
102nd	(1991–1993)	8	1[9]	1[9]	1[9]	–	–
103rd	(1993–1995)	26	2[9]	2[9]	2[9]	1	1[6]
104th	(1995–1997)	15	–	–	–	–	–
105th	(1997–1999)	8	–	–	–	–	–
106th	(1999–2001)	11	–	–	–	–	–
107th	(2001–2003)	12	1	–	–	–	–
108th	(2003–2005)	16	–	–	–	–	–
109th	(2005–2007)	18	–	–	–	–	–
110th	(2007–2009)	18	–	–	–	–	–
111th	(2009–2011)	13	–	–	–	–	–
112th	(2011–2013)	6	–	–	–	–	–
113th	(2013–2015)	12	–	–	–	–	–
114th	(2015–2017)	6	–	–	–	–	–
Totals		652	47	31	26	19	4

SOURCES: Richard S. Beth, "The Discharge Rule in the House: Recent Use in Historical Context," Congressional Research Service, Library of Congress, September 15, 1997; update provided by CRS, September 1999, April 2000, December 2005. Clerk of the House, March 2010, http://clerk.house.gov/legislative/legvotes.aspx.

[1] A discharge motion is "entered" when the petition receives a sufficient number of member signatures for it to be entered on the Calendar of Motions to Discharge Committees. This number was 145 in the 72nd and 73rd Congresses, 219 in the 86th and 87th Congresses, and 218 for all other Congresses in the table.

[2] A discharge motion may be offered on the floor on any second or fourth Monday falling at least seven legislative days after the discharge petition is entered. Each day on which the House convenes is usually a legislative day.

[3] A discharge petition may be filed to bring to the floor either a substantive measure in committee or a "special rule" from the Committee on Rules providing for House consideration of such a measure that is either in committee or previously reported. The last two columns of this table reflect action on the underlying, substantive measure, not on the special rule, if any, on which discharge was directly sought.

[4] Includes bills and joint resolutions becoming law; constitutional amendments submitted to the states for ratification; resolutions agreed to by the House; and concurrent resolutions finally agreed to by both chambers.

[5] During this Congress, the Rules Committee was discharged from a special rule for consideration of one measure, and the measure was taken up but then recommitted. Subsequently, the Rules Committee was discharged from a second special rule for consideration of the measure. This measure accordingly appears twice under "Committee discharged" and earlier columns, but only once under "Passed House" and subsequently.

[6] Resolution attempting to change House Rules.

[7] Includes one petition entered with respect to a special rule on a measure and another on the same measure directly.

[8] Includes one petition filed on a special rule for considering two measures.

[9] Includes one measure in the 102nd Congress and two in the 103rd from which the committee was discharged, and which were brought to the floor, by unanimous consent after the discharge petition was entered.

Congressional Reapportionment, 1789–2010

	Constitution	Year of Census [1]																				
	(1789)[2]	1790	1800	1810	1820	1830	1840	1850	1860	1870	1880	1890	1900	1910	1930[3]	1940	1950	1960	1970	1980	1990	2000	2010
Alabama				1[4]	3	5	7	7	6	8	8	9	9	10	9	9	9	8	7	7	7	7	7
Alaska																	1[4]	1	1	1	1	1	1
Arizona														1[4]	1	2	3	4	5	6	6	8	9
Arkansas						1[4]	1	2	3	4	5	6	7	7	7	7	6	4	4	4	4	4	4
California							2[4]	2	3	4	6	7	8	11	20	23	30	38	43	45	52	53	53
Colorado										1[4]	1	2	3	4	4	4	4	4	5	6	6	7	7
Connecticut	5	7	7	7	6	6	4	4	4	4	4	4	5	5	6	6	6	6	6	6	6	5	5
Delaware	1	1	1	2	1	1	1	1	1	1	1	1	1	1	1	1	1	1	1	1	1	1	1
Florida							1[4]	1	1	2	2	2	3	4	5	6	8	12	15	19	23	25	27
Georgia	3	2	4	6	7	9	8	8	7	9	10	11	11	12	10	10	10	10	10	10	11	13	14
Hawaii																	1[4]	2	2	2	2	2	2
Idaho											1[4]	1	1	2	2	2	2	2	2	2	2	2	2
Illinois				1[4]	1	3	7	9	14	19	20	22	25	27	27	26	25	24	24	22	20	19	18
Indiana				1[4]	3	7	10	11	11	13	13	13	13	13	12	11	11	11	11	10	10	9	9
Iowa							2[4]	2	6	9	11	11	11	11	9	8	8	7	6	6	5	5	4
Kansas									1	3	7	8	8	8	7	6	6	5	5	5	4	4	4
Kentucky		2	6	10	12	13	10	10	9	10	11	11	11	11	9	9	8	7	7	7	6	6	6
Louisiana				1[4]	3	3	4	4	5	6	6	6	7	8	8	8	8	8	8	8	7	7	6
Maine				7[4]	7	8	7	6	5	5	4	4	4	4	3	3	3	2	2	2	2	2	2
Maryland	6	8	9	9	9	8	6	6	5	6	6	6	6	6	6	6	7	8	8	8	8	8	8
Massachusetts	8	14	17	13[5]	13	12	10	11	10	11	12	13	14	16	15	14	14	12	12	11	10	10	9
Michigan						1[4]	3	4	6	9	11	12	12	13	17	17	18	19	19	18	16	15	14
Minnesota								2[4]	2	3	5	7	9	10	9	9	9	8	8	8	8	8	8
Mississippi				1[4]	1	2	4	5	5	6	7	7	8	8	7	7	6	5	5	5	5	4	4
Missouri					1	2	5	7	9	13	14	15	16	16	13	13	11	10	10	9	9	9	8
Montana											1[4]	1	1	2	2	2	2	2	2	2	2	1	1
Nebraska									1[4]	1	3	6	6	6	5	4	4	3	3	3	3	3	3
Nevada									1[4]	1	1	1	1	1	1	1	1	1	1	2	2	3	4
New Hampshire	3	4	5	6	6	5	4	3	3	3	2	2	2	2	2	2	2	2	2	2	2	2	2
New Jersey	4	5	6	6	6	6	5	5	5	7	7	8	10	12	14	14	14	15	15	14	13	13	12
New Mexico														1[4]	1	2	2	2	2	3	3	3	3
New York	6	10	17	27	34	40	34	33	31	33	34	34	37	43	45	45	43	41	39	34	31	29	27
North Carolina	5	10	12	13	13	13	9	8	7	8	9	9	10	10	11	12	12	11	11	11	12	13	13
North Dakota											1[4]	1	2	3	2	2	2	2	1	1	1	1	1
Ohio			1[4]	6	14	19	21	21	19	20	21	21	21	22	24	23	23	24	23	21	19	18	16
Oklahoma													5[4]	8	9	8	6	6	6	6	6	5	5
Oregon								1[4]	1	1	1	2	2	3	3	4	4	4	4	5	5	5	5
Pennsylvania	8	13	18	23	26	28	24	25	24	27	28	30	32	36	34	33	30	27	25	23	21	19	18
Rhode Island	1	2	2	2	2	2	2	2	2	2	2	2	2	3	2	2	2	2	2	2	2	2	2
South Carolina	5	6	8	9	9	9	7	6	4	5	7	7	7	7	6	6	6	6	6	6	6	6	7
South Dakota											2[4]	2	2	3	2	2	2	2	2	1	1	1	1
Tennessee		1[4]	3	6	9	13	11	10	8	10	10	10	10	10	9	10	9	9	8	9	9	9	9
Texas							2[4]	2	4	6	11	13	16	18	21	21	22	23	24	27	30	32	36
Utah												1[4]	1	2	2	2	2	2	2	3	3	3	4
Vermont		2	4	6	5	5	4	3	3	3	2	2	2	2	1	1	1	1	1	1	1	1	1
Virginia	10	19	22	23	22	21	15	13	11	9	10	10	10	10	9	9	10	10	10	10	11	11	11
Washington											1[4]	2	3	5	6	6	7	7	7	8	9	9	10
West Virginia										3	4	4	5	6	6	6	6	5	4	4	3	3	3
Wisconsin							2[4]	3	6	8	9	10	11	11	10	10	10	10	9	9	9	8	8
Wyoming											1[4]	1	1	1	1	1	1	1	1	1	1	1	1
Total	65	106	142	186	213	242	232	237	243	293	332	357	391	435	435	435	437[6]	435	435	435	435	435	435

SOURCES: *Biographical Directory of the American Congress* and Bureau of the Census.

[1] Apportionment effective with congressional election two years after census.

[2] Original apportionment made in Constitution, pending first census.

[3] No apportionment was made in 1920.

[4] These figures are not based on any census, but indicate the provisional representation accorded newly admitted states by Congress, pending the next census.

[5] Twenty members were assigned to Massachusetts, but seven of these were credited to Maine when that area became a state.

[6] Normally 435, but temporarily increased two seats by Congress when Alaska and Hawaii became states.

The Presidency

Selected Presidential Texts

President Obama's Second Inaugural Address

Following is the White House transcript of the second inaugural address of Barack Obama, the nation's forty-fourth president, delivered on January 21, 2013.

Thank you. Thank you so much.

Vice President Biden, Mr. Chief Justice, Members of the United States Congress, distinguished guests, and fellow citizens:

Each time we gather to inaugurate a President we bear witness to the enduring strength of our Constitution. We affirm the promise of our democracy. We recall that what binds this Nation together is not the colors of our skin or the tenets of our faith or the origins of our names. What makes us exceptional—what makes us American—is our allegiance to an idea articulated in a declaration made more than two centuries ago:

We hold these truths to be self-evident, that all men are created equal; that they are endowed by their Creator with certain unalienable rights; that among these are life, liberty, and the pursuit of happiness.

Today we continue a never-ending journey to bridge the meaning of those words with the realities of our time. For history tells us that while these truths may be self-evident, they've never been self-executing; that while freedom is a gift from God, it must be secured by His people here on Earth. The patriots of 1776 did not fight to replace the tyranny of a king with the privileges of a few or the rule of a mob. They gave to us a republic, a government of and by and for the people, entrusting each generation to keep safe our founding creed.

And for more than 200 years, we have.

Through blood drawn by lash and blood drawn by sword, we learned that no union founded on the principles of liberty and equality could survive half-slave and half-free. We made ourselves anew, and vowed to move forward together.

Together, we determined that a modern economy requires railroads and highways to speed travel and commerce, schools and colleges to train our workers.

Together, we discovered that a free market only thrives when there are rules to ensure competition and fair play.

Together, we resolved that a great nation must care for the vulnerable and protect its people from life's worst hazards and misfortune.

Through it all, we have never relinquished our skepticism of central authority nor have we succumbed to the fiction that all society's ills can be cured through government alone. Our celebration of initiative and enterprise, our insistence on hard work and personal responsibility, these are constants in our character.

But we have always understood that when times change, so must we; that fidelity to our founding principles requires new responses to new challenges; that preserving our individual freedoms ultimately requires collective action. For the American people can no more meet the demands of today's world by acting alone than American soldiers could have met the forces of fascism or communism with muskets and militias. No single person can train all the math and science teachers we'll need to equip our children for the future, or build the roads and networks and research labs that will bring new jobs and businesses to our shores. Now more than ever, we must do these things together, as one nation and one people.

This generation of Americans has been tested by crises that steeled our resolve and proved our resilience. A decade of war is now ending. An economic recovery has begun. America's possibilities are limitless, for we possess all the qualities that this world without boundaries demands: youth and drive; diversity and openness; an endless capacity for risk and a gift for reinvention. My fellow Americans, we are made for this moment and we will seize it—so long as we seize it together.

For we, the people, understand that our country cannot succeed when a shrinking few do very well and a growing many barely make it. We believe that America's prosperity must rest upon the broad shoulders of a rising middle class. We know that America thrives when every person can find independence and pride in their work; when the wages of honest labor liberate families from the brink of hardship. We are true to our creed when a little girl born into the bleakest poverty knows that she has the same chance to succeed as anybody else, because she is an American; she is free and she is equal, not just in the eyes of God, but also in our own.

We understand that outworn programs are inadequate to the needs of our time. So we must harness new ideas and technology to remake our government, revamp our Tax Code, reform our schools, and empower our citizens with the skills they need to work harder, learn more, reach higher. But while the means will change, our purpose endures: a nation that rewards the effort and determination of every single American. That is what this moment requires. That is what will give real meaning to our creed.

We, the people, still believe that every citizen deserves a basic measure of security and dignity. We must make the hard choices to reduce the cost of health care and the size of our deficit. But we reject the belief that America must choose between caring for the generation that built this country and investing in the generation that will build its future. For we remember the lessons of our past, when twilight years were spent in poverty and parents of a child with a disability had nowhere to turn.

We do not believe that in this country freedom is reserved for the lucky, or happiness for the few. We recognize that no matter how responsibly we live our lives, any one of us at any time may face a job loss or a sudden illness or a home swept away in a terrible storm. The commitments we make to each other through Medicare and Medicaid and Social Security, these things do not sap our initiative, they strengthen us. They do not make us a nation of takers; they free us to take the risks that make this country great.

We, the people, still believe that our obligations as Americans are not just to ourselves, but to all posterity. We will respond to the threat of climate change, knowing that the failure to do so would betray our children and future generations. Some may still deny the overwhelming judgment of science, but none can avoid the devastating impact of raging fires and crippling drought and more powerful storms.

The path towards sustainable energy sources will be long and sometimes difficult. But America cannot resist this transition, we must lead it. We cannot cede to other nations the technology that will power new jobs and new industries, we must claim its promise. That's how we will maintain our economic vitality and our national treasure—our forests and waterways, our crop lands and snow-capped peaks. That is how we will preserve our planet, commanded to our care by God. That's what will lend meaning to the creed our fathers once declared.

We, the people, still believe that enduring security and lasting peace do not require perpetual war. Our brave men and women in uniform, tempered by the flames of battle, are unmatched in skill and courage. Our citizens, seared by the memory of those we have lost, know too well the price that is paid for liberty. The knowledge of their sacrifice will keep us forever vigilant against those who would do us harm. But we are also heirs to those who won the peace and not just the war; who turned sworn enemies into the surest of friends—and we must carry those lessons into this time as well.

We will defend our people and uphold our values through strength of arms and rule of law. We will show the courage to try and resolve our differences with other nations peacefully—not because we are naive about the dangers we face, but because engagement can more durably lift suspicion and fear.

America will remain the anchor of strong alliances in every corner of the globe. And we will renew those institutions that extend our capacity to manage crisis abroad, for no one has a greater stake in a peaceful world than its most powerful nation. We will support democracy from Asia to Africa, from the Americas to the Middle East, because our interests and our conscience compel us to act on behalf of those who long for freedom. And we must be a source of hope to the poor, the sick, the marginalized, the victims of prejudice—not out of mere charity, but because peace in our time requires the constant advance of those principles that our common creed describes: tolerance and opportunity, human dignity and justice.

We, the people, declare today that the most evident of truths—that all of us are created equal—is the star that guides us still; just as it guided our forebears through Seneca Falls and Selma and Stonewall; just as it guided all those men and women, sung and unsung, who left footprints along this great Mall, to hear a preacher say that we cannot walk alone; to hear a King proclaim that our individual freedom is inextricably bound to the freedom of every soul on Earth.

It is now our generation's task to carry on what those pioneers began. For our journey is not complete until our wives, our mothers and daughters can earn a living equal to their efforts. Our journey is not complete until our gay brothers and sisters are treated like anyone else under the law—for if we are truly created equal, then surely the love we commit to one another must be equal as well. Our journey is not complete until no citizen is forced to wait for hours to exercise the right to vote. Our journey is not complete until we find a better way to welcome the striving, hopeful immigrants who still see America as a land of opportunity—until bright young students and engineers are enlisted in our workforce rather than expelled from our country. Our journey is not complete until all our children, from the streets of Detroit to the hills of Appalachia, to the quiet lanes of Newtown, know that they are cared for and cherished and always safe from harm.

That is our generation's task—to make these words, these rights, these values of life and liberty and the pursuit of happiness real for every American. Being true to our founding documents does not require us to agree on every contour of life. It does not mean we all define liberty in exactly the same way or follow the same precise path to happiness. Progress does not compel us to settle centuries-long debates about the role of government for all time, but it does require us to act in our time.

For now decisions are upon us and we cannot afford delay. We cannot mistake absolutism for principle or substitute spectacle for politics or treat name-calling as reasoned debate. We must act, knowing that our work will be imperfect. We must act, we must act knowing that today's victories will be only partial and that it will be up to those who stand here in 4 years and 40 years and 400 years hence to advance the timeless spirit once conferred to us in a spare Philadelphia hall.

My fellow Americans, the oath I have sworn before you today, like the one recited by others who serve in this Capitol, was an oath to God and country, not party or faction. And we must faithfully execute that pledge during the duration of our service. But the words I spoke today are not so different from the oath that is taken each time a soldier signs up for duty or an immigrant realizes her dream. My oath is not so different from the pledge we all make to the flag that waves above and that fills our hearts with pride.

They are the words of citizens and they represent our greatest hope. You and I, as citizens, have the power to set this country's course. You and I, as citizens, have the obligation to shape the debates of our time—not only with the votes we cast, but with the voices we lift in defense of our most ancient values and enduring ideals.

Let us, each of us, now embrace with solemn duty and awesome joy what is our lasting birthright. With common effort and common purpose, with passion and dedication, let us answer the call of history and carry into an uncertain future that precious light of freedom.

Thank you. God bless you, and may He forever bless these United States of America.

Executive Office of the President. "Inaugural Address." January 21, 2013. *Compilation of Presidential Documents* 2013, no. 00032 (January 21, 2013). http://www.gpo.gov/fdsys/pkg/DCPD-201300032/pdf/DCPD-201300032.pdf.

President Obama's 2013 State of the Union Address

Following is the White House transcript of President Obama's address before a joint session of Congress on the state of the union delivered on February 12, 2013.

Please, everybody, have a seat. Mr. Speaker, Mr. Vice President, Members of Congress, fellow Americans: Fifty-one years ago, John F. Kennedy declared to this Chamber that "the Constitution makes us not rivals for power, but partners for progress." "It is my task," he said, "to report the state of the Union; to improve it is the task of us all."

Tonight, thanks to the grit and determination of the American people, there is much progress to report. After a decade of grinding war, our brave men and women in uniform are coming home. After years of grueling recession, our businesses have created over 6 million new jobs. We buy more American cars than we have in 5 years and less foreign oil than we have in 20. Our housing market is healing, our stock market is rebounding, and consumers, patients, and homeowners enjoy stronger protections than ever before.

So together, we have cleared away the rubble of crisis, and we can say with renewed confidence that the state of our Union is stronger.

But we gather here knowing that there are millions of Americans whose hard work and dedication have not yet been rewarded. Our economy is adding jobs, but too many people still can't find full-time employment. Corporate profits have skyrocketed to all-time highs, but for more than a decade, wages and incomes have barely budged.

It is our generation's task, then, to reignite the true engine of America's economic growth: a rising, thriving middle class.

It is our unfinished task to restore the basic bargain that built this country: the idea that if you work hard and meet your responsibilities, you can get ahead, no matter where you come from, no matter what you look like or who you love. It is our unfinished task to make sure that this Government works on behalf of the many, and not just the few; that it encourages free enterprise, rewards individual initiative, and opens the doors of opportunity to every child across this great Nation.

The American people don't expect government to solve every problem. They don't expect those of us in this Chamber to agree on every issue. But they do expect us to put the Nation's interests before party. They do expect us to forge reasonable compromise where we can. For they know that America moves forward only when we do so together and that the responsibility of improving this Union remains the task of us all.

BUDGET AND DEFICIT REDUCTION

Now, our work must begin by making some basic decisions about our budget, decisions that will have a huge impact on the strength of our recovery.

Over the last few years, both parties have worked together to reduce the deficit by more than $2.5 trillion, mostly through spending cuts, but also by raising tax rates on the wealthiest 1 percent of Americans. As a result, we are more than halfway towards the goal of $4 trillion in deficit reduction that economists say we need to stabilize our finances.

Now we need to finish the job. And the question is, how?

In 2011, Congress passed a law saying that if both parties couldn't agree on a plan to reach our deficit goal, about a trillion dollars' worth of budget cuts would automatically go into effect this year. These sudden, harsh, arbitrary cuts would jeopardize our military readiness. They'd devastate priorities like education and energy and medical research. They would certainly slow our recovery and cost us hundreds of thousands of jobs. And that's why Democrats, Republicans, business leaders, and economists have already said that these cuts—known here in Washington as the sequester—are a really bad idea.

Now, some in Congress have proposed preventing only the defense cuts by making even bigger cuts to things like education and job training, Medicare, and Social Security benefits. That idea is even worse.

Yes, the biggest driver of our long-term debt is the rising cost of health care for an aging population. And those of us who care deeply about programs like Medicare must embrace the need for modest reforms; otherwise, our retirement programs will crowd out the investments we need for our children and jeopardize the promise of a secure retirement for future generations.

But we can't ask senior citizens and working families to shoulder the entire burden of deficit reduction while asking nothing more from the wealthiest and the most powerful. We won't grow the middle class simply by shifting the cost of health care or college onto families that are already struggling or by forcing communities to lay off more teachers and more cops and more firefighters. Most Americans—Democrats, Republicans, and Independents— understand that we can't just cut our way to prosperity. They know that broad-based economic growth requires a balanced approach to deficit reduction, with spending cuts and revenue and with everybody doing their fair share. And that's the approach I offer tonight.

On Medicare, I'm prepared to enact reforms that will achieve the same amount of health care savings by the beginning of the next decade as the reforms proposed by the bipartisan Simpson-Bowles Commission. Already, the Affordable Care Act is helping to slow the growth of health care costs. And the reforms I'm proposing go even further. We'll reduce taxpayer subsidies to prescription drug companies and ask more from the wealthiest seniors. We'll bring down costs by changing the way our Government pays for Medicare, because our medical bills shouldn't be based on the number of tests ordered or days spent in the hospital; they should be based on the quality of care that our seniors receive. And I am open to additional reforms from both parties, so long as they don't violate the guarantee of a secure retirement. Our Government shouldn't make promises we cannot keep, but we must keep the promises we've already made.

To hit the rest of our deficit reduction target, we should do what leaders in both parties have already suggested and save hundreds of billions of dollars by getting rid of tax loopholes and deductions for the well-off and the well-connected. After all, why would we choose to make deeper cuts to education and Medicare just to protect special interest tax breaks? How is that fair? Why is it that deficit reduction is a big emergency justifying making cuts in Social Security benefits, but not closing some loopholes? How does that promote growth?

TAX REFORM

Now is our best chance for bipartisan, comprehensive tax reform that encourages job creation and helps bring down the deficit. We can get this done. The American people deserve a Tax Code that helps small businesses spend less time filling out complicated forms and more time expanding and hiring; a Tax Code that ensures billionaires with high-powered accountants can't work the system and pay a lower rate than their hard-working secretaries; a Tax Code that lowers incentives to move jobs overseas and lowers tax rates for businesses and manufacturers that are creating jobs right here in the United States of America. That's what tax reform can deliver. That's what we can do together.

I realize that tax reform and entitlement reform will not be easy. The politics will be hard for both sides. None of us will get a hundred percent of what we want. But the alternative will cost us jobs, hurt our economy, visit hardship on millions of hard-working Americans. So let's set party interests aside and work to pass a budget that replaces reckless cuts with smart savings and wise investments in our future. And let's do it without the brinksmanship that stresses consumers and scares off investors. The greatest nation on Earth cannot keep conducting its business by drifting from one manufactured crisis to the next. We can't do it.

Let's agree right here, right now to keep the people's Government open and pay our bills on time and always uphold the full faith and credit of the United States of America. The American people have worked too hard, for too long, rebuilding from one crisis to see their elected officials cause another.

Now, most of us agree that a plan to reduce the deficit must be part of our agenda. But let's be clear: Deficit reduction alone is not an economic plan. A growing economy that creates good, middle class jobs, that must be the north star that guides our efforts. Every day, we should ask ourselves three questions as a nation: How do we attract more jobs to our shores? How do we equip our people with the skills they need to get those jobs? And how do we make sure that hard work leads to a decent living?

JOBS

Now, a year and a half ago, I put forward an American Jobs Act that independent economists said would create more than 1 million new jobs. And I thank the last Congress for passing some of that agenda. I urge this Congress to pass the rest. But tonight I'll lay out additional proposals that are fully paid for and fully consistent with the budget framework both parties agreed to just 18 months ago. Let me repeat: Nothing I'm proposing tonight should increase our deficit by a single dime. It is not a bigger Government we need, but a smarter Government that sets priorities and invests in broad-based growth. That's what we should be looking for.

Our first priority is making America a magnet for new jobs and manufacturing. After shedding jobs for more than 10 years, our manufacturers have added about 500,000 jobs over the past 3. Caterpillar is bringing jobs back from Japan. Ford is bringing jobs back from Mexico. And this year, Apple will start making Macs in America again.

There are things we can do right now to accelerate this trend. Last year, we created our first manufacturing innovation institute in Youngstown, Ohio. A once-shuttered warehouse is now a state-of-the-art lab where new workers are mastering the 3-D printing that has the potential to revolutionize the way we make almost everything. There's no reason this can't happen in other towns.

So tonight I'm announcing the launch of three more of these manufacturing hubs, where businesses will partner with the Department of Defense and Energy to turn regions left behind by globalization into global centers of high-tech jobs. And I ask this Congress to help create a network of 15 of these hubs and guarantee that the next revolution in manufacturing is made right here in America. We can get that done.

Now, if we want to make the best products, we also have to invest in the best ideas. Every dollar we invested to map the human genome returned $140 to our economy—every dollar. Today, our scientists are mapping the human brain to unlock the answers to Alzheimer's. They're developing drugs to regenerate damaged organs, devising new materials to make batteries 10 times more powerful. Now is not the time to gut these job-creating investments in science and innovation, now is the time to reach a level of research and development not seen since the height of the space race. We need to make those investments.

Today, no area holds more promise than our investments in American energy. After years of talking about it, we're finally poised to control our own energy future. We produce more oil at home than we have in 15 years. We have doubled the distance our cars will go on a gallon of gas and the amount of renewable energy we generate from sources like wind and solar, with tens of thousands of good American jobs to show for it. We produce more natural gas than ever before, and nearly everyone's energy bill is lower because of it. And over the last 4 years, our emissions of the dangerous carbon pollution that threatens our planet have actually fallen.

CLIMATE CHANGE

But for the sake of our children and our future, we must do more to combat climate change. Now, it's true that no single event makes a trend. But the fact is, the 12 hottest years on record have all come in the last 15. Heat waves, droughts, wildfires, floods—all are now more frequent and more intense. We can choose to believe that Superstorm Sandy and the most severe drought in decades and the worst wildfires some States have ever seen were all just a freak coincidence. Or we can choose to believe in the overwhelming judgment of science and act before it's too late.

Now, the good news is we can make meaningful progress on this issue while driving strong economic growth. I urge this Congress to get together, pursue a bipartisan, market-based solution to climate change, like the one John McCain and Joe Lieberman worked on together a few years ago. But if Congress won't act soon to protect future generations, I will. I will direct my Cabinet to come up with executive actions we can take, now and in the future, to reduce pollution, prepare our communities for the consequences of climate change, and speed the transition to more sustainable sources of energy.

ENERGY

And 4 years ago, other countries dominated the clean energy market and the jobs that came with it. And we've begun to change that. Last year, wind energy added nearly half of all new power capacity in America. So let's generate even more. Solar energy gets cheaper by the year; let's drive down costs even further. As long as countries like China keep going all in on clean energy, so must we.

Now, in the meantime, the natural gas boom has led to cleaner power and greater energy independence. We need to encourage that. And that's why my administration will keep cutting redtape and speeding up new oil and gas permits. That's got to be part of an all-of-the-above plan. But I also want to work with this Congress to encourage the research and technology that helps natural gas burn even cleaner and protects our air and our water. In fact, much of our new-found energy is drawn from lands and waters that we, the public, own together. So tonight I propose we use some of our oil and gas revenues to fund an energy security trust that will drive new research and technology to shift our cars and trucks off oil for good. If a nonpartisan coalition of CEOs and retired generals and admirals can get behind this idea, then so can we. Let's take their advice and free our families and businesses from the painful spikes in gas prices we've put up with for far too long.

I'm also issuing a new goal for America: Let's cut in half the energy wasted by our homes and businesses over the next

20 years. We'll work with the States to do it. Those States with the best ideas to create jobs and lower energy bills by constructing more efficient buildings will receive Federal support to help make that happen.

America's energy sector is just one part of an aging infrastructure badly in need of repair. Ask any CEO where they'd rather locate and hire, a country with deteriorating roads and bridges or one with high-speed rail and Internet, high-tech schools, self-healing power grids. The CEO of Siemens America—a company that brought hundreds of new jobs to North Carolina—said that if we upgrade our infrastructure, they'll bring even more jobs. And that's the attitude of a lot of companies all around the world. And I know you want these job-creating projects in your district. I've seen all those ribbon-cuttings. *[Laughter]*

So tonight I propose a Fix-It-First program to put people to work as soon as possible on our most urgent repairs, like the nearly 70,000 structurally deficient bridges across the country. And to make sure taxpayers don't shoulder the whole burden, I'm also proposing a partnership to rebuild America that attracts private capital to upgrade what our businesses need most: modern ports to move our goods, modern pipelines to withstand a storm, modern schools worthy of our children. Let's prove there's no better place to do business than here in the United States of America, and let's start right away. We can get this done.

HOUSING INITIATIVES

And part of our rebuilding effort must also involve our housing sector. The good news is, our housing market is finally healing from the collapse of 2007. Home prices are rising at the fastest pace in 6 years. Home purchases are up nearly 50 percent, and construction is expanding again.

But even with mortgage rates near a 50-year low, too many families with solid credit who want to buy a home are being rejected. Too many families who never missed a payment and want to refinance are being told no. That's holding our entire economy back. We need to fix it.

Right now there's a bill in this Congress that would give every responsible homeowner in America the chance to save $3,000 a year by refinancing at today's rates. Democrats and Republicans have supported it before, so what are we waiting for? Take a vote and send me that bill. Why are—why would we be against that? Why would that be a partisan issue, helping folks refinance? Right now overlapping regulations keep responsible young families from buying their first home. What's holding us back? Let's streamline the process and help our economy grow.

These initiatives in manufacturing, energy, infrastructure, housing, all these things will help entrepreneurs and small-business owners expand and create new jobs. But none of it will matter unless we also equip our citizens with the skills and training to fill those jobs.

EDUCATION AND JOB TRAINING

And that has to start at the earliest possible age. Study after study shows that the sooner a child begins learning, the better he or she does down the road. But today, fewer than 3 in 10 4-year-olds are enrolled in a high-quality preschool program. Most middle class parents can't afford a few hundred bucks a week for a private preschool. And for poor kids who need help the most, this lack of access to preschool education can shadow them for the rest of their lives. So tonight I propose working with States to make high-quality preschool available to every single child in America. That's something we should be able to do.

Every dollar we invest in high-quality early childhood education can save more than 7 dollars later on: by boosting graduation rates, reducing teen pregnancy, even reducing violent crime. In States that make it a priority to educate our youngest children, like Georgia or Oklahoma, studies show students grow up more likely to read and do math at grade level, graduate high school, hold a job, form more stable families of their own. We know this works. So let's do what works and make sure none of our children start the race of life already behind. Let's give our kids that chance.

Let's also make sure that a high school diploma puts our kids on a path to a good job. Right now countries like Germany focus on graduating their high school students with the equivalent of a technical degree from one of our community colleges. So those German kids, they're ready for a job when they graduate high school. They've been trained for the jobs that are there. Now at schools like P–TECH in Brooklyn, a collaboration between New York Public Schools and City University of New York and IBM, students will graduate with a high school diploma and an associate's degree in computers or engineering. We need to give every American student opportunities like this.

And 4 years ago, we started Race to the Top, a competition that convinced almost every State to develop smarter curricula and higher standards, all for about 1 percent of what we spend on education each year. Tonight I'm announcing a new challenge to redesign America's high schools so they better equip graduates for the demands of a high-tech economy. And we'll reward schools that develop new partnerships with colleges and employers and create classes that focus on science, technology, engineering, and math: the skills today's employers are looking for to fill the jobs that are there right now and will be there in the future.

Now, even with better high schools, most young people will need some higher education. It's a simple fact: The more education you've got, the more likely you are to have a good job and work your way into the middle class. But today, skyrocketing costs price too many young people out of a higher education or saddle them with unsustainable debt.

Through tax credits, grants, and better loans, we've made college more affordable for millions of students and families over the last few years. But taxpayers can't keep on subsidizing higher and higher and higher costs for higher education. Colleges must do their part to keep costs down, and it's our job to make sure that they do.

So tonight I ask Congress to change the Higher Education Act so that affordability and value are included in determining which colleges receive certain types of Federal aid. And tomorrow my administration will release a new college scorecard that parents and students can use to compare schools based on a simple criterion: where you can get the most bang for your educational buck.

Now, to grow our middle class, our citizens have to have access to the education and training that today's jobs require. But we also have to make sure that America remains a place where everyone who's willing to work—everybody who's willing to work hard—has the chance to get ahead.

Our economy is stronger when we harness the talents and ingenuity of striving, hopeful immigrants. And right now leaders from the business, labor, law enforcement, faith communities, they all agree that the time has come to pass comprehensive immigration reform. Now is the time to do it. Now is the time to get it done. [Applause] Now is the time to get it done.

IMMIGRATION REFORM

Real reform means stronger border security, and we can build on the progress my administration has already made: putting more boots on the southern border than at any time in our history and reducing illegal crossings to their lowest levels in 40 years.

Real reform means establishing a responsible pathway to earned citizenship, a path that includes passing a background check, paying taxes and a meaningful penalty, learning English, and going to the back of the line behind the folks trying to come here legally.

And real reform means fixing the legal immigration system to cut waiting periods and attract the highly skilled entrepreneurs and engineers that will help create jobs and grow our economy.

In other words, we know what needs to be done. And as we speak, bipartisan groups in both Chambers are working diligently to draft a bill, and I applaud their efforts. So let's get this done. Send me a comprehensive immigration reform bill in the next few months, and I will sign it right away. And America will be better for it. Let's get it done. [Applause] Let's get it done.

LABOR INITIATIVES

But we can't stop there. We know our economy is stronger when our wives, our mothers, our daughters can live their lives free from discrimination in the workplace and free from the fear of domestic violence. Today the Senate passed the "Violence Against Women's Act" that Joe Biden originally wrote almost 20 years ago. And I now urge the House to do the same. Good job, Joe. And I ask this Congress to declare that women should earn a living equal to their efforts, and finally pass the "Paycheck Fairness Act" this year.

We know our economy is stronger when we reward an honest day's work with honest wages. But today, a full-time worker making the minimum wage earns $14,500 a year. Even with the tax relief we put in place, a family with two kids that earns the minimum wage still lives below the poverty line. That's wrong. That's why, since the last time this Congress raised the minimum wage, 19 States have chosen to bump theirs even higher.

Tonight let's declare that in the wealthiest nation on Earth, no one who works full-time should have to live in poverty and raise the Federal minimum wage to $9 an hour. We should be able to get that done.

This single step would raise the incomes of millions of working families. It could mean the difference between groceries or the food bank, rent or eviction, scraping by or finally getting ahead. For businesses across the country, it would mean customers with more money in their pockets. And a whole lot of folks out there would probably need less help from government. In fact, working folks shouldn't have to wait year after year for the minimum wage to go up while CEO pay has never been higher. So here's an idea that Governor Romney and I actually agreed on last year: Let's tie the minimum wage to the cost of living so that it finally becomes a wage you can live on.

Tonight let's also recognize that there are communities in this country where no matter how hard you work, it is virtually impossible to get ahead: factory towns decimated from years of plants packing up; inescapable pockets of poverty, urban and rural, where young adults are still fighting for their first job. America is not a place where the chance of birth or circumstance should decide our destiny. And that's why we need to build new ladders of opportunity into the middle class for all who are willing to climb them.

Let's offer incentives to companies that hire Americans who've got what it takes to fill that job opening, but have been out of work so long that no one will give them a chance anymore. Let's put people back to work rebuilding vacant homes in rundown neighborhoods. And this year, my administration will begin to partner with 20 of the hardest hit towns in America to get these communities back on their feet. Now, we'll work with local leaders to target resources at public safety and education and housing.

We'll give new tax credits to businesses that hire and invest. And we'll work to strengthen families by removing the financial deterrents to marriage for low-income couples and do more to encourage fatherhood, because what makes you a man isn't the ability to conceive a child, it's having the courage to raise one. And we want to encourage that. We want to help that.

Stronger families. Stronger communities. A stronger America. It is this kind of prosperity—broad, shared, built on a thriving middle class—that has always been the source of our progress at home. It's also the foundation of our power and influence throughout the world.

COUNTERTERRORISM

Tonight we stand united in saluting the troops and civilians who sacrifice every day to protect us. Because of them, we can say with confidence that America will complete its mission in Afghanistan and achieve our objective of defeating the core of Al Qaida.

Already, we have brought home 33,000 of our brave service men and women. This spring, our forces will move into a support role, while Afghan security forces take the lead. Tonight I can announce that over the next year, another 34,000 American troops will come home from Afghanistan. This drawdown will continue, and by the end of next year, our war in Afghanistan will be over.

Beyond 2014, America's commitment to a unified and sovereign Afghanistan will endure, but the nature of our commitment will change. We're negotiating an agreement with the Afghan Government that focuses on two missions: training and equipping Afghan forces so that the country does not again slip into chaos and counterterrorism efforts that allow us to pursue the remnants of Al Qaida and their affiliates.

Today, the organization that attacked us on 9/11 is a shadow of its former self. It's true, different Al Qaida affiliates and extremist groups have emerged, from the Arabian Peninsula to Africa. The threat these groups pose is evolving. But to meet this threat, we don't need to send tens of thousands of our sons and daughters abroad or occupy other nations. Instead, we'll need to help countries like Yemen and Libya and Somalia provide for their own security and help allies who take the fight to terrorists, as we have in Mali. And where necessary, through a range of capabilities, we will continue to take direct action against those terrorists who pose the gravest threat to Americans.

Now, as we do, we must enlist our values in the fight. That's why my administration has worked tirelessly to forge a durable legal and policy framework to guide our counterterrorism efforts. Throughout, we have kept Congress fully informed of our efforts. I recognize that in our democracy, no one should just take my word for it that we're doing things the right way. So, in the months ahead, I will continue to engage Congress to ensure not only that our targeting, detention, and prosecution of terrorists remains consistent with our laws and system of checks and balances, but that our efforts are even more transparent to the American people and to the world.

Of course, our challenges don't end with Al Qaida. America will continue to lead the effort to prevent the spread of the world's most dangerous weapons. The regime in North Korea must know they will only achieve security and prosperity by meeting their international obligations. Provocations of the sort we saw last night will only further isolate them, as we stand by our allies, strengthen our own missile defense, and lead the world in taking firm action in response to these threats.

Likewise, the leaders of Iran must recognize that now is the time for a diplomatic solution, because a coalition stands united in demanding that they meet their obligations, and we will do what is necessary to prevent them from getting a nuclear weapon.

At the same time, we'll engage Russia to seek further reductions in our nuclear arsenals and continue leading the global effort to secure nuclear materials that could fall into the wrong hands, because our ability to influence others depends on our willingness to lead and meet our obligations.

America must also face the rapidly growing threat from cyber attacks. Now, we know hackers steal people's identities and infiltrate private e-mails. We know foreign countries and companies swipe our corporate secrets. Now our enemies are also seeking the ability to sabotage our power grid, our financial institutions, our air traffic control systems. We cannot look back years from now and wonder why we did nothing in the face of real threats to our security and our economy.

And that's why, earlier today, I signed a new Executive order that will strengthen our cyber defenses by increasing information sharing and developing standards to protect our national security, our jobs, and our privacy.

But now Congress must act as well, by passing legislation to give our Government a greater capacity to secure our networks and deter attacks. This is something we should be able to get done on a bipartisan basis.

INTERNATIONAL RELATIONS

Now, even as we protect our people, we should remember that today's world presents not just dangers, not just threats, it presents opportunities. To boost American exports, support American jobs and level the playing field in the growing markets of Asia, we intend to complete negotiations on a Trans-Pacific Partnership. And tonight I'm announcing that we will launch talks on a comprehensive transatlantic trade and investment partnership with the European Union, because trade that is fair and free across the Atlantic supports millions of good-paying American jobs.

We also know that progress in the most impoverished parts of our world enriches us all, not only because it creates new markets, more stable order in certain regions of the world, but also because it's the right thing to do. In many places, people live on little more

than a dollar a day. So the United States will join with our allies to eradicate such extreme poverty in the next two decades by connecting more people to the global economy, by empowering women, by giving our young and brightest minds new opportunities to serve and helping communities to feed and power and educate themselves, by saving the world's children from preventable deaths, and by realizing the promise of an AIDS-free generation, which is within our reach.

You see, America must remain a beacon to all who seek freedom during this period of historic change. I saw the power of hope last year in Rangoon, in Burma, when Aung San Suu Kyi welcomed an American President into the home where she had been imprisoned for years; when thousands of Burmese lined the streets, waving American flags, including a man who said: "There is justice and law in the United States. I want our country to be like that."

In defense of freedom, we'll remain the anchor of strong alliances from the Americas to Africa, from Europe to Asia. In the Middle East, we will stand with citizens as they demand their universal rights and support stable transitions to democracy.

We know the process will be messy, and we cannot presume to dictate the course of change in countries like Egypt, but we can and will insist on respect for the fundamental rights of all people. We'll keep the pressure on a Syrian regime that has murdered its own people and support opposition leaders that respect the rights of every Syrian. And we will stand steadfast with Israel in pursuit of security and a lasting peace.

These are the messages I'll deliver when I travel to the Middle East next month. And all this work depends on the courage and sacrifice of those who serve in dangerous places at great personal risk: our diplomats, our intelligence officers, and the men and women of the United States Armed Forces. As long as I'm Commander in Chief, we will do whatever we must to protect those who serve their country abroad, and we will maintain the best military the world has ever known.

We'll invest in new capabilities, even as we reduce waste and wartime spending. We will ensure equal treatment for all service members and equal benefits for their families, gay and straight. We will draw upon the courage and skills of our sisters and daughters and moms, because women have proven under fire that they are ready for combat.

We will keep faith with our veterans, investing in world-class care—including mental health care—for our wounded warriors, supporting our military families, giving our veterans the benefits and education and job opportunities that they have earned. And I want to thank my wife Michelle and Dr. Jill Biden for their continued dedication to serving our military families as well as they have served us. Thank you, honey. Thank you, Jill.

Defending our freedom, though, is not just the job of our military alone. We must all do our part to make sure our God-given rights are protected here at home. That includes one of the most fundamental rights of a democracy: the right to vote. Now, when any American, no matter where they live or what their party, are denied that right because they can't afford to wait for 5 or 6 or 7 hours just to cast their ballot, we are betraying our ideals.

So tonight I'm announcing a nonpartisan commission to improve the voting experience in America. And it definitely needs improvement. I'm asking two long-time experts in the field— who, by the way, recently served as the top attorneys for my campaign and for Governor Romney's campaign—to lead it. We can fix this, and we will. The American people demand it, and so does our democracy.

GUN CONTROL

Of course, what I've said tonight matters little if we don't come together to protect our most precious resource: our children. It has been 2 months since Newtown. I know this is not the first time this country has debated how to reduce gun violence. But this time is different. Overwhelming majorities of Americans— Americans who believe in the Second Amendment— have come together around commonsense reform, like background checks that will make it harder for criminals to get their hands on a gun. Senators of both parties are working together on tough new laws to prevent anyone from buying guns for resale to criminals. Police chiefs are asking our help to get weapons of war and massive ammunition magazines off our streets, because these police chiefs, they're tired of seeing their guys and gals being outgunned.

Each of these proposals deserves a vote in Congress. Now, if you want to vote no, that's your choice. But these proposals deserve a vote. Because in the 2 months since Newtown, more than a thousand birthdays, graduations, anniversaries have been stolen from our lives by a bullet from a gun—more than a thousand.

One of those we lost was a young girl named Hadiya Pendleton. She was 15 years old. She loved Fig Newtons and lip gloss. She was a majorette. She was so good to her friends, they all thought they were her best friend. Just 3 weeks ago, she was here, in Washington, with her classmates, performing for her country at my Inauguration. And a week later, she was shot and killed in a Chicago park after school, just a mile away from my house.

Hadiya's parents, Nate and Cleo, are in this Chamber tonight, along with more than two dozen Americans whose lives have been torn apart by gun violence. They deserve a vote. They deserve a vote. [Applause] They deserve a vote. Gabby Giffords deserves a vote. The families of Newtown deserve a vote. The families of Aurora deserve a vote. The families of Oak Creek and Tucson and Blacksburg, and the countless other communities ripped open by gun violence, they deserve a simple vote. They deserve a simple vote.

Our actions will not prevent every senseless act of violence in this country. In fact, no laws, no initiatives, no administrative acts will perfectly solve all the challenges I've outlined tonight. But we were never sent here to be perfect.

We were sent here to make what difference we can, to secure this Nation, expand opportunity, uphold our ideals through the hard, often frustrating, but absolutely necessary work of self-government. We were sent here to look out for our fellow Americans the same way they look out for one another, every single day, usually without fanfare, all across this country.

We should follow their example. We should follow the example of a New York City nurse named Menchu Sanchez. When Hurricane Sandy plunged her hospital into darkness, she wasn't thinking about how her own home was faring. Her mind was on the 20 precious newborns in her care and the rescue plan she devised that kept them all safe.

We should follow the example of a North Miami woman named Desiline Victor. When Desiline arrived at her polling place, she was told the wait to vote might be 6 hours. And as time ticked by, her concern was not with her tired body or aching feet, but whether folks like her would get to have their say. And hour after hour, a throng of people stayed in line to support her, because Desiline is 102 years old. And they erupted in cheers when she finally put on a sticker that read, "I voted." [Applause] There's Desiline.

We should follow the example of a police officer named Brian Murphy. When a gunman opened fire on a Sikh temple in Wisconsin and Brian was the first to arrive—and he did not consider his own safety. He fought back until help arrived and ordered his fellow officers to protect the safety of the Americans worshiping inside, even as he lay bleeding from 12 bullet wounds. And when asked how he did that, Brian said, "That's just the way we're made."

That's just the way we're made. We may do different jobs and wear different uniforms and hold different views than the person beside us. But as Americans, we all share the same proud title: We are citizens. It's a word that doesn't just describe our nationality or legal status. It describes the way we're made. It describes what we believe. It captures the enduring idea that this country only works when we accept certain obligations to one another and to future generations; that our rights are wrapped up in the rights of others; and that well into our third century as a nation, it remains the task of us all, as citizens of these United States, to be the authors of the next great chapter of our American story.

Thank you. God bless you, and God bless these United States of America.

Executive Office of the President. "Address Before a Joint Session of Congress on the State of the Union." February 12, 2013. *Compilation of Presidential Documents* 2013, no. 00090 (February 12, 2013). http://www.gpo.gov/fdsys/pkg/DCPD-201300090/pdf/DCPD-201300090.pdf.

President Obama's Speech on Gun Control Legislation

Following is the White House transcript of President Obama's April 17, 2013, remarks on gun control legislation.

A few months ago, in response to too many tragedies, including the shootings of a United States Congresswoman, Gabby Giffords, who's here today, and the murder of 20 innocent schoolchildren and their teachers, this country took up the cause of protecting more of our people from gun violence.

Families that know unspeakable grief summoned the courage to petition their elected leaders, not just to honor the memory of their children, but to protect the lives of all of our children. A few minutes ago, a minority in the United States Senate decided it wasn't worth it. They blocked commonsense gun reforms even while these families looked on from the Senate gallery.

By now, it's well known that 90 percent of the American people support universal background checks that make it harder for a dangerous person to buy a gun. We're talking about convicted felons, people convicted of domestic violence, people with a severe mental illness. Ninety percent of Americans support that idea. Most Americans think that's already the law.

And a few minutes ago, 90 percent of Democrats in the Senate voted for that idea. But it's not going to happen, because 90 percent of Republicans in the Senate just voted against that idea. A majority of Senators voted yes to protecting more of our citizens with smarter background checks. But by this continuing distortion of Senate rules, a minority was able to block it from moving forward.

Now, I'm going to speak plainly and honestly about what's happened here, because the American people are trying to figure out: How can something have 90 percent support and yet not happen? We had a Democrat and a Republican—both gun owners, both fierce defenders of our Second Amendment, with A grades from the NRA—come together and work together to write a commonsense compromise on background checks. And I want to thank Joe Manchin and Pat Toomey for their courage in doing that. That was not easy given their traditional strong support for Second Amendment rights.

As they said, nobody could honestly claim that the package they put together infringed on our Second Amendment rights. All it did was extend the same background check rules that already apply to guns purchased from a dealer to guns purchased at gun shows or over the Internet. So 60 percent of guns are already purchased through a background check system; this would have covered a lot of the guns that are currently outside that system.

Their legislation showed respect for gun owners, and it showed respect for the victims of gun violence. And Gabby Giffords, by the way, is both; she's a gun owner and a victim of gun violence. She is a Westerner and a moderate. And she supports these background checks.

In fact, even the NRA used to support expanded background checks. The current leader of the NRA used to support these background checks. So while this compromise didn't contain everything I wanted or everything that these families wanted, it did represent progress. It represented moderation and common sense. That's why 90 percent of the American people supported it.

But instead of supporting this compromise, the gun lobby and its allies willfully lied about the bill. They claimed that it would create some sort of big brother gun registry, even though the bill did the opposite. This legislation, in fact, outlawed any registry. Plain and simple, right there in the text. But that didn't matter.

And unfortunately, this pattern of spreading untruths about this legislation served a purpose, because those lies upset an intense minority of gun owners, and that in turn intimidated a lot of Senators. And I talked to several of these Senators over the past few weeks, and they're all good people. I know all of them were shocked by tragedies like Newtown. And I also understand that they come from States that are strongly pro-gun. And I have consistently said that there are regional differences when it comes to guns and that both sides have to listen to each other.

But the fact is most of these Senators could not offer any good reason why we wouldn't want to make it harder for criminals and those with severe mental illnesses to buy a gun. There were no coherent arguments as to why we wouldn't do this. It came down to politics: the worry that that vocal minority of gun owners would come after them in future elections. They worried that the gun lobby would spend a lot of money and paint them as anti–Second Amendment.

And obviously, a lot of Republicans had that fear, but Democrats had that fear too. And so they caved to the pressure, and they started looking for an excuse—any excuse—to vote no.

One common argument I heard was that this legislation wouldn't prevent all future massacres. And that's true. As I said from the start, no single piece of legislation can stop every act of violence and evil. We learned that tragically just 2 days ago. But if action by Congress could have saved one person, one child, a few hundred, a few thousand, if it could have prevented those people from losing their lives to gun violence in the future while preserving our Second Amendment rights, we had an obligation to try. And this legislation met that test. And too many Senators failed theirs.

I've heard some say that blocking this step would be a victory. And my question is, a victory for who? A victory for what? All that happened today was the preservation of the loophole that lets dangerous criminals buy guns without a background check. That didn't make our kids safer. Victory for not doing something that 90 percent of Americans, 80 percent of Republicans, the vast majority of your constituents wanted to get done? It begs the question, who are we here to represent?

I've heard folks say that having the families of victims lobby for this legislation was somehow misplaced. "A prop," somebody called them. "Emotional blackmail," some outlets said. Are they serious? Do we really think that thousands of families whose lives have been shattered by gun violence don't have a right to weigh in on this issue? Do we think their emotions, their loss is not relevant to this debate? So all in all, this was a pretty shameful day for Washington.

But this effort is not over. I want to make it clear to the American people: We can still bring about meaningful changes that reduce gun violence, so long as the American people don't give up on it. Even without Congress, my administration will keep doing everything it can to protect more of our communities. We're going to address the barriers that prevent States from participating in the existing background check system. We're going to give law enforcement more information about lost and stolen guns so it can do its job. We're going to help to put in place emergency plans to protect our children in their schools.

But we can do more if Congress gets its act together. And if this Congress refuses to listen to the American people and pass commonsense gun legislation, then the real impact is going to have to come from the voters.

To all the people who supported this legislation—law enforcement and responsible gun owners, Democrats and Republicans, urban moms, rural hunters, whoever you are—you need to let your Representatives in Congress know that you are disappointed and that if they don't act this time, you will remember come election time.

To the wide majority of NRA households who supported this legislation, you need to let your leadership and lobbyists in Washington know they didn't represent your views on this one.

The point is, those who care deeply about preventing more and more gun violence will have to be as passionate and as organized and as vocal as those who blocked these commonsense steps to help keep our kids safe. Ultimately, you outnumber those who argued the other way. But they're better organized. They're better financed. They've been at it longer. And they make sure to stay focused on this one issue during election time. And that's the reason why you can have something that 90 percent of Americans support and you can't get it through the Senate or the House of Representatives.

So to change Washington, you, the American people, are going to have to sustain some passion about this. And when necessary, you've got to send the right people to Washington. And that requires strength, and it requires persistence.

And that's the one thing that these families should have inspired in all of us. I still don't know how they have been able to muster up the strength to do what they've doing over the last several weeks, last several months.

And I see this as just round one. When Newtown happened, I met with these families and I spoke to the community, and I said, something must be different right now. We're going to have to change. That's what the whole country said. Everybody talked about how we were going to change something to make sure this didn't happen again, just like everybody talked about how we needed to do something after Aurora. Everybody talked about, we needed to change something after Tucson.

And I'm assuming that the emotions that we've all felt since Newtown, the emotions that we've all felt since Tucson and Aurora and Chicago—the pain we share with these families and families all across the country who've lost a loved one to gun violence—I'm assuming that's not a temporary thing. I'm assuming our expressions of grief and our commitment to do something different—to prevent these things from happening—are not empty words.

I believe we're going to be able to get this done. Sooner or later, we are going to get this right. The memories of these children demand it. And so do the American people.

Thank you very much, everybody.

Executive Office of the President. "Remarks on Senate Action on Gun Control Legislation." April 17, 2013. *Compilation of Presidential Documents* 2013, no. 00252 (April 17, 2013). http://www.gpo.gov/fdsys/pkg/DCPD-201300252/pdf/DCPD-201300252.pdf.

President Obama's Speech to the United Nations General Assembly

Following is the White House transcript of President Obama's speech delivered to the United Nations General Assembly on September 24, 2013.

Mr. President, Mr. Secretary General, fellow delegates, ladies and gentlemen: Each year, we come together to reaffirm the founding vision of this institution. For most of recorded history, individual aspirations were subject to the whims of tyrants and empires. Divisions of race and religion and tribe were settled through the sword and the clash of armies. The idea that nations and peoples could come together in peace to solve their disputes and advance common prosperity seemed unimaginable.

It took the awful carnage of two world wars to shift our thinking. The leaders who built the United Nations were not naive; they did not think this body could eradicate all wars. But in the wake of millions dead and continents in rubble, and with the development of nuclear weapons that could annihilate a planet, they understood that humanity could not survive the course it was on. And so they gave us this institution, believing that it could allow us to resolve conflicts, enforce rules of behavior, and build habits of cooperation that would grow stronger over time.

Now, for decades, the United Nations has in fact made a difference, from helping to eradicate disease to educating children, to brokering peace. But like every generation of leaders, we face new and profound challenges, and this body continues to be tested. The question is whether we possess the wisdom and the courage, as nation-states and members of an international community, to squarely meet those challenges, whether the United Nations can meet the tests of our time.

For much of my tenure as President, some of our most urgent challenges have revolved around an increasingly integrated global economy and our efforts to recover from the worst economic crisis of our lifetime. Now, 5 years after the global economy collapsed and thanks to coordinated efforts by the countries here today, jobs are being created, global financial systems have stabilized, and people are once again being lifted out of poverty. But this progress is fragile and unequal, and we still have work to do together to assure that our citizens can access the opportunities that they need to thrive in the 21st century.

Together, we've also worked to end a decade of war. Five years ago, nearly 180,000 Americans were serving in harm's way, and the war in Iraq was the dominant issue in our relationship with the rest of the world. Today, all of our troops have left Iraq. Next year, an international coalition will end its war in Afghanistan, having achieved its mission of dismantling the core of Al Qaida that attacked us on 9/11.

For the United States, these new circumstances have also meant shifting away from a perpetual war footing. Beyond bringing our troops home, we have limited the use of drones so they target only those who pose a continuing, imminent threat to the United States where capture is not feasible and there is a near certainty of no civilian casualties. We're transferring detainees to other countries and trying terrorists in courts of law, while working diligently to close the prison at Guantanamo Bay. And just as we reviewed how we deploy our extraordinary military capabilities in a way that lives up to our ideals, we've begun to review the way that we gather intelligence so that we properly balance the legitimate security concerns of our citizens and allies with the privacy concerns that all people share.

As a result of this work and cooperation with allies and partners, the world is more stable than it was 5 years ago. But even a glance at today's headlines indicates that dangers remain. In Kenya, we've seen terrorists target innocent civilians in a crowded shopping mall, and our hearts go out to the families of those who have been affected. In Pakistan, nearly 100 people were recently killed by suicide bombers outside a church. In Iraq, killings and car bombs continue to be a terrible part of life. And meanwhile, Al Qaida has splintered into regional networks and militias, which doesn't give them the capacity at this point to carry out attacks like 9/11, but does pose serious threats to governments and diplomats, businesses and civilians, all across the globe.

SYRIA

Just as significantly, the convulsions in the Middle East and North Africa have laid bare deep divisions within societies, as an old order is upended and people grapple with what comes next. Peaceful movements have too often been answered by violence, from those resisting change and from extremists trying to hijack change. Sectarian conflict has reemerged. And the potential spread of weapons of mass destruction continues to cast a shadow over the pursuit of peace.

Nowhere have we seen these trends converge more powerfully than in Syria. There, peaceful protests against an authoritarian regime were met with repression and slaughter. In the face of such carnage, many retreated to their sectarian identity—Alawite and Sunni, Christian and Kurd—and the situation spiraled into civil war.

The international community recognized the stakes early on, but our response has not matched the scale of the challenge. Aid cannot keep pace with the suffering of the wounded and displaced. A peace process is stillborn. America and others have worked to bolster the moderate opposition, but extremist groups have still taken root to exploit the crisis. Asad's traditional allies have propped him up, citing principles of sovereignty to shield his regime. And on August 21, the regime used chemical weapons in an attack that killed more than 1,000 people, including hundreds of children.

Now, the crisis in Syria, and the destabilization of the region, goes to the heart of broader challenges that the international community must now confront. How should we respond to conflicts in the Middle East and North Africa—conflicts between countries, but also conflicts within them? How do we address the choice of standing callously by while children are subjected to nerve gas or embroiling ourselves in someone else's civil war? What's the role of force in resolving disputes that threaten the stability of the region and undermine all basic standards of civilized conduct? And what's the role of the United Nations and international law in meeting cries for justice?

Today I want to outline where the United States of America stands on these issues. With respect to Syria, we believe that as a starting point, the international community must enforce the ban on chemical weapons. When I stated my willingness to order a limited strike against the Asad regime in response to the brazen use of chemical weapons, I did not do so lightly. I did so because I believe it is in the security interest of the United States and in the interests of the world to meaningfully enforce a prohibition whose origins are older than the United Nations itself. The ban against the use of chemical weapons, even in war, has been agreed to by 98 percent of humanity. It is strengthened by the searing memories of soldiers suffocating in the trenches, Jews slaughtered in gas chambers, Iranians poisoned in the many tens of thousands.

The evidence is overwhelming that the Asad regime used such weapons on August 21. U.N. inspectors gave a clear accounting that advanced rockets fired large quantities of sarin gas at civilians. These rockets were fired from a regime-controlled neighborhood and landed in opposition neighborhoods. It's an insult to human reason—and to the legitimacy of this institution—to suggest that anyone other than the regime carried out this attack.

Now, I know that in the immediate aftermath of the attack, there were those who questioned the legitimacy of even a limited strike in the absence of a clear mandate from the Security Council. But without a credible military threat, the Security Council had demonstrated no inclination to act at all. However, as I've discussed with President Putin for over a year, most recently in St. Petersburg, my preference has always been a diplomatic resolution to this issue. And in the past several weeks, the United States, Russia, and our allies have reached an agreement to place Syria's chemical weapons under international control and then to destroy them.

The Syrian Government took a first step by giving an accounting of its stockpiles. Now there must be a strong Security Council resolution to verify that the Asad regime is keeping its commitments, and there must be consequences if they fail to do so. If we cannot agree even on this, then it will show that the United Nations is incapable of enforcing the most basic of international laws. On the other hand, if we succeed, it will send a powerful message that the use of chemical weapons has no place in the 21st century and that this body means what it says.

Now, agreement on chemical weapons should energize a larger diplomatic effort to reach a political settlement within Syria. I do not believe that military action—by those within Syria, or by external powers—can achieve a lasting peace. Nor do I believe that America or any nation should determine who will lead Syria; that is for the Syrian people to decide. Nevertheless, a leader who slaughtered his citizens and gassed children to death cannot regain the legitimacy to lead a badly fractured country. The notion that Syria can somehow return to a prewar status quo is a fantasy.

So it's time for Russia and Iran to realize that insisting on Asad's rule will lead directly to the outcome that they fear: an increasingly violent space for extremists to operate. In turn, those of us who continue to support the moderate opposition must persuade them that the Syrian people cannot afford a collapse of state institutions and that a political settlement cannot be reached without addressing the legitimate fears and concerns of Alawites and other minorities.

We are committed to working this political track. And as we pursue a settlement, let's remember, this is not a zero-sum endeavor. We're no longer in a cold war. There's no great game to be won, nor does America have any interest in Syria beyond the well-being of its people, the stability of its neighbors, the elimination of chemical weapons, and ensuring that it does not become a safe haven for terrorists.

I welcome the influence of all nations that can help bring about a peaceful resolution of Syria's civil war. And as we move the Geneva process forward, I urge all nations here to step up to meet humanitarian needs in Syria and surrounding countries. America has committed over a billion dollars to this effort, and today I can announce that we will be providing an additional $340 million. No aid can take the place of a political resolution that gives the Syrian people the chance to rebuild their country, but it can help desperate people to survive.

What broader conclusions can be drawn from America's policy towards Syria? I know there are those who have been frustrated by our unwillingness to use our military might to depose Asad and believe that a failure to do so indicates a weakening of American resolve in the region. Others have suggested that my willingness to direct even limited military strikes to deter the further use of chemical weapons shows we've learned nothing from Iraq and that America continues to seek control over the Middle East for our own purposes. In this way, the situation in Syria mirrors a contradiction that has persisted in the region for decades: the United States is chastised for meddling in the region, accused of having a hand in all manner of conspiracy; at the same time, the United States is blamed for failing to do enough to solve the region's problems and for showing indifference toward suffering Muslim populations.

I realize some of this is inevitable, given America's role in the world. But these contradictory attitudes have a practical impact on the American people's support for our involvement in the region and allow leaders in the region—as well as the international community sometimes—to avoid addressing difficult problems themselves.

So let me take this opportunity to outline what has been U.S. policy towards the Middle East and North Africa and what will be my policy during the remainder of my Presidency.

The United States of America is prepared to use all elements of our power, including military force, to secure our core interests in the region. We will confront external aggression against our allies and partners, as we did in the Gulf war.

We will ensure the free flow of energy from the region to the world. Although America is steadily reducing our own dependence on imported oil, the world still depends on the region's energy supply, and a severe disruption could destabilize the entire global economy.

We will dismantle terrorist networks that threaten our people. Wherever possible, we will build the capacity of our partners, respect the sovereignty of nations, and work to address the root causes of terror. But when it's necessary to defend the United States against terrorist attack, we will take direct action.

And finally, we will not tolerate the development or use of weapons of mass destruction. Just as we consider the use of chemical weapons in Syria to be a threat to our own national security, we reject the development of nuclear weapons that could trigger a nuclear arms race in the region and undermine the global non-proliferation regime.

IRAN

Now, to say that these are America's core interests is not to say that they are our only interests. We deeply believe it is in our interests to see a Middle East and North Africa that is peaceful and prosperous, and we'll continue to promote democracy and human rights and open markets, because we believe these practices achieve peace and prosperity. But I also believe that we can rarely achieve these objectives through unilateral American action, particularly through military action. Iraq shows us that democracy cannot simply be imposed by force. Rather, these objectives are best achieved when we partner with the international community and with the countries and peoples of the region.

So what does this mean going forward? In the near term, America's diplomatic efforts will focus on two particular issues: Iran's pursuit of nuclear weapons and the Arab-Israeli conflict. While these issues are not the cause of all the region's problems, they have been a major source of instability for far too long, and resolving them can help serve as a foundation for a broader peace.

The United States and Iran have been isolated from one another since the Islamic Revolution of 1979. This mistrust has deep roots. Iranians have long complained of a history of U.S. interference in their affairs and of America's role in overthrowing an Iranian Government during the cold war. On the other hand, Americans see an Iranian Government that has declared the United States an enemy and directly—or through proxies—taken American hostages, killed U.S. troops and civilians, and threatened our ally Israel with destruction.

I don't believe this difficult history can be overcome overnight; the suspicions run too deep. But I do believe that if we can resolve the issue of Iran's nuclear program, that can serve as a major step down a long road towards a different relationship, one based on mutual interests and mutual respect.

Now, since I took office, I've made it clear in letters to the Supreme Leader in Iran and more recently to President Rouhani that America prefers to resolve our concerns over Iran's nuclear program peacefully, although we are determined to prevent Iran from developing a nuclear weapon. We are not seeking regime change, and we respect the right of the Iranian people to access peaceful nuclear energy. Instead, we insist that the Iranian Government meet its responsibilities under the Nuclear Non-Proliferation Treaty and U.N. Security Council resolutions.

Now, meanwhile, the Supreme Leader has issued a fatwa against the development of nuclear weapons, and President Rouhani has just recently reiterated that the Islamic Republic will never develop a nuclear weapon.

So these statements made by our respective Governments should offer the basis for a meaningful agreement. We should be able to achieve a resolution that respects the rights of the Iranian people, while giving the world confidence that the Iranian program is peaceful. But to succeed, conciliatory words will have to be matched by actions that are transparent and verifiable. After all, it's the Iranian Government's choices that have led to the comprehensive sanctions that are currently in place. And this not—this is not simply an issue between the United States and Iran. The world has seen Iran evade its responsibilities in the past and has an abiding interest in making sure that Iran meets its obligations in the future.

But I want to be clear: We are encouraged that President Rouhani received from the Iranian people a mandate to pursue a more moderate course. And given President Rouhani's stated commitment to reach an agreement, I am directing John Kerry to pursue this effort with the Iranian Government, in close cooperation with the European Union, the United Kingdom, France, Germany, Russia, and China.

The roadblocks may prove to be too great, but I firmly believe the diplomatic path must be tested. For while the status quo will only deepen Iran's isolation, Iran's genuine commitment to go down a different path will be good for the region and the world and will help the Iranian people meet their extraordinary potential: in commerce and culture, in science and education.

ARAB-ISRAELI CONFLICT

We are also determined to resolve a conflict that goes back even further than our differences with Iran, and that is the conflict between Palestinians and Israelis. I've made it clear that the United States will never compromise our commitment to Israel's security, nor our support for its existence as a Jewish state. Earlier this year, in Jerusalem, I was inspired by young Israelis who stood up for the belief that peace was necessary, just, and possible. And I believe there is a growing recognition within Israel that the occupation of the West Bank is tearing at the democratic fabric of the Jewish State. But the children of Israel have the right to live in a world where the nations assembled in this body fully recognize their country and where we unequivocally reject those who fire rockets at their homes or incite others to hate them.

Likewise, the United States remains committed to the belief that the Palestinian people have a right to live with security and dignity in their own sovereign state. On the same trip, I had the opportunity to meet with young Palestinians in Ramallah whose ambition and incredible potential are matched by the pain they feel in having no firm place in the community of nations. They are understandably cynical that real progress will ever be made, and they're frustrated by their families enduring the daily indignity of occupation. But they, too, recognize that two states is the only real path to peace, because just as the Palestinian people must not be displaced, the State of Israel is here to stay.

So the time is now ripe for the entire international community to get behind the pursuit of peace. Already, Israeli and Palestinian leaders have demonstrated a willingness to take significant political risks. President Abbas has put aside efforts to short-cut the pursuit of peace and come to the negotiating table. Prime Minister Netanyahu has released Palestinian prisoners and reaffirmed his commitment to a Palestinian state. Current talks are focused on final status issues of borders and security, refugees and Jerusalem.

So now the rest of us must be willing to take risks as well. Friends of Israel, including the United States, must recognize that Israel's security as a Jewish and democratic state depend on the realization of a Palestinian state, and we should say so clearly. Arab States, and those who have supported the Palestinians, must recognize that stability will only be served through a two-state solution and a secure Israel.

All of us must recognize that peace will be a powerful tool to defeat extremists throughout the region and embolden those who are prepared to build a better future. And moreover, ties of trade and commerce between Israelis and Arabs could be an engine of growth and opportunity at a time when too many young people in the region are languishing without work. So let's emerge from the familiar corners of blame and prejudice. Let's support Israeli and Palestinian leaders who are prepared to walk the difficult road to peace.

Now, real breakthroughs on these two issues—Iran's nuclear program, and Israeli–Palestinian peace—would have a profound and positive impact on the entire Middle East and North Africa. But the current convulsions arising out of the Arab Spring remind us that a just and lasting peace cannot be measured only by agreements between nations. It must also be measured by our ability to resolve conflict and promote justice within nations. And by that measure, it's clear that all of us have a lot more work to do.

When peaceful transitions began in Tunisia and Egypt, the entire world was filled with hope. And although the United States—like others—was struck by the speed of transition, and although we did not—and in fact could not—dictate events, we chose to support those who called for change. And we did so based on the belief that while these transitions will be hard and take time, societies based upon democracy and openness and the dignity of the individual will ultimately be more stable, more prosperous, and more peaceful.

EGYPT

Over the last few years, particularly in Egypt, we've seen just how hard this transition will be. Muhammad Mursi was democratically elected, but proved unwilling or unable to govern in a way that was fully inclusive. The Interim Government that replaced him responded to the desires of millions of Egyptians who believed the revolution had taken a wrong turn, but it, too, has made decisions inconsistent with inclusive democracy, through an emergency law and restrictions on the press and civil society and opposition parties.

Of course, America has been attacked by all sides of this internal conflict, simultaneously accused of supporting the Muslim Brotherhood and engineering their removal of power. In fact, the United States has purposely avoided choosing sides. Our overriding interest throughout these past few years has been to encourage a government that legitimately reflects the will of the Egyptian people and recognizes true democracy as requiring a respect for minority rights and the rule of law, freedom of speech and assembly, and a strong civil society.

That remains our interest today. And so, going forward, the United States will maintain a constructive relationship with the Interim Government that promotes core interests like the Camp David Accords and counterterrorism. We'll continue support in areas like education that directly benefit the Egyptian people. But we have not proceeded with the delivery of certain military systems, and our support will depend upon Egypt's progress in pursuing a more democratic path.

And our approach to Egypt reflects a larger point: The United States will at times work with Governments that do not meet, at least in our view, the highest international expectations, but who work with us on our core interests. Nevertheless, we will not stop asserting principles that are consistent with our ideals, whether that means opposing the use of violence as a means of suppressing dissent or supporting the principles embodied in the Universal Declaration of Human Rights.

DEMOCRACY

We will reject the notion that these principles are simply Western exports, incompatible with Islam or the Arab World. We believe they are the birthright of every person. And while we recognize that our influence will at times be limited, although we will be wary of efforts to impose democracy through military force, and although we will at times be accused of hypocrisy and inconsistency, we will be engaged in the region for the long haul. For the hard work of forging freedom and democracy is the task of a generation.

And this includes efforts to resolve sectarian tensions that continue to surface in places like Iraq, Bahrain, and Syria. We understand such longstanding issues cannot be solved by outsiders; they must be addressed by Muslim communities themselves. But we've seen grinding conflicts come to an end before—most recently in Northern Ireland, where Catholics and Protestants finally recognized that an endless cycle of conflict was causing both communities to fall behind a fast-moving world. And so we believe those same sectarian conflicts can be overcome in the Middle East and North Africa.

To summarize, the United States has a hard-earned humility when it comes to our ability to determine events inside other countries. The notion of American empire may be useful propaganda, but it isn't borne out by America's current policy or by public opinion. Indeed, as recent debates within the United States over Syria clearly showed, the danger for the world is not an America that is too eager to immerse itself in the affairs of other countries or to take on every problem in the region as its own. The danger for the world is that the United States, after a decade of war—rightly concerned about issues back home, aware of the hostility that our engagement in the region has engendered throughout the Muslim world—may disengage, creating a vacuum of leadership that no other nation is ready to fill.

Now, I believe such disengagement would be a mistake. I believe America must remain engaged for our own security. But I also believe the world is better for it. Some may disagree, but I believe America is exceptional, in part because we have shown a willingness through the sacrifice of blood and treasure to stand up not only for our own narrow self-interests, but for the interests of all.

I must be honest though. We're far more likely to invest our energy in those countries that want to work with us, that invest in their people instead of a corrupt few, that embrace a vision of society where everyone can contribute: men and women; Shia or Sunni; Muslim, Christian, or Jew. Because from Europe to Asia, from Africa to the Americas, nations that have persevered on a democratic path have emerged more prosperous, more peaceful, and more invested in upholding our common security and our common humanity. And I believe that the same will hold true for the Arab world.

HUMAN RIGHTS

And this leads me to a final point. There will be times when the breakdown of societies is so great, the violence against civilians so substantial, that the international community will be called upon to act. This will require new thinking and some very tough choices. While the United Nations was designed to prevent wars between states, increasingly we face the challenge of preventing slaughter within states. And these challenges will grow more pronounced as we are confronted with states that are fragile or failing, places where horrendous violence can put innocent men, women, and children at risk, with no hope of protection from their national institutions.

I have made it clear that even when America's core interests are not directly threatened, we stand ready to do our part to prevent mass atrocities and protect basic human rights. But we cannot and should not bear that burden alone. In Mali, we supported both the French intervention that successfully pushed back Al Qaida and the African forces who are keeping the peace. In Eastern Africa, we are working with partners to bring the Lord's Resistance Army to an end. And in Libya, when the Security Council provided a mandate to protect civilians, America joined a coalition that took action. And because of what we did there, countless lives were saved, and a tyrant could not kill his way back to power.

I know that some now criticize the action in Libya as an object lesson. They point to the problems that the country now confronts: a democratically elected Government struggling to provide security; armed groups, in some places extremists, ruling parts of a fractured land. And so these critics argue that any intervention to protect civilians is doomed to fail: "Look at Libya." Now, no one is more mindful of these problems than I am, for they resulted in the death of four outstanding U.S. citizens who were committed to the Libyan people, including Ambassador Chris Stevens, a man whose courageous efforts helped save the city of Benghazi. But does anyone truly believe that the situation in Libya would be better if Qadhafi had been allowed to kill, imprison, or brutalize his people into submission? It's far more likely that without international action, Libya would now be engulfed in civil war and bloodshed.

So we live in a world of imperfect choices. Different nations will not agree on the need for action in every instance, and the principle of sovereignty is at the center of our international order. But sovereignty cannot be a shield for tyrants to commit wanton murder or an excuse for the international community to turn a blind eye. While we need to be modest in our belief that we can remedy every evil, while we need to be mindful that the world is full of unintended consequences, should we really accept the notion that the world is powerless in the face of a Rwanda or Srebrenica? If that's the world that people want to live in, they should say so and reckon with the cold logic of mass graves.

But I believe we can embrace a different future. And if we don't want to choose between inaction and war, we must get better—all of us—at the policies that prevent the breakdown of basic order: through respect for the responsibilities of nations and the rights of individuals; through meaningful sanctions for those who break the rules; through dogged diplomacy that resolves the root causes of conflict, not merely its aftermath; through development assistance that brings hope to the marginalized. And yes, sometimes—although this will not be enough—there are going to be moments where the international community will need to acknowledge that the multilateral use of military force may be required to prevent the very worst from occurring.

Ultimately, this is the international community that America seeks, one where nations do not covet the land or resources of other nations, but one in which we carry out the founding purpose of this institution and where we all take responsibility; a world in which the rules established out of the horrors of war can help us resolve conflicts peacefully and prevent the kinds of wars that our forefathers fought; a world where human beings can live with dignity and meet their basic needs, whether they live in New York or Nairobi, in Peshawar or Damascus.

These are extraordinary times, with extraordinary opportunities. Thanks to human progress, a child born anywhere on Earth today can do things today that 60 years ago would have been out of reach for the mass of humanity. I saw this in Africa, where nations moving beyond conflict are now poised to take off. And America is with them, partnering to feed the hungry and care for the sick and to bring power to places off the grid.

I see it across the Pacific region, where hundreds of millions have been lifted out of poverty in a single generation. I see it in the faces of young people everywhere who can access the entire world with the click of a button and who are eager to join the cause of eradicating extreme poverty and combating climate change, starting businesses, expanding freedom, and leaving behind the old ideological battles of the past. That's what's happening in Asia and Africa. It's happening in Europe and across the Americas. That's the future that the people of the Middle East and North Africa deserve as well, one where they can focus on opportunity, instead of whether they'll be killed or repressed because of who they are or what they believe.

Time and again, nations and people have shown our capacity to change—to live up to humanity's highest ideals, to choose our better history. Last month, I stood where, 50 years ago, Martin Luther King Jr. told America about his dream, at a time when many people of my race could not even vote for President. Earlier this year, I stood in the small cell where Nelson Mandela endured decades cut off from his own people and the world. Who are we to believe that today's challenges cannot be overcome, when we've seen what changes the human spirit can bring? Who in this hall can argue that the future belongs to those who seek to repress that spirit rather than those who seek to liberate it?

I know what side of history I want the United States of America to be on. We're ready to meet tomorrow's challenges with you, firm in the belief that all men and women are in fact created equal, each individual possessed with a dignity and inalienable rights that cannot be denied. That is why we look to the future not with fear, but with hope. And that's why we remain convinced that this community of nations can deliver a more peaceful, prosperous, and just world to the next generation.

Thank you very much.

Executive Office of the President. "Remarks to the United Nations General Assembly in New York City." September 24, 2013. *Compilation of Presidential Documents* 2013, no. 00655 (September 24, 2013). http://www.gpo.gov/fdsys/pkg/DCPD-201300655/pdf/DCPD-201300655.pdf.

President Obama's 2014 State of the Union Address

Following is the White House transcript of President Obama's address before a joint session of Congress on the state of the union delivered on January 28, 2014.

Mr. Speaker, Mr. Vice President, Members of Congress, my fellow Americans: Today in America, a teacher spent extra time with a student who needed it and did her part to lift America's graduation rate to its highest levels in more than three decades. An entrepreneur flipped on the lights in her tech startup and did her part to add to the more than 8 million new jobs our businesses have created over the past 4 years. An autoworker fine-tuned some of the best, most fuel-efficient cars in the world and did his part to help America wean itself off foreign oil.

A farmer prepared for the spring after the strongest 5-year stretch of farm exports in our history. A rural doctor gave a young child the first prescription to treat asthma that his mother could afford. A man took the bus home from the graveyard shift, bone-tired, but dreaming big dreams for his son. And in tight-knit communities all across America, fathers and mothers will tuck in their kids, put an arm around their spouse, remember fallen comrades, and give thanks for being home from a war that after 12 long years is finally coming to an end.

Tonight this Chamber speaks with one voice to the people we represent: It is you, our citizens, who make the state of our Union strong.

And here are the results of your efforts: the lowest unemployment rate in over 5 years; a rebounding housing market; a manufacturing sector that's adding jobs for the first time since the 1990s; more oil produced at home than we buy from the rest of the world, the first time that's happened in nearly 20 years; our deficits cut by more than half. And for the first time in over a decade, business leaders around the world have declared that China is no longer the world's number-one place to invest, America is.

That's why I believe this can be a breakthrough year for America. After 5 years of grit and determined effort, the United States is better positioned for the 21st century than any other nation on Earth.

The question for everyone in this Chamber, running through every decision we make this year, is whether we are going to help or hinder this progress. For several years now, this town has been consumed by a rancorous argument over the proper size of the Federal Government. It's an important debate, one that dates back to our very founding. But when that debate prevents us from carrying out even the most basic functions of our democracy—when our differences shut down Government or threaten the full faith and credit of the United States— then we are not doing right by the American people.

Now, as President, I'm committed to making Washington work better and rebuilding the trust of the people who sent us here. And I believe most of you are too. Last month, thanks to the work of Democrats and Republicans, Congress finally produced a budget that undoes some of last year's severe cuts to priorities like education. Nobody got everything they wanted, and we can still do more to invest in this country's future while bringing down our deficit in a balanced way, but the budget compromise should leave us freer to focus on creating new jobs, not creating new crises.

And in the coming months, let's see where else we can make progress together. Let's make this a year of action. That's what most Americans want: for all of us in this Chamber to focus on their lives, their hopes, their aspirations. And what I believe unites the people of this Nation—regardless of race or region or party, young or old, rich or poor—is the simple, profound belief in opportunity for all: the notion that if you work hard and take responsibility, you can get ahead in America.

Now, let's face it, that belief has suffered some serious blows. Over more than three decades, even before the great recession hit, massive shifts in technology and global competition had eliminated a lot of good, middle class jobs and weakened the economic foundations that families depend on.

Today, after 4 years of economic growth, corporate profits and stock prices have rarely been higher, and those at the top have never done better. But average wages have barely budged. Inequality has deepened. Upward mobility has stalled. The cold, hard fact is that even in the midst of recovery, too many Americans are working more than ever just to get by, let alone to get ahead. And too many still aren't working at all.

So our job is to reverse these trends. It won't happen right away, and we won't agree on everything. But what I offer tonight is a set of concrete, practical proposals to speed up growth, strengthen the middle class, and build new ladders of opportunity into the middle class. Some require congressional action, and I am eager to work with all of you. But America does not stand still, and neither will I. So wherever and whenever I can take steps without legislation to expand opportunity for more American families, that's what I'm going to do.

As usual, our First Lady sets a good example. *[Applause]* Well—*[applause]*. Michelle's "Let's Move!" partnership with schools, businesses, local leaders has helped bring down childhood obesity rates for the first time in 30 years. And that's an achievement that will improve lives and reduce health care costs for decades to come. The Joining Forces alliance that Michelle and Jill Biden launched has already encouraged employers to hire or train nearly 400,000 veterans and military spouses.

Taking a page from that playbook, the White House just organized a College Opportunity Summit, where already, 150 universities, businesses, nonprofits have made concrete commitments to reduce inequality in access to higher education and to help every hardworking kid go to college and succeed when they get to campus. And across the country, we're partnering with mayors, Governors, and State legislatures on issues from homelessness to marriage equality.

The point is, there are millions of Americans outside of Washington who are tired of stale political arguments and are moving this country forward. They believe—and I believe—that here in America, our success should depend not on accident of birth, but the strength of our work ethic and the scope of our dreams. That's what drew our forebears here. That's how the daughter of a factory worker is CEO of America's largest automaker; how the son of a barkeep is Speaker of the House; how the son of a single mom can be President of the greatest nation on Earth.

Opportunity is who we are. And the defining project of our generation must be to restore that promise. We know where to start: The best measure of opportunity is access to a good job. With the economy picking up speed, companies say they intend to hire more people this year. And over half of big manufacturers say they're thinking of insourcing jobs from abroad.

So let's make that decision easier for more companies. Both Democrats and Republicans have argued that our Tax Code is riddled with wasteful, complicated loopholes that punish businesses investing here and reward companies that keep profits abroad. Let's flip that equation. Let's work together to close those loopholes, end those incentives to ship jobs overseas, and lower tax rates for businesses that create jobs right here at home.

Moreover, we can take the money we save from this transition to tax reform to create jobs rebuilding our roads, upgrading our ports, unclogging our commutes, because in today's global economy, first-class jobs gravitate to first-class infrastructure. We'll need Congress to protect more than 3 million jobs by finishing transportation and waterways bills this summer. That can happen. But I'll act on my own to slash bureaucracy and streamline the permitting process for key projects so we can get more construction workers on the job as fast as possible.

We also have the chance, right now, to beat other countries in the race for the next wave of high-tech manufacturing jobs. My administration has launched two hubs for high-tech manufacturing in Raleigh, North Carolina, and Youngstown, Ohio, where we've connected businesses to research universities that can help America lead the world in advanced technologies. Tonight I'm announcing, we'll launch six more this year. Bipartisan bills in both Houses could double the number of these hubs and the jobs they create. So get those bills to my desk. Put more Americans back to work.

Let's do more to help the entrepreneurs and small-business owners who create most new jobs in America. Over the past 5 years, my administration has made more loans to small business owners than any other. And when 98 percent of our exporters are small businesses, new trade partnerships with Europe and Asia—the Asia-Pacific will help them create more jobs. We need to work together on tools like bipartisan trade promotion authority to protect our workers, protect our environment, and open new markets to new goods stamped "Made in the U.S.A."

Listen, China and Europe aren't standing on the sidelines, and neither should we. We know that the nation that goes all-in on innovation today will own the global economy tomorrow. This is an edge America cannot surrender. Federally funded research helped lead to the ideas and inventions behind Google and smartphones. And that's why Congress should undo the damage done by last year's cuts to basic research so we can unleash the next great American discovery.

There are entire industries to be built based on vaccines that stay ahead of drug-resistant bacteria or paper-thin material that's stronger than steel. And let's pass a patent reform bill that allows our businesses to stay focused on innovation, not costly and needless litigation.

Now, one of the biggest factors in bringing more jobs back is our commitment to American energy. The all-of-the-above energy strategy I announced a few years ago is working, and today, America is closer to energy independence than we have been in decades.

One of the reasons why is natural gas. If extracted safely, it's the bridge fuel that can power our economy with less of the carbon pollution that causes climate change. Businesses plan to invest almost $100 billion in new factories that use natural gas. I'll cut red tape to help States get those factories built and put folks to work, and this Congress can help by putting people to work building fueling stations that shift more cars and trucks from foreign oil to American natural gas.

Meanwhile, my administration will keep working with the industry to sustain production and jobs growth while strengthening protection of our air, our water, our communities. And while we're at it, I'll use my authority to protect more of our pristine Federal lands for future generations.

Well, it's not just oil and natural gas production that's booming, we're becoming a global leader in solar too. Every 4 minutes, another American home or business goes solar, every panel pounded into place by a worker whose job cannot be outsourced. Let's continue that progress with a smarter tax policy that stops giving $4 billion a year to fossil fuel industries that don't need it so we can invest more in fuels of the future that do.

And even as we've increased energy production, we've partnered with businesses, builders, and local communities to reduce the energy we consume. When we rescued our automakers, for example, we worked with them to set higher fuel efficiency standards for our cars. In the coming months, I'll build on that success by setting new standards for our trucks so we can keep driving down oil imports and what we pay at the pump.

And taken together, our energy policy is creating jobs and leading to a cleaner, safer planet. Over the past 8 years, the United States has reduced our total carbon pollution more than any other nation on Earth. But we have to act with more urgency, because a changing climate is already harming Western communities struggling with drought and coastal cities dealing with floods. That's why I directed my administration to work with States, utilities, and others to set new standards on the amount of carbon pollution our power plants are allowed to dump into the air.

The shift to a cleaner energy economy won't happen overnight, and it will require some tough choices along the way. But the debate is settled. Climate change is a fact. And when our children's children look us in the eye and ask if we did all we could to leave them a safer, more stable world, with new sources of energy, I want us to be able to say, yes, we did.

Finally, if we're serious about economic growth, it is time to heed the call of business leaders, labor leaders, faith leaders, law enforcement and fix our broken immigration system. Republicans and Democrats in the Senate have acted, and I know that members of both parties in the House want to do the same. Independent economists say immigration reform will grow our economy and shrink our deficits by almost $1 trillion in the next two decades. And for good reason: When people come here to fulfill their dreams—to study, invent, contribute to our culture—they make our country a more attractive place for businesses to locate and create jobs for everybody. So let's get immigration reform done this year. [Applause] Let's get it done. It's time.

The ideas I've outlined so far can speed up growth and create more jobs. But in this rapidly changing economy, we have to make sure that every American has the skills to fill those jobs. The good news is, we know how to do it.

Two years ago, as the auto industry came roaring back, Andra Rush opened up a manufacturing firm in Detroit. She knew that Ford needed parts for the best selling truck in America, and she knew how to make those parts. She just needed the workforce. So she dialed up what we call an American Job Center, places where folks can walk in to get the help or training they need to find a new job or a better job. She was flooded with new workers. And today, Detroit Manufacturing Systems has more than 700 employees. And what Andra and her employees experienced is how it should be for every employer and every job seeker.

So tonight I've asked Vice President Biden to lead an across-the-board reform of America's training programs to make sure they have one mission: train Americans with the skills employers need and match them to good jobs that need to be filled right now.

That means more on-the-job training and more apprenticeships that set a young worker on an upward trajectory for life. It means connecting companies to community colleges that can help design training to fill their specific needs. And if Congress wants to help, you can concentrate funding on proven programs that connect more ready-to-work Americans with ready-to-be-filled jobs.

I'm also convinced we can help Americans return to the workforce faster by reforming unemployment insurance so that it's more effective in today's economy. But first, this Congress needs to restore the unemployment insurance you just let expire for 1.6 million people.

Let me tell you why. Misty DeMars is a mother of two young boys. She'd been steadily employed since she was a teenager, put herself through college. She'd never collected unemployment benefits, but she'd been paying taxes. In May, she and her husband used their life savings to buy their first home. A week later, budget cuts claimed the job she loved. Last month, when their unemployment insurance was cut off, she sat down and wrote me a letter, the kind I get every day. "We are the face of the unemployment crisis," she wrote. "I'm not dependent on the government. Our country depends on people like us who build careers, contribute to society, care about our neighbors. I'm confident that in time, I will find a job, I will pay my taxes, and we will raise our children in their own home in the community we love. Please give us this chance."

Congress, give these hard-working, responsible Americans that chance. Give them that chance. *[Applause]* Give them the chance. They need our help right now. But more important, this country needs them in the game. That's why I've been asking CEOs to give more long-term unemployed workers a fair shot at new jobs, a new chance to support their families. And in fact, this week, many will come to the White House to make that commitment real. Tonight I ask every business leader in America to join us and to do the same, because we are stronger when America fields a full team.

Of course, it's not enough to train today's workforce. We also have to prepare tomorrow's workforce, by guaranteeing every child access to a world-class education. Estiven Rodriguez couldn't speak a word of English when he moved to New York City at age 9. But last month, thanks to the support of great teachers and an innovative tutoring program, he led a march of his classmates through a crowd of cheering parents and neighbors from their high school to the post office, where they mailed off their college applications. And this son of a factory worker just found out, he's going to college this fall.

Five years ago, we set out to change the odds for all our kids. We worked with lenders to reform student loans, and today, more young people are earning college degrees than ever before. Race to the Top, with the help of Governors from both parties, has helped States raise expectations and performance. Teachers and principals in schools from Tennessee to Washington, DC, are making big strides in preparing students with the skills for the new economy: problem solving, critical thinking, science, technology, engineering, math.

Now, some of this change is hard. It requires everything from more challenging curriculums and more demanding parents to better support for teachers and new ways to measure how well our kids think, not how well they can fill in a bubble on a test. But it is worth it, and it is working. The problem is, we're still not reaching enough kids, and we're not reaching them in time. And that has to change.

Research shows that one of the best investments we can make in a child's life is high-quality early education. Last year, I asked this Congress to help States make high-quality pre-K available to every 4-year-old. And as a parent as well as a President, I repeat that request tonight. But in the meantime, 30 States have raised pre-K funding on their own. They know we can't wait. So just as we worked with States to reform our schools, this year, we'll invest in new partnerships with States and communities across the country in a Race to the Top for our youngest children. And as Congress decides what it's going to do, I'm going to pull together a coalition of elected officials, business leaders, and philanthropists willing to help more kids access the high-quality pre-K that they need. It is right for America. We need to get this done.

Last year, I also pledged to connect 99 percent of our students to high-speed broadband over the next 4 years. Tonight I can announce that with the support of the FCC and companies like Apple, Microsoft, Sprint, and Verizon, we've got a down payment to start connecting more than 15,000 schools and 20 million students over the next 2 years, without adding a dime to the deficit.

We're working to redesign high schools and partner them with colleges and employers that offer the real-world education and hands-on training that can lead directly to a job and career. We're shaking up our system of higher education to give parents more information and colleges more incentive to offer better value so that no middle class kid is priced out of a college education.

We're offering millions the opportunity to cap their monthly student loan payments to 10 percent of their income, and I want to work with Congress to see how we can help even more Americans who feel trapped by student loan debt. And I'm reaching out to some of America's leading foundations and corporations on a new initiative to help more young men of color facing especially tough odds to stay on track and reach their full potential.

The bottom line is, Michelle and I want every child to have the same chance this country gave us. But we know our opportunity agenda won't be complete, and too many young people entering the workforce today will see the American Dream as an empty promise, unless we also do more to make sure our economy honors the dignity of work and hard work pays off for every single American.

Today, women make up about half our workforce, but they still make 77 cents for every dollar a man earns. That is wrong, and in 2014, it's an embarrassment. Women deserve equal pay for equal work. She deserves to have a baby without sacrificing her job. A mother deserves a day off to care for a sick child or a sick parent without running into hardship. And you know what, a father does too. It is time to do away with workplace policies that belong in a "Mad Men" episode. *[Laughter]* This year, let's all come together—Congress, the White House, businesses from Wall Street to Main Street—to give every woman the opportunity she deserves. Because I believe when women succeed, America succeeds.

Now, women hold a majority of lower wage jobs, but they're not the only ones stifled by stagnant wages. Americans understand that some people will earn more money than others, and we don't resent those who, by virtue of their efforts, achieve incredible success. That's what America is all about. But Americans overwhelmingly agree that no one who works full time should ever have to raise a family in poverty.

In the year since I asked this Congress to raise the minimum wage, five States have passed laws to raise theirs. Many businesses have done it on their own. Nick Chute is here today with his boss, John Soranno. John's an owner of Punch Pizza in Minneapolis, and Nick helps make the dough. *[Laughter]* Only now he makes more of it. *[Laughter]* John just gave his employees a raise to 10 bucks an hour, and that's a decision that has eased their financial stress and boosted their morale.

Tonight I ask more of America's business leaders to follow John's lead: Do what you can to raise your employees' wages. It's good for the economy. It's good for America. To every mayor, Governor, State legislator in America, I say: You don't have to wait for Congress to act; Americans will support you if you take this on.

And as a chief executive, I intend to lead by example. Profitable corporations like Costco see higher wages as the smart way to boost productivity and reduce turnover. We should too. In the coming weeks, I will issue an Executive order requiring Federal contractors to pay their federally funded employees a fair wage of at least 10 dollars and 10 cents an hour. Because if you cook our troops' meals or wash their dishes, you should not have to live in poverty.

Of course, to reach millions more, Congress does need to get on board. Today, the Federal minimum wage is worth about 20 percent less than it was when Ronald Reagan first stood here. And Tom Harkin and George Miller have a bill to fix that by lifting the minimum wage to 10 dollars and 10 cents. It's easy to remember: 10-10. This will help families. It will give businesses customers with more money to spend. It does not involve any new bureaucratic program. So join the rest of the country. Say yes. Give America a raise. Give them a raise.

There are other steps we can take to help families make ends meet, and few are more effective at reducing inequality and helping families pull themselves up through hard work than the earned-income tax credit. Right now it helps about half of all parents at some point. Think about that: It helps about half of all parents in America at some point in their lives. But I agree with Republicans like Senator Rubio that it doesn't do enough for single workers who don't have kids. So let's work together to strengthen the credit, reward work, help more Americans get ahead.

Let's do more to help Americans save for retirement. Today, most workers don't have a pension. A Social Security check often isn't enough on its own. And while the stock market has doubled over the last 5 years, that doesn't help folks who don't have 401(k)s. That's why, tomorrow, I will direct the Treasury to create a new way for working Americans to start their own retirement savings: MyI—MyRA.

It's a new savings bond that encourages folks to build a nest egg. MyRA guarantees a decent return with no risk of losing what you put in. And if this Congress wants to help, work with me to fix an upside-down Tax Code that gives big tax breaks to help the wealthy save, but does little or nothing for middle class Americans. Offer every American access to an automatic IRA on the job so they can save at work just like everybody in this Chamber can.

And since the most important investment many families make is their home, send me legislation that protects taxpayers from footing the bill for a housing crisis ever again and keeps the dream of home ownership alive for future generations.

One last point on financial security: For decades, few things exposed hard-working families to economic hardship more than a broken health care system. And in case you haven't heard, we're in the process of fixing that. Now, a preexisting condition used to mean that someone like Amanda Shelley, a physician's assistant and single mom from Arizona, couldn't get health insurance. But on January 1, she got covered. On January 3, she felt a sharp pain. On January 6, she had emergency surgery. Just one week earlier, Amanda said, and that surgery would have meant bankruptcy.

That's what health insurance reform is all about: the peace of mind that if misfortune strikes, you don't have to lose everything. Already, because of the Affordable Care Act, more than 3 million Americans under age 26 have gained coverage under their parents' plan. More than 9 million Americans have signed up for private health insurance or Medicaid coverage. Nine million.

And here's another number: zero. Because of this law, no American—none, zero—can ever again be dropped or denied coverage for a preexisting condition like asthma or back pain or cancer. No woman can ever be charged more just because she's a woman. And we did all this while adding years to Medicare's finances, keeping Medicare premiums flat, and lowering prescription costs for millions of seniors.

Now, I do not expect to convince my Republican friends on the merits of this law. *[Laughter]* But I know that the American people are not interested in refighting old battles. So again, if you have specific plans to cut costs, cover more people, increase choice, tell America what you'd do differently. Let's see if the numbers add up. But let's not have another 40-something votes to repeal a law that's already helping millions of Americans like Amanda. The first 40 were plenty. *[Laughter]*

We all owe it to the American people to say what we're for, not just what we're against. And if you want to know the real impact this law is having, just talk to Governor Steve Beshear of Kentucky, who's here tonight. Now, Kentucky is not the most liberal part of the country. That's not where I got my highest vote totals. *[Laughter]* But he's like a man possessed when it comes to covering his Commonwealth's families. They're our neighbors and our friends, he said: "They're people we shop and go to church with, farmers out on the tractor, grocery clerks. They're people who go to work every morning praying they don't get sick. No one deserves to live that way."

Steve's right. That's why tonight I ask every American who knows someone without health insurance to help them get covered by March 31. *[Applause]* Help them get covered. Moms, get on your kids to sign up. Kids, call your mom and walk her through the application. It will give her some peace of mind, and plus, she'll appreciate hearing from you. *[Laughter]*

After all, that's the spirit that has always moved this Nation forward. It's the spirit of citizenship, the recognition that through hard work and responsibility, we can pursue our individual dreams, but still come together as one American family to make sure the next generation can pursue its dreams as well.

Citizenship means standing up for everyone's right to vote. Last year, part of the Voting Rights Act was weakened, but conservative Republicans and liberal Democrats are working together to strengthen it. And the bipartisan Commission I appointed, chaired by my campaign lawyer and Governor Romney's campaign lawyer, came together and have offered reforms so that no one has to wait more than a half hour to vote. Let's support these efforts. It should be the power of our vote, not the size of our bank accounts, that drives our democracy.

Citizenship means standing up for the lives that gun violence steals from us each day. I've seen the courage of parents, students, pastors, police officers all over this country who say, "We are not afraid." And I intend to keep trying, with or without Congress, to help stop more tragedies from visiting innocent Americans in our movie theaters, in our shopping malls, or schools like Sandy Hook.

Citizenship demands a sense of common purpose, participation in the hard work of self-government, an obligation to serve our communities. And I know this Chamber agrees that few Americans give more to their country than our diplomats and the men and women of the United States Armed Forces. Thank you.

Tonight, because of the extraordinary troops and civilians who risk and lay down their lives to keep us free, the United States is more secure. When I took office, nearly 180,000 Americans were serving in Iraq and Afghanistan. Today, all our troops are out of Iraq. More than 60,000 of our troops have already come home from Afghanistan. With Afghan forces now in the lead for their own security, our troops have moved to a support role. Together with our allies, we will complete our mission there by the end of this year, and America's longest war will finally be over.

After 2014, we will support a unified Afghanistan as it takes responsibility for its own future. If the Afghan Government signs a security agreement that we have negotiated, a small force of Americans could remain in Afghanistan with NATO allies to carry out two narrow missions: training and assisting Afghan forces and counterterrorism operations to pursue any remnants of Al Qaida. For while our relationship with Afghanistan will change, one thing will not: our resolve that terrorists do not launch attacks against our country.

The fact is, that danger remains. While we've put Al Qaida's core leadership on a path to defeat, the threat has evolved as Al Qaida affiliates and other extremists take root in different parts of the world. In Yemen, Somalia, Iraq, Mali, we have to keep working with partners to disrupt and disable those networks. In Syria, we'll support the opposition that rejects the agenda of terrorist networks. Here at home, we'll keep strengthening our defenses and combat new threats like cyber attacks. And as we reform our defense budget, we will have to keep faith with our men and women in uniform and invest in the capabilities they need to succeed in future missions.

We have to remain vigilant. But I strongly believe our leadership and our security cannot depend on our outstanding military alone. As Commander in Chief, I have used force when needed to protect the American people, and I will never hesitate to do so as long as I hold this office. But I will not send our troops into harm's way unless it is truly necessary, nor will I allow our sons and daughters to be mired in open-ended conflicts. We must fight the battles that need to be fought, not those that terrorists prefer from us: large-scale deployments that drain our strength and may ultimately feed extremism.

So even as we actively and aggressively pursue terrorist networks through more targeted efforts and by building the capacity of our foreign partners, America must move off a permanent war footing. That's why I've imposed prudent limits on the use of drones. For we will not be safer if people abroad believe we strike within their countries without regard for the consequence.

That's why, working with this Congress, I will reform our surveillance programs, because the vital work of our intelligence community depends on public confidence, here and abroad, that privacy of ordinary people is not being violated.

And with the Afghan war ending, this needs to be the year Congress lifts the remaining restrictions on detainee transfers and we close the prison at Guantanamo Bay. Because we counter terrorism not just through intelligence and military actions, but by remaining true to our constitutional ideals and setting an example for the rest of the world.

You see, in a world of complex threats, our security, our leadership, depends on all elements of our power, including strong and principled diplomacy. American diplomacy has rallied more than 50 countries to prevent nuclear materials from falling into the wrong hands and allowed us to reduce our own reliance on cold war stockpiles. American diplomacy, backed by the threat of force, is why Syria's chemical weapons are being eliminated.

And we will continue to work with the international community to usher in the future the Syrian people deserve, a future free of dictatorship, terror, and fear. As we speak, American diplomacy is supporting Israelis and Palestinians as they engage in the difficult but necessary talks to end the conflict there, to achieve dignity and an independent state for Palestinians and lasting peace and security for the State of Israel, a Jewish state that knows America will always be at their side.

And it is American diplomacy, backed by pressure, that has halted the progress of Iran's nuclear program and rolled back parts of that program for the very first time in a decade. As we gather here tonight, Iran has begun to eliminate its stockpile of higher levels of enriched uranium. It's not installing advanced centrifuges. Unprecedented inspections help the world verify every day that Iran is not building a bomb. And with our allies and partners, we're engaged in negotiations to see if we can peacefully achieve a goal we all share: preventing Iran from obtaining a nuclear weapon.

These negotiations will be difficult. They may not succeed. We are clear eyed about Iran's support for terrorist organizations like Hizballah, which threatens our allies. And we're clear about the mistrust between our nations, mistrust that cannot be wished away. But these negotiations don't rely on trust. Any long-term deal we agree to must be based on verifiable action that convinces us and the international community that Iran is not building a nuclear bomb. If John F. Kennedy and Ronald Reagan could negotiate with the Soviet Union, then surely a strong and confident America can negotiate with less powerful adversaries today.

The sanctions that we put in place helped make this opportunity possible. But let me be clear: If this Congress sends me a new sanctions bill now that threatens to derail these talks, I will veto it. For the sake of our national security, we must give diplomacy a chance to succeed. If Iran's leaders do not seize this opportunity, then I will be the first to call for more sanctions and stand ready to exercise all options to make sure Iran does not build a nuclear weapon. But if Iran's leaders do seize the chance—and we'll know soon enough—then Iran could take an important step to rejoin the community of nations, and we will have resolved one of the leading security challenges of our time without the risks of war.

Now, finally, let's remember that our leadership is defined not just by our defense against threats, but by the enormous opportunities to do good and promote understanding around the globe: to forge greater cooperation, to expand new markets, to free people from fear and want. And no one is better positioned to take advantage of those opportunities than America.

Our alliance with Europe remains the strongest the world has ever known. From Tunisia to Burma, we're supporting those who are willing to do the hard work of building democracy. In Ukraine, we stand for the principle that all people have the right to express themselves freely and peacefully and to have a say in their country's future. Across Africa, we're bringing together businesses and governments to double access to electricity and help end extreme poverty. In the Americas, we're building new ties of commerce, but we're also expanding cultural and educational exchanges among young people. And we will continue to focus on the Asia-Pacific, where we support our allies, shape a future of greater security and prosperity, and extend a hand to those devastated by disaster, as we did in the Philippines, when our Marines and civilians rushed to aid those battered by a typhoon, and who were greeted with words like, "We will never forget your kindness" and "God bless America."

We do these things because they help promote our long-term security, and we do them because we believe in the inherent dignity and equality of every human being, regardless of race or religion, creed or sexual orientation. And next week, the world will see one expression of that commitment, when Team U.S.A. marches the red, white, and blue into the Olympic Stadium and brings home the gold. *[Laughter]*

Audience members. U.S.A.! U.S.A.! U.S.A.!

The President. My fellow Americans, no other country in the world does what we do. On every issue, the world turns to us, not simply because of the size of our economy or our military might, but because of the ideals we stand for and the burdens we bear to advance them. No one knows this better than those who serve in uniform.

As this time of war draws to a close, a new generation of heroes returns to civilian life. We'll keep slashing that backlog so our veterans receive the benefits they've earned and our wounded warriors receive the health care—including the mental health care—that they need. We'll keep working to help all our veterans translate their skills and leadership into jobs here at home. And we will all continue to join forces to honor and support our remarkable military families.

Let me tell you about one of those families I've come to know. I first met Cory Remsburg, a proud Army Ranger, at Omaha Beach on the 65th anniversary of D-day. Along with some of his fellow Rangers, he walked me through the program and the ceremony. He was a strong, impressive young man, had an easy manner, he was sharp as a tack. And we joked around and took pictures, and I told him to stay in touch.

A few months later, on his 10th deployment, Cory was nearly killed by a massive roadside bomb in Afghanistan. His comrades found him in a canal, face down, underwater, shrapnel in his brain. For months, he lay in a coma. And the next time I met him, in the hospital, he couldn't speak, could barely move. Over the years, he's endured dozens of surgeries and procedures, hours of grueling rehab every day.

Even now, Cory is still blind in one eye, still struggles on his left side. But slowly, steadily, with the support of caregivers like his dad Craig and the community around him, Cory has grown stronger. And day by day, he's learned to speak again and stand again and walk again. And he's working toward the day when he can serve his country again. "My recovery has not been easy," he says. "Nothing in life that's worth anything is easy."

Cory is here tonight. And like the Army he loves, like the America he serves, Sergeant First Class Cory Remsburg never gives up, and he does not quit. Cory.

My fellow Americans, men and women like Cory remind us that America has never come easy. Our freedom, our democracy, has never been easy. Sometimes, we stumble, we make mistakes; we get frustrated or discouraged. But for more than 200 years, we have put those things aside and placed our collective shoulder to the wheel of progress: to create and build and expand the possibilities of individual achievement, to free other nations from tyranny and fear, to promote justice and fairness and equality under the law so that the words set to paper by our Founders are made real for every citizen. The America we want for our kids—a rising America where honest work is plentiful and communities are strong, where prosperity is widely shared and opportunity for all lets us go as far as our dreams and toil will take us—none of it is easy. But if we work together—if we summon what is best in us, the way Cory summoned what is best in him—with our feet planted firmly in today, but our eyes cast toward tomorrow, I know it is within our reach. Believe it.

God bless you, and God bless the United States of America.

Executive Office of the President. "Address Before a Joint Session of the Congress on the State of the Union." January 28, 2014. *Compilation of Presidential Documents* 2014, no. 00050 (January 28, 2014). http://www.gpo.gov/fdsys/pkg/DCPD-201400050/pdf/DCPD-201400050.pdf.

President Obama's Remarks on Immigration Reform

Following is the White House transcript of President Obama's address to the nation on immigration reform on November 20, 2014.

My fellow Americans, tonight I'd like to talk with you about immigration.

For more than 200 years, our tradition of welcoming immigrants from around the world has given us a tremendous advantage over other nations. It's kept us youthful, dynamic, and entrepreneurial. It has shaped our character as a people with limitless possibilities, people not trapped by our past, but able to remake ourselves as we choose. But today, our immigration system is broken, and everybody knows it.

Families who enter our country the right way and play by the rules watch others flout the rules. Business owners who offer their workers good wages and benefits see the competition exploit undocumented immigrants by paying them far less. All of us take offense to anyone who reaps the rewards of living in America without taking on the responsibilities of living in America. And undocumented immigrants who desperately want to embrace those responsibilities see little option but to remain in the shadows or risk their families being torn apart. It's been this way for decades. And for decades, we haven't done much about it.

When I took office, I committed to fixing this broken immigration system. And I began by doing what I could to secure our borders. Today, we have more agents and technology deployed to secure our southern border than at any time in our history. And over the past 6 years, illegal border crossings have been cut by more than half. Although this summer there was a brief spike in unaccompanied children being apprehended at our border, the number of such children is now actually lower than it's been in nearly 2 years. Overall, the number of people trying to cross our border illegally is at its lowest level since the 1970s. Those are the facts.

Meanwhile, I worked with Congress on a comprehensive fix, and last year, 68 Democrats, Republicans, and Independents came together to pass a bipartisan bill in the Senate. It wasn't perfect. It was a compromise. But it reflected common sense. It would have doubled the number of border patrol agents while giving undocumented immigrants a pathway to citizenship if they paid a fine, started paying their taxes, and went to the back of the line. And independent experts said that it would help grow our economy and shrink our deficits.

Had the House of Representatives allowed that kind of bill a simple yes-or-no vote it would have passed with support from both parties, and today, it would be the law. But for a year and a half now, Republican leaders in the House have refused to allow that simple vote.

Now, I continue to believe that the best way to solve this problem is by working together to pass that kind of commonsense law. But until that happens, there are actions I have the legal authority to take as President—the same kinds of actions taken by Democratic and Republican Presidents before me—that will help make our immigration system more fair and more just.

Tonight I am announcing those actions. First, we'll build on our progress at the border with additional resources for our law enforcement personnel so that they can stem the flow of illegal crossings and speed the return of those who do cross over. Second, I'll make it easier and faster for high-skilled immigrants, graduates, and entrepreneurs to stay and contribute to our economy, as so many business leaders have proposed. Third, we'll take steps to deal responsibly with the millions of undocumented immigrants who already live in our country.

I want to say more about this third issue, because it generates the most passion and controversy. Even as we are a nation of immigrants, we're also a nation of laws. Undocumented workers broke our immigration laws, and I believe that they must be held accountable, especially those who may be dangerous. That's why, over the past 6 years, deportations of criminals are up 80 percent. And that's why we're going to keep focusing enforcement resources on actual threats to our security: felons, not families; criminals, not children; gang members, not a mom who's working hard to provide for her kids. We'll prioritize, just like law enforcement does every day.

But even as we focus on deporting criminals, the fact is, millions of immigrants in every State, of every race and nationality, still live here illegally. And let's be honest: Tracking down, rounding up, and deporting millions of people isn't realistic. Anyone who suggests otherwise isn't being straight with you. It's also not who we are as Americans. After all, most of these immigrants have been here a long time. They work hard, often in tough, low-paying jobs. They support their families. They worship at our churches. Many of their kids are American-born or spent most of their lives here, and their hopes, dreams, and patriotism are just like ours. As my predecessor President Bush once put it, "They are a part of American life."

Now, here's the thing: We expect people who live in this country to play by the rules. We expect that those who cut the line will not be unfairly rewarded. So we're going to offer the following deal: If you've been in America for more than 5 years; if you have children who are American citizens or legal residents;

if you register, pass a criminal background check, and you're willing to pay your fair share of taxes, you'll be able to apply to stay in this country temporarily without fear of deportation. You can come out of the shadows and get right with the law. That's what this deal is.

Now, let's be clear about what it isn't. This deal does not apply to anyone who has come to this country recently. It does not apply to anyone who might come to America illegally in the future. It does not grant citizenship or the right to stay here permanently or offer the same benefits that citizens receive. Only Congress can do that. All we're saying is, we're not going to deport you.

I know some of the critics of this action call it amnesty. Well, it's not. Amnesty is the immigration system we have today: millions of people who live here without paying their taxes or playing by the rules, while politicians use the issue to scare people and whip up votes at election time.

That's the real amnesty: leaving this broken system the way it is. Mass amnesty would be unfair. Mass deportation would be both impossible and contrary to our character. What I'm describing is accountability, a commonsense, middle-ground approach: If you meet the criteria, you can come out of the shadows and get right with the law. If you're a criminal, you'll be deported. If you plan to enter the U.S. illegally, your chances of getting caught and sent back just went up.

The actions I'm taking are not only lawful, they're the kinds of actions taken by every single Republican President and every single Democratic President for the past half century. And to those Members of Congress who question my authority to make our immigration system work better or question the wisdom of me acting where Congress has failed, I have one answer: Pass a bill.

I want to work with both parties to pass a more permanent legislative solution. And the day I sign that bill into law, the actions I take will no longer be necessary. Meanwhile, don't let a disagreement over a single issue be a deal breaker on every issue. That's not how our democracy works, and Congress certainly shouldn't shut down our Government again just because we disagree on this. Americans are tired of gridlock. What our country needs from us right now is a common purpose, a higher purpose.

Most Americans support the types of reforms I've talked about tonight. But I understand the disagreements held by many of you at home. Millions of us, myself included, go back generations in this country, with ancestors who put in the painstaking work to become citizens. So we don't like the notion that anyone might get a free pass to American citizenship.

I know some worry, immigration will change the very fabric of who we are or take our jobs or stick it to middle class families at a time when they already feel like they've gotten the raw deal for over a decade. I hear those concerns. But that's not what these steps would do. Our history and the facts show that immigrants are a net plus for our economy and our society. And I believe it's important that all of us have this debate without impugning each other's character.

Because for all the back and forth of Washington, we have to remember that this debate is about something bigger. It's about who we are as a country and who we want to be for future generations.

Are we a nation that tolerates the hypocrisy of a system where workers who pick our fruit and make our beds never have a chance to get right with the law? Or are we a nation that gives them a chance to make amends, take responsibility, and give their kids a better future?

Are we a nation that accepts the cruelty of ripping children from their parents' arms? Or are we a nation that values families and works together to keep them together?

Are we a nation that educates the world's best and brightest in our universities, only to send them home to create businesses in countries that compete against us? Or are we a nation that encourages them to stay and create jobs here, create businesses here, create industries right here in America?

That's what this debate is all about. We need more than politics as usual when it comes to immigration. We need reasoned, thoughtful, compassionate debate that focuses on our hopes, not our fears. I know the politics of this issue are tough. But let me tell you why I have come to feel so strongly about it.

Over the past years, I have seen the determination of immigrant fathers who worked two or three jobs without taking a dime from the government and at risk any moment of losing it all, just to build a better life for their kids. I've seen the heartbreak and anxiety of children whose mothers might be taken away from them just because they didn't have the right papers. I've seen the courage of students who, except for the circumstances of their birth, are as American as Malia or Sasha, students who bravely come out as undocumented in hopes they could make a difference in the country they love.

These people—our neighbors, our classmates, our friends—they did not come here in search of a free ride or an easy life. They came to work and study and serve in our military and, above all, contribute to America's success.

Tomorrow I'll travel to Las Vegas and meet with some of these students, including a young woman named Astrid Silva. Astrid was brought to America when she was 4 years old. Her only possessions were a cross, her doll, and the frilly dress she had on. When she started school, she didn't speak any English. She caught up to other kids by reading newspapers and watching PBS, and she became a good student. Her father worked in landscaping. Her mom cleaned other people's homes. They wouldn't let Astrid apply to a technology magnet school, not because they didn't love her, but because they were afraid the paperwork would out her as an undocumented immigrant. So she applied behind their back and got in. Still, she mostly lived in the shadows, until her grandmother, who visited every year from Mexico, passed away, and she couldn't travel to the funeral without risk of being found out and deported. It was around that time she decided to begin advocating for herself and others like her, and today, Astrid Silva is a college student working on her third degree.

Are we a nation that kicks out a striving, hopeful immigrant like Astrid, or are we a nation that finds a way to welcome her in? Scripture tells us that we shall not oppress a stranger, for we know the heart of a stranger; we were strangers once too.

My fellow Americans, we are and always will be a nation of immigrants. We were strangers once too. And whether our forebears were strangers who crossed the Atlantic or the Pacific or the Rio Grande, we are here only because this country welcomed them in and taught them that to be an American is about something more than what we look like or what our last names are or how we worship. What makes us Americans is our shared commitment to an ideal: that all of us are created equal and all of us have the chance to make of our lives what we will.

That's the country our parents and grandparents and generations before them built for us. That's the tradition we must uphold. That's the legacy we must leave for those who are yet to come.

Thank you. God bless you, and God bless this country we love.

Executive Office of the President. "Address to the Nation on Immigration Reform." November 20, 2014. *Compilation of Presidential Documents* 2014, no. 00877 (November 20, 2014). http://www.gpo.gov/fdsys/pkg/DCPD-201400877/pdf/DCPD-201400877.pdf.

President Obama's Address on U.S.–Cuba Policies

Following is the White House transcript of President Obama's address to the nation on changes to U.S. policy toward Cuba on December 17, 2014.

Good afternoon. Today the United States of America is changing its relationship with the people of Cuba.

In the most significant changes in our policy in more than 50 years, we will end an outdated approach that, for decades, has failed to advance our interests, and instead, we will begin to normalize relations between our two countries. Through these changes, we intend to create more opportunities for the American and Cuban people and begin a new chapter among the nations of the Americas.

There's a complicated history between the United States and Cuba. I was born in 1961, just over 2 years after Fidel Castro took power in Cuba and just a few months after the Bay of Pigs invasion, which tried to overthrow his regime. Over the next several decades, the relationship between our countries played out against the backdrop of the cold war and America's steadfast opposition to communism. We are separated by just over 90 miles. But year after year, an ideological and economic barrier hardened between our two countries.

Meanwhile, the Cuban exile community in the United States made enormous contributions to our country: in politics and business, culture and sports. Like immigrants before, Cubans helped remake America, even as they felt a painful yearning for the land and families they left behind. All of this bound America and Cuba in a unique relationship, at once family and foe.

Proudly, the United States has supported democracy and human rights in Cuba through these five decades. We've done so primarily through policies that aimed to isolate the island, preventing the most basic travel and commerce that Americans can enjoy anyplace else. And though this policy has been rooted in the best of intentions, no other nation joins us in imposing these sanctions, and it has had little effect beyond providing the Cuban Government with a rationale for restrictions on its people. Today, Cuba is still governed by the Castros and the Communist Party that came to power half a century ago.

Neither the American nor Cuban people are well served by a rigid policy that's rooted in events that took place before most of us were born. Consider that for more than 35 years, we've had relations with China, a far larger country also governed by a Communist Party.

Nearly two decades ago, we reestablished relations with Vietnam, where we fought a war that claimed more Americans than any cold war confrontation.

That's why, when I came into office, I promised to reexamine our Cuba policy. As a start, we lifted restrictions for Cuban Americans to travel and send remittances to their families in Cuba. These changes, once controversial, now seem obvious. Cuban Americans have been reunited with their families and are the best possible ambassadors for our values. And through these exchanges, a younger generation of Cuban Americans has increasingly questioned an approach that does more to keep Cuba closed off from an interconnected world.

While I've been prepared to take additional steps for some time, a major obstacle stood in our way: the wrongful imprisonment, in Cuba, of a U.S. citizen and USAID subcontractor, Alan Gross, for 5 years. Over many months, my administration has held discussions with the Cuban Government about Alan's case and other aspects of our relationship. His Holiness Pope Francis issued a personal appeal to me, and to Cuba's President Raul Castro, urging us to resolve Alan's case and to address Cuba's interest in the release of three Cuban agents who've been jailed in the United States for over 15 years.

Today Alan returned home, reunited with his family at long last. Alan was released by the Cuban Government on humanitarian grounds. Separately, in exchange for the three Cuban agents, Cuba today released one of the most important intelligence agents that the United States has ever had in Cuba, and who has been imprisoned for nearly two decades. This man, whose sacrifice has been known to only a few, provided America with the information that allowed us to arrest the network of Cuban agents that included the men transferred to Cuba today, as well as other spies in the United States. This man is now safely on our shores.

Having recovered these two men who sacrificed for our country, I'm now taking steps to place the interests of the people of both countries at the heart of our policy.

First, I've instructed Secretary Kerry to immediately begin discussions with Cuba to reestablish diplomatic relations that have been severed since January of 1961. Going forward, the United States will reestablish an Embassy in Havana, and high-ranking officials will visit Cuba.

Where we can advance shared interests, we will: on issues like health, migration, counterterrorism, drug trafficking, and disaster response. Indeed, we've seen the benefits of cooperation between our countries before. It was a Cuban, Carlos Finlay, who discovered that mosquitoes carry yellow fever; his work helped Walter Reed fight it. Cuba has sent hundreds of health care workers to Africa to fight Ebola, and I believe American and Cuban health care workers should work side by side to stop the spread of this deadly disease.

Now, where we disagree, we will raise those differences directly, as we will continue to do on issues related to democracy and human rights in Cuba. But I believe that we can do more to support the Cuban people and promote our values through engagement. After all, these 50 years have shown that isolation has not worked. It's time for a new approach.

Second, I've instructed Secretary Kerry to review Cuba's designation as a state sponsor of terrorism. This review will be guided by the facts and the law. Terrorism has changed in the last several decades. At a time when we are focused on threats from Al Qaida to ISIL, a nation that meets our conditions and renounces the use of terrorism should not face this sanction.

Third, we are taking steps to increase travel, commerce, and the flow of information to and from Cuba. This is fundamentally about freedom and openness and also expresses my belief in the power of people-to-people engagement. With the changes I'm announcing today, it will be easier for Americans to travel to Cuba, and Americans will be able to use American credit and debit cards on the island. Nobody represents America's values better than the American people, and I believe this contact will ultimately do more to empower the Cuban people.

I also believe that more resources should be able to reach the Cuban people. So we're significantly increasing the amount of money that can be sent to Cuba and removing limits on remittances that support humanitarian projects, the Cuban people, and the emerging Cuban private sector.

I believe that American businesses should not be put at a disadvantage and that increased commerce is good for Americans and for Cubans. So we will facilitate authorized transactions between the United States and Cuba. U.S. financial institutions will be allowed to open accounts at Cuban financial institutions. And it will be easier for U.S. exporters to sell goods in Cuba.

I believe in the free flow of information. Unfortunately, our sanctions on Cuba have denied Cubans access to technology that has empowered individuals around the globe. So I've authorized increased telecommunications connections between the United States and Cuba. Businesses will be able to sell goods that enable Cubans to communicate with the United States and other countries.

These are the steps that I can take as President to change this policy. The embargo that's been imposed for decades is now codified in legislation. As these changes unfold, I look forward to engaging Congress in an honest and serious debate about lifting the embargo.

Yesterday I spoke with Raul Castro to finalize Alan Gross's release and the exchange of prisoners and to describe how we will move forward. I made clear my strong belief that Cuban society is constrained by restrictions on its citizens. In addition to the return of Alan Gross and the release of our intelligence agent, we welcome Cuba's decision to release a substantial number of prisoners whose cases were directly raised with the Cuban Government by my team. We welcome Cuba's decision to provide more access to the Internet for its citizens and to continue increasing engagement with international institutions like the United Nations and the International Committee of the Red Cross that promote universal values.

But I'm under no illusion about the continued barriers to freedom that remain for ordinary Cubans. The United States believes that no Cuban should face harassment or arrest or beatings simply because they're exercising a universal right to have their voices heard, and we will continue to support civil society there. While Cuba has made reforms to gradually open up its economy, we continue to believe that Cuban workers should be free to form unions, just as their citizens should be free to participate in the political process.

Moreover, given Cuba's history, I expect it will continue to pursue foreign policies that will at times be sharply at odds with American interests. I do not expect the changes I'm announcing today to bring about a transformation of Cuban society overnight. But I am convinced that through a policy of engagement, we can more effectively stand up for our values and help the Cuban people help themselves as they move into the 21st century.

To those who oppose the steps I'm announcing today, let me say that I respect your passion and share your commitment to liberty and democracy. The question is how we uphold that commitment. I do not believe we can keep doing the same thing for over five decades and expect a different result. Moreover, it does not serve America's interests or the Cuban people to try to push Cuba towards collapse. Even if that worked—and it hasn't for 50 years—we know from hard-earned experience that countries are more likely to enjoy lasting transformation if their people are not subjected to chaos. We are calling on Cuba to unleash the potential of 11 million Cubans by ending unnecessary restrictions on their political, social, and economic activities. In that spirit, we should not allow U.S. sanctions to add to the burden of Cuban citizens that we seek to help.

To the Cuban people, America extends a hand of friendship. Some of you have looked to us as a source of hope, and we will continue to shine a light of freedom. Others have seen us as a former colonizer intent on controlling your future. José Martí once said, "Liberty is the right of every man to be honest." Today I'm being honest with you. We can never erase the history between us, but we believe that you should be empowered to live with dignity and self-determination. Cubans have a saying about daily life: *"No es fácil"*—it's not easy. Today, the United States wants to be a partner in making the lives of ordinary Cubans a little bit easier, more free, more prosperous.

To those who have supported these measures, I thank you for being partners in our efforts. In particular, I want to thank His Holiness Pope Francis, whose moral example shows us the importance of pursuing the world as it should be, rather than simply settling for the world as it is; the Government of Canada, which hosted our discussions with the Cuban Government; and a bipartisan group of Congressmen who've worked tirelessly for Alan Gross's release and for a new approach to advancing our interests and values in Cuba.

Finally, our shift in policy towards Cuba comes at a moment of renewed leadership in the Americas. This April, we are prepared to have Cuba join the other nations of the hemisphere at the Summit of the Americas. But we will insist that civil society join us so that citizens, not just leaders, are shaping our future. And I call on all of my fellow leaders to give meaning to the commitment to democracy and human rights at the heart of the Inter-American Charter. Let us leave behind the legacy of both colonization and communism, the tyranny of drug cartels, dictators, and sham elections. A future of greater peace, security, and democratic development is possible if we work together, not to maintain power, not to secure vested interests, but instead to advance the dreams of our citizens.

My fellow Americans, the city of Miami is only 200 miles or so from Havana. Countless thousands of Cubans have come to Miami, on planes and makeshift rafts, some with little but the shirt on their back and hope in their hearts. Today, Miami is often referred to as the capital of Latin America. But it is also a profoundly American city, a place that reminds us that ideals matter more than the color of our skin or the circumstances of our birth, a demonstration of what the Cuban people can achieve and the openness of the United States to our family to the South. *Todos somos Americanos.*

Change is hard, in our own lives and in the lives of nations. And change is even harder when we carry the heavy weight of history on our shoulders. But today we are making these changes because it is the right thing to do. Today America chooses to cut loose the shackles of the past so as to reach for a better future, for the Cuban people, for the American people, for our entire hemisphere, and for the world.

Thank you. God bless you, and God bless the United States of America.

Executive Office of the President. "Address to the Nation on United States Policy Toward Cuba." December 17, 2014. *Compilation of Presidential Documents* 2014, no. 00937 (December 17, 2014). http://www.gpo.gov/fdsys/pkg/DCPD-201400937/pdf/DCPD-201400937.pdf.

President Obama's 2015 State of the Union Address

Following is the White House transcript of President Obama's address before a joint session of Congress on the state of the union given on January 20, 2015.

The President. Mr. Speaker, Mr. Vice President, Members of Congress, my fellow Americans: We are 15 years into this new century. Fifteen years that dawned with terror touching our shores, that unfolded with a new generation fighting two long and costly wars, that saw a vicious recession spread across our Nation and the world. It has been and still is a hard time for many.

But tonight we turn the page. Tonight, after a breakthrough year for America, our economy is growing and creating jobs at the fastest pace since 1999. Our unemployment rate is now lower than it was before the financial crisis. More of our kids are graduating than ever before. More of our people are insured than ever before. And we are as free from the grip of foreign oil as we've been in almost 30 years.

Tonight, for the first time since 9/11, our combat mission in Afghanistan is over. Six years ago, nearly 180,000 American troops served in Iraq and Afghanistan. Today, fewer than 15,000 remain. And we salute the courage and sacrifice of every man and woman in this 9/11 generation who has served to keep us safe. We are humbled and grateful for your service.

America, for all that we have endured, for all the grit and hard work required to come back, for all the tasks that lie ahead, know this: The shadow of crisis has passed, and the State of the Union is strong.

At this moment—with a growing economy, shrinking deficits, bustling industry, booming energy production—we have risen from recession freer to write our own future than any other nation on Earth. It's now up to us to choose who we want to be over the next 15 years and for decades to come.

Will we accept an economy where only a few of us do spectacularly well? Or will we commit ourselves to an economy that generates rising incomes and chances for everyone who makes the effort?

Will we approach the world fearful and reactive, dragged into costly conflicts that strain our military and set back our standing? Or will we lead wisely, using all elements of our power to defeat new threats and protect our planet?

Will we allow ourselves to be sorted into factions and turned against one another? Or will we recapture the sense of common purpose that has always propelled America forward?

In 2 weeks, I will send this Congress a budget filled with ideas that are practical, not partisan. And in the months ahead, I'll crisscross the country making a case for those ideas. So tonight I want to focus less on a checklist of proposals and focus more on the values at stake in the choices before us.

It begins with our economy. Seven years ago, Rebekah and Ben Erler of Minneapolis were newlyweds. [*Laughter*] She waited tables. He worked construction. Their first child Jack was on the way. They were young and in love in America. And it doesn't get much better than that. "If only we had known," Rebekah wrote to me last spring, "what was about to happen to the housing and construction market."

As the crisis worsened, Ben's business dried up, so he took what jobs he could find, even if they kept him on the road for long stretches of time. Rebekah took out student loans and enrolled in community college and retrained for a new career. They sacrificed for each other. And slowly, it paid off. They bought their first home. They had a second son Henry. Rebekah got a better job and then a raise. Ben is back in construction and home for dinner every night.

"It is amazing," Rebekah wrote, "what you can bounce back from when you have to. . . . We are a strong, tight-knit family who has made it through some very, very hard times." We are a strong, tight-knit family who has made it through some very, very hard times.

America, Rebekah and Ben's story is our story. They represent the millions who have worked hard and scrimped and sacrificed and retooled. You are the reason that I ran for this office. You are the people I was thinking of 6 years ago today, in the darkest months of the crisis, when I stood on the steps of this Capitol and promised we would rebuild our economy on a new foundation. And it has been your resilience, your effort that has made it possible for our country to emerge stronger.

We believed we could reverse the tide of outsourcing and draw new jobs to our shores.

And over the past 5 years, our businesses have created more than 11 million new jobs.

We believed we could reduce our dependence on foreign oil and protect our planet. And today, America is number one in oil and gas. America is number one in wind power. Every 3 weeks, we bring online as much solar power as we did in all of 2008. And thanks to lower gas prices and higher fuel standards, the typical family this year should save about $750 at the pump.

We believed we could prepare our kids for a more competitive world. And today, our younger students have earned the highest math and reading scores on record. Our high school graduation rate has hit an all-time high. More Americans finish college than ever before.

We believed that sensible regulations could prevent another crisis, shield families from ruin, and encourage fair competition. Today, we have new tools to stop taxpayer-funded bailouts and a new consumer watchdog to protect us from predatory lending and abusive credit card practices. And in the past year alone, about 10 million uninsured Americans finally gained the security of health coverage.

At every step, we were told our goals were misguided or too ambitious, that we would crush jobs and explode deficits. Instead, we've seen the fastest economic growth in over a decade, our deficits cut by two-thirds, a stock market that has doubled, and health care inflation at its lowest rate in 50 years. This is good news, people. [*Laughter*]

So the verdict is clear. Middle class economics works. Expanding opportunity works. And these policies will continue to work as long as politics don't get in the way. We can't slow down businesses or put our economy at risk with Government shutdowns or fiscal showdowns. We can't put the security of

families at risk by taking away their health insurance or unraveling the new rules on Wall Street or refighting past battles on immigration when we've got to fix a broken system. And if a bill comes to my desk that tries to do any of these things, I will veto it. It will have earned my veto.

Today, thanks to a growing economy, the recovery is touching more and more lives. Wages are finally starting to rise again. We know that more small-business owners plan to raise their employees' pay than at any time since 2007. But here's the thing: Those of us here tonight, we need to set our sights higher than just making sure Government doesn't screw things up—[*laughter*]—that Government doesn't halt the progress we're making. We need to do more than just do no harm. Tonight, together, let's do more to restore the link between hard work and growing opportunity for every American.

Because families like Rebekah's still need our help. She and Ben are working as hard as ever, but they've had to forego vacations and a new car so that they can pay off student loans and save for retirement. Friday night pizza, that's a big splurge. Basic childcare for Jack and Henry costs more than their mortgage and almost as much as a year at the University of Minnesota. Like millions of hard-working Americans, Rebekah isn't asking for a handout, but she is asking that we look for more ways to help families get ahead.

And in fact, at every moment of economic change throughout our history, this country has taken bold action to adapt to new circumstances and to make sure everyone gets a fair shot. We set up worker protections, Social Security, Medicare, Medicaid to protect ourselves from the harshest adversity. We gave our citizens schools and colleges, infrastructure and the Internet, tools they needed to go as far as their efforts and their dreams will take them.

That's what middle class economics is: the idea that this country does best when everyone gets their fair shot, everyone does their fair share, everyone plays by the same set of rules. We don't just want everyone to share in America's success, we want everyone to contribute to our success.

So what does middle class economics require in our time? First, middle class economics means helping working families feel more secure in a world of constant change. That means helping folks afford childcare, college, health care, a home, retirement. And my budget will address each of these issues, lowering the taxes of working families and putting thousands of dollars back into their pockets each year.

Here's one example. During World War II, when men like my grandfather went off to war, having women like my grandmother in the workforce was a national security priority, so this country provided universal childcare. In today's economy, when having both parents in the workforce is an economic necessity for many families, we need affordable, high-quality childcare more than ever.

It's not a nice-to-have, it's a must-have. So it's time we stop treating childcare as a side issue, or as a women's issue, and treat it like the national economic priority that it is for all of us. And that's why my plan will make quality childcare more available and more affordable for every middle class and low-income family with young children in America, by creating more slots and a new tax cut of up to $3,000 per child, per year.

Here's another example. Today, we are the only advanced country on Earth that doesn't guarantee paid sick leave or paid maternity leave to our workers. Forty-three million workers have no paid sick leave—43 million. Think about that. And that forces too many parents to make the gut-wrenching choice between a paycheck and a sick kid at home. So I'll be taking new action to help States adopt paid leave laws of their own. And since paid sick leave won where it was on the ballot last November, let's put it to a vote right here in Washington. Send me a bill that gives every worker in America the opportunity to earn 7 days of paid sick leave. It's the right thing to do. [*Applause*] It's the right thing to do.

Of course, nothing helps families make ends meet like higher wages. That's why this Congress still needs to pass a law that makes sure a woman is paid the same as a man for doing the same work. I mean, it's 2015. [*Laughter*] It's time. We still need to make sure employees get the overtime they've earned. And to everyone in this Congress who still refuses to raise the minimum wage, I say this: If you truly believe you could work full time and support a family on less than $15,000 a year, try it. If not, vote to give millions of the hardest working people in America a raise.

Now, these ideas won't make everybody rich, won't relieve every hardship. That's not the job of government. To give working families a fair shot, we still need more employers to see beyond next quarter's earnings and recognize that investing in their workforce is in their company's long-term interest. We still need laws that strengthen rather than weaken unions, and give American workers a voice.

But you know, things like childcare and sick leave and equal pay, things like lower mortgage premiums and a higher minimum wage—these ideas will make a meaningful difference in the lives of millions of families. That's a fact. And that's what all of us, Republicans and Democrats alike, were sent here to do.

Now, second, to make sure folks keep earning higher wages down the road, we have to do more to help Americans upgrade their skills. America thrived in the 20th century because we made high school free, sent a generation of GIs to college, trained the best workforce in the world. We were ahead of the curve. But other countries caught on. And in a 21st-century economy that rewards knowledge like never before, we need to up our game. We need to do more.

By the end of this decade, two in three job openings will require some higher education— two in three. And yet we still live in a country where too many bright, striving Americans are priced out of the education they need. It's not fair to them, and it's sure not smart for our future. And that's why I'm sending this Congress a bold new plan to lower the cost of community college to zero.

Keep in mind, 40 percent of our college students choose community college. Some are young and starting out. Some are older and looking for a better job. Some are veterans and single parents trying to transition back into the job market. Whoever you are, this plan is your chance to graduate ready for the new economy without a load of debt. Understand, you've got to earn it. You've got to keep your grades up and graduate on time.

Tennessee, a State with Republican leadership, and Chicago, a city with Democratic leadership, are showing that free community college is possible. I want to spread that idea all across America so that 2 years of college becomes as free and universal in America as high school is today. Let's stay ahead of the curve. And I want to work with this Congress to make sure those already burdened with student loans can reduce their monthly payments so that student debt doesn't derail anyone's dreams.

Thanks to Vice President Biden's great work to update our job training system, we're connecting community colleges with local employers to train workers to fill high-paying jobs like coding and nursing and robotics. Tonight I'm also asking more businesses to follow the lead of companies like CVS and UPS and offer more educational benefits and paid apprenticeships, opportunities that give workers the chance to earn higher paying jobs even if they don't have a higher education.

And as a new generation of veterans comes home, we owe them every opportunity to live the American Dream they helped defend. Already, we've made strides towards ensuring that every veteran has access to the highest quality care. We're slashing the backlog that had too many veterans waiting years to get the benefits they need. And we're making it easier for vets to translate their training and experience into civilian jobs. And Joining Forces, the national campaign launched by Michelle and Jill Biden—[*applause*]—thank you, Michelle; thank you, Jill—has helped nearly 700,000 veterans and military spouses get a new job. So to every CEO in America, let me repeat: If you want somebody who's going to get the job done and done right, hire a veteran.

Finally, as we better train our workers, we need the new economy to keep churning out high-wage jobs for our workers to fill. Since 2010, America has put more people back to work than Europe, Japan, and all advanced economies combined.

Our manufacturers have added almost 800,000 new jobs. Some of our bedrock sectors, like our auto industry, are booming. But there are also millions of Americans who work in jobs that didn't even exist 10 or 20 years ago, jobs at companies like Google and eBay and Tesla.

So no one knows for certain which industries will generate the jobs of the future. But we do know we want them here in America. We know that. And that's why the third part of middle class economics is all about building the most competitive economy anywhere, the place where businesses want to locate and hire.

Twenty-first century businesses need 21st-century infrastructure: modern ports and stronger bridges, faster trains and the fastest Internet. Democrats and Republicans used to agree on this. So let's set our sights higher than a single oil pipeline. Let's pass a bipartisan infrastructure plan that could create more than 30 times as many jobs per year and make this country stronger for decades to come. Let's do it. Let's get it done. [*Applause*] Let's get it done.

Twenty-first century businesses, including small businesses, need to sell more American products overseas. Today, our businesses export more than ever, and exporters tend to pay their workers higher wages. But as we speak, China wants to write the rules for the world's fastest growing region. That would put our workers and our businesses at a disadvantage. Why would we let that happen? We should write those rules. We should level the playing field. And that's why I'm asking both parties to give me trade promotion authority to protect American workers, with strong new trade deals from Asia to Europe that aren't just free, but are also fair. It's the right thing to do.

Look, I'm the first one to admit that past trade deals haven't always lived up to the hype, and that's why we've gone after countries that break the rules at our expense. But 95 percent of the world's customers live outside our borders. We can't close ourselves off from those opportunities. More than half of manufacturing executives have said they're actively looking to bring jobs back from China. So let's give them one more reason to get it done.

Twenty-first century businesses will rely on American science and technology, research and development. I want the country that eliminated polio and mapped the human genome to lead a new era of medicine, one that delivers the right treatment at the right time.

In some patients with cystic fibrosis, this approach has reversed a disease once thought unstoppable. So tonight I'm launching a new precision medicine initiative to bring us closer to curing diseases like cancer and diabetes and to give all of us access to the personalized information we need to keep ourselves and our families healthier. We can do this.

I intend to protect a free and open Internet, extend its reach to every classroom and every community and help folks build the fastest networks so that the next generation of digital innovators and entrepreneurs have the platform to keep reshaping our world.

I want Americans to win the race for the kinds of discoveries that unleash new jobs: converting sunlight into liquid fuel; creating revolutionary prosthetics so that a veteran who gave his arms for his country can play catch with his kids again; pushing out into the solar system not just to visit, but to stay. Last month, we launched a new spacecraft as part of a reenergized space program that will send American astronauts to Mars. And in 2 months, to prepare us for those missions, Scott Kelly will begin a year-long stay in space. So good luck, Captain. Make sure to Instagram it. We're proud of you.

Now, the truth is, when it comes to issues like infrastructure and basic research, I know there's bipartisan support in this Chamber. Members of both parties have told me so. Where we too often run onto the rocks is how to pay for these investments. As Americans, we don't mind paying our fair share of taxes as long as everybody else does too. But for far too long, lobbyists have rigged the Tax Code with loopholes that let some corporations pay nothing while others pay full freight. They've riddled it with giveaways that the super-rich don't need, while denying a break to middle class families who do.

This year, we have an opportunity to change that. Let's close loopholes so we stop rewarding companies that keep profits abroad and reward those that invest here in America. Let's use those savings to rebuild our infrastructure and to make it more attractive for companies to bring jobs home. Let's simplify the system and let a small-business owner file based on her actual bank statement, instead of the number of accountants she can afford. And let's close the loopholes that lead to inequality by allowing the top 1 percent to avoid paying taxes on their accumulated wealth. We can use that money to help more families pay for childcare and send their kids to college. We need a Tax Code that truly helps working Americans trying to get a leg up in the new economy, and we can achieve that together. [*Applause*] We can achieve it together.

Helping hard-working families make ends meet, giving them the tools they need for good-paying jobs in this new economy, maintaining the conditions of growth and competitiveness— this is where America needs to go. I believe it's where the American people want to go. It will make our economy stronger a year from now, 15 years from now, and deep into the century ahead.

Of course, if there's one thing this new century has taught us, it's that we cannot separate our work here at home from challenges beyond our shores. My first duty as Commander in Chief is to defend the United States of America. In doing so, the question is not whether America leads in the world, but how. When we make rash decisions, reacting to the headlines instead of using our heads, when the first response to a challenge is to send in our military, then we risk getting drawn into unnecessary conflicts and neglect the broader strategy we need for a safer, more prosperous world. That's what our enemies want us to do.

I believe in a smarter kind of American leadership. We lead best when we combine military power with strong diplomacy, when we leverage our power with coalition building, when we don't let our fears blind us to the opportunities that this new century presents. That's exactly what we're doing right now. And around the globe, it is making a difference.

First, we stand united with people around the world who have been targeted by terrorists, from a school in Pakistan to the streets of Paris. We will continue to hunt down terrorists and dismantle their networks, and we reserve the right to act unilaterally, as we have done relentlessly since I took office, to take out terrorists who pose a direct threat to us and our allies.

At the same time, we've learned some costly lessons over the last 13 years. Instead of Americans patrolling the valleys of Afghanistan, we've trained their security forces, who have now taken the lead, and we've honored our troops' sacrifice by supporting that country's first democratic transition. Instead of sending large ground forces overseas, we're partnering with nations from South Asia to North Africa to deny safe haven to terrorists who threaten America.

In Iraq and Syria, American leadership—including our military power—is stopping ISIL's advance. Instead of getting dragged into another ground war in the Middle East, we are leading a broad coalition, including Arab nations, to degrade and ultimately destroy this terrorist group. We're also supporting a moderate opposition in Syria that can help us in this effort and assisting people everywhere who stand up to the bankrupt ideology of violent extremism.

Now, this effort will take time. It will require focus. But we will succeed. And tonight I call on this Congress to show the world that we are united in this mission by passing a resolution to authorize the use of force against ISIL. We need that authority.

Second, we're demonstrating the power of American strength and diplomacy. We're upholding the principle that bigger nations can't bully the small, by opposing Russian aggression and supporting Ukraine's democracy and reassuring our NATO allies.

Last year, as we were doing the hard work of imposing sanctions along with our allies, as we were reinforcing our presence with frontline states, Mr. Putin's aggression, it was suggested, was a masterful display of strategy and strength. That's what I heard from some folks. [*Laughter*] Well, today, it is America that stands strong and united with our allies, while Russia is isolated with its economy in tatters. That's how America leads: not with bluster, but with persistent, steady resolve.

In Cuba, we are ending a policy that was long past its expiration date. When what you're doing doesn't work for 50 years, it's time to try something new. [*Laughter*] And our shift in Cuba policy has the potential to end a legacy of mistrust in our hemisphere. It removes a phony excuse for restrictions in Cuba. It stands up for democratic values and extends the hand of friendship to the Cuban people. And this year, Congress should begin the work of ending the embargo.

As His Holiness Pope Francis has said, diplomacy is the work of "small steps." And these small steps have added up to new hope for the future in Cuba. And after years in prison, we are overjoyed that Alan Gross is back where he belongs. Welcome home, Alan. We're glad you're here.

Our diplomacy is at work with respect to Iran, where, for the first time in a decade, we've halted the progress of its nuclear program and reduced its stockpile of nuclear material.

Between now and this spring, we have a chance to negotiate a comprehensive agreement that prevents a nuclear-armed Iran, secures America and our allies, including Israel, while avoiding yet another Middle East conflict. There are no guarantees that negotiations will succeed, and I keep all options on the table to prevent a nuclear Iran.

But new sanctions passed by this Congress, at this moment in time, will all but guarantee that diplomacy fails: alienating America from its allies, making it harder to maintain sanctions, and ensuring that Iran starts up its nuclear program again. It doesn't make sense. And that's why I will veto any new sanctions bill that threatens to undo this progress. The American people expect us only to go to war as a last resort, and I intend to stay true to that wisdom.

Third, we're looking beyond the issues that have consumed us in the past to shape the coming century. No foreign nation, no hacker, should be able to shut down our networks, steal our trade secrets, or invade the privacy of American families, especially our kids. So we're making sure our Government integrates intelligence to combat cyber threats, just as we have done to combat terrorism.

And tonight I urge this Congress to finally pass the legislation we need to better meet the evolving threat of cyber attacks, combat identity theft, and protect our children's information. That should be a bipartisan effort. If we don't act, we'll leave our Nation and our economy vulnerable. If we do, we can continue to protect the technologies that have unleashed untold opportunities for people around the globe.

In West Africa, our troops, our scientists, our doctors, our nurses, our health care workers are rolling back Ebola, saving countless lives and stopping the spread of disease. I could not be prouder of them, and I thank this Congress for your bipartisan support of their efforts. But the job is not yet done, and the world needs to use this lesson to build a more effective global effort to prevent the spread of future pandemics, invest in smart development, and eradicate extreme poverty.

In the Asia-Pacific, we are modernizing alliances while making sure that other nations play by the rules: in how they trade, how they resolve maritime disputes, how they participate in meeting common international challenges like nonproliferation and disaster relief. And no challenge—no challenge—poses a greater threat to future generations than climate change.

Two thousand fourteen was the planet's warmest year on record. Now, 1 year doesn't make a trend, but this does: 14 of the 15 warmest years on record have all fallen in the first 15 years of this century.

Now, I've heard some folks try to dodge the evidence by saying they're not scientists, that we don't have enough information to act. Well, I'm not a scientist, either. But you know what, I know a lot of really good scientists—[laughter]—at NASA and at NOAA and at our major universities. And the best scientists in the world are all telling us that our activities are changing the climate, and if we don't act forcefully, we'll continue to see rising oceans, longer, hotter heat waves, dangerous droughts and floods, and massive disruptions that can trigger greater migration and conflict and hunger around the globe. The Pentagon says that climate change poses immediate risks to our national security. We should act like it.

And that's why, over the past 6 years, we've done more than ever to combat climate change, from the way we produce energy to the way we use it. That's why we've set aside more public lands and waters than any administration in history. And that's why I will not let this Congress endanger the health of our children by turning back the clock on our efforts. I am determined to make sure that American leadership drives international action.

In Beijing, we made a historic announcement: The United States will double the pace at which we cut carbon pollution. And China committed, for the first time, to limiting their emissions. And because the world's two largest economies came together, other nations are now stepping up and offering hope that this year the world will finally reach an agreement to protect the one planet we've got.

And there's one last pillar of our leadership, and that's the example of our values. As Americans, we respect human dignity, even when we're threatened, which is why I have prohibited torture and worked to make sure our use of new technology like drones is properly constrained. It's why we speak out against the deplorable anti-Semitism that has resurfaced in certain parts of the world. It's why we continue to reject offensive stereotypes of Muslims, the vast majority of whom share our commitment to peace. That's why we defend free speech and advocate for political prisoners and condemn the persecution of women or religious minorities or people who are lesbian, gay, bisexual, or transgender. We do these things not only because they are the right thing to do, but because ultimately, they will make us safer.

As Americans, we have a profound commitment to justice. So it makes no sense to spend $3 million per prisoner to keep open a prison that the world condemns and terrorists use to recruit. Since I've been President, we've worked responsibly to cut the population of Gitmo in half. Now it is time to finish the job. And I will not relent in my determination to shut it down. It is not who we are. It's time to close Gitmo.

As Americans, we cherish our civil liberties, and we need to uphold that commitment if we want maximum cooperation from other countries and industry in our fight against terrorist networks. So while some have moved on from the debates over our surveillance programs, I have not. As promised, our intelligence agencies have worked hard, with the recommendations of privacy advocates, to increase transparency and build more safeguards against potential abuse. And next month, we'll issue a report on how we're keeping our promise to keep our country safe while strengthening privacy.

Looking to the future instead of the past, making sure we match our power with diplomacy and use force wisely, building coalitions to meet new challenges and opportunities, leading always with the example of our values—that's what makes us exceptional. That's what keeps us strong. That's why we have to keep striving to hold ourselves to the highest of standards: our own.

You know, just over a decade ago, I gave a speech in Boston where I said there wasn't a liberal America or a conservative America, a Black America or a White America, but a United States of America. I said this because I had seen it in my own life, in a nation that gave someone like me a chance; because I grew up in Hawaii, a melting pot of races and customs; because I made Illinois my home, a State of small towns, rich farmland, one of the world's great cities, a microcosm of the country where Democrats and Republicans and Independents, good people of every ethnicity and every faith, share certain bedrock values.

Over the past 6 years, the pundits have pointed out more than once that my Presidency hasn't delivered on this vision. How ironic, they say, that our politics seems more divided than ever. It's held up as proof not just of my own flaws—of which there are many—but also as proof that the vision itself is misguided, naive, that there are too many people in this town who actually benefit from partisanship and gridlock for us to ever do anything about it.

I know how tempting such cynicism may be. But I still think the cynics are wrong. I still believe that we are one people. I still believe that together, we can do great things, even when the odds are long.

I believe this because over and over in my 6 years in office, I have seen America at its best.

I've seen the hopeful faces of young graduates from New York to California and our newest officers at West Point, Annapolis, Colorado Springs, New London. I've mourned with grieving families in Tucson and Newtown, in Boston, in West, Texas, and West Virginia. I've watched Americans beat back adversity from the Gulf Coast to the Great Plains, from Midwest assembly lines to the Mid-Atlantic seaboard. I've seen something like gay marriage go from a wedge issue used to drive us apart to a story of freedom across our country, a civil right now legal in States that 7 in 10 Americans call home.

So I know the good and optimistic and big-hearted generosity of the American people who every day live the idea that we are our brother's keeper and our sister's keeper. And I know they expect those of us who serve here to set a better example.

So the question for those of us here tonight is how we, all of us, can better reflect America's hopes. I've served in Congress with many of you. I know many of you well. There are a lot of good people here on both sides of the aisle. And many of you have told me that this isn't what you signed up for: arguing past each other on cable shows, the constant fundraising, always looking over your shoulder at how the base will react to every decision.

Imagine if we broke out of these tired old patterns. Imagine if we did something different. Understand, a better politics isn't one where Democrats abandon their agenda or Republicans simply embrace mine. A better politics is one where we appeal to each other's basic decency instead of our basest fears. A better politics is one where we debate without demonizing each other, where we talk issues and values and principles and facts rather than "gotcha" moments or trivial gaffes or fake controversies that have nothing to do with people's daily lives.

A politics—a better politics is one where we spend less time drowning in dark money for ads that pull us into the gutter and spend more time lifting young people up with a sense of purpose and possibility, asking them to join in the great mission of building America.

If we're going to have arguments, let's have arguments, but let's make them debates worthy of this body and worthy of this country. We still may not agree on a woman's right to choose, but surely we can agree it's a good thing that teen pregnancies and abortions are nearing all-time lows and that every woman should have access to the health care that she needs.

Yes, passions still fly on immigration, but surely we can all see something of ourselves in the striving young student and agree that no one benefits when a hard-working mom is snatched from her child and that it's possible to shape a law that upholds our tradition as a nation of laws and a nation of immigrants.

I've talked to Republicans and Democrats about that. That's something that we can share.

We may go at it in campaign season, but surely we can agree that the right to vote is sacred, that it's being denied to too many, and that on this 50th anniversary of the great march from Selma to Montgomery and the passage of the Voting Rights Act, we can come together, Democrats and Republicans, to make voting easier for every single American.

We may have different takes on the events of Ferguson and New York. But surely we can understand a father who fears his son can't walk home without being harassed. And surely we can understand the wife who won't rest until the police officer she married walks through the front door at the end of his shift. And surely we can agree that it's a good thing that for the first time in 40 years, the crime rate and the incarceration rate have come down together, and use that as a starting point for Democrats and Republicans, community leaders and law enforcement, to reform America's criminal justice system so that it protects and serves all of us.

That's a better politics. That's how we start rebuilding trust. That's how we move this country forward. That's what the American people want. And that's what they deserve.

I have no more campaigns to run.

[*At this point, some audience members applauded.*]

My only agenda—[*laughter*].

Audience member. [Inaudible]

The President. I know because I won both of them. [*Laughter*] My only agenda for the next 2 years is the same as the one I've had since the day I swore an oath on the steps of this Capitol: to do what I believe is best for America. If you share the broad vision I outlined tonight, I ask you to join me in the work at hand. If you disagree with parts of it, I hope you'll at least work with me where you do agree. And I commit to every Republican here tonight that I will not only seek out your ideas, I will seek to work with you to make this country stronger.

Because I want this Chamber, I want this city to reflect the truth: that for all our blind spots and shortcomings, we are a people with the strength and generosity of spirit to bridge divides, to unite in common effort, to help our neighbors, whether down the street or on the other side of the world.

I want our actions to tell every child in every neighborhood, your life matters, and we are committed to improving your life chances, as committed as we are to working on behalf of our own kids. I want future generations to know that we are a people who see our differences as a great gift, that we're a people who value the dignity and worth of every citizen: man and woman, young and old, Black and White, Latino, Asian, immigrant, Native American, gay, straight, Americans with mental illness or physical disability. Everybody matters. I want them to grow up in a country that shows the world what we still know to be true: that we are still more than a collection of red States and blue States, that we are the United States of America.

I want them to grow up in a country where a young mom can sit down and write a letter to her President with a story that sums up these past 6 years: "It's amazing what you can bounce back from when you have to. . . . We are a strong, tight-knit family who's made it through some very, very hard times."

My fellow Americans, we too are a strong, tight-knit family. We too have made it through some hard times. Fifteen years into this new century, we have picked ourselves up, dusted ourselves off, and begun again the work of remaking America. We have laid a new foundation. A brighter future is ours to write. Let's begin this new chapter together, and let's start the work right now.

Thank you. God bless you. God bless this country we love. Thank you.

Executive Office of the President. "Address Before a Joint Session of the Congress on the State of the Union." January 20, 2015. *Compilation of Presidential Documents* 2015, no. 00036 (January 20, 2015). www.gpo .gov/fdsys/pkg/DCPD-201500036/pdf/DCPD-201500036.pdf.

President Obama's Remarks on Authorizing Military Action against ISIL

Following is the White House transcript of President Obama's remarks to the nation given on February 11, 2015, on U.S. military strategy.

Good afternoon. Today, as part of an international coalition of some 60 nations, including Arab countries, our men and women in uniform continue the fight against ISIL in Iraq and in Syria.

More than 2,000 coalition airstrikes have pounded these terrorists. We're disrupting their command and control and supply lines, making it harder for them to move. We're destroying their fighting positions, their tanks, their vehicles, their barracks, their training camps, and the oil and gas facilities and infrastructure that fund their operations. We're taking out their commanders, their fighters, and their leaders.

In Iraq, local forces have largely held the line and, in some places, have pushed ISIL back.

In Syria, ISIL failed in its major push to take the town of Kobani, losing countless fighters in the process, fighters who will never again threaten innocent civilians. And we've seen reports of sinking morale among ISIL fighters as they realize the futility of their cause.

Now, make no mistake, this is a difficult mission, and it will remain difficult for some time.

It's going to take time to dislodge these terrorists, especially from urban areas. But our coalition is on the offensive, ISIL is on the defensive, and ISIL is going to lose. Its barbaric murders of so many people, including American hostages, are a desperate and revolting attempt to strike fear in the hearts of people it can never possibly win over by its ideas or its ideology, because it offers nothing but misery and death and destruction. And with vile groups like this, there is only one option: With our allies and partners, we are going to degrade and ultimately destroy this terrorist group.

And when I announced our strategy against ISIL in September, I said that we are strongest as a nation when the President and Congress work together. Today my administration submitted a draft resolution to Congress to authorize the use of force against ISIL. I want to be very clear about what it does and what it does not do.

This resolution reflects our core objective to destroy ISIL. It supports the comprehensive strategy that we've been pursuing with our allies and our partners: a systemic and sustained campaign of airstrikes against ISIL in Iraq and Syria; support and training for local forces on the ground, including the moderate Syrian opposition; preventing ISIL attacks in the region and beyond, including by foreign terrorist fighters who try to threaten

our countries; regional and international support for an inclusive Iraqi Government that unites the Iraqi people and strengthens Iraqi forces against ISIL; humanitarian assistance for the innocent civilians of Iraq and Syria, who are suffering so terribly under ISIL's reign of horror.

I want to thank Vice President Biden, Secretaries Kerry and Hagel, and General Marty Dempsey for their leadership in advancing our strategy. Even as we meet this challenge in Iraq and Syria, we all agree that one of our weapons against terrorists like ISIL—a critical part of our strategy—is the values we live here at home. One of the best antidotes to the hateful ideologies that try to recruit and radicalize people to violent extremism is our own example as diverse and tolerant societies that welcome the contributions of all people, including people of all faiths.

The resolution we've submitted today does not call for the deployment of U.S. ground combat forces to Iraq or Syria. It is not the authorization of another ground war, like Afghanistan or Iraq. The 2,600 American troops in Iraq today largely serve on bases, and yes, they face the risks that come with service in any dangerous environment. But they do not have a combat mission. They are focused on training Iraqi forces, including Kurdish forces.

As I've said before, I'm convinced that the United States should not get dragged back into another prolonged ground war in the Middle East. That's not in our national security interest, and it's not necessary for us to defeat ISIL. Local forces on the ground who know their countries best are best positioned to take the ground fight to ISIL, and that's what they're doing.

At the same time, this resolution strikes the necessary balance by giving us the flexibility we need for unforeseen circumstances. For example, if we had actionable intelligence about a gathering of ISIL leaders, and our partners didn't have the capacity to get them, I would be prepared to order our Special Forces to take action, because I will not allow these terrorists to have a safe haven. So we need flexibility, but we also have to be careful and deliberate. And there is no heavier decision than asking our men and women in uniform to risk their lives on our behalf. As Commander in Chief, I will only send our troops into harm's way when it is absolutely necessary for our national security.

Finally, this resolution repeals the 2002 authorization of force for the invasion of Iraq and limits this new authorization to 3 years. I do not believe America's interests are served by endless war or by remaining on a perpetual war footing. As a nation, we need to ask the difficult and necessary questions about when, why, and how we use military force. After all, it is our troops who bear the costs of our decisions, and we owe them a clear strategy and the support they need to get the job done. So this resolution will give our Armed Forces and our coalition the continuity we need for the next 3 years.

It is not a timetable. It is not announcing that the mission is completed at any given period. What it is saying is that Congress should revisit the issue at the beginning of the next President's term. It's conceivable that the mission is completed earlier. It's conceivable that after deliberation, debate, and evaluation, that there are additional tasks to be carried out in this area. And the people's representatives, with a new President, should be able to have that discussion.

In closing, I want to say that in crafting this resolution we have consulted with, and listened to, both Republicans and Democrats in Congress. We have made a sincere effort to address difficult issues that we've discussed together. In the days and weeks ahead, we'll continue to work closely with leaders and Members of Congress on both sides of the aisle. I believe this resolution can grow even stronger with the thoughtful and dignified debate that this moment demands. I'm optimistic that it can win strong bipartisan support and that we can show our troops and the world that Americans are united in this mission.

Now, today, our men and women in uniform continue the fight against ISIL, and we salute them for their courageous service. We pray for their safety. We stand with their families who miss them and who are sacrificing here at home. But know this: Our coalition is strong, our cause is just, and our mission will succeed. And long after the terrorists we face today are destroyed and forgotten, America will continue to stand free and tall and strong.

May God bless our troops, and may God bless the United States of America. Thank you very much, everybody.

Executive Office of the President. "Remarks on Proposed Legislation Submitted to the Congress to Authorize the Use of Military Force Against the Islamic State of Iraq and the Levant (ISIL) Terrorist Organization." February 11, 2015. *Compilation of Presidential Documents 2015*, no. 00092 (February 11, 2015). www.gpo.gov/fdsys/pkg/DCPD-201500092/pdf/DCPD-201500092.pdf.

President Obama's 2016 State of the Union Address

Following is the White House transcript of President Obama's address before a joint session of Congress on the state of the union given on January 12, 2016.

Thank you. Mr. Speaker, Mr. Vice President, Members of Congress, my fellow Americans: Tonight marks the eighth year that I've come here to report on the State of the Union. And for this final one, I'm going to try to make it a little shorter. I know some of you are antsy to get back to Iowa. [*Laughter*] I've been there. I'll be shaking hands afterwards if you want some tips. [*Laughter*]

Now, I understand that because it's an election season, expectations for what we will achieve this year are low. But, Mr. Speaker, I appreciate the constructive approach that you and other leaders took at the end of last year to pass a budget and make tax cuts permanent for working families. So I hope we can work together this year on some bipartisan priorities like criminal justice reform and helping people who are battling prescription drug abuse and heroin abuse. So, who knows, we might surprise the cynics again.

But tonight I want to go easy on the traditional list of proposals for the year ahead. Don't worry, I've got plenty—[*laughter*]—from helping students learn to write computer code to personalizing medical treatments for patients. And I will keep pushing for progress on the work that I believe still needs to be done: fixing a broken immigration system, protecting our kids from gun violence, equal pay for equal work, paid leave, raising the minimum wage. All these things still matter to hard-working families. They're still the right thing to do. And I won't let up until they get done.

But for my final address to this Chamber, I don't want to just talk about next year. I want to focus on the next 5 years, the next 10 years, and beyond. I want to focus on our future.

We live in a time of extraordinary change, change that's reshaping the way we live, the way we work, our planet, our place in the world. It's change that promises amazing medical breakthroughs, but also economic disruptions that strain working families. It promises this education for girls in the most remote villages, but also connects terrorists plotting an ocean away. It's change that can broaden opportunity or widen inequality. And whether we like it or not, the pace of this change will only accelerate.

America has been through big changes before: wars and depression, the influx of new immigrants, workers fighting for a fair deal, movements to expand civil rights. Each time, there have been those who told us to fear the future; who claimed we could slam the brakes on change; who promised to restore past glory if we just got some group or idea that was threatening America under control. And each time, we overcame those fears. We did not, in the words of Lincoln, adhere to the "dogmas of the quiet past." Instead, we thought anew and acted anew. We made change work for us, always extending America's promise outward, to the next frontier, to more people. And because we did, because we saw opportunity with a—where others saw peril, we emerged stronger and better than before.

What was true then can be true now. Our unique strengths as a nation—our optimism and work ethic, our spirit of discovery, our diversity, our commitment to rule of law—these things give us everything we need to ensure prosperity and security for generations to come.

In fact, it's in that spirit that we have made progress these past 7 years. That's how we recovered from the worst economic crisis in generations. That's how we reformed our health care system and reinvented our energy sector. That's how we delivered more care and benefits to our troops coming home and our veterans. That's how we secured the freedom in every State to marry the person we love.

But such progress is not inevitable. It's the result of choices we make together. And we face such choices right now. Will we respond to the changes of our time with fear, turning inward as a nation, turning against each other as a people? Or will we face the future with confidence in who we are, in what we stand for, in the incredible things that we can do together?

So let's talk about the future and four big questions that I believe we as a country have to answer, regardless of who the next President is or who controls the next Congress. First, how do we give everyone a fair shot at opportunity and security in this new economy? Second, how do we make technology work for us and not against us, especially when it comes to solving urgent challenges like climate change? Third, how do we keep America safe and lead the world without becoming its policeman? And finally, how can we make our politics reflect what's best in us and not what's worst?

Let me start with the economy and a basic fact: The United States of America right now has the strongest, most durable economy in the world. We're in the middle of the longest streak of private sector job creation in history. More than 14 million new jobs, the strongest 2 years of job growth since the 1990s, an unemployment rate cut in half. Our auto industry just had its best year ever. That's just part of a manufacturing surge that's created nearly 900,000 new jobs in the past 6 years. And we've done all this while cutting our deficits by almost three-quarters.

Anyone claiming that America's economy is in decline is peddling fiction. Now, what is true—and the reason that a lot of

Americans feel anxious—is that the economy has been changing in profound ways, changes that started long before the great recession hit, changes that have not let up.

Today, technology doesn't just replace jobs on the assembly line, but any job where work can be automated. Companies in a global economy can locate anywhere, and they face tougher competition. As a result, workers have less leverage for a raise. Companies have less loyalty to their communities. And more and more wealth and income is concentrated at the very top.

All these trends have squeezed workers, even when they have jobs, even when the economy is growing. It's made it harder for a hard-working family to pull itself out of poverty, harder for young people to start their careers, tougher for workers to retire when they want to. And although none of these trends are unique to America, they do offend our uniquely American belief that everybody who works hard should get a fair shot.

For the past 7 years, our goal has been a growing economy that also works better for everybody. We've made progress, but we need to make more. And despite all the political arguments that we've had these past few years, there are actually some areas where Americans broadly agree.

We agree that real opportunity requires every American to get the education and training they need to land a good-paying job. The bipartisan reform of No Child Left Behind was an important start, and together, we've increased early childhood education, lifted high school graduation rates to new highs, boosted graduates in fields like engineering. In the coming years, we should build on that progress, by providing pre-K for all and offering every student the hands-on computer science and math classes that make them job-ready on day one. We should recruit and support more great teachers for our kids.

And we have to make college affordable for every American. No hard-working student should be stuck in the red. We've already reduced student loan payments by—to 10 percent of a borrower's income. And that's good. But now we've actually got to cut the cost of college. Providing 2 years of community college at no cost for every responsible student is one of the best ways to do that, and I'm going to keep fighting to get that started this year. It's the right thing to do.

But a great education isn't all we need in this new economy. We also need benefits and protections that provide a basic measure of security. It's not too much of a stretch to say that some of the only people in America who are going to work the same job, in the same place, with a health and retirement package for 30 years are sitting in this Chamber. [*Laughter*] For everyone else, especially folks in their forties and fifties, saving for retirement or bouncing back from job loss has gotten a lot tougher. Americans understand that at some point in their careers, in this new economy, they may have to retool, they may have to retrain. But they shouldn't lose what they've already worked so hard to build in the process.

That's why Social Security and Medicare are more important than ever. We shouldn't weaken them, we should strengthen them. And for Americans short of retirement, basic benefits should be just as mobile as everything else is today. That, by the way, is what the Affordable Care Act is all about. It's about filling the gaps in employer-based care so that when you lose a job or you go back to school or you strike out and launch that new business, you'll still have coverage. Nearly 18 million people have gained coverage so far. And in the process, health care inflation has slowed. And our businesses have created jobs every single month since it became law.

Now, I'm guessing we won't agree on health care anytime soon, but—[*laughter*]—a little applause back there. [*Laughter*] Just a guess. But there should be other ways parties can work together to improve economic security. Say a hard-working American loses his job. We shouldn't just make sure that he can get unemployment insurance, we should make sure that program encourages him to retrain for a business that's ready to hire him. If that new job doesn't pay as much, there should be a system of wage insurance in place so that he can still pay his bills. And even if he's going from job to job, he should still be able to save for retirement and take his savings with him. That's the way we make the new economy work better for everybody.

I also know Speaker Ryan has talked about his interest in tackling poverty. America is about giving everybody willing to work a chance, a hand up. And I'd welcome a serious discussion about strategies we can all support, like expanding tax cuts for low-income workers who don't have children.

But there are some areas where—we just have to be honest—it has been difficult to find agreement over the last 7 years. And a lot of them fall under the category of what role the Government should play in making sure the system's not rigged in favor of the wealthiest and biggest corporations. And it's an honest disagreement, and the American people have a choice to make.

I believe a thriving private sector is the lifeblood of our economy. I think there are outdated regulations that need to be changed. There is redtape that needs to be cut. [*Applause*] There you go! Yes! See? But after years now of record corporate profits, working families won't get more opportunity or bigger paychecks just by letting big banks or big oil or hedge funds make their own rules at everybody else's expense. Middle class families are not going to feel more secure because we allowed attacks on collective bargaining to go unanswered. Food stamp recipients did not cause the financial crisis; recklessness on Wall Street did. Immigrants aren't the principal reason wages haven't gone up; those decisions are made in the boardrooms that all too often put quarterly earnings over long-term returns. It's sure not the average family watching tonight that avoids paying taxes through offshore accounts. [*Laughter*]

The point is, I believe that in this new economy, workers and startups and small businesses need more of a voice, not less. The rules should work for them. And I'm not alone in this. This year, I plan to lift up the many businesses who have figured out that doing right by their workers or their customers or their communities ends up being good for their shareholders. And I want to spread those best practices across America. That's part of a brighter future.

In fact, it turns, out many of our best corporate citizens are also our most creative. And this brings me to the second big question we as a country have to answer: How do we reignite that spirit of innovation to meet our biggest challenges?

Sixty years ago, when the Russians beat us into space, we didn't deny *Sputnik* was up there. [*Laughter*] We didn't argue about the science or shrink our research and development budget. We built a space program almost overnight. And 12 years later, we were walking on the Moon.

Now, that spirit of discovery is in our DNA. America is Thomas Edison and the Wright Brothers and George Washington Carver. America is Grace Hopper and Katherine Johnson and Sally Ride. America is every immigrant and entrepreneur from Boston to Austin to Silicon Valley, racing to shape a better future. That's who we are.

And over the past 7 years, we've nurtured that spirit. We've protected an open Internet and taken bold new steps to get more students and low-income Americans online. We've launched next-generation manufacturing hubs and online tools that give an entrepreneur everything he or she needs to start a business in a single day. But we can do so much more.

Last year, Vice President Biden said that with a new moonshot, America can cure cancer. Last month, he worked with this Congress to give scientists at the National Institutes of Health the strongest resources that they've had in over a decade. Well—so tonight I'm announcing a new national effort to get it done. And because he's gone to the mat for all of us on so many issues over the past 40 years, I'm putting Joe in charge of mission control. For the loved ones we've all lost, for the families that we can still save, let's make America the country that cures cancer once and for all. What do you say, Joe? Let's make it happen.

Now, medical research is critical. We need the same level of commitment when it comes to developing clean energy sources. Look, if anybody still wants to dispute the science around climate change, have at it. [*Laughter*] You will be pretty lonely, because you'll be debating our military, most of America's business leaders, the majority of the American people, almost the entire scientific community, and 200 nations around the world who agree it's a problem and intend to solve it. But even if the planet wasn't at stake, even if 2014 wasn't the warmest year on record—until 2015 turned out to be even hotter—why would we want to pass up the chance for American businesses to produce and sell the energy of the future?

Listen, 7 years ago, we made the single biggest investment in clean energy in our history. Here are the results. In fields from Iowa to Texas, wind power is now cheaper than dirtier, conventional power. On rooftops from Arizona to New York, solar is saving Americans tens of millions of dollars a year on their energy bills and employs more Americans than coal in jobs that pay better than average. We're taking steps to give homeowners the freedom to generate and store their own energy, something, by the way, that environmentalists and Tea Partiers have teamed up to support. And meanwhile, we've cut our imports of foreign oil by nearly 60 percent and cut carbon pollution more than any other country on Earth. Gas under 2 bucks a gallon ain't bad either. [*Laughter*]

Now we've got to accelerate the transition away from old, dirtier energy sources. Rather than subsidize the past, we should invest in the future, especially in communities that rely on fossil fuels. We do them no favor when we don't show them where the trends are going. And that's why I'm going to push to change the way we manage our oil and coal resources so that they better reflect the costs they impose on taxpayers and our planet. And that way, we put money back into those communities and put tens of thousands of Americans to work building a 21st-century transportation system.

Now, none of this is going to happen overnight. And yes, there are plenty of entrenched interests who want to protect the status quo. But the jobs we'll create, the money we'll save, the planet we'll preserve—that is the kind of future our kids and our grandkids deserve. And it's within our grasp.

Now, climate change is just one of many issues where our security is linked to the rest of the world. And that's why the third big question that we have to answer together is how to keep America safe and strong without either isolating ourselves or trying to nation-build everywhere there's a problem.

Now, I told you earlier all the talk of America's economic decline is political hot air. Well, so is all the rhetoric you hear about our enemies getting stronger and America getting weaker. Let me tell you something: The United States of America is the most powerful nation on Earth. Period. [*Applause*] Period. It's not even close. [*Applause*] It's not even close. It's not even close. We spend more on our military than the next eight nations combined. Our troops are the finest fighting force in the history of the world. [*Applause*] All right. No nation attacks us directly, or our allies, because they know that's the path to ruin. Surveys show our standing around the world is higher than when I was elected to this office, and when it comes to every important international issue, people of the world do not look to Beijing or Moscow to lead.

They call us. So I think it's useful to level set here, because when we don't, we don't make good decisions.

Now, as someone who begins every day with an intelligence briefing, I know this is a dangerous time. But that's not primarily because of some looming superpower out there, and it's certainly not because of diminished American strength. In today's world, we're threatened less by evil empires and more by failing states.

The Middle East is going through a transformation that will play out for a generation, rooted in conflicts that date back millennia. Economic headwinds are blowing in from a Chinese economy that is in significant transition. Even as their economy severely contracts, Russia is pouring resources in to prop up Ukraine and Syria, client states that they saw slipping away from their orbit. And the international system we built after World War II is now struggling to keep pace with this new reality. It's up to us, the United States of America, to help remake that system. And to do that well, it means that we've got to set priorities.

Priority number one is protecting the American people and going after terrorist networks. Both Al Qaida and now ISIL pose a direct threat to our people, because in today's world, even a handful of terrorists who place no value on human life, including their own, can do a lot of damage. They use the Internet to poison the minds of individuals inside our country. Their actions undermine and destabilize our allies. We have to take them out.

But as we focus on destroying ISIL, over-the-top claims that this is World War III just play into their hands. Masses of fighters on the back of pickup trucks, twisted souls plotting in apartments or garages, they pose an enormous danger to civilians; they have to be stopped. But they do not threaten our national existence. That is the story ISIL wants to tell. That's the kind of propaganda they use to recruit. We don't need to build them up to show that we're serious, and we sure don't need to push away vital allies in this fight by echoing the lie that ISIL is somehow representative of one of the world's largest religions. We just need to call them what they are: killers and fanatics who have to be rooted out, hunted down, and destroyed.

And that's exactly what we're doing. For more than a year, America has led a coalition of more than 60 countries to cut off ISIL's financing, disrupt their plots, stop the flow of terrorist fighters, and stamp out their vicious ideology. With nearly 10,000 airstrikes, we're taking out their leadership, their oil, their training camps, their weapons. We're training, arming, and supporting forces who are steadily reclaiming territory in Iraq and Syria.

If this Congress is serious about winning this war and wants to send a message to our troops and the world, authorize the use of military force against ISIL. Take a vote. [*Applause*] Take a vote. But the American people should know that with or without congressional action, ISIL will learn the same lessons as terrorists before them. If you doubt America's commitment—or mine—to see that justice is done, just ask Usama bin Laden. Ask the leader of Al Qaida in Yemen, who was taken out last year, or the perpetrator of the Benghazi attacks, who sits in a prison cell. When you come after Americans, we go after you. And it may take time, but we have long memories, and our reach has no limits.

Our foreign policy has to be focused on the threat from ISIL and Al Qaida, but it can't stop there. For even without ISIL, even without Al Qaida, instability will continue for decades in many parts of the world: in the Middle East, in Afghanistan and parts of Pakistan, in parts of Central America, in Africa and Asia. Some of these places may become safe havens for new terrorist networks. Others will just fall victim to ethnic conflict or famine, feeding the next wave of refugees. The world will look to us to help solve these problems, and our answer needs to be more than tough talk or calls to carpet-bomb civilians. That may work as a TV sound bite, but it doesn't pass muster on the world stage.

We also can't try to take over and rebuild every country that falls into crisis, even if it's done with the best of intentions. That's not leadership; that's a recipe for quagmire, spilling American blood and treasure that ultimately will weaken us. It's the lesson of Vietnam; it's the lesson of Iraq. And we should have learned it by now.

Now, fortunately there is a smarter approach: a patient and disciplined strategy that uses every element of our national power. It says America will always act, alone if necessary, to protect our people and our allies, but on issues of global concern, we will mobilize the world to work with us and make sure other countries pull their own weight. That's our approach to conflicts like Syria, where we're partnering with local forces and leading international efforts to help that broken society pursue a lasting peace.

That's why we built a global coalition, with sanctions and principled diplomacy, to prevent a nuclear-armed Iran. And as we speak, Iran has rolled back its nuclear program, shipped out its uranium stockpile, and the world has avoided another war.

That's how we stopped the spread of Ebola in West Africa. Our military, our doctors, our development workers—they were heroic; they set up the platform that then allowed other countries to join in behind us and stamp out that epidemic. Hundreds of thousands, maybe a couple million, lives were saved.

That's how we forged a Trans-Pacific Partnership to open markets and protect workers and the environment and advance American leadership in Asia. It cuts 18,000 taxes on products made in America, which will then support more good jobs here in America. With TPP, China does not set the rules in that region, we do. You want to show our strength in this new century? Approve this agreement. Give us the tools to enforce it. It's the right thing to do.

Let me give you another example. Fifty years of isolating Cuba had failed to promote democracy. It set us back in Latin America. That's why we restored diplomatic relations, opened the door to travel and commerce, positioned ourselves to improve the lives of the Cuban people. So if you want to consolidate our leadership and credibility in the hemisphere, recognize that the cold war is over. Lift the embargo.

The point is, American leadership in the 21st century is not a choice between ignoring the rest of the world—except when we kill terrorists—or occupying and rebuilding whatever society is unraveling. Leadership means a wise application of military power and rallying the world behind causes that are right. It means seeing our foreign assistance as a part of our national security, not something separate, not charity.

When we lead nearly 200 nations to the most ambitious agreement in history to fight climate change, yes, that helps vulnerable countries, but it also protects our kids. When we help Ukraine defend its democracy or Colombia resolve a decades-long war, that strengthens the international order we depend on. When we help African countries feed their people and care for the sick, it's the right thing to do, and it prevents the next pandemic from reaching our shores. Right now we're on track to end the scourge of HIV/AIDS. That's within our grasp.

And we have the chance to accomplish the same thing with malaria, something I'll be pushing this Congress to fund this year.

That's American strength. That's American leadership. And that kind of leadership depends on the power of our example. That's why I will keep working to shut down the prison at Guantanamo. It is expensive, it is unnecessary, and it only serves as a recruitment brochure for our enemies. There's a better way.

And that's why we need to reject any politics—any politics—that targets people because of race or religion. Let me just say this. This is not a matter of political correctness, this is a matter of understanding just what it is that makes us strong. The world respects us not just for our arsenal, it respects us for our diversity and our openness and the way we respect every faith.

His Holiness Pope Francis told this body from the very spot that I'm standing on tonight that "to imitate the hatred and violence of tyrants and murderers is the best way to take their place." When politicians insult Muslims, whether abroad or our fellow citizens, when a mosque is vandalized or a kid is called names, that doesn't make us safer. That's not telling it what—telling it like it is. It's just wrong. It diminishes us in the eyes of the world. It makes it harder to achieve our goals. It betrays who we are as a country.

"We the People." Our Constitution begins with those three simple words, words we've come to recognize mean all the people, not just some; words that insist we rise and fall together, that that's how we might perfect our Union. And that brings me to the fourth and maybe most important thing that I want to say tonight.

The future we want—all of us want—opportunity and security for our families, a rising standard of living, a sustainable, peaceful planet for our kids—all that is within our reach. But it will only happen if we work together. It will only happen if we can have rational, constructive debates. It will only happen if we fix our politics.

A better politics doesn't mean we have to agree on everything. This is a big country: different regions, different attitudes, different interests. That's one of our strengths too. Our Founders distributed power between States and branches of government and expected us to argue, just as they did, fiercely, over the size and shape of government, over commerce and foreign relations, over the meaning of liberty and the imperatives of security.

But democracy does require basic bonds of trust between its citizens. It doesn't work if we think the people who disagree with us are all motivated by malice. It doesn't work if we think that our political opponents are unpatriotic or trying to weaken America. Democracy grinds to a halt without a willingness to compromise or when even basic facts are contested or when we listen only to those who agree with us. Our public life withers when only the most extreme voices get all the attention. And most of all, democracy breaks down when the average person feels their voice doesn't matter, that the system is rigged in favor of the rich or the powerful or some special interest.

Too many Americans feel that way right now. It's one of the few regrets of my Presidency: that the rancor and suspicion between the parties has gotten worse instead of better. I have no doubt, a President with the gifts of Lincoln or Roosevelt might have better bridged the divide, and I guarantee, I'll keep trying to be better so long as I hold this office.

But, my fellow Americans, this cannot be my task—or any President's—alone. There are a whole lot of folks in this Chamber, good people, who would like to see more cooperation, would like to see a more elevated debate in Washington, but feel trapped by the imperatives of getting elected, by the noise coming out of your base. I know; you've told me. It's the worst kept secret in Washington. And a lot of you aren't enjoying being trapped in that kind of rancor.

But that means if we want a better politics—and I'm addressing the American people now—if we want a better politics, it's not enough just to change a Congressman or change a Senator or even change a President. We have to change the system to reflect our better selves.

I think we've got to end the practice of drawing our congressional districts so that politicians can pick their voters and not the other way around. Let a bipartisan group do it.

I believe we've got to reduce the influence of money in our politics so that a handful of families or hidden interests can't bankroll our elections. And if our existing approach to campaign finance reform can't pass muster in the courts, we need to work together to find a real solution. Because it's a problem. And most of you don't like raising money. [Laughter] I know. I've done it.

We've got to make it easier to vote, not harder. We need to modernize it for the way we live now. This is America: We want to make it easier for people to participate. And over the course of this year, I intend to travel the country to push for reforms that do just that.

But I can't do these things on my own. Changes in our political process—in not just who gets elected, but how they get elected—that will only happen when the American people demand it. It depends on you. That's what's meant by a government of, by, and for the people.

What I'm suggesting is hard. It's a lot easier to be cynical; to accept that change is not possible and politics is hopeless and the problem is, all the folks who are elected don't care; and to believe that our voices and our actions don't matter. But if we give up now, then we forsake a better future. Those with money and power will gain greater control over the decisions that could send a young soldier to war or allow another economic disaster or roll back the equal rights and voting rights that generations of Americans have fought, even died, to secure. And then, as frustration grows, there will be voices urging us to fall back into our respective tribes, to scapegoat fellow citizens who don't look like us or pray like us or vote like we do or share the same background.

We can't afford to go down that path. It won't deliver the economy we want. It will not produce the security we want. But most of all, it contradicts everything that makes us the envy of the world.

So, my fellow Americans, whatever you may believe, whether you prefer one party or no party, whether you supported my agenda or fought as hard as you could against it, our collective futures depends on your willingness to uphold your duties as a citizen. To vote. To speak out. To stand up for others, especially the weak, especially the vulnerable, knowing that each of us is only here because somebody, somewhere, stood up for us. We need every American to stay active in our public life—and not just during election time—so that our public life reflects the goodness and the decency that I see in the American people every single day.

It is not easy. Our brand of democracy is hard. But I can promise that a little over a year from now, when I no longer hold this office, I will be right there with you as a citizen, inspired by those voices of fairness and vision, of grit and good humor and kindness, that have helped America travel so far. Voices that help us see ourselves not, first and foremost, as Black or White or Asian or Latino, not as gay or straight, immigrant or native born, not Democrat or Republican, but as Americans first, bound by a common creed. Voices Dr. King believed would have the final word: voices of "unarmed truth and unconditional love."

And they're out there, those voices. They don't get a lot of attention; they don't seek a lot of fanfare; but they're busy doing the work this country needs doing. I see them everywhere I travel in this incredible country of ours. I see you, the American people. And in your daily acts of citizenship, I see our future unfolding.

I see it in the worker on the assembly line who clocked extra shifts to keep his company open and the boss who pays him higher wages instead of laying him off. I see it in the dreamer who stays up late at night to finish her science project and the teacher who comes in early, maybe with some extra supplies that she bought because she knows that that young girl might someday cure a disease.

I see it in the American who served his time, made bad mistakes as a child, but now is dreaming of starting over. And I see it in the business owner who gives him that second chance. The protester determined to prove that justice matters and the young cop walking the beat, treating everybody with respect, doing the brave, quiet work of keeping us safe.

I see it in the soldier who gives almost everything to save his brothers, the nurse who tends to him till he can run a marathon, the community that lines up to cheer him on. It's the son who finds the courage to come out as who he is and the father whose love for that son overrides everything he's been taught.

I see it in the elderly woman who will wait in line to cast her vote as long as she has to, the new citizen who casts his vote for the first time, the volunteers at the polls who believe every vote should count. Because each of them, in different ways, know how much that precious right is worth.

That's the America I know. That's the country we love: clear eyed, big hearted, undaunted by challenge. Optimistic that unarmed truth and unconditional love will have the final word.

That's what makes me so hopeful about our future. I believe in change because I believe in you, the American people. And that's why I stand here as confident as I have ever been that the state of our Union is strong.

Thank you. God bless you. God bless the United States of America. Thank you.

Executive Office of the President. "Address Before a Joint Session of Congress on the State of the Union." January 12, 2016. *Compilation of Presidential Documents* 2016, no. 00012 (January 12, 2016). http://www.gpo.gov/fdsys/pkg/DCPD-201600012/pdf/DCPD-201600012.pdf.

President Obama's
Speech in Hiroshima, Japan

Following is the White House transcript of President Obama's speech in Hiroshima, Japan, with Japan's Prime Minister, Shinzo Abe, on May 27, 2016.

President Obama. Seventy-one years ago, on a bright, cloudless morning, death fell from the sky, and the world was changed. A flash of light and a wall of fire destroyed a city and demonstrated that mankind possessed the means to destroy itself.

Why do we come to this place, to Hiroshima? We come to ponder a terrible force unleashed in a not-so-distant past. We come to mourn the dead, including over 100,000 Japanese men, women, and children; thousands of Koreans; a dozen Americans held prisoner. Their souls speak to us. They ask us to look inward, to take stock of who we are and what we might become.

It is not the fact of war that sets Hiroshima apart. Artifacts tell us that violent conflict appeared with the very first man. Our early ancestors, having learned to make blades from flint and spears from wood, used these tools not just for hunting, but against their own kind. On every continent, the history of civilization is filled with war, whether driven by scarcity of grain or hunger for gold, compelled by nationalist fervor or religious zeal. Empires have risen and fallen. Peoples have been subjugated and liberated. And at each juncture, innocents have suffered, a countless toll, their names forgotten by time.

The World War that reached its brutal end in Hiroshima and Nagasaki was fought among the wealthiest and most powerful of nations. Their civilizations had given the world great cities and magnificent art. Their thinkers had advanced ideas of justice and harmony and truth. And yet the war grew out of the same base instinct for domination or conquest that had caused conflicts among the simplest tribes, an old pattern amplified by new capabilities and without new constraints. In the span of a few years, some 60 million people would die: men, women, children no different than us, shot, beaten, marched, bombed, jailed, starved, gassed to death.

There are many sites around the world that chronicle this war: memorials that tell stories of courage and heroism; graves and empty camps that echo of unspeakable depravity. Yet in the image of a mushroom cloud that rose into these skies, we are most starkly reminded of humanity's core contradiction; how the very spark that marks us as a species—our thoughts, our imagination, our language, our tool-making, our ability to set ourselves apart from nature and bend it to our will—those very things also give us the capacity for unmatched destruction.

How often does material advancement or social innovation blind us to this truth. How easily we learn to justify violence in the name of some higher cause. Every great religion promises a pathway to love and peace and righteousness, and yet no religion has been spared from believers who have claimed their faith as a license to kill. Nations arise, telling a story that binds people together in sacrifice and cooperation, allowing for remarkable feats, but those same stories have so often been used to oppress and dehumanize those who are different.

Science allows us to communicate across the seas and fly above the clouds, to cure disease and understand the cosmos. But those same discoveries can be turned into ever-more efficient killing machines.

The wars of the modern age teach this truth. Hiroshima teaches this truth. Technological progress without an equivalent progress in human institutions can doom us. The scientific revolution that led to the splitting of an atom requires a moral revolution as well.

That is why we come to this place. We stand here, in the middle of this city, and force ourselves to imagine the moment the bomb fell. We force ourselves to feel the dread of children confused by what they see. We listen to a silent cry. We remember all the innocents killed across the arc of that terrible war and the wars that came before and the wars that would follow.

Mere words cannot give voice to such suffering, but we have a shared responsibility to look directly into the eye of history and ask what we must do differently to curb such suffering again. Someday the voices of the *hibakusha* will no longer be with us to bear witness. But the memory of the morning of August 6, 1945, must never fade. That memory allows us to fight complacency. It fuels our moral imagination. It allows us to change.

And since that fateful day, we have made choices that give us hope. The United States and Japan forged not only an alliance, but a friendship that has won far more for our people than we could ever claim through war. The nations of Europe built a Union that replaced battlefields with bonds of commerce and democracy. Oppressed peoples and nations won liberation. An international community established institutions and treaties that worked to avoid war and aspire to restrict and roll back and ultimately eliminate the existence of nuclear weapons.

Still, every act of aggression between nations, every act of terror and corruption and cruelty and oppression that we see around the world shows, our work is never done. We may not be able to eliminate man's capacity to do evil, so nations—and the alliances that we've formed—must possess the means to defend ourselves. But among those nations like my own that hold nuclear stockpiles, we must have the courage to escape the logic of fear and pursue a world without them.

We may not realize this goal in my lifetime. But persistent effort can roll back the possibility of catastrophe. We can chart a course that leads to the destruction of these stockpiles. We can stop the spread to new nations and secure deadly materials from fanatics.

And yet that is not enough. For we see around the world today how even the crudest rifles and barrel bombs can serve up violence on a terrible scale. We must change our mindset about war itself: to prevent conflict through diplomacy and strive to end conflicts after they've begun; to see our growing interdependence as a cause for peaceful cooperation and not violent competition; to define our nations not by our capacity to destroy, but by what we build.

And perhaps above all, we must reimagine our connection to one another as members of one human race. For this, too, is what makes our species unique. We're not bound by genetic code to repeat the mistakes of the past. We can learn. We can choose. We can tell our children a different story: one that describes a common humanity, one that makes war less likely and cruelty less easily accepted.

We see these stories in the *hibakusha*: the woman who forgave a pilot who flew the plane that dropped the atomic bomb, because she recognized that what she really hated was war itself; the man who sought out families of Americans killed here, because he believed their loss was equal to his own.

My own Nation's story began with simple words: All men are created equal and endowed by our Creator with certain unalienable rights, including life, liberty, and the pursuit of happiness. Realizing that ideal has never been easy, even within our own borders, even among our own citizens.

But staying true to that story is worth the effort. It is an ideal to be strived for, an ideal that extends across continents and across oceans. The irreducible worth of every person, the insistence that every life is precious, the radical and necessary notion that we are part of a single human family—that is the story that we all must tell.

That is why we come to Hiroshima. So that we might think of people we love: the first smile from our children in the morning, the gentle touch from a spouse over the kitchen table, the comforting embrace of a parent. We can think of those things and know that those same precious moments took place here 71 years ago. Those who died, they are like us. Ordinary people understand this, I think. They do not want more war. They would rather that the wonders of science be focused on improving life and not eliminating it.

When the choices made by nations, when the choices made by leaders, reflect this simple wisdom, then the lesson of Hiroshima is done.

The world was forever changed here. But today, the children of this city will go through their day in peace. What a precious thing that is. It is worth protecting and then extending to every child. That is the future we can choose, a future in which Hiroshima and Nagasaki are known not as the dawn of atomic warfare, but as the start of our own moral awakening.

[The speech given by Prime Minster Abe has been omitted.]

Executive Office of the President. "Remarks With Prime Minister Shinzo Abe of Japan at Hiroshima Peace Memorial Park in Hiroshima, Japan." May 27, 2016. *Compilation of Presidential Documents* 2016, no. 00357 (May 27, 2016). http://www.gpo.gov/fdsys/pkg/DCPD-201600357/pdf/DCPD-201600357.pdf.

President Obama's Speech on Military Strategy in Afghanistan

Following is the White House transcript of President Obama's address before a joint session of Congress on military strategy in Afghanistan given on July 6, 2016.

Good morning, everybody.

More than 14 years ago, after Al Qaida attacked our nation on 9/11, the United States went to war in Afghanistan against these terrorists and the Taliban that harbored them. Over the years—and thanks to heroic efforts by our military, our intelligence community, our diplomats, and our development professionals—we pushed Al Qaida out of its camps, helped the Afghan people topple the Taliban and helped them establish a democratic government. We dealt crippling blows to the Al Qaida leadership. We delivered justice to Usama bin Laden.

And we trained Afghan forces to take responsibility for their own security.

And given that progress, a year and a half ago, in December 2014, America's combat mission in Afghanistan came to a responsible end. Compared to the 100,000 troops we once had there,

today, fewer than 10,000 remain. And compared to their previous mission—helping to lead the fight—our forces are now focused on two narrow missions: training and advising Afghan forces and supporting counterterrorist operations against the remnants of Al Qaida as well as other terrorist groups, including ISIL. In short, even as we've maintained a relentless case against those who are threatening us, we are no longer engaged in a major ground war in Afghanistan.

But even these narrow missions continue to be dangerous. Over the past year and a half, 38 Americans—military and civilian—have lost their lives in Afghanistan on behalf of our security. And we honor their sacrifice. We stand with their families in their grief and in their pride. And we resolve to carry on the mission for which they gave their last full measure of devotion.

This is also not America's mission alone. In Afghanistan, we're joined by 41 allies and partners, a coalition that contributes more than 6,000 troops of their own. We have a partner in the Afghan Government and the Afghan people, who support a long-term strategic partnership with the United States. And in fact, Afghans continue to step up. For the second year now, Afghan forces are fully responsible for their own security. Every day, nearly 320,000 Afghan soldiers and police are serving and fighting, and many are giving their lives to defend their country.

To their credit—and in the face of a continued Taliban insurgency and terrorist networks—Afghan forces remain in control of all the major population centers, provincial capitals, major transit routes and most district centers. Afghan forces have beaten back attacks, and they've pushed the Taliban out of some areas. And meanwhile, in another milestone, we recently removed the leader of the Taliban, Akhtar Mohammad Mansur.

Nevertheless, the security situation in Afghanistan remains precarious. Even as they improve, Afghan security forces are still not as strong as they need to be. With our help, they're still working to improve critical capabilities such as intelligence, logistics, aviation, and command and control. At the same time, the Taliban remains a threat. They have gained ground in some cases. They've continued attacks and suicide bombings, including in Kabul.

Because the Taliban deliberately target innocent civilians, more Afghan men, women, and children are dying. And often overlooked in the global refugee crisis, millions of Afghans have fled their homes and many have been fleeing their country.

Now, as President and Commander in Chief, I've made it clear that I will not allow Afghanistan to be used as safe haven for terrorists to attack our Nation again. That's why I constantly review our strategy with my national security team, including our commanders in Afghanistan. In all these reviews, we're guided by the facts—what's happening on the ground—to determine what's working and what needs to be changed. And that's why, at times, I've made adjustments, for example, by slowing the drawdown of our forces and, more recently, by giving U.S. forces more flexibility to support Afghan forces on the ground and in the air. And I strongly believe that it is in our national security interest—especially after all the blood and treasure we've invested in Afghanistan over the years—that we give our Afghan partners the very best opportunity to succeed.

Upon taking command of coalition forces this spring, General Nicholson conducted a review of the security situation in Afghanistan and our military posture. It was good to get a fresh set of eyes. And based on the recommendation of General Nicholson, as well as Secretary Carter and Chairman Dunford, and following extensive consultations with my national security team, as well as Congress and the Afghan Government and our international partners, I'm announcing an additional adjustment to our posture.

Instead of going down to 5,500 troops by the end of this year, the United States will maintain approximately 8,400 troops in Afghanistan into next year, through the end of my administration. The narrow missions assigned to our forces will not change. They remain focused on supporting Afghan forces and going after terrorists. But maintaining our forces at this specific level, based on our assessment of the security conditions and the strength of Afghan forces, will allow us to continue to provide tailored support to help Afghan forces continue to improve. From coalition bases in Jalalabad and Kandahar, we'll be able to continue supporting Afghan forces on the ground and in the air. And we continue supporting critical counterterrorism operations.

Now, in reaffirming the enduring commitment of the United States to Afghanistan and its people, the decision I'm making today can help our allies and partners align their own commitments. As you know, tomorrow I depart for the NATO summit in Warsaw, where I'll meet with our coalition partners and Afghan President Ghani and Chief Executive Abdullah. Many of our allies and partners have already stepped forward with commitments of troops and funding so that we can keep strengthening Afghan forces through the end of this decade. The NATO summit will be an opportunity for more allies and partners to affirm their contributions, and I'm confident they will, because all of us have a vital interest in the security and stability of Afghanistan.

My decision today also sends a message to the Taliban and all those who have opposed Afghanistan's progress. You have now been waging war against the Afghan people for many years. You've been unable to prevail. Afghan security forces continue to grow stronger. And the commitment of the international community, including the United States, to Afghanistan and its people will endure. I will say it again: The only way to end this conflict and to achieve a full drawdown of foreign forces from Afghanistan is through a lasting political settlement between the Afghan Government and the Taliban. That's the only way. And that is why the United States will continue to strongly support an Afghan-led reconciliation process and why we call on all countries in the region to end safe havens for militants and terrorists.

Finally, today's decision best positions my successor to make future decisions about our presence in Afghanistan. In January, the next U.S. President will assume the most solemn responsibility of the Commander in Chief: the security of the United States and the safety of the American people. The decision I'm making today ensures that my successor has a solid foundation for continued progress in Afghanistan as well as the flexibility to address the threat of terrorism as it evolves.

So, in closing, I want to address directly what I know is on the minds of many Americans, especially our troops and their families who have borne a heavy burden for our security. When we first sent our forces into Afghanistan 14 years ago, few Americans imagined we'd be there— in any capacity—this long. As President,

I focused our strategy on training and building up Afghan forces. It has been continually my belief that it is up to Afghans to defend their country. Because we have emphasized training their capabilities, we've been able to end our major ground war there and bring 90 percent of our troops back home.

But even as we work for peace, we have to deal with the realities of the world as it is. And we can't forget what's at stake in Afghanistan. This is where Al Qaida is trying to regroup. This is where ISIL continues to try to expand its presence. If these terrorists succeed in regaining areas and camps where they can train and plot, they will attempt more attacks against us. And we cannot allow that to happen. I will not allow that to happen.

This September will mark 15 years since the attacks of 9/11. And once more, we'll pause to remember the lives we lost, Americans and peoples from around the world. We'll stand with their families, who still grieve. We'll stand with survivors, who still bear the scars of that day.

We'll thank the first responders who rushed to save others. And perhaps most importantly, we'll salute our men and women in uniform—our 9/11 generation—who have served in Afghanistan and beyond for our security. We'll honor the memory of all those who've made the ultimate sacrifice, including more than 2,200 American patriots who have given their lives in Afghanistan. As we do, let's never forget the progress their service has made possible.

Afghanistan is not a perfect place. It remains one of the poorest countries in the world. It is going to continue to take time for them to build up military capacity that we sometimes take for granted. And given the enormous challenges they face, the Afghan people will need the partnership of the world, led by the United States, for many years to come. But with our support, Afghanistan is a better place than it once was. Millions of Afghan children—boys and girls—are in school. Dramatic improvements in public health have saved the lives of mothers and children. Afghans have cast their ballots in democratic elections and seen the first democratic transfer of power in their country's history. The current National Unity Government continues to pursue reforms—including record revenues last year—to strengthen their country and, over time, help decrease the need for international support.

That Government is a strong partner with us in combating terrorism. That's the progress we've helped make possible. That's the progress that our troops have helped make possible, and our diplomats and our development personnel. That's the progress we can help sustain, in partnership with the Afghan people and our coalition partners. And so I firmly believe the decision I'm announcing today is the right thing to do: for Afghanistan, for the United States, and for the world.

May God bless our troops and all who serve to protect us. May God bless the United States of America.

Executive Office of the President. "Remarks on United States Military Strategy in Afghanistan." July 6, 2016. *Compilation of Presidential Documents* 2016, no. 00450 (July 6, 2016). http://www.gpo.gov/fdsys/pkg/DCPD-201600450/pdf/DCPD-201600450.pdf.

Presidential Vetoes and Veto Messages, 2013–2016

President Barack Obama vetoed ten bills in his second term, all of them after Republicans strengthened their hold on the House and won control of the Senate in the 2014 midterm elections. In contrast, he had issued just two vetoes during his first term.

Several of Obama's vetoes blocked legislation that would have scaled back environmental and labor regulations, as well as ended key provisions of the Affordable Care Act. Congress overrode just one of his vetoes, of the Justice Against Sponsors of Terrorism Act, which allowed U.S. courts to hear cases against foreign governments accused of aiding terrorist acts in the United States even if those governments were not designated as state sponsors of terrorism.

Obama's twelve vetoes were tied with John F. Kennedy, who served less than three years, for the fewest vetoes of any recent president (see table, below).

Obama's predecessor, President George W. Bush, did not veto any legislation during his first four years in office, from 2001 through 2004. He was the first president since John Quincy Adams in the 1820s to go through a full term without issuing a veto. But Bush's second term was quite different with Democrats in control of Congress for two of the four years: he cast twelve vetoes from 2005 through 2008 (Congress and the Nation Vol XII, p. 1039).

By contrast, several presidents in the second half of the twentieth century issued dozens of vetoes. Dwight Eisenhower, faced with a Democratic Congress throughout his eight years in the White House, vetoed many more than any of his successors. But only two were overridden. Bill Clinton, who faced a Republican Congress for six of his eight years, issued thirty-seven vetoes but also had just two overridden. Gerald Ford, who faced an overwhelmingly Democratic and assertive Congress in the wake of the Watergate scandal, saw twelve out of his sixty-six vetoes overridden even though he served only a little more than two years.

Presidential Vetoes

President	Congress vetoes	Regular vetoes	Pocket vetoes	Total	Overridden
Dwight D. Eisenhower	83rd–86th	73	108	181	2
John F. Kennedy	87th–88th	12	9	21	0
Lyndon B. Johnson	88th–90th	16	14	30	0
Richard M. Nixon	91st–93rd	26	17	43	7
Gerald R. Ford	93rd–94th	48	18	66	12
Jimmy Carter	95th–96th	13	18	31	2
Ronald Reagan	97th–100th	39	39	78	9
George H. W. Bush[1]	101st–102nd	29	15	44	1
Bill Clinton[2]	103rd–106th	36	1	37	2
George W. Bush	107th–108th	12	0	12	4
Barack Obama[3]	109th–114th	12	0	12	1

1. President George H. W. Bush attempted to pocket veto two bills during recess periods. Congress considered the two bills enacted into law because of the president's failure to return the legislation. The bills are not counted as pocket vetoes in this table.

2. Does not include line-item vetoes, which were permitted under a 1996 law that was struck down by the Supreme Court.

3. President Barack Obama considered one of his vetoes from 2009, one from 2010, and three from 2015 to be pocket vetoes, but since he returned the parchments to Congress, the Senate considers them regular vetoes.

Grover Cleveland issued the most vetoes in one term, 414. Franklin D. Roosevelt, who served as president for three full terms and into a fourth, vetoed the most measures, 635. Seven presidents before Bush vetoed no bills.

Following is a list of bill vetoed by President Barack Obama in his second term, 2013–2017, and his messages to Congress on the vetoes.

2015

1. S.1 (Keystone XL Pipeline Approval Act)
Vetoed Feb. 24, 2015 S.Doc. 114-2
The Senate sustained the veto on March 4, 2015: 62–37.

2. S.J.Res.8 (National Labor Relations Board Union Election Rule)
Vetoed March 31, 2015
The Senate did not challenge the veto.

3. H.R.1735 (National Defense Authorization Act for Fiscal Year 2016)
Vetoed Oct. 22, 2015
The House did not challenge the veto.

4. S.J.Res.23 (Standards of Performance for Greenhouse Gas Emissions)
Vetoed Dec. 18, 2015
The Senate did not challenge the veto.

5. S.J.Res.24 (Carbon Pollution Emission Guidelines)
Vetoed Dec. 18, 2015
The Senate did not challenge the veto.

2016

1. H.R.3762 (Restoring Americans' Healthcare Freedom Reconciliation Act of 2015)
Vetoed Jan. 8, 2016
The House sustained the veto on Feb. 2, 2016: 241–186.

2. S.J.Res.22 (Rule clarifying the jurisdictional boundaries of the Clean Water Act)
Vetoed Jan. 19, 2016
The Senate did not challenge the veto.

3. H.J.Res.88 (Nullifying the Department of Labor's final conflict of interest rule)
Vetoed June 8, 2016
The House sustained the veto on June 22, 2016: 239–180.

4. H.R.1777 (Presidential Allowance Modernization Act of 2016)
Vetoed July 22, 2016
The House did not challenge the veto.

5. S.2040 (Justice Against Sponsors of Terrorism Act)
Vetoed Sept. 23, 2016
Veto overridden by the House on Sept. 28, 2016: 348–77.
Veto overridden by the Senate on Sept. 28, 2016: 97–1.

President Obama's Veto of the Keystone XL Pipeline Approval Act

Following is the text of President Obama's February 24, 2015, veto message on S.1, authorizing the Keystone XL pipeline.

To the Senate of the United States:
I am returning herewith without my approval S. 1, the "Keystone XL Pipeline Approval Act." Through this bill, the United States Congress attempts to circumvent longstanding and proven processes for determining whether or not building and operating a cross-border pipeline serves the national interest.

The Presidential power to veto legislation is one I take seriously. But I also take seriously my responsibility to the American people. And because this act of Congress conflicts with established executive branch procedures and cuts short thorough consideration of issues that could bear on our national interest—including our security, safety, and environment—it has earned my veto.

> BARACK OBAMA.
> THE WHITE HOUSE
> February 24, 2015

President Obama's Veto of the National Labor Relations Board Union Election Rule

Following is the text of President Obama's March 31, 2015, veto message on S.J.Res.8, nullifying the submitted by the NLRB.

To the Senate of the United States:

S.J. Res. 8 would overturn the National Labor Relations Board's recently issued "representation case procedures" rule and block modest but overdue reforms to simplify and streamline private sector union elections. Accordingly, I am withholding my approval of this resolution. (The Pocket Veto Case, 279 U.S. 655 (1929)).

Workers need a strong voice in the workplace and the economy to protect and grow our Nation's middle class. Unions have played a vital role in giving workers that voice, allowing workers to organize together for higher wages, better working conditions, and the benefits and protections that most workers take for granted today. Workers deserve a level playing field that lets them freely choose to make their voices heard, and this requires fair and streamlined procedures for determining whether to have unions as their bargaining representative. Because this resolution seeks to undermine a streamlined democratic process that allows American workers to freely choose to make their voices heard, I cannot support it.

To leave no doubt that the resolution is being vetoed, in addition to withholding my signature, I am returning S.J. Res. 8 to the Secretary of the Senate, along with this Memorandum of Disapproval.

> BARACK OBAMA.
> THE WHITE HOUSE
> March 31, 2015

President Obama's Veto of the National Defense Authorization Act for Fiscal Year 2016

Following is the text of President Obama's October 22, 2015, veto message on H.R.1735, authorizing national defense funding.

To The House of Representatives:

I am returning herewith without my approval H.R. 1735, the "National Defense Authorization Act for Fiscal Year 2016." While there are provisions in this bill that I support, including the codification of key interrogation-related reforms from Executive Order 13491 and positive changes to the military retirement system, the bill would, among other things, constrain the ability of the Department of Defense to conduct multi-year defense planning and align military capabilities and force structure with our national defense strategy, impede the closure of the detention facility at Guantanamo Bay, and prevent the implementation of essential defense reforms.

This bill fails to authorize funding for our national defense in a fiscally responsible manner. It underfunds our military in the base budget, and instead relies on an irresponsible budget gimmick that has been criticized by members of both parties. Specifically, the bill's use of $38 billion in Overseas Contingency Operations funding—which was meant to fund wars and is not subject to budget caps—does not provide the stable, multi-year budget upon which sound defense planning depends. Because this bill authorizes base budget funding at sequestration levels, it threatens the readiness and capabilities of our military and fails to provide the support our men and women in uniform deserve. The decision reflected in this bill to circumvent rather than reverse sequestration further harms our national security by locking in unacceptable funding cuts for crucial national security activities carried out by non-defense agencies.

I have repeatedly called upon the Congress to work with my Administration to close the detention facility at Guantanamo Bay, Cuba, and explained why it is imperative that we do so. As I have noted, the continued operation of this facility weakens our national security by draining resources, damaging our relationships with key allies and partners, and emboldening violent extremists. Yet in addition to failing to remove unwarranted restrictions on the transfer of detainees, this bill seeks to impose more onerous ones. The executive branch must have the flexibility, with regard to those detainees who remain at Guantanamo, to determine when and where to prosecute them, based on the facts and circumstances of each case and our national security interests, and when and where to transfer them consistent with our national security and our humane treatment policy. Rather than taking steps to bring this chapter of our history to a close, as I have repeatedly called upon the Congress to do, this bill aims to extend it.

The bill also fails to adopt many essential defense reforms, including to force structure, weapons systems, and military health care. Our defense strategy depends on investing every dollar where it will have the greatest effect. My Administration's proposals will accomplish this through critical reforms that divest unneeded force structure, slow growth in compensation, and reduce wasteful overhead. The restrictions in the bill would require the Department of Defense to retain unnecessary force structure and weapons systems that we cannot afford in today's fiscal environment, contributing to a military that will be less capable of responding effectively to future challenges.

Because of the manner in which this bill would undermine our national security, I must veto it.

> BARACK OBAMA.
> THE WHITE HOUSE
> October 22, 2015

President Obama's Veto of the Standards of Performance for Greenhouse Gas Emissions

Following is the text of President Obama's December 18, 2015, veto message on S.J.Res.23, providing relaxation of EPA carbon pollution standards for new power plants.

To the Senate of the United States:

S.J. Res. 23 is a joint resolution providing for congressional disapproval under chapter 8 of title 5 of the United States Code of a rule submitted by the Environmental Protection Agency (EPA) relating to "Standards of Performance for Greenhouse Gas Emissions from New, Modified, and Reconstructed Stationary Sources: Electric Utility Generating Units." This resolution would nullify EPA's carbon pollution standards for new, modified, and reconstructed power plants. Accordingly, I am withholding my approval of this resolution. (The Pocket Veto Case, 279 U.S. 655 (1929)).

Climate change poses a profound threat to our future and future generations. Atmospheric levels of carbon dioxide, a primary greenhouse gas, are higher than they have been in at least 800,000 years. In 2009, EPA determined that greenhouse gas pollution endangers Americans' health and welfare by causing long-lasting changes in the climate that can have, and are already having, a range of negative effects on human health, the climate, and the environment. We are already seeing the impacts of climate change, and established science confirms that we will experience stronger storms, deeper droughts, longer wildfire seasons, and other intensified impacts as the planet warms. The Pentagon has determined that climate change poses immediate risks to our national security.

Power plants are the largest source of greenhouse gas pollution in our country. Although we have limits on other dangerous pollutants from power plants, the carbon pollution standards and the Clean Power Plan ensure that we will finally have national standards to reduce the amount of carbon pollution that our power plants can emit.

The carbon pollution standards will ensure that, when we make major investments in power generation infrastructure, we also deploy available technologies to make that infrastructure as low-emitting as possible. By blocking these standards from taking effect, S.J. Res. 23 would delay our transition to cleaner electricity generating technologies by enabling continued build-out of outdated, high-polluting infrastructure. Because it would overturn carbon pollution standards that are critical to protecting against climate change and ensuring the health and well-being of our Nation, I cannot support the resolution.

To leave no doubt that the resolution is being vetoed, in addition to withholding my signature, I am returning S.J. Res. 23 to the Secretary of the Senate, along with this Memorandum of Disapproval.

BARACK OBAMA.
THE WHITE HOUSE
December 18, 2015

President Obama's Veto of the Carbon Pollution Emission Guidelines

Following is the text of President Obama's December 18, 2015, veto message on S.J.Res.24, nullifying the Clean Power Plan.

To the Senate of the United States:

S.J. Res. 24 is a joint resolution providing for congressional disapproval under chapter 8 of title 5 of the United States Code of a rule submitted by the Environmental Protection Agency (EPA) relating to "Carbon Pollution Emission Guidelines for Existing Stationary Sources: Electric Utility Generating Units."

This resolution would nullify the Clean Power Plan, the first national standards to address climate-destabilizing greenhouse gas pollution from existing power plants. Accordingly, I am withholding my approval of this resolution. (The Pocket Veto Case, 279 U.S. 655 (1929)).

Climate change poses a profound threat to our future and future generations. Atmospheric levels of carbon dioxide, a primary greenhouse gas, are higher than they have been in at least 800,000 years. In 2009, EPA determined that greenhouse gas pollution endangers Americans' health and welfare by causing long-lasting changes in the climate that can have, and are already having, a range of negative effects on human health, the climate, and the environment. We are already seeing the impacts of climate change, and established science confirms that we will experience stronger storms, deeper droughts, longer wildfire seasons, and other intensified impacts as the planet warms. The Pentagon has determined that climate change poses immediate risks to our national security.

The Clean Power Plan is a tremendously important step in the fight against global climate change. It is projected to reduce carbon pollution from power plants by 32 percent from 2005 levels by 2030. It builds on progress States and the power sector are already making to move toward cleaner energy production, and gives States the time and flexibility they need to develop tailored, cost-effective plans to reduce their emissions. By nullifying the Clean Power Plan, S.J. Res. 24 not only threatens ongoing progress toward cleaner energy, but would also eliminate public health and other benefits of up to $54 billion per year by 2030, including thousands fewer premature deaths from air pollution and thousands fewer childhood asthma attacks each year.

The Clean Power Plan is essential in addressing the largest source of greenhouse gas pollution in our country. It is past time to act to mitigate climate impacts on American communities. Because the resolution would overturn the Clean Power Plan, which is critical to protecting against climate change and ensuring the health and well-being of our Nation, I cannot support it.

To leave no doubt that the resolution is being vetoed, in addition to withholding my signature, I am returning S.J. Res. 24 to the Secretary of the Senate, along with this Memorandum of Disapproval.

BARACK OBAMA.
THE WHITE HOUSE
December 18, 2015

President Obama's Veto of the Restoring Americans' Healthcare Freedom Reconciliation Act of 2015

Following is the text of President Obama's January 8, 2016, veto message on H.R.3762, repealing parts of the Affordable Care Act and defunding Planned Parenthood.

To the House of Representatives:

I am returning herewith without my approval H.R. 3762, which provides for reconciliation pursuant to section 2002 of the concurrent resolution on the budget for fiscal year 2016, herein referred to as the Reconciliation Act. This legislation would not only repeal parts of the Affordable Care Act, but would reverse the significant progress we have made in improving health care in

America. The Affordable Care Act includes a set of fairer rules and stronger consumer protections that have made health care coverage more affordable, more attainable, and more patient centered. And it is working. About 17.6 million Americans have gained health care coverage as the law's coverage provisions have taken effect. The Nation's uninsured rate now stands at its lowest level ever, and demand for Marketplace coverage during December 2015 was at an all-time high. Health care costs are lower than expected when the law was passed, and health care quality is higher—with improvements in patient safety saving an estimated 87,000 lives. Health care has changed for the better, setting this country on a smarter, stronger course.

The Reconciliation Act would reverse that course. The Congressional Budget Office estimates that the legislation would increase the number of uninsured Americans by 22 million after 2017. The Council of Economic Advisers estimates that this reduction in health care coverage could mean, each year, more than 900,000 fewer people getting all their needed care, more than 1.2 million additional people having trouble paying other bills due to higher medical costs, and potentially more than 10,000 additional deaths. This legislation would cost millions of hard-working middle-class families the security of affordable health coverage they deserve. Reliable health care coverage would no longer be a right for everyone: it would return to being a privilege for a few.

The legislation's implications extend far beyond those who would become uninsured. For example, about 150 million Americans with employer-based insurance would be at risk of higher premiums and lower wages. And it would cause the cost of health coverage for people buying it on their own to skyrocket.

The Reconciliation Act would also effectively defund Planned Parenthood. Planned Parenthood uses both Federal and nonfederal funds to provide a range of important preventive care and health services, including health screenings, vaccinations, and check-ups to millions of men and women who visit their health centers annually. Longstanding Federal policy already prohibits the use of Federal funds for abortions, except in cases of rape or incest or when the life of the woman would be endangered. By eliminating Federal Medicaid funding for a major provider of health care, H.R. 3762 would limit access to health care for men, women, and families across the Nation, and would disproportionately impact low-income individuals.

Republicans in the Congress have attempted to repeal or undermine the Affordable Care Act over 50 times. Rather than refighting old political battles by once again voting to repeal basic protections that provide security for the middle class, Members of Congress should be working together to grow the economy, strengthen middle-class families, and create new jobs. Because of the harm this bill would cause to the health and financial security of millions of Americans, it has earned my veto.

BARACK OBAMA.
THE WHITE HOUSE
January 8, 2016

President Obama's Veto of the Clean Water Act Jurisdiction Boundaries Rule

Following is the text of President Obama's January 19, 2016, veto message on S.J.Res.22, redefining "Waters of the United States" under the Federal Water Pollution Control Act.

To the Senate of the United States:

I am returning herewith without my approval S.J. Res. 22, a resolution that would nullify a rule issued by the Environmental Protection Agency and the Department of the Army to clarify the jurisdictional boundaries of the Clean Water Act. The rule, which is a product of extensive public involvement and years of work, is critical to our efforts to protect the Nation's waters and keep them clean; is responsive to calls for rulemaking from the Congress, industry, and community stakeholders; and is consistent with decisions of the United States Supreme Court.

We must protect the waters that are vital for the health of our communities and the success of our businesses, agriculture, and energy development. As I have noted before, too many of our waters have been left vulnerable. Pollution from upstream sources ends up in the rivers, lakes, reservoirs, and coastal waters near which most Americans live and on which they depend for their drinking water, recreation, and economic development. Clarifying the scope of the Clean Water Act helps to protect these resources and safeguard public health. Because this resolution seeks to block the progress represented by this rule and deny businesses and communities the regulatory certainty and clarity needed to invest in projects that rely on clean water, I cannot support it. I am therefore vetoing this resolution.

BARACK OBAMA.
THE WHITE HOUSE
January 19, 2016

President Obama's Veto of the Department of Labor's Conflict of Interest Rule

Following is the text of President Obama's June 8, 2016, veto message on H.J.Res.88, nullifying the Department of Labor's final conflict of interest rule.

To the House of Representatives:

I am returning herewith without my approval H.J. Res. 88, a resolution that would nullify the Department of Labor's final conflict of interest rule. This rule is critical to protecting Americans' hardearned savings and preserving their retirement security.

The outdated regulations in place before this rulemaking did not ensure that financial advisers act in their clients' best interests when giving retirement investment advice. Instead, some firms have incentivized advisers to steer clients into products that have higher fees and lower returns—costing America's families an estimated $17 billion a year.

The Department of Labor's final rule will ensure that American workers and retirees receive retirement advice that is in their best interest, better enabling them to protect and grow their savings. The final rule reflects extensive feedback from industry, advocates, and Members of Congress, and has been streamlined to reduce the compliance burden and ensure continued access to advice, while maintaining an enforceable best interest standard that protects consumers. It is essential that these critical protections go into effect. Because this resolution seeks to block the progress represented by this rule and deny retirement savers investment advice in their best interest, I cannot support it. I am therefore vetoing this resolution.

BARACK OBAMA.
THE WHITE HOUSE
June 8, 2016

President Obama's Veto of the Presidential Allowance Modernization Act of 2016

Following is the text of President Obama's July 22, 2016, veto message on H.R.1777, reforming pensions and allowances for former presidents.

To the House of Representatives:

I am returning herewith without my approval H.R. 1777, the "Presidential Allowance Modernization Act of 2016," which would amend the Former Presidents Act of 1958.

I agree with H.R. 1777's goal of reforming the pensions and allowances provided to former Presidents so as to reduce unnecessary costs to taxpayers. But if implemented as drafted, the bill would have unintended consequences. It would impose onerous and unreasonable burdens on the offices of former Presidents, including by requiring the General Services Administration to immediately terminate salaries and benefits of office employees and to remove furnishings and equipment from offices. It would withdraw the General Services Administration's ability to administer leases and negatively impact operations, with unanticipated implications for the protection and security of former Presidents.

My Administration will work with the authors of the bill and other leaders in the Congress, in consultation with the offices of former Presidents, to explore the best ways to achieve these goals going forward. If the Congress returns the bill having appropriately addressed these concerns, I will sign it. For now, I must veto the bill.

BARACK OBAMA.
THE WHITE HOUSE
July 22, 2016

President Obama's Veto of the Justice Against Sponsors of Terrorism Act

Following is the text of President Obama's September 23, 2016, veto message on S.2040, narrowing the scope of foreign sovereign immunity.

To the Senate of the United States:

I am returning herewith without my approval S. 2040, the "Justice Against Sponsors of Terrorism Act: (JASTA), which would, among other things, remove sovereign immunity in U.S. courts from foreign governments that are not designated state sponsors of terrorism.

I have deep sympathy for the families of the victims of the terrorist attacks of September 11, 2001 (9/11), who have suffered grievously. I also have a deep appreciation of these families' desire to pursue justice and am strongly committed to assisting them in their efforts.

Consistent with this commitment, over the past 8 years, I have directed my Administration to pursue relentlessly al-Qa'ida, the terrorist group that planned the 9/11 attacks. The heroic efforts of our military and counterterrorism professionals have decimated al-Qa'ida's leadership and killed Osama bin Laden. My Administration also strongly supported, and I signed into law, legislation which ensured that those who bravely responded on that terrible day and other survivors of the attacks will be able to receive treatment for any injuries resulting from the attacks. And my Administration also directed the Intelligence Community to perform a declassification review of "Part Four of the Joint Congressional Inquiry into Intelligence Community Activities Before and After the Terrorist Attacks of September 11," so that the families of 9/11 victims and broader public can better understand the information investigators gathered following that dark day of our history.

Notwithstanding these significant efforts, I recognize that there is nothing that could ever erase the grief the 9/11 families have endured. My Administration therefore remains resolute in its commitment to assist these families in their pursuit of justice and do whatever we can to prevent another attack in the United States. Enacting JASTA into law, however, would neither protect Americans from terrorist attacks nor improve the effectiveness of our response to such attacks. As drafted, JASTA would allow private litigation against foreign governments in U.S. courts based on allegations that such foreign governments' actions abroad made them responsible for terrorism-related injuries on U.S. soil. This legislation would permit litigation against countries that have neither been designated by the executive branch as state sponsors of terrorism nor taken direct actions in the United States to carry out an attack here. The JASTA would be detrimental to U.S. national interests more broadly, which is why I am returning it without my approval.

First, JASTA threatens to reduce the effectiveness of our response to indications that a foreign government has taken steps outside our borders to provide support for terrorism, by taking such matters out of the hands of national security and foreign policy professionals and placing them in the hands of private litigants and courts.

Any indication that a foreign government played a role in a terrorist attack on U.S. soil is a matter of deep concern and merits a forceful, unified Federal Government response that considers the wide range of important and effective tools available. One of these tools is designating the foreign government in question as a state sponsor of terrorism, which carries with it a litany of repercussions, including the foreign government being stripped of its sovereign immunity before U.S. courts in certain terrorism-related cases and subjected to a range of sanctions. Given these serious consequences, state sponsor of terrorism designations are made only after national security, foreign policy, and intelligence professionals carefully review all available information to determine whether a country meets the criteria that the Congress established.

In contrast, JASTA departs from longstanding standards and practice under our Foreign Sovereign Immunities Act and threatens to strip all foreign governments of immunity from judicial process in the United States based solely upon allegations by private litigants that a foreign government's overseas conduct had some role or connection to a group or person that carried out a terrorist attack inside the United States. This would invite consequential decisions to be made based upon incomplete information and risk having different courts reaching different conclusions about the culpability of individual foreign governments and their role in terrorist activities directed against the United States—which is neither an effective nor a coordinated way for us to respond to indications that a foreign government might have been behind a terrorist attack.

Second, JASTA would upset longstanding international principles regarding sovereign immunity, putting in place rules that, if applied globally, could have serious implications for U.S. national interests. The United States has a larger international presence, by far, than any other country, and sovereign immunity principles protect our Nation and its Armed Forces, officials, and assistance professionals, from foreign court proceedings. These principles also protect U.S. Government assets from attempted seizure by private litigants abroad. Removing sovereign immunity in U.S. courts from foreign governments that are not designated as state sponsors of terrorism, based solely on allegations that such foreign governments' actions abroad had a connection to terrorism-related injuries on U.S. soil, threatens to undermine these longstanding principles that protect the United States, our forces, and our personnel.

Indeed, reciprocity plays a substantial role in foreign relations, and numerous other countries already have laws that allow for the adjustment of a foreign state's immunities based on the treatment their governments receive in the courts of the other state. Enactment of JASTA could encourage foreign governments to act reciprocally and allow their domestic courts to exercise jurisdiction over the United States or U.S. officials—including our men and women in uniform—for allegedly causing injuries overseas via U.S. support to third parties. This could lead to suits against the United States or U.S. officials for actions taken by members of an armed group that received U.S. assistance, misuse of U.S. military equipment by foreign forces, or abuses committed by police units that received U.S. training, even if the allegations at issue ultimately would be without merit. And if any of these litigants were to win judgments—based on foreign domestic laws as applied by foreign courts—they would begin to look to the assets of the U.S. Government held abroad to satisfy those judgments, with potentially serious financial consequences for the United States.

Third, JASTA threatens to create complications in our relationships with even our closest partners. If JASTA were enacted, courts could potentially consider even minimal allegations accusing U.S. allies or partners of complicity in a particular terrorist attack in the United States to be sufficient to open the door to litigation and wide-ranging discovery against a foreign country—for example, the country where an individual who later committed a terrorist act traveled from or became radicalized. A number of our allies and partners have already contacted us with serious concerns about the bill. By exposing these allies and partners to this sort of litigation in U.S. courts, JASTA threatens to limit their cooperation on key national security issues, including counterterrorism initiatives, at a crucial time when we are trying to build coalitions, not create divisions.

The 9/11 attacks were the worst act of terrorism on U.S. soil, and they were met with an unprecedented U.S. Government response. The United States has taken robust and wide-ranging actions to provide justice for the victims of the 9/11 attacks and keep Americans safe, from providing financial compensation for victims and their families to conducting worldwide counterterrorism programs to bringing criminal charges against culpable individuals. I have continued and expanded upon these efforts, both to help victims of terrorism gain justice for the loss and suffering of their loved ones and to protect the United States from future attacks. The JASTA, however, does not contribute to these goals, does not enhance the safety of Americans from terrorist attacks, and undermines core U.S. interests.

For these reasons, I must veto the bill.

BARACK OBAMA.
THE WHITE HOUSE
September 23, 2016

Political Charts

Summary of Presidential Elections, 1789–2016

Year	No. of states	Candidates	Party	Electoral vote	Popular vote
1789[1]	10	**George Washington**	Fed.	69	—[2]
		John Adams	Fed.	34	
1792[1]	15	**George Washington**	Fed.	132	—[2]
		John Adams	Fed.	77	
1796[1]	16	**John Adams**	Fed.	71	—[2]
		Thomas Jefferson	Dem.-Rep.	68	
1800[1]	16	**Thomas Jefferson**	Dem.-Rep.	73	—[2]
		Aaron Burr	Dem.-Rep.	73	
		John Adams	Fed.	65	
		Charles Cotesworth Pinckney	Fed.	64	
1804	17	**Thomas Jefferson**	Dem.-Rep.	162	—[2]
		George Clinton			
		Charles Cotesworth Pinckney	Fed.	64	
		Rufus King			
1808	17	**James Madison**	Dem.-Rep.	122	—[2]
		George Clinton			
		Charles Cotesworth Pinckney	Fed.	64	
		Rufus King			
1812	18	**James Madison**	Dem.-Rep.	128	—[2]
		Elbridge Gerry			
		George Clinton	Fed.	89	
		Jared Ingersoll			
1816	19	**James Monroe**	Dem.-Rep.	183	—[2]
		Daniel D. Tompkins			
		Rufus King	Fed.	34	
		John Howard			
1820	24	**James Monroe**	Dem.-Rep.	231[3]	—[2]
		Daniel D. Tompkins			
1824[4]	24	**John Quincy Adams**	Dem.-Rep.	99	113,122 (30.9%)
		John C. Calhoun			
		Andrew Jackson	Dem.-Rep.	84	151,271 (41.3%)
		Nathan Sanford			
1828	24	**Andrew Jackson**	Dem.-Rep.	178	642,553 (56.0%)
		John C. Calhoun			
		John Quincy Adams	Nat.-Rep.	83	500,897 (43.6%)
		Richard Rush			
1832[5]	24	**Andrew Jackson**	Dem.	219	701,780 (54.2%)
		Martin Van Buren			
		Henry Clay	Nat.-Rep.	49	484,205 (37.4%)
		John Sergeant			
1836[6]	26	**Martin Van Buren**	Dem.	170	764,176 (50.8%)
		Richard M. Johnson			
		William Henry Harrison	Whig	73	550,816 (36.6%)
		Francis Granger			
1840	26	**William Henry Harrison**	Whig	234	1,275,390 (52.9%)
		John Tyler			
		Martin Van Buren	Dem.	60	1,128,854 (46.8%)
		Richard M. Johnson			
1844	26	**James K. Polk**	Dem.	170	1,339,494 (49.5%)
		George M. Dallas			
		Henry Clay	Whig	105	1,300,004 (48.1%)
		Theodore Frelinghuysen			
1848	30	**Zachary Taylor**	Whig	163	1,361,393 (47.3%)
		Millard Fillmore			
		Lewis Cass	Dem.	127	1,223,460 (42.5%)
		William O. Butler			
1852	31	**Franklin Pierce**	Dem.	254	1,607,510 (50.8%)
		William R. King			
		Winfield Scott	Whig	42	1,386,942 (43.9%)
		William A. Graham			
1856[7]	31	**James Buchanan**	Dem.	174	1,836,072 (45.3%)
		John C. Breckinridge			
		John C. Frémont	Rep.	114	1,342,345 (33.1%)
		William L. Dayton			
1860[8]	33	**Abraham Lincoln**	Rep.	180	1,865,908 (39.8%)
		Hannibal Hamlin			
		Stephen A. Douglas	Dem.	12	1,380,202 (29.5%)
		Herschel V. Johnson			
1864[9]	36	**Abraham Lincoln**	Rep.	212	2,218,388 (55.0%)
		Andrew Johnson			
		George B. McClellan	Dem.	21	1,812,807 (45.0%)
		George H. Pendleton			
1868[10]	37	**Ulysses S. Grant**	Rep.	214	3,013,650 (52.7%)
		Schuyler Colfax			
		Horatio Seymour	Dem.	80	2,708,744 (47.3%)
		Francis P. Blair Jr.			
1872	37	**Ulysses S. Grant**	Rep.	286	3,598,235 (55.6%)
		Henry Wilson			
		Horace Greeley	Dem.	—[11]	2,834,761 (43.8%)
		Benjamin Gratz Brown			
1876	38	**Rutherford B. Hayes**	Rep.	185	4,034,311 (47.9%)
		William A. Wheeler			
		Samuel J. Tilden	Dem.	184	4,288,546 (51.0%)
		Thomas A. Hendricks			
1880	38	**James A. Garfield**	Rep.	214	4,446,158 (48.3%)
		Chester A. Arthur			
		Winfield S. Hancock	Dem.	155	4,444,260 (48.2%)
		William H. English			
1884	38	**Grover Cleveland**	Dem.	219	4,874,621 (48.5%)
		Thomas A. Hendricks			
		James G. Blaine	Rep.	182	4,848,936 (48.2%)
		John A. Logan			
1888	38	**Benjamin Harrison**	Rep.	233	5,443,892 (47.8%)
		Levi P. Morton			
		Grover Cleveland	Dem.	168	5,534,488 (48.6%)
		Allen G. Thurman			
1892[12]	44	**Grover Cleveland**	Dem.	277	5,551,883 (46.1%)
		Adlai E. Stevenson			
		Benjamin Harrison	Rep.	145	5,179,244 (43.0%)
		Whitelaw Reid			

Year	No. of states	Candidates	Party	Electoral vote	Popular vote	Year	No. of states	Candidates	Party	Electoral vote	Popular vote
1896	45	**William McKinley** *Garret A. Hobart*	**Rep.**	**271**	**7,108,480 (51.0%)**	1952	48	Dwight D. Eisenhower *Richard M. Nixon*	Rep.	442	33,936,137 (55.1%)
		William J. Bryan *Arthur Sewall*	Dem.	176	6,511,495 (46.7%)			Adlai E. Stevenson II *John J. Sparkman*	Dem.	89	27,314,649 (44.4%)
1900	45	**William McKinley** *Theodore Roosevelt*	**Rep.**	**292**	**7,218,039 (51.7%)**	1956[16]	48	Dwight D. Eisenhower *Richard M. Nixon*	Rep.	457	35,585,245 (57.4%)
		William J. Bryan *Adlai E. Stevenson*	Dem.	155	6,358,345 (45.5%)			Adlai E. Stevenson II *Estes Kefauver*	Dem.	73	26,030,172 (42.0%)
1904	45	**Theodore Roosevelt** *Charles W. Fairbanks*	**Rep.**	**336**	**7,626,593 (56.4%)**	1960[17]	50	John F. Kennedy *Lyndon B. Johnson*	Dem.	303	34,221,344 (49.7%)
		Alton B. Parker *Henry G. Davis*	Dem.	140	5,028,898 (37.6%)			Richard Nixon *Henry Cabot Lodge*	Rep.	219	34,106,671 (49.5%)
1908	46	**William Howard Taft** *James S. Sherman*	**Rep.**	**321**	**7,676,258 (51.6%)**	1964	50*	Lyndon B. Johnson *Hubert H. Humphrey*	Dem.	486	43,126,584 (61.1%)
		William J. Bryan *John W. Kern*	Dem.	162	6,406,801 (43.0%)			Barry Goldwater *William E. Miller*	Rep.	52	27,177,838 (38.5%)
1912[13]	48	**Woodrow Wilson** *Thomas R. Marshall*	**Dem.**	**435**	**6,293,152 (41.8%)**	1968[18]	50*	Richard Nixon *Spiro T. Agnew*	Rep.	301	31,785,148 (43.4%)
		William Howard Taft *James S. Sherman*	Rep.	8	3,486,333 (23.2%)			Hubert H. Humphrey *Edmund S. Muskie*	Dem.	191	31,274,503 (42.7%)
1916	48	**Woodrow Wilson** *Thomas R. Marshall*	**Dem.**	**277**	**9,126,300 (49.2%)**	1972[19]	50*	Richard Nixon *Spiro T. Agnew*	Rep.	520	47,170,179 (60.7%)
		Charles E. Hughes *Charles W. Fairbanks*	Rep.	254	8,546,789 (46.1%)			George McGovern *Sargent Shriver*	Dem.	17	29,171,791 (37.5%)
1920	48	**Warren G. Harding** *Calvin Coolidge*	**Rep.**	**404**	**16,133,314 (60.3%)**	1976[20]	50*	Jimmy Carter *Walter F. Mondale*	Dem.	297	40,830,763 (50.1%)
		James M. Cox *Franklin D. Roosevelt*	Dem.	127	9,140,884 (34.2%)			Gerald R. Ford *Robert Dole*	Rep.	240	39,147,793 (48.0%)
1924[14]	48	**Calvin Coolidge** *Charles G. Dawes*	**Rep.**	**382**	**15,717,553 (54.1%)**	1980	50*	Ronald Reagan *George Bush*	Rep.	489	43,904,153 (50.7%)
		John W. Davis *Charles W. Bryan*	Dem.	136	8,386,169 (28.8%)			Jimmy Carter *Walter F. Mondale*	Dem.	49	35,483,883 (41.0%)
1928	48	**Herbert C. Hoover** *Charles Curtis*	**Rep.**	**444**	**21,411,991 (58.2%)**	1984	50*	Ronald Reagan *George Bush*	Rep.	525	54,455,074 (58.8%)
		Alfred E. Smith *Joseph T. Robinson*	Dem.	87	15,000,185 (40.8%)			Walter F. Mondale *Geraldine Ferraro*	Dem.	13	37,577,137 (40.6%)
1932	48	**Franklin D. Roosevelt** *John N. Garner*	**Dem.**	**472**	**22,825,016 (57.4%)**	1988[21]	50*	George Bush *Dan Quayle*	Rep.	426	48,881,278 (53.4%)
		Herbert C. Hoover *Charles Curtis*	Rep.	59	15,758,397 (39.6%)			Michael S. Dukakis *Lloyd Bentsen*	Dem.	111	41,805,374 (45.6%)
1936	48	**Franklin D. Roosevelt** *John N. Garner*	**Dem.**	**523**	**27,747,636 (60.8%)**	1992	50*	Bill Clinton *Al Gore*	Dem.	370	44,908,233 (43.0%)
		Alfred M. Landon *Frank Knox*	Rep.	8	16,679,543 (36.5%)			George Bush *Dan Quayle*	Rep.	168	39,102,282 (37.4%)
1940	48	**Franklin D. Roosevelt** *Henry A. Wallace*	**Dem.**	**449**	**27,263,448 (54.7%)**	1996	50*	Bill Clinton *Al Gore*	Dem.	379	47,402,357 (49.2%)
		Wendell L. Willkie *Charles L. McNary*	Rep.	82	22,336,260 (44.8%)			Bob Dole *Jack Kemp*	Rep.	159	39,198,755 (40.7%)
1944	48	**Franklin D. Roosevelt** *Harry S. Truman*	**Dem.**	**432**	**25,611,936 (53.4%)**	2000[22]	50*	George W. Bush *Richard B. Cheney*	Rep.	271	50,455,156 (47.9%)
		Thomas E. Dewey *John W. Bricker*	Rep.	99	22,013,372 (45.9%)			Al Gore *Joseph I. Lieberman*	Dem.	266	50,992,335 (48.4%)
1948[15]	48	**Harry S. Truman** *Alben W. Barkley*	**Dem.**	**303**	**24,105,587 (49.5%)**						
		Thomas E. Dewey *Earl Warren*	Rep.	198	21,970,017 (45.1%)						

Year	No. of states	Candidates	Party	Electoral vote	Popular vote	Year	No. of states	Candidates	Party	Electoral vote	Popular vote
2004[23]	50*	**George W. Bush** *Richard B. Cheney*	**Rep.**	**286**	**62,040,610 (50.7%)**	2012	50*	**Barack Obamna** *Joseph R. Biden Jr.*	**Dem.**	**332**	**65,915,796 (51.1%)**
		John Kerry *John Edwards*	Dem.	251	59,028,439 (48.3%)			Mitt Romney *Paul Ryan*	Rep.	206	60,933,500 (47.2%)
2008[24]	50*	**Barack Obama** *Joseph R. Biden Jr.*	**Dem.**	**365**	**69,498,516 (52.9%)**	2016[25]	50*	**Donald J. Trump** *Mike Pence*	**Rep.**	**304**	**62,984,828 (46.1%)**
		John McCain *Sarah Palin*	Rep.	173	59,948,323 (45.7%)			Hilary R. Clinton *Tim Kaine*	Dem.	227	65,853,514 (48.2%)

SOURCE: Harold W. Stanley and Richard G. Niemi, *Vital Statistics on American Politics*, 5th ed. (Washington, DC.: CQ Press, 1995), Table 3-13; Richard M. Scammon, Alice V. McGillivray, and Rhodes Cook, *America Votes 24, 30, 32* (Washington, DC.: Sage/CQ Press, 2009, 2013, 2016).

NOTE: Bold indicates victors. In the elections of 1789, 1792, 1796, and 1800, each candidate ran for the office of president. The candidate with the second-highest number of electoral votes became vice president. For elections after 1800, italic indicates vice presidential candidates.

1. Elections of 1789–1800 were held under rules that did not allow separate voting for president and vice president.

2. Popular vote returns are not shown before 1824 because consistent, reliable data are not available.

3. Monroe ran unopposed. One electoral vote was cast for John Adams and Richard Stockton, who were not candidates.

4. 1824: All four candidates represented Democratic-Republican factions. William H. Crawford received 41 electoral votes, and Henry Clay received 37 votes. Since no candidate received a majority, the election was decided (in Adams's favor) by the House of Representatives.

5. 1832: Two electoral votes were not cast.

6. 1836: Other Whig candidates receiving electoral votes were Hugh L. White, who received 26 votes, and Daniel Webster, who received 14 votes.

7. 1856: Millard Fillmore, Whig-American, received 8 electoral votes.

8. 1860: John C. Breckinridge, Southern Democrat, received 72 electoral votes. John Bell, Constitutional Union, received 39 electoral votes.

9. 1864: Because of the Civil War, 81 electoral votes were not cast.

10. 1868: Because of Reconstruction, 23 electoral votes were not cast.

11. 1872: Horace Greeley, Democrat, died after the election. In the electoral college, Democratic electoral votes went to Thomas Hendricks, 42 votes; Benjamin Gratz Brown, 18 votes; Charles J. Jenkins, 2 votes; and David Davis, 1 vote. Seventeen electoral votes were not cast.

12. 1892: James B. Weaver, People's Party, received 22 electoral votes.

13. 1912: Theodore Roosevelt, Progressive Party, received 86 electoral votes.

14. 1924: Robert M. La Follette, Progressive Party, received 13 electoral votes.

15. 1948: J. Strom Thurmond, States' Rights Party, received 39 electoral votes.

16. 1956: Walter B. Jones, Democrat, received 1 electoral vote.

17. 1960: Harry Flood Byrd, Democrat, received 15 electoral votes.

18. 1968: George C. Wallace, American Independent Party, received 46 electoral votes.

19. 1972: John Hospers, Libertarian Party, received 1 electoral vote.

20. 1976: Ronald Reagan, Republican, received 1 electoral vote.

21. 1988: Lloyd Bentsen, the Democratic vice-presidential nominee, received 1 electoral vote for president.

22. 2000: One District of Columbia elector did not vote.

23. 2004: A Democratic elector in Minnesota cast a vote for Edwards rather than Kerry.

24. 2008: Nebraska split its five electoral votes, with four going to John McCain and one to Barack Obama. Nebraska is one of two states, along with Maine, that splits electoral votes between congressional districts. Nebraska has three. The winner of each district receives that district's vote; the statewide winner receives the other two. The 2008 election was the first time that split electoral vote occurred in either state.

25. 2016: Due to faithless electors, the following individuals received electoral votes: Colin Powell (3), Faith Spotted Eagle (1), John Kasich (1), Ron Paul (1), Bernard Sanders (1).

*Fifty states plus the District of Columbia.

Victorious Party in Presidential Races, 1860–2016

State	1860	1864	1868	1872	1876	1880	1884	1888	1892	1896	1900	1904	1908	1912	1916	1920	1924	1928	1932	1936
Alabama	SD	2	R	R	D	D	D	D	D	D	D	D	D	D	D	D	D	D	D	D
Alaska																				
Arizona														D	D	R	R	R	D	D
Arkansas	SD	2	R	4	D	D	D	D	D	D	D	D	D	D	D	D	D	D	D	D
California	R	R	R	R	R	D6	R	R	D7	R12	R	R	R	PR	D	R	R	R	D	D
Colorado					R	R	R	R	PP	D	D	R	D	D	D	R	R	R	D	D
Connecticut	R	R	R	R	D	R	D	D	D	R	R	R	R	D	R	R	R	R	R	D
Delaware	SD	D	D	R	D	D	D	D	D	R	R	R	R	D	R	R	R	R	R	D
Dist. of Columbia																				
Florida	SD	2	R	R	R	D	D	D	D	D	D	D	D	D	D	D	D	R	D	D
Georgia	SD	2	D	D5	D	D	D	D	D	D	D	D	D	D	D	D	D	D	D	D
Hawaii																				
Idaho									PP	D	D	R	R	D	D	R	R	R	D	D
Illinois	R	R	R	R	R	R	R	R	D	R	R	R	R	D	R	R	R	R	D	D
Indiana	R	R	R	R	D	R	D	R	D	R	R	R	R	D	R	R	R	R	D	D
Iowa	R	R	R	R	R	R	R	R	R	R	R	R	R	D	R	R	R	R	D	D
Kansas		R	R	R	R	R	R	R	PP	D	R	R	R	D	D	R	R	R	D	D
Kentucky	CU	D	D	D	D	D	D	D	D	R13	D	D	D	D	D	D	R	R	D	D
Louisiana	SD	2	D	4	R	D	D	D	D	D	D	D	D	D	D	D	D	D	D	D
Maine	R	R	R	R	R	R	R	R	R	R	R	R	R	D	R	R	R	R	R	R
Maryland	SD	R	D	D	D	D	D	D	D	R	R	D14	D15	D	D	R	R	R	D	D
Massachusetts	R	R	R	R	R	R	R	R	R	R	R	R	R	D	R	R	R	D	D	D
Michigan	R	R	R	R	R	R	R	R	R8	R	R	R	R	PR	R	R	R	R	D	D
Minnesota	R	R	R	R	R	R	R	R	R	R	R	R	R	PR	R	R	R	R	D	D
Mississippi	SD	2	3	R	D	D	D	D	D	D	D	D	D	D	D	D	D	D	D	D
Missouri	D	R	R	D	D	D	D	D	D	D	D	R	D	D	D	R	R	R	D	D
Montana									R	D	D	R	R	D	D	R	R	R	D	D
Nebraska			R	R	R	R	R	R	R	D	D	R	D	D	D	R	R	R	D	D
Nevada		R	R	R	R	D	R	R	PP	D	D	R	D	D	D	R	R	R	D	D
New Hampshire	R	R	R	R	R	R	R	R	R	R	R	R	R	D	D	R	R	R	R	D
New Jersey	R1	D	D	R	D	D	D	D	D	R	R	R	R	D	R	R	R	R	D	D
New Mexico														D	D	R	R	R	D	D
New York	R	R	D	R	D	R	D	R	D	R	R	R	R	D	R	R	R	R	D	D
North Carolina	SD	2	R	R	D	D	D	D	D	D	D	D	D	D	D	D	D	R	D	D
North Dakota									9	R	R	R	R	D	D	R	R	R	D	D
Ohio	R	R	R	R	R	R	R	R	R10	R	R	R	R	D	D	R	R	R	D	D
Oklahoma													D	D	D	R	D	R	D	D
Oregon	R	R	D	R	R	R	R	R	R11	R	R	R	R	D	R	R	R	R	D	D
Pennsylvania	R	R	R	R	R	R	R	R	R	R	R	R	R	PR	R	R	R	R	R	D
Rhode Island	R	R	R	R	R	R	R	R	R	R	R	R	R	D	R	R	R	D	D	D
South Carolina	SD	2	R	R	R	D	D	D	D	D	D	D	D	D	D	D	D	D	D	D
South Dakota									R	D	R	R	R	PR	R	R	R	R	D	D
Tennessee	CU	2	R	D	D	D	D	D	D	D	D	D	D	D	D	R	D	R	D	D
Texas	SD	2	3	D	D	D	D	D	D	D	D	D	D	D	D	D	D	R	D	D
Utah										D	R	R	R	R	D	R	R	R	D	D
Vermont	R	R	R	R	R	R	R	R	R	R	R	R	R	R	R	R	R	R	R	R
Virginia	CU	2	3	R	D	D	D	D	D	D	D	D	D	D	D	D	D	R	D	D
Washington									R	D	R	R	R	PR	D	R	R	R	D	D
West Virginia		R	R	R	D	D	D	D	D	R	R	R	R	D	R16	R	R	R	D	D
Wisconsin	R	R	R	R	R	R	R	R	D	R	R	R	R	D	R	R	PR	R	D	D
Wyoming									R	D	R	R	R	D	D	R	R	R	D	D
Winning Party	R	R	R	R	R	R	D	R	D	R	R	R	R	D	D	R	R	R	D	D

NOTE: With the exception of the District of Columbia, blanks indicate states not yet admitted to the Union. The District of Columbia received the presidential vote in 1961.

KEY: AI-American Independent Party; CU-Constitutional Union Party; D-Democratic Party; PP-People's Party; PR-Progressive (Bull Moose) Party; R-Republican Party; SD-Southern Democratic Party; SR-States' Rights Democratic Party.

1. Four electors voted Republican; three, Democratic.
2. Confederate states did not vote in 1864.
3. Did not vote in 1868.
4. Votes were not counted.
5. Three votes for Greeley not counted.
6. Five electors voted Democratic; one, Republican.
7. Eight electors voted Democratic; one, Republican.
8. Nine electors voted Republican; five, Democratic.
9. One vote each for Democratic, Republican, and People's parties.
10. Twenty-two electors voted Republican; one, Democratic.
11. Three electors voted Republican; one, People's Party.
12. Eight electors voted Republican; one, Democratic.

1940	1944	1948	1952	1956	1960	1964	1968	1972	1976	1980	1984	1988	1992	1996	2000	2004	2008	2012	2016	Dems	Reps	Other
D	D	SR	D	D[18]	D[19]	R	AI	R	D	R	R	R	R	R	R	R	R	R	R	22	14	0
					R	D	R	R	R	R	R	R	R	R	R	R	R	R	R	1	14	0
D	D	D	R	R	R	R	R	R	R	R	R	R	D	R	R	R	R	R	R	8	19	0
D	D	D	D	D	D	D	AI	R	D	R	R	R	D	D	R	R	R	R	R	26	10	0
D	D	D	R	R	R	D	R	R	R	R	R	R	D	D	D	D	D	D	D	16	23	0
R	R	D	R	R	R	D	R	R	R	R	R	R	D	R	R	R	D	D	D	13	22	0
D	D	R	R	R	D	D	D	R	R	R	R	R	D	D	D	D	D	D	D	18	22	0
D	D	R	R	R	D	D	R	R	D	R	R	R	D	D	D	D	D	D	D	21	18	0
						D	D	D	D	D	D	D	D	D	D[26]	D	D	D	D	14	0	0
D	D	D	R	R	R	D	R	R	D	R	R	R	R	D	R	R	D	D	R	22	16	0
D	D	D	D	D	D	R	AI	R	D	D	R	R	D	R	R	R	R	R	R	27	19	0
					D	D	D	R	D	D	R	D	D	D	D	D	D	D	D	13	2	0
D	D	D	R	R	R	D	R	R	R	R	R	R	R	R	R	R	R	R	R	10	21	0
D	D	D	R	R	D	D	R	R	R	R	R	R	D	D	D	D	D	D	D	16	24	0
R	R	R	R	R	R	D	R	R	R	R	R	R	R	R	R	R	D	R	R	8	32	0
R	R	D	R	R	R	D	R	R	R	R	R	D	D	D	D	R	D	D	R	11	29	0
R	R	R	R	R	R	D	R	R	R	R	R	R	R	R	R	R	R	R	R	6	32	0
D	D	D	D	R	R	D	R	R	D	R	R	R	D	D	R	R	R	R	R	24	15	0
D	D	SR	D	R	D	R	AI	R	D	R	R	R	D	D	R	R	R	R	R	23	12	0
R	R	R	R	R	R	D	D	R	R	R	R	R	D	D	D	D	D	D	D	10	30	0
D	D	D	R	R	D	D	R	R	D	D	R	R	D	D	D	D	D	D	D	27	12	0
D	D	D	R	R	D	D	D	D	D	R	R	D	D	D	D	D	D	D	D	20	20	0
D	D	R	R	R	D	D	D	R	R	R	R	R	D	D	D	D	D	D	R	12	27	0
D	D	D	R	R	D	D	D	R	D	D	D	D	D	D	D	D[27]	D	D	D	19	20	0
D	D	SR	D	D	[20]	R	AI	R	D	R	R	R	R	R	R	R	R	R	R	21	13	0
D	D	D	R	R	D	D	R	R	D	R	R	R	D	D	R	R	R	R	R	22	18	0
D	D	D	R	R	R	D	R	R	R	R	R	R	D	R	R	R	R	R	R	11	21	0
R	R	R	R	R	R	D	R	R	R	R	R	R	R	R	R	R	R[28]	R	R	7	31	0
D	D	D	R	R	D	D	R	R	R	R	R	R	D	D	R	R	D	D	D	18	20	0
R	R	R	R	R	R	D	R	R	R	R	R	R	D	D	R	D	D	D	D	12	28	0
D	D	R	R	R	D	D	R	R	R	R	R	R	D	D	D	D	D	D	D	21	19	0
D	D	D	R	R	D	D	R	R	R	R	R	R	D	D	D	R	D	D	D	15	12	0
D	D	R	R	R	D	D	D	R	D	R	R	D	D	D	D	D	D	D	D	21	19	0
D	D	D	D	D	D	D	R[22]	R	D	R	R	R	R	R	R	R	D	R	R	24	14	0
R	R	R	R	R	R	D	R	R	R	R	R	R	R	R	R	R	R	R	R	5	26	0
D	D	D	R	R	R	D	R	R	D	R	R	R	D	D	R	R	D	D	R	12	28	0
D	D	D	R	R	R[21]	D	R	R	R	R	R	R	R	R	R	R	R	R	R	10	18	0
R	R	R	R	R	R	D	R	R	R	R	R	D	D	D	D	D	D	D	D	15	25	0
D	D	R	R	R	D	D	D	R	D	R	R	R	D	D	D	D	D	D	R	13	26	0
D	D	D	R	R	D	D	D	R	D	D	R	D	D	D	D	D	D	D	D	20	20	0
D	D	SR	D	D	D	R	R	R	D	R	R	R	R	R	R	R	R	R	R	21	16	0
R	R	R	R	R	R	D	R	R	R	R	R	R	R	R	R	R	R	R	R	4	27	0
D	D	D[17]	R	R	R	D	R	R	D	R	R	R	D	D	R	R	R	R	R	22	16	0
D	D	D	R	R	D	D	D	R	D	R	R	R	R	R	R	R	R	R	R	23	14	0
D	D	D	R	R	R	D	R	R	R	R	R	R	R	R	R	R	R	R	R	8	23	0
R	R	R	R	R	R	D	R	R	R	R	R	R	D	D	D	D	D	D	D	8	32	0
D	D	D	R	R	R	D	R	R[23]	R	R	R	R	R	R	R	R	D	D	D	22	15	0
D	D	D	R	R	R	D	R	R	R[24]	R	R	D	D	D	D	D	D	D	D	17	14	0
D	D	D	D	R	D	D	D	R	D	D	R	D[25]	D	D	R	R	R	R	R	20	19	0
D	D	D	R	R	D	D	R	R	D	R	R	D	D	D	D	D	D	D	R	15	24	0
D	D	D	R	R	R	D	R	R	R	R	R	R	R	R	R	R	R	R	R	8	24	0
D	D	D	R	R	D	D	R	R	R	R	R	D	D	D	R	D	D	D	R	16	24	0

13. Twelve electors voted Republican; one, Democratic.

14. Seven electors voted Democratic; one, Republican.

15. Six electors voted Democratic; two, Republican.

16. Seven electors voted Republican; one, Democratic.

17. Eleven electors voted Democratic; one, States' Rights.

18. One elector voted for Walter B. Jones.

19. Six of eleven electors voted for Harry F. Byrd.

20. Eight independent electors voted for Byrd.

21. One vote cast for Byrd.

22. Twelve electors voted Republican; one, American Independent.

23. One elector voted Libertarian.

24. One elector voted for Ronald Reagan.

25. One elector voted for Lloyd Bentsen.

26. One elector did not vote.

27. One elector voted for John Edwards.

28. Obama won the vote of one elector.

2012 Presidential Election

State	Total vote	Barack Obama (Democrat)		Mitt Romney (Republican)		Other			Dem.-Rep. Plurality
		Votes	%	Votes	%	Votes	%		
Alabama	2,074,338	759,696	38.4	1,255,925	60.6	22,717	1.1	R	460,229
Alaska	300,495	122,640	40.8	164,676	54.8	13,179	4.4	R	42,036
Arizona	2,299,254	1,025,232	44.6	1,233,654	53.6	40,368	1.8	R	208,422
Arkansas	1,069,468	394,409	36.9	647,744	60.6	27,315	2.6	R	253,335
California	13,038,547	7,854,285	60.2	4,839,958	37.1	344,304	2.6	D	3,014,327
Colorado	2,569,522	1,323,102	51.5	1,185,243	46.1	61,177	2.4	D	137,858
Connecticut	1,558,960	905,083	58.1	634,892	40.7	18,985	1.2	D	270,191
Delaware	413,921	242,584	58.6	165,484	40.0	5,822	1.4	D	77,100
Florida	8,474,179	4,237,756	50.0	4,163,447	49.1	72,976	0.9	D	74,309
Georgia	3,900,050	1,773,827	45.5	2,078,688	53.3	47,535	1.2	R	304,861
Hawaii	434,697	306,658	70.5	121,015	27.8	7,024	1.6	D	185,643
Idaho	652,346	212,787	32.6	420,911	64.5	18,648	2.9	R	208,124
Illinois	5,242,014	3,019,512	57.6	2,135,216	40.7	87,286	1.7	D	884,286
Indiana	2,624,534	1,152,887	43.9	1,420,543	54.1	51,104	2.0	R	267,656
Iowa	1,582,180	822,544	52.0	730,617	46.2	29,019	1.8	D	91,927
Kansas	1,159,971	440,726	38.0	692,634	59.7	26,611	2.3	R	251,908
Kentucky	1,797,212	679,370	37.8	1,087,190	60.5	30,652	1.7	R	407,820
Louisiana	1,994,065	809,141	40.6	1,152,262	57.8	32,662	1.6	R	343,121
Maine	713,180	401,306	56.3	292,276	41.0	19,598	2.8	D	109,030
Maryland	2,707,327	1,677,844	62.0	971,869	35.9	57,614	2.1	D	705,975
Massachusetts	3,167,767	1,921,290	60.7	1,188,314	37.5	58,163	1.8	D	732,976
Michigan	4,730,961	2,564,569	54.2	2,115,256	44.7	51,136	1.1	D	449,313
Minnesota	2,936,561	1,546,167	52.7	1,320,225	45.0	70,169	2.4	D	225,942
Mississippi	1,285,584	562,949	43.8	710,746	55.3	11,889	0.9	R	147,797
Missouri	2,757,323	1,223,323	44.4	1,482,440	53.8	51,087	1.9	R	258,644
Montana	484,048	201,839	41.7	267,928	55.4	14,281	3.0	R	66,089
Nebraska	794,379	302,081	38.0	475,064	59.8	17,234	2.2	R	172,983
Nevada	1,014,918	531,373	52.4	463,567	45.7	19,978	2.0	D	67,806
New Hampshire	710,972	369,561	52.0	329,918	46.4	11,493	1.6	D	39,643
New Jersey	3,640,292	2,125,101	58.4	1,477,568	40.6	37,623	1.0	D	647,533
New Mexico	783,757	415,335	53.0	335,788	42.8	32,635	4.2	D	79,547
New York	7,081,159	4,480,244	63.3	2,489,569	35.2	104,910	1.5	D	1,990,675
North Carolina	4,505,372	2,178,391	48.4	2,270,395	50.4	56,586	1.3	R	92,004
North Dakota	322,627	124,966	58.3	188,320	58.3	9,646	3.0	R	63,354
Ohio	5,580,840	2,827,710	50.7	2,661,433	47.7	91,697	1.6	D	166,277
Oklahoma	1,334,872	443,547	33.2	891,325	66.8	–	–	R	447,778
Oregon	1,789,270	970,488	54.2	754,175	42.1	64,607	3.6	D	216,313
Pennsylvania	5,753,670	2,990,274	52.0	2,680,434	46.6	82,962	1.4	D	309,840
Rhode Island	446,049	279,677	62.7	157,204	35.2	9,168	2.1	D	122,473
South Carolina	1,964,118	865,941	44.1	1,071,645	54.6	26,532	1.4	R	205,704
South Dakota	363,815	145,039	39.9	210,610	57.9	8,166	2.2	R	65,571
Tennessee	2,458,577	960,709	39.1	1,462,330	59.5	35,538	1.5	R	501,621
Texas	7,993,851	3,308,124	41.4	4,569,843	57.2	115,884	1.5	R	1,261,719
Utah	1,017,440	251,813	24.8	740,600	72.8	25,027	2.5	R	488,787
Vermont	299,290	199,239	66.6	92,698	31.0	7,353	2.5	D	106,541
Virginia	3,854,489	1,971,820	51.2	1,822,522	47.3	60,147	1.6	D	149,298
Washington	3,125,516	1,755,369	56.2	1,290,670	41.3	79,450	2.5	D	464,726
West Virginia	670,438	238,269	35.5	417,655	62.3	14,514	2.2	R	179,386
Wisconsin	3,068,434	1,620,985	52.8	1,407,966	45.9	39,483	1.3	D	213,019
Wyoming	249,061	69,286	27.8	170,962	68.6	8,813	3.5	R	101,676
District of Columbia	293,764	267,070	90.9	21,371	7.3	5,313	1.8	D	245,689
Totals	129,085,474	65,915,796	51.1	60,933,500	47.2	2,236,178	1.7	D	4,738,804

NOTE: Percentages are of the total vote.

2012 Electoral Votes and Map

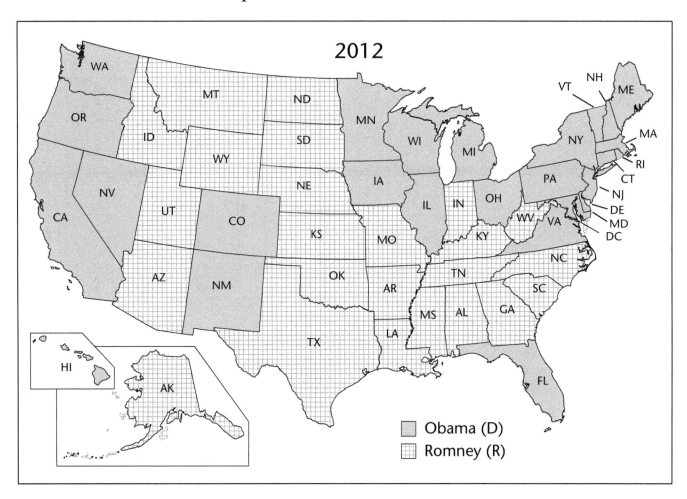

2012

Obama (D)
Romney (R)

KEY: D—Democrat; R—Republican

States	Electoral votes	Obama	Romney	States	Electoral votes	Obama	Romney
Alabama	9	—	9	Montana	3	—	3
Alaska	3	—	3	Nebraska	5	—	5
Arizona	11	—	11	Nevada	6	6	—
Arkansas	6	—	6	New Hampshire	4	4	—
California	55	55	—	New Jersey	14	14	—
Colorado	9	9	—	New Mexico	5	5	—
Connecticut	7	7	—	New York	29	29	—
Delaware	3	3	—	North Carolina	15	—	15
District of Columbia	3	3	—	North Dakota	3	—	3
Florida	29	29	—	Ohio	18	18	—
Georgia	16	—	16	Oklahoma	7	—	7
Hawaii	4	4	—	Oregon	7	7	—
Idaho	4	—	4	Pennsylvania	20	20	—
Illinois	20	20	—	Rhode Island	4	4	—
Indiana	11	—	11	South Carolina	9	—	9
Iowa	6	6	—	South Dakota	3	—	3
Kansas	6	—	6	Tennessee	11	—	11
Kentucky	8	—	8	Texas	38	—	38
Louisiana	8	—	8	Utah	6	—	6
Maine	4	4	—	Vermont	3	3	—
Maryland	10	10	—	Virginia	13	13	—
Massachusetts	11	11	—	Washington	12	12	—
Michigan	16	16	—	West Virginia	5	—	5
Minnesota	10	10	—	Wisconsin	10	10	—
Mississippi	6	—	6	Wyoming	3	—	3
Missouri	10	—	10	Totals	538	332	206

2016 Presidential Election

State	Total vote	Donald J. Trump (Republican)		Hillary Clinton (Democrat)		Other			Dem.-Rep. Plurality
		Votes	%	Votes	%	Votes	%		
Alabama	2,069,514	1,318,255	62.1%	729,547	34.4%	21,712	1.0%	R	588,708
Alaska	289,042	163,387	51.3	116,454	36.6	9,201	2.9	R	46,933
Arizona	2,463,985	1,252,401	48.1	1,161,167	44.6	50,417	1.9	R	91,234
Arkansas	1,087,551	684,872	60.6	380,494	33.7	22,185	2.0	R	304,378
California	13,480,727	4,483,810	31.5	8,753,788	61.5	243,129	1.7	D	4,269,978
Colorado	2,597,689	1,202,484	43.3	1,338,870	48.2	56,335	2.0	R	136,386
Connecticut	1,573,403	673,215	40.9	897,572	54.6	2,616	0.2	D	224,357
Delaware	422,954	185,127	41.7	235,603	53.1	2,224	0.5	D	50,476
Florida	9,204,592	4,617,886	48.6	4,504,975	47.4	81,731	0.9	R	112,911
Georgia	4,016,139	2,089,104	50.4	1,877,963	45.3	49,072	1.2	R	211,141
Hawaii	400,246	128,847	30.0	266,891	62.2	4,508	1.1	D	138,044
Idaho	615,626	409,055	59.2	189,765	27.5	16,806	2.4	R	219,290
Illinois	5,308,022	2,146,015	38.4	3,090,729	55.2	71,278	1.3	D	944,714
Indiana	2,623,835	1,557,286	56.5	1,033,126	37.5	33,423	1.2	R	524,160
Iowa	1,474,644	800,983	51.1	653,669	41.7	19,992	1.3	R	147,314
Kansas	1,115,843	671,018	56.2	427,005	35.7	17,820	1.5	R	244,013
Kentucky	1,847,617	1,202,971	62.5	628,854	32.7	15,792	0.8	R	574,117
Louisiana	1,977,023	1,178,638	58.1	780,154	38.4	18,231	0.9	R	398,484
Maine	695,571	335,593	44.9	357,735	47.8	2,243	0.3	D	22,142
Maryland	2,665,896	943,169	33.9	1,677,928	60.3	44,799	1.6	D	734,759
Massachusetts	3,139,367	1,090,893	32.8	1,995,196	60.0	53,278	1.6	D	904,303
Michigan	4,600,661	2,279,543	47.3	2,268,839	47.0	52,279	1.1	R	10,704
Minnesota	2,779,166	1,323,232	44.9	1,367,825	46.4	88,109	3.0	D	44,593
Mississippi	1,192,666	700,714	57.9	485,131	40.1	6,821	0.6	R	215,583
Missouri	2,691,803	1,594,511	56.4	1,071,068	37.9	26,224	0.9	R	523,443
Montana	465,815	279,240	55.6	177,709	35.4	8,866	1.8	R	101,531
Nebraska	796,506	495,961	58.7	284,494	33.7	16,051	1.9	R	211,467
Nevada	1,080,181	512,058	45.5	539,260	47.9	28,863	2.6	D	27,202
New Hampshire	706,345	345,790	46.5	348,526	46.8	12,029	1.6	D	2,736
New Jersey	3,796,474	1,601,933	41.0	2,148,278	55.0	46,263	1.2	D	546,345
New Mexico	713,899	319,667	40.0	385,234	48.3	8,998	1.1	D	65,567
New York	7,436,921	2,819,534	36.5	4,556,124	59.0	61,263	0.8	D	1,736,590
North Carolina	4,611,438	2,362,631	49.8	2,189,316	46.2	59,491	1.3	R	173,315
North Dakota	316,949	216,794	63.0	93,758	27.2	6,397	1.9	R	123,036
Ohio	5,291,524	2,841,005	51.3	2,394,164	43.2	56,355	1.0	R	446,841
Oklahoma	1,452,992	949,136	65.3	420,375	28.9	83,481	5.7	R	528,761
Oregon	1,857,103	782,403	39.1	1,002,106	50.1	72,594	3.6	D	219,703
Pennsylvania	5,948,480	2,970,733	48.2	2,926,441	47.5	51,306	0.8	R	44,292
Rhode Island	442,507	180,543	38.9	252,525	54.4	9,439	2.0	D	71,982
South Carolina	2,032,807	1,155,389	54.9	855,373	40.7	22,045	1.0	R	300,016
South Dakota	349,243	227,721	61.5	117,458	31.7	4,064	1.1	R	110,263
Tennessee	2,421,637	1,522,925	60.7	870,695	34.7	28,017	1.1	R	652,230
Texas	8,614,176	4,685,047	52.2	3,877,868	43.2	51,261	0.6	R	807,179
Utah	860,303	515,231	45.1	310,676	27.2	34,396	3.0	R	204,555
Vermont	282,090	95,369	30.3	178,573	56.7	8,148	2.6	D	83,204
Virginia	3,810,424	1,769,443	44.4	1,981,473	49.8	59,508	1.5	D	212,030
Washington	3,048,335	1,221,747	36.8	1,742,718	52.5	83,870	2.5	D	520,971
West Virginia	686,345	489,371	67.9	188,794	26.2	8,180	1.1	R	300,577
Wisconsin	2,822,970	1,405,284	47.2	1,382,536	46.5	35,150	1.2	R	22,748
Wyoming	237,296	174,419	68.2	55,973	21.9	6,904	2.7	R	118,446
District of Columbia	302,104	12,723	4.1	282,830	90.9	6,551	2.1	D	270,107
Total	130,718,446	62,985,106		65,853,625		1,879,715			19,417,451

NOTE: Percentages are of the total vote.

2016 Electoral Votes and Map

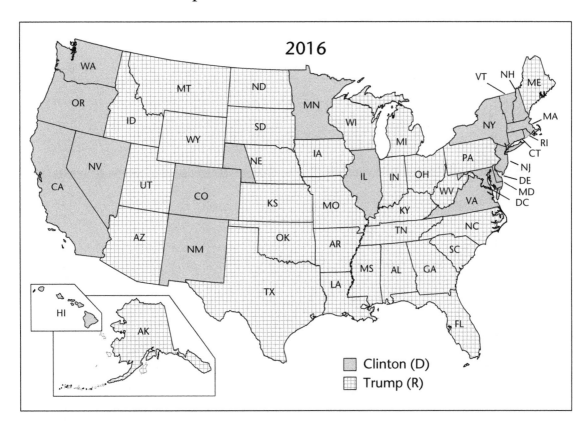

2016

Clinton (D)
Trump (R)

States	Electoral votes	Trump	Clinton	States	Electoral votes	Trump	Clinton
Alabama	9	9	—	Montana	3	3	—
Alaska	3	3	—	Nebraska	5	5	—
Arizona	11	11	—	Nevada	6	—	6
Arkansas	6	6	—	New Hampshire	4	—	4
California	55	—	55	New Jersey	14	—	14
Colorado	9	—	9	New Mexico	5	—	5
Connecticut	7	—	7	New York	29	—	29
Delaware	3	—	3	North Carolina	15	15	—
District of Columbia	3	—	3	North Dakota	3	3	—
Florida	29	29	—	Ohio	18	18	—
Georgia	16	16	—	Oklahoma	7	7	—
Hawaii[1]	4	—	3	Oregon	7	—	7
Idaho	4	4	—	Pennsylvania	20	20	—
Illinois	20	—	20	Rhode Island	4	—	4
Indiana	11	11	—	South Carolina	9	9	—
Iowa	6	6	—	South Dakota	3	3	—
Kansas	6	6	—	Tennessee	11	11	—
Kentucky	8	8	—	Texas[3]	38	36	—
Louisiana	8	8	—	Utah	6	6	—
Maine[2]	4	1	3	Vermont	3	—	3
Maryland	10	—	10	Virginia	13	—	13
Massachusetts	11	—	11	Washington[4]	12	—	8
Michigan	16	16	—	West Virginia	5	5	—
Minnesota	10	—	10	Wisconsin	10	10	—
Mississippi	6	6	—	Wyoming	3	3	—
Missouri	10	10	—	Totals	538	304	227

1. Hawaii does not appoint its electors proportionally. Due to faithless voting, the electoral votes for Hawaii were: for Clinton 3 and Bernie Sanders 1.

2. Maine appoints its electors proportionally. Although Clinton/Kaine won in the First Congressional District and took the state, Trump/Pence won the Second Congressional District. Maine's electoral votes were proportionally awarded accordingly: for Clinton 3 and Trump 1.

3. Texas does not appoint its electors proportionally. Due to faithless voting, the electoral votes for Texas were: for Trump 36, Ron Paul 1, and John Kasich 1.

4. Washington does not appoint its electors proportionally. Due to faithless voting, the electoral votes for Washington were: for Clinton 8, Colin Powell 3, and Faith Spotted Eagle 1.

Distribution of House Seats and Electoral Votes

State	US House Seats							
	1963–1973	1973 Census changes	1973–1983	1980 Census changes	1983–1993	1990 Census changes	1993–2003	2000 Census changes
Alabama	8	−1	7	—	7	—	7	—
Alaska	+ (1)	—	+ (1)	—	+ (1)	—	+ (1)	—
Arizona	3	+ (1)	4	+ (1)	5	+ (1)	6	+ (2)
Arkansas	4	—	4	—	4	—	4	—
California	38	+ (5)	43	+ (2)	45	+ (7)	52	+ (1)
Colorado	4	+ (1)	5	+ (1)	6	—	6	+ (1)
Connecticut	6	—	6	—	6	—	6	−1
Delaware	+ (1)	—	+ (1)	—	+ (1)	—	+ (1)	—
District of Columbia	—	—	—	—	—	—	—	—
Florida	12	+ (3)	15	+ (4)	19	+ (4)	23	+ (2)
Georgia	10	—	10	—	10	+ (1)	11	+ (2)
Hawaii	2	—	2	—	2	—	2	—
Idaho	2	—	2	—	2	—	2	—
Illinois	24	—	24	−2	22	−2	20	−1
Indiana	11	—	11	−1	10	—	10	−1
Iowa	7	−1	6	—	6	−1	5	—
Kansas	5	—	5	—	5	−1	4	—
Kentucky	7	—	7	—	7	−1	6	—
Louisiana	8	—	8	—	8	−1	7	—
Maine	2	—	2	—	2	—	2	—
Maryland	8	—	8	—	8	—	8	—
Massachusetts	12	—	12	−1	11	−1	10	—
Michigan	19	—	19	−1	18	−2	16	−1
Minnesota	8	—	8	—	8	—	8	—
Mississippi	5	—	5	—	5	—	5	−1
Missouri	10	—	10	−1	9	—	9	—
Montana	2	—	2	—	2	−1	+ (1)	—
Nebraska	3	—	3	—	3	—	3	—
Nevada	+ (1)	—	+ (1)	+ (1)	2	—	2	+ (1)
New Hampshire	2	—	2	—	2	—	2	—
New Jersey	15	—	15	−1	14	−1	13	—
New Mexico	2	—	2	+ (1)	3	—	3	—
New York	41	−2	39	+ (5)	34	−3	31	−2
North Carolina	11	—	11	—	11	+ (1)	12	+ (1)
North Dakota	2	−1	+ (1)	—	+ (1)	—	+ (1)	—
Ohio	24	−1	23	−2	21	−2	19	−1
Oklahoma	6	—	6	—	6	—	6	−1
Oregon	4	—	4	+ (1)	5	—	5	—
Pennsylvania	27	−2	25	−2	23	−2	21	−2
Rhode Island	2	—	2	—	2	—	2	—
South Carolina	6	—	6	—	6	—	6	—
South Dakota	2	—	2	−1	+ (1)	—	+ (1)	—
Tennessee	9	−1	8	+ (1)	9	—	9	—
Texas	23	+ (1)	24	+ (3)	27	3	30	+ (2)
Utah	2	—	2	+ (1)	3	—	3	—
Vermont	+ (1)	—	+ (1)	—	+ (1)	—	+ (1)	—
Virginia	10	—	10	—	10	+ (1)	11	—
Washington	7	—	7	+ (1)	8	+ (1)	9	—
West Virginia	5	−1	4	—	4	+ (1)	3	—
Wisconsin	10	−1	9	—	9	—	9	−1
Wyoming	+ (1)	—	+ (1)	—	+ (1)	—	+ (1)	—

NOTE: Table was constructed by CQ Press editors based on the censuses of 1950, 1960, 1970, 1980, 1990, 2000, and 2010.

2003–2013	2010 Census changes	2013–2023	Electoral Votes						
			1952, 1956, 1960	1964, 1968	1972, 1976, 1980	1984, 1988	1992, 1996, 2000	2004, 2008	2012, 2016, 2020
7	—	7	11	10	9	9	9	9	9
+(1)	—	+(1)	3	3	3	3	3	3	3
8	+(1)	9	4	5	6	7	8	10	11
4	—	4	8	6	6	6	6	6	6
53	—	53	32	40	45	47	54	55	55
7	—	7	6	6	7	8	8	9	9
5	—	5	8	8	8	8	8	7	7
+(1)	—	+(1)	3	3	3	3	3	3	3
—	—	—	—	3	3	3	3	3	3
25	+(2)	27	10	14	17	21	25	27	29
13	+(1)	14	12	12	12	12	13	15	16
2	—	2	3	4	4	4	4	4	4
2	—	2	4	4	4	4	4	4	4
19	−1	18	27	26	26	24	22	21	20
9	—	9	13	13	13	12	12	11	11
5	−1	4	10	9	8	8	7	7	6
4	—	4	8	7	7	7	6	6	6
6	—	6	10	9	9	9	8	8	8
7	−1	6	10	10	10	10	9	9	8
2	—	2	5	4	4	4	4	4	4
8	—	8	9	10	10	10	10	10	10
10	−1	9	16	14	14	13	12	12	11
15	−1	14	20	21	21	20	18	17	16
8	—	8	11	10	10	10	10	10	10
4	—	4	8	7	7	7	7	6	6
9	−1	8	13	12	12	11	11	11	10
+(1)	—	1	4	4	4	4	3	3	3
3	—	3	6	5	5	5	5	5	5
3	+(1)	4	3	3	3	4	4	5	6
2	—	2	4	4	4	4	4	4	4
13	−1	12	16	17	17	16	15	15	14
3	—	3	4	4	4	5	5	5	5
29	−2	27	45	43	41	36	33	31	29
13	—	13	14	13	13	13	14	15	15
+(1)	—	1	4	4	3	3	3	3	3
18	−2	16	25	26	25	23	21	20	18
5	—	5	8	8	8	8	8	7	7
5	—	5	6	6	6	7	7	7	7
19	−1	18	32	29	27	25	23	21	20
2	—	2	4	4	4	4	4	4	4
6	+(1)	7	8	8	8	8	8	8	9
+(1)	—	1	4	4	4	3	3	3	3
9	—	9	11	11	10	11	11	11	11
32	+(4)	36	24	25	26	29	32	34	38
3	+(1)	4	4	4	4	5	5	5	6
+(1)	—	1	3	3	3	3	3	3	3
11	—	11	12	12	12	12	13	13	13
9	+(1)	10	9	9	9	10	11	11	12
3	—	3	8	7	6	6	5	5	5
8	—	8	12	12	11	11	11	10	10
+(1)	—	+(1)	3	3	3	3	3	3	3

Party Affiliations in Congress and the Presidency, 1789–2017

Year	Congress	House Majority party	House Principal minority party	Senate Majority party	Senate Principal minority party	President
1789–1791	1st	AD–38	Op–26	AD–17	Op–9	F (Washington)
1791–1793	2nd	F–37	DR–33	F–16	DR–13	F (Washington)
1793–1795	3rd	DR–57	F–48	F–17	DR–13	F (Washington)
1795–1797	4th	F–54	DR–52	F–19	DR–13	F (Washington)
1797–1799	5th	F–58	DR–48	F–20	DR–12	F (J. Adams)
1799–1801	6th	F–64	DR–42	F–19	DR–13	F (J. Adams)
1801–1803	7th	DR–69	F–36	DR–18	F–13	DR (Jefferson)
1803–1805	8th	DR–102	F–39	DR–25	F–9	DR (Jefferson)
1805–1807	9th	DR–116	F–25	DR–27	F–7	DR (Jefferson)
1807–1809	10th	DR–118	F–24	DR–28	F–6	DR (Jefferson)
1809–1811	11th	DR–94	F–48	DR–28	F–6	DR (Madison)
1811–1813	12th	DR–108	F–36	DR–30	F–6	DR (Madison)
1813–1815	13th	DR–112	F–68	DR–27	F–9	DR (Madison)
1815–1817	14th	DR–117	F–65	DR–25	F–11	DR (Madison)
1817–1819	15th	DR–141	F–42	DR–34	F–10	DR (Monroe)
1819–1821	16th	DR–156	F–27	DR–35	F–7	DR (Monroe)
1821–1823	17th	DR–158	F–25	DR–44	F–4	DR (Monroe)
1823–1825	18th	DR–187	F–26	DR–44	F–4	DR (Monroe)
1825–1827	19th	AD–105	J–97	AD–26	J–20	DR (J. Q. Adams)
1827–1829	20th	J–119	AD–94	J–28	AD–20	DR (J. Q. Adams)
1829–1831	21st	D–139	NR–74	D–26	NR–22	DR (Jackson)
1831–1833	22nd	D–141	NR–58	D–25	NR–21	D (Jackson)
1833–1835	23rd	D–147	AM–53	D–20	NR–20	D (Jackson)
1835–1837	24th	D–145	W–98	D–27	W–25	D (Jackson)
1837–1839	25th	D–108	W–107	D–30	W–18	D (Van Buren)
1839–1841	26th	D–124	W–118	D–28	W–22	D (Van Buren)
1841–1843	27th	W–133	D–102	W–28	D–22	W (W. Harrison); W (Tyler)
1843–1845	28th	D–142	W–79	W–28	D–25	W (Tyler)
1845–1847	29th	D–143	W–77	D–31	W–25	D (Polk)
1847–1849	30th	W–115	D–108	D–36	W–21	D (Polk)
1849–1851	31st	D–112	W–109	D–35	W–25	W (Taylor); W (Fillmore)
1851–1853	32nd	D–140	W–88	D–35	W–24	W (Fillmore)
1853–1855	33rd	D–159	W–71	D–38	W–22	D (Pierce)
1855–1857	34th	R–108	D–83	D–40	R–15	D (Pierce)
1857–1859	35th	D–118	R–92	D–36	R–20	D (Buchanan)
1859–1861	36th	R–114	D–92	D–36	R–26	D (Buchanan)
1861–1863	37th	R–105	D–43	R–31	D–10	R (Lincoln)
1863–1865	38th	R–102	D–75	R–36	D–9	R (Lincoln)
1865–1867	39th	U–149	D–42	U–42	D–10	R (Lincoln); R (A. Johnson)
1867–1869	40th	R–143	D–49	R–42	D–11	R (A. Johnson)
1869–1871	41st	R–149	D–63	R–56	D–11	R (Grant)
1871–1873	42nd	R–134	D–104	R–52	D–17	R (Grant)
1873–1875	43rd	R–194	D–92	R–49	D–19	R (Grant)
1875–1877	44th	D–169	R–109	R–45	D–29	R (Grant)
1877–1879	45th	D–153	R–140	R–39	D–36	R (Hayes)
1879–1881	46th	D–149	R–130	D–42	R–33	R (Hayes)
1881–1883	47th	R–147	D–135	R–37	D–37	R (Garfield); R (Arthur)
1883–1885	48th	D–197	R–118	R–38	D–36	R (Arthur)
1885–1887	49th	D–183	R–140	R–43	D–34	D (Cleveland)
1887–1889	50th	D–169	R–152	R–39	D–37	D (Cleveland)
1889–1891	51st	R–166	D–159	R–39	D–37	R (B. Harrison)
1891–1893	52nd	D–235	R–88	R–47	D–39	R (B. Harrison)
1893–1895	53rd	D–218	R–127	D–44	R–38	D (Cleveland)
1895–1897	54th	R–244	D–105	R–43	D–39	D (Cleveland)
1897–1899	55th	R–204	D–113	R–47	D–34	R (McKinley)
1899–1901	56th	R–185	D–163	R–53	D–26	R (McKinley)
1901–1903	57th	R–197	D–151	R–55	D–31	R (McKinley); R (T. Roosevelt)
1903–1905	58th	R–208	D–178	R–57	D–33	R (T. Roosevelt)
1905–1907	59th	R–250	D–136	R–57	D–33	R (T. Roosevelt)
1907–1909	60th	R–222	D–164	R–61	D–31	R (T. Roosevelt)
1909–1911	61st	R–219	D–172	R–61	D–32	R (Taft)
1911–1913	62nd	D–228	R–161	R–51	D–41	R (Taft)
1913–1915	63rd	D–291	R–127	D–51	R–44	D (Wilson)
1915–1917	64th	D–230	R–196	D–56	R–40	D (Wilson)
1917–1919	65th	D–216	R–210	D–53	R–42	D (Wilson)
1919–1921	66th	R–240	D–190	R–49	D–47	D (Wilson)
1921–1923	67th	R–301	D–131	R–59	D–37	R (Harding)
1923–1925	68th	R–225	D–205	R–51	D–43	R (Coolidge)
1925–1927	69th	R–247	D–183	R–56	D–39	R (Coolidge)

Year	Congress	House		Senate		President
		Majority party	Principal minority party	Majority party	Principal minority party	
1927–1929	70th	R–237	D–195	R–49	D–46	R (Coolidge)
1929–1931	71st	R–267	D–167	R–56	D–39	R (Hoover)
1931–1933	72nd	D–220	R–214	R–48	D–47	R (Hoover)
1933–1935	73rd	D–310	R–117	D–60	R–35	D (F. Roosevelt)
1935–1937	74th	D–319	R–103	D–69	R–25	D (F. Roosevelt)
1937–1939	75th	D–331	R–89	D–76	R–16	D (F. Roosevelt)
1939–1941	76th	D–261	R–164	D–69	R–23	D (F. Roosevelt)
1941–1943	77th	D–268	R–162	D–66	R–28	D (F. Roosevelt)
1943–1945	78th	D–218	R–208	D–58	R–37	D (F. Roosevelt)
1945–1947	79th	D–242	R–190	D–56	R–38	D (F. Roosevelt); D (Truman)
1947–1949	80th	R–245	D–188	R–51	D–45	D (Truman)
1949–1951	81st	D–263	R–171	D–54	R–42	D (Truman)
1951–1953	82nd	D–234	R–199	D–49	R–47	D (Truman)
1953–1955	83rd	R–221	D–211	R–48	D–47	R (Eisenhower)
1955–1957	84th	D–232	R–203	D–48	R–47	R (Eisenhower)
1957–1959	85th	D–233	R–200	D–49	R–47	R (Eisenhower)
1959–1961	86th	D–283	R–153	D–64	R–34	R (Eisenhower)
1961–1963	87th	D–263	R–174	D–65	R–35	D (Kennedy)
1963–1965	88th	D–258	R–177	D–67	R–33	D (Kennedy); D (L. Johnson)
1965–1967	89th	D–295	R–140	D–68	R–32	D (L. Johnson)
1967–1969	90th	D–247	R–187	D–64	R–36	D (L. Johnson)
1969–1971	91st	D–243	R–192	D–57	R–43	R (Nixon)
1971–1973	92nd	D–254	R–180	D–54	R–44	R (Nixon)
1973–1975	93rd	D–239	R–192	D–56	R–42	R (Nixon); R (Ford)
1975–1977	94th	D–291	R–144	D–60	R–37	R (Ford)
1977–1979	95th	D–292	R–143	D–61	R–38	D (Carter)
1979–1981	96th	D–276	R–157	D–58	R–41	D (Carter)
1981–1983	97th	D–243	R–192	R–53	D–46	R (Reagan)
1983–1985	98th	D–269	R–165	R–54	D–46	R (Reagan)
1985–1987	99th	D–252	R–182	R–53	D–47	R (Reagan)
1987–1989	100th	D–258	R–177	D–55	R–45	R (Reagan)
1989–1991	101st	D–259	R–174	D–55	R–45	R (G. H.W. Bush)
1991–1993	102nd	D–267	R–167	D–56	R–44	R (G. H.W. Bush)
1993–1995	103rd	D–258	R–176	D–57	R–43	D (Clinton)
1995–1997	104th	R–230	D–204	R–53	D–47	D (Clinton)
1997–1999	105th	R–227	D–207	R–55	D–45	D (Clinton)
1999–2001	106th	R–222	D–211	R–55	D–45	D (Clinton)
2001–2003	107th	R–221	D–212	R–50	D–50	R (G.W. Bush)
2003–2005	108th	R–229	D–205	R–51	D–48	R (G.W. Bush)
2005–2007	109th	R–232	D–202	R–55	D–44	R (G.W. Bush)
2007–2009	110th	D–233	R–202	D–49*	R–49	R (G.W. Bush
2009–2011	111th	D–236	R–199	D–57*	R–41	D (Obama)
2011–2013	112th	R–242	D–193	D–51*	R–47	D (Obama)
2013–2015	113th	R–234	D–201	D–53*	R–45	D (Obama)
2015–2017	114th	R–248	D–192	R–54	D–44*	D (Obama)

SOURCES: U.S. Bureau of the Census, *Historical Statistics of the United States, Colonial Times to 1970* (Washington, DC: Government Printing Office, 1975); and U.S. Congress, Joint Committee on Printing, *Official Congressional Directory* (Washington, DC: Government Printing Office, 1967–); and *America Votes 26–31* (Washington, DC: CQ Press, 2007, 2009, 2011, 2013, 2015).

NOTE: Figures are for the beginning of the first session of each Congress. Key to abbreviations: AD—Administration; AM—Anti-Masonic; D—Democratic; DR—Democratic-Republican; F—Federalist; J—Jacksonian; NR—National Republican; Op—Opposition; R—Republican; U—Unionist; W—Whig.

*The 110th Congress had two independent senators who caucused with the Democrats, giving them control of the chamber that otherwise would have been in Republican control because the vice president at the time was Republican, allowing him to cast a deciding vote in case of a tie. The 111th, 112th, 113th, and 114th Congresses had two independent senators who caucused with the Democrats, thereby increasing their total in the chamber.

113th Congress Special Elections, 2013 Gubernatorial Elections

Special House Elections, 113th Congress

	Vote total	Percent		Vote total	Percent
Illinois 2nd CD—April 9, 2013			**Florida 13th CD—March 11, 2014**		
Robin Kelly (D)	58,834	70.7	David Jolly (R)	88,294	48.5
Paul McKinley (R)	18,387	22.1	Alex Sink (D)	84,877	46.6
South Carolina 1st CD—May 7, 2013			**Florida 19th CD—June 24, 2014**		
Mark Sanford (R)	77,600	54.0	Curt Clawson (R)	66,887	67.0
Elizabeth Colbert-Busch (D)	64,961	45.2	April Freeman (D)	29,294	29.3
Missouri 8th CD—June 4, 2013			**North Carolina 12th CD—November 4, 2014**		
Jason T. Smith (R)	42,141	67.1	Alma Adams (D)	130,096	75.3
Steve Hodges (D)	17,207	27.4	Vince Coakley (R)	42,568	24.7
Louisiana 5th CD—November 16, 2013			**Virginia 7th CD—November 4, 2014**		
Vance McAllister (R)	54,450	59.6	David Brat (R)	148,841	61.7
Neil Riser (R)	36,840	40.4	Jack Trammell (D)	91,236	37.8
Massachusetts 5th CD—December 10, 2013			**New Jersey 1st CD—November 4, 2014**		
Katherine Clark (D)	40,303	66.0	Donald Norcross (D)	93,315	57.4
Frank Addivinola (R)	19,328	31.6	Garry Cobb (R)	64,073	39.4
Alabama 1st CD—December 10, 2013					
Bradley Byrne (R)	36,042	71.0			
Burton LeFlore (D)	14,968	29.0			

Special Senate Elections, 113th Congress

	Vote total	Percent		Vote total	Percent
Massachusetts—June 25, 2013			**South Carolina—November 4, 2014**		
Ed Markey (D)	645,429	54.9	Tim Scott (R)	757,215	61.1
Gabriel Gomez (R)	525,307	44.7	Joyce Dickerson (D)	459,583	37.1
New Jersey—October 16, 2013			**Oklahoma—November 4, 2014**		
Cory Booker (D)	740,742	54.9	James Lankford (R)	557,002	67.9
Steve Lonegan (R)	593,684	44.0	Constance Johnson (D)	237,923	29.0
Hawaii—November 4, 2014					
Brian Schatz (D)	246,770	66.8			
Cam Cavasso (R)	97,983	26.5			

2013 Gubernatorial Elections

	Vote total	Percent		Vote total	Percent
New Jersey			**Virginia**		
Chris Christie (R)	1,278,932	60.3	Terry McAuliffe (D)	1,069,789	47.8
Barbara Buono (D)	809,978	38.2	Ken Cuccinelli (R)	1,013,354	45.2

NOTE: Vote totals are included for all candidates listed on the ballot who received 5 percent or more of the total vote.

2014 Election Returns for Governor, Senate, and House

Following are the official vote returns for the gubernatorial, Senate, and House contests based on figures supplied by the fifty state election boards.

Vote totals are included for all candidates listed on the ballot who received 5 percent or more of the total vote. For candidates who received under 5 percent, consult *America Votes 31 (2013–2014)*, published by CQ Press. The percent column shows the percentage of the total vote cast.

An asterisk (*) indicates an incumbent.

An "X" denotes candidates without major part opposition; no votes were tallied.

KEY: AC—American Constitution; AMI—American Independent; C—Conservative; CNSTP—Constitution; D—Democratic; G—Green; I—Independent; INDC—Independence; L—Liberal; LIBERT—Libertarian; MDE—Moderate; NPA—No Party Affiliation; R—Republican; REF—Reform; WRI—Write-in

An AL indicates an at-large member of Congress in a state with a single congressional district.

		Vote total	Percent
Alabama			
Governor.			
	Robert J. Bentley (R)	750,231	63.6
	Parker Griffith (D)	427,787	36.2
Senate			
	Jeff Sessions (R) *	795,606	97.2
House			
1	Bradley Byrne (R) *	103,320	68.0
	Burton LeFlore (D)	47,913	32.0
2	Martha Roby (R) *	95,073	67.3
	Erick Wright (D)	48,789	34.0
3	Mike Rogers (R) *	103,558	66.0
	Jesse Smith (D)	52,816	34.0
4	Robert Aderholt (R) *	132,831	99.0
5	Mo Brooks (R) *	115,338	74.0
	Mark Bray (Ind)	39,305	26.0
6	Gary Palmer (R)	135,935	76.2
	Mark Lester (D)	42,291	23.7
7	Terri Sewell (D)*	133,687	98.0
Alaska			
Governor.			
	Bill Walker (D)	134,658	48.1
	Sean Parnell (R)	128,435	45.9
Senate			
	Dan Sullivan (R)	135,445	48.0
	Mark Begich (D)	129,431	45.8
House			
AL	Don Young (R)	142,260	50.9
	Forrest Dunbar (D)	114,317	40.9
	Jim McDermott (LIBERT)	21,373	7.6
Arizona			
Governor.			
	Doug Ducey (R)	805,062	53.4
	Fred DuVal (D)	626,921	41.5
Senate			
	John McCain (R)	1,359,267	53.7
	Ann Kirkpatrick (D)	1,031,245	40.8
	Gary Swing (GREEN)	138,634	5.5
House			
1	Ann Kirkpatrick (D) *	97,391	52.6
	Andy Tobin (R)	87,723	47.4
2	Martha McSally (R)	109,704	50.0
	Ron Barber (D) *	109,543	49.9
3	Raúl Grijalva (D) *	58,192	55.7
	Gabby Saucedo Mercer (R)	46,185	44.2
4	Paul Gosar (R) *	122,560	70.0
	Mike Weisser (D)	45,179	25.8
5	Matt Salmon (R) *	124,867	69.6
	James Woods (D)	54,596	30.4
6	David Schweikert (R) *	129,578	64.9
	W. John Williamson (D)	70,198	35.1
7	Ruben Gallego (D)	54,235	74.9
	Joe Cobb (LIBERT)	10,715	14.8
	Rebecca Dewitt (AE)	3,858	5.3

		Vote total	Percent
8	Trent Franks (R) *	128,710	75.4
	Stephen Dolgos (AE)	41,066	24.0
9	Kyrsten Sinema (D) *	88,609	54.7
	Wendy Rogers (R)	67,841	41.9
Arkansas			
Governor.			
	Asa Hutchinson (R)	470,429	55.4
	Mike Ross (D)	352,115	41.5
Senate			
	Tom Cotton (R)	478,819	56.5
	Mark Pryor (D)	334,174	39.4
House			
1	Rick Crawford (R) *	124,139	63.3
	Jackie McPherson (D)	63,555	32.4
2	French Hill (R)	123,073	51.9
	Pat Hays (D)	103,477	43.6
3	Steve Womack (R)	151,630	79.4
	Grant Brand (LIBERT)	39,305	20.6
4	Bruce Westerman (R)	110,789	53.8
	James Lee Witt (D)	87,742	42.6
California			
Governor.			
	Jerry Brown (D)	4,388,368	60.0
	Neel Kashkari (R)	2,929,213	40.0
Senate			
	Kevin de León (D)	1,760,892	56.2
	Bob Huff (R)	1,371,020	43.7
House			
1	Doug LaMalfa (R) *	132,052	61.0
	Heidi Hall (D)	84,320	39.0
2	Jared Huffman (D) *	163,124	75.0
	Dale K. Mensing (R)	54,400	25.0
3	John Garamendi (D) *	79,224	52.7
	Dan Logue (R)	71,036	47.3
4	Tom McClintock (R) *	126,784	60.0
	Art Moore (R)	84,350	40.0
5	Mike Thompson (D) *	129,613	75.7
	James Hinton (NPA)	41,535	24.3
6	Doris Matsui (D) *	97,008	72.7
	Joseph McCray Sr. (R)	36,448	27.3
7	Ami Bera (D) *	92,521	50.4
	Doug Ose (R)	91,066	49.6
8	Paul Cook (R) *	77,480	67.6
	Bob Conaway (D)	37,056	32.4
9	Jerry McNerney (D)*	63,475	52.4
	Antonio "Tony" Amador (R)	57,729	47.6
10	Jeff Denham (R) *	70,582	56.1
	Michael Eggman (D)	55,123	43.9
11	Mark DeSaulnier (D)	117,502	67.3
	Tue Phan (R)	57,160	32.7
12	Nancy Pelosi (D)*	160,067	83.3
	John Dennis (R)	32,197	16.7
13	Barbara Lee (D)*	168,491	88.5
	Dakin Sundeen (R)	21,940	11.5
14	Jackie Speier (D) *	114,389	76.7

		Vote total	Percent
	Robin Chew (R)	34,757	23.3
15	Eric Swalwell (D)*	99,756	69.8
	Hugh Bussell (R)	43,150	30.2
16	Jim Costa (D)*	46,277	50.7
	Johnny Tacherra (R)	44,943	49.3
17	Mike Honda (D)*	69,561	51.8
	Ro Khanna (D)	64,847	48.2
18	Anna Eshoo (D)*	133,060	67.8
	Richard B. Fox (R)	63,326	32.2
19	Zoe Lofgren (D)*	85,888	67.2
	Robert Murray (D)	41,900	32.8
20	Sam Farr (D)*	106,034	75.2
	Ronald Paul Kabat (NPA)	35,010	24.8
21	David Valadao (R) *	45,907	57.8
	Amanda Renteria (D)	33,470	42.2
22	Devin Nunes (R)*	96,053	72.0
	Suzanna "Sam" Aguilera-Marreno (D)	37,289	28.0
23	Kevin McCarthy (R)*	100,317	74.8
	Raul Garcia (D)	33,726	25.2
24	Lois Capps (D)*	103,228	51.9
	Christopher Mitchum (R)	95,566	48.1
25	Steve Knight (R)	60,847	53.3
	Tony Strickland (R)	53,225	46.7
26	Julia Brownley (D)*	87,176	51.3
	Jeff Gorell (R)	82,653	48.7
27	Judy Chu (D)*	75,728	59.4
	Jack Orswell (R)	51,852	40.6
28	Adam Schiff (D)*	91,996	76.5
	Steve Stokes (NPA)	28,268	23.5
29	Tony Cardenas (D)*	50,096	74.6
	William O'Callaghan Leader (R)	17,045	25.6
30	Brad Sherman (D)*	86,568	65.6
	Mark S. Reed (R)	45,315	34.4
31	Pete Aguilar (D)	51,622	51.7
	Paul Chabot (R)	48,162	48.3
32	Grace Napolitano (D)*	50,353	59.7
	Arturo Enrique Alas (R)	34,053	40.3
33	Ted Lieu (D)	108,331	59.2
	Elan Carr (R)	74,700	40.8
34	Xavier Becerra (D)*	44,697	72.5
	Adrienne Nicole Edwards (D)	16,924	27.5
35	Norma Torres (D)	39,502	63.5
	Christina Gagnier (D)	22,753	36.5
36	Raul Ruiz (D)*	72,682	54.2
	Brian Nestande (R)	61,457	45.8
37	Karen Bass (D)*	96,787	84.3
	R. Adam King (D)	18,051	15.7
38	Linda Sánchez (D)*	58,192	59.1
	Benjamin Campos (R)	40,288	40.9

		Vote total	Percent
39	Ed Royce (R)*	91,319	68.5
	Peter O. Anderson (D)	41,906	31.4
40	Lucille Roybal-Allard (D)*	30,208	61.2
	David Sanchez (D)	19,171	38.8
41	Mark Takano (D)*	46,948	56.6
	Steve Adams (R)	35,936	43.4
42	Ken Calvert (R)*	74,540	65.7
	Tim Sheridan (D)	38,850	34.3
43	Maxine Waters (D)*	69,681	71.0
	John Wood Jr. (R)	28,521	29.0
44	Janice Hahn (D)*	59,670	86.7
	Adam Shbeita (PFP)	9,192	13.3
45	Mimi Walters (R)*	106,083	65.1
	Drew E. Leavens (D)	56,819	34.9
46	Loretta Sanchez (D)*	49,738	59.7
	Adam Nick (R)	33,577	40.3
47	Alan Lowenthal (D)*	69,061	56.0
	Andy Whallon (R)	54,309	44.0
48	Dana Rohrabacher (R)*	112,082	64.1
	Suzanne Joyce Savary (D)	62,713	35.9
49	Darrell Issa (R)*	98,161	60.2
	Dave Peiser (D)	64,981	39.8
50	Duncan D. Hunter (R)*	111,997	71.2
	James H. Kimber (D)	45,302	28.8
51	Juan Vargas (D)*	56,373	68.8
	Stephen Meade (R)	25,577	32.2
52	Scott Peters (D)*	98,826	51.6
	Carl DeMaio (R)	92,746	48.4
53	Susan Davis (D)*	87,104	58.8
	Larry A. Wilske (R)	60,940	41.2

Colorado

Governor.

	Vote total	Percent
John Hickenlooper (D)	1,006,433	49.3
Bob Beauprez (R)	938,195	46.0

Senate

Cory Gardner (R)	983,891	48.2
Mark Udall (D)	944,203	46.3

House

1	Diana DeGette (D)*	183,281	65.8
	Martin Walsh (R)	80,682	29.0
	Danny Stroud (I)	5,236	1.9
2	Jared Polis (D)*	196,300	56.7
	George Leing (R)	149,645	43.3
3	Scott Tipton (R)*	163,011	58.0
	Abel Tapia (D)	100,364	35.7
4	Ken Buck (R)	185,292	64.7
	Vic Meyers (D)	83,727	29.2
5	Doug Lamborn (R)*	157,182	59.8
	Irv Halter (D)	105,673	40.2
6	Mike Coffman (R)*	143,467	51.9
	Andrew Romanoff (D)	118,847	43.0
7	Ed Perlmutter (D)*	148,225	55.1
	Don Ytterberg (R)	120,918	44.9

Connecticut

Governor.

Dannel Malloy (D)	554,314	50.8
Thomas C. Foley (R)*	526,295	48.2

Senate

Chris Murphy (D)	815,077	55.1
Linda McMahon (R)	637,857	43.3

House

1	John B. Larson (D)*	135,825	62.3
	Matthew Corey (R)	78,609	36.1
2	Joe Courtney (D)*	141,948	62.3
	Lori Hopkins-Cavanagh (R)	80,837	35.5

		Vote total	Percent
3	Rosa DeLauro (D)*	140,485	66.9
	James E. Brown (R)	69,454	33.1
4	Jim Himes (D)*	106,873	53.8
	Dan Debicella (R)	91,922	46.2
5	Elizabeth Esty (D)*	113,564	53.2
	Mark Greenberg (R)	97,767	45.8

Delaware

Governor.

John Carney (D)	248,404	58.3
Colin Bonini (R)	166,852	39.2

Senate

Chris Coons (D)	130,655	55.8
Kevin Wade (R)	98,823	42.2

House

AL	John Carney (D)*	137,251	59.3
	Rose Izzo (R)	85,146	36.8

Florida

Governor.

Rick Scott (R)	2,865,343	48.1
Charlie Crist (D)	2,801,198	47.1

Senate

Marco Rubio (R)*	4,835,191	52.0
Patrick Murphy (D)	4,122,088	44.3

House

1	Jeff Miller (R)	165,086	70.2
	Jim Bryan (D)	54,976	23.4
	Mark Wichern (NPA)	15,281	6.5
2	Gwen Graham (D)	126,096	50.5
	Steve Southerland (R)*	123,262	49.4
3	Ted Yoho (R)	148,691	65.0
	Marihelen Wheeler (D)	73,910	32.3
4	Ander Crenshaw (R)	177,877	78.3
	Paula Moser-Bartlett (NPA)	35,663	15.7
	Gary L. Koniz (NPA)	13,690	6.0
5	Corrine Brown (D)	112,340	65.5
	Glo Smith (R)	59,237	34.5
6	Ron DeSantis (R)	166,254	62.5
	David Cox (D)	99,563	37.5
7	John Mica (R)	144,474	63.6
	Wes Neuman (D)	73,011	32.1
8	Bill Posey (R)	180,728	65.8
	Gabriel Rothblatt (D)	93,724	34.1
9	Alan Grayson (D)	93,850	54.0
	Carol Platt (R)	74,963	43.1
10	Daniel Webster (R)	143,128	61.5
	Michael McKenna (D)	89,426	38.5
11	Rich Nugent (R)	181,508	66.7
	Dave Koller (D)	90,786	33.3
12	Gus Bilirakis (R)*	X	X
13	David Jolly (R)	168,172	75.2
	Lucas Overby (LIBERT)	55,318	24.7
14	Kathy Castor (D)*	X	X
15	Dennis A. Ross (R)	128,750	60.3
	Alan Cohn (D)	84,832	39.7
16	Vern Buchanan (R)	169,126	61.5
	Henry Lawrence (D)	105,483	38.4
17	Tom Rooney (R)	141,493	63.2
	Will Bronson (D)	82,263	36.8
18	Patrick Murphy (D)	151,478	59.8
	Carl J. Domino (R)	101,896	40.2
19	Curt Clawson (R)	159,354	64.6
	April Freeman (D)	80,824	32.7
20	Alcee Hastings (D)	128,498	81.6
	Jay Bonner (R)	28,968	18.4
21	Ted Deutch (D)	153,395	99.6
22	Lois Frankel (D)	125,404	58.0
	Paul Spain (R)	90,685	42.0
23	Debbie Wasserman Schultz (D)	103,269	62.7

		Vote total	Percent
	Joseph "Joe" Kaufman (R)	61,519	37.3
24	Frederica Wilson (D)	129,192	86.2
	Dufirstson Julio Neree (R)	15,239	10.2
25	Mario Diaz-Balart (R)*	X	X
26	Carlos Curbelo (R)	83,031	51.5
	Joe García (D)*	78,306	48.5
27	Ileana Ros-Lehtinen (R)*	X	X

Georgia

Governor.

Nathan Deal (R)*	1,341,161	52.8
Jason Carter (D)	1,138,476	44.8

Senate

David Perdue (R)	1,358,088	52.9
Michelle Nunn (D)	1,160,811	45.2

House

1	Buddy Carter (R)	95,337	60.9
	Brian Reese (D)	61,175	39.1
2	Sanford Bishop (D)*	96,363	59.2
	Greg Duke (R)	66,357	40.9
3	Lynn Westmoreland (R)*	156,277	100.0
4	Hank Johnson (D)*	161,211	100.0
5	John Lewis (D)*	170,236	100.0
6	Tom Price (R)*	139,018	66.0
	Robert Montigel (D)	71,486	34.0
7	Rob Woodall (R)*	113,557	65.4
	Thomas Wight (D)	60,112	34.6
8	Austin Scott (R)*	129,938	100.0
9	Doug Collins (R)*	146,039	80.7
	David Vogel (D)	34,988	19.3
10	Jody Hice (R)	130,703	66.5
	Ken Dious (D)	65,777	33.5
11	Barry Loudermilk (R)	161,532	100.0
12	Rick Allen (R)	91,336	54.8
	John Barrow (D)*	75,478	45.3
13	David Scott (D)*	159,445	100.0
14	Tom Graves (R)	118,782	100.0

Hawaii

Governor.

David Ige (D)	181,106	49.0
Duke Aiona (R)	135,775	36.7
Mufi Hannemann (I)	42,934	11.6

Senate

Brian Schatz (D)	246,827	69.8
Campbell Cavasso (R)	98,006	27.8

House

1	Mark Takai (D)	93,390	51.2
	Charles Djou (R)	86,454	47.4
2	Tulsi Gabbard (D)*	142,010	78.7
	Kawika Crowley (R)	33,630	18.6

Idaho

Governor.

C. L. "Butch" Otter (R)*	235,405	53.5
A. J. Balukoff (D)	169,556	38.6

Senate

Jim Risch (R)	285,596	65.3
Nels Mitchell (D)	151,574	34.7

House

1	Raúl Labrador (R)*	143,580	65.01
	Shirley Ringo (D)	77,277	34.99
2	Mike Simpson (R)*	131,492	61.36
	Richard H. Stallings (D)	82,801	38.6

Illinois

Governor.

Bruce Rauner (R)	1,823,627	50.3
Pat Quinn (D)*	1,681,343	46.4

NOTE: *In Florida in a district where a candidate had no opposition, including write-ins, no vote was taken.*

		Vote total	Percent
Senate			
	Dick Durbin (D)	1,929,637	53.5
	Jim Oberweis (R)	1,538,522	42.7
House			
1	Bobby Rush (D)*	162,268	73.1
	Jimmy Lee Tillman (R)	59,749	26.9
2	Robin Kelly (D)*	160,337	78.5
	Eric Wallace (R)	43,799	21.4
3	Dan Lipinski (D)*	116,764	64.6
	Sharon Brannigan (R)	64,091	35.4
4	Luis Gutiérrez (D)*	79,666	78.2
	Hector Concepción (R)	22,278	21.9
5	Mike Quigley (D)*	116,364	63.2
	Vince Kolber (R)	56,350	30.6
	Nancy Wade (GREEN)	11,305	6.1
6	Peter Roskam (R)*	160,287	67.1
	Michael Mason (D)	78,465	32.9
7	Danny K. Davis (D)*	155,110	85.1
	Robert Bumpers (R)	27,168	14.9
8	Tammy Duckworth (D)*	84,178	55.7
	Larry Kaifesh (R)	66,878	44.3
9	Jan Schakowsky (D)*	141,000	66.1
	Susanne Atanus (R)	72,384	33.9
10	Robert Dold (R)	95,992	51.3
	Brad Schneider (D)*	91,136	48.7
11	Bill Foster (D)*	93,436	53.5
	Darlene Senger (R)	81,335	46.5
12	Mike Bost (R)	110,038	52.5
	William Enyart (D)*	87,860	41.9
	Paula Bradshaw (GREEN)	11,840	5.7
13	Rodney Davis (R)*	123,337	58.7
	Ann Callis (D)	86,935	41.3
14	Randy Hultgren (R)*	145,369	65.4
	Dennis Anderson (D)	76,861	34.6
15	John Shimkus (R)*	166,274	74.9
	Eric Thorsland (D)	55,652	25.1
16	Adam Kinzinger (R)*	153,388	70.6
	Randall Olsen (D)	63,810	29.4
17	Cheri Bustos (D)*	110,560	55.5
	Bobby Schilling (R)	88,785	44.5
18	Aaron Schock (R)*	184,363	74.7
	Darrel Miller (D)	62,377	25.3

Indiana

		Vote total	Percent
House			
1	Pete Visclosky (D)*	86,579	60.9
	Mark Leyva (R)	51,000	35.8
2	Jackie Walorski (R)*	85,583	58.9
	Joe Bock (D)	55,590	38.3
3	Marlin Stutzman (R)*	97,892	65.8
	Justin Kuhnle (D)	39,771	26.7
	Scott Wise (LIBERT)	11,130	7.5
4	Todd Rokita (R)*	94,998	66.9
	John Dale (D)	47,056	33.1
5	Susan Brooks (R)*	105,277	65.2
	Shawn Denney (D)	49,756	30.8
6	Luke Messer (R)*	102,187	65.9
	Susan Hall Heitzman (D)	45,509	29.4
7	Andre Carson (D)*	61,443	54.7
	Catherine Ping (R)	46,887	41.8
8	Larry Bucshon (R)*	103,344	60.3
	Tom Spangler (D)	61,384	35.8
9	Todd Young (R)*	101,594	62.2
	Bill Bailey (D)	55,016	33.7

Iowa

		Vote total	Percent
Governor.			
	Terry Branstad (R)*	666,023	59.0
	Jack Hatch (D)	420,778	37.3

		Vote total	Percent
Senate			
	Joni Ernst (R)	588,575	52.1
	Bruce Braley (D)	494,370	43.8
House			
1	Rod Blum (R)	147,762	51.1
	Pat Murphy (D)	141,145	48.8
2	Dave Loebsack (D)*	143,431	52.5
	Mariannette Miller-Meeks (R)	129,455	47.4
3	David Young (R)	148,814	52.8
	Staci Appel (D)	119,109	42.2
4	Steve King (R)*	169,834	61.6
	Jim Mowrer (D)	105,504	38.3

Kansas

		Vote total	Percent
Governor.			
	Sam Brownback (R)*	433,196	49.8
	Paul Davis (D)	401,100	46.1
Senate			
	Pat Roberts (R)	460,350	53.1
	Greg Orman (I)	368,372	42.5
House			
1	Tim Huelskamp (R)*	138,764	68.0
	James Sherow (D)	65,397	32.0
2	Lynn Jenkins (R)*	128,742	57.0
	Margie Wakefield (D)	87,153	38.6
3	Kevin Yoder (R)*	134,493	60.0
	Kelly Kultala (D)	89,584	40.0
4	Mike Pompeo (R)*	138,757	66.7
	Perry Schuckman (D)	69,396	33.3

Kentucky

		Vote total	Percent
Senate			
	Mitch McConnell (R)	806,787	56.2
	Alison Lundergan Grimes (D)	584,698	40.7
House			
1	Ed Whitfield (R)*	173,022	73.1
	Charles Kendall Hatchett (D)	63,596	26.9
2	Brett Guthrie (R)*	156,936	69.2
	Ron Leach (D)	69,898	30.8
3	John Yarmuth (D)*	157,056	63.5
	Michael MacFarlane (R)	87,981	35.6
4	Thomas Massie (R)*	150,464	67.7
	Peter Newberry (D)	71,694	32.3
5	Hal Rogers (R)*	171,350	78.3
	Kenneth Stepp (D)	47,617	21.7
6	Andy Barr (R)*	147,404	60.0
	Elisabeth Jensen (D)	98,290	40.0

Louisiana

		Vote total	Percent
Senate			
	Bill Cassidy (R)	712,379	55.9
	Mary Landrieu (D)	561,210	44.1
House			
1	Steve Scalise (R)*	189,250	77.6
	M. V. "Vinny" Mendoza (D)	24,761	10.2
	Lee A. Dugas (D)	21,286	8.7
2	Cedric Richmond (D)*	152,201	68.7
	Gary Landrieu (D)	37,805	17.1
	David Brooks (I)	16,327	7.4
	Samuel Davenport (LIBERT)	15,237	6.9
3	Charles Boustany (R)*	185,867	78.7
	Russell Richard (I)	28,342	12.0
	Bryan Barrilleaux (R)	22,059	9.3
4	John Fleming (R)*	152,683	73.4
	Randall Lord (LIBERT)	55,236	26.6

		Vote total	Percent
5	Ralph Abraham (R)	134,616	64.2
	Jamie Mayo (D)	75,006	35.8
6	Garret Graves (R)	139,209	62.4
	Edwin Edwards (D)	83,781	37.6

Maine

		Vote total	Percent
Governor.			
	Paul LePage (R)*	294,533	48.2
	Mike Michaud (D)	265,125	43.4
	Eliot Cutler (I)	51,518	8.4
Senate			
	Susan Collins (R)*	413,495	68.5
	Shenna Bellows (D)	190,244	31.5
House			
1	Chellie Pingree (D)*	186,674	60.4
	Isaac J. Misiuk (R)	94,751	30.7
	Richard P. Murphy (I)	27,410	8.9
2	Bruce Poliquin (R)	133,320	47.0
	Emily Ann Cain (D)	118,568	41.8
	Blaine Richardson (I)	31,337	11.1

Maryland

		Vote total	Percent
Governor.			
	Larry Hogan (R)	884,400	51.0
	Anthony G. Brown (D)	818,890	47.2
House			
1	Andrew P. Harris (R)*	176,342	70.4
	Bill Tilghman (D)	73,843	29.5
2	Dutch Ruppersberger (D)*	120,412	61.3
	David Banach (R)	70,411	35.8
3	John Sarbanes (D)*	128,594	59.5
	Charles A. Long (R)	87,029	40.3
4	Donna Edwards (D)*	134,628	70.1
	Nancy Hoyt (R)	54,217	28.2
5	Steny Hoyer (D)*	144,725	64.0
	Chris Chaffee (R)	80,752	35.7
6	John Delaney (D)*	94,704	49.7
	Dan Bongino (R)	91,930	48.2
7	Elijah Cummings (D)*	144,639	69.7
	Corrogan R. Vaughn (R)	55,860	27.2
8	Chris Van Hollen (D)*	136,722	60.7
	Dave Wallace (R)	87,859	39.0

Massachusetts

		Vote total	Percent
Governor.			
	Charlie Baker (R)	1,044,573	48.4
	Martha Coakley (D)	1,004,408	46.5
Senate			
	Ed Markey (D)*	1,289,944	61.9
	Brian Herr (R)	791,950	38.0
House			
1	Richard Neal (D)*	167,612	98.0
2	Jim McGovern (D)*	169,640	98.2
3	Niki Tsongas (D)*	139,104	63.0
	Ann Wofford (R)	81,638	37.0
4	Joseph P. Kennedy III (D)*	184,158	97.9
5	Katherine Clark (D)*	182,100	98.3
6	Seth Moulton (D)	149,638	55.0
	Richard Tisei (R)	111,989	41.1
7	Mike Capuano (D)*	142,133	98.3
8	Stephen Lynch (D)*	200,644	98.7
9	Bill Keating (D)*	140,413	55.0
	John Chapman (R)	114,971	45.0

Michigan

		Vote total	Percent
Governor.			
	Rick Snyder (R)*	1,605,034	50.9
	Mark Schauer (D)	1,476,904	46.8
Senate			
	Gary Peters (D)	1,704,936	54.6
	Terri Lynn Land (R)	1,290,199	41.3

NOTE: *Iowa's 5th district became obsolete for the 113th Congress in 2013.*

		Vote total	Percent
House			
1	Dan Benishek (R)*	130,414	52.1
	Jerry Cannon (D)	113,263	45.3
2	Bill Huizenga (R)*	135,568	63.6
	Dean Vanderstelt (D)	70,851	33.3
3	Justin Amash (R)*	125,754	57.9
	Bob Goodrich (D)	84,720	39.0
4	John Moolenaar (R)	123,962	56.5
	Jeff Holmes (D)	85,777	39.1
5	Dan Kildee (D)*	148,182	66.7
	Allen Hardwick (R)	69,222	31.2
6	Fred Upton (R)*	116,801	55.9
	Paul Clements (D)	84,391	40.4
7	Tim Walberg (R)*	119,564	53.5
	Pam Byrnes (D)	92,083	41.2
8	Mike Bishop (R)	132,739	54.6
	Eric Schertzing (D)	102,269	42.1
9	Sander Levin (D)*	136,342	60.4
	George Brikho (R)	81,470	36.1
10	Candice Miller (R)*	157,069	68.7
	Chuck Stadler (D)	67,143	29.4
11	Dave Trott (R)	140,435	55.9
	Bobby McKenzie (D)	101,681	40.5
12	Debbie Dingell (D)	134,346	65.0
	Terry Bowman (R)	64,716	31.3
13	John Conyers (D)*	132,710	79.5
	Jeff Gorman (R)	27,234	16.3
14	Brenda Lawrence (D)	165,272	77.8
	Christina Barr (R)	41,801	19.7

Minnesota

		Vote total	Percent
Governor.			
	Mark Dayton (D)*	989,113	50.1
	Jeff Johnson (R)	879,257	44.5
Senate			
	Al Franken (D)	1,053,205	53.2
	Mike McFadden (R)	850,227	42.9
House			
1	Tim Walz (D)*	122,851	54.2
	Jim Hagedorn (R)	103,536	45.7
2	John Kline (R)*	137,778	56.0
	Mike Obermueller (D)	95,565	38.9
	Paula Overby (I)	12,319	5.0
3	Erik Paulsen (R)*	167,515	62.1
	Sharon Sund (D)	101,846	37.8
4	Betty McCollum (D)*	147,857	61.2
	Sharna Wahlgren (R)	79,492	32.2
	Dave Thomas (I)	14,059	5.8
5	Keith Ellison (D)*	167,079	70.8
	Doug Daggett (R)	56,577	24.0
	Lee Bauer (I)	12,001	5.1
6	Tom Emmer (R)	133,328	56.3
	Joe Perske (D)	90,926	38.4
	John Denney (I)	12,457	5.3
7	Collin Peterson (D)*	130,546	54.2
	Torrey Westrom (R)	109,955	45.7
8	Rick Nolan (D)*	129,090	48.5
	Stewart Mills III (R)	125,358	47.1

Mississippi

		Vote total	Percent
Senate			
	Thad Cochran (R)*	378,481	59.9
	Travis Childers (D)	239,439	37.9
House			
1	Alan Nunnelee (R)*	102,622	67.9
	Ron Dickey (D)	43,713	28.9
2	Bennie Thompson (D)*	100,688	67.7
	Troy Ray (I)	36,465	24.5
	Shelley Shoemaker (REF)	11,493	7.7
3	Gregg Harper (R)*	117,771	68.9
	Doug Magee (D)	47,744	27.9
4	Steven Palazzo (R)*	108,776	69.9
	Matt Moore (D)	37,869	24.3

Missouri

		Vote total	Percent
House			
1	Lacy Clay (D)*	119,315	73.0
	Daniel J. Elder (R)	35,273	21.6

		Vote total	Percent
	Robb E. Cunningham (LIBERT)	8,906	5.5
2	Ann Wagner (R)*	148,191	64.1
	Arthur Lieber (D)	75,384	32.6
3	Blaine Luetkemeyer (R)*	130,940	68.3
	Courtney Denton (D)	52,021	27.2
4	Vicky Hartzler (R)*	120,014	68.1
	Nate Irvin (D)	46,464	26.4
	Herschel L. Young (LIBERT)	9,793	5.6
5	Emanuel Cleaver II (D)*	79,256	51.6
	Jacob Turk (R)	69,071	45.0
6	Sam Graves (R)*	124,616	66.7
	W. A. "Bill" Hedge (D)	55,157	29.5
7	Billy Long (R)*	104,054	63.5
	Jim Evans (D)	47,282	28.8
	Kevin Craig (LIBERT)	12,584	7.7
8	Jason Smith (R)*	106,124	66.7
	Barbara Stocker (D)	38,721	24.3

Montana

		Vote total	Percent
Senate			
	Steve Daines (R)	210,863	57.9
	Amanda Curtis (D)	145,601	40.0
House			
AL	Ryan Zinke (R)	203,871	55.4
	John Lewis (D)	148,690	40.4

Nebraska

		Vote total	Percent
Governor.			
	Pete Ricketts (R)	308,751	57.2
	Chuck Hassebrook (D)	211,905	38.9
Senate			
	Ben Sasse (R)	347,636	64.5
	David Domina (D)	170,127	31.5
House			
1	Jeff Fortenberry (R)*	123,219	68.8
	Dennis Crawford (D)	55,838	31.2
2	Brad Ashford (D)	83,872	49.0
	Lee Terry (R)*	78,157	45.7
3	Adrian Smith (R)*	139,440	75.4
	Mark Sullivan (D)	45,524	24.6

Nevada

		Vote total	Percent
Governor.			
	Brian Sandoval (R)	386,340	70.6
	Bob Goodman (D)	130,722	23.9
House			
1	Dina Titus (D)*	45,643	57.0
	Annette Teijeiro (R)	30,413	38.0
2	Mark Amodei (R)*	122,402	66.0
	Kristen Spees (D)	52,016	28.0
3	Joe Heck (R)*	88,528	61.0
	Erin Bilbray (D)	52,644	36.0
4	Cresent Hardy (R)	63,466	49.0
	Steven Horsford (D)*	59,844	46.0

New Hampshire

		Vote total	Percent
Governor.			
	Maggie Hassan (D)*	254,666	52.5
	Walt Havenstein (R)	229,610	47.3
Senate			
	Jeanne Shaheen (D)*	251,184	51.5
	Scott Brown (R)	235,347	48.2
House			
1	Frank Guinta (R)	125,508	51.7
	Carol Shea-Porter (D)*	116,769	48.1
2	Ann McLane Kuster (D)*	130,679	54.9
	Marilinda Garcia (R)	106,857	44.9

New Jersey

		Vote total	Percent
Senate			
	Cory Booker (D)*	1,043,866	55.8
	Jeff Bell (R)	791,297	42.3
House			
1	Donald Norcross (D)	93,315	57.4
	Garry Cobb (R)	64,073	39.4
2	Frank LoBiondo (R)*	108,875	61.5
	Bill Hughes (D)	66,026	37.3

		Vote total	Percent
3	Tom MacArthur (R)	100,471	54.0
	Aimee Belgard (D)	82,537	44.4
4	Chris Smith (R)*	118,826	68.0
	Ruben M. Scolavino (D)	54,415	31.1
5	Scott Garrett (R)*	104,678	55.4
	Roy Cho (D)	81,808	43.3
6	Frank Pallone (D)*	72,190	59.9
	Anthony E. Wilkinson (R)	46,891	38.9
7	Leonard Lance (R)*	104,287	59.3
	Janice E. Kovach (D)	68,232	38.8
8	Albio Sires (D)*	61,510	77.4
	Jude Anthony Tiscornia (R)	15,141	19.0
9	Bill Pascrell (D)*	82,498	68.5
	Dierdre G. Paul (R)	36,246	30.1
10	Donald Payne Jr. (D)*	95,734	85.4
	Yolanda Dentley (R)	14,154	12.6
11	Rodney Frelinghuysen (R)*	109,455	62.6
	Mark Dunec (D)	65,477	37.4
12	Bonnie Watson Coleman (D)	90,430	61.0
	Alieta Eck (R)	54,168	36.5

New Mexico

		Vote total	Percent
Governor.			
	Susana Martinez (R)*	288,549	57.3
	Gary King (D)	214,636	42.7
Senate			
	Tom Udall (D)*	286,409	55.6
	Allen Weh (R)	229,097	44.4
House			
1	Michelle Lujan Grisham (D)*	105,474	58.6
	Michael Frese (R)	74,558	41.4
2	Steve Pearce (R)	95,209	64.4
	Rocky Lara (D)	52,499	35.5
3	Ben R. Lujan (D)*	113,249	61.5
	Jefferson Byrd (R)	70,775	38.5

New York

		Vote total	Percent
Governor.			
	Andrew Cuomo (D)*	2,069,480	54.2
	Rob Astorino (R)	1,537,077	40.3
House			
1	Lee Zeldin (R)	94,035	53.2
	Tim Bishop (D)*	78,722	44.6
2	Peter T. King (R)*	95,177	64.9
	Patricia Maher (D)	41,814	28.5
3	Steve Israel (D)*	90,032	52.6
	Grant M. Lally (R)	74,269	43.4
4	Kathleen Rice (D)	89,793	51.2
	Bruce A. Blakeman (R)	80,127	45.7
5	Gregory W. Meeks (D)*	75,712	80.2
6	Grace Meng (D)*	55,368	71.6
7	Nydia Velazquez (D)*	56,593	82.6
	Jose Luis Fernandez (R)	5,713	8.3
8	Hakeem Jeffries (D)*	77,255	81.2
	Alan Bellone (C)	6,673	7.0
9	Yvette Clarke (D)*	82,659	81.4
	Daniel J. Cavanagh (C)	9,727	9.6
10	Jerrold Nadler (D)*	89,080	78.7
	Ross Brady (C)	12,042	10.6
11	Michael Grimm (R)*	58,886	53.1
	Domenic M. Recchia Jr. (D)	45,244	40.8
12	Carolyn Maloney (D)*	90,603	77.2
	Nicholas S. Di Iorio (R)	22,731	19.4
13	Charles B. Rangel (D)*	68,396	74.5
	Daniel Vila Rivera (GREEN)	9,806	10.7
14	Joseph Crowley (D)*	50,352	74.7
	Elizabeth Perri (C)	6,735	10.0
15	Jose E. Serrano (D)*	54,906	89.6
16	Eliot Engel (D)*	99,658	71.9

		Vote total	Percent
17	Nita Lowey (D)*	98,150	54.0
	Christopher E. Day (R)	75,781	41.7
18	Sean Patrick Maloney (D)*	88,993	47.7
	Nan Hayworth (R)	85,660	45.9
19	Chris Gibson (R)*	131,594	62.6
	Sean S. Eldridge (D)	72,470	34.5
20	Paul D. Tonko (D)*	125,111	59.0
	James M. Fischer (R)	79,104	37.3
21	Elise M. Stefanik (R)	96,226	53.0
	Aaron G. Woolf (D)	59,063	32.5
	Matthew J. Funiciello (GREEN)	19,238	10.6
22	Richard L. Hanna (R)*	129,851	74.0
23	Thomas W. Reed II (R)*	113,130	59.4
	Martha Robertson (D)	70,242	36.9
24	John M. Katko (R)	118,474	58.2
	Daniel B. Maffei (D)*	80,304	39.5
25	Louise M. Slaughter (D)*	96,803	49.3
	Mark W. Assini (R)	95,932	48.8
26	Brian Higgins (D)*	113,210	65.1
	Kathleen A. Weppner (R)	52,909	30.4
27	Chris Collins (R)*	144,675	67.2
	James D. O'Donnell (D)	58,911	27.4

North Carolina

Senate

		Vote total	Percent
	Thom Tillis (R)	1,423,259	48.8
	Kay Hagan (D)*	1,377,651	47.3

House

		Vote total	Percent
1	G. K. Butterfield (D)*	154,333	73.4
	Arthur Rich (R)	55,990	26.6
2	Renee Ellmers (R)*	122,128	58.8
	Clay Aiken (D)	85,479	41.2
3	Walter B. Jones Jr. (R)*	139,415	67.8
	Marshall Adame (D)	66,182	32.2
4	David Price (D)*	169,946	74.3
	Paul Wright (R)	57,416	25.3
5	Virginia Foxx (R)*	139,279	61.0
	Joshua Brannon (D)	88,973	39.0
6	Mark Walker (R)	147,312	58.7
	Laura Fjeld (D)	103,758	41.3
7	David Rouzer (R)	134,431	59.4
	Jonathan Barfield Jr. (D)	84,054	37.1
8	Richard Hudson (R)*	121,568	64.9
	Antonio Blue (D)	65,854	35.1
9	Robert Pittenger (R)*	163,080	93.9
10	Patrick McHenry (R)*	133,504	61.0
	Tate MacQueen (D)	85,292	39.0
11	Mark Meadows (R)*	144,682	62.9
	Tom Hill (D)	85,342	37.1
12	Alma Adams (D)	130,096	75.4
	Vince Coakley (R)	42,568	24.7
13	George Holding (R)	153,991	57.3
	Brenda Cleary (D)	114,718	42.7

North Dakota

House

		Vote total	Percent
AL	Kevin Cramer (R)*	138,100	55.5
	George B. Sinner (D)	95,678	38.5
	Jack Seaman (LIBERT)	14,531	5.8

Ohio

Governor.

	Vote total	Percent
John Kasich (R)*	1,944,848	63.6
Ed FitzGerald (D)	1,009,359	33.0

House

		Vote total	Percent
1	Steve Chabot (R)*	124,779	63.2
	Fred Kundrata (D)	72,604	36.8
2	Brad Wenstrup (R)*	132,658	66.0
	Marek Tyszkiewicz (D)	68,453	34.0
3	Joyce Beatty (D)*	91,769	64.1
	John Adams (R)	51,475	35.9
4	Jim Jordan (R)*	125,907	67.7
	Janet Garrett (D)	60,165	32.3
5	Bob Latta (R)*	134,449	66.5
	Robert Fry (D)	58,507	28.8
6	Bill Johnson (R)*	111,026	58.2
	Jennifer Garrison (D)	73,561	38.6
7	Bob Gibbs (R)*	143,959	100.0
8	John Boehner (R)*	126,539	67.2
	Tom Poetter (D)	51,534	27.4
	James J. Condit Jr. (CNSTP)	10,257	5.5
9	Marcy Kaptur (D)*	108,870	67.7
	Richard May (R)	51,704	32.2
10	Mike Turner (R)*	130,752	65.2
	Robert Klepinger (D)	63,249	31.5
11	Marcia Fudge (D)*	137,105	79.5
	Mark Zetzer (R)	35,461	20.6
12	Pat Tiberi (R)*	150,573	68.1
	David Arthur Tibbs (D)	61,360	27.8
13	Tim Ryan (D)*	120,230	68.5
	Thomas Pekarek (R)	55,233	31.5
14	David Joyce (R)*	135,736	63.3
	Michael Wager (D)	70,856	33.0
15	Steve Stivers (R)*	128,496	66.0
	Scott Wharton (D)	66,125	34.0
16	Jim Renacci (R)*	132,176	63.7
	Pete Crossland (D)	75,199	36.3

Oklahoma

Governor.

	Vote total	Percent
Mary Fallin (R)*	460,298	55.8
Joe Dorman (D)	338,239	41.0

Senate

	Vote total	Percent
Jim Inhofe (R)*	558,166	68.0
Matt Silverstein (D)	234,307	28.5

House

		Vote total	Percent
1	Jim Bridenstine (R)*	X	X
2	Markwayne Mullin (R)*	110,925	70.0
	Earl Everett (D)	38,964	24.6
	Jon Douthitt (I)	8,518	5.4
3	Frank Lucas (R)*	133,335	78.6
	Frankie Robbins (D)	36,270	21.4
4	Tom Cole (R)*	117,721	70.8
	Bert Smith (D)	40,998	24.7
5	Steve Russell (R)	95,632	60.1
	Al McAffrey (D)	57,790	36.3

Oregon

Governor.

	Vote total	Percent
John Kitzhaber (D)*	733,230	49.9
Dennis Richardson (R)	648,542	44.1

Senate

	Vote total	Percent
Jeff Merkley (D)*	814,537	55.7
Monica Wehby (R)	538,847	36.9

House

		Vote total	Percent
1	Suzanne Bonamici (D)*	160,038	57.3
	Jason Yates (R)	96,245	34.5
2	Greg Walden (R)*	202,374	70.4
	Aelea Christofferson (D)	73,785	25.7
3	Earl Blumenauer (D)*	211,748	72.3
	James Buchal (R)	57,424	19.6
4	Peter DeFazio (D)*	181,624	58.6
	Art Robinson (R)	116,534	37.6
5	Kurt Schrader (D)*	150,944	53.7
	Tootie Smith (R)	110,332	39.3

Pennsylvania

Governor.

	Vote total	Percent
Tom Wolf (R)*	1,920,355	54.9
Tom Corbett (D)	1,575,511	45.1

House

		Vote total	Percent
1	Bob Brady (D)*	131,248	82.8
	Megan Rath (R)	27,193	17.2
2	Chaka Fattah (D)*	181,141	87.7
	Armond James (R)	25,397	12.3
3	Mike Kelly (R)*	113,859	60.6
	Dan LaVallee (D)	73,931	39.4
4	Scott Perry (R)*	147,090	74.5
	Linda D. Thompson (D)	50,250	25.5
5	Glenn Thompson (R)*	115,018	63.6
	Kerith Strano Taylor (D)	65,839	36.4
6	Ryan Costello (R)	119,643	56.3
	Manan Trivedi (D)	92,901	43.7
7	Pat Meehan (R)*	145,869	62.0
	Mary Ellen Balchunis (D)	89,256	38.0
8	Mike Fitzpatrick (R)*	137,731	61.9
	Kevin Strouse (D)	84,767	38.1
9	Bill Shuster (R)*	110,094	63.5
	Alanna Hartzok (D)	63,223	36.5
10	Tom Marino (R)*	112,851	62.6
	Scott Brion (D)	44,737	24.8
	Nicholas Troiano (I)	22,734	12.6
11	Lou Barletta (R)*	122,464	66.3
	Andrew Ostrowski (D)	62,228	33.7
12	Keith Rothfus (R)*	127,993	59.3
	Erin McClelland (D)	87,928	40.7
13	Brendan F. Boyle (D)	123,601	67.1
	Carson "Dee" Adcock (R)	60,549	32.9
14	Michael F. Doyle (D)*	148,351	100.0
15	Charlie Dent (R)*	128,285	100.0
16	Joe Pitts (R)*	101,722	57.7
	Tom Houghton (D)	74,513	42.3
17	Matt Cartwright (D)*	93,680	56.8
	David Moylan (R)	71,371	43.9
18	Timothy F. Murphy (R)*	166,076	100.0

Rhode Island

Governor.

	Vote total	Percent
Gina Raimondo (D)	131,452	40.7
Allan Fung (R)	117,106	36.2
Robert J. Healey (MDE)	69,070	21.4

Senate

	Vote total	Percent
Jack Reed (D)*	223,675	70.6
Mark Zaccaria (R)	92,684	29.2

House

		Vote total	Percent
1	David Cicilline (D)	87,060	59.5
	Cormick Lynch (R)	58,877	40.2
2	James Langevin (D)	105,716	62.2
	Rhue Reis (R)	63,844	37.6

South Carolina

Governor.

	Vote total	Percent
Nikki Haley (R)*	696,645	55.9
Vincent Sheheen (D)	516,166	41.4

Senate

	Vote total	Percent
Lindsey Graham (R)*	672,942	55.3
Brad Hutto (D)	480,933	38.8

House

		Vote total	Percent
1	Mark Sanford (R)*	119,392	93.4
2	Joe Wilson (R)*	121,649	62.5
	Phil Black (D)	68,719	35.3
3	Jeff Duncan (R)*	116,741	71.2
	Barbara Jo Mullis (D)	47,181	28.8
4	Trey Gowdy (R)*	126,452	84.8
	Curtis E. McLaughlin Jr. (LIBERT)	21,969	14.7
5	Mick Mulvaney (R)*	103,078	58.9
	Tom Adams (D)	71,985	41.1
6	Jim Clyburn (D)*	125,747	72.5
	Anthony Culler (R)	44,311	25.6
7	Tom Rice (R)*	102,833	60.0
	Gloria Bromell-Tinubu (D)	68,576	40.0

South Dakota

Governor.

	Vote total	Percent
Dennis Daugaard (R)*	195,477	70.5
Susan Wismer (D)	70,549	25.4

Senate

	Vote total	Percent
Mike Rounds (R)	140,741	50.4
Rick Weiland (D)	82,456	29.5
Larry Pressler (I)	47,741	17.1

House

		Vote total	Percent
AL	Kristi Noem (R)*	183,834	66.5
	Corinna Robinson (D)	92,485	33.5

Vote total *Percent*

Tennessee

Governor.

Candidate	Vote total	Percent
Bill Haslam (R)*	951,796	70.3
Charles Brown (D)	309,237	22.8

Senate

Candidate	Vote total	Percent
Lamar Alexander (R)*	849,629	61.9
Gordon Ball (D)	437,251	31.8

House

Dist	Candidate	Vote total	Percent
1	Phil Roe (R)	115,533	82.8
	Robert N. Smith (GREEN)	9,869	7.1
2	John J. Duncan Jr. (R)	120,833	72.5
	Bob Scott (D)	37,612	22.6
3	Chuck Fleischmann (R)	97,344	62.4
	Mary M. Headrick (D)	53,983	34.6
4	Scott DesJarlais (R)	84,815	58.3
	Lenda Sherrell (D)	51,357	35.3
	Robert Rankin Doggart (I)	9,246	6.4
5	Jim Cooper (D)	96,148	62.3
	Bob Ries (R)	55,078	35.7
6	Diane Black (R)	115,231	71.1
	Amos Scott Powers (D)	37,232	23.0
7	Marsha Blackburn (R)	110,534	70.0
	Daniel Cramer (D)	42,280	26.8
8	Stephen Fincher (R)	122,255	70.8
	Wes Bradley (D)	42,433	24.6
9	Steve Cohen (D)	87,376	75.0
	Charlotte Bergmann (R)	27,173	23.3

Texas

Governor.

Candidate	Vote total	Percent
Greg Abbott (R)	2,796,547	59.3
Wendy Davis (D)	1,835,596	38.9

Senate

Candidate	Vote total	Percent
John Cornyn (R)*	2,855,068	61.6
David Alameel (D)	1,594,252	34.4

House

Dist	Candidate	Vote total	Percent
1	Louie Gohmert (R)*	115,084	77.5
	Shirley McKellar (D)	33,476	22.5
2	Ted Poe (R)*	101,936	68.0
	Niko Letsos (D)	44,462	29.6
3	Sam Johnson (R)*	113,404	82.0
	Paul Blair (GREEN)	24,876	18.0
4	John Ratcliffe (R)	115,085	100.0
5	Jeb Hensarling (R)*	88,998	85.4
	Ken Ashby (LIBERT)	15,264	14.6
6	Joe Barton (R)*	92,334	61.2
	David Cozad (D)	55,027	36.4
7	John Culberson (R)*	90,606	63.3
	James Cargas (D)	49,478	34.6
8	Kevin Brady (R)*	125,066	89.3
	Ken Petty (LIBERT)	14,947	10.7
9	Al Green (D)*	78,109	90.8
	Johnny Johnson (LIBERT)	7,894	9.2
10	Michael McCaul (R)*	109,726	62.2
	Tawana Walter-Cadien (D)	60,243	34.1
11	Mike Conaway (R)*	107,939	90.3
	Ryan T. Lange (LIBERT)	11,635	9.7
12	Kay Granger (R)*	113,186	71.3
	Mark Greene (D)	41,757	26.3
13	Mac Thornberry (R)*	110,842	84.3
	Mike Minter (D)	16,822	12.8
14	Randy Weber (R)*	90,116	61.9
	Donald Brown (D)	52,545	36.1
15	Ruben Hinojosa (D)*	48,708	54.0
	Eddie Zamora (R)	39,016	43.3
16	Beto O'Rourke (D)*	49,338	67.5
	Corey Roen (R)	21,324	29.2
17	Bill Flores (R)*	85,807	64.6
	Nick Haynes (D)	43,049	32.4
18	Sheila Jackson Lee (D)*	76,097	71.8
	Sean Seibert (R)	26,249	24.8
19	Randy Neugebauer (R)*	90,160	77.2
	Neal Marchbanks (D)	21,458	18.4
20	Joaquin Castro (D)*	66,554	75.7
	Jeffrey C. Blunt (LIBERT)	21,410	24.3
21	Lamar Smith (R)*	135,660	71.8
	Antonio Diaz (GREEN)	27,831	14.7
	Ryan Shields (LIBERT)	25,505	13.5
22	Pete Olson (R)*	100,861	66.6
	Frank Briscoe (D)	47,844	31.6
23	Will Hurd (R)	57,459	49.8
	Pete Gallego (D)*	55,037	47.7
24	Kenny Marchant (R)*	93,712	65.0
	Patrick McGehearty (D)	46,548	32.3
25	Roger Williams (R)*	107,120	60.2
	Marco Montoya (D)	64,463	36.2
26	Michael Burgess (R)*	116,944	82.7
	Mark Boler (LIBERT)	24,526	17.3
27	Blake Farenthold (R)*	83,342	63.6
	Wesley Reed (D)	44,152	33.7
28	Henry Cuellar (D)*	62,508	82.1
	William Aikens (LIBERT)	10,153	13.3
29	Gene Green (D)*	41,321	79.6
	James Stanczak (LIBERT)	4,822	10.5
30	Eddie Bernice Johnson (D)*	93,041	88.0
	Max W. Koch III (LIBERT)	7,154	6.8
	Eric LeMonte Williams (I)	5,598	5.3
31	John Carter (R)*	91,607	64.1
	Louie Minor (D)	45,715	32.0
32	Pete Sessions (R)*	96,495	61.8
	Frank Perez (D)	55,325	35.4
33	Marc Veasey (D)*	43,769	86.5
	Jason Reeves (LIBERT)	6,823	13.5
34	Filemon Vela (D)*	47,503	59.5
	Larry Smith (R)	30,811	38.6
35	Lloyd Doggett (D)*	60,124	62.5
	Susan Narvaiz (R)	32,040	33.3
36	Brian Babin (R)*	101,663	76.0
	Michael Cole (D)	29,543	22.1

Utah

House

Dist	Candidate	Vote total	Percent
1	Rob Bishop (R)*	84,231	64.7
	Donna McAleer (D)	36,422	28.0
2	Chris Stewart (R)*	88,915	60.8
	Luz Robles (D)	47,585	32.5
3	Jason Chaffetz (R)*	102,952	72.2
	Brian Wonnacott (D)	32,059	22.4
4	Mia Love (R)	74,936	50.9
	Doug Owens (D)	67,425	45.8

Vermont

Governor.

Candidate	Vote total	Percent
Peter Shumlin (D)*	89,509	46.4
Scott Milne (R)	87,075	45.1

House

Dist	Candidate	Vote total	Percent
AL	Peter Welch (D)*	123,349	64.4
	Mark Donka (R)	59,432	31.0

Virginia

Senate

Candidate	Vote total	Percent
Mark Warner (D)*	1,073,667	49.1
Ed Gillespie (R)	1,055,940	48.3

House

Dist	Candidate	Vote total	Percent
1	Rob Wittman (R)*	131,861	62.9
	Norm Mosher (D)	72,059	34.4
2	Scott Rigell (R)*	101,558	58.7
	Suzanne Patrick (D)	71,178	41.1
3	Bobby Scott (D)*	139,197	94.4
4	Randy Forbes (R)*	120,684	60.2
	Elliott Fausz (D)	75,270	37.5
5	Robert Hurt (R)*	124,735	60.9
	Lawrence Gaughan (D)	73,482	35.9
6	Bob Goodlatte (R)*	133,898	74.5
	Will Hammer (LIBERT)	22,161	12.3
	Elaine Hildebrandt (I)	21,447	11.9
7	Dave Brat (R)	148,026	60.8
	Jack Trammell (D)	89,914	37.0
8	Don Beyer (D)	128,102	63.1
	Micah Edmond (R)	63,810	31.4
9	Morgan Griffith (R)*	117,465	72.2
	William Carr (I)	39,412	24.2
10	Barbara Comstock (R)	125,914	56.5
	John Foust (D)	89,957	40.4
11	Gerry Connolly (D)*	106,780	56.9
	Suzanne Scholte (R)	75,796	40.4

Washington

House

Dist	Candidate	Vote total	Percent
1	Suzan DelBene (D)*	124,151	55.0
	Pedro Celis (R)	101,428	45.0
2	Rick Larsen (D)*	122,173	60.6
	B. J. Guillot (R)	79,518	39.4
3	Jaime Herrera Beutler (R)*	124,796	61.5
	Bob Dingethal (D)	78,018	38.5
4	Dan Newhouse (R)	77,772	50.8
	Clint Didier (R)	75,307	49.2
5	Cathy McMorris Rodgers (R)*	135,470	60.7
	Joseph Pakootas (D)	87,772	39.3
6	Derek Kilmer (D)*	141,265	63.0
	Marty McClendon (R)	83,025	37.0
7	Jim McDermott (D)*	203,954	81.0
	Craig Keller (R)	47,921	19.0
8	Dave Reichert (R)*	125,741	63.3
	Jason Ritchie (D)	73,003	36.7
9	Adam Smith (D)*	118,132	70.8
	Doug Basler (R)	48,662	29.2
10	Denny Heck (D)*	99,279	54.7
	Joyce McDonald (R)	82,213	45.3

West Virginia

Senate

Candidate	Vote total	Percent
Shelley Moore Capito (R)	280,123	62.1
Natalie Tennant (D)	155,456	34.5

House

Dist	Candidate	Vote total	Percent
1	David McKinley (R)*	92,491	63.9
	Glen Gainer, III (D)	52,109	36.0
2	Alex X. Mooney (R)	72,619	47.1
	Nick Casey (D)	67,687	43.9
3	Evan Jenkins (R)	77,713	55.4
	Nick Rahall II (D)*	62,688	44.7

Wisconsin

Governor.

Candidate	Vote total	Percent
Scott Walker (R)*	1,259,706	52.3
Mary Burke (D)	1,122,913	46.6

House

Dist	Candidate	Vote total	Percent
1	Paul Ryan (R)*	182,316	63.3
	Rob Zerban (D)	105,552	36.6
2	Mark Pocan (D)*	224,920	68.4
	Peter Theron (R)	103,619	31.5
3	Ron Kind (D)*	155,368	56.5
	Tony Kurtz (R)	119,540	43.4
4	Gwen Moore (D)*	179,045	70.2
	Dan Sebring (R)	68,490	26.9
5	Jim Sensenbrenner (R)*	231,160	69.5
	Chris Rockwood (D)	101,190	30.4
6	Glenn Grothman (R)	169,767	56.8
	Mark Harris (D)	122,212	40.9
7	Sean Duffy (R)*	169,891	59.3
	Kelly Westlund (D)	112,949	39.4
8	Reid Ribble (R)*	188,553	65.0
	Ron Gruett (D)	101,345	34.9

Wyoming

Governor.

Candidate	Vote total	Percent
Matt Mead (R)*	99,700	58.3
Pete Gosar (D)	45,752	26.7
Don Wills (I)	9,895	5.8

Senate

Candidate	Vote total	Percent
Mike Enzi (R)*	121,554	72.2
Charlie Hardy (D)	29,377	17.5
Curt Gottshall (I)	13,311	7.9

House

Dist	Candidate	Vote total	Percent
AL	Cynthia Lummis (R)	113,038	68.5
	Richard Grayson (D)	37,803	22.9

114th Congress Special Elections, 2015 Gubernatorial Elections

Special House Elections, 114th Congress

	Vote total	Percent		Vote total	Percent
New York 11th CD—May 5, 2015			**Ohio 8th CD—June 7, 2016**		
Daniel Donovan (R)	23,409	58.9	Warren Davidson (R)	21,618	76.8
Vincent Gentile (D)	15,808	39.8	Corey Foister (D)	5,937	21.1
Mississippi 1st CD—May 12, 2015			**Pennsylvania 2nd CD—November 8, 2016**		
Walter Zinn (D)	15,385	17.4	Dwight Evans (D)	271,098	90.3
Trent Kelly (R)	14,418	16.3	James Jones (R)	29,173	9.7
Mike Tagert (R)	11,231	12.7			
Greg Pirkle (R)	7,142	8.1	**Hawaii 1st CD—November 8, 2016**		
Starner Jones (R)	6,993	7.9	Colleen Hanabusa (D)	129,083	65.1
Chip Mills (R)	6,929	7.8	Shirlene Ostrov (R)	44,090	22.2
Special Election Runoff—June 2, 2015			**Kentucky 1st CD—November 8, 2016**		
Trent Kelly (R)	69,516	70.0	James Comer (R)	209,807	72.2
Walter Zinn (D)	29,831	30.0	Sam Gaskins (D)	80,813	27.8
Illinois 18th CD—September 10, 2015					
Darin LaHood (R)	33,319	68.8			
Robert Mellon (D)	15,127	31.2			

2015 Gubernatorial Elections

	Vote total	Percent		Vote total	Percent
Kentucky			**Louisiana**		
Matt Bevin (R)	511,374	52.5	John Bel Edwards (D)	646,924	56.1
Jack Conway (D)	426,620	43.8	David Vitter (R)	505,940	43.9
Mississippi					
Phil Bryant (R)	472,197	66.6			
Robert Gray (D)	227,400	32.1			

NOTE: Vote totals are included for all candidates listed on the ballot who received 5 percent or more of the total vote.

2016 Election Returns for Governor, Senate, and House

Following are the official vote returns for the gubernatorial, Senate, and House contests based on figures supplied by the fifty state election boards.

Vote totals are included for all candidates listed on the ballot who received 5 percent or more of the total vote. For candidates who received under 5 percent, consult *America Votes 31 (2013–2014)*, published by CQ Press. The percent column shows the percentage of the total vote cast.

An asterisk (*) indicates an incumbent.

An "X" denotes candidates without major part opposition; no votes were tallied.

KEY: AC—American Constitution; AMI—American Independent; C—Conservative; CNSTP—Constitution; D—Democratic; G—Green; I—Independent; INDC—Independence; L—Liberal; LIBERT—Libertarian; MDE—Moderate; NPA—No Party Affiliation; R—Republican; REF—Reform; WRI—Write-in

		Vote total	Percent
Alabama			
Senate			
	Richard Shelby (R)*	1,335,104	63.9
	Ron Crumpton (D)	748,709	35.8
House			
1	Bradley Byrne (R)*	208,083	96.3
2	Martha Roby (R)*	134,886	48.7
	Nathan Mathis (D)	112,089	40.5
	Rebecca "Becky" Gerritson (WRI)	25,027	9.1
3	Mike Rogers (R)*	192,164	66.9
	Jesse Smith (D)	94,549	32.9
4	Robert Aderholt (R)*	235,925	98.5
5	Mo Brooks (R)*	205,647	66.7
	Will Boyd Jr. (D)	102,234	33.1
6	Gary Palmer (R)*	245,313	74.4
	David J. Putman (D)	83,709	25.4
7	Terri Sewell (D)*	229,330	98.4
Alaska			
Senate			
	Lisa Murkowski (R)*	138,149	44.4
	Joe Miller (D)	90,825	29.2
House			
AL	Don Young (R)*	155,088	50.3
	Steve Lindbeck (D)	111,019	36.0
	Jim McDermott (LIBERT)	31,770	10.3
Arizona			
Senate			
	John McCain (R)*	1,359,267	53.7
	Ann Kirkpatrick (D)	1,031,245	40.8
	Gary Swing (GREEN)	138,634	5.5
House			
1	Tom O'Halleran (D)	142,219	50.7
	Paul Babeu (R)	121,745	43.4
	Ray Parrish (GREEN)	16,746	6.0
2	Martha McSally (R)*	179,806	57.0
	Matt Heinz (D)	135,873	43.0
3	Raúl Grijalva (D)*	148,973	100.0
4	Paul Gosar (R)*	203,487	71.5
	Mikel Weisser (D)	81,296	28.6
5	Andy Biggs (R)	205,184	64.1
	Talia Fuentes (D)	114,940	35.9
6	David Schweikert (R)*	201,578	62.1
	W. John Williamson (D)	122,866	37.9
7	Ruben Gallego (D)*	119,465	75.3
	Eve Nunez (R)	39,286	24.8
8	Trent Franks (R)*	204,942	68.6
	Mark Salazar (GREEN)	93,954	31.3
9	Kyrsten Sinema (D)	169,055	60.9
	Dave Giles (R)	108,350	39.1
Arkansas			
Senate			
	John Boozman (R)*	661,984	59.8
	Conner Eldridge (D)	400,602	36.2

		Vote total	Percent
House			
1	Rick Crawford (R)*	183,866	76.3
	Mark West (LIBERT)	57,181	23.7
2	French Hill (R)*	176,472	58.4
	Dianne Curry (D)	111,347	36.8
3	Steve Womack (R)*	217,192	77.3
	Steve Isaacson (LIBERT)	63,715	22.7
4	Bruce Westerman (R)*	182,885	74.9
	Kerry Hicks (LIBERT)	61,274	25.1
California			
Senate			
	Kamala Harris (D)	7,542,753	61.6
	Loretta Sanchez (D)	4,701,417	38.4
House			
1	Doug LaMalfa (R)*	185,448	59.1
	Jim Reed (D)	128,588	40.9
2	Jared Huffman (D)*	254,194	76.9
	Dale K. Mensing (R)	76,572	23.1
3	John Garamendi (D)*	152,513	59.4
	N. Eugene Cleek (R)	104,453	40.6
4	Tom McClintock (R)*	220,133	62.7
	Robert W. Derlet (D)	130,845	37.3
5	Mike Thompson (D)*	224,526	76.9
	Carlos Santamaria (R)	67,565	23.1
6	Doris Matsui (D)*	177,565	75.4
	Robert "Bob" Evans (R)	57,848	24.6
7	Ami Bera (D)*	152,133	51.2
	Scott Jones (R)	145,168	48.8
8	Paul Cook (R)*	136,972	62.3
	Rita Ramirez (D)	83,035	37.7
9	Jerry McNerney (D)*	133,163	57.4
	Antonio C. "Tony" Amador (R)	98,992	42.6
10	Jeff Denham (R)*	124,671	51.7
	Michael Eggman (D)	116,470	48.3
11	Mark DeSaulnier (D)*	214,868	72.1
	Roger Allen Petersen (R)	83,341	27.9
12	Nancy Pelosi (D)*	274,035	80.9
	Preston Picus (NPA)	64,810	19.1
13	Barbara Lee (D)*	293,117	90.8
	Sue Caro (R)	29,754	9.2
14	Jackie Speier (D)*	231,630	80.9
	Angel Cardenas (R)	54,817	19.1
15	Eric Swalwell (D)*	198,578	73.8
	Danny R. Turner (R)	70,619	26.2
16	Jim Costa (D)*	97,473	58.0
	Johnny M. Tacherra (R)	70,483	42.0
17	Ro Khanna (D)	142,268	61.0
	Mike Honda (D)*	90,924	39.0
18	Anna Eshoo (D)*	230,460	71.1
	Richard B. Fox (R)	93,470	28.9
19	Zoe Lofgren (D)*	181,802	73.9
	G. Burt Lancaster (R)	64,061	26.1
20	Jimmy Panetta (D)	180,980	70.8
	Casey Lucius (R)	74,811	29.2

		Vote total	Percent
21	David Valadao (R)*	75,126	56.7
	Emilio Huerta (D)	57,282	43.3
22	Devin Nunes (R)*	158,755	67.6
	Louie J. Campos (D)	76,211	32.4
23	Kevin McCarthy (R)*	167,116	69.2
	Wendy Reed (D)	74,468	30.8
24	Salud Carbajal (D)	166,034	53.4
	Justin Fareed (R)	144,780	46.6
25	Steve Knight (R)*	138,755	53.1
	Bryan Caforio (D)	122,406	46.9
26	Julia Brownley (D)*	169,248	60.4
	Rafael A. Dagnesses (R)	111,059	39.6
27	Judy Chu (D)*	168,977	67.4
	Jack Orswell (R)	81,655	32.6
28	Adam Schiff (D)*	210,883	78.0
	Lenore Solis (R)	59,526	22.0
29	Tony Cardenas (D)*	128,407	74.7
	Richard Alarcon (D)	43,417	25.3
30	Brad Sherman (R)*	205,279	72.6
	Mark Reed (R)	77,325	27.4
31	Pete Aguilar (D)*	121,070	56.1
	Paul Chabot (R)	94,866	43.9
32	Grace Napolitano (D)*	114,926	61.6
	Roger Hernández (D)	71,720	38.4
33	Ted Lieu (D)*	219,397	66.4
	Kenneth W. Wright (R)	110,822	33.6
34	Xavier Becerra (D)*	122,842	77.2
	Adrienne Nicole Edwards (D)	36,314	22.8
35	Norma Torres (D)*	124,044	72.4
	Tyler Fischella (R)	47,309	27.6
36	Raul Ruiz (D)*	144,348	62.1
	Jeff Stone (R)	88,269	37.9
37	Karen Bass (D)*	192,490	81.1
	Chris Blake Wiggins (D)	44,782	18.9
38	Linda Sánchez (D)*	163,590	70.5
	Ryan Downing (R)	68,524	29.5
39	Ed Royce (R)*	150,777	57.6
	Brett Murdock (D)	112,679	42.4
40	Lucille Roybal-Allard (D)*	106,554	71.4
	Roman Gabriel Gonzalez (NPA)	42,743	28.6
41	Mark Takano (D)*	128,164	65.0
	Doug Shepherd (R)	69,159	35.0
42	Ken Calvert (R)*	149,547	58.8
	Tim Sheridan (D)	104,689	41.2
43	Maxine Waters (D)*	167,017	76.1
	Omar Navarro (R)	52,499	23.9
44	Nanette Barragán (D)	93,124	52.2
	Isadore Hall III (D)	85,289	47.8
45	Mimi Walters (R)*	182,618	58.6
	Ron Varasteh (D)	129,231	41.4
46	Lou Correa (D)	115,248	70.0
	Bao Nguyen (D)	49,345	30.0

		Vote total	Percent
47	Alan Lowenthal (D)*	154,759	63.7
	Andy Whallon (R)	88,109	36.3
48	Dana Rohrabacher (R)*	178,701	58.5
	Suzanne Savary (D)	127,715	41.5
49	Darrell Issa (R)*	155,888	50.3
	Doug Applegate (D)	154,267	49.7
50	Duncan D. Hunter (R)*	179,937	63.5
	Patrick Malloy (D)	103,646	36.5
51	Juan Vargas (D)*	145,162	72.2
	Juan M. Hidalgo Jr. (R)	54,362	27.8
52	Scott Peters (D)*	181,253	56.5
	Denise Gitsham (R)	139,403	43.5
53	Susan Davis (D)*	198,988	67.0
	James Veltmeyer (R)	97,968	33.0

Colorado

Senate

		Vote total	Percent
	Michael Bennet (D)*	1,370,710	50.0
	Darryl Glenn (R)	1,215,318	44.3

House

		Vote total	Percent
1	Diana DeGette (D)*	257,254	67.9
	Charles "Casper" Stockham (R)	105,030	27.7
2	Jared Polis (D)*	260,175	56.9
	Nicholas Morse (R)	170,001	37.2
	Richard Longstreth (LIBERT)	27,136	5.9
3	Scott Tipton (R)*	204,220	54.6
	Gail Schwartz (D)	150,914	40.4
	Gaylon Kent (LIBERT)	18,903	5.1
4	Ken Buck (R)*	248,230	63.6
	Bob Seay (D)	123,642	31.7
5	Doug Lamborn (R)*	225,445	62.3
	Misty Plowright (D)	111,676	30.9
6	Mike Coffman (R)*	191,626	50.9
	Morgan Carroll (D)	160,372	42.6
7	Ed Perlmutter (D)*	199,758	55.2
	George Athanasopoulos (R)	144,066	39.8

Connecticut

Senate

		Vote total	Percent
	Richard Blumenthal (D)*	1,008,714	63.2
	Dan Carter (R)	552,621	34.6

House

		Vote total	Percent
1	John B. Larson (D)*	200,686	63.9
	Matthew M. Corey (R)	105,674	33.8
2	Joe Courtney (D)*	208,818	63.2
	Daria Novak (R)	111,149	33.7
3	Rosa DeLauro (D)*	207,515	69.0
	Angel Cadena (R)	95,786	31.0
4	Jim Himes (D)*	187,811	59.9
	John Shaban (R)	125,724	40.1
5	Elizabeth Esty (D)*	179,252	57.9
	Clay Cope (R)	129,801	42.0

Delaware

Governor.

		Vote total	Percent
	John Carney (D)	248,404	58.3
	Colin Bonini (R)	166,852	39.2

House

		Vote total	Percent
AL	Lisa Blunt Rochester (D)	233,554	55.5
	Hans Reigle (R)	172,301	40.9

Florida

Senate

		Vote total	Percent
	Marco Rubio (R)*	4,835,191	52.0
	Patrick Murphy (D)	4,122,088	44.3

House

		Vote total	Percent
1	Matt Gaetz (R)	255,107	69.1
	Steven Specht (D)	114,079	30.9
2	Neal Dunn (R)	231,163	67.3
	Walter Dartland (D)	102,801	29.9

		Vote total	Percent
3	Ted Yoho (R)*	193,843	56.6
	Kenneth "Ken" McGurn (D)	136,338	39.8
4	John Rutherford (R)	287,509	70.2
	David E. Bruderly (D)	113,088	27.6
5	Al Lawson (D)	194,549	64.2
	Glo Smith (R)	108,325	35.8
6	Ron DeSantis (R)	213,519	58.6
	Bill McCullough (D)	151,051	41.4
7	Stephanie Murphy (D)	182,039	51.5
	John Mica (R)*	171,583	48.5
8	Bill Posey (R)	246,483	63.1
	Corry Westbrook (D)	127,127	32.6
9	Darren Soto (D)	195,311	57.5
	Wayne Liebnitzky (R)	144,450	42.5
10	Val Demings (D)	198,491	64.9
	Thuy Lowe (R)	107,498	35.1
11	Daniel Webster (R)	258,016	65.4
	Dave Koller (D)	124,713	31.6
12	Gus Bilirakis (R)	253,559	68.6
	Robert Matthew Tager (D)	116,110	31.4
13	Charlie Crist (D)	184,693	51.9
	David Jolly (R)	171,149	48.1
14	Kathy Castor (D)*	195,789	61.8
	Christine Quinn (R)	121,088	38.2
15	Dennis A. Ross (R)*	182,999	57.5
	Jim Lange (D)	135,475	42.5
16	Vern Buchanan (R)*	230,654	59.8
	Jan Schneider (D)	155,262	40.2
17	Tom Rooney (R)*	209,348	61.8
	April Freeman (D)	115,974	34.2
18	Brian Mast (R)	201,488	53.6
	Randy Perkins (D)	161,918	43.1
19	Francis Rooney (R)	239,225	65.9
	Robert Neeld (D)	123,812	34.1
20	Alcee Hastings (D)*	222,914	80.3
	Gary Stein (R)	54,646	19.7
21	Ted Deutch (D) *	199,113	58.9
	Andrea Leigh McGee (R)	138,737	41.1
22	Lois Frankel (D)*	210,606	62.7
	Paul Spain (R)	118,038	35.1
23	Debbie Wasserman Schultz (D)*	183,225	56.7
	Joe Kaufman (R)	130,818	40.5
24	Frederica Wilson (D)*	X	X
25	Mario Diaz-Balart (R)*	157,921	62.4
	Alina Valdes (D)	95,319	37.6
26	Carlos Curbelo (R)*	148,547	53.0
	Joe Garcia (D)	115,493	41.2
27	Ileana Ros-Lehtinen (R)*	157,917	54.9
	Scott Fuhrman (D)	129,760	45.1

Georgia

Senate

		Vote total	Percent
	Johnny Isakson (R)*	2,135,806	54.8
	Jim Barksdale (D)	1,599,726	41.0

House

		Vote total	Percent
1	Buddy Carter (R)*	210,243	100.0
2	Sanford Bishop (D)*	148,543	61.2
	Greg Duke (R)	94,056	38.7
3	Drew Ferguson (R)*	207,218	68.3
	Angela Pendley (D)	95,969	31.6
4	Hank Johnson (D)*	220,146	75.7
	Victor Armendariz (R)	70,593	24.2
5	John Lewis (D)*	253,781	84.4
	Douglas Bell (R)	46,768	15.5
6	Tom Price (R)*	201,088	61.7
	Rodney Stooksbury (D)	124,917	38.3
7	Rob Woodall (R)*	174,081	60.4
	Rashid Malik (D)	114,220	39.6

		Vote total	Percent
8	Austin Scott (R)*	173,983	67.6
	James Neal Harris (D)	83,225	32.4
9	Doug Collins (R)*	256,535	100.0
10	Jody Hice (R)*	243,725	100.0
11	Barry Loudermilk (R)*	217,935	67.4
	Don Wilson (D)	105,383	32.6
12	Rick Allen (R)*	159,492	61.6
	Patricia C. McCracken (D)	99,420	38.4
13	David Scott (D)*	252,833	100.0
14	Tom Graves (R)*	216,743	100.0

Hawaii

Senate

		Vote total	Percent
	Brian Schatz (D)*	306,604	70.1
	John Carroll (R)	92,653	21.2

House

		Vote total	Percent
1	Colleen Hanabusa (D)	145,417	68.1
	Shirlene D. "Shirl" Ostrov (R)	45,958	21.5
2	Tulsi Gabbard (D)*	170,848	76.2
	Angela Aulani Kaaihue (R)	39,668	17.7

Idaho

Senate

		Vote total	Percent
	Mike Crapo (R)*	449,017	66.1
	Jerry Sturgill (D)	188,249	27.7
	Ray Writz (CNSTP)	41,677	6.1

House

		Vote total	Percent
1	Raul Labrador (R)*	242,252	68.2
	James Piotrowski (D)	113,052	31.8
2	Mike Simpson (R)*	205,292	62.9
	Jennifer Martinez (D)	95,940	29.4
	Anthony Tomkins (CNSTP)	25,005	7.7

Illinois

Senate

		Vote total	Percent
	Tammy Duckworth (D)	3,012,940	54.9
	Mark Kirk (R)*	2,184,693	39.8

House

		Vote total	Percent
1	Bobby Rush (D)*	234,037	74.1
	August Deuser (R)	81,817	25.9
2	Robin Kelly (D)*	235,051	79.8
	John Morrow (R)	59,471	20.2
3	Dan Lipinski (D)*	225,320	100.0
4	Luis Gutiérrez (D)*	171,297	100.0
5	Mike Quigley (D)*	212,842	67.8
	Vince Kolber (R)	86,222	27.5
6	Peter Roskam (R)*	208,555	59.2
	Amanda Howland (D)	143,591	40.8
7	Danny K. Davis (D)*	250,584	84.2
	Jeffrey Leef (R)	46,882	15.8
8	Raja Krishnamoorthi (D)	144,954	58.3
	Pete DiCianni (R)	103,617	41.7
9	Jan Schakowsky (D)*	217,306	66.5
	Joan McCarthy Lasonde (R)	109,550	33.5
10	Brad Schneider (D)	150,435	52.6
	Bob Dold (R)*	135,535	47.4
11	Bill Foster (D)*	166,578	60.4
	Tonia Khouri (R)	108,995	39.6
12	Mike Bost (R)*	169,976	54.3
	C. J. Baricevic (D)	124,246	39.7
	Paula Bradshaw (GREEN)	18,780	6.0
13	Rodney L. Davis (R)*	187,583	59.7
	Mark Wicklund (D)	126,811	40.3
14	Randy Hultgren (R)*	200,508	59.3
	Jim Walz (D)	137,589	40.7
15	John Shimkus (R)*	274,554	100.0
16	Adam Kinzinger (R)*	259,722	100.0

		Vote total	Percent
17	Cheri Bustos (D)*	173,125	60.3
	Patrick Harlan (R)	113,943	39.7
18	Darin LaHood (R)*	250,506	72.1
	Junius Rodriguez (D)	96,770	27.9

Indiana

Governor.

	Vote total	Percent
Eric Holcomb (R)	1,397,396	51.4
John R. Gregg (D)	1,235,503	45.4

Senate

		Vote total	Percent
	Todd Young (R)	1,423,991	52.1
	Evan Bayh (D)	1,158,974	42.4
	Lucy Brenton (LIBERT)	149,481	5.5
1	Pete Visclosky (D)*	207,515	81.5
	Donna Dunn (LIBERT)	47,051	18.5
2	Jackie Walorski (R)*	164,355	59.3
	Lynn Coleman (D)	102,401	36.9
3	Jim Banks (R)	201,396	70.1
	Thomas Schrader (D)	66,023	23.0
	Pepper Snyder (LIBERT)	19,828	6.9
4	Todd Rokita (R)*	193,412	64.6
	John Dale (D)	91,256	30.5
5	Susan Brooks (R)*	221,957	61.5
	Angela Demaree (D)	123,849	34.3
6	Luke Messer (R)*	204,920	69.1
	Barry A. Welsh (D)	79,135	26.7
7	Andre Carson (D)*	158,739	60.0
	Catherine "Cat" Ping (R)	94,456	35.7
8	Larry Bucshon (R)*	187,702	63.7
	Ronald L. Drake (D)	93,356	31.7
9	Trey Hollingsworth (R)	174,791	54.1
	Shelli Yoder (D)	130,627	40.5
	Russell Brooksbank (LIBERT)	17,425	5.4

Iowa

Senate

		Vote total	Percent
	Chuck Grassley (R)*	926,007	60.1
	Patty Judge (D)	549,460	35.7

House

1	Rod Blum (R)*	206,903	53.7
	Monica Vernon (D)	177,403	46.1
2	David Loebsack (D)*	198,571	53.7
	Christopher Peters (R)	170,933	46.2
3	David Young (R)*	208,598	53.45
	Jim Mowrer (D)	155,002	39.71

Kansas

Senate

		Vote total	Percent
	Jerry Moran (R)*	732,376	62.2
	Patrick Wiesner (D)	379,740	32.2
	Robert Garrard (LIBERT)	65,760	5.6

House

1	Roger Marshall (R)	169,992	65.9
	Alan LaPolice (I)	67,739	26.3
	Kerry Burt (LIBERT)	19,366	7.5
2	Lynn Jenkins (R)*	181,228	60.9
	Britani Potter (D)	96,840	32.6
	James Houston Bales (LIBERT)	19,333	6.5
3	Kevin Yoder (R)*	176,022	51.3
	Jay Sidie (D)	139,300	40.6
	Steve Hohe (LIBERT)	27,791	8.1
4	Mike Pompeo (R)*	166,998	60.7
	Daniel B. Giroux (D)	81,495	29.6
	Miranda Allen (I)	19,021	6.9

Kentucky

Senate

		Vote total	Percent
	Rand Paul (R)*	1,090,177	57.3
	Jim Gray (D)	813,246	42.7

House

		Vote total	Percent
1	James Comer (R)	216,959	72.6
	Sam Gaskins (D)	81,710	27.3
2	Brett Guthrie (R)*	251,825	100.0
3	John Yarmuth (D)*	212,401	63.5
	Harold Bratcher (R)	122,093	36.5
4	Thomas Massie (R)*	233,922	71.3
	Calvin Sidle (D)	94,065	28.7
5	Hal Rogers (R)*	221,242	100.0
6	Andy Barr (R)*	202,099	61.1
	Nancy Jo Kemper (D)	128,728	38.9

Louisiana

Senate

		Vote total	Percent
	John Kennedy (R)	536,191	60.7
	Foster Campbell (D)	347,816	39.3

House

1	Steve Scalise (R)*	243,645	74.6
	Lee Ann Dugas (D)	41,840	12.8
2	Cedric Richmond (D)*	198,289	69.8
	Kip Holden (D)	57,125	20.1
	Kenneth Cutno (D)	28,855	10.2
3	Clay Higgins (R)	77,671	56.0
	Scott A. Angelle (R)	60,762	44.0
4	Mike Johnson (R)	87,370	65.0
	Marshall Jones (D)	46,579	35.0
5	Ralph Abraham (R)*	208,545	81.6
	Billy Burkette (R)	47,117	18.4
6	Garret Graves (R)*	207,483	62.7
	Richard Lieberman (D)	49,380	14.9
	Bob Bell (R)	33,592	10.2
	Jermaine Sampson (D)	29,822	9.0

Maine

House

1	Chellie Pingree (D)	227,546	58.0
	Mark Holbrook (R)	164,569	41.9
2	Bruce Poliquin (R)	192,878	54.8
	Emily Cain (D)	159,081	45.2

Maryland

Senate

		Vote total	Percent
	Chris Van Hollen (D)	1,659,907	60.9
	Kathy Szeliga (R)	972,557	35.7

House

1	Andy Harris (R)*	242,574	67.0
	Joe Werner (D)	103,622	28.6
2	Dutch Ruppersberger (D)*	192,183	62.1
	Pat McDonough (R)	102,577	33.1
3	John Sarbanes (D)*	214,640	63.2
	Mark Plaster (R)	115,048	33.9
4	Anthony G. Brown (D)	237,501	74.1
	George E. McDermott (R)	68,670	21.4
5	Steny Hoyer (D)*	242,989	67.4
	Mark Arness (R)	105,931	29.4
6	John Delaney (D)*	185,770	56.0
	Amie Hoeber (R)	133,081	40.1
7	Elijah Cummings (D)*	238,838	74.9
	Corrogan R. Vaughn (R)	69,556	21.8
8	Jamie Raskin (D)	220,657	60.6
	Dan Cox (R)	124,651	34.2

Massachusetts

House

1	Richard Neal (D)*	235,803	73.3
	Frederick O. Mayock (I)	57,504	17.9
	Thomas T. Simmons (LIBERT)	27,511	8.6
2	Jim McGovern (D)*	275,487	98.2
3	Niki Tsongas (D)*	236,713	68.7
	Ann Wofford (R)	107,519	31.2

		Vote total	Percent
4	Joseph P. Kennedy III (D)*	265,823	70.1
	David A. Rosa (R)	113,055	29.8
5	Katherine Clark (D)*	285,606	98.6
6	Seth Moulton (D)*	308,923	98.4
7	Mike Capuano (D)*	253,354	98.6
8	Stephen Lynch (D)*	271,019	72.4
	William Burke (R)	102,744	27.5
9	William Keating (D)*	211,790	55.7
	Mark Alliegro (R)	127,803	33.6
	Paul Harrington (I)	26,233	6.9

Michigan

House

1	Jack Bergman (R)	197,777	54.9
	Lon Johnson (D)	144,334	40.1
2	Bill Huizenga (R)*	212,508	62.6
	Dennis Murphy (D)	110,391	32.5
3	Justin Amash (R)*	203,545	59.5
	Douglas Smith (D)	128,400	37.5
4	John Moolenaar (R)*	194,572	61.6
	Debra Wirth (D)	101,277	32.1
5	Dan Kildee (D)*	195,279	61.2
	Al Hardwick (R)	112,102	35.1
6	Fred Upton (R)*	193,259	58.6
	Paul Clements (D)	119,980	36.4
7	Tim Walberg (R)*	184,321	55.1
	Gretchen Driskell (D)	134,010	40.0
8	Mike Bishop (R)*	205,629	56.0
	Suzanna Shkreli (D)	143,791	39.2
9	Sander Levin (D)*	199,661	57.9
	Christopher Morse (R)	128,937	37.4
10	Paul Mitchell (R)	215,132	63.1
	Frank Accavitti Jr. (D)	110,112	32.3
11	Dave Trott (R)*	200,872	52.9
	Anil Kumar (D)	152,461	40.2
	Kerry Bentivolio (I)	16,610	4.4
12	Debbie Dingell (D)*	211,378	64.3
	Jeff Jones (R)	96,104	29.3
13	John Conyers (D)*	198,771	77.1
	Jeff Gorman (R)	40,541	15.7
14	Brenda Lawrence (D)*	244,135	78.5
	Howard Klausner (R)	58,103	18.7

Mississippi

House

1	Trent Kelly (R)*	206,455	68.7
	Jacob Owens (D)	83,947	27.9
2	Bennie G. Thompson (D)*	192,343	67.1
	John Boule II (R)	83,542	29.2
3	Gregg Harper (R)*	209,490	66.2
	Dennis C. Quinn (D)	96,101	30.4
4	Steven Palazzo (R)*	181,323	65.0
	Mark Gladney (D)	77,505	27.8
	Richard Blake	14,687	5.3
	McCluskey (LIBERT)		

Missouri

Governor.

	Vote total	Percent
Eric Greitens (R)	1,433,397	51.1
Chris Koster (D)	1,277,360	45.5

Senate

	Vote total	Percent
Roy Blunt (R)*	1,378,458	49.2
Jason Kander (D)	1,300,200	47.4

House

1	Lacy Clay (D)*	236,993	75.5
	Steven Bailey (R)	62,714	20.0
2	Ann Wagner (R)*	241,954	58.5
	Bill Otto (D)	155,689	37.7
	Jim Higgins (LIBERT)	11,758	2.9
3	Blaine Luetkemeyer (R)*	249,865	67.8
	Kevin Miller (D)	102,891	27.9

		Vote total	Percent
4	Vicky Hartzler (R)*	225,348	67.8
	Gordon Christensen (D)	92,510	27.9
5	Emanuel Cleaver (D)*	190,766	58.8
	Jacob Turk (R)	123,771	38.2
6	Sam Graves (R)*	238,388	68.0
	David Blackwell (D)	99,692	28.5
7	Billy Long (R)*	228,692	67.5
	Genevieve Williams (D)	92,756	27.4
	Benjamin T. Brixey (LIBERT)	17,153	5.1
8	Jason Smith (R)*	229,792	74.4
	Dave Cowell (D)	70,009	22.7

Montana

Governor.

	Vote total	Percent
Steve Bullock (D)*	255,933	50.2
Greg Gianforte (R)	236,115	46.4

House

		Vote total	Percent
AL	Ryan Zinke (R)*	285,358	56.2
	Denise Juneau (D)	205,919	40.6

Nebraska

House

		Vote total	Percent
1	Jeff Fortenberry (R)*	189,771	69.5
	Daniel Wik (D)	83,467	30.6
2	Don Bacon (R)	141,066	48.9
	Brad Ashford (D)*	137,602	47.7
3	Adrian Smith (R)*	226,720	100.0

Nevada

Senate

	Vote total	Percent
Catherine Cortez Masto (D)	521,994	47.1
Joe Heck (R)	495,079	44.7

House

		Vote total	Percent
1	Dina Titus (D)*	116,537	61.8
	Mary Perry (R)	54,174	28.7
	Reuben D'Silva (I)	13,897	7.4
2	Mark Amodei (R)*	182,676	58.3
	H. D. Evans (D)	115,722	36.9
3	Jacky Rosen (D)	146,869	47.2
	Danny Tarkanian (R)	142,926	45.9
4	Ruben Kihuen (D)	128,985	48.5
	Cresent Hardy (R)*	118,328	44.5

New Hampshire

Governor.

	Vote total	Percent
Chris Sununu (R)	354,040	48.8
Colin Van Ostern (D)	337,589	46.6

Senate

	Vote total	Percent
Maggie Hassan (D)	354,649	48.0
Kelly Ayotte (R)*	353,632	47.8

House

		Vote total	Percent
1	Carol Shea-Porter (D)	162,080	44.3
	Frank Guinta (R)*	157,176	43.0
	Shawn O'Connor (I)	34,735	9.5
2	Ann McLane Kuster (D)*	174,371	49.8
	Jim Lawrence (R)	158,825	45.3

New Jersey

House

		Vote total	Percent
1	Donald Norcross (D)	183,231	60.0
	Bob Patterson (R)	112,388	36.8
2	Frank LoBiondo (R)	176,338	59.2
	David H. Cole (D)	110,838	37.2
3	Tom MacArthur (R)	194,596	59.3
	Frederick John Lavergne (D)	127,526	38.9
4	Chris Smith (R)	211,992	63.7
	Lorna Phillipson (D)	111,532	33.5
5	Josh Gottheimer (D)	172,587	51.1
	Scott Garrett (R)*	157,690	46.7
6	Frank Pallone (D)*	167,895	63.7
	Brent Sonnek-Schmelz (R)	91,908	34.9

		Vote total	Percent
7	Leonard Lance (R)*	185,850	54.1
	Peter Jacob (D)	148,188	43.1
8	Albio Sires (D)*	134,733	77.0
	Agha Khan (R)	32,337	18.5
9	Bill Pascrell (D)*	162,642	69.7
	Hector L. Castillo (R)	65,376	28.0
10	Donald Payne Jr. (D)*	190,856	85.7
	David H. Pinckney (R)	26,450	11.9
11	Rodney Frelinghuysen (R)*	194,299	58.0
	Joseph M. Wenzel (D)	130,162	38.9
12	Bonnie Watson Coleman (D)*	181,430	62.9
	Steven J. Uccio (R)	92,407	32.0

New Mexico

House

		Vote total	Percent
1	Michelle Grisham (D)*	181,088	65.2
	Richard Priem (R)	96,879	34.9
2	Steve Pearce (R)*	143,514	62.7
	Merrie Lee Soules (D)	85,232	37.3
3	Ben Ray Lujan (D)*	170,612	62.4
	Michael H. Romero (R)	102,730	37.6

New York

Senate

	Vote total	Percent
Chuck Schumer (D)*	5,221,945	70.6
Wendy Long (R)	2,009,355	27.2

House

		Vote total	Percent
1	Lee Zeldin (R)	188,499	55.1
	Anna Throne-Holst (D)	135,278	39.6
2	Peter T. King (R)*	181,221	57.2
	DuWayne Gregory (D)	110,812	34.9
3	Thomas Suozzi (D)	167,758	48.8
	Jack Martins (R)	149,577	43.5
4	Kathleen Rice (D)*	185,286	54.4
	David H. Gurfein (R)	125,865	36.9
5	Gregory Meeks (D)*	199,552	80.1
	Michael A. O'Reilly (R)	30,257	12.2
6	Grace Meng (D)*	136,506	64.8
	Danniel S. Maio (R)	50,617	24.1
7	Nydia Velazquez (D)*	172,146	83.1
	Allan E. Romaguera (R)	17,478	8.4
8	Hakeem Jeffries (D)	214,595	83.3
	Daniel J. Cavanagh (C)	15,401	5.9
9	Yvette Clarke (D)	214,189	83.3
	Alan Bellone (C)	17,576	6.8
10	Jerrold Nadler (D)*	192,371	72.1
	Philip Rosenthal (R)	53,857	20.2
11	Dan Donovan (R)*	142,934	56.7
	Richard A. Reichard (D)	85,257	33.8
12	Carolyn Maloney (D)*	244,358	78.2
	Robert Ardini (R)	49,398	15.8
13	Adriano Espaillat (D)	207,194	81.1
	Robert A. Evans Jr. (R)	16,089	6.3
14	Joseph Crowley (D)*	147,587	74.8
	Frank J. Spotorno (R)	30,545	15.4
15	Jose E. Serrano (D)*	165,688	85.5
16	Eliot Engel (D)*	209,857	72.9
17	Nita Lowey (D)*	214,530	65.89
18	Sean Patrick Maloney (D)*	162,060	50.7
	Phil Oliva (R)	129,369	40.5
19	John Faso (R)	164,800	51.0
	Zephyr Teachout (D)	138,800	43.0
20	Paul Tonko (D)*	213,021	64.0
	Joe Vitollo (R)	100,738	30.2
21	Elise Stefanik (R)*	177,886	61.6
	Mike Derrick (D)	82,161	28.4
22	Claudia Tenney (R)	129,444	43.7
	Kim A. Myers (D)	114,266	38.5
	Martin Babinec (REF)	34,638	11.7

		Vote total	Percent
23	Tom Reed (R)*	161,050	54.3
	John F. Plumb (D)	118,584	40.0
24	John Katko (R)*	182,761	57.9
	Colleen Deacon (D)	119,040	37.7
25	Louise Slaughter (D)*	182,950	54.3
	Mark Assini (R)	142,650	42.4
26	Brian Higgins (D)*	215,289	69.2
	Shelly Schratz (R)	73,377	23.6
27	Chris Collins (R)*	220,885	62.3
	Diana K. Kastenbaum (D)	107,832	30.4

North Carolina

Governor.

	Vote total	Percent
Roy Cooper (D)	2,309,157	49.0
Pat McCrory (R)*	2,298,880	48.8

Senate

	Vote total	Percent
Richard Burr (R)*	2,395,376	51.1
Deborah K. Ross (D)	2,128,165	45.4

House

		Vote total	Percent
1	G. K. Butterfield (D)*	240,661	68.6
	H. Powell Dew Jr. (R)	101,567	29.0
2	George Holding (R)	221,485	56.7
	John P. McNeil (D)	169,082	43.3
3	Walter B. Jones (R)*	217,531	67.2
	Ernest T. Reeves (D)	106,170	32.8
4	David Price (D)*	279,380	68.2
	Sue Googe (R)	130,161	31.8
5	Virginia Foxx (R)*	207,625	58.4
	Josh Brannon (D)	147,887	41.6
6	Mark Walker (R)*	207,983	59.2
	Pete Glidewell (D)	143,167	40.8
7	David Rouzer (R)*	211,801	60.9
	J. Wesley Casteen (D)	135,905	39.1
8	Richard Hudson (R)*	189,863	58.8
	Thomas Mills (D)	133,182	41.2
9	Robert Pittenger (R)*	193,452	58.2
	Christian Cano (D)	139,041	41.8
10	Patrick McHenry (R)*	220,825	63.1
	Andy Millard (D)	128,919	36.9
11	Mark Meadows (R)*	230,405	64.1
	Rick Bryson (D)	129,103	35.9
12	Alma Adams (D)*	234,115	67.0
	Leon Threatt (R)	115,185	33.0
13	Ted Budd (R)	199,443	56.1
	Bruce Davis (D)	156,049	43.9

North Dakota

Governor.

	Vote total	Percent
Doug Burgum (R)	259,863	76.5
Marvin Nelson (D)	65,855	19.4

Senate

	Vote total	Percent
John Hoeven (R)*	268,788	78.5
Eliot Glassheim (D)	58,116	17.0

House

		Vote total	Percent
AL	Kevin Cramer (R)*	233,980	69.1
	Chase Iron Eyes (D)	80,377	23.7
	Jack Seaman (LIBERT)	23,528	7.0

Ohio

Senate

	Vote total	Percent
Rob Portman (R)*	3,118,567	58.0
Ted Strickland (D)	1,996,908	37.2

House

		Vote total	Percent
1	Steve Chabot (R)*	210,014	59.2
	Michele Young (D)	144,644	40.8
2	Brad Wenstrup (R)*	221,193	65.0
	William R. Smith (D)	111,694	32.8
3	Joyce Beatty (D)*	199,791	68.6
	John Adams (R)	91,560	31.4
4	Jim Jordan (R)*	210,227	68.0
	Janet Garrett (D)	98,981	32.0
5	Bob Latta (R)*	244,599	70.9
	James L. Neu Jr. (D)	100,392	29.1
6	Bill Johnson (R)*	213,975	70.7
	Michael L. Lorentz (D)	88,780	29.3

		Vote total	Percent
7	Bob Gibbs (R)*	198,221	64.0
	Roy Rich (D)	89,638	29.0
	Dan Phillip (I)	21,694	7.0
8	Warren Davidson (R)*	223,833	68.8
	Steven Fought (D)	87,794	27.0
9	Marcy Kaptur (D)*	193,966	68.7
	Donald P. Larson (R)	88,427	31.3
10	Mike Turner (R)*	215,724	64.1
	Robert Klepinger (D)	109,981	32.7
	Tom McMasters (I)	10,890	3.2
	David A. Harlow (WRI)	7	0.0
11	Marcia Fudge (D)*	242,917	80.3
	Beverly Goldstein (R)	59,769	19.8
12	Pat Tiberi (R)*	251,266	66.6
	Ed Albertson (D)	112,638	29.8
13	Tim Ryan (D)*	208,610	67.7
	Richard A. Morckel (R)	99,377	32.3
14	David Joyce (R)*	219,191	62.6
	Michael Wager (D)	130,907	37.4
15	Steve Stivers (R)*	222,847	66.2
	Scott Wharton (D)	113,960	33.8
16	Jim Renacci (R)*	225,794	65.3
	Keith Mundy (D)	119,830	34.7

Oklahoma

Senate

		Vote total	Percent
	James Lankford (R)*	980,892	67.7
	Mike Workman (D)	355,911	24.6

House

		Vote total	Percent
1	Jim Bridenstine (R)*	X	X
2	Markwayne Mullin (R)*	189,839	70.1
	Joshua Harris-Till (D)	62,387	23.2
	John McCarthy (I)	16,644	6.2
3	Frank Lucas (R)*	227,525	78.3
	Frankie Robbins (D)	63,090	21.7
4	Tom Cole (R)*	204,143	69.6
	Christina Owen (D)	76,472	26.1
5	Steve Russell (R)*	160,184	57.1
	Al McAffrey (D)	103,273	36.8
	Zachary Knight (LIBERT)	17,113	6.1

Oregon

Governor.

		Vote total	Percent
	Kate Brown (D)*	985,027	50.9
	Bud Pierce (R)	845,609	43.1

Senate

		Vote total	Percent
	Ron Wyden (D)*	1,105,119	56.6
	Mark Callahan (R)	651,106	33.4

House

		Vote total	Percent
1	Suzanne Bonamici (D)*	225,391	59.6
	Brian Heinrich (R)	139,756	36.9
2	Greg Walden (R)*	272,952	71.6
	James "Jim" Crary (D)	106,640	28.0
3	Earl Blumenauer (D)*	274,687	71.8
	David W. Walker (I)	78,154	20.4
	David Delk (Progressive)	27,978	7.3
4	Peter A. DeFazio (D)*	220,628	55.4
	Art Robinson (R)	157,743	39.6
5	Kurt Schrader (D)*	199,505	53.4
	Colm Willis (R)	160,443	43.0

Pennsylvania

Senate

		Vote total	Percent
	Pat Toomey (R)*	2,951,702	48.8
	Katie McGinty (D)	2,865,012	47.3

House

		Vote total	Percent
1	Bob Brady (D)*	245,791	82.2
	Debbie Williams (R)	53,219	17.8
2	Dwight E. Evans (D)	322,514	90.2
	James Jones (R)	35,131	9.8
3	Mike Kelly (R)*	244,893	100.0
4	Scott Perry (R)*	220,628	66.1
	Josh Burkholder (D)	113,372	33.9
5	Glenn Thompson (R)*	206,761	67.2

		Vote total	Percent
	Kerith Strano Taylor (D)	101,082	32.8
6	Ryan Costello (R)*	207,469	57.2
	Mike Parrish (D)	155,000	42.8
7	Pat Meehan (R)*	225,678	59.5
	Mary Ellen Balchunis (D)	153,824	40.5
8	Brian Fitzpatrick (R)	207,263	54.4
	Steve Santarsiero (D)	173,555	45.6
9	Bill Shuster (R)*	186,580	63.3
	Arthur L Halvorson (D)	107,985	36.7
10	Tom Marino (R)*	211,282	70.2
	Mike Molesevich (D)	89,823	29.8
11	Lou Barletta (R)*	199,421	63.7
	Michael Marsicano (D)	113,800	36.3
12	Keith Rothfus (R)*	221,851	61.8
	Erin Mcclelland (D)	137,353	38.2
13	Brendan Boyle (D)*	239,316	100.0
14	Michael F. Doyle (D)*	255,293	74.4
	Lenny McAllister (R)*	87,999	25.6
15	Charlie Dent (R)*	190,618	58.4
	Rick Daugherty (D)	124,129	38.0
16	Lloyd Smucker (R)	168,669	53.8
	Christina Hartman (D)	134,586	42.9
17	Matt Cartwright (D)*	157,734	53.8
	Matt Connolly (R)	135,430	46.2
18	Timothy F. Murphy (R)*	293,684	100.0

Rhode Island

House

		Vote total	Percent
1	David Cicilline (D)*	130,540	64.5
	Harold Russell Taub (R)	71,023	35.1
2	James Langevin (D)*	133,108	58.1
	Rhue R. Reis (R)	70,301	30.7

South Carolina

Senate

		Vote total	Percent
	Tim Scott (R)*	1,241,609	60.6
	Thomas Dixon (D)	757,022	39.6

House

		Vote total	Percent
1	Mark Sanford (R)*	190,410	58.5
	Dimitri Cherny (D)	119,779	36.8
2	Joe Wilson (R)*	183,746	60.2
	Arik Bjorn (D)	109,452	35.8
3	Jeff Duncan (R)*	196,325	72.8
	Hosea Cleveland (D)	72,933	27.1
4	Trey Gowdy (R)*	198,648	67.2
	Chris Fedalei (D)	91,676	31.0
5	Mick Mulvaney (R)*	161,669	59.2
	Fran Person (D)	105,772	38.7
6	Jim Clyburn (D)*	177,947	70.1
	Laura Sterling (R)	70,099	27.6
7	Tom Rice (R)*	176,468	61.0
	Mal Hyman (D)	112,744	39.0

South Dakota

Senate

		Vote total	Percent
	John Thune (R)*	265,516	71.8
	Jay Williams (D)	104,140	28.2

House

		Vote total	Percent
AL	Kristi Noem (R)*	237,163	64.1
	Paula Hawks (D)	132,810	35.9

Tennessee

House

		Vote total	Percent
1	Phil Roe (R)*	198,067	78.4
	Alan Bohms (D)	38,988	15.4
	Robert Franklin (I)	15,673	6.2
2	John J. Duncan Jr. (R)*	212,313	75.6
	Stuart Starr (D)	68,373	24.4
3	Chuck Fleischmann (R)*	176,448	66.4
	Melody Shekari (D)	76,665	28.9
4	Scott DesJarlais (R)*	165,594	65.0
	Steven Reynolds (D)	89,018	35.0

		Vote total	Percent
5	Jim Cooper (D)*	170,729	62.6
	Stacy Ries Snyder (R)	102,220	37.5
6	Diane Black (R)*	202,038	71.1
	David Kent (D)	61,940	21.8
	David Ross (I)	20,241	7.1
7	Marsha Blackburn (R)*	200,252	72.3
	Tharon Chandler (D)	64,973	23.5
8	David Kustoff (R)	194,155	68.8
	Rickey Hobson (D)	70,828	25.1
9	Steve Cohen (D)*	171,070	78.7
	Wayne Alberson (R)	41,021	18.9

Texas

House

		Vote total	Percent
1	Louie Gohmert (R)*	192,434	73.9
	Shirley J. McKellar (D)	62,847	24.1
2	Ted Poe (R)*	168,692	60.6
	Pat Bryan (D)	100,231	36.0
3	Sam Johnson (R)*	193,684	61.2
	Adam P. Bell (D)	109,420	34.6
4	John Ratcliffe (R)*	216,643	88.0
	Cody Wommack (LIBERT)	29,577	12.0
5	Jeb Hensarling (R)*	155,469	80.6
	Ken Ashby (LIBERT)	37,406	19.4
6	Joe Barton (R)*	159,444	58.3
	Ruby Faye Woolridge (D)	106,667	39.0
7	John Culberson (R)*	143,542	56.2
	James Cargas (D)	111,991	43.8
8	Kevin Brady (R)*	236,379	100.0
9	Al Green (D)*	152,032	80.6
	Jeff Martin (R)	36,491	19.4
10	Michael McCaul (R)*	179,221	57.3
	Tawana W. Cadien (D)	120,170	38.4
11	Mike Conaway (R)*	201,871	89.5
	Nicholas Landholt (LIBERT)	23,677	10.5
12	Kay Granger (R)*	196,482	69.4
	Bill Bradshaw (D)	76,029	26.9
13	Mac Thornberry (R)*	199,050	90.0
	Calvin DeWeese (LIBERT)	14,725	6.7
14	Randy Weber (R)*	160,631	61.9
	Michael Cole (D)	99,054	38.1
15	Vicente Gonzalez (D)	101,712	57.3
	Tim Westley (R)	66,877	37.7
16	Beto O'Rourke (D)*	150,228	85.7
	Jaime O. Perez (LIBERT)	17,491	10.0
17	Bill Flores (R)*	149,417	60.8
	William Matta (D)	86,603	35.2
18	Sheila Jackson Lee (D)*	150,157	73.5
	Lori Bartley (R)	48,306	23.6
19	Jodey Arrington (R)	176,314	86.7
	Troy Bonar (LIBERT)	17,376	8.5
20	Joaquin Castro (D)*	149,640	79.7
	Jeffrey C. Blunt (LIBERT)	29,055	15.5
21	Lamar S. Smith (R)*	202,967	57.0
	Tom Wakely (D)	129,765	36.5
22	Pete Olson (R)*	181,864	59.5
	Mark Gibson (D)	123,679	40.5
23	Will Hurd (R)*	110,577	48.3
	Pete P. Gallego (D)	107,526	47.0
24	Kenny Marchant (R)*	154,845	56.2
	Jan McDowell (D)	108,389	39.3
25	Roger Williams (R)*	180,988	58.4
	Kathi Thomas (D)	117,073	37.7
26	Michael C. Burgess (R)*	211,730	66.4
	Eric Mauck (D)	94,507	29.6
27	Blake Farenthold (R)*	142,251	61.7
	Raul (Roy) Barrera (D)	88,329	38.3

	Vote total	Percent
28 Henry Cuellar (D)*	122,086	66.2
Zeffen Hardin (R)	57,740	31.3
29 Gene Green (D)*	95,649	72.5
Julio Garza (R)	31,646	24.0
30 Eddie Bernice Johnson	170,502	77.9
(D)*		
Charles Lingerfelt (R)	41,518	19.0
31 John Carter (R)*	166,060	58.4
Mike Clark (D)	103,852	36.5
Scott Ballard (LIBERT)	14,676	5.2
32 Pete Sessions (R)*	162,868	71.1
Ed Rankin (LIBERT)	43,490	19.0
Gary Stuard (GREEN)	22,813	10.0
33 Marc Veasey (D)*	93,147	73.7
M. Mark Mitchell (R)	33,222	26.3
34 Filemon Vela Jr. (D)*	104,638	62.7
Rey Gonzalez Jr. (R)	62,323	37.3
35 Lloyd Doggett (D)*	124,612	63.1
Susan Narvaiz (R)	62,384	31.6
36 Brian Babin (R)*	193,675	88.6
Hal J. Ridley Jr.	24,890	11.4
(GREEN)		

Utah

Governor.

	Vote total	Percent
Gary Herbert (R)*	750,850	66.7
Mike Weinholtz (D)	323,349	28.7

Senate

Mike Lee (R)*	760,241	68.2
Misty Snow (D)	301,860	27.1

House

1 Rob Bishop (R)*	182,928	65.9
Peter Clemens (D)	73,381	26.4
Craig Bowden	16,296	5.9
(LIBERT)		
2 Chris Stewart (R)*	170,542	61.6
Charlene Albarran (D)	93,780	33.9
3 Jason Chaffetz (R)*	209,589	73.5
Stephen P. Tryon (D)	75,716	26.5
4 Mia Love (R)*	147,597	53.8
Doug Owens (D)	113,413	41.3

Vermont

Governor.

Phil Scott (R)	166,817	52.1
Sue Minter (D)	139,253	44.5

Senate

Patrick Leahy (D)*	192,243	60.0
Scott Milne (R)	103,637	32.3

House

AL Peter Welch (D)	264,414	82.5

	Vote total	Percent
Erica Clawson (LUP)	29,410	9.2

Virginia

House

	Vote total	Percent
1 Rob Wittman (R)*	230,213	59.8
Matt Rowe (D)	140,785	36.6
2 Scott Taylor (R)	190,475	61.3
Shaun D. Brown (D)	119,440	38.4
3 Bobby Scott (D)*	208,337	66.7
Marty Williams (R)	103,289	33.1
4 Donald McEachin (D)	200,136	57.7
Mike Wade (R)	145,731	42.0
5 Tom Garrett (R)	207,758	58.2
Jane Dittmar (D)	148,339	41.5
6 Bob Goodlatte (R)*	225,471	66.6
Kai Degner (D)	112,170	33.1
7 David Brat (R)*	218,057	57.7
Eileen Bedell (D)	160,159	42.2
8 Don Beyer (D)*	246,653	68.3
Charles Hernick (R)	98,387	27.2
9 Morgan Griffith (R)*	212,838	68.5
Derek Kitts (D)	87,877	28.3
10 Barbara Jean	210,791	52.6
Comstock (R)*		
LuAnn L. Bennett (D)	187,712	46.9
11 Gerry Connolly (D)*	247,818	87.9

Washington

Governor.

Jay Inslee (D)*	1,760,520	54.4
Bill Bryant (R)	1,476,346	45.6

Senate

Patty Murray (D)*	1,913,979	59.0
Chris Vance (R)	1,329,338	41.0

House

1 Suzan DelBene (D)*	193,619	55.4
Robert J. Sutherland (R)	155,779	44.6
2 Rick Larsen (D)*	208,314	64.0
Marc Hennemann (R)	117,094	36.0
3 Jaime Herrera Beutler	193,457	61.8
(R)*		
Jim Moeller (D)	119,820	38.3
4 Dan Newhouse (R)*	132,517	57.6
Clint Didier (R)	97,402	42.4
5 Cathy McMorris	192,959	59.6
Rodgers (R)*		
Joe Pakootas (D)	130,575	40.4
6 Derek Kilmer (D)*	201,718	61.5
Todd A. Bloom (R)	126,116	38.5
7 Pramila Jayapal (D)	212,010	56.0
Brady Walkinshaw (D)	166,744	44.0

	Vote total	Percent
8 Dave Reichert (R)*	193,145	60.2
Tony Ventrella (D)	127,720	39.8
9 Adam Smith (D)*	205,165	72.9
Doug Basler (R)	76,317	27.1
10 Dennis Heck (D)*	170,460	58.7
Jim Postma (R)	120,104	41.3

West Virginia

Governor.

Jim Justice (D)	350,408	49.1
Bill Cole (R)	301,987	42.3
Charlotte Pritt	42,068	5.9
(Mountain Party)		

House

1 David McKinley (R)*	163,469	69.0
Mike Manypenny (D)	73,534	31.0
2 Alex Mooney (R)*	140,807	58.2
Mark Hunt (D)	101,207	41.8
3 Evan Jenkins (R)*	140,741	67.9
Matt Detch (D)	49,708	24.0
Zane Lawhorn	16,883	8.1
(LIBERT)		

Wisconsin

Senate

Ron Johnson (R)*	1,479,471	50.2
Russ Feingold (D)	1,380,335	46.8

House

1 Paul Ryan (R)*	230,072	65.0
Ryan Solen (D)	107,003	30.2
2 Mark Pocan (D)*	273,537	68.7
Peter Theron (R)	124,044	31.2
3 Ron Kind (D)*	257,401	98.9
4 Gwen Moore (D)*	220,181	76.7
Robert Raymond (I)	33,494	11.7
Andy Craig (LIBERT)	32,183	11.2
5 James Sensenbrenner	260,706	66.7
(R)*		
Khary Penebaker (D)	114,477	29.3
6 Glenn Grothman (R)*	204,147	57.2
Sarah Lloyd (D)	133,072	37.3
Jeff Dahlke (I)	19,716	5.5
7 Sean Duffy (R)*	223,418	61.7
Mary Hoeft (D)	138,643	38.3
8 Mike Gallagher (R)	227,892	62.7
Tom Nelson (D)	135,682	37.3

Wyoming

House

AL Liz Cheney (R)	156,141	60.4
Ryan Greene (D)	75,449	29.2

Results of House Elections, 1928–2016

	1928	1930	1932	1934	1936	1938	1940	1942	1944	1946	1948	1950	1952	1954	1956	1958	1960	1962	1964	1966	1968
Totals																					
Democrats	165	217	313	322	334	262	268	222	242	188	263	235	213	232	234	283	263	259	295	248	243
Republicans	269	217	117	103	88	169	162	209	191	246	171	199	221	203	201	153	174	176	140	187	192
Alabama																					
Democrats	10	10	9[1]	9	9	9	9	9	9	9	9	9	9	9	9	9	9	8[1]	3	5	5
Republicans	0	0	0	0	0	0	0	0	0	0	0	0	0	0	0	0	0	0	5	3	3
Alaska																					
Democrats	—	—	—	—	—	—	—	—	—	—	—	—	—	—	—	1	1	1	1	0	0
Republicans	—	—	—	—	—	—	—	—	—	—	—	—	—	—	—	0	0	0	0	1	1
Arizona																					
Democrats	1	1	1	1	1	1	1	2[2]	2	2	2	2	1	1	1	1	1	2[2]	2	1	1
Republicans	0	0	0	0	0	0	0	0	0	0	0	0	1	1	1	1	1	1	1	2	2
Arkansas																					
Democrats	7	7	7	7	7	7	7	7	7	7	7	7	6[1]	6	6	6	6	4[1]	4	3	3
Republicans	0	0	0	0	0	0	0	0	0	0	0	0	0	0	0	0	0	0	0	1	1
California																					
Democrats	1	1	11[2]	13	15	12	11	12[2]	16	9	10	10	11[2]	11	13	16	16	25[2,3]	23	21	21
Republicans	10	10	9	7	4	8	9	11	7	14	13	13	19	19	17	14	14	13	15	17	17
Colorado																					
Democrats	1	1	4	4	4	4	2	1	0	1	3	2	2	2	2	3	2	2	4	3	3
Republicans	3	3	0	0	0	0	2	3	4	3	1	2	2	2	2	1	2	2	0	1	1
Connecticut																					
Democrats	0	2	2[2]	4	6	2	6	0	4	0	3	2	1	1	0	6	4	5	6	5	4
Republicans	5	3	4	2	0	4	0	6	2	6	3	4	5	5	6	0	2	1	0	1	2
Delaware																					
Democrats	0	0	1	0	1	0	1	0	1	0	0	0	0	1	0	1	1	1	1	0	0
Republicans	1	1	0	1	0	1	0	1	0	1	1	0	1	0	0	0	0	0	0	1	1
Florida																					
Democrats	4	4	5[2]	5	5	5	5	6[2]	6	6	6	6	8[2]	7	7	7	7	10[2]	10	9	9
Republicans	0	0	0	0	0	0	0	0	0	0	0	0	0	1	1	1	1	2	2	3	3
Georgia																					
Democrats	12	12	10[1]	10	10	10	10	10	10	10	10	10	10	10	10	10	10	10	9	8	8
Republicans	0	0	0	0	0	0	0	0	0	0	0	0	0	0	0	0	0	0	1	2	2
Hawaii																					
Democrats	—	—	—	—	—	—	—	—	—	—	—	—	—	—	—	—	1	2[2]	2	2	2
Republicans	—	—	—	—	—	—	—	—	—	—	—	—	—	—	—	—	0	0	0	0	0
Idaho																					
Democrats	0	0	2	2	2	1	1	1	1	0	1	0	1	1	1	1	2	2	1	0	0
Republicans	2	2	0	0	0	1	1	1	1	2	1	2	1	1	1	1	0	0	1	2	2
Illinois																					
Democrats	6	13[4]	19	21	21	17	11	7[1]	11	6	12	8	9[1]	12	11	14	14	12[1]	13	12	12
Republicans	21	14	8	6	6	10	16	19	15	20	14	18	16	13	14	11	11	12	11	12	12
Indiana																					
Democrats	3	9	12[1]	11	11	5	4	2[1]	2	2	7	2	1	2	2	8	4[4]	4	6	5	4
Republicans	10	4	0	1	1	7	8	9	9	9	4	9	10	9	9	3	7	7	5	6	7
Iowa																					
Democrats	0	1	6[1]	6	5	2	2	1	0	0	0	0	0	0	1	4	2	1[1]	6	2	2
Republicans	11	10	3	3	4	7	7	8	8	8	8	8	8	8	7	4	6	6	1	5	5
Kansas																					
Democrats	1	1	3[1]	3	2	1	1	1	0	0	0	0	1	0	1	3	1	1	0	0	0
Republicans	7	7	4	4	5	6	6	6	6	6	6	6	5	6	5	3	5	5	5	5	5
Kentucky																					
Democrats	2	9	9[1]	8	8	8	8	8	8	6	7	7	6[1]	6	6	7	7	5[1]	6	4	4
Republicans	9	2	0	1	1	1	1	1	1	3	2	2	2	2	2	1	1	2	1	3	3
Louisiana																					
Democrats	8	8	8	8	8	8	8	8	8	8	8	8	8	8	8	8	8	8	8	8	8
Republicans	0	0	0	0	0	0	0	0	0	0	0	0	0	0	0	0	0	0	0	0	0
Maine																					
Democrats	0	0	2[1]	2	0	0	0	0	0	0	0	0	0	0	1	2	0	1	1	2	2
Republicans	4	4	1	1	3	3	3	3	3	3	3	3	3	3	2	1	3	2	1	0	0
Maryland																					
Democrats	4	6	6	6	6	6	6	4	5	4	4	3	3[2]	4	4	7	6	6[2]	6	5	4
Republicans	2	0	0	0	0	0	0	2	1	2	2	3	4	3	3	0	1	2	2	3	4
Massachusetts																					
Democrats	3	4	5[1]	7	5	5	6	4[1]	4	5	4	6	6	7	7	8	8	7[1]	7	7	7
Republicans	13	12	10	8	10	10	9	10	10	9	8	8	8	7	7	6	6	5	5	5	5

1970	1972	1974	1976	1978	1980	1982	1984	1986	1988	1990	1992	1994	1996	1998	2000	2002	2004	2006	2008	2010	2012	2014	2016
255	243	291	292	277	243	269	253	258	260	267	258	204	207	211	212	205	202	233	255	193	201	188	194
180	192	144	143	158	192	166	182	177	175	167	176	230	227	223	221	229	232	202	180	242	234	247	241
5	4[1]	4	4	4	4	5	5	5	5	5	4	4	2	2	2	2	2	2	3	1	1	1	1
3	3	3	3	3	3	2	2	2	2	2	3	3	5	5	5	5	5	5	4	6	6	6	6
1	1[3]	0	0	0	0	0	0	0	0	0	0	0	0	0	0	0	0	0	0	0	0	0	0
0	0	1	1	1	1	1	1	1	1	1	1	1	1	1	1	1	1	1	1	1	1	1	1
1	1[2]	1	2	2	2	2[2]	1	1	1	1	3[2]	1	1	1	1	2	2	4	3	3	5[2]	4	4
2	3	3	2	2	2	3	4	4	4	4	3	5	5	5	5	6	6	4	5	5	4	5	5
3	3	3	3	2	2	2	3	3	3	3	2	2	2	2	3	3	3	3	3	1	0	0	0
1	1	1	1	2	2	2	1	1	1	1	2	2	2	2	1	1	1	1	1	3	4	4	4
20	23[2]	28	29	26	22	28[2]	27	27	27	26	30[2]	27	29	28	32	33	33	34	34	34	38	39	39
18	20	15	14	17	21	17	18	18	18	19	22	25	23	24	20	20	20	19	19	19	15	14	14
2	2[2]	3	3	3	3	3[2]	2	3	3	3	2	2	2	2	2	2	3	4	5	3	3	3	3
2	3	2	2	2	2	3	4	3	3	3	4	4	4	4	4	5	4	3	2	4	4	4	4
3	3	4	4	5	4	4	3	3	3	3	3	3	4	4	3	2	2	4	5	5	5	5	5
2	3	2	2	1	2	2	3	3	3	3	3	3	2	2	3	3	3	1	0	0	0	0	0
0	0	0	0	0	0	1	1	1	1	1	0	0	0	0	0	0	0	0	0	1	1	1	1
1	1	1	1	1	1	0	0	0	0	0	1	1	1	1	1	1	1	1	1	0	0	0	0
9	11[2]	10	10	12	11	13[2]	12	12	10	9	10[2]	8	8	8	8	7	7	9	10	6	10[2]	10	11
3	4	5	5	3	4	6	7	7	9	10	13	15	15	15	15	18	18	16	15	19	17	17	16
8	9	10	10	9	9	9	8	8	9	9	7[2]	4	3	3	3	5	6	7	6	5	5[2]	4	4
2	1	0	0	1	1	1	2	2	1	1	4	7	8	8	8	8	7	6	7	8	9	10	10
2	2	2	2	2	2	2	2	1	1	2	2	2	2	2	2	2	2	2	2	2	2	2	2
0	0	0	0	0	0	0	0	1	1	0	0	0	0	0	0	0	0	0	0	0	0	0	0
0	0	0	0	0	0	0	1	1	1	2	1	0	0	0	0	0	0	2	1	0	0	0	0
2	2	2	2	2	2	2	1	1	1	0	1	2	2	2	2	2	2	0	1	2	2	2	2
12	10	13	12	11	10	12[1]	13	13	14	15	12[1]	10	10	10	10	9	10	10	12	8	12[1]	10	11
12	14	11	12	13	14	10	9	9	8	7	8	10	10	10	10	10	9	9	7	11	6[8]	8	7
5	4	9	8	7	6	5[1]	5[4]	6	6	8	7	4	4	4	4	3	2	5	5	3	2	2	2
6	7	2	3	4	5	5	5	4	4	2	3	6	6	6	6	6	7	4	4	6	7	7	7
2	3[1]	5	4	3	3	3	2	2	2	2	1[1]	0	1	1	1	1	1	3	3	3	2[1]	1	1
5	3	1	2	3	3	3	4	4	4	4	4	5	4	4	4	4	4	2	2	2	2	3	3
1	1	1	2	1	1	2	2	2	2	2	2[1]	0	0	1	1	1	1	2	1	0	0	0	0
4	4	4	3	4	4	3	3	3	3	3	2	4	4	3	3	3	3	2	3	4	4	4	4
5	5	5	5	4	4	4	4	4	4	4	4[1]	2	1	1	1	1	1	2	2	2	1	1	1
2	2	2	2	3	3	3	3	3	3	3	2	4	5	5	5	5	5	4	4	4	5	5	5
8	7[3]	6[5]	6	5	6	6	6	5	4	4	4[1]	4	2	2	2	3	2	2	1	1	1[1]	1	1
0	1	2	2	3	2	2	2	3	4	4	3	3	5	5	5	4	5	5	6	6	5	5	5
2	1	0	0	0	0	0	1	1	1	1	1	2	2	2	2	2	2	2	2	2	2	1	1
0	1	2	2	2	2	2	2	1	1	1	1	1	0	0	0	0	0	0	0	0	0	1	1
5	4	5	5	6	7	7	6	6	6	5	4	4	4	4	4	6	6	6	7	6	7	7	7
3	4	3	3	2	1	1	2	2	2	3	4	4	4	4	4	2	2	2	1	2	1	1	1
8	9[6]	10	10	10	10	10[1]	10	10	10	10	8[1]	8	10	10	10	10	10	10	10	10	9	9	9
4	3	2	2	2	2	1	1	1	1	1	2	2	0	0	0	0	0	0	0	0	0	0	0

	1928	1930	1932	1934	1936	1938	1940	1942	1944	1946	1948	1950	1952	1954	1956	1958	1960	1962	1964	1966	1968
Michigan																					
Democrats	0	0	10²	6	8	5	6	5	6	3	5	5	5²	7	6	7	7	8²	12	7	7
Republicans	13	13	7	11	9	12	11	12	11	14	12	12	13	11	12	11	11	11	7	12	12
Minnesota																					
Democrats	0	0	1¹	1	1	1	0	0	2	1	4	4	4	5	5	4	3	4¹	4	3	3
Republicans	9	9	3	5	3	7	8	8	7	8	5	5	5	4	4	5	6	4	4	5	5
Mississippi																					
Democrats	8	8	7¹	7	7	7	7	7	7	7	7	7	6¹	6	6	6	6	5¹	4	5	5
Republicans	0	0	0	0	0	0	0	0	0	0	0	0	0	0	0	0	0	0	1	0	0
Missouri																					
Democrats	6	12	13¹	12	12	12	10	5	7	4	12	10	7	9	10	10	9	8¹	8	8	9
Republicans	10	4	0	1	1	1	3	8	6	9	1	3	4	2	1	1	2	2	2	2	1
Montana																					
Democrats	1	1	2	2	2	1	1	2	1	1	1	1	1	1	2	2	1	1	1	1	1
Republicans	1	1	0	0	0	1	1	0	1	1	1	1	1	1	0	0	1	1	1	1	1
Nebraska																					
Democrats	2	4	5¹	4	4	2	2	1	0	0	1	0	0	0	0	2	0	1	1	0	0
Republicans	4	2	0	1	1	3	3	4	4	4	3	4	4	4	4	2	4	3	2	3	3
Nevada																					
Democrats	0	0	1	1	1	1	1	1	1	0	1	1	0	0	1	1	1	1	1	1	1
Republicans	1	1	0	0	0	0	0	0	0	1	0	0	1	1	0	0	0	0	0	0	0
New Hampshire																					
Democrats	0	0	1	1	1⁴	0	0	0	0	0	0	0	0	0	0	0	0	0	0	1	0	0
Republicans	2	2	1	1	1	2	2	2	2	2	2	2	2	2	2	2	2	2	1	2	2
New Jersey																					
Democrats	2	3	4²	4	7	3	4	3	2	2	5	5	5	6	4	5	6	7²	11	9	9
Republicans	10	9	10	10	7	11	10	11	12	12	9	9	9	8	10	9	8	8	4	6	6
New Mexico																					
Democrats	0	1	1	1	1	1	1	2²	2	2	2	2	2	2	2	2	2	2	2	2	0
Republicans	1	0	0	0	0	0	0	0	0	0	0	0	0	0	0	0	0	0	0	0	2
New York																					
Democrats	23	23	29²	29	29	25	25	23	22	16	24	23	16¹	17	17	19	22	20¹	27	26	26
Republicans	20	20	16	16	16	19	19	21	22	28	20	22	27	26	26	24	21	21	14	15	15
North Carolina																					
Democrats	8	10	11²	11	11	11	11	12²	12	12	12	12	11	11	11	11	11	9¹	9	8	7
Republicans	2	0	0	0	0	0	0	0	0	0	0	0	1	1	1	1	1	2	2	3	4
North Dakota																					
Democrats	0	0	1	0	0	0	0	0	0	0	0	0	0	0	0	1	0	0	1	0	0
Republicans	3	3	2	2	2	2	2	2	2	2	2	2	2	2	2	1	2	2	1	2	2
Ohio																					
Democrats	3	9	18²	18	22	9	12	3¹	6	4	12	7	6	6	6	9	7	6²	10	5	6
Republicans	19	13	6	6	2	15	12	20	17	19	11	15	16	17	17	14	16	18	14	19	18
Oklahoma																					
Democrats	5	7	9²	9	9	9	8	7¹	6	6	8	6	5¹	5	5	5	5	5	5	4	4
Republicans	3	1	0	0	0	0	1	1	2	2	0	2	1	1	1	1	1	1	1	2	2
Oregon																					
Democrats	0	1	2	1	2	1	1	2	0	0	0	0	0	1	3	3	2	3	3	2	2
Republicans	3	2	1	2	1	2	2	4	4	4	4	4	4	3	1	1	2	1	1	2	2
Pennsylvania																					
Democrats	1	3	11¹	23	27	15	19	14¹	15	5	16	13	11¹	14	13	16	14	13¹	15	14	14
Republicans	35	33	23	11	7	9	15	19	18	28	19	20	19	16	17	14	16	14	12	13	13
Rhode Island																					
Democrats	1	1	2¹	2	2	0	2	2	2	2	2	2	2	2	2	2	2	2	2	2	2
Republicans	2	2	0	0	0	2	0	0	0	0	0	0	0	0	0	0	0	0	0	0	0
South Carolina																					
Democrats	7	7	6¹	6	6	6	6	6	6	6	6	6	6	6	6	6	6	6	6	5	5
Republicans	0	0	0	0	0	0	0	0	0	0	0	0	0	0	0	0	0	0	0	1	1
South Dakota																					
Democrats	0	0	2¹	2	1	0	0	0	0	0	0	0	0	0	0	1	1	0	0	0	0
Republicans	3	3	0	0	1	2	2	2	2	2	2	2	2	2	1	1	2	2	2	2	2
Tennessee																					
Democrats	8	8	7¹	7	7	7	7	8²	8	8	8	8	7¹	7	7	7	7	7	6	5	5
Republicans	2	2	2	2	2	2	2	2	2	2	2	2	2	2	2	2	2	3	3	4	4
Texas																					
Democrats	17	17	21²	21	21	21	21	21	21	21	21	21	22²	21	21	21	21	21²	23	21	20
Republicans	17⁷	1	0	0	0	0	0	0	0	0	0	0	0	1	1	1	1	2	0	2	3
Utah																					
Democrats	0	0	2	2	2	2	2	2	2	1	2	2	0	0	0	1	2	0	1	0	0
Republicans	2	2	0	0	0	0	0	0	0	1	0	0	2	2	2	1	0	2	1	2	2

1970	1972	1974	1976	1978	1980	1982	1984	1986	1988	1990	1992	1994	1996	1998	2000	2002	2004	2006	2008	2010	2012	2014	2016
7	7	12	11	13	12	12[1]	11	11	11	11	10[1]	9	10	10	9	6	6	6	8	6	5[1]	5	5
12	12	7	8	6	7	6	7	7	7	7	6	7	6	6	7	9	9	9	7	9	9	9	9
4	4	5	5	4	3	5	5	5	5	6	6	6	6	6	5	4	4	5	5	4	5	5	5
4	4	3	3	4	5	3	3	3	3	2	2	2	2	2	3	4	4	3	3	4	3	3	3
5	3	3	3	3	3	3	3	4	4	5	5	4	2	3	3	2	2	2	3	1	1	1	1
0	2	2	2	2	2	2	2	1	1	0	0	1	3	2	2	2	2	2	1	3	3	3	3
9	9	9	8	8	6	6[1]	6	5	5	6	6	6	5	5	4	4	4	4	4	3	2[1]	2	2
1	1	1	2	2	4	3	3	4	4	3	3	3	4	4	5	5	5	5	5	6	6	6	6
1	1	2	1	1	1	1	1	1	1	1	1[1]	1	1	0	0	0	0	0	0	0	0	0	0
1	1	0	1	1	1	1	1	1	1	1	0	0	0	1	1	1	1	1	1	1	1	1	1
0	0	0	1	1	0	0	0	0	1	1	1	0	0	0	0	0	0	0	0	0	0	1	0
3	3	3	2	2	3	3	3	3	2	2	2	3	3	3	3	3	3	3	3	3	3	2	3
1	0	1	1	1	1	1[2]	1	1	1	1	1	0	0	1	1	1	1	1	2	1	2	1	3
0	1	0	0	0	0	1	1	1	1	1	1	2	2	1	1	2	2	2	1	2	2	3	1
0	0	1	1	1	1	1	0	0	0	1	1	0	0	0	0	0	0	2	2	0	2	1	2
2	2	1	1	1	1	1	2	2	2	1	1	2	2	2	2	2	2	0	0	2	0	1	0
9	8	12	11	10	8	9[1]	8	8	8	8	7[1]	5	6	7	7	7	7	7	8	7	6[1]	6	7
6	7	3	4	5	7	5	6	6	6	6	6	8	7	6	6	6	6	6	5	6	6	6	5
1	1	1	1	1	0	1[2]	1	1	1	1	1	1	1	1	1	1	1	1	3	2	2	2	2
1	1	1	1	1	2	2	2	2	2	2	2	2	2	2	2	2	2	2	0	1	1	1	1
24	22[1]	27	28	26	22	20[1]	19	20	21	21	18[1]	17	18	18	19	19	20	23	26	21	21[1]	18	18
17	17	12	11	13	17	14	15	14	13	13	13	14	13	13	12	10	9	6	3	8	6	9	9
7	7	9	9	9	7	9	6	8	8	7	8[2]	4	6	5	5	6	6	7	8	7	4	3	3
4	4	2	2	2	4	2	5	3	3	4	4	8	6	7	7	7	7	6	5	6	9	10	10
1	1	0	0	0	1	1	1	1	1	1	1	1	1	1	1	1	1	1	1	0	0	0	0
1	1	1	1	1	0	0	0	0	0	0	0	0	0	0	0	0	0	0	0	1	1	1	1
7	7[1]	8	10	10	11	10[1]	11	11	11	11	10[1]	6	8	8	8	6	6	7	10	5	41	4	4
17	16	15	13	13	12	11	10	10	10	10	9	13	11	11	11	12	12	11	8	13	12	12	12
4	5	6	5	5	5	5	5	4	4	4	4	1	0	0	1	1	1	1	1	1	0	0	0
2	1	0	1	1	1	1	1	2	2	2	2	5	6	6	5	4	4	4	4	4	5	5	5
2	2	4	4	4	3	3[2]	3	3	3	4	4	3	4	4	4	4	4	4	4	4	4	4	4
2	2	0	0	0	1	2	2	2	2	1	1	2	1	1	1	1	1	1	1	1	1	1	1
14	13[1]	14	17	15	13[6]	13[1]	13	12	12	11	11[1]	11	11	11	10	7	7	11	12	7	5[1]	5	5
13	12	11	8	10	12	10	10	11	11	12	10	10	10	10	11	12	12	8	7	12	13	13	13
2	2	2	2	2	1	1	1	1	0	1	1	2	2	2	2	2	2	2	2	2	2	2	2
0	0	0	0	0	1	1	1	1	1	2	1	1	0	0	0	0	0	0	0	0	0	0	0
5	4	5	5	4	2	3	3	4	4	4	3	2	2	2	2	2	2	2	2	1	1[2]	1	1
1	2	1	1	2	4	3	3	2	2	2	3	4	4	4	4	4	4	4	4	5	6	6	6
2	1	0	0	1	1	1[1]	1	1	1	1	1	1	0	0	0	0	1	1	1	0	0	0	0
0	1	2	2	1	1	0	0	0	0	0	0	0	1	1	1	1	0	0	0	1	1	1	1
5	31	5	5	5	5	6[2]	6	6	6	6	6	4	4	4	4	5	5	5	5	2	2	2	2
4	5	3	3	3	3	3	3	3	3	3	3	5	5	5	5	4	4	4	4	7	7	7	7
20	20[2]	21	22	20	19	22[2]	17	17	19	19	21[2]	19	17	17	17	17	11	13	12	9	12[2]	11	11
3	4	3	2	4	5	5	10	10	8	8	9	11	13	13	13	15	21	19	20	23	24	25	25
1	2	2	1	1	0	2	0	1	1	2	2	1	0	0	1	1	1	1	1	1	12	0	0
1	0	0	1	1	2	3	3	2	2	1	1	2	3	3	2	2	2	2	2	3	4	4	4

	1928	1930	1932	1934	1936	1938	1940	1942	1944	1946	1948	1950	1952	1954	1956	1958	1960	1962	1964	1966	1968
Vermont																					
Democrats	0	0	1	0	0	0	0	0	0	0	0	0	0	0	0	1	0	0	0	0	0
Republicans	2	2	1	1	1	1	1	1	1	1	1	1	1	1	1	0	1	1	1	1	1
Virginia																					
Democrats	8	9	9[1]	9	9	9	9	9	9	9	9	9	7[2]	8	8	8	8	8	8	6	5
Republicans	2	1	0	0	0	0	0	0	0	0	0	0	3	2	2	2	2	2	2	4	5
Washington																					
Democrats	1	1	6[2]	6	6	6	6	3	4	1	2	2	1[2]	1	1	1	2	1	5	5	5
Republicans	4	4	0	0	0	0	0	3	2	5	4	4	6	6	6	6	5	6	2	2	2
West Virginia																					
Democrats	1	2	6	6	6	5	6	3	5	2	6	6	5	6	4	5	5	4[1]	4	4	5
Republicans	5	4	0	0	0	1	0	3	1	4	0	0	1	0	2	1	1	1	1	1	0
Wisconsin																					
Democrats	0	1	5[1]	3	3	0	1	3	2	0	2	1	1	3	3	5	4	4	5	3	3
Republicans	11	10	5	0	0	8	6	5	7	10	8	9	9	7	7	5	6	6	5	7	7
Wyoming																					
Democrats	0	0	0	1	1	0	1	0	0	0	0	0	0	0	0	0	0	1	0	0	1
Republicans	1	1	1	0	0	1	0	1	1	1	1	1	1	1	1	1	1	1	0	1	1

1. State lost seats due to reapportionment.

2. State gained seats due to reapportionment.

3. Alaska 1972, California 1962, and Louisiana 1972: national and state totals reflect the reelection of a Democrat who died before the election but whose name remained on the ballot.

4. Illinois 1930, Indiana 1960 and 1984, and New Hampshire 1936: national and state totals reflect the final outcome of a contested election in which a Republican was first certified the winner, but the House decided to seat the Democrat.

5. Louisiana 1974: national and state totals reflect the final outcome of a contested election in which no winner was declared, followed by a special election won by the Republican.

6. Massachusetts 1972 and Pennsylvania 1980: national and state Democratic totals reflect the election of an Independent candidate who previously announced he would serve as a Democrat.

7. Texas 1928: national and state totals reflect the final outcome of a contested election in which a Democrat was at first certified the winner, but the House decided to seat the Republican.

8. At the time of the 2012 elections, Illinois had 18 House seats divided between 12 Democrats and 6 Republicans. However, following the election one Democrat—Jesse Jackson Jr.—resigned his seat, citing health and other issues. A special election to fill the vacancy was scheduled in 2013. For purposes of this table, that contest has been assigned to Democrats because Jackson's seat in Chicago is one of the safest Democratic seats in the nation. If a Democrat wins, as expected, the Illinois ratio of Democrats to Republicans will be 12 to 6.

NOTES: State totals reflect the number of Democrats and Republicans in each House delegation at the start of each Congress. The above totals do not include "other" representatives elected as independent or third-party candidates. Those numbers are California: Progressive 1936 (1). (No formal party. The representative became a Democrat in 1938.) Minnesota: Farmer-Labor 1928–1930 (1), 1932 (5), 1934 (3), 1936 (5), 1938–1942 (1). (Merged with D in 1944.) New York: American Labor 1938–1948 (1). (Party disbanded after 1954.) Ohio: Independent 1950–1952 (1). (Defeated by Democrat in 1954.) Vermont: Independent 1990–2000 (1). Virginia: Independent 2000 (1). Wisconsin: Progressive 1934 (7), 1936–1938 (2), 1940 (3), 1942 (2), and 1944 (1). (Disbanded after 1944. The last Progressive became a Republican in 1946.) National totals: 1928–1930 (1), 1932 (5), 1934 (10), 1936 (13), 1938 (4), 1940 (5), 1942 (4), 1944 (2), 1946–1952 (1), 1990–1998 (1), and 2000 (2).

1970	1972	1974	1976	1978	1980	1982	1984	1986	1988	1990	1992	1994	1996	1998	2000	2002	2004	2006	2008	2010	2012	2014	2016
0	0	0	0	0	0	0	0	0	0	0	0	0	0	0	0	0	0	1	1	1	1	1	1
1	1	1	1	1	1	1	1	1	1	0	0	0	0	0	0	0	0	0	0	0	0	0	0
4	3	5	4	4	1	4	4	5	5	6	7^2	6	6	6	4	3	3	3	6	3	3	3	4
6	7	5	6	6	9	6	6	5	5	4	4	5	5	5	6	8	8	8	5	8	8	8	7
6	6	6	6	6	5	5^2	5	5	5	5	8^2	2	3	5	6	6	6	6	6	5	6^2	6	6
1	1	1	1	1	2	3	3	3	3	3	1	7	6	4	3	3	3	3	3	4	4	4	4
5	4^1	4	4	4	2	4	4	4	4	4	3^1	3	3	3	2	2	2	2	2	1	1	0	0
0	0	0	0	0	2	0	0	0	0	0	0	0	0	0	1	1	1	1	1	2	2	3	3
5	5^1	7	7	6	5	5	5	5	5	4	4	3	5	4	5	4	4	5	5	3	3	3	3
5	4	2	2	3	4	4	4	4	4	5	5	6	4	5	4	4	4	3	3	5	5	5	5
1	1	1	0	0	0	0	0	0	0	0	0	0	0	0	0	0	0	0	0	0	0	0	0
0	0	0	0	1	1	1	1	1	1	1	1	1	1	1	1	1	1	1	1	1	1	1	1

Governors, 2013–2017

Following is a list of governors who served during the period of President Barack Obama's second term, 2013–2017; multiple governors who began their service in 2018 are also listed. All governors serve four-year terms except those who served as acting governors or those representing New Hampshire and Vermont; they serve two-year terms. Party designations appear in parentheses following the governor's name. The following abbreviations were used: (D) Democrat; (R) Republican.

	Dates of Service		*Dates of Service*
Alabama		**Maine**	
Robert Bentley (R)	January 17, 2011 – April 10, 2017	Paul R. LePage (R)	January 5, 2011 –
Kay Ivey (R)	April 10, 2017 –	**Maryland**	
Alaska		Martin O'Malley (D)	January 17, 2007 – January 21, 2015
Bill Walker (R)	December 1, 2014 –	Larry Hogan (R)	January 21, 2015 –
Arizona		**Massachusetts**	
Jan Brewer (R)	January 21, 2009 – January 5, 2015	Deval Patrick (D)	January 4, 2007 – January 8, 2015
Doug Ducey (R)	January 5, 2015 –	Charlie Baker (R)	January 8, 2015 –
Arkansas		**Michigan**	
Mike Beebe (D)	January 9, 2007 – January 13, 2015	Rick Snyder (R)	January 1, 2011 –
Asa Hutchinson (R)	January 13, 2015 –	**Minnesota**	
California		Mark Dayton (D)	January 3, 2011 –
Jerry Brown (D)	January 3, 2011 –	**Mississippi**	
Colorado		Phil Bryant (R)	January 10, 2012 –
John W. Hickenlooper (D)	January 11, 2011 –	**Missouri**	
Conneticut		Jay Nixon (D)	January 12, 2009 – January 9, 2017
Dannel P. Malloy (D)	January 5, 2011 –	Eric Greitens (R)	January 9, 2017 – June 1, 2018
Delaware		Mike Parson (R)	June 1, 2018 –
Jack Markell (D)	January 20, 2009 – January 17, 2017	**Montana**	
John Carney (D)	January 17, 2017 –	Steve Bullock (D)	January 7, 2013 –
Florida		**Nebraska**	
Rick Scott (R)	January 4, 2011 –	Dave Heineman (R)	January 20, 2005 – January 8, 2015
Georgia		Pete Ricketts (R)	January 8, 2015 –
Nathan Deal (R)	January 10, 2011 –	**Nevada**	
Hawaii		Brian Sandoval (R)	January 3, 2011 –
David Ige (D)	December 1, 2014 –	**New Hampshire**	
Idaho		Maggie Hassan (D)	January 3, 2013 – January 2, 2017
C. L. "Butch" Otter (R)	January 1, 2007 –	Chuck Morse (R)	January 3, 2017 – January 5, 2017
Illinois		Chris Sununu (R)	January 5, 2017 –
Pat Quinn (D)	January 29, 2009 – January 12, 2015	**New Jersey**	
Bruce Rauner (R)	January 12, 2015 –	Chris Christie (R)	January 19, 2010 – January 16, 2018
Indiana		Phil Murphy (D)	January 16, 2018 –
Mike Pence (R)	January 14, 2013 – January 9, 2017	**New Mexico**	
Eric Holcomb (R)	January 9, 2017 –	Susana Martinez (R)	January 1, 2011 –
Iowa		**New York**	
Terry E. Branstad (R)	July 12, 2017 –	Andrew M. Cuomo (D)	January 1, 2011 –
Kansas		**North Carolina**	
Sam Brownback (R)	January 10, 2011 – January 31, 2018	Pat McCrory (R)	January 5, 2013 – January 1, 2017
Jeff Colyer (R)	January 31, 2018 –	Roy Cooper (D)	January 1, 2017 –
Kentucky		**North Dakota**	
Steven L. Beshear (D)	December 11, 2007 – December 8, 2015	Jack Dalrymple (R)	December 7, 2010 – December 15, 2016
		Doug Burgum (R)	December 15, 2016 –
Matt Bevin (D)	December 8, 2015 –	**Ohio**	
Louisiana		John R. Kasich (R)	January 10, 2011 –
Bobby Jindal (R)	January 14, 2008 – January 11, 2016	**Oklahoma**	
John Bel Edwards (D)	January 11, 2016 –	Mary Fallin (R)	January 10, 2011 –

Dates of Service

Oregon

John Kitzhaber (D)   January 10, 2011 – February 18, 2015
Kate Brown (D)   February 18, 2015 –

Pennsylvania

Tom Corbett (R)   January 18, 2011 – January 20, 2015
Tom Wolf (D)   January 20, 2015 –

Rhode Island

Lincoln Chafee (D)   January 4, 2011 – January 6, 2015
Gina Raimondo (D)   January 6, 2015 –

South Carolina

Nikki R. Haley (R)   January 12, 2011 – January 24, 2017
Henry McMaster (R)   January 24, 2017 –

South Dakota

Dennis Daugaard (R)   January 8, 2011 –

Tennessee

Bill Haslam (R)   January 15, 2011 –

Texas

Rick Perry (R)   December 21, 2000 – January 20, 2015
Greg Abbott (R)   January 20, 2015 –

Dates of Service

Utah

Gary R. Herbert (R)   August 11, 2009 –

Vermont

Peter Shumlin (D)   January 6, 2011 – January 5, 2017
Phil Scott (R)   January 5, 2017 –

Virginia

Bob McDonnell (R)   January 16, 2010 – January 11, 2014
Terry McAuliffe (D)   January 11, 2014 – January 13, 2018
Ralph Northam (D)   January 13, 2018 –

Washington

Jay Inslee (D)   January 16, 2013 –

West Virginia

Earl Ray Tomblin (D)   November 15, 2010 – January 16, 2017
Jim Justice (R)   January 16, 2017 –

Wisconsin

Scott Walker (R)   January 3, 2011 –

Wyoming

Matt Mead (R)   January 3, 2011 –

Index

Note: Page references with (fig.) or (table) refer to figures and tables, respectively.

CPSIA information can be obtained
at www.ICGtesting.com
Printed in the USA
JSHW021216101219
2894JS00003B/10

9 781544 350660